PERIODIC TABLE OF THE ELEMENTS

Main groups

Group	Legend
Metals	
Nonmetals	
Noble gases	

Transition metals

Main groups

1 1A[a][b]	2 2A	3 3B	4 4B	5 5B	6 6B	7 7B	8	9 8B	10	11 1B	12 2B	13 3A	14 4A	15 5A	16 6A	17 7A	18 8A
1 **H** Hydrogen 1.00794																	2 **He** Helium 4.002602
3 **Li** Lithium 6.941	4 **Be** Beryllium 9.012182											5 **B** Boron 10.811	6 **C** Carbon 12.0107	7 **N** Nitrogen 14.00674	8 **O** Oxygen 15.9994	9 **F** Fluorine 18.998403	10 **Ne** Neon 20.1797
11 **Na** Sodium 22.989770	12 **Mg** Magnesium 24.3050											13 **Al** Aluminum 26.981538	14 **Si** Silicon 28.0855	15 **P** Phosphorus 30.973762	16 **S** Sulfur 32.066	17 **Cl** Chlorine 35.4527	18 **Ar** Argon 39.948
19 **K** Potassium 39.0983	20 **Ca** Calcium 40.078	21 **Sc** Scandium 44.95591	22 **Ti** Titanium 47.867	23 **V** Vanadium 50.9415	24 **Cr** Chromium 51.9961	25 **Mn** Manganese 54.938049	26 **Fe** Iron 55.845	27 **Co** Cobalt 58.933200	28 **Ni** Nickel 58.6934	29 **Cu** Copper 63.546	30 **Zn** Zinc 65.39	31 **Ga** Gallium 69.723	32 **Ge** Germanium 72.61	33 **As** Arsenic 74.92160	34 **Se** Selenium 78.96	35 **Br** Bromine 79.904	36 **Kr** Krypton 83.80
37 **Rb** Rubidium 85.4678	38 **Sr** Strontium 87.62	39 **Y** Yttrium 88.90585	40 **Zr** Zirconium 91.224	41 **Nb** Niobium 92.90638	42 **Mo** Molybdenum 95.94	43 **Tc** Technetium [98]	44 **Ru** Ruthenium 101.07	45 **Rh** Rhodium 102.90550	46 **Pd** Palladium 106.42	47 **Ag** Silver 107.8682	48 **Cd** Cadmium 112.411	49 **In** Indium 114.818	50 **Sn** Tin 118.710	51 **Sb** Antimony 121.760	52 **Te** Tellurium 127.60	53 **I** Iodine 126.90447	54 **Xe** Xenon 131.29
55 **Cs** Cesium 132.90545	56 **Ba** Barium 137.327	57 ***La** Lanthanum 138.9055	72 **Hf** Hafnium 178.49	73 **Ta** Tantalum 180.9479	74 **W** Tungsten 183.84	75 **Re** Rhenium 186.207	76 **Os** Osmium 190.23	77 **Ir** Iridium 192.217	78 **Pt** Platinum 195.078	79 **Au** Gold 196.96655	80 **Hg** Mercury 200.59	81 **Tl** Thallium 204.3833	82 **Pb** Lead 207.2	83 **Bi** Bismuth 208.98038	84 **Po** Polonium [209]	85 **At** Astatine [210]	86 **Rn** Radon [222]
87 **Fr** Francium [223]	88 **Ra** Radium 226.025	89 **†Ac** Actinium 227.028	104 **Rf** Rutherfordium [261]	105 **Db** Dubnium [262]	106 **Sg** Seaborgium [266]	107 **Bh** Bohrium [267]	108 **Hs** Hassium [269]	109 **Mt** Meitnerium [268]	110 **Ds** Darmstadtium [281]	111 **Rg** Roentgenium [272]	112 **Cn** Copernicum [285]	113[c] [286]	114 **Fl** [289]	115 [288]	116 **Lv** [293]	117 [294]	118 [294]

*Lanthanide series

58 **Ce** Cerium 140.116	59 **Pr** Praseodymium 140.90765	60 **Nd** Neodymium 144.24	61 **Pm** Promethium [145]	62 **Sm** Samarium 150.36	63 **Eu** Europium 151.964	64 **Gd** Gadolinium 157.25	65 **Tb** Terbium 158.92534	66 **Dy** Dysprosium 162.50	67 **Ho** Holmium 164.93032	68 **Er** Erbium 167.26	69 **Tm** Thulium 168.93421	70 **Yb** Ytterbium 173.04	71 **Lu** Lutetium 174.967

†Actinide series

90 **Th** Thorium 232.0381	91 **Pa** Protactinium 231.03588	92 **U** Uranium 238.0289	93 **Np** Neptunium 237.048	94 **Pu** Plutonium [244]	95 **Am** Americium [243]	96 **Cm** Curium [247]	97 **Bk** Berkelium [247]	98 **Cf** Californium [251]	99 **Es** Einsteinium [252]	100 **Fm** Fermium [257]	101 **Md** Mendelevium [258]	102 **No** Nobelium [259]	103 **Lr** Lawrencium [262]

Atomic masses in brackets are the masses of the longest-lived or most important isotope of certain radioactive elements.

[a] The labels on top (1, 2, 3 ... 18) are the group numbers recommended by the International Union of Pure and Applied Chemistry.

[b] The labels on the bottom (1A, 2A, ... 8A) are the group numbers commonly used in the United States and the ones we use in this text.

[c] The names and symbols of elements 113, 115, 117, and 118 have not been assigned.

Further information is available at the Web site of WebElements™.

TABLE OF ATOMIC MASSES BASED ON CARBON-12

Name	Symbol	Atomic Number	Atomic Mass	Name	Symbol	Atomic Number	Atomic Mass
Actinium	Ac	89	227.028	Manganese	Mn	25	54.9380
Aluminum	Al	13	26.9815	Meitnerium	Mt	109	(268)
Americium	Am	95	(243)	Mendelevium	Md	101	(258)
Antimony	Sb	51	121.760	Mercury	Hg	80	200.59
Argon	Ar	18	39.948	Molybdenum	Mo	42	95.94
Arsenic	As	33	74.9216	Neodymium	Nd	60	144.24
Astatine	At	85	(210)	Neon	Ne	10	20.1797
Barium	Ba	56	137.327	Neptunium	Np	93	237.048
Berkelium	Bk	97	(247)	Nickel	Ni	28	58.6934
Beryllium	Be	4	9.01218	Niobium	Nb	41	92.9064
Bismuth	Bi	83	208.980	Nitrogen	N	7	14.0067
Bohrium	Bh	107	(267)	Nobelium	No	102	(259)
Boron	B	5	10.811	Osmium	Os	76	190.23
Bromine	Br	35	79.904	Oxygen	O	8	15.9994
Cadmium	Cd	48	112.411	Palladium	Pd	46	106.42
Calcium	Ca	20	40.078	Phosphorus	P	15	30.9738
Californium	Cf	98	(251)	Platinum	Pt	78	195.078
Carbon	C	6	12.0107	Plutonium	Pu	94	(244)
Cerium	Ce	58	140.116	Polonium	Po	84	(209)
Cesium	Cs	55	132.905	Potassium	K	19	39.0983
Chlorine	Cl	17	35.4527	Praseodymium	Pr	59	140.908
Chromium	Cr	24	51.9961	Promethium	Pm	61	(145)
Cobalt	Co	27	58.9332	Protactinium	Pa	91	231.036
Copernicium	Cn	112	(285)	Radium	Ra	88	226.025
Copper	Cu	29	63.546	Radon	Rn	86	(222)
Curium	Cm	96	(247)	Rhenium	Re	75	186.207
Darmstadtium	Ds	110	(281)	Rhodium	Rh	45	102.906
Dubnium	Db	105	(262)	Roentgenium	Rg	111	(272)
Dysprosium	Dy	66	162.50	Rubidium	Rb	37	85.4678
Einsteinium	Es	99	(252)	Ruthenium	Ru	44	101.07
Erbium	Er	68	167.26	Rutherfordium	Rf	104	(261)
Europium	Eu	63	151.964	Samarium	Sm	62	150.36
Fermium	Fm	100	(257)	Scandium	Sc	21	44.9559
Fluorine	F	9	18.9984	Seaborgium	Sg	106	(266)
Flerovium	Fl	114	(289)	Selenium	Se	34	78.96
Francium	Fr	87	(223)	Silicon	Si	14	28.0855
Gadolinium	Gd	64	157.25	Silver	Ag	47	107.868
Gallium	Ga	31	69.723	Sodium	Na	11	22.9898
Germanium	Ge	32	72.61	Strontium	Sr	38	87.62
Gold	Au	79	196.967	Sulfur	S	16	32.066
Hafnium	Hf	72	178.49	Tantalum	Ta	73	180.948
Hassium	Hs	108	(269)	Technetium	Tc	43	(98)
Helium	He	2	4.00260	Tellurium	Te	52	127.60
Holmium	Ho	67	164.930	Terbium	Tb	65	158.925
Hydrogen	H	1	1.00794	Thallium	Tl	81	204.383
Indium	In	49	114.818	Thorium	Th	90	232.038
Iodine	I	53	126.904	Thulium	Tm	69	168.934
Iridium	Ir	77	192.217	Tin	Sn	50	118.710
Iron	Fe	26	55.845	Titanium	Ti	22	47.867
Krypton	Kr	36	83.80	Tungsten	W	74	183.84
Lanthanum	La	57	138.906	Uranium	U	92	238.029
Lawrencium	Lr	103	(262)	Vanadium	V	23	50.9415
Lead	Pb	82	207.2	Xenon	Xe	54	131.29
Lithium	Li	3	6.941	Ytterbium	Yb	70	173.04
Lutetium	Lu	71	174.967	Yttrium	Y	39	88.9059
Livermorium	Lv	116	(293)	Zinc	Zn	30	65.39
Magnesium	Mg	12	24.3050	Zirconium	Zr	40	91.224

Atomic masses in this table are relative to carbon-12 and limited to six significant figures, although some atomic masses are known more precisely. For certain radioactive elements the numbers listed (in parentheses) are the mass numbers of the most stable isotopes.

CHEMISTRY

FOR CHANGING TIMES

CHEMISTRY

FOR CHANGING TIMES

John W. Hill
University of Wisconsin–River Falls

Terry W. McCreary
Murray State University

Robert and Elzbieta Cook, Louisiana State University
Ricardo Delgado, Lindenwood University
Marilyn Duerst, University of Wisconsin-River Falls
Steven R. Gwaltney, Mississippi State University
Andrew Jorgensen, The University of Toledo
Jeremy Mason, Texas Tech University
Rill Ann Reuter, Winona State University

PEARSON

Acquisitions Editor: Chris Hess
Editor in Chief: Jeanne Zalesky
Product Marketing Manager: Will Moore
Project Manager: Lisa Pierce
Program Manager: Jessica Moro
Development Editor: Donald Gecewicz
Editorial Assistant: Caitlin Falco
Director of Development: Jennifer Hart
Program Management Team Lead: Kristen Flathman
Project Management Team Lead: David Zielonka
Production Management: Francesca Monaco, codeMantra

Compositor: codeMantra
Design Manager: Derek Bacchus
Interior Designer: Tani Hasegawa
Cover Designer: Tani Hasegawa
Art Coordinator/Illustrator: Andrew Troutt, Precision Graphics
Text Permissions Manager: Timothy Nicholls
Rights & Permissions Management: Rachel Youdelman
Photo Researcher: Carolyn Arcabascio, Lumina Datamatics
Senior Specialist, Manufacturing: Maura Zaldivar-Garcia
Cover Photo Credit: Shutterstock; Getty Images; NASA (see Credits page for full list)

Library of Congress Cataloging-in-Publication Data

Hill, John William, 1933-
    Chemistry for changing times. -- Fourteenth edition / John W. Hill, University of Wisconsin--River Falls, Terry W. McCreary, Murray State University, Doris K. Kolb.
        pages cm
    ISBN 978-0-321-97202-6
    1. Chemistry--Textbooks. I. McCreary, Terry Wade, 1955- II. Kolb, Doris K. III. Title.
QD33.2.H54 2016
540--dc23
                                                            2013035235

www.pearsonhighered.com

ISBN 10: 0-321-97202-3; ISBN 13: 978-0-321-97202-6 (Student edition)

2 3 4 5 6 7 8 9 10–V382–18 17 16 15

BRIEF CONTENTS

CONTENTS

5 Chemical Accounting   136

6 Gases, Liquids, Solids ... and Intermolecular Forces   164

7 Acids and Bases   189

8 Oxidation and Reduction   216

14 Water 410

15 Energy 437

16 Biochemistry 478

17 Food 516

GREEN CHEMISTRY

The fourteenth edition of *Chemistry for Changing Times* is pleased to present the green chemistry essays listed below. The topics have been carefully chosen to introduce students to the concepts of green chemistry—a new approach to designing chemicals and chemical transformations that are beneficial for human health and the environment. The green chemistry essays in this edition highlight cutting-edge research by chemists, molecular scientists, and engineers to explore the fundamental science and practical applications of chemistry that is "benign by design." These examples emphasize the responsibility of chemists for the consequences of the new materials they create and the importance of building a sustainable chemical enterprise.

PREFACE

Chemistry for Changing Times is now in its fourteenth edition. Times have changed immensely since the first edition appeared in 1972 and continue to change more rapidly than ever—especially in the vital areas of biochemistry (neurochemistry, molecular genetics), the environment (sustainable practices, climate change), energy, materials, drugs, and health and nutrition. This book has changed accordingly. We have thoroughly updated the text and further integrated green chemistry throughout. There is a new or revised green chemistry essay in each chapter. Learning objectives and end-of-chapter problems are correlated to each essay. In preparing this new edition, we have responded to suggestions from users and reviewers of the thirteenth edition, as well as used our own writing, teaching, and life experiences. The text has been fully revised and updated to reflect the latest scientific developments in a fast-changing world.

New to This Edition

- New! Chemistry@Home experiments have been added to the end of each chapter. These simple experiments give students the opportunity to apply the information learned in each chapter through experimentation that is easily done at home. Live demonstrations with assessment questions are also available in MasteringChemistry.

- We have placed greater focus on incorporating new data, statistics, and the latest scientific findings. Examples include:

  - In Chapter 2, we reworked the coverage of the laws of conservation of mass and of definite proportions.

  - Chapter 4 has been heavily revised to reflect new thinking on how to describe chemical bonding, stressing some important underlying concepts such as the octet rule and electronegativity.

  - Chapter 13 has been rewritten to incorporate the latest data captured during the constant monitoring of air quality and makeup of the atmosphere.

- Green chemistry coverage has been increased and further integrated into the text:

  - A greater emphasis is placed on sustainability—both in the green essays and within chapter application.

  - All essays have been carefully reviewed. Of the 22 essays, 11 are entirely new and the remaining have been rewritten extensively. Each essay identifies the principles of green chemistry that are applied in it.

  - In each chapter, there are two to five end-of-chapter problems that relate to the green chemistry essay. These have been vetted and renewed as necessary.

- Updated! Content has been streamlined throughout to expand coverage on topics where students struggle most. Some examples include:

  - In Chapter 1, we reduced historical content in favor of a greater emphasis on fundamental ideas, including the scientific method, green chemistry, and data assessment.

  - We developed a more intuitive feel for stoichiometry in Chapter 5, a concept that nonmajors often find to be the most challenging in this course.

  - Chapter 6 now includes coverage of Gay-Lussac's law.

  - We adjusted coverage of stability of isotopes in Chapter 11 (another topic that frequently provides a challenge) and the workings of catalytic converters in Chapter 13. We also added coverage of heat capacity and specific heat to Chapter 14.

- Learning objectives, located at the beginning of each chapter and at the start of each section, have been revised as needed for clarity. They are linked to end-of-chapter problems to assist students and professors when assessing mastery of concepts.

- Updated! At least 25% of the Critical Thinking Exercises have been revised or replaced in all chapters. These exercises require students to apply concepts learned in the chapter and stress that critical thinking is a regular part of the work of students and scientists.

- Self-Assessment Questions at the end of each section facilitate student interaction with topics just learned. These multiple-choice items provide immediate feedback to test students' understanding of the material and serve as quick checks during reading of the chapter.

- We have revised or replaced more than 25% of the end-of-chapter problems to highlight the constant changes taking place in chemistry. Between editions, we are constantly sketching out new and interesting problems, which then are incorporated into the following edition's problem sets.

- Many of the worked-out examples and their accompanying exercises in the chapters have also been modified or revised to reflect current thinking, applications, and even some novelty. This is especially the case in the first 12 chapters—the core of the course.

- Updated! Each chapter starts with compelling images and a set of questions called "Have You Ever Wondered?" These real-life questions engage students in the chapter's content. Many have been changed as we listen to students and the questions they bring up. We watch for new developments that interest the general public, too. Answers to the questions are found in the outer column within the chapter, near the related text content.

- Updated! Collaborative Group Projects, which follow the end-of-chapter problems, have been revised or replaced in many chapters. These projects can extend the students' learning of chemistry far beyond the textbook.

TO THE INSTRUCTOR

Our knowledge base has expanded enormously since this book's first edition, never more so than in the last few years. We have faced tough choices in deciding what to include and what to leave out. We now live in what has been called the Information Age. Unfortunately, information is not knowledge; the information may or may not be valid. Our focus, more than ever, is on helping students evaluate information. May we all someday gain the gift of wisdom.

A major premise of this book is that a chemistry course for students who are not majoring in science should be quite different from a course offered to science majors. It must present basic chemical concepts with intellectual honesty, but it need not—probably should not—focus on esoteric theories or rigorous mathematics. It should include lots of modern everyday applications. The textbook should be appealing to look at, easy to understand, and interesting to read.

A large proportion of the legislation considered by the U.S. Congress involves questions having to do with science or technology, yet only rarely does a scientist or engineer enter politics. Most of the people who make important decisions regarding our health and our environment are not trained in science, but it is critical that these decision makers be scientifically literate. In the judicial system, decisions often depend on scientific evidence, but judges and jurors frequently have little education in the sciences. A chemistry course for students who are not science majors should emphasize practical applications of chemistry to problems involving, most notably, environmental pollution, radioactivity, energy sources, and human health. The students who take liberal arts chemistry courses include future teachers, business leaders, lawyers, legislators, accountants, artists, journalists, jurors, and judges.

Objectives

Our main objectives for a chemistry course for students who are not majoring in science are as follows:

- To attract lots of students from a variety of disciplines. If students do not enroll in the course, we can't teach them.

- To help students become literate in science. We want our students to develop a comfortable knowledge of science so that they may become productive, creative, ethical, and engaged citizens.

- To use topics of current interest to illustrate chemical principles. We want students to appreciate the importance of chemistry in the real world.

- To relate chemical problems to the everyday lives of our students. Chemical problems become more significant to students when they can see a personal connection.

- To acquaint students with scientific methods. We want students to be able to read about science and technology with some degree of critical judgment. This is especially important because many scientific problems are complex and controversial.

- To show students, by addressing the concepts of sustainability and green chemistry, that chemists seek better, safer, and more environmentally friendly processes and products.

- To instill an appreciation for chemistry as an open-ended learning experience. We hope that our students will develop a curiosity about science and will want to continue learning throughout their lives.

Questions and Problems

Worked-out Examples and accompanying exercises are given within most chapters.

Each Example carefully guides students through the process for solving a particular type of problem. It is then followed by one or more exercises that allow students to check their comprehension right away. Many Examples are followed by two exercises, labeled A and B. The goal in an A exercise is to apply to a similar situation the method outlined in the Example. In a B exercise, students must often combine that method with other ideas previously learned. Many of the B exercises provide a context closer to that in which chemical knowledge is applied, and they thus serve as a bridge between the Worked Examples and the more challenging problems at the end of the chapter. The A and B exercises provide a simple way for the instructor to assign homework that is closely related to the Examples. Answers to all the in-chapter exercises are given in the Answers section at the back of the book.

Answers to all odd-numbered end-of-chapter problems, identified by blue numbers, are given in the Answers section at the back of the book. The end-of chapter problems include the following:

- Review Questions for the most part simply ask for a recall of material in the chapter.

- A set of matched-pair problems is arranged according to subject matter in each chapter.

- Additional Problems are not grouped by type. Some of these are more challenging than the matched-pair problems and often require a synthesis of ideas from more than one chapter. Others pursue an idea further than is done in the text or introduce new ideas.

Acknowledgments

For more than four decades, we have greatly benefited from hundreds of helpful reviews. It would take far too many pages to list all of those reviewers here, but they should know that their contributions are deeply appreciated. For the fourteenth edition, we are especially grateful to the following reviewers:

Accuracy Reviewers

Guy Patrick Meier, *Spokane Falls Community College*
Christine Seppanen, *Riverland Community College*
Alice Suroviec, *Berry College*
Paloma Valverde, *Wentworth Institute of Technology*

Reviewers of This Edition

Meltem Arikan, *University of Massachusetts-Dartmouth*
Debe Bell, *Metropolitan State University of Denver*
Terrence Black, *Nassau Community College*

Bruce Burnham, *Rider University*
Leticia Colmenares, *Winward Community College*
Matthew Crawford, *Frostburg State University*
Ricardo Delgado, *Lindenwood University*
Jeremiah Duncan, *Plymouth State University*
Jeannine Eddleton, *Virginia Tech*
Bradley Fahlman, *Central Michigan University*
Eric Goll, *Brookdale Community College of Monmouth*
Ellen Kehres, *Bloomsburg University*
Irvin Levy, *Gordon College*
Aiye Liang, *Charleston Southern University*
Sedef Maloy, *University of Hawaii at Manoa*
Gary Martinie, *University of North Carolina Greensboro*
Guy Patrick Meier, *Spokane Falls Community College*
Julie Peller, *Indiana University Northwest*
Albert Plaush, *Saginaw Valley State University*
Douglas Raynie, *South Dakota State University*
Mark Rockley, *Oklahoma State University*
Phil Silverman, *University of Missouri Columbia*
David Smith, *New Mexico State University*
Patricia Stan, *Taylor University*
Susanne Swanker, *American International College*
Jeffrey Webb, *Southern Connecticut State University*
Brian Zoltowski, *Southern Methodist University*

Green Chemistry Contributors

We are enormously grateful to Jennifer MacKellar, program manager at the American Chemical Society's Green Chemistry Institute®, who coordinated the development of the new and revised green chemistry essays and correlated the content of these essays. We thank her for her dedication to this project. We also thank the team of green chemists listed below who contributed the green essays and helped to integrate each essay's content into the chapter with learning objectives, end-of-chapter problems, summaries, and section references.

Eric Beckman, *University of Pittsburgh*
Amy Cannon, *Beyond Benign*
David Constable, *ACS Green Chemistry Institute*
Scott Cummings, *Kenyon College*
Joseph Fortunak, *Howard University*
Tom Goodwin, *Hendrix College*
Michael Heben, *University of Toledo*
Phil Jessop, *Queen's University*
Margaret Kerr, *Worcester State University*
Karen Larson, *Clarke University*
Irv Levy, *Gordon College*
Doris Lewis, *Suffolk University*

Jennifer MacKellar, *ACS Green Chemistry Institute*
Alex Mayer, *Michigan Technological University*
Lallie C. McKenzie, *Chem11 LLC*
Martin Mulvihill, *University of California–Berkeley*
Katie Privett, *Green Chemistry Centre of Excellence York, UK*
Douglas Raynie, *South Dakota State University*
Robert Sheldon, *Delft University of Technology*
Galen Suppes, *University of Missouri*
David Vosburg, *Harvey Mudd College*
John Warner, *Warner Babcock Institute*
Rich Williams; *Environmental Science & Green Chemistry Consulting, LLC*

Reviewers of Previous Editions

Debe Bell, *Metro State College*
Mark Blazer, *Shasta College*
Michelle Boucher, *Utica College*
Kirsten Casey, *Anne Arundel Community College*
Roxanne Finney, *Skagit Valley College*
Luther Giddings, *Salt Lake Community College*
Todd Hamilton, *Georgetown College*
Alice Harper, *Berry College*

Alton Hassell, *Baylor University*
Scott Hewitt, *California State University, Fullerton*
Sherell Hickman, *Brevard Community College, Cocoa*
Beth Hixon, *Tulsa Community College*
Donna K. Howell, *Park University*
James L. Klino, *SUNY College of Agriculture and Technology, Cobleskill*
Meghan Knapp, *Georgetown College*

David Lippman, *University of Texas-Austin*

Kim Loomis, *Century College*

James L. Marshall, *University of North Texas*

Jeremy Mason, *Texas Technical University*

Douglas Mulford, *Emory University*

David S. Newman, *Bowling Green State University*

Charlotte A. Ovechka, *University of St. Thomas*

James K. Owen, *The Art Institute of Tennessee*

Lois Schadenwald, *Normandale Community College*

Christine Seppanen, *Riverland Community College*

Michael Dennis Seymour, *Hope College*

Shirish K. Shah, *Towson University*

Joseph Sinski, *Bellarmine University*

Kelli M. Slunt, *University of Mary Washington*

Julianne Smist, *Springfield College*

Jie Song, *University of Michigan, Flint*

Wayne M. Stalick, *University of Central Missouri*

Durwin Striplin, *Davidson College*

Shashi Unnithan, *Front Range Community College*

Mona Uppal, *Tarrant County College, Nebraska*

Paloma Valverde, *Wentworth Institute of Technology*

Edward Vitz, *Kutztown University*

Dan Wacks, *University of Redlands*

Elizabeth Wallace, *Western Oklahoma State College*

Matthew E. Wise, *University of Colorado, Boulder*

We also appreciate the many people who have called, written, or e-mailed with corrections and other helpful suggestions. Cynthia S. Hill prepared much of the original material on biochemistry, food, and health and fitness.

We owe a special debt of gratitude to Doris K. Kolb (1927–2005), who was an esteemed coauthor from the seventh through the eleventh editions. Doris and her husband Ken were friends and helpful supporters long before Doris joined the author team. She provided much of the spirit and flavor of the book. Doris's contributions to *Chemistry for Changing Times*—and indeed to all of chemistry and chemical education—will live on for many years to come, not only in her publications, but in the hearts and minds of her many students, colleagues, and friends.

Throughout her career as a teacher, scientist, community leader, poet, and much more, Doris was blessed with a wonderful spouse, colleague, and companion, Kenneth E. Kolb. Over the years, Ken did chapter reviews, made suggestions, and gave invaluable help for many editions. All who knew Doris miss her greatly. Those of us who had the privilege of working closely with her miss her wisdom and wit most profoundly. Let us all dedicate our lives, as Doris did hers, to making this world a better place.

We also want to thank our colleagues at the University of Wisconsin–River Falls, Murray State University, and Bradley University for all their help and support through the years. We are thankful to the contributors who revised all chapters for this new edition, Robert and Elzbieta Cook, Louisiana State University; Ricardo Delgado, Lindenwood University; Marilyn Duerst, University of Wisconsin-River Falls; Steven R. Gwaltney, Mississippi State University Andrew Jorgensen, The University of Toledo; Jeremy Mason, Texas Tech University; Rill Ann Reuter, Winona State University. Thank you to Amy Cannon and Kate Anderson who coordinated the Chemistry @ Home experiments. The Chemistry @ Home demonstrations help bring the subject matter to life for students.

We also owe a debt of gratitude to the many creative people at Pearson who have contributed their talents to this edition. Jessica Moro, program manager, has been a delight to work with, providing valuable guidance throughout the project. She showed extraordinary skill and diplomacy in coordinating all the many facets of this project. Director of Development Jennifer Hart and Development Editor Donald Gecewicz contributed greatly to this project, especially in challenging us to be better authors in every way. We treasure their many helpful suggestions of new material and better presentation of all the subject matter. We are grateful to Acquisitions Editor Chris Hess for his overall guidance and to Project Managers Francesca Monaco and Lisa Pierce for their diligence and patience in bringing all the parts together to yield a finished work. We are indebted to our copyeditor Betty Pessagno, whose expertise helped improve the consistency of the text; and to proofreaders and accuracy checkers whose sharp eyes caught many of our errors and typos. We also salute our art specialist, Andrew Troutt, for providing outstanding illustrations, and our photo researcher, Carolyn Arcabascio, who vetted hundreds of images in the search for quality photos.

John W. Hill owes a very special kind of thanks to his wonderful spouse, Ina, who over the years has done typing, library research, and so many other things that allow him time to concentrate on writing. Most of all, he is grateful for her boundless patience, unflagging support, understanding, and enduring love. He is also grateful to his beloved daughter Cindy for her help with the house and the yard and so many other things. Terry W. McCreary would like to thank his wife, Geniece, and children, Corinne and Yvette, for their unflagging support, understanding, and love.

Finally, we also thank all those many students whose enthusiasm has made teaching such a joy. It is gratifying to have students learn what you are trying to teach them, but it is a supreme pleasure to find that they want to learn even more. And, of course, we are grateful to all of you who have made so many helpful suggestions. We welcome and appreciate all your comments, corrections, and criticisms.

John W. Hill
jwhill602@comcast.net

Terry W. McCreary
terry.mccreary@murraystate.edu

TO THE STUDENT

Tell me, what is it you plan to do
with your one wild and precious life?
—American poet Mary Oliver (b. 1935)
"The Summer Day," from *New and Selected Poems*
(Boston, MA: Beacon Press, 1992)

Welcome to Our Chemical World!

Learning chemistry will enrich your life—now and long after this course is over—through a better understanding of the natural world, the scientific and technological questions now confronting us, and the choices you will face as citizens in a scientific and technological society.

Skills gained in this course can be exceptionally useful in many aspects of your life. Learning chemistry involves thinking logically, critically, and creatively. You will learn how to use the language of chemistry: its symbols, formulas, and equations. More importantly, you will learn how to obtain meaning from information. The most important thing you will learn is how to learn. Memorized material quickly fades into oblivion unless it is arranged on a framework of understanding.

Chemistry Directly Affects Our Lives

How does the human body work? How does aspirin cure headaches, reduce fevers, and lessen the chance of a heart attack or stroke? How does penicillin kill bacteria without harming our healthy body cells? Is ozone a good thing or a threat to our health? Do we really face climate change, and if so, how severe will it be? Do humans contribute to climate change, and if so, to what degree? Why do most weight-loss diets seem to work in the short run but fail in the long run? Why do our moods swing from happy to sad? Chemists have found answers to questions such as these and continue to seek the knowledge that will unlock other secrets of our universe. As these mysteries are resolved, the direction of our lives often changes—sometimes dramatically. We live in a chemical world—a world of drugs, biocides, food additives, fertilizers, fuels, detergents, cosmetics, and plastics. We live in a world with toxic wastes, polluted air and water, and dwindling petroleum reserves. Knowledge of chemistry will help you better understand the benefits and hazards of this world and will enable you to make intelligent decisions in the future.

We Are All Chemically Dependent

Even in the womb we are chemically dependent. We need a constant supply of oxygen, water, glucose, amino acids, triglycerides, and a multitude of other chemical substances.

Chemistry is everywhere. Our world is a chemical system—and so are we. Our bodies are durable but delicate systems with innumerable chemical reactions occurring constantly within us that allow our bodies to function properly. Learning, exercising, feeling, gaining or losing weight, and virtually all life processes are made possible by these chemical reactions. Everything that we ingest is part of a complex process that determines whether our bodies work effectively. The consumption of some substances can initiate chemical reactions that will stop body functions. Other substances, if consumed, can cause permanent handicaps, and still others can make living less comfortable. A proper balance of the right foods provides the chemicals that fuel the reactions we need in order to function at our best. Learning chemistry will help you better understand how your body works so that you will be able to take proper care of it.

Changing Times

We live in a world of increasingly rapid change. Isaac Asimov (1920–1992), Russian-born American biochemist and famous author of popular science and science fiction books, once said that "The only constant is change, continuing change, inevitable change, that is the dominant factor in society today. No sensible decision can be made any longer without taking into account not only the world as it is, but the world as it will be." We now face some of the greatest problems that humans have ever encountered, and these dilemmas seem to have no perfect solutions. We are sometimes forced to make a best choice among only bad alternatives, and our decisions often provide only temporary solutions. Nevertheless, if we are to choose properly, we must understand what our choices are. Mistakes can be costly, and they cannot always be rectified. It is easy to pollute, but cleaning up pollution is enormously expensive. We can best avoid mistakes by collecting as much information as possible and evaluating it carefully before making critical decisions. Science is a means of gathering and evaluating information, and chemistry is central to all the sciences.

Chemistry and the Human Condition

Above all else, our hope is that you will learn that the study of chemistry need not be dull and difficult. Rather, it can enrich your life in so many ways—through a better understanding of your body, your mind, your environment, and the world in which you live. After all, the search to understand the universe is an essential part of what it means to be human. We offer you a challenge first issued by American educator Horace Mann (1796–1859) in his 1859 address at Antioch College: "Be ashamed to die until you have won some victory for humanity."

ABOUT THE AUTHORS

John W. Hill

John Hill received his Ph.D. from the University of Arkansas. As an organic chemist, he has published more than 50 papers, most of which have an educational bent. He has authored or coauthored several introductory-level chemistry textbooks, all of which have been published in multiple editions. He has also presented over 60 papers at national conferences, many relating to chemical education. He has received several awards for outstanding teaching and has long been active in the American Chemical Society, both locally and nationally. Now professor emeritus at the University of Wisconsin–River Falls, he authored the first edition of *Chemistry for Changing Times* in 1972. Revising and updating this book has been a major focus of his life for four decades.

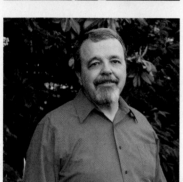

Terry W. McCreary

Terry McCreary received his B.S. from St. Francis University, his M.S. from the University of Georgia, and his Ph.D. from Virginia Tech. He has taught chemistry at Murray State University since 1988 and was presented with the Regents Excellence in Teaching Award in 2008. He is a member of the American Chemical Society and the Kentucky Academy of Science and has served as technical editor for the *Journal of Pyrotechnics*. In his spare time, he designs, builds, and flies rockets with the Tripoli Rocketry Association; he was elected president of the association in 2010. McCreary is the author of several laboratory manuals: *General Chemistry* with John Hill, Ralph Petrucci, and Scott Perry; and *Experimental Composite Propellant*, a fundamental treatise on the preparation and properties of solid rocket propellant.

Without the help of several chapter contributors, the fourteenth edition would not exist. We are grateful to the following people who updated all 22 chapters of this new edition to make it more current.

Chapter Contributors of the Fourteenth Edition

Robert and Elzbieta Cook, Louisiana State University
Ricardo Delgado, Lindenwood University
Marilyn Duerst, University of Wisconsin-River Falls
Steven R. Gwaltney, Mississippi State University
Andrew Jorgensen, The University of Toledo
Jeremy Mason, Texas Tech University
Rill Ann Reuter, Winona State University

ABOUT OUR SUSTAINABILITY INITIATIVES

Pearson recognizes the environmental challenges facing this planet, as well as acknowledges our responsibility in making a difference. This book is carefully crafted to minimize environmental impact. The binding, cover, and paper come from facilities that minimize waste, energy consumption, and the use of harmful chemicals. Pearson closes the loop by recycling every out-of-date text returned to our warehouse.

Along with developing and exploring digital solutions to our market's needs, Pearson has a strong commitment to achieving carbon-neutrality. As of 2009, Pearson became the first carbon- and climate-neutral publishing company. Since then, Pearson remains strongly committed to measuring, reducing, and offsetting our carbon footprint.

The future holds great promise for reducing our impact on Earth's environment, and Pearson is proud to be leading the way. We strive to publish the best books with the most up-to-date and accurate content, and to do so in ways that minimize our impact on Earth. To learn more about our initiatives, please visit https://www.pearson.com/social-impact.html

Green Chemistry Emphasis

The fourteenth edition emphasizes green chemistry through a framework of twelve principles. Each chapter contains a **Green Essay**, written by an expert in the field, which identifies the principles within the application. Chapter **Learning Objectives**, **End-of-Chapter Summaries**, and **Problems** now include green chemistry content to reinforce the principles for students.

- -

Green Chemistry Essays

Green chemistry essays, written by experts in the field, introduce students to one or more of the twelve principles of green chemistry, while highlighting references to the chapter when applicable.

Learning Objectives

Learning Objectives for each section in the text and related green chemistry have been added to every chapter and link to end-of-chapter problems in the textbook and in MasteringChemistry®.

Learning Objectives	
> Explain the electrical properties of an atom. (3.1)	Problems 1, 20
> Describe how the properties of electricity explain the structure of atoms. (3.1)	Problems 4, 18
> Describe the experiments that led to the discovery of X-rays and an explanation of radioactivity. (3.2)	Problems 2, 21
> Distinguish the three main kinds of radioactivity: alpha, beta, and gamma. (3.3)	Problems 3, 19
> Sketch the nuclear model of the atom, and identify its parts. (3.4)	Problems 5, 9
> List the particles that make up the nucleus of an atom, and give their relative masses and electric charges. (3.5)	Problems 6–8, 16, 17, 22
> Identify elements and isotopes from their nuclear particles. (3.5)	Problems 10, 11, 15, 23–27, 29
> Define *quantum*. (3.6)	Problems 12, 13, 48
> Arrange the electrons in a given atom in energy levels (shells). (3.6)	Problems 45, 50–52
> Relate the idea of a quantum of energy to an orbital. (3.7)	Problems 14, 28
> Write an electron configuration (in subshell notation) for a given atom. (3.7)	Problems 30–36, 49
> Describe how an element's electron configuration relates to its location in the periodic table. (3.8)	Problems 37–44, 46, 47
> Distinguish the conversion of solar energy into electrical energy in a solar cell from the conversion of solar energy into the chemical-bond energy of a solar fuel.	Problems 54–56
> Explain why splitting water into the elements hydrogen and oxygen requires an energy input and producing water by the reaction of hydrogen and oxygen releases energy.	Problem 53

End-of-Chapter Summaries

Each chapter includes end-of-chapter summaries, with key terms highlighted in blue, as well as a section summarizing the green chemistry highlighted within each chapter essay.

SUMMARY

Section 3.1—Davy, Faraday, and others showed that matter is electrical in nature. They were able to decompose compounds into elements by electrolysis or by passing electricity through molten salts. Electrodes are carbon rods or metal strips that carry electricity into the electrolyte, the solution or compound that conducts electricity. The electrolyte contains ions—charged atoms or groups of atoms. The anode is the positive electrode, and anions (negatively charged ions) move toward it. The cathode is the negative electrode, and cations (positively charged ions) move toward it. Experiments with cathode rays in gas-discharge tubes showed that matter contained negatively charged particles, which were called electrons. Thomson determined the mass-to-charge ratio for the electron. Goldstein's experiment showed that matter also contained positively charged particles. Millikan's oil-drop experiment measured the charge on the electron, so its mass could then be calculated.

Section 3.2—In his studies of cathode rays, Roentgen accidentally discovered X-rays, a highly penetrating form of radiation now used in medical diagnosis. Becquerel accidentally discovered another type of radiation that comes from certain unstable elements. Marie Curie named this new discovery radioactivity and studied it extensively.

Section 3.3—Radioactivity was soon classified as three different types of radiation: Alpha particles have four times the mass of a hydrogen atom and a positive charge twice that of an electron. Beta particles are energetic electrons. Gamma rays are a form of energy like X-rays but more penetrating.

another by a quantum, or discrete unit of energy. An atom drops to the lowest energy state, or ground state, after being in a higher energy state, or excited state. The energy emitted when electrons move to lower energy levels manifests as a line spectrum characteristic of the particular element, with the lines corresponding to specific wavelengths (colors) of light. Bohr also deduced that the energy levels of an atom could hold at most $2n^2$ electrons, where n is the number of the energy level, or shell. A description of the shells occupied by the electrons of an atom is one way of giving the atom's electron configuration, or arrangement of electrons.

Section 3.7—de Broglie hypothesized that electrons have wave properties. Schrödinger developed equations that described each electron's location in terms of an orbital, a volume of space that the electron usually occupies. Each orbital holds at most two electrons. Orbitals in the same shell and with the same energy make up a subshell, or sublevel, each of which is designated by a letter. An *s* orbital is spherical and a *p* orbital is dumbbell-shaped. The *d* and *f* orbitals have more complex shapes. The first main shell can hold only one *s* orbital; the second can hold one *s* and three *p* orbitals; and the third can hold one *s*, three *p*, and five *d* orbitals. In writing an electron configuration using subshell notation, we give the shell number and subshell letter, followed by a superscript indicating the number of electrons in that subshell. The order of the shells and subshells can be remembered with a chart or by looking at the periodic table.

End-of-Chapter Questions

Each chapter includes two to five end-of-chapter problems that relate to the green chemistry in that chapter.

71. Sulfuric acid is produced from elemental sulfur by a three-step process: (1) Sulfur is burned to produce sulfur dioxide. (2) Sulfur dioxide is oxidized to sulfur trioxide using oxygen and a vanadium (V) oxide catalyst. (3) Finally, the sulfur trioxide is reacted with water to produce 98% sulfuric acid. Write equations for the three reactions.

72. When carbon dioxide mixes with water a weak acid called carbonic acid is formed. Will CO_2 reduce the pH of the water, increase the pH of the water, or leave the pH of the water unchanged?

73. Suppose a certain company has an alkaline waste stream that requires 1 mL of concentrated HCl to neutralize 1 liter of waste. If that company chooses to switch to CO_2 to neutralize their annual 1 million liter waste stream, how many liters of concentrated HCl are replaced annually by this choice?

74. Carbonated water (pure water in which CO_2 is dissolved) has a slightly sour taste. What does this hint indicate about the pH of carbonated water?

75. An important type of chemical substance called an ester can be prepared by heating two chemicals in the presence of a strong mineral acid. No water is used in this reaction. Suggest a greener alternative to the strong mineral acid.

Critical Thinking

In order to help students improve their critical thinking skills, Chapter One introduces the principles used to test a claim (falsifiability, logic, replicability, and sufficiency; identified by the acronym FLaReS). Each end-of-chapter section reinforces their importance by including a section of Critical Thinking questions, allowing students to use these principles to test each of the claims. Instructors can assign Critical Thinking questions in MasteringChemistry, which provide wrong answer feedback to help students learn from their mistakes and ultimately gain a stronger grasp of the process of science.

CRITICAL THINKING EXERCISES

Apply knowledge that you have gained in this chapter and one or more of the FLaReS principles (Chapter 1) to evaluate the following statements or claims.

3.1 Suppose you read in the newspaper that a chemist in South America claims to have discovered a new element with an atomic mass of 34. Extremely rare, it was found in a sample taken from the Andes Mountains. Unfortunately, the chemist has used all of the sample in his analyses.

3.2 Some aboriginal tribes have rain-making ceremonies in which they toss pebbles of gypsum up into the air. (Gypsum is the material used to make plaster of Paris by heating the rock to remove some of its water.) Sometimes it does rain several days after these rain-making ceremonies.

3.3 Some scientists think that life on other planets might be based on silicon rather than carbon. Evaluate this possibility.

3.4 You come across a website selling water made from only single isotopes of hydrogen and oxygen. A testimonial on the website claims that drinking only the isotopically pure water helps a person feel more refreshed throughout the day.

Worked Examples

Worked examples within each chapter guide students through the process of solvings particular types of problems. Examples are followed by one or more exercises allowing students to immediately check their problem-solving skills.

Example 3.1	Number of Neutrons

How many neutrons are there in the $^{235}_{92}U$ nucleus?

Solution

We simply subtract the atomic number Z (number of protons) from the mass number A (number of protons plus number of neutrons).

$$A - Z = \text{number of neutrons}$$
$$235 - 92 = 143$$

There are 143 neutrons in the $^{235}_{92}U$ nucleus.

■ EXERCISE 3.1A
How many neutrons are there in the $^{60}_{27}Co$ nucleus?

■ EXERCISE 3.1B
An iodine isotope has 78 neutrons in its nucleus. What are the mass number and the name of the isotope?

Exercise A allows students to apply the problem-solving method just explained to a similar situation.

Exercise B prompts the student to combine the specific problem-solving method just taught with concepts learned in previous sections.

Applications

Emulsions

When oil and water are vigorously shaken together, the oil is broken up into tiny, microscopic droplets and dispersed throughout the water, a mixture called an *emulsion*. Unless a third substance has been added, the emulsion usually breaks down rapidly, as the oil droplets recombine and float to the surface of the water.

Emulsions can be stabilized by adding a type of gum, a soap, or a protein that can form a protective coating around the oil droplets and prevent them from coming together. Lecithin in egg yolks keeps mayonnaise from separating, while casein in milk keeps fat droplets suspended. Compounds called *bile salts* keep tiny fat droplets suspended in aqueous media during human digestion. This greatly aids the digestive process. The tiny emulsified droplets provide a much greater surface area on which the water-soluble lipase enzymes can break down the triacylglycerides to glycerol and fatty acids.

▲ Many foods are emulsions. Milk is an emulsion of butterfat in water. The stabilizing agent is a protein called *casein*. Mayonnaise is an emulsion of vegetable oil in water, stabilized by egg yolk.

Current and Relevant Applications

Essays throughout the new edition focus on interesting, relevant applications to help students connect the chemistry covered in a particular chapter or section to the world around them.

It DOES Matter!

When light hits a photovoltaic "solar" cell, photons are absorbed, promoting electrons to excited states. Those excited state electrons are captured by the photovoltaic cell to produce an electrical current. Scientists are working to create new materials that will absorb more of the sun's photons and more efficiently convert those photons into electrical energy. Scientists are also working on creating new materials that will lower the cost to make solar cells. Depending on where you live and how much sunlight you get, solar electricity may already be cheaper than the electricity you buy from the power company.

It DOES Matter!

Marginal boxes briefly discuss a specific application or phenomenon and show students how the material being studied relates to their world.

NEW! Chemistry@Home

The Chemistry@Home experiments located at the end of each chapter give students the opportunity to apply the information learned in each chapter through experimentation they can easily do at home.

CHEMISTRY@HOME   How Sweet It Is to Be Fermented by You!

Materials required

- Yeast (jar)
- Large measuring cup: 2 cup or larger capacity
- Measuring spoons (teaspoon and tablespoon)
- 6 resealable plastic bags
- 1 tablespoon of sugar
- 1 tablespoon of sweetener (Equal®, Sweet'N Low®)
- 1 tablespoon of flour
- 2 breakfast cereal samples (each with sugar listed as ingredient)
- Lukewarm water
- Paper towels (for clean-up)

What does yeast need to survive and thrive? Can yeast also digest artificial sweeteners and flour?

Yeast is most commonly used in the kitchen to make dough rise. Have you ever watched pizza crust or a loaf of bread swell in the oven? Yeast makes the dough expand. But what is yeast exactly and how does it work? Yeast strains are made up of living eukaryotic microbes, meaning that they contain cells with nuclei and are classified as fungi. In this experiment, we will watch yeast come to life as it breaks down sugar, also known as sucrose, through a process called fermentation.

To begin, create a data table for your experiment results. The data table should include columns for 6 bags, their contents, and your observations. Label bags 1 through 6.

Bag 1 will be your control.
–To bag 2, add 1 tablespoon of sugar.
–To bag 3, add 1 tablespoon of sweetener (Sweet'N Low® or Equal®).
–To bag 4, add 1 tablespoon of flour.
–To bag 5, add 1 tablespoon of breakfast cereal A, crushed.
–To bag 6, add 1 tablespoon of breakfast cereal B, crushed.

Next add $\frac{1}{4}$ cup of lukewarm water and 2 teaspoons of yeast to each bag.

▶ Figure 2

Carefully, without spilling any of the contents, squeeze out as much air as possible and seal each bag. Put the bags in a warm place for 20 minutes. (Either a window or a large bowl with warm water works well.) Observe the bags periodically. After 20 minutes, remove the bags from the warm place and observe them.

▶ Figure 3

What changes have occurred? Which bag has grown in size the most?

To measure the volume of the bags, fill the large measuring cup with 1 cup water and lower the bag into the large measuring cup. To find the estimated volume, you will use displacement measurement. Record the volume of the water with the bag in it and subtract the initial starting volume of 1 cup of water to obtain your volume. (Don't forget to account for any volume change of your control bag.)

Resources

Resource	Available in Print	Available Online	Instructor or Student Resource	Description
Study Guide and Selected Solutions Manual ISBN: 0133889041	✓		Resource for Students	The Study Guide and Selected Solutions Manual assists students with the text material. It contains learning objectives, chapter outlines, key terms, additional problems with self-tests and answers, and answers to odd-numbered problems in the text.
Chemical Investigations for Changing Times ISBN: 0133891852	✓		Resource for Students	This resource contains over 60 laboratory experiments that correspond to topics covered in *Chemistry for Changing Times, 14th edition.*
Online Instructor Resource Center ISBN: 013388922X		✓	Resource for Instructor	This resource contains the following: • All illustrations, tables, and photos from the text in JPEG format • Four pre-built PowerPoint Presentations (lecture, worked examples, images, CRS/ clicker questions) • TestGen computerized software with the TestGen version of the Testbank • Word files of the Test Item File
Instructor's Manual (Download Only) ISBN: 0133889025		✓	Resource for Instructor	Organized by chapter, this useful guide includes objectives, lecture outlines, references to figures and solved problems, as well as teaching demonstrations.
Instructor Manual for Lab Manual (Download Only) ISBN: 0133901459		✓	Resource for Instructor	The Instructor Manual for the Lab Manual provides instructors with useful tips, lab notes, and answers to lab report questions and pre- and post-lab questions.
Test Bank ISBN: 0133888991		✓	Resource for Instructor	The Test Bank contains more than 2500 multiple choice, true/false, and matching questions.

MasteringChemistry®

MasteringChemistry® from Pearson is the leading online teaching and learning system designed to improve results by engaging students before, during, and after class with powerful content. Ensure that students arrive ready to learn by assigning educationally effective content before class, and encourage critical thinking and retention with in-class resources such as Learning Catalytics. Students can further master concepts after class through traditional homework assignments that provide hints and answer-specific feedback. The Mastering gradebook records scores for all automatically graded assignments while diagnostic tools give instructors access to rich data that helps assess student understanding and identifies class-wide misconceptions. Mastering brings learning full circle by continuously adapting to each student and making learning more personal than ever—before, during, and after class.

- -

BEFORE CLASS

Reading Quizzes

Reading Quizzes give you the opportunity to assign reading and test students on their comprehension of chapter content before they come to class, empowering you to assume a certain baseline level of knowledge and helping you to spend more time on the toughest topics that require your expertise.

Dynamic Study Modules

Help students quickly learn chemistry!
Now assignable, Dynamic Study Modules (DSMs) enable your students to study on their own and be better prepared to achieve higher scores on their tests. When your students use DSMs outside of class, you can take knowledge transfer out of the classroom, allowing class time to be spent on higher-order learning. The mobile app is available for iOS and Android devices for study on the go.

DURING CLASS

Learning Catalytics

Learning Catalytics "is a "bring your own device" student engagement, assessment, and classroom intelligence system. With Learning Catalytics you can:

- Assess students in real time, using open-ended tasks to probe student understanding.
- Understand immediately where students are and adjust your lecture accordingly.
- Improve your students' critical-thinking skills.
- Access rich analytics to understand student performance.
- Add your own questions to make Learning Catalytics fit your course exactly.
- Manage student interactions with intelligent grouping and timing.

AFTER CLASS

Student Tutorials

Tutorials, featuring specific wrong-answer feedback, hints, and a wide variety of educationally effective content, guide your students through the toughest topics in chemistry. The hallmark Hints and Feedback offer scaffolded instruction similar to what students would experience in an office hour, allowing them to learn from their mistakes without being given the answer.

The interactive Chemistry@Home demonstrations bring the subject matter to life and are assignable with follow-up assessments in MasteringChemistry.

CHEMISTRY

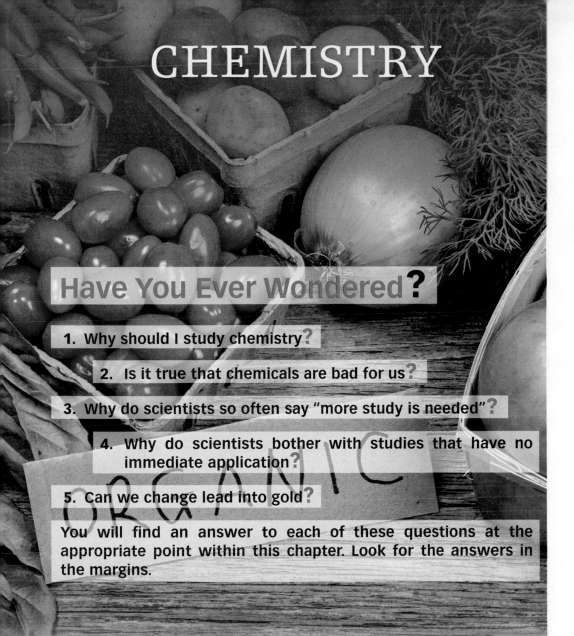

Have You Ever Wondered?

1. **Why should I study chemistry?**

2. **Is it true that chemicals are bad for us?**

3. **Why do scientists so often say "more study is needed"?**

4. **Why do scientists bother with studies that have no immediate application?**

5. **Can we change lead into gold?**

You will find an answer to each of these questions at the appropriate point within this chapter. Look for the answers in the margins.

Learning Objectives

> Define science, chemistry, technology, and alchemy. (1.1)

> Describe the importance of green chemistry and sustainable chemistry. (1.1)

> Define *hypothesis, scientific law, scientific theory,* and *scientific model,* and explain their relationships in science. (1.2)

> Define *risk* and *benefit,* and give an example of each. (1.3)

> Estimate a desirability quotient from benefit and risk data. (1.3)

> Distinguish basic research from applied research. (1.4)

> Differentiate: mass and weight; physical and chemical change; and physical and chemical properties. (1.5)

> Classify matter according to state and as mixture, substance, compound, and/or element. (1.6)

> Assign proper units of measurement to observations, and manipulate units in conversions. (1.7)

> Calculate the density, mass, or volume of an object given the other two quantities. (1.8)

> Distinguish between heat and temperature. (1.9)

> Explain how the temperature scales are related. (1.9)

> Use critical thinking to evaluate claims and statements. (1.10)

> Define green chemistry.

> Describe how *green chemistry* reduces risk and prevents environmental problems.

A SCIENCE FOR ALL SEASONS We invite you to join us on a journey toward a horizon of infinite possibilities. We will be exploring chemistry, a field of endeavor that pervades every aspect of our lives. Look around you. Everything you see is made of chemicals: the food we eat, the air we breathe, the clothes we wear, the buildings that shelter us, the vehicles we ride in, and the medicines that help keep us healthy.

Everything we *do* also involves chemistry. Whenever we eat a sandwich, bathe, listen to music, drive a car, or ride a bicycle, we use chemistry. Even when we are asleep, chemical reactions go on constantly throughout our bodies.

Chemistry is everywhere, not just in laboratories. Chemistry occurs in soil and rocks, in waters, in clouds, and in us. Knowledge of chemistry enhances our understanding of climate change, helps to provide food for Earth's increasing population, and is crucial to the development and production of sustainable fuels.

▲ Organic foods are not chemical-free. In fact, they are made entirely of chemicals!

Chemistry also affects society as a whole. Developments in health and medicine involve a lot of chemistry. The astounding advances in biotechnology—such as genetic engineering, new drugs, improvements to nutrition, and much more—have a huge chemical component. Understanding and solving environmental problems require knowledge and application of chemistry. The worldwide issues of climate change and ozone depletion involve chemistry.

So what is chemistry anyway? We explore that question in some detail in Section 1.5. And just what is a chemical? The word *chemical* may sound ominous, but it is simply a name for any material. Gold, water, salt, sugar, air, coffee, ice cream, a computer, a pencil—all are chemicals or are made entirely of chemicals.

Material things undergo changes. Sometimes these changes occur naturally—maple leaves turn yellow and red in autumn. Often, we change material things intentionally, to make them more useful, as when we light a candle or cook an egg. Most of these changes are accompanied by changes in energy. For example, when we burn gasoline, the process releases energy that we can use to propel an automobile. Chemistry helps to define life. How do we differentiate a living collection of chemicals from the same assembly of chemicals in a dead organism or sample of inanimate matter that was never alive? A living set of molecules can replicate itself and has a way to harvest energy from its surroundings.

Our bodies are marvelous chemical factories. They take the food we eat and turn it into skin, bones, blood, and muscle, while also generating energy for all of our activities. This amazing chemical factory operates continuously 24 hours a day for as long as you live. Chemistry affects your own life every moment, and it also transforms society as a whole. Chemistry shapes our civilization.

1.1 Science and Technology: The Roots of Knowledge

Learning Objectives ❯ Define science, chemistry, technology, and alchemy.
❯ Describe the importance of green chemistry and sustainable chemistry.

1. Why should I study chemistry?
Chemistry is a part of many areas of study and affects everything you do. Knowledge of chemistry helps you to understand many facets of modern life.

Chemistry is a *science*, but what is science? **Science** is the primary means by which we obtain new knowledge. It is an accumulation of knowledge about nature and our physical world and of theories that we use to explain that knowledge. **Chemistry** is that area of knowledge that deals with the behavior of matter.

Science and technology often are confused with one another. **Technology** is the application of knowledge for practical purposes. Technology arose in prehistoric times, long before science. The discovery of fire was quickly followed by cooking, baking pottery, and smelting ores to produce metals such as copper. The discovery of fermentation led to beer and winemaking. Such tasks were accomplished without an understanding of the scientific principles involved.

About 2500 years ago, Greek philosophers attempted to formulate *theories* of chemistry—rational explanations of the behavior of matter. Those philosophers generally did not test their theories by experimentation. Nevertheless, their view of nature—attributed mainly to Aristotle—dominated Western thinking about the workings of the material world for the next 20 centuries.

The experimental roots of chemistry lie in **alchemy**, a primitive form of chemistry that flourished in Europe from about 500 to 1500 C.E. Alchemists searched for a "philosopher's stone" that would turn cheaper metals into gold and for an elixir that would bring eternal life. Although they never achieved these goals, alchemists discovered many new chemical substances and perfected techniques such as distillation and extraction that are still used today.

Toward the end of the Middle Ages, a real science of chemistry began to see light. The behavior of matter began to be examined by experimentation. Theories that arose from that experimentation gradually pushed aside the authority of early philosophers. The 1800s saw a virtual explosion of knowledge as more scientists studied the behavior of matter in breadth and depth. Through the 1950s and early 1960s, science in general and chemistry in particular saw increasing relevance in our lives. Laboratory-developed fertilizers, alloys, drugs, and plastics were incorporated into everyday living. DuPont, one of the largest chemical companies in the world, used its slogan "Better Living Through Chemistry" with great effect through the 1970s.

For most of human history, people exploited Earth's resources, giving little thought to the consequences. Rachel Carson, a biologist, was an early proponent of environmental awareness. The main theme of her book *Silent Spring* (1962) was that our use of chemicals to control insects was threatening to destroy all life—including ourselves. People in the pesticide industries and their allies roundly denounced Carson as a propagandist, though some scientists rallied to support her. By the late 1960s, however, the threatened extinction of several species of birds and the disappearance of fish from many rivers, lakes, and areas of the ocean caused many scientists to move into Carson's camp. Popular support for Carson's views became overwhelming.

In response to growing public concern, chemists have in recent years developed the concept of **green chemistry**, which uses materials and processes that are intended to prevent or reduce pollution at its source. This approach was further extended in the first decade of the twenty-first century to include the idea of **sustainable chemistry**—chemistry designed to meet the needs of the present generation without compromising the needs of future generations. Sustainability preserves resources and aspires to produce environmentally friendly products from renewable resources.

Chemicals themselves are neither good nor bad. Their misuse can indeed cause problems, but properly used, chemicals have saved countless millions of lives and have improved the quality of life for the entire planet. Chlorine and ozone kill bacteria that cause dreadful diseases. Drugs and vaccinations relieve pain and suffering. Fertilizers such as ammonia increase food production, and petroleum provides fuel for heating, cooling, lighting, and transportation. In short, chemistry has provided ordinary people with luxuries that were not available even to the mightiest rulers in ages past. Chemicals are essential to our lives—life itself would be impossible without chemicals.

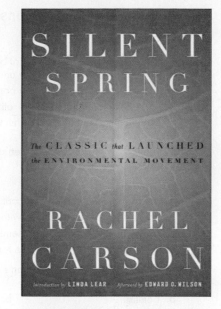

▲ Rachel Carson's *Silent Spring* was one of the first publications to point out a number of serious environmental issues.

2. Is it true that chemicals are bad for us?

Everything you can see, smell, taste, or touch is either a chemical or is made of chemicals. Chemicals are neither good nor bad in themselves. They can be put to good use, bad use, or anything in between.

▲ A century ago, contaminated drinking water was often the cause of outbreaks of cholera and other diseases. Modern water treatment uses chemicals to remove solid matter and kill disease-causing bacteria, making water safe to drink.

SELF-ASSESSMENT Questions

Select the best answer or response.

1. Which of the following would not be a technological advancement made possible by understanding chemistry?
   a. Cooking pans coated with a nonstick surface like Teflon®
   b. The ability to change lead or other metals into gold
   c. Lengthening the life span of human beings using medicines
   d. Alternate fuel sources to lessen our dependence on petroleum

2. Alchemy is
   a. philosophical speculation about nature
   b. chemistry that is concerned with environmental issues
   c. the beginnings of modern chemistry
   d. the application of knowledge for practical purposes

3. The main theme of Rachel Carson's *Silent Spring* was that life on Earth would be destroyed by
   a. botulism   b. nuclear war
   c. overpopulation   d. pesticides

4. A goal of green chemistry is to
   a. produce cheap green dyes
   b. provide great wealth for corporations
   c. reduce pollution
   d. turn deserts into forests and grasslands

5. Which best exemplifies sustainable chemistry?
   a. Toluene, extracted from coal, is used to make TNT, an explosive.
   b. Paper is made from hardwood trees.
   c. Minerals mined in South America are used in China to make LCD screens.
   d. Plastic bottles are made from both petroleum and recycled plastic.

Answers: 1, b; 2, c; 3, d; 4, c; 5, b

1.2 Science: Reproducible, Testable, Tentative, Predictive, and Explanatory

Learning Objectives ❯ Define *hypothesis, scientific law, scientific theory,* and *scientific model,* and explain their relationships in science.

We have defined science, but science has certain characteristics that distinguish it from other studies.

Scientists often disagree about what is and what will be, but does that make science merely a guessing game in which one guess is as good as another? Not at all. Science is based on observations and experimental tests of our assumptions. However, it is not a collection of unalterable facts. We cannot force nature to fit our preconceived ideas. Science is good at correcting errors, but it is not especially good at establishing truths. Science is an unfinished work. The things we have learned from science fill millions of books and scholarly journals, but what we know pales in comparison to what we do not yet know.

Scientific Data Must Be Reproducible

Scientists collect data by making careful observations. Data must be *reproducible*—the data reported by a scientist must also be observable by other scientists. Careful measurements are required, and conditions are thoroughly controlled and described. Scientific work is not fully accepted until it has undergone *peer review* and has been verified by other scientists.

Observations, though, are just the beginning of the intellectual processes of science. There are many different paths to scientific discovery, and there is no general set of rules. Science is not a straightforward process for cranking out discoveries.

Scientific Hypotheses Are Testable

Scientists do not merely state what they feel may be true. They develop *testable* **hypotheses** (educated guesses, *hypothesis* in the singular) as tentative explanations of observed data. They test these hypotheses by designing and performing experiments. Experimentation distinguishes science from the arts and humanities. In the humanities, people still argue about some of the same questions that were debated thousands of years ago: What is truth? What is beauty? These arguments persist because the proposed answers cannot be tested and confirmed objectively.

Like artists and poets, scientists are often imaginative and creative. The tenets of science, however, are *testable*. Experiments can be devised to answer most scientific questions. Ideas can be tested and thereby either verified or rejected. Some ideas may be accepted for a while, but rejected when further studies are performed. For example, it was long thought that exercise caused muscles to tire and become sore from a buildup of lactic acid. Recent findings suggest instead that lactic acid *delays* muscle tiredness and that the cause of tired, sore muscles may be related to other factors, including leakage of calcium ions inside muscle cells, which weakens contractions. Through many experiments, scientists have established a firm foundation of knowledge, allowing each new generation to build on the past.

Large amounts of scientific data are often summarized in brief verbal or mathematical statements called **scientific laws**. For example, Robert Boyle (1627–1691), an Irishman, conducted many experiments on gases. In each experiment, he founded *Boyle's law*, which said that the volume of the gas decreased when the pressure applied to the gas was increased. Mathematically, Boyle's law can be written as $PV = k$, where P is the pressure on a gas, V is its volume, and k is a constant. If P is doubled, V will be cut in half. Scientific laws are *universal*. Under the specified conditions, they hold everywhere in the observable universe.

Scientific Theories Are Tentative and Predictive

Scientists organize the knowledge they accumulate on a framework of detailed explanations called theories. A **theory** represents the best current explanation for a phenomenon, but it is always *tentative*. In the future, a theory may have to be modified or even discarded as a result of new observations, for the body of knowledge that is science is rapidly growing and always changing.

Theories organize scientific knowledge and are also useful for their *predictive* value. Predictions based on theories are tested by further experiments. Theories that make successful predictions are usually widely accepted by the scientific community. A theory developed in one area is often found to apply in others.

3. Why do scientists so often say "more study is needed"?
More data help scientists refine a hypothesis so that it is better defined, clearer, or more applicable.

A Possible Scientific Process

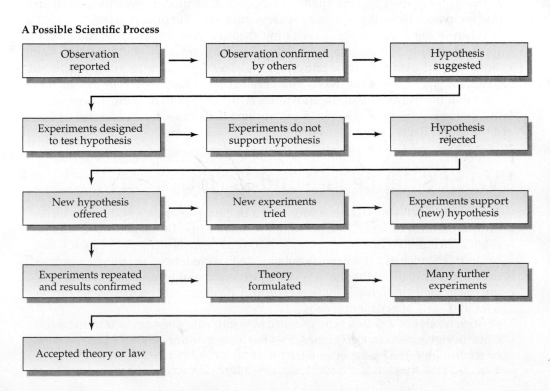

Observation reported → Observation confirmed by others → Hypothesis suggested →

Experiments designed to test hypothesis → Experiments do not support hypothesis → Hypothesis rejected →

New hypothesis offered → New experiments tried → Experiments support (new) hypothesis →

Experiments repeated and results confirmed → Theory formulated → Many further experiments →

Accepted theory or law

▲ A molecular model of diamond shows the tightly linked, rigid structure that explains why diamonds are so hard.

Scientific Models Are Explanatory

Scientists often use models to help *explain* complicated phenomena. A *scientific model* uses tangible items or pictures to represent invisible processes. For example, the invisible particles of a gas can be visualized as billiard balls, or as dots or circles on paper. We know that when a glass of water is left standing for a period of time, the water disappears through the process of evaporation (Figure 1.1).

▶ **Figure 1.1** The evaporation of water. (a) When a container of water is left standing open to the air, the water slowly disappears. (b) Scientists explain evaporation in terms of the motion of molecules.

● = Water molecule

● = Air (nitrogen or oxygen) molecule

Scientists explain evaporation with the *kinetic-molecular theory*, which proposes that a liquid is composed of tiny particles called molecules that are in constant motion and are held together by forces of attraction. The molecules collide with one another like billiard balls on a playing table. Sometimes, a "hard break" of billiard balls causes one ball to fly off the table. Likewise, some of the molecules of a liquid gain enough energy through collisions to overcome the attraction to their neighbors, escape from the liquid, and disperse among the widely spaced molecules in air. The water in the glass gradually disappears. This model gives us more than a name for evaporation. It gives us an understanding of the phenomenon.

When doing experiments, developing theories, and constructing models, it is important to note that an apparent connection—a *correlation*—between two items is not necessarily evidence that one *causes* the other. For example, many people suffer from allergies in the fall when goldenrod is in bloom. However, research has shown that the main cause of these allergies is ragweed pollen. There is a correlation between the blooming of goldenrod and autumnal allergies, but goldenrod pollen is not the cause. Ragweed happens to bloom at the same time.

What Science is—and is Not

Responsible news media generally try to be fair, presenting both sides of an issue regardless of where the prevailing evidence lies. In science, the evidence often indicates that one side is simply wrong. Scientists strive for accuracy, not balance. The idea of a flat Earth is not given equal credence to a (roughly) spherical Earth. Only ideas that have survived experimental testing and peer review are considered valid. Ideas that are beautiful, elegant, or even sacrosanct can be invalidated by experimental data.

Science is not a democratic process. Majority rule does not determine what constitutes sound science. Science does not accept notions that are proven false or remain untested by experiment.

The Limitations of Science

Some people say that we could solve many of our problems if we would only attack them using the methods of science. Why can't the procedures of the scientist be applied to social, political, ethical, and economic problems? And why do scientists disagree over environmental, social, and political issues?

Disagreement often results from the inability to control *variables*. A **variable** is something that can change over the course of an experiment. If, for example, we wanted to study in the laboratory how the volume of a gas varies with changes in pressure, we could hold constant such factors as temperature and the amount and kind of gas. If, on the other hand, we wanted to determine the effect of low levels of a particular pollutant on the health of a human population, we would find it almost impossible to control such variables as individuals' diets, habits, and exposure to other substances, all of which affect health. Although we could make observations, formulate hypotheses, and conduct experiments on the health effect of the pollutant, interpretation of the results would be difficult and subject to disagreement.

SELF-ASSESSMENT Questions

Select the best answer or response.

1. To gather information to support or discredit a hypothesis, a scientist
   a. conducts experiments
   b. consults an authority
   c. establishes a scientific law
   d. formulates a scientific theory

2. The statement that mass is always conserved when chemical changes occur is an example of a scientific
   a. experiment
   b. hypothesis
   c. law
   d. theory

3. A successful theory
   a. can be used to make predictions
   b. eventually becomes a scientific law
   c. is not subject to further testing
   d. is permanently accepted as true

4. Which of the following is *not* a hypothesis?
   a. UFOs frequent the Bermuda Triangle, which accounts for all of the oddities in the region.
   b. Ice floats on water because of the air bubbles that get trapped during the freezing process.
   c. Oxygen reacts with silver to form rust.
   d. Synthetic hormones have the same effect in an organism as the naturally occurring ones.

5. Which of the following is a requirement of scientific research?
   a. It must be approved by a committee of scientists and politicians.
   b. It must benefit the Earth and improve human life.
   c. It must be experimentally tested and peer reviewed for validity.
   d. It must be balanced and weigh the pros and cons of the results.

6. Social problems are difficult to solve because it is difficult to
   a. control variables
   b. discount paranormal events
   c. form hypotheses
   d. formulate theories

Answers: 1, a; 2, c; 3, a; 4, a; 5, c; 6, a

1.3 Science and Technology: Risks and Benefits

Learning Objectives ❯ Define *risk* and *benefit*, and give an example of each.
❯ Estimate a desirability quotient from benefit and risk data.

Most people recognize that society has benefited from science and technology, but many seem not to realize that there are risks associated with every technological advance. How can we determine when the benefits outweigh the risks? One approach, called **risk–benefit analysis**, involves the estimation of a desirability quotient (DQ).

$$DQ = \frac{Benefits}{Risks}$$

A *benefit* is anything that promotes well-being or has a positive effect. Benefits may be economic, social, or psychological. A *risk* is any hazard that leads to loss or injury. Some of the risks associated with modern technology have led to disease,

It DOES Matter!

For most people of northern European ancestry, milk is a wholesome food. Milk's benefits far outweigh its risks. Other ethnic groups have high rates of lactose intolerance among adults, and the desirability quotient for milk is much smaller.

death, economic loss, and environmental deterioration. Risks and benefits may involve one individual, a group, or society as a whole.

Every technological advance has both benefits and risks. For example, a car provides the benefit of rapid, convenient transportation. But driving a car involves risk—individual risks of injury or death in a traffic accident and societal risks such as pollution and climate change. Most people consider the benefits of driving a car to outweigh the risks.

Weighing the benefits and risks connected with a product is more difficult when considering a group of people. For example, pasteurized low-fat milk is a safe, nutritious beverage for many people of northern European descent. Some people in this group can't tolerate lactose, the sugar in milk. And some are allergic to milk proteins. But since these problems are relatively uncommon among people of northern European descent, the benefits of milk are large and the risks are small, resulting in a large DQ for this group. However, adults of other ethnic backgrounds often are lactose-intolerant, and for them, milk has a small DQ. Thus, milk is not always suitable for use in programs to relieve malnutrition.

Other technologies provide large benefits and present large risks. For these technologies the DQ is uncertain. An example is the conversion of coal to liquid fuels. Most people find liquid fuels to be very beneficial in transportation, home heating, and industry. There are great risks associated with coal conversion, however, including risks to coal-mine workers, air and water pollution, and exposure of conversion plant workers to toxic chemicals. The result, again, is an uncertain DQ and political controversy.

There are yet other problems in risk–benefit analysis. Some technologies benefit one group of people while presenting a risk to another. For example, gold plating and gold wires in computers and other consumer electronics benefit the consumer, providing greater reliability and longer life. But when the devices are scrapped, small-scale attempts to recover the gold often produce serious pollution in the area of recovery. Difficult political decisions are needed in such cases.

Other technologies provide current benefits but present future risks. For example, although nuclear power now provides useful electricity, improperly stored wastes from nuclear power plants might present hazards for centuries. Thus, the use of nuclear power is controversial.

Science and technology obviously involve *both* risks and benefits. The determination of benefits is almost entirely a social judgment. Although risk assessment also involves social and personal decisions, it can often be greatly aided by scientific investigation. Understanding the chemistry behind many of the technological advancements will help you make a more accurate risk–benefit analysis for you, your family, your community, and the world.

CONCEPTUAL Example 1.1 | Risk–Benefit Analysis

Heroin is thought by some to be more effective than other drugs for the relief of severe pain. For example, heroin is a legal prescription drug in the United Kingdom. People can become addicted to heroin with continued use in as little as three days, and recreational use often renders addicts unable to function in society. Do a risk–benefit analysis of the use of heroin in treating the pain of **(a)** a young athlete with a broken leg and **(b)** a terminally ill cancer patient.

Solution
a. The heroin would provide the benefit of pain relief, but its use for such purposes has been judged to be too risky by the U.S. Food and Drug Administration. The DQ is low.
b. The heroin would provide the benefit of pain relief. The risk of addiction in a dying person is irrelevant. Heroin is banned for any purpose in the United States. The DQ is uncertain. (Both answers involve judgments that are not clearly scientific; people can differ in their assessments of each.)

▪ EXERCISE 1.1A

Chloramphenicol is a powerful antibacterial drug that often destroys bacteria unaffected by other drugs. It is highly dangerous to some individuals, however, causing fatal aplastic anemia in about 1 in 30,000 people. Do a risk–benefit analysis of administering chloramphenicol to **(a)** sick farm animals, whose milk or meat might contain residues of the drug, and **(b)** a person with Rocky Mountain spotted fever facing a high probability of death or permanent disability.

▪ EXERCISE 1.1B

The drug thalidomide was introduced in the 1950s as a sleeping aid. It was found to be a *teratogen*, a substance that causes birth defects, and it was removed from the market after children in Europe whose mothers took it during pregnancy were born with deformed limbs. Recently, thalidomide has been investigated as an effective treatment for the lesions caused by leprosy and for Kaposi's sarcoma (a form of cancer often suffered by AIDS patients). Do a risk–benefit analysis of prescribing thalidomide to **(a)** all women and **(b)** women with AIDS.

Risks of Death

Our perception of risk often differs from the actual risk we face. Some people fear flying but readily assume the risk of an automobile trip. The odds of dying from various causes are listed in Table 1.1.

Table 1.1	Approximate Lifetime Risks of Death in the United States		
Action	Lifetime Risk[a]	Approximate Lifetime Odds	Details/Assumptions
All causes	1	1 in 1	We all die of something.
Cigarettes	0.25	1 in 4	Cigarette smoking, 1 pack/day
Heart disease	0.20	1 in 5	Heart attacks, congestive heart failure
All cancers	0.14	1 in 7	All cancers
Motor vehicles	0.01	1 in 100	Death in motor vehicle accident
Home accidents	0.010	1 in 100	Home accident death
Natural forces	0.0003	1 in 3360	Heat, cold, storm, quakes, etc.
Peanut butter (aflatoxin)	0.00060	1 in 1700	4 tablespoons peanut butter a day
Airplane accidents	0.00005	1 in 20,000	Death in aircraft crashes
Terrorist attack[b]	0.00077	1 in 1300	One 9/11-level attack per year
Terrorist attack[c]	0.000077	1 in 13,000	One 9/11-level attack every 10 years

[a] The odds of dying of a particular cause in a given year are calculated by dividing the population by the number of deaths by that cause in that year. Lifetime odds of dying of a specific cause are calculated by dividing the one-year odds by the life expectancy of a person born in that year.

[b] Unlikely scenario

[c] More reasonable scenario

Science is a unified whole. Common scientific laws apply everywhere and on all levels of organization. The various areas of science interact and support one another. Accordingly, chemistry is not only useful in itself but also fundamental to other scientific disciplines. The application of chemical principles has revolutionized biology and medicine, has provided materials for powerful computers used in mathematics, and has profoundly influenced other fields such as psychology. The social goals of better health, nutrition, and housing are dependent to a large extent on the knowledge and techniques of chemists. Recycling of basic materials—paper, glass, and metals—involves chemical processes.

▶ **Figure 1.2** Chemistry has a central role among the sciences.

Chemistry is indeed a central science (Figure 1.2). There is no area of our daily lives that is not affected by chemistry. Many modern materials have been developed by chemists, and even more amazing materials are in the works.

Chemistry is also important to the *economy* of industrial nations. In the United States, the chemical industry makes thousands of consumer products, including personal-care products, agricultural products, plastics, coatings, soaps, and detergents. It produces 80% of the materials used to make medicines. The U.S. chemical industry is one of the country's largest industries, with sales of almost $700 billion per year, accounting for 10% of all U.S. exports. It employs 800,000 workers, including scientists, engineers, and technicians, and generates nearly 11% of all U.S. patents. Despite widespread fear of chemicals, workers in the chemical industry are five times safer than the average worker in the U.S. manufacturing sector.

SELF-ASSESSMENT Questions

Select the best answer or response.

1. Our perception of risk is
   a. always based on sound science
   b. always higher than actual risk
   c. always lower than actual risk
   d. often different from actual risk

2. Among the following, the highest risk of death (see Table 1.1) is associated with
   a. heart disease   b. peanut butter
   c. cancer   d. car wreck

3. Chemistry is called the central science because
   a. the chemical industry is based mainly in the U.S. Midwest
   b. it is the core course in all college curricula
   c. it is fundamental to other scientific disciplines
   d. it is the source of many environmental problems

4. The U.S. chemical industry is
   a. patently unsafe
   b. the source of nearly all pollution
   c. the source of many consumer products
   d. unimportant to the U.S. economy

Answers: 1, d; 2, a; 3, c; 4, c

1.4 Solving Society's Problems: Scientific Research

Learning Objective › Distinguish basic research from applied research.

Chemistry is a powerful force in shaping society today. Chemical research not only plays a pivotal role in other sciences, but it also has a profound influence on society as a whole. Chemists, like other scientists, do one of two categories of research: *applied research* or *basic research*. The two often overlap, and it isn't always possible to label a particular project as one or the other.

Applied Research

Some chemists test polluted soil, air, and water. Others analyze foods, fuels, cosmetics, detergents, and drugs. Still others synthesize new substances for use as drugs or pesticides or formulate plastics for new applications. These activities are examples of **applied research**—work oriented toward the solution of a particular problem in an industry or the environment.

Among the most monumental accomplishments in applied research were those of George Washington Carver. Born in slavery, Carver attended Simpson College and later graduated from Iowa State University. A botanist and agricultural chemist, Carver taught and did research at Tuskegee Institute. He developed more than 300 products from peanuts, from peanut butter to hand cleaner to insulating board. He created other new products from sweet potatoes, pecans, and clay. Carver also taught Southern farmers to rotate crops and to use legumes to replenish the nitrogen removed from the soil by cotton crops. Carver's work helped to revitalize the economy of the South.

▲ George Washington Carver (1864–1943), research scientist, in his laboratory at Tuskegee Institute.

Basic Research: The Search for Knowledge

Many chemists are involved in **basic research**, the search for knowledge for its own sake. Some chemists work out the fine points of atomic and molecular structure. Others measure the intricate energy changes that accompany complex chemical reactions. Some synthesize new compounds and determine their properties. Done for the sheer joy of unraveling the secrets of nature and discovering order in our universe, basic research is characterized by the absence of any predictable, marketable product.

Lack of a product doesn't mean that basic research is useless. Far from it! Findings from basic research often *are* applied at a later time. This may be the hope, but it is not the main goal of the researcher. In fact, most of our modern technology is based on results obtained in basic research. Without this base of factual information, technological innovation would be haphazard and slow.

Applied research is carried out mainly by industries seeking to gain a competitive edge by developing a novel, better, or more salable product. The ultimate aim of such research is usually profit for the stockholders. Basic research is conducted mainly at universities and research institutes. Most support for this research comes from federal and state governments and foundations, although some larger industries also support it.

One example of basic research that was later applied to improving human welfare is the work of Gertrude Elion and George Hitchings, who in the 1940s and 1950s studied compounds called *purines* in an attempt to understand their role in the chemistry of the cell. This basic research at Burroughs Wellcome Research Laboratories in North Carolina led to the discovery of a number of valuable new drugs that facilitate organ transplants and treat various diseases such as gout, malaria, herpes, and cancer. Elion and Hitchings shared the 1988 Nobel Prize in Physiology or Medicine, and in 1991, Elion became the first woman to be inducted into the National Inventors Hall of Fame.

Another example involves the work of two physicists. In the 1920s, Otto Stern and Walther Gerlach of Germany determined that certain atomic nuclei (Chapter 3) have a property called *spin*, which causes these nuclei to act as tiny magnets. Isidor Isaac Rabi at Columbia University later developed a method for recording the magnetic properties of atomic nuclei. For their basic research in studying and measuring these minuscule magnetic fields, Stern and Rabi won the Nobel Prize in Physics in 1943 and 1944, respectively.

In the 1940s, teams led by Edward M. Purcell and Felix Bloch used nuclear spins to work out the structure of complicated molecules. Their technique, called *nuclear magnetic resonance* (NMR), has become a major tool of chemists for determining molecular structure. Purcell and Bloch shared the Nobel Prize in Physics in 1952 for their research. Still later, in the 1960s, Paul Lauterbur, Peter Mansfield, and other scientists applied the principles of NMR to performing scans of the human body.

4. Why do scientists bother with studies that have no immediate application?
The results of basic research may not have an immediate practical use. However, basic research extends our understanding of the world and can be considered an investment in the future. And basic research often *finds* a practical application. For example, *zone refining* is a method developed in the early twentieth century for producing extremely pure solids. It had little practical application until the advent of integrated circuits. Zone refining is now used to produce the ultrapure silicon needed for every electronic device on Earth.

It DOES Matter!

Gertrude Elion won a Nobel Prize for her basic research on purines. Her work has led to many applications in pharmaceuticals and medicine. Many important modern applications started out with basic research.

This noninvasive diagnostic technique, called *magnetic resonance imaging* (MRI), has replaced many exploratory surgical operations and made other surgical procedures much more precise. Lauterbur and Mansfield won the 2003 Nobel Prize in Physiology or Medicine for their work.

Importance of Basic Research

"There are two compelling reasons why society must support basic science. One is substantial: The theoretical physics of yesterday is the nuclear defense of today; the obscure synthetic chemistry of yesterday is curing disease today. The other reason is cultural. The essence of our civilization is to explore and analyze the nature of man and his surroundings. As proclaimed in the Bible in the Book of Proverbs: 'Where there is no vision, the people perish.'"

Arthur Kornberg (1918–2007), American biochemist and recipient of Nobel Prize in Physiology or Medicine, 1959

SELF-ASSESSMENT Questions

Classify each of the following as (a) basic research or (b) applied research.

1. A chemist develops a better, longer lasting, pain reliever.
2. A researcher investigates the responses a plant has to drought conditions.
3. A scientist seeks to extract biologically active compounds from sea sponges.
4. Scientists create rBST to improve milk production in cows.

Answers: 1, b; 2, a; 3, a; 4, b

1.5 Chemistry: A Study of Matter and Its Changes

Learning Objective ❯ Differentiate: mass and weight; physical and chemical changes; and physical and chemical properties.

As we have noted, chemistry is often defined as the study of matter and the changes it undergoes. Because the entire physical universe is made up of matter and energy, the field of chemistry extends from atoms to stars, from rocks to living organisms. Now let's look at matter a little more closely.

Matter is the stuff that makes up all material things. It is anything that occupies space and has mass. Matter has *mass*. You can weigh it. Wood, sand, water, air, and people have mass and are, therefore, matter. **Mass** is a measure of the quantity of matter that an object contains. The greater the mass of an object, the more difficult it is to change its velocity. You can easily deflect a fist-sized tennis ball coming toward you at 30 meters per second, but you would have difficulty stopping an iron cannonball of that size moving at the same speed. A cannonball has more mass than a tennis ball of equal size.

The mass of an object does not vary with location. An astronaut has the same mass on the moon as on Earth. In contrast, **weight** measures a force. On Earth, it measures the force of attraction between our planet and the mass in question. On the moon, where gravity is one-sixth that on Earth, an astronaut weighs only one-sixth as much as on Earth (Figure 1.3). Weight varies with gravity. Mass does not.

▲ **Figure 1.3** Astronaut John W. Young leaps from the lunar surface, where gravity pulls at him with only one-sixth as much force as on Earth.

Q: *If an astronaut has a mass of 72 kg, what would be his mass on the moon? If an astronaut weighs 180 lb on Earth, what would he weigh on the moon?*

CONCEPTUAL **Example 1.2**	Mass and Weight

Gravity on the planet Mercury is 3/8th that on Earth. **(a)** What would be the mass on Mercury of a person who has a mass of 80 kilograms (kg) on Earth? **(b)** What would be the weight on Mercury of a person who weighs 160 pounds (lb) on Earth?

Solution

a. The person's mass would be the same as on Earth (80 kg). The quantity of matter has not changed.

b. The person would weigh only 0.375 × 160 lb = 60 lb; the force of attraction between Mercury and the person would be only 0.375 times that between Earth and the person.

▪ EXERCISE 1.2

At the surface of Venus, the force of gravity is 0.903 times that at Earth's surface. **(a)** What would be the mass of a 1.00-kg object on Venus? **(b)** How much would a man who weighs 198 lb on Earth weigh on the surface of Venus?

Physical and Chemical Properties

We can use our knowledge of chemistry to change matter to make it more useful. Chemists can change crude oil into gasoline, plastics, pesticides, drugs, detergents, and thousands of other products. Changes in matter are accompanied by changes in energy. Often, we change matter to extract part of its energy. For example, we burn gasoline to get energy to propel our automobiles.

To distinguish between samples of matter, we can compare their properties (Figure 1.4). A **physical property** of a substance is a characteristic or behavior that

 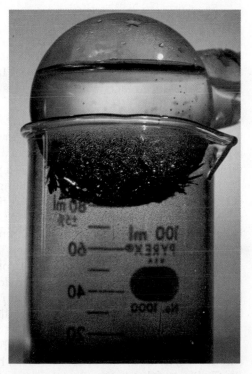

▲ **Figure 1.4** A comparison of the physical properties of two elements. Copper (left), obtained as pellets, can be hammered into thin foil or drawn into wire. Iodine (right) consists of brittle gray crystals that crumble into a powder when struck.

Q: *What additional physical properties of copper and iodine are apparent from the photographs?*

Table 1.2 Some Examples of Physical Properties

Property	Examples
Temperature	0 °C for ice water, 100 °C for boiling water.
Mass	A nickel weighs 5 g. A penny weighs 2.5 g.
Color	Sulfur is yellow. Bromine is reddish-brown.
Taste	Acids are sour. Bases are bitter.
Odor	Benzyl acetate smells like jasmine. Hydrogen sulfide smells like rotten eggs.
Boiling point	Water boils at 100 °C. Ethyl alcohol boils at 78.5 °C.
Hardness	Diamond is exceptionally hard. Sodium metal is soft.
Density	1.00 g/mL for water, 19.3 g/cm^3 for gold.

Table 1.3 Some Examples of Chemical Properties

Substance	Typical Chemical Property
Iron	rusts (combines with oxygen to form iron oxide).
Carbon	burns (combines with oxygen to form carbon dioxide).
Silver	tarnishes (combines with sulfur to form silver sulfide).
Nitroglycerin	explodes (decomposes to produce a mixture of gases).
Carbon monoxide	is toxic (combines with hemoglobin, causing anoxia).
Neon	is inert (does not react with anything).

can be observed or measured without generating new types of matter. Color, odor, and hardness are physical properties (Table 1.2). A **chemical property** describes how a substance reacts with other types of matter—how its basic building blocks can change (Table 1.3).

A **physical change** involves an alteration in the physical appearance of matter without changing its chemical identity or composition. An ice cube can melt to form a liquid, but it is still water. Melting is a physical change, and the temperature at which it occurs—the melting point—is a physical property.

A **chemical change** involves a change in the chemical identity of matter into other substances that are chemically different. In exhibiting a chemical property, matter undergoes a chemical change. At least one substance in the original matter is replaced by one or more new substances. Iron metal reacts with oxygen from the air to form rust (iron oxide). When sulfur burns in air, sulfur, which is made up of one type of atom, and oxygen (from air), which is made up of another type of atom, combine to form sulfur dioxide, which is made up of molecules that have sulfur and oxygen atoms in the ratio 1:2. A *molecule* is a group of atoms bound together as a single unit. (You'll learn more about atoms and molecules later.)

It is difficult at times to determine whether a change is physical or chemical. We can decide, though, on the basis of what happens to the composition or structure of the matter involved as well as the reversibility of the change. Physical changes are usually reversible while chemical changes are not. *Composition* refers to the types of atoms that are present and their relative proportions, and *structure* refers to the arrangement of those atoms with respect to one another or in space. A chemical change results in a change in composition or structure, whereas a physical change does not.

CONCEPTUAL Example 1.3 | Chemical Change and Physical Change

Which of the following events involve chemical changes, and which involve physical changes?

a. You trim your fingernails.
b. Lemon juice converts milk to curds and whey.
c. Molten aluminum is poured into a mold, where it solidifies.
d. Sodium chloride (table salt) is broken down into sodium metal and chlorine gas.

Solution

We examine each change and determine whether there has been a change in composition or structure. In other words, we ask, "Have any substances that are chemically different been created?" If so, the change is chemical; if not, it is physical.

a. Physical change: The composition of a fingernail is not changed by cutting.
b. Chemical change: The compositions of curds and whey are different from the composition of milk.
c. Physical change: Whether it is solid or liquid, aluminum is the same substance with the same composition.
d. Chemical change: New substances, sodium and chlorine, are formed.

■ EXERCISE 1.3

Which of the following events involve chemical changes, and which involve physical changes?

a. A steel wrench left out in the rain becomes rusty.
b. A stick of butter melts.
c. Charcoal briquettes are burned.
d. Peppercorns are ground into flakes.

SELF-ASSESSMENT Questions

Select the best answer or response.

1. Which of the following is *not* an example of matter?
   a. methane gas   **b.** steam
   c. silver   **d.** a rainbow

2. Which of the following is an example of matter?
   a. sunlight   **b.** air pollution
   c. magnetic field   **d.** ultraviolet light

3. Two identical items are taken from Earth to Mars, where they have
   a. both the same mass and the same weight as on Earth
   b. neither the same mass nor the same weight as on Earth
   c. the same mass but not the same weight as on Earth
   d. the same weight but not the same mass as on Earth

4. What kind of change alters the identity of a material.
   a. temperature
   b. physical
   c. pressure
   d. The other 3 do not change the identity

5. Bending glass tubing in a hot flame involves
   a. applied research   **b.** a chemical change
   c. an experiment   **d.** a physical change

6. Creating solid ice from liquid water involves
   a. adding energy to the water
   b. a physical change
   c. a chemical change
   d. creating a new substance

7. Which of the following is a chemical property?
   a. iodine vapor is purple
   b. copper tarnishes
   c. salt dissolves in water
   d. balsa wood is easily carved

8. Which of the following is an example of a physical change?
   a. A cake is baked from flour, baking powder, sugar, eggs, shortening, and milk.
   b. Milk left outside a refrigerator overnight turns sour.
   c. Sheep are sheared, and the wool is spun into yarn.
   d. Spiders eat flies and make silk.

9. Which of the following is an example of a chemical change?
   a. An egg is broken and poured into an eggnog mix.
   b. A tree is pruned, shortening some branches.
   c. A tree is watered and fertilized, and it grows larger.
   d. Frost forms on a cold windowpane.

Answers: 1. d; 2. b; 3. c; 4. b; 5. d; 6. b; 7. b; 8. c; 9. c

1.6 Classification of Matter

Learning Objective ❯ Classify matter according to state and as mixture, substance, compound, and/or element.

In this section, we examine three of the many ways of classifying matter. First, we look at the physical forms or *states of matter*.

The States of Matter

There are three familiar states of matter: solid, liquid, and gas (Figure 1.5). They can be classified by bulk properties (a *macro* view) or by arrangement of the particles that comprise them (a *molecular*, or *micro*, view). A **solid** object maintains its shape and volume regardless of its location. A **liquid** occupies a definite volume but assumes the shape of the portion of a container that it occupies. If you have 355 milliliters (mL) of a soft drink, you have 355 mL whether the soft drink is in a can, in a bottle, or, through a mishap, on the floor—which demonstrates another property of liquids. Unlike solids, liquids flow readily. A **gas** maintains neither shape nor volume. It expands to fill completely whatever container it occupies. Gases flow and are easily compressed. For example, enough air for many minutes of breathing can be compressed into a steel tank for SCUBA diving.

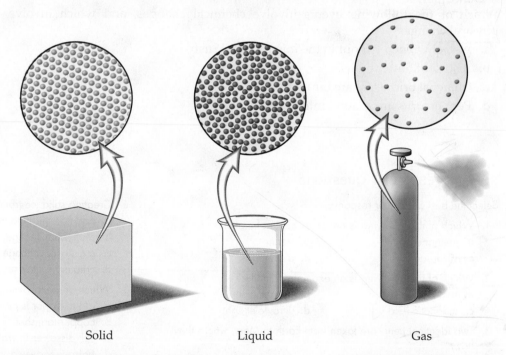

Solid   Liquid   Gas

▲ **Figure 1.5** The kinetic-molecular theory can be used to interpret (or explain) the bulk properties of *solids, liquids,* and *gases.* In solids, the particles are close together and in fixed positions. In liquids, the particles are close together, but they are free to move about. In gases, the particles are far apart and are in rapid random motion.

Q: *Based on this figure, why does a quart of water vapor weigh so much less than a quart of liquid water?*

Bulk properties of solids, liquids, and gases are explained using the kinetic-molecular theory. In solids, the particles are close together and in fixed positions. In liquids, the particles are close together, but they are free to move about. In gases, the particles are far apart and are in rapid random motion. We discuss the states of matter in more detail in Chapter 5.

Substances and Mixtures

Matter can be either pure or mixed (Figure 1.6). Pure matter is considered to be a **substance**, defined as having a definite, or fixed, composition that does not vary from one sample to another. Pure gold (24-karat gold) consists entirely of gold atoms. It is a substance. All samples of pure water are comprised of molecules consisting of two hydrogen atoms and one oxygen atom. Water is a substance.

The composition of a **mixture** of two or more substances is variable. The substances retain their identities. They do not change chemically; they simply mix. Mixtures can be separated by physical means. Mixtures can be either *homogeneous* or *heterogeneous*. All parts of a homogeneous mixture have the same composition (Section 6.4) and the same appearance. A solution of salt in water is a homogeneous mixture. The proportions of salt and water can vary from one solution to another, but the water is still water and the salt remains salt. The two substances can be separated by physical means. For example, the water can be boiled away, leaving the salt behind.

Sand and water form a heterogeneous mixture. The appearance is not the same throughout. The grains of sand are different from the liquid water. Most things we deal with each day are heterogeneous mixtures. All you have to do is look at a computer, a book, a pen, or a person to see that different parts of those mixtures have different compositions. (Your hair is quite different from your skin, for example.)

Elements and Compounds

A *substance* is either an element or a compound. An **element** is one of the fundamental substances from which all material things are constructed. Elements cannot be broken down into simpler substances by any chemical process. There are more than 100 known elements, of which this book deals with only about a third. A list of all

▲ **Figure 1.6** A scheme for classifying matter. The "molecular-level" views are of gold, an *element*; water, a *compound*; 12-karat gold, a *homogeneous mixture* of silver and gold; and the contents of a prospector's pan, a *heterogeneous mixture* of gold flakes in water.

elements appears on the inside front cover. Oxygen, carbon, sulfur, aluminum, and iron are familiar elements.

A **compound** is a substance made up of two or more elements chemically combined in a fixed ratio. For example, water is a compound because it has fixed proportions of hydrogen (H) and oxygen (O). Aluminum oxide (the "sand" on sandpaper), carbon dioxide, and iron disulfide (FeS_2, "fool's gold") are other compounds.

Because elements are so fundamental to our study of chemistry, we find it useful to refer to them in a shorthand form. Each element can be represented by a **chemical symbol** made up of one or two letters derived from the name of the element. Symbols for the elements are listed in the Table of Atomic Masses (inside front cover). The first letter of a symbol is always capitalized. The second (if there are two) is always lowercase. It makes a difference. For example, Co is the symbol for cobalt, a metallic element, but CO is the formula for carbon monoxide, a poisonous compound.

A chemical symbol in a formula stands for one atom of the element. If more than one atom is included in a formula, a subscript number is used after the symbol. For example, the formula H_2 represents two atoms of hydrogen, and the formula CH_4 stands for one atom of carbon and four atoms of hydrogen. Mixtures do not have such formulas because a mixture does not have a fixed composition.

The elements' symbols are the alphabet of chemistry. Most are based on the English names of the elements, but a few are based on Latin and Greek names. For example, the symbol for gold is Au from the Latin word *aurum*, and lead's symbol is Pb from the Latin *plumbum*. (The latter is also the origin of the word *plumbing*, because lead was used for plumbing pipes and fittings until the 1960s.)

5. Can we change lead into gold?

One element cannot be changed into another element by chemical reactions. An element cannot be created or destroyed, although an element can be extracted from a mixture or compound containing the element.

CONCEPTUAL Example 1.4 | Elements and Compounds

Which of the following represent elements and which represent compounds?

C   Cu   HI   BN   In   HBr

Solution

The periodic table shows that C, Cu, and In represent elements (each is a single symbol). HI, BN, and HBr are each composed of two symbols and represent compounds.

▪ **EXERCISE 1.4A**

Which of the following represent elements, and which represent compounds?

He   CuO   No   NO   KF   Os

▪ **EXERCISE 1.4B**

How many *different* elements are represented in the list in Exercise 1.4A?

Atoms and Molecules

An **atom** is the smallest characteristic part of an element. Each element is composed of atoms of a particular kind. For example, the element copper is made up of copper atoms, and gold is made up of gold atoms. All copper atoms are alike in a fundamental way and are different from gold atoms.

The smallest characteristic part of most compounds is a molecule. A **molecule** is a group of atoms bound together as a unit. All the molecules of a given compound have the same atoms in the same proportions. For example, all water molecules have two hydrogen atoms and one oxygen atom, as indicated by the formula, H_2O. We will discuss atoms in some detail in Chapter 2, and much of the focus of many later chapters is on molecules.

SELF-ASSESSMENT Questions

1. Which state of matter has a definite volume but not a definite shape?
   a. gas   **b.** compound   **c.** liquid   **d.** solid

2. Which of the following is a mixture?
   a. carbon   **b.** copper   **c.** silver   **d.** soda water

3. Which of the following is *not* an element?
   a. aluminum   **b.** brass   **c.** lead   **d.** sulfur

4. A compound can be separated into its elements
   a. by chemical means   **b.** by mechanical means
   c. by physical means   **d.** using a magnet

5. The smallest part of an element is a(n)
   a. atom   **b.** corpuscle   **c.** mass   **d.** molecule

6. The symbol for sodium is
   a. S   **b.** Na   **c.** Sd   **d.** So

7. Ar is the symbol for
   a. air   **b.** argon   **c.** aluminum   **d.** arsenic

Answers: 1, c; 2, d; 3, b; 4, a; 5, a; 6, b; 7, b

1.7 The Measurement of Matter

Learning Objective ❯ Assign proper units of measurement to observations, and manipulate units in conversions.

Accurate measurements of such properties as mass, volume, time, and temperature are essential to the compilation of dependable scientific data. Such data are of critical importance in all science-related fields. Measurements of temperature and blood pressure are routinely made in medicine, and modern medical diagnosis depends on a whole battery of other measurements, including careful chemical analyses of blood and urine.

The measurement system agreed on by scientists since 1960 is the *International System of Units*, or **SI units** (from the French *Système International*), a modernized version of the metric system established in France in 1791. Most countries use metric measures in everyday life. In the United States, these units are used mainly in science laboratories, although they are increasingly being used in commerce, especially in businesses with an international component. One-liter and two-liter bottled beverages are found everywhere, and sporting events often use metric measurements, such as the 100-meter dash. Figure 1.7 compares some metric and customary units.

▲ **Figure 1.7** Comparisons of metric and customary units of measure. The meter stick is 100 centimeters long and is slightly longer than the yardstick below it (1 m = 1.09 yd).

Q: *From this figure, approximately how many pounds are in a kilogram? Which two units are closer in size, the inch and centimeter or the quart and the liter?*

Because SI units are based on the decimal system, it is easy to convert from one unit to another. All measured quantities can be expressed in terms of the seven base units listed in Table 1.4. We use the first six in this text.

Table 1.4	The Seven SI Base Units	
Physical Quantity	Name of Unit	Symbol of Unit
Length	meter[a]	m
Mass	kilogram	kg
Time	second	s
Temperature	kelvin	K
Amount of substance	mole	mol
Electric current	ampere	A
Luminous intensity	candela	cd

[a] Spelled *metre* in most countries.

Exponential Numbers: Powers of Ten

Scientists deal with objects smaller than atoms and as large as the universe. We usually use exponential notation to describe the sizes of such objects. A number is in *exponential notation* when it is written as the product of a coefficient and a power of ten, such as 1.6×10^{-19} or 35×10^6. A number is said to be expressed in *scientific notation* when the coefficient has a value between 1 and 10.

An electron has a diameter of about 10^{-15} meter (m) and a mass of about 10^{-30} kilogram (kg). At the other extreme, a galaxy typically measures about 10^{23} m across and has a mass of about 10^{41} kg. It is difficult even to imagine numbers so small and so large. The accompanying figure offers some perspectives on size. Appendix A.2 provides a more detailed discussion of scientific notation.

Because measurements using the basic SI units can be of awkward magnitude, we often use exponential numbers. However, it is sometimes more convenient to use prefixes (Table 1.5) to indicate units larger and smaller than the base unit. The following examples show how prefixes and powers of ten are interconverted.

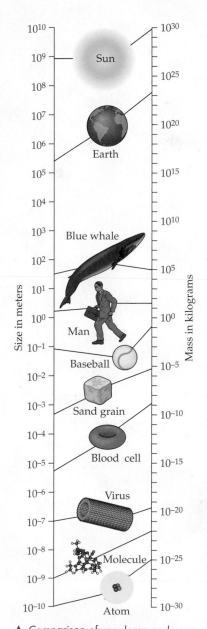

▲ Comparison of very large and very small objects is much easier with exponential notation.

Example 1.5 Prefixes and Powers of Ten

Convert each of the following measurements to a unit that replaces the power of ten by a prefix.

a. 2.89×10^{-6} g   **b.** 4.30×10^3 m

Solution

Our goal is to replace each power of ten with the appropriate prefix from Table 1.5. For example, $10^{-3} = 0.001$ corresponds to milli (unit). (It doesn't matter what the unit is; here we are dealing only with the prefixes.)

a. 10^{-6} corresponds to the prefix *micro-*, that is, $10^{-6} \times$ (unit) = micro (unit); so we have 2.89 microgram (μg).

b. 10^3 corresponds to the prefix *kilo-*, that is, $10^3 \times$ (unit) = kilo (unit); so we have 4.30 km.

▪ EXERCISE 1.5

Convert each of the following measurements to a unit that replaces the power of ten by a prefix.

a. 7.24×10^3 g   **b.** 4.29×10^{-6} m   **c.** 7.91×10^{-3} s

d. 2.29×10^{-2} g   **e.** 7.90×10^6 m

Table 1.5	Approved Numerical Prefixes[a]				
Exponential Expression	Decimal Equivalent	Prefix	Pronounced	Symbol
10^{12}	1,000,000,000,000	*tera-*	TER-uh	T
10^{9}	1,000,000,000	*giga-*	GIG-uh	G
10^{6}	1,000,000	*mega-*	MEG-uh	M
10^{3}	1,000	*kilo-*	KIL-oh	k
10^{2}	100	*hecto-*	HEK-toe	h
10^{1}	10	*deka-*	DEK-uh	da
10^{-1}	0.1	*deci-*	DES-ee	d
10^{-2}	0.01	*centi-*	SEN-tee	c
10^{-3}	0.001	*milli-*	MIL-ee	m
10^{-6}	0.000001	*micro-*	MY-kro	μ
10^{-9}	0.000000001	*nano-*	NAN-oh	n
10^{-12}	0.000000000001	*pico-*	PEE-koh	p
10^{-15}	0.000000000000001	*femto-*	FEM-toe	f

[a] The most commonly used prefixes are shown in color.

Example 1.6   Prefixes and Powers of Ten

Express each of the following measurements in terms of an SI base unit in both decimal and exponential form.

a. 4.12 cm   **b.** 947 ms   **c.** 3.17 nm

Solution

a. Our goal is to find the power of ten that relates the given unit to the SI base unit. That is, centi (base unit) $= 10^{-2} \times$ (base unit)

$$4.12 \text{ cm} = 4.12 \text{ centimeter} = 4.12 \times 10^{-2} \text{ m} = 0.0412 \text{ m}$$

b. To change millisecond (ms) to the base unit second, we replace the prefix *milli-* by 10^{-3}; as a shortcut you can move the decimal place to the left for each negative power or to the right for each positive power:

$$947 \text{ ms} = 0.947 \text{ s}$$

c. To change nanometer (nm) to the base unit meter, we replace the prefix *nano-* by 10^{-9}. The answer in exponential form is 3.17×10^{-9} m, and in decimal notation, it is 0.00000000317.

▪ EXERCISE 1.6

Convert the following measurements to an SI base unit.

a. 7.45 nm   **b.** 5.25 μs   **c.** 1.415 km
d. 2.06 mm   **e.** 6.19×10^{6} mm

Mass

The SI base unit for mass is the **kilogram (kg)**, about 2.2 pounds (lb) or the mass of a 1-L soft drink. This base unit is unusual in that it already has a prefix. A more convenient mass unit for most laboratory work is the gram (g), about the mass of a large paperclip.

$$1 \text{ kg} = 1000 \text{ g} = 10^{3} \text{ g}$$

The milligram (mg) is a suitable unit for small quantities of materials, such as some drug dosages or spices added while cooking food. Other drugs or vitamins that we take require a very small amount such as a microgram (μg), which is commonly abbreviated as mcg on the label.

$$1 \text{ mg} = 10^{-3} \text{ g} = 0.001 \text{ g}$$

Chemists can now detect masses in the nanogram (ng), picogram (pg), and even femtogram (fg) ranges.

Length, Area, and Volume

The SI base unit of length is the **meter (m)**, a unit about 10% longer than 1 yard (yd). The kilometer (km) is used to measure distances along highways.

$$1 \text{ km} = 1000 \text{ m}$$

In the laboratory, we usually find lengths smaller than the meter to be more convenient. For example, we use the centimeter (cm), which is about the width of a typical calculator button, or the millimeter (mm), which is about the thickness of the cardboard backing in a notepad.

$$1 \text{ cm} = 0.01 \text{ m} \qquad 1 \text{ mm} = 0.001 \text{ m}$$

For measurements at the atomic and molecular level, we use the micrometer (μm), the nanometer (nm), and the picometer (pm). For example, a hemoglobin molecule, which is nearly spherical, has a diameter of 5.5 nm or 5500 pm, and the diameter of a sodium atom is 372 pm.

The units for area and volume are derived from the base unit of length. The SI unit of area is the square meter (m^2), but we often find square centimeters (cm^2) or square millimeters (mm^2) to be more convenient for laboratory work.

$$1 \text{ cm}^2 = (10^{-2} \text{ m})^2 = 10^{-4} \text{ m}^2 \qquad 1 \text{ mm}^2 = (10^{-3} \text{ m})^2 = 10^{-6} \text{ m}^2$$

Similarly, the SI unit of volume is the cubic meter (m^3), but two units more likely to be used in the laboratory are the cubic centimeter (cm^3 or cc) and the cubic decimeter (dm^3). A cubic centimeter is about the volume of a sugar cube, and a cubic decimeter is slightly larger than 1 quart (qt).

$$1 \text{ cm}^3 = (10^{-2} \text{ m})^3 = 10^{-6} \text{ m}^3 \qquad 1 \text{ dm}^3 = (10^{-1} \text{ m})^3 = 10^{-3} \text{ m}^3$$

The cubic decimeter is commonly called a liter. A **liter (L)** is 1 cubic decimeter or 1000 cubic centimeters.

$$1 \text{ L} = 1 \text{ dm}^3 = 1000 \text{ cm}^3$$

The milliliter (mL) or cubic centimeter is frequently used in laboratories. A milliliter is about one "squirt" from a medicine dropper.

$$1 \text{ mL} = 1 \text{ cm}^3$$

Time

The SI base unit for measuring intervals of time is the second (s). Extremely short time periods are expressed using SI prefixes: millisecond (ms), microsecond (μs), nanosecond (ns), and picosecond (ps).

$$1 \text{ ms} = 10^{-3} \text{ s} \qquad 1 \mu\text{s} = 10^{-6} \text{ s} \qquad 1 \text{ ns} = 10^{-9} \text{ s} \qquad 1 \text{ ps} = 10^{-12} \text{ s}$$

Long time intervals, in contrast, are usually expressed in traditional, non-SI units: minute (min), hour (h), day (d), and year (y).

$$1 \text{ min} = 60 \text{ s} \qquad 1 \text{ h} = 60 \text{ min} \qquad 1 \text{ d} = 24 \text{ h} \qquad 1 \text{ y} = 365 \text{ d}$$

Problem Solving: Estimation

Many chemistry problems require calculations that yield numerical answers. When you use a calculator, it will always give you an answer—but the answer may not be correct. You may have punched a wrong number or used the wrong function. You can learn to estimate answers so you can tell whether your calculated answers are reasonable. At times an estimated answer is good enough, as the following Example and Exercises illustrate. This ability to estimate answers can be important in everyday life as well as in a chemistry course. Note that estimation does *not* require a detailed calculation. Only a rough calculation—or none at all—is required.

1 mm

1 cm

1 cm^2

1 mm^2

▲ Units of area such as mm^2 and cm^2 are derived from units of length.

Q: *How many mm are in 1 cm? How many mm^2 are in 1 cm^2?*

Example 1.7	Mass, Length, Area, Volume

Without doing detailed calculations, determine which of the following is a reasonable (a) mass (weight) and (b) height for a typical two-year-old child.

Mass:	10 mg	10 g	10 kg	100 g
Height:	85 mm	85 cm	850 cm	8.5 m

Solution

a. In customary units, a two-year-old child should weigh about 20–25 lb. Since 1 kg is a little more than 2 lb, the only reasonable answer is 10 kg.

b. In customary units, a two-year-old child should be about 30–36 in. tall. Since 1 cm is a little less than 0.5 in., the answer must be a little more than twice that range, or a bit over 60–72 cm. Thus the only reasonable answer is 85 cm.

■ **EXERCISE 1.7A**

Without doing a detailed calculation, determine which of the following is a reasonable area for the front cover of your textbook.

$$500 \text{ mm}^2 \quad 50 \text{ cm}^2 \quad 500 \text{ cm}^2 \quad 50 \text{ m}^2$$

■ **EXERCISE 1.7B**

Without doing a detailed calculation, determine which of the following is a reasonable volume for your textbook.

$$1600 \text{ mm}^3 \quad 16 \text{ cm}^3 \quad 1600 \text{ cm}^3 \quad 1.6 \text{ m}^3$$

Problem Solving: Unit Conversions

It is easy to convert from one metric unit to another using the *unit conversion* method of problem solving. If you are not familiar with this method, you should study it now in Appendix A.3, which also discusses the conversion of common units to metric units.

You can find a discussion of *significant figures*, a way of indicating the precision of measurements, in Appendix A.4. In the following problems and throughout the text, we will simply carry three digits in most calculations.

Example 1.8	Unit Conversions

Convert

(a) 1.83 kg to grams and (b) 729 microliters to milliliters.

Solution

a. We start with the given quantity, 1.83 kg, and use the equivalence 1 kg = 1000 g to form a conversion factor (see Appendix A.3) that allows us to cancel the unit kg and end with the unit g.

$$1.83 \text{ kg} \times \frac{1000 \text{ g}}{1 \text{ kg}} = 1830 \text{ g}$$

b. Here we start with the given quantity, 729 μL, and we want the unit to be in mL. So we need to find the ratio of μL to mL. According to Table 1.5, micro is 10^{-6} and milli is 10^{-3}. This is a difference of 10^3 or 1000 units. We know that 1 mL is equivalent to 1000 μL. Set up the conversion with mL (desired unit) on top and μL (starting unit) on the bottom, leaving us with an answer in the correct unit.

$$729 \text{ } \mu\text{L} \times \frac{1 \text{ mL}}{1000 \text{ } \mu\text{L}} = 0.729 \text{ mL}$$

▪ **EXERCISE 1.8**
Convert

a. 0.755 m to millimeters

b. 205.6 mL to liters

c. 0.206 g to micrograms

d. 7.38 cm to millimeters

SELF-ASSESSMENT Questions

1. The SI unit of length is the
   a. foot b. kilometer c. pascal d. meter

2. The SI unit of mass is the
   a. dram b. gram c. grain d. kilogram

3. The prefix that means 10^{-2} is
   a. centi- b. deci- c. micro- d. milli-

4. An inch is about 250% longer than a
   a. meter b. centimeter
   c. millimeter d. decimeter

5. One cubic centimeter is equal to one
   a. deciliter b. dram
   c. liter d. milliliter

6. One quart is slightly less than one
   a. deciliter b. kiloliter
   c. liter d. milliliter

7. A rope is 5.775 cm long. What is its length in millimeters?
   a. 0.05775 mm b. 0.5775 mm
   c. 5.775 mm d. 57.75 mm

8. Which of the following has a mass of roughly 1 g?
   a. an ant b. an orange
   c. a peanut d. a watermelon

9. Your doctor recommends that you take 1000 μg of vitamin B_{12}. That is the same as
   a. 1 centigram b. 1 decigram
   c. 1 gram d. 1 milligram

10. Which of the following has a thickness of roughly 1 cm?
    a. a brick b. a cell phone
    c. a knife blade d. this textbook

11. Which of the following has a volume of roughly 250 mL (0.250 L)?
    a. 1 cup b. 1 gallon
    c. 1 pint d. 1 tablespoon

Answers: 1. d; 2. d; 3. a; 4. b; 5. d; 6. c; 7. d; 8. c; 9. d; 10. b; 11. a

Nanoworld

For over two centuries, chemists have been able to rearrange atoms to make molecules, which have dimensions in the *picometer* (10^{-12} m) range. This ability has led to revolutions in the design of drugs, plastics, and many other materials. Over the last several decades, scientists have made vast strides in handling materials with dimensions in the *micrometer* (10^{-6} m) range. The revolution in electronic devices—computers, cell phones, and so on—was spurred by the ability of scientists to produce computer chips by photolithography on a micrometer scale.

Now many scientists focus on *nanotechnology*. The prefix *nano-* means one-billionth (10^{-9}). Nanotechnology bridges the gap between picometer-sized molecules and micrometer-sized electronics. A nanometer-sized object contains just a few hundred to a few thousand atoms or molecules, and such objects often have different properties than large objects of the same substance. For example, bulk gold is yellow, but a ring made up of nanometer-sized gold particles appears red. Carbon in the form of graphite (pencil lead) is quite weak and soft, but carbon nanotubes can be 100 times stronger than steel. Nanotubes, so called because of their size (only one 10,000th the thickness of a human hair) and their

shape (hollow tube), have thousands of potential uses but are extremely expensive to make. Scientists can now manipulate matter on every scale, from nanometers to meters, greatly increasing the scope of materials design. We will examine some of the many practical applications of nanotechnology in subsequent chapters.

▲ Molecular view of a carbon nanotube—stronger than steel and more expensive than gold.

1.8 Density

Learning Objective ❯ Calculate the density, mass, or volume of an object given the other two quantities.

In everyday life, we might speak of lead as "heavy" or aluminum as "light," but such descriptions are imprecise at best. Scientists use the term *density* to describe this important property. The **density**, *d*, of a substance is the quantity of mass, *m*, per unit of volume, *V*.

$$d = \frac{m}{V}$$

For substances that don't mix, such as oil and water, the concept of density allows us to predict which will float on the other. It isn't just the mass of each material, but the *mass per unit volume*—the density—that determines the result. Density is the property that explains why oil (lower density) floats on water (higher density) in a bottle of Italian salad dressing. Figure 1.8 shows other examples.

We can rearrange the equation for density to give

$$m = d \times V \quad \text{and} \quad V = \frac{m}{d}$$

These equations are useful for calculations. Densities of some common substances are listed in Table 1.6. They are customarily reported in grams per milliliter (g/mL) for liquids and grams per cubic centimeter (g/cm³) for solids. Values listed in the table are used in some of the following Examples and Exercises and in some of the end-of-chapter problems.

As with problems involving mass, length, area, and volume (Example 1.7 on page 23), it is often sufficient to estimate answers to problems involving densities, for example, in determining relative volumes of materials or whether or not a material will float or sink in water. Such estimation is illustrated in the following Example and Exercises. Note again that estimation does *not* require a detailed calculation.

▲ One cubic centimeter of copper weighs 8.94 g, so the density of copper is 8.94 g/cm³.

Q: *What is the mass of 2 cm³ of copper? What is the density of 2 cm³ of copper?*

▲ **Figure 1.8** At room temperature, the density of water is approximately 1.00 g/mL. A coin sinks in water, but a cork floats on water.

Q: *Is the density of these coins less than, equal to, or greater than 1.00 g/mL? Is the density of the corks less than, equal to, or greater than 1.00 g/mL?*

Table 1.6	Densities of Some Common Substances at Specified Temperatures	
Substance*	Density	Temperature
Solids		
Copper (Cu)	8.94 g/cm³	25 °C
Gold (Au)	19.3 g/cm³	25 °C
Magnesium (Mg)	1.738 g/cm³	20 °C
Water (ice) (H_2O)	0.917 g/cm³	0 °C
Liquids		
Ethanol (CH_3CH_2OH)	0.789 g/mL	20 °C
Hexane ($CH_3CH_2CH_2CH_2CH_2CH_3$)	0.660 g/mL	20 °C
Mercury (Hg)	13.534 g/mL	25 °C
Urine (a mixture)	1.003–1.030 g/mL	25 °C
Water (H_2O)	0.998 g/mL	0 °C
	1.000 g/mL	4 °C
	0.998 g/mL	20 °C

*Formulas are provided for possible future reference.

| **Example 1.9** | Mass, Volume, and Density |

Density can provide a wealth of information without even doing a detailed calculation. The following problems can be worked without using a calculator. During the gold rush, prospectors would often find fool's gold, iron pyrite, which looks exactly like gold. However, it has a density of approximately 3.3 g/ml. Using Table 1.6, find the density of gold. If a miner found a nugget of fool's gold that fit in the palm of his hand, **(a)** would there be a significant difference in mass compared to a similar sized nugget of pure gold? **(b)** if the fool's gold weighed the same as the gold nugget would you see a difference in size?

Solution

a. From Table 1.6, we can see that the density of gold is 19.3 g/ml. That means gold is nearly 6 times heavier than a similarly sized piece of iron pyrite. This allowed prospectors to easily identify which ore they had found.

b. As seen above, the density of gold is 6 times that of iron pyrite. Because gold is denser, it can pack in tighter and take up less space. Comparing two ore samples of equal mass, we find that the gold would be 1/6th as large as the pyrite.

| **Example 1.10** | Density, Mass, or Volume |

Mass and volume give density. What is the density of iron if 156 g of iron occupies a volume of 20.0 cm³?

Solution
The given quantities are

$$m = 156 \text{ g} \quad \text{and} \quad V = 20.0 \text{ cm}^3$$

We use the equation that defines density.

$$d = \frac{m}{V} = \frac{156 \text{ g}}{20.0 \text{ cm}^3} = 7.80 \text{ g/cm}^3$$

Likewise, density and mass give you volume; volume and density give you mass according to the follow rearrangements of our original density equation.

$$V = \frac{m}{d} \quad \text{or} \quad m = dV$$

▪ EXERCISE 1.10A
Find the density of a salt solution if 210 mL of solution has a mass of 234 g.

▪ EXERCISE 1.10B
What metal do you have if a 10 cm³ piece weighs 17.38 g? (See Table 1.6.)

▪ EXERCISE 1.10C
Find the volume of a solution if you have 3 g and a density of 0.67 g/mL.

▪ EXERCISE 1.10D
You need 700 g of hexane. Will it fit in a 1.00-L container? (See Table 1.6.)

▪ EXERCISE 1.10E
Find the mass of a sample of rock that has a density of 9.7 g/mL and occupies 5 mL of space.

▪ EXERCISE 1.10F
What is the mass in kilograms of the ethanol that fills a 16-gallon "gas tank"? (1 gallon = 3.78 L; also see Table 1.6.)

You can do your own demonstration of a density difference. Make a classic French vinaigrette salad dressing by adding 10 mL of red wine vinegar to 30–40 mL of extra virgin olive oil. Add seasonings such as salt, pepper, oregano, thyme, Dijon mustard, and garlic. Which material, oil or vinegar, forms the top layer? Enjoy!

SELF-ASSESSMENT Questions

1. The density of a wood plank floating on a lake is
   a. less than that of air
   b. less than that of water
   c. more than that of water
   d. the same as that of water

2. A pebble and a lead sinker both sink when dropped into a pond. This shows that the two objects
   a. are both less dense than water
   b. are both more dense than water
   c. have different densities
   d. have the same density

3. Ice floats on liquid water. A reasonable value for the density of ice is
   a. 0.92 g/cm^3
   b. 1.08 g/cm^3
   c. 1.98 g/cm^3
   d. 4.90 g/cm^3

4. A prospector panning for gold swirls a mixture of mud, gravel, and water in a pan. He looks for gold at the bottom because gold
   a. dissolves in water and sinks
   b. has a high density and sinks
   c. is less dense than rocks
   d. is repelled by the other minerals

5. Which of the following metals will sink in a pool of mercury (d = 13.534 g/cm^3)?
   a. aluminum (d = 2.6 g/cm^3)
   b. iron (d = 7.9 g/cm^3)
   c. lead (d = 11.34 g/cm^3)
   d. uranium (d = 19.5 g/cm^3)

6. If the volume of a rock is 80.0 cm^3 and its mass is 160.0 g, its density is
   a. 0.05 g/cm^3
   b. 0.50 g/cm^3
   c. 2.0 g/cm^3
   d. 20 g/cm^3

1.9 Energy: Heat and Temperature

Learning Objectives ❯ Distinguish between heat and temperature. ❯ Explain how the temperature scales are related.

The physical and chemical changes that matter undergoes are almost always accompanied by changes in energy. **Energy** is required to make something happen that wouldn't happen by itself. Energy is the ability to change matter, either physically or chemically.

Two important concepts in science that are related, and sometimes confused, are *temperature* and *heat*. When two objects at different temperatures are brought together, heat flows from the warmer to the cooler object until both are at the same temperature. **Heat** is energy on the move, the energy that flows from a warmer object to a cooler one. **Temperature** is a measure of how hot or cold an object is. Temperature tells us the direction in which heat will flow. Heat flows from more

▶ **Figure 1.9** Temperature and heat are different phenomena. Both the baby's bathtub and the hot tub are at roughly the same temperature—about 40 °C—but it took much more heat to warm the hot tub to that temperature than it did the baby's bathtub.

energetic (higher-temperature) to less energetic (lower-temperature) atoms or molecules. For example, if you touch a hot test tube, heat will flow from the tube to your hand. If the tube is hot enough, your hand will be burned.

The SI base unit of temperature is the **kelvin (K)**. For laboratory work, we often use the more familiar **Celsius scale**. On this temperature scale, the freezing point of water is 0 degrees Celsius (°C) and the boiling point is 100 °C. The interval between these two reference points is divided into 100 equal parts, each a *degree Celsius*. The Kelvin scale is called an *absolute scale* because its zero point is the coldest temperature possible, or absolute zero. (This fact was determined by theoretical considerations and has been confirmed by experiment, as we will see in Chapter 6.)

The zero point on the Kelvin scale, 0 K, is equal to −273.15 °C, which we often round to −273 °C. A kelvin is the same size as a degree Celsius, so the freezing point of water on the Kelvin scale is 273 K. The Kelvin scale has no negative temperatures, and we don't use a degree sign with the K. To convert from degrees Celsius to kelvins, simply add 273.15 to the Celsius temperature.

$$K = {}°C + 273.15$$

Example 1.11 | **Temperature Conversions**

Diethyl ether boils at 36 °C. What is the boiling point of this liquid on the Kelvin scale?

Solution

$$K = {}°C + 273.15$$
$$K = 36 + 273.15 = 309 \text{ K}$$

▪ **EXERCISE 1.11A**
What is the boiling point of ethanol (78 °C) expressed in kelvins?

▪ **EXERCISE 1.11B**
At atmospheric pressure, liquid nitrogen boils at −196 °C. Express that temperature in kelvins.

The Fahrenheit temperature scale is widely used in the United States. Figure 1.10 compares the three temperature scales. Note that on the Fahrenheit scale, there are 180 Fahrenheit degrees between the freezing point and the boiling point of water. On the Celsius scale, there are 100 Celsius degrees between these two points. Thus, one Celsius degree equals 1.8 Fahrenheit degrees. Conversions between Fahrenheit and Celsius temperatures use this relationship, which is discussed in Appendix A.5.

The SI-derived unit of energy is the **joule (J)**, but the **calorie (cal)** is the more familiar unit in everyday life.

$$1 \text{ cal} = 4.184 \text{ J}$$

A calorie is the amount of heat required to raise the temperature of 1 g of water by 1 °C.

The "calorie" used for expressing the energy content of foods is actually a **kilocalorie (kcal)**.

$$1000 \text{ cal} = 1 \text{ kcal} = 4184 \text{ J}$$

A dieter might be aware that a banana split contains 1500 "calories." If the dieter realized that this was really 1500 *kilo*calories, or 1,500,000 calories, giving up the banana split might be easier! The concept of heat is discussed further in Appendix A.5.

Example 1.12	Energy Conversions

When 1.00 g of gasoline burns, it yields about 10.3 kcal of energy. What is this quantity of energy in kilojoules (kJ)?

Solution

$$10.3 \text{ kcal} \times \frac{1000 \text{ kcal}}{1 \text{ kcal}} \times \frac{4.184 \text{ J}}{1 \text{ cal}} \times \frac{1 \text{ kJ}}{1000 \text{ J}} = 43.1 \text{ kJ}$$

▪ EXERCISE 1.12A
Each day, the average European woman consumes food with an energy content of 7525 kJ. What is this daily intake in kilocalories (food calories)?

▪ EXERCISE 1.12B
It takes about 12 kJ of energy to melt a single ice cube. How much energy in kilocalories does it take to melt a tray of 12 ice cubes?

SELF-ASSESSMENT Questions

1. Heat is
   a. an element
   b. the energy flow from a hot object to a cold one
   c. a measure of energy intensity
   d. a temperature above room temperature

2. The SI scale for temperature is known as the
   a. Celsius scale
   b. Fahrenheit scale
   c. Kelvin scale
   d. Richter scale

3. Water boils at
   a. 0 °C   b. 100 °F
   c. 273 °C   d. 373 K

4. To convert a temperature on the Kelvin scale to degrees Celsius, we
   a. add 100   b. add 273
   c. subtract 100   d. subtract 273

5. The SI unit of energy is the
   a. calorie   b. coulomb
   c. joule   d. watt

Answers: 1, b; 2, c; 3, d; 4, d; 5, c

Normal Body Temperature

Carl Wunderlich (1815–1877), a German physician, first recognized that fever is a symptom of disease. He recorded thousands of temperature measurements from healthy people and reported the average value as 37 °C. When this value was converted to the Fahrenheit scale, it somehow (improperly) acquired an extra significant figure, and 98.6 °F became widely (and incorrectly) known as the *normal body temperature*. In recent years, millions of measurements have revealed that *average* normal body temperature is actually 98.2 °F and that body temperatures in healthy people range from 97.7 °F to 99.5 °F.

1.10 Critical Thinking

Learning Objective   ❯ Use critical thinking to evaluate claims and statements.

One of the hallmarks of science is the ability to think critically—to evaluate statements and claims in a rational, objective fashion. For example, a diet-plan advertisement shows people who have lost a lot of weight. Somewhere in the ad, in tiny print, you may find a statement such as "results may vary" or "results not typical." Such ads also often advise combining the plan with diet and exercise.

Does an ad like this prove that a diet plan works? You can use critical thinking to evaluate the ad's claim. Critical thinking involves gathering facts, assessing them, using logic to reach a conclusion, and then evaluating the conclusion. The ability to think critically can be learned, and it will serve you well in everyday life as well as in science courses. Critical thinking is important for workers in all types of professions and employees in all kinds of industries. We will use an approach adapted from one developed by James Lett.[1] This approach is outlined below and followed by several examples.

You can use the acronym **FLaReS** (ignore the vowels) to remember four principles used to test a claim: *f*alsifiability, *l*ogic, *r*eplicability, and *s*ufficiency.

- **Falsifiability:** Can any conceivable evidence show the claim to be false? It must be possible to think of evidence that would prove the claim false. A hypothesis that cannot be falsified is of no value. Science cannot prove anything true in an absolute sense, although it can provide overwhelming evidence. Science *can* prove something false.

[1] Lett used the acronym FiLCHeRS (ignore the vowels) as a mnemonic for six rules: falsifiability, logic, comprehensiveness, honesty, replicability, and sufficiency. See Lett, James, "A Field Guide to Critical Thinking," *The Skeptical Inquirer*, Winter 1990, pp. 153–160.

- **Logic:** Any argument offered as evidence in support of a claim must be sound. An argument is sound if its conclusion follows inevitably from its premises and if its premises are true. It is unsound if a premise is false, and it is unsound if there is a single exception in which the conclusion does not necessarily follow from the premises.

- **Replicability:** If the evidence for a claim is based on an experimental result, it is necessary that the evidence be replicable in subsequent experiments or trials. Scientific research is almost always reviewed by other qualified scientists. The peer-reviewed research is then published in a form that enables others to repeat the experiment. Sometimes, bad science slips through the peer-review process, but such results eventually fail the test of replicability. For example, in May 2005 the journal *Science* published research by Korean biomedical scientist Hwang Woo-suk in which he claimed to have tailored embryonic stem cells so that every patient could receive custom treatment. Others were unable to reproduce Hwang's findings, and evidence emerged that he had intentionally fabricated results. *Science* retracted the article in January 2006. Research results published in media that are not peer reviewed have little or no standing in the scientific community—nor should you rely on them.

- **Sufficiency:** The evidence offered in support of a claim must be adequate to establish the truth of that claim, with these stipulations: (1) The burden of evidence for any claim rests on the claimant, (2) extraordinary claims demand extraordinary evidence, and (3) evidence based on an authority figure or on testimony is never adequate.

If a claim passes all four FLaReS tests, then it *might* be true. On the other hand, it could still be proven false. However, if a claim fails even one of the FLaReS tests, it is likely to be false. The FLaReS method is a good starting point for evaluating the myriad claims that you will find on the Internet and elsewhere. We apply one or more of the FLaReS principles to evaluate a claim in each of the following examples.

CRITICAL THINKING Examples

1.1. A practitioner claims outstanding success in curing cancer with a vaccine made from a patient's own urine. However, the vaccine works only if the patient's immune system is still sufficiently strong. Is the claim falsifiable?

Solution

    No. The practitioner can always say that the patient's immune system was no longer sufficiently strong.

1.2. A website claims, "The medical-industrial complex suppresses natural treatments because they cure the patient. A cured patient no longer needs a doctor, and the doctor loses income." Is the claim logical?

Solution

    No. Doctors do not cure all patients. Many remain ill and some die.

1.3. Many "psychics" claim to be able to predict the future. These predictions are often made near the end of one year and concern the next year. Apply all the FLaReS tests to evaluate this claim.

Solution

1. *Is the claim falsifiable? Yes. You could write down a prediction and then check it yourself at the end of the year.*
2. *Is the claim logical? No. If psychics could really predict the future, they could readily win lotteries, ward off all kinds of calamities by providing advance warning, and so on.*
3. *Is the claim reproducible? No. Psychics often make broad, general predictions, such as "tornadoes will hit Oklahoma in April and May." (It would be a rare year when there were no tornadoes in Oklahoma in those months.) The psychics later make claim-specific references to "hits" while ignoring "misses."*
4. *Is the claim sufficient? No. Any such claim is extraordinary; it would require extraordinary evidence. The burden of proof for the claim rests on the claimant.*

Jennifer MacKellar and David Constable, *ACS Green Chemistry Institute®*

Green Chemistry: Reimagining Chemistry for a Sustainable World

Learning Objectives ❯ Define green chemistry. ❯ Describe how green chemistry reduces risk and prevents environmental problems.

The famous naturalist, John Muir, once said, "When one tugs at a single thing in nature, he finds it attached to the rest of the world." In a world of shifting climate and unprecedented environmental disasters, we realize that nothing could be truer. But what can we do to change the current path? What would a sustainable planet look like?

Imagine a community where human society lives in harmony with nature. People enjoy good health without diminishing the resources that support them. Land, water, and air are managed in ways that retain the ecological value of the environment. Sustainable communities realize the importance of balancing economic, environmental, and social issues and thrive because of it.

The twentieth century saw enormous technical advances in medicine, manufacturing, and chemical processing that led to an increased quality of life in the United States. However, this standard of living has taken a significant toll on the environment and human health. Improper chemical use and disposal and general environmental pollution have significantly degraded the world's ecosystems, threatening the security of future generations. Since the publication of Rachel Carson's *Silent Spring* in 1962 (Section 1.1) and the birth of the environmental movement, an increasing number of governmental regulations focus on pollution prevention and environmental protection.

But what if we could prevent hazardous waste altogether? What if we could design chemicals that would meet our needs and desires without destroying our environment? Sustainable and green chemistry, in simple terms, is just a different way of thinking about how chemistry and chemical engineering can be done. Over the years, different principles have been proposed that can be used when thinking about the design, development, and implementation of chemical products and processes. These principles enable scientists and engineers to protect and benefit the economy, people, and the planet by finding creative and innovative ways to reduce waste, conserve energy, and replace hazardous substances. (See the inside front cover.)

It is important to note that green chemistry and engineering principles should be applied across the life of a product. Doing so means the use of more sustainable or renewable feedstocks all the way through to designing for end of life or the final disposition of the product. Green chemistry is applicable across all chemistry disciplines including organic, inorganic, analytical, and physical chemistry and biochemistry.

Governments and scientific communities throughout the world recognize that the practice of green chemistry leads not only to a cleaner and more sustainable Earth but also to economic benefits and positive social impacts. These benefits encourage businesses and government to support development of greener products and processes. The United States, specifically, has recognized green chemistry innovations since 1996 through an annual Presidential Green Chemistry Challenge Award program.

In 2012, Elevance Renewable Sciences won the Presidential Green Chemistry Challenge Award for Greener Synthetic Pathways by using Nobel Prize–winning chemistry known as metathesis to break down natural oils and recombine the fragments into high-performance chemicals. The company makes specialty chemicals for many uses, such as highly concentrated cold-water detergents that provide better cleaning with reduced energy costs.

The use of green-chemistry practices makes a more sustainable future possible, but it is important to consider, too, that today's crises call for innovative thinking and a willingness to change. Albert Einstein said it best, "Problems cannot be solved at the same level of awareness that created them." Despite all of the research advances in green chemistry, mainstream business has yet to fully embrace greener and more sustainable technology. Today, more than 98% of all organic chemicals are still derived from petroleum. Green chemists are working very hard to take their innovations out of the lab and into the boardroom by creating products that can be embraced by today's industry leaders and consumers.

Sustainability and the health of our environment have an impact on all of us. The environment spans age, race, income levels, and cultural differences, producing an impact on all of life. Green chemistry is a solutions-based approach to addressing some of our pressing global challenges.

▲ In 2013, the Elevance biorefinery in Gresik, Indonesia, began producing specialty-chemical products commercially. The feedstocks for the biorefinery are renewable—mainly vegetable oils.

SUMMARY

Section 1.1—**Technology** is the practical application of knowledge, while **science** is an accumulation of knowledge about nature and our physical world along with our explanations of that knowledge. The roots of chemistry lie in **natural philosophy**, philosophical speculation about nature, and in **alchemy**, a mixture of chemistry and magic practiced in Europe in the Middle Ages. **Green chemistry** uses materials and processes that are intended to prevent or reduce pollution at its source. **Sustainable chemistry** is designed to meet the needs of the present generation without compromising the needs of future generations.

Section 1.2—Science is *reproducible, testable, predictive, explanatory,* and *tentative.* A set of confirmed observations about nature may lead to a **hypothesis**—a tentative explanation of the observations. A **scientific law** is a brief statement that summarizes large amounts of data and is universally true. There are very few laws and many theories. If a hypothesis stands up to testing and further experimentation, it may become a **theory**—the best current explanation for a phenomenon. A theory is always tentative and can be rejected if it does not continue to stand up to further testing. A valid theory can be used to predict new scientific facts. Scientists disagree over social and political issues partly because of the inability to control **variables**, factors that can change during an experiment.

Section 1.3—Science and technology have provided many benefits for our world, but they have also introduced new risks. A **risk–benefit analysis** can help us decide which outweighs the other.

Section 1.4—Most chemists are involved in some kind of research. The purpose of **applied research** is to make useful products or to solve a particular problem, while **basic research** is carried out simply to obtain new knowledge or to answer a fundamental question. Basic research often also leads to a useful product or process.

Section 1.5—**Chemistry** is the study of matter and the changes it undergoes. **Matter** is anything that has mass and takes up space. **Mass** is a measure of the amount of matter in an object, while **weight** represents the gravitational force of attraction for an object. **Physical properties** of matter can be observed without making new substances. When **chemical properties** are observed, new substances are formed. A **physical change** does not entail a change in chemical composition. A **chemical change** does involve such a change.

Section 1.6—Matter can be classified according to physical state. A **solid** has definite shape and volume. A **liquid** has definite volume but takes the shape of its container. A **gas** takes both the shape and the volume of its container. Matter also can be classified according to composition. A **sub**stance always has the same composition, no matter how it is made or where it is found. A **mixture** can have different compositions depending on how it is prepared. Substances are either elements or compounds. An **element** is composed of atoms of one type, an **atom** being the smallest characteristic particle of an element. There are over a hundred elements, each of which is represented by a **chemical symbol** consisting of one or two letters derived from the element's name. A **compound** is made up of two or more elements, chemically combined in a fixed ratio. Most compounds exist as **molecules**, groups of atoms bound together as a unit.

Section 1.7—Scientific measurements are expressed with **SI units**, which comprise an agreed-on standard version of the metric system. Base units include the **kilogram (kg)** for mass and the **meter (m)** for length. Although it is not the SI standard unit of volume, the **liter (L)** is widely used. Prefixes make basic units larger or smaller by factors of ten.

Section 1.8—**Density** can be thought of as "how heavy something is for its size." It is the amount of mass per unit volume.

$$d = \frac{m}{V}$$

Density can be used as a conversion factor. The density of water is almost exactly 1 g/mL.

Section 1.9—When matter undergoes a physical or chemical change, a change in **energy** is involved. Energy is the *ability* to cause these changes. **Heat** is energy flow from a warmer object to a cooler one. **Temperature** is a measure of how hot or cold an object is. The **kelvin (K)** is the SI base unit of temperature, but the **Celsius scale (°C)** is more commonly used. On the Celsius scale, water boils at 100 °C and freezes at 0 °C. The SI unit of heat is the **joule (J)**. A more familiar unit, the **calorie (cal)**, is the amount of heat needed to raise the temperature of 1 g of water by 1 °C. The food "calorie" is actually a **kilocalorie (kcal)**, or 1000 calories.

Section 1.10—Claims may be tested by applying critical thinking. The acronym **FLaReS** represents four principles used to test a claim: *f*alsifiability, *l*ogic, *r*eplicability, and *s*ufficiency.

GREEN CHEMISTRY Green chemistry means preventing waste, using nonhazardous chemicals and renewable resources, conserving energy, and making products that degrade after use. Green chemistry takes into account the sources and ultimate destinations of chemicals, and the impact they will have on humans and the planet.

Learning Objectives

❯ Define science, chemistry, technology, and alchemy. (1.1)	Problems 1, 4
❯ Describe the importance of green chemistry and sustainable chemistry (1.1)	Problems 43, 44
❯ Define *hypothesis, scientific law, scientific theory,* and *scientific model,* and explain their relationships in science. (1.2)	Problems 2, 3, 71, 72, 74, 75
❯ Define *risk* and *benefit,* and give an example of each. (1.3)	Problem 5
❯ Estimate a desirability quotient from benefit and risk data. (1.3)	Problems 7, 13–18
❯ Distinguish basic research from applied research. (1.4)	Problems 8, 9
❯ Differentiate: mass and weight; physical and chemical change; and physical and chemical properties. (1.5)	Problems 29–32
❯ Classify matter in three ways. (1.6)	Problems 33–44
❯ Assign proper units of measurement to observations, and manipulate units in conversions. (1.7)	Problems 10–12, 19–28, 45–52, 69, 70, 73, 78–80
❯ Calculate the density, mass, or volume of an object given the other two quantities. (1.8)	Problems 53–64, 76, 77, 81–88
❯ Distinguish between heat and temperature. (1.9)	Problems 67, 68
❯ Explain how the temperature scales are related. (1.9)	Problems 65, 66
❯ Use critical thinking to evaluate claims and statements. (1.10)	Problem 6
❯ Define green chemistry.	Problem 89
❯ Describe how green chemistry reduces risk and prevents environmental problems.	Problems 90–92

REVIEW QUESTIONS

1. State five distinguishing characteristics of science. Which characteristic best serves to distinguish science from other disciplines?

2. Why do experiments have to be done to support a hypothesis?

3. Why can't scientific methods always be used to solve social, political, ethical, and economic problems?

4. How does technology differ from science?

5. What is risk–benefit analysis?

6. What sorts of judgments go into (a) the evaluation of benefits and (b) the evaluation of risks?

7. What is a DQ? What does a large DQ mean? Why is it often difficult to estimate a DQ?

8. What derived units of (a) mass and (b) length are commonly used in the laboratory?

9. What is the SI-derived unit for volume? What volume units are more often used in the laboratory?

10. Following is an incomplete table of SI prefixes, their symbols, and their meanings. Fill in the blank cells. The first row is completed as an example.

Prefix	Symbol	Definition
tera-	T	10^{12}
_____	M	_____
centi-	_____	_____
_____	μ	_____
milli-	_____	_____
_____	_____	10^{-1}
_____	K	_____
nano-	_____	_____

11. Identify the following research projects as either applied or basic.
    a. A Virginia Tech chemist tests a method for analyzing coal powder in less than a minute, before the powder goes into a coal-fired energy plant.
    b. A Purdue engineer develops a method for causing aluminum to react with water to generate hydrogen for automobiles.
    c. A worker at University of Illinois Urbana-Champaign examines the behavior of atoms at high temperatures and low pressures.

12. Identify the following work as either applied research or basic research.
    a. An engineer determines the strength of a titanium alloy that will be used to construct notebook-computer cases.
    b. A biochemist runs experiments to determine how oxygen binds to the blood cells of lobsters.
    c. A biologist determines the number of eagles that nest annually in Kentucky's Land Between the Lakes area over a six-year period.

PROBLEMS

A Word of Advice You cannot learn to work problems by reading them or by watching your instructor work them, just as you cannot become a piano player solely by reading about piano-playing skills or by attending performances. Working problems will help you improve your understanding of the ideas presented in the chapter and your ability to synthesize concepts as well as allow you to practice your estimation skills. Plan to work through the great majority of these problems.

Risk–Benefit Analysis

13. Penicillin kills bacteria, thus saving the lives of thousands of people who otherwise might die of infectious diseases. Penicillin causes allergic reactions in some people, which can lead to death if the resulting condition is not treated. Do a risk–benefit analysis of the use of penicillin by society as a whole.

14. Sodium sulfite is a compound sometimes added to dried fruit, some fruit juices, and wines as a preservative. About 1% of the population is sensitive to sulfites. Consider the use of sulfites in **(a)** fruit juice and **(b)** wine. How might these uses differ in risk–benefit analysis?

15. Paints used on today's automobiles are often composed of two components and harden several hours after mixing. One component is an *isocyanate* that can sensitize a person, causing an allergic reaction, if it is breathed (even in small amounts) over a long time period. Do a risk–benefit analysis of the use of these paints by **(a)** an automotive factory worker and **(b)** a hobbyist who is restoring a 1965 Mustang. How might the DQ for both of these people be increased?

16. X-rays are widely used in medicine and dentistry. Do a risk–benefit analysis for **(a)** a dental patient who has one set of x-rays done per year and **(b)** a dentist who stays in the room with a patient while x-rays are taken, three times each day.

17. MRSA (methicillin resistant *staphylococcus aureus* bacteria) infections are becoming more common as the prescribing of antibiotics increases. **(a)** Is the DQ for the use of antibiotics to routinely treat sore throats high or low? Justify your answer briefly. **(b)** How does this DQ differ from the DQ for the use of antibiotics to treat influenza (higher or lower)? Justify your answer briefly.

18. The virus called HIV causes AIDS, a devastating and often deadly disease. Several drugs are available to treat HIV infection, but all are expensive. Used separately and in combination, these drugs have resulted in a huge drop in AIDS deaths. An expensive new drug shows promise for treating HIV/AIDS patients, especially in preventing passage of the HIV virus from a pregnant woman to her fetus. What is the DQ for administering this drug to **(a)** a man who thinks he may be infected with HIV, **(b)** a pregnant woman who is HIV positive, and **(c)** an unborn child whose mother has AIDS?

Mass and Weight

19. Which are realistic masses for a cellular telephone and a laptop computer, respectively?

    100 mg, 100 g   100 g, 100 mg   100 g, 2 kg   1 kg, 2 kg

20. In Europe, A2 sized paper measures 594 mm × 420 mm. Is this larger or smaller than the standard 8½ in. × 11 in. paper used in the United States?

21. Which one(s) of the following are likely to be paired incorrectly? Add or remove zeroes to the incorrect masses to make them more reasonable **(a)** large paper clip, 1000 mg; **(b)** pair of wire-frame glasses, 20 g; **(c)** carpet covering a large living room, 10 kg; **(d)** case of bottled water, 1 kg.

22. Sample X on the moon has exactly the same mass as Sample Y on Earth. Do the two samples weigh the same? Explain.

Length, Area, and Volume

23. Which of the following is a reasonable volume for a teacup?

    25 mL   250 mL   2.5 L   25 L

24. Which of the following is a reasonable approximation for the area of a credit card?

    $4\ cm^2$ $40\ cm^2$ $400\ cm^2$ $4\ m^2$

25. Earth's oceans contain $3.50 \times 10^8\ mi^3$ of water and cover an area of $1.40 \times 10^8\ mi^2$. What is the volume of ocean water in cubic kilometers?

26. What is the area of Earth's oceans in square kilometers? See Problem 25.

27. Consider the two tubes shown below. The aluminum tube has an outside diameter of 0.998 in. and an inside diameter of 0.782 in. Without doing a detailed calculation, determine whether the aluminum tube will fit inside another aluminum tube with an inside diameter of 26.3 mm.

28. Which one(s) of the following could be the inside diameter of the paper tube shown above (with Problem 27): 19.9 mm; 24.9 mm, 18.7 mm?

Physical and Chemical Properties and Changes

29. Identify the following as physical or chemical properties.
   a. The glass on a tablet computer is cracked when a child sits on it.
   b. Bread becomes moldy when it is allowed to stand in the open.
   c. Gold and copper melt at almost the same temperature.
   d. A dessert custard is prepared by cooking a mixture of eggs, sugar, and milk.

30. Identify the following as physical or chemical properties.
    a. Milk chocolate melts in the mouth.
    b. An iron nail rusts when it gets wet.
    c. Titanium chips burn with a brilliant white light.
    d. Yogurt is made by allowing a bacterial culture to ferment in warm milk.

31. Identify the following changes as physical or chemical.
    a. Bits of yellow plastic are melted and forced into a mold to make a yellow toy.
    b. Waste oil from restaurants is converted to biodiesel fuel that burns differently from cooking oil.
    c. Orange juice is prepared by adding three cans of water to one can of orange-juice concentrate.

32. Identify the following changes as physical or chemical.
    a. Bacteria are killed by chlorine added to a swimming pool.
    b. Brown print is created in an inkjet printer by mixing cyan, magenta, and yellow inks.
    c. Sugar is dissolved in water to make syrup.

Substances and Mixtures

33. Identify each of the following as a substance or a mixture.
    a. helium gas used to fill a balloon
    b. the juice squeezed from an orange
    c. distilled water
    d. carbon dioxide gas

34. Identify each of the following as a substance or a mixture.
    a. oxygen   b. sodium sulfite
    c. smog   d. a carrot
    e. pure milk chocolate   f. rabbit fur

35. Which of the following mixtures are homogeneous, and which are heterogeneous?
    a. copper water pipe   b. distilled water
    c. liquid oxygen   d. chicken noodle soup

36. Which of the following mixtures are homogeneous, and which are heterogeneous?
    a. gasoline   b. Italian salad dressing
    c. rice pudding   d. an intravenous glucose solution

37. Every sample of the sugar glucose (no matter where on Earth it comes from) consists of 8 parts (by mass) oxygen, 6 parts carbon, and 1 part hydrogen. Is glucose a substance or a mixture? Explain.

38. An advertisement for shampoo says, "Pure shampoo, with nothing artificial added." Is this shampoo a substance or a mixture? Explain.

Elements and Compounds

39. Which of the following represent elements, and which represent compounds?
    a. Ir   b. I   c. InN   d. IF_7

40. Which of the following represent elements, and which represent compounds?
    a. Li   b. CO   c. Cf   d. CF_4

41. Without consulting tables, name each of the following.
    a. Fe   b. Mg   c. He   d. N

42. Without consulting tables, write a symbol for each of the following.
    a. oxygen   b. phosphorus
    c. potassium   d. argon

43. In his 1789 textbook, *Traité élémentaire de Chimie*, Antoine Lavoisier (Chapter 2) listed 33 known elements, one of which was baryte. Which of the following observations best shows that baryte cannot be an element?
    a. Baryte is insoluble in water.
    b. Baryte melts at 1580 °C.
    c. Baryte has a density of 4.48 g/cm^3.
    d. Baryte is formed in hydrothermal veins and around hot springs.
    e. Baryte is formed as a solid when sulfuric acid and barium hydroxide are mixed.
    f. Baryte is formed as a sole product when a particular metal is burned in oxygen.

44. In 1774 Joseph Priestley isolated a gas that he called "dephlogisticated air." Which of the following observations best shows that dephlogisticated air is an element?
    a. Dephlogisticated air combines with charcoal to form "fixed air."
    b. Dephlogisticated air combines with "inflammable air" to form water.
    c. Dephlogisticated air combines with a metal to form a solid called a "calx."
    d. Dephlogisticated air has never been separated into simpler substances.
    e. Dephlogisticated air and "mephitic air" are the main components of the atmosphere.

The Metric System: Measurement and Unit Conversion

45. Change the unit for each of the following measurements by replacing the power of ten with an appropriate SI prefix.
    a. 1.0×10^{-1} L   b. 8.5×10^{-12} g
    c. 1.05×10^{-3} m

46. Convert each of the following measurements to the SI base unit.
    a. 45 mg   b. 125 ns   c. 10.7 μL   d. 12.5346 kg

47. Carry out the following conversions.
    a. 5.52×10^4 mL to L   b. 325 mg to g
    c. 27 cm to m   d. 27 mm to cm
    e. 78 μs to ms

48. Carry out the following conversions.
    a. 546 mm to m   b. 65 ns to μs
    c. 87.6 mg to kg   d. 46.3 dm^3 to L
    e. 181 pm to μm

49. Indicate which is the larger unit in each pair.
    a. mm or cm   b. kg or g   c. dL or μL

50. There are about 7,000,000,000,000,000,000,000,000,000,000 (7 octillion) atoms in an adult human body. What is this quantity in scientific notation?

51. Express the length of a 31-cm ruler in **(a)** mm, **(b)** meters, and **(c)** nm.

52. What is the volume in liters of **(a)** a 352-mL soft drink, **(b)** a 26 kL tank of gasoline?

Density

(You may need data from Table 1.6 for some of these problems.)

53. A silver ingot has a volume of 53.6 cm^3 and weighs 500.0 g. What is the density, in grams per cubic centimeter, of silver?

54. What is the density, in grams per milliliter, of hand sanitizer gel if 25.0 mL of the gel has a mass of 22.4 g?

55. A student measures 49.1 mL of concentrated nitric acid, which has a density of 1.51 g/mL. What is the mass of the acid?

56. The rubber in a pencil eraser has a density of 1.43 g/cm^3. What is the mass of an eraser with a volume of 13.2 cm^3?

57. What is the volume of **(a)** 227 g of hexane (in milliliters) and **(b)** a 454-g block of ice (in cubic centimeters)?

58. What is the volume of **(a)** a 475-g piece of copper (in cubic centimeters) and **(b)** a 253-g sample of mercury (in milliliters)?

59. A 40-mL quantity each of mercury and hexane, as well as 80 mL of water, is placed in the 250-mL beaker shown below. The three liquids do not mix with one another. Sketch the relative locations and levels of the three liquids in the container.

60. A piece of red maple wood ($d = 0.49$ g/cm^3), a piece of balsa wood ($d = 0.11$ g/cm^3), a copper coin, a gold coin, and a piece of ice are dropped into the mixture of Problem 59. Where will each solid end up in the beaker?

61. A metal stand specifies a maximum load of 450 lb. Will it support an aquarium that weighs 59.5 lb and is filled with 37.9 L of seawater ($d = 1.03$ g/mL)?

62. E85 fuel is a mixture of 85% ethanol and 15% gasoline by volume. What mass in kilograms of E85 ($d = 0.758$ g/mL) can be contained in a 14.0-gal tank?

63. A "crystal ball" is 148 mm in diameter and is made of glass that has a density of 3.18 g/cm^3. What is the mass of this object? (The volume of a sphere is $4\pi r^3/3$ where r is the radius.)

64. The base of a paper carton of skim milk is 77×77 mm. Skim milk has a density of 1.031 g/mL. How tall must the carton be to hold 0.500 kg of skim milk?

Energy: Heat and Temperature

65. Liquid nitrogen, used for freezing sperm samples, has a temperature of 77 K. What is this temperature in Celsius?

66. Normal body temperature is about 37 °C. What is this temperature in kelvins?

67. The label on a 100-mL container of orange juice packaged in New Zealand reads in part, "energy . . . 161 kJ." What is that value in kilocalories (food "calories")?

68. To vaporize 1.00 g of sweat (water) from your skin, the water must absorb 584 calories. What is that value in kilojoules?

ADDITIONAL PROBLEMS

69. A certain chemistry class is 1.00 microcentury (μ cen) long. What is its length in minutes?

70. A unit of beauty, a *helen*, thought to have been invented by British mathematician W.A.H. Rushton, is based on Helen of Troy (from Christopher Marlowe's play *Doctor Faustus*), who is widely known as having "the face that launched a thousand ships." How many ships could be launched by a face with 1.00 millihelen of beauty?

71. English chemist William Henry studied the amounts of gases absorbed by water at different temperatures and under different pressures. In 1803, he stated a formula, $p = k_{\mathrm{H}}c$, which related the concentration of the dissolved gas at a constant temperature to the partial pressure of

that gas in equilibrium with that liquid. This relationship describes a scientific

a. hypothesis
b. law
c. observation
d. theory

72. A classmate is planning to try a new diet. On this diet, he can eat anything he wants, but he must swallow a spoonful of crushed ice with each bite of food. His reasoning is (a) it takes about 79 calories of heat to melt one gram of ice, and (b) swallowing the ice and allowing it to melt in his stomach "uses up" that same amount of food energy. Although both (a) and (b) are correct, the diet does

not work. Explain. (*Hint*: See page 29 for a discussion of energy units, then calculate the amount of energy in food calories needed to melt a kilogram of ice.)

73. American writer Cullen Murphy coined a unit of fame, the warhol, based on artist Andy Warhol's claim that "everyone will be famous for fifteen minutes."

   1 warhol = 15 min of fame

   Entertainer Herbert Khaury (stage name Tiny Tim) was famous, starting in 1962, for about 200 kilowarhols. How long was that in years?

For Problems 74 and 75, classify each of the numbered statements as (a) an experiment, (b) a hypothesis, (c) a scientific law, (d) an observation, or (e) a theory. (It is not necessary to understand the science involved to do these problems.)

74. In the early 1800s, many scientific advances came from the study of gases. (1) For example, Joseph Gay-Lussac reacted hydrogen and oxygen to produce water vapor, and he reacted nitrogen and oxygen to form either dinitrogen oxide (N_2O) or nitrogen monoxide (NO). Gay-Lussac found that hydrogen and oxygen react in a 2:1 volume ratio and that nitrogen and oxygen can react in 2:1 or 1:1 volume ratios depending on the product. (2) In 1808, Gay-Lussac published a paper in which he stated that the relative volumes of gases in a chemical reaction are present in the ratio of small integers provided that all gases are measured at the same temperature and pressure. (3) In 1811, Amedeo Avogadro proposed that equal volumes of all gases measured at the same temperature and pressure contain the same number of molecules. (4) By midcentury, Rudolf Clausius, James Clerk Maxwell, and others had developed a detailed rationalization of the behavior of gases in terms of molecular motions.

75. Potassium bromate acts as a conditioner in dough made from wheat flour. Flour contains a protein called *gluten*. Proteins consist of amino-acid units linked in long chains. (1) Dough to which potassium bromate has been added rises better, producing a lighter, larger volume loaf. (2) Potassium bromate acts by oxidizing the gluten and cross-linking tyrosine (an amino acid) units of the protein molecules, enabling the dough to retain gas better. (3) A scientist wonders if sodium bromate might cross-link separate tyrosine molecules, forming a dimer (a molecule consisting of two subunits). (4) She adds sodium bromate to a solution of tyrosine. (5) She notes that a precipitate (solid falling out of solution) is formed.

76. A glass container weighs 48.462 g. A sample of 8.00 mL of antifreeze solution is added, and the container and the antifreeze together weigh 60.562 g. Calculate the density of the antifreeze solution.

77. A block of balsa wood ($d = 0.11$ g/cm^3) is 7.6 cm × 7.6 cm × 94 cm. What is the mass of the block in grams?

78. Arrange the following in order of increasing length (shortest first): (1) a 1.21-m chain, (2) a 75-in. board, (3) a 3-ft 5-in. rattlesnake, (4) a yardstick.

79. Arrange the following in order of increasing mass (lightest first): (1) a 5-lb bag of potatoes, (2) a 1.65-kg cabbage, (3) 2500 g of sugar.

80. One of the people in the photo has a mass of 47.2 kg and a height of 1.53 m. Which one is it likely to be?

81. Some metal chips having a volume of 3.29 cm^3 are placed on a piece of paper and weighed. The combined mass is found to be 18.43 g. The paper itself weighs 1.21 g. Calculate the density of the metal.

82. A 10.5-in. (26.7-cm) iron skillet has a mass of 7.00 lb (3180 g). How many cubic centimeters of iron does it contain? (See Table 1.6.)

83. A 5.79-mg piece of gold is hammered into gold leaf of uniform thickness with an area of 44.6 cm^2. What is the thickness of the gold leaf? (See Table 1.6.)

84. A bundle of cylindrical stainless steel ($d = 7.48$ g/cm^3) rods weighs 1850 kg. Each rod is 6.1 m long and 25.4 mm in diameter. How many rods are in the bundle? The volume of a cylinder $= \pi r^2 h$, where r is the radius and h is the height.

85. What is the mass, in metric tons, of a cube of gold that is 36.1 cm on each side? (1 metric ton = 1000 kg) (See Table 1.6.)

86. A collection of gold-colored metal beads has a mass of 425 g. The volume of the beads is found to be 48.0 cm^3. Using the given densities and those in Table 1.6, identify the metal: bronze ($d = 9.87$ g/cm^3), copper, gold, or nickel silver ($d = 8.86$ g/cm^3).

87. The density of a planet can be approximated from its radius and estimated mass. Calculate the approximate average density, in grams per cubic centimeter, of **(a)** Jupiter, which has a radius of about 7.0×10^4 and a mass of 1.9×10^{27} kg; **(b)** Earth, radius of 6.4×10^3 km and mass of 5.98×10^{24} kg; and **(c)** Saturn, radius 5.82×10^4 km and mass of 5.68×10^{26} kg. The volume of a sphere is $4\pi r^3/3$ where r = radius. How does the density of each planet compare to that of water?

88. The extrasolar planet HAT-P-1 orbits a star 450 light-years from Earth. The planet has about half the mass of Jupiter, and its radius is about 1.38 times that of Jupiter (see Problem 87). Calculate the approximate average density, in grams per cubic centimeter, of HAT-P-1. How does this density compare to that of water?

89. Define green chemistry.
90. List six of the Twelve Principles of Green Chemistry.
91. How does green chemistry reduce risk? (Choose one.)
    a. by reducing hazard and exposure
    b. by avoiding the use of chemicals
    c. by increasing exposures to higher levels
    d. by reducing human errors

92. For companies implementing green chemistry, how does green chemistry save money?
    a. by lowering costs
    b. by using less energy
    c. by creating less waste
    d. all of the above

 CRITICAL THINKING EXERCISES

Apply knowledge that you have gained in this chapter and one or more of the FLaReS principles to evaluate the following statements or claims.

1.1 An alternative health practitioner claims that a nuclear power plant releases radiation at a level so low that it cannot be measured, but that this radiation is harmful to the thyroid gland. He sells a thyroid extract that he claims can prevent the problem.

1.2 A doctor claims that she can cure a patient of arthritis by simply massaging the affected joints. If she has the patient's complete trust, she can cure the arthritis within a year. Several of her patients have testified that the doctor has cured their arthritis.

1.3 German physicist Jan Hendrik Schön of Bell Labs claimed in 2001 that he had produced a molecular scale transistor. Others scientists noted that his data contained irregulari-

ties. Attempts to perform experiments similar to Schön's did not give similar results.

1.4 A mercury-containing preservative called thiomersal was used to prevent bacterial and fungal contamination in vaccines from the 1930s until its use was phased out starting in 1999. In the United States, a widespread concern arose that these vaccines caused autism. There was no such concern in the United Kingdom, although the vaccine with the same preservative was used there. Is the concern valid?

1.5 A woman claims that she has memorized the New Testament. She offers to quote any chapter of any book entirely from memory.

1.6 The label on a bag of Morton solar salt crystals has the statement "No chemicals or additives."

 COLLABORATIVE GROUP PROJECTS

Prepare a PowerPoint, poster, or other presentation (as directed by your instructor) to share with the class.

1. The Global University Leadership Forum has developed a Sustainable Campus Charter by which a school's core mission is aligned with sustainable development, facilities, research, and education. Is your school committed to sustainability? If so, in what way is it working toward sustainability? If not, consult with administrative, faculty, and student groups on how to get such a program started.

2. Prepare a brief biographical report on one of the following.
    a. Frederick Sanger
    b. Rachel Carson
    c. Albert Einstein
    d. George Washington Carver

(The following problem is best done in a group of four students.)

3. Make copies of the following form. Student 1 should write a word from the list in the first column of the form and its definition in the second column. Then, she or he should fold the first column under to hide the word and pass the

sheet to Student 2, who uses the definition to determine what word was defined and place that word in the third column. Student 2 then folds the second column under to hide it and passes the sheet to Student 3, who writes a definition for the word in the third column and then folds the third column under and passes the form to Student 4. Finally, Student 4 writes the word corresponding to the definition given by Student 3.

Compare the word in the last column with that in the first column. Discuss any differences in the two definitions. If the word in the last column differs from that in the first column, determine what went wrong in the process.

a. hypothesis
b. theory
c. mixture
d. substance

Text Entry	Student 1	Student 2	Student 3	Student 4
Word	Definition	Word	Definition	Word

CHEMISTRY@HOME   Rainbow Density Column

Materials Needed:

- $\frac{1}{4}$ cup dark corn syrup
- $\frac{1}{4}$ cup dishwashing liquid
- $\frac{1}{4}$ cup water
- $\frac{1}{4}$ cup vegetable oil
- $\frac{1}{4}$ cup rubbing alcohol
- A tall 12-ounce glass or clear plastic cup
- Food coloring
- Measuring cup

When you drop an ice cube into your glass of water, what happens? Everyone knows that ice floats. . . but, why? The simple answer is density.

Water and ice, even though they are made of the same substance, have different *densities*. Density is a measurement of the ratio of the mass of something to its volume. Remember the density equation (Density = Mass/volume).

For this experiment you will need to locate different liquids that can be found in kitchen and bathroom cabinets. One way you could determine which liquids have higher or lower densities would be to weigh them, but this experiment involves layering the liquids to learn something about the densities of these common household items.

Before you start your experiment, prepare $\frac{1}{4}$ cup of rubbing alcohol with a few drops of food coloring (either blue or green) and prepare $\frac{1}{4}$ cup of water with food coloring (red or orange).

Take the 12-ounce clear glass (slim ones work best). Being careful not to get syrup on the side of the glass, pour the syrup into the center of the bottom of the glass. Pour enough syrup to fill the glass one-sixth of the way.

After you have added the syrup, tip the glass slightly and pour an equal amount of the dishwashing liquid slowly down the side of the glass. Be careful to add the next liquids slowly. Tip the glass slightly, and pouring slowly down the side of the glass, add first the colored water, then the vegetable oil, and finally the colored rubbing alcohol.

Questions

1. Why do the liquids stay separated?
2. Can you determine what the relationship is between the density of a liquid and its position in the glass?
3. Stir up the liquids in the glass and watch what happens to the layers. Have any of the layers mixed?
4. Did you notice a change after a few minutes? Why?
5. Why is it useful to know a substance's density?

ATOMS

Have You Ever Wondered?

1. **What are atoms and why do we care what they are?**

2. **How do we know atoms are not figments of our imaginations?**

3. **Why is it often difficult to destroy hazardous wastes?**

4. **Is light made of atoms?**

5. **Why is the table of elements called the "periodic table"?**

6. **What's the difference between atoms and molecules?**

Learning Objectives

> Explain the ancient Greeks' ideas about the characteristics of matter. (2.1)

> Describe the significance of the laws of conservation of mass and definite proportions. (2.2)

> Calculate the amounts of elements from the composition of a compound. (2.2)

> Explain why the idea that matter is made of atoms is a theory. (2.3)

> Know how atomic theory explains the laws of multiple proportions and conservation of mass. (2.3)

> Describe what a mole is and how it is used. (2.4)

> Convert between the masses and the moles of a substance. (2.4)

> Describe how the elements are arranged in the periodic table and why the arrangement is important. (2.5)

> Distinguish atoms from molecules. (2.6)

> Identify elements that could be classified as hazardous or rare.

> Explain how green chemistry can change technologies that rely on hazardous or rare elements.

ARE THEY FOR REAL? We hear something about atoms almost every day. The twentieth century saw the start of the so-called Atomic Age. The terms *atomic power*, *atomic energy*, and *atomic clock* are a part of our ordinary vocabulary. But just what are atoms?

Every material thing in the world, including you the reader, is made up of atoms, and atoms determine how matter behaves. Because chemistry studies the behavior of matter, it is necessary for anyone studying chemistry to understand atoms to gain insights into how everything works.

At the heart of every "high-tech" device, including cars, refrigerators, printers, smart phones, and tablet computers, lies a wafer of silicon (above right) in one or more integrated circuits (ICs or "chips"). The silicon used for electronics must be so pure that these devices could not be manufactured until zone-refining purification was developed in the early 1950s. Silicon is an *element* made of a single type of atom. For making ICs, only about one atom of impurity can be present for every billion atoms of silicon. But how do we even know that atoms exist? The false-color image at the right shows individual silicon atoms in a hexagonal arrangement, using a recently developed technique called *scanning tunneling microscopy* (STM). However, the behavior of matter led scientists to the atomic nature of matter over two hundred years ago. In this chapter, we will see some of that history, and we will explore the properties of atoms.

So how do chemists define atoms? Atoms are the smallest portion of an element with the properties of that element. For example, one carbon atom—if you could see it in action—would behave the same way as an entire chunk of diamond. Note that a pure diamond is made only of carbon atoms.

Atoms are not all alike. Each element has its own kinds of atoms. On Earth, about 90 elements occur in nature. About two dozen more have been synthesized by scientists. As far as we know, the entire universe is made up of these same few elements.

So how small are atoms? The smallest speck of matter that can be detected by the human eye is made up of many billions of atoms. For example, the United States' Silver Eagle dollar coin contains more than 100,000,000,000,000,000,000,000 (10^{23}) silver atoms. Figure 2.1 tries to place this wondrously large number into context.

Carbon Atom — Multiplied by 3.115×10^{25} → Uncut Cullinan Diamond — Multiplied by 9.611×10^{24} → Planet Earth

59.7 kg
Mountain Lion — Multiplied by ? → 5.97 × 10^{25} kg
Planet Earth

▲ **Figure 2.1** There are more atoms in the largest known raw (uncut) diamond—the Cullinan diamond, which was 3106.75 carats or 621.35 g—than the number of such diamonds that it would take to equal the mass of Planet Earth. In fact, you would have to more than triple the number of Cullinan diamonds.

Q: *An average mountain lion weighs 59.7 kg. How many mountain lions would it take to equal the mass of Planet Earth of 5.97 × 10^{25} kg?*

2.1 Atoms: Ideas from the Ancient Greeks

Learning Objective ❯ Explain the ancient Greeks' ideas about the characteristics of matter.

Ancient Greek philosophers broke our planet—not literally, of course—into four main components or elements: air, water, earth, and fire (Figure 2.2). You can imagine that two of these philosophers, namely Leucippus, who lived in the fifth century B.C.E., and his student Democritus (ca. 460–ca. 370 B.C.E.), might have been looking at a pool of water and thinking about the water being separated into drops, and then each drop being split into smaller and smaller drops, even after they became much too small to see. Is water infinitely divisible? Would you eventually get a drop, or particle, that, if divided, would no longer be water?

Leucippus reasoned that there must ultimately be tiny particles of water that could not be divided any further. After all, from a distance, the sand on the beach looked continuous, but closer inspection showed it to be made up of tiny grains (Figure 2.3).

1. What are atoms and why do we care what they are?

Atoms are the basic building blocks of matter and control the behavior of all matter.

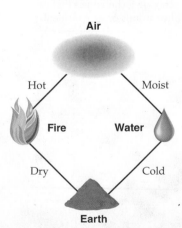

▲ **Figure 2.2** The Greek view of matter was that there were only four elements (in bold) connected by four "principles." The Chinese further broke down the earth component into wood and metal.

▲ **Figure 2.3** A sandy beach.

Q: *Sand looks continuous—infinitely divisible—when you look at a beach from a distance. Is it really continuous? Pavement appears continuous from a moving car, but is this perception correct? Water looks continuous, even when viewed up close. Is it really continuous? Is a cloud continuous? Is air?*

Democritus expanded on Leucippus' idea. He called the particles *atomos* (meaning "cannot be cut"), from which we derive the modern name *atom* for the tiny, discrete particle of an element. Democritus thought that each kind of atom was distinct in shape and size (Figure 2.4). He thought that real substances were mixtures of various kinds of atoms.

Unfortunately for Democritus, along came the famous Greek philosopher Aristotle (ca. 384–ca. 322 B.C.E.), who declared that matter was continuous (infinitely divisible) rather than discrete (consisting of tiny indivisible particles). The people of that time had no way of determining which view was correct. To most of them, Aristotle's continuous view of matter seemed more logical and reasonable. So, this view prevailed for 2000 years, even though it was wrong.

SELF-ASSESSMENT Questions

1. Consider how the qualities *discrete* and *continuous* apply to materials at the macroscopic (visible to the unaided eye) level. Which of the following is continuous?
   a. coffee (the beverage)
   b. a bag of coffee beans
   c. a pile of leaves
   d. a tiled floor

2. The view that matter is continuous rather than atomic prevailed for centuries because it was
   a. actually correct
   b. easy to understand
   c. tested by faulty experiments
   d. tested and found to be true

Answers: 1, a; 2, b

2.2 Scientific Laws: Conservation of Mass and Definite Proportions

Learning Objectives > Describe the significance of the laws of conservation of mass and definite proportions. > Calculate the amounts of elements from the composition of a compound.

Little progress was made in chemistry, especially the atomic view, until the Age of Enlightenment beginning in the 1700s. During this period, a cascade of some colorful, committed, and, by and large, self-funded science "hobbyists" studied gases and developed quantitative methods. These methods led to the beginning of modern chemistry as we know it today.

▲ **Figure 2.4** Democritus imagined that "atoms" of water might be smooth, round balls and that atoms of fire might have sharp edges.

Most notably, we need to go back to Robert Boyle (Anglo-Irish, 1627–1691), a very religious man who wrote the famous book *The Sceptical Chymist*, as well as books on morality. Boyle worked on gases and proposed that elements were made up of various types and sizes of "corpuscles" (atoms), which could organize into groups to create different chemical substances. He also distinguished compounds from mixtures. Boyle stated that if a substance could be broken down into simpler substances, then it was not an element.

Boyle's work led to further study by Joseph Black (France and Scotland, 1728–1799) who showed that air was not a single substance but a mixture. This idea was followed by the work of Joseph Priestley (England, 1733–1804) and Carl Scheele (Sweden, 1742–1786) both of whom discovered oxygen at about the same time. There is evidence that, while Scheele arrived at the discovery first, Priestley had formally published his discovery ahead of Scheele. In the days before e-mail and the Internet, information flowed very slowly, making an exact chronology of discoveries difficult to establish. It should be noted that Priestley, while not particularly strong in theory, was a wonderful experimentalist and discovered nine additional new gases.

Henry Cavendish (England, 1731–1810), a contemporary of Priestley, was a detail-oriented person but was painfully shy and slow to publish, which resulted in a lack of recognition for his work. Yet it was Cavendish's concern for accuracy that led to the development of quantitative methods that yielded the 2:1 volume ratio of hydrogen to oxygen gases in water within 2%.

Building on the work of his predecessors, Antoine-Laurent Lavoisier (France, 1743–1794) was the first to weigh all the substances present before and after the reaction and found that matter was *conserved*—the amount remained constant. He was also the first to interpret the meaning of these results correctly, in modern terms. Accordingly, some consider Lavoisier the father of modern chemistry. In a historical twist, while Lavoisier, a tax collector by day, was being executed during the French Revolution, Joseph Priestley was at sea, in exile, on his way to America. Already a friend of Benjamin Franklin, Priestley became a resident of Pennsylvania.

Chemistry was a collective—but not necessarily collaborative—achievement of a number of contemporaries. This era of chemistry was only possible by the development of ideas and written communication of those developments. Simply stated, scientists always have built knowledge on the knowledge of those who came before them.

▲ Lavoisier is considered by many to be the father of modern chemistry. Here, Lavoisier is shown with his wife, Marie, in a painting by Jacques Louis David in 1788. In her own right, Marie was also a very good scientist.

The Law of Conservation of Mass

Lavoisier summarized his findings as the **law of conservation of mass**, which states that matter is neither created nor destroyed during a chemical change (Figure 2.5).

100.00 grams of mercuric oxide		92.61 grams of mercury		7.39 grams of oxygen
100.00	=	92.61	+	7.39

▲ **Figure 2.5** Although mercuric oxide (a red solid) has none of the properties of mercury (a silver liquid) or oxygen (a colorless gas), when 100.00 g of mercuric oxide is decomposed by heating, the products are 92.61 g of mercury and 7.39 g of oxygen. Properties are completely changed in this reaction, but there is no change in mass.

Q: *When 20.00 g of mercuric oxide decomposes, 1.478 g of oxygen forms. What mass of mercury forms?*

The total mass of the reaction products is always equal to the total mass of the reactants (starting materials). We will discuss chemical reactions in more detail beginning with Chapter 4. For now, some simple examples and discussion will illustrate the conservation of mass.

The law of conservation of mass is the basis for many chemical calculations. This law states that we cannot create materials from nothing. We can make new materials only by changing the way atoms are combined. For example, we can obtain iron metal from iron ore only because the ore contains iron atoms (as we will see in Chapter 12). Furthermore, we cannot get rid of wastes by the destruction of matter. We must put wastes somewhere. However, through chemical reactions, we can change some kinds of potentially hazardous wastes to less harmful forms. Such transformations of matter from one form to another are what chemistry is all about.

2. How do we know atoms are not figments of our imaginations?

If matter had no "smallest particles," the law of conservation of mass, the law of definite proportions, and the law of multiple proportions would be almost impossible to explain. Atomic theory provides a simple explanation for these laws and for many others.

The Law of Definite Proportions

By the end of the eighteenth century, Lavoisier and other scientists noted that many substances were compounds, composed of two or more elements. Each compound had the same elements in the same proportions, regardless of where it came from or who prepared it. The painstaking work of Joseph Louis Proust (France, 1754–1826) convinced most chemists of the general validity of these observations. In one set of experiments, for example, Proust found that basic copper carbonate, whether prepared in the laboratory or obtained from natural sources, was always composed of 57.48% by mass copper, 5.43% carbon, 0.91% hydrogen, and 36.18% oxygen (Figure 2.6).

(a)   (b)   (c)

▲ **Figure 2.6** The compound known as *basic copper carbonate* has the formula $Cu_2(OH)_2CO_3$ and occurs in nature as the mineral *malachite* (a). It is formed as a patina on copper roofs (b). It can also be synthesized in the laboratory (c). Regardless of its source, basic copper carbonate always has the same composition. Analysis of this compound led Proust to formulate the law of definite proportions.

To summarize these and many other experiments, Proust formulated a new scientific law in 1799. The **law of definite proportions** (also known as Proust's law of constant combination, constant composition, or defined proportions) states that a compound always contains the same elements in certain definite proportions and in no others. This law explains Cavendish's 2:1 ratio of hydrogen to oxygen in water and is an example of theory catching up to experimental data. In other cases, experiments have been used to confirm theory, as will be seen later.

Although Jöns Jakob Berzelius (Sweden, 1779–1848) may have been a hypochondriac, he had time to carry out experiments much like the ones illustrated in Figure 2.7. In these experiments, a defined amount of lead (a grayish soft metal) was heated with various amounts of sulfur (a yellow solid) to form lead sulfide (a shiny black solid). Excess sulfur was washed away with carbon disulfide, a solvent that dissolves sulfur but not lead sulfide. As long as he used at least 1.55 g of sulfur with 10.00 g of lead, Berzelius got exactly 11.55 g of lead sulfide. Any sulfur in excess of

▲ **Figure 2.7** An example showing how Berzelius's experiments illustrate the law of definite proportions.

Q: *What mass of lead would completely react with 3.10 g of sulfur? What mass of lead sulfide forms?*

▲ **Figure 2.8** Electrolysis of water. Hydrogen and oxygen are always produced in a volume ratio of 2:1.

Q: *If 24 cubic feet of hydrogen gas are produced by electrolysis, how much oxygen gas will be produced?*

1.55 g was left over. It did not react. If Berzelius used more than 10.00 g of lead with 1.55 g of sulfur, he got 11.55 g of lead sulfide, with some lead left over.

Although Cavendish's 2:1 ratio of hydrogen to oxygen for water was a volume ratio (using an apparatus similar to that shown in Figure 2.8) and Berzelius's experiment gave a mass ratio, both substantiate the law of definite proportions. This scientific law led to rapid developments in chemistry and dealt a deathblow to the ancient Greek idea of water as an element. It is also important to note that the large amount of carefully obtained data provided a depository to be used in testing of other theories, such as Dalton's atomic theory of matter.

The law of definite proportions is the basis for chemical formulas (Chapter 4), such as H_2O for water. Constant composition also means that substances have constant properties. Pure water always dissolves salt or sugar, and at normal pressure, it always freezes at 0 °C and boils at 100 °C.

SELF-ASSESSMENT Questions

1. If a chemical alteration takes place in a sealed container, the mass of the container and its contents
   a. increases
   b. decreases
   c. remains unchanged
   d. is unpredictable

2. When diamond—a pure form of carbon—is burned in an oxygen atmosphere, each carbon atom combines with two oxygen atoms. If a 2.000 g (10.00 carat) diamond is burned in a closed container with only 6.000 g of oxygen, how much will the container's contents weigh after the burning process?
   a. 2.000 g   b. 6.000 g   c. 8.000 g   d. uncertain

3. The ancient Greeks thought that water was an element. In 1800, William Nicholson and Anthony Carlisle decomposed water into hydrogen and oxygen. Their experiment proved that
   a. electricity causes decomposition
   b. the Greeks were correct
   c. hydrogen and oxygen are elements
   d. water is not an element

4. Jim and Jane are husband and wife who like clothes: so much so that each time Jim buys a new hat he also buys a pair (two) of gloves, while every time Jane buys a new purse she also buys a pair of shoes. This one-to-two ratio of hats to gloves and purses to shoes is best described by:
   a. Dalton's atomic theory
   b. Democritus' atomic theory
   c. the law of definite proportions
   d. the law of conservation of mass

5. The composition of water (solid [ice], liquid, or gas [water vapor]) always yields 88.81% oxygen and 11.19% hydrogen by mass, which illustrates:
   a. Dalton's atomic theory
   b. Democritus' atomic theory
   c. the law of definite proportions
   d. the law of conservation of mass

6. In collaboration, Joseph Louis Gay-Lussac (France, 1778–1850) and his friend Alexander von Humboldt (Germany, 1769–1859) passed electric sparks through a mixture of oxygen and hydrogen gases to produce water vapor. They noticed that their experiments always required exactly twice as much volume of hydrogen as oxygen. This finding is best described by:
   a. Dalton's atomic theory
   b. the law of diminishing returns
   c. the law of definite proportions
   d. the law of conservation of mass

7. When 60.0 g of carbon is burned in 160.0 g of oxygen, 220.0 g of carbon dioxide is formed. What mass of carbon dioxide is formed when 60.0 g of carbon is burned in 750.0 g of oxygen?
   a. 60.0 g
   b. 160.0 g
   c. 220.0 g
   d. 810.0 g

Answers: 1, c; 2, c; 3, d; 4, c; 5, c; 6, c; 7, c

2.3 John Dalton and the Atomic Theory of Matter

Learning Objectives > Explain why the idea that matter is made of atoms is a theory.
> Know how atomic theory explains the laws of multiple proportions and conservation of mass.

John Dalton (England, 1766–1844) was not the first to come up with the concept of atoms. This honor goes to Greek philosophers like Democritus. The Greek philosophers, however, were not encumbered with experimental data, and hence, they came up with some wonderfully creative but completely incorrect atomic models. For example, it was their belief that vinegar was composed of spiky atoms and olive oil was made of smooth atoms. While other predecessors of Dalton—like the already mentioned Boyle—wrote about the particulate nature of matter, Dalton's contribution was that he placed the concept of atoms in the framework of the law of definite proportions. He stated that the unvarying ratios come from matter being made of atoms.

As Dalton continued his work, he discovered another law that his theory would have to explain. Proust had stated that a compound contains elements in certain proportions and only those proportions. Dalton's new law, called the **law of multiple proportions**, stated that elements might combine in *more* than one set of proportions, with each set corresponding to a different compound. For example, carbon combines with oxygen in a mass ratio of 1.00:2.66 (or 3.00:8.00) to form carbon dioxide, a gas that is a product of respiration and of the burning of coal or wood. But Dalton found that carbon also combines with oxygen in a mass ratio of 1.00:1.33 (or 3.00:4.00) to form carbon monoxide, a poisonous gas produced when a fuel is burned in the presence of a limited air supply. In short, when elements combine in different proportions, the compounds they form have very different properties.

▲ John Dalton, in addition to developing the atomic theory, carried out important investigations of the behavior of gases. All of his contributions to science were made in spite of the fact that he was color-blind.

Dalton's Atomic Theory	Modern Modifications
1. All matter is composed of extremely small and indestructible particles called atoms.	1. Dalton assumed atoms to be indivisible, but atoms are divisible as we will see in Chapter 3.
2. Elements are made of just one type of atom that is unique to that element.	2. Dalton assumed that all the atoms of a given element were identical in all respects, including mass. We now know this to be incorrect, due to subtleties at the subatomic scale, as we will see on page 49.
3. Compounds are formed when atoms of different elements combine in fixed proportions.	3. Unmodified. Chemists still agree with Dalton. For example, carbon monoxide (carbonic oxide in Dalton's day) has a 1:1 ratio of carbon to oxygen, and carbon dioxide (carbonic acid in Dalton's day) has a 2:1 ratio of carbon to oxygen.
4. A chemical reaction involves a *rearrangement* of atoms, but there is no breaking, destroying, or creating of atoms.	4. Unmodified for *chemical* reactions (Chapter 5), but it does not hold for nuclear reactions (Chapter 11).

3. Why is it often difficult to destroy hazardous wastes?
Hazardous wastes that are compounds or mixtures can be converted to other compounds or mixtures—but the elements from those compounds or mixtures are still present and may be hazardous as well. For example, insecticide containing arsenic oxide can be broken down into the elements arsenic and oxygen—but the element arsenic is poisonous and can't be broken down into something else.

Dalton then used his **atomic theory** to explain the various laws. On the preceding page are the important points of Dalton's atomic theory, with some modern modifications that we will consider later.

Explanations Using Atomic Theory

Dalton's theory clearly explains the difference between elements and compounds. *Elements* are composed of only one kind of atom. For example, a sample of the element phosphorus contains only phosphorus atoms. *Compounds* are made up of two or more kinds of atoms chemically combined in definite proportions (We will see exactly what *kind* means in Section 3.5). For example, water—a compound—contains both hydrogen and oxygen, in the fixed ratio of 2:1.

At this moment, we should formally introduce the concept of a molecule. In the simplest possible terms, a molecule is a combination of two or more atoms. When two or more atoms of the same element combine, a homogeneous compound is formed, such as molecular (or diatomic, meaning 2 atoms) oxygen, O_2, or molecular hydrogen, H_2. This is, in fact, the way both oxygen and hydrogen exist in the atmosphere (air). When two or more atoms of different elements combine, a heterogeneous compound is formed, such as water, H_2O, which combines atoms of oxygen and hydrogen. In fact, you can think of chemical reactions as the rearrangements of atoms through the breaking up and formation of molecules.

Figure 2.9 illustrates how atomic theory can be applied to the law of definite proportions. The figure illustrates that water is formed from 2 hydrogen atoms and 1 oxygen atom; that is, hydrogen and oxygen combine in the defined proportion of 2:1. In addition, note that any unreacted oxygen atoms are still present (left over). In other words, we have the same overall number of hydrogen and oxygen atoms on both sides of the arrow. Thus, this figure illustrates that the atomic theory upholds the law of conservation of mass, as both the right side and left side (separated by the arrow) have the same mass.

▲ **Figure 2.9** The law of definite proportions and the law of conservation of mass interpreted in terms of Dalton's atomic theory.

Q: *If 10 molecules of diatomic oxygen (O_2) and 28 molecules of diatomic hydrogen (H_2) react, how many molecules of H_2O (water) can form? Which element is left over? How many molecules of the leftover element are there?*

The central part of Dalton's atomic theory and its application to the law of definite proportions was the concept that each element was made up of atoms with a single unique weight. In modern times, the concept of weights has been replaced by *relative atomic masses* or, simply, *atomic masses*. You will find a table of atomic masses on the front endpaper of this book. We will use these modern values in some examples showing how Dalton's atomic theory explains the various laws.

Finally, atomic theory explains the law of multiple proportions. For example, 1.00 g of carbon combines with 1.33 g of oxygen to form carbon monoxide or with

2.66 g of oxygen to form carbon dioxide. Carbon dioxide has twice the mass of oxygen per gram of carbon as carbon monoxide does. This is because one atom of carbon combines with *one* atom of oxygen to form carbon monoxide, whereas one atom of carbon combines with *two* atoms of oxygen to form carbon dioxide.

Using modern values, we assign an oxygen atom a relative mass of 16.0 and a carbon atom a relative mass of 12.0. One atom of carbon combined with one atom of oxygen (in carbon monoxide) means a mass ratio of 12.0 parts carbon to 16.0 parts oxygen, or 3.00:4.00. One atom of carbon combined with two atoms of oxygen (in carbon dioxide) gives a mass ratio of 12.0 parts carbon to $2 \times 16.0 = 32.0$ parts oxygen, or 3.00:8.00. Because all oxygen atoms have the same average mass, and all carbon atoms have the same average mass, the ratio of oxygen in carbon dioxide to oxygen in carbon monoxide is 8.00 to 4.00 or 2:1. The same law holds true for other compounds formed from the same two elements. Table 2.1 shows another example of the law of multiple proportions, involving nitrogen and oxygen.

It DOES Matter!

A molecule with one carbon (C) atom and two oxygen (O) atoms is carbon dioxide (CO_2), a gas that you exhale and that provides the "fizz" in soft drinks. Cooled to about −80 °C, it becomes dry ice (shown above), used to keep items frozen during shipping. But a molecule with one less O atom is deadly carbon monoxide, CO. Just 0.2% CO in the air is enough to kill. Unfortunately, most fuels produce a little CO when they burn, which is why a car engine should never be left running in a closed garage.

Table 2.1	The Law of Multiple Proportions		
Compound	Representation[a]	Mass of N per 1.000 g of O	Ratio of the Masses of N[b]
Nitrous oxide		1.750 g	$(1.750 \div 0.4375) = 4.000$
Nitric oxide		0.8750 g	$(0.8750 \div 0.4375) = 2.000$
Nitrogen dioxide		0.4375 g	$(0.4375 \div 0.4375) = 1.000$

[a] ⬤ = nitrogen atom and ⬤ = oxygen atom

[b] We obtain the ratio of the masses of N that combine with a given mass of O by dividing each quantity in the third column by the smallest (0.4375 g).

Isotopes: Atoms of an Element with Different Masses

In Chapter 3, we will explain the reasons for using the word *average* in the discussion above, as this is where part of Dalton's atomic theory has hit a snag. As we have noted, Dalton's second assumption, that all atoms of an element are alike, has been modified.

Atoms of an element *can* have different masses, and such atoms are called *isotopes*. For example, most carbon atoms have a relative atomic mass of 12 (carbon-12), but 1.1% of carbon atoms have a relative atomic mass of 13 (carbon-13).

2.4 The Mole and Molar Mass

Learning Objectives ❯ Describe what a mole is and how it is used. ❯ Convert between the masses and the moles of a substance.

The Mole and Avogadro's Number

At this point in our conversation, some house cleaning is required so that we can use the modern concept of the mole. We started off by asking just how small an atom was and stating that it was amazingly small. However, we are now talking about grams of elements. The reason is that, as a whole, we are more comfortable working in grams than atoms in the chemistry laboratory. This raises the question of exactly how many atoms there are in x grams of an element. To answer this question requires that we measure the same entity at both the incredibly small atomic scale and the more tangible macroscopic (gram) scale.

Modern scientific instrumentation allows us to measure the same entity on both atomic and macroscopic scales. In fact, modern instrumentation can measure exactly how much space a carbon atom in a diamond occupies. We can do this because, in a crystal, which a diamond is, atoms are highly ordered. In a diamond, the carbon atoms are spaced equally apart from each other. This means that for a diamond of known dimensions we know how many carbon atoms it contains. By also knowing the mass of the diamond, we know how many atoms are needed to make up this mass.

Using this approach, we can determine that a diamond weighing 12.011 g, the molecular weight of carbon, contains 6.022×10^{23} atoms of carbon. The quantity, 6.022×10^{23} atoms, is known as *Avogadro's number*, and 6.022×10^{23} atoms of carbon equal one *mole* of carbon. This concept applies to all elements, so that 6.022×10^{23} atoms of any element equal one mole of that element.

Avogadro's number is very large and best imagined using analogies. For example, a mole—that is, the Avogadro's number—of bowling balls weighs more than Earth (1.314×10^{25} lb or 5.972×10^{24} kg), or a mole of great white sharks (2200 lb or 1000 kg each) would equal 100 Earths in mass.

Chemists use the concept of a mole just as a baker and egg farmer use the term *dozen*. Rather than 12, however, chemists use 6.022×10^{23} (a rounded Avogadro's number).

Molar Mass

So how much does a mole of 6.022×10^{23} atoms or molecules weigh? As stated previously, the answer will depend on the element (or elements, in the case of molecules). We also have to pick one element to be used as a point of reference. Here, the choice was easy—carbon. Carbon is rather common, central to the existence of living organisms on Earth, and has a very simple isotopic composition—nearly 99 out of 100 carbon atoms found in nature are carbon-12 isotopes. (Again, you will find out more about isotopes in Chapter 3.) So 1 mole, or 6.022×10^{23} atoms, of pure carbon-12 isotope has a mass of exactly 12.0000 grams, and therefore, the molar mass of carbon-12 is 12.0000 grams per mole. The mass of a sample and the number of atoms or molecules in a sample can be transformed into one another using the concept of a mole (Figure 2.10).

▲ **Figure 2.10** Connecting mass to mole to molecules (and other building blocks of matter) and back highlights the central role of the mole. The number of atoms or molecules is converted to moles through Avogadro's number. The mass of an element or a compound is converted to moles by molar mass. This means, as illustrated, that moles serve as a "hub" while going between the number of atoms (and molecules) and the mass of those atoms (and molecules) and vice versa.

Q: *Using Figure 2.10, determine the mass of 1.807×10^{24} molecules of water. With the aid of Figure 2.10, determine the number of carbon atoms in a 3 g diamond.*

Stated differently, the molar mass of an element is the mass of 6.022×10^{23} atoms of that element, while the molar mass of a compound is the mass of 6.022×10^{23} molecules of that compound. Because carbon-12 is used as a reference, molar masses of all other elements (and compounds) are related to it. Similarly, all elements' atomic masses are expressed relative to carbon-12, and typically, they are expressed in **atomic mass units (amu)**, commonly referred to as *units (u)*.

It is worthwhile to warn you at this time not to confuse two words: molar and molecular, as in *molar* mass and *molecular* weight. Pay attention to the units. For instance, molar mass of atomic hydrogen is 1.0079 grams per mole, molar mass of diatomic hydrogen is $2 \times 1.0079 = 2.0158$ grams per mole, while molecular weight of a single molecule of H_2 is 2.0158 amu.

Problem Solving: Mass, Atom Ratios, and Moles

We can use proportions, such as those determined by Dalton, or moles to calculate the amount of a substance needed to combine with (or form) a given quantity of another substance. To learn how to do this, let's look at some examples.

CONCEPTUAL Example 2.1 | Mass Ratios, Atom Ratios and Moles

Hydrogen gas for fuel cells can be made by decomposing *methane* (CH_4), which is the main component of natural gas. The decomposition gives carbon (C) and hydrogen (H) in a ratio of 3.00 parts by mass of carbon to 1.00 part by mass of hydrogen. How much hydrogen can be made from 90.0 g of methane?

Using Mass Ratios

Solution
We can express the ratio of parts by mass in any units we choose—pounds, grams, kilograms—as long as it is the same for both elements. Using grams as the units, we see that 3.00 g of C and 1.00 g of H would be produced if 4.00 g of CH_4 were decomposed. To convert g CH_4 to g H, we have to find a conversion factor that includes 1.00 g H and 4.00 g CH_4.

We start with the given quantity.

We multiply by the conversion factor, expressed in grams.

$$90.0 \text{ g } CH_4 \times \frac{1.00 \text{ g H}}{4.00 \text{ g } CH_4} = 22.5 \text{ g H}$$

the number   the unit

Using Atom Ratios

Solution
If we look at the formula of methane, CH_4, we can see that for each carbon atom there are four hydrogen atoms. This means that, in methane, the carbon-to-hydrogen atom ratio is always 1:4. From the periodic table, we can see that carbon is about 12 times more massive than hydrogen. This means that if we convert the 1:4 atom ratio to the mass ratio we will get 12:4. Thus, for every 1.0 g of hydrogen produced, there will be 3.0 g of carbon produced. Note that we have arrived at the same conclusion as when pursuing the mass-ratio solution above.

Using Moles

Solution
According to the chemical formula for methane, CH_4, for every one mole of carbon, methane also contains four moles of hydrogen. If we now look at the periodic table, we can see that each mole of carbon weighs 12.0107 g (molar mass of carbon) and that a mole of hydrogen weighs 1.0079 g. For methane, this means that for every one mole (or 12.0107 grams or 6.022×10^{23} atoms) of carbon, we have four moles (equivalent to 4.0316 g or to 24.092×10^{23} atoms) of hydrogen. Thus, once again, we have come very close to the carbon-to-hydrogen mass ratio of 3 to 1 and to an exact 1 to 4 atomic ratio for carbon to hydrogen. The mass ratio is slightly off the 3:1 ratio (2.9791:1.0000 to be exact) because of the presence of isotopes.

4. Is light made of atoms?
Light is not matter and is not made of atoms. Light is a form of energy. Energy—including chemical energy, electrical energy, and nuclear energy—is defined as the ability to do work. We will learn more about energy in Chapter 15.

▪ EXERCISE 2.1A

Phosphine gas can be decomposed to give phosphorus and hydrogen in a mass ratio of 10.3:1.00. If the relative mass of phosphorus is 31.0 when the mass of hydrogen is taken to be 1.00, how many hydrogen atoms are combined with each phosphorus atom in the gas?

▪ EXERCISE 2.1B

Nitrous oxide can be decomposed to give 7.00 parts by mass of nitrogen and 4.00 parts by mass of oxygen. What mass of nitrogen is obtained if enough nitrous oxide is decomposed to yield 36.0 g of oxygen?

CONCEPTUAL Example 2.2 Mass, Atom, or Mole Ratios

Diamonds (just like graphite) can be burned in pure oxygen, and if the temperature is high enough, this reaction produces only carbon dioxide (CO_2). At first, scientists thought that the diamond had simply *disappeared*. This reaction, though, was a critical step in providing evidence that diamonds were simply a pure form of carbon. If we were to completely burn a 10.0000 carat (2.00000 g) diamond with enough pure oxygen, how much CO_2 would be produced?

Using Mass Ratios

Solution

Because diamonds are a pure form of carbon, a 2.00000 g diamond is, in reality, 2.00000 g of carbon. In CO_2, the product of the reaction, for every carbon atom there are two oxygen atoms. The relative mass of oxygen to carbon is 15.9994 to 12.0107. For CO_2 this means that for every 12.0107 g of carbon we will have the following amount of oxygen:

$$2 \times 15.9994 \text{ g} = 31.9988 \text{ g}.$$

Thus, for 2.00000 g of carbon, we will have the following amount of oxygen:

$$2 \times 31.9988 \text{ g}/12.0107 \text{ g} = 5.32838 \text{ g}.$$

If we add the mass of carbon and the mass of oxygen, we get a total mass of 7.32838 g of CO_2.

Using Atom Ratios

Solution

In burning a diamond, two atoms of oxygen are consumed for every one atom of carbon. Therefore, we get the carbon-to-oxygen atom ratio of 1:2. If we now look at the periodic table, it can be seen that oxygen is 15.9994/12.0107 times more massive than carbon. This means that the 1:2 atom ratio gives a mass ratio of:

$$1.00000:2(15.9994/12.0107) = 1.00000:2.66419.$$

Thus, 2.00000 g of carbon commands the use of 5.32838 g of oxygen, and a total mass of the produced CO_2 is 7.32838 g.

Using Moles

Solution

The burning of a diamond yields one mole of CO_2 for every one mole of C (carbon) burned. This means that we have a simple 1:1 molar ratio between C and CO_2. The molar mass of carbon is 12.0107, while the molar mass for CO_2 is the molar mass of carbon plus two times the molar mass of oxygen, which is

$$12.0107 + (2 \times 15.9994) = 44.0095 \text{ g/mole}.$$

A 10.0000 carat diamond has the following moles of carbon

$$2.00000 \text{ g}/12.0107 \text{ g/mole} = 0.66518 \text{ moles.}$$

Therefore, 0.66518 moles of CO_2 weighs (which is how much CO_2 is produced)

$$0.66518 \text{ moles} \times 44.0095 \text{ g/mole} = 7.32838 \text{ g.}$$

Conceptual Example 2.2 shows that more than one method exists when it comes to solving problems. Of course, correct conversions between ratios of atoms, masses, and moles must be applied. In the end, all three alternate solutions presented resulted in the same answer. Scientists often have personal preferences for the methods they use.

■ **EXERCISE 2.2**

When one mole of limestone ($CaCO_3$) is heated, one mole of quicklime (CaO) and one mole of carbon dioxide (CO_2) are formed. What mass of quicklime will be obtained from 200 grams of limestone?

Dalton arrived at his atomic theory by basing his reasoning on experimental findings, and with modest modification, the theory has stood the test of time and of modern, highly sophisticated instrumentation. Formulation of so successful a theory was quite a triumph for a Quaker schoolteacher in 1803. With that said, it can be seen from the above examples that the concept of moles greatly aids in our application of Dalton's atomic theory to common chemical calculations. The importance of the mole will be further highlighted in Chapter 5 (Chemical Accounting).

SELF-ASSESSMENT Questions

1. Consider carbon monoxide (CO) and carbon dioxide (CO_2). They both contain carbon and oxygen. If a sample of CO contains 36.0321 g of C and 47.9982 g of O, how many grams of O would there be in CO_2 if it contained 36.0321 g C?
   a. 15.9994
   b. 47.9982
   c. 36.0321
   d. 95.9964

2. According to Dalton, elements are distinguished from each other by
   a. density in the solid state
   b. nuclear charge
   c. shapes of their atoms
   d. weights of their atoms

3. Dalton postulated that atoms were indestructible to explain why
   a. the same two elements can form more than one compound
   b. no two elements have the same atomic mass
   c. mass is conserved in chemical reactions
   d. nuclear fission (splitting) is impossible

4. Dalton viewed chemical change as
   a. a change of atoms from one type into another
   b. creation and destruction of atoms
   c. a rearrangement of atoms
   d. a transfer of electrons

5. How many types of atoms are present in a given compound?
   a. at least two
   b. hundreds
   c. three or more
   d. depends on the mass of the compound

6. Which statement in regards to a mole of carbon is incorrect?
   a. It contains the Avogadro's number of carbon atoms
   b. It is a quantity of carbon
   c. It weighs 12.0107 g
   d. It contains 12 atoms of carbon

7. Which statement in regards to molar mass is incorrect?
   a. The molar mass of carbon-12 is 12.0000 g/mole
   b. It is the mass of 6.022×10^{23} atoms of an element
   c. It is the mass of 6.022×10^{23} molecules of a compound
   d. It can only be applied to atoms of an element

Questions 8–10 refer to the following figures:

a.

b.

c.

8. Which figure represents an element?

9. Which figure represents a single compound?

10. Which figure represents a mixture?

Answers: 1. d; 2. d; 3. c; 4. c; 5. a; 6. d; 7. d; 8. b; 9. a; 10. c

2.5 Mendeleev and the Periodic Table

Learning Objective ❯ Describe how the elements are arranged in the periodic table and why the arrangement is important.

During the eighteenth and nineteenth centuries, new elements were discovered with surprising frequency. By 1830, there were 55 known elements, all with different properties that demonstrated no apparent order. Dalton had set up a table of relative atomic masses in his 1808 book *A New System of Chemical Philosophy*. Dalton's rough values were improved in subsequent years, notably by Berzelius, who, in 1828, published a table of atomic weights containing 54 elements. Most of Berzelius's values agree well with modern values.

Emerging Patterns and Periodicity within the Known Elements

As early as 1816, Johann Wolfgang Döbereiner (Germany, 1780–1849) found a triadic relationship between elements based on their atomic masses. The average mass of the lighter and heavier atoms of the triad equaled the mass of the middle element of the triad. Some examples of the triads he found are Li/Na/K; Ca/Sr/Ba; Cl/Br/I; and S/Se/Te. You can check to see how well these triads work with the modern periodic table at the front cover of the textbook. Although useful at the time, these types of relationships have been replaced by the relationship present in the modern-day periodic table.

CONCEPTUAL Example 2.3 Predicting Periodic Properties

Solution
The atomic mass of lithium (Li) is 6.941 u and that of potassium (K) is 39.098 u. The average of the two is (6.941 u + 39.098 u) ÷ 2 = 23.020 u, quite close to the modern value for sodium (Na) of 22.989 u.

▪ **EXERCISE 2.3**
One of Döbereiner's triads included the *salt formers*: chlorine, bromine, and iodine. Show that the relative atomic mass of the middle element in this triad is close to the average of the relative atomic masses of the other two elements.

▲ Dmitri Mendeleev, the Russian chemist who arranged the 63 known elements into a periodic table similar to the one we use today, was considered one of the great teachers of his time. Unable to find a suitable chemistry textbook, he wrote his own, *The Principles of Chemistry*. Mendeleev also studied the nature and origin of petroleum and made many other contributions to science. Element 101 is named mendelevium (Md) in his honor.

The next trend noticed in the available atomic masses was that atomic masses were separated by regular intervals of eight times the atomic mass of hydrogen. This pattern was discovered by both the English chemist John Newlands (1837–1898) and French mineralogist Alexandre Béguyer de Chancourtois (1820–1886). It is sometimes referred to as Newlands's law of octaves, even though Béguyer de Chancourtois was the first to publish his idea in 1863, two years before Newlands did.

The Periodic Table: Mendeleev and Meyer

The patterns discovered by these scientists were followed by the work of Julius Lothar Meyer (Germany, 1830–1895) and Dmitri Ivanovich Mendeleev (Russia, 1834–1907). They both linked chemical properties to atomic mass and, in doing so, developed the periodic law. In 1862, Meyer published his periodic table of 28 elements, while in 1869 Mendeleev published his *first* periodic table for all the known

63 elements (with some corrected atomic masses), as well as spaces where he predicted the yet undiscovered elements should be! He even predicted the properties of these elements, based on the periodic law.

Three of the missing elements were soon discovered and named scandium, gallium, and germanium. As can be seen in Table 2.2, Mendeleev's predictions for germanium—called eka-silicon at the time—were amazingly successful. Mendeleev's great genius lay in his ability to connect the *knowns* as well as to *fill in the blanks* and predict the existence of the *unknowns*. The predictive value of his periodic table led to its wide acceptance. This is why Mendeleev tends to be given almost sole credit for developing the periodic table.

Mendeleev continued to tinker with the periodic table for much of his life, eventually placing silver, gold, and several other metals slightly out of the previously proposed order. Doing so allowed sulfur, selenium, and tellurium, which have similar chemical properties, to appear in the same column. This rearrangement also put iodine in the same column as chlorine and bromine, which iodine resembles chemically.

5. Why is the table of elements called the "periodic table"?

Periodic indicates that something occurs regularly. The physical and chemical properties of the elements are periodic. That is, many of those properties are similar for elements in a given column of the table.

Table 2.2 **Properties of Germanium: Predicted and Observed**

Property	Predicted by Mendeleev for Eka-Silikon (1871)	Observed by Winkler for Germanium (1886)
Atomic mass	72	72.6
Density (g/cm^3)	5.5	5.47
Color	Dirty gray	Grayish white
Density of oxide (g/cm^3)	EsO_2:4.7	GeO_2:4.703
Boiling point of chloride	$EsCl_4$:below 100 °C	$GeCl_4$:86 °C

Tabelle II.

Reihen	Gruppe I. — R^2O	Gruppe II. — RO	Gruppe III. — R^2O^3	Gruppe IV. RH^4 RO^2	Gruppe V. RH^3 R^2O^5	Gruppe VI. RH^2 RO^3	Gruppe VII. RH R^2O^7	Gruppe VIII. — RO^4
1	H = 1							
2	Li = 7	Be = 9,4	B = 11	C = 12	N = 14	O = 16	F = 19	
3	Na = 23	Mg = 24	Al = 27,3	Si = 28	P = 31	S = 32	Cl = 35,5	
4	K = 39	Ca = 40	— = 44	Ti = 48	V = 51	Cr = 52	Mn = 55	Fe = 56, Co = 59, Ni = 59, Cu = 63.
5	(Cu = 63)	Zn = 65	— = 68	— = 72	As = 75	Se = 78	Br = 80	
6	Rb = 85	Sr = 87	?Yt = 88	Zr = 90	Nb = 94	Mo = 96	— = 100	Ru = 104, Rh = 104, Pd = 106, Ag = 108.
7	(Ag = 108)	Cd = 112	In = 113	Sn = 118	Sb = 122	Te = 125	J = 127	
8	Cs = 133	Ba = 137	?Di = 138	?Ce = 140	—	—	—	— — — —
9	(—)			—		—	—	
10	—	—	?Er = 178	?La = 180	Ta = 182	W = 184	—	Os = 195, Ir = 197, Pt = 198, Au = 199.
11	(Au = 199)	Hg = 200	Ti = 204	Pb = 207	Bi = 208	—	—	
12	—	—	—	Th = 231	—	U = 240	—	— — — —

der chemischen Elemente.

▲ **Figure 2.11** Mendeleev's periodic table. In this 1898 version, he wrongly "corrected" the atomic weight of tellurium to be less than that of iodine.

▲ **Figure 2.12** Representation of an element on the modern periodic table.

The modern periodic table contains 118 elements, some of which have reportedly been observed or synthesized but have not yet been verified or named. Each element is represented by a box in the periodic table, as shown in Figure 2.12. We will discuss the periodic table and its theoretical basis in Chapter 3.

SELF-ASSESSMENT Questions

1. Which of the following is *not* true of Mendeleev's periodic table?
   a. It includes new elements that he had just discovered.
   b. The elements are arranged generally in order of increasing atomic mass.
   c. He left gaps for predicted new elements.
   d. He placed some heavier elements before lighter ones.

2. Meyer and Mendeleev arranged elements in their periodic tables
   a. alphabetically
   b. according to their chemical properties
   c. in the order they were discovered
   d. using the Eastern philosophical system of Feng Shui

3. Relative masses in the modern periodic table are based on the value for
   a. the carbon-12 isotope
   b. the hydrogen atom
   c. naturally occurring oxygen
   d. the oxygen-16 isotope

4. The number of elements known today is approximately
   a. 12
   b. 100
   c. 1000
   d. 30 million

Answers: 1, a; 2, b; 3, a; 4, b

▲ An image of atoms of manganese obtained using STM.

6. What's the difference between atoms and molecules?

A molecule is made of atoms that are combined in fixed proportions. A carbon atom is the smallest particle of the element carbon, and a carbon dioxide molecule is the smallest particle of the compound carbon dioxide. As you have probably figured out, molecules can be broken down into their atoms.

2.6 Atoms and Molecules: Real and Relevant

Learning Objective ❯ Distinguish atoms from molecules.

Are atoms real? Certainly they are real as a concept, a highly useful concept. And scientists today can observe computer-enhanced images of individual atoms. These portraits provide powerful (though still indirect) evidence that atoms exist.

Are atoms relevant? Much of modern science and technology—including the production of new materials and the technology of pollution control—is based on the concept of atoms. We have seen that atoms are conserved in chemical reactions. Thus, material things—things made of atoms—can be recycled, for the atoms are not destroyed no matter how we use them. The one way we might "lose" a material from a practical standpoint is to spread its atoms so thinly that it would take too much time and energy to put them back together again. The essay on recycling (page 57) describes a real-world example of such loss.

Now back to Leucippus and Democritus and their musings on that Greek beach. We now know that if we keep dividing drops of water, we will ultimately obtain a small particle—called a *molecule*—that is still water. A **molecule** is a group of atoms chemically bonded, or connected, to one another. Molecules are represented by chemical formulas. The symbol H represents an *atom* of hydrogen. The formula H_2 represents a *molecule* of hydrogen, which is composed of two hydrogen atoms. The formula H_2O represents a molecule of water, which is composed of two hydrogen atoms and one oxygen atom. If we divide a water molecule, we will obtain *two atoms* of hydrogen and *one atom* of oxygen.

And if we divide those atoms . . . but that is a story for another time.

Dalton regarded the atom as indivisible, as did his successors up until the discovery of radioactivity in 1895. We examine the evolving concept of the atom in Chapter 3.

Recycling

Because it is an element, iron cannot be created or destroyed in a chemical reaction, but that does not mean it always exists in its elemental state. Let's consider two different pathways for the recycling of iron.

1. Hematite, an iron ore, is obtained from a mine and converted into pig iron, which is used to make steel cans. Once discarded, the cans rust. Iron ions (ions are explained in Chapter 4) slowly leach from the rust into groundwater and eventually wind up in the ocean. These dissolved ions can be absorbed by and incorporated into marine plants. Marine creatures that eat the plants will in turn absorb and incorporate iron ions. The original iron atoms are now widely separated in space. Some of them might even become part of the hemoglobin in your blood. The iron has been recycled, but it will never again resemble the original pig iron. This means that for new products to be made of iron, more iron must be mined. Mining makes it a nonsustainable practice in the long run. It is also not a chemically green approach due to the environmental damage caused by iron-mining practices.

2. Iron ore is taken from a mine and converted to pig iron and then into steel. The steel is used in making an automobile, which is driven for a decade and then sent to the junkyard. There, it is compacted and sent to a recycling plant, where the steel is recovered and ultimately used again in a new automobile. Once the iron was removed from its ore, it was conserved in its elemental metallic form. In this form of recycling, the iron continues to be useful for a long time. This is a sustainable practice because it allows the mined iron to be reused over and over again. It is also a chemically green practice because recycling iron places much less stress on the environment than iron-mining practices do.

SELF-ASSESSMENT Questions

1. We can recycle materials because atoms
   a. always combine in the same way
   b. are conserved
   c. are indivisible
   d. combine in multiple portions

2. A molecule is
   a. a collection of like atoms
   b. conserved in chemical reactions
   c. a group of atoms chemically bonded to one another
   d. indivisible

3. Which statement is correct in regards to recycling?
   a. Compounds are never altered.
   b. New elements may be created, except for gold.
   c. Elements remain unaltered.
   d. Only iron can be recycled.

Answers: 1, b; 2, c; 3, c

GREEN CHEMISTRY

Lallie C. McKenzie, *Chem11 LLC*

It's Elemental

Learning objectives ❯ Identify elements that could be classified as hazardous or rare. ❯ Explain how green chemistry can change technologies that rely on hazardous or rare elements.

In this chapter, you learned that everything is made up of atoms and that an atom is the smallest particle that is characteristic of a given element. Although the universe is composed of an uncountable number of compounds and mixtures, the basic building blocks are elements. The periodic table (Section 2.4) organizes the elements by relative mass and, more importantly, by their predictable chemical properties.

What do elements have to do with green chemistry? When chemists design products and processes, they take advantage of the entire periodic table, including elements used rarely or not at all in nature or our bodies. It is important to think about impacts of the chosen elements on human health and the environment. Two important factors to evaluate are inherent hazard and natural abundance. Hazard can be different for the element itself or when it is in a compound, so the element's form can determine whether it causes harm. For example, elemental sodium is very reactive with water, but sodium chloride is a compound that we eat. Also, as you learned from the law of conservation of mass (Section 2.2), elements cannot be created or destroyed. Therefore, the amounts on the planet are limited and may be scarce.

Green chemistry principles #3, #7, and #10 apply to products and processes that involve hazardous and rare elements. Understanding the impacts of toxic elements and compounds on human health and the environment helps us to develop safer alternatives and reduce or eliminate the use of these materials. Also, designing new technologies that rely on earth-abundant elements can prevent depletion of resources. Finally, reclaiming materials after use is critical if they can cause harm or are scarce.

The use of three hazardous elements – lead, cadmium, and mercury – has been reduced through green chemistry. These elements are known to harm systems of the human body and have a negative impact on children's development. Although they are important in many products, the urgent need to limit exposure to these elements has led to developing safer alternatives. For example, lead is no longer in paint, compounds with lower toxicity now substitute for lead stabilizers and cadmium pigments in plastics, and new chemicals are being used instead of traditional solder in electronics. Substitution of metal hydrides for cadmium in batteries has

diminished cadmium use. In addition, a variety of new efficient light bulbs are available that contain no mercury, and electronic or nonhazardous thermometers and switches have replaced mercury-based versions. Because coal-fired power plants emit mercury, advances in alternative energy sources also reduce our exposure to this element.

Many current technologies may be limited by their need for scarce elements, but green chemistry can promote new opportunities. Although almost all of the elements are found in the earth's crust, eight account for more than 98% of the total. In fact, almost three-quarters of the earth's crust is comprised of two elements, silicon and oxygen. Currently, the permanent magnets in computer hard drives, wind turbines, and hybrid cars include the scarce elements neodymium and dysprosium. Also, many products depend on cerium, yttrium, neodymium, and lanthanum. These elements are drawn from a single source and can be hard to separate from other materials. Current supplies are much lower than needed to support projected growth. Approaches based on earth-abundant elements (such as silicon, iron, and aluminum) would support technology and protect resources.

Green chemistry supports the design of materials where the individual elemental components can be recycled easily. Atoms of a material can be reclaimed directly through recycling or spread through the environment. If released, hazardous materials can have a negative effect on health and the environment, so recycling of these elements should be a priority. Reclaiming raw materials reduces the demand for natural resources, including scarce elements.

Green chemistry approaches are especially important when products and processes present health or environmental risks. Identifying and replacing hazardous and rare elements can lead to greener technologies and a sustainable future for everyone.

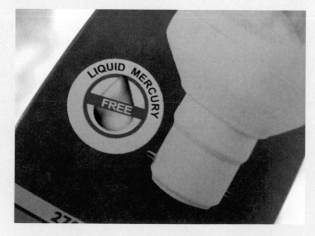

◀ New technologies have led to mercury-free efficient light bulbs like this one. These products save energy and do not contain toxic elements that were used for traditional fluorescent lighting.

SUMMARY

Section 2.1—The concept of atoms was first suggested in ancient Greece by Leucippus and Democritus. However, this idea was rejected for almost 2000 years in favor of Aristotle's view that matter was continuous.

Section 2.2—The **law of conservation of mass** resulted from careful experiments by Cavendish, Lavoisier, and others, who weighed all the reactants and products for a number of chemical reactions and found that no change in mass occurred. Boyle said that a proposed element must be tested. If it could be broken down into simpler substances, it was not an element. The **law of definite proportions** (law of constant composition, constant combinations, or defined proportions) was formulated by Proust, based on his experiments and on those of Berzelius. It states that a given compound always contains the same elements in exactly the same proportions by mass.

Section 2.3—In 1803, Dalton explained the laws of definite proportions and conservation of mass with his **atomic theory**, which had four main points: (1) Matter is made up of tiny particles called atoms; (2) atoms of the same element are alike; (3) compounds are formed when atoms of different elements combine in certain proportions; and (4) during chemical reactions, atoms are rearranged, not destroyed.

Dalton also discovered the **law of multiple proportions**, which states that different elements might combine in two or more different sets of proportions, each set corresponding to a different compound. His atomic theory also explained this new law. These laws can be used to perform calculations to find the amounts of elements that combine or are present in a compound or reaction. In more than two centuries, atomic theory has undergone only minor modifications. The most significant change has been due to the recognition that not all atoms of an element are identical, with some having slightly different masses; such atoms are known as **isotopes**.

Section 2.4—A **mole** of X consists of 6.022×10^{23} particles (atoms, molecules, or compounds) of X. The figure 6.022×10^{23} is known as **Avogadro's number**. The mass of 6.022×10^{23} atoms or molecules is known as the **molar mass**. Both the atomic masses reported in the periodic table (in **atomic mass units, amu**), and the molar masses we use in calculations (in grams per mole) are relative to the atomic mass and the molar mass of carbon-12.

Section 2.5—Berzelius published a table of atomic weights in 1828, and his values agree well with modern ones. In 1869, Mendeleev published his version of the **periodic table**, a systematic arrangement of the elements that allowed him to predict the existence and properties of undiscovered elements. In the modern periodic table, each element is listed, along with its symbol and the average mass of an atom of that element.

Section 2.6—Because atoms are conserved in chemical reactions, matter (which is made of atoms) can always be recycled. Atoms can be lost, in effect, if they are scattered in the environment. A **molecule** is a group of atoms chemically bonded together. Just as an atom is the smallest particle of an element, a molecule is the smallest particle of most compounds.

GREEN CHEMISTRY   When chemists design products and processes, potential impacts on human health and the environment of the incorporated elements should be considered. Identifying and replacing toxic and rare elements can lead to greener technologies and enhance sustainability.

Learning Objectives

› Explain the ancient Greeks' ideas about the characteristics of matter. (2.1)	Problems 1–3
› Describe the significance of the laws of conservation of mass and definite proportions. (2.2)	Problems 4–6, 15–28, 47, 48
› Calculate the amounts of elements from the composition of a compound. (2.2)	Problems 7, 49–51
› Explain why the idea that matter is made of atoms is a theory. (2.3)	Problem 8
› Know how atomic theory explains the laws of multiple proportions and conservation of mass. (2.3)	Problems 9–11, 29–40, 52, 53
› Describe what a mole is and how it is used. (2.4)	Problems 12, 41–44, 54
› Convert between the masses and the moles of a substance. (2.4)	Problems 12, 41–43
› Describe how the elements are arranged in the periodic table and why the arrangement is important. (2.5)	Problems 13, 55
› Distinguish atoms from molecules. (2.6)	Problems 14, 45, 46
› Identify elements that can be classified as hazardous or rare.	Problem 56
› Explain how green chemistry can change technologies that rely on hazardous or rare elements.	Problems 57, 58

REVIEW QUESTIONS

1. Distinguish between **(a)** the atomic view and the continuous view of matter and **(b)** the ancient Greek definition of an element and the modern one.

2. What was Democritus' contribution to atomic theory? Why did the idea that matter was continuous (rather than atomic) prevail for so long? What discoveries finally refuted the idea?

3. Consider the following *macroscopic* (visible to the unaided eye) objects. Which are best classified as *discrete* (like Democritus' description of matter), and which are *continuous* (like Aristotle's description)?
   a. people   b. cloth
   c. calculators   d. milk chocolate
   e. M&M's candies

4. What were Boyle's contributions to modern chemistry?

5. Cavendish found that water was composed of two hydrogen atoms for every one oxygen atom, Explain how this supports the law of definite proportions.

6. Describe Lavoisier's contribution to the development of modern chemistry.

7. Fructose (fruit sugar) is always composed of 40.0% carbon, 53.3% oxygen, and 6.7% hydrogen regardless of the fruit that it comes from. What law does this illustrate?

8. Outline the main points of Dalton's atomic theory, and apply them to the following laws: **(a)** conservation of mass, **(b)** definite proportions, and **(c)** multiple proportions.

9. What law does the following list of compounds illustrate? N_2O, NO, NO_2, N_2O_4

10. State the law of multiple proportions. For a fixed mass of the first element in each of the following compounds, what is the relationship between (ratio of) the
    a. masses of oxygen in ClO_2 and in ClO?
    b. masses of fluorine in ClF_3 and ClF?
    c. masses of oxygen in P_4O_6 and P_4O_{10}?

11. In the figure, the blue spheres represent phosphorus atoms, and the red ones represent oxygen atoms. The box labeled

"Initial" represents a mixture. Which one of the other three boxes (A, B, or C) could *not* represent that mixture after a chemical reaction occurred? Explain briefly.

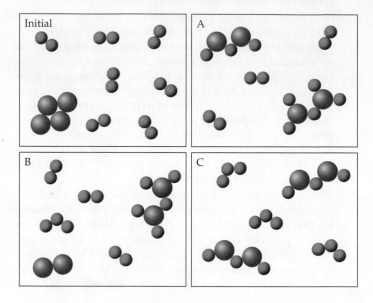

12. **a.** How is Avogadro's number linked with the concept of the mole? **b.** How many atoms are in a mole of oxygen? **c.** How many molecules are in a mole of caffeine? **d.** How much does a mole of diatomic nitrogen (N_2) weigh?

13. Explain how the periodic law allowed Mendeleev to construct his periodic table and to predict the existence and properties of elements yet to be discovered.

14. Lavoisier considered *alumina* an element. In 1825, the Danish chemist Hans Christian Oersted (1777–1851) isolated aluminum metal by reacting aluminum chloride with potassium. Later experiments showed that alumina is formed by reacting aluminum metal with oxygen. What did these experiments prove?

PROBLEMS

Conservation of Mass

15. **a.** If a closed container contains a mouse as well as enough food, water, and oxygen for the mouse to live for three weeks, how much will the container weigh 1 and 2 weeks later after the mouse has eaten, drunk, and exercised (respiration is CO_2 emission), and why? **b.** If the mouse was in a wire cage and only the weights of the mouse, food, and water were considered, would you come to the same answer as in **a.** and why?

16. An iron nail dissolves in a solution of hydrochloric acid. The nail disappears. Have the iron atoms been destroyed? If so, how? If not, where are they?

17. If you place a 4.00 g effervescent antacid pill into 100 mL (100 g) of water in a 100 g glass, how much will the

glass of water weigh once the antacid pill has dissolved and why?
   a. 104 g   b. 204 g
   c. less than 204 g   d. more than 204 g

18. Please explain how the following two combustion (burning) reactions appear to disobey the law of conservation of mass:
   a. When a diamond is burned, the mass that remains is zero.
   b. When a piece of wood is burned, the leftover ashes weigh less than the wood.
   Upon further investigation, it is noted that CO_2 is vented off from both reactions. With this additional information, state how you can prove the diamond is made of pure carbon and yet the wood is not.

19. Acetylene, used for welding, contains 24.02 g of carbon for every 2.02 g of hydrogen. If you have 78.5 g of carbon that can be converted to acetylene, what mass of hydrogen will be needed for the conversion?

20. Nitrous oxide (N_2O, "laughing gas") contains 28.01 g of nitrogen in every 44.01 g of nitrous oxide. What mass of nitrous oxide can be formed from 48.7 g of nitrogen?

21. An overly enthusiastic chemistry student burns 88.20 g of propane (C_3H_8; 36.03 g C for each to 8.07 g H) and states that 300.06 g of CO_2 (12.01 g C for each 32.00 g O) was produced. Explain to the student why her answer is impossible.

22. A student heats 2.796 g of zinc powder with 2.414 g of sulfur. He reports that he obtains 4.169 g of zinc sulfide and recovers 1.041 g of unreacted sulfur. Show by calculation whether or not his results obey the law of conservation of mass.

23. When 1.00 g zinc and 0.80 g sulfur are allowed to react, all the zinc is used up, 1.50 g of zinc sulfide is formed, and some unreacted sulfur remains. What is the mass of *unreacted* sulfur (choose one)?
    a. 0.20 g
    b. 0.30 g
    c. 0.50 g
    d. impossible to determine from this information alone

24. A city has to come up with a plan to dispose of its solid wastes. The solid wastes consist of many different kinds of materials, and the materials consist of many different kinds of atoms. The options for disposal include burying the wastes in a landfill, incinerating them, and dumping them at sea. Which method, if any, will get rid of the atoms that make up the wastes? Which method, if any, will immediately change the chemical form of the wastes?

Definite Proportions

25. When 18.02 g of water is decomposed by electrolysis, 16.00 g of oxygen and 2.02 g of hydrogen are formed. According to the law of definite proportions, what masses, in grams, of **(a)** hydrogen and **(b)** oxygen will be formed by the electrolysis of 775 g of water?

26. Hydrogen from the decomposition of water has been promoted as the fuel of the future (Chapter 15). What mass of water, in kilograms, would have to be electrolyzed to produce 125 kg of hydrogen? (See Problem 25.)

27. Given a plentiful supply of air, 3.0 parts carbon will react with 8.0 parts oxygen by mass to produce carbon dioxide. Use this mass ratio to calculate the mass of carbon required to produce 14 kg of carbon dioxide.

28. If a diamond is burned in an oxygen-containing atmosphere, the carbon in the diamond is converted to CO_2. How much CO_2 will be produced if a 0.4 g (2 carat) diamond is burned? (See Problem 27.)

Dalton's Atomic Theory

29. Are the following findings, expressed to the nearest atomic mass unit, in agreement with Dalton's atomic theory? Explain your answers.
    a. An atom of calcium has a mass of 40 u; an atom of vanadium, 1 u.
    b. An atom of calcium has a mass of 40 u; an atom of potassium, 40 u.

30. The Greeks thought that atoms had different shapes, with water and oil atoms being smooth and atoms associated with fire and spiciness having sharp edges. Does this view agree with Dalton's atomic theory? Explain your answer.

31. Use Dalton's atomic theory to explain what is happening to the carbon atoms when a diamond is burned and to oxygen and hydrogen atoms when water is electrolyzed.

32. According to Dalton's atomic theory, when elements react, their atoms combine in (choose one)
    a. a simple whole-number ratio that is unique for each set of elements
    b. exactly a 1:1 ratio
    c. one or more simple whole-number ratios
    d. pairs
    e. random proportions

33. Hydrogen and oxygen combine in a mass ratio of about 1:8 to form water. If every water molecule consists of two atoms of hydrogen and one atom of oxygen, what fraction or multiple of the mass of a hydrogen atom is the mass of an oxygen atom?
    a. $\frac{1}{16}$ b. $\frac{1}{8}$
    c. 8 times   d. 16 times

34. The elements fluorine and nitrogen combine in a mass ratio of 57:14 to form a compound. If every molecule of the compound consists of three atoms of fluorine and one atom of nitrogen, what fraction or multiple of the mass of a fluorine atom is the mass of a nitrogen atom?
    a. $\frac{19}{14}$ b. 3 times
    c. $\frac{14}{19}$ d. 14 times

Multiple Proportions

35. Carbon combines with oxygen in a mass ratio of 1.000:2.664 to form carbon dioxide (CO_2) and in a mass ratio of 1.000:1.332 to form carbon monoxide (CO). A third carbon–oxygen compound, called carbon suboxide, is 52.96% C by mass and 47.04% O by mass. Show that these compounds follow the law of multiple proportions.

36. A compound containing only oxygen and rubidium has 0.187 g of O per 1.00 g of Rb. The relative atomic masses are 16.0 for O and 85.5 for Rb. What is a possible O-to-Rb mass ratio for a different oxide of rubidium (choose one)?
    a. 8.0:85.5   b. 16.0:85.5
    c. 32.0:85.5   d. 16.0:171

37. A sample of an oxide of tin with the formula SnO consists of 0.742 g of tin and 0.100 g of oxygen. A sample of another oxide of tin consists of 0.555 g of tin and 0.150 g of oxygen. What is the formula of the second oxide?

38. Consider three oxides of nitrogen, X, Y, and Z. Oxide X has an oxygen-to-nitrogen mass ratio of 2.28:1.00, oxide Y has an oxygen-to-nitrogen mass ratio of 1.14:1.00, and oxide Z has an oxygen-to-nitrogen mass ratio of 0.57:1.00. What is the whole-number ratio of masses of oxygen in these compounds given a fixed mass of nitrogen?

39. Iron forms a number of oxides in nature. A sample of wüstite (FeO) contains 0.558 g of Fe and 0.160 g O, while samples of hematite and magnetite contain 0.558 g of Fe and 0.240 g O and 3.35 g Fe and 1.28 O, respectively. Given what we know about wüstite, what are the iron-to-oxygen ratios for hematite and magnetite? Do your conclusions agree with the law of multiple proportions? Explain your answer.

40. Two compounds, V and W, are composed only of hydrogen and carbon. Compound V is 80.0% carbon by mass and 20.0% hydrogen by mass. Compound W is 83.3% carbon by mass and 16.7% hydrogen by mass. What is the ratio of masses of hydrogen in these compounds given a fixed mass of carbon?

Moles and Molecular Mass

41. A pure diamond is made only of carbon atoms. How many moles of carbon are there in a 1.000 g (5.000 carat) diamond? From how many atoms of carbon is this diamond composed?

42. A water molecule is made up of one oxygen atom and two hydrogen atoms. What is the mass of one mole of water? How many atoms of oxygen and hydrogen are there in one mole of water?

43. What is the mass of 5 moles of carbon-12? What is the mass of 5 moles of carbon?

44. What is the mass of hydrogen relative to carbon-12? What is the mass of hydrogen relative to carbon?

Chemical Compounds

45. A blue solid called *azulene* is thought to be a pure compound. Analyses of three samples of the material yield the following results.

	Mass of Sample	Mass of Carbon	Mass of Hydrogen
Sample 1	1.000 g	0.937 g	0.0629 g
Sample 2	0.244 g	0.229 g	0.0153 g
Sample 3	0.100 g	0.094 g	0.0063 g

Could the material be a pure compound?

46. A colorless liquid is thought to be a pure compound. Analyses of three samples of the material yield the following results.

	Mass of Sample	Mass of Carbon	Mass of Hydrogen
Sample 1	1.000 g	0.862 g	0.138 g
Sample 2	1.549 g	1.295 g	0.254 g
Sample 3	0.988 g	0.826 g	0.162 g

Could the material be a pure compound? Explain.

 ADDITIONAL PROBLEMS

47. A compound of uranium and fluorine is used to generate uranium for nuclear power plants. The gas can be decomposed to yield 2.09 parts by mass of uranium for every 1 part by mass of fluorine. If the relative mass of a uranium atom is 238 and the relative mass of a fluorine atom is 19, calculate the number of fluorine atoms that are combined with one uranium atom.

48. In one experiment, 3.06 g hydrogen was allowed to react with an excess of oxygen to form 27.35 g water. In a second experiment, electric current broke down a sample of water into 1.45 g hydrogen and 11.51 g oxygen. Are these results consistent with the law of definite proportions? Show why or why not.

49. Two experiments were performed in which sulfur was burned completely in pure oxygen gas, producing sulfur dioxide and leaving some unreacted oxygen. In the first experiment, burning 0.312 g of sulfur produced 0.623 g of sulfur dioxide. In the second experiment, 1.305 g of sulfur was burned. What mass of sulfur dioxide was produced?

50. Use Figure 2.5 to calculate the mass of mercuric oxide that would be needed to produce 100.0 g of mercury metal.

51. See Table 2.1. Another compound of nitrogen and oxygen contains 0.5836 g of nitrogen per 1.000 g of oxygen. Calculate the ratio of mass of N in this compound to mass of N in nitrogen dioxide. What *whole-number* ratio does this value represent?

52. Gasoline can be approximated by the formula C_8H_{18}. An environmental advocate points out that burning one gallon (about 7 lb) of gasoline produces about 19 lb of carbon dioxide, a greenhouse gas that raises the temperature of the atmosphere. Explain this seeming contradiction of the law of conservation of mass.

53. In an experiment shown in the illustration, about 15 mL of hydrochloric acid solution was placed in a flask and approximately 3 g of sodium carbonate was put into a balloon. The opening of the balloon was then carefully stretched over the top of the flask, taking care not to allow the sodium carbonate to fall into the acid in the flask. The flask was placed on an electronic balance, and the mass of the flask and its contents was found to be 38.61 g. The sodium carbonate was then slowly shaken into the acid. The balloon began to fill with gas. When the reaction was complete, the mass of the flask and its contents, including the gas in the balloon, was found to be 38.61 g. What law does this experiment illustrate? Explain.

54. Fritz Haber was awarded a Nobel Prize for the processes he invented in which nitrogen and hydrogen gases are combined to make ammonia (NH_3), a valuable chemical and a vital nutrient in modern agriculture.
   a. If 28.0 g of nitrogen with 6.05 g of hydrogen are combined in a closed system, what mass of ammonia will be produced?

b. How much nitrogen is required to fully consume 11.0 g of hydrogen, and how much ammonia will be produced?

c. If we had 11.0 g of nitrogen and 2 g of hydrogen, how much nitrogen would remain if all the hydrogen was consumed?

55. Using Döbereiner's triadic relationship, calculate the mass of Se:

a. based on Mendeleev's values from his periodic table (Figure 2.11)

b. based on values in the modern periodic table in the inside front cover of this book

56. Identify whether the following elements are hazardous, rare, or neither.

a. silicon
b. neodymium
c. mercury
d. oxygen
e. lead

57. Give two examples of how green chemistry has helped to reduce the use of cadmium in consumer products.

58. Why is it important to recycle mercury-based fluorescent light bulbs instead of putting them in landfills?

 # CRITICAL THINKING EXERCISES

Apply knowledge that you have gained in this chapter and one or more of the FLaReS principles (Chapter 1) to evaluate the following statements or claims.

2.1 In a science fiction movie, a woman proceeds through nine months of pregnancy in minutes. She takes in no nutrients during this time. She dies during labor and an emergency C-section is performed to save the child. The child lives for only a matter of hours, rapidly aging, and dies a withered old man. A classmate claims that the movie is based on a documented, secret alien encounter.

2.2 When water is electrolyzed, from each one molecule of water you always get 1 atom of oxygen and 2 atoms of hydrogen. However, when 1,000,000 U.S. dollars are exchanged for Canadian dollars, the amount of Canadian dollars may vary.

2.3 A health-food store has a large display of bracelets made of copper metal. Some people claim that wearing such a bracelet will protect the wearer from arthritis or rheumatoid diseases.

2.4 An old cookbook claims that cooking acidic food, such as spaghetti sauce, in an iron pot provides more nutrients than cooking the same food in an aluminum pot.

2.5 A company markets a device it calls a "water ener-oxizer." It claims the device can supply so much energy to drinking water that the mass of oxygen in the water is increased, thereby providing more oxygen to the body.

2.6 According to a mystic, one can tell whether someone is guilty or innocent by using a diamond. His claim is that, in a guilty person's hand, the diamond appears dull, while it sparkles when handled by an innocent person due to the person's goodness.

 # COLLABORATIVE GROUP PROJECTS

Prepare a PowerPoint, poster, or other presentation (as directed by your instructor) to share with the class.

1. Prepare a brief report on early Greek contributions to and ideas in the field of science, focusing on the work of one of the following: Aristotle, Leucippus, Democritus, Thales, Anaximander, Anaximenes of Miletus, Heraclitus, Empedocles, or another Greek philosopher of the time before 300 B.C.E.

2. Prepare a brief biographical report on one of the following.

a. Henry Cavendish
b. Joseph Proust
c. John Newlands
d. Lothar Meyer
e. Dmitri Mendeleev
f. John Dalton
g. Antoine Lavoisier
h. Marie-Anne Pierrette Paulze

3. Prepare a brief report on the *phlogiston theory*. Describe what the theory was, how it explained changes in mass when something is burned, and why it was finally abandoned.

4. Discuss why the concept of a mole ratio is more useful than the concept of atom or mass ratios.

5. Write a brief essay on recycling of one of the following: metals, paper, plastics, glass, food wastes, or grass clippings. Contrast a recycling method that maintains the properties of an element with one that changes them.

CHEMISTRY@HOME

Reaction in a Bag: Demonstrating the Law of Conservation of Matter

Materials Needed:

- Alka-Seltzer tablets (8)
- $1/4$ cup of water
- 2 small plastic cups
- Sealable plastic bag (1)
- Kitchen scale

Can you observe the law of conservation of matter if a gas is produced in a chemical reaction?

The law of conservation of matter states that atoms are not created or destroyed during a chemical reaction. For your experiment, we are challenging you to demonstrate this law through the dissolution of Alka-Seltzer tablets in water.

Alka-Seltzer tablets function as an antacid and pain reliever, with aspirin as the analgesic. When the tablets are dissolved in water, citric acid and sodium bicarbonate are dissolved and react to form water and carbon dioxide. The formed sodium citrate and aspirin are dissolved in the water and can be consumed to help with heartburn and pain relief. In this experiment, you can observe whether or not atoms are lost in the reaction, and, therefore, you are observing the law of conservation of matter.

First, measure $1/8$ cup of water into a small plastic cup. Record the weight of the water and the cup using a kitchen scale.

(Hint: set it to grams.) Drop 4 Alka-Seltzer tablets into the water and immediately record the total weight. Write down your observations as the tablets dissolve in the water. What observations can you make about the mixture?

After the reaction is completed, measure the final weight of the mixture. Did you see a difference in the weight before and after the reaction?

For the next step, run the reaction again, but this time, place both the $1/8$ cup of water and the 4 Alka-Seltzer tablets on opposite sides of the plastic bag. Seal the bag and then move the Alka-Seltzer tablets into the cup of water. Be sure to record the total weight of the mixture in the bag before and after the reaction.

Questions

1. What observations can be made about the mixture in the bag as compared to the mixture that was not in the bag?
2. Did you see a change in the weight of the mixture in the sealed bag? Why or why not?
3. What does this experiment tell you about the law of conservation of matter?

ATOMIC STRUCTURE

Have You Ever Wondered?

1. **If we can't see atoms, how do we know they are made of even smaller particles?**

2. **Why are accidental discoveries so common in science?**

3. **What is radioactivity?**

4. **Most light bulbs produce white light. Why does a neon light appear orange?**

5. **What does the word *quantum* mean?**

6. **What is "periodic" about the periodic table?**

Learning Objectives

> Explain the electrical properties of an atom. (3.1)

> Describe how the properties of electricity explain the structure of atoms. (3.1)

> Describe the experiments that led to the discovery of X-rays and an explanation of radioactivity. (3.2)

> Distinguish the three main kinds of radioactivity: alpha, beta, and gamma. (3.3)

> Sketch the nuclear model of the atom, and identify its parts. (3.4)

> List the particles that make up the nucleus of an atom, and give their relative masses and electric charges. (3.5)

> Identify elements and isotopes from their nuclear particles. (3.5)

> Define *quantum*. (3.6)

> Arrange the electrons in a given atom in energy levels (shells). (3.6)

> Relate the idea of a quantum of energy to an orbital. (3.7)

> Write an electron configuration (in subshell notation) for a given atom. (3.7)

> Describe how an element's electron configuration relates to its location in the periodic table. (3.8)

> Distinguish the conversion of solar energy into electrical energy in a solar cell from the conversion of solar energy into the chemical-bond energy of a solar fuel.

> Explain why splitting water into the elements hydrogen and oxygen requires an energy input and why producing water by the reaction of hydrogen and oxygen releases energy.

IMAGES OF THE INVISIBLE

Atoms are exceedingly tiny particles, much too small to see even with an optical microscope. It is true that scientists can obtain images of individual atoms, but they use special instruments such as a scanning tunneling microscope (STM, page 41). Even so, we can see only outlines of atoms and their arrangements in a substance. If atoms are so small, how can we possibly know anything about their inner structures?

Although scientists have never examined the interior of an atom directly, they have been able to obtain a great deal of *indirect* information. By designing clever experiments and exercising their powers of deduction, scientists have been able to develop amazingly detailed information about what an atom's interior is like.

Neon lights—the signature of entertainment, restaurants, bars, and the big city. Interestingly enough, most of the flickering illumination seen on signs like these from Times Square and Las Vegas is not from the element neon. The liquid fire of real neon lights is a characteristic orange-red color, and neon cannot be made to glow in any other color. Other colors are created by coating the inside of the tubing with a phosphor that glows in a specific color when current is applied to the tube. But why will neon only give off orange-red light? The answer lies in the structure of its atoms—the subject of this chapter.

Why do we care about the structure of particles as tiny as atoms? The reason is that the arrangement of the various parts of atoms determines the properties of different kinds of atoms and the matter they make up. Only by understanding atomic structure can we learn how atoms combine to make millions of different substances. With such knowledge, we can modify and synthesize materials to meet our needs more precisely.

Perhaps of greater interest to you is the fact that your understanding of chemistry (as well as much of biology and other sciences) depends, at least in part, on your knowledge of atomic structure. Let's begin by going back to the time of John Dalton.

▲ In addition to his work in electrochemistry, Michael Faraday also devised methods for liquefying gases such as chlorine and invented the electrical transformer.

3.1 Electricity and the Atom

Learning Objectives > Explain the electrical properties of an atom. > Describe how the properties of electricity explain the structure of atoms.

Dalton, who set forth his atomic theory in 1803, regarded the atom as hard and indivisible. However, it wasn't long before evidence accumulated to show that matter has electrical properties. Indeed, the electrolytic decomposition of water by Nicholson and Carlisle in 1800 (see Section 2.2) had already indicated this. Electricity played an important role in unraveling the structure of the atom.

Static electricity has been known since ancient times, but continuous electric current was born with the nineteenth century. In 1800, Alessandro Volta invented an electrochemical cell much like a modern battery. If the poles of such a cell are connected by a wire, current flows through the wire. The current is sustained by chemical reactions inside the cell. Volta's invention soon was applied in many areas of science and everyday life.

Electrolysis

Electricity source

(+)   (−)

Anode   Cathode

▲ **Figure 3.1** An electrolysis apparatus. The electricity source (for example, a battery) directs electrons through wires from the anode to the cathode. Cations (+) are attracted to the cathode (−), and anions (−) are attracted to the anode (+). This migration of ions is the flow of electricity through the solution.

Soon after Volta's invention, Humphry Davy (1778–1829), a British chemist, built a powerful battery that he used to pass electricity through molten (melted) salts. Davy quickly discovered several new elements. In 1807, he liberated highly reactive potassium metal from molten potassium hydroxide. Shortly thereafter, he produced sodium metal by passing electricity through molten sodium hydroxide. Within a year, Davy had also produced magnesium, strontium, barium, and calcium metals for the first time. The science of electrochemistry was born. (We will study electrochemistry in more detail in Chapter 8.)

Davy's protégé, Michael Faraday (1791–1867), greatly extended this new science. Lacking in formal education, Faraday consulted others to define many of the terms we still use today. His physician helped coin the term **electrolysis** for chemical reactions caused by electricity (Figure 3.1) and the name **electrolyte** for a compound that conducts electricity when melted or dissolved in water.

Another friend of Faraday, a classical scholar, suggested the names for the parts of the electrolytic apparatus. The carbon rods or metal strips inserted into a molten compound or a solution to carry the electric current are called **electrodes**. The electrode that bears a positive charge is the **anode**, and the negatively charged electrode is the **cathode**. The entities that carry the electric current through a melted compound or a solution are called *ions*. An **ion** is an atom or a group of atoms bonded together that has an electric charge. An ion with a negative charge is an **anion**; it travels toward the anode. A positively charged ion is a **cation**; it moves toward the cathode.

Faraday's work established that atoms have electrical properties, but further details of atomic structure had to wait several decades for more powerful sources of electricity and better vacuum pumps.

Cathode-Ray Tubes

In 1875, William Crookes (1832–1919), an English chemist, was able to construct a low-pressure gas-discharge tube that would allow electricity to pass through it. Crookes's tube is the forerunner of neon tubes used for signs and of cathode-ray tubes used in old television sets and computer monitors. Metal electrodes are sealed in the tube, which is connected to a vacuum pump so that most of the air can be removed from it. A beam of current produces a green fluorescence when it strikes a screen coated with zinc sulfide. This beam, which seems to leave the cathode and travel to the anode, was called a **cathode ray**.

(a)   (b)

▲ **Figure 3.2** Thomson's apparatus, showing deflection of the cathode rays (a beam of electrons). Cathode rays are invisible but can be observed because they produce a green fluorescence when they strike a zinc sulfide-coated screen. The diagram (a) shows deflection of the beam in an electric field. Notice the direction that the beam deflects. The photograph (b) shows the deflection in a magnetic field. Cathode rays travel in straight lines unless some kind of external field is applied.

Thomson's Experiment: Mass-to-Charge Ratio

Considerable speculation arose about the nature of cathode rays, and many experiments were undertaken. Were these rays beams of particles, or did they consist of a wavelike form of energy much like visible light? The answer came (as scientific answers should) from an experiment performed by the English physicist Joseph John Thomson in 1897. His experiment is shown in Figure 3.2. J. J. Thomson showed that cathode rays were deflected in an electric field (look at Figure 3.2a). The beam was attracted to the positive plate and repelled by the negative plate. Thomson concluded that cathode rays consisted of negatively charged particles. His experiments also showed that the particles were the same no matter from what material the electrodes were made or what type of gas was in the tube. He concluded that all atoms have these negative particles in them. Thomson named these negatively charged units **electrons**. Cathode rays, then, are beams of electrons emanating from the cathode of a gas-discharge tube.

Cathode rays are deflected in magnetic fields as well as in electric fields. The greater the charge on a particle, the more it is deflected in an electric (or magnetic) field. The heavier the particle, the less it is deflected by the field. By measuring the amount of deflection in fields of known strength, Thomson was able to calculate the *ratio* of the mass of the electron to its charge. (He could not measure either the mass or the charge separately.) Thomson was awarded the Nobel Prize in Physics in 1906.

1. If we can't see atoms, how do we know they are made of even smaller particles?

The existence of electrons and other subatomic particles was deduced from the behavior of electricity. The existence and behavior of the subatomic particles make atoms behave the way they do.

Goldstein's Experiment: Positive Particles

In 1886, German scientist Eugen Goldstein performed experiments with gas-discharge tubes that had perforated cathodes (Figure 3.3). He found that although electrons were formed and sped off toward the anode as usual, positive particles were also formed and shot in the opposite direction, toward the cathode. Some of these positive particles went through the holes in the cathode. In 1907, a study of the deflection of these positive particles in a magnetic field indicated that the mass of these particles depended on the gas in the cathode. The lightest particles, formed when there was a little hydrogen gas in the tube, were later shown to have a mass 1837 times that of an electron.

▲ **Figure 3.3** Goldstein's apparatus for the study of positive particles. This apparatus, with holes in the cathode, is a modification of the cathode-ray tube in Figure 3.2. Some positive ions, attracted toward the cathode, pass through the holes in the cathode. The deflection of these particles (not shown) in a magnetic field can be studied in the region to the left of the cathode.

Millikan's Oil-Drop Experiment: Electron Charge

The charge on the electron was determined in 1909 by Robert A. Millikan (1868–1953), a physicist at the University of Chicago. Millikan observed electrically charged oil drops in an electric field. A diagram of his apparatus is shown in Figure 3.4. A spray bottle is used to form tiny droplets of oil. Some acquire negative charges, either from irradiation with X-rays or from the friction generated as the particles rub against the opening of the spray nozzle and against each other. (The charge is static electricity, just like the charge you get from walking across a nylon carpet.) Either way, the droplets acquire one or more extra electrons.

Some of the oil droplets pass into a chamber where they can be viewed through a telescope. The negative plate at the bottom of the chamber repels the negatively charged droplets, and the positive plate attracts them. By manipulating the charge on each plate and observing the behavior of the droplets, the charge on each droplet can be determined. Millikan took the smallest possible difference in charge between two droplets to be the charge of an individual electron. For his research, he received the Nobel Prize in Physics in 1923.

From Millikan's value for the charge and Thomson's value for the mass-to-charge ratio, the mass of the electron was readily calculated. That mass was found to be only 9.1×10^{-28} g. To have a mass of 1 g would require more than 1×10^{27} electrons—that's a 1 followed by 27 zeros, or a billion billion billion electrons. More important, the electron's mass is much smaller than that of the lightest atom.

In practice, we seldom use the actual mass and charge of the electron. For many purposes, the electron is considered the unit of electrical charge. The charge is shown as a superscript minus sign (meaning $1-$). In indicating charges on ions, we use $^-$ to indicate a net charge due to one "extra" electron, $^{2-}$ to indicate a charge due to two "extra" electrons, and so on.

▶ **Figure 3.4** The Millikan oil-drop experiment. Oil drops irradiated with X-rays pick up electrons and become negatively charged. Their fall due to gravity can be balanced by adjusting the voltage of the electric field. The charge on the oil drop can be determined from the applied voltage and the mass of the oil drop. The charge on each drop is that of some whole number of electrons.

SELF-ASSESSMENT Questions

1. The use of electricity to cause a chemical reaction is called
   a. anodizing
   b. corrosion
   c. electrolysis
   d. hydrolysis

2. During electrolysis of molten sodium chloride, chloride anions move to the
   a. anode, which is negatively charged
   b. anode, which is positively charged
   c. cathode, which is negatively charged
   d. cathode, which is positively charged

3. Cathode rays are
   a. composed of positively charged particles
   b. composed of particles with a mass of 1 u
   c. deflected by electric fields
   d. different for every element

4. J. J. Thomson measured the electron's
   a. atomic number
   b. charge
   c. mass
   d. mass-to-charge ratio

5. In his oil-drop experiment, Millikan determined the charge of an electron by
   a. measuring the diameters of the tiniest drops
   b. noting that the drops had either a certain minimum charge or multiples of that charge
   c. using an atomizer that could spray out individual electrons
   d. viewing the smallest charged drops microscopically and noting that they had one extra electron

Answers: 1, c; 2, b; 3, c; 4, d; 5, b

3.2 Serendipity in Science: X-Rays and Radioactivity

Learning Objective ❯ Describe the experiments that led to the discovery of X-rays and an explanation of radioactivity.

Let's take a look at two serendipitous discoveries of the last years of the nineteenth century that profoundly changed the world and are related to atomic structure.

Roentgen: The Discovery of X-Rays

In 1895, German scientist Wilhelm Conrad Roentgen (1845–1923) was working in a dark room, studying the glow produced in certain substances by cathode rays. To his surprise, he noted this glow on a chemically treated piece of paper some distance from the cathode-ray tube. The paper even glowed when a wall separated the tube from the paper. This type of ray could travel through walls. When he waved his hand between the radiation source and the glowing paper, he was able to see an image of the bones of his hand in darker shades on the paper. He called these mysterious rays **X-rays**. He found, in general, that X-rays were absorbed more by bone or other hard and fairly dense materials than by soft, less dense tissues.

X-rays are a form of electromagnetic radiation—energy with electric and magnetic components. Among other types, electromagnetic radiation also includes visible light, radio waves, microwaves, infrared radiation, ultraviolet light, and gamma rays (Section 3.3). These forms differ in energy, with radio waves lowest in energy, followed by microwaves, infrared radiation, visible light, ultraviolet light, X-rays, and, the most energetic, gamma rays.

Today, X-rays are one of the most widely used tools in the world for medical diagnosis. Not only are they employed for examining decayed teeth, broken bones, and diseased lungs, but they are also the basis for such procedures as mammography and computerized tomography (Chapter 11). How ironic that Roentgen himself made no profit at all from his discovery. He considered X-rays a "gift to humanity" and refused to patent any part of the discovery. However, he did receive much popular acclaim and in 1901 was awarded the first Nobel Prize in Physics.

2. Why are accidental discoveries so common in science?

Serendipity—a "happy accident" like drilling for water and striking oil—happens to everyone at times. Scientists, however, are trained observers. When something unexpected happens, they often wonder why and investigate. The same accident might happen to an untrained person and go unnoticed—though even scientists often miss important finds at first. Or, if something unusual is noticed, its significance might not be grasped.

Fig. 20.—The first roentgen photograph. (Mrs. Roentgen's hand.)

▲ The use of X-rays in medical diagnosis began shortly after they were discovered by Wilhelm Roentgen in 1895. In fact, the first known X-ray photograph is the one seen here—of Mrs. Roentgen's hand!

▲ Marie Sklodowska Curie and Pierre Curie in their laboratory. They shared the 1903 Nobel Prize in Physics with Becquerel.

The Discovery of Radioactivity

Certain chemicals exhibit *fluorescence* after exposure to strong sunlight. They continue to glow even when taken into a dark room. In 1895, Antoine Henri Becquerel (1852–1908), a French physicist, was studying fluorescence by wrapping photographic film in black paper, placing a few crystals of the fluorescing chemical on top of the paper, and then placing the package in strong sunlight. If the glow was like ordinary light, it would not pass through the paper. On the other hand, if it was similar to X-rays, it would pass through the black paper and fog the film.

While working with a uranium compound, Becquerel made an important accidental discovery. When placed in sunlight, the compound fluoresced and fogged the film. On several cloudy days when exposure to sunlight was not possible, he prepared samples and placed them in a drawer. To his great surprise, the photographic film was fogged even though the uranium compound had not been exposed to sunlight. Further experiments showed that the radiation coming from the uranium compound was unrelated to fluorescence but was a characteristic of the element uranium.

Other scientists immediately began to study this new radiation. Becquerel's graduate student from Poland, Marie Sklodowska, gave the phenomenon a name: radioactivity. **Radioactivity** is the spontaneous emission of radiation from certain unstable elements. Marie later married Pierre Curie, a French physicist. Together they discovered the radioactive elements polonium and radium.

After her husband's death in 1906, Marie Curie continued to work with radioactive substances, winning the Nobel Prize in Chemistry in 1911. For more than 50 years, she was the only person ever to have received two Nobel Prizes.

SELF-ASSESSMENT Questions

1. When Roentgen saw an X-ray image of his hand, the bones were darker than the glowing paper because the X-rays were
   a. absorbed more by bone than by flesh
   b. radiation that is less energetic than visible light
   c. made up of fast-moving atoms
   d. a type of radioactivity

2. Radioactivity arises from elements that
   a. absorb radio waves and release stronger radiation
   b. are unstable and emit radiation
   c. fluoresce
   d. undergo fission (splitting) of their atoms when they absorb energy

Answers: 1, a; 2, b

3.3 Three Types of Radioactivity

3. What is radioactivity?
Radioactivity is the spontaneous decay (occurring without a cause) of an atom into one or more other atoms. Exposure to the radiation—alpha, beta, or gamma rays—given off by radioactive material can be hazardous.

Learning Objective ❯ Distinguish the three main kinds of radioactivity: alpha, beta, and gamma.

Scientists soon showed that three types of radiation emanated from various radioactive elements. Ernest Rutherford (1871–1937), a New Zealander who early in his career worked under J. J. Thomson (Section 3.1), chose the names *alpha*, *beta*, and *gamma* for the three types of radioactivity. When passed through a strong magnetic or electric field, the alpha type was deflected in a manner indicating that it consisted of a beam of positive particles (Figure 3.5). Later experiments showed that an **alpha particle** has a mass four times that of a hydrogen atom and a charge twice the magnitude of, but opposite in sign, to that of an electron. An alpha par-

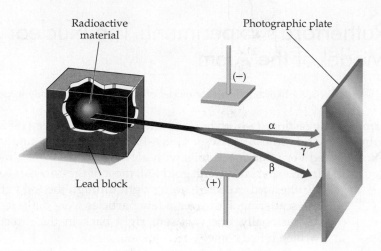

▲ **Figure 3.5** Behavior of a beam of radioactivity in an electric field.

Q: *Why are alpha rays deflected upward in this figure? Why are beta rays deflected downward?*

ticle is in fact identical to the nucleus (Section 3.4) of a helium atom and is often symbolized by He^{2+}.

The beta radiation was shown to be made up of negatively charged particles identical to those of cathode rays. Therefore, a **beta particle** is an electron, although it has much more energy than an electron in an atom. **Gamma rays** are not deflected by a magnetic field. They are a form of electromagnetic radiation, much like the X-rays used in medical work but even more energetic and more penetrating. The three types of radioactivity are summarized in Table 3.1.

The discoveries of the late nineteenth century paved the way for an entirely new picture of the atom, which developed rapidly during the early years of the twentieth century.

Table 3.1	Types of Radioactivity		
Name	Greek Letter	Mass (u)	Charge
Alpha	α	4	2+
Beta	β	$\dfrac{1}{1837}$	1−
Gamma	γ	0	0

SELF-ASSESSMENT Questions

1. The mass of an alpha particle is about
   a. four times that of a hydrogen atom
   b. the same as that of an electron
   c. the same as that of a hydrogen atom
   d. the same as that of a beta particle

2. Compared to the charge on an electron (designated 1−), the charge on an alpha particle is
   a. 4−   b. 1−   c. 1+   d. 2+   e. 4+

3. A beta particle is a(n)
   a. boron atom   b. electron   c. helium nucleus   d. proton

4. The mass of a gamma ray is
   a. −1 u   b. 0 u   c. 1 u   d. 4 u

It DOES Matter!

It is important to distinguish between the *rays* given off by a radioactive element and the radioactive element itself. Like light, alpha, beta, and gamma rays can be absorbed by materials and do not generally cause problems thereafter. In fact, sometimes gamma rays are used to kill harmful microorganisms in food, making the food safer. The main danger from radioactivity is from radioactive atoms. Those atoms can lodge on or be absorbed by materials and give off damaging alpha, beta, or gamma rays. After the Fukushima Daiichi nuclear disaster in March 2011, a large amount of radioactive material was released from the damaged nuclear reactors. Some of the radioactive material continues to escape into the ocean around the plant. Cleaning up the radioactive material from the accident will likely take decades and cost billions of dollars. In the picture workers from the Fukushima plant are being checked for radioactive particles on their clothing. These topics are covered in more detail in Chapter 11.

3.4 Rutherford's Experiment: The Nuclear Model of the Atom

Learning Objective ❯ Sketch the nuclear model of the atom, and identify its parts.

At Rutherford's suggestion, two of his coworkers—Hans Geiger (1882–1945), a German physicist, and Ernest Marsden (1889–1970), an English undergraduate student—bombarded very thin metal foils with alpha particles from a radioactive source (Figure 3.6). In an experiment with gold foil, most of the particles behaved as Rutherford expected, going right through the foil with little or no scattering. However, a few particles were deflected sharply. Occasionally, one was sent right back in the direction from which it had come!

Alpha source

Zinc sulfide screen for detecting radiation

Alpha radiation

Gold foil

▲ **Figure 3.6** Rutherford's gold-foil experiment. Most alpha particles passed right through the gold foil, but now and then a particle was deflected.

Rutherford had assumed that positive charge was spread evenly over all the space occupied by the atom, but obviously it was not. To explain the results, Rutherford concluded that all the positive charge and nearly all the mass of an atom are concentrated at the center of the atom in a tiny core called the **nucleus**.

When an alpha particle, which is positively charged, directly approached the positively charged nucleus, it was strongly repelled and therefore sharply deflected (Figure 3.7). Because only a few alpha particles were deflected, Rutherford concluded that the nucleus must occupy only a tiny fraction of the volume of an atom. Most of the alpha particles passed right through because most of an atom is empty space. The space outside the nucleus isn't completely empty, however. It contains the negatively charged electrons. Rutherford concluded that the electrons had so little mass that they were no match for the alpha particle "bullets." It would be analogous to a mouse trying to stop a charging hippopotamus.

Rutherford's nuclear theory of the atom, set forth in 1911, was revolutionary. He postulated that all the positive charge and nearly all the mass of an atom are concentrated in a tiny, tiny nucleus. The negatively charged electrons have almost no mass, yet they occupy nearly all the volume of an atom. To picture Rutherford's model, visualize a sphere as big as the largest covered football stadium. The nucleus at the middle of the sphere is as small as a pea but weighs several million tons. A few flies flitting here and there throughout the sphere represent the electrons.

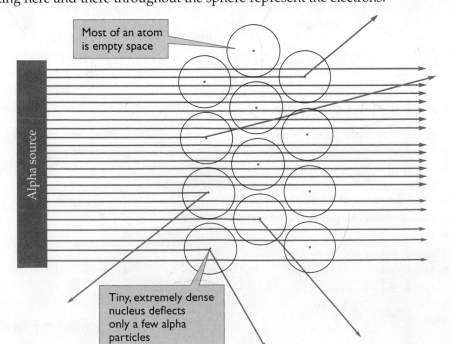

Most of an atom is empty space

Alpha source

Tiny, extremely dense nucleus deflects only a few alpha particles

▶ **Figure 3.7** Model explaining the results of Rutherford's gold-foil experiment. Most of the alpha particles pass right through the foil because the gold atoms are mainly empty space. But some alpha particles are deflected as they pass close to a dense, positively charged atomic nucleus. Once in a while, an alpha particle encounters an atomic nucleus head-on and is knocked back in the direction from which it came.

SELF-ASSESSMENT Questions

1. The most persuasive evidence from Rutherford's gold-foil experiment was that
   a. all the alpha particles were deflected a bit
   b. most of the alpha particles went right through the foil, but a tiny fraction were deflected right back toward the source
   c. some gold atoms were converted to lead atoms
   d. some gold atoms were split

2. Rutherford's gold-foil experiment showed that
   a. gold atoms consisted of electrons in a "pudding" of positive charge
   b. the nucleus was huge and positively charged
   c. the nucleus was tiny and positively charged
   d. some gold atoms were shattered by alpha particles

3. From his gold-foil experiment, Rutherford concluded that atoms consist mainly of
   a. electrons
   b. empty space
   c. neutrons
   d. protons

4. The positively charged part of the atom is its
   a. cation
   b. nucleus
   c. outer electrons
   d. widespread cloud of electrons

Answers: 1, b; 2, c; 3, b; 4, b

3.5 The Atomic Nucleus

Learning Objectives ❯ List the particles that make up the nucleus of an atom, and give their relative masses and electric charges. ❯ Identify elements and isotopes from their nuclear particles.

In 1914, Rutherford suggested that the smallest positive particle (the one formed when there is hydrogen gas in Goldstein's apparatus—see Section 3.1) is the unit of positive charge in the nucleus. This particle, called a **proton**, has a charge equal in magnitude to that of the electron and has nearly the same mass as a hydrogen atom. Rutherford's suggestion was that protons constitute the positively charged matter in all atoms. The nucleus of a hydrogen atom consists of one proton, and the nuclei of larger atoms contain greater numbers of protons.

But most atomic nuclei are heavier than is indicated by the number of positive charges (number of protons). For example, the helium nucleus has a charge of 2+ (and therefore two protons, according to Rutherford's theory), but its mass is *four* times that of hydrogen. This excess mass puzzled scientists at first. Then, in 1932, English physicist James Chadwick (1891–1974) discovered a particle with about the same mass as a proton but with no electrical charge. It was called a **neutron**, and its existence explains the unexpectedly high mass of the helium nucleus. Whereas the hydrogen nucleus contains only one proton of mass 1 u, the helium nucleus contains not only two protons (2 u) but also two neutrons (2 u), giving it a total mass of 4 u.

With the discovery of the neutron, the list of "building blocks" that we use for "constructing" atoms is complete. The properties of these particles are summarized in Table 3.2. (There are dozens of other subatomic particles, but most exist only momentarily and are not important to our discussion.)

Atomic Number

The number of protons in the nucleus of an atom of any element is the **atomic number** (Z) of that element. This number determines the kind of atom—that is, the identity of the element—and it is found on any periodic table or list of the elements.

Table 3.2 Subatomic Particles

Particle	Symbol	Mass (u)	Charge	Location in Atom
Proton	p^+	1	1+	Nucleus
Neutron	n	1	0	Nucleus
Electron	e^-	$\dfrac{1}{1837}$	1−	Outside nucleus

Dalton thought that the mass of an atom determines the element. We now know it is not the mass but the number of protons that determines the identity of an element. For example, every atom with 26 protons is an atom of iron (Fe), whose atomic number $Z = 26$. Any atom with 50 protons is an atom of tin (Sn), which has $Z = 50$. In a neutral atom (one with no electrical charge), the positive charge of the protons is exactly neutralized by the negative charge of the electrons. The attractive forces between the unlike charges help hold the atom together.

A proton and a neutron have almost the same mass, 1.0073 u and 1.0087 u, respectively. This difference is so small that it usually can be ignored. Thus, for many purposes, we can assume that the masses of the proton and the neutron are the same, 1 u. The proton has a charge equal in magnitude but opposite in sign to that of an electron. This charge on a proton is written as 1+. The electron has a charge of 1− and a mass of 0.00055 u. The electrons in an atom contribute so little to its total mass that their mass is usually disregarded (treated as if it were 0).

Isotopes

We can now more precisely define *isotopes*, a term we mentioned in Section 2.3. Atoms of a given element can have different numbers of neutrons in their nuclei. For example, most hydrogen atoms have a nucleus consisting of a single proton and no neutrons. However, about 1 hydrogen atom in 6700 has a neutron as well as a proton in its nucleus. This heavier hydrogen atom is called *deuterium*. A third, rare isotope of hydrogen is *tritium*, which has two neutrons and one proton in the nucleus.

Whether it has one neutron, two neutrons, or no neutrons, any atom with $Z = 1$—that is, with one proton—is a hydrogen atom. Atoms that have this sort of relationship—having the same number of protons but different numbers of neutrons—are called **isotopes** (Figure 3.8).

Most, but not all, elements exist in nature in isotopic forms. For example, tin is present in nature in 10 different isotopic forms. It also has 15 radioactive isotopes that do not occur in nature. Aluminum, on the other hand, has only one naturally occurring isotope.

Isotopes usually have little or no effect on ordinary chemical reactions. For example, all three hydrogen isotopes react with oxygen to form water. Because these isotopes differ in mass, compounds formed with them have different physical properties, but such differences are usually slight. For example, water in which both hydrogen atoms are deuterium is called *heavy water*, often represented as D_2O. Heavy water boils at 101.4 °C (instead of 100 °C) and freezes at 3.8 °C (instead of 0 °C). In nuclear reactions, however, isotopes are of the utmost importance, as we shall see in Chapter 11.

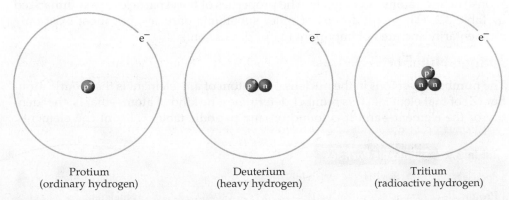

Protium
(ordinary hydrogen)

Deuterium
(heavy hydrogen)

Tritium
(radioactive hydrogen)

▲ **Figure 3.8** The three isotopes of hydrogen. Each has one proton and one electron, but they differ in the number of neutrons in the nucleus.

Q: *What is the atomic number and mass number of each of the isotopes? What is the mass of each, in atomic mass units, to the nearest whole number?*

Symbols for Isotopes

Collectively, the two main nuclear particles, protons and neutrons, are called **nucleons**. Isotopes are represented by symbols with subscripts and superscripts.

$$_Z^A X$$

In this general symbol, Z is the nuclear charge (atomic number, or number of protons), and A is the **mass number**, or the **nucleon number** because it is the number of nucleons. (*Nucleon number* is the term recommended by the International Union of Pure and Applied Chemistry.) As an example, the isotope with the symbol

$$_{17}^{35} Cl$$

has 17 protons and 35 nucleons. The number of neutrons is therefore $35 - 17 = 18$.

Isotopes often are named by adding the mass number as a suffix to the name of the element. The three hydrogen isotopes are represented as

$$_1^1 H \quad _1^2 H \quad _1^3 H$$

and named hydrogen-1, hydrogen-2, and hydrogen-3, respectively.

Example 3.1   Number of Neutrons

How many neutrons are there in the $_{92}^{235}U$ nucleus?

Solution

We simply subtract the atomic number Z (number of protons) from the mass number A (number of protons plus number of neutrons).

$$A - Z = \text{number of neutrons}$$
$$235 - 92 = 143$$

There are 143 neutrons in the $_{92}^{235}U$ nucleus.

▪ EXERCISE 3.1A

How many neutrons are there in the $_{27}^{60}Co$ nucleus?

▪ EXERCISE 3.1B

An iodine isotope has 78 neutrons in its nucleus. What are the mass number and the name of the isotope?

CONCEPTUAL Example 3.2   Isotopes

Refer to the following isotope symbols, in which the letter X replaces each element symbol. **(a)** Which represent isotopes of the same element? **(b)** Which have the same mass number? **(c)** Which have the same number of neutrons?

$$_8^{16}X \quad _7^{16}X \quad _7^{14}X \quad _6^{14}X \quad _6^{12}X$$

Solution

a. Isotopes of the same element have the same atomic number (subscript). Therefore, $_7^{16}X$ and $_7^{14}X$ are isotopes of nitrogen (N), and $_6^{14}X$ and $_6^{12}X$ are isotopes of carbon (C).

b. The mass number is the superscript, so $_8^{16}X$ and $_7^{16}X$ have the same mass number. The first is an isotope of oxygen, and the second an isotope of nitrogen. $_7^{14}X$ and $_6^{14}X$ also have the same mass number. The first is an isotope of nitrogen, and the second an isotope of carbon.

c. To determine the number of neutrons, we subtract the atomic number from the mass number. We find that $_8^{16}X$ and $_6^{14}X$ each have eight neutrons ($16 - 8 = 8$ and $14 - 6 = 8$, respectively).

▪ EXERCISE 3.2A

Which of the following represent isotopes of the same element?

$$_{37}^{90}X \quad _{35}^{90}X \quad _{37}^{88}X \quad _{38}^{88}X \quad _{38}^{93}X$$

▪ EXERCISE 3.2B

How many different elements are represented in Exercise 3.2A?

SELF-ASSESSMENT Questions

1. The three basic components of an atom are
   a. protium, deuterium, and tritium
   b. protons, neutrinos, and ions
   c. protons, neutrons, and electrons
   d. protons, neutrons, and ions

2. The identity of an element is determined by its
   a. atomic mass
   b. number of atoms
   c. number of electrons
   d. number of protons

3. How many electrons are required to equal the mass of one proton?
   a. 1   b. 18   c. about 1800   d. 1×10^{27}

4. Which particles have approximately the same mass?
   a. electrons and neutrons
   b. electrons and protons
   c. electrons, neutrons, and protons
   d. neutrons and protons

5. A change in the number of protons in an atom produces a(n)
   a. compound
   b. atom of a different element
   c. ion
   d. different isotope of the same element

6. A change in the number of neutrons in an atom produces a(n)
   a. compound
   b. atom of a different element
   c. ion
   d. different isotope of the same element

7. The number of protons plus neutrons in an atom is its
   a. atomic mass
   b. atomic number
   c. isotope number
   d. nucleon number

8. How many protons (p) and how many neutrons (n) are there in a $^{15}_{7}N$ nucleus?
   a. 7 p, 7 n   b. 7 p, 8 n   c. 7 p, 15 n   d. 8 p, 8 n

9. A neutral atom has 19 electrons and 20 neutrons. Its atomic number is
   a. 1   b. 19   c. 20   d. 39

10. An atom has 16 neutrons. It is
    a. definitely phosphorus
    b. definitely potassium
    c. definitely sulfur
    d. not possible to identify the element from the number of neutrons

11. The symbol for the isotope potassium-40 is
    a. $^{21}_{9}K$ b. $^{39}_{19}K$ c. $^{40}_{19}K$ d. $^{19}_{40}K$

3.6 Electron Arrangement: The Bohr Model

Learning Objectives ❯ Define *quantum.* ❯ Arrange the electrons in a given atom in energy levels (shells).

Let's turn our attention once more to electrons. Rutherford demonstrated that atoms have a tiny, positively charged nucleus with electrons outside it. Evidence soon accumulated that the electrons were not randomly distributed but were arranged in an ordered fashion. We will examine that evidence soon. But first, let's take a side trip into some colorful chemistry and physics to provide a background for our study of the arrangement of electrons in atoms.

Fireworks and Flame Tests

Chemists of the eighteenth and nineteenth centuries developed flame tests that used the colors of flames to identify several elements (Figure 3.9). Sodium salts produce a persistent yellow flame, potassium salts a fleeting lavender flame, and lithium salts a brilliant red flame. It was not until the structure of atoms was better understood, however, that scientists could explain why each element emits a distinctive color of light.

Fireworks originated earlier than flame tests, in ancient China. The brilliant colors of aerial displays still mark our celebrations of patriotic holidays. The colors of fireworks are attributable to specific elements. Brilliant reds are produced by strontium compounds, whereas barium compounds are used to produce green, sodium com-

▲ The brilliant colors of a fireworks display come from compounds added to the fireworks. Strontium compounds produce red, copper compounds produce blue or violet, and barium compounds produce green.

Lithium, Li	Sodium, Na	Potassium, K	Calcium, Ca	Strontium, Sr

▲ **Figure 3.9** Certain chemical elements can be identified by the characteristic colors their compounds impart to flames. Five examples are shown here.

pounds yield yellow, and copper salts produce blue or violet. However, the colors of fireworks and flame tests are not as simple as they seem to the unaided eye.

Continuous and Line Spectra

When white light from an incandescent lamp is passed through a prism, it produces a continuous spectrum, or rainbow of colors (Figure 3.10). A similar phenomenon occurs when sunlight passes through raindrops. The different colors of light correspond to different wavelengths. Blue light has shorter wavelengths than red light, but there is no sharp transition in moving from one color to the next. All wavelengths are present in a continuous spectrum (Figure 3.11, top). White light is simply a combination of all the various colors.

If the light from a colored flame test or a gas-discharge tube containing a particular element is passed through a prism, only narrow colored lines are observed (Figure 3.11). Each line corresponds to light of a particular wavelength. The pattern of lines emitted by an element is called its *line spectrum*. The line spectrum of an element is characteristic of that element and can be used to identify it. Not all the lines in the spectrum of an atom are visible; some are infrared or ultraviolet radiation.

4. Most light bulbs produce white light. Why does a neon light appear orange?

When a solid, like the filament in an incandescent lamp, is heated, it goes through a stage of red heat, then yellow. Finally, white light is emitted, which consists of all wavelengths. When a gas such as neon is heated, we get a line spectrum (Figure 3.11), which gives a specific color to the light. Fluorescent and LED lamps mix several colors together to make their light appear white.

▲ **Figure 3.10** A glass prism separates white light into a continuous spectrum, or rainbow, of colors just as sunlight passing through raindrops causes a rainbow in the sky.

CONTINUOUS SPECTRUM

4000 4500 5000 5500 6000 6500 7000 7500

EMISSION (BRIGHT LINE) SPECTRA

Cd

4000 4500 5000 5500 6000 6500 7000 7500

Sr

4000 4500 5000 5500 6000 6500 7000 7500

Ba

4000 4500 5000 5500 6000 6500 7000 7500

Ca

4000 4500 5000 5500 6000 6500 7000 7500

H

4000 4500 5000 5500 6000 6500 7000 7500

Na

4000 4500 5000 5500 6000 6500 7000 7500

◀ **Figure 3.11** Line spectra of selected elements. Some of the components of the light emitted by excited atoms appear as colored lines. A continuous spectrum is shown at the top for comparison. The numbers are wavelengths of light given in ångström units (1Å = 10^{-10} m). Each element has its own characteristic line spectrum that differs from all others and can be used to identify the element.

5. What does the word *quantum* mean?

Just as an atom is the smallest unit of an element, a quantum is the smallest unit of energy in a system. In atoms and molecules energy is produced or consumed in discrete rather than continuous amounts. A quantum of energy is too small to notice in daily life, but from lasers to transistors, the fact that energy is quantized is central to much of modern technology. A "quantum leap" comes from the idea suggested by Figure 3.12, where an electron can "leap" from one energy level to another.

The visible line spectrum of hydrogen is fairly simple, consisting of four lines in that portion of the electromagnetic spectrum. To explain the hydrogen spectrum, Danish physicist Niels Bohr (1885–1962) worked out a model for the electron arrangement of the hydrogen atom.

Bohr's Explanation of Line Spectra

Niels Bohr presented his explanation of line spectra in 1913. He suggested that electrons cannot have just any amount of energy but can have only certain specified amounts; that is, the energy of an electron is *quantized*. A **quantum** (plural: *quanta*) is a tiny unit of energy whose value depends on the frequency of the radiation. A specified energy value for an electron is called its **energy level**.

By absorbing a quantum of energy (for example, when atoms of the element are heated), an electron is elevated to a higher energy level (Figure 3.12). By giving up a quantum of energy, the electron can return to a lower energy level. The energy released shows up as a line spectrum. Each line has a specific wavelength corresponding to a quantum of energy. An electron moves practically instantaneously from one energy level to another, and there are no intermediate stages.

Consider the analogy of a person on a ladder. A person can stand on the first rung, the second rung, the third rung, and so on, but is unable to stand between rungs. As the person goes from one rung to another, the potential energy (energy due to position) changes by definite amounts. As an electron moves from one energy level to another, its total energy (both potential and kinetic) also changes by definite amounts, or quanta.

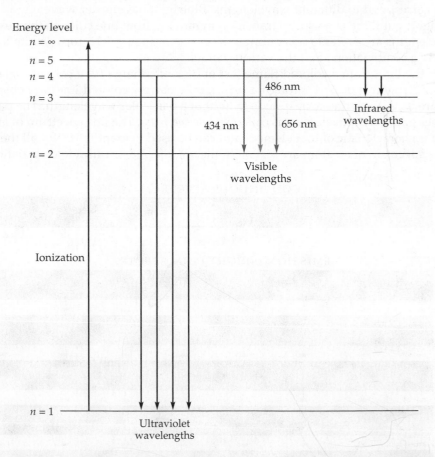

▲ **Figure 3.12** Possible electron shifts between energy levels in atoms to produce the lines found in spectra. Not all of the lines are in the visible portion of the spectrum. The three colored arrows correspond to three of the colored lines in the hydrogen spectrum seen in Figure 3.11.

Q: *Which transition involves the greater change in energy, a drop from energy level 4 to energy level 2, or a drop from energy level 5 to energy level 4? What color of light is absorbed when an electron in a hydrogen atom is boosted from energy level 2 to energy level 3?*

Bohr based his model of the atom on the laws of planetary motion that had been set down by the German astronomer Johannes Kepler (1571–1630) three centuries before. Bohr imagined the electrons to be orbiting about the nucleus much as planets orbit the sun (Figure 3.13). Different energy levels were pictured as different orbits. Bohr received the 1922 Nobel Prize in Physics for his planetary model of the atom with its quantized electron energy levels. Element 107 is named bohrium (Bh) in his honor.

As it turns out, the electrons in an atom don't really move around the nucleus in fixed paths. The modern understanding of the structure of an atom is different, as we will see in the next section. But Bohr's model does help explain why elements produce line spectra.

Ground States and Excited States

The electron in a hydrogen atom is usually in the first, or lowest, energy level. Electrons tend to stay in their lowest possible energy levels (those nearest the nucleus). Atoms with their electrons thus situated are said to be in their **ground state**. When a flame or other source supplies energy to an atom (of hydrogen, for example) and an electron jumps from the lowest possible level to a higher level, the atom is said to be in an **excited state**. An atom in an excited state eventually emits a quantum of energy—often a *photon*, or "particle," of light—as the electron jumps back down to one of the lower levels and ultimately reaches the ground state.

Bohr's theory was spectacularly successful in explaining the line spectrum of hydrogen. It established the important idea of energy levels in atoms.

Atoms larger than hydrogen have more than one electron, and Bohr was also able to deduce that a given energy level of an atom could contain at most only a certain number of electrons. The maximum number of electrons that can be in a given level is indicated by the formula

$$\text{Maximum number of electrons} = 2n^2$$

where n is the energy level being considered. For the first energy level ($n = 1$), the maximum number of electrons is $2 \times 1^2 = 2 \times 1 = 2$. For the second energy level ($n = 2$), the maximum number is $2 \times 2^2 = 2 \times 4 = 8$. For the third level, the maximum number is $2 \times 3^2 = 2 \times 9 = 18$.

The various energy levels are often called **shells**. The first energy level ($n = 1$) is the first shell, the second energy level ($n = 2$) is the second shell, and so on.

Example 3.3   Electron-Shell Capacity

What is the maximum number of electrons in the fifth shell (fifth energy level)?

Solution
The maximum number of electrons in a given shell is given by $2n^2$. For the fifth level, $n = 5$, so we have

$$2 \times 5^2 = 2 \times 25 = 50 \quad \text{electrons}$$

▪ EXERCISE 3.3A
What is the maximum number of electrons in the fourth shell (fourth energy level)?

▪ EXERCISE 3.3B
What is the lowest energy level that can hold 18 electrons?

Building Atoms: Main Shells

Imagine building up atoms by adding one electron to the proper shell as *each* proton is added to the nucleus, keeping in mind that electrons will go to the lowest energy level (shell) available. For hydrogen, with a nucleus containing only one proton ($Z = 1$), the single electron goes into the first shell. For helium, with a nucleus having two protons ($Z = 2$), both electrons go into the first shell. According to Bohr,

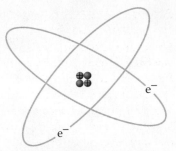

▲ **Figure 3.13** The nuclear atom, as envisioned by Bohr. Most of its mass is in an extremely small nucleus. Bohr thought that electrons orbited about the nucleus in the same way that planets orbit the sun. However, the real electron movements are more complicated, as seen in Figure 3.14.

It DOES Matter!

When light hits a photovoltaic "solar" cell, photons are absorbed, promoting electrons to excited states. Those excited state electrons are captured by the photovoltaic cell to produce an electrical current. Scientists are working to create new materials that will absorb more of the sun's photons and more efficiently convert those photons into electrical energy. Scientists are also working on creating new materials that will lower the cost to make solar cells. Depending on where you live and how much sunlight you get, solar electricity may already be cheaper than the electricity you buy from the power company.

two electrons is the maximum population of the first shell, and that level is filled in the helium atom. (We can ignore the neutrons in the nucleus because they are not involved in this process.)

With lithium ($Z = 3$), two electrons go into the first shell, and the third must go into the second shell. This process of adding electrons is continued until the second shell is filled with 8 electrons, as in a neon atom ($Z = 10$), which has 2 of its 10 electrons in the first shell and the remaining 8 in the second shell.

A sodium atom ($Z = 11$) has 11 electrons. Two are in the first shell, the second shell is filled with eight electrons, and the remaining electron is in the third shell. We can represent the **electron configuration** (or arrangement) of the first 11 elements as follows:

Element	1st shell	2nd shell	3rd shell
H	1		
He	2		
Li	2	1	
⋮	⋮	⋮	
Ne	2	8	
Na	2	8	1

Sometimes the main-shell electron configuration is abbreviated by writing the symbol for the element followed by the number of electrons in each shell, separated by commas, starting with the lowest energy level. Following the color scheme from the preceding table, the main-shell configuration for sodium is simply

$$\text{Na } 2, 8, 1$$

We can continue to add electrons to the third shell until we get to argon. The main-shell configuration for argon is

$$\text{Ar } 2, 8, 8$$

After argon, the notation for electron configurations is enhanced with more detail. This notation is discussed in greater detail in Section 3.8. Meanwhile, Example 3.4 shows how to determine a few main-shell configurations.

Example 3.4 | Main-Shell Electron Configurations

What is the main-shell electron configuration for fluorine?

Solution
Fluorine has the symbol F ($Z = 9$). It has nine electrons. Two of these electrons go into the first shell, and the remaining seven go into the second shell.

$$\text{F } 2, 7$$

▪ EXERCISE 3.4
Write the main-shell electron configurations for **(a)** beryllium and **(b)** magnesium. These elements are in the same column of the periodic table. What do you notice about the number of electrons in their outermost shells?

SELF-ASSESSMENT Questions

1. When electrified in a gas-discharge tube, different elements emit light that forms narrow lines that are
   a. characteristic of each particular element
   b. the same as those of the hydrogen spectrum
   c. dependent on the amount of gas present in the tube
   d. the same for all elements but with differing intensities

2. When an electron in an atom goes from a higher energy level to a lower one, the electron
   a. absorbs energy
   b. changes its volume
   c. changes its charge
   d. releases energy

3. An atom in an excited state is one with an electron that has
   a. moved to a higher energy level
   b. been removed
   c. bonded to another atom to make a molecule
   d. combined with a proton to make a neutron

4. The maximum number of electrons in the first shell of an atom is
   a. 2   b. 6   c. 8   d. unlimited

5. The maximum number of electrons in the third shell of an atom is
   a. 6   b. 8   c. 18   d. 32

6. The main-shell electron configuration of aluminum is
   a. 2, 8, 1
   b. 2, 8, 3
   c. 2, 8, 13
   d. 2, 8, 8, 8, 1

7. The main-shell electron configuration of sulfur is
   a. 2, 8, 4
   b. 2, 8, 6
   c. 2, 8, 8, 8, 6
   d. 2, 8, 18, 4

3.7 Electron Arrangement: The Quantum Model

Learning Objectives   ❯ Relate the idea of a quantum of energy to an orbital.   ❯ Write an electron configuration (in subshell notation) for a given atom.

Although Bohr's simple planetary model of the atom explained the spectrum of the hydrogen atom, it could never explain the spectra of any other elements. It was eventually replaced by more sophisticated models in which electrons are treated as *both* particles and waves. The electrons have characteristic wavelengths, and their locations are indicated as probabilities. The hypothesis that the electron should have wavelike properties was first suggested in 1924 by Louis de Broglie (1892–1987), a young French physicist. Although it was hard to accept because of Thomson's evidence that electrons are particles, de Broglie's hypothesis was experimentally verified within a few years.

Erwin Schrödinger (1887–1961), an Austrian physicist, used highly mathematical *quantum mechanics* in the 1920s to develop equations that describe the properties of electrons in atoms. Fortunately, we can make use of some of Schrödinger's results without understanding his elaborate equations. The solutions to these equations express an electron's location in terms of the probability of finding that electron in a given volume of space. These variously shaped volumes of space, called **orbitals**, replace the planetary orbits of the Bohr model.

Suppose you had a camera that could photograph electrons and you left the shutter open while an electron zipped about the nucleus. The developed picture would give a record of where the electron had been. (Doing the same thing with an electric fan would give a blurred image of the rapidly moving blades, an image resembling a disk.) The electrons in the first shell would appear as a fuzzy ball (often referred to as a *charge cloud* or an *electron cloud* [Figure 3.14]).

An *s* orbital

A *p* orbital

▲ **Figure 3.14** The modern charge-cloud representation of an atomic orbital is more accurate than the Bohr model (Figure 3.13). An electron cloud is the "fuzzy" region around an atomic nucleus where an electron is likely to be. The type of orbital determines the general shape of the cloud, as seen here.

Building Atoms by Orbital Filling

Scientists realized that each electron orbital could contain a maximum of two electrons and that some shells could contain more than one orbital. The first shell contains a single spherical orbital called 1*s*. The second shell contains four orbitals: 2*s* is spherical, and the other three orbitals, called 2*p*, are dumbbell-shaped (Figure 3.15). Orbitals in the same shell that have the same letter designation make up a **subshell (sublevel)**. The second shell has two subshells, the 2*s* subshell with only one orbital and the 2*p* subshell with three orbitals. The third shell contains nine orbitals distributed among three subshells: a spherical 3*s* orbital in the 3*s* subshell,

▶ **Figure 3.15** Electron orbitals of the second main shell. In these drawings, the nucleus of the atom is located at the intersection of the axes. The eight electrons that would be placed in the second shell of Bohr's model are distributed among these four orbitals in the current model of the atom, with two electrons per orbital.

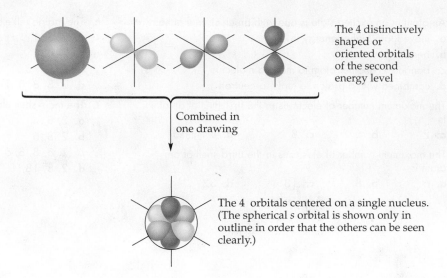

The 4 distinctively shaped or oriented orbitals of the second energy level

Combined in one drawing

The 4 orbitals centered on a single nucleus. (The spherical *s* orbital is shown only in outline in order that the others can be seen clearly.)

three dumbbell-shaped $3p$ orbitals in the $3p$ subshell, and five $3d$ orbitals with more complicated shapes in the $3d$ subshell.

In building up the electron configurations of atoms of the various elements, the lower sublevels (subshells) are filled first.

Hydrogen ($Z = 1$) has only one electron in the s orbital of the first shell. The electron configuration is

H $1s^1$

Helium ($Z = 2$) has two electrons and its electron configuration is

He $1s^2$

Electrons are in an *s* subshell.

Two electrons are in the 1*s* subshell.

Electrons are in the first shell.

Lithium ($Z = 3$) has three electrons—two in the first shell and one in the second shell. Because the s subshell is slightly lower in energy than the p subshell of the same shell, the third electron goes into the $2s$ orbital, and lithium's electron configuration is

Li $1s^2 2s^1$

Skipping to nitrogen ($Z = 7$), we fill the $1s$ and $2s$ subshells first. The remaining electrons go into the $2p$ subshell, and the seven electrons are arranged as follows:

N $1s^2 2s^2 2p^3$

Let's review what this notation means:

Two electrons in the first main shell

Two electrons in the *s* subshell of the second main shell

Three electrons in the *p* subshell of the second main shell

N $1s^2 2s^2 2p^3$

First main shell

Second main shell

For argon ($Z = 18$), with its 18 electrons, the configuration is

Ar $1s^2 2s^2 2p^6 3s^2 3p^6$

◄ **Figure 3.16** An order-of-filling chart for determining the electron configurations of atoms.

Note that the highest occupied subshell, $3p$, is filled. However, the order of subshell filling for elements with Z greater than 18 is not intuitively obvious. In potassium ($Z = 19$), for example, the $4s$ subshell fills before the $3d$ subshell. The order in which the various subshells are filled is shown in Figure 3.16. Table 3.3 gives the electron configurations for the first 20 elements. The electrons in the outermost main shell, called *valence electrons* (Section 3.8), are shown in color.

Table 3.3	Electron Configurations for Atoms of the First 20 Elements	
Name	Atomic Number	Electron Configuration
Hydrogen	1	$1s^1$
Helium	2	$1s^2$
Lithium	3	$1s^2 2s^1$
Beryllium	4	$1s^2 2s^2$
Boron	5	$1s^2 2s^2 2p^1$
Carbon	6	$1s^2 2s^2 2p^2$
Nitrogen	7	$1s^2 2s^2 2p^3$
Oxygen	8	$1s^2 2s^2 2p^4$
Fluorine	9	$1s^2 2s^2 2p^5$
Neon	10	$1s^2 2s^2 2p^6$
Sodium	11	$1s^2 2s^2 2p^6 3s^1$
Magnesium	12	$1s^2 2s^2 2p^6 3s^2$
Aluminum	13	$1s^2 2s^2 2p^6 3s^2 3p^1$
Silicon	14	$1s^2 2s^2 2p^6 3s^2 3p^2$
Phosphorus	15	$1s^2 2s^2 2p^6 3s^2 3p^3$
Sulfur	16	$1s^2 2s^2 2p^6 3s^2 3p^4$
Chlorine	17	$1s^2 2s^2 2p^6 3s^2 3p^5$
Argon	18	$1s^2 2s^2 2p^6 3s^2 3p^6$
Potassium	19	$1s^2 2s^2 2p^6 3s^2 3p^6 4s^1$
Calcium	20	$1s^2 2s^2 2p^6 3s^2 3p^6 4s^2$

Example 3.5	Subshell Notation

Without referring to Table 3.3, use subshell notation to write the electron configurations for **(a)** oxygen and **(b)** sulfur. What do the electron configurations of these two elements have in common?

Solution

a. Oxygen (Z = 8) has eight electrons. We place them in subshells, starting with the lowest energy level. Two go into the 1s orbital and two into the 2s orbital. That leaves four electrons to be placed in the 2p subshell. The electron configuration is $1s^2 2s^2 2p^4$.

b. Sulfur (Z = 16) atoms have 16 electrons each. The electron configuration is $1s^2 2s^2 2p^6 3s^2 3p^4$. Note that the total of the superscripts is 16 and that we have not exceeded the maximum capacity for any sublevel.

Both O and S have electron configurations, with four electrons in the highest energy sublevel (outermost subshell).

▪ **EXERCISE 3.5A**

Without referring to Table 3.3, use subshell notation to write out the electron configurations for **(a)** chlorine and **(b)** bromine. What do the electron configurations for these two elements have in common?

▪ **EXERCISE 3.5B**

Use Figure 3.16 to write the electron configurations for **(a)** titanium (Ti) and **(b)** tin (Sn).

SELF-ASSESSMENT Questions

1. The shape of a 1s orbital is
   a. circular
   b. a dumbbell
   c. spherical
   d. variable

2. The maximum number of electrons in an atomic orbital
   a. depends on the main shell
   b. depends on the subshell
   c. is always 2
   d. is always 8

3. Which of the following subshells has the highest energy?
   a. 2p   **b.** 2s   **c.** 3p   **d.** 3s

4. What is the lowest-numbered main shell to have d orbitals?
   a. 1   **b.** 2   **c.** 3   **d.** 4

5. Which of the following atoms has a half-filled subshell in the ground state?
   a. beryllium
   b. nitrogen
   c. oxygen
   d. neon

6. Which subshell has a total of three orbitals?
   a. s   **b.** p   **c.** d   **d.** f

7. In what main shell is a 3d subshell located?
   a. 1   **b.** 3   **c.** 5   **d.** none

8. The electron capacity of the 4p subshell is
   a. 3   **b.** 4   **c.** 6   **d.** 10

Answers: 1, c; 2, c; 3, c; 4, c; 5, b; 6, b; 7, b; 8, c

3.8 Electron Configurations and the Periodic Table

Learning Objective ❯ Describe how an element's electron configuration relates to its location in the periodic table.

In general, the properties of elements can be correlated with their electron configurations. Because the number of electrons equals the number of protons, the periodic table tells us about electron configuration as well as atomic number. (We will explore bond formation using electron configurations in Chapter 4.)

The modern periodic table (inside front cover) has horizontal rows and vertical columns.

- Each vertical column is a **group** or *family*. Elements in a group have similar chemical properties.
- A horizontal row of the periodic table is called a **period**. The properties of elements change in a recurring manner across a period.

In the United States, the groups are often indicated by a numeral followed by the letter A or B.

- An element in an A group is a **main-group element**.
- An element in a B group is a **transition element**.

The International Union of Pure and Applied Chemistry (IUPAC) recommends numbering the groups from 1 to 18. Both systems are indicated on the periodic table on the inside front cover, but this book uses the traditional U.S. system.

Family Features: Outer Electron Configurations

The period in which an element appears in the periodic table tells us how many main shells an atom of that element has. Phosphorus, for example, is in the third period, so the phosphorus atom has three main shells. The U.S. group number (for main-group elements) tells us how many electrons are in the outermost shell. An electron in the outermost shell of an atom is called a **valence electron**. From the fact that phosphorus is in group 5A, we can deduce that it has five valence electrons. Two of these are in an s orbital, and the other three are in p orbitals. We can indicate the outer electron configuration of the phosphorus atom as

$$P \quad 3s^2 3p^3$$

The valence electrons determine most of the chemistry of an atom. Because all the elements in the same group of the periodic table have the same number of valence electrons, they should have similar chemistry, and they do.

Figure 3.17 relates the subshell configurations to the groups in the periodic table. On the left is the s block, consisting of the first two groups. For the atoms in these two groups the last electron added goes into an s orbital. On the far right is the p block. Its six groups correspond to the six electrons that can go into a p subshell. Between these blocks are the transition metals, whose 10 groups correspond to the five d orbitals in a d subshell, and the inner transition metals, where the seven f orbitals in the f subshell get filled.

6. What is periodic about the periodic table?

Figure 3.17 shows why there are periodic, or recurring, trends in the periodic table. Elements in the same column have similar electron configurations and often have similar chemical and physical characteristics as well.

▲ **Figure 3.17** Valence-shell electron configurations and the periodic table.

Family Groups

Elements within a group have similar properties. All the elements in group 1A have one valence electron, and all except hydrogen are very reactive metals (hydrogen is a nonmetal). All group 1A elements have the outer electron configuration ns^1, where n denotes the number of the outermost main shell.

The metals in group 1A are called **alkali metals**. They react vigorously with water, producing hydrogen gas. There are noticeable trends in properties within this family. For example, lithium is the hardest metal in the group. Sodium is softer than lithium; potassium is softer still; and so on down the group. Lithium is also the least reactive toward water. Sodium, potassium, rubidium, and cesium are progressively more reactive. Francium is highly radioactive and extremely rare. Few of its properties have been measured.

Hydrogen is the odd one in group 1A. It is not an alkali metal but rather a typical nonmetal. Based on its properties, hydrogen probably should be put in a group of its own.

Group 2A elements are known as **alkaline earth metals**. The metals in this group have the outer electron configuration ns^2. Most are fairly soft and moderately reactive with water. Beryllium is the odd member of the group in that it is rather hard and does not react with water. As in other families, there are trends in properties within the group. For example, magnesium, calcium, strontium, barium, and radium are progressively more reactive toward water.

Group 7A elements, often called **halogens**, also consist of reactive elements. All have seven valence electrons with the configuration ns^2np^5. Halogens react vigorously with alkali metals to form crystalline solids (this is discussed further in Chapter 4). There are trends in the halogen family as you move down the group. Fluorine is most reactive toward alkali metals, chlorine is the next most reactive, and so on. Fluorine and chlorine are gases at room temperature, bromine is a liquid, and iodine is a solid. (Astatine, like francium, is highly radioactive and extremely rare; few of its properties have been determined.)

Members of group 8A, to the far right on the periodic table, have a complete set of valence electrons and therefore undergo few, if any, chemical reactions. They are called **noble gases**, for their lack of chemical reactivity.

▲ (Upper) Lithium, an alkali metal, reacts with water to form hydrogen gas. (Lower) Potassium, another alkali metal, undergoes the same reaction but much more vigorously.

Example 3.6 | Valence-Shell Electron Configurations

Use subshell notation to write the electron configurations for the outermost main shell of **(a)** strontium (Sr) and **(b)** arsenic (As).

Solution

a. Strontium is in group 2A and thus has two valence electrons in an s subshell. Because strontium is in the fifth period of the periodic table, its outer main shell is $n = 5$. Its outer electron configuration is therefore $5s^2$.

b. Arsenic is in group 5A and the fourth period. Its five outer (valence) electrons are in the $n = 4$ shell, and the configuration is $4s^24p^3$.

▪ EXERCISE 3.6A

Use subshell notation to write the configurations for the outermost main shell of **(a)** rubidium (Rb), **(b)** selenium (Se), and **(c)** germanium (Ge).

▪ EXERCISE 3.6B

The valence electrons in aluminum have the configuration $3s^23p^1$. In the periodic table, gallium is directly below aluminum, and indium is directly below gallium. Use only this information to write the configurations for the valence electrons in **(a)** gallium and **(b)** indium.

Metals and Nonmetals

Elements in the periodic table are divided into two classes by a heavy, stepped line (see inside front cover). Those to the left of the line are *metals*. A **metal** has a characteristic luster (shininess) and generally is a good conductor of heat and electricity. Except for mercury, which is a liquid, all metals are solids at room temperature. Metals generally are *malleable*; that is, they can be hammered into thin sheets. Most also are *ductile*, which means that they can be drawn into wires.

Elements to the right of the stepped line are *nonmetals*. A **nonmetal** lacks metallic properties. Several nonmetals are gases (oxygen, nitrogen, fluorine, and chlorine). Others are solids (e.g., carbon, sulfur, phosphorus, and iodine). Bromine is the only nonmetal that is a liquid at room temperature.

Some of the elements bordering the stepped line are called *semimetals*, or *metalloids*, and these have intermediate properties that may resemble those of both metals and nonmetals. There is a lack of agreement on just which elements fit in this category.

▲ (Upper) Metals such as gold are easily shaped, and they conduct heat and electricity well. (Lower) Nonmetals such as sulfur are usually brittle, melt at low temperatures, and often are good insulators.

Which Model to Use

For some purposes in this text, we use only main-shell configurations of atoms to picture the distribution of electrons in atoms. At other times, the electron clouds of the quantum-mechanical model are more useful. Even Dalton's model sometimes proves to be the best way to describe certain phenomena (the behavior of gases, for example). The choice of model is always based on which one is most helpful in understanding a particular concept. This, after all, is the purpose of scientific models.

SELF-ASSESSMENT Questions

1. Which pair of elements has the most similar chemical properties?
   a. Ca and Cd   **b.** Cl and Br   **c.** P and S   **d.** Sb and Sc

2. Elements within a period of the periodic table have the same number of
   a. electrons in the outermost shell   **b.** neutrons in the nucleus
   c. occupied main shells   **d.** protons in the nucleus

3. The valence-shell electron configuration of the halogens is
   a. ns^1 **b.** ns^2np^3
   c. ns^2np^5 **d.** ns^2np^6

4. The alkali metals are members of group
   a. 1A   **b.** 2A   **c.** 7A   **d.** 8A

5. What is the total number of valence electrons in an atom of bromine?
   a. 5   **b.** 7   **c.** 17   **d.** 35

6. Which of the following sets of elements exhibits the most similar chemical properties?
   a. Ca, Zn, Kr   **b.** Pt, Au, Hg
   c. Li, Na, K   **d.** N, O, F

7. In the ground state, atoms of a fourth period element must have
   a. a 3d sublevel
   b. electrons in the fourth shell
   c. four valence electrons
   d. properties similar to those of other elements in the fourth period

Answers: 1, b; 2, c; 3, c; 4, a; 5, b; 6, c; 7, b

Scott Cummings, *Kenyon College*

Clean Energy from Solar Fuels

Learning Objectives ➤ Distinguish the conversion of solar energy into electrical energy in a solar cell from the conversion of solar energy into the chemical bond energy of a solar fuel. ➤ Explain why splitting water into the elements hydrogen and oxygen requires an energy input and why producing water by the reaction of hydrogen and oxygen releases energy.

Imagine a world powered by a clean fuel manufactured using sunlight and water that produces no carbon dioxide emissions when used. This has been the dream of chemists around the world, who have been working for many years to develop a "solar fuel" that might someday replace some of the fossil fuels (oil, coal, and natural gas) that are so important to modern society.

Sunlight is a free and abundant power source. The amount of solar energy reaching the Earth's surface in *one hour* is as much as all of the fossil fuel energy humans use in *one year*. The goal for chemists is to develop efficient methods to capture just a tiny part of this sunlight and convert it into a useful form. Of course, the most common approach is to convert solar energy into electricity using solar panels, devices constructed from photovoltaic cells that are usually made of silicon. But sunshine is intermittent, so this solar electricity is only available on sunny days.

A different approach is to use the energy of sunlight to promote a chemical change, converting radiant solar energy into chemical energy in the form of fuel that can be stored and used even when the sun has gone down. One idea for a solar fuel is hydrogen. Using sunlight to make hydrogen is one of the grand challenges of chemistry.

A full hydrogen energy cycle uses solar energy to split water (H_2O) into hydrogen (H_2) and oxygen (O_2) and then uses the hydrogen as a clean fuel to produce either heat (when burned) or electricity (using a fuel cell). Splitting water requires energy input to break the chemical bonds that hold together the O and H atoms in water molecules. One of the simplest ways to do this is by electrolysis (Section 3.1), which requires electrical energy. If the electricity is produced using a solar panel, then the hydrogen formed is a solar fuel. This approach is currently expensive, and much research in chemistry is aimed at discovering new and inexpensive photovoltaic materials—including plastics—from which to construct solar panels. Chemists also seek ways to make the electrodes and other components from abundant elements instead of from the precious metal platinum (Pt).

For a different approach to hydrogen production, chemists are turning to green plants for inspiration. Plants absorb energy from the sun and store it in the form of chemical bonds of compounds known

solar energy

water (H_2O)

hydrogen (H_2) and oxygen (O_2)

heat or electricity

Clean energy cycle. Solar energy is used to produce hydrogen and oxygen from water (top). Hydrogen fuel reacts with oxygen to produce water and releases energy as either heat or electricity.

as carbohydrates (Section 8.10). This photosynthetic reaction, which is essential to sustain life on the planet, relies on the ability of molecules in the plant to split water using sunlight. Chemists are hoping to unlock the secrets of the leaf to develop "artificial photosynthesis," which uses solar energy to produce hydrogen fuel from water.

In natural photosynthesis, plants employ many different molecules to capture and convert solar energy. Chlorophyll molecules absorb part of the solar spectrum, giving a leaf its green color. To mimic this process, chemists are designing colorful synthetic dyes to capture photons from the sun. When a dye absorbs light, one of its electrons is excited, which generates an excited-state molecule. The challenge is to harness this excitation energy to split water before it is simply emitting as a photon (Section 3.6). Plants also employ a cluster of manganese, calcium, and oxygen atoms to crack apart water molecules and produce oxygen. Chemists have been active in trying to mimic this reaction as well, using compounds made in the laboratory.

Solar fuels such as hydrogen embody several green chemistry principles. Hydrogen fuel is only as green as the method used to make it. If produced using sunlight as the energy source and water as the chemical feedstock, though, the fuel can be clean and renewable (Principle 7). Unlike fossil fuels, hydrogen is a carbon-free fuel that, if produced using sunlight, can prevent carbon dioxide emissions (Principle 1). A solar-hydrogen system relies on compounds that increase efficiency and facilitate both the water-splitting chemistry and the use of hydrogen (Principle 9). If these materials are earth-abundant and do not cause harm to the environment, this process closes the clean-fuel cycle.

PHOTOSYNTHESIS

carbon dioxide + water + sunlight →
carbohydrate + oxygen

ARTIFICIAL PHOTOSYNTHESIS

water → hydrogen + oxygen

Two ways to make solar fuels. Green plants use photosynthesis to produce carbohydrate fuels. Chemists are trying to produce hydrogen fuel. Both reactions use water and solar energy.

SUMMARY

Section 3.1—Davy, Faraday, and others showed that matter is electrical in nature. They were able to decompose compounds into elements by **electrolysis** or by passing electricity through molten salts. **Electrodes** are carbon rods or metal strips that carry electricity into the **electrolyte**, the solution or compound that conducts electricity. The electrolyte contains **ions**—charged atoms or groups of atoms. The **anode** is the positive electrode, and **anions** (negatively charged ions) move toward it. The **cathode** is the negative electrode, and **cations** (positively charged ions) move toward it. Experiments with **cathode rays** in gas-discharge tubes showed that matter contained negatively charged particles, which were called **electrons**. Thomson determined the mass-to-charge ratio for the electron. Goldstein's experiment showed that matter also contained positively charged particles. Millikan's oil-drop experiment measured the charge on the electron, so its mass could then be calculated.

Section 3.2—In his studies of cathode rays, Roentgen accidentally discovered **X-rays**, a highly penetrating form of radiation now used in medical diagnosis. Becquerel accidentally discovered another type of radiation that comes from certain unstable elements. Marie Curie named this new discovery **radioactivity** and studied it extensively.

Section 3.3—Radioactivity was soon classified as three different types of radiation: **Alpha particles** have four times the mass of a hydrogen atom and a positive charge twice that of an electron. **Beta particles** are energetic electrons. **Gamma rays** are a form of energy like X-rays but more penetrating.

Section 3.4—Rutherford's experiments with alpha particles and gold foil showed that most of the alpha particles emitted toward the foil passed through it. A few were deflected or, occasionally, bounced back almost directly toward the source. This indicated that all the positive charge and most of the mass of an atom must be in a tiny core, which Rutherford called the **nucleus**.

Section 3.5—Rutherford called the smallest unit of positive charge the **proton**; it has about the mass of a hydrogen atom and a charge equal in size but opposite in sign to the electron. In 1932, Chadwick discovered the **neutron**, a nuclear particle as massive as a proton but with no charge. The number of protons in an atom is the **atomic number** (Z). Atoms of the same element have the same number of protons but may have different numbers of neutrons; such atoms are called **isotopes**. Different isotopes of an element are nearly identical chemically. Protons and neutrons collectively are called **nucleons**, and the number of nucleons is called the **mass number** or **nucleon number**. The difference between the mass number and the atomic number is the number of neutrons. The general symbol for an isotope of element X is written $_Z^A X$, where A is the mass number and Z is the atomic number.

Section 3.6—Light from the sun or from an incandescent lamp produces a continuous spectrum, containing all colors. Light from a gas-discharge tube produces a line spectrum, containing only certain colors. Bohr explained line spectra by proposing that an electron in an atom resides only at certain discrete **energy levels**, which differ from one another by a **quantum**, or discrete unit of energy. An atom drops to the lowest energy state, or **ground state**, after being in a higher energy state, or **excited state**. The energy emitted when electrons move to lower energy levels manifests as a line spectrum characteristic of the particular element, with the lines corresponding to specific wavelengths (colors) of light. Bohr also deduced that the energy levels of an atom could hold at most $2n^2$ electrons, where n is the number of the energy level, or **shell**. A description of the shells occupied by the electrons of an atom is one way of giving the atom's **electron configuration**, or arrangement of electrons.

Section 3.7—de Broglie hypothesized that electrons have wave properties. Schrödinger developed equations that described each electron's location in terms of an **orbital**, a volume of space that the electron usually occupies. Each orbital holds at most two electrons. Orbitals in the same shell and with the same energy make up a **subshell**, or sublevel, each of which is designated by a letter. An s orbital is spherical and a p orbital is dumbbell-shaped. The d and f orbitals have more complex shapes. The first main shell can hold only one s orbital; the second can hold one s and three p orbitals; and the third can hold one s, three p, and five d orbitals. In writing an electron configuration using subshell notation, we give the shell number and subshell letter, followed by a superscript indicating the number of electrons in that subshell. The order of the shells and subshells can be remembered with a chart or by looking at the periodic table.

Section 3.8—Elements in the periodic table are arranged vertically in **groups** and horizontally in **periods**. Electrons in the outermost shell of an atom, called **valence electrons**, determine the reactivity of that atom. Elements in a group usually have the same number of valence electrons and similarities in properties. We designate groups by a number and the letter A or B. The A-group elements are **main-group elements**. The B-group elements are **transition elements**. Group 1A elements are the **alkali metals**. Except for hydrogen, they are all soft, low-melting, highly reactive metals. Group 2A consists of the **alkaline earth metals**, fairly soft and reactive metals. Group 7A elements, the **halogens**, are reactive nonmetals. Group 8A elements, the **noble gases**, react very little or not at all. A stepped line divides the periodic table into **metals**, which conduct electricity and heat and are shiny, malleable, and ductile, and **nonmetals**, which tend to lack the properties of metals. Some elements bordering the stepped line, called *metalloids*, have properties intermediate between those of metals and nonmetals.

GREEN CHEMISTRY Hydrogen is a promising clean fuel because it can be manufactured using sunlight and water and because using it does not produce carbon dioxide as waste. Using a solar cell, energy from sunlight can be converted into electricity, which can then be used to split water into hydrogen and oxygen; this splitting of water can also be accomplished by a process that mimics photosynthesis. The hydrogen can be burned to produce heat or used in a fuel cell to produce electricity.

Learning Objectives

❯ Explain the electrical properties of an atom. (3.1)	Problems 1, 20
❯ Describe how the properties of electricity explain the structure of atoms. (3.1)	Problems 4, 18
❯ Describe the experiments that led to the discovery of X-rays and an explanation of radioactivity. (3.2)	Problems 2, 21
❯ Distinguish the three main kinds of radioactivity: alpha, beta, and gamma. (3.3)	Problems 3, 19
❯ Sketch the nuclear model of the atom, and identify its parts. (3.4)	Problems 5, 9
❯ List the particles that make up the nucleus of an atom, and give their relative masses and electric charges. (3.5)	Problems 6–8, 16, 17, 22
❯ Identify elements and isotopes from their nuclear particles. (3.5)	Problems 10, 11, 15, 23–27, 29
❯ Define *quantum*. (3.6)	Problems 12, 13, 48
❯ Arrange the electrons in a given atom in energy levels (shells). (3.6)	Problems 45, 50–52
❯ Relate the idea of a quantum of energy to an orbital. (3.7)	Problems 14, 28
❯ Write an electron configuration (in subshell notation) for a given atom. (3.7)	Problems 30–36, 49
❯ Describe how an element's electron configuration relates to its location in the periodic table. (3.8)	Problems 37–44, 46, 47
❯ Distinguish the conversion of solar energy into electrical energy in a solar cell from the conversion of solar energy into the chemical-bond energy of a solar fuel.	Problems 54–56
❯ Explain why splitting water into the elements hydrogen and oxygen requires an energy input and producing water by the reaction of hydrogen and oxygen releases energy.	Problem 53

REVIEW QUESTIONS

1. What did each of the following scientists contribute to our knowledge of the atom?
   a. William Crookes
   b. Eugen Goldstein
   c. Michael Faraday
   d. J. J. Thomson
   e. Ernest Rutherford
   f. James Chadwick

2. What is radioactivity? How did the discovery of radioactivity contradict Dalton's atomic theory?

3. How are X-rays and gamma rays similar? How are they different?

4. How was Goldstein's experiment different from Thomson's, and how did it reveal different information about the atom?

5. In Rutherford's model of the atom, where are the protons, the neutrons, and the electrons found?

6. Define or identify each of the following.
   a. deuterium
   b. tritium
   c. photon

7. The following table describes four atoms.

	Atom A	Atom B	Atom C	Atom D
Number of protons	17	18	18	17
Number of neutrons	18	17	18	17
Number of electrons	17	18	18	17

Are atoms A and B isotopes? A and C? A and D? B and C? C and D?

8. Which two atoms in Question 7 have about the same mass?

9. Compare Dalton's model of the atom with the nuclear model of the atom.

10. What are the symbol, name, and atomic number of the element with $Z = 76$? You may use the periodic table and a table of atomic masses.

11. What are the symbol, name, and atomic number of the element that has 44 protons in the nuclei of its atoms?

12. Explain what is meant by the term *quantum*.

13. Which atom absorbs more energy, one in which an electron moves from the second shell to the third shell or an otherwise identical atom in which an electron moves from the first to the third shell?

14. How did Bohr and Schrödinger refine the model of the atom?

15. What theory uses wave properties to describe the motion of particles at the atomic and subatomic levels?

16. Use the periodic table to determine the number of protons in an atom of each of the following elements.
    a. beryllium
    b. sodium
    c. sulfur
    d. selenium
    e. copper
    f. uranium

17. How many electrons are there in each neutral atom of the elements listed in Question 16?

 PROBLEMS

Components of Atoms

18. What subatomic particle makes up cathode rays?

19. Rank the three types of radioactivity by charge and by mass.

20. An atom with an electric charge is
    a. an ion   b. a molecule
    c. a nucleus   d. radioactive

21. Radioactive elements
    a. are those essential to the electronics industry
    b. readily form ionic bonds
    c. split into nearly equal fragments
    d. spontaneously give off particles or rays

Nuclear Symbols and Isotopes

22. A neutral atom with 9 protons will have how many electrons?

23. Give the symbol and name for **(a)** an isotope with a mass number of 37 and an atomic number of 17 and **(b)** an isotope with 30 neutrons and 25 protons.

24. Fill in the table:

Element	Mass Number	Number of Protons	Number of Neutrons
Nickel	60		
	108	46	
		7	7
Iodine			74

25. How many different elements are listed here?
    $^{23}_{11}X$ $^{22}_{10}X$ $^{11}_{5}X$ $^{24}_{11}X$ $^{25}_{12}X$

26. How many different isotopes of silver are listed here? (The X does not necessarily represent any specific element.)
    $^{108}_{47}X$ $^{108}_{48}X$ $^{110}_{47}X$ $^{109}_{46}X$ $^{107}_{47}X$

27. The most likely mass number of atom with an atomic number of 14 is _____.

28. A beryllium atom has four protons, four electrons, and five neutrons. What is the atom's mass number?

29. When an atom loses two electrons, the charge on its ion is _____.

Subshell Notation for Electron Configurations

30. Which subshell can be occupied by a maximum of 10 electrons?

31. Without referring to the periodic table, give the atomic numbers of the elements with the following electron configurations.
    a. $1s^2 2s^2 2p^4$
    b. $1s^2 2s^2 2p^6 3s^2 3p^2$
    c. $1s^2 2s^2 2p^6 3s^2 3p^6 3d^8 4s^2$

32. Without referring to the periodic table, give the atomic numbers of the elements with the following electron configurations.
    a. $1s^2 2s^2 2p^5$
    b. $1s^2 2s^2 2p^6 3s^2 3p^6 4s^1$
    c. $1s^2 2s^2 2p^6 3s^2 3p^6 3d^{10} 4s^2$

33. Indicate whether each electron configuration represents an atom in the ground state or in a possible excited state or is incorrect. In each case, explain why.
    a. $1s^1 2s^1$ b. $1s^2 2s^2 2p^7$
    c. $1s^2 2p^2$ d. $1s^2 2s^2 2p^2$

34. Indicate whether each electron configuration represents an atom in the ground state or in a possible excited state or is incorrect. In each case, explain why.
    a. $1s^2 2s^2 3s^2$ b. $1s^2 2s^2 2p^3 3s^1$
    c. $1s^2 2s^2 2p^6 2d^5$ d. $1s^2 2s^4 2p^2$

35. Suppose that one electron is added to the outermost shell of a fluorine atom. What element's electron configuration would the atom then have?

36. Suppose that each of the following changes is made. Give the symbol for the element whose electron configuration matches the result.
    a. Two electrons are added to an oxygen atom.
    b. Two electrons are removed from a calcium atom.
    c. Three electrons are removed from an aluminum atom.

37. Referring only to the periodic table, tell how the electron configurations of silicon (Si) and germanium (Ge) are similar. How are they different?

38. Referring only to the periodic table, tell how the electron configurations of fluorine (F) and chlorine (Cl) are similar. How are they different? How do you expect the electron configurations of bromine (Br) and iodine (I) to be similar to those of fluorine and chlorine?

39. Refer to the periodic table to identify each element as a metal or a nonmetal.
    a. manganese
    b. strontium
    c. cesium
    d. argon

Use the following list of elements to answer Problems 40–44:

Mg, Cs, Ne, P, Kr, K, Ra, N, Fe, Ca, Mo

40. Which element(s) is (are) alkali metals?

41. Which element(s) is (are) noble gases?

42. Which element(s) is (are) transition metals?

43. How many of the elements are nonmetals?

44. All elements with more than 83 protons are *radioactive*, as we shall see in Chapter 11. Are any of the elements in the list above necessarily radioactive? If so, which one(s)? Could radioactive isotopes of any of the others exist?

 ADDITIONAL PROBLEMS

45. An atom of an element has two electrons in the first shell, eight electrons in the second shell, and five electrons in the third shell. From this information, give the element's **(a)** atomic number, **(b)** name, **(c)** total number of electrons in each of its atoms, **(d)** total number of *s* electrons, and **(e)** total number of *d* electrons.

46. Refer to Problem 36. Explain how you can answer the three parts of that problem just by looking at a periodic table and without writing electron structures.

47. Without referring to any tables in the text, color the *s*, *p*, and *d* blocks and mark an appropriate location for each of the following in the blank periodic table provided: **(a)** the fourth period noble gas, **(b)** the third period alkali metal, **(c)** the fourth period halogen, and **(d)** a metal in the fourth period and in group 3B.

48. Look again at Figure 3.11. A patient is found to be suffering from heavy-metal poisoning. An emission spectrum is obtained from a sample of the patient's blood, by spraying a solution of the blood into a flame. The brightest emission lines are found at 5520, 5540, 5890, and 5900 Å. What two elements are likely to be present? Which one is more likely to be the culprit?

49. Refer to Figure 3.16 and write the electron configurations of **(a)** iron (Fe), **(b)** tin (Sn), and **(c)** lead (Pb).

50. Atoms of two adjacent elements in the third period are in the ground state. An atom of element A has only *s* electrons in its valence shell. An atom of element B has at least one *p* electron in its valence shell. Identify elements A and B.

51. Atoms of two adjacent elements in the fifth period are in the ground state. An atom of element L has only *s* electrons in its valence shell. An atom of element M has at least one *d* electron in an unfilled shell. Identify elements L and M.

52. Atoms of two elements, one above the other in the same group, are in the ground state. An atom of element Q has two *s* electrons in its outer shell and no *d* electrons. An atom of element R has *d* electrons in its configuration. Identify elements Q and R.

53. Which of the following is true of the water-splitting reaction on page 88?
    a. It produces energy, for example, electricity or heat.
    b. It requires an energy input, for example, electricity or sunlight.
    c. It produces twice as much oxygen as hydrogen.
    d. It occurs inside a fuel cell.

54. What is produced when solar energy is converted into chemical-bond energy in the water-splitting reaction?
    a. hydrogen and nitrogen
    b. oxygen and carbon
    c. hydrogen and oxygen
    d. oxygen and calcium

55. Which of the following is *not* a benefit of using a solar fuel such as hydrogen?
    a. A solar fuel can store the energy of sunlight, which is intermittent.
    b. A solar fuel can replace some fossil fuels.
    c. Using a solar fuel such as hydrogen produces no carbon dioxide emissions.
    d. Electrodes used in electrolysis rely on platinum metal.

56. Isotopes played an important role in one of the most important experiments investigating photosynthesis, the chemical reaction that converts water (H_2O) and carbon dioxide (CO_2) into glucose ($C_6H_{12}O_6$) and oxygen (O_2). For most of the early twentieth century, scientists thought that the oxygen produced by photosynthetic plants and algae came from carbon dioxide they absorbed. To investigate this question, in the early 1940s, chemists at Stanford University used an isotope of oxygen to study the mechanism of the photosynthetic reaction. The researchers fed photosynthesizing algae with water enriched with oxygen-18 and discovered that the oxygen produced was enriched with oxygen-18. Did this result support or refute the hypothesis that the O_2 produced by photosynthesis comes from CO_2?

CRITICAL THINKING EXERCISES

Apply knowledge that you have gained in this chapter and one or more of the FLaReS principles (Chapter 1) to evaluate the following statements or claims.

3.1 Suppose you read in the newspaper that a chemist in South America claims to have discovered a new element with an atomic mass of 34. Extremely rare, it was found in a sample taken from the Andes Mountains. Unfortunately, the chemist has used all of the sample in his analyses.

3.2 Some aboriginal tribes have rain-making ceremonies in which they toss pebbles of gypsum up into the air. (Gypsum is the material used to make plaster of Paris by heating the rock to remove some of its water.) Sometimes it does rain several days after these rain-making ceremonies.

3.3 Some scientists think that life on other planets might be based on silicon rather than carbon. Evaluate this possibility.

3.4 You come across a website selling water made from only single isotopes of hydrogen and oxygen. A testimonial on the website claims that drinking only the isotopically pure water helps a person feel more refreshed throughout the day.

COLLABORATIVE GROUP PROJECTS

Prepare a PowerPoint, poster, or other presentation (as directed by your instructor) to share with the class.

1. Prepare a brief biographical report on one of the following.
   a. Humphry Davy
   b. Antoine Henri Becquerel
   c. Wilhelm Roentgen
   d. Marie Curie
   e. Robert Millikan
   f. Niels Bohr
   g. Alessandro Volta
   h. Ernest Rutherford
   i. Michael Faraday
   j. J. J. Thomson

2. Draw a grid containing 16 squares, in two rows of 8, representing the 16 elements in the periodic table from lithium to argon. For each of the elements, give **(a)** the main-shell electron configuration and **(b)** the subshell notation for the electron configuration.

3. Prepare a brief report on one of the **(a)** alkali metals, **(b)** alkaline earth metals, **(c)** halogens, or **(d)** noble gases. List sources and commercial uses.

4. Many different forms of the periodic table have been generated. Prepare a brief report showing at least three different versions of the periodic table, and comment on their usefulness.

CHEMISTRY@HOME Birthday Candle Flame Test

Materials required:

- Colorflame birthday candles (available in party supply stores or online)
- Matches or lighter
- Play dough or an aluminum pan of sand (container big enough to stand 5 candles in a row)
- Diffraction grating film (available as 8.5 × 11 inch or 12 × 6 inch sheets through online scientific education suppliers: 225 lines/mm or 500 lines/mm grating films work the best; the sheets can be cut in to smaller pieces for use by multiple investigators)

What if you could test your ability to identify and describe elements by burning a birthday candle? Would you do it?

Traditionally, labs creating flame-emission spectra use solutions of hazardous metal salts and Bunsen burners. Even when used in tiny amounts, the metal ions in the salt solutions become volatized (airborne), causing a risk of inhalation. We can reduce the hazards by using birthday candles that burn at a much lower temperature than a Bunsen burner and eliminate the preparation and disposal of solutions of metal salts.

Your objective will be to compare and contrast the emission spectra from the colored birthday candles. Keep in mind that white light is composed of the multiple wavelengths of light that produce the whole rainbow. When individual atoms are heated, they absorb energy that causes transitions from lower to higher energy states. When the electrons return to the ground state, this energy is released as visible light. Every element has its own, unique emission spectrum that can be used as its "fingerprint" for identification.

To perform this experiment, gather your materials and find a room that can easily be darkened. Place the five candles in the sand or play dough about an inch apart, pressing them in about a quarter inch to steady them.

Create a small data table to record your findings. The order of the candles should match the data table, for instance, red, purple, green, blue, orange.

Light the candles using the match or lighter, and darken the room to observe them better. First observe the flames with your naked eye. Write down the color of each flame. Next, hold the diffraction film 6 to 12 inches away from the flames and observe the dominant colors for each flame. Make a note about those colors. Blow out the candles. What did you see? How do the colors seen by the naked eye compare to the emission spectra emitted by each flame?

To validate your observations check out the emission-spectra websites such as: http://webmineral.com/help/FlameTest.shtml to identify the element in each flame. Which element is in each candle? Write down your answer in the data table.

Light individual candles again and compare your new and old observations. Are you able to justify your identifications of elements based on your observations? Why or why not? Brainstorm to find any mistake you might have made with this experiment.

Questions

1. How do the colors seen by the naked eye compare to the emission spectra emitted by each flame?
2. Why did the flames produce different colors?
3. Explain what happened within the atoms to produce the emission spectra.
4. Suggest potential sources of error in the analysis of the flames.
5. Justify your metal identifications based upon your observations.

CHEMICAL BONDS

Have You Ever Wondered?

1. **Why is there no such thing as a jar of chloride ions only?**

2. **Why does chlorine in a swimming pool have an odor but chlorine in salt does not?**

3. **My father is on a low-sodium diet. What exactly does that mean?**

4. **If there is iron in blood, why aren't we magnetic?**

5. **Both oxygen and hydrogen are gases at room temperatures. How come water—which combines them—is a liquid?**

Learning Objectives

> Determine the number of electrons in an ion. (4.1)

> Write the Lewis symbol for an atom or ion. (4.2)

> Distinguish between an ion and an atom. (4.3)

> Describe the nature of the attraction that leads to formation of an ionic bond. (4.3)

> Write symbols for common ions, and determine their charges. (4.4)

> Describe the relationship between the octet rule and the charge on an ion. (4.4)

> Name and write formulas for binary ionic compounds. (4.5)

> Explain the difference between a covalent bond and an ionic bond. (4.6)

> Name and write formulas for covalent compounds. (4.6)

> Classify a covalent bond as polar or nonpolar. (4.7)

> Use electronegativities of elements to determine bond polarity. (4.7)

> Predict the number of bonds formed by common nonmetals (the HONC rules). (4.8)

> Recognize common polyatomic ions and be able to use them in naming and writing formulas for compounds. (4.9)

> Write Lewis formulas for simple molecules and polyatomic ions. (4.10)

> Identify free radicals. (4.10)

> Predict the shapes of simple molecules from their Lewis formulas. (4.11)

> Classify a simple molecule as polar or nonpolar from its shape and the polarity of its bonds. (4.12)

> Describe the concept of molecular recognition.

> Explain the green chemistry advantages of using production methods based on molecular recognition.

THE TIES THAT BIND The element carbon is commonly found as soft, black soot formed by incomplete combustion. By heating that soot under tremendous pressure, we can make the hardest material known—diamond. We have not changed the carbon in soot to a different element in this process, so why is diamond so different from soot? The answer lies in the bonds that hold the carbon atoms together.

The same holds true for a sheet of graphene when rolled up into carbon nanotube. By carbon–carbon bonding along the long edge of the graphene sheet, a new class of substances results. To start understanding why these things happen, we have already learned a bit about the structure of the atom. Now we are ready to consider chemical bonds, the ties that bind atoms together.

Atoms combine by forming chemical bonds. These bonds determine, to a great extent, the properties of the substance. Here we see carbon in the form of a diamond, but it can also form graphite (pencil lead) or soot. The only difference between the forms of carbon is the bonds between the carbon atoms. The arrangement and number of these bonds in diamond make it by far the hardest natural material in the world.

Chemical bonds are the forces that hold atoms together in molecules and hold ions together in ionic crystals. The vast number and incredible variety of chemical compounds—tens of millions are known—result from the fact that atoms can form bonds with many other types of atoms. Further, chemical bonds determine the three-dimensional shapes of molecules. Some important consequences of chemical structure and bonding include

- Whether a substance is a solid, liquid, or gas at room temperature
- The strengths of materials (as well as adhesives that hold materials together) used for building bridges, houses, and many other structures
- Whether a liquid is light and volatile (like gasoline) or heavy and viscous (like corn syrup)
- The optical properties of the substance (think of the "dusty" appearance of soot versus that of a shiny diamond)
- The taste, odor, and drug activity of chemical compounds
- The structural integrity of skin, muscles, bones, and teeth
- The toxicity of certain molecules to living organisms

Chemical bonding is related to the arrangement of electrons in compounds. In this chapter, we look at different types of chemical bonds and some of the unusual properties of compounds that result.

4.1 The Art of Deduction: Stable Electron Configurations

Learning Objective   ❯ Determine the number of electrons in an ion.

In our discussion of the atom and its structure (Chapters 2 and 3), we followed the historical development of some of the more important atomic concepts. Continuing to look at chemistry this way would require several volumes of print—and perhaps more of your time than you care to spend. We won't abandon the historical approach entirely but will emphasize another important aspect of scientific endeavor: deduction.

The art of deduction works something like this.

- **Fact:** Noble gases, such as helium, neon, and argon, are inert; they undergo few, if any, chemical reactions.
- **Theory:** The inertness of noble gases results from their electron configurations. Each (except helium) has an octet of electrons in its outermost shell.
- **Deduction:** Other elements that can alter their electron configurations to become like those of noble gases would become less reactive by doing so.

We can use an example to illustrate this deductive argument. Sodium has 11 electrons, one of which is in the third shell. Recall that electrons in the outermost shell are called **valence electrons**, while those in all the other shells are lumped together as **core electrons**. The outermost shell is filled when it contains eight electrons, two in an *s* orbital and six in a *p* orbital. The first shell is an exception: It holds only two electrons in the 1*s* orbital.

If the sodium atom got rid of its valence electron, its remaining core electrons would have the same electron configuration as an atom of the noble gas neon. Using main-shell configurations (Chapter 3), we can represent this as

Similarly, if a chlorine atom gained an electron, it would have the same electron configuration as argon. The drive to have an electron configuration like a noble gas is strong (we will see more in the subsection titled The Octet Rule on pages 102 and 103).

The sodium atom, having lost an electron, becomes positively charged. It has 11 protons (11+) and only 10 electrons (10−). It is symbolized by Na^+ and is called a *sodium ion*. The chlorine atom, having gained an electron, becomes negatively charged. It has 17 protons (17+) and 18 electrons (18−). It is symbolized by Cl^- and is called a *chloride ion*. Note that a positive charge, as in Na^+, indicates that one electron has been lost. Similarly, a negative charge, as in Cl^-, indicates that one electron has been gained.

It is important to note that even though Cl^- and Ar are **isoelectronic** (i.e., they have the same electron configuration), they are *different* chemical species, because their nuclei are different. In the same way, a sodium atom does not *become* an atom of neon when it loses an electron; the sodium ion is simply isoelectronic with neon.

1. Why is there no such thing as a jar of chloride ions only?
Formation of an anion, such as a chloride ion, is only possible when another atom or group of atoms gives up an electron and forms a cation. The presence of an anion is predicated on the presence of a cation in the same jar. Otherwise, there would be the need for a balance, and in all probability a very violent one, of positive and negative charges.

SELF-ASSESSMENT Questions

1. Which group of elements in the periodic table is characterized by an especially stable electron arrangement?
   a. 2A **b.** 2B **c.** 8A **d.** 8B

2. The structural difference between a sodium atom and a sodium ion is that the sodium ion has one
   a. less proton than the sodium atom
   b. less electron than the sodium atom
   c. more proton and one less electron than the sodium atom
   d. more proton than the sodium atom

3. Which of the following are isoelectronic?
   a. S^{2-} and Ar
   b. Al^{3+} and Ar
   c. Kr and Cl^-
   d. Ne and Ar

4. Which of the following cations is isoelectronic with S^{2-}?
   a. Na^+ **b.** Rb^+ **c.** Mg^{2+} **d.** Ca^{2+}

Answers: 1, c; 2, b; 3, a; 4, d

4.2 Lewis (Electron-Dot) Symbols

Learning Objective ❯ Write the Lewis symbol for an atom or ion.

In forming ions, the cores of the sodium and chlorine atoms do not change. It is convenient therefore to let the element symbol represent the *core* of the atom (nucleus plus inner electrons). This approach allows us then to focus on the valence electrons only, which we will represent as dots when writing equations *drawn* in the preceding section:

$$Na\cdot \longrightarrow Na^+ + 1\,e^-$$

▲ Electron-dot symbols are called *Lewis symbols* after G. N. Lewis, the famous American chemist (1875–1946) who invented them. Lewis also made important contributions to our understanding of thermodynamics, acids and bases, and spectroscopy.

and

$$\cdot \ddot{\underset{..}{Cl}}\colon \quad + \quad 1\,e^- \longrightarrow \colon\!\ddot{\underset{..}{Cl}}\colon^-$$

These electron-dot symbols are usually called Lewis dot symbols or **Lewis symbols** for short. In writing a Lewis dot symbol, consider that a chemical symbol has four sides (right, left, top, and bottom). Starting on *any side,* place single dots until each side has one dot before adding another one (if needed). There should be no more than two dots on any given side of the chemical symbol.

Table 4.1	Lewis Dot Symbols for Selected Main Group Elements						
Group 1A	Group 2A	Group 3A	Group 4A	Group 5A	Group 6A	Group 7A	Noble Gases
H·							He:
Li·	·Be·	·Ḃ·	·Ċ·	:Ṅ·	:Ö·	:Ḟ:	:Ṅe:
Na·	·Mg·	·Al·	·Ṡi·	:Ṗ·	:Ṡ·	:Ċl·	:Ar:
K·	·Ca·				:Se·	:Br·	:Kr:
Rb·	·Sr·				:Te·	:İ·	:Xe:
Cs·	·Ba·						

Lewis Dot Symbols and the Periodic Table

It is especially easy to write Lewis dot symbols for most of the main-group elements. The number of valence electrons for most of these elements is equal to the group number (Table 4.1). Because of their more complicated electron configurations, elements in the central part of the periodic table (the transition metals) cannot easily be represented by electron-dot symbols.

Example 4.1	Writing Lewis Symbols

Without referring to Table 4.1, but using the periodic table, write Lewis dot symbols for magnesium, oxygen, and phosphorus. In what respect was the periodic table useful?

Solution

According to the periodic table, magnesium is in group 2A, oxygen is in group 6A, and phosphorus is in group 5A. The Lewis dot symbols, therefore, have two, six, and five dots, respectively. They are

$$\cdot Mg\cdot \qquad :\ddot{\underset{..}{O}}: \qquad :\dot{\underset{.}{P}}\cdot$$

■ **EXERCISE 4.1**

Without referring to Table 4.1, write Lewis symbols for each of the following elements. You may use the periodic table.

   a. Kr   **b.** Ba   **c.** I   **d.** N   **e.** K   **f.** S

SELF-ASSESSMENT Questions

1. How many dots surround B in the Lewis dot symbol for boron?
     a. 2   **b.** 3   **c.** 5   **d.** 9

2. How many dots surround Br in the Lewis dot symbol for Br^-?
     a. 1   **b.** 8
     c. 7   **d.** 9

3. Which of the following Lewis dot symbols is *incorrect*?
     a. ·Ċ·   **b.** :Ċl·   **c.** Li: **d.** :Ṅ·

4. Which of the following Lewis dot symbols is *incorrect*?
     a. ·As·   **b.** :Ö·   **c.** Rb·   **d.** ·Ṡi·

4.3 The Reaction of Sodium and Chlorine

Learning Objectives › Distinguish between an ion and an atom. › Describe the nature of the attraction that leads to formation of an ionic bond.

Sodium (Na) is a highly reactive metal. It is soft enough to be cut with a knife. When freshly cut, it is bright and silvery, but it dulls rapidly because it reacts with oxygen in the air. It reacts so readily in air that it is usually stored away from oxygen under oil. Sodium reacts violently with water, too, becoming so hot that it melts. A small piece forms a spherical bead after melting and races around on the surface of the water as it reacts. All other alkali metals react vigorously to violently with water, as shown on page 84.

(a)   (b)   (c)

▲ **Figure 4.1** (a) Sodium, a soft, silvery metal, and chlorine, a greenish gas (b). The two react violently to form sodium chloride (ordinary table salt), a white crystalline solid (c).

Q: *What kinds of particles, ions or molecules, make up sodium chloride?*

Chlorine (Cl_2) is a greenish-yellow gas and is extremely irritating to the eyes and nose. In fact, it was used as a poisonous gas, bertholite, in World War I. These same properties also make it a common disinfectant for drinking water and swimming pools. (The actual substance added is often a compound that reacts with water to form chlorine.) When a piece of sodium is dropped into a flask containing chlorine gas, a violent reaction ensues, producing beautiful white crystals of sodium chloride, table salt, that you might sprinkle on your food at the dinner table (Figure 4.1). Clearly, sodium chloride has very few properties in common with either of its parent materials, sodium or chlorine.

The Reaction of Sodium and Chlorine: Theory

A sodium atom achieves a filled valence shell by losing one electron. A chlorine atom achieves a filled valence shell by adding one electron. What happens when sodium atoms come into contact with chlorine atoms? The obvious answer: A chlorine atom takes an electron from a sodium atom.

2. Why does chlorine in a swimming pool have an odor, but chlorine in salt does not?

Chlorine used in water treatment is often the element, Cl_2, while the chlorine in salt exists as chlor*ide* ions, Cl^-. An element is chemically quite different from its ions.

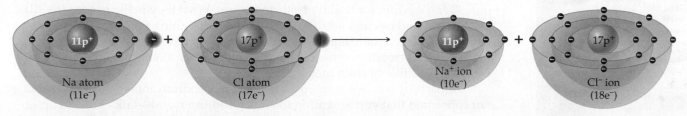

Na atom (11e⁻) + Cl atom (17e⁻) → Na⁺ ion (10e⁻) + Cl⁻ ion (18e⁻)

With Lewis symbols, this reaction is written as

$$Na\cdot \; + \; :\ddot{C}l\cdot \longrightarrow Na^+ + \; :\ddot{C}l:^-$$

3. My father is on a low-sodium diet. What exactly does that mean and why?

It means that he must restrict his intake of sodium *ions*. For many people, too many sodium ions in the body can increase blood pressure. This is because salt increases the amount of water in your kidneys, which use osmosis to remove water from blood and then expel it. Osmosis requires a delicate balance between the amount of sodium and potassium ions in your body. Too much of either and things go badly. Many low-sodium seasonings have replaced some sodium-based salts with potassium-based salts.

But wait a minute! Chlorine gas is composed of diatomic molecules of Cl_2 and not separate Cl atoms, so how can *one* chlorine atom combine with a sodium atom to form NaCl? It turns out that each chlorine atom in a diatomic chlorine molecule takes one electron from each of the two sodium atoms to fill its electron shell; Cl^- and Na^+ ions are formed as a result:

$$Cl_2 + 2\ Na \longrightarrow 2\ Cl^- + 2\ Na^+$$

Since Cl^- and Na^+ have different electronic configurations from chlorine and sodium atoms, the compound they form—sodium chloride—has very different properties from their parent atoms.

Ionic Bonds

The Na^+ and Cl^- ions formed from sodium and chlorine atoms have opposite charges and are strongly attracted to one another. These ions arrange themselves in an orderly fashion. Each sodium ion attracts (and is attracted to) six chloride ions (above and below, front and back, left and right), as shown in Figure 4.2a. The arrangement is repeated many times in all directions (Figure 4.2b). The result is a **crystal** of sodium chloride. The orderly microscopic arrangement of the ions is reflected in the macroscopic shape, a cube of a salt crystal (Figure 4.2c). Even the tiniest grain of salt has billions and billions of ions of each type. The forces holding the crystal together—the attractive forces between positive and negative ions—are called **ionic bonds**.

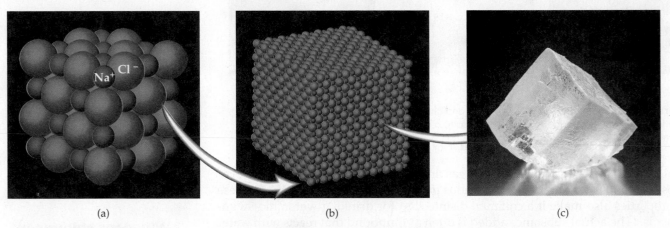

(a) (b) (c)

▲ **Figure 4.2** Molecular and macroscopic views of a sodium chloride crystal. (a) Each Na^+ ion (small purple spheres) is surrounded by six Cl^- ions (large green spheres), and each Cl^- ion by six Na^+ ions. (b) This arrangement repeats itself many, many times. (c) The highly ordered pattern of alternating Na^+ and Cl^- ions is observed in the macroscopic world as a crystal of sodium chloride.

Atoms and Ions: Distinctively Different

Ions are emphatically different from the atoms from which they are made, much as cars with and without an engine differ greatly. The names and symbols of an atom and its ion may look a lot alike, especially the positively charged ions, called cations, but the actual entities are very different (Figure 4.3). Unfortunately, the situation is confusing because people talk about needing iron to perk up "tired blood" and calcium for healthy teeth and bones. What they really need is iron(II) *ions* (Fe^{2+}) and calcium *ions* (Ca^{2+}). You wouldn't think of eating iron nails to get iron (although some enriched cereals do indeed have powdered iron added; the iron metal is readily converted to Fe^{2+} cations in the stomach). Nor would you eat highly reactive calcium metal.

Similarly, if you are warned to reduce your sodium intake, your doctor is not concerned that you are eating too much sodium metal—talk about an upset

◄ **Figure 4.3** Forms of iron and calcium that are useful to the human body are the ions (usually Fe^{2+} and Ca^{2+}) in ionic compounds such as $FeSO_4$ and $CaCO_3$. The elemental forms (Fe and Ca) are chemically very different from the forms found in ionic compounds.

stomach—but that your intake of Na^+ *ions*—usually as sodium chloride—may be too high. Although the names are similar, the atom and the cation are quite different chemically. This is why it is important to make careful distinctions and use precise terminology. Thankfully, there is less room for confusion when it comes to naming the negatively charged ions, called anions. As you will see in Section 4.5, the names of anions, while based on the names of the atoms they come from, are made to sound different through the use of suffixes (or endings), such as *-ide* in chlor*ide*.

SELF-ASSESSMENT Questions

1. A potassium ion and an argon atom have the same
   a. electron configuration
   b. net charge
   c. nuclear charge
   d. properties

2. How many dots are shown on the Lewis symbol for chloride ion, and what is the ion's charge?
   a. five dots, no charge
   b. six dots, positive charge
   c. seven dots, negative charge
   d. eight dots, negative charge

3. The bonding between Li^+ ions and F^- ions in lithium fluoride is
   a. covalent   **b.** ionic   **c.** nonpolar   **d.** polar

4. Which group of elements will form stable ions with a 2− charge?
   a. 2A   **b.** 2B   **c.** 6A   **d.** 8A

4.4 Using Lewis Symbols for Ionic Compounds

Learning Objectives ❯ Write symbols for common ions and determine their charges.
❯ Describe the relationship between the octet rule and the charge on an ion.

Potassium, a metal in the same family as sodium and therefore similar to sodium in properties, also reacts with chlorine. The reaction yields potassium chloride (KCl), a stable white crystalline solid.

$$K\cdot \; + \; \cdot \ddot{\underset{\cdot\cdot}{Cl}}: \longrightarrow K^+ \; + \; :\ddot{\underset{\cdot\cdot}{Cl}}:^-$$

Potassium also reacts with bromine, a reddish-brown liquid in the same family as chlorine and therefore similar to chlorine in properties. The product, potassium bromide (KBr), again, is a stable white crystalline solid.

$$K\cdot \; + \; \cdot \ddot{\underset{\cdot\cdot}{Br}}: \longrightarrow K^+ \; + \; :\ddot{\underset{\cdot\cdot}{Br}}:^-$$

Example 4.2 Electron Transfer to Form Ions

Use Lewis dot symbols to show the transfer of electrons from sodium atoms to bromine atoms to form ions with noble gas configurations.

Solution
Sodium has one valence electron, and bromine has seven. Transfer of the single valence electron from sodium to bromine leaves each with a noble gas configuration.

$$Na\cdot \; + \; \cdot \ddot{\underset{\cdot\cdot}{Br}}: \longrightarrow Na^+ \; + \; :\ddot{\underset{\cdot\cdot}{Br}}:^-$$

Q: Would you hypothesize that sodium bromide is a white crystalline solid in pure form, and why?

▪ EXERCISE 4.2A
Use Lewis symbols to show the transfer of electrons from lithium atoms to fluorine atoms to form ions with noble gas configurations.

▪ EXERCISE 4.2B
Use Lewis dot symbols to show the transfer of electrons from cesium atoms to fluorine atoms. Does cesium now have a noble gas configuration?

Magnesium, a group 2A metal, is less reactive than sodium. When an atom of magnesium reacts with an atom of oxygen, a group 6A element that forms a colorless diatomic gas, O_2, a stable, white, crystalline solid called magnesium oxide (MgO) is formed:

$$\cdot Mg \cdot \; + \; \cdot \ddot{\underset{..}{O}} : \longrightarrow Mg^{2+} + \; : \ddot{\underset{..}{O}} :^{2-}$$

When an Mg atom loses two electrons, it becomes an Mg^{2+} ion and its second shell becomes its outermost shell. On the other hand, when an oxygen atom gains two electrons, it fills its current outermost shell. These are the *same* two electrons changing hands! Both the Mg^{2+} and O^{2-} ions become isoelectronic with the Ne atom and have the same stable main-shell electron configurations: 2, 8.

An atom such as oxygen, which needs two electrons to achieve a noble gas configuration, may react with potassium atoms, which have only one electron each to give. In this case, two atoms of potassium are needed for each one oxygen atom. The product is potassium oxide (K_2O).

$$\begin{array}{l} K\cdot \\ \\ K\cdot \end{array} \; + \; \cdot \ddot{\underset{..}{O}} : \longrightarrow \begin{array}{l} K^+ \\ \\ K^+ \end{array} \; + \; : \ddot{\underset{..}{O}} :^{2-}$$

Through this reaction, each potassium atom achieves the electron configuration of argon. As before, oxygen ends up with the neon configuration.

Example 4.3 Electron Transfer to Form Ions

Use Lewis symbols to show the transfer of electrons from magnesium atoms to nitrogen atoms to form ions with noble gas configurations.

Solution

$$\begin{array}{ccc} \cdot Mg \cdot & \ddot{\underset{.}{N}} \cdot & Mg^{2+} \quad :\ddot{\underset{..}{N}}:^{3-} \\ \cdot Mg \cdot \; + & \ddot{\underset{..}{N}} \longrightarrow & Mg^{2+} + \\ \cdot Mg \cdot & \cdot \ddot{\underset{.}{N}} \cdot & Mg^{2+} \quad :\ddot{\underset{..}{N}}:^{3-} \end{array}$$

Each of the three magnesium atoms gives up two electrons (a total of six), and each of the two nitrogen atoms acquires three electrons (a total of six). Notice that the total positive and negative charges on the products are equal (6+ and 6−). Magnesium reacts with nitrogen to yield magnesium nitride Mg_3N_2.

▪ EXERCISE 4.3

Aluminum is a very reactive metal, but in the Earth's atmosphere, the outside surface of aluminum is converted to the rather unreactive aluminum oxide. Use Lewis symbols to show the transfer of electrons from aluminum atoms to oxygen atoms to form ions with noble gas configurations.

It DOES Matter!

Loss of electrons is known as *oxidation*, and gain of electrons is called *reduction*. Oxidation by oxygen gas is both useful and destructive. Oxygen gas oxidizes fuels to produce energy, but it also oxidizes iron metal into familiar orange or red rust (Fe_2O_3), which causes billions of dollars of damage each year. We explore the concepts of oxidation and reduction in greater detail in Chapter 8.

Generally speaking, metallic elements in groups 1A and 2A (those from the left side of the periodic table) react with nonmetallic elements in groups 6A and 7A (those from the right side) to form ionic compounds. These products are stable crystalline solids.

The Octet Rule: The Drive for Eight

Each atom of a metal tends to give up electrons from its outer shell, and each atom of a nonmetal tends to take on enough electrons to *complete, or close, its valence shell* (s^2p^6). In other words, atoms are driven toward becoming ions to have eight—an *octet* of—electrons in their valence shells. An octet of electrons is characteristic of all noble gases except helium. When atoms react with each other, they often tend to attain this very stable electron configuration of a noble gas closest to them. Thus, they are said to follow the **octet rule**, or the "rule of eight." (In the case of helium, a maximum of two electrons can occupy its single electron shell. Consequently, such small atoms as hydrogen (in metal hydrides) or lithium, often follow the "rule of two" or the "duet rule" to obtain the electron configuration of their nearest noble gas—helium).

In following the octet rule, atoms of group 1A metals give up one electron to form 1+ ions, those of group 2A metals give up two electrons to form 2+ ions, and those of group 3A metals give up three electrons to form 3+ ions. Group 7A non-metal atoms take on one electron to form 1− ions, and group 6A atoms tend to pick up two electrons to form 2− ions. See how this information is encoded in the periodic table, as shown in Figure 4.4. Atoms of B group metals can give up various numbers of electrons to form positive ions with various charges. These periodic relationships are summarized in Figure 4.4.

1A	2A	3B	4B	5B	6B	7B	8B			1B	2B	3A	4A	5A	6A	7A	Noble gases
Li^+														N^{3-}	O^{2-}	F^-	
Na^+	Mg^{2+}											Al^{3+}		P^{3-}	S^{2-}	Cl^-	
K^+	Ca^{2+}						Fe^{2+} Fe^{3+}			Cu^+ Cu^{2+}	Zn^{2+}					Br^-	
Rb^+	Sr^{2+}									Ag^+						I^-	
Cs^+	Ba^{2+}																

▲ **Figure 4.4** Periodic relationships of some simple ions. Many of the transition elements (B groups) can form different ions with different charges.

Q: *Can you write a formula for the simple ion formed from tellurium (Te)? For the simple ion formed from gallium (Ga)?*

Example 4.4 **Determining Formulas by Electron Transfer**

What is the formula of the compound formed by the reaction of sodium and sulfur?

Solution
Sodium is in group 1A; the sodium atom has one valence electron. Sulfur is in group 6A; the sulfur atom has six valence electrons.

$$Na\cdot \quad \cdot \ddot{S} \cdot$$

Sulfur needs two electrons to gain an argon configuration, but sodium has only one to give. The sulfur atom therefore must react with two sodium atoms.

$$\begin{matrix} Na\cdot \\ \\ Na\cdot \end{matrix} + \cdot\ddot{S}\cdot \longrightarrow \begin{matrix} Na^+ \\ \\ Na^+ \end{matrix} + :\ddot{S}:^{2-}$$

The formula of the compound, called sodium sulfide, is Na_2S.

■ **EXERCISE 4.4A**
What are the formulas of the compounds formed by the reaction of **(a)** calcium with fluorine and **(b)** lithium with oxygen?

■ **EXERCISE 4.4B**
Use Figure 4.4 to predict the formulas of the two compounds that can be formed from iron (Fe) and chlorine.

4. If there is iron in blood, why aren't we magnetic?
Iron metal is magnetic, but compounds—such as the hemoglobin in blood—usually contain iron(II) or iron(III) ions. The ions differ chemically and physically from the metal and are not magnetic.

SELF-ASSESSMENT Questions

1. Which of the following pairs of elements would be most likely to form an ionic compound with each other?
   - **a.** K and Ca
   - **b.** Se and Cl
   - **c.** Cs and Se
   - **d.** Ne and Na

2. Oxygen forms a simple (monatomic) ion with a charge of
   - **a.** 6−
   - **b.** 2−
   - **c.** 2+
   - **d.** 6+

3. Strontium forms a simple (monatomic) ion with a charge of
   - **a.** 2−
   - **b.** 2+
   - **c.** 4+
   - **d.** 8+

4. Ca and P react to form Ca_3P_2, an ionic compound. How many electrons are there in the valence shell of the P^{3-} (phosphide) ion?
   - **a.** 2
   - **b.** 8
   - **c.** 10
   - **d.** 16

5. The formula of the ionic compound formed by lithium and nitrogen is (this is the only stable nitride of an alkali metal)
   - **a.** LiN
   - **b.** Li_3N
   - **c.** LiN_3
   - **d.** Li_6N_2

6. The formula of the ionic compound formed by magnesium and bromine is
   - **a.** MgBr
   - **b.** Mg_2Br
   - **c.** $MgBr_2$
   - **d.** Mg_2Br_3

7. Only one of the following ions is likely to be formed in an ordinary chemical reaction; it is
   - **a.** Ar^{3-}
   - **b.** Br^-
   - **c.** K^{2+}
   - **d.** S^-

Answers: 1, c; 2, b; 3, b; 4, b; 5, b; 6, c; 7, b

4.5 Formulas and Names of Binary Ionic Compounds

Learning Objective ❯ Name and write formulas for binary ionic compounds.

Names of simple positive ions (*cations*) are derived from those of their parent elements by simply adding the word *ion*. For example, when a sodium atom loses an electron, it becomes a *sodium ion* (Na^+). A magnesium atom (Mg), on losing two electrons, becomes a *magnesium ion* (Mg^{2+}). When a metal forms more than one ion, the charges on the different ions are denoted by Roman numerals in parentheses. For example, Fe^{2+} is iron(II) ion and Fe^{3+} is iron(III) ion.

Names of simple negative ions (*anions*) are derived from those of their parent elements by replacing the usual ending with a suffix *-ide* and adding the word *ion*. For instance, when a chlor*ine* atom gains an electron, it becomes a chlor*ide* *ion* (Cl^-).

Table 4.2 lists symbols and names for some ions formed when atoms gain or lose electrons. You can calculate the charge on the negative ions in the table by subtracting 8 from the group number. For example, and using Figure 4.4, you can see

A Compound by Any Other Name ...

As you read labels on foodstuffs and pharmaceuticals, you will see some names that are beginning to sound familiar and some that are confusing or mysterious. For example, why do we have two names for Fe^{2+}? Some names are historical: iron, copper, gold, silver, and other elements have been known for thousands of years. In naming compounds of these elements, the ending *-ous* came to be used for the ion of smaller charge and the ending *-ic* for the ion of larger charge. The modern system uses Roman numerals to indicate ionic charge. Although the new system is more logical and easier to apply, the old names persist, especially in everyday life and in some of the biomedical sciences.

POTASSIUM.................... mg 108   water
CHLORIDE .... mg 63   powde
GETABLE OIL (PALM OLEIN, COCONUT, SOY AND
OTEIN CONCENTRATE, GALACTOOLIGOSACCHA-
1%: MORTIERELLA ALPINA OIL**, CRYPTHECO-
ATE, POTASSIUM CITRATE, FERROUS SULFATE,
DE, SODIUM CHLORIDE, ZINC SULFATE, CUPRIC
SELENITE, SOY LECITHIN, CHOLINE CHLORIDE,
NTOTHENATE, VITAMIN A PALMITATE, VITAMIN B_{12},
CHLORIDE, VITAMIN B_6 HYDROCHLORIDE, FOLIC

To Ma
2 fl oz
4 fl oz
8 fl o

▲ Labels for dietary supplements often use older, Latin-derived names.

Table 4.2 Symbols and Names for Some Simple (Monatomic) Ions

Group	Element	Name of Ion	Symbol for Ion
1A	Hydrogen	Hydrogen ion	H^+
	Lithium	Lithium ion	Li^+
	Sodium	Sodium ion	Na^+
	Potassium	Potassium ion	K^+
2A	Magnesium	Magnesium ion	Mg^{2+}
	Calcium	Calcium ion	Ca^{2+}
3A	Aluminum	Aluminum ion	Al^{3+}
5A	Nitrogen	Nitride ion	N^{3-}
	Phosphorus	Phosphide ion	P^{3-}
6A	Oxygen	Oxide ion	O^{2-}
	Sulfur	Sulfide ion	S^{2-}
7A	Fluorine	Fluoride ion	F^-
	Chlorine	Chloride ion	Cl^-
	Bromine	Bromide ion	Br^-
	Iodine	Iodide ion	I^-
1B	Copper	Copper(I) ion (cuprous ion)	Cu^+
		Copper(II) ion (cupric ion)	Cu^{2+}
	Silver	Silver ion	Ag^+
2B	Zinc	Zinc ion	Zn^{2+}
8B	Iron	Iron(II) ion (ferrous ion)	Fe^{2+}
		Iron(III) ion (ferric ion)	Fe^{3+}

that the charge on the oxide ion (oxygen is in group 6A) is $6 - 8 = -2$. The nitride ion (nitrogen is in group 5A) has a charge of $5 - 8 = -3$.

Simple ions of opposite charge can be combined to form **binary** (two-element) ionic **compounds**. To get the correct formula for a binary ionic compound, (1) write each ion with its charge (positive ion to the left), (2) swap the charge numbers (but not the plus and minus signs), (3) confirm that the transposed (swapped) numbers are in the lowest possible integers, while maintaining the original atomic ratio, and (4) write them as subscripts. The process is best learned by practice, which is provided in the following examples, exercises, and end-of-chapter problems.

Example 4.5 Determining Formulas from Ionic Charges

Write the formulas for **(a)** calcium chloride and **(b)** aluminum oxide.

Solution

a. First, we write the symbols for the ions. (We write the charge on chloride ion explicitly as "1−" to illustrate the method. You may omit the "1" when you are comfortable with the process.)

$$Ca^{2+} \ Cl^{1-}$$

We cross over the charge numbers (without the charges) as subscripts.

Then we write the formula. The formula for calcium chloride is

$$Ca_1Cl_2 \quad \text{or} \quad (\text{dropping the "1"}) \text{ simply } CaCl_2$$

b. We write the symbols for the ions.

$$Al^{3+}O^{2-}$$

We cross over the charge numbers as subscripts.

We write the formula for aluminum oxide as

$$Al_2O_3$$

▪ EXERCISE 4.5

Write the formulas for **(a)** potassium oxide, **(b)** calcium nitride, **(c)** magnesium phosphide (a fumigant), and **(d)** aluminum phosphide (another fumigant).

The method just described, called the *crossover method*, works because it is based on the transfer of electrons and the conservation of charge. Two Al atoms lose three electrons each (a total of six electrons lost), and three O atoms gain two electrons each (a total of six electrons gained). The electrons lost must equal the electrons gained. Similarly, two Al^{3+} ions have six positive charges (three each), and three O^{2-} ions have six negative charges (two each). The net charge on Al_2O_3 is zero, just as it should be.

Now you are able to translate chemical names, such as aluminum oxide, into a chemical formula, Al_2O_3. You also can translate in the other direction, as shown in Example 4.6.

Example 4.6	Naming Ionic Compounds

What are the names of **(a)** MgS and **(b)** $FeCl_3$?

Solution

a. From Table 4.2, we can determine that MgS is made up of Mg^{2+} (magnesium ion) and S^{2-} (sulfide ion). The name is simply magnesium sulfide.

b. From Table 4.2, we can determine that the ions in $FeCl_3$ are

$$Fe^{3+} \quad Cl^-$$

How do we know the iron ion in $FeCl_3$ is Fe^{3+} and not Fe^{2+}? Because there are three Cl^- ions, each with a $1-$ charge, the single Fe ion must have a $3+$ charge since the compound, $FeCl_3$, is neutral. The names of these ions are iron(III) ion (or ferric ion) and chloride ion. Therefore, the compound is iron(III) chloride (or, by the older system, ferric chloride).

▪ EXERCISE 4.6

What are the names of **(a)** CaF_2 and **(b)** $CuBr_2$?

Handle with Care ...

The dark side of aluminum phosphide is that it is highly toxic. It is toxic because, when it is ingested, it reacts with water and phosphine (PH_3) gas is liberated. Phosphine gas is a cytotoxic compound, meaning that it causes damage to tissues within the body. However, the good side of aluminum phosphide is that it is highly effective in preserving cereal grains. For safety, during grain processing, the aluminum phosphate is diluted to nontoxic levels.

SELF-ASSESSMENT Questions

1. The formula for the binary ionic compound of barium and sulfur is
   a. BaS
   b. Ba_2S
   c. BaS_2
   d. Ba_2S_3

2. Which of the following formulas is correct?
   a. ZnCl
   b. Zn_2Cl
   c. $ZnCl_2$
   d. Zn_2Cl_5

3. Which of the following formulas is incorrect?
   a. $AlCl_3$
   b. Al_3P_2
   c. CaS
   d. Cs_2S

4. The correct name for KCl is
   a. krypton chloride
   b. krypton chlorite
   c. potassium chloride
   d. potassium chlorine

5. The correct name for Al_2S_3 is
   a. aluminum sulfide
   b. dialuminum trisulfite
   c. antimony sulfide
   d. antimony trisulfide

6. The correct name for LiBr is
   a. bromide lithide
   b. bromine lithide
   c. lithium bromium
   d. lithium bromide

7. The correct name for ZnI_2 is
   a. diiodomonozircon
   b. zinc iodide
   c. zincocide chloride
   d. zirconium iodide

Answers: 1, a; 2, c; 3, b; 4, c; 5, a; 6, d; 7, b

4.6 Covalent Bonds: Shared Electron Pairs

Learning Objectives ❯ Explain the difference between a covalent bond and an ionic bond. ❯ Name and write formulas for covalent compounds.

In Chapter 2, we stated that some elements form diatomic molecules. You now have the tools to understand why this is so. Let's start with hydrogen. Because hydrogen follows the duet rule, it tends to have two electrons in order to complete its valence shell. The problem is that each hydrogen atom has only one electron. However, when two hydrogen atoms combine and share their electrons, each atom *gains access* to two electrons and a complete valence shell. Both hydrogen atoms come to this compromise because all hydrogen atoms have an equal attraction for electrons. This leads to the two hydrogen atoms *sharing a pair* of electrons.

$$\text{H} \cdot + \cdot \text{H} \longrightarrow \text{H} \colon \text{H}$$

By sharing electrons, the two hydrogen atoms form a *diatomic* hydrogen molecule. The bond formed when atoms share electrons is called a **covalent bond**. When one pair of electrons is shared, the bond is a **single bond**.

H:H

└─ covalent bond (shared pair of electrons)

A covalent bond is usually represented as a *dash*, so that the Lewis dot structure for H_2 becomes H—H.

Let's consider chlorine next. A chlorine atom readily takes an extra electron from anything willing to give one up. In this case, it is the octet rule that is at play so that the chlorine atom can fully fill its valence electron shell. Thus, chlorine atoms can also attain a more stable arrangement by sharing a pair of electrons.

$$\ddot{\underset{..}{Cl}}\cdot + \cdot\ddot{\underset{..}{Cl}}\colon \longrightarrow \ddot{\underset{..}{Cl}}\colon\ddot{\underset{..}{Cl}}\colon$$

The shared pair of electrons in the chlorine molecule is another example of a covalent bond; they are called a **bonding pair**. The electrons that stay on one atom and are not shared are called *nonbonding pairs*, or **lone pairs**.

$$\ddot{\underset{..}{Cl}}\colon\ddot{\underset{..}{Cl}}\colon$$

For simplicity, the *diatomic* hydrogen molecule is often represented as H_2, and the *diatomic* chlorine molecule as Cl_2. The word *diatomic* is usually dropped, and we refer to H_2 as simply a hydrogen molecule, while Cl_2 becomes a chlorine molecule, as already seen in Section 4.3. In each case, the covalent bond between the atoms is implied. Sometimes the covalent bond is indicated by a dash: H—H and Cl—Cl. Lone pairs of electrons often are not shown. Each chlorine atom in a chlorine molecule has eight electrons around it, an arrangement like that of the noble gas argon. Thus, the atoms involved in a covalent bond follow the octet rule by sharing electrons, just as those linked by an ionic bond follow it by giving up or accepting electrons.

Multiple Bonds

In some cases, atoms may share more than one pair of electrons. An example would be oxygen. An oxygen atom has six valence electrons and seeks out two more electrons to complete its valence shell with an octet of electrons. When one oxygen atom finds another, they create a diatomic molecule by equally sharing two pairs of electrons:

$$\ddot{\underset{..}{O}}\colon\colon\ddot{\underset{..}{O}}\colon \quad \boxed{\begin{array}{c}\text{Bonding} \\ \text{Representation}\end{array}}\!\!\!\!\Rightarrow \quad \ddot{\underset{..}{O}}{=}\ddot{\underset{..}{O}}\colon$$

The covalent bond that forms from two pairs of electrons being shared between two atoms is called a **double bond** and is indicated by a double dash between atoms.

Two atoms also can even share three pairs of electrons so that both atoms fill their valence shells. In the nitrogen (N_2) molecule, for example, each nitrogen atom equally shares three pairs of electrons with the other.

$$\colon N \colon\colon\colon N \colon$$

The atoms are joined by a **triple bond**, a covalent linkage in which two atoms share three pairs of electrons ($N{\equiv}N$). Note that each of the nitrogen atoms has an octet of electrons around it.

The number of bonds between two atoms is known as the *bond multiplicity* (or *bond order*). The more bonds between the two atoms, the higher the bond multiplicity.

CONCEPTUAL **Example 4.7**	Predicting Bond Multiplicity (Number of Bonds Between Two Atoms)

Predict the bond multiplicity between two atoms of the same element with the valence-shell electron configuration of 2, 4.

Solution

The valence-shell electron configuration of 2, 4 means that each atom has a total of six valence electrons and thus needs to obtain two more electrons to satisfy the octet rule. With two such atoms needing access to two additional electrons, and with both atoms being of the same element, a total of four electrons will be *equally* shared. Since each bond requires two shared electrons, four shared electrons will yield a double bond (and bond multiplicity of two).

SELF-ASSESSMENT Questions

1. A bond formed when two atoms share one pair of electrons is
   a. single covalent   **b.** double covalent
   c. triple covalent   **d.** ionic

2. What type of a bond forms when two atoms in group 7A combine to form a diatomic molecule?
   a. single covalent   **b.** double covalent
   c. triple covalent   **d.** ionic

3. How many pairs of nonbonding electrons does an atom of oxygen have when it forms a double covalent bond with another atom of oxygen?
   a. 0   **b.** 1   **c.** 2   **d.** 4

Answers: 1, a; 2, a; 3, c

4.7 Unequal Sharing: Polar Covalent Bonds

Learning Objectives ❯ Classify a covalent bond as polar or nonpolar.
❯ Use electronegativities of elements to determine bond polarity.

So far, we have seen that atoms combine in two different ways to fill their valence shells. Atoms that are quite different in electron configuration (from opposite sides of the periodic table) react by the complete transfer of one or more electrons from one atom to another to form an ionic bond. Some identical nonmetal atoms (such as two chlorine atoms or two hydrogen atoms) combine by equally sharing a pair of electrons to form a covalent bond. Now let's consider bond formation between atoms that are different, yet not so different as to form ionic bonds.

Hydrogen Chloride

Hydrogen and chlorine react to form a colorless gas called *hydrogen chloride*. This reaction may be represented as

$$\text{H·} + \text{·}\overset{\cdot\cdot}{\underset{\cdot\cdot}{\text{Cl}}}\text{:} \longrightarrow \text{H}\overset{\cdot\cdot}{\underset{\cdot\cdot}{\text{Cl}}}\text{:}$$

Ignoring the lone pairs of electrons and using a dash to represent the covalent bond, we can write the hydrogen chloride molecule as H—Cl. Both hydrogen and chlorine need an electron to achieve a noble gas configuration (filled valence shell)—a helium configuration for hydrogen and an argon configuration for chlorine. They achieve these configurations by sharing a pair of electrons and, in doing so, form a covalent bond.

In reality, when hydrogen and chlorine react to form hydrogen chloride, they do so as diatomic hydrogen and chlorine. For convenience and simplicity, the reaction is often represented, as follows:

$$\text{H}_2 + \text{Cl}_2 \longrightarrow 2\ \text{HCl}$$

The bonds between the atoms and the lone pairs on the chlorine atoms are not shown explicitly, but remember that they are there.

Example 4.8   Homonuclear and Heteronuclear Covalent Bonds from Lewis Symbols

Use Lewis symbols to show the formation of a covalent bond **(a)** between two fluorine atoms and **(b)** between a fluorine atom and a hydrogen atom.

Solution

$$:\overset{\cdot\cdot}{\underset{\cdot\cdot}{\text{F}}}\text{·} + \text{·}\overset{\cdot\cdot}{\underset{\cdot\cdot}{\text{F}}}: \longrightarrow :\overset{\cdot\cdot}{\underset{\cdot\cdot}{\text{F}}}\text{:}\overset{\cdot\cdot}{\underset{\cdot\cdot}{\text{F}}}: \quad \text{bonding pair}$$

$$\text{H·} + \text{·}\overset{\cdot\cdot}{\underset{\cdot\cdot}{\text{F}}}: \longrightarrow \text{H}\text{:}\overset{\cdot\cdot}{\underset{\cdot\cdot}{\text{F}}}: \quad \text{bonding pair}$$

■ **EXERCISE 4.8**
Use Lewis symbols to show how a covalent bond is formed between **(a)** two bromine atoms, **(b)** a lithium atom and a bromine atom, and **(c)** a fluorine atom and a chlorine atom.

1A																	Noble gases
H 2.1	2A											3A	4A	5A	6A	7A	
Li 1.0	Be 1.5											B 2.0	C 2.5	N 3.0	O 3.5	F 4.0	
Na 0.9	Mg 1.2	3B	4B	5B	6B	7B		8B		1B	2B	Al 1.5	Si 1.8	P 2.1	S 2.5	Cl 3.0	
K 0.8	Ca 1.0													As 2.0	Se 2.4	Br 2.8	
																I 2.5	

▲ **Figure 4.5** Pauling electronegativity values are given for several common elements.

Q: *Can you estimate a value for the electronegativity of germanium (Ge)? For the electronegativity of rubidium (Rb)?*

You might be asking why a chlorine atom would leave an equally attractive chlorine atom for a hydrogen atom, and the same for hydrogen. The answer lies in stability. There is stable, and there is *more* stable. The chlorine molecule represents a more stable arrangement than two separate chlorine atoms. However, given the opportunity, a chlorine atom selectively forms a bond with a hydrogen atom rather than with another chlorine atom.

Each molecule of hydrogen chloride consists of one atom of hydrogen and one atom of chlorine sharing a pair of electrons. *Sharing,* however, does not necessarily mean "equal" sharing. In fact, chlorine attracts the electron pair more strongly, making it the "electron hog" of the two atoms. The reason for this is that chlorine is more *electronegative.*

Electronegativity

The **electronegativity** of an element can be viewed as its ability to attract electrons *in a molecule.* The more electronegative an atom is, the greater its tendency to pull the electrons toward its end of the covalent bond. The atoms to the right in the periodic table are, in general, more electronegative than those to the left. The ones on the right are precisely the atoms that, in forming ions, tend to gain electrons and form negatively charged ions (anions). The ones on the left—metals—tend to give up electrons and become positively charged ions (cations). Within a column, electronegativity tends to be higher at the top and lower at the bottom of the column.

The American chemist Linus Pauling (1901–1994) devised a scale of relative electronegativity values by assigning fluorine, the most electronegative element, a value of 4.0. Figure 4.5 displays the electronegativity values for some of the common elements that we will encounter in this text. Within the periodic table, electronegativity follows two trends: It increases as one goes left to right along a period, and it decreases for the elements as one goes down the group.

Let's now take a closer look at HCl. Chlorine has an electronegativity of 3.0, while hydrogen has an electronegativity of 2.1. This means that chlorine is more electronegative. As a result, the shared electron pair will be closer to chlorine, making the chlorine end of the bond more negative compared to the hydrogen end. An unequal sharing of an electron pair (or pairs) leads to bond polarity, and the bond is called a **polar covalent bond.** By comparison, the bonds where the electron pairs are shared equally, such as those you have already seen in the diatomic molecules of hydrogen, chlorine, oxygen, and nitrogen, are **nonpolar covalent bonds.**

A polar covalent bond is not an ionic bond. In an ionic bond, one atom completely loses an electron. In a polar covalent bond, the atom at the positive end of the bond (hydrogen in HCl) still has a partial share of the bonding pair of electrons

▲ Chlorine hogs the electron blanket, leaving hydrogen partially, but positively, exposed.

(Figure 4.6). To distinguish this kind of bond from an ionic bond or a nonpolar covalent bond, we use the following notation:

$$\overset{\delta+}{H}-\overset{\delta-}{Cl}$$

The line between the atoms represents the covalent bond, a pair of shared electrons. The $\delta+$ and $\delta-$ (read "delta plus" and "delta minus") signify which end of the bond is partially positive and which is partially negative. (The word *partially* is used to distinguish these charges from the full charges on ions.)

Though not 100% foolproof, electronegativity values for the two atoms joined by a bond can be used to predict the type of bonding.

Electronegativity Difference	Bonding Type
< 0.5	Nonpolar covalent
0.5–2.0	Polar covalent
> 2.0	Ionic

▲ **Figure 4.6** Representation of the polar hydrogen chloride molecule. (a) The electron-dot formula, with the symbols $\delta+$ and $\delta-$ indicating the partial positive and partial negative charge, respectively. (b) An *electrostatic potential diagram* depicting the unequal distribution of electron density in the hydrogen chloride molecule.

Example 4.9 Using Electronegativities to Classify Bonds

Use data from Figure 4.5 to classify the bond between each of the following pairs of atoms as nonpolar covalent, polar covalent, or ionic:

a. H, H   b. C, F   c. C, H   d. C, O

Solution

a. Two H atoms have exactly the same electronegativity. The electronegativity difference is 0. The bond is nonpolar covalent.
b. The electronegativity difference is $4.0 - 2.5 = 1.5$. The bond is polar covalent.
c. The electronegativity difference is $2.5 - 2.1 = 0.4$. The bond is nonpolar covalent.
d. The electronegativity difference is $3.5 - 2.5 = 1.0$. The bond is polar covalent.

■ **EXERCISE 4.9A**

Use data from Figure 4.5 to classify the bond between each of the following pairs of atoms as nonpolar covalent, polar covalent, or ionic:

a. H, Br   b. Na, O   c. C, C   d. B, F

■ **EXERCISE 4.9B**

Use the periodic table to classify the following bonds as nonpolar covalent or polar covalent:

a. N—H   b. C—N   c. C—O   d. C=C

■ **EXERCISE 4.9C**

Rank the following bond between each of the following pairs of atoms in terms of increasing polarity:

a. C, O   b. N, O   c. Si, F   d. As, O

Names of Covalent Compounds

Covalent, or *molecular*, compounds are those in which electrons are shared, not transferred. Such compounds generally have molecules that consist of two or more nonmetal atoms. Many covalent compounds have common and widely used names. Examples are water (H_2O), ammonia (NH_3), and methane (CH_4).

However, when naming most covalent compounds, systematic rules apply. The prefixes *mono-*, *di-*, *tri-*, and so on are used to indicate the number of atoms of each element in the molecule. Prefixes for up to 10 atoms are given in Table 4.3. For example, the compound N_2O_4 is called *dinitrogen tetroxide*. (The ending vowel is often dropped from *tetra-* and other prefixes when they precede another vowel.) We leave off the prefix *mono-* in front of the first atom in a formula but include it in front of the second atom (for instance, NO is nitrogen monoxide).

Table 4.3 Prefixes That Indicate the Number of Atoms of an Element in a Covalent Compound

Prefix	Number of Atoms
Mono-	1
Di-	2
Tri-	3
Tetra-	4
Penta-	5
Hexa-	6
Hepta-	7
Octa-	8
Nona-	9
Deca-	10

You can have fun with chemical names, as with water. Some compounds have strange—even funny—common names. Curious? Curium(III) chloride is curious chloride. Titanium(IV) chloride ($TiCl_4$) is titanic chloride.

Example 4.10 Naming Covalent Compounds

What are the systematic names of **(a)** $AsCl_3$, **(b)** P_4S_3, and **(c)** H_2O?

Solution

a. With one arsenic atom and three chlorine atoms, $AsCl_3$ is arsenic trichloride.

b. With four phosphorus and three sulfur atoms, P_4S_3 is tetraphosphorus trisulfide.

c. With two hydrogen atoms and one oxygen atom, H_2O is dihydrogen monoxide. A glass of dihydrogen monoxide sounds much more dangerous to the general public than a glass of water.

▪ **EXERCISE 4.10**

What are the names of **(a)** BrF_3, **(b)** BrF_5, **(c)** N_2O, and **(d)** NO_2?

Example 4.11 Formulas of Covalent Compounds

Write the formula for triphosphorus pentaiodide.

Solution

The prefix *tri-* indicates three phosphorus atoms, and *penta-* specifies five iodine atoms. The formula is P_3I_5.

▪ **EXERCISE 4.11**

Write the formulas for **(a)** carbon dioxide, **(b)** dichlorine heptoxide, **(c)** nitrogen triiodide, and **(d)** disulfur decafluoride.

SELF-ASSESSMENT Questions

1. The bond in Br_2 is
   a. nonpolar double covalent
   b. ionic
   c. nonpolar single covalent
   d. polar triple covalent

2. Carbon monoxide possesses a _____ bond.
   a. polar double covalent
   b. trisingle ionic
   c. nonpolar triple covalent
   d. polar triple covalent

3. When HCl is formed,
   a. a Cl atom gives one valence electron to an H atom
   b. an H atom gives one valence electron to a Cl atom
   c. a pair of valence electrons is shared, one each from the H atom and the Cl atom
   d. a pair of valence electrons is shared, none from the H atom and two from the Cl atom

4. Which of the following bonds is the most polar?
   a. C—Br   b. C—Cl   c. C—F   d. H—H

5. In which of the following pairs does carbon have the smallest share of electrons?
   a. C—C   b. C—F   c. C—O   d. C—N

6. In a polar covalent bond, the atom with the partial negative charge is
   a. less electronegative
   b. has no electronegativity
   c. more electronegative
   d. ionized

7. For an ionic bond to exist between two atoms, their difference in electronegativity should be
   a. between 0 and 0.5
   b. between 0.5 and 2.0
   c. greater than 2.0
   d. zero

8. The formula for phosphorus trichloride is
   a. KCl_3 b. K_3Cl c. PCl_3 d. P_3Cl

9. The formula for sulfur hexafluoride is
   a. S_5F b. SF c. SF_6 d. S_6F_6

10. The correct name for N_2S_4 is
    a. dinitrogen disulfide
    b. dinitrogen tetrasulfide
    c. tetrasulfodinitrogen
    d. tetrasulfur dinitride

11. The correct name for I_2O_5 is
    a. diiodine pentoxide
    b. diiodopentoxide
    c. iridium pentoxide
    d. pentaoxodiiodine

Answers: 1. c; 2. d; 3. c; 4. c; 5. b; 6. c; 7. c; 8. c; 9. c; 10. b; 11. a

4.8 Polyatomic Molecules: Water, Ammonia, and Methane

Learning Objective ❯ Predict the number of bonds formed by common nonmetals (the HONC rules).

To obtain an octet of electrons, an oxygen atom must share electrons with two hydrogen atoms, a nitrogen atom must share electrons with *three* hydrogen atoms, and a carbon atom must share electrons with *four* hydrogen atoms. In general, nonmetals tend to form a number of covalent bonds that is equal to eight minus the number of valence electrons they have. The way that the periodic table is laid out means that this equates to eight minus the group number. Oxygen, which is in group 6A, forms $8 - 6 = 2$ covalent bonds in most molecules. The same holds for sulfur because it also is in group 6A. Nitrogen, in group 5A, forms $8 - 5 = 3$ covalent bonds in most molecules. Carbon, in group 4A, forms $8 - 4 = 4$ covalent bonds in most molecules. This fact is central to a host of organic compounds (Chapter 9) including the compounds of life (Chapter 18). The following simple guidelines—sometimes called the HONC rules—will enable you to write formulas for many molecules.

- Hydrogen forms 1 bond.
- Oxygen forms 2 bonds.
- Nitrogen forms 3 bonds.
- Carbon forms 4 bonds.

Water

Water has fascinated humankind for a long time, especially because it is essential to life on our planet. The electrolysis experiment of Nicholson and Carlisle (Chapter 2) and subsequent experiments have shown that the molecular formula for water is H_2O. Oxygen needs two electrons to complete its octet, but each hydrogen only has one electron to share. Therefore, for oxygen to satisfy its octet, it must share electrons with two hydrogen atoms. This means that oxygen fulfills its octet by sharing two pairs of electrons—one pair of electrons per hydrogen. This is how a *polyatomic* molecule is formed—a molecule containing more than two atoms.

$$\ddot{\underset{\cdot}{O}}\colon + \; 2\,H\cdot \;\longrightarrow\; H\colon\!\ddot{\underset{\cdot\cdot}{O}}\colon \; \text{ or } \; \underset{\underset{H}{|}}{H\!-\!O}$$

This arrangement completes the valence-shell octet of the oxygen atom, giving it the neon configuration. It also completes the outer shell of each hydrogen atom, giving each of these atoms the helium configuration. Oxygen is more electronegative (3.5) than hydrogen (2.1), so the H—O bonds formed are *polar covalent*.

Ammonia

A nitrogen atom has five electrons in its valence shell. It can attain the neon configuration by sharing three pairs of electrons with *three* hydrogen atoms. The result is the compound ammonia.

$$\cdot\ddot{N}\cdot + \; 3\,H\cdot \;\longrightarrow\; H\colon\!\underset{\underset{H}{\cdot\cdot}}{\ddot{N}}\!\colon\!H \; \text{ or } \; \underset{\underset{H}{|}}{H\!-\!N\!-\!H}$$

In ammonia, the bond arrangement resembles that of a tripod (see Figure 4.10, page 127) with a hydrogen atom at the end of each leg and the nitrogen atom with its unshared pair of electrons centrally at the top. (We will see why it has this shape in Section 4.11.) The electronegativity of N is 3.0, and that of H is 2.1, so all three N—H bonds are *polar covalent*.

Methane

A carbon atom has four electrons in its valence shell. It can achieve the neon configuration by sharing pairs of electrons with four hydrogen atoms, forming the compound methane.

$$\cdot \overset{\displaystyle \cdot}{\underset{\displaystyle \cdot}{C}} \cdot \; + \; 4\,H\cdot \;\longrightarrow\; H : \overset{\displaystyle H}{\underset{\displaystyle \ddot{\underset{}{H}}}{\ddot{C}}} : H \quad \text{or} \quad H - \overset{\displaystyle H}{\underset{\displaystyle H}{\overset{|}{\underset{|}{C}}}} - H$$

The methane molecule, as shown above, appears to be planar (flat) but actually it is not—as we shall see in Section 4.11. The electronegativity difference between H and C is so small, less than 0.5, that the C—H bonds are considered nonpolar.

SELF-ASSESSMENT Questions

1. When two H atoms each share an electron with an O atom to form H_2O, the bonding is
   a. diatomic
   b. ionic
   c. nonpolar covalent
   d. polar covalent

2. How many electrons are in the valence shell of the C atom in a methane molecule?
   a. 2   b. 5   c. 6   d. 8

3. In which of the following molecules does hydrogen satisfy the duet rule?
   a. H_2 b. H_2O c. CH_4 d. all

4.9 Polyatomic Ions

Learning Objective ❯ Recognize common polyatomic ions and be able to use them in naming and writing formulas for ionic compounds.

Many compounds contain both ionic and covalent bonds. Sodium hydroxide, commonly known as caustic soda or lye, consists of sodium ions (Na^+) and hydroxide ions (OH^-). The hydroxide ion contains an oxygen atom covalently bonded to a hydrogen atom, plus an "extra" electron, which gives it the negative charge. That extra electron is needed so that both the O and the H atoms have their valence shells filled.

$$e^- \; + \; \cdot \ddot{O} \cdot \; + \; \cdot H \;\longrightarrow\; [:\ddot{O}:H]^-$$

The chemical formula for sodium hydroxide is NaOH. For each sodium ion, there is one hydroxide ion, so that NaOH is neutral. The bond between the sodium and hydroxide ions is ionic, just like the ionic bonds you have already seen between sodium and chloride ions in Section 4.3.

There are many groups of atoms that (like hydroxide ion) remain together, as ions, through most chemical reactions. **Polyatomic ions** are charged particles containing two or more covalently bonded atoms. Table 4.4 lists some common polyatomic ions. By combining the ions listed in Tables 4.2 and 4.4, you can determine formulas for many ionic compounds.

Table 4.4 **Some Common Polyatomic Ions**

Charge	Name	Formula
1+	Ammonium ion	NH_4^+
	Hydronium ion	H_3O^+
1–	Hydrogen carbonate (bicarbonate) ion	HCO_3^-
	Hydrogen sulfate (bisulfate) ion	HSO_4^-
	Acetate ion	$CH_3CO_2^-$ (or $C_2H_3O_2^-$)
	Nitrite ion	NO_2^-
	Nitrate ion	NO_3^-
	Cyanide ion	CN^-
	Hydroxide ion	OH^-
	Dihydrogen phosphate ion	$H_2PO_4^-$
	Permanganate ion	MnO_4^-
2–	Carbonate ion	CO_3^{2-}
	Sulfate ion	SO_4^{2-}
	Chromate ion	CrO_4^{2-}
	Hydrogen (monohydrogen) phosphate ion	HPO_4^{2-}
	Oxalate ion	$C_2O_4^{2-}$
	Dichromate ion	$Cr_2O_7^{2-}$
3–	Phosphate ion	PO_4^{3-}

Acetate ion

Ammonium ion

Hydrogen carbonate ion
(bicarbonate ion)

Carbonate ion   Nitrite ion

Example 4.12 Formulas with Polyatomic Ions

What is the formula for ammonium sulfide?

Solution
Ammonium ion is found in Table 4.4. Sulfide ion is a sulfur atom (group 6A) with two additional electrons. The ions are

$$NH_4^+ \quad S^{2-}$$

Crossing over gives

$$NH_4^{①\,+} \quad \times\!\!\!\times \quad S^{②\,-}$$

The formula for ammonium sulfide is $(NH_4)_2S$. (Note the parentheses.)

▪ EXERCISE 4.12A
What are the formulas for **(a)** calcium carbonate, **(b)** potassium phosphate, and **(c)** ammonium sulfide?

▪ EXERCISE 4.12B
(a) How many hydrogen atoms are there in the formula of ammonium sulfide, and **(b)** how many oxygen atoms are there in calcium carbonate and potassium phosphate, respectively?

Example 4.13	Naming Compounds with Polyatomic Ions

What are the names of **(a)** NaCN, **(b)** $Fe(OH)_2$, and **(c)** $FePO_4$?

Solution

As with compounds containing only monatomic ions, we name the cation and then the anion.

   a. The cation is sodium ion, and the anion is cyanide ion (Table 4.4). The compound is sodium cyanide.

   b. The cation is an iron ion, and the anion is hydroxide ion (Table 4.4). There are two hydroxide ions, each with a charge of 1−, so the iron ion must be a 2+ ion [iron(II) or ferrous]. The compound is iron(II) hydroxide or ferrous hydroxide.

   c. Again, the cation is an iron ion and the anion is phosphate ion. Phosphate has a charge of 3−. Since there is one iron ion in this neutral compound, the iron ion must have a 3+ charge [iron(III) or ferric]. The compound is iron(III) phosphate or ferric phosphate.

■ EXERCISE 4.13A

What are the names of **(a)** $MgCO_3$, **(b)** $Ca_3(PO_4)_2$, and **(c)** $NH_4C_2H_3O_2$?

■ EXERCISE 4.13B

What are the names of **(a)** $(NH_4)_2SO_4$, **(b)** KH_2PO_4, and **(c)** $CuCr_2O_7$?

SELF-ASSESSMENT Questions

1. Which of the following compounds incorporates a polyatomic ion?
   a. CO_2 **b.** $C_6H_{12}O_6$ **c.** K_2SO_3 **d.** $SrBr_2$

2. The formula for ammonium phosphate is
   a. NH_4PO_3 **b.** $NH_4(PO_4)_2$
   c. $(NH_4)_2PO_4$ **d.** $(NH_4)_3PO_4$

3. The formula for sodium hydrogen carbonate is
   a. $NaHCO_3$ **b.** Na_2HCO_3
   c. NaH_2CO_3 **d.** $NaHCO_4$

4. The formula for copper(I) hydrogen sulfate is
   a. $CuHSO_4$ **b.** Cu_2HSO_3
   c. Cu_2HSO_4 **d.** $Cu(HSO_4)_2$

5. The formula for ammonium dichromate is
   a. $NH_4Cr_2O_7$ **b.** NH_4CrO_4
   c. $(NH_4)_2Cr_2O_7$ **d.** $(NH_4)_2CrO_4$

6. The correct name for NH_4HCO_3 is
   a. ammonium acetate
   b. ammonium carbonate
   c. ammonium hydrogen carbonate
   d. ammonium cyanide

7. Sodium cyanide can be used in the extraction of gold according to the processes shown:

   $$4\,Au + 8\,NaCN + O_2 + 2\,H_2O$$
   $$\rightarrow 4\,Na[Au(CN)_2] + 4\,NaOH$$

   Which compound (or compounds) contain a polyatomic ion?
   a. NaCN   **b.** NaOH
   c. $Na[Au(CN)_2]$ **d.** all

8. In the chemical equation shown in Question 7, what is the correct name for NaCN?
   a. sodium carbonic nitrogen
   b. sodium cyanite
   c. sodium cyanide
   d. sodium monocyanide

Answers: 1, c; 2, d; 3, a; 4, a; 5, c; 6, c; 7, d; 8, c

4.10 Rules for Writing Lewis Formulas

Learning Objectives ❯ Write Lewis formulas for simple molecules and polyatomic ions. ❯ Identify free radicals.

As we have seen, electrons are transferred or shared in ways that leave most atoms with octets (or a duet for hydrogen) of electrons in their outermost shells. In this section, we describe how to write **Lewis formulas** for molecules and polyatomic ions. To write a Lewis formula, we first put the atoms of the molecule or ion in their proper places, and then we place all the valence electrons so that each atom has a filled shell.

The *skeletal structure* of a molecule tells us the order in which the atoms are attached to one another. Drawing a skeletal structure takes some practice. However, if there is no experimental evidence, the following guidelines help us to devise likely skeletal structures:

- Hydrogen atoms form only single bonds. They are always at the end of a sequence of atoms. Hydrogen is often bonded to carbon, nitrogen, or oxygen.
- Oxygen tends to form two bonds, nitrogen usually forms three bonds, and carbon forms four bonds (recall the HONC rule).
- Polyatomic molecules and ions often consist of a central atom surrounded by atoms of higher electronegativity. (Hydrogen is an exception; it is always on the outside, even when bonded to a more electronegative element.) The central atom of a polyatomic molecule or ion is often the *least* electronegative atom.

After choosing a skeletal structure for a polyatomic molecule or ion, we can use the following steps to write the Lewis formula:

1. Determine the total number of valence electrons. This total is the sum of the valence electrons for all the atoms in the molecule or ion. You must also account for the charge(s) on a polyatomic ion.
   a. For a polyatomic anion, *add* to its total number of valence electrons the number of negative charges.
   b. For a polyatomic cation, *subtract* the number of positive charges from the total number of valence electrons.

Examples:

N_2O_4 has $[2 \times 5] + [4 \times 6] = 34$ valence electrons.

NO_3^- has $[1 \times 5] + [3 \times 6] + 1 = 24$ valence electrons.

NH_4^+ has $[1 \times 5] + [4 \times 1] - 1 = 8$ valence electrons.

2. Write a reasonable skeletal structure and connect bonded pairs of atoms by a dash (one dash per each shared electron pair).
3. Starting with the most electronegative atom in the polyatomic molecule or ion, place electrons in pairs around outer atoms so that each has an octet, except for hydrogen, which will have a duet.
4. Subtract the number of electrons assigned so far (both in bonds and as lone pairs) from the total calculated in step 1. Any electrons that remain are assigned in pairs to the central atom(s).
5. If a central atom has fewer than eight electrons after step 4, one or more multiple bonds are likely. Move one or more lone pairs from an outer atom to the space between the atoms to form a double or triple bond. A deficiency of two electrons suggests a double bond, and a shortage of four electrons indicates either two double bonds or a triple bond to the central atom.

Example 4.14   Writing Lewis Formulas

Write Lewis formulas for **(a)** methanol (CH_3OH), **(b)** the BF_4^- ion, and **(c)** carbon dioxide (CO_2).

Solution

We start by following the preceding rules:

1. The total number of valence electrons is $4 + (4 \times 1) + 6 = 14$.
2. The skeletal structure must have all the H atoms on the outside. That means the C and O atoms must be bonded to each other. A reasonable skeletal structure is

$$
\begin{array}{c}
\text{H} \\
| \\
\text{H} - \text{C} - \text{O} - \text{H} \\
| \\
\text{H}
\end{array}
$$

3. Now, we count five bonds with two electrons each, making a total of ten electrons. Thus, four of the fourteen valence electrons are left to be assigned. They are placed (as two lone pairs) on the oxygen atom.

$$
\begin{array}{c}
\text{H} \\
| \\
\text{H}-\text{C}-\ddot{\text{O}}-\text{H} \\
| \\
\text{H}
\end{array}
$$

(The remaining steps are not necessary. Both carbon and oxygen now have octets of electrons.)

Again, we start by applying the preceding rules:

1. There are $3 + (4 \times 7) + 1 = 32$ valence electrons.
2. The skeletal structure is

$$
\begin{array}{c}
\text{F} \\
| \\
\text{F}-\text{B}-\text{F} \\
| \\
\text{F}
\end{array}
$$

3. Placing three lone pairs on each fluorine atom gives

$$
\left[
\begin{array}{c}
:\ddot{\text{F}}: \\
| \\
:\ddot{\text{F}}-\text{B}-\ddot{\text{F}}: \\
| \\
:\ddot{\text{F}}:
\end{array}
\right]^{-}
$$

4. We have assigned 32 electrons. None remains to be assigned. Brackets and a negative sign are added to show that this is the structure for an anion, not a molecule. The charge is written outside the brackets to indicate the charge is on the ion as a whole, not necessarily on any particular atom.

Again, we start by applying the rules:

1. There are $4 + (2 \times 6) = 16$ valence electrons.
2. The skeletal structure is O—C—O.
3. First, we place three lone pairs on each oxygen atom.

$$
:\ddot{\text{O}}-\text{C}-\ddot{\text{O}}:
$$

4. We have assigned 16 electrons. None remains to be placed.
5. The central carbon atom has only four electrons. It needs to have two double bonds to achieve an octet. We move a lone pair from each oxygen atom to the space between the atoms to form a double bond on each side of the carbon atom.

$$
:\ddot{\text{O}}=\text{C}=\ddot{\text{O}}:
$$

▪ **EXERCISE 4.14A**

Write Lewis formulas for **(a)** carbon monoxide, CO, **(b)** oxygen difluoride, OF_2, and **(c)** methyl chloride, CH_3Cl.

▪ **EXERCISE 4.14B**

Write Lewis formulas for **(a)** the azide ion, N_3^-, **(b)** the ammonium ion, NH_4^+, and **(c)** the nitryl fluoride molecule, NO_2F (O—N—O—F skeleton).

The rules we have used here lead to the results for selected elements that are summarized in Table 4.5. Figure 4.7 relates the number of covalent bonds that a particular element forms to its position on the periodic table.

Table 4.5 **Number of Bonds Formed by Selected Elements**

Lewis Symbol	Bond Picture	Number of Bonds	Representative Molecules	Ball-and-Stick Models
H·	H—	1	H—H H—Cl	HCl
He:		0	He	He
·Ċ·	—Ċ—	4	$\begin{array}{c} H \\ H-C-H \\ H \end{array}$ $\begin{array}{c} O \\ \| \\ H-C-F \end{array}$	CH₄
·N̈·	—N̈—	3	$\begin{array}{c} H-N-H \\ H \end{array}$ $\begin{array}{c} N-O-H \\ \| \\ H-C-H \end{array}$	NH₃
·Ö:	—Ö—	2	$\begin{array}{c} H-O \\ H \end{array}$ $\begin{array}{c} O \\ \| \\ H-C-H \end{array}$	H₂O
·F̈:	—F̈	1	H—F F—F	F₂
·C̈l:	—C̈l	1	Cl—Cl $\begin{array}{c} H \\ H-C-Cl \\ H \end{array}$	CH₃Cl

▲ **Figure 4.7** Covalent bonding of representative elements on the periodic table.

Q: *What is the relationship between an atom's position on the periodic table and the number of covalent bonds it tends to form? Why are the group 1A and most of the group 2A elements omitted from the table?*

Odd-Electron Molecules: Free Radicals

There are some classes of molecules in which atoms do not conform to the octet rule. *Free radicals* are one such class. (See Problems 70 and 71 for two other types.) Molecules with odd numbers of valence electrons obviously cannot satisfy the octet rule. We only need to look at the valence electrons because filled core shells and subshells contain only paired electrons, having placed two electrons in each orbital (Section 3.7).

Examples of such molecules are nitrogen monoxide (NO, also called nitric oxide), with $5 + 6 = 11$ valence electrons; nitrogen dioxide (NO_2), with 17 valence electrons; and chlorine dioxide (ClO_2), with 19 valence electrons. Lewis formulas of NO, NO_2, and ClO_2 each have one atom with an unpaired electron. The more electronegative the atom, the more likely it is to obey the octet rule. Therefore, it is usually the less electronegative atom that ends up with an unpaired electron and, as a consequence, remains short of the octet.

$$:\!\overset{..}{N}\!:\!:\!\overset{..}{O}\!: \qquad :\!\overset{..}{O}\!:\!\overset{..}{N}\!:\!:\!\overset{..}{O}\!: \qquad :\!\overset{..}{O}\!:\!\overset{..}{Cl}\!:\!\overset{..}{O}\!:$$

Useful Applications of Free Radicals

Moses Gomberg discovered free radicals at the University of Michigan in 1900. The very reactive nature of free radicals does not preclude their importance and use in a variety of natural, medical, and industrial applications.

- Nitrogen monoxide (NO) has been shown to be a signaling molecule in the human cardiovascular system. American scientists Robert F. Furchgott, Louis J. Ignarro, and Ferid Murad won the Nobel Prize in Physiology or Medicine in 1998 for that discovery. Interestingly, one of the physiological effects of sildenafil citrate (Viagra®) is the production of small quantities of NO in the bloodstream.

- Small radical molecules are used in biochemistry to gain insight into how proteins—large biomolecules essential to life—function in our bodies. These studies also include biomedical research into drug design and other promising therapies.

- Hydroxyl radicals (·OH) are produced in the body in the process of oxidation of foods and by radiation. The decomposition of hydrogen peroxide (HOOH) and other peroxides produces ·OH. These radicals inflict havoc on DNA and other essential substances and have been implicated in the formation of cancerous cells due to their rapid reaction with DNA. Hydroxyl radicals also play a role in air pollution (Chapter 13). Among beneficial applications of the ·OH radicals is their use in the treatment of municipal wastewater and contaminated soils.

- Many plastics, including polyethylene and polyvinyl chloride (PVC), are made using free radicals to initiate the reactions. Liquid polyester resin is used to repair automobiles and to construct small boats and surfboards. The resin is converted to hard plastic by the addition of a free radical catalyst called *methyl ethyl ketone peroxide.*

- The free radical chlorine dioxide (ClO_2) is widely used to bleach paper and other products, including flour. Unbleached flour (left) is a pale cream color; bleached flour (right) is whiter and is considered more attractive to consumers. Chlorine radicals also play a role in ozone destruction, especially in the formation of the Antarctic ozone hole.

▲ Chlorine dioxide (ClO_2) is used to bleach flour. Unbleached flour (left) and bleached flour (right).

An atom or molecule with unpaired electrons is called a **free radical**. Most free radicals are highly reactive and exist for only a very brief time before reacting with another species. Any atom or molecule with an odd number of electrons must have one unpaired electron, so such atoms or molecules are free radicals.

Nitrogen oxides are major components of smog (Chapter 13). Chlorine atoms from the breakdown of chlorofluorocarbons in the stratosphere lead to depletion of the ozone layer (Chapter 13). Some free radicals are quite stable, however, and have important functions in the body as well as in industrial processes.

SELF-ASSESSMENT Questions

1. How many lone pairs of electrons are there in the Lewis formula of CF_4?
   - **a.** 4
   - **b.** 12
   - **c.** 14
   - **d.** 16

2. How many lone pairs of electrons are there in the Lewis formula of CF_2Cl_2?
   - **a.** 4
   - **b.** 12
   - **c.** 14
   - **d.** 16

3. How many unshared electrons are there in the Lewis formula of H_2O_2?
   - **a.** 3
   - **b.** 8
   - **c.** 14
   - **d.** 18

4. How many unpaired electrons are there on S in SCl_2?
   - **a.** 0
   - **b.** 1
   - **c.** 2
   - **d.** 3

5. The Lewis formula for CCl_4 has
   - **a.** 0 lone pairs
   - **b.** 1 double bond
   - **c.** 4 ionic bonds
   - **d.** 24 unshared electrons

6. The correct Lewis formula for carbon dioxide is
   - **a.** O—C—O
   - **b.** :O—C—O:
   - **c.** :Ö—C—Ö:
   - **d.** :Ö=C=Ö:

7. The correct Lewis formula for the Cl_2O molecule is
   - **a.** :Ċl—Ċl—Ö:
   - **b.** :Ċl=O=Ċl
   - **c.** :Ö—Ċl—Ö:
   - **d.** :Ċl—Ö—Ċl:

8. In the Lewis formula for SO_2, the number of lone pairs of electrons in the outer shell of the central atom is
   - **a.** 0
   - **b.** 1
   - **c.** 2
   - **d.** 4

9. Which of the following species does not have a triple bond in its Lewis formula?
   - **a.** N_2
   - **b.** CN^-
   - **c.** CO
   - **d.** O_2

10. The Lewis formula for the SO_3^{2-} ion that follows the octet rule is
    - **a.** $\left[:\ddot{O}-S-\ddot{O}: \atop :\ddot{O}:\right]^{2-}$
    - **b.** $\left[:\ddot{O}-S=\ddot{O}: \atop :\ddot{O}:\right]^{2-}$
    - **c.** $\left[:\ddot{O}=S=\ddot{O}: \atop :\ddot{O}:\right]^{2-}$
    - **d.** $\left[:\ddot{O}-S-\ddot{O}: \atop :\ddot{O}:\right]^{2-}$

4.11 Molecular Shapes: The VSEPR Theory

Learning Objective ❭ Predict the shapes of simple molecules from their Lewis formulas.

It is now time to *lift* polyatomic molecules and ions—represented so far as flat—off the two-dimensional (2D) paper and give them three-dimensional (3D) shapes. This third dimension is important in determining molecular properties. For example, the shapes of the molecules that make up gasoline determine its octane rating (Chapter 15), while drug molecules must have the right atoms in the right places to be effective (Chapter 18).

We can use Lewis formulas as the initial step and then apply **valence-shell electron pair repulsion (VSEPR) theory** to predict the arrangement of atoms about a central atom in a molecule. In applying the VSEPR theory to predict molecular shapes, we will use the term *electron set* to refer to either a lone pair on a central atom or a bond—single, double, or triple—between the central atom and another atom. The basis of the VSEPR theory is that electron sets arrange themselves as far away from each other as possible so as to minimize repulsions between these like-charged particles. To do this, molecules follow some simple geometric arrangements.

When there are only two electron sets on the central atom to consider, then their arrangement is *linear* (see Figure 4.8a and Table 4.6 for the geometric representation and chemical examples, respectively). This arrangement allows for the largest possible angle between electron sets, namely, $360°/2 = 180°$. This arrangement is one-dimensional (1D), that is, one in which all atoms are aligned. When three electron sets are in play, we must expand into 2D space, where all atoms are arranged in one plane. In principle, the angles between electron sets could all be different as long as their sum is 360°; however, the three identical $360°/3 = 120°$ angles ensure the maximum separation of the electron sets and minimize repulsions among them. This geometric arrangement is called *trigonal planar* (see Figure 4.8b and Table 4.6).

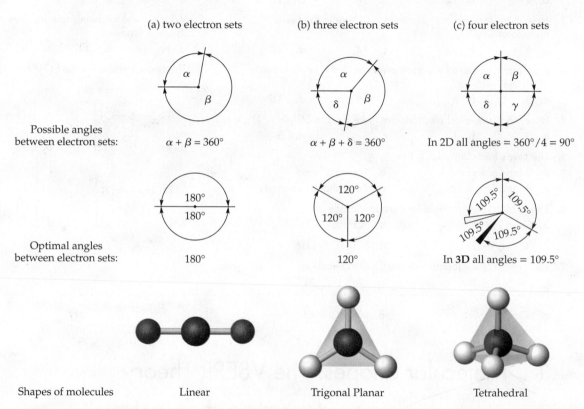

(a) two electron sets	(b) three electron sets	(c) four electron sets

Possible angles between electron sets: $\alpha + \beta = 360°$ $\alpha + \beta + \delta = 360°$ In 2D all angles = $360°/4 = 90°$

Optimal angles between electron sets: 180°   120°   In **3D** all angles = 109.5°

Shapes of molecules   Linear   Trigonal Planar   Tetrahedral

▲ **Figure 4.8** Determination of the arrangement of electron sets in molecules based on maximum separation and minimum repulsion among them. (a) In a *linear* molecule, the bond angle is 180°. (b) In a *trigonal planar* molecule, bond angles are 120°. (c) In a *tetrahedral* molecule, bond angles are 109.5°. In the absence of lone pairs (LPs) of electrons on the central atom, the three basic arrangements of electron sets—*linear*, *trigonal planar*, and *tetrahedral*—lend their names to the shapes of molecules.

Using similar logic, we would expect four electron sets to be separated by $360°/4 = 90°$ angles, as shown in the top portion of Figure 4.8c. Well, upon exploration of the 3D space, it is possible for the four electron sets to be separated by even larger angles of 109.5°. The corresponding *tetrahedral* geometry is shown in the bottom portion of Figure 4.8c, and several chemical examples are listed in Table 4.6.

We can determine the shapes of many molecules (and polyatomic ions) by following this simple procedure:

1. Draw a Lewis formula in which a shared electron pair (bonding pair) is indicated by a line. Use dots to show any unshared pairs (lone pairs) of electrons.

Table 4.6 **Bonding and the Shapes of Molecules**

Number of Bonded Atoms	Number of Lone Pairs	Number of Electron Sets	Molecular Shape	Examples of Molecules	Ball-and-Stick Models
2	0	2	Linear	$BeCl_2$ $HgCl_2$ CO_2 HCN	BeCl₂
3	0	3	Trigonal Planar	BF_3 $AlBr_3$ CH_2O	BF₃
4	0	4	Tetrahedral	CH_4 CBr_4 $SiCl_4$	CH₄
3	1	4	Trigonal Pyramidal	NH_3 PCl_3	NH₃
2	2	4	Bent	H_2O H_2S SCl_2	H₂O
2	1	3	Bent	SO_2 O_3	SO₂

2. To determine shape, count the number of electron sets around the *central* atom. Recall that a multiple bond counts only as one electron set. Examples are

H—Ö: | H Four sets (2 atoms, 2 LPs)	H—N̈—H | H Four sets (3 atoms, 1 LP)	H | H—C—H | H Four sets (4 atoms)

H—C≡N: Two sets (2 atoms)	:Ö=C=Ö: Two sets (2 atoms)	H | H—B—H Three sets (3 atoms)	[:Ö—N̈=Ö:]⁻ Three sets (2 atoms, 1 LP)

3. Using the number of electron sets determined in step 2, draw a shape *as if* all the sets were bonding pairs and place these electron sets as far apart as possible (Table 4.6).

4. If there are *no* lone pairs, the shape from step 3 is the shape of the molecule. If there *are* lone pairs, remove them, leaving the bonding pairs exactly as they were. (This may seem strange, but it stems from the fact that *all* the sets determine the geometry, even though only the arrangement of bonded atoms is considered in the shape of the molecule.)

5. The presence of lone pairs of electrons on the central atom decreases the angles between the bonds, as lone pairs require more space than bonding pairs of electrons. Likewise, double and triple bonds command more space and push remaining

bonds away. While somewhat distorted, most molecules maintain their predicted arrangement of electron sets (Table 4.6). The actual (distorted) angles must be measured experimentally, and you will *not* be asked to memorize or figure them out!

Example 4.15 **Shapes of Molecules**

What are the shapes of **(a)** the H_2CO molecule and **(b)** the SCl_2 molecule?

Solution

a. follow the preceding rules, starting with the Lewis formula.
   1. The Lewis formula for H_2CO is

$$
\begin{array}{c}
\text{H} \\
| \\
\text{C}=\ddot{\text{O}} \\
| \\
\text{H}
\end{array}
$$

   2. There are three sets of electrons: two C—H single bonds and one C=O double bond.
   3. A trigonal planar arrangement puts the three electron sets as far apart as possible.

$$
\begin{array}{c}
\text{H} \\
\diagdown \\
\quad \text{C}=\ddot{\text{O}}: \\
\diagup \\
\text{H}
\end{array}
$$

   4. All the electron sets are bonding pairs; the molecular shape is trigonal planar, the same as the arrangement of the electron sets.
   5. Due to the presence of a double bond, the actual angles, while based on the ideal 120° angles, will be somewhat distorted.

$$
\begin{array}{c}
\text{H} \quad > 120° \\
\diagdown \\
\quad \text{C}=\ddot{\text{O}}: \\
\diagup \\
\text{H}
\end{array}
$$

b. Again, we follow the rules, starting with the Lewis formula.
   1. The Lewis formula for SCl_2 is

$$
\begin{array}{c}
:\ddot{\text{S}}-\ddot{\text{C}}\text{l}: \\
| \\
:\ddot{\text{C}}\text{l}:
\end{array}
$$

   2. There are four sets of electrons on the sulfur atom.
   3. A tetrahedral arrangement around the central atom puts the four sets of electrons as far apart as possible.

A tetrahedral arrangement with a bond angle of less than 109.5°

   4. Two of the electron sets are bonding pairs and two are lone pairs. The molecular shape is *bent*.
   5. The two lone pairs of electrons require more space, which decreases the Cl-S-Cl bond angle from the ideal 109.5° to 103°.

▪ **EXERCISE 4.15A**

What are the shapes of **(a)** the PI_3 molecule and **(b)** $SiCl_4$?

■ EXERCISE 4.15B
What are the shapes of **(a)** the carbonate ion (CO_3^{2-}) and **(b)** the hydrogen peroxide (H_2O_2) molecule?

■ EXERCISE 4.15C
A student drew the following molecular shapes of several molecules. In the corresponding Lewis dot formula, which of the central atoms had **(a)** one, and which one had **(b)** two lone pairs of electrons?

SELF-ASSESSMENT Questions

1. Which of the following molecular shapes *cannot* be formed from the tetrahedral arrangement of the electron sets?

   a. linear **b.** bent **c.** trigonal pyramidal

2. Which of the following molecular shapes *can* be formed from the trigonal planar arrangement of the electron sets?

   a. linear **b.** bent **c.** tetrahedral
   d. trigonal pyramidal

3. Which of the following molecules and polyatomic ion has the smallest O—S—O bond angle?

   a. SO_2 **b.** SO_3^{2-} **c.** SO_3

Answer the next four questions by matching the formula in the left column with the molecular shape in the right column.

4. CS_2 **a.** bent

5. OF_2 **b.** linear

6. SiF_4 **c.** trigonal pyramidal

7. NH_3 **d.** tetrahedral

Answers: 1, a; 2, b; 3, b; 4, b; 5, a; 6, d; 7, c

4.12 Shapes and Properties: Polar and Nonpolar Molecules

Learning Objective ❯ Classify a simple molecule as polar or nonpolar from its shape and the polarity of its bonds.

Section 4.7 discussed polar and nonpolar bonds. A diatomic molecule is nonpolar if its bond is nonpolar, as in H_2 or Cl_2, and polar if its bond is polar, as in HCl. Recall from Section 4.7 that the partial charges in a polar bond are indicated by $\delta+$ and $\delta-$. In the case of a **dipole**, a molecule with a positive end and a negative end, the polarity is commonly indicated with an arrow with a plus sign at the tail end (↔).

(a)

(b)

(c)

▲ **Figure 4.9** The methane molecule. In (a), black lines indicate covalent bonds; the red lines outline a tetrahedron; and all bond angles are 109.5°. The slightly polar C—H bonds cancel each other (b), resulting in a nonpolar, tetrahedral molecule (c).

Q: *How does the electrostatic potential diagram in (c) look different from the one in Figure 4.6?*

5. Both oxygen and hydrogen are gases. How come water—which combines them—is a liquid at room temperature?

When atoms of different elements bond with each other to form compounds, they lose their elemental characteristics. Along come changes in chemical and physical properties, including state of matter.

The plus sign indicates the part of the molecule with a partial positive charge, and the head of the arrow signifies the end of the molecule with a partial negative charge.

$$H—H \text{ and } Cl—Cl \qquad\qquad \overset{\delta+}{H}—\overset{\delta-}{Cl} \text{ or } \overset{\longmapsto}{H—Cl}$$

Nonpolar   Polar

For a molecule with three or more atoms, we must consider the polarity of the individual bonds as well as the overall geometry of the molecule to determine whether or not the molecule as a whole is polar. A **polar molecule** has separate centers of positive and negative charge, just as a magnet has north and south poles. Many properties of compounds—such as melting point, boiling point, and solubility—depend on the polarity of their molecules.

Methane: A Tetrahedral Molecule

There are four electron sets around the central carbon atom in methane, CH_4. Using the VSEPR theory, we would expect a tetrahedral arrangement and bond angles of 109.5° (Figure 4.9a). The actual bond angles are 109.5°, as predicted by the theory. All four electron sets are shared with hydrogen atoms and, therefore, occupy identical volumes. Since the electronegativity difference between carbon and hydrogen is only 0.4 (< 0.5), carbon to hydrogen bonds are essentially nonpolar. Moreover, since the methane molecule is symmetric, these negligible bond polarities (Figure 4.9b) cancel out anyway leaving the methane molecule, as a whole, nonpolar (Figure 4.9c).

Ammonia: A Trigonal Pyramidal Molecule

In ammonia, NH_3, the central nitrogen atom has three bonds and a lone pair around it. The N—H bonds of ammonia are more polar than the C—H bonds of methane. More important, the NH_3 molecule has a different geometry as a result of the lone pair on the nitrogen atom. The VSEPR theory predicts a tetrahedral arrangement of the four sets of electrons, giving bond angles of 109.5° (Figure 4.10a). However, the lone pair of electrons occupies a greater volume than a bonding pair, pushing the bonding pairs slightly closer together and resulting in actual bond angles of about 107°. The trigonal pyramidal geometry can be envisioned as a tripod with a hydrogen atom at the end of each leg and the nitrogen atom with its lone pair sitting at the top. Each nitrogen-to-hydrogen bond is somewhat polar (Figure 4.10b). The asymmetric structure makes the ammonia molecule polar, with a partial negative charge on the nitrogen atom and partial positive charges on the three hydrogen atoms (Figure 4.10c).

Water: A Bent Molecule

The O—H bonds in water are even more polar than the N—H bonds in ammonia because oxygen is more electronegative than nitrogen. (Recall that electronegativity increases from left to right in the periodic table.) Just because a molecule contains polar bonds, however, does not mean that the molecule as a whole is polar. If the atoms in the water molecule were in a straight line (that is, in a linear arrangement, as in CO_2), the two polar bonds would cancel one another and the molecule would be nonpolar.

In its physical and chemical properties, however, water acts like a polar molecule. Molecules such as water and ammonia, in which the polar bonds do not cancel out, act as dipoles. Such molecules have a positive end and a negative end.

We can understand the dipole in the water molecule by using the VSEPR theory. The two bonds and two lone pairs should form a tetrahedral arrangement of electron sets (Figure 4.11a). Ignoring the lone pairs, we see that the molecular shape has the atoms in a bent arrangement, with a bond angle of about 104.5° (instead of 109.5°). As with ammonia, the actual angle is slightly smaller than the predicted angle because of the greater volume of space occupied by the two lone pairs compared to the bonding pairs. The larger space occupied by the lone pairs reduces the space in which the bonding pairs reside, pushing them closer together. The two polar O—H bonds do not cancel each other (Figure 4.11b), making the bent water molecule polar (Figure 4.11c).

◀ **Figure 4.10** The ammonia molecule. In (a), black lines indicate covalent bonds. The red lines outline a tetrahedron. The polar N—H bonds do not cancel each other completely in (b), resulting in a polar, trigonal pyramidal molecule (c).

(a)

(b)

δ⁻

δ⁺   δ⁺

δ⁺

(c)

Q: *How does the electrostatic potential diagram in Figure 4.10c resemble the one in Figure 4.6?*

◀ **Figure 4.11** The water molecule. In (a), black lines indicate covalent bonds, and the red lines outline a tetrahedron. The polar O—H bonds do not cancel each other in (b), resulting in a polar, bent molecule (c).

(a)

(b)

δ⁻

δ⁺   δ⁺

(c)

CONCEPTUAL **Example 4.16**	Polarity of Molecules

Which of these arrangements of water molecules is the most probable? Explain your answer.

● Oxygen
◐ Hydrogen

a.   b.   c.   d.

Solution

Due to electronegativity differences between the O and H atoms, bonds within water molecules are polar. Since the water molecule is bent, the bond polarities add up to render water molecules polar, with the partially negative oxygen atom at one end and the partially positive hydrogen atoms at the other. In liquid, water molecules arrange themselves so that the partially negative oxygen atom in one water molecule faces the partially positively charged hydrogen atoms in another water molecule. While greatly idealized, answer **b** is correct. The partially negative oxygen ends of water dipoles repel each other. Likewise, the partially positive hydrogen ends of water dipoles repel each other, making answers **a**, **c**, and **d** very unlikely.

SELF-ASSESSMENT Questions

1. Which of the following molecules is polar?
   a. H_2 **b.** CH_4 **c.** CO_2 **d.** NH_3

2. Which of the following molecules is nonpolar?
   a. HF   **b.** H_2O **c.** CCl_4 **d.** PF_3

3. Which of the following molecules is polar?
   a. CF_4 **b.** BF_3 **c.** HCN   **d.** F_2

4. Which of the following molecules has polar bonds but is nonpolar?
   a. SiF_4 **b.** Cl_2 **c.** NCl_3 **d.** OF_2

GREEN CHEMISTRY

John C. Warner, *Warner Babcock Institute for Green Chemistry*

Amy S. Cannon, *Beyond Benign*

Green Chemistry and Chemical Bonds

Learning Objectives ❯ Describe the concept of molecular recognition. ❯ Explain the green chemistry advantages of using production methods based on molecular recognition.

You learned in this chapter that atoms bond together to form compounds and these new compounds have properties that differ greatly from the component elements. In molecular compounds (molecules), atoms join by forming covalent bonds that cause the molecules to adopt specific geometric shapes (Sections 4.6, 4.7, 4.12). Each atom is held in a specific position relative to other atoms in the molecule. In ionic compounds, atoms are held together through ionic bonds (Section 4.3).

Molecular shape and composition of compounds control reactivity and interactions with other substances. As a chemist manipulates the geometry and composition of molecules, the properties can change drastically. A wonderful example of how shape impacts the design of molecules is seen in medicine. Within our bodies, biological molecules have particular shapes that are recognized by enzymes and other receptors, in the same way that a key matches a lock (Chapter 16). The molecule and the receptor fit together to form complexes through *noncovalent forces* (intermolecular forces, Section 6.3).

Medicinal chemists design new medicines and drug molecules (Chapter 18) so that they will resemble biological molecules and bind to enzymes or receptors in our body. But these molecule–receptor complexes must behave differently from the biological molecule. The binding triggers a response in our bodies and helps us to heal. Medicinal chemists use the shapes of molecules and forces between them to create new life-saving or life-changing medicines. Interaction between molecules caused by the geometric orientations of their atoms is called **molecular recognition**. The 1987 Nobel Prize in Chemistry was awarded to Donald J. Cram, Jean-Marie Lehn, and Charles J. Pedersen for pioneering work in this area. Scientists are now learning to use molecular recognition to control molecular properties and create not only new medicines but also new materials.

What does this have to do with green chemistry? The processes that chemists rely on to make materials often use large amounts of energy or highly reactive and toxic chemicals. New production methods that take advantage of molecular recognition typically use lower energy, solvent-free processes that do not require harsh conditions.

This way of making materials takes advantage of several of the 12 principles of green chemistry. Principles 3, 5, 6, and 8 focus on the choices we make as chemists as we design new molecules and materials. For example, using less hazardous chemicals to make new medicines means we can reduce the environmental impact of the manufacturing process for these compounds. Doing so ensures that they can change the lives of sick patients as well as provide safer workplaces for the workers making the new medicines.

Typical reactions carried out in laboratories use solvents that dissolve the molecules (solutes) (Section 5.5) and allow them to react to form new molecules. Many solvents can be hazardous to human health and the environment. Processes for making new noncovalent complexes that rely on molecular recognition often do not require solvents. This drastically reduces the environmental impact of these processes.

Many traditional processes require high temperatures, which translates to high energy use. Noncovalent complexes created through molecular recognition function in much the same way as molecules interact within our bodies at moderate temperatures. Therefore, these new approaches use very little energy, which benefits the environment and reduces the manufacturing cost. Also, many processes that generate new molecules and materials are quite complex. By understanding how molecules interact by shape and noncovalent forces, we can reduce the complexity in these processes and avoid the generation of waste and the reliance on hazardous materials.

By understanding molecular shape, the nature of chemical bonds, and how molecules interact with other molecules through noncovalent forces, chemists are able to design new medicines, molecules, and materials that benefit society and, at the same time, have minimal impact on the environment and human health. Green chemistry allows chemists to use these skills combined with new innovative techniques to design chemicals that do not harm our environment in the process.

▲ The antibiotic *vancomysin* carries out its function using molecular recognition. Vancomysin undergoes strong, selective hydrogen bonding with *peptides* (small protein chains) of bacteria, preventing formation of the cell wall.

A Chemical Vocabulary

Learning chemical symbolism is much like learning a foreign language. Once you have learned the basic "vocabulary," the rest is a lot easier. At first, the task is complicated because different chemical species or definitions sound a lot alike (sodium atoms versus sodium ions). Another complication is that we have several different ways to represent the *same* chemical species (Figure 4.12).

Ammonia $\longrightarrow$ NH_3 $\longrightarrow$ H—N̈—H $\longrightarrow$ (molecular geometry diagram)
                                            |
                                            H

Name   Chemical   Lewis formula   Molecular
        formula   geometry

◀ **Figure 4.12** Several representations of the ammonia molecule.

In Chapter 1, we introduced symbols for the chemical elements. Chapter 3 discussed the structure of the nucleus and the symbolism for distinguishing different isotopes. This chapter covered chemical names and chemical formulas. Now you also know how to write Lewis symbols and formulas using dots to represent valence electrons, and you can predict the shapes of thousands of different molecules with the VSEPR theory. In the next chapter, you will add the mathematics of chemistry to your toolbox.

✦ SUMMARY

Section 4.1—Outermost shell electrons are called **valence electrons**; those in all other shells are **core electrons**. The noble gases are inert because they have an octet of valence electrons. Helium is the exception, but it is also inert as it has a duet of valence electrons. Atoms of other elements become more stable by gaining or losing electrons to attain an electron configuration that makes them **isoelectronic** with (having the same electron configuration as) a noble gas.

Section 4.2—The number of valence electrons for most main group elements is the same as the group number. Electron-dot symbols, or **Lewis symbols**, use dots singly or in pairs to represent valence electrons of an atom or ion.

Section 4.3—The element sodium reacts violently with elemental chlorine to give sodium chloride, or table salt. In this reaction, an electron is transferred from a sodium atom to a chlorine atom, forming ions.

The ions formed have opposite charges and are strongly attracted to one another; this attraction results in an **ionic bond**. The positive and negative ions arrange themselves in a regular array, forming a **crystal** of sodium chloride. The ions of an element have very different properties from the atoms of that element.

Section 4.4—Metal atoms tend to give up their valence electrons to become positively charged ions, and nonmetal atoms tend to accept (8 – group number) electrons to become negatively charged ions. In either case, the ions formed tend to have eight valence electrons. Small atoms, such as lithium, are an exception and tend to form ions with two valence electrons. The formation of ions is thus said to follow the **octet (or duet) rule**. The symbol for an ion is the element symbol with a superscript that indicates the number and type (+ or −) of charge. Some elements, especially the transition metals, can form ions of different charges. The formula of an ionic compound always has the same number of positive charges as negative charges.

Section 4.5—A **binary ionic compound** contains two different elements; it has a cation of a metal and an anion of a nonmetal. The formula of a binary ionic compound represents the numbers and types of ions in the compound. The formula is found by crossing over the charge numbers of the ions (without the plus and minus signs).

Binary ionic compounds are named by naming the cation first and then putting an -*ide* ending on the stem of the anion name. Examples are calcium chloride, potassium oxide, aluminum nitride, and so on. Differently charged cations of a metal are named with Roman numerals to indicate the charge: Fe^{2+} is iron(II) ion and Fe^{3+} is iron(III) ion.

Section 4.6—Nonmetal atoms can bond by sharing one or more pairs of electrons, forming a **covalent bond**. A **single bond** is one pair of shared electrons; a **double bond** is two pairs; and a **triple bond** is three pairs. Shared pairs of electrons are called **bonding pairs**, and unshared pairs are called nonbonding pairs, or **lone pairs**.

Section 4.7—Bonding pairs are shared equally when the two atoms are the same but may be unequally shared when the atoms are different. The **electronegativity** of an element is the attraction of an atom in a molecule for a bonding pair. Electronegativity generally increases toward the right and up on the periodic table, so fluorine is the most electronegative element. When electrons of a covalent bond are shared unequally, the more electronegative atom takes on a partial negative charge ($\delta-$), the other atom takes on a partial positive charge ($\delta+$), and the bond is said to be a **polar covalent bond**. The greater the difference in electronegativity, the more polar is the bond. A bonding pair shared equally is a **nonpolar covalent bond**. Most binary covalent compounds are named by naming the first element in the formula, followed by the stem of the second element with an *-ide* ending. Prefixes such as *mono-*, *di-*, *tri-*, and so on, are used to indicate the number of atoms of each element.

Section 4.8—Carbon tends to form four covalent bonds, nitrogen three, and oxygen two; hydrogen can form only one bond. A water molecule has two bonding pairs (O—H bonds) and two lone pairs, an ammonia molecule has three bonding pairs (N—H bonds) and one lone pair, and a methane molecule has four bonding pairs (C—H bonds).

Section 4.9—A **polyatomic ion** is a charged particle containing two or more covalently bonded atoms. Compounds containing polyatomic ions are named, and their formulas written, in the same fashion as compounds containing monatomic ions, except that parentheses are placed around the formula for a polyatomic ion if there is more than one of it in the compound. Names of polyatomic ions often end in *-ate* or *-ite*.

Section 4.10—A **Lewis formula** shows the arrangement of atoms, bonds, and lone pairs in a molecule or polyatomic ion. To draw a Lewis formula, we (a) count the valence electrons; (b) draw a reasonable skeletal structure, showing the arrangement of atoms; (c) connect bonded atoms with a dash (one electron pair); (d) place electron pairs around outer atoms to give each an octet; and (e) place remaining electrons in pairs on the central atom. A multiple bond is formed if there are not enough electrons to give each atom an octet (except small atoms, such as hydrogen, which require only two electrons). There are exceptions to the octet rule. Atoms and molecules with unpaired electrons are called **free radicals**. They are highly reactive and short-lived. Examples of free radicals are NO and ClO_2.

Section 4.11—The shape of a molecule can be predicted with the **VSEPR theory**, which assumes that sets of electrons (either lone pairs or electrons in a bond) around a central atom will get as far away from each other as possible. Two sets of electrons are 180° apart, three sets are about 120° apart, and four sets are about 109° apart. The presence of lone pairs of electrons on the central atom will somewhat decrease the angle between the bonds within the molecule. Once these angles have been established, we determine the shape of the molecule by examining only the bonded atoms. Simple molecules have shapes described as linear, bent, trigonal planar, trigonal pyramidal, or tetrahedral.

Section 4.12—Like a polar bond, a **polar molecule** has separation between its centers of positive charge and negative charge. A molecule with nonpolar bonds is nonpolar. A molecule with polar bonds is nonpolar if its shape causes the polar bonds to cancel one another. If the polar bonds do not cancel, the molecule is polar or is said to be a **dipole**. The water molecule has polar O—H bonds and is bent, so it is polar.

GREEN CHEMISTRY Chemists manipulate the geometry and composition of molecules to change the properties of both molecules and materials. Typical methods for making these molecules and materials use highly reactive and toxic chemicals and high-energy processes. Greener approaches that take advantage of molecular recognition can instead use low energy, solvent-free processes that do not require harsh conditions.

Learning Objectives

› Determine the number of electrons in an ion. (4.1)	Problems 1–3, 7
› Write the Lewis symbol for an atom or ion. (4.2)	Problems 10–12
› Distinguish between an ion and an atom. (4.3)	Problems 1–3, 79, 82
› Describe the nature of the attraction that leads to formation of an ionic bond. (4.3)	Problems 53, 54
› Write symbols for common ions, and determine their charges. (4.4)	Problems 5, 16–22
› Describe the relationship between the octet rule and the charge on an ion. (4.4)	Problems 4, 6, 7, 81
› Name and write formulas for binary ionic compounds. (4.5)	Problems 13–15, 23–26, 74, 87
› Explain the difference between a covalent bond and an ionic bond. (4.6)	Problems 30–37, 53, 54, 80
› Name and write formulas for covalent compounds. (4.6)	Problems 30–40
› Classify a covalent bond as polar or nonpolar. (4.7)	Problems 45–54
› Use electronegativities of elements to determine bond polarity. (4.7)	Problems 45–55, 77
› Predict the number of bonds formed by common nonmetals (the HONC rules). (4.8)	Problems 8, 9, 83
› Recognize common polyatomic ions and be able to use them in naming and writing formulas for compounds. (4.9)	Problems 27–29, 85
› Write Lewis formulas for simple molecules and polyatomic ions. (4.10)	Problems 41–44, 76, 78, 86
› Identify free radicals. (4.10)	Problems 68–70
› Predict the shapes of simple molecules from their Lewis formulas. (4.11)	Problems 56–58, 75, 88, 89
› Classify a simple molecule as polar or nonpolar from its shape and the polarity of its bonds. (4.12)	Problems 59–63, 73
› Describe the concept of molecular recognition.	Problems 90, 91
› Explain the green chemistry advantages of using production methods based on molecular recognition.	Problems 92, 93

REVIEW QUESTIONS

1. How does sodium metal differ from sodium ions (in sodium chloride, for example) in properties?

2. Why is potassium metal so much more reactive than potassium ion (KOH, for example)?

3. What are the structural differences among chlorine atoms, chlorine molecules, and chloride ions? How do their properties differ?

4. How many electrons are in a duet, and how many electrons are in an octet?

5. What are the charges on simple ions formed from atoms of the following?
   a. group 1A elements   b. group 6A elements
   c. group 5A elements   d. group 2A elements

6. How many electrons are needed for the elements below to complete their octet?
   a. group 1A elements   b. group 6A elements
   c. group 5A elements   d. group 2A elements

7. In what group of the periodic table would elements that form ions with the following charges likely be found?
   a. 2−   b. 3+   c. 1+   d. 2+

8. How many covalent bonds do each of the following usually form? You may refer to the periodic table.
   a. H   b. Cl   c. S
   d. F   e. N   f. P

9. Of the elements H, O, N, and C, which one(s) can readily form triple bonds?

PROBLEMS

Lewis Symbols for Elements

10. Write Lewis symbols for each of the following elements. You may use the periodic table.
    a. calcium   b. sulfur   c. silicon

11. Write Lewis symbols for each of the following elements. You may use the periodic table.
    a. phosphorus   b. fluorine   c. boron

12. Write the Lewis symbol for each species in the following pairs.
    a. Na, Na$^+$ b. Ca, Ca^{2+} c. Cl, Cl$^-$

Lewis Formulas for Ionic Compounds

13. Write Lewis formulas for each of the following.
    a. sodium iodide   b. potassium sulfide
    c. calcium chloride   d. aluminum fluoride

14. Write Lewis formulas for each of the following.
    a. lithium bromide   b. strontium sulfide
    c. sodium nitride   d. aluminum oxide

15. Which of the following statements regarding Lewis dot symbols of ions is false?
    a. In magnesium oxide, O^{2-} has eight electrons.
    b. Mg^{2+} always has one electron around it.
    c. In sodium chloride, Na$^+$ has no electrons around it.
    d. In ionic compounds containing chloride, ions, Cl$^-$ is isoelectronic with Ar.

Names and Symbols for Simple Ions

16. Pair (match) the names and symbols for the ions below:
    a. nitride ion   b. Fe^{2+}
    c. cuprous ion   d. N^{3-}
    e. ferrous ion   f. Cu$^+$
    g. silver ion   h. Ag$^+$

17. Without referring to Table 4.2, supply a symbol given the name or a name given the symbol for each of the following ions:
    a. sulfide ion   b. K$^+$
    c. Br$^-$ d. fluoride ion
    e. Ca^{2+} f. iron(III) ion

18. Refer to the beginning paragraphs of Section 4.5, then use that information to name the following ions:
    a. Cr^{2+} b. Cr^{3+} c. Cr^{6+}

19. Refer to the beginning paragraphs of Section 4.5, then use that information to name the following ions.
    a. Mo^{4+} b. Mo^{6+}

20. Refer to the beginning paragraphs of Section 4.5, then write symbols for:
    a. vanadium(II) ion   b. titanium(II) ion
    c. titanium(IV) ion

21. Refer to the beginning paragraphs of Section 4.5, then write symbols for:
    a. manganese(II) ion   b. manganese(III) ion
    c. manganese(VII) ion

22. For copper and iron ions, we sometimes use the *-ic* and *-ous* endings. Which ending indicates the more positively charged ion?

Names and Formulas for Binary Ionic Compounds

23. Pair (match) the names and formulas for the following binary ionic compounds:
    a. iron(II) chloride   b. FeBr$_3$
    c. silver fluoride   d. FeCl$_2$
    e. iron(III) bromide   f. Na$_2$O
    g. sodium oxide   h. AgF

24. Write a formula to match the name or a name to match the formula of the following binary ionic compounds:
    a. LiF   b. calcium chloride
    c. MgS   d. silver iodide
    e. CuO   f. copper(I) sulfide

25. There are two common binary ionic compounds formed from chromium and oxygen. One of them contains chromium(III) ions; the other contains chromium(VI) ions. Write the formulas for the two compounds, and name them.

26. One of two binary ionic compounds is often added to toothpaste. One of these compounds contains sodium and fluorine; the other contains tin(II) ions and fluorine. Write the formulas for these two compounds, and name them.

Names and Formulas for Ionic Compounds with Polyatomic Ions

27. Pair (match) the names and formulas for the following polyatomic ionic compounds:
   a. ammonium nitrate   **b.** $FePO_4$
   c. calcium carbonate   **d.** NH_4NO_3
   e. iron(III) phosphate   **f.** $Ca(CH_3CO_2)_2$
   g. calcium acetate   **h.** $CaCO_3$

28. Supply a formula to match the name or a name to match the formula for the following:
   a. potassium hydroxide   **b.** $MgCO_3$
   c. iron(III) cyanide   **d.** iron(II) oxalate
   e. $CuSO_4$ **f.** $Na_2Cr_2O_7$

29. Supply a formula to match the name or a name to match the formula for the following:
   a. $AgNO_2$
   b. lithium chromate
   c. $(NH_4)_2SO_3$
   d. magnesium hydrogen carbonate
   e. copper(I) phosphate
   f. $Al(MnO_4)_3$

Molecules: Covalent Bonds

30. How is a covalent bond different from an ionic bond?

31. Use Lewis dot symbols to show the sharing of electrons between a hydrogen atom and a fluorine atom.

32. Use Lewis dot symbols to show the sharing of electrons between two bromine atoms to form a bromine (Br_2) molecule. Label all electron pairs as bonding pairs (BPs) or lone pairs (LPs).

33. Use Lewis dot symbols to show the sharing of electrons between a phosphorus atom and hydrogen atoms to form a molecule in which phosphorus has an octet of electrons.

34. Use Lewis dot symbols to show the sharing of electrons between a silicon atom and hydrogen atoms to form a molecule in which silicon has an octet of electrons.

35. Use Lewis dot symbols to show the sharing of electrons between a carbon atom and chlorine atoms to form a molecule in which each atom has an octet of electrons.

36. Use Lewis dot symbols to show the sharing of electrons between a nitrogen atom and fluorine atoms to form a molecule in which each atom has an octet of electrons.

37. When a hydrogen atom covalently bonds to another atom, how many electrons associated with this hydrogen atom become involved in such a bond? (Explain your answer.)

Names and Formulas for Covalent Compounds

38. Pair (match) the names and formulas for the following binary covalent compounds:
   a. dichlorine monoxide   **b.** ClO
   c. chlorine monoxide   **d.** Cl_2O_7
   e. dichlorine trioxide   **f.** Cl_2O
   g. dichlorine heptoxide   **h.** Cl_2O_3

39. Supply a formula for the name or a name for the formula for the following covalent compounds:
   a. dinitrogen tetroxide   **b.** bromine trichloride
   c. OF_2 **d.** nitrogen triiodide
   e. CBr_4 **f.** N_2S_4

40. Supply a formula for the name or a name for the formula for the following covalent compounds:
   a. carbon disulfide   **b.** chlorine trifluoride
   c. PF_5 **d.** CI_4
   e. tricarbon dioxide   **f.** P_4S_3

Lewis Formulas for Molecules and Polyatomic Ions

41. Write Lewis formulas that follow the octet rule for the following covalent molecules:
   a. SiH_4 **b.** N_2F_4
   c. CH_5N **d.** H_2CO
   e. NOH_3 **f.** H_3PO_3

42. Write Lewis formulas that follow the octet rule for the following covalent molecules:
   a. NH_2Cl **b.** C_2H_4
   c. H_2SO_4 **d.** C_2N_2
   e. $COCl_2$ **f.** SCl_2

43. Write Lewis formulas that follow the octet rule for the following ions:
   a. ClO^- **b.** HPO_4^{2-} **c.** BrO_3^-

44. Write Lewis formulas that follow the octet rule for the following ions:
   a. CN^- **b.** ClO_2^- **c.** HSO_4^{2-}

Electronegativity: Polar Covalent Bonds

45. If element A bonds covalently with element B, then what must the electronegativity difference between A and B be for this bond to be polar?

46. If element X bonds covalently with element Y, then what must the electronegativity difference between X and Y be for this bond to be nonpolar?

47. Classify the following covalent bonds as polar or nonpolar.
   a. H—O   **b.** N—F   **c.** Cl—B

48. Classify the following covalent bonds as polar or nonpolar.
   a. H—N   **b.** O—Be   **c.** P—F

49. Use the symbol $\leftrightarrow$ to indicate the direction of the dipole in each polar bond in Problem 47.

50. Use the symbol $\leftrightarrow$ to indicate the direction of the dipole in each polar bond in Problem 48.

51. Use the symbols $\delta+$ and $\delta-$ to indicate partial charges, if any, on the following bonds.
   a. Si—O   **b.** F—F   **c.** F—N

52. Use the symbols $\delta+$ and $\delta-$ to indicate partial charges, if any, on the following bonds.
   a. O—H   **b.** C—F   **c.** C=C

Classifying Bonds

53. Classify the bonds in the following as ionic or covalent. For bonds that are covalent, indicate whether they are polar or nonpolar.
   a. K_2O **b.** $BrCl$ **c.** MgF_2 **d.** I_2

54. Classify the bonds in the following as ionic or covalent. For bonds that are covalent, indicate whether they are polar or nonpolar.
   a. Na_2O **b.** $CaCl_2$ **c.** NBr_3 **d.** CS_2

55. Rank the following bonds in terms of increasing polarity.
   a. H—F   **b.** N—F
   c. B—F   **d.** Si—F
   e. Si—Cl   **f.** P—Cl

VSEPR Theory: The Shapes of Molecules

56. Pair (match) the VSEPR predicted shape to the listed molecules:
- **a.** $AlCl_3$
- **b.** linear
- **c.** CSe_2
- **d.** trigonal planar
- **e.** SeH_2
- **f.** bent
- **g.** SiI_4
- **h.** tetrahedral

57. Use the VSEPR theory to predict the shape of each of the following molecules:
- **a.** silane (SiH_4)
- **b.** hydrogen selenide (H_2Se)
- **c.** phosphine (PH_3)
- **d.** silicon tetrafluoride (SiF_4)
- **e.** oxygen difluoride (OF_2)
- **f.** formaldehyde (H_2CO)

58. Use VSEPR theory to predict the shape of each of the following molecules:
- **a.** chloroform ($CHCl_3$)
- **b.** boron trichloride (BCl_3)
- **c.** carbon tetrafluoride (CF_4)
- **d.** sulfur difluoride (SF_2)
- **e.** nitrogen triiodide (NI_3)
- **f.** dichlorodifluoromethane (CCl_2F_2)

Polar and Nonpolar Molecules

59. Despite the large electronegativity difference between fluorine and beryllium atoms, BeF_2 forms linear molecules in gas phase. Are these molecules polar or nonpolar? Explain.

60. The molecule SF_2 is bent. Is it polar or nonpolar? Explain.

61. Is BCl_2F polar or nonpolar? Explain.

62. Look again at the molecules in Problem 57. For each one, are the bonds polar? What are the approximate bond angles? Is the molecule as a whole polar?

63. Look again at the molecules in Problem 58. For each one, are the bonds polar? What are the approximate bond angles? Is the molecule as a whole polar?

64. What makes the molecule of SO_2 polar?

65. What makes the molecule of SO_3 nonpolar?

66. Is it possible for a molecule of CH_2Cl_2 to be nonpolar (C is the central atom)? Explain.

67. Is H_2O more or less polar than SCl_2?

Molecules That Are Exceptions to the Octet Rule

68. Which of the following species (atoms or molecules) are free radicals?
- **a.** Br
- **b.** F_2
- **c.** CCl_3

69. Which of the following species (atoms or molecules) are free radicals?
- **a.** S
- **b.** NO_2
- **c.** N_2O_4

70. Free radicals are one class of molecules in which atoms do not conform to the octet rule. Another exception involves atoms with fewer than eight electrons, as seen in elements of group 3 and in beryllium. In some covalent molecules, these atoms can have six or four electrons, respectively. Write Lewis structures for the following covalent molecules:
- **a.** $AlBr_3$
- **b.** BeH_2
- **c.** BH_3

71. Exceptions to the octet rule include molecules that have atoms with more than 8 valence electrons, most typically 10 or 12. Atoms heavier than Si can expand their valence shell, meaning that they can accommodate the "extra" electrons in unoccupied, higher-energy orbitals. Draw Lewis structures for the following molecules or ions:
- **a.** XeF_4
- **b.** I_3^-
- **c.** SF_4
- **d.** KrF_2

ADDITIONAL PROBLEMS

72. Why does neon tend not to form chemical bonds?

73. Draw an electrostatic potential diagram of the H_2S molecule. Use the symbols $\delta+$ and $\delta-$ to indicate the polarity of the molecule.

74. The gas phosphine (PH_3) is used as a fumigant to protect stored grain and other durable produce from pests. Phosphine is generated where it is to be used by adding water to aluminum phosphide or magnesium phosphide. Give formulas for these two phosphides.

75. Explain why the angle between Cl—S—Cl is less than $109.5°$ in SCl_2.

76. There are two different covalent molecules with the formula C_2H_6O. Write Lewis formulas for the two molecules.

77. Solutions of iodine chloride (ICl) are used as disinfectants. Is the compound ICl ionic, polar covalent, or nonpolar covalent?

78. Consider the hypothetical elements X, Y, and Z, which have the following Lewis symbols:

$$:\ddot{X}\cdot \qquad :\dot{Y}\cdot \qquad :\dot{Z}\cdot$$

- **a.** To which group in the periodic table would each element belong?
- **b.** Write the Lewis formula for the simplest compound each would form with hydrogen.

- **c.** Write Lewis formulas for the ions that would be formed when X reacted with sodium and when Y reacted with sodium.

79. Potassium is a soft, silvery metal that reacts violently with water and ignites spontaneously in air. Your doctor recommends that you take a potassium supplement. Would you take potassium metal? If not, what would you take?

80. What is wrong with the phrase "just a few molecules of potassium iodide"?

81. Use subshell notation to write an electron configuration for the most stable simple ion formed by each of the following elements.
- **a.** Ca
- **b.** Rb
- **c.** S
- **d.** I
- **e.** N
- **f.** Se

82. Why is Na^+ smaller than Na? Why is Cl^- larger than Cl?

83. The halogens (F, Cl, Br, and I) tend to form only one single bond in binary molecules. Explain.

84. A science magazine for the general public contains this statement: "Some of these hydrocarbons are very light, like methane gas—just a single carbon molecule attached to three hydrogen molecules." Evaluate the statement, and correct any inaccuracies.

85. Sodium tungstate is Na_2WO_4. What is the formula for aluminum tungstate?

86. Scientists estimate that the atmosphere of Titan (a moon of Saturn) consists of about 98.4% nitrogen and 1.6% methane. They have also found traces of organic molecules with the molecular formulas C_2H_4, C_3H_4, C_4H_2, HCN, HC_3N, and C_2N_2. Write possible Lewis formulas for each of these molecules.

87. What is the formula for the compound formed by the imaginary ions Q^{2+} and ZX_4^{3-}?

88. Why are the 120° angles optimal in a trigonal planar geometry?

89. Why are the 109.5° angles optimal in a tetrahedral geometry?

90. Give two design criteria that chemists use to design new medicines.

91. What is the term for the science that explains how molecules interact through geometric orientation of atoms?

92. Give three ways that molecular recognition approaches can support greener methods for making molecules and materials.

93. How can an understanding of enzymes and biological receptors guide medicinal chemists?

CRITICAL THINKING EXERCSISES

Apply knowledge that you have gained in this chapter and one or more of the FLaReS principles (Chapter 1) to evaluate the following statements or claims.

4.1 Some people believe that crystals have special powers. Crystal therapists claim that they can use quartz crystals to restore balance and harmony to a person's spiritual energy.

4.2 A "fuel-enhancer" device is being sold by an entrepreneur. The device contains a powerful magnet and is placed on the fuel line of an automobile. The inventor claims that the device "separates the positive and negative charges in the hydrocarbon fuel molecules, increasing their polarity and allowing them to react more readily with oxygen."

4.3 Sodium chloride (NaCl) is a metal–nonmetal compound held together by ionic bonds. A scientist has studied mercury(II) chloride ($HgCl_2$) and says that its atoms are held together by covalent bonds. The scientist says that since a solution of this substance in water does not conduct an electric current, it does not contain an appreciable amount of ions.

4.4 Another scientist, noting that the noble gas xenon does not contain any ions, states that xenon atoms must be held together by covalent bonds.

4.5 A webpage claims, "Fifty years ago, the hydrogen bond angle in water was 108° and you rarely heard of anyone with cancer. Today, it's only 104° and, as a result, cancer is an epidemic!"

4.6 In the 1960s the concept of polywater came into fashion. The idea was that under the right circumstances, water could be made into a polymer, that is, a large molecule in which a number of water molecules would be covalently bonded with each other.

4.7 It was claimed that a compound containing a pentavalent carbon atom (a C atom with five bonds attached to it) was synthesized. This report was received with great skepticism by the scientific community.

4.8 A football coach claims that his players have more stamina since they drink atomic O-saturated water rather than O_2-saturated water.

4.9 A fertilizer company is marketing a new form of garden fertilizer. It is made of thin flakes and is claimed to work better because it contains flat ammonia molecules, which have greater surface area and dissolve better in water.

4.10 A scientist claims to have detected HeH^+ and HeH_2.

COLLABORATIVE GROUP PROJECTS

Prepare a PowerPoint, poster, or other presentation (as directed by your instructor) for presentation to the class. Projects 1 and 2 are best done by a group of four students.

1. Make a form like that in Project 3 on page 39 but replace the column headings "Word" and "Definition" with "Name" and "Lewis Formula." Student 1 should write the name from the list below in the first column of the form and its Lewis formula in the second column. Proceed as in Project 3 on page 39 , ending by comparing the name in the last column with that in the first column. Discuss any differences in the two names. If the name in the last column differs from that in the first column, determine what went wrong in the process.
   a. bromide ion   **b.** calcium fluoride
   c. phosphorus trifluoride   **d.** carbon disulfide

2. Make a form like that in Project 3 on page 39, using the column headings "Name" and "Structure." Then student 1 should write a name from the following list in the first column of the form and its structure in the second column.

Proceed as in Project 3 on page 39 , ending by comparing the name in the last column with that in the first column. Discuss any differences in the two names. If the name in the last column differs from that in the first column, determine what went wrong in the process.
   a. ammonium nitrate   **b.** potassium phosphate
   c. lithium carbonate   **d.** copper(I) chloride

3. Starting with 20 balloons, blown up to about the same size and tied, tie two balloons together. Next, tie three balloons together. Repeat this with four, five, and six balloons. (*Suggestion*: Three sets of two balloons can be twisted together to form a six-balloon set, and so on.) Show how these balloon sets can be used to illustrate the VSEPR theory.

4. Prepare a brief biographical report on one of the following:
   a. Gilbert N. Lewis   **b.** Linus Pauling

5. There are several different definitions and scales for electronegativity. Search for information on these, and write a brief compare-and-contrast essay about two of them.

CHEMISTRY @ HOME   Molecular Shapes: Please Don't Eat the Atoms!

Materials Needed

- Large gumdrops (2)
- Small gumdrops (8)
- Toothpicks (10)

Molecules can be written out as formulas or drawn in bond-line format. However, molecules are actually three-dimensional. Can you use household items to create your own 3D models of molecules?

In this experiment, you will have the opportunity to visualize the geometric shapes defined by VSEPR theory, and you will be practicing writing Lewis formulas and predicting molecular geometry.

Using your gumdrops and toothpicks, you will create a series of molecules and observe their geometry.

a. First, connect two small gumdrops with one toothpick. This geometry is called linear and is similar to any diatomic molecule, such as oxygen (O_2). Sketch the three-dimensional shape and write the Lewis formula.

b. Next, connect two small gumdrops to one large central gumdrop. Keep the gumdrops in one line. This geometry is also called linear and is similar to carbon dioxide (CO_2). Sketch the three-dimensional shape and write the Lewis formula.

c. Now connect three small gumdrops to one large central gumdrop. Place them all in the same plane but spread them out equally. This geometry is called triangular and is similar to a nitrate ion (NO_3^{-1}). Sketch the three-dimensional shape and write the Lewis formula.

d. Remove one of the toothpicks and small gumdrops. The remaining two small gumdrops and one large gumdrop define a "bent" or "angular" molecule similar to sulfur dioxide (SO_2). Sketch the three-dimensional shape and write the Lewis formula.

e. Now connect four small gumdrops to one central large gumdrop in the shape of a tetrahedron. This geometry is similar to methane (CH_4). Sketch the three-dimensional shape and write the Lewis formula.

f. Remove one of the small gumdrops and toothpicks. The remaining system is called pyramidal. This shape is the same as that of an ammonia molecule (NH_3). Sketch the three-dimensional structure and write the Lewis formula.

g. Remove another small gumdrop and toothpick. You should have two small gumdrops connected to one large gumdrop. This is another "bent" or "angular" geometry. Notice that it is different from the geometry in c. (In c, the small–large–small angle was 120°; in this case, the single is about 109.5°, the tetrahedral angle.) This geometry is similar to that of water (H_2O). Sketch the three-dimensional structure and write the Lewis formula.

Questions

1. Why do the SO_2 and H_2O molecules have a bent or angular geometry? Why are they not linear geometries?

2. Using your gumdrops and toothpicks, create a titanium tetrachloride ($TiCl_4$) molecule. Write the Lewis formula to predict the geometry.

3. Dichlorocarbene (CCl_2) has a "bent" geometry. Using the Lewis formula, predict the angle of the "bent" geometry.

5

Learning Objectives

> Identify balanced and unbalanced chemical equations, and balance equations by inspection. (5.1)

> Determine volumes of gases that react, using a balanced equation for a reaction. (5.2)

> Calculate the formula mass, molecular mass, or molar mass of a substance. (5.3)

> Use Avogadro's number to determine the number of particles of different types in a mass of a substance (5.3)

> Convert from mass to moles and from moles to mass of a substance. (5.4)

> Calculate the mass or number of moles of a reactant or product from the mass or number of moles of another reactant or product. (5.4)

> Calculate the concentration (molarity, percent by volume, or percent by mass) of a solute in a solution. (5.5)

> Calculate the amount of solute or solution given the concentration and the other amount. (5.5)

> Explain how the concept of atom economy can be applied to pollution prevention and environmental protection.

> Calculate the atom economy for chemical reactions.

CHEMICAL ACCOUNTING

Have You Ever Wondered?

1. How can a car make more pollution than the gasoline it uses?

2. What's the difference between .925 silver and .800 silver?

3. Does 2% milk have just 2% of the calories of whole milk?

4. What does a toxicity rating (LD$_{50}$) of 100 ppm mean?

MASS AND VOLUME RELATIONSHIPS

We can look at or represent chemical phenomena on three levels:

1. Macro and tangible: for example, a sample of yellow powder or a blue solution in a beaker.

2. Particle (atom, molecule, or ion) and invisible: for example, a sulfur atom, a carbon dioxide molecule, or a chloride ion.

3. Symbolic and mathematical: for example, S, CO_2, Cl, or $d = m/V$.

Macro-level representations of chemicals are familiar from everyday life.

It is easy to visualize salt crystals in a shaker, gold in jewelry, baking soda in a box, aspirin in tablets, and many other common substances because they are tangible. We can see them and touch them. The other representations were introduced in earlier chapters. You may have recognized the

Everything that burns fuel requires oxygen, and the human body is no exception. At the top of Mount Everest, there is not enough oxygen in the air to keep people alive, so climbers making the ascent must bring oxygen with them. But how much oxygen should each climber bring? A knowledge of chemistry allows this question to be answered, thus promoting the safety of the climbers and the success of their venture.

mathematical equation for density from Chapter 1. We employed symbols when discussing atoms in Chapters 2 and 3 and formulas in our discussion of molecules and ions in Chapter 4. In this chapter, we consider symbolic and mathematical descriptions of chemical changes.

Why Chemical "Accounting"

Much chemistry can be discussed and understood with little or no mathematics, but the quantitative aspects can shed a great deal of light on properties of matter. In this chapter, we will consider some of the basic calculations used in chemistry and related fields such as biology and medicine. This type of algebra is not limited to these fields but can also be applied to business, social sciences, and even art. Chemists use many kinds of mathematics, from simple arithmetic to sophisticated calculus and complicated computer algorithms, but our calculations here will require at most a bit of algebra.

The aspect of chemistry in this chapter, often called *stoichiometry*, is extremely important in learning the science of chemistry. The name comes from two words, *stoicheion*, which is the Greek word for element, and *metria*, referring to measurement. Literally, it means the measurement of elements. There is more to this field than just measuring, however. Like a financial accountant, who must do more than just count money but must also make an account of where the funds go and how they are used, a chemist must also account for the matter involved in a chemical reaction. As we will see later in this chapter and in other parts of this text, Dalton's laws demand that we keep track of all the movements and locations of matter.

5.1 Chemical Sentences: Equations

Learning Objective ❯ Identify balanced and unbalanced chemical equations, and balance equations by inspection.

Studying science, like studying a language, means that the student has to learn the vocabulary and grammar of that specific language. A beginner cannot launch directly into speaking that language. Chemistry is a study of matter and its changes as it interacts with energy. The symbols and formulas we have used to represent elements and compounds make up the letters (symbols) and words (formulas) of our chemical language. Using them, we can write sentences (chemical equations), but we must understand the rules for speaking the chemical language. A **chemical equation** uses symbols and formulas to represent the elements and compounds involved in the change.

At the macro level, we can describe a chemical reaction in words. For example,

Carbon reacts with oxygen to form carbon dioxide.

We can describe the same reaction symbolically.

$$C + O_2 \longrightarrow CO_2$$

The plus sign (+) indicates that carbon and oxygen are added together or combined in some way. The arrow ($\longrightarrow$) is read "yield(s)" or "react(s) to produce." Substances on the left of the arrow (C and O_2 in this case) are **reactants**, or *starting materials*. Those on the right (here, CO_2) are the **products** of the reaction. Reactants and products need not be written in any particular order in a chemical equation, except that all reactants must be to the left of the arrow and all products to the right. In other words, we could also write the preceding equation as

$$O_2 + C \longrightarrow CO_2$$

At the atomic or molecular level, the equation means that one carbon (C) atom reacts with one oxygen (O_2) molecule to produce one carbon dioxide (CO_2) molecule. It is important to note that chemical substances sometimes can be found as elemental atoms, like the carbon, while others, like the oxygen, are only obtained in a molecular state.

Sometimes, we indicate the physical states of the reactants and products by writing the initial letter of the state immediately following the formula: (g) indicates a gaseous substance, (l) a liquid, and (s) a solid. The label (aq) indicates that the substance is in an aqueous (water) solution. Using state labels, we see that the above equation becomes

$$C(s) + O_2(g) \longrightarrow CO_2(g)$$

Balancing Chemical Equations

We can represent some reactions quite simply, like the previous reaction of carbon and oxygen to form carbon dioxide, but many other chemical reactions require more thought. For example, hydrogen reacts with oxygen to form water. Using formulas, we can represent this reaction as

However, this representation shows two oxygen atoms in the reactants (as O_2), but only one in the product (in H_2O). Because matter is neither created nor destroyed in a chemical reaction (the law of conservation of mass, Section 2.2), the equation must be *balanced* to represent the chemical reaction correctly. Because we are interpreting the equation to mean that each symbol represents multiples of a single atom or molecule, we cannot simply assume that we are using one-half of the oxygen molecule. Instead, we will need to maintain the relationships between the whole particles. Also, we must be sure that the same number of each of the different types of atom appears on both sides of the arrow. To balance the oxygen atoms, we need only place the coefficient 2 in front of the formula for water.

This coefficient means that two whole molecules of water are produced. As is the case with a subscript of 1, a coefficient of 1 is understood when there is no number in front of a formula. *Everything* in a formula is multiplied by the coefficient in front of it. In the preceding equation, adding the coefficient 2 before H_2O not only increases the total number of oxygen atoms on the product side to two but also increases the total number of hydrogen atoms to four.

But the equation is still not balanced. There are now four hydrogen atoms on the product side of the equation but only two on the left side of the equation. As we fixed the number of oxygen atoms in the product, we unbalanced the number of hydrogen atoms. To balance the hydrogen, we must now place a coefficient 2 in front of H_2.

● = hydrogen
● = oxygen

▲ **Figure 5.1** To balance the equation for the reaction of hydrogen and oxygen to form water, the same number of each kind of atom must appear on each side (atoms are conserved). When the equation is balanced, there are four H atoms and two O atoms on each side.

Q: *Why can't you balance the equation by removing one of the oxygen atoms from the left side of the first balance?*

Now there are four hydrogen atoms and two oxygen atoms on each side of the equation. Atoms are conserved: The equation is balanced (Figure 5.1), and the law of conservation of mass is obeyed. Figure 5.2 illustrates two common pitfalls in the process of balancing equations, as well as the correct method. You cannot simply gain or lose substances on the product side of the equation, as it may represent an invalid reaction. Also, if you change the subscript of a specific chemical formula, you create either a different substance or an invalid formula.

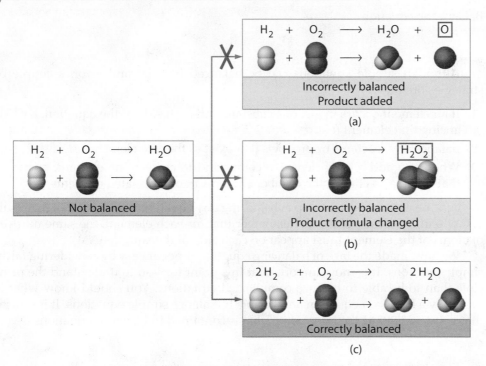

◀ **Figure 5.2** Balancing the equation for the reaction between hydrogen and oxygen to form water. (a) Incorrect. There is no atomic oxygen (O) as a product. Other products cannot be introduced simply to balance an equation. (b) Incorrect. The product of the reaction is water (H_2O), not hydrogen peroxide (H_2O_2). A formula can't be changed simply to balance an equation. (c) Correct. An equation can be balanced only by using the correct formulas and adjusting the coefficients.

Example 5.1 | **Balancing Equations**

Balance the following chemical equation, which represents the reaction that occurs when an airbag in a car deploys.

$$NaN_3 \longrightarrow Na + N_2$$

Solution

The sodium (Na) atoms are balanced, but the nitrogen (N) atoms are not. To balance this equation, we can use the concept of the least common multiple. There are three nitrogen atoms on the left (reactant side) and two on the right (product side). The least common multiple of 2 and 3 is 6. To get *six* nitrogen atoms on each side, we need *three* N_2 and *two* NaN_3:

$2 \times 3 = 6$ N atoms $3 \times 2 = 6$ N atoms

$$2\,NaN_3 \longrightarrow Na + 3\,N_2 \qquad \text{(not balanced)}$$

$2 \times 1 = 2$ Na atoms   1 Na atom

We now have *two* sodium atoms on the left. We can get two on the right by placing the coefficient 2 in front of Na.

$$2 \, NaN_3 \longrightarrow 2 \, Na + 3 \, N_2 \quad \text{(balanced)}$$

Checking, we count two Na atoms and six N atoms on each side. The equation is balanced.

▪ EXERCISE 5.1A

The reaction between hydrogen and nitrogen to give ammonia, called the *Haber process*, is typically the first step in the industrial production of nitrogen fertilizers.

$$H_2 + N_2 \longrightarrow NH_3$$

Balance the equation.

▪ EXERCISE 5.1B

Metal ores such as Fe_2O_3 are *smelted* by reaction with carbon to produce metallic iron and carbon dioxide.

$$Fe_2O_3 + C \longrightarrow CO_2 + Fe$$

Balance the equation.

Although simple equations can be balanced by trial and error, a couple of strategies often help:

1. If an element occurs in just one substance on each side of the equation, try balancing that element *first*.
2. Balance any reactants or products that exist as the free element *last*.
3. When you add a coefficient to a compound to correct one element, be aware that it will also change the number of atoms in other related elements.

Perhaps the most important step in balancing any equation is to check that the result you obtain is indeed balanced. Remember that for each element, the same number of atoms of the element must appear on each side of the equation.

We have made the task of balancing equations appear easy by considering fairly simple reactions. It is more important at this point for you to understand the principle than to be able to balance complicated equations. You should know what is meant by a balanced equation and be able to balance simple equations. It is crucial that you understand the information that is contained in balanced equations.

SELF-ASSESSMENT Questions

1. Which of the following equations are balanced? (You need not balance the equations. Just determine whether or not they are balanced as written.)

   I. $Mg + 2 \, H_2O \longrightarrow Mg(OH)_2 + H_2$
   II. $4 \, LiH + AlCl_3 \longrightarrow 2 \, LiAlH_4 + 2 \, LiCl$
   III. $2 \, KOH + CO_2 \longrightarrow K_2CO_3 + H_2O$
   IV. $2 \, Sn + 2 \, H_2SO_4 \longrightarrow 2 \, SnSO_4 + SO_2 + 2 \, H_2O$

   a. I and II   **b.** I and III
   c. II and III   **d.** II and IV

2. Consider the equation for the reaction of phosphine with oxygen to form tetraphosphorus decoxide and water:

   $$PH_3 + O_2 \longrightarrow P_4O_{10} + H_2O \quad \text{(not balanced)}$$

   When the equation is balanced, how many molecules of water are produced for each molecule of P_4O_{10} formed?
   a. 1   **b.** 4   **c.** 6   **d.** 12

Items 3–5 refer to the following equation for the reaction of magnesium hydroxide $[Mg(OH)_2]$ with phosphoric acid (H_3PO_4).

$$Mg(OH)_2 + H_3PO_4 \longrightarrow H_2O + Mg_3(PO_4)_2 \quad \text{(not balanced)}$$

3. When the equation is balanced, how many H_3PO_4 molecules must react to produce one $Mg_3(PO_4)_2$ formula unit?
   a. 1   **b.** 2   **c.** 3   **d.** 6

4. When the equation is balanced, how many H_2O molecules will be produced for each H_3PO_4 molecule that reacts?
   a. 1   **b.** 2   **c.** 3   **d.** 6

5. When the equation is balanced, how many $Mg(OH)_2$ formula units are needed to react with six H_3PO_4 molecules? (Just as a molecule is the smallest unit of a molecular compound, a *formula unit* is the smallest unit of an ionic compound.)
   a. 1   **b.** 1.5   **c.** 6   **d.** 9

5.2 Volume Relationships in Chemical Equations

Learning Objective ❯ Determine volumes of gases that react, using a balanced equation for a reaction.

One challenge in dealing with chemical reactions is that they seldom occur in reactions between just a few atoms or molecules. In the real world, chemists work with quantities of matter that contain billions of billions of atoms.

John Dalton postulated that atoms of different elements have different masses. Therefore, equal masses of different elements must contain different numbers of atoms. In Section 5.1, we used hydrogen and oxygen atoms to make water molecules. Oxygen molecules have a significantly different mass from hydrogen molecules. Similarly, a kilogram of golf balls contains a smaller number of balls than a kilogram of Ping-Pong balls because a golf ball is heavier than a Ping-Pong ball. While you might determine the number of balls in each case simply by counting them, it is not possible to count individual atoms. The smallest visible particle of matter contains more atoms than could be counted in 10 lifetimes! There are other ways, however, to determine the number of atoms in a substance, as you will learn in this chapter.

Ironically, it was studies of gases, which are also difficult to observe, that advanced our understanding of how to account for atoms involved in chemical reactions. These studies, which occurred in the 1700s, revealed the interesting nature and behavior of gases. (These behaviors are explored in Chapter 6.)

Here we focus on some historical experiments with gases that revealed how chemical equations can be balanced. French scientist Joseph Louis Gay-Lussac (1778–1850) performed experiments that led to an approach to quantifying atoms. In 1808, he announced the results of some chemical reactions that he had carried out with gases and summarized these experiments in a new law. The **law of combining volumes** states that when all measurements are made at the same temperature and pressure, the volumes of gaseous reactants and products are in small whole-number ratios.

One such experiment is illustrated in Figure 5.3. Hydrogen gas will react with nitrogen gas to create ammonia. In practice, three volumes of hydrogen will combine with one volume of nitrogen to yield two volumes of ammonia. The small whole-number ratio is 3:1:2.

Gay-Lussac thought there must be some direct relationship between the numbers of molecules and the volumes of gaseous reactants and products. It was Italian mathematician and scientist, Amedeo Avogadro, who first explained the law of combining volumes in 1811. **Avogadro's hypothesis**, based on a shrewd interpretation of experimental facts, was that equal volumes of all gases, when

| Hydrogen gas | Nitrogen gas | Ammonia gas |
| (three volumes) | (one volume) | (two volumes) |

▲ **Figure 5.3** Gay-Lussac's law of combining volumes. Three volumes of hydrogen gas react with one volume of nitrogen gas to yield two volumes of ammonia gas, when measured at the same temperature and pressure.

Q: *Can you sketch a similar figure for the reaction* $2\ SO_2(g) + O_2(g) \longrightarrow 2\ SO_3(g)$?

Hydrogen gas
(three volumes)

Nitrogen gas
(one volume)

Ammonia
(two volumes)

▲ **Figure 5.4** Avogadro's explanation of Gay-Lussac's law of combining volumes. Equal volumes of all the gases contain the same number of molecules.

Q: *Can you sketch a similar figure for the reaction* $2 NO(g) + O_2(g) \longrightarrow 2 NO_2(g)$?

▲ Amedeo Avogadro (1776–1856) and his hypothesis. The quotation reads, "Equal volumes of gases under the same conditions of temperature and of pressure contain the same number of molecules."

measured at the same temperature and pressure, contain the same number of molecules (Figure 5.4).

The equation then for the combination of hydrogen and nitrogen to form ammonia is

$$3 H_2(g) + N_2(g) \longrightarrow 2 NH_3(g)$$

Note that the coefficients of the molecules correlate with the combining ratio of the gas volumes, 3:1:2 (Figure 5.3). The equation says that three H_2 molecules react with one N_2 molecule to produce two NH_3 molecules. The balanced equation then provides equivalent ratios that can be scaled for the size of the reaction, regardless of how much or how little you need to use. If you had 3 million H_2 molecules, you would need 1 million N_2 molecules to produce 2 million NH_3 molecules. According to the equation, three volumes of hydrogen react with one volume of nitrogen to produce two volumes of ammonia because each volume of hydrogen contains the same number of molecules as that same volume of nitrogen.

Example 5.2   Volume Relationships of Gases

What volume of oxygen is required to burn 2.000 L of propane in the following combustion reaction, assuming that both gases are measured at the same temperature and pressure?

$$C_3H_8(g) + 5 O_2(g) \longrightarrow 3 CO_2(g) + 4 H_2O(g)$$

Solution

The coefficients in the equation indicate that each volume of $C_3H_8(g)$ requires five volumes of O_2 gas. Thus, we use 5 L $O_2(g)$/1 L $C_3H_8(g)$ as a conversion factor to find the volume of oxygen required. (Conversion factors are explained in Section A.3 of the Appendix.) Note x-ref. App A3 is on unit conversions.

$$? L\ O_2(g) = 2.000\ L\ \cancel{C_3H_8(g)} \times \frac{5\ L\ O_2(g)}{1\ L\ \cancel{C_3H_8(g)}} = 10.00\ L\ O_2(g)$$

▪ **EXERCISE 5.2A**

Using the equation in Example 5.2, calculate the volume of $CO_2(g)$ produced when 0.553 L of propane is burned if the two gases are compared at the same temperature and pressure.

▪ **EXERCISE 5.2B**

If 4.00 L each of propane and oxygen are combined at the same temperature and pressure, which gas will be left over after reaction? What volume of that gas will remain?

SELF-ASSESSMENT Questions

1. In the reaction $2 H_2(g) + O_2(g) \longrightarrow 2 H_2O(g)$, with all substances at the same temperature and pressure, the ratio of volumes, for H_2, O_2, and H_2O, respectively, is
   a. 1:0:1 **b.** 1:1:1 **c.** 2:0:2 **d.** 2:1:2

2. How many CO_2 molecules are produced in the following reaction if 75 O_2 molecules react?

   $$2 C_8H_{18}(l) + 25 O_2(g) \longrightarrow 16 CO_2(g) + 18 H_2O(l)$$

   a. 50 molecules   **b.** 100 molecules
   c. 48 molecules   **d.** 32 molecules

3. In the reaction $N_2(g) + 3 H_2(g) \longrightarrow 2 NH_3(g)$, with all substances at the same temperature and pressure, what volume of ammonia is produced when 4.50 L of nitrogen reacts with excess hydrogen?
   a. 3.00 L   **b.** 9.00 L   **c.** 6.75 L   **d.** 4.50 L

Answers: 1. d; 2. c; 3. b

5.3 Avogadro's Number and the Mole

Learning Objectives ❯ Calculate the formula mass, molecular mass, or molar mass of a substance. ❯ Use Avogadro's number to determine the number of particles of different types in a mass of a substance.

Avogadro's hypothesis, which has been verified many times and in several ways over the years, states that equal volumes of gases at the same temperature and pressure contain equal numbers of molecules. This means that if we weigh equal volumes of different gases, the gases won't weigh the same. The ratio of their masses should be the same as the mass ratio of the molecules themselves. The challenge is that there is not always the option of using gases only when performing reactions. We need to extend this relationship to other forms of matter.

Avogadro's Number: 6.02×10^{23}

Avogadro had no way of knowing how many molecules were in a given volume of gas. Scientists since his time have determined the number of atoms in various weighed samples of substances. Atoms are so incredibly small that these numbers are extremely large, even for tiny samples. Recall that the mass of a carbon-12 atom is exactly 12 atomic mass units (u) (Section 2.4, page 49) because the carbon-12 atom sets the standard for atomic mass. The number of carbon-12 atoms in a 12-g sample of carbon-12 is called **Avogadro's number** and has been determined experimentally to be 6.0221367×10^{23}. We usually round this number to three significant figures: 6.02×10^{23}.

The Mole: "A Dozen Eggs and a Mole of Sugar, Please"

We buy socks by the pair (2 socks), eggs by the dozen (12 eggs), pencils by the gross (144 pencils), and paper by the ream (500 sheets of paper). We use these quantitative terms as constant measures and are comfortable with them. A dozen is the same number whether we are counting eggs or oranges. But a dozen eggs and a dozen oranges do not weigh the same. If an orange weighs five times as much as an egg, a dozen oranges will weigh five times as much as a dozen eggs. Furthermore, when we need to obtain large numbers of these items, we can do so easily. No one would want to purchase 2000 individual sheets of paper if it meant counting them out, but buying 4 reams of paper is easily done. Likewise, a baker might need to make hundreds of cakes and therefore need many dozens of eggs and can obtain them in multiples of a dozen.

   The sellers of many of those items will not want to sell them in fragments, however, so even if staff in an office wanted to buy 500 pencils, they would not typically be able to buy the exact number. They would instead have to purchase 4 gross of pencils (576 pencils) and have a surplus. Similarly, sometimes we have to deal with an excess amount of chemical components due to the whole-number ratios used in chemical equations.

   In the same way that an office manager may purchase paper by the ream and pencils by the gross, a chemist counts atoms and molecules by the *mole*. A single carbon atom is much too small to see or weigh, but a mole of carbon atoms fills a tablespoon and weighs 12 g. A mole of carbon and a mole of titanium each contain

► How big is Avogadro's number?

6.02 × 10²³ baseballs   roughly equals   Mass of the earth

6.02 × 10²³ drops of water   roughly equals   Mass of the oceans

the same number of atoms. But a titanium atom has a mass four times that of a carbon atom, so a mole of titanium has a mass four times that of a mole of carbon.

A **mole (mol)** is an amount of any substance or item that contains the same number of elementary units as there are atoms in exactly 12 g of carbon-12. That number is 6.02×10^{23}, Avogadro's number. The elementary units may be atoms (such as S or Ca), molecules (such as O_2 or CO_2), ions (such as K^+ or SO_4^{2-}), or any other kind of formula unit. A mole of NaCl, for example, contains 6.02×10^{23} NaCl formula units, which means that it contains 6.02×10^{23} Na^+ ions and 6.02×10^{23} Cl^- ions.

Formula Masses

Each element has a characteristic atomic mass. Because chemical compounds are made up of two or more elements, the masses of compounds are combinations of atomic masses. For any substance, the **formula mass** is the sum of the masses of the atoms represented in the formula. If the formula represents a molecule, the term *molecular mass* is often used. For example, because the formula CO_2 specifies one carbon atom and two oxygen atoms per molecule of carbon dioxide, the formula (or molecular) mass of carbon dioxide (CO_2) is the atomic mass of carbon plus twice the atomic mass of oxygen.

$$\text{Formula mass } CO_2 = 1 \times \text{atomic mass of C} + 2 \times \text{atomic mass of O}$$
$$= 1 \times 12.0\,u + 2 \times 16.0\,u = 44.0\,u$$

Example 5.3	Calculating Molecular Masses

Calculate **(a)** the molecular mass of sulfur dioxide (SO_2), a yellow-brown gas that is often associated with coal-burning power plants, and **(b)** the formula mass of ammonium sulfate [$(NH_4)_2SO_4$], a fertilizer commonly used by home gardeners.

Solution

a. We start with the molecular formula: SO_2. Then, to determine the molecular mass, we simply add the atomic mass of sulfur to twice the atomic mass of oxygen.

$$1 \times \text{atomic mass of S} = 1 \times 32.1\,u = 32.1\,u$$
$$2 \times \text{atomic mass of O} = 2 \times 16.0\,u = \underline{32.0\,u}$$
$$\text{Formula mass of } SO_2 = 64.1\,u$$

b. The formula $(NH_4)_2SO_4$ signifies two nitrogen atoms, eight hydrogen atoms, one sulfur atom, and four oxygen atoms. Combining the atomic masses, we have

$$(2 \times 14.0 \text{ u}) + (8 \times 1.01 \text{ u}) + (1 \times 32.0 \text{ u}) + (4 \times 16.0 \text{ u}) = 132.1 \text{ u}$$

■ EXERCISE 5.3

Calculate the formula mass of **(a)** sodium azide (NaN_3), used in automobile airbags, **(b)** propylene glycol $C_3H_8O_2$, used as a food preservative, **(c)** *para*-dichlorobenzene $(C_6H_4Cl_2)$, used as a moth repellent, and **(d)** calcium dihydrogen phosphate $[Ca(H_2PO_4)_2]$, used as a leavening agent in baked goods and pancake mixes.

Percent Composition of a Compound from Formula Masses

A chemical formula represents the ratio of atoms as well as a ratio of mass. This relationship allows us to be able to relate the mass to the number of particles and be able to express the information in a meaningful way for a variety of applications. For example, the mass of 1.00 mol CO_2 is 44.0 g, of which 12.0 g is carbon and 32.0 g is oxygen. The composition of CO_2 can be expressed as percentages by mass of carbon and of oxygen:

$$\% \text{ by mass C} = \frac{\text{mass C}}{\text{mass } CO_2} \times 100\% = \frac{12.0 \text{ g}}{44.0 \text{ g}} \times 100\% = 27.3\%$$

Because oxygen is the only other element in CO_2, its percent by mass is $100\% - 27.3\% = 72.7\%$ oxygen.

The idea of percent composition by mass is useful in several applications. Dietary sodium limits are usually indicated in milligrams of Na^+. We consume Na^+ mainly as sodium chloride. The American Heart Association (AHA) recommends a maximum intake of 2400 mg Na^+ per day. Example 5.4 shows how we can relate this amount to the NaCl in one teaspoon of table salt.

Example 5.4	Calculating Percent Composition from a Formula

What mass of Na^+ is present in one teaspoon (6.0 g) of NaCl? How does this compare to the maximum intake of 2400 mg Na^+ per day recommended by the AHA?

Solution
A mole of sodium chloride has 1 mole (23.0 g) Na^+ and 1 mole (35.5 g) Cl^-. The percent by mass of Na^+ is

$$\% \text{ by mass Na} = \frac{\text{mass Na}}{\text{mass NaCl}} \times 100\% = \frac{23.0 \text{ g}}{58.5 \text{ g}} \times 100\% = 39.3\%$$

So in 100 g of NaCl there are 39.3 g of Na^+. One teaspoon (6.0 g) of NaCl has

$$6.0 \text{ g NaCl} \times \frac{39.3 \text{ g Na}^+}{100 \text{ g NaCl}} = 2.4 \text{ g Na}^+$$

That is 2400 mg Na^+, the maximum recommended for one day's intake.

■ EXERCISE 5.4

Calculate the percent by mass of nitrogen in **(a)** $NaNO_3$ and **(b)** $(NH_4)_2S$.

Many environmental pollutants are reported as elements even when the actual pollutant is a compound or a mixture of compounds. For example, nitrates (NO_3^-) in groundwater (Chapter 14) are reported as parts per million nitrogen, and carbon dioxide emissions (Chapter 13) often are reported as tons of carbon. The idea of percent by mass is useful in understanding these reported quantities.

SELF-ASSESSMENT Questions

1. How many oxygen-16 atoms are there in exactly 16 g of oxygen-16?
   a. 1   **b.** 16   **c.** 256   **d.** 6.02×10^{23}

2. The mass of 1 mol of carbon-12 atoms is
   a. 12 g   **b.** 12.011 g   **c.** 12 u   **d.** 12.011 u

3. Which of the following has the smallest molecular mass?
   a. CH_4 **b.** HCl   **c.** H_2O **d.** PH_3

4. How many moles of sulfur atoms are in 1 mol $Cr(SO_4)_3$?
   a. 1 mol   **b.** 3 mol   **c.** 15 mol   **d.** 17 mol

5. How many moles of hydrogen atoms are present in 2.00 mol of water H_2O?
   a. 2.00 mol   **b.** 4.00 mol   **c.** 6.00 mol   **d.** 8.00 mol

6. Sodium chloride, by mass, is
   a. about 40% Na^+ and 60% Cl^-
   b. 50% Na^+ and 50% Cl^-
   c. about 60% Na^+ and 40% Cl^-
   d. 23.0% Na^+ and 35.5% Cl^-

5.4 Molar Mass: Mole-to-Mass and Mass-to-Mole Conversions

Learning Objectives ❯ Convert from mass to moles and from moles to mass of a substance. ❯ Calculate the mass or number of moles of a reactant or product from the mass or number of moles of another reactant or product.

By now, you should be able to see the usefulness of the relationship of moles to mass. Our ability to take a measurement of the mass of a substance and convert that value to a number of particles means that the chemical equation can be used not just as a guide to the reaction between equal volumes of gases or equal numbers of individual molecules. We can also scale the equation to any amount of a given substance. We just have to know how to apply the equations.

The **molar mass** of a substance is just what the name implies: the mass of 1 mole of that substance. The molar mass is numerically equal to the atomic mass, molecular mass, or formula mass, but it is expressed in the unit *grams per mole* (g/mol). The atomic mass of sodium is 23.0 u, so its molar mass is 23.0 g/mol. The molecular mass of carbon dioxide is 44.0 u; its molar mass is 44.0 g/mol. The formula mass of ammonium sulfate is 132.1 u; its molar mass is 132.1 g/mol. We can use these facts, together with the definition of the mole, to write the following relationships.

$$1 \text{ mol Na} = 23.0 \text{ g Na}$$

$$1 \text{ mol CO}_2 = 44.0 \text{ g CO}_2$$

$$1 \text{ mol (NH}_4)_2\text{SO}_4 = 132.1 \text{ g (NH}_4)_2\text{SO}_4$$

These relationships supply the conversion factors we need to convert between mass in grams and amount in moles, as illustrated in the following examples. It is important to note that these conversion factors represent equalities, which means that we can always invert them in the equations so that the units cancel appropriately.

Example 5.5 Conversions Involving Moles and Mass

(a) What mass in grams of CH_4 is 0.400 mole CH_4? **(b)** Calculate the number of moles of Na in a 62.5 g sample of sodium metal.

Solution

a. The molecular mass of CH_4 is 12.0 u + (4 × 1.0 u) = 16.0 u. The molar mass of CH_4 is therefore 16.0 g/mol. Using this molar mass as a conversion factor (red), we have

$$? \text{ g CH}_4 = 0.400 \text{ mol CH}_4 \times \frac{16.0 \text{ g CH}_4}{1 \text{ mol CH}_4} = 6.4 \text{ g CH}_4$$

b. The molar mass of Na is 23.0 g/mol. To convert from mass to moles, we must use the *inverse* of the molar mass as a conversion factor (1 mol Na/23.0 g Na) to cancel units of mass. When we start with grams, we must have grams in the denominator of our conversion factor (red).

$$? \text{ mol Na} = 62.5 \text{ g Na} \times \frac{1 \text{ mol Na}}{23.0 \text{ g Na}} = 2.72 \text{ mol Na}$$

▪ EXERCISE 5.5A

Calculate the mass, in grams, of **(a)** 0.0728 mol carbon, **(b)** 55.5 mol H_2O, and **(c)** 0.0728 mol $Ca(HSO_4)_2$.

▪ EXERCISE 5.5B

Calculate the amount, in moles, of **(a)** 3.71 g Fe, **(b)** 165 g C_5H_{12}, and **(c)** 0.100 g $Mg(NO_3)_2$.

Figure 5.5 shows 1-mole samples of several different substances. Each container holds Avogadro's number of formula units of the substance. That is, there are just as many sugar molecules in the largest dish as there are helium atoms in the balloon.

Mole and Mass Relationships in Chemical Equations

It is now time to put these important ideas together. We have learned the basics of balancing equations, and we have learned the importance of mole/mass conversions. Now, we can apply them in realistic situations.

Chemists, other scientists, and engineers are often confronted with questions such as "How much iron can be obtained from 1.0 ton of Fe_2O_3?" or "How much carbon dioxide is produced by burning 1000 g of propane?" There is no simple way to calculate the mass of one substance directly from the mass of another in the same reaction. Because chemical reactions involve atoms and molecules, quantities in reactions are calculated in moles of atoms, ions, or molecules. To do such calculations, it is necessary to convert grams of a substance to moles, as we did in Example 5.5. We also must write balanced equations to determine the relationship between moles.

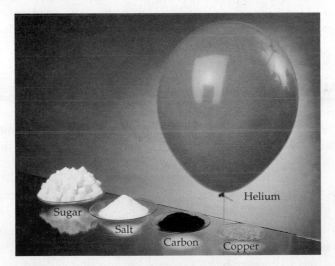

▲ **Figure 5.5** One mole of each of several familiar substances. From left to right on the table are sugar, salt, carbon, and copper. Behind them, the balloon contains helium. Each container holds Avogadro's number of elementary units of the substance. There are 6.02×10^{23} molecules of sugar, formula units of NaCl, and atoms of carbon, copper, and helium in the respective samples.

Q: *How many Na^+ ions and how many Cl^- ions are there in the dish of salt? If the balloon was filled with oxygen gas (O_2), how many oxygen atoms would it contain?*

▶ **Figure 5.6** We cannot weigh single atoms or molecules, but we can weigh equal numbers of these tiny particles.

One carbon atom (12 u) + One oxygen molecule (32 u) ⟶ One carbon dioxide molecule (44 u)

1.0 mol of carbon atoms
6.02×10^{23} carbon atoms
(12 g of carbon)

1.0 mol of oxygen molecules
6.02×10^{23} oxygen molecules
(32 g of oxygen)

1.0 mol of carbon dioxide molecules
6.02×10^{23} carbon dioxide molecules
(44 g of carbon dioxide)

We always start a problem of these types with our chemical equation. The balanced chemical equation is the recipe or guideline that we follow to solve the new and unknown equation. Recall that chemical equations provide ratios of atoms and molecules as well as ratios of moles. For example, the equation

$$C + O_2 \longrightarrow CO_2$$

tells us not only that one C atom reacts with one O_2 molecule (two atoms) to form one CO_2 molecule (one C atom and two O atoms). The equation also means that 1 mol (6.02×10^{23} atoms) of carbon reacts with 1 mol (6.02×10^{23} molecules) of oxygen to yield 1 mol (6.02×10^{23} molecules) of carbon dioxide. Because the molar mass in grams of a substance is numerically equal to the formula mass of the substance in atomic mass units, the equation can also tell us (indirectly) that 12.0 g (1 mol) C reacts with 32.0 g (1 mol) O_2 to yield 44.0 g (1 mol) CO_2 (Figure 5.6).

The crucial task is to maintain the *ratio* of masses. If the ratios are fixed, then we can always predict the outcomes. In the preceding reaction, the mass ratio of oxygen to carbon is 32.0:12.0, which could be simplified to 8.0:3.0 by reducing those values by a factor of 4. Likewise, the product would also be reduced by a factor of 4. Thus, 8.0 g O and 3.0 g C will produce 11.0 g CO_2. In fact, to calculate the amount of oxygen needed to react with a given amount of carbon, we need only multiply the amount of carbon by the factor 32.0:12.0. The following examples illustrate these relationships.

It DOES Matter!

If there is not enough oxygen gas to react completely with burning carbon, some of the carbon will be incompletely oxidized and deadly carbon monoxide will form. From 1999 to 2010, there were an average of 430 deaths per year from unintentional carbon monoxide poisoning in the United States. Many of these are caused by improperly ventilated heat sources used indoors, including fireplaces and wood-burning stoves.

CONCEPTUAL Example 5.6 ‖ Molecular, Molar, and Mass Relationships

Nitrogen monoxide (nitric oxide), an air pollutant discharged by internal combustion engines, combines with oxygen to form nitrogen dioxide, a yellowish-brown gas that irritates our respiratory systems and eyes. The equation for this reaction is

$$2\,NO + O_2 \longrightarrow 2\,NO_2$$

State the molecular, molar, and mass relationships indicated by this equation.

Solution

The molecular and molar relationships can be obtained directly from the equation; no calculation is necessary. The mass relationship requires a little simple calculation.

Molecular: Two molecules of NO react with one molecule of O_2 to form two molecules of NO_2.

Molar: 2 mol NO react with 1 mol O_2 to form 2 mol NO_2.

Mass: 60.0 g NO (2 mol NO $\times$ 30.0 g/mol) react with 32.0 g (1 mol O_2 $\times$ 32.0 g/mol) O_2 to form 92.0 g (2 mol NO_2 $\times$ 46.0 g/mol) NO_2.

▪ **EXERCISE 5.6**

Hydrogen sulfide, a gas that smells like rotten eggs, burns in air to produce sulfur dioxide and water according to the equation

$$2 H_2S + 3 O_2 \longrightarrow 2 SO_2 + 2 H_2O$$

State the molecular, molar, and mass relationships indicated by this equation.

Molar Relationships in Chemical Equations

As was mentioned earlier in the chapter, the quantitative relationship between reactants and products in a chemical reaction is called **stoichiometry**. The ratio of moles of reactants and products is given by the coefficients in a balanced chemical equation. Consider the combustion of butane, a common fuel for lighters

$$2 C_4H_{10} + 13 O_2 \longrightarrow 8 CO_2 + 10 H_2O$$

The coefficients in the balanced equation allow us to make statements such as

- 2 mol C_4H_{10} react with 13 mol O_2.
- 8 mol CO_2 are produced for every 2 mol C_4H_{10} that react.
- 10 mol H_2O are produced for every 8 mol CO_2 produced.

We can turn these statements into conversion factors known as stoichiometric factors. A **stoichiometric factor** relates the amounts, in *moles*, of any two substances involved in a chemical reaction. Note that we can set up stoichiometric factors for any two substances involved in a reaction. Also note that stoichiometric factors, because they come from the balanced equation for a reaction, involve small whole numbers. In the examples that follow, stoichiometric factors are shown in color.

Example 5.7 **Molar Relationships**

When 0.105 mol of propane is burned in a plentiful supply of oxygen, how many moles of oxygen are consumed?

$$C_3H_8 + 5 O_2 \longrightarrow 3 CO_2 + 4 H_2O$$

Solution

The balanced equation tells us that 5 mol O_2 are required to burn 1 mol C_3H_8. From this relationship, we can construct conversion factors to relate moles of oxygen to moles of propane. The possible conversion factors are

$$\frac{1 \text{ mol } C_3H_8}{5 \text{ mol } O_2} \quad \text{and} \quad \frac{5 \text{ mol } O_2}{1 \text{ mol } C_3H_8}$$

Which one do we use? Only if we multiply the given quantity (0.105 mol C_3H_8) by the factor on the *right* will the answer be expressed in the units requested (moles of oxygen).

$$? \text{ mol } O_2 = 0.105 \text{ mol } C_3H_8 \times \frac{5 \text{ mol } O_2}{1 \text{ mol } C_3H_8} = 0.525 \text{ mol } O_2$$

▪ **EXERCISE 5.7A**

Consider the combustion (burning) of propane presented in Example 5.7. **(a)** How many moles of CO_2 are formed when 1.250 mol C_3H_8 is burned? **(b)** How many moles of CO_2 are produced when 0.059 mol O_2 is consumed?

▪ EXERCISE 5.7B

For the combustion of propane in Example 5.7, suppose that 25.0 mol O_2 and 12.0 mol propane are combined. After reaction, which reactant will be used up, and how many moles of the other reactant will be left over? (*Hint:* Calculate the number of moles of propane that will react with the oxygen given. Is there enough propane?)

Mass Relationships in Chemical Equations

A chemical equation defines the stoichiometric relationship in terms of moles, but because we cannot directly measure moles in the laboratory, problems are seldom presented in terms of moles. Typically, you are given the mass (grams) of one substance and asked to calculate the mass of another substance that will react or can be produced. Such calculations involve several steps:

1. Write a balanced chemical equation for the reaction.
2. Determine the molar masses of the substances involved in the calculation.
3. Write down the given quantity and use the molar mass to convert this quantity to moles.
4. Use coefficients (stoichiometric relationship) from the balanced chemical equation to convert moles of the given substance to moles of the desired substance.
5. Use the molar mass to convert moles of the desired substance to grams of the desired substance.

If we know the quantity of any substance in an equation, we can determine the quantities of all the other substances. The conversion process is diagrammed in Figure 5.7. It is best learned by studying examples and working exercises.

▲ **Figure 5.7** We can use a chemical equation to relate the number of *moles* of any two substances represented in the equation. These substances may be a reactant and a product, two reactants, or two products. We cannot directly relate the mass of one substance to the mass of another substance involved in the same reaction. To obtain *mass* relationships, we must convert the mass of each substance to moles, relate moles of one substance to moles of the other through a stoichiometric factor, and then convert moles of the second substance to its mass.

Example 5.8	Mass Relationships

Calculate the mass of oxygen needed to react with 5.00 g of carbon in the reaction that forms carbon dioxide.

Solution

Step 1. The balanced equation is

$$C + O_2 \longrightarrow CO_2$$

Step 2. The molar masses are 12.0 g/mol for C and $2 \times 16.0 = 32.0$ g/mol for O_2.

Step 3. We convert the given mass of carbon to an amount in moles.

$$5.0 \text{ g C} \times \frac{1 \text{ mol C}}{12.0 \text{ g C}} = 0.417 \text{ mol C}$$

Step 4. We use coefficients from the balanced equation to establish the stoichiometric factor (red) that relates the amount of oxygen to that of carbon.

$$0.417 \text{ mol C} \times \frac{1 \text{ mol O}_2}{1 \text{ mol C}} = 0.417 \text{ mol O}_2$$

Step 5. We convert from moles of oxygen to grams of oxygen.

$$0.417 \text{ mol O}_2 \times \frac{32.0 \text{ g O}_2}{1 \text{ mol O}_2} = 13.3 \text{ g O}_2$$

We can also combine the five steps into a single setup. Note that the units in the denominators of the conversion factors are chosen so that each cancels the unit in the numerator of the preceding term.

We start here	This converts g C to mol C	This relates mol C to mol O$_2$	This converts mol O$_2$ to g O$_2$	The answer: the number and the unit

$$5.0 \text{ g C} \times \frac{1 \text{ mol C}}{12.0 \text{ g C}} \times \frac{1 \text{ mol O}_2}{1 \text{ mol C}} \times \frac{32.0 \text{ g O}_2}{1 \text{ mol O}_2} = 13.3 \text{ g O}_2$$

■ EXERCISE 5.8A

Calculate the mass of oxygen (O$_2$) needed to react with 1.505 g nitrogen (N$_2$) in the reaction that forms nitrogen dioxide.

■ EXERCISE 5.8B

Calculate the mass of carbon dioxide formed by burning 355 g each of **(a)** methane (CH$_4$) and **(b)** pentane (C$_5$H$_{12}$) in oxygen gas. (*Hint:* The reaction in Example 5.7 may help in balancing the equations.)

1. How can a car make more pollution than the gasoline it uses?

A mole of carbon (12 g) combines with oxygen from the atmosphere to form a mole of carbon dioxide (44 g). Gasoline is mostly carbon by weight, so the mass of carbon dioxide formed is greater than the mass of gasoline burned. Carbon dioxide is a major greenhouse gas (Chapter 13).

SELF-ASSESSMENT Questions

1. The mass of 4.65 mol H$_2$SO$_4$ is
   a. 314 g
   b. 456 g
   c. 466 g
   d. 564 g

2. For which of the following would a 10.0-g sample contain the most moles?
   a. Co   b. F   c. Se   d. P

3. How many moles of CO$_2$ are there in 1 lb (453.6 g) CO$_2$?
   a. 0.0969 mol
   b. 9.20 mol
   c. 10.3 mol
   d. 14.2 mol

4. How many moles of benzene (C$_6$H$_6$) are there in a 7.8-g sample of benzene?
   a. 0.100 mol
   b. 1.00 mol
   c. 7.81 mol
   d. 610 mol

Items 5–7 refer to the equation 2 H$_2$ + O$_2$ ⟶ 2 H$_2$O.

5. At the molar level, the equation means that
   a. 2 mol H react with 1 mol O to form 2 mol H$_2$O
   b. 4 mol H react with 2 mol O to form 4 mol H$_2$O
   c. 2 mol H$_2$ react with 1 mol O$_2$ to form 2 mol H$_2$O
   d. 2 mol O$_2$ react with 1 mol H$_2$ to form 2 mol H$_2$O

6. How many moles of water can be formed from 0.500 mol H$_2$?
   a. 0.500 mol
   b. 1.00 mol
   c. 2.00 mol
   d. 4.00 mol

7. How many moles of oxygen (O$_2$) are required to form 0.222 mol H$_2$O?
   a. 0.111 mol
   b. 0.222 mol
   c. 0.444 mol
   d. 1.00 mol

Answers: 1. b; 2. b; 3. c; 4. a; 5. c; 6. a; 7. a

It DOES Matter!

The ethanol content of a beverage is almost always expressed by *volume* (see Example 5.13A). This may be done partly as a marketing ploy. Ethanol is about 20% less dense than water, so a beverage that is labeled "12% alcohol by volume" is only about 10% ethanol by weight. The higher percent by volume may make purchasers think they are getting "more for the money."

5.5 Solutions

Learning Objectives ❯ Calculate the concentration (molarity, percent by volume, or percent by mass) of a solute in a solution. ❯ Calculate the amount of solute or solution given the concentration and the other amount.

Many chemical reactions take place in solutions because the chemical components are more readily exchanged. A **solution** is a homogeneous mixture of two or more substances. The substance being dissolved is the *solute*, and the substance doing the dissolving is the *solvent*. The solvent is usually present in greater quantity than the solute. There are many solvents: Kerosene dissolves grease; ethanol dissolves many drugs; isopentyl acetate, a component of banana oil, is a solvent for model airplane glue.

Water is no doubt the most familiar solvent, dissolving as it does many common substances such as sugar, salt, and ethanol. We focus our discussion here on **aqueous solutions**, those in which water is the solvent, and we take a more quantitative look at the relationship between solute and solvent.

Solution Concentrations

We say that some substances, such as sugar and salt, are *soluble* in water. Of course, there is a limit to the quantity of sugar or salt that we can dissolve in a given volume of water. Yet we still find it convenient to say that they are soluble in water because an appreciable quantity dissolves. Other substances, such as a copper penny or glass (silicon dioxide), we consider to be *insoluble* because their solubility in water is near zero. Such terms as *soluble* and *insoluble* are useful, but they are imprecise and must be used with care.

Two other roughly estimated but sometimes useful terms are *dilute* and *concentrated*. A **dilute solution** is one that contains a relatively small amount of solute in lots of solvent. For example, a pinch of sugar in a cup of tea makes a dilute, faintly sweet, sugar solution. A **concentrated solution** is one with a relatively large amount of solute dissolved in a small amount of solvent. Pancake syrup, with lots of sugar solute in a relatively small amount of water, is a concentrated, and very sweet, solution.

Scientific work generally requires more precise concentration units than "a pinch of sugar in a cup of tea." Further, quantitative work often requires the *mole* unit because substances enter into chemical reactions according to *molar* ratios.

Molarity

A concentration unit that chemists often use is *molarity*. For reactions involving solutions, the amount of solute is usually measured in moles and the quantity of solution in liters or milliliters. The **molarity (M)** is the amount of solute, in moles, per liter of solution.

$$\text{Molarity (M)} = \frac{\text{moles of solute}}{\text{liters of solution}}$$

Example 5.9	Solution Concentration: Molarity and Moles

Calculate the molarity of a solution made by dissolving 3.50 mol NaCl in enough water to produce 2.00 L of solution.

Solution

$$\text{Molarity (M)} = \frac{\text{moles of solute}}{\text{liters of solution}} = \frac{3.50 \text{ mol NaCl}}{2.00 \text{ L solution}} = 1.75 \text{ M NaCl}$$

We read 1.75 M NaCl as "1.75 molar sodium chloride."

■ EXERCISE 5.9A

Calculate the molarity of a solution that has 0.0400 mol NH_3 in 5.95 L of solution.

■ EXERCISE 5.9B

Calculate the molarity of a solution made by dissolving 0.850 mol H_2SO_4 in enough water to produce 775 mL of solution.

Usually, when preparing a solution, we must *weigh* the solute. Balances do not display units of moles, so we usually work with a given mass and divide by the molar mass of the substance, as illustrated in Example 5.10.

Example 5.10	Solution Concentration: Molarity and Mass

What is the molarity of a solution in which 333 g potassium hydrogen carbonate is dissolved in enough water to make 10.0 L of solution?

Solution

First, we must convert grams of $KHCO_3$ to moles of $KHCO_3$.

$$333 \text{ g } \cancel{KHCO_3} \times \frac{1 \text{ mol KHCO}_3}{100.1 \text{ g } \cancel{KHCO_3}} = 3.33 \text{ mol KHCO}_3$$

Next, we use this value as the numerator in the defining equation for molarity. The solution volume, 10.0 L, is the denominator.

$$\text{Molarity} = \frac{3.33 \text{ mol KHCO}_3}{10.0 \text{ L solution}} = 0.333 \text{ M KHCO}_3$$

■ EXERCISE 5.10A

Calculate the molarity of **(a)** 18.0 g H_3PO_4 in 2.00 L of solution and **(b)** 3.00 g KCl in 2.39 L of solution.

■ EXERCISE 5.10B

Calculate the molarity of 0.309 g HF in 1752 mL of solution. HF is used for etching glass.

Often, we need to know the *mass* of solute required to prepare a given volume of a solution of a particular molarity. In such calculations, we can use molarity as a conversion factor between moles of solute and liters of solution. For instance, in Example 5.11, the expression "0.15 M NaCl" means 0.15 mol NaCl per liter of solution, expressed as the conversion factor

$$\frac{0.15 \text{ mol NaCl}}{1 \text{ L solution}}$$

Example 5.11	Solution Preparation: Molarity

What mass in grams of NaCl is required to prepare 0.500 L of typical over-the-counter saline solution (about 0.15 M NaCl)?

Solution

First, we use the molarity as a conversion factor to calculate moles of NaCl.

$$0.500 \text{ L } \cancel{\text{solution}} \times \frac{0.15 \text{ mol NaCl}}{1 \text{ L } \cancel{\text{solution}}} = 0.075 \text{ mol NaCl}$$

Then, we use the molar mass to calculate grams of NaCl.

$$0.75 \text{ mol NaCl} \times \frac{58.5 \text{ g NaCl}}{1 \text{ mol NaCl}} = 44 \text{ g NaCl}$$

■ EXERCISE 5.11

What mass in grams of potassium hydroxide is required to prepare **(a)** 1.500 L of 4.00 M KOH and **(b)** 200.0 mL of 1.00 M KOH?

2. What's the difference between .925 silver and .800 silver?

The purity of silver is rated as an expression of a decimal part of 1 representing pure silver. Greater than .925 silver is often referred to as *sterling* silver. 92.5% silver has .925 g of silver atoms for every 1.000 g of the alloy. 80.0% silver has .800 g of silver for every 1.000 g of the alloy. Items made of silver alloys are different from silver-plated items.

▲ Rubbing alcohol is a water–isopropyl alcohol solution that is 70% isopropyl alcohol [(CH$_3$)$_2$CHOH] by volume.

Quite often, solutions of known molarity are available commercially. For example, concentrated hydrochloric acid is 12 M. How would you determine the *volume* of this solution that contains a certain number of moles of solute? We can again rearrange the definition of molarity to obtain the volume.

$$\text{Liters of solution} = \frac{\text{moles of solute}}{\text{molarity}}$$

Example 5.12 Moles from Molarity and Volume

Concentrated hydrochloric acid is 12.0 M HCl. What volume in milliliters of this solution contains 0.425 mol HCl?

Solution

$$\text{Liters of solution} = \frac{\text{moles of solute}}{\text{molarity}} = \frac{0.425 \text{ mol HCl}}{12.0 \text{ M HCl}}$$

$$= \frac{0.425 \text{ mol HCl}}{12.0 \text{ mol HCl/L}} = 0.0354 \text{ L}$$

In this case, 0.0354 L (35.4 mL) of the solution contains 0.425 mol of the solute. Remember that molarity is moles per liter of *solution*, not per liter of solvent.

■ EXERCISE 5.12A

What volume in milliliters of 18.0 M glacial acetic acid (HC$_2$H$_3$O$_2$) solution contains 0.445 mol (HC$_2$H$_3$O$_2$)?

■ EXERCISE 5.12B

What mass in grams of HNO$_3$ is in 500 mL of acid rain that has a concentration of 2.00×10^{-5} M HNO$_3$?

Percent Concentrations

For many practical applications, including those in medicine and pharmacy, solution concentrations are often expressed in percentages. There are different ways to express percentages, depending on whether mass or volume is being measured. If both solute and solvent are liquids, **percent by volume** is often used because liquid volumes are easily measured.

$$\text{Percent by volume} = \frac{\text{volume of solute}}{\text{volume of solution}} \times 100\%$$

In calculating percent by volume, we can measure the solute and solution in any unit of volume as long as we use the same unit for both. For example, we can measure both volumes in milliliters or in gallons. Ethanol (CH$_3$CH$_2$OH) for medicinal purposes is 95% by volume. That is, it consists of 95 mL CH$_3$CH$_2$OH per 100 mL of aqueous solution.

Example 5.13 Percent by Volume

Two-stroke engines, commonly used in such equipment as chainsaws and lawn-mowers, use a mixture of 120 mL of oil dissolved in enough gasoline to make 4.0 L of fuel. What is the percent by volume of oil in this mixture?

Solution

$$\text{Percent by volume} = \frac{120 \text{ mL oil}}{4000 \text{ mL solution}} \times 100\% = 3.0\%$$

■ EXERCISE 5.13A
What is the volume percent of ethanol in a solution of 845 mL of an ethanol–water solution that contains 90.0 mL of water?

■ EXERCISE 5.13B
Determine the volume percent of toluene ($C_6H_5CH_3$) in a solution made by mixing 35.5 mL of toluene with 80.0 mL of benzene (C_6H_6). Assume that the volumes are additive.

Many commercial solutions are labeled with the concentration in **percent by mass**. For example, sulfuric acid is sold in several concentrations: 35.7% H_2SO_4 for use in storage batteries, 77.7% H_2SO_4 for the manufacture of phosphate fertilizers, and 93.2% H_2SO_4 for pickling steel. Each of these percentages is by mass: 35.7 g of H_2SO_4 per 100 g of sulfuric acid solution, and so on.

$$\text{Percent by mass} = \frac{\text{mass of solute}}{\text{mass of solution}} \times 100\%$$

As with percent by volume, we can express the masses of solute and solution in any mass unit, as long as we use the same unit for both.

▲ "Reagent grade" concentrated hydrochloric acid is a 38% by mass solution of HCl in water.

Example 5.14 Percent by Mass

What is the percent by mass of NaCl if 25.5 g of it is dissolved in 425 g (425 mL) of water?

Solution
We use these values in the above percent-by-mass equation:

$$\text{Percent by mass} = \frac{25.5 \text{ g NaCl}}{(25.5 + 425) \text{ g solution}} \times 100\% = 5.66\% \text{ NaCl}$$

■ EXERCISE 5.14A
Hydrogen peroxide solution for home use is 3.0% by mass of H_2O_2 in water. What is the percent by mass of a solution of 8.95 g H_2O_2 dissolved in 425 g (425 mL) of water?

■ EXERCISE 5.14B
Sodium hydroxide (NaOH, lye) is used to make soap and is quite soluble in water. What is the percent by mass of NaOH in a solution that contains 1.00 kg NaOH in 1025 mL water?

3. Does 2% milk have just 2% of the calories of whole milk?
No. Whole milk contains at least 3.25% butterfat by mass. Some of the butterfat is removed to make 2% milk, which is 2% butterfat by mass. Actually, 2% milk has about 75% of the calories of whole milk.

It DOES Matter!

An isotonic, or "normal," intravenous solution must have the proper concentration of solute to avoid damage to blood cells.

4. What does a toxicity rating (LD$_{50}$) of 100 ppm mean?

The LD$_{50}$ designation means the median lethal dose, the dosage of a substance that would result in fatality for 50% of the organisms tested. A 100 ppm or parts per million measurement means that there would only have to be 100 milligrams of the toxic substance per 1 kilogram of an organism's body weight.

Example 5.15 Solution Preparation: Percent by Mass

Describe how to make 430 g of an aqueous solution that is 4.85% by mass NaNO$_3$.

Solution

We begin by rearranging the equation for percent by mass to solve for mass of solute.

$$\text{Mass of solute} = \frac{\text{percent by mass} \times \text{mass of solution}}{100\%}$$

Substituting, we have

$$\frac{4.85\% \times 430\ g}{100\%} = 20.9\ g$$

We would weigh out 20.9 g NaNO$_3$ and add enough water to make 430 g of solution.

▪ **EXERCISE 5.15A**

Describe how you would prepare 250 g of an aqueous solution that is 4.50% glucose by mass.

▪ **EXERCISE 5.15B**

Describe how you would prepare 1250 g of *isotonic saline*, a commonly used intravenous (IV) solution that is 0.89% sodium chloride by mass.

Note that for percent concentrations, the mass or volume of the solute needed doesn't depend on what the solute is. A 10% by mass solution of NaOH contains 10 g NaOH per 100 g of solution. Similarly, 10% HCl and 10% (NH$_4$)$_2$SO$_4$ and 10% C$_{110}$H$_{190}$N$_3$O$_2$Br each contain 10 g of the specified solute per 100 g of solution. For *molar* solutions, however, the mass of solute in a solution of specified molarity is different for different solutes. A liter of 0.10 M solution requires 4.0 g (0.10 mol) NaOH, 3.7 g (0.10 mol) HCl, 13.2 g (0.10 mol) (NH$_4$)$_2$SO$_4$, or 166 g (0.10 mol) C$_{110}$H$_{190}$N$_3$O$_2$Br.

SELF-ASSESSMENT Questions

1. In a solution of 85.0 g water and 5.0 g sucrose (C$_{12}$H$_{22}$O$_{11}$), the
   a. solute is sucrose and the solution is the solvent
   b. solute is sucrose and the solvent is water
   c. solute is water and sucrose is the solvent
   d. water and sucrose are both solutes

2. What is the molarity of a sodium hydroxide solution having 0.500 mol NaOH in 62.5 mL of solution?
   a. 0.00200 M
   b. 0.200 M
   c. 2.00 M
   d. 8.00 M

3. How many moles of sugar are required to make 2.00 L of 0.600 M sugar solution?
   a. 1.20 mol   b. 2.40 mol   c. 24.0 mol   d. 6.67 mol

4. What mass of NaCl in grams is needed to prepare 2.500 L of a 0.800 M NaCl solution?
   a. 2.00 g   b. 4.00 g   c. 58.5 g   d. 117 g

5. What volume of 6.00 M HCl solution contains 1.80 mol HCl?
   a. 250 mL   b. 300 mL   c. 900 mL   d. 9.00 L

6. What is the percent by volume of ethanol in a solution made by adding 50.0 mL of pure ethanol to enough water to make 250 mL of solution?
   a. 16.7%   b. 20.0%   c. 25.0%   d. 80.0%

7. A solution contains 15.0 g sucrose and 60.0 g of water. What is the percent by mass of sucrose in the solution?
   a. 15.0%   b. 20.0%   c. 25.0%   d. 80.0%

8. What volume of water should be added to 23.4 g NaCl to make 100.0 mL of 4.00 M NaCl solution?
   a. 76.6 mL
   b. 96.0 mL
   c. 100.0 mL
   d. enough to make 100.0 mL of solution

Answers: 1, b; 2, d; 3, a; 4, d; 5, b; 6, b; 7, b; 8, d

GREEN CHEMISTRY

Margaret Kerr, *Worcester State University*

Atom Economy

Learning Objectives ❯ Explain how the concept of atom economy can be applied to pollution prevention and environmental protection. ❯ Calculate the atom economy for chemical reactions.

Imagine yourself in the future. Your job is related to environmental protection, which requires that you provide information to practicing chemists as they design new processes and reactions. Waste management is one of your top concerns. Although waste typically has been addressed only after production of desired commodities, you realize that a greener approach can mean minimizing the waste from the start. What methods would you use in this job? What topics are important? How can chemists provide new products while protecting the environment?

Intrinsic in greener approaches to waste management is the concept of *atom economy*, a calculation of the number of atoms conserved in the desired product rather than gone in waste. In 1998, Barry Trost of Stanford University won a Presidential Green Chemistry Challenge Award for his work in developing this concept. By calculating the number of atoms that will not become part of the desired product and, therefore, will enter the waste stream, chemists can precisely determine the minimum amount of waste that will be produced by chemicals used in a reaction before even running the reaction.

You have learned how to write and balance chemical equations (Section 5.1) and you also can calculate molar mass, convert from mass to moles, and determine the amount of product formed from given amounts of reactants (Sections 5.3, 5.4). Other ways of calculating the efficiency of a reaction have traditionally been expressed using *theoretical yield*, *experimental yield*, and *percent yield*. The theoretical yield is the maximum amount of desired product that can be produced by the amounts of reactants used. Under laboratory conditions, the theoretical yield of a reaction is not usually obtained. The actual amount of desired product collected is called the experimental yield. Chemists often express their experimental results in percent yield, which is simply the experimental yield divided by the theoretical yield, then multiplied by 100%.

$$\% \text{ yield} = \frac{\text{experimental yield}}{\text{theoretical yield}} = 100\%$$

A report of a 100% yield for a reaction seems good, but the percent yield considers only the desired product. Any other substance formed (for instance, a by-product) is not counted in the percent yield. By-products often become part of the chemical waste stream. Some reactions produce more by-products than desired products.

Atom economy is a better way to measure reaction efficiency. Percent atom economy (% A.E.) measures the proportion of the atoms in the reaction mixture that actually become part of the desired product. Reactant atoms that do not appear in the product are considered waste. The % A.E. is given by the following relationship:

$$\% \text{ A.E.} = \frac{\text{molar mass of desired product}}{\text{molar masses of all reactants}} \times 100\%$$

A reaction can have a poor atom economy even when the percent yield is near 100%.

Consider the following two ways to make butene (C_4H_8), a compound that is an important chemical feedstock in the plastics industry. First, butene can be made using butylbromide (C_4H_9Br) and sodium hydroxide (NaOH).

$$C_4H_9Br + NaOH \longrightarrow C_4H_8 + H_2O + NaBr$$

In this reaction, a Br atom and a H atom are eliminated from the butylbromide to form the final product. Generally, in reactions like this one, only one product is desired and all other products are not used.

We can calculate the atom economy for this reaction.

$$\% \text{ A.E.} = \frac{\text{molar mass } C_4H_8}{\text{molar mass } C_4H_9Br + \text{molar mass NaOH}} \times 100\%$$

$$\% \text{ A.E.} = \frac{56.11 \text{ g/mol}}{137.02 \text{ g/mol} + 40.00 \text{ g/mol}} \times 100\% = 31.7\%$$

These elimination reactions never have 100% atom economy because there is always a by-product. This results in some atoms going into the waste stream.

Butene can also be made using butyne (C_4H_6) and hydrogen gas (H_2):

$$C_4H_6 + H_2 \longrightarrow C_4H_8$$

In this reaction, all of the atoms in both reactants appear in the desired product and none go into the waste stream. The percent atom economy is 100%.

$$\% \text{ A.E.} = \frac{\text{molar mass } C_4H_8}{\text{molar mass } C_4H_6 + \text{molar mass } H_2} = 100\%$$

$$\% \text{ A.E.} = \frac{56.11 \text{ g/mol}}{54.09 \text{ g/mol} + 2.02 \text{ g/mol}} \times 100\% = 100\%$$

Because the concept of atom economy offers a way to predict waste, it can lead to innovative design processes that eliminate or minimize waste. By focusing on waste from the beginning of the reaction, we reduce or eliminate cleanup at the end.

157

SUMMARY

Section 5.1—A **chemical equation** is shorthand for a chemical change, using symbols and formulas instead of words: for example, $C + O_2 \longrightarrow CO_2$. Substances to the left of the arrow are starting materials, or **reactants**; those to the right of the arrow are **products**, or what the reaction produces. Physical states may be indicated with (s), (l), or (g). Because matter is conserved, a chemical equation must be balanced. It must have the same numbers and types of atoms on each side. Equations are balanced by placing coefficients in front of the formula for each reactant or product; we do *not* balance an equation by changing the formulas of reactants or products. The balanced equation $2\ NaN_3 \longrightarrow 2\ Na + 3\ N_2$ means that two formula units of NaN_3 react to give two atoms of Na and three molecules of N_2.

Section 5.2—Gay-Lussac's experiments led him to the **law of combining volumes**: At a given temperature and pressure, the volumes of gaseous reactants and products are in a small whole-number ratio (such as 1:1, 2:1, 4:3). **Avogadro's hypothesis** explained this law by stating that equal volumes of all gases contain the same number of molecules at fixed temperature and pressure.

Section 5.3—**Avogadro's number** is defined as the number of ^{12}C atoms in exactly 12 g of ^{12}C, that is, 6.02×10^{23} atoms. A **mole (mol)** is the amount of a substance that contains Avogadro's number of elementary units—atoms, molecules, or formula units, depending on the substance. The **formula mass** is the sum of masses of the atoms represented in the formula of a substance. If the formula represents a molecule, the term *molecular mass* often is used. A formula represents a mass ratio as well as an atom ratio, and the composition by mass of a compound may be calculated from the formula.

Section 5.4—The **molar mass** is the mass of one mole of a substance. Molar mass has the same number as formula mass, molecular mass, or atomic mass but is expressed in units of grams per mole (g/mol). Molar mass is used to convert from grams to moles of a substance, and vice versa. A balanced equation can be read in terms of atoms and molecules or in terms of moles. **Stoichiometry**, or mass relationships in chemical reactions, can be found by using **stoichiometric factors**, which relate moles of one substance to moles of another. Stoichiometric factors can be obtained without calculation, directly from the balanced equation. To evaluate mass relationships in chemical reactions, molar masses and stoichiometric factors are both used as conversion factors.

Section 5.5—A **solution** is a homogeneous mixture of two or more substances, often consisting of a solute dissolved in a solvent. A substance is soluble in a solvent if some appreciable quantity of the substance dissolves in the solvent. Any substance that does not dissolve significantly in a solvent is insoluble in that solvent. An **aqueous solution**, indicated by the label (aq), has water as the solvent. The concentration of a solution can be expressed in many ways. A **concentrated solution** has a relatively large amount of solute compared to solvent, and a **dilute solution** has only a little solute in a large amount of solvent. One quantitative unit of concentration is **molarity (M)**, moles of solute dissolved per liter of solution.

$$\text{Molarity (M)} = \frac{\text{moles of solute}}{\text{liters of solution}}$$

There are several ways to express concentration using percentages. Two important ones are **percent by volume** and **percent by mass**.

$$\text{Percent by volume} = \frac{\text{volume of solute}}{\text{volume of solution}} \times 100\%$$

$$\text{Percent by mass} = \frac{\text{mass of solute}}{\text{mass of solution}} \times 100\%$$

For each concentration unit, if we know two of the three terms in the equation, we can solve for the third.

GREEN CHEMISTRY Atom economy is an important component of green chemistry and waste prevention. By strategically designing reactions to maximize the number of atoms used, a chemist has the ability to reduce waste production.

Learning Objectives

› Identify balanced and unbalanced chemical equations, and balance equations by inspection. (5.1)	Problems 4, 11–16, 51–53, 62
› Determine volumes of gases that react, using a balanced equation for a reaction. (5.2)	Problems 2, 3, 17–22, 55
› Calculate the formula mass, molecular mass, or molar mass of a substance. (5.3)	Problems 27–34
› Use Avogadro's number to determine the number of particles of different types in a mass of a substance. (5.3)	Problems 23–26
› Convert from mass to moles and from moles to mass of a substance. (5.4)	Problem 71
› Calculate the mass or number of moles of a reactant or product from the mass or number of moles of another reactant or product. (5.4)	Problems 35–38, 54, 56–58, 62, 69
› Calculate the concentration (molarity, percent by volume, or percent by mass) of a solute in a solution. (5.5)	Problems 39–50, 60, 61
› Calculate the amount of solute or solution given the concentration and the other amount. (5.5)	Problems 59, 64, 65
› Explain how the concept of atom economy can be applied to pollution prevention and environmental protection.	Problem 73
› Calculate the atom economy for chemical reactions.	Problems 72–75

REVIEW QUESTIONS

1. Define or illustrate each of the following.
   a. formula unit   b. formula mass
   c. mole   d. Avogadro's number
   e. molar mass   f. molar volume (of a gas)

2. Explain the difference between the atomic mass of chlorine and the formula mass of chlorine gas.

3. What is Avogadro's hypothesis? How does it explain Gay-Lussac's law of combining volumes?

4. Referring to the law of conservation of mass, explain why we must work with balanced chemical equations.

5. Define or explain and illustrate the following terms.
   a. solution   b. solvent
   c. solute   d. aqueous solution

6. Define or explain and illustrate the following terms.
   a. concentrated solution   b. dilute solution
   c. soluble   d. insoluble

 PROBLEMS

Interpreting Formulas

7. How many oxygen atoms does each of the following contain?
   a. $Al(H_2PO_4)_3$ b. $HOC_6H_4COOCH_3$
   c. $(BiO)_2SO_4$

8. How many carbon atoms does each of the following contain?
   a. $Fe_2(C_2O_4)_3$ b. $Al(CH_3COO)_3$
   c. $(CH_3)_3CCH(CH_3)_2$

9. How many atoms of each element (N, P, H, and O) does the notation $3 (NH_4)_2HPO_4$ indicate?

10. How many atoms of each element (Fe, C, H, and O) does the notation $4 Fe(HOOCCH_2COO)_3$ indicate?

Interpreting Chemical Equations

11. Consider the following equation. (a) Explain its meaning at the molecular level. (b) Interpret it in terms of moles. (c) State the mass relationships conveyed by the equation.
$$2 H_2O_2 \longrightarrow 2 H_2O + O_2$$

12. Express each chemical equation in terms of moles.
   a. $2 Mg + O_2 \longrightarrow 2 MgO$
   b. $2 C_2H_6 + 7 O_2 \longrightarrow 4 CO_2 + 6 H_2O$

Balancing Chemical Equations

13. Balance the following equations.
   a. $Mg + O_2 \longrightarrow MgO$
   b. $C_3H_8 + O_2 \longrightarrow CO_2 + H_2O$
   c. $H_2 + Ta_2O_3 \longrightarrow Ta + H_2O$

14. Balance the following equations.
   a. $K + O_2 \longrightarrow K_2O_2$
   b. $FeCl_2 + Na_2SiO_3 \longrightarrow NaCl + FeSiO_3$
   c. $F_2 + AlCl_3 \longrightarrow AlF_3 + Cl_2$

15. Write balanced equations for the following processes.
   a. Nitrogen gas and oxygen gas react to form nitrogen oxide (NO).
   b. Ozone (O_3) decomposes into oxygen gas.
   c. Uranium(IV) oxide reacts with hydrogen fluoride (HF) to form uranium(IV) fluoride and water.

16. Write balanced equations for the following processes.
   a. Aluminum metal reacts with oxygen gas to form aluminum oxide.
   b. Calcium carbonate (the active ingredient in many antacids) reacts with stomach acid (HCl) to form calcium chloride, water, and carbon dioxide.
   c. Hexane (C_6H_{14}) burns in oxygen gas to form carbon dioxide and water.

Volume Relationships in Chemical Equations

17. Make a sketch similar to Figure 5.3 to show the reaction of hydrogen gas with oxygen gas to form steam [$H_2O(g)$] at 100 °C.

18. Make a sketch similar to Figure 5.3 to show that when hydrogen reacts with oxygen to form steam at 100 °C, each volume of gas—hydrogen, oxygen, or steam—contains the same number of molecules.

19. Consider the following equation, which represents the combustion (burning) of heptane (C_7H_{16}).
$$C_7H_{16}(g) + 11 O_2(g) \longrightarrow 7 CO_2(g) + 8 H_2O(g)$$
   a. What volume, in liters, of $CO_2(g)$ is formed when 20.6 L of $C_7H_{16}(g)$ is burned? Assume that both gases are measured under the same conditions.
   b. What volume, in milliliters, of $C_7H_{16}(g)$ has to burn to react with 29.0 mL $O_2(g)$? Assume that both gases are measured under the same conditions.

20. Consider the following equation, which represents the combustion of ammonia.
$$4 NH_3(g) + 3 O_2(g) \longrightarrow 2 N_2(g) + 6 H_2Og)$$
   a. What volume, in liters, of $N_2(g)$ is formed when 125 L of $NH_3(g)$ is burned? Assume that both gases are measured under the same conditions.
   b. What volume, in liters, of $O_2(g)$ is required to form 36 L of $H_2O(g)$? Assume that both gases are measured under the same conditions.

21. Using the equation in Problem 19, determine the ratio of volume of $CO_2(g)$ formed to volume of $C_7H_{16}(g)$ that reacts, assuming that both gases are measured under the same conditions.

22. Using the equation in Problem 20, determine the ratio of volume of $H_2O(g)$ formed to volume of $NH_3(g)$ that reacts, assuming that both gases are measured under the same conditions.

Avogadro's Number

23. How many **(a)** sulfur *molecules* and how many **(b)** sulfur *atoms* are there in 1.00 mol S_8?

24. How many **(a)** calcium ions and how many **(b)** nitride ions are there in 1.00 mol Ca_3N_2?

25. Choose one of the following to complete this statement correctly: One *mole* of bromine (Br_2) gas _____.
    a. has a mass of 79.9 g
    b. contains 6.02×10^{23} Br atoms
    c. contains 12.04×10^{23} Br atoms
    d. has a mass of 6.02×10^{23} g

26. **(a)** How many barium ions and how many nitrate ions are there in 1.00 mol $Ba(NO_3)_2$? **(b)** How many nitrogen atoms and how many oxygen atoms are there in 1.00 mol $Ba(NO_3)_2$?

Formula Masses and Molar Masses

You may round atomic masses to one decimal place.

27. Calculate the molar mass of each of the following compounds.
    a. $AgNO_3$ **b.** $Mg(ClO)_2$
    c. $Zn(lO_4)_2$ **d.** $CH_3(CH_2)_3COF$

28. Calculate the molar mass of each of the following compounds.
    a. Bi_2O_3 **b.** $FeSO_4$
    c. $Ca(CH_3COO)_2$ **d.** $(NH_4)_2Cr_2O_7$

29. Calculate the mass, in grams, of each of the following.
    a. 7.57 mol $BaSO_4$ **b.** 0.0472 mol
    c. 0.250 mol $C_{12}H_{22}O_{11}$

30. Calculate the mass, in grams, of each of the following.
    a. 4.61 mol PCl_3 **b.** 6.15 mol Cr_2O_3
    c. 0.158 mol IF_5

31. Calculate the amount, in moles, of each of the following.
    a. 6.63 g Sb_2S_3 **b.** 19.1 g MoO_3
    c. 434 g $AlPO_4$

32. Calculate the amount, in moles, of each of the following.
    a. 16.3 g SF_6 **b.** 25.4 g $Pb(C_2H_3O_2)_2$
    c. 15.6 g

33. Calculate the percent by mass of N in **(a)** $NaNO_3$, and **(b)** NH_4Cl.

34. Calculate the percent by mass of C, H, and O in glucose ($C_6H_{12}O_6$).

Mole and Mass Relationships in Chemical Equations

35. Consider the reaction for the combustion of butane (C_4H_{10}), a component of liquefied petroleum (LP) gas.

    $$2\,C_4H_{10}(g) + 13\,O_2(g) \longrightarrow 8\,CO_2(g) + 10\,H_2O(g)$$

    a. How many moles of CO_2 are produced when 0.845 mol of butane are burned?
    b. How many moles of oxygen are required to burn 2.54 mol of butane?

36. Consider the reaction for the combustion of octane (C_8H_{18}).

    $$2\,C_8H_{18} + 25\,O_2 \longrightarrow 16\,CO_2 + 18\,H_2O$$

    a. How many moles of H_2O are produced when 0.281 mol of octane is burned?
    b. How many moles of CO_2 are produced when 8.12 mol of oxygen reacts with octane?

37. What mass in grams **(a)** of ammonia can be made from 250 g of H_2 and **(b)** of hydrogen is needed to react completely with 923 g N_2?

    $$N_2 + H_2 \longrightarrow NH_3 \quad \text{(not balanced)}$$

38. Toluene (C_7H_8) and nitric acid (HNO_3) are used in the production of trinitrotoluene (TNT, $C_7H_5N_3O_6$), an explosive.

    $$C_7H_8 + HNO_3 \longrightarrow C_7H_5N_3O_6 + H_2O \quad \text{(not balanced)}$$

    What mass in grams **(a)** of nitric acid is required to react with 454 g and **(b)** of TNT can be made from 829 g C_7H_8?

Molarity of Solutions

39. Calculate the molarity of each of the following solutions.
    a. 23.4 mol HCl in 10.0 L of solution
    b. 0.0875 mol Li_2CO_3 in 632 mL of solution

40. Calculate the molarity of each of the following solutions.
    a. 8.82 mol H_2SO_4 in 7.50 L of solution
    b. 1.22 mol C_2H_5OH in 96.3 mL of solution

41. What mass in grams of solute is needed to prepare **(a)** 3.50 L of 0.500 M NaOH and **(b)** 65.0 mL of 1.45 M $C_6H_{12}O_6$?

42. What mass in grams of solute is needed to prepare **(a)** 0.250 L of 0.167 M $K_2Cr_2O_7$ and **(b)** 625 mL of 0.0200 M $KMnO_4$?

43. What volume in liters of **(a)** 6.00 M NaOH contains 2.50 mol NaOH and **(b)** 0.0500 M KH_2AsO_4 contains 8.10 g KH_2AsO_4?

44. What volume in liters of **(a)** 0.250 M NaOH contains 2.50 M NaOH and **(b)** 4.25 M $H_2C_2O_4$ contains 0.225 g $H_2C_2O_4$?

Percent Concentrations of Solutions

45. What is the percent by volume concentration of **(a)** 58.0 mL of water in 625 mL of an acetic acid–water solution and **(b)** 79.1 mL of methanol in 755 mL of a methanol–water solution?

46. What is the percent by volume concentration of **(a)** 35.0 mL of water in 725 mL of an ethanol–water solution and **(b)** 78.9 mL of acetone in 1550 mL of an acetone–water solution?

47. Describe how you would prepare 3375 g of an aqueous solution that is 8.2% NaCl by mass.

48. Describe how you would prepare 2.44 kg of an aqueous solution that is 16.3% KOH by mass.

49. Describe how you would prepare 2.00 L of an aqueous solution that is 2.00% acetic acid by volume.

50. Describe how you would prepare 600.0 mL of an aqueous solution that is 30.0% isopropyl alcohol by volume.

ADDITIONAL PROBLEMS

51. Both magnesium and aluminum react with hydrogen ions in aqueous solution to produce hydrogen. Why is it that only one of the following equations correctly describes the reaction?

$$Mg(s) + 2\,H^+(aq) \longrightarrow Mg^{2+}(aq) + H_2(g)$$
$$Al(s) + 2\,H^+(aq) \longrightarrow Al^{3+}(aq) + H_2(g)$$

52. Which of the following correctly represents the decomposition of potassium chlorate to produce potassium chloride and oxygen gas?
   a. $KClO_3(s) \longrightarrow KClO_3(s) + O_2(g) + O(g)$
   b. $2\,KClO_3(s) \longrightarrow 2\,KCl(s) + 3\,O_2(g)$
   c. $KClO_3(s) \longrightarrow KClO(s) + O_2(g)$
   d. $KClO_3(s) \longrightarrow KCl(s) + O_3(g)$

53. Write a balanced chemical equation to represent **(a)** the decomposition, by heating, of solid mercury(II) nitrate to produce pure liquid mercury, nitrogen dioxide gas, and oxygen gas, and **(b)** the reaction of aqueous sodium carbonate with aqueous hydrochloric acid (hydrogen chloride) to produce water, carbon dioxide gas, and aqueous sodium chloride.

54. Joseph Priestley discovered oxygen in 1774 by heating "red calx of mercury" [mercury(II) oxide]. The calx decomposed to its elements. The equation is

$$HgO \longrightarrow Hg + O_2 \quad \text{(not balanced)}$$

What mass of oxygen is produced by the decomposition of 18.0 g HgO?

55. Consider 1.00 mol $H_2(g)$, 2.00 mol $He(g)$, and 0.50 mol $C_2H_2(g)$ at the same temperature and pressure. **(a)** Do the three samples have the same number of atoms? **(b)** Which sample has the greatest mass?

56. What mass in grams of the magnetic oxide of iron (Fe_3O_4) can be made from 50.0 g of pure iron and an excess of oxygen? The equation is

$$Fe + O_2 \longrightarrow Fe_3O_4 \quad \text{(not balanced)}$$

57. When heated above ~900 °C, limestone (calcium carbonate) decomposes to quicklime (calcium oxide), which is used to make cement, and carbon dioxide. What mass in grams of quicklime can be produced from 2.5×10^5 g of limestone?

58. Ammonia reacts with oxygen to produce nitric acid (HNO_3) and water. What mass of nitric acid, in grams, can be made from 549 g of ammonia?

59. Hydrogen peroxide solution sold in drugstores is 3.0% H_2O_2 by mass dissolved in water. How many moles of H_2O_2 are in a typical 16-fl. oz bottle of this solution? (1 fl. oz = 29.6 mL; density = 1.00 g/mL)

60. What is the mass percent of **(a)** NaOH in a solution of 2.59 g NaOH in 100.0 g of water and **(b)** ethanol in a solution of 5.25 mL of ethanol (density = 0.789 g/mL) in 50.0 g of water?

61. What is the volume percent of **(a)** ethanol in 355 mL of an ethanol–water solution that contains 18.0 mL of water and **(b)** acetone in 1.55 L of an acetone–water solution that contains 4.00 mL of acetone?

62. Laughing gas (dinitrogen monoxide, N_2O; also called nitrous oxide) can be made by very carefully heating ammonium nitrate. The other product is water.
   a. Write a balanced equation for the process.
   b. Draw the Lewis structure for N_2O.
   c. What mass in grams of N_2O can be made from 150.0 g of ammonium nitrate?

63. In Table 1.6 we listed some multiplicative prefixes used with SI base units. In the 1990s, some new prefixes were recommended:

   zetta- (Z, 10^{21})   *yotta-* (Y, 10^{24})
   zepto- (z, 10^{-21})   *yocto-* (y, 10^{-24})

   a. What is the mass of 1.50 ymol of uranium in yoctograms?
   b. How many atoms are in 1.20 zmol of uranium?

64. What volume of 0.859 M oxalic acid contains 31.7 g of oxalic acid ($H_2C_2O_4$)?

65. In tests for intoxication, blood alcohol levels are expressed as percentages by volume. A blood alcohol level of 0.080% by volume means 0.080 mL of ethanol per 100 mL of blood and is considered proof of intoxication. If a person's total blood volume is 5.0 L, what volume of alcohol in the blood gives a blood alcohol level of 0.165% by volume?

66. Homeopathic remedies are prepared by using a process of dilution, starting with a substance that causes symptoms of the illness being treated. Some homeopaths use a scale (X) in which the substance is diluted by a factor of ten at each stage. For example, for a 6X remedy, the original substance is diluted tenfold six times, for a total dilution of 10^6. (Many homeopathic remedies are diluted far more than six times.)
   a. If the original substance is in the form of a 1.00 M solution, what would be the yoctomolar concentration of a 24X remedy? (Few starting solutions are 1 M; most are far less concentrated.)
   b. How many molecules of the original substance remain in 1.00 L of a 24X remedy?

67. Evaluate this statement: "One cup of water has more molecules than there are cups of water in all of Earth's oceans" (1 cup = 236 mL = 236 cm³). For the volume of the oceans, use 3.50×10^8 cubic miles.

68. If a Neanderthal excreted 500 mL of urine into the ocean 50,000 years ago, how many molecules in 500 mL of water you drink today are from that urine? Refer to Problem 67, and assume complete mixing of the waters of Earth over 50,000 years.

69. A truck carrying about 50,000 kg of sulfuric acid (H_2SO_4) is involved in an accident, spilling the acid. What mass of sodium bicarbonate ($NaHCO_3$) is needed to react with and neutralize the sulfuric acid? The products of the reaction are sodium sulfate (Na_2SO_4), water, and carbon dioxide.

70. Referring to Problem 69, determine the mass of sodium carbonate (Na_2CO_3) needed to neutralize the acid. (The products of the reaction are the same.)

71. How many moles of H_2O are in 2.00 L of water? (d = 1.00 g/mL)

72. Consider the following equation for the reaction of sodium azide that forms nitrogen gas in airbags. **(a)** What is the atom economy for the production of N_2? **(b)** What is the mass in grams of N_2 that is formed if 5.74 g of NaN_3 are reacted?

$$2\,NaN_3 \longrightarrow 2\,Na + 3\,N_2$$

73. Ethanol (C_2H_5OH) is a very important chemical. In addition to being widely used as an industrial solvent, a gasoline additive, and an alternative fuel, it is well known as the alcohol in alcoholic beverages. A common name for ethanol is *grain alcohol* because it is formed by the fermentation of glucose ($C_6H_{12}O_6$) and other sugars in grains such as corn, wheat, and barley:

$$C_6H_{12}O_6 \longrightarrow C_2H_5OH + CO_2$$

The previous reaction has been carried out for many centuries and is one of the oldest manufacturing processes. In a more recent development, ethanol can be prepared by reacting ethylene (found in petroleum) with water:

$$C_2H_4 + H_2O \longrightarrow C_2H_5OH$$

a. Write the *balanced* equation for each of the two reactions above.
b. Calculate the % A.E. (for the product ethanol) for each of the two reactions.
c. Explain how you can determine which reaction has the higher atom economy without doing the calculation in part (b) above.

d. Is either method sustainable? Which one? Justify your answer.
e. Given the results from parts (b) and (d) above, select one of the two methods as the better candidate overall for preparing ethanol. Justify your selection.

74. Consider the following equation for the formation of carbon dioxide CO_2, a known greenhouse gas, from the combustion of hydrocarbons.

$$C_5H_{12} + O_2 \longrightarrow CO_2 + H_2O \quad \text{(not balanced)}$$

a. What is the percent atom economy based on carbon dioxide as the target product?
b. How many grams of CO_2 form if 12.0 g C_5H_{12} is burned?
c. What is the percent yield of the reaction if 15.2 g CO_2 are formed at the end of the reaction? (Hint: Use the information in the Atom Economy essay for this calculation.)

75. Balance each reaction and calculate the percent atom economy based on the underlined molecule as your desired product.
a. $CuCl_2(aq) + Na_2CO_3(aq) \longrightarrow \underline{CuCO_3}(s) + NaCl(aq)$
b. $NH_3(g) + O_2(g) \longrightarrow \underline{NO}(g) + H_2O(g)$
c. $KMnO_4(aq) + KOH(aq) + KI(aq) \longrightarrow$
$\underline{K_2MnO_4}(aq) + KIO_3(aq) + H_2O(l)$

CRITICAL THINKING EXERCISES

Apply knowledge that you have gained in this chapter and one or more of the FLaReS principles (Chapter 1) to evaluate the following statements or claims.

5.1. Suppose that someone has published a paper claiming to have established a new value for Avogadro's number. The author says that he has made some very careful laboratory measurements and his calculations indicate that the true value for Avogadro's number is 3.0187×10^{23}. Is this claim credible in your opinion? What questions would you ask the author about his claim?

5.2. A chemistry teacher asked her students, "What is the mass, in grams, of a mole of chlorine?" One student answered 35; another said 70; and several others gave answers of 36, 37, 72, and 74. The teacher stated that all of these answers were correct. Do you believe her statement?

5.3. A website on fireworks provides directions for preparing potassium nitrate, KNO_3 (molar mass = 101 g/mol),

using potassium carbonate (138 g/mol) and ammonium nitrate (80 g/mol), according to the following equation:

$$K_2CO_3 + 2\,NH_4NO_3 \longrightarrow 2\,KNO_3 + CO_2 + H_2O + NH_3$$

The directions state: "Mix one kilogram of potassium carbonate with two kilograms of ammonium nitrate. The carbon dioxide and ammonia come off as gases, and the water can be evaporated, leaving two kilograms of pure potassium nitrate." Use information from this chapter to evaluate this statement.

5.4. A manufacturer of fuel cells claims that his hydrogen fuel cells are lighter than rechargeable batteries for use in electric cars because the batteries use metals like lead, nickel, and cadmium, and his fuel cell is powered by hydrogen, which has a lighter atomic mass.

5.5. After working Problem 66 of Additional Problems, evaluate the claim that homeopathy is a valid alternative medical treatment.

COLLABORATIVE GROUP PROJECTS

Prepare a PowerPoint, poster, or other presentation (as directed by your instructor) to share with the class.

1. Prepare a brief biographical report on Amedeo Avogadro.
2. In the view of many scientists, hydrogen holds great promise as a source of clean energy. A 2008 report by the U.S. National Research Council suggested that a government subsidy of roughly $4 billion per year through 2023

could make hydrogen cars competitive with petroleum-powered vehicles. Search the web to explore the proposals for using hydrogen as a fuel. Write a brief summary of what you find, and use an appropriate balanced equation to explain why hydrogen is considered a clean, renewable source. More discussion of hydrogen as a fuel is found in Chapter 15.

CHEMISTRY@HOME   Cookie Equations

Materials Needed:

- Sandwich cookies (Oreo style with approximately 32 cookies in a package)
  - 1 package dark cookies with white filling (6 cookies)
  - 1 package yellow cookies with brown filling (3 cookies)
- *double stuff is easier to manipulate
- Butter knife
- Napkin

How many cookies does it take to balance a chemical equation? Wait, wait, don't eat the molecules!

Let's practice writing chemical equations using cookies as manipulatives. Remember that chemical equations use symbols and formulas to represent the elements and compounds in the change. Whatever elements are on the left side of the equation will be in the final product on the right side of the equation. The combinations may be different, but the amount on the left must equal the amount on the right. "What goes in must come out."

The law of the conservation of matter states that matter is neither created nor destroyed during the course of a chemical reaction. Although atoms may be combined differently, the mass of the atoms in the reactants must equal the mass of the atoms in the product.

Use the cookies to construct a model of the following reaction. Separate the cookies from the fillings using the knife. Follow the key to match up the crackers with the elements. How many atoms do you start with? How many atoms do you end up with? How many molecules do you end up with?

> **Key**
> Cracker #1 = H
> Cracker #2 = C
> Cracker #3 = O

$$CH_4 + 2\,O_2 \longrightarrow CO_2 + 2\,H_2O$$

> **Key**
> Cracker #1 = H
> Cracker #2 = Na
> Cracker #3 = O
> Cracker #4 = Cl

$$NaOH + HCl \longrightarrow NaCl + H_2O$$

Exercise 5.1B

To follow up on the assignment in the text, balance this equation. Use the crackers and rewrite the equation so that it is balanced.

> **Key**
> Cracker #1 = Fe
> Cracker #2 = C
> Cracker #3 = O

$$Fe_2O_3 + C \longrightarrow CO_2 + Fe$$

Questions

1. What natural process does formula A show?
2. What is created that is hazardous? Why?
3. Why is it important to balance equations?

6

GASES, LIQUIDS, SOLIDS ... AND INTERMOLECULAR FORCES

Learning Objectives

> Explain how the different properties of solids, liquids, and gases are related to the motion and spacing of atoms, molecules, or ions. (6.1)

> Identify some differences between ionic and molecular substances, and explain why these differences exist. (6.2)

> Classify forces between molecules as dipole–dipole forces, dispersion forces, or hydrogen bonds. (6.3)

> Explain the effects that intermolecular forces have on melting and boiling points. (6.3)

> Explain why nonpolar solutes tend to dissolve in nonpolar solvents and polar and ionic solutes tend to dissolve in polar solvents. (6.4)

> List the five basic concepts of the kinetic–molecular theory of gases. (6.5)

> State the four simple gas laws by name and mathematically. (6.6)

> Use any gas law to find the value of one variable if the other values are given. (6.6)

> State the ideal gas law, and use it to calculate one of the quantities if the others are given. (6.7)

> Describe how Green Chemistry Principle 3 must be considered in designing chemical reactions and processes.

> Identify the properties that make supercritical fluids applicable in greener chemical processes.

Have You Ever Wondered?

1. Why does Silly Putty® have such strange properties?

2. What does "5W30" on a bottle of motor oil mean?

3. What keeps oil and water from mixing?

4. Why doesn't creamy Italian dressing separate like ordinary Italian dressing?

5. How cold can it possibly get, and how hot can it possibly get?

6. Why is it recommended that tire pressure be measured when tires are cold?

WE INTRODUCED THE THREE STATES OF MATTER—gas, liquid, and solid—in Chapter 1. Water is the

most familiar substance that we experience in all three states: as Earth's most common liquid, as a solid (ice), and as a gas (steam). Many other substances can exist in the three states, depending on conditions. An understanding of those conditions is important for our understanding of matter. The state that a substance exhibits depends on the physical properties of that substance, on the pressure, and especially on the temperature. When it is very cold, water exists as solid ice. When it is warmer, water is a liquid. At still higher temperatures, water boils and becomes steam.

Water is an unusual substance in a number of ways. It is the only common substance that exists in all three states—solid ice, liquid water, and gaseous steam—in Earth's biosphere. A small amount of solid water (left) can cool a relatively large amount of liquid water very quickly. Liquid water is also a good cooling agent, and it dissolves many substances both ionic and covalent. Interestingly, the visible cloud often referred to as steam (top) is many microscopic droplets of liquid water; steam is an invisible gas. The properties mentioned here are largely due to the *intermolecular forces* that exist in water. We will learn about those forces in this chapter.

Chapter 4 described the forces called *chemical bonds* that bind atoms together within molecules. Chemical bonds are *intra*molecular forces that determine such molecular properties as geometry and polarity. Forces *between* molecules—*inter*molecular forces—determine the macroscopic physical properties of liquids and solids. Intermolecular forces are also related to the kinds of bonds found in substances. Figure 6.1 compares intermolecular and intramolecular forces. Attractive intermolecular forces hold molecules together in liquids and solids. If there were no intermolecular attractive forces, there would be no liquids or solids—everything would be in a gaseous state.

The shape, size, and polarity of molecules determine how they interact with each other. The physical state of a material depends on the strength of the intermolecular forces that hold the molecules or ions together, relative to the thermal energy (temperature) that acts to separate them.

Forces *between* molecules are *inter*molecular forces.

A covalent bond is an *intra*molecular force.

▲ **Figure 6.1** Intramolecular and intermolecular forces. The gray "sticks" represent covalent bonds in water molecules—*intra*molecular forces, or pairs of shared electrons. The dotted red lines represent forces between water molecules—*inter*molecular forces.

6.1 Solids, Liquids, and Gases

Learning Objective ❯ Explain how the different properties of solids, liquids, and gases are related to the motion and spacing of atoms, molecules, or ions.

Most solids are highly ordered assemblies of atoms, molecules, or ions in close contact with one another, as suggested by Figure 6.2a. This makes it difficult to compress solids. The motion of these particles is mainly vibration. Table salt (sodium chloride) is a typical crystalline solid. In this solid, ionic bonds hold the Na^+ and Cl^- ions in position and maintain the orderly arrangement (look again at Figure 4.2).

In liquids, the particles are still in close contact, but they are randomly arranged and are freer to move about (Figure 6.2b). Like solids, liquids are difficult to compress, but they are able to flow and to conform to the shape of their container. To get a better image of a liquid at the molecular level, think of a box of marbles being shaken continuously. The marbles move back and forth, rolling over one another. The particles of a liquid (like the marbles) are not held in place as rigidly as the particles in a solid are. Even so, there must be some force attracting the particles in a liquid to one another. Otherwise, they would not stay close together.

In gases, the particles are separated by relatively great distances and are moving quite rapidly in random directions (Figure 6.2c). In this state, the atoms or molecules have no interactions with one another. We will look more closely at gases in Section 6.5.

▲ Most solids are made up of highly ordered particles. Glass is an exception. The atoms in glass (Chapter 12) are randomly arrayed.

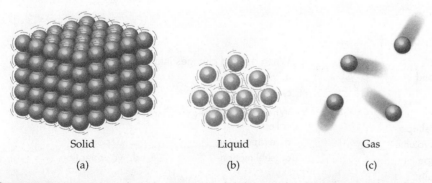

Solid	Liquid	Gas
(a)	(b)	(c)

▲ **Figure 6.2** Three states of matter. (a) Most solids have molecules (or atoms) that vibrate around fixed positions. (b) In liquids, the molecules are still close together but are free to move about like people in a crowded room. (c) Molecules of gases are widely spaced and move freely and randomly.

1. Why does Silly Putty® have such strange properties?

Although it appears to be a solid, Silly Putty® is a liquid—a very thick, slow-flowing (viscous) liquid.

▲ The reverse of sublimation is *deposition*, a process that occurs on cold mornings. Water vapor deposits directly onto the grass as solid frost.

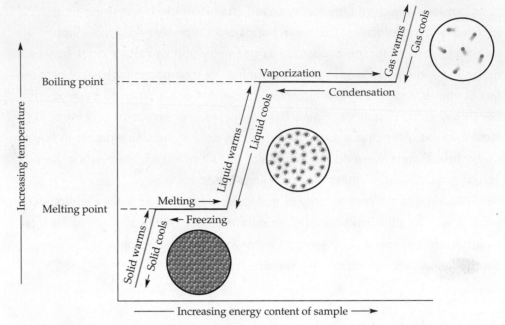

▲ **Figure 6.3** Diagram of changes in state of a substance on heating or cooling.

Most solids can be changed to liquids; that is, they can be *melted*. When a solid is heated, the thermal energy is absorbed by the particles of the solid. The energy causes the particles to vibrate more vigorously until, finally, the forces holding the particles in their regular arrangement are overcome. The solid becomes a liquid. The temperature at which this happens is the **melting point** of the solid. A high melting point indicates that the forces holding a solid together are very strong.

Many liquids can change to gases in a process called **vaporization**. Again, all that is needed to achieve this change is enough heat. Energy is absorbed by the liquid particles, which move faster and faster as a result. Finally, this increasingly violent motion overcomes the attractive forces holding the liquid particles close to one another, and the particles fly apart. The liquid becomes a gas. The temperature at which this happens is the **boiling point** of the liquid.

Removing energy from the gas and slowing down the particles can reverse the sequence of changes. A gas changes to a liquid in a process called **condensation**; a liquid changes to a solid in a process called *freezing*. Figure 6.3 presents a diagram of the changes in state that occur as energy is added to or removed from a sample. Some substances go directly from the solid state to the gaseous state, a process called **sublimation**. For example, ice cubes left in a freezer for a long time shrink, and solid mothballs slowly disappear in a drawer or closet. In each case, the solid undergoes sublimation.

SELF-ASSESSMENT Questions

1. Molecules are farthest apart in a(n)
   a. ionic solid
   b. covalent solid
   c. liquid
   d. gas

2. Liquids are
   a. difficult to compress and have no definite shape
   b. difficult to compress and have no definite volume
   c. easy to compress and have a definite shape
   d. easy to compress and have a definite volume

3. When a liquid changes into a gas, the process is called
   a. condensation
   b. sublimation
   c. gasification
   d. vaporization

4. When a liquid changes into a solid, the process is called
   a. condensation
   b. freezing
   c. fusion
   d. melting

5. When a solid changes directly into a gas, the process is called
   a. evaporation
   b. deposition
   c. sublimation
   d. vaporization

6.2 Comparing Ionic and Molecular Substances

Learning Objective ❯ Identify some differences between ionic and molecular substances, and explain why these differences exist.

Recall that Figure 6.1 illustrates *intermolecular* forces. Ionic substances such as sodium chloride (recall Figure 4.2) are made of ions, not molecules, so the term *intermolecular forces* really doesn't apply to them. Nevertheless, there are attractive forces between ions, and we can compare them to the forces between molecules. First, let's consider some differences between ionic and molecular substances.

- Almost all ionic compounds, such as NaCl, KBr, CaCO$_3$, and NH$_4$NO$_3$, are solids at room temperature. Some molecular substances are liquids or gases at room temperature, although many are solids. Ethane (CH$_3$CH$_3$), hydrogen sulfide (H$_2$S,) and chlorine (Cl$_2$) are gases. Ethanol (CH$_3$CH$_2$OH), bromine (Br$_2$), and phosphorus trichloride (PCl$_3$) are liquids. Sulfur (S$_8$), glucose (C$_6$H$_{12}$O$_6$), and iodine (I$_2$) are solids.

- Ionic compounds generally have much higher melting points and boiling points than molecular compounds. High temperatures are necessary to overcome the strong ionic bonds (Section 4.3) in ionic compounds. Less energy is required to overcome the much weaker attractions between molecules (Section 6.3). For example, sodium chloride (NaCl) must be heated to 801 °C before it melts, but the molecular compound ethane (CH$_3$CH$_3$) melts at −184 °C.

- It generally takes between 10 and 100 times as much energy to melt one mole of a typical ionic compound as it does to melt one mole of a typical molecular

It DOES Matter!

A salt lamp has a light bulb mounted in a large piece of sodium chloride. Some vendors claim that the heat from the lamp causes negative ions to be emitted from the salt. But ionic compounds like sodium chloride have extremely high melting and boiling points, far above the temperature of an ordinary light bulb. No significant quantity of ions can be produced from such a lamp, and there is no conclusive evidence that such ions would be beneficial anyway.

1 M NaCl(aq)
Strong electrolyte.
Solute consists of ions:

⊕ Na$^+$ ⬤ Cl$^-$

1 M CH$_3$OH(aq)
Nonelectrolyte.
Solute consists of molecules;
no ions

◀ **Figure 6.4** (Left) The bulb lights because the solution of sodium chloride contains ions. The ions carry current, and the solution conducts electricity. (Right) A solution of methanol contains no ions and does not conduct electricity.

compound. To melt one mole of sodium chloride requires almost 30 kJ, while it takes only about 3 kJ to melt one mole of ethane.

- Many familiar ionic compounds dissolve in water; those that do dissolve form solutions that conduct electricity. The dissociated ions carry the electric current through the solution. Most molecular compounds, even those that dissolve in water, do not dissociate into ions and thus do not form conducting solutions. A solution of sodium chloride conducts electricity, as seen in Figure 6.4, while a solution of methanol (CH$_3$OH) does not.

- As solids, most ionic compounds are crystalline, hard, and often quite brittle. Solid molecular compounds are usually much softer than ionic ones.

Next, we consider some other interactions that hold the particles of solids and liquids together.

SELF-ASSESSMENT Questions

1. Which of the following is not composed of particles that exhibit intermolecular forces?
   a. HCN   b. HF
   c. NaBr   d. CH_4

2. Which of the following solids is likely to require the greatest input of energy to melt?
   a. $C_6H_{12}O_6$ b. N_2O
   c. KBr   d. Kr

Answers: 1, c; 2, c

(a)

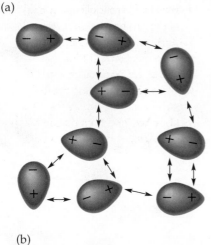

(b)

▲ **Figure 6.5** An idealized representation of dipole–dipole forces in (a) a solid and (b) a liquid. In a real liquid or solid, the interactions between particles are more complex.

6.3 Forces between Molecules

Learning Objectives ❯ Classify forces between molecules as dipole–dipole forces, dispersion forces, or hydrogen bonds. ❯ Explain the effects that intermolecular forces have on melting and boiling points.

As we have noted, many substances, such as water and carbon dioxide, do not consist of ions but instead are molecular compounds. Molecular compounds are characterized by covalent bonds—*intra*molecular forces. For example, in a hydrogen chloride molecule, a covalent bond holds the hydrogen and chlorine *atoms* together. These atoms share a pair of electrons. But what makes one HCl molecule interact with another? In this section, we examine several types of *inter*molecular forces—forces *between* molecules.

Dipole–Dipole Forces

Recall that the hydrogen chloride molecule is a *dipole*: a molecule with a positive end and a negative end (see Figure 4.6). When oppositely charged ends of two dipoles are nearby, they attract one another. In solid HCl, the molecules line up so that the positive end of one molecule attracts the negative end of neighboring molecules, as suggested by Figure 6.5a. If we heat the solid sufficiently, the orderly arrangement is undone, and the solid melts. In the liquid state, the oppositely charged dipoles in the liquid still attract one another, but more randomly, as shown in Figure 6.5b. These **dipole–dipole forces** occur between any two polar molecules. Generally, these forces are much weaker than ionic bonds, but they are stronger than the forces between nonpolar molecules of comparable size. The more polar the molecules, the stronger the dipole–dipole forces are.

Dispersion Forces

It is easy enough to understand how ions or polar molecules maintain contact with one another. After all, opposite charges attract. But how can we explain the fact that *nonpolar* substances can exist in the liquid and solid states? Even hydrogen (H_2) can exist as a liquid or a solid if the temperature is low enough (its melting point is −259 °C). Some force must be holding nonpolar molecules close to one another in the liquid and solid states.

Figure 6.6a suggests that the electrons in a covalent bond are evenly distributed between the two atoms sharing the bond. Recall, however, that electrons are *not* stationary but move continuously. Within a covalent bond, electrons are moving around the nuclei. On *average*, the two electrons in a nonpolar bond are evenly distributed around the two nuclei. But, at any given instant, it is possible for more electrons in a molecule to be at one end than at the other [Figure 6.6b], causing a temporary negative charge at that end. This causes electrons in an adjacent molecule to move toward the opposite end of that molecule, as in Figure 6.6c. Thus,

1. Electrons are evenly distributed about the molecules.

2. Electrons in the left-hand molecule are momentarily clustered on the left.

3. The temporary dipole of the left-hand molecule attracts electrons in the right-hand molecule.

(a) (b) (c)

▲ **Figure 6.6** The mechanism underlying dispersion forces.

an attractive force is created between the electron-rich end of one molecule and the electron-poor end of the next. This attractive force only lasts for an instant before the electrons redistribute themselves evenly.

These momentary, usually weak, attractive forces between molecules are called **dispersion forces**. Because the electrons are in constant motion, dispersion forces can be thought of as dipole–dipole forces in which the dipoles are constantly shifting. Generally, the bigger the molecule, the stronger the dispersion forces are because more electrons are available to cause these momentary dipole forces. To a large extent, dispersion forces determine the physical properties of nonpolar compounds. However, dispersion forces exist between *any* two particles, whether polar, nonpolar, or ionic.

Hydrogen Bonds

Certain polar molecules exhibit stronger attractive forces than would be expected from ordinary dipole–dipole interactions. These forces are strong enough to be given a special name, *hydrogen bonds*. The name is a bit misleading because it emphasizes only one of the two atoms in the interaction. The name is also misleading because hydrogen bonds are not bonds at all; no electrons are shared in a hydrogen bond. Not all compounds containing hydrogen exhibit this kind of attractive force. In most cases, the hydrogen atom *must* be attached to a small, very electronegative atom, namely, nitrogen, oxygen, or fluorine. The high electronegativity of such atoms leaves the hydrogen with a large partial positive charge. A hydrogen bond forms when this hydrogen comes near a nitrogen, oxygen, or fluorine on another molecule. The positively charged hydrogen is strongly attracted to the negatively charged N, O, or F.

In hydrogen fluoride (HF), for example, the hydrogen–fluorine bond is strongly polar, with a negative fluorine end and a positive hydrogen end. Both hydrogen and fluorine are small atoms, so the electrons on the fluorine end of one molecule can approach very closely to the hydrogen end of a second molecule. This unusually strong interaction is the **hydrogen bond**. Hydrogen bonds are often explicitly represented by *dotted* lines (see Figure 6.7) to emphasize that their strength is much greater than that of other intermolecular forces.

Water has both an unusually high melting point (0 °C) and an unusually high boiling point (100 °C) for a compound with such small molecules. These abnormal values are attributed to the water molecules' ability to form hydrogen bonds. Remember, however, that during melting and boiling, only the hydrogen bonds *between water molecules* are overcome. The covalent bonds between the hydrogen atoms and the oxygen atom in each water molecule remain intact. No chemical change occurs when there is a change in state because covalent bonds are much stronger than hydrogen bonds.

The unique properties of water resulting from hydrogen bonding are discussed in Chapter 14. Hydrogen bonding also plays an important role in biological molecules.

2. What does "5W30" on a bottle of motor oil mean?

Oil must have the proper *viscosity* or thickness—which depends on the strength of its intermolecular forces—to lubricate an engine properly. As the engine gets hot, the high temperature makes the oil flow more easily, so a thicker oil (viscosity of 30) is needed. However, when the engine is first started, especially on a cold winter morning, the engine needs a thinner oil (viscosity of 5) to work properly. Oil labeled "5W30" has molecules with intermolecular forces that are about the same whether the oil is cold or hot, and such oil can be used in both summer and winter.

Hydrogen bond

Hydrogen fluoride

Water

▲ **Figure 6.7** Hydrogen bonding in hydrogen fluoride and in water. See also Figure 6.1.

The three-dimensional structures of proteins and enzymes and the arrangement of DNA (Chapter 16) are dependent on the presence and strength of hydrogen bonds.

Strength of Intermolecular Forces

For molecules of similar size and shape, intermolecular forces range in strength from dispersion forces (the weakest), to dipole–dipole forces, to hydrogen bonds (the strongest). Stronger attractions between molecules lead to higher melting points and boiling points. Melting requires weakening the forces between molecules, while boiling requires completely breaking them. So, the stronger the intermolecular forces, the more energy in the form of a higher temperature that must be applied before a compound can melt or boil. These effects can be seen in Figure 6.8. The boiling points of the group 4A compounds (CH_4 to SnH_4), which are all nonpolar, increase with mass as you go down the group. The same trend with mass is seen in the group 5A, 6A, and 7A compounds. However, since these molecules are polar, the boiling point trend lines for these compounds lie above the line for the group 4A compounds. The dipole–dipole forces present in these compounds give them higher boiling points than their group 4A analogs.

Three compounds in Figure 6.8 don't follow these trends. H_2O, HF, and NH_3 have much higher boiling points than their third row equivalents. These three compounds have hydrogen bonds. In fact, the hydrogen bonds in water are so strong that they raise the boiling point by almost 200 °C!

▶ **Figure 6.8** Boiling points of some hydrogen-containing covalent compounds.

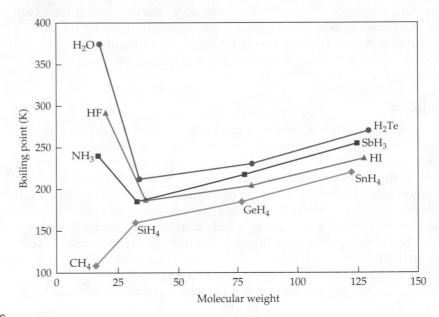

SELF-ASSESSMENT Questions

1. What intermolecular forces are most significant in accounting for the high boiling point of liquid water relative to other substances of similar molecular weight?
   a. dispersion forces
   b. dipolar attractions
   c. hydrogen bonds
   d. ionic bonds

2. Which one of the following interactions is the strongest?
   a. covalent bonds
   b. dipole–dipole forces
   c. dispersion forces
   d. hydrogen bonds

3. In ethanol (CH_3CH_2OH), the attractions between neighboring molecules are
   a. covalent bonds and dispersion forces only
   b. dipole–dipole forces and hydrogen bonds only
   c. covalent bonds only
   d. hydrogen bonds, dipole–dipole forces, and dispersion forces only

4. The molecules of liquid water in a beaker are held to each other by
   a. covalent bonds
   b. intramolecular forces
   c. intermolecular forces
   d. ionic bonds

5. Of CH_3OH, H_2, HF, and H_2O, which molecule(s) can form hydrogen bonds?
   a. H_2 only
   b. H_2O only
   c. CH_3OH, HF, and H_2O
   d. all four

6. Which one of the following molecules does *not* form hydrogen bonds?
   a. ammonia (NH_3)
   b. chloroform ($CHCl_3$)
   c. methyl alcohol (CH_3OH)
   d. ethylene glycol ($HOCH_2CH_2OH$)

6.4 Forces in Solutions

Learning Objective ❯ Explain why nonpolar solutes tend to dissolve in nonpolar solvents and polar and ionic solutes tend to dissolve in polar solvents.

To complete our look at intermolecular forces, let's briefly examine the interactions that occur in solutions. A **solution** is an intimate, homogeneous mixture of two or more substances. Here *intimate* means that mixing occurs down to the level of individual ions and molecules, as suggested in Figure 6.9. For example, a sugar-in-water solution has separate sugar molecules randomly distributed among water molecules. *Homogeneous* means that all parts of the solution have the same distribution of components. A sugar solution is equally sweet at the top, bottom, and middle of the solution. The substance being dissolved, and present in a lesser amount, is called the **solute**. The substance doing the dissolving, and present in a greater amount, is the **solvent**. In a sugar-in-water solution, sugar is the solute and water is the solvent.

Ordinarily, solutions form most readily when the substances involved have *similar* strengths of forces between their molecules (or atoms or ions). An old chemical adage is, "Like dissolves like." Nonpolar solutes dissolve best in nonpolar solvents. For example, oil and gasoline, both nonpolar, mix [Figure 6.10a], but oil and vinegar do not [Figure 6.10b]. Vinegar is mostly water, and the strong hydrogen bonds between water molecules do not allow nonpolar oil molecules (which only have the much weaker dispersion forces) to mix freely with them. On the other hand, both ethyl alcohol molecules and water molecules can form hydrogen bonds. Thus, ethyl alcohol readily dissolves in water [Figure 6.10c]. In general, a solute dissolves when attractive forces between it and the solvent are at least almost as strong as the attractive forces operating in the pure solute and in the pure solvent.

● = Solvent molecule
● = Solute molecule

▲ **Figure 6.9** In a solution, solute molecules (orange spheres) are randomly distributed among solvent molecules (purple spheres).

3. What keeps oil and water from mixing?

Oil molecules are nonpolar, and water molecules are very polar. The weak forces between oil and water molecules aren't strong enough to overcome the strong forces between the water molecules. Thus, oil and water don't mix.

(a)   (b)   (c)

▲ **Figure 6.10** (a) Lawn mowers with two-cycle engines are fueled and lubricated with a solution of nonpolar lubricating oil in nonpolar gasoline. (b) In a salad dressing, polar vinegar and nonpolar olive oil are mixed. However, the two liquids do not form a solution and separate on standing. (c) Wine is a solution of polar ethyl alcohol in polar water.

Q: *What are some other examples of mixtures of polar and nonpolar substances?*

Why, then, does salt dissolve in water? Ionic solids are held together by strong ionic bonds. We have already seen that high temperatures are required to melt ionic solids and break these bonds. Yet if we simply place sodium chloride in water at room temperature, the salt dissolves. And when such a solid dissolves, its bonds *are* broken. The difference between the two processes is the difference between brute force and persuasion. In the melting process, we simply put in enough energy (as heat) to break the crystal down. In the dissolving process, we offer the ions an attractive alternative to their ionic interactions in the crystal.

When a salt crystal dissolves, water molecules first surround the crystal. The molecules that approach a negative ion align themselves so that the positive ends

4. Why doesn't creamy Italian dressing separate like ordinary Italian dressing?

Both kinds of dressings contain oil and vinegar. However, proteins (from egg yolk or other sources) are mixed into the creamy dressing. The protein molecules have both polar parts and nonpolar parts and keep tiny droplets of oil suspended in the vinegar.

of their dipoles point toward the ion, as shown in Figure 6.11. The molecules that approach a positive ion align themselves so that the negative ends of their dipoles point toward the ion. Although the attraction between a dipole and an ion is not as strong as that between two ions, several water molecules surround each ion, and the many *ion–dipole* interactions that are formed as the crystal dissolves overcome the ionic bonds.

In an ionic solid, the positive and negative ions are strongly bonded together in an orderly crystalline arrangement. In solution, cations and anions move about more or less independently, each surrounded by a cage of solvent molecules. Water—including the water in our bodies—is an excellent solvent for many ionic compounds. Water also dissolves many molecules that are polar covalent like itself. These solubility principles explain how nutrients reach the cells of our bodies (dissolved in blood, which is mostly water) and how many kinds of pollutants get into our water supplies.

▶ **Figure 6.11** An ionic solid (sodium chloride) dissolving in a polar solvent (water). The hydrogen ends of the water molecules surround the negatively charged chloride ions, while the oxygen ends of the water molecules surround the positively charged sodium ions.

SELF-ASSESSMENT Questions

1. A solution is a mixture that is
   a. heterogeneous
   b. homogeneous
   c. homologous
   d. humectic

2. Which of the following pairs of substances is *least likely* to form a solution?
   a. an ionic compound in a nonpolar solvent
   b. an ionic compound in a polar solvent
   c. a nonpolar compound in a nonpolar solvent
   d. a polar compound in a polar solvent

3. A positive test for iodine is the purple color of a solution of I_2 in hexane (C_6H_{14}). What type of solute–solvent interaction is most important in a solution of nonpolar I_2 in nonpolar C_6H_{14}?
   a. dipole–dipole forces
   b. dispersion forces
   c. ion–dipole interactions
   d. hydrogen bonds

4. What type of solute–solvent interaction is most important in a solution of calcium chloride ($CaCl_2$) in water?
   a. dipole–dipole forces
   b. ion–dipole interactions
   c. ionic bonds
   d. dispersion forces

5. What type of solute–solvent interaction is most important in a solution of acetic acid (CH_3COOH) in water?
   a. dipole–dipole forces
   b. dipole–hydrogen bonds
   c. hydrogen bonds
   d. dispersion forces

6. Which of the following solutes is most likely to dissolve in octane (C_8H_{18}), a component of gasoline?
   a. $CH_3(CH_2)_4CH_3$
   b. $CaCl_2$
   c. KCl
   d. MgO

6.5 Gases: The Kinetic–Molecular Theory

Learning Objective   › List the five basic concepts of the kinetic–molecular theory of gases.

At the macroscopic level, gases may seem more difficult to understand than liquids and solids—perhaps because most gases are invisible, while we can see and feel liquids and solids. However, at the microscopic level, gases are more readily treated mathematically. Gas molecules are so far apart that intermolecular forces can be ignored. Therefore, the behavior of a gas normally doesn't depend on the composition of the gas, so the description of gases that appears in the rest of the chapter can be applied to almost any gas. On the other hand, in liquids and solids, the intermolecular forces are stronger, and they vary depending on the type of molecules and the distance between them. This variation complicates any theoretical treatment.

Experiments with gases were instrumental in developing the concepts of Avogadro's number and of molar ratios in reactions. Let's look at the behavior of gases more closely, using a model known as the **kinetic–molecular theory** (Figure 6.12). There are five basic concepts of this theory.

1. Particles of a gas (usually *molecules*, but *atoms* in the case of noble gases) are in rapid, constant motion and move in straight lines.
2. The particles of a gas are tiny compared with the distances between them.
3. Because the particles of a gas are so far apart, there is very little interaction between them.
4. Particles of a gas collide with one another. Energy is *conserved* in these collisions; energy lost by one particle is gained by the other.
5. Temperature is a measure of the average kinetic energy (energy of motion) of the gas particles.

Section 6.3 described how intermolecular forces hold molecules together in solids and liquids. In gases, the particles are separated by relatively great distances and are moving about randomly. Although these particles can collide, they seldom interact. We can use the kinetic–molecular *theory* to explain the gas *laws* presented in the next section.

▲ **Figure 6.12** According to the kinetic–molecular theory, particles (molecules or atoms) of a gas are in constant, random motion. They move in straight lines and undergo collisions with each other and with the walls of the container.

SELF-ASSESSMENT Questions

1. Which of the following is *not* a concept of the kinetic–molecular theory of gases?
   a. Particles of a gas are in constant motion.
   b. The pressure and volume of a gas are inversely related.
   c. Temperature is a measure of the average kinetic energy of the gas particles.
   d. The particles are very small compared to the distances between them.

2. According to the kinetic–molecular theory of gases, a gas particle
   a. will collide with another gas particle with no loss of kinetic energy for either
   b. will stick to a wall of its container
   c. is tiny compared to the volume occupied by the gas
   d. repels another gas particle when the two are nearby each other

3. In collisions between gas particles, the total energy
   a. decreases slightly
   b. decreases considerably
   c. increases slightly
   d. remains the same

6.6 The Simple Gas Laws

Learning Objectives ❯ State the four simple gas laws, by name and mathematically.
❯ Use any gas law to find the value of one variable if the other values are given.

The behavior of gases can be described by mathematical relationships called *gas laws*. These equations use four variables to specify properties of a sample of gas: its amount in moles (*n*), its volume (*V*), its temperature (*T*), and its pressure (*P*). These variables are related through simple laws that show how one of the variables (for example, *V*) changes as a second variable (for example, *P*) changes and the other two (for example, *n* and *T*) remain constant.

4.00 atm   2.00 atm   1.00 atm

▲ **Figure 6.13** The kinetic–molecular theory and Boyle's law. As the pressure is reduced from 4.00 atm to 2.00 atm and then to 1.00 atm, the volume of the gas doubles and then doubles again.

Q: *What would happen to the volume of the gas if the pressure were changed to 0.500 atm?*

Boyle's Law: Pressure and Volume

The first gas law was discovered by Robert Boyle in 1662. It describes the relationship between the pressure and the volume of a gas. **Boyle's law** states that *for a given amount of gas at a constant temperature, the volume of the gas varies inversely with its pressure.* That is, when the pressure in a closed container of gas increases, the volume decreases; when the pressure decreases, the volume increases.

A bicycle pump illustrates Boyle's law. When you push down on the plunger, you decrease the volume of the air in the pump. The pressure of the air increases, and the higher-pressure air flows into the bicycle tire.

Think of gases as pictured by the kinetic–molecular theory. A gas exerts a particular pressure because its molecules bounce against the container walls with a certain frequency and speed. If the volume of the container is increased while the amount of gas remains fixed, the number of molecules per unit volume decreases (Figure 6.13). The frequency with which molecules strike a unit area of the container walls decreases, and the gas pressure decreases. Thus, as the volume of a gas is increased, its pressure decreases.

Mathematically, for a given amount of gas at a constant temperature, Boyle's law is written

$$V \propto \frac{1}{P}$$

where the symbol $\propto$ means "is proportional to." This relationship can be changed to an equation by inserting a proportionality constant, *a*.

$$V = \frac{a}{P}$$

Multiplying both sides of the equation by *P*, we get

$$PV = a\,(\,\text{at constant temperature and amount of gas}\,)$$

Another way to state Boyle's law, then, is that for a given amount of gas at a constant temperature, the product of the pressure and the volume is a constant. This is an elegant and precise way of summarizing a lot of experimental data. If the product $P \times V$ is constant, then, when *V* increases, *P* must decrease, and vice versa. This relationship is illustrated in Figure 6.14 by a pressure–volume graph.

Boyle's law has a number of practical applications, which are perhaps best introduced through some examples. In Example 6.1, we see how to estimate an answer. Sometimes an estimate is all we need. Even when we need a quantitative answer, however, an estimate helps us determine whether or not the answer we get is reasonable.

▲ **Figure 6.14** A graphic representation of Boyle's law. As the pressure is increased, the volume of a gas decreases. When the pressure is doubled ($P_2 = 2 \times P_1$), the volume of the gas decreases to one-half of its original value ($V_2 = \frac{1}{2} \times V_1$). The pressure–volume product is a constant ($PV = a$).

Q: *What would happen to the volume of the gas if the pressure were quadrupled?*

Example 6.1	Boyle's Law: Pressure–Volume Relationships

A gas is enclosed in a cylinder fitted with a piston. The volume of the gas is 2.00 L at 0.524 atm. The piston is moved to increase the pressure to 5.15 atm. Which of the following is a reasonable value for the volume of the gas at the greater pressure if the temperature of the gas stays the same?

0.20 L   0.40 L   1.00 L   16.0 L

Solution

The pressure increase from 0.524 atm to 5.15 atm is almost tenfold. The volume should drop to about one-tenth of the initial value. Thus, we estimate a volume of 0.20 L. (The calculated value is 0.203 L.)

▪ EXERCISE 6.1

Argon gas is enclosed in a 10.2-L tank at 1208 mmHg (*mmHg* is a pressure unit: 760 mmHg = 1 atm). Which of the following is a reasonable value for the pressure when the argon is transferred to a 30.0-L tank at a constant temperature?

300 mmHg   400 mmHg   3600 mmHg   12,000 mmHg

Example 6.2 illustrates quantitative calculations using Boyle's law. For a given confined sample of a gas at a constant temperature, the initial pressure (P_1) times the initial volume (V_1) is equal to the final pressure (P_2) times the final volume (V_2). That is, Boyle's law can be written as the following equation.

$$P_1V_1 = a = P_2V_2$$

Example 6.2	Boyle's Law: Pressure–Volume Relationships

A cylinder of oxygen has a volume of 2.25 L. The pressure in the cylinder is 1470 pounds per square inch (psi) at 20 °C. What volume will the oxygen occupy at standard atmospheric pressure (14.7 psi), assuming no temperature change?

Solution

We find it helpful to first separate the initial and final conditions.

Initial	Final	Change
$P_1 = 1470$ psi	$P_2 = 14.7$ psi	The pressure goes down; therefore, the volume goes up.
$V_1 = 2.25$ L	$V_2 = ?$	

Next, we solve the equation $P_1V_1 = P_2V_2$ for the desired volume or pressure. In this case, we solve for V_2. Finally, we substitute the given values for P_1, V_1, and P_2.

$$V_2 = \frac{P_1V_1}{P_2}$$

$$V_2 = \frac{1470 \text{ psi} \times 2.25 \text{ L}}{14.7 \text{ psi}} = 225 \text{ L}$$

Note how the units for pressure cancel. It doesn't matter what units we use for pressure and volume, as long as we use the same ones throughout the calculation. Because the final pressure (14.7 psi) is *less than* the initial pressure (1470 psi), we expect the final volume (225 L) to be *larger than* the original volume (2.25 L), and we see that it is.

▪ EXERCISE 6.2A

A sample of air occupies 73.3 mL at 98.7 atm and 0 °C. What volume will the air occupy at 4.02 atm and 0 °C?

▪ EXERCISE 6.2B

A sample of helium occupies 535 mL at 988 mmHg and 25 °C. If the sample is transferred to a 1.05-L flask at 25 °C, what will the gas pressure in the flask be?

5. How cold can it possibly get, and how hot can it possibly get?
Quantum mechanics (Section 3.7) says that all atoms must always keep moving, at least a little bit. At 0 K (absolute zero, −273.15 °C), atomic motion is the minimum allowed. Because atoms cannot move any slower than this, no lower temperature is possible. Theoretically, atoms have no upper limit on the amount of kinetic energy they can have. However, at such high values, temperature ceases to have much meaning.

Charles's Law: Temperature and Volume

In 1787, the French physicist Jacques Charles (1746–1823), a pioneer hot-air balloonist, studied the relationship between volume and temperature of gases. He found that when a fixed mass of gas is cooled at constant pressure, its volume decreases. When the gas is heated, its volume increases. Temperature and volume vary directly; that is, they rise or fall together. But this relationship is a bit more complex. If a quantity of gas that occupies 1.00 L is heated from 100 °C to 200 °C at constant pressure, the volume does not double but increases only to about 1.27 L. The relationship between temperature and volume is not as simple as it may seem at first.

For most measurements and quantities, "zero" means "none." A measured pressure of 0 atm means no measurable pressure, and it is not possible to have a lower pressure than 0 atm. On the other hand, zero degrees Celsius (0 °C) merely signifies the freezing point of water. Temperatures below 0 °C are often encountered. Decreasing the temperature of 1 L of a gas from 20 °C to 0 °C does not cause the volume to decrease to zero. Instead, the volume decreases only to about 0.92 L.

Charles noted that for each degree Celsius that the temperature rises, the volume of a gas increases by $\frac{1}{273}$ of its volume at 0 °C. A plot of volume against temperature is a straight line (Figure 6.15). We can extrapolate (extend) the line to the temperature at which the volume of the gas should become zero. This temperature is −273.15 °C. In 1848, William Thomson (Lord Kelvin) made this temperature the zero point on an absolute temperature scale now called the Kelvin scale. As noted in Chapter 1, the unit on this temperature scale is the kelvin (K).

A modern statement of **Charles's law** is that *the volume of a fixed amount of a gas at a constant pressure is directly proportional to its absolute temperature.* Mathematically, this relationship is expressed as

$$V = bT \quad \text{or} \quad \frac{V}{T} = b$$

▲ **Figure 6.15** Charles's law relates gas volume to temperature at constant pressure. In the case shown, when the gas is at about 70 °C, its volume is 60 mL. As the temperature is lowered from about 70 °C to −100 °C the volume drops to 30.0 mL. The volume continues to fall as the temperature is lowered. The extrapolated (dashed) line intersects the temperature axis (corresponding to a volume of zero) at about −273 °C.

Q: *What would be the approximate volume of the gas at a temperature of −150 °C?*

where b is a proportionality constant. To keep V/T at a constant value, when the temperature increases, the volume must also increase. When the temperature decreases, the volume must decrease accordingly (Figure 6.16).

With a given sample of trapped gas at a constant pressure, the initial volume (V_1) divided by the initial absolute temperature (T_1) is equal to the final volume (V_2) divided by the final absolute temperature (T_2). We can therefore use the following equation to solve problems involving Charles's law.

$$\frac{V_1}{T_1} = \frac{V_2}{T_2}$$

The kinetic–molecular model readily explains the relationship between gas volume and temperature. When we heat a gas, the gas molecules absorb energy and move faster. These speedier molecules strike the walls of the container harder and more often. For the pressure to stay the same, the volume of the container must increase so that the increased molecular motion will be distributed over a greater space.

(a)

(b)

▲ **Figure 6.16** A dramatic illustration of Charles's law. (a) Liquid nitrogen (boiling point, −196 °C) cools the balloon and its contents to a temperature far below room temperature. (b) As the balloon warms back to room temperature, the volume of air increases proportionately (about fourfold).

Example 6.3 Charles's Law: Temperature–Volume Relationship

In a room at 27 °C, a balloon has a volume of 2.00 L. What would its volume be **(a)** in a sauna, where the temperature is 47 °C, and **(b)** outdoors, where the temperature is –23 °C? Assume that there is no change in pressure in either case.

Solution

First, and most important, we convert all temperatures to the Kelvin scale:

$$T(\text{K}) = t(\text{°C}) + 273$$

The initial temperature (T_1) in each case is $27 + 273 = 300$ K, and the final temperatures are **(a)** $47 + 273 = 320$ K and **(b)** $-23 + 273 = 250$ K.

a. We start by separating the initial from the final condition.

Initial	Final	Change
$T_1 = 300$ K	$T_2 = 320$ K	⇑
$V_1 = 2.00$ L	$V_2 = ?$	⇑

Solving the equation

$$\frac{V_1}{T_1} = \frac{V_2}{T_2}$$

for V_2, we have

$$V_2 = \frac{V_1 T_2}{T_1}$$

Substituting the known values gives

$$V_2 = \frac{2.00\ \text{L} \times 320\ \text{K}}{300\ \text{K}} = 2.13\ \text{L}$$

As expected, because the temperature increases, the volume must also increase.

b. We have the same initial conditions as in **(a)** but different final conditions.

Initial	Final	Change
$T_1 = 300$ K	$T_2 = 250$ K	⇓
$V_1 = 2.00$ L	$V_2 = ?$	⇓

Again, using Charles's law, we solve the equation for V_2 and substitute the known quantities.

$$V_2 = \frac{V_1 T_2}{T_1}$$

$$V_2 = \frac{2.00 \text{ L} \times 250 \text{ K}}{300 \text{ K}} = 1.67 \text{ L}$$

As expected, the volume decreases because the temperature decreases.

■ EXERCISE 6.3A

A sample of ethane gas occupies a volume of 16.8 L at 25 °C. What volume will this sample occupy at 109 °C? (Assume no change in pressure.)

■ EXERCISE 6.3B

At what Celsius temperature will the initial volume of ethane in Exercise 6.3A occupy 0.750 L? (Assume no change in pressure.)

Example 6.4	Gay-Lussac's Law: Temperature and Pressure Relationship

In addition to Boyle's law, which describes the relationship between the pressure and volume, and Charles's law, relating volume and temperature, another simple gas law, called Gay-Lussac's law, relates temperature and pressure. **Gay-Lussac's law** states that *the pressue of a fixed amount of a gas at a constant volume is directly proportional to its absolute temperature.* If a 20.0 L cylinder containing a gas at 6.00 atm pressure at 27 °C is heated to 77 °C, what would the pressure of the gas be?

Solution

The cylinder's volume remains unchanged. Gay-Lussac's law can be expressed as

$$\frac{P_1}{T_1} = \frac{P_2}{T_2}$$

Whenever working with the gas laws, first convert all temperatures to the Kelvin scale:

The initial temperature (T_1) is (27 + 273) = 300 K and the final temperature is (77 + 273) = 350 K.

We start by separating the initial from the final condition.

Initial	Final	Change
$t_1 = 27 \text{ °C}$	$t_2 = 77 \text{ °C}$	⇑
$T_1 = 300 \text{ K}$	$T_2 = 350 \text{ K}$	⇑
$P_1 = 6.00 \text{ atm}$	$P_2 = ?$	⇑

Solving the Gay-Lussac equation for P_2

$$P_2 = \frac{P_1 T_2}{T_1}$$

$$P_2 = \frac{6.00 \text{ atm} \times 350 \text{ K}}{300 \text{ K}} = 7.00 \text{ atm}$$

■ EXERCISE 6.4A

A tire has a pressure of 32 psi at 35 °C. What will the tire pressure be if the temperature drops to 5 °C? (Assume no change in tire volume.)

■ EXERCISE 6.4B

A weather balloon has a pressure of 1.00 atm at 23 °C. At what temperature will the pressure of the balloon reach 0.600 atm if the volume of the balloon doesn't change?

Molar Volume

As Section 5.2 described, Amedeo Avogadro proposed a hypothesis to explain the volume ratios in which gases combine during chemical reactions. His hypothesis states that equal numbers of molecules of different gases at the same temperature and pressure occupy equal volumes. Thus, Avogadro's hypothesis relates an amount of gas (numbers of molecules or moles) to the gas volume when temperature and pressure remain constant. We call the simple gas law implied by this relationship **Avogadro's law**: *At a fixed temperature and pressure, the volume of a gas is directly proportional to the amount of gas (that is, to the number of moles of gas, n, or to the number of molecules of gas).* If we double the number of moles of gas at a fixed temperature and pressure, the volume of the gas doubles. Mathematically, we can state Avogadro's law as

$$V \propto n \quad \text{or} \quad V = cn \quad (\text{where } c \text{ is a constant})$$

A mole of gas contains Avogadro's number of molecules (or atoms if it is a noble gas). Furthermore, a gas sample consisting of Avogadro's number of molecules occupies the same volume (at a given temperature and pressure) regardless of the size or mass of the individual molecules. The volume occupied by one mole of gas is the **molar volume** of a gas.

Because the volume of a gas is altered by changes in temperature or pressure, a particular set of conditions has been chosen as the standard set for reference purposes. Standard pressure is 1 atmosphere (atm), which is the normal pressure of the air at sea level. Standard temperature is 0 °C, which is the freezing point of water. A mole of any gas at **standard temperature and pressure (STP)** occupies a volume of about 22.4 L, slightly more than a five-gallon water bottle (Figure 6.17). This is known as the *standard molar volume* of a gas. At a temperature of 0 °C and 1 atm pressure, a 22.4-L container holds one mole (28.0 g) of N_2, one mole (32.0 g) of O_2, one mole (44.0 g) of CO_2, and so on.

We can readily calculate the density (g/L) of a gas at STP. We begin with the molar mass of the gas (g/mol) and use the conversion factor 1 mol gas = 22.4 L. Because the conversion factor can be inverted, we can also use it to calculate molar mass from density.

▲ **Figure 6.17** An "empty" bottle from an office water cooler is not really empty. It holds five gallons of air, slightly less than 22.4 L— the volume of one mole of a gas at STP.

Q: *About how many C_2H_6 molecules would the bottle hold at STP?*

Example 6.5 Density of a Gas at STP

Calculate the density of **(a)** nitrogen gas and **(b)** methane (CH_4) gas, both at STP.

Solution

a. The molar mass of N_2 gas is 28.0 g/mol. We multiply by the conversion factor 1 mol N_2 = 22.4 L, arranged to cancel units of *moles*.

$$\frac{28.0 \text{ g } N_2}{1 \text{ mol } N_2} \times \frac{1 \text{ mol } N_2}{22.4 \text{ L } N_2} = 1.25 \text{ g/L}$$

b. The molar mass of CH_4 gas is (1×12.0) g/mol + (4×1.01) g/mol = 16.0 g/mol. Again, we use the conversion factor 1 mol CH_4 = 22.4 L.

$$\frac{16.0 \text{ g } CH_4}{1 \text{ mol } CH_4} \times \frac{1 \text{ mol } CH_4}{22.4 \text{ L } CH_4} = 0.714 \text{ g/L}$$

▪ EXERCISE 6.5A
Calculate the density of xenon gas at STP.

▪ EXERCISE 6.5B
Estimate the density of air at STP (assume that air is 78% N_2 and 22% O_2), and compare this value to the value you calculated for xenon in Exercise 6.5A.

6. Why is it recommended that tire pressure be measured when tires are cold?

Tire pressure is measured when the tires are cold because a tire has nearly constant volume. According to Gay-Lussac's law, as the temperature increases (by friction from the road), the pressure increases, too. If the tire pressure were adjusted right after a long drive, the tires might be soft and underpressurized the next morning. Air temperature also affects tire pressure. So, it's a good idea to check your car's tire pressure any time the temperature changes significantly.

SELF-ASSESSMENT Questions

1. Gas pressure is caused by
   a. gas molecules colliding with each other
   b. gas molecules colliding with vessel walls
   c. gas molecules condensing to form a liquid
   d. measurement with a barometer

2. Boyle's law states that the pressure of a gas is inversely proportional to its
   a. amount
   b. mass
   c. temperature
   d. volume

3. A gas sample occupies 6.00 L at 2.00 atm pressure. At what pressure would the volume be 1.50 L if the temperature remains constant?
   a. 0.500 atm
   b. 8.00 atm
   c. 9.00 atm
   d. 12.0 atm

4. In an experiment, as the temperature is changed at constant pressure, the volume of a gas is halved. How is the final temperature related to the initial temperature?
   a. The Celsius temperature is doubled.
   b. The Celsius temperature is halved.
   c. The Kelvin temperature is doubled.
   d. The Kelvin temperature is halved.

5. One 1.00-L flask (Flask A) contains NO gas, and another 1.00-L flask (Flask B) contains NO_2 gas, both at STP. Flask A contains
   a. less mass and fewer molecules than Flask B
   b. less mass but the same number of molecules as Flask B
   c. less mass but more molecules than Flask B
   d. more mass and more molecules than Flask B

6. How many moles are there in 5.60 L of a gas at STP?
   a. 0.250 mol
   b. 0.500 mol
   c. 4.00 mol
   d. 125 mol

Answers: 1. b; 2. d; 3. b; 4. d; 5. b; 6. a

6.7 The Ideal Gas Law

Learning Objective ❭ State the ideal gas law, and use it to calculate one of the quantities if the others are given.

Boyle's law, Charles's law, Gay-Lussac's law, and Avogadro's law are useful when two variables of the four (P, V, n, and T) are held constant. Often, however, the temperature, pressure, and volume all change at the same time. In such cases, the simple gas laws can be incorporated into a single relationship called the **combined gas law**. Mathematically, this law is written as

$$\frac{PV}{T} = k \quad \text{or} \quad PV = kT$$

where k is a constant. For comparing the same sample of gas under two different sets of conditions, the combined gas law can be written as

$$\frac{P_1 V_1}{T_1} = \frac{P_2 V_2}{T_2}$$

Because the amount of gas, n, may change as well, incorporating this variable gives an expression called the **ideal gas law**, which involves all four variables.

$$\frac{PV}{nT} = R \quad \text{or} \quad PV = nRT$$

In this equation, R is a constant (called the *gas constant*), which can be calculated from the fact that one mole of gas occupies 22.4 L at 273 K (0 °C) and 1 atm (Section 6.6). If P is in atmospheres, V in liters, and T in kelvins, then R has a value of

$$0.0821 \frac{\text{L} \cdot \text{atm}}{\text{mol} \cdot \text{K}}$$

The ideal gas equation can be used to calculate the value of any of the four variables—P, V, n, or T—if the other three values are known.

Example 6.6	The Combined Gas Law

A balloon used for underwater salvage is inflated to 50.0 L at a depth of 200 ft, where the pressure is 6.89 atm and the temperature is 3 °C. The balloon rises to the surface (22 °C and 0.988 atm). What is the new volume of the balloon?

Solution

We start by solving the combined gas law equation for V_2.

$$\frac{P_1 V_1}{T_1} = \frac{P_2 V_2}{T_2}$$

$$V_2 = \frac{P_1 V_1 T_2}{T_1 P_2}$$

We have $T_1 = 3 + 273 = 276$ K, and $T_2 = 22 + 273 = 295$ K.

$$V_2 = \frac{6.89 \text{ atm} \times 50.0 \text{ L} \times 295 \text{ K}}{276 \text{ K} \times 0.988 \text{ atm}} = 373 \text{ L}$$

▪ **EXERCISE 6.6A**

What will be the final volume of a 425 mL sample of a gas initially at 22.0 °C and 760 mmHg pressure when the temperature is changed to 30.0 °C and the pressure to 360 mmHg?

▪ **EXERCISE 6.6B**

What will be the final pressure of a 2.34 L sample of a gas initially at 28.0 °C and pressure of 823 torr (1 torr = 1 mmHg) if the temperature is changed to 44.0 °C and the volume to 4.76 L?

Example 6.7	Ideal Gas Law

Use the ideal gas law to calculate **(a)** the volume occupied by 1.00 mol N_2 gas at 244 K and 1.00 atm pressure and **(b)** the pressure exerted by 0.500 mol O_2 gas in a 15.0-L container at 303 K.

Solution

a. We solve the ideal gas equation for V and substitute the known quantities. It's important when using the ideal gas law always to express volume in L, pressure in atm, and temperature in K.

$$V = \frac{nRT}{P}$$

$$V = \frac{1.00 \text{ mol}}{1.00 \text{ atm}} \times \frac{0.0821 \text{ L} \cdot \text{atm}}{\text{mol} \cdot \text{K}} \times 244 \text{ K} = 20.0 \text{ L}$$

b. Here we solve the ideal gas equation for P and substitute the known quantities.

$$P = \frac{nRT}{V}$$

$$P = \frac{0.500 \text{ mol}}{15.0 \text{ L}} \times \frac{0.0821 \text{ L} \cdot \text{atm}}{\text{mol} \cdot \text{K}} \times 303 \text{ K} = 0.829 \text{ atm}$$

▪ **EXERCISE 6.7A**

Determine **(a)** the pressure exerted by 0.0450 mol O_2 gas in a 22.0-L container at 313 K and **(b)** the volume occupied by 0.400 mol N_2 gas at 298 K and 0.980 atm.

▪ **EXERCISE 6.7B**

Determine the volume occupied by 132 g N_2 gas at 25 °C and 1.03 atm.

Doug Raynie, *South Dakota State University*

Supercritical Fluids

Learning Objectives ⟩ Describe how green chemistry principle 3 must be considered in designing chemical reactions and processes. ⟩ Identify the properties that make supercritical fluids applicable in greener chemical processes.

Many chemical reactions take place in solution (Section 5.5), and most chemical processes involve a separation of components at some stage. Water is an excellent solvent for many substances, but some substances do not dissolve in water under ordinary conditions (Section 6.4). Chemists have traditionally used organic solvents such as benzene (C_6H_6), a cancer-causing aromatic hydrocarbon (Section 9.2), and methylene chloride (CH_2Cl_2), a toxic chlorinated hydrocarbon (Section 9.3), to dissolve nonpolar and slightly polar substances. Wouldn't it be nice to have a nontoxic, benign solvent that could be recycled readily?

Let's look again at the states of matter and changes of state (Section 6.1), particularly the change from liquid to gas. Have you ever used a pressure cooker, or tried to cook food while backpacking in the mountains? If you have, you've probably noticed that boiling point changes with pressure. In a pressure cooker, the increase in pressure lets us cook at higher temperatures. In the mountains, where the air pressure is lower, water boils at a lower temperature, so it takes longer to prepare a meal. This behavior is shown in the following graph called a *phase* diagram:

▲ A phase diagram shows the physical state of a material at given temperatures and pressures. As the temperature and pressure increase, the material shown in the graph changes from a solid to a liquid or gas. Above a certain temperature and pressure (the critical point C), the material is neither gas nor liquid but becomes a supercritical fluid.

The curve *AC* slopes upward, showing that the boiling point increases with increasing pressure. Notice that the line *AC* does not continue forever. Eventually, continued heating will take a substance to point *C*, called the *critical* point. Above the critical point, matter exists as neither a gas nor a liquid but as a kind of a hybrid called

a **supercritical fluid**. We can think of supercritical fluids as having properties of both gases and liquids. Most importantly, they can dissolve things as liquids do, but they flow rapidly like gases. We can vary these properties to make the fluid more liquid-like or more gas-like by changing the temperature or pressure.

The most commonly used supercritical fluid is carbon dioxide (scCO$_2$), an inexpensive, convenient-to-use, nonflammable, and nontoxic substance. Carbon dioxide becomes a supercritical fluid at temperatures greater than 31 °C and pressures greater than 73 atm. As a solvent, carbon dioxide (nonpolar) is a complement to water (polar), giving us two environmentally friendly solvents with different properties and uses. Individually or combined, these supercritical fluids can dissolve a wide range of chemical compounds. Also, because they can flow like gases, supercritical fluids can often make processes occur more quickly.

Supercritical water and scCO$_2$ are "generally regarded as safe" by the U.S. Food and Drug Administration and are often used in the food industry (see Chapter 17). For example, coffee is sometimes decaffeinated using scCO$_2$ extraction. After the extraction, the scCO$_2$ is decompressed and returned to a gaseous state, leaving the caffeine behind. The gaseous CO$_2$ is cooled and compressed to return it to a liquid form to be used again. This process is much greener than the older one using toxic methylene chloride, a liquid that had to be removed from the coffee by distillation. In the green chemistry essay "Practicing Green Chemistry at Home" in Chapter 21, you will see that carbon dioxide can also be used to replace perchloroethylene (C_2Cl_4), another toxic chlorinated hydrocarbon long used in dry cleaning.

Flavors and fragrances are often isolated using scCO$_2$. In the cosmetics industry, oils such as palm oil or jojoba oil are isolated from their plant sources using scCO$_2$. Supercritical fluids are used to clean or degrease precision parts in electronic instruments and medical devices. In more specialized cases, chemical reactions are carried out using supercritical fluid solvents. The main drawback to the use of supercritical fluids is that special equipment is needed to control the temperatures and high pressures required for these processes. The generation of specialty materials as nanoparticles (Section 20.4) or low-density aerogels, very strong insulators with nanoscale structures, is also favored in scCO$_2$.

Nearly all chemical processes require the separation of one chemical from a mixture of others by dissolving the compound of interest in a separate phase. Water and scCO$_2$ give us a pair of inexpensive and safe solvents that dissolve a wide range of chemical compounds—an excellent application of Green Chemistry Principle 5, which urges the use of safer reaction conditions and less toxic solvents.

SELF-ASSESSMENT Questions

1. In the ideal gas equation, $PV = nRT$, the variable n stands for
   a. a constant
   b. the number of atoms
   c. the number of moles
   d. the principal quantum number

2. At STP, 1.00 mol of an ideal gas occupies 22.4 L. What volume does 1.00 mol of an ideal gas occupy at 20 °C and 1.50 atm?
   a. 13.9 L b. 22.4 L c. 16.0 L d. 672 L

3. The molar volume of an ideal gas at 2.00 atm and 546 K is
   a. 5.60 L b. 22.4 L c. 44.8 L d. 89.6 L

Answers: 1, c; 2, c; 3, b

SUMMARY

Section 6.1—When a substance is melted or vaporized, the forces that hold its particles (molecules, atoms, or ions) close to one another are overcome. Several properties are related to the strengths of those forces. The **melting point** of a solid is the temperature at which the forces holding the particles together in a regular arrangement are overcome. The reverse of the melting process, a liquid changing to a solid, is called *freezing*. **Vaporization** is the conversion of a liquid to a gas; the reverse process is called **condensation**. The temperature at which a substance vaporizes is called its **boiling point**. Some substances undergo **sublimation**, a conversion directly from the solid to the gaseous state.

Section 6.2—Ionic solids have very strong forces holding the ions to one another, so most ionic compounds have higher melting points and higher boiling points than molecular compounds.

Section 6.3—**Dipole–dipole forces** are due to the attraction of the positive end of one dipole for the negative end of another dipole. Nonpolar molecules also have forces between them. These **dispersion forces** result from electron motions within molecules, which cause tiny, short-lived dipoles. Dispersion forces are generally weak. An especially strong type of dipolar force occurs when the positive end of a dipole is a hydrogen atom attached to N, O, or F and the negative end is a second N, O, or F atom. Such a force is called a **hydrogen bond**. Generally, hydrogen bonds are much stronger than dipole–dipole forces, which are stronger than dispersion forces.

Section 6.4—A **solution** is a homogeneous mixture of two (or more) substances. The substance that is dissolved is called the **solute**, and the dissolving substance is called the **solvent**. Nonpolar solutes dissolve in nonpolar solvents. Polar and ionic solutes dissolve in polar solvents.

Section 6.5—The behavior of gases is explained using **kinetic–molecular theory**, which describes gas particles: (1) They move rapidly and constantly and in straight lines; (2) they are far apart; (3) there is little interaction among them; (4) when they collide, energy is conserved; (5) temperature is a measure of their average kinetic energy.

Section 6.6—**Boyle's law** says that the volume of a fixed amount of a gas varies inversely with pressure at constant temperature, or $P_1V_1 = P_2V_2$. **Charles's law** says that the volume of a fixed amount of a gas varies directly with absolute (Kelvin) temperature at constant pressure, or $V_1/T_1 = V_2/T_2$. **Gay-Lussac's law** says that the pressure of a fixed amount of a gas varies directly with absolute (Kelvin) temperature at constant volume, or $P_1/T_1 = P_2/T_2$. **Avogadro's law** states that at constant temperature and pressure the volume of a gas is directly proportional to the number of moles of gas, $V = cn$. The **molar volume** of any gas is the volume occupied by 1 mol of the gas. At 0 °C and 1 atm, known as **standard temperature and pressure (STP)**, the molar volume is 22.4 L for any gas. We can use that molar volume to convert from moles of gas to volume, and vice versa.

Section 6.7—The simple gas laws can be incorporated into a single relationship called the **combined gas law**. The **ideal gas law** shows the relationship among pressure (P), volume (V), number of moles (n), and absolute temperature (T): $PV = nRT$. When P is in atmospheres, V is in liters, n is moles of gas, and T is in kelvins, the value of the constant R is 0.0821 liter · atm/(mol · K).

GREEN CHEMISTRY—While we are familiar with gases, liquids, and solids, a fourth phase of matter, **supercritical fluid**, exists at higher temperatures and pressures. Supercritical fluids have solubility properties similar to liquids, yet they flow like gases. The most common of these fluids, scCO$_2$, is considered an environmentally friendly solvent and is replacing more toxic solvents in laboratories and industrial processes.

Learning Objectives

❯ Explain how the different properties of solids, liquids, and gases are related to the motion and spacing of atoms, molecules, or ions. (6.1)	Problems 1–4
❯ Identify some differences between ionic and molecular substances, and explain why these differences exist. (6.2)	Problems 8–9
❯ Classify forces between molecules as dipole–dipole forces, dispersion forces, or hydrogen bonds. (6.3)	Problems 5, 10–12
❯ Explain the effects that intermolecular forces have on melting and boiling points. (6.3)	Problems 6, 13

❯ Explain why nonpolar solutes tend to dissolve in nonpolar solvents and polar and ionic solutes tend to dissolve in polar solvents. (6.4)	Problems 14, 15
❯ List the five basic concepts of the kinetic–molecular theory of gases. (6.5)	Problems 47, 48
❯ State the four simple gas laws, by name and mathematically. (6.6)	Problems 49, 50
❯ Use any gas law to find the value of one variable if the other values are given. (6.6)	Problems 7, 16–34, 51–59
❯ State the ideal gas law, and use it to calculate one of the quantities if the others are given. (6.7)	Problems 35–46, 60–63
❯ Describe how Green Chemistry principle 3 must be considered in designing chemical reactions and processes.	Problems 64, 65
❯ Identify the properties that make supercritical fluids applicable in greener chemical processes.	Problems 66, 67

 ## REVIEW QUESTIONS

1. In what ways are liquids and solids similar? In what ways are they different?

2. Define each of the following terms.
   a. melting   b. vaporization
   c. condensation   d. freezing

3. Label each arrow with the correct term from Question 2 that identifies the process.

solid   liquid   gas

4. In which process is energy absorbed by the substance undergoing the change of state?
   a. melting or freezing
   b. condensation or vaporization

5. List four types of interactions between the particles of a substance in the liquid and solid states from weakest to strongest. Give an example of each type.

6. What intermolecular forces or combinations of intermolecular forces are likely to lead to
   a. the higest melting point?
   b. the lowest boiling point?

7. In the combined gas law, is the volume of a gas directly proportional or inversely proportional to the pressure? Is the volume directly or inversely proportional to the absolute temperature?

 ## PROBLEMS

Intermolecular Forces

8. What type of intermolecular interaction predominates in each substance?
   a. ammonia (NH_3)   b. ethane (C_2H_6)
   c. helium (He)   d. potassium chloride (KCl)

9. Which of the following have ionic bonds: N_2, NBr_3, NaBr?

10. For which of the following would hydrogen bonding be an important intermolecular force?

   a. H—S with H below (H—S—H)

   b.
   $$\text{H}\!-\!\overset{\displaystyle \text{H}}{\underset{\displaystyle \text{H}}{\text{C}}}\!-\!\overset{}{\underset{\displaystyle \text{H}}{\text{N}}}\!-\!\text{H}$$

   c.
   $$\text{H}\!-\!\overset{\displaystyle \text{H}}{\underset{\displaystyle \text{H}}{\text{C}}}\!-\!\text{F}$$

   d.
   $$\text{H}\!-\!\overset{\displaystyle \text{H}}{\underset{\displaystyle \text{H}}{\text{C}}}\!-\!\text{O}$$

   e.
   $$\text{H}\!-\!\overset{\displaystyle \text{H}}{\underset{\displaystyle \text{H}}{\text{C}}}\!-\!\overset{\displaystyle \text{H}}{\underset{\displaystyle \text{H}}{\text{C}}}\!-\!\text{H}$$

11. In which of the following are dispersion forces the only type of intermolecular force: N_2, NH_3, NCl_3?

12. In which of the following substances are dipole–dipole forces an important intermolecular force: Br_2, HBr, NaBr?

13. Order the chemicals in Question 8 by expected melting point.

14. Hexane (C_6H_{14}) is a nonpolar solvent. Would you expect KNO_3 to dissolve in hexane? Explain.

15. Which of the following would you expect to dissolve in water and which in carbon tetrachloride (CCl_4)?
   a. NaCl   b. C_5H_{12} c. C_8H_{18} d. Li_2CO_3

Boyle's Law

16. A sample of helium occupies 1820 mL at 719 mmHg. Assume that the temperature is held constant and determine **(a)** the volume of the helium at 752 mmHg and **(b)** the pressure, in mmHg, if the volume is changed to 345 mL.

17. A decompression chamber used by deep-sea divers has a volume of 10.1 m^3 and operates at an internal pressure of 4.25 atm. What volume, in cubic meters, would the air in the chamber occupy if it were at 1.00 atm pressure, assuming no temperature change?

18. Oxygen used in respiratory therapy is stored at room temperature under a pressure of 150 atm in a gas cylinder with a volume of 60.0 L.
   a. What volume would the oxygen occupy at 0.925 atm? Assume no temperature change.

b. If the oxygen flow to the patient is adjusted to 6.00 L/min at room temperature and 0.925 atm, how long will the tank of gas last?

19. The pressure within a 4.50-L balloon is 1.10 atm. If the volume of the balloon increases to 9.95 L, what will the final pressure within the balloon be if the temperature does not change?

20. A gas sample has a volume of 0.954 L at a pressure of 764 mmHg. What would be the pressure of the gas if the volume is changed to 477 mL? Assume that the amount and the temperature of the gas remain constant.

21. A balloon filled with air at a pressure of 0.994 atm has a volume of 1.88 L. What will be the volume of the balloon if the pressure is changed to 0.497 atm? Assume that the temperature and the amount of the gas remain constant.

Charles's Law

22. A balloon is filled with helium. Its volume is 5.90 L at 26 °C. What will its volume be at 78 °C, assuming no pressure change?

23. A gas at a temperature of 100 °C occupies a volume of 154 mL. What will the volume be at 10 °C, assuming no change in pressure?

24. A sample of gas at STP is to be heated at constant pressure until its volume triples. What will the final gas temperature be?

25. A normal breath of air is about 1.00 L. If the air is drawn in at 18 °C and is warmed to 37 °C, what will be the new volume of the air? Assume that the pressure and amount of the gas remain constant.

26. A normal breath of air is about 1.00 L. If the air is drawn in at −10 °C and is warmed to 37 °C, what will be the new volume of the air? Assume that the pressure and the amount of the gas remain constant.

27. A 567-mL sample of a gas at 305 °C and 1.20 atm is cooled at constant pressure until its volume becomes 425 mL. What is the final gas temperature?

28. An air/gasoline vapor mix in an automobile cylinder has an initial temperature of 177 °C and a volume of 12.7 cm^3. If the mixture is heated to 565 °C with the pressure and amount held constant, what will be the final volume of the gas in cubic centimeters?

Molar Volume and Gas Densities

29. What is the volume of each of the following samples of gas at STP?
   a. 1.00 mol Kr   **b.** 1.75 mol H_2 **c.** 0.225 mol C_2H_4

30. What is the mass in grams of one molar volume of each of the gases in Problem 29?

31. Calculate the density, in grams per liter, of radon (Rn) gas at STP.

32. Calculate the density, in grams per liter, of carbon dioxide (CO_2) gas at STP.

33. Calculate the molar mass of **(a)** a gas that has a density of 2.12 g/L at STP and **(b)** an unknown liquid, whose vapor has a density of 2.97 g/L at STP.

34. Calculate the molar mass of **(a)** a gas that has a density of 1.98 g/L at STP and **(b)** an unknown liquid for which 3.33 L of its vapor at STP weighs 10.88 g.

The Ideal Gas Law

35. Will the volume of a fixed amount of a gas increase, decrease, or remain unchanged with
   a. an increase in pressure at constant temperature?
   b. a decrease in temperature at constant pressure?
   c. a decrease in pressure coupled with an increase in temperature?

36. Will the pressure of a fixed amount of a gas increase, decrease, or remain unchanged with
   a. an increase in temperature at constant volume?
   b. a decrease in volume at constant temperature?
   c. an increase in temperature coupled with a decrease in volume?

37. According to the kinetic–molecular theory, **(a)** what change in temperature occurs if the particles of a gas begin to move more slowly, on average, and **(b)** what change in pressure occurs when the particles of a gas strike the walls of the container less often?

38. For each of the following, indicate whether a given gas will have the same or different densities in the two containers. If the densities are different, in which container is the density greater?
   a. Containers A and B have the same volume and are at the same temperature, but the gas in A is at a higher pressure.
   b. Containers A and B are at the same pressure and temperature, but the volume of A is greater than that of B.
   c. Containers A and B are at the same pressure and volume, but the gas in A is at a higher temperature.

39. Calculate **(a)** the volume, in liters, of 0.00600 mol of a gas at 31 °C and 0.870 atm and **(b)** the pressure, in atmospheres, of 0.0108 mol $CH_4(g)$ in a 0.265-L flask at 37 °C.

40. Calculate **(a)** the volume, in liters, of 1.12 mol $H_2S(g)$ at 62 °C and 1.38 atm and **(b)** the pressure, in atmospheres, of 4.64 mol CO(g) in a 3.96-L tank at 29 °C.

41. How many moles of Kr(g) are there in 0.555 L of the gas at 0.918 atm and 25 °C?

42. How many grams of CO(g) are there in 74.5 mL of the gas at 0.933 atm and 30 °C?

43. How many moles of gas are there in a 660 mL sample at 298 K and a pressure of 0.154 atm?

44. A 0.334 mol sample of xenon gas has a volume of 20.0 L at a pressure of 0.555 atm. What is the temperature of the gas in degrees Celsius?

45. What must the volume be for a 4.55 mol of a gas at 7.32 atm 285 K?

46. What is the pressure of 0.0456 mol of CO_2 gas contained in a 7.50 L volume at 29° C?

ADDITIONAL PROBLEMS

47. What are the five basic postulates of the kinetic–molecular theory? Which postulate best explains why a gas can be compressed?

48. Which of the postulates of the kinetic–molecular theory explain why the same gas laws can be used to describe most gases?

49. What conditions of a gas sample ought to remain constant for **(a)** Boyle's law to be used? **(b)** For Charles's law to be used? **(c)** For Avogadro's law to be used?

50. Which simple gas law has the form $P_1V_1 = P_2V_2$?

51. What mass of He(g) will occupy the same volume at STP as 0.75 mol H_2 at STP? (*Hint:* It is not necessary to find the volume of the H_2 at STP.)

52. Which of the following gases has the greatest density at STP? Explain how this question may be answered *without* calculating the densities.
    a. BF_3 b. SO_3
    c. OF_2 d. PF_3

53. Look again at Figure 6.16. If the balloon has a volume of a 1.50 L at 20 °C, what will its final volume be in part **(a)**, assuming that the air in the balloon reaches the temperature of the liquid nitrogen? You may ignore the stretching forces in the rubber.

54. Three 2.00-L flasks, labeled X, Y, and Z, each at 758 mmHg and 21 °C, contain neon (Flask X), argon (Flask Y), and krypton (Flask Z). **(a)** Which flask holds the most atoms of gas? **(b)** In which flask does the gas have the greatest density? **(c)** If Flask X is heated and Flask Y is cooled, which of the flasks will have the highest pressure? **(d)** If the temperature of Flask X is lowered and that of Flask Z is raised, which of the three flasks will contain the largest number of moles of gas?

55. A 14.4-g sample of an unknown gas has a volume of 8.00 L at 760 mmHg and 25 °C. What is the molar mass of the gas?

56. If a basketball is inflated to an internal pressure of 1.32 atm at 25 °C and then taken outside, where the temperature is 10 °C, what will be the final pressure in the ball?

57. What is the volume **(a)** in cubic meters and **(b)** in liters of a room that is 4.6 m × 4.9 m × 3.0 m? **(c)** What mass in kg of CO_2(g) at STP will the room hold?

58. A gas at 750 mmHg and 27 °C has a density of 2.32 g/L. Which of the following could it be: CO_2, Kr, H_2S, or C_4H_{10}?

59. The density (mass per unit volume) of air in the atmosphere is proportional to the atmospheric pressure. At sea level, mean atmospheric pressure is 760 mmHg. Boyle's law, which relates the pressure of a given amount of gas to its volume, indicates that density decreases with altitude in the atmosphere. As altitude increases, there is less mass of air above a given point; thus, less pressure is exerted. About half the mass of the atmosphere lies below an altitude of about 5.5 km, about 95% of the mass lies below 25 km, and 99% below 30 km. What is the approximate pressure at an altitude of **(a)** 5.5 km, **(b)** 25 km, and **(c)** 30 km?

60. How many liters of hydrogen gas (at STP) are produced from the electrolysis of 1.00 L H_2O(l)? (Hint: 1.00 L H_2O weighs 1.00 kg.)

61. Which of the following will *not* result in an increase in the volume of a gas?
    a. an increase in temperature
    b. an increase in pressure
    c. a decrease in temperature
    d. a threefold increase in pressure together with a twofold reduction in Kelvin temperature

62. Choose the answer that correctly completes the statement: At 0 °C and 0.500 atm, 4.48 L NH_3(g) **(a)** contains 0.20 mol NH_3; **(b)** has a mass of 3.40 g; **(c)** contains 6.02×10^{22} molecules; **(d)** contains 0.40 mol NH_3.

63. Butane (C_4H_{10}), a gas at room temperature, is compressed to a liquid and used as a fuel in cigarette lighters and camping stoves. If the 5.00 mL of liquid butane ($d = 0.601$ g/mL at 20 °C) in a lighter vaporizes, about what volume will the gas occupy at STP?

64. Which of the following properties must be considered when selecting a solvent for a chemical process?
    a. solute and solvent polarity
    b. ease of isolation of solute
    c. flammability
    d. toxicity
    e. all of the above

65. Many of the Presidential Green Chemistry Challenge Awards have involved the use of liquid or supercritical carbon dioxide. What properties of $scCO_2$ support its use in greener chemical processing?

66. Give two examples of solvents previously used in industrial processes that have been replaced by $scCO_2$.

67. In addition to Green Chemistry Principles 3 and 5, how else might the use of an environmentally friendly solvent like $scCO_2$ impact green chemistry?

CRITICAL THINKING EXERCISES

Apply knowledge that you have gained in this chapter and one or more of the FLaReS principles (Chapter 1) to evaluate the following statements or claims.

6.1. Some tire stores claim that filling your car tires with pure, dry nitrogen is much better than using plain air. They make the following claims: **(1)** The pressure inside N_2-filled tires does not rise or fall with temperature changes. **(2)** Nitrogen leaks out of tires much more slowly than air because the N_2 molecules are bigger. **(3)** Nitrogen is not very reactive, and moisture and O_2 in air cause corrosion that shortens tire life by 25–30%.

6.2. A researcher claims to have discovered why the gecko can walk on walls and ceilings. His claim is that the lizard's feet have many microscopic hairlike protrusions that get close enough to the wall or ceiling surface to allow intermolecular forces to "take over" and hold the gecko to the surface.

6.3. A microbrewery claims to have prepared "hydrogen beer." This beer is reportedly "carbonated" with H_2 gas instead of CO_2 gas. A chemist at the brewery claims that the H_2 gas molecules engage in hydrogen bonding with the water molecules in the beer, so that more gas can dissolve in the beer.

6.4. A student in an advanced chemistry course has been assigned to determine the density of the vapor from an unknown liquid. She claims that the density is 0.053 g/L.

 COLLABORATIVE GROUP PROJECTS

Prepare a PowerPoint, poster, or other presentation (as directed by your instructor) to share with the class.

1. Look ahead to Table 9.3 and consider this series of compounds: methane (CH_4), ethane (CH_3CH_3), propane ($CH_3CH_2CH_3$), butane ($CH_3CH_2CH_2CH_3$), and pentane ($CH_3CH_2CH_2CH_2CH_3$). For each compound: **(a)** Indicate whether its molecules are polar or nonpolar. **(b)** Indicate the predominant type of intermolecular forces in the liquid state. **(c)** Calculate the molar mass. **(d)** Convert each boiling point from Celsius degrees to kelvins. **(e)** Plot a graph of boiling point (in K) versus molar mass. **(f)** Is there any discernible relationship between molar mass and boiling point?

2. Consider this series of compounds: methane (CH_4), fluoromethane (CH_3F), chloromethane (CH_3Cl), bromomethane (CH_3Br), and iodomethane (CH_3I). Repeat parts **(a)** through **(e)** of Project 1 for these compounds. Boiling points may be found in a printed reference work, such as the *CRC Handbook* or *Merck Index*, or on a website such as that of the National Institute for Standards and Technology (NIST). Is there any discernible relationship between molar mass and boiling point? How does the graph for these compounds differ from that in Project 1? Suggest a reason for the difference.

3. Most ionic compounds are solids, but *ionic liquids* have recently been made and have found many uses. Search the Web for information on ionic liquids. In particular, find out why they are liquids rather than solids, and report on some of their current and potential applications.

CHEMISTRY@HOME   **Blow Up My Balloon**

Materials required

- 1 Small balloon
- 1 Container with lid large enough to hold the balloon (for instance, a pot and a lid)
- Warm water
- Ice
- Measuring tape, or a piece of string and a ruler (Hint: Use the string to measure the circumference of the balloon, then measure the length using the ruler)

For this exercise, we will blow up a small balloon and observe the volume of the gas upon heating or cooling. You will be applying your knowledge of Charles's law in this experiment.

First, inflate the balloon and secure it so that the air cannot escape. Measure and record the circumference of the balloon (the distance around the outside of the balloon).

Next, place the balloon in a container that is filled with warm tap water. Make sure your container has enough water to cover much of the balloon, but not too much water so that it spills out. Now, cover the container and allow the balloon to warm up to the temperature of the water (about 5 minutes).

Take the balloon out of the container and measure and record the circumference of the hot balloon. Allow the balloon to cool to room temperature for about 2 to 3 minutes. While the balloon is cooling, pour the warm water out of the container and replace it with ice water.

Then, place the balloon into the container with the ice water and cover the container with the lid. Allow the balloon to cool for about 5 minutes. Remove the balloon from the container and measure and record the circumference of the cold balloon. What do you notice about the size of the cold and warm balloon? Now, place your hands on the cold balloon as it is warming up. What do you notice about the balloon?

Questions

1. What was the overall change in the circumference of the balloon after heating?
2. What was the overall change in the circumference of the balloon after cooling?
3. Why did the balloon change in size when you heated or cooled the balloon?
4. What can you conclude about the dependence of temperature and volume of a gas?
5. What would happen if you had a rigid container that did not expand or contract like the balloon? Would you expect the pressure to rise or fall if heated or cooled?

ACIDS AND BASES

7

Have You Ever Wondered?

1. **Are all acids corrosive?**

2. **What is an amino acid?**

3. **What is the difference between salt and sodium?**

4. **What is meant by "pH-balanced shampoo"?**

PLEASE PASS THE PROTONS

Have you ever tasted a lemon or a grapefruit? Or felt a burning sensation on your arm after using a cleaning solution containing ammonia? These are but two examples of acids (citric acid in lemons and grapefruit) and bases (ammonia in cleaning solutions) that we encounter in our daily lives. Other familiar acids are vinegar (acetic acid), vitamin C (ascorbic acid), and battery acid (sulfuric acid). Some familiar bases are drain cleaners (sodium hydroxide), baking soda (sodium bicarbonate), and antacids.

From "acid indigestion" to "acid rain," the word *acid* appears frequently in the news and in advertisements. Air and water pollution often

The chemical substances we call acids and bases are all around us. Acids are used in steel production and metal plating, as well as in chemical analysis. Acids are even found in the food we eat. Pancakes and muffins rise because of acids and bases in the ingredients, and the tart taste of fruit comes from the different acids in its flesh. If you get too much acid in your stomach, antacids (bases) can provide relief.

Learning Objectives

> Distinguish between acids and bases using their chemical and physical properties. (7.1)

> Explain how an acid–base indicator works. (7.1)

> Identify Arrhenius and Brønsted–Lowry acids and bases. (7.2)

> Write a balanced equation for a neutralization or an ionization. (7.2)

> Identify acidic and basic anhydrides, and write equations showing their reactions with water. (7.3)

> Define and identify strong and weak acids and bases. (7.4)

> Identify the reactants and predict the products in a neutralization reaction. (7.5)

> Describe the relationship between the pH of a solution and its acidity or basicity. (7.6)

> Find the molar concentration of hydrogen ion, $[H^+]$, from a pH value or the pH value from $[H^+]$. (7.6)

> Write the formula for the conjugate base of an acid or for the conjugate acid of a base. (7.7)

> Describe the action of a buffer. (7.7)

> Describe everyday uses of acids and bases and how they affect daily life. (7.8)

> Recognize carbon dioxide in water as a useful, safe source of acid.

> Describe alternate choices for greener reaction conditions when using acids and bases.

involve acids and bases. Acid rain, for example, is a serious environmental problem. In arid areas, alkaline (basic) water is sometimes undrinkable.

Did you know that our senses recognize four tastes related to acid–base chemistry? Acids taste sour, bases taste bitter, and the compounds formed when acids react with bases (salts) taste salty. The sweet taste is more complicated. To taste sweet, a compound must have both an acidic part and a basic part, plus just the right geometry to fit the sweet-taste receptors of our taste buds.

In this chapter, we discuss some of the chemistry of acids and bases. You use them every day. Your body processes them continuously. You will probably hear and read about them as long as you live. What you learn here can help you gain a better understanding of these important classes of compounds.

7.1 Acids and Bases: Experimental Definitions

Learning Objectives ❯ Distinguish between acids and bases using their chemical and physical properties. ❯ Explain how an acid–base indicator works.

Acids and bases are chemical opposites, and so their properties are quite different—often opposite. Let's begin by listing a few of these properties.

An *acid* is a compound that

- tastes sour.
- causes litmus indicator dye to turn red.
- dissolves active metals such as zinc and iron, producing hydrogen gas.
- reacts with bases to form water and ionic compounds called *salts*.

A *base* is a compound that

- tastes bitter.
- causes litmus indicator dye to turn blue.
- feels slippery on the skin.
- reacts with acids to form water and salts.

We can identify foods that are acidic by their sour taste. Vinegar and lemon juice are examples. Vinegar is a solution of acetic acid (about 5%) in water. Lemons, limes, and other citrus fruits contain citric acid. Lactic acid gives yogurt its tart taste, and

▲ **Figure 7.1** Some common acids (left), bases (center), and salts (right). Acids, bases, and salts are components of many familiar consumer products.

Q: *How would each of the three classes of compounds affect the indicator dye litmus? (See Figure 7.2.)*

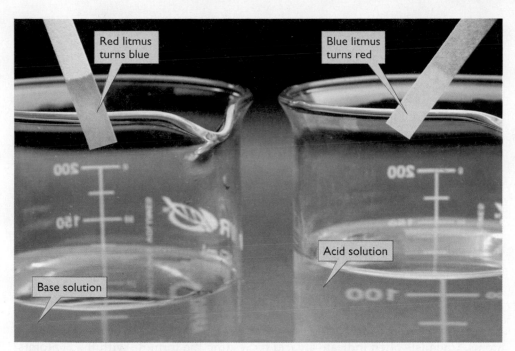

Red litmus turns blue

Blue litmus turns red

Acid solution

Base solution

▲ **Figure 7.2** Strips of paper impregnated with litmus dye (extracted from a fungus) are often used to distinguish between acids and bases. The sample on the left turns litmus blue and is therefore basic. The sample on the right turns litmus red and is acidic.

It DOES Matter!

Hydrangea is one of many types of flowers that may show different colors depending on the acidity of the soil in which it is grown. Some varieties are blue (top) when planted in slightly acidic soil but pink (bottom) when planted in more basic soil.

phosphoric acid is often added to carbonated drinks to impart tartness. The bitter taste of tonic water, on the other hand, comes in part from quinine, a base. Figure 7.1 shows some common acids and bases.

A litmus test is a common way to identify a substance as an acid or a base. Litmus (Figure 7.2) is an **acid–base indicator**, one of many such compounds. If you dip a strip of neutral (violet-colored) litmus paper into an unknown solution and the strip turns pink, the solution is acidic. If it turns blue, the solution is basic. If the strip does not turn pink or blue, the solution is neither acidic nor basic. Many substances, such as those that give the colors to grape juice, red cabbage, blueberries, and many flower petals, are acid–base indicators.

SELF-ASSESSMENT Questions

1. Which of the following is *not* a property of acids?
   a. feel slippery on the skin
   b. react with Zn to form hydrogen gas
   c. taste sour
   d. turn litmus red

2. Which of the following is *not* a property of bases?
   a. feel slippery on the skin
   b. react with salts to form acids
   c. taste bitter
   d. turn litmus blue

3. In general, when an acid and a base are mixed,
   a. a new acid and a salt are formed
   b. a new base and a salt are formed
   c. no reaction occurs
   d. water and a salt are formed

4. A common substance that contains lactic acid is
   a. olive oil   b. soap   c. vinegar   d. yogurt

5. The sour taste of grapefruit is due to
   a. acetic acid   b. ammonia   c. sodium chloride   d. citric acid

▲ You can make your own indicator dye. Chop about 2 cups of red cabbage. Cover with boiling water. Stir. After about 10 min, filter out the solids with a coffee filter. Add a few mL of the liquid to various household chemicals (vinegar, baking soda, ammonia, and so on) to test for pH. The indicator changes from red at about pH 2 to purple at pH 4, violet at pH 6, blue at pH 8, blue-green at pH 10, and greenish-yellow at pH 12. Other plant materials that contain indicators include blackberries, black raspberries, red radish peels, red rose petals, and turmeric. See Chemistry @ Home box on p. 215.

Answers: 1, *a*; 2, *b*; 3, *d*; 4, *d*; 5, *d*

7.2 Acids, Bases, and Salts

Learning Objectives ❭ Identify Arrhenius and Brønsted–Lowry acids and bases.
❭ Write a balanced equation for a neutralization or an ionization.

Acids and bases have certain characteristic properties. But why do they have these properties? We use several different theories to explain them.

The Arrhenius Theory

Svante Arrhenius developed the first successful theory of acids and bases in 1887. According to Arrhenius's concept, an **acid** is a molecular substance that breaks up in aqueous solution into hydrogen ions (H^+) and an anion. (Because a hydrogen ion is a hydrogen atom from which the sole electron has been removed, H^+ ions are also called *protons*.) The acid is said to *ionize*. For example, nitric acid ionizes in water.

$$HNO_3(aq) \longrightarrow H^+(aq) + NO_3^-(aq)$$

In water, the properties of acids are those of the H^+ ion. It is the hydrogen ion that turns litmus red, tastes sour, and reacts with bases and active metals. Table 7.1 lists some common acids. Notice that each formula contains one or more hydrogen atoms. Chemists often indicate an acid by writing the formula with the H atom(s) first. HCl, H_2SO_4, and HNO_3 are acids; NH_3 and CH_4 are not. The formula $HC_2H_3O_2$ (acetic acid) indicates that one H atom ionizes when this compound is in aqueous solution, and three do not.

An Arrhenius **base** is defined as a substance that releases hydroxide ions (OH^-) in aqueous solution. Some bases are ionic solids that contain OH^-, such as sodium hydroxide (NaOH) and calcium hydroxide $[Ca(OH)_2]$. These compounds simply release hydroxide ions into the solution when the solid is dissolved in water:

$$NaOH(s) \xrightarrow{H_2O} Na^+(aq) + OH^-(aq)$$

We write H_2O over the arrow to indicate that it is a solvent, not a reactant.

Other bases are molecular substances such as ammonia that ionize to produce OH^- when placed in water (see page 195).

Experimental evidence indicates that the properties of bases in water are due to OH^-. Table 7.2 lists some common bases. Most of these are ionic compounds containing positively charged metal ions, such as Na^+ or Ca^{2+}, and negatively charged hydroxide ions. When these compounds dissolve in water, they all provide OH^- ions, and thus they are all bases. The properties of bases are those of hydroxide ions, just as the properties of acids are those of hydrogen ions.

▲ Swedish chemist Svante Arrhenius (1859–1927) proposed the theory that acids, bases, and salts in water are composed of ions. He also was the first to relate carbon dioxide in the atmosphere to the greenhouse effect (Chapter 13).

1. Are all acids corrosive?

It is clear from Table 7.1 that acid does not necessarily mean "corrosive." Many acids are harmless enough to be included in foods we eat, and some are necessary for life.

Table 7.1	Some Common Acids		
Name	Formula	Acid Strength	Common Uses/Notes
Sulfuric acid	H_2SO_4	Strong	Battery acid; ore processing, fertilizer manufacturing, oil refining
Hydrochloric acid	HCl	Strong	Cleaning of metals and bricks, removing scale from boilers
Phosphoric acid	H_3PO_4	Moderate	Used in colas and rust removers
Lactic acid	$CH_3CHOHCOOH$	Weak	Yogurt; acidulant (food additive to increase tartness), lotion additive
Acetic acid	CH_3COOH	Weak	Vinegar; acidulant
Boric acid	H_3BO_3	Very weak	Antiseptic eyewash, roach poison
Hydrocyanic acid	HCN	Very weak	Plastics manufacture; extremely toxic

Table 7.2	Some Common Bases		
Name	Formula	Classification	Common Uses/Notes
Sodium hydroxide	NaOH	Strong	Acid neutralization; soap making
Potassium hydroxide	KOH	Strong	Making liquid soaps and biodiesel fuels
Lithium hydroxide	LiOH	Strong	Alkaline storage batteries
Calcium hydroxide	Ca(OH)$_2$	Strong[a]	Plaster, cement; soil neutralizer
Magnesium hydroxide	Mg(OH)$_2$	Strong[a]	Antacid, laxative
Ammonia	NH$_3$	Weak	Fertilizer, household cleansers

[a]Although these bases are classified as strong, they are not very soluble in water. Calcium hydroxide is only slightly soluble, and magnesium hydroxide is practically insoluble.

Arrhenius further proposed that the essential reaction between an acid and a base, **neutralization**, is the combination of H^+ and OH^- to form water. The cation that was originally associated with the OH^- combines with the anion that was associated with the H^+ to form an ionic compound, a **salt**.

$$\text{An acid} + \text{a base} \longrightarrow \text{a salt} + \text{water}$$

▲ Many skin-peel preparations used by cosmetologists contain alpha-hydroxy acids such as glycolic acid or lactic acid.

CONCEPTUAL Example 7.1   Ionization of Acids and Bases

Write equations showing **(a)** the ionization of sulfuric acid (H_2SO_4) in water and **(b)** the ionization of solid potassium hydroxide (KOH) in water.

Solution

a. An H_2SO_4 molecule ionizes to form *two* hydrogen ions and a sulfate ion. Because this reaction occurs in water, we can use the label "(aq)" to indicate that the substances involved are in aqueous solution.

$$H_2SO_4(aq) \longrightarrow 2\,H^+(aq) + SO_4^{2-}(aq)$$

b. Potassium hydroxide (KOH), an ionic solid, simply dissolves in the water, forming separate $K^+(aq)$ and $OH^-(aq)$ ions.

$$KOH(s) \xrightarrow{H_2O} K^+(aq) + OH^-(aq)$$

■ **EXERCISE 7.1A**

Write equations showing **(a)** the ionization of HI (hydroiodic acid) in water and **(b)** the ionization of solid calcium hydroxide in water.

■ **EXERCISE 7.1B**

Historically, formulas for carboxylic acids (compounds containing a —COOH group; see Chapter 9) are often written with the ionizable hydrogen *last*. For example, instead of writing the formula for acetic acid as $HC_2H_3O_2$, it can be written as CH_3COOH. Write an equation showing the ionization of CH_3COOH in water.

2. What is an amino acid?

An amino acid is a molecule that contains both —COOH, which is acidic, and —NH$_2$ (an *amino group*; see Sections 9.8 and 9.9), which is basic. Amino acids link together to form the proteins in living tissue.

Limitations of the Arrhenius Theory

The Arrhenius theory is limited in several ways.

▪ A simple free proton does not exist in water solution. The H^+ ion has such a high positive charge density that it is immediately attracted to a lone pair of electrons on an O atom of an H_2O molecule, forming a *hydronium ion*, H_3O^+.

$$H\!:\!\overset{\cdot\cdot}{\underset{\cdot\cdot}{O}}\!:\;+\;H^+\;\longrightarrow\;\left[H\!:\!\overset{\cdot\cdot}{\underset{\cdot\cdot}{O}}\!:\!H\right]^+$$
$$\quad\;\;\underset{\text{Water}}{\overset{|}{H}}\qquad\qquad\qquad\quad\underset{\text{Hydronium ion}}{\overset{|}{H}}$$

- It does not explain the basicity of ammonia and related compounds. Ammonia seems out of place in Table 7.2 because it contains no hydroxide ions.
- It applies only to reactions in aqueous solution.

As with many scientific theories, a better one based on newer data has supplanted Arrhenius's theory.

The Brønsted–Lowry Acid–Base Theory

The shortcomings of the Arrhenius theory were largely overcome by a theory proposed in 1923 by J. N. Brønsted in Denmark and T. M. Lowry in Great Britain, who were working independently. In the Brønsted–Lowry theory,

- an acid is a *proton donor*, and
- a base is a *proton acceptor*.

The theory portrays the ionization of hydrogen chloride in this way:

$$HCl(aq) + H_2O \longrightarrow H_3O^+(aq) + Cl^-(aq)$$

Here, water is a reactant. The acid molecules donate hydrogen ions (protons) to the water molecules, so the acid (HCl) acts as a proton donor.

Acid
(proton donor)

Hydrochloric acid

The HCl molecule donates a proton to a water molecule, producing a hydronium ion and a chloride ion and forming a solution called *hydrochloric acid*. Other acids react similarly. They donate hydrogen ions to water molecules to produce hydronium ions. If we let HA represent any acid, the reaction is written as

$$HA(aq) + H_2O \longrightarrow H_3O^+(aq) + A^-(aq)$$

Even in solvents other than water, acids still act as proton donors, transferring H^+ ions to the solvent molecules.

> In water, an H^+ ion is associated with several H_2O molecules—for example, four H_2O molecules in the ion $H(H_2O)_4{}^+$, or $H_9O_4{}^+$. For many purposes, we simply use H^+ and ignore the associated water molecules. However, keep in mind that the notation H^+ is a simplification of the real situation: Protons in water are always associated with water molecules.

CONCEPTUAL Example 7.2 | Brønsted–Lowry Acids

Write an equation showing the reaction with water of HNO_3 as a Brønsted–Lowry acid. What is the role of water in the reaction?

Solution
As a Brønsted–Lowry acid, HNO_3 donates a proton to a water molecule, forming a hydronium ion and a nitrate ion.

$$HNO_3(aq) + H_2O \longrightarrow H_3O^+(aq) + NO_3{}^-(aq)$$

Water is a Brønsted–Lowry base in this reaction; it accepts the proton from the HNO_3.

▪ EXERCISE 7.2A
Write an equation showing the reaction with water of HBr as a Brønsted–Lowry acid.

▪ EXERCISE 7.2B
Write an equation showing the reaction with methanol (CH_3OH) of $HClO_4$ as a Brønsted–Lowry acid.

Where does the OH^- come from when bases such as ammonia (NH_3) are dissolved in water? The Arrhenius theory proved inadequate in answering this question, but the Brønsted–Lowry theory explains how ammonia acts as a base in water.

Ammonia is a gas at room temperature. When it is dissolved in water, some of the ammonia molecules react as shown by the following equation.

$$NH_3(aq) + H_2O \longrightarrow NH_4^+(aq) + OH^-(aq)$$

An ammonia molecule accepts a proton from a water molecule; NH_3 acts as a Brønsted–Lowry base. (Recall that the N atom of ammonia has a lone pair of electrons, which it can share with a proton.) The water molecule acts as a proton donor—an acid. The ammonia molecule accepts the proton and becomes an ammonium ion. When a proton leaves a water molecule, it leaves behind the electron pair that it shared with the O atom. The water molecule becomes a negatively charged hydroxide ion.

In general, then, *a base is a proton acceptor* (Figure 7.3). This definition includes not only hydroxide ions but also neutral molecules such as ammonia and *amines* (organic compounds such as CH_3NH_2 that are derived from ammonia). It also includes other negative ions such as the oxide (O^{2-}), carbonate (CO_3^{2-}), and bicarbonate (HCO_3^-) ions. The idea of an acid as a proton donor and a base as a proton acceptor greatly expands our concept of acids and bases.

Acid   Base

▲ **Figure 7.3** A Brønsted–Lowry acid is a proton donor. A base is a proton acceptor.

Q: *Can you write an equation in which the acid is represented as HA and the base as B⁻?*

Salts

Salts, formed from the neutralization reactions of acids and bases, are ionic compounds composed of cations and anions. These ions can be simple ions, such as sodium ion (Na^+) or chloride ion (Cl^-), or they can be polyatomic ions, such as ammonium ion (NH_4^+), sulfate ion (SO_4^{2-}), or acetate ion (CH_3COO^-). Sodium chloride, ordinary table salt, is probably the most familiar salt, but many different salts exist.

Salts that conduct electricity when dissolved in water are called *electrolytes*. Various electrolytes, in certain amounts, are critical for many bodily functions including nerve conduction, heartbeat, and fluid balance. Medical blood tests often check levels of Na^+, K^+, Cl^-, HCO_3^-, and other electrolyte ions (Chapter 19).

There are many common salts with familiar uses. Sodium chloride and calcium chloride are used to melt ice on roads and sidewalks in winter. Copper(II) sulfate is used to kill tree roots in sewage lines. We will encounter many other examples in later chapters as dietary minerals (Chapter 17), fertilizers (Chapter 20), and more. Table 7.3 lists some salts used in medicine.

Table 7.3	Some Salts with Present or Past Uses in Medicine	
Name	Formula	Uses
Silver nitrate	$AgNO_3$	Germicide and antiseptic
Stannous fluoride [tin(II) fluoride]	SnF_2	Toothpaste additive to prevent dental cavities
Calcium sulfate (plaster of Paris)	$(CaSO_4)_2 \cdot \frac{1}{2} H_2O^a$	Plaster casts
Magnesium sulfate (Epsom salts)	$MgSO_4 \cdot 7\,H_2O^a$	Laxative, foot baths
Potassium permanganate	$KMnO_4$	Cauterizing agent, antiseptic
Ferrous sulfate [iron(II) sulfate]	$FeSO_4$	Prescribed for iron deficiency (anemia)
Zinc sulfate	$ZnSO_4$	Skin treatment (eczema)
Barium sulfate	$BaSO_4$	Provides the contrast material in "barium cocktail" given for gastrointestinal X-rays
Mercurous chloride [mercury(I) chloride; calomel]	Hg_2Cl_2	Laxative; no longer used

ªThese compounds are hydrates, substances containing water molecules combined in a definite ratio as an integral part of the compound.

SELF-ASSESSMENT Questions

For Questions 1–5, match each formula with the compound's application.

1. CH_3COOH
2. H_3BO_3
3. HCl
4. H_2SO_4
5. NaOH

a. battery acid
b. soap making
c. antiseptic eyewash
d. remove boiler scale
e. vinegar

6. Which of the following equations best represents what happens when hydrogen bromide dissolves in water?

a. $2 \ HBr \xrightarrow{H_2O} Br_2 + H_2$
b. $HBr(g) \xrightarrow{H_2O} H(aq) + Br(aq)$
c. $HBr(g) \xrightarrow{H_2O} H^+(aq) + Br^-(aq)$
d. $HBr(g) + H_2O \longrightarrow Br^-(aq) + H_3O^+(aq)$

For Questions 7–10, match each term with the correct definition.

7. Arrhenius acid
8. Arrhenius base
9. Brønsted acid
10. Brønsted base

a. proton acceptor
b. proton donor
c. produces H^+ in water
d. produces OH^- in water

Answers: 1. e; 2. c; 3. d; 4. a; 5. b; 6. d; 7. c; 8. d; 9. b; 10. a

7.3 Acidic and Basic Anhydrides

Learning Objective ❯ Identify acidic anhydrides and basic anhydrides, and write equations showing their reactions with water.

Certain metal and nonmetal oxides are well known for their ability to produce or to neutralize acids or bases. For example, nitrogen dioxide (NO_2) and sulfur dioxide (SO_2) are notorious for producing acid rain. Calcium oxide (quicklime, CaO) is widely used to neutralize acidic soils. In the Brønsted–Lowry view, many metal oxides act directly as bases because the oxide ion can accept a proton. These metal oxides also react with water to form metal hydroxides, compounds that are bases in the Arrhenius sense. And many nonmetal oxides react with water to form acids.

Nonmetal Oxides: Acidic Anhydrides

Many acids are made by reacting nonmetal oxides with water. For example, sulfur trioxide reacts with water to form sulfuric acid.

$$SO_3 + H_2O \longrightarrow H_2SO_4$$

Similarly, carbon dioxide reacts with water to form carbonic acid.

$$CO_2 + H_2O \longrightarrow H_2CO_3$$

In general, nonmetal oxides react with water to form acids.

$$\text{Nonmetal oxide} + H_2O \longrightarrow \text{acid}$$

Nonmetal oxides that act in this way are called **acidic anhydrides**. *Anhydride* means "without water." These reactions explain why rainwater is acidic (Section 7.8).

CONCEPTUAL **Example 7.3**	Acidic Anhydrides

Give the formula for the acid formed when sulfur dioxide reacts with water.

Solution

The formula for the acid, H_2SO_3, is obtained by adding the two H atoms and one O atom of water to SO_2. The equation for the reaction is simply

$$SO_2 + H_2O \longrightarrow H_2SO_3$$

■ **EXERCISE 7.3A**
Give the formula for the acid formed when selenium dioxide (SeO_2) reacts with water.

■ **EXERCISE 7.3B**
Give the formula for the acid formed when dinitrogen pentoxide (N_2O_5) reacts with water. (*Hint:* Two molecules of acid are formed.)

It DOES Matter!
Slaked lime is inexpensive, easily made from cheap raw materials, and low in toxicity. These properties make it the most widely used base for neutralizing acids. It is an ingredient in such diverse materials as bricklayer's mortar, plaster, glues, and even pickles and corn tortillas. The whitewash made famous in Mark Twain's *Adventures of Tom Sawyer* was a simple mixture of slaked lime and water.

Metal Oxides: Basic Anhydrides

Just as acids can be made from nonmetal oxides, many common hydroxide bases can be made from metal oxides. For example, calcium oxide reacts with water to form calcium hydroxide ("slaked lime").

$$CaO + H_2O \longrightarrow Ca(OH)_2$$

Another example is the reaction of lithium oxide with water to form lithium hydroxide.

$$Li_2O + H_2O \longrightarrow 2\,LiOH$$

In general, metal oxides react with water to form bases (Figure 7.4). These metal oxides are called **basic anhydrides**.

$$\text{Metal oxide} + H_2O \longrightarrow \text{base}$$

O^{2-} H_2O OH^- OH^-

▲ **Figure 7.4** Metal oxides are basic because the oxide ion reacts with water to form two hydroxide ions.

Q: *Can you write an equation that shows how solid sodium oxide (Na_2O) reacts with water to form sodium hydroxide?*

| CONCEPTUAL **Example 7.4** | Basic Anhydrides |

Give the formula for the base formed by the addition of water to barium oxide (BaO).

Solution
Again, we add the atoms of a water molecule to BaO. Because a barium ion has a 2+ charge, the formula for the base has *two* hydroxide (1−) ions.

$$BaO + H_2O \longrightarrow Ba(OH)_2$$

■ **EXERCISE 7.4A**
Give the formula for the base formed by the addition of water to strontium oxide (SrO).

■ **EXERCISE 7.4B**
What base is formed by the addition of water to potassium oxide K_2O? (*Hint:* Two moles of base are formed for each mole of potassium oxide.)

1. Selenic acid (H_2SeO_4) is an extremely corrosive acid that when heated is capable of dissolving gold. It is quite soluble in water. The anhydride of selenic acid is
   a. SeO   **b.** SeO_2 **c.** SeO_3 **d.** SeO_4

2. Zinc hydroxide [$Zn(OH)_2$] is used as an absorbent in surgical dressings. The anhydride of zinc hydroxide is
   a. ZnO   **b.** ZnOH   **c.** ZnO_2 **d.** ZnH_2

Answers: 1, c; 2, a

7.4 Strong and Weak Acids and Bases

Learning Objective ⟩ Define and identify strong and weak acids and bases.

One of the most important acid–base reactions occurs between two water molecules. As shown in Figure 7.5, it is possible for one water molecule to transfer a proton to another water molecule.

$$2\,H_2O(l) \longrightarrow H_3O^+(aq) + OH^-(aq)$$

▶ **Figure 7.5** A water molecule can transfer a proton to another water molecule to create a hydroxide and a hydronium ion. A hydronium ion can donate a proton back to a hydroxide ion to make two water molecules. Both reactions occur constantly, and the reactants and products are in equilibrium.

Hydroxide ion

Hydronium ion

Hydrogen-bonded water molecules

Formation of hydronium and hydroxide ions from hydrogen-bonded molecules

This is the opposite reaction of neutralization.

$$H_3O^+(aq) + OH^-(aq) \longrightarrow 2\,H_2O(l)$$

Both reactions occur simultaneously all the time. So, instead of writing both reactions, we use arrows pointing both ways to indicate that both the forward reaction and the backward reaction occur.

$$2\,H_2O(l) \rightleftharpoons H_3O^+(aq) + OH^-(aq)$$

Chemists read an equation like this with the double arrows as water is "in equilibrium" with hydronium and hydroxide ions. A chemical system at equilibrium does not change over time. When a system is in equilibrium, chemical reactions are occurring, but the concentrations of reactants and products stay the same. In some equilibria, a lot of product is produced. For others, like the dissociation of water, very little product is produced. At any given time in neutral water, only about one in 500 million water molecules are dissociated into hydroxide ions and hydronium ions. In this reaction, one of the water molecules is acting as an acid by donating a proton; the other is acting as a base by accepting the proton. A substance such as water that can either donate a proton or accept a proton is said to be *amphiprotic* (see also Additional Problem 66).

We can also express the autoionization of water as

$$H_2O(l) \rightleftharpoons H^+(aq) + OH^-(aq)$$

This equation focuses on the dissociation of a water molecule, and (aq) is used to indicate a solution in water. Of course, a free hydrogen ion never exists in a water solution.

Many acids participate in similar equilibria. The poisonous gas hydrogen cyanide (HCN) ionizes in water to produce hydrogen ions and cyanide ions. HCN also ionizes only to a slight extent. In a solution that has 1 mol of HCN in 1 L of water, only one HCN molecule in 40,000 ionizes to produce a hydrogen ion.

$$HCN(aq) \rightleftharpoons H^+(aq) + CN^-(aq)$$

Remember, the opposite-pointing arrows indicate that the reaction is reversible; the ions can also combine to form HCN molecules. Here, a short arrow points to the right and a longer arrow points to the left to remind us that most of the HCN remains intact as HCN molecules.

On the other hand, when gaseous hydrogen chloride (HCl) reacts with water, it reacts completely to form hydronium ions and chloride ions.

$$HCl(aq) \longrightarrow H^+(aq) + Cl^-(aq)$$

This time, only a single arrow is used because effectively 100% of the HCl molecules ionize. The opposite reaction doesn't occur.

Acids can be classified according to their extent of ionization.

- An acid such as HCl that ionizes completely in (reacts completely with) water is called a **strong acid**.
- An acid such as HCN that ionizes only slightly in water is a **weak acid**.

There are only a few strong acids. The first two acids listed in Table 7.1 (sulfuric and hydrochloric) are the most common ones. The other strong acids are nitric acid (HNO_3), hydrobromic acid (HBr), hydroiodic acid (HI), and perchloric acid ($HClO_4$). Most acids are weak acids.

Bases are also classified as strong or weak.

- A **strong base** is completely ionized in water.
- A **weak base** is only slightly ionized in water.

The word *strong* does not refer to the *amount* of acid or base in a solution. As mentioned in Section 5.5, a solution that contains a relatively large amount of an acid or a base, whether strong or weak, as the solute in a given volume of solution is called a *concentrated* solution. A solution with only a little solute in that same volume of solution is a *dilute* solution.

Perhaps the most familiar strong base is sodium hydroxide (NaOH), commonly called *lye*. It exists as sodium ions and hydroxide ions even as a solid. Other strong bases include potassium hydroxide (KOH) and the hydroxides of all the other group 1A metals. Except for $Be(OH)_2$, the hydroxides of group 2A metals are also strong bases. However, $Ca(OH)_2$ is only slightly soluble in water, and $Mg(OH)_2$ is nearly insoluble. The concentration of hydroxide ions in a solution of $Ca(OH)_2$ or $Mg(OH)_2$ is, therefore, not very high.

The most familiar weak base is ammonia (NH_3). It reacts with water to a slight extent to produce ammonium ions (NH_4^+) and hydroxide ions (Figure 7.6).

$$NH_3 + H_2O \rightleftharpoons NH_4^+ + OH^-$$

In its reaction with HCl (page 194), water acts as a base (proton acceptor). In its reaction with NH_3, water acts as an acid (proton donor).

SELF-ASSESSMENT Questions

For Questions 1–7, select the correct classification (more than one substance may fit into a given classification).

1. $Ca(OH)_2$
2. HCN
3. HF
4. HNO_3
5. NH_3
6. KOH
7. CH_3NH_2

a. strong acid
b. strong base
c. weak acid
d. weak base

8. Acetic acid reacts with water to form
   a. $CH_3COO^- + H_2O$
   b. $CH_3COOH + OH^-$
   c. $CH_3COO^- + H_3O^+$
   d. $CH_3COO^+ + OH^-$

9. Ammonia reacts with water to form
   a. $NH_3 + H_2O$
   b. $NH_4^+ + OH^-$
   c. $NH_2^- + H_3O^+$
   d. $NH_3 + OH^-$

NH₃   H₂O   NH₄⁺   OH⁻

▲ **Figure 7.6** Ammonia is a base because it accepts a proton from water. A solution of ammonia in water contains ammonium ions and hydroxide ions. Only a small fraction of the ammonia molecules react, however; most remain unchanged. Ammonia is therefore a *weak* base.

Q: *Amines are related to ammonia; in an amine, one or more of the H atoms of NH₃ is replaced by a carbon-containing group. Amines react in the same way as ammonia does. Can you write an equation that shows how the amine CH₃NH₂ reacts with water? One product is hydroxide ion.*

7.5 Neutralization

Learning Objective   ❯ Identify the reactants and predict the products in a neutralization reaction.

When an acid reacts with a base, the products are water and a salt. If a solution containing hydrogen ions (an acid) is mixed with another solution containing exactly the same amount of hydroxide ions (a base), the resulting solution does not change the color of litmus, dissolve zinc or iron, or feel slippery on the skin. It is no longer either acidic or basic. It is neutral. As was mentioned earlier, the reaction of an acid with a base is called *neutralization* (Figure 7.7).

$$H^+ + OH^- \longrightarrow H_2O$$

(a)   (b)   (c)

▲ **Figure 7.7** The amount of acid (or base) in a solution is determined by careful neutralization. Here a 5.00-mL sample of vinegar, some water, and a few drops of phenolphthalein (an acid–base indicator) are placed in a flask (a). A solution of 0.1000 M NaOH is added to the flask slowly from a buret (a device for precise measurement of volumes of solutions) (b). As long as the acid is in excess, the solution is colorless. When the acid has been neutralized and a tiny excess of base is present, the phenolphthalein indicator turns pink (c).

Q: *Can you write an equation for the reaction of acetic acid (CH₃COOH), the acid in vinegar, with aqueous NaOH?*

If sodium hydroxide is neutralized by hydrochloric acid, the products are water and sodium chloride (ordinary table salt)

A base	An acid	A salt	Water

NaOH(aq)   +   HCl(aq) ⟶ NaCl(aq)   +   H₂O

Example 7.5	Neutralization Reactions

Potassium nitrate, a component of black powder gunpowder and some fertilizers, was obtained from the late Middle Ages through the nineteenth century by precipitation from urine. Commonly called *saltpeter*, it can be prepared by the reaction of nitric acid with potassium hydroxide. Write the equation for this neutralization reaction.

Solution

The OH^- from the base and the H^+ from the acid combine to form water. The cation of the base (K^+) and the anion of the acid (NO_3^-) form a solution of the salt (potassium nitrate, KNO_3).

$$KOH(aq) + HNO_3(aq) \longrightarrow KNO_3(aq) + H_2O(l)$$

▪ **EXERCISE 7.5A**
Countertop spills of lye solutions (aqueous sodium hydroxide) can be neutralized with vinegar (aqueous acetic acid; see Table 7.1). Write the equation for the neutralization reaction.

▪ **EXERCISE 7.5B**
A toilet-bowl cleaner contains hydrochloric acid. An emergency first-aid treatment for accidental ingestion is a teaspoon of milk of magnesia (magnesium hydroxide). Write the equation for the neutralization reaction between magnesium hydroxide and hydrochloric acid. (*Hint:* Be sure to write the correct formulas for the reactants and the salt before attempting to balance the equation.)

3. What is the difference between salt and sodium?
A salt is any ionic compound formed by reacting an acid and a base. In everyday life, *salt* usually refers to table salt—sodium chloride (NaCl). Sodium is a highly reactive metal element. Sodium ions are essential for life, but you wouldn't want to eat sodium metal. It reacts violently with water.

SELF-ASSESSMENT Questions

1. When equal amounts of acids and bases are mixed
   a. the acid becomes more concentrated
   b. the base becomes more concentrated
   c. no reaction occurs
   d. they neutralize each other

2. How many moles of hydrochloric acid are needed to neutralize 1.5 mol of sodium hydroxide?
   a. 1.0 mol   b. 1.5 mol
   c. 3.0 mol   d. 4.5 mol

3. How many moles of hydrochloric acid are needed to neutralize 2.4 mol of calcium hydroxide?
   a. 1.2 mol   b. 2.4 mol
   c. 3.6 mol   d. 4.8 mol

4. How many moles of strontium hydroxide are needed to neutralize 2.0 mol of phosphoric acid? Be careful to write the balanced chemical equation first.
   a. 1.0 mol   b. 2.0 mol
   c. 3.0 mol   d. 6.0 mol

Answers: 1, d; 2, b; 3, d; 4, c

7.6 The pH Scale

Learning Objectives ❯ Describe the relationship between the pH of a solution and its acidity or basicity. ❯ Find the molar concentration of hydrogen ion, $[H^+]$, from a pH value or the pH value from $[H^+]$.

In solutions, the concentrations of ions are expressed in moles per liter (molarity; see Section 5.5). Because hydrogen chloride is completely ionized in water, a 1 molar solution of hydrochloric acid (1 M HCl), for example, contains 1 mol H^+ ions per liter of solution. Likewise, 1 L of 3 M HCl contains 3 mol H^+ ions, and 0.500 L of 0.00100 M HCl contains 0.500 L $\times$ 0.00100 mol/L = 0.000500 mol H^+ ions.

We can describe the acidity of a particular solution in moles per liter of hydrogen ions: The hydrogen ion concentration of a 0.00100 M HCl solution is 1×10^{-3} mol/L. However, exponential notation isn't very convenient. More often, the acidity of this solution is reported simply as pH 3.

We usually use the **pH** scale, first proposed in 1909 by the Danish biochemist S. P. L. Sørensen, to describe the degree of acidity or basicity of a solution. Most solutions have a pH that lies in the range of 0 to 14. The neutral point on the scale is 7, with values below 7 indicating increasing acidity and those above 7 increasing basicity. Thus, pH 6 is slightly acidic, whereas pH 12 is very basic (Figure 7.8).

▲ **Figure 7.8** The pH scale. A change in pH of one unit means a tenfold change in the hydrogen ion concentration.

Q: *Are tomatoes more acidic or less acidic than oranges? About how many times more (or less) acidic?*

The numbers on the pH scale are directly related to the hydrogen ion concentration. In Section 7.4 we saw how, at any given time in pure water, about 1 out of every 500 million water molecules is split into H^+ and OH^- ions. This gives a concentration of hydrogen ions and of hydroxide ions in pure water of 0.0000001 mol/L, or 1×10^{-7} M each. Can you see why 7 is the pH of pure water? It is simply the power of 10 for the molar concentration of H^+, with the negative sign removed. (The H in pH stands for "hydrogen," and the p for "power.") Thus, pH is defined as the negative logarithm of the molar concentration of hydrogen ion (refer to Table 7.4):

$$pH = -\log[H^+]$$

The brackets around H^+ mean "molar concentration." The relationship between pH and $[H^+]$ is perhaps easier to see when the equation is written in the following form. $[H^+] = 10^{-pH}$

Although pH is an acidity scale, note that its value goes down when acidity goes up. Not only is the relationship an inverse one, but it is also logarithmic. A decrease of one pH unit represents a tenfold increase in acidity, and when pH goes down by two units, acidity increases by a factor of 100. This relationship may seem strange at first, but once you understand the pH scale, you will appreciate its convenience.

Table 7.4 summarizes the relationship between hydrogen ion concentration and pH. A pH of 4 means a hydrogen ion concentration of 1×10^{-4} mol/L, or 0.0001 M. If the concentration of hydrogen ions is 0.01 M, or 1×10^{-2} M, the pH is 2. Typical pH values for various common solutions are listed in Table 7.5.

Table 7.4	Relationship between pH and Concentration of H^+ Ion	
Concentration of H^+(mol/L)		pH
1×10^{-0}		0
1×10^{-1}		1
1×10^{-2}		2
1×10^{-3}		3
1×10^{-4}		4
1×10^{-5}		5
1×10^{-6}		6
1×10^{-7}		7
1×10^{-8}		8
1×10^{-9}		9
1×10^{-10}		10
1×10^{-11}		11
1×10^{-12}		12
1×10^{-13}		13
1×10^{-14}		14

Example 7.6 pH from Hydrogen Ion Concentration

What is the pH of a solution that has a hydrogen ion concentration of 1×10^{-5} M?

Solution
The hydrogen ion concentration is 1×10^{-5} M. The exponent is -5; the pH is, therefore, the negative of this exponent: $-(-5)$ or 5.

▪ **EXERCISE 7.6A**
What is the pH of a solution that has a hydrogen ion concentration of 1×10^{-9} M?

▪ **EXERCISE 7.6B**
What is the pH of a solution that is 0.010 M HNO_3? (*Hint:* HNO_3 is a strong acid.)

Table 7.5	Approximate pH Values of Some Common Solutions
Solution	pH
Hydrochloric acid (4%)	0
Gastric juice	1.6–1.8
Soft drink	2.0–4.0
Lemon juice	2.1
Vinegar (4%)	2.5
Urine	5.5–7.0
Rainwater[a]	5.6
Saliva	6.2–7.4
Milk	6.3–6.6
Pure water	7.0
Blood	7.4
Fresh egg white	7.6–8.0
Bile	7.8–8.6
Milk of magnesia	10.5
Washing soda	12.0
Sodium hydroxide (4%)	13.0

[a] Saturated with carbon dioxide from the atmosphere but unpolluted.

▲ A pH meter is a device for determining pH quickly and accurately.

Q: *Is the solution in the beaker more basic or less basic than household ammonia? (Refer to Figure 7.8.)*

Example 7.7	Finding Hydrogen Ion Concentration from pH

What is the hydrogen ion concentration of a solution that has a pH of 4?

Solution
A pH value of 4 means that the exponent of 10 is −4. The hydrogen ion concentration is, therefore, 1×10^{-4} M.

■ EXERCISE 7.7A
What is the hydrogen ion concentration of a solution that has a pH of 2?

■ EXERCISE 7.7B
What is the concentration of an HI solution that has a pH of 3? (*Hint:* HI is a strong acid.)

CONCEPTUAL Example 7.8	Estimating pH from Hydrogen Ion Concentration

Which of the following is a reasonable pH for a solution that is 8×10^{-4} M in H^+?
   a. 2.9
   b. 3.1
   c. 4.2
   d. 4.8

Solution
The $[H^+]$ is greater than 1×10^{-4} M, so the pH must be less than 4. That rules out answers **(c)** and **(d)**. The $[H^+]$ is less than 10×10^{-4} (or 1×10^{-3} M), so the pH must be greater than 3. That rules out answer **(a)**. The only reasonable answer is **(b)**, a value between 3 and 4.

4. What is meant by "pH-balanced shampoo"?
Shampoo on either end of the pH scale would damage hair (and probably skin as well!). Most shampoos are formulated to be neutral (pH 7) or slightly basic.

(With a scientific calculator, you can calculate the actual pH, usually with the following keystrokes: (8)(exp)(4)(±)(log). This gives a value of −3.1 for the log of 8×10^{-4}. Because pH is the *negative* log of the H^+ concentration, the pH value is 3.1.)

▪ **EXERCISE 7.8**
Which of the following is a reasonable pH for a solution that is 2×10^{-10} M in H^+?
   a. 2.0   **b.** 8.7   **c.** 9.7   **d.** 10.2

In a neutral solution, the hydrogen ion and the hydroxide ion concentrations are both 1×10^{-7} M. Multiplying the two together gives 1×10^{-14}. It turns out that in an aqueous solution at 25 °C, $[H^+] \times [OH^-]$ always equals 1×10^{-14}. So, if the hydrogen ion concentration is greater than 1×10^{-7} M, the hydroxide ion concentration must be less than 1×10^{-7} M. For example, a solution with a pH of 4 has 1×10^{-4} M of H^+ ions but only 1×10^{-10} M of OH^- ions. On the other hand, basic solutions have more than 1×10^{-7} M OH^- ions and, therefore, must have less than 1×10^{-7} M of H^+ ions. Hence, a basic solution with 1×10^{-2} M of OH^- ions must have 1×10^{-12} M of H^+ ions and a pH of 12. This is why a pH greater than 7 means the solution is basic.

CONCEPTUAL Example 7.9	Hydrogen and Hydroxide Ions in Acids and Bases

Classify the three aqueous solutions shown below as acidic, basic, or neutral. (Water molecules are not shown.)

I   II   III

⊕ = H^+
● = K^+
🔴 = NO_3^-
⊖ = OH^-

Solution
Beaker I contains equal numbers of OH^- ions and H^+ ions—six of each—so that solution is neutral. Beaker II contains more OH ions (seven) than H^+ ions (one), so its solution is basic. Beaker III contains six H^+ ions and one OH ion; the solution is acidic.

▪ **EXERCISE 7.9**
What is the formula of the compound that was dissolved in Beaker III of Example 7.9? What is the formula of the compound that was dissolved in Beaker II?

SELF-ASSESSMENT Questions

1. The hydrogen ion concentration, $[H^+]$, of a 0.0010 M HNO_3 solution is
   a. 1.0×10^{-4} M   **b.** 1.0×10^{-3} M
   c. 1.0×10^{-2} M   **d.** 10 M

2. What is the pH of a solution that has a hydrogen ion concentration of 1.0×10^{-11} M?
   a. 1.0   **b.** 3   **c.** 10   **d.** 11

3. What is the pH of a solution that has a hydroxide ion concentration of 1.0×10^{-5} M?
   a. 1.0   **b.** 5   **c.** 9   **d.** 14

4. Swimming pool water with a pH of 8 has a hydrogen ion concentration of
   a. 8.0 M   **b.** 8.0×10^{-8} M
   c. 1.0×10^{-8} M   **d.** 1.0×10^8 M

5. The pH of pure water is
    a. 0   **b.** 1   **c.** 7   **d.** 10   **e.** 14

6. Which of the following is a reasonable pH for 0.015 M HCl?
    a. 0.015   **b.** 1.82   **c.** 8.24   **d.** 12.18

7. Which of the following is a reasonable pH for 0.015 M NaOH?
    a. 0.015   **b.** 1.82   **c.** 8.24   **d.** 12.18

8. Physiological pH (7.4) is the average pH of blood. Which of the following is a reasonable hydrogen ion concentration of a solution at physiological pH?
    a. −7.4 M   **b.** 0.6 M
    c. 6×10^{-7} M   **d.** 1×10^{-8} M
    e. 4×10^{-8} M

Answers: 1, b; 2, d; 3, c; 4, c; 5, c; 6, b; 7, d; 8, e

7.7 Buffers and Conjugate Acid–Base Pairs

Learning Objectives > Write the formula for the conjugate base of an acid or for the conjugate acid of a base. > Describe the action of a buffer.

In the Brønsted–Lowry theory, a pair of compounds or ions that differ by one proton (H^+) is called a **conjugate acid–base pair**. HF and F^- are a conjugate acid–base pair, as are NH_3 and NH_4^+. When a base (for example, NH_3) accepts a proton, it becomes an acid because it now has a proton that it can donate. NH_4^+ is an acid; it can donate its "extra" proton. Similarly, when an acid (for example, HF) donates a proton, it becomes a base because it can now accept a proton. F^- is a base; it can accept a proton.

CONCEPTUAL Example 7.10   Conjugate Acid–Base Pairs

What is the conjugate base **(a)** of HBr and **(b)** of H_3PO_4? What is the conjugate acid **(c)** of OH^- and **(d)** of HSO_4^-?

Solution

a. Removing a proton from HBr leaves Br^-; the conjugate base of HBr is Br^-.

b. Removing a proton from H_3PO_4 leaves $H_2PO_4^-$; the conjugate base of H_3PO_4 is $H_2PO_4^-$.

c. Adding a proton to OH^- gives H_2O; the conjugate acid of OH^- is H_2O.

d. Adding a proton to HSO_4^- gives H_2SO_4; the conjugate acid of HSO_4^- is H_2SO_4.

■ EXERCISE 7.10

What is the conjugate base **(a)** of HCN and **(b)** of H_3O^+? What is the conjugate acid **(c)** of SO_4^{2-} and **(d)** of HCO_3^-?

Buffer Solutions

A **buffer solution** maintains an almost constant pH when small amounts of a strong acid or a strong base are added to it. Buffer solutions have many important applications in industry, in the laboratory, and in living organisms because some chemical reactions consume acids, others produce acids, and many are catalyzed by acids. A *catalyst* is a substance or mixture that speeds up a reaction. Unlike a reactant, a catalyst can be recovered unchanged after the reaction is complete, and ordinarily it can be reused. A buffer solution consists of a weak acid and its conjugate base (for example, $HC_2H_3O_2$ and $C_2H_3O_2^-$) or a weak base and its conjugate acid (for example, NH_3 and NH_4^+).

Consider the equation for the ionization of acetic acid, in which the double arrow indicates the slight extent to which the acid ionizes.

$$HC_2H_3O_2(aq) \rightleftharpoons H^+(aq) + C_2H_3O_2^-(aq)$$

If we add sodium acetate to a solution of acetic acid, we are adding the conjugate base of acetic acid—that is, acetate ion—thus forming a buffer solution. If we add a little strong base to this solution, it will react with the weak acid to produce its conjugate weak base.

$$OH^+ + HC_2H_3O_2 \longrightarrow H_2O + C_2H_3O_2^-$$

Do you see that the solution no longer contains the strong base? Instead, it has a little more weak base and a little less weak acid than it did before the strong base was added. The pH remains very nearly constant. Likewise, if a little strong acid is added, it will react with the weak base to produce its conjugate weak acid.

$$H^+ + C_2H_3O_2^- \longrightarrow HC_2H_3O_2$$

The strong acid is consumed, extra weak acid is formed, and the solution pH decreases only slightly. This behavior of buffered solutions contrasts sharply with that of unbuffered solutions, in which any added strong acid or strong base changes the pH greatly.

A dramatic and essential example of the action of buffers is found in our blood. Blood must maintain a pH very close to 7.4, or it cannot carry oxygen from the lungs to cells. The most important buffer for maintaining acid–base balance in the blood is the carbonic acid–bicarbonate ion (H_2CO_3/HCO_3^-) buffer.

SELF-ASSESSMENT Questions

1. Which of the following pairs is a conjugate acid–base pair?
   a. CH_3COOH and OH^-
   b. HCN and CN^-
   c. HCN and OH^-
   d. HCl and OH^-

2. Which of the following is *not* a conjugate acid–base pair?
   a. CH_3COO^- and CH_3COOH
   b. F^- and HF
   c. H_2O and H_3O^+
   d. NH_3 and H_3O^+

3. A buffer solution is made from formic acid (HCOOH) and sodium formate (HCOONa). Added acid will react with
   a. $HCOO^-$
   b. HCOOH
   c. Na^+
   d. OH^-

4. Which of the following pairs could form a buffer?
   a. C_6H_5COOH and C_6H_5COONa
   b. HCl and NaCl
   c. HCl and NaOH
   d. NH_3 and H_3BO_3

Answers: 1, b; 2, d; 3, a; 4, a

7.8 Acids and Bases in Industry and in Daily Life

Learning Objective ❯ Describe everyday uses of acids and bases and how they affect daily life.

Acids and bases play an important role in our bodies, in medicine, in our homes, and in industry; they are useful products in many ways. However, as industrial by-products, they can damage the environment. Their use requires caution, and their misuse can be dangerous to human health.

▲ **Figure 7.9** Claims that antacids are "fast acting" are almost meaningless because most common acid–base reactions are almost instantaneous. Some tablets may dissolve a little more slowly than others. You can speed their action by chewing them.

Antacids: A Basic Remedy

The stomach secretes hydrochloric acid to aid in the digestion of food. Sometimes overindulgence or emotional stress leads to *hyperacidity* (too much acid is secreted). Hundreds of brands of antacids (Figure 7.9) are sold in the United States to treat this condition. Despite the many brand names, there are only a few different antacid ingredients, all of which are bases. Common ingredients are sodium bicarbonate, calcium carbonate, aluminum hydroxide, magnesium carbonate, and magnesium hydroxide. Even a single brand name often encompasses a variety of products. For example, there are more than a dozen varieties of Alka-Seltzer®.

Sodium bicarbonate ($NaHCO_3$), commonly called *baking soda*, was one of the first antacids and is still used occasionally. It is the principal antacid in most forms of Alka-Seltzer for heartburn relief. The bicarbonate ions react with the acid in the stomach to form carbonic acid, which then breaks down to carbon dioxide and water.

$$HCO_3^-(aq) + H^+(aq) \longrightarrow H_2CO_3(aq)$$

$$H_2CO_3(aq) \longrightarrow CO_2(g) + H_2O(l)$$

The $CO_2(g)$ is largely responsible for the burps that bicarbonate-containing antacids produce. Overuse of sodium bicarbonate can make the blood too alkaline, a condition called **alkalosis**. Also, antacids that contain sodium ion are not recommended for people with hypertension (high blood pressure).

You can make your own aspirin-free "Alka-Seltzer." Simply place half a teaspoon of baking soda in a glass of orange juice. (What is the acid and what is the base in this reaction?)

Why Doesn't Stomach Acid Dissolve the Stomach?

We know that strong acids are corrosive to skin. Look back at Table 7.1 and you will see that the gastric juice in your stomach is extremely acidic. Gastric juice is a solution containing about 0.5% hydrochloric acid. Why doesn't the acid in your stomach destroy your stomach lining? The cells that line the stomach are protected by a layer of mucus, a viscous solution of a sugar–protein complex called *mucin* and other substances in water. The mucus serves as a physical barrier, but its role is broader than that. The mucin acts like a sponge that soaks up bicarbonate ions from the cells lining the stomach and hydrochloric acid from within the stomach. The bicarbonate ions neutralize the acid within the mucus.

It used to be thought that too much stomach acid was the cause of ulcers, but it is now known that the acid plays only a minor role in ulcer formation. Research has shown that most ulcers develop as a result of infection with a bacterium called *Helicobacter pylori* (*H. pylori*) that damages the mucus, exposing cells in the stomach lining to the harsh stomach acid. Other agents, such as aspirin and alcohol, may be contributing factors to the development of ulcers. Treatment usually involves antibiotics that kill *H. pylori*.

Another ingredient found in antacids, calcium carbonate ($CaCO_3$), is safe in small amounts, but regular use can cause constipation. Also, taking large amounts of calcium carbonate can actually result in increased acid secretion after a few hours. Tums® and many store brands of antacids have calcium carbonate as the only active ingredient.

Aluminum hydroxide [$Al(OH)_3$], like calcium carbonate, can cause constipation. There is also some concern that antacids containing aluminum ions can deplete the body of essential phosphate ions. Aluminum hydroxide is the active ingredient in Amphojel®.

A suspension of magnesium hydroxide [$Mg(OH)_2$] in water is sold as *milk of magnesia*. Magnesium carbonate ($MgCO_3$) is also used as an antacid. These magnesium compounds act as antacids in small doses but as laxatives in large doses.

Many antacid products have a mixture of antacids. Rolaids® and Mylanta® contain calcium carbonate and magnesium hydroxide. Maalox® liquid has aluminum hydroxide and magnesium hydroxide. These products balance the tendency of magnesium compounds to cause diarrhea with that of aluminum and calcium compounds to cause constipation.

Although antacids are generally safe for occasional use, they can interact with other medications. Anyone who has severe or repeated attacks of indigestion should consult a physician. Self-medication can sometimes be dangerous.

Acids and Bases in Industry and at Home

Sulfuric acid is the leading chemical product in the United States (average production of about 40 billion kg each year), with a worldwide production of over 200 billion kg annually. Most of it is used for making fertilizers and other industrial chemicals. Around the home, we use sulfuric acid in automobile batteries and in some special kinds of drain cleaners.

▲ Drugs such as ranitidine (Zantac™), famotidine (Pepcid AC™), cimetidine (Tagamet HB™), and omeprazole (Prilosec) are not antacids. Rather than neutralizing stomach acid, these drugs act on cells in the lining of the stomach, reducing the amount of acid that is produced.

Hydrochloric acid is used in industry to remove rust from metal, in construction to remove excess mortar from bricks and to etch concrete for painting, and in the home to remove lime deposits from fixtures and toilet bowls. The product used in the home is often called *muriatic acid*, an old name for hydrochloric acid. Concentrated solutions (about 38% HCl) cause severe burns, but dilute solutions can be used safely in the home if handled carefully. Yearly production of hydrochloric acid is more than 4 billion kg in the United States and about 20 billion kg worldwide.

Lime (CaO) is the cheapest and most widely used commercial base. It is made by heating limestone ($CaCO_3$) to drive off CO_2.

$$CaCO_3(s) + heat \longrightarrow CaO(s) + CO_2(g)$$

Yearly production of calcium oxide is about 22 billion kg in the United States and about 230 billion kg worldwide. Adding water to lime forms calcium hydroxide [$Ca(OH)_2$], or slaked lime, which is generally safer to handle. Slaked lime is used in agriculture and to make mortar and cement.

Sodium hydroxide (NaOH, *lye*) is the strong base most often used in the home. It is employed in products such as Easy Off® for cleaning ovens, in products such as Drano® for unclogging drains, and to make both commercial and homemade soaps. Yearly U.S. production of sodium hydroxide is about 9 billion kg.

Ammonia (NH_3) is produced in huge volume, mainly for use as fertilizer. Yearly U.S. production is nearly 11 billion kg. Ammonia is used around the home in a variety of cleaning products (Chapter 21).

Acids and Bases in Health and Disease

When they are misused, acids and bases can be damaging to human health. Concentrated strong acids and bases are corrosive poisons (Chapter 22) that can cause serious chemical burns. Once the chemical agents are removed, these injuries resemble burns caused by heat and are often treated in the same way. Besides being a strong acid, sulfuric acid is also a powerful dehydrating agent that can react with water in the cells.

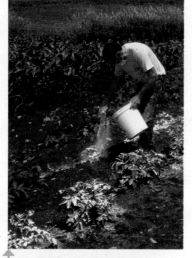

↑ It DOES Matter!
The proper pH is as important for plant growth as fertilizer is. Soil that is "sour," or too acidic, is "sweetened" by adding slaked lime (calcium hydroxide). A few plants, such as blueberries and citrus fruit, require acidic soil, and an acid such as vinegar may have to be periodically added to the soil they grow in.

Acid Rain

Carbon dioxide is the anhydride of carbonic acid (Section 7.3). Raindrops falling through the air absorb CO_2, which is converted to H_2CO_3 in the drops. Rainwater is thus a dilute solution of carbonic acid, a weak acid. Rain saturated with carbon dioxide has a pH of 5.6. In many areas of the world, particularly those downwind from industrial centers, rainwater is much more acidic, with a pH as low as 3 or less. Rain with a pH below 5.6 is called **acid rain**.

Acid rain is due to acidic pollutants in the air. As we shall see in Chapter 13, several air pollutants are acid anhydrides. These include sulfur dioxide (SO_2) and sulfur trioxide (SO_3), mainly from the burning of high-sulfur coal in power plants and metal smelters, and nitrogen dioxide (NO_2) and nitrogen monoxide (NO), from automobile exhaust fumes.

Some acid rain is due to natural pollutants, such as those resulting from volcanic eruptions and lightning. Volcanoes give off sulfur oxides and sulfuric acid, and lightning produces nitrogen oxides and nitric acid from nitrogen, oxygen, and water in the air.

Acid rain is an important environmental problem that involves both air pollution (Chapter 13) and water pollution (Chapter 14). It can have serious effects on plant and animal life.

Irvin J. Levy, Gordon College, Wenham, MA

Acids and Bases–Greener Alternatives

Learning Objectives › Recognize carbon dioxide in water as a useful, safe source of acid. › Describe alternate choices for greener reaction conditions when using acids and bases.

Acids and bases are among the most common types of chemical substances. We find them everywhere. Although you may not identify acids and bases by their technical terms, we are in contact with them every moment of our lives. For example, a healthy person's blood is very slightly basic (pH ~ 7.4), also referred to as alkaline, while that person's stomach is rather acidic (pH ~ 2–3) (Section 7.6). Acids and bases also are found in many food ingredients. For instance, vinegar and orange juice are slightly acidic solutions, and baking soda is an alkaline solid.

Although acids and bases are important chemicals, concentrated solutions can be hazardous. Some industrial processes produce large quantities of highly basic or acidic waste. Those waste streams, if untreated, are dangerous to human health and the environment if unintended exposure occurs. Neutralization of acidic and alkaline waste is necessary as part of its proper disposal. Acids and bases also are used in many chemical reactions and, therefore, must be transported, stored, and used in large quantities. These corrosive substances can harm the equipment and storage containers where they are handled and, potentially, the people who work with them. As described below, chemical processes that include acids and bases provide opportunities for developing greener alternatives.

One example is the conversion of brine (sodium chloride solution) into important chemicals, including chlorine and sodium hydroxide. The process produces millions of tons of these useful chemicals every year but also results in a vast amount of alkaline waste. For the waste to be handled safely, an acid must be added to reduce the pH to between 6 and 9. Typically, mineral acid—hydrochloric or sulfuric acid—is added to the waste stream to neutralize the waste (Section 7.2). Yet that method has several disadvantages.

First, the amount of added acid is significant, and it represents a wasteful use of chemicals. Further, the amount must be very carefully controlled or the process could "over-neutralize" the waste (Section 7.5). This would convert the hazardous alkaline waste stream into a hazardous acidic waste stream, which would hardly be very helpful. Also, the unwanted products produced when the neutralizing acid comes together with the alkaline waste can cause additional problems. Lastly, and maybe most importantly, mineral acids are hazardous substances that pose threats during production, transport, storage, and use at the end site. There must be a greener way to handle these waste streams.

Indeed, companies are beginning to neutralize alkaline waste with a much greener substance, carbon dioxide (CO_2). CO_2 often is seen as a danger to the environment because the large amounts that we release from burning fossil fuels contribute to global climate changes. However, there are many good uses for the CO_2 that is already in our atmosphere. For example, a weakly acidic solution is formed when carbon dioxide dissolves in water, so it is possible to neutralize alkaline waste streams by simply bubbling CO_2 through them. The solutions cannot be "over-neutralized" with CO_2 because it will not lower the pH of the solution below 7 in practical use, and excess CO_2 simply bubbles out of the water. This method replaces mineral acids, prevents waste, relies on a renewable resource, and leads to the same outcome with safer chemicals (Principles 1, 3, 7, and 12).

Chemistry is a very lively field and the Principles of Green Chemistry remind chemists of many opportunities to develop methods that are safer for human health and the environment, more cost-effective, and work as well as—or even better than—more hazardous alternatives. One area of research is replacing acids in chemical processes with naturally occurring safer substances. For example, a common chemical reaction that converts an alcohol (a molecule with a carbon bonded to an OH group) to a different chemical substance requires a high concentration of very strong mineral acid and high temperature:

$$\underset{\substack{|\quad| \\ }}{-\underset{|}{\overset{H}{C}}-\underset{|}{\overset{OH}{C}}-} \xrightarrow[\text{high temp}]{\text{strong acid}} \overset{}{\underset{}{C}}=\overset{}{\underset{}{C}} + H_2O$$

Recently, it has been learned that the sulfuric and phosphoric acids used in this chemical transformation can be replaced by a much safer substance—a type of clay called montmorillonite. Clay catalysts are finding many uses in the chemical industry and significantly improve the safety of those processes.

Many methods that have been in place in the chemical industry for decades are now again areas of active research by chemists who are dedicated to using green chemistry's guiding principles to develop safer substances and methods. You might say that's a really "basic" idea. (And acidic, too!)

Strong acids and bases, even in dilute solutions, break down, or *denature*, the protein molecules in living cells, much as cooking does. Generally, the fragments are not able to carry out the functions of the original proteins. If exposure to the acid or base is sustained, this fragmentation continues until the tissue has been completely destroyed.

Acids and bases affect human health in more subtle ways. A delicate balance between acids and bases must be maintained in the blood, other body fluids, and cells. If the acidity of the blood changes too much, the blood loses its capacity to carry oxygen. In living cells, proteins function properly only at an optimal pH. If the pH changes too much in either direction, the proteins can't carry out their functions. Fortunately, the body has a complex but efficient mechanism for maintaining a proper acid–base balance (Section 7.7).

SELF-ASSESSMENT Questions

1. Which of the following is a common ingredient in antacids?
   a. $CaCO_3$
   b. $Ca(OH)_2$
   c. HCl
   d. KOH

2. When a person with excess stomach acid takes an antacid, the pH of the person's stomach changes
   a. from a low value to a value nearer 7
   b. from 7 to a much higher value
   c. from a low value to an even lower value
   d. from a high value to a lower value

3. The leading chemical product of U.S. industry is
   a. ammonia
   b. lime
   c. plastics
   d. sulfuric acid

4. The acid used in automobile batteries is
   a. citric acid
   b. hydrochloric acid
   c. nitric acid
   d. sulfuric acid

5. The base often used in soap making is
   a. $Ca(OH)_2$
   b. KOH
   c. NaOH
   d. NH_3

Answers: 1, a; 2, a; 3, d; 4, d; 5, c

SUMMARY

Section 7.1—Acids taste sour, turn litmus red, and react with active metals to form hydrogen. Bases taste bitter, turn litmus blue, and feel slippery to the skin. Acids and bases react to form salts and water. An **acid–base indicator** such as litmus has different colors in acid and in base and is used to determine whether solutions are acidic or basic.

Section 7.2—According to Arrhenius's definition an *acid* produces hydrogen ions (H^+), also called protons, in aqueous solution, and a *base* produces hydroxide ions (OH^-). **Neutralization** is the combination of H^+ and OH^- to form water. The anion and cation that were associated with H^+ and OH^- ions combine to form an ionic **salt**. In the more general Brønsted–Lowry acid–base theory, an **acid** is a proton donor and a **base** is a proton acceptor. When a Brønsted–Lowry acid dissolves in water, H_2O molecules pick up H^+ to form hydronium ions (H_3O^+). A Brønsted–Lowry base in water accepts a proton from a water molecule, forming OH^-.

Section 7.3—Some nonmetal oxides (such as CO_2 and SO_3) are **acidic anhydrides** in that they react with water to form acids. Some metal oxides (such as Li_2O and CaO) are **basic anhydrides**; they react with water to form bases.

Section 7.4—A **strong acid** is one that ionizes completely in water to form H^+ ions and anions. A **weak acid** ionizes only slightly in water; most of the acid exists as intact

molecules. Common strong acids are sulfuric, hydrochloric, and nitric acids. Likewise, a **strong base** is completely ionized in water, and a **weak base** is only slightly ionized. Sodium hydroxide and potassium hydroxide are common strong bases.

Section 7.5—The reaction between an acid and a base is called *neutralization*. In aqueous solution, it is the combination of H^+ and OH^- to form water. The other anions and cations form an ionic salt.

Section 7.6—The **pH** scale indicates the degree of acidity or basicity; pH is defined as pH $= -\log[H^+]$, where $[H^+]$ is the molar concentration of hydrogen ion. A pH of 7 ($[H^+] = 1 \times 10^{-7}$ M) is neutral; pH values lower than 7 represent increasing acidity, and pH values greater than 7 represent increasing basicity. A change in pH of one unit represents a tenfold change in $[H^+]$.

Section 7.7—A pair of compounds or ions that differ by one proton (H^+) is called a **conjugate acid–base pair**. A **buffer solution** is a mixture of a weak acid and its conjugate base or a weak base and its conjugate acid. A buffer maintains a nearly constant pH when a small amount of a strong acid or a strong base is added.

Section 7.8—An antacid is a base such as sodium bicarbonate, magnesium hydroxide, aluminum hydroxide, or calcium carbonate that is taken to relieve hyperacidity. Overuse of some antacids can make the blood too alkaline (basic), a condition called **alkalosis**. Sulfuric acid is the number one chemical produced in the United States and is used for making fertilizers and other industrial chemicals. Hydrochloric acid is used for rust removal and etching mortar and concrete. Lime (calcium oxide) is made from limestone and is the cheapest and most widely used base. It is an ingredient in plaster and cement and is used in agriculture. Sodium hydroxide is used to make many industrial products, as well as soap. Ammonia is a weak base produced mostly for use as fertilizer. **Acid rain** is rain with a pH less than 5.6. The acidity is due to sulfur oxides and nitrogen oxides from natural sources as well as industrial air pollution and automobile

exhaust fumes. Acid rain can have serious effects on plant and animal life. Concentrated strong acids and bases are corrosive poisons that can cause serious burns. Living cells have an optimal pH that is necessary for the proper functioning of proteins.

GREEN CHEMISTRY—Acids can be used for many purposes, including neutralizing basic waste streams or promoting chemical reactions. The Twelve Principles of Green Chemistry can guide us in the selection of acids and bases in chemical processes that are safer than the ones that were once considered standard choices. Replacements of hazardous mineral acids by carbon dioxide in water and montmorillonite clay are two examples.

Learning Objectives

Objective	Problems
› Distinguish between acids and bases using their chemical and physical properties. (7.1)	Problems 1, 2, 57
› Explain how an acid–base indicator works. (7.1)	Problems 3, 58
› Identify Arrhenius and Brønsted–Lowry acids and bases. (7.2)	Problems 4–6, 13–28, 59
› Write a balanced equation for a neutralization or an ionization. (7.2)	Problems 7, 39–42, 60–62
› Identify acidic and basic anhydrides, and write equations showing their reactions with water. (7.3)	Problems 8, 29, 30
› Define and identify strong and weak acids and bases. (7.4)	Problems 9–11, 31–38
› Identify the reactants and predict the products in a neutralization reaction. (7.5)	Problems 43–46
› Describe the relationship between the pH of a solution and its acidity or basicity. (7.6)	Problems 43, 44
› Find the molar concentration of hydrogen ion, [H$^+$], from a pH value or the pH value from [H$^+$]. (7.6)	Problems 45–52, 63–65
› Write the formula for the conjugate base of an acid or for the conjugate acid of a base. (7.7)	Problems 53, 54
› Describe the action of a buffer. (7.7)	Problems 66, 67
› Describe everyday uses of acids and bases and how they affect daily life. (7.8)	Problems 12, 55, 56, 68–71
› Recognize carbon dioxide in water as a useful, safe source of acid.	Problems 72, 73, 74
› Describe alternate choices for greener reaction conditions when using acids and bases.	Problems 73, 75

REVIEW QUESTIONS

1. Define the following terms, and give an example of each.
   a. acid   **b.** base   **c.** salt

2. List four general properties **(a)** of acidic solutions and **(b)** of basic solutions.

3. Describe the effect on litmus and the action on iron or zinc of a solution that has been neutralized.

4. Can a substance be a Brønsted–Lowry acid if it does not contain H atoms? Are there any characteristic atoms that must be present in a Brønsted–Lowry base?

5. What is meant by a proton in acid–base chemistry? How does it differ from a nuclear proton (Chapter 3)?

6. According to the Arrhenius theory, all acids have one element in common. What is that element? Are all compounds containing that element acids? Explain.

7. Describe the neutralization of an acid or a base.

8. What is an acidic anhydride? A basic anhydride? What is meant by the word *anhydride*?

9. Both strong bases and weak bases have properties characteristic of hydroxide ions. How do strong bases and weak bases differ?

10. Magnesium hydroxide is completely ionic, even in the solid state, yet it can be taken internally as an antacid. Explain why taking it does not cause injury although taking sodium hydroxide would.

11. What are the effects of strong acids and strong bases on the skin?

12. What is alkalosis? What antacid ingredient might cause alkalosis if taken in excess?

PROBLEMS

Acids and Bases: The Arrhenius Theory

13. Write equations that represent the action in water **(a)** of perchloric acid as an Arrhenius acid and **(b)** of rubidium hydroxide as an Arrhenius base.

14. Write equations that represent the action in water **(a)** of hydroiodic acid as an Arrhenius acid and **(b)** of barium hydroxide as an Arrhenius base. (Be sure to include the correct charges for ions.)

15. Write an equation that represents the action in water of dihydrogen phosphate ion as an Arrhenius acid. (Be sure to include the correct charges for ions.)

16. Write equations that represent the action in water **(a)** of hydrobromic acid as an Arrhenius acid and **(b)** of strontium hydroxide as an Arrhenius base.

Acids and Bases: The Brønsted–Lowry Acid–Base Theory

17. Use the Brønsted–Lowry definitions to identify the first compound in each equation as an acid or a base. (*Hint:* What is produced by the reaction?)
   a. $(CH_3)_2NH + H_2O \longrightarrow (CH_3)_2NH_2^+ + OH^-$
   b. $C_6H_5NH_2 + H_2O \longrightarrow C_6H_5NH_3^+ + OH^-$
   c. $C_6H_5CH_2NH_2 + H_2O \longrightarrow C_6H_5CH_2NH_3^+ + OH^-$

18. Use the Brønsted–Lowry definitions to identify the first compound in each equation as an acid or a base.
   a. $CH_3NH_2 + H_2O \longrightarrow CH_3NH_3^+ + OH^-$
   b. $H_2O_2 + H_2O \longrightarrow H_3O^+ + HO_2^-$
   c. $NH_2Cl + H_2O \longrightarrow NH_3Cl^+ + OH^-$

19. Write equations that represent the action in water **(a)** of formic acid (HCOOH) as a Brønsted–Lowry acid and **(b)** of pyridine (C_5H_5N) as a Brønsted–Lowry base.

20. Write equations that represent the action in water **(a)** of hypochlorous acid (HOCl) as a Brønsted–Lowry acid and **(b)** of diethylamine ($CH_3CH_2)_2NH$ as a Brønsted–Lowry base.

21. Write the equation that shows how ammonia acts as a Brønsted–Lowry base in water.

22. Hydroxylamine ($HONH_2$) is not an Arrhenius base, even though it contains OH, but it *is* a Brønsted–Lowry base. Write an equation that shows how hydroxylamine acts as a Brønsted–Lowry base in water.

Acids and Bases: Names and Formulas

23. For the following acids and bases, supply a formula to match the name or a name to match the formula.
   a. HCl
   b. strontium hydroxide
   c. KOH
   d. boric acid

24. For the following acids and bases, supply a formula to match the name or a name to match the formula.
   a. rubidium hydroxide
   b. $Al(OH)_3$
   c. hydrocyanic acid
   d. HNO_3

25. Name the following, and classify each as an acid or a base.
   a. H_3PO_4
   b. CsOH
   c. H_2CO_3

26. Name the following, and classify each as an acid or a base.
   a. $Mg(OH)_2$
   b. NH_3
   c. CH_3COOH

27. When an acid name ends in -*ic acid*, there is often a related acid whose name ends in -*ous acid*. The formula of the -*ous* acid has one fewer oxygen atom than that of the -*ic* acid. With this information, write formulas for **(a)** nitrous acid and **(b)** phosphorous acid.

28. Refer to Problem 27 and Table 7.1. Tellurium is in the same group as sulfur. Use this information to write the formulas for **(a)** telluric acid and **(b)** tellurous acid.

Acidic and Basic Anhydrides

29. Give the formula for the compound formed when **(a)** sulfur trioxide reacts with water and **(b)** magnesium oxide reacts with water. In each case, is the product an acid or a base?

30. Give the formula for the compound formed when **(a)** potassium oxide reacts with water and **(b)** carbon dioxide reacts with water. In each case, is the product an acid or a base?

Strong and Weak Acids and Bases

31. When 1.0 mol of hydrogen iodide (HI) gas is dissolved in a liter of water, the resulting solution contains 1.0 mol of hydronium ions and 1.0 mol of iodide ions. Classify HI as a strong acid, a weak acid, a weak base, or a strong base.

32. Thallium hydroxide (TlOH) is a water-soluble ionic compound. Classify TlOH as a strong acid, a weak acid, a weak base, or a strong base.

33. A solution made by adding 1.300 mol of methylamine (CH_3NH_2) gas to 1.00 L of water contains 0.00936 mol each of methylammonium ions ($CH_3NH_3^+$) and hydroxide ions (OH^-) and 1.291 mol of CH_3NH_2 molecules. Classify CH_3NH_2 as a strong acid, weak acid, weak base, or strong base.

34. A solution made by adding 1.000 mol of HOCN to 1.00 L of water contains 0.055 mol each of H^+ ions and OCN^- ions and 0.945 mol of HOCN molecules. Classify HOCN as a strong acid, weak acid, weak base, or strong base.

35. Identify each of the following substances as a strong acid, a weak acid, a strong base, a weak base, or a salt.
   a. LiOH
   b. HBr
   c. HNO_2
   d. $CuSO_4$

36. Identify each of the following substances as a strong acid, a weak acid, a strong base, a weak base, or a salt.
   a. K_3PO_4
   b. $CaBr_2$
   c. $Mg(OH)_2$
   d. NH_4Cl

37. Which of the following aqueous solutions has the highest concentration of H^+ ions? Which has the lowest?
    a. 0.10 M HNO_3
    b. 0.10 M NH_3
    c. 0.10 M CH_3COOH

38. Consider 0.10 M solutions of acetic acid, ammonia, hydrochloric acid, and sodium hydroxide. Rank these solutions in order of increasing pH.

Neutralization

39. Write equations for the reaction (a) of potassium hydroxide with hydrochloric acid and (b) of lithium hydroxide with nitric acid.

40. Write equations for the reaction (a) of 1 mol of calcium hydroxide with 2 mol of hydrochloric acid and (b) of 1 mol of sulfuric acid with 2 mol of potassium hydroxide.

41. Write the equation for the reaction of 1 mol of sulfurous acid (H_2SO_3) with 1 mol of magnesium hydroxide.

42. Write the equation for the reaction of 1 mol of phosphoric acid with 1 mol of aluminum hydroxide.

The pH Scale

43. Indicate whether each of the following pH values represents an acidic, basic, or neutral solution.
    a. 4
    b. 7
    c. 3.5
    d. 9

44. Lime juice is quite sour. Which of the following is a reasonable pH for lime juice?
    a. 2
    b. 6
    c. 7.8
    d. 12

45. What is the pH of a solution that has a hydrogen ion concentration of 1.0×10^{-5} M?

46. What is the pH of a solution that has a hydrogen ion concentration of 1.0×10^{-9} M?

47. What is the pH of a solution that has a hydroxide ion concentration of 1.0×10^{-5} M?

48. What is the pH of a solution that has a hydroxide ion concentration of 1.0×10^{-9} M?

49. What is the hydrogen ion concentration of a solution that has a pH of 3?

50. What is the hydrogen ion concentration of a solution that has a pH of 11?

51. Milk of magnesia has a hydrogen ion concentration between 1.0×10^{-10} M and 1.0×10^{-11} M. The pH of milk of magnesia is between which two whole numbers?

52. Oven cleaner has a pH between 13 and 14. What two whole-number values of x should be used in 1.0×10^{-x} M to express the range of hydrogen ion concentration?

Conjugate Acid–Base Pairs

53. In the following reaction in aqueous solution, identify (a) which of the reactants is the acid and which is the base, (b) the conjugate base of the acid, and (c) the conjugate acid of the base.

$$HNO_3(aq) + NH_3(aq) \longrightarrow NO_3^-(aq) + NH_4^+(aq)$$

54. In the following reaction in aqueous solution, identify (a) which of the reactants is the acid and which is the base, (b) the conjugate base of the acid, and (c) the conjugate acid of the base.

$$CH_3CH_2COOH + H_2O \longrightarrow CH_3CH_2COO^- + H_3O^+$$

Antacids

55. Mylanta liquid has 200 mg of $Al(OH)_3$ and 200 mg of $Mg(OH)_2$ per teaspoonful. Write the equation for the neutralization of stomach acid [represented as HCl(aq)] by each of these substances.

56. What is the Brønsted–Lowry base in each of the following compounds? Which are ingredients in antacids?
    a. $NaHCO_3$ b. $Mg(OH)_2$
    c. $MgCO_3$ d. $CaCO_3$

ADDITIONAL PROBLEMS

57. Most soaps have a bitter taste. What does this hint indicate about the pH of most soaps?

58. What color will litmus paper turn if placed in a solution of citric acid? What will happen to the color of the litmus paper as sodium hydroxide is added to the citric acid solution?

59. According to the Arrhenius theory, is every compound that contains OH a base? Explain.

60. Lime deposits on brass faucets are mostly $CaCO_3$. The deposits can be removed by soaking the faucets in hydrochloric acid. Write an equation for the reaction that occurs.

61. Strontium iodide can be made by the reaction of solid strontium carbonate ($SrCO_3$) with an acid. Identify the acid, and write the balanced equation for the reaction.

62. When a well is drilled into rock that contains sulfide minerals, some of the minerals may dissolve in the well water, yielding "sulfur water" that smells like rotten eggs. The water from these wells feels slightly slippery, contains HS^- ions, and turns litmus paper blue. From this information, write an equation representing the reaction of HS^- ions with water.

63. The pOH is related to $[OH^-]$ just as pH is related to $[H^+]$. What is the pOH (a) of a solution that has a hydroxide ion concentration of 1.0×10^{-3} M? (b) of a 0.01 M KOH solution? (c) of a 0.01 M HCl solution?

64. Rank 0.1 M solutions of (a) acetic acid ($HC_2H_3O_2$), (b) ammonia (NH_3), (c) nitric acid (HNO_3), (d) sodium chloride (NaCl), and (e) sodium hydroxide (NaOH) from the highest pH to the lowest pH.

65. Calculate the pH of a 0.50 M Ba[OH]$_2$ solution.

66. Human blood contains buffers that minimize changes in pH. One blood buffer is the hydrogen phosphate ion (HPO_4^{2-}). Like water, HPO_4^{2-} is amphiprotic. That is, it can act either as a Brønsted–Lowry acid or as a Brønsted–Lowry base. Write equations that illustrate the reaction with water of HPO_4^{2-} as an acid and as a base.

67. Which is likely to be a better buffer, a solution of ammonia with ammonium acetate or a solution of sodium hydroxide with sodium acetate? Why?

68. Three varieties of Tums have calcium carbonate as the only active ingredient: Regular Tums tablets have 500 mg; Tums E-X, 750 mg; and Tums ULTRA, 1000 mg. How many regular Tums would you have to take to get the same quantity of calcium carbonate as you would get with two Tums E-X? With two Tums ULTRA tablets?

69. The active ingredient in the antacid Basaljel is a gel of solid aluminum carbonate. Write the equation for the neutralization of aluminum carbonate by stomach acid (aqueous HCl).

70. Milk of magnesia has 400 mg of Mg(OH)$_2$ per teaspoon. Calculate the mass of stomach acid that can be neutralized by 1.00 teaspoon of milk of magnesia, assuming that the stomach acid is 0.50% HCl by mass.

71. Sulfuric acid is produced from elemental sulfur by a three-step process: (1) Sulfur is burned to produce sulfur dioxide. (2) Sulfur dioxide is oxidized to sulfur trioxide using oxygen and a vanadium (V) oxide catalyst. (3) Finally, the sulfur trioxide is reacted with water to produce 98% sulfuric acid. Write equations for the three reactions.

72. When carbon dioxide mixes with water a weak acid called carbonic acid is formed. Will CO_2 reduce the pH of the water, increase the pH of the water, or leave the pH of the water unchanged?

73. Suppose a certain company has an alkaline waste stream that requires 1 mL of concentrated HCl to neutralize 1 liter of waste. If that company chooses to switch to CO_2 to neutralize their annual 1 million liter waste stream, how many liters of concentrated HCl are replaced annually by this choice?

74. Carbonated water (pure water in which CO_2 is dissolved) has a slightly sour taste. What does this hint indicate about the pH of carbonated water?

75. An important type of chemical substance called an ester can be prepared by heating two chemicals in the presence of a strong mineral acid. No water is used in this reaction. Suggest a greener alternative to the strong mineral acid.

CRITICAL THINKING EXERCISES

Apply knowledge that you have gained in this chapter and one or more of the FLaReS principles (Chapter 1) to evaluate the following statements or claims.

7.1. A television advertisement claimed that the antacid Maalox neutralizes stomach acid faster and, therefore, relieves heartburn faster than Pepcid AC®, a drug that inhibits the release of stomach acid. To illustrate this claim, two flasks of acid were shown. In one, Maalox rapidly neutralized the acid. In the other, Pepcid AC did not neutralize the acid.

7.2. Testifying in a court case, a witness makes the following statement: "Although runoff from our plant did appear to contaminate a stream, the pH of the stream before the contamination was 6.4, and after contamination it was 5.4. So the stream is now only slightly more acidic than before."

7.3. A Jamaican fish recipe calls for adding the juice of several limes to the fish, but no heat is used to cook the fish. The directions state that the lime juice in effect "cooks" the fish.

7.4. An advertisement claims that vinegar in a glass-cleaning product will remove the spots left on glasses by tap water. The spots are largely calcium carbonate deposits.

7.5. A Web page on making biodiesel claims that any water in the waste oil must be removed before starting the reaction.

COLLABORATIVE GROUP PROJECTS

Prepare a PowerPoint, poster, or other presentation (as directed by your instructor) to share with the class.

1. Prepare a brief report on one of the following acids or bases. List sources (including local sources for the acid or base, if available) and commercial uses.
   a. ammonia
   b. hydrochloric acid
   c. phosphoric acid
   d. nitric acid
   e. sodium hydroxide
   f. sulfuric acid

2. Examine the labels of at least five antacid preparations. Make a list of the ingredients in each. Look up the properties (medical use, side effects, toxicity, and so on) of each ingredient on the Web or in a reference book such as *The Merck Index*.

3. Examine the labels of at least five toilet-bowl cleaners and five drain cleaners. Make a list of the ingredients in each. Look up the formulas and properties of each ingredient on the Web or in a reference book such as *The Merck Index*. Which ingredients are acids? Which are bases?

CHEMISTRY@HOME   Acids and Bases and pH, Oh My!

Materials required

- Red cabbage
- Water
- Container (for strained cabbage juice indicator)
- Measuring cup
- Lemon juice
- Vinegar
- Ammonia
- Orange juice
- Borax solution (1 tsp in ¼ cup water); stir until mostly dissolved
- Baking soda solution (1 tsp in ¼ cup water); stir until mostly dissolved
- Milk of magnesia
- Clear shampoo
- Seltzer water
- Clear plastic cups, 10
- Tablespoon or dropper

Think of all of the products that we use every day. Is everything that we use pH neutral? How do we test if something is acidic or basic?

You can rank how acidic or basic something is by using the pH scale. Recall that the number of hydrogen (H^+) or hydroxide (OH^-) ions in a solution affects how acidic or basic (alkaline) it is. pH is measured using chemicals that change color when they bind to the extra hydrogen or hydroxyl ions in water. So, for example, the more acidic a solution, the more hydrogen ions there are, and the more the color will change. The more basic (alkaline) hydroxyl ions there are, the more basic (alkaline) a solution and the more the color will change.

In this lab, you will be using a natural indicator from red cabbage to test the pH of different substances that can be found in your local grocery store or pharmacy. The chemicals responsible for the red color in red cabbage and many other vegetables, fruits, and flower petals belong to the anthocyanin family. Over 300 kinds of anthocyanin have been discovered so far. They are also powerful antioxidants, that have been shown to be very beneficial to human health. The red cabbage indicator has its own pH color change chart.

Red Cabbage Color Changes with pH Chart (Figure 1).

pH	0	2	4	6	8	10	12	14
color	red	light pink	dark pink	purple	blue	aqua	green	yellow

Begin by preparing your indicator from red cabbage.

–First, peel off leaves from a head of red cabbage and finely chop 2 cups worth of red cabbage (you can also use a blender).

–Meanwhile, boil 8 cups of water.

–Add the chopped cabbage leaves to the pot, lower the heat, and let it simmer for 20 minutes.

–Pour the mixture through a strainer into a large container. Let the liquid cool to room temperature, and use the cabbage juice as your indicator.

Once you have prepared your cabbage-juice indicator and gathered your supplies, you are ready for the experiment. Set out 10 clear plastic cups, and fill them halfway with indicator juice. For each household item, add one tablespoon of the liquid to the indicator juice and stir. Be sure to leave one cup with only red cabbage indicator and add tap water to another. This will give you 10 samples to examine. Be sure to record your observations.

Does the indicator change color? Create a data table to track the chemical tested, color change, and pH. Once you've finished, arrange the cups from most acidic, to most basic.

Questions

1. Did the pH of any of the products surprise you?
2. Which substances were acidic?
3. Which substances were basic?
4. How would you go about neutralizing a particularly acidic solution?
5. What would account for any of your pH measurements not matching the actual pH?

8

OXIDATION AND REDUCTION

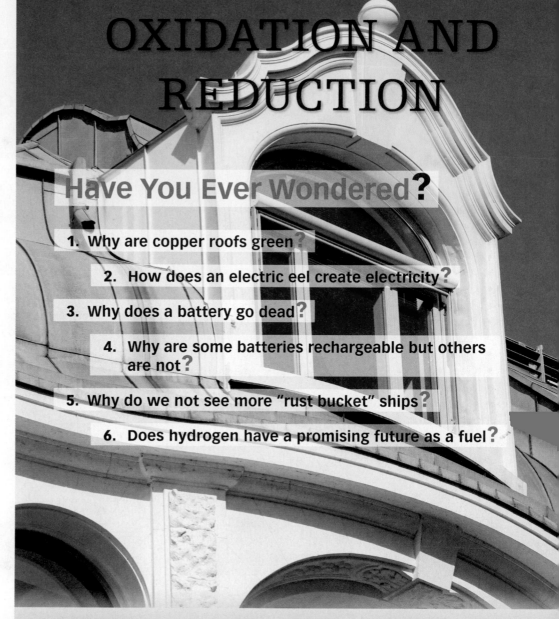

Have You Ever Wondered?

1. **Why are copper roofs green?**

2. **How does an electric eel create electricity?**

3. **Why does a battery go dead?**

4. **Why are some batteries rechargeable but others are not?**

5. **Why do we not see more "rust bucket" ships?**

6. **Does hydrogen have a promising future as a fuel?**

Learning Objectives

> Classify a particular change within a redox reaction as either oxidation or reduction. (8.1)

> Identify an oxidation–reduction reaction. (8.1)

> Identify the oxidizing agent and the reducing agent in a redox reaction. (8.2)

> Balance redox equations. (8.3)

> Identify and write the half-reactions in an electrochemical cell. (8.3)

> Describe the reactions that occur when iron rusts. (8.4)

> Explain why an explosive reaction is so energetic. (8.4)

> Write equations for reactions in which oxygen is an oxidizing agent. (8.5)

> List some of the common oxidizing agents encountered in daily life. (8.5)

> Identify some common reducing agents. (8.6)

> Write the overall equations for the metabolism of glucose and for photosynthesis. (8.7)

> Use a balanced reaction to calculate the atom economy and E factor of the reaction

> Describe the role of catalysts in minimizing waste in the chemical and allied industries.

BURN AND UNBURN From the conversion of sunlight to food to looking up a recipe on a smart phone to cook the food, to metabolizing the food to gain energy so we can look up the next recipe, to the simple act of breathing oxygen in and carbon dioxide out, we depend on an important group of reactions called *oxidation–reduction reactions*, or *redox reactions* (a shortening of *reduction–oxidation*). These reactions are extremely diverse: charcoal burns, iron rusts, bleach removes stains. Redox reactions are employed in pollution remediation, wastewater treatment, and determination of blood-sugar levels by diabetics. Even the generation of a shock of 600 volts by an electric eel is due to redox processes.

Corrosion is a fundamental process that takes place over time. The cost to the economy of the United States has been estimated to be approximately 3.1% of the gross domestic product, or more than $275 billion each year. The estimated corrosion cost to the Department of Defense is about $20 billion annually. Producing and purifying metals for various applications consumes energy, and corrosion is nature's way of returning these metals to their native energy levels. Metal corrosion nearly always involves redox reactions. Other redox reactions are desirable, or even necessary, to life itself. In this chapter, we will examine the nature of redox reactions, and we will look at some of their applications in life and in modern technology.

Oxidation and reduction always take place together. They represent opposite directions of a single process, a redox reaction. When one substance is oxidized, another is reduced. In other words, you can't have one without the other (Figure 8.1). However, it is sometimes convenient to discuss only a part of the process—the oxidation part or the reduction part.

Reduced forms of matter—foods, coal, and gasoline—are high in energy. *Oxidized* forms—carbon dioxide and water—are low in energy. The energy in foods and fossil fuels is released when these materials are oxidized. In this chapter, we examine the processes of oxidation and reduction in some detail to better understand the chemical reactions that keep us alive and maintain our civilization.

▲ **Figure 8.1** Oxidation and reduction always occur together. Pictured on the left is a reaction called the ammonium dichromate volcano. In the reaction, the ammonium ion (NH_4^+) is oxidized and the dichromate ion ($Cr_2O_7^{2-}$) is reduced. Considerable heat and light are evolved. The equation for the reaction is

$$(NH_4)_2Cr_2O_7 \longrightarrow Cr_2O_3 + N_2 + 4 H_2O$$

The water is driven off as vapor, and the nitrogen gas escapes, leaving pure Cr_2O_3 as the visible product (right).

8.1 Oxidation and Reduction: Four Views

Learning Objectives ❯ Classify a particular change within a redox reaction as either oxidation or reduction. ❯ Identify an oxidation–reduction reaction.

One of the most important redox reactions is combustion, that is, the burning of a substance in oxygen. The term **oxidation** came from the observation that during combustion, oxygen was added. The opposite process would require the removal of oxygen, and thus, it was called **reduction**.

Originally, the term *oxidation* was limited to reactions involving combination with oxygen. As chemists came to realize that combination with chlorine (or bromine or another active nonmetal) was not all that different from combination with oxygen, they broadened the definition of oxidation to include reactions involving these other substances—as we shall shortly see.

Let's take a look at the simplest combustion reaction, the combustion (oxygen present) of hydrogen to form water.

$$2 H_2 + O_2 \longrightarrow 2 H_2O$$

In this reaction, oxygen is added to hydrogen, oxidizing it. At the same time, the oxygen is reduced. Whenever oxidation occurs, reduction must also occur in an exactly equivalent amount, and vice versa.

Because oxidation and reduction are chemical opposites and constant companions, their definitions are linked. We can view oxidation and reduction in four different ways (Figure 8.2).

▶ **Figure 8.2** Four different views of oxidation and reduction.

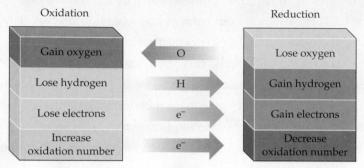

1. *Oxidation* is a gain of oxygen atoms.
   Reduction is a loss of oxygen atoms.

At high temperatures (such as those in automobile engines), nitrogen, which is normally quite unreactive, combines with oxygen to form nitric oxide.

$$N_2 + O_2 \longrightarrow 2\,NO$$

Nitrogen gains oxygen atoms; there are no O atoms in the N_2 molecule and one O atom in each of the NO molecules. Therefore, nitrogen is oxidized.

Now consider what happens when methane is burned to form carbon dioxide and water. Both carbon and hydrogen gain oxygen atoms, and so both elements are oxidized.

When lead dioxide is heated at high temperatures, it decomposes as follows:

$$2\,PbO_2 \longrightarrow 2\,PbO + O_2$$

| This Pb atom has two O atoms attached | This Pb atom has only one O atom attached |

The lead dioxide loses oxygen, so it is reduced.

| **CONCEPTUAL Example 8.1** | Redox Processes—Gain or Loss of Oxygen Atoms |

In each of the following changes, is the reactant undergoing oxidation or reduction? (These are not complete chemical equations.)

a. $Pb \longrightarrow PbO_2$ **b.** $SnO_2 \longrightarrow SnO$

c. $KClO_3 \longrightarrow KCl$ **d.** $Cu_2O \longrightarrow 2\,CuO$

Solution

a. Lead gains oxygen atoms (it has none on the left and two on the right); it is oxidized.

b. Tin loses an oxygen atom (it has two on the left and only one on the right); it is reduced.

c. There are three O atoms on the left and none on the right. The compound loses oxygen; it is reduced.

d. The two copper atoms on the left share a single oxygen atom, that is, half an oxygen atom each. On the right, each Cu atom has an O atom all to itself. Cu has gained oxygen; it is oxidized.

▪ EXERCISE 8.1

In each of the following changes, is the reactant undergoing oxidation or reduction? (These are not complete chemical equations.)

a. $3 Fe \longrightarrow Fe_3O_4$ b. $NO \longrightarrow NO_2$

c. $CrO_3 \longrightarrow Cr_2O_3$ d. $C_3H_6O \longrightarrow C_3H_6O_2$

A second view of oxidation and reduction involves hydrogen atoms.

2. *Oxidation* is a loss of hydrogen atoms.
   Reduction is a gain of hydrogen atoms.
   Look once more at the burning of methane:

$$CH_4 + 2 O_2 \longrightarrow CO_2 + 2 H_2O$$

The oxygen gains hydrogen to form water, so the oxygen is reduced. Methane loses hydrogen and is oxidized. (We see that the carbon and hydrogen atoms in CH_4 also gain oxygen, so our two views of oxidation and reduction are consistent with one another.)

Methyl alcohol (CH_3OH), when passed over hot copper gauze, forms formaldehyde and hydrogen gas.

$$CH_3OH \longrightarrow CH_2O + H_2$$

| The C and O atoms have four H atoms attached | The C and O atoms have only two H atoms attached |

Because the methyl alcohol loses hydrogen, it is oxidized in this reaction.

Methyl alcohol can be made by reaction of carbon monoxide with hydrogen.

$$CO + 2 H_2 \longrightarrow CH_3OH$$

Because the carbon monoxide gains hydrogen atoms, it is reduced.

Biochemists often find the gain or loss of hydrogen atoms a useful way to look at oxidation–reduction processes. For example, a substance called NAD^+ is changed to NADH in a variety of biochemical redox reactions. The actual molecules are rather complex, but we can write the equation for the oxidation of ethyl alcohol to acetaldehyde, one step in the metabolism of the alcohol, as follows.

$$CH_3CH_2OH + NAD^+ \longrightarrow CH_3CHO + NADH + H^+$$

We can see that ethyl alcohol is oxidized (loses hydrogen) and NAD^+ is reduced (gains hydrogen).

| CONCEPTUAL **Example 8.2** | Redox Processes—Gain or Loss of Hydrogen Atoms |

In each of the following changes, is the reactant undergoing oxidation or reduction? (These are not complete chemical equations.)

a. $C_2H_6O \longrightarrow C_2H_4O$ b. $C_2H_2 \longrightarrow C_2H_6$

Solution

a. There are six H atoms in the reactant on the left and only four in the product on the right. The reactant loses H atoms; it is oxidized.

b. There are two H atoms in the reactant on the left and six in the product on the right. The reactant gains H atoms; it is reduced.

Oxidation
number

+4

+3

+2

+1

0

−1

−2

−3

Reduction

Oxidation

▲ **Figure 8.3** An increase in oxidation number means a loss of electrons and is therefore oxidation. A decrease in oxidation number means a gain of electrons and is therefore reduction.

■ **EXERCISE 8.2**
In each of the following changes, is the reactant undergoing oxidation or reduction? (These are not complete chemical equations.)

a. $C_3H_6O \longrightarrow C_3H_8O$
b. $C_3H_6 \longrightarrow C_3H_4$

A third view of oxidation and reduction involves gain or loss of electrons.

3. *Oxidation* is a loss of electrons.
   Reduction is a gain of electrons.
   When magnesium metal reacts with chlorine, magnesium ions and chloride ions are formed.

$$Mg + Cl_2 \longrightarrow Mg^{2+} + 2\,Cl^-$$

Because the magnesium atom loses electrons (two), it is oxidized, and because the chlorine atoms gain electrons (one each), they are reduced.

A redox reaction also takes place when zinc is placed in an acidic solution.

$$Zn + 2\,H^+ \longrightarrow Zn^{2+} + H_2$$

In this reaction, it can be seen that zinc loses two electrons, which means it is oxidized. Each of the two hydrogen atoms, on the other hand, gains an electron and is thus reduced.

There are two popular mnemonics for remembering the link between oxidation/reduction and electron loss/gain:

CONCEPTUAL Example 8.3 | Redox Processes—Gain or Loss of Electrons

In each of the following changes, is the reactant undergoing oxidation or reduction? (These are not complete chemical equations.)

a. $Zn \longrightarrow Zn^{2+}$
b. $Fe^{3+} \longrightarrow Fe^{2+}$
c. $S^{2-} \longrightarrow S$
d. $F_2 \longrightarrow 2\,F^-$

Solution

a. In forming a 2+ ion, a Zn atom loses two electrons: $Zn \longrightarrow Zn^{2+} + 2\,e^-$, so zinc is oxidized.

b. To change from a 3+ ion to a 2+ ion, Fe gains an electron: $Fe^{3+} + 1e^- \longrightarrow Fe^{2+}$. This means that Fe ion is reduced.

c. To change from an S^{2-} ion to an atom with no charge, S loses two electrons: $S^{2-} \longrightarrow S + 2e^-$. So, the sulfide ion is oxidized.

d. Here two F^- ions are formed from neutral diatomic F_2, so an electron is gained by each fluorine atom in F_2: $F_2 + 2e^- \longrightarrow 2\,F^-$. In other words, F is reduced.

■ **EXERCISE 8.3**
In each of the following changes, is the reactant undergoing oxidation or reduction? (These are not complete chemical equations.)

a. $Cr^{6+} \longrightarrow Cr^{3+}$
b. $Sn^{2+} \longrightarrow Sn^{4+}$
c. $2\,H^+ \longrightarrow H_2$
d. $Hg^{2+} \longrightarrow Hg$

At this stage, it would be highly beneficial to introduce the concept of oxidation numbers (or oxidation states) and how it is applied. The fourth view of oxidation and reduction involves an increase or decrease in oxidation number (see Figure 8.3).

4. *Oxidation* increases the oxidation number.
   Reduction decreases the oxidation number.

For monoatomic ions, the oxidation number can be defined as the number of unit charges on the atom. For instance, in Fe^{3+} and S^{2-} the oxidation numbers of iron and sulfur atoms are +3 and −2, respectively.

As you already know from Chapter 4, for an atom in a molecule (or a polyatomic ion), the situation is a little more complicated due to the sharing of electrons through bonds. This means that usually the oxidation number for atoms within a molecule is the charge that an atom would have *if the bonding was ionic* and not covalent.

When an oxidation number increases, the actual or perceived charge of an atom becomes more positive or less negative as a result of an electron (or electrons) being lost. The opposite is true for a reduction: The charge of an atom becomes less positive or more negative as a result of an electron (or electrons) being gained.

The following set of rules *generally* yields correct oxidation numbers:

1. An atom in its elemental form has an oxidation number of 0.
2. An atom in a monoatomic ion has an oxidation number equal to the charge of the ion.
3. Hydrogen and oxygen in compounds have oxidation numbers of +1 and −2, respectively. (Exceptions: −1 for oxygen in peroxides, e.g., H_2O_2; −1 for hydrogen in hydrides, e.g., CaH_2)
4. The sum of the oxidation numbers of the atoms in a polyatomic ion (or molecule) equals the charge of the ion (or molecule).

Note the placement of the sign (+ or −):
Fe^{3+} (sign after the number in the charge of an ion)
and: +3 (sign before the number in the oxidation number)

CONCEPTUAL **Example 8.4**	Determining Oxidation Numbers in Molecules and Polyatomic Ions

What are the oxidation numbers of atoms in the following molecules and ions?

a. SO_2 **b.** HNO_2 **c.** NH_4^+ **d.** $Cr_2O_7^{2-}$

Solution

a.

$\boxed{}_S + 2\,\boxed{}_{O_2}$ Step 1: Place boxes above elements. Multiply each box by the number of atoms of that element in a molecule. Boxes *will* hold oxidation numbers.

$\boxed{}_S + 2\,\boxed{}_{O_2} = 0$ Step 2: Set up an "equation" in which the sum of the oxidation numbers of all atoms equals 0.

$\boxed{}_S + 2\,\boxed{-2}_{O_2} = 0$ Step 3: Follow oxidation number assignment rules for oxygen (−2).

$\boxed{+4}_S + 2\,\boxed{-2}_{O_2} = 0$ Step 4: Determine the oxidation number for sulfur (+4).

b.

$\boxed{}_H + \boxed{}_N + 2\,\boxed{}_{O_2}$ Step 1: Place boxes above elements. Multiply each box by the number of atoms of that element in a molecule. Boxes *will* hold oxidation numbers.

$\boxed{}_H + \boxed{}_N + 2\,\boxed{}_{O_2} = 0$ Step 2: Set up an "equation" in which the sum of the oxidation numbers of all atoms equals 0.

$\boxed{+1}_H + \boxed{}_N + 2\,\boxed{-2}_{O_2} = 0$ Step 3: Follow oxidation number assignment rules for oxygen (−2) and hydrogen (+1).

$\boxed{+1}_H + \boxed{+3}_N + 2\,\boxed{-2}_{O_2} = 0$ Step 4: Determine the oxidation number for nitrogen (+3).

c.

Step 1: Place boxes above elements. Multiply each box by the number of atoms of that element in a molecule. Boxes *will* hold oxidation numbers.

Step 2: Set up an "equation" in which the sum of the oxidation numbers of all atoms equals the ion's charge, here +1.

Step 3: Follow oxidation number assignment rules for hydrogen (+1).

Step 4: Determine the oxidation number for nitrogen (–3).

d.

Step 1: Place boxes above elements. Multiply each box by the number of atoms of that element in a molecule. Boxes *will* hold oxidation numbers.

Step 2: Set up an "equation" in which the sum of the oxidation numbers of all atoms equals 0 (for a molecule) or the ion's charge (for an ion), here –2.

Step 3: Follow oxidation number assignment rules for oxygen (–2).

Step 4: Determine the oxidation number for chromium (+6).

■ **EXERCISE 8.4**

In each of the following examples, determine the oxidation number of the chlorine atom.

a. Cl_2 **b.** HCl   **c.** ClO_3^- **d.** Cl_2O_3

CONCEPTUAL Example 8.5	Redox Processes—Oxidation Number as Applied to Reactions

In the following change, is the reactant undergoing oxidation or reduction? (This is not a complete chemical equation.)

$$C_2H_6O \longrightarrow C_2H_4O$$

Note that we have previously looked at this case in Conceptual Example 8.4b in terms of the hydrogen removal. This time, however, let's do so in terms of the oxidation numbers:

Solution

C_2H_6O: Each of the six hydrogen atoms has an oxidation number of +1, thus contributing the "charge" of +6. Oxygen has an oxidation number of −2. This means that the overall "charge" due to hydrogen and oxygen is +6 − 2 = +4. The overall charge of the molecule is 0. This means that the two carbon atoms must cancel the +4 "charge." Because there are two carbon atoms, each carbon must have the oxidation number of −2.

C_2H_4O: Each of the four hydrogen atoms has an oxidation number of +1, for a total "charge" of +4. When combined with the oxidation number of the oxygen atom equal to −2, the overall "charge" of +4 − 2 = +2. Because all molecules are neutral, each of the two carbon atoms must have the oxidation number of −1.

This means that the oxidation number for carbon has changed from −2 to −1 (it became less negative in this case) and an electron was lost. In other words, carbon was reduced.

■ EXERCISE 8.5

In each of the following changes, is the reactant undergoing oxidation or reduction? (These are not complete chemical equations.)

a. $ClO_3^- \longrightarrow Cl^-$ **b.** $Br_2 \longrightarrow BrO_3^-$

Using oxidation numbers to determine whether a substance underwent an oxidation or reduction as a result of electron loss or gain of electrons, respectively, is especially useful in electrochemistry, as we will see in Section 8.3.

It is now time to apply what we have just learned to a real chemical reaction. The following reaction is of great importance within the environment, as it greatly alters chromium's toxicity.

$$Cr_2O_7^{2-}(aq) + 3\,Sn^{2+}(aq) + 14\,H^+(aq) \rightleftharpoons 2\,Cr^{3+}(aq) + 3\,Sn^{4+}(aq) + 7\,H_2O(l)$$

Putting it all together, we get the following, where it is easy to see what element has been oxidized and what has been reduced.

Why do we have different ways to look at oxidation and reduction? Oxidation as a gain of oxygen is historical and specific, but the definition in terms of electrons applies more broadly. Which one should we use? Ordinarily, the definitions are consistent with one another, so we use the most convenient one. For the combustion (burning) of carbon,

$$C + O_2 \longrightarrow CO_2$$

it is most convenient to see that carbon is oxidized by gaining oxygen atoms. Similarly, for the reaction

$$CH_2O + H_2 \longrightarrow CH_4O$$

it is easy to see that the reactant CH_2O gains hydrogen atoms and is thereby reduced. Finally, in the case of the reaction

$$3\,Sn^{2+} + 2\,Bi^{3+} \longrightarrow 3\,Sn^{4+} + 2\,Bi$$

it is clear that tin is oxidized because it loses electrons, increasing its oxidation number from +2 to +4. Similarly, we see that bismuth is reduced because it gains electrons, decreasing its oxidation number from +3 to 0. While viewing redox reactions through the prism of oxygen and hydrogen gain or loss is useful in organic chemistry (Chapter 9) and for some simple reactions, it is the electron loss or gain analysis that is universally applicable to all redox processes, and in particular to those not involving any oxygen or hydrogen-containing species. The oxidation number approach is the method of choice for analyzing and studying redox processes ranging from oxygen transport in our bodies to powering nearly all high performance electronic devices, from cell phones to glucose meters.

1. Why are copper roofs green?

Copper is a versatile roofing material, highly regarded for its appearance as well as its economical heat-conducting properties. One interesting aspect of copper roofs is that they turn green (as in the chapter-opening photo). The name for this desired green coating is patina. This change in copper's appearance is due to a number of chemical reactions. The first of these reactions is the oxidation of Cu^0 to Cu^+ by oxygen:

$$4\,Cu + O_2 \longrightarrow 2\,Cu_2O$$

Copper is then further oxidized to Cu^{2+}, forming black CuO and CuS. Further reactions with sulfur dioxide and carbon dioxide present in the air, aided by moisture, yield azurite (blue), $Cu_3(CO_3)_2(OH)_2$; brochantite (green), $Cu_4SO_4(OH)_6$; and malachite (green), $2\,Cu_2CO_3(OH)_2$. These three minerals combine to give patina its unique green hues.

SELF-ASSESSMENT Questions

1. Which of the following is *not* one of the ways we can view oxidation?
   a. electrons gained
   b. electrons lost
   c. hydrogen atoms lost
   d. oxygen atoms gained

2. Which of the following partial equations represents an oxidation of nitrogen?
   a. $NH_3 \longrightarrow NH_4^+$
   b. $N_2O_4 \longrightarrow NI_3$
   c. $NO_3^- \longrightarrow NO$
   d. $NO_2 \longrightarrow N_2O_5$

3. When CrO_4^- reacts to form Cr^{3+}, the chromium in CrO_4^- is
   a. reduced; it loses electrons
   b. reduced; it loses oxygen
   c. oxidized; its oxidation number increases
   d. oxidized; it gains positive charge

4. Which of the following equations best represents a reduction of molybdenum?

   a. $MoO_2 + H_2O \longrightarrow H_2MoO_3$

   b. $MoO_2 + 4 H_2 \longrightarrow Mo + 2 H_2O$

   c. $2 MoO_2 + O_2 \longrightarrow 2 MoO_3$

   d. $MoO_2 + 4 H^+ \longrightarrow Mo^{4+} + 2 H_2O$

5. According to the following equation, Cl_2 is

   $$3 Cl_2 + 2 Al \longrightarrow 2 AlCl_3$$

   a. both oxidized and reduced

   b. neither oxidized nor reduced

   c. oxidized, only

   d. reduced only

6. According to the following partial equation, manganese

   $$Mn \longrightarrow Mn^{2+} + 2 e^-$$

   a. gains electrons and is oxidized

   b. gains electrons and is reduced

   c. loses electrons and is oxidized

   d. loses electrons and is reduced

7. When an element is oxidized, its oxidation number

   a. decreases, as electrons are gained

   b. decreases, as electrons are lost

   c. increases, as electrons are gained

   d. increases, as electrons are lost

8. What are the oxidation numbers of sodium and oxygen atoms in Na_2O, respectively?

   a. 0, 0   b. +1, +1   c. +1, −2   d. +1, −1

9. What is the oxidation number of manganese in $KMnO_4$?

   a. +7   b. +8   c. +1   d. +6

10. Which of the following statements is correct in regards to assigning oxidation numbers?

    a. Alkali metals can have an oxidation number of either +1 or −1.

    b. Halogens can never have an oxidation number of −1.

    c. Oxygen must always have an oxidation number of −2, even in its elemental form.

    d. The oxidation number of alkaline earth metals in ionic compounds is always +2.

11. What is the charge of the $PO_4{}^{n-}$ ion, in which phosphorus has the oxidation number of +5 and each of the oxygen atoms has the oxidation number of −2?

    a. 0   b. 1−   c. 2−   d. 3−

8.2 Oxidizing and Reducing Agents

Learning Objective ❯ Identify the oxidizing agent and the reducing agent in a redox reaction.

It is often convenient to focus attention on one reactant at a time to see how this reactant affects the entire redox reaction. When a reactant causes another reactant to become oxidized, it is known as the **oxidizing agent**. When a reactant causes another reactant to become reduced, it is known as the **reducing agent**. Stated differently, the reducing agent is the substance being oxidized; the oxidizing agent is the substance being reduced. For example, in the reaction

$$\boxed{+2} \xrightarrow{\text{reduction}} \boxed{0}$$
$$CuO + H_2 \longrightarrow Cu + H_2O$$
$$\boxed{0} \xrightarrow[\text{oxidation}]{} \boxed{+1}$$

we see that copper in copper oxide is reduced and hydrogen is oxidized. Since CuO brought about the oxidation of H_2, CuO is the *oxidizing agent*. On the other hand, since H_2 brought about the reduction of CuO, H_2 is the *reducing agent*. Each oxidation–reduction reaction has an oxidizing agent and a reducing agent among the reactants. The reducing agent is the substance being oxidized; the oxidizing agent is the substance being reduced.

CONCEPTUAL **Example 8.6**	Oxidizing and Reducing Agents

Identify the oxidizing and reducing agents in the following reactions.

   a. $2 C + O_2 \longrightarrow 2 CO$

   b. $N_2 + 3 H_2 \longrightarrow 2 NH_3$

   c. $3 Mg + N_2 \longrightarrow Mg_3N_2$

   d. $2 H_2S + 8 NO_3{}^- \longrightarrow SO_4{}^{2-} + 4 N_2 + 4 H_2O + 2 H^+$

Solution

We can determine the answers by applying the various definitions of oxidation and reduction.

a. C gains oxygen and is oxidized, so it must be the reducing agent. O_2 is therefore the oxidizing agent.

b. N_2 gains hydrogen and is reduced, so it is the oxidizing agent. H_2 therefore is the reducing agent.

c. The oxidation number of magnesium increases from 0 to +2 as a result of magnesium losing two electrons. In other words, Mg is oxidized and is the reducing agent. As a result, N_2 is the oxidizing agent, gaining electrons by decreasing the oxidation number of the nitrogen atom from 0 to −3. Note that the argument involving oxygen gain or hydrogen loss for oxidation would not have worked in this case! Neither of these elements is in this reaction.

d. S in H_2S increases its oxidation number from −2 to +6 by losing eight electrons and becoming oxidized, so H_2S is the reducing agent. The oxidation number of the nitrogen atom in the NO_3^- ion decreases from +5 to 0: N is reduced. Consequently, NO_3^- is the oxidizing agent.

■ **EXERCISE 8.6**

Identify the oxidizing agents and reducing agents in the following reactions.

a. $Se + O_2 \longrightarrow SeO_2$

b. $2\ K + Br_2 \longrightarrow 2\ K^+ + 2\ Br^-$

c. $4\ Fe(s) + 3\ O_2(g) \longrightarrow 2\ Fe_2O_3(s)$

d. $V_2O_5 + 2\ H_2 \longrightarrow V_2O_3 + 2\ H_2O$

SELF-ASSESSMENT Questions

1. A reducing agent
   a. gains electrons
   b. gains protons
   c. loses electrons
   d. loses protons

2. When a compound gains two electons, it is
   a. an oxidizing agent
   b. a reducing agent
   c. oxidized
   d. a double-reducing agent

3. If an oxidation number of an atom in a compound increases from +2 to +4, the compound
   a. is a reducing agent
   b. is an oxidizing agent
   c. gains electrons
   d. gains protons

4. Which substance is the oxidizing agent in the following reaction?

   $$Cu(s) + 2\ Ag^+(aq) \longrightarrow Cu^{2+}(aq) + 2\ Ag(s)$$

   a. Ag   b. Ag^+ c. Cu   d. Cu^{2+}

5. In the following reaction, the reducing agent is

   $$Al(s) + Cr^{3+}(aq) \longrightarrow Al^{3+}(aq) + Cr(s)$$

   a. Al(s)
   b. $Al^{3+}(aq)$
   c. $Cr^{3+}(aq)$
   d. Cr(s)

6. What is the oxidizing agent in the following reaction?

   $$Zn(s) + 2\ Tl^+(aq) \longrightarrow Zn^{2+}(aq) + 2\ Tl(s)$$

   a. Tl(s)
   b. $Tl^+(aq)$
   c. Zn(s)
   d. $Zn^{2+}(aq)$

7. What is the reducing agent in the following reaction?

   $$12\ H^+(aq) + 2\ IO_3^-(aq) + 10\ Fe^{2+}(aq)$$
   $$\longrightarrow 10\ Fe^{3+}(aq) + I_2(s) + 6\ H_2O(l)$$

   a. $Fe^{2+}(aq)$
   b. $H^+(aq)$
   c. $I_2(s)$
   d. $IO_3^-(aq)$

Answers: 1. c; 2. a; 3. a, b; 4. b; 5. a; 6. b; 7. a

8.3 Electrochemistry: Cells and Batteries

Learning Objectives ❯ Balance redox equations. ❯ Identify and write the half-reactions in an electrochemical cell.

We saw in Chapter 3 that electricity can effect chemical change; such a process is called *electrolysis*. For example, an electric current passed through water produces

Colorless
Ag⁺ ions

Cu metal

(a)

Blue
Cu^{2+} ions

Ag metal

(b)

▲ **Figure 8.4** A coil of copper wire is immersed in a colorless solution of Ag^+ ions (a). As the reaction progresses, the more active copper displaces the less active silver from solution, producing needle-like crystals of silver metal (b) and a blue solution of Cu^{2+} ions. The equation for the reaction is
$2\ Ag^+(aq) + Cu(s) \longrightarrow$
$2\ Ag(s) + Cu^{2+}(aq)$.

hydrogen and oxygen gases. In Sections 8.1 and 8.2, we have seen that oxidation–reduction reactions can induce electron transfer. This electron transfer can be harnessed to produce electricity. An electric current in a wire is simply a flow of electrons.

The study of this natural phenomenon has a long history. It all started off with the desire to understand how muscles work. An Italian scientist by the name of Luigi Galvani (1737–1798), a lecturer of anatomy, discovered that amputated frog legs suspended by a brass hook twitched when the hook was dragged along an iron rail or when lightning struck close by (or so the story goes. . .). He concluded that the electricity came from the frog's leg.

Another Italian scientist, Alessandro Volta (1745–1827)—a very good professor of experimental physics—did not agree with Galvani's conclusion. Instead, Volta set up a number of experiments in which he tried to connect a number of metals through brine (saltwater) solutions. He used his tongue (the best detector of the day) to detect if electricity was formed and how much. He settled on the combination of silver and zinc. To make his device as portable as possible, and to prove his idea in the process, he piled up alternating silver and zinc discs separated by brine-soaked cardboard discs. This was the first battery and is almost the same technology that is used in nearly all modern-day portable electronics. The brine was the original electrolyte—a solution that can conduct electricity. All this from the fundamental question of why muscles move.

When a coil of copper wire is placed in a solution of silver nitrate (Figure 8.4a), the copper atoms give up their outer electrons to the silver ions. (We can omit the nitrate ions from the equation because they do not change.) The copper metal dissolves, going into solution as copper(II) ions that color the solution blue. The silver ions come out of solution as beautiful needles of silver metal (Figure 8.4b). The copper is oxidized; the silver ions are reduced.

So far so good, but how can we go about harnessing electricity? Because the reaction involves only the transfer of electrons, it can occur even when the silver ions are separated from the copper metal. If we place the reactants in separate compartments and connect them with a wire, the electrons will flow through the wire from the copper side, where the electrons are lost due to the oxidation, to the silver side, where the electrons are simultaneously taken up in the reduction process. This flow of electrons constitutes an electric current, and it can be used to run a motor or light a lamp.

In the **electrochemical cell** pictured in Figure 8.5, there are two separate compartments. One contains copper metal in a blue solution of copper(II) sulfate, and the other contains silver metal in a colorless solution of silver nitrate. Copper atoms give up electrons much more readily than silver atoms do, so electrons flow away from the copper compartment and toward the silver. The copper bar (Cu^0) slowly dissolves as copper atoms give up electrons to form Cu^{2+} ions. The electrons flow through the wire to the silver compartment, where silver ions (Ag^+) pick them up to become silver atoms and add to the mass of the silver bar (Ag^0).

But hold on! Isn't the copper side getting more positive and the silver side more negative as the electrons flow from the copper side to the silver side? This is when the nitrate anions, originally present in the silver nitrate solution, come into play. In all electrochemical cells, the transfer of electrons is balanced by the transfer of anions in the opposite direction. For this anion transfer to take place, the two sides (or halves) of the electrochemical cell must be connected by a porous medium that allows for the transport of the anions, much as wire allows the transfer of electrons. This porous barrier is usually called a *salt bridge* and can take many forms, but it always has a medium (electrolyte) in which ions are present and can be transported. In the case of Volta's electrochemical cell (battery) the salt bridge was the brine-soaked cardboard. In the electrochemical cell in Figure 8.5, each copper atom gives up two electrons, two silver ions pick up one electron each, and two nitrate ions move from the right compartment to the left compartment.

The two pieces of metal where electrons are transferred are called **electrodes**. The electrode where oxidation occurs is called the **anode**. The one where reduction occurs is the **cathode**. In our example cell, copper gives up electrons, it is oxidized, and the copper bar is therefore the anode. Silver ions gain electrons and are reduced, so the silver bar is the cathode.

Dry Cells

The familiar *dry cell* (Figure 8.6) is used in flashlights and a large number of remote controls. The cylindrical zinc case serves as an anode, while the cathode is a carbon rod in the center of the cell. The space between the cathode and the anode contains a moist paste of graphite powder (carbon), manganese(IV) oxide (MnO_2), and ammonium chloride (NH_4Cl) in contact with the carbon cathode. This paste is separated from the zinc anode (case) by a porous spacer. The reaction on the anode is the oxidation of the zinc cylinder to zinc ions:

$$Oxidation \text{ (anode): } Zn(s) \longrightarrow Zn^{2+} + 2\,e^-$$

The reaction on the cathode involves reduction of manganese(IV) oxide:

$$Reduction \text{ (cathode): } 2\,MnO_2(s) + H_2O(l) + 2\,e^- \longrightarrow Mn_2O_3(s) + 2\,OH^-(aq)$$

A simplified version of the overall reaction is

$$Zn + 2\,MnO_2 + H_2O \longrightarrow Zn^{2+} + Mn_2O_3 + 2\,OH^-$$

In alkaline cells, potassium hydroxide (NaOH) is used instead of NH_4Cl. While somewhat more expensive, alkaline cells are preferred because zinc-corroding ammonium ions are not present. They also last longer—both in storage and in use.

(+)
— Graphite rod (cathode)
— Spacer (porous)
— Zinc case (anode)
— Moist paste of MnO_2, NH_4Cl, and graphite powder
(−)

▲ **Figure 8.6** Cross section of a zinc–carbon cell.

Lead-Storage Batteries

Although we often refer to dry cells as batteries, a **battery** is actually a collection of electrochemical cells (recall Volta's battery). The 12-volt (V) storage battery used in automobiles, for example, is a series of six 2-V cells. Each cell (Figure 8.7) contains a pair of electrodes, one lead and the other lead(IV) oxide, in a chamber filled with sulfuric acid. Lead–acid batteries have been known for 150 years.

An important feature of the lead-storage battery is that it can be recharged. A car battery discharges while supplying electricity for the ignition or when the engine is off but the lights or the radio are on. The net reaction during discharge is:

$$Pb + PbO_2 + 2\,H_2SO_4 \longrightarrow 2\,PbSO_4 + 2\,H_2O$$

The battery is recharged when the car is moving, and an electric current created by the mechanical action of the car is supplied back to the battery. The reaction during recharge is the reverse:

$$2\,PbSO_4 + 2\,H_2O \longrightarrow Pb + PbO_2 + 2\,H_2SO_4$$

Lead-storage batteries are durable, but they are heavy, they contain corrosive sulfuric acid, and lead is a toxic environmental problem. In fact, the vast majority of battery technologies are not friendly to the environment.

↟ **It DOES Matter!**
Batteries labeled "Heavy Duty" or "Super" may be ordinary dry cells and may not have the longer shelf life and operating life of alkaline cells. Usually, alkaline cells are labeled as such and are only slightly higher in cost, making them a better buy.

e⁻   e⁻

Discharge   Charge

Charge   Discharge
e⁻

PbO_2 cathode

Pb anode

$H_2SO_4(aq)$

◄ **Figure 8.7** One cell of a lead-storage battery has two anode plates and two cathode plates. Six such cells make up the common 12-V car battery. The half-reactions are

Oxidation (anode):

$$Pb(s) + SO_4{}^{2-}(aq) \longrightarrow PbSO_4(s) + 2\,e^-$$

Reduction (cathode):

$$PbO_2(s) + 4\,H^+(aq) + SO_4{}^{2-}(aq) + 2\,e^- \longrightarrow PbSO_4(s) + 2\,H_2(l)$$

3. Why does a battery go dead?

When one or more of the reactants (zinc and MnO_2 in a dry cell) is used up, the cell can no longer provide useful energy.

4. Why are some batteries rechargeable but others are not?

A rechargeable battery uses a *reversible* redox reaction. The normal, forward reaction provides electrical energy. Applying electrical energy in the opposite direction using a charger reverses the reaction, and the starting materials are reformed. Not all redox reactions can be reversed in this manner.

▲ Some carbon monoxide detectors use an electrochemical cell in which carbon monoxide is oxidized to carbon dioxide at the anode, and oxygen is consumed at the cathode. Sulfuric acid serves as the electrolyte. The cell produces current related to the CO concentration in the air, and the current triggers an alarm or produces a readout of the CO concentration.

Other Batteries

Rechargeable batteries are one of the most important classes of batteries in today's marketplace. Over their lifetime, these batteries are more economical and environmentally friendly then their nonrechargeable counterparts. They are also more convenient in most applications—you can have your cake and eat it too—with the correct science, of course. Several rechargeable-battery technologies are on the market today. They utilize different chemical combinations, with the most common being: lead–acid, nickel cadmium (NiCd), nickel metal hydride (NiMH), lithium ion (Li-ion), and lithium-ion polymer (Li-ion polymer).

Much of the current battery technology involves the use of lithium, which has an extraordinarily low density and yet provides higher voltage than other metals. They are very popular despite some well-publicized issues, including bursting and causing fires. In fact, nearly all high-performance lightweight electronic devices, such as smartphones, tablets, and laptop computers, were made possible due to their use of lithium-ion batteries. Lithium-ion polymer batteries are the current technology of choice, as they can be made into nearly any shape imaginable. Lithium–SO_2 cells are used in submarines and rockets; lithium–iodine cells are used in pacemakers; and lithium–FeS_2 batteries are used in cameras, radios, and compact disc players.

Button batteries used in hearing aids and hand calculators formerly contained mercury (zinc anode, HgO cathode), but these cells are gradually being phased out and replaced with zinc–air cells. Tiny silver oxide cells (zinc anode, Ag_2O cathode) are used mainly in watches and cameras.

Rhubarb: No Longer Just for Pies!

Although rhubarb has been added to pie fillings for decades, it has now been successfully added to batteries! Why? To answer this question, some background is needed.

A number of house owners are adding solar cells to their roofs. The idea here is that, during the day, the solar panel collects more electricity than the household uses, and this excess electricity is sent back to the electric utility company. The house owner gets credit for this extra electricity and the utilities can lower their electrical production capacity and the costs associated with it.

On paper this looks like a win–win situation. However, any excess electricity must be stored... you guessed it... in rechargeable batteries. On the scale needed by electric utility companies, this battery technology is too expensive. Enter the flow battery. In a flow battery, separate liquid tanks are used to store energy. By removing some of the electrolyte from the battery, flow batteries can be tuned to deliver the needed capacity. This type of battery can be scaled up and down, which makes it more cost-effective than traditional batteries.

Traditionally, flow batteries have used expensive metals in the electrolyte, raising both the cost and environmental concerns. However, recently it has been found that inexpensive, nontoxic organic molecules can be used instead of metals. At the moment, one of the most promising candidates for such organic molecules is obtained from rhubarb.

Fuel Cells

An interesting kind of battery is the fuel cell. In a **fuel cell**, the oxidizing agent (usually oxygen) and the reducing agent are supplied continuously to the cell. Unlike other cells, a fuel cell does not "go dead" as long as the reactants are supplied. Moreover, when fossil fuels such as coal are burned to generate electricity, at most 35–40% of the energy from the combustion is actually harnessed. In a fuel cell, the fuel is oxidized and oxygen is reduced with 70–75% efficiency. As we shall see in Chapter 15, most present-day fuel cells use hydrogen as the fuel with platinum, nickel, or rhodium electrodes, in a solution of potassium hydroxide.

Electrolysis

Dry cells and fuel cells produce electricity from chemical reactions. Sometimes, we can reverse the process. In electrolysis (discussed briefly in Section 3.1), electricity supplied externally causes a chemical reaction to occur. The charging reaction of the lead-storage cell shown in Figure 8.7 is one type of electrolysis. The car's alternator provides electric current, causing lead(II) sulfate to be converted back to lead metal and PbO_2. Other rechargeable cells undergo the reverse of their electricity-producing reaction when they are recharged.

Electrolysis is very important in industry. About 1% of all of the electricity in the United States is used to convert aluminum oxide to the aluminum metal we use for pots, foil, and cans. Chrome plating is performed by passing electricity through a solution of chromium ions (Cr^{6+}); electrons convert the ions to shiny chromium metal. Crude copper metal is purified by electrolysis, which converts the copper metal at the anode into copper(II) ions and then deposits nearly pure copper metal at the cathode. Many other materials—including sodium hydroxide, chlorine bleach, and magnesium metal—are produced by electrolysis.

SELF-ASSESSMENT Questions

1. In an electrochemical cell, electrons flow from the
   a. anode to the cathode
   b. cathode to the anode
   c. anode to the salt bridge
   d. salt bridge to the cathode

2. In the electrochemical cell whose overall reaction is represented by the following equation, the negative electrode is
$$Zn(s) + Cu^{2+}(aq) \longrightarrow Zn^{2+}(aq) + Cu(s)$$
   a. $Cu(s)$ b. $Cu^{2+}(aq)$ c. $Zn(s)$ d. $Zn^{2+}(aq)$

3. In the zinc-carbon cell, the anode is _____ and the cathode is _____.
   a. Zn, MnO_2 b. Zn, C c. C, Zn d. C, MnO_2

4. In an electrochemical cell composed of two half-cells, ions flow from one half-cell to another through
   a. electrodes   b. air   c. a salt bridge   d. a wire

5. For the following reaction, the oxidation half-reaction is
$$Mg + CuO \longrightarrow MgO + Cu$$
   a. $Cu^{2+} + 2\ e^- \longrightarrow CuO$ b. $CuO \longrightarrow Cu^{2+} + 2\ e^-$
   c. $Mg^{2+} + 2\ e^- \longrightarrow MgO$ d. $Mg \longrightarrow Mg^{2+} + 2\ e^-$

6. In a lead-storage battery, the product of both cathode and anode half-reactions is
   a. H_2SO_4 b. Pb c. PbO_2 d. $PbSO_4$

7. Which statement is not true in regards to lithium batteries?
   a. are low density
   b. are used in laptop computers
   c. provide high voltage
   d. are nonrechargeable

8. The overall electricity-producing reaction in the H_2/O_2 fuel cell is
$$2\ H_2(g) + O_2(g) \longrightarrow 2\ H_2O(g)$$
   The half-reaction at the cathode is
   a. $H_2 \longrightarrow 2\ H^+ + 2\ e^-$
   b. $2\ H^+ + 2\ e^- \longrightarrow H_2$
   c. $O_2 + 4\ H^+ + 4\ e^- \longrightarrow 2\ H_2O$
   d. $2\ H_2O \longrightarrow O_2 + 4\ H^+ + 4\ e^-$

Answers: 1. a; 2. c; 3. b; 4. c; 5. d; 6. d; 7. d; 8. c

8.4 Corrosion and Explosion

Learning Objectives ❭ Describe the reactions that occur when iron rusts.
❭ Explain why an explosive reaction is so energetic.

You might think *corrosion* and *explosion* have little in common except that they rhyme. However, both processes involve redox reactions. Corrosion of metals is of great economic importance. In the United States alone, corrosion costs about $275 billion a year, as already mentioned in the introduction to this chapter. Perhaps as much as 20% of all the iron and steel produced in the United States each year goes to replace corroded items. Explosions can bring economic benefit when used in mining, road building, demolition jobs, and removing ice dams to reduce flooding during the spring melt. They can also cause enormous loss in war and accidents.

5. Why don't we see more "rust bucket" ships?

Most ship hulls are made of steel (mostly iron) and, according to Figure 8.8, when a ship sails the ocean (lots of electrolyte present!) it should simply rust away. So, why is this not the case?

For rust to form, iron must give up its electrons and get oxidized. Some metals give up electrons more easily than others. For instance, zinc is more easily oxidized than iron. By simply attaching a block of zinc to the steel hull, the zinc is oxidized instead of the iron. The zinc block acts as the so-called *sacrificial anode*. More recently, paints have been developed that contain chemicals that react with rust to form a tough protective polymer coating. The same approach is taken to preserve oil rigs and other steel-containing ocean structures.

The Rusting of Iron

In moist air, iron is oxidized, particularly at a nick or scratch.

$$Fe(s) \longrightarrow Fe^{2+}(aq) + 2\ e^-$$

As iron is oxidized, oxygen is reduced.

$$O_2(g) + 2\ H_2O(l) + 4\ e^- \longrightarrow 4\ OH^-(aq)$$

The net result, initially, is the formation of insoluble iron(II) hydroxide, which appears dark green or black.

$$2\ Fe(s) + O_2(g) + 2\ H_2O(l) \longrightarrow 2\ Fe(OH)_2(s)$$

This product is usually further oxidized to iron(III) hydroxide.

$$4\ Fe(OH)_2(s) + O_2(g) + 2\ H_2O(l) \longrightarrow 4\ Fe(OH)_3(s)$$

Iron(III) hydroxide $[Fe(OH)_3]$, sometimes written as $Fe_2O_3 \cdot 3\ H_2O$, is the familiar iron rust.

Oxidation and reduction often occur at separate points on the metal's surface. Electrons are transferred through the iron metal. The circuit is completed by an electrolyte in aqueous solution. In the Snow Belt, this solution is often the slush from road salt and melting snow. The metal is pitted in an anodic area, where iron is oxidized to Fe^{2+}. These ions migrate to the cathodic area, where they react with hydroxide ions formed by the reduction of oxygen.

$$Fe^{2+}(aq) + 2\ OH^-(aq) \longrightarrow Fe(OH)_2(s)$$

As noted previously, the iron(II) hydroxide is then oxidized to $Fe(OH)_3$, or rust. This process is diagrammed in Figure 8.8. Note that the anodic area is protected from oxygen by a water film, while the cathodic area is exposed to air.

▲ **Figure 8.8** The corrosion of iron requires water, oxygen, and an electrolyte.

Protection of Aluminum

Aluminum is more reactive than iron, yet corrosion is not a serious problem with aluminum. We use aluminum foil, we cook with aluminum pots, and we buy beverages in aluminum cans. Even after many years, they do not corrode. How is this possible? The aluminum at the surface reacts with oxygen in the air to form a thin layer of oxide:

$$4\ Al(s) + 3\ O_2(g) \longrightarrow 2\ Al_2O_3(s)$$

Instead of being porous and flaky like iron oxide in rust, aluminum oxide is hard and tough and adheres strongly to the surface of the metal, protecting it from further oxidation.

Nonetheless, corrosion can sometimes be an issue with aluminum. Certain substances, such as salt, can interfere with the protective oxide coating on aluminum, allowing the metal to oxidize. This problem can have some serious consequences, such as when the wheels in the aluminum landing gear of some planes shear off.

Silver Tarnish

The tarnish on silver results from oxidation of the silver surface by hydrogen sulfide (H_2S) in the air or from food. It produces a film of black silver sulfide (Ag_2S) on the metal surface.

$$2\ Ag(s) + H_2S(g) \longrightarrow Ag_2S(s) + H_2(g)$$

You can use silver polish to remove the tarnish, but in doing so, you also lose part of the silver. An alternative method involves the use of aluminum metal. The overall equation is:

$$3\ Ag_2S(s)\ +\ 2\ Al(s)\ \longrightarrow\ 6\ Ag(s)\ +\ Al_2S_3(s)$$

Since sulfur does not contribute to the above redox reaction (its oxidation number does not change), the reaction can be written only in terms of silver, which gets reduced (its oxidation number decreases from +1 to 0) and aluminum, which gets oxidized (its oxidation number increases from 0 to +3.)

$$3\ Ag^+(aq)\ +\ Al(s)\ \longrightarrow\ 3\ Ag(s)\ +\ Al^{3+}(aq)$$

This reaction also requires an electrolyte, and sodium bicarbonate ($NaHCO_3$) is usually used. The tarnished silver is placed in contact with aluminum metal (often in the form of foil) and covered with a hot solution of sodium bicarbonate. The silver ions are reduced to silver metal at the expense of the cheaper metal.

Explosive Reactions

Corrosive reactions are often quite slow. A chemical explosion (that is, not one based on nuclear fission or fusion) is usually an extremely rapid redox reaction, often accompanied by a considerable increase in volume. This volume increase is due to the conversion of a solid or liquid explosive into a number of gaseous products in a course of a redox reaction. Such a reaction often involves a compound of nitrogen, such as nitroglycerin (the active ingredient in dynamite), ammonium nitrate (NH_4NO_3, a common fertilizer), or trinitrotoluene (TNT). These compounds can decompose readily, yielding nitrogen gas as one of the products. As you already know from Chapter 6, molar volume of gas at STP conditions is 22.4 L. For instance, when TNT detonates, depending on conditions, it decomposes into:

$$2\ C_7H_5N_3O_6(s)\ \longrightarrow\ 3\ N_2(g)\ +\ 5\ H_2O(g)\ +\ 7\ CO(g)\ +\ 7\ C(s)$$

$$2\ C_7H_5N_3O_6(s)\ \longrightarrow\ 3\ N_2(g)\ +\ 5\ H_2(g)\ +\ 12\ CO(g)\ +\ 2\ C(s)$$

This means that each one mole of TNT, about 0.14 L, yields either 169 L (7.5×22.4 L) or 224 L (10×22.4 L) for the top and bottom reaction, respectively, at STP conditions. In both cases, the expansion is greater than 1000-fold!

Nitroglycerin has a very interesting history. Alfred Nobel, who established the Nobel Prize, made his fortune in nitroglycerin as an explosive, including inventing dynamite. The motivation behind establishing this prize was born out of the sense of guilt because commercial explosives afforded by Nobel's invention, mainly for mining and public works, had been used as a weapon, with very tragic consequences. Somewhat ironically, in the later part of his life, Nobel used nitroglycerin to treat his heart condition. This application of nitroglycerin is still in use to this day.

Explosive mixtures are used for mining, earth-moving projects, and the demolition of buildings. *ANFO* (*A*mmonium *N*itrate mixed with *F*uel *O*il) is an inexpensive and effective explosive, widely used for mining salt, coal, and other minerals. When ANFO explodes, ammonium ion is the reducing agent and nitrate ion is the oxidizing agent. The fuel oil provides additional oxidizable material. Using $C_{17}H_{36}$ as the formula for a typical molecule in fuel oil, we can write the equation for the explosive reaction.

$$52\ NH_4NO_3(s)\ +\ C_{17}H_{36}(l)\ \longrightarrow\ 52\ N_2(g)\ +\ 17\ CO_2(g)\ +\ 122\ H_2O(g)$$

Once again, notice that the starting materials, 53 moles of solid and liquid reactants, generate 191 mol of gaseous products. This reaction produces a huge volume increase, which becomes part of the explosive force.

Unfortunately, ANFO has also been used in terrorist attacks around the world. Ammonium nitrate is a widely used fertilizer, and fuel oil is used in many home furnaces. The fact that both of these materials are readily accessible to potential terrorists is cause for some concern.

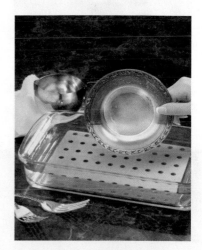

▲ Silver tarnish (Ag_2S) is readily removed from silver metal brought into contact with aluminum metal in a baking soda solution. Working in a sink, add about 1 cup of baking soda to 1 gal of hot water. Immerse a piece of aluminum and then the tarnished silver object so that it touches the aluminum.

SELF-ASSESSMENT Questions

1. When iron rusts, it is being
   a. converted to gold
   b. oxidized
   c. reduced
   d. neutralized

2. Corrosion of aluminum is not as big a problem as corrosion of iron because aluminum
   a. forms an oxide layer that adheres to the metal's surface
   b. is less reactive than Fe
   c. needs water to corrode
   d. has a higher oxidation number

3. When silver is tarnished by H_2S, hydrogen is
   a. reduced
   b. dissolved
   c. oxidized
   d. evaporated

4. In a typical explosive reaction, which of the following usually occurs?
   a. Gases are converted from one form to another.
   b. Liquids or solids are converted to aqueous solutions.
   c. Liquids or solids are converted to gases.
   d. Nitrogen nuclei are split.

5. Black powder is a mixture of charcoal (carbon), potassium nitrate, and sulfur. The oxidizing agent in black powder is
   a. charcoal
   b. nitroglycerin
   c. potassium nitrate
   d. sulfur

Answers: 1, b; 2, a; 3, a; 4, c; 5, c

8.5 Oxygen: An Abundant and Essential Oxidizing Agent

Learning Objectives ❯ Write equations for reactions in which oxygen is an oxidizing agent. ❯ List some of the common oxidizing agents encountered in daily life.

Oxygen itself is the most common oxidizing agent. Many other oxidizing agents—sometimes called *oxidants*—are important in the laboratory, in industry, and in the home. They are used as antiseptics, disinfectants, and bleaches and play a role in many chemical syntheses.

Oxygen: Occurrence and Properties

The structure and chemistry of Earth are discussed in Chapter 12, of the atmosphere in Chapter 13, and of water in Chapter 14.

Certainly one of the most important elements on Earth, oxygen is one of about two dozen elements essential to life. Making up one-fifth of the air, it oxidizes the wood in our campfires and the gasoline in our automobiles. It is found in most compounds that are important to living organisms. Foodstuffs—carbohydrates, fats, and proteins—all contain oxygen. The human body is approximately 65% water (by mass). Because water is 89% oxygen by mass and many other compounds in your body also contain oxygen, almost two-thirds of your body mass is oxygen.

Oxygen comprises about half of the accessible portion of Earth by mass. It occurs in all three subdivisions of Earth's outermost structure. Oxygen occurs as (O_2) molecules in the atmosphere (the gaseous mass surrounding Earth). In the hydrosphere (the oceans, seas, rivers, and lakes), oxygen is combined with hydrogen in water. In the lithosphere (the outer solid portion of the Earth's crust), oxygen is combined with silicon (sand is SiO_2), aluminum (in clays), and other elements.

The atmosphere is about 21% elemental oxygen (O_2) by volume. The rest is about 78% nitrogen (N_2) and 1% argon (Ar), both of which are quite unreactive. The free, uncombined oxygen in the air is taken into our lungs, passes into our bloodstreams, is carried to our body tissues, and reacts with the food we eat. This is the process that provides us with energy to move and think.

Fuels such as natural gas, gasoline, and coal also need oxygen to burn and release their stored energy. Oxidation, or combustion, of these fossil fuels currently supplies about 86% of the energy that turns the wheels of civilization.

Pure oxygen is obtained by liquefying air and then letting the nitrogen and argon boil off. Nitrogen boils at $-196°C$, argon at $-186°C$, and oxygen at $-183°C$. About 20 billion kg of oxygen is produced annually in the United States, but most of it is used directly by industry, much of it in steel plants. About 1% is compressed into tanks for use in welding, hospital respirators, and other purposes.

Not everything that oxygen does is desirable. Besides causing corrosion (Section 8.4), it promotes food spoilage and wood decay.

It DOES Matter!

Physical activity under conditions in which plenty of oxygen is available to body tissues is called *aerobic* exercise. When the available oxygen is insufficient, the exercise is called *anaerobic*, and it often leads to weakness and pain resulting from "oxygen debt." (See Chapter 19.)

Oxygen: Reactions with Other Elements

Many oxidation reactions involving atmospheric oxygen are quite complicated, but we can gain some understanding by looking at some of the simpler ones. For example, as we have seen, oxygen combines with many metals to form metal oxides and with nonmetals to form nonmetal oxides.

▲ Fuels burn more rapidly in pure oxygen than in air. Huge quantities of liquid oxygen are used to burn the fuels that blast rockets into orbit.

| Example 8.9 | Writing Equations: Reaction of Oxygen with Other Elements |

Magnesium combines readily with oxygen when ignited in air. Write the equation for this reaction.

Solution

Magnesium is a group 2A metal. Oxygen occurs as diatomic molecules (O_2). The two react to form MgO. The reaction is

$$Mg(s) + O_2(g) \longrightarrow MgO(s) \text{ (not balanced)}$$

To balance the equation, we need 2 Mg and 2 MgO.

$$2\,Mg(s) + O_2(g) \longrightarrow 2\,MgO(s)$$

▪ **EXERCISE 8.9**

Write equations for the following reactions.
  a. Zinc burns in air to form zinc oxide (ZnO).
  b. Selenium (Se) burns in air to form selenium dioxide.
  c. Diamond (C) burns in air to form CO_2.

Oxygen: Reactions with Compounds

Oxygen reacts with many compounds, oxidizing one or more of the elements in the compound. As we have seen, combustion of a fuel is oxidation and produces oxides. There are many other examples. Hydrogen sulfide, a gaseous compound with a rotten-egg odor, burns to produce oxides of hydrogen (water) and of sulfur (sulfur dioxide).

$$2\,H_2S(g) + 3\,O_2(g) \longrightarrow 2\,H_2O(l) + 2\,SO_2(g)$$

| Example 8.10 | Writing Equations: Reaction of Oxygen with Compounds |

Carbon disulfide, a highly flammable liquid, combines readily with oxygen, burning with a blue flame. What products are formed? Write the equation.

Solution

Carbon disulfide is CS_2. The products are oxides of carbon (carbon dioxide) and of sulfur (sulfur dioxide). The balanced equation is

$$CS_2(g) + 3\,O_2(g) \longrightarrow CO_2(g) + 2\,SO_2(g)$$

▪ **EXERCISE 8.10A**

When heated in air, lead sulfide (PbS) combines with oxygen to form lead(II) oxide (PbO) and sulfur dioxide. Write a balanced equation for the reaction.

▪ **EXERCISE 8.10B**

Write a balanced equation for the combustion (reaction with oxygen) of ethanol (C_2H_5OH).

Ozone: Another Form of Oxygen

In addition to diatomic O_2, oxygen also has a triatomic form (O_3) called *ozone*. Ozone is a powerful oxidizing agent. In fact, it is a more powerful oxidizer than any

▲ Hydrogen peroxide is a powerful oxidizing agent. Dilute solutions are used as disinfectant and to bleach hair.

chlorine-based disinfectant or antiseptic. This has made ozone a major chemical in water treatment, especially in Europe. Ozone can completely break down urea, through oxidation, as follows:

$$(NH_2)_2CO(aq) + O_3(g) \longrightarrow N_2(g) + CO_2(g) + 2\ H_2O(l)$$

In the reaction above, the oxidation number of nitrogen has changed from −3 to 0. This oxidation is caused by ozone.

In the following reaction

$$2\ Mn^{2+}(aq) + 2\ O_3(g) + 4\ H_2O(l) \longrightarrow 2\ MnO(OH)_2(s) + 2\ O_2(g) + 4\ H^+(aq)$$

ozone increases the oxidation number of manganese from +2 to +4 and, most importantly, removes manganese—a potential toxin causing psychiatric and motor disorders—from solution by forming a poorly soluble solid called manganite.

Ozone can also be a harmful air pollutant. It can be extremely irritating to both plants and animals and is especially destructive to rubber. On the other hand, a layer of ozone in the upper stratosphere serves as a shield that protects life on Earth from ultraviolet radiation from the sun (Chapter 13). Ozone clearly illustrates that the same substance can be extremely beneficial or quite harmful, depending on the context.

Other Common Oxidizing Agents

Oxidizing agents used around the home include antiseptics, disinfectants, and bleaches. Many others are used in workplaces and in laboratories.

Disinfectants and antiseptics are alike in that both are materials used to destroy microorganisms (that is, they are germicidal), but antiseptics are applied mainly to living tissue and disinfectants to nonliving things. A good example of a disinfectant is chlorine, which is used to kill disease-causing microorganisms in drinking water and some swimming pools. The actual disinfecting agent is hypochlorous acid (HOCl), formed by the reaction of chlorine with water.

$$Cl_2(g) + H_2O(l) \longrightarrow HOCl(aq) + HCl(aq)$$

▲ Pure water (left) has little effect on a dried tomato sauce stain. Sodium hypochlorite bleach (right) removes the stain by oxidizing the colored tomato pigments to colorless products.

SAFETY ALERT

Strong oxidizing agents such as 30% aqueous hydrogen peroxide can cause severe burns. In general, strong oxidizing agents are corrosive, and many are highly toxic. They can also initiate a fire or increase the severity of a fire when brought into contact with combustible materials.

In recent years, concern has been raised about by-products that form when chlorine is used to disinfect water containing certain impurities. Although chlorine kills harmful microorganisms, it can also oxidize certain small molecules to form harmful by-products, such as chloroform.

Swimming pools are often chlorinated with calcium hypochlorite [$Ca(OCl)_2$]. Because calcium hypochlorite is alkaline, it also raises the pH of the water. (When a pool becomes too alkaline, the pH is lowered by adding hydrochloric acid. Swimming pools are usually maintained at pH 7.2–7.8.)

Solutions of potassium permanganate ($KMnO_4$), a common laboratory oxidizing agent, are also good disinfectants. Such solutions are a deep purplish pink. Highly diluted solutions are pale pink (called "pinky water" in India) and are used in developing countries to disinfect foods. Their use is limited because the permanganate ion is reduced to brown manganese dioxide, leaving a brown stain on the treated substance.

Hydrogen peroxide (H_2O_2) is a common oxidizing agent that has the advantage of being converted to water in most reactions. Pure hydrogen peroxide is a syrupy liquid. It is available (in laboratories) as a dangerous 30% solution that has powerful oxidizing power or as a 3% solution (sold in stores) for various uses around the home. When combined with a specially designed catalyst, hydrogen peroxide can be used to oxidize colored compounds and water impurities.

As a dilute aqueous solution, hydrogen peroxide is used to bleach hair (which gave rise to the phrase "peroxide blonde"). Dilute H_2O_2 is used medically to clean and deodorize wounds and ulcers.

Iodine is used as an antiseptic, either in an alcoholic solution (called *tincture of iodine*) or in Lugol's iodine solution (which contains no alcohol).

An oxidizing agent sometimes used in the laboratory is potassium dichromate ($K_2C_2O_7$). It is an orange substance that turns green when it is reduced to chromium(III) compounds. One of the compounds that potassium dichromate oxidizes is ethyl alcohol. The early Breathalyzer test for intoxication made use of a dichromate solution. The exhaled breath of the person being tested was mixed with the acidic dichromate, and the degree of color change indicated the level of alcohol.

Ointments for treating acne often contain 5–10% benzoyl peroxide, a powerful antiseptic and also a skin irritant. It causes old skin to slough off and be replaced by new, fresher-looking skin. When used on areas exposed to sunlight, however, benzoyl peroxide may promote skin cancer.

Bleaches are oxidizing agents, too. A **bleach** removes unwanted color from fabrics or other material. Most bleaches work by oxidizing carbon–carbon double bonds in the colored substances to single bonds. This renders the stain colorless or nearly so. Almost any oxidizing agent could do the job, but some might be unsafe to use, or harmful to fabrics, or perhaps too expensive.

Bleaches (Chapter 21) are usually sodium hypochlorite (NaOCl) in aqueous solution (in laundry products such as Purex® and Clorox®), often called *chlorine bleaches*, or calcium hypochlorite [$Ca(OCl)_2$], known as *bleaching powder*. The powder is usually preferred for large industrial operations, such as the whitening of paper or fabrics. Nonchlorine bleaches, often called *oxygen bleaches*, contain sodium percarbonate (a combination of Na_2CO_3 and H_2O_2) or sodium perborate (a combination of $NaBO_3$ and H_2O_2).

Stain removal is more complicated than bleaching. A few stain removers are oxidizing agents, but some are reducing agents, some are solvents or detergents, and some have quite different action. Stains often require rather specific stain removers.

SELF-ASSESSMENT Questions

1. When CH_4 is burned in plentiful air, the products are
   a. $C + H_2$
   b. $CH_2 + H_2O$
   c. $CO_2 + H_2$
   d. $CO_2 + H_2O$

2. When sulfur burns in plentiful air, the product is
   a. CO_2 b. H_2S c. H_2SO_4 d. SO_2

3. Which of the following is a common oxidizing agent?
   a. HCl   b. H_2O_2 c. NaOH   d. NaCl

4. Which of the following is a common oxidizing agent?
   a. Cl_2 b. H_2 c. HCl   d. KOH

5. The main active ingredient in common household bleach, often called *chlorine bleach*, is
   a. HCl   b. NaOCl   c. NaOH   d. NaCl

6. Bleach for hair usually contains
   a. ammonia
   b. hydrochloric acid
   c. hydrogen peroxide
   d. sodium hypochlorite

7. Many disinfectants are
   a. oxidizing agents
   b. reducing agents
   c. strong acids
   d. strong bases

8. Potassium permanganate is a powerful oxidizing agent. In acidic solutions, the permanganate anion turns into Mn^{2+} cation, while in basic solution, it becomes a solid MnO_2. How many electrons are involved in these processes, respectively?
   a. 6, 2   b. 6, 3   c. 4, 5   d. 5, 3

8.6 Some Common Reducing Agents

Learning Objective   ❯ Identify some common reducing agents.

In every reaction involving oxidation, the oxidizing agent is reduced, and the substance undergoing oxidation acts as a reducing agent. Let's now consider reactions in which the purpose of the reaction is reduction.

Metals

Most metals occur in nature as compounds. To prepare the free metals, the compounds must be reduced. Metals are often freed from their ores by using coal or *coke* (elemental carbon obtained by heating coal to drive off volatile matter). Tin(IV) oxide is one of the many ores that can be reduced with coal or coke.

$$SnO_2(s) + C(s) \longrightarrow Sn(s) + CO_2(g)$$

Sometimes a metal can be obtained by heating its ore with a more active metal. Chromium(III) oxide, for example, can be reduced by heating it with aluminum.

$$Cr_2O_3(s) + 2\ Al(s) \longrightarrow Al_2O_3(s) + 2\ Cr(s)$$

Antioxidants

In food chemistry, certain reducing agents are called **antioxidants**. Ascorbic acid (vitamin C) can prevent the browning of fruit (such as sliced apples or pears) by inhibiting air oxidation. Vitamin C is water soluble, but tocopherol (vitamin E) and beta-carotene (a precursor of vitamin A) are fat-soluble antioxidants. All these vitamins are believed to retard various oxidation reactions that are potentially damaging to vital components of living cells (Chapter 17).

Hydrogen as a Reducing Agent

Hydrogen is an excellent reducing agent that can free many metals from their ores, but it is generally used to produce more expensive metals, such as tungsten (W).

$$WO_3(s) + 3\ H_2(g) \longrightarrow W(s) + 3\ H_2O(l)$$

Hydrogen can be used to reduce many kinds of chemical compounds. Ethylene, for example, can be reduced to ethane.

$$C_2H_4(g) + H_2(g) \longrightarrow C_2H_6(g)$$

The reaction requires a **catalyst**, a substance that increases the rate of a chemical reaction without itself being used up. Nickel is the catalyst used in this case. (Catalysts lower the *activation energy*—the minimum energy needed to get a reaction started; they are further explored in Chapter 15.)

Hydrogen also reduces nitrogen, from air, in the industrial production of ammonia.

$$N_2(g) + 3\ H_2(g) \longrightarrow 2\ NH_3(g)$$

A nickel catalyst is also used in converting unsaturated fats to saturated fats (Chapter 17). Unsaturated fats ordinarily react very slowly with hydrogen, but in the presence of nickel metal, the reaction proceeds readily. The nickel increases the rate of the reaction, but it does not increase the amount of product formed.

Ammonia is the source of most nitrogen fertilizers in modern agriculture. The reaction that produces ammonia employs an iron catalyst.

A stream of pure hydrogen burns quietly in air with an almost colorless flame, but when a mixture of hydrogen and oxygen is ignited by a spark or a flame, an explosion results. The product in both cases is water.

$$2\ H_2(g) + O_2(g) \longrightarrow 2\ H_2O(l)$$

Certain metals, including platinum and palladium, have an unusual affinity for hydrogen. They absorb large volumes of the gas. Palladium can absorb up to 900 times its own volume of hydrogen. It is interesting to note that hydrogen and oxygen can be mixed at room temperature with no perceptible reaction. If a piece of platinum gauze is added to the mixture, however, the gases react violently. The platinum acts as a catalyst. The heat from the initial reaction heats up the platinum, making it glow; it then ignites the hydrogen–oxygen mixture, causing an explosion.

Nickel, platinum, and palladium are often used as catalysts for reactions involving hydrogen. These metals have the greatest catalytic activity when they are finely divided and have lots of active surface area. Hydrogen adsorbed on the surface of these metals is more reactive than ordinary hydrogen gas.

Catalysts are an important area of research in green chemistry. Chemists are able to develop more energy-efficient and sustainable processes by designing catalysts that enable chemical reactions to occur at lower temperatures or pressures. Using a catalyst can also allow a reaction to occur using milder reactants, such as oxygen or hydrogen peroxide instead of chlorine for oxidizing stains on clothes or destroying harmful microorganisms in drinking water.

6. Does hydrogen have a promising future as a fuel?

Gram for gram, hydrogen provides more energy than any other chemical fuel. Also, when hydrogen is oxidized by oxygen, the product is ordinary water. Unfortunately, it takes more energy to produce hydrogen than we get from burning the hydrogen. Until we can use renewable energy to generate hydrogen, its future as a fuel will remain in question.

A Closer Look at Hydrogen

Unlike oxygen, hydrogen is rarely found as a free, uncombined element on Earth. Most of it is combined with oxygen in water. Some is combined with carbon in petroleum and natural gas, which are mixtures of hydrocarbons. Nearly all compounds derived from plants and animals contain hydrogen.

Small amounts of elemental hydrogen can be made for laboratory use by reacting zinc with hydrochloric acid (Figure 8.9).

$$Zn(s) + 2\ HCl(aq) \longrightarrow ZnCl_2(aq) + H_2(g)$$

Commercial quantities of hydrogen are obtained as by-products of petroleum refining or from the reaction of natural gas with steam. About 8 billion kg of hydrogen is produced each year in the United States. At present, hydrogen is used mainly to make ammonia and methanol. Its possible use as a fuel in the future is discussed in Chapter 15.

SELF-ASSESSMENT Questions

1. Which of the following is a common reducing agent?
   a. Cl_2 **b.** F_2 **c.** H_2 **d.** I_2

2. Which of the following is a common reducing agent?
   a. C   **b.** O_2 **c.** CO_2 **d.** $KMnO_4$

3. All the following metals are used as catalysts for reactions involving hydrogen gas *except*
   a. aluminum   **b.** nickel   **c.** palladium   **d.** platinum

4. A catalyst changes the rate of a chemical reaction by
   a. changing the products of the reaction
   b. changing the reactants involved in the reaction
   c. increasing the frequency of molecular collisions
   d. lowering the activation energy

Answers: 1, c; 2, a; 3, a; 4, d

▲ **Figure 8.9** Hydrogen gas can be prepared in the laboratory by the reaction of zinc metal with hydrochloric acid.

Q: *Is the reaction between H_2 and Zn a redox reaction? Explain.*

8.7 Oxidation, Reduction, and Living Things

Learning Objective   ❯ Write the overall equations for the metabolism of glucose and for photosynthesis.

Perhaps the most important oxidation–reduction processes are the ones that maintain life on this planet. We obtain energy for all our physical and mental activities by metabolizing food in a process called *cellular respiration*. The process has many steps, but eventually the food we eat is converted mainly into carbon dioxide, water, and energy.

Bread and many of the other foods we eat are largely made up of carbohydrates, composed of carbon, hydrogen, and oxygen (Chapter 17). If we represent carbohydrates with the simple example of glucose ($C_6H_{12}O_6$), we can write the overall equation for their metabolism as follows.

$$C_6H_{12}O_6 + 6\ O_2 \longrightarrow 6\ CO_2 + 6\ H_2O + energy$$

This process occurs constantly in animals, including humans. The carbohydrate is oxidized in the process.

Meanwhile, plants need carbon dioxide, water, and energy from the sun to produce carbohydrates. The process by which plants synthesize carbohydrates is called **photosynthesis** (Figure 8.11). The overall chemical equation is

$$6\ CO_2 + 6\ H_2O + energy \longrightarrow C_6H_{12}O_6 + 6\ O_2$$

Notice that this process in plant cells is exactly the reverse of the process going on inside animals. In food metabolism in animals, we focus on an oxidation process. In photosynthesis, we focus on a reduction process.

The carbohydrates produced by photosynthesis are the ultimate source of all our food because fish, fowl, and other animals either eat plants or eat other animals

▲ **Figure 8.11** Photosynthesis occurs in green plants. The chlorophyll pigments that catalyze the photosynthesis process give the green color to much of the land area of Earth.

GREEN CHEMISTRY

Roger A. Sheldon, *Delft University of Technology, Netherlands*

Green Redox Catalysis

Learning Objectives ❯ Use a balanced reaction to calculate the atom economy and E factor of the reaction. ❯ Describe the role of catalysts in minimizing waste in the chemical and allied industries.

Oxidation and reduction processes always occur together in what is called a redox reaction (Section 8.1). When one substance is oxidized, another is always reduced. Oxidation and reduction reactions are extremely important in the chemical and allied industries. The simplest and least expensive reducing agent and oxidizing agent are molecular hydrogen and oxygen, respectively. Hydrogen is used in catalytic reductions (hydrogenations), and oxygen is used in catalytic oxidations. Both types of reactions produce a variety of bulk industrial chemicals in the petrochemical and other large industries. The catalyst increases the reaction rate or the selectivity to the product. In contrast, the manufacture of specialty chemicals, such as pharmaceuticals, generally involves the use of complicated reducing and oxidizing agents that are usually more expensive and also generate large amounts of waste.

A main goal of green chemistry is to minimize or eliminate waste, which is defined as everything formed in the process except the desired product (Principle 1). Comparing different reactions can illustrate how greener redox reactions can reduce waste and improve efficiency. To compare the greenness of processes, it is necessary to use meaningful green metrics. Two such metrics were developed in the early 1990s. These are *atom economy* (see the essay "Atom Economy" in Chapter 5) and the *E factor* (kilograms of waste per kilogram of product). As discussed in the green chemistry essay in Chapter 5, the ideal atom economy is 100%, which means that all of the atoms end up in the product, and the ideal E factor is zero–no waste (Principle 2).

In Scheme 1, we compare the reduction of acetone to an alcohol using one equivalent of sodium borohydride or hydrogen in the presence of catalytic amounts of palladium-on-charcoal. Reduction with sodium borohydride produces the desired isopropyl alcohol product and one equivalent each of boric acid and sodium hydroxide as waste. In the catalytic hydrogenation, in contrast, no waste product is formed (Principle 9).

You might ask, however, what is important about the catalyst? Since a catalyst is defined as a substance that changes the rate of a reaction (by lowering its activation energy) without itself being changed in the process, it can, in principle, be recycled indefinitely and no waste is generated (Section 8.6).

As shown in Scheme 1, the atom economy of the sodium borohydride reduction is 70% and the theoretical E factor is 0.42. However, in practice, the E factor is generally higher than predicted by the atom economy because the chemical yield is not 100%.

(1) Stoichiometric reduction of a ketone with sodium borohydride

$$\text{atom economy} = \frac{\text{product MW}}{\text{total MW of all reactants}} = \frac{240}{232 + 38 + 72} = 70\%$$

$$\text{theoretical E factor} = \frac{\text{kg waste}}{\text{kg product}} = \frac{102}{240} = 0.42$$

(2) Palladium-on-charcoal catalyzed hydrogenation of a ketone

$$\text{atom economy} = \frac{78}{78} = 100\%$$

$$\text{theoretical E factor} = 0$$

Scheme 1. Atom economies and theoretical E factors of stoichiometric vs catalytic reduction.

Reagents, including sodium borohydride, are generally used in excess amounts to obtain complete conversion of the starting material in a reasonable time. Also, some waste is not contained in the stoichiometric equation, for example, solvents. In stark contrast, the atom economy of the catalytic hydrogenation is 100%, and the theoretical E factor is zero.

Similarly, in Scheme 2, we compare the reverse reaction, the oxidation of an alcohol to acetone. One option is to use a classical stoichiometric reagent, potassium dichromate. The other route is a catalytic oxidation with molecular oxygen in the presence of a palladium catalyst. The atom economies are 20% and 76%, and the theoretical E factors are 3.98 and 0.31, respectively. In practice, the E factor for the first reaction is substantially higher than 4 because dichromate and sulfuric acid are used in large excess.

Yet it is not only the amount of waste formed that is important. Chromium(VI) is a suspected carcinogen and, hence, chromium-containing waste is potentially toxic. In contrast, the byproduct in the catalytic oxidation is one equivalent of water, which is harmless (Principle 3). Replacement of chromium(VI) as the oxidant is important from another green chemistry viewpoint, avoiding the use of toxic or hazardous reagents. In short, catalysis is the key to green and sustainable redox chemistry.

(1) Stoichiometric oxidation with potassium dichromate

$$\text{atom economy} = \frac{174}{180 + 294 + 392} = \frac{174}{866} = 20\%$$

$$\text{theoretical E factor} = \frac{692}{174} = 3.98$$

(2) Catalytic oxidation with molecular oxygen (air)

$$\text{atom economy} = \frac{58}{76} = 76\%$$

$$\text{theoretical E factor} = \frac{18}{58} = 0.31$$

Scheme 2. Atom economies and theoretical E factors of stoichiometric vs catalytic oxidation.

that eat plants. Note that the photosynthesis process not only makes carbohydrates but also yields free elementary oxygen (O_2). In other words, photosynthesis does not just provide the food we eat—it also provides the oxygen we breathe.

There are many oxidation reactions that occur in nature (with oxygen being reduced in the process). The net photosynthesis reaction is unique in that it is a natural reduction of carbon dioxide (with oxygen being oxidized). Many processes in nature use oxygen. Photosynthesis is the only natural process that produces it.

SELF-ASSESSMENT Questions

1. The main process by which animals obtain energy from food is
   a. acidification
   b. cellular respiration
   c. photosynthesis
   d. reduction of CO_2

2. The only natural process that produces O_2 is
   a. acidification of carbonates
   b. photosynthesis
   c. oxidation of CO_2
   d. reduction of metal oxide

3. In photosynthesis and cellular respiration carbon is _____ and _____, respectively.
   a. reduced, reduced
   b. reduced, oxidized
   c. oxidized, oxidized
   d. oxidized, reduced

Answers: 1, b; 2, b; 3, b

SUMMARY

Section 8.1—Oxidation and reduction are processes that occur together. They may be defined in three ways. **Oxidation** occurs when a substance gains oxygen atoms or loses hydrogen atoms or loses electrons or when its oxidation number increases. **Reduction** is the opposite of oxidation; it occurs when a substance loses oxygen atoms or gains hydrogen atoms or gains electrons or when its oxidation number decreases. We usually use the definition that is most convenient for the situation.

Section 8.2—In an oxidation–reduction (or redox) reaction, the substance that causes oxidation is the **oxidizing agent**. The substance that causes reduction is the **reducing agent**. In a redox reaction, the oxidizing agent is reduced, and the reducing agent is oxidized.

Section 8.3—A redox reaction involves a transfer of electrons. That transfer can be made to take place in an **electrochemical cell**, which has two solid **electrodes** where the electrons are transferred. The electrode where oxidation occurs is the **anode**, and the one where reduction occurs is the **cathode**. Electrons are transferred from anode to cathode through a wire; their flow is an electric current. When the oxidation half-reaction is added to the reduction half-reaction, the electrons in the half-reactions cancel and we get the overall cell reaction. Knowing this, we can balance many redox reactions.

A dry cell (flashlight battery) has a zinc case and a central carbon rod and contains a paste of manganese dioxide with graphite powder and ammonium chloride. Alkaline cells are similar but contain potassium hydroxide instead of ammonium chloride. A **battery** is a series of connected cells. An automobile's lead-storage battery contains six cells. Each cell contains lead and lead(IV) oxide electrodes in sulfuric acid, and the battery can be recharged. A **fuel cell** generates electricity by oxidizing a fuel in a cell to which the fuel and oxygen are supplied continuously.

Section 8.4—Corrosion of metals is ordinarily an undesirable redox reaction. When iron corrodes, the iron is first oxidized to Fe^{2+} ions, and oxygen gas is reduced to hydroxide ions. The $Fe(OH)_2$ that forms is further oxidized to $Fe(OH)_3$, or rust. Oxidation and reduction often occur in separate places on the metal surface, and an electrolyte (such as salt) on the surface can intensify the corrosion reaction. Aluminum corrodes, but the oxide layer is tough and adherent and protects the underlying metal. Silver corrodes in the presence of sulfur compounds, forming black silver sulfide, which can be removed electrochemically. An explosive reaction is a redox reaction that occurs rapidly and with a considerable increase in volume (due to the formation of gases).

Section 8.5—Oxygen is an oxidizing agent that is essential to life. It makes up about one-fifth of the air and about two-thirds of our body mass. Our food is "burned" in oxygen as we breathe, and fuels such as coal react with oxygen when they burn and release most of the energy used in civilization. Pure oxygen is obtained from liquefied air, and most of it is used in industry. Oxygen reacts with metals and nonmetals to form oxides. It reacts with many compounds to form oxides of the elements in the compound. Ozone, O_3, is a form of oxygen that is an air pollutant in the lower atmosphere but provides a shield from ultraviolet radiation in the upper atmosphere. Other oxidizing agents include hydrogen peroxide, potassium dichromate, benzoyl peroxide, and chlorine. A **bleach** is an oxidizing agent that removes unwanted color from fabric or other material.

Section 8.6—Most metals are reducing agents. An **antioxidant** is a reducing agent that retards damaging oxidation reactions in living cells. Vitamins C and E and beta-carotene are antioxidants. Common reducing agents include carbon, hydrogen, and active metals. Carbon in the form of coal or coke is often used as a reducing agent to obtain metals from their oxides. Active metals such as aluminum are also used for this purpose. Hydrogen can free many metals from their ores. Some reactions of hydrogen require a **catalyst**, which speeds up a reaction without itself being used up. Formation of ammonia from hydrogen and nitrogen uses a catalyst.

Section 8.7—Oxidation of carbohydrates and other substances in foods produces the energy humans and other animals need to survive. The reduction of carbon dioxide in **photosynthesis** is the most important reduction process on Earth. We could not exist without it. Photosynthesis provides the food we eat and the oxygen we breathe.

GREEN CHEMISTRY—In organic synthesis, it is important to use methods where most of the materials end up in the product (high atom economy). This process minimizes the amount of waste generated (low E factor). It is also important to avoid, where possible, the use of hazardous or toxic reagents and solvents, thereby minimizing the environmental impact of reagents used and waste generated.

Learning Objectives

› Classify a particular change within a redox reaction as either oxidation or reduction. (8.1)	Problems 1, 16–18, 21, 41–43, 45, 57, 49, 51, 58, 61, 65–68, 72, 76
› Identify an oxidation–reduction reaction. (8.1)	Problems 16–18
› Identify the oxidizing agent and the reducing agent in a redox reaction. (8.2)	Problems 3, 22–31, 38–40, 44, 46, 48, 50–51, 58, 69, 71, 73, 80
› Balance redox equations. (8.3)	Problems 35–37, 60–62, 73
› Identify and write the half-reactions in an electrochemical cell. (8.3)	Problems 3, 6, 33, 34
› Describe the reactions that occur when iron rusts. (8.4)	Problems 12, 59
› Explain why an explosive reaction is so energetic. (8.4)	Problem 70

❯ Write equations for reactions in which oxygen is an oxidizing agent. (8.5)	Problems 52–54, 63, 64
❯ List some of the common oxidizing agents encountered in daily life. (8.5)	Problem 14
❯ Identify some common reducing agents. (8.6)	Problems 44, 48
❯ Write the overall equations for the metabolism of glucose and for photosynthesis. (8.7)	Problems 15, 65–67
❯ Use a balanced reaction to calculate the atom economy and E factor of the reaction.	Problems 77–78
❯ Describe the role of catalysts in minimizing waste in the chemical and allied industries.	Problems 79–80

REVIEW QUESTIONS

1. What happens to the oxidation number of one of its elements when a compound is oxidized? When it is reduced?

2. What is an electrochemical cell? A battery?

3. What happens at the anode and the cathode of an electrochemical cell? Why do electrons flow from the anode to the cathode?

4. How does a fuel cell differ from batteries?

5. What is the purpose of a porous partition between the two electrode compartments in an electrochemical cell?

6. What is a half-reaction? How are half-reactions combined to give an overall cell reaction?

7. From what material is the case of a zinc–carbon dry cell made? What purpose does this material serve? What happens to it as the cell discharges?

8. How does an alkaline cell differ from a zinc–carbon dry cell, and why are alkaline cells preferred?

9. How does a lead-storage battery become recharged?

10. Describe what happens when a lead-storage battery discharges.

11. Why are most modern high-performance electronic devices powered by lithium-based batteries?

12. Describe what happens when iron corrodes. Why does road salt intensify this process?

13. How does silver tarnish? How can the tarnish be removed without the loss of silver?

14. Describe how a bleaching agent, such as hypochlorite (ClO^-), works.

15. Relate the chemistry of photosynthesis to the chemical process that provides energy for your heartbeat.

PROBLEMS

Recognizing Oxidation and Reduction

16. Indicate whether the reactant in each of the following partial equations is being oxidized or reduced. Explain.
    a. $Fe \longrightarrow Fe^{3+}$
    b. $H_2O \longrightarrow O_2$
    c. $Sr \longrightarrow Sr^{2+}$
    d. $P_4 \longrightarrow 4\ P^{3-}$
    e. $CH_4O \longrightarrow CH_2O$

17. In the following reaction, identify whether carbon has underdone reduction or oxidation, and determine how the oxidation number of carbon has changed.
    a. $C + 2\ Cl_2 \longrightarrow CCl_4$
    b. $2\ C + O_2 \longrightarrow 2\ CO$
    c. $C + O_2 \longrightarrow CO_2$
    d. $C_2H_2 + I_2 \longrightarrow C_2H_2I_2$
    e. $C + 2\ H_2 \longrightarrow CH_4$

18. In which of the following changes is the reactant undergoing oxidation? Explain.
    a. $C_2H_4 \longrightarrow C_2H_6$
    b. $CrO_3 \longrightarrow Cr$
    c. $Fe^{3+} \longrightarrow Fe^{2+}$
    d. $C_{27}H_{33}N_9O_{15}P_2 \longrightarrow C_{27}H_{35}N_9O_{15}P_2$
    e. $2\ Cl^- \longrightarrow Cl_2$

19. Write a balanced oxidation half-reaction similar to $Na \longrightarrow Na^+ + e^-$ for each of the following metals.
    a. Ca   b. Al   c. Cu (two different equations)

20. Write a balanced reduction half-reaction similar to $Cl_2 + 2\ e^- \longrightarrow 2\ Cl^-$ for each of the following nonmetals.
    a. I_2 b. N_2 c. S_8

21. In the following reaction identify the atom that has undergone oxidation and reduction.
    a. $4\ Cu + O_2 \longrightarrow 2\ Cu_2O$
    b. $Mg + 2\ H^+ \longrightarrow Mg^{2+} + H_2$
    c. $Br_2 + H_2O_2 \longrightarrow O_2 + 2\ H^+ + 2\ Br^-$
    d. $4\ S_2O_3^{2-} + O_2 + 2\ H^+ \longrightarrow 2\ S_4O_6^{2-} + 2\ H_2O$

22. Discuss what happens to copper in photochromic lenses from a redox perspective.

Oxidizing Agents and Reducing Agents

23. Identify the oxidizing agent and the reducing agent in each reaction.
    a. $3\ C + Fe_2O_3 \longrightarrow 3\ CO + 2\ Fe$
    b. $P_4 + 5\ O_2 \longrightarrow P_4O_{10}$
    c. $C + H_2O \longrightarrow CO + H_2$
    d. $H_2SO_4 + Zn \longrightarrow ZnSO_4 + H_2$

24. Identify the oxidizing agent and the reducing agent in each reaction.
    a. $CuS + H_2 \longrightarrow Cu + H_2S$
    b. $4 K + CCl_4 \longrightarrow C + 4 KCl$
    c. $C_3H_4 + 2 H_2 \longrightarrow C_3H_8$
    d. $Fe^{3+} + Ce^{3+} \longrightarrow Fe^{2+} + Ce^{4+}$

25. Look again at Figure 8.4. What is the reducing agent?

26. What is the oxidizing agent in Figure 8.4?

27. Look again at Figure 8.6. Identify the oxidizing and reducing agents.

28. Look again at Figure 8.7 **(a)** Is SO_4^{2-} the oxidizing agent, the reducing agent, both, or neither? **(b)** When the cell is being charged, the discharge half-reactions are reversed. During charging, is Pb^{2+} being oxidized, reduced, both, or neither?

29. In an electrochemical cell, electrons flow from the anode to the cathode. How would you classify the anode and cathode in terms of oxidizing and reducing agents?

30. When aluminum is placed in contact with copper, electrons flow from the aluminum to the copper. Which of the two metals is the oxidizing agent?

31. In a modern glucose meter, glucose is oxidized by an enzyme, Is the enzyme acting as a reducing or oxidizing agent?

32. Why is oxygen such a good oxidizing agent? (*Hint*: Use knowledge you have gained in this chapter and Chapter 4.)

Half-Reactions

33. Separate the following redox reactions into half-reactions, and label each half-reaction as oxidation or reduction.
    a. $Fe(s) + 2 H^+(aq) \longrightarrow Fe^{2+}(aq) + H_2(g)$
    b. $2 Al(s) + 3 Cr^{2+}(aq) \longrightarrow 3 Cr(s) + 2 Al^{3+}(aq)$

34. Separate the following redox reactions into half-reactions, and label each half-reaction as oxidation or reduction.
    a. $2 Al(s) + 6 H^+(aq) \longrightarrow 2 Al^{3+}(aq) + 3 H_2(g)$
    b. $2 Cu^+(aq) + Mg(s) \longrightarrow Mg^{2+}(aq) + 2 Cu(s)$

35. Label each of the following half-reactions as oxidation or reduction, and then combine them to obtain a balanced overall redox reaction.
    a. $Cu^{2+} + 2 e^- \longrightarrow Cu(s)$ and
       $Fe(s) \longrightarrow Fe^{2+} + 2 e^-$
    b. $2 H_2O_2 \longrightarrow 2 O_2 + 4 H^+ + 4 e^-$ and
       $Fe^{3+} + e^- \longrightarrow Fe^{2+}$
    c. $WO_3 + 6 H^+ + 6 e^- \longrightarrow W + 3 H_2O$ and
       $C_2H_6O \longrightarrow C_2H_4O + 2 H^+ + 2 e^-$

36. Label each of the following half-reactions as oxidation or reduction, and then combine them to obtain a balanced overall redox reaction.
    a. $2 I^- \longrightarrow I_2 + 2 e^-$ and $Cl_2 + 2 e^- \longrightarrow 2 Cl^-$
    b. $HNO_3 + H^+ + e^- \longrightarrow NO_2 + H_2O$ and
       $SO_2 + 2 H_2O \longrightarrow H_2SO_4 + 2 H^+ + 2 e^-$

37. The following half-reactions are of environmental importance. Label each of the reactions as oxidation or reduction, and then combine them to obtain a balanced overall redox reaction.
    a. $Mn^{2+} \longrightarrow Mn^{5+} + 5 e^-$ and $Pb^{4+} + 2 e^- \longrightarrow Pb^{2+}$
    b. $2 S^{2+} \longrightarrow 2 S^{2.5+} + e^-$ and $O + 2 e^- \longrightarrow O^{2-}$

Oxidation and Reduction: Chemical Reactions

38. In the following reactions, which substance is oxidized? Which is the oxidizing agent?
    a. $2 NHO_3 + SO_2 \longrightarrow H_2SO_4 + 2 NO_2$
    b. $2 CrO_3 + 6 HI \longrightarrow Cr_2O_3 + 3 I_2 + 3 H_2O$

39. In the following reactions, which element is oxidized and which is reduced?
    a. $CH_3CHO + H_2O_2 \longrightarrow CH_3COOH + H_2O$
    b. $5 C_2H_6O + 4 MnO_4^- + 12 H^+ \longrightarrow$
       $\qquad\qquad 5 C_2H_4O_2 + 4 Mn^{2+} + 11 H_2O$

40. In which reaction is nitrogen being reduced, and in which is it being oxidized?
    a. $2 MnO_2 + NO_2^- + 2H^+ \longrightarrow Mn_2O_3 + NO_3^-$
    b. $3 MnO_2 + 2 NH_4^+ + 4 H^+ \longrightarrow 3 Mn^{2+} + N_2 + 6 H_2O$

41. Is manganese reduced or oxidized in Equations a and b in Question 40?

42. Ethylene (C_2H_4) reacts with hydrogen to form ethane (C_2H_6). Is the ethylene oxidized or reduced? Explain.

43. Unsaturated vegetable oils react with hydrogen to form saturated fats. A typical reaction is
    $$C_{57}H_{104}O_6 + 3 H_2 \longrightarrow C_{57}H_{110}O_6$$
    Is the unsaturated oil oxidized or reduced? Explain.

44. Tantalum, a metal used in electronic devices such as cellular phones and computers, can be manufactured by the reaction of its oxide with molten sodium metal.
    $$Ta_2O_5 + 10 Na \longrightarrow 2 Ta + 5 Na_2O$$
    Which substance is reduced? Which is the reducing agent?

45. To test for iodide ions (for example, in iodized salt), a solution is treated with chlorine to liberate iodine.
    $$2 I^- + Cl_2 \longrightarrow I_2 + 2 Cl^-$$
    Which substance is oxidized? Which is reduced?

46. In the Fukushima nuclear reactor that failed in March 2011, zirconium metal reacted with steam to produce hydrogen gas.
    $$Zr + 2 H_2O \longrightarrow ZrO_2 + 2 H_2$$
    What substance was oxidized in the reaction? What was the oxidizing agent?

47. Unripe grapes are exceptionally sour because of a high concentration of tartaric acid ($C_4H_6O_6$). As the grapes ripen, this compound is converted to glucose ($C_4H_{12}O_6$). Is the tartaric acid oxidized or reduced?

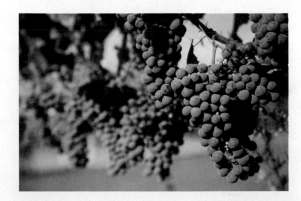

48. Vitamin C (ascorbic acid) is thought to protect our stomachs from the carcinogenic effect of nitrite ions (NO_2^-) by converting the ions to nitric oxide (NO). Is the nitrite ion oxidized or reduced? Is ascorbic acid an oxidizing agent or a reducing agent?

49. In the reaction in Problem 48, ascorbic acid ($C_6H_8O_6$) is converted to dehydroascorbic acid ($C_6H_6O_6$). Is ascorbic acid oxidized or reduced in this reaction?

50. Bacteria are able to drive energy for growth utilizing Mn in the following manner:

$$C_6H_{12}O_6 + 12\,MnO_2 + 24\,H^+ \longrightarrow$$
$$6\,CO_2 + 12\,Mn^{2+} + 18\,H_2O$$

In the above equation, which element is being reduced and which element is being oxidized? Which compound is the oxidizing agent? What changes in oxidation numbers do carbon and manganese undergo?

51. Bacteria are able to drive energy for growth utilizing Fe in the following manner:

$$C_6H_{12}O_6 + 24\,Fe(OH)_3 + 48\,H^+ \longrightarrow$$
$$6\,CO_2 + 24\,Fe^{2+} + 66\,H_2O$$

In the above equation, which element is being reduced and which element is being oxidized? What compound is the oxidation agent? What changes in oxidation numbers do carbon and iron undergo?

Combination with Oxygen

52. Write formula(s) for the product(s) formed when each of the following substances reacts with oxygen (O_2).
    a. S
    b. CH_3OH
    c. C_3H_6O

53. Write formula(s) for the product(s) formed when each of the following substances reacts with oxygen (O_2). (There may be more than one correct answer.)
    a. N_2
    b. CS_2
    c. C_5H_{12}

54. What is the oxidation number of oxygen on the reactant side in the following examples?
    a. $C + O_2 \longrightarrow CO_2$
    b. $O_2 + H_2 \longrightarrow H_2O_2$
    c. $O_2 + 2\,F_2 \longrightarrow 2\,F_2O$

ADDITIONAL PROBLEMS

55. What is the oxidation number of carbon in the following compounds?
    a. CO b. CO_2 c. CH_4 d. CCl_4 e. CH_2F_2

56. Rank the following elements in terms of their ability to act as reducing agents.
    a. Na b. Ca c. O d. Cl

57. Rank the following elements in terms of their ability to act as oxidizing agents.
    a. F b. Cl c. Br d. I

58. The dye indigo (used to color blue jeans) is formed by exposure of indoxyl to air.

$$2\,C_8H_7ON + O_2 \longrightarrow C_{16}H_{10}N_2O_2 + 2\,H_2O$$

Indoxyl   Indigo

What substance is oxidized? What is the oxidizing agent?

59. Why do some mechanics lightly coat their tools with grease or oil before storing them?

60. When an aluminum wire is placed in a blue solution of copper(II) chloride, the blue solution turns colorless and reddish-brown copper metal comes out of solution. Write an equation for the reaction. (Chloride ion is not involved in the reaction.)

61. Researchers led by Elisabeth Bouwman, a chemist at Leiden University in the Netherlands, discovered a copper-based catalyst that can convert CO_2 from the air to oxalate ion ($C_2O_4^{2-}$). Write the equation for the half-reaction. Is the CO_2 oxidized or reduced?

62. When exposed to air containing hydrogen sulfide, lead-based paints turn black because the Pb^{2+} ions react with the H_2S to form black lead sulfide (PbS). This has caused the darkening of old oil-based paintings. Hydrogen peroxide lightens the paints by oxidizing the black sulfide (S^{2-}) to white sulfates (SO_4^{2-}). **(a)** Write the equation for the darkening reaction. **(b)** Write the equation for this reaction that lightens the paints.

63. The oxidizing agent that our bodies use to obtain energy from food is oxygen (from the air). If you breathe 15 times a minute (at rest), taking in and exhaling 0.5 L of air with each breath, what volume of air do you breathe each day? Air is 21% oxygen by volume. What volume of oxygen do you breathe each day?

64. To oxidize 1.0 kg of fat, our bodies require about 2000 L of oxygen. A healthy diet contains not more than about 80 g of fat per day. What volume (at STP) of oxygen is required to oxidize that fat?

65. The photosynthesis reaction (Section 8.7) can be expressed as the net result of two processes, one of which requires light and is called the *light reaction*. This reaction may be written as

$$12\,H_2O \xrightarrow{\text{light}} 6\,O_2 + 24\,H^+ + 24\,e^-$$

    a. Is the light reaction an oxidation or reduction?
    b. Write the equation for the other half-reaction, called the *dark reaction*, for photosynthesis.

66. In cellular respiration, the average oxidation number of carbon changes from _____ to _____.

67. In photosynthesis, the oxidation number of carbon changes from _____ to _____.

68. Indicate whether the first-named substance in each change undergoes an oxidation, a reduction, or neither. Explain your reasoning.
    a. A violet solution of vanadium(II) ions, V^{2+} (aq), is converted to a green solution of V^{3+} (aq).
    b. Nitrogen dioxide converts to dinitrogen tetroxide when cooled.
    c. Carbon monoxide reacts with hydrogen to form methanol.

69. As a rule, metallic elements act as reducing agents, not as oxidizing agents. Explain. (Hint: Consider the charges on metal ions.) Do nonmetals act only as oxidizing agents and not as reducing agents? Explain your answer.

70. Why are TNT explosions so powerful?

71. If a stream of hydrogen gas is ignited in air, the flame can be immersed in a jar of chlorine gas and it will still burn. Write the balanced equation for the reaction that occurs in the jar. What is the oxidizing agent in the reaction?

72. Consider the following reaction of calcium hydride (CaH_2) with molten sodium metal. Identify the species being oxidized and the species being reduced according to (a) the second definition shown in Figure 8.2 and (b) the third definition in Figure 8.2. What difficulty arises?

    $$CaH_2(s) + 2\ Na(l) \longrightarrow 2\ NaH(s) + Ca(l)$$

73. Aluminum metal can react with water, but the oxide coating normally found on the metal prevents that reaction. In 2007, a Purdue University researcher found that adding gallium to aluminum prevented the formation of the oxide coating, allowing the aluminum to react with water to form hydrogen gas. This process might lead to a compact source of hydrogen gas for fuel. Write a balanced equation for the reaction of aluminum with water (aluminum hydroxide is the other product), and identify the oxidizing and reducing agents in the reaction.

74. Refer to Problem 73. Aluminum has a density of 2.70 g/cm³. What volume in cubic centimeters of aluminum metal would be needed to produce 2.0×10^4 L of hydrogen gas at STP? How many times smaller is this volume of aluminum than is the volume of hydrogen gas? (Recall that at STP, 1 mol of gas occupies 22.4 L.)

75. Consider the oxidation of ethanol (CH_3CH_2OH) to acetaldehyde (CH_3CHO) by NAD^+ (page 219). (a) Write half-reactions for the process. (b) NADH is a biochemical reducing agent, in the reverse of the oxidation reaction. Write half-reactions for the reduction of pyruvic acid ($CH_3COCOOH$) to lactic acid ($CH_3CHOHCOOH$) by NADH, and then combine these two half-reactions to get the equation for the overall reaction.

76. Following are so organic chemistry processes. Classify each as an oxidation or a reduction. R represents a hydrocarbon group and does not change in the process.
    a. RCH_3 (alkane) $\longrightarrow$ RCH_2OH (alcohol)
    b. RCHO (aldehyde) $\longrightarrow$ RCH_2OH (alcohol)
    c. RCHO (aldehyde) $\longrightarrow$ RCOOH (carboxylic acid)
    d. RCOOH (carboxylic acid) $\longrightarrow$ RCHO (aldehyde)
    e. RCH_2OH (alcohol) $\longrightarrow$ RCHO (aldehyde)

77. The traditional process for producing propylene oxide involves reaction of propylene with hypochlorous acid (HOCl), which is formed by absorbing chlorine gas in water, to form propylene chlorohydrin. In a second step, the propylene chlorohydrin is treated with calcium hydroxide to form propylene oxide (see reaction below). Recently, an alternative process involving hydrogen peroxide as the oxidant, and titanium silicalite as the catalyst, has been commercialized.

    a. Write down the stochiometric equation for both processes.
    b. Calculate the atom economy and the E factor of both processes.
    c. Compare the two processes with regard to reagents used and waste generated.

78. A green catalyst is one that
    a. contains earth-abundant elements
    b. makes reagents react more efficiently
    c. decreases the cost of producing a chemical
    d. does all of the above

79. Give one reason why it can be difficult to design a long-lived oxidation catalyst.

80. Identify the oxidizing agent and the substance that is oxidized in the following reaction.
    $$3\ C_2H_6O + Cr_2O_7^{2-} + 8\ H^+ \longrightarrow$$
    $$3\ C_2H_4O + 2\ Cr^{3+} + 7\ H_2O$$

CRITICAL THINKING EXERCISES

Apply knowledge that you have gained in this chapter and one or more of the FLaReS principles (Chapter 1) to evaluate the following statements or claims.

8.1. Over the years, some people have claimed that someone has invented an automobile engine that burns water instead of gasoline. They say that we have not heard about it because the oil companies have bought the rights to the engine from the inventor so that they can keep it from the public and people will continue to burn gasoline in their cars.

8.2. In January 2011, Italian scientists claimed to have constructed an apparatus to produce energy. The apparatus uses hydrogen and nickel and is supposed to give several hundred times as much energy as would be obtained by merely burning the hydrogen.

8.3. A website claims that electricity can remove rust. The procedure is described as follows: Connect a wire to the object to be derusted, and immerse in a bath of sodium carbonate (washing soda) solution. Immerse a second wire in the bath. Connect the wires to a battery so that the object to be derusted is the cathode. The site claims that hydrogen gas is produced at the cathode and oxygen at the anode. The hydrogen then changes the rust back to iron metal.

8.4. You have just moved to a colder climate. A car salesperson tries to sell you zinc undercoating for your car. He claims that, due to salt being spread on the roads in winter months, the zinc undercoating will protect your car's iron frame from corrosion.

8.5. A co-worker states that the reason behind explosions being so destructive is the release of heat, which expands air.

8.6. A friend claims that an automobile can be kept free of rust simply by connecting the negative pole of the car's battery to the car's body. He reasons that this action makes the car the cathode, and oxidation does not occur at the cathode. He claims that for years he has kept his car from rusting by doing this.

8.7. A salesman claims that your tap water is contaminated. As evidence, he connects a battery to a pair of "special electrodes" and dips the electrodes in a glass of your tap water. Within a few minutes, white and brown "gunk" appears in the water. The salesman sells a special purifying filter that he claims will remove the contaminants and leave the water pure and clear.

 COLLABORATIVE GROUP PROJECTS

Prepare a PowerPoint, poster, or other presentation (as directed by your instructor) to share with the class.

1. Prepare a brief report on one of the following types of electrochemical cells or batteries. If possible, give the half-reactions, the overall reaction, and typical uses.
   a. lithium–SO_2 cell
   b. lithium–iodine cell
   c. lithium–FeS_2 battery
   d. Ni–Cad cell
   e. silver oxide cell
   f. nickel–metal hydride cell

2. Prepare a brief report on one of the following methods of protecting steel from corrosion. Identify the chemical reactions involved in the process, and tell how the process is related to oxidation and reduction.
   a. galvanization
   b. coating with tin
   c. cathodic protection

3. Batteries contain toxic substances and should be recycled rather than thrown in the trash. Prepare a brief report on battery recycling. Are there facilities in your area for recycling batteries?

4. Military personnel, outdoor recreation enthusiasts such as wilderness campers and trekkers, and others often have to drink water from untreated streams or lakes. People who temporarily lack safe drinking water after a natural disaster also need a way to purify water. A variety of water purification tablets are available to treat contaminated water. Research several such tablets, and list their ingredients.

5. Visit one or more websites about fuel cells. Write the reactions that occur in the different types of fuel cells in development. Prepare a brief report on one of the following topics:
   a. a cost–benefit analysis of using fuel cells in automobiles versus using gasoline, electricity from batteries, or natural gas
   b. safety considerations about the hydrogen–oxygen fuel cell
   c. political–economic factors that may be hindering or promoting fuel cell research

CHEMISTRY@HOME   Light My Fruit

Materials Required

- 2 lemons
- 2 kiwis
- Copper wire (or a penny)
- Zinc strip (galvanized nail)
- Voltmeter
- 2 connection wires with alligator clips
- A 2 milliamp, 1.5 volt diode (LED)

Can fruits make electricity? Do you think comparing lemons and kiwis will show how redox reactions work?

In this experiment, you will compare a lemon and a kiwi. Both the lemon and kiwi have juicy and acidic characteristics that make for the exact properties needed in a conductive solution, or electrolyte, which is any acid, base, or salt solution that is rich in ions. The chemical bath within these fruits allows the transference of electrons from different elements and, thus, makes a single cell electric battery. This means the charge "wants to" move from one metal to the other—creating electric potential.

Begin by gathering your supplies. Start by squeezing the fruit gently so the juice goes to the middle. Be careful not to burst the skin.

Poke your copper wire (or penny) into one side of the fruit. Push your zinc strip (or nail) in as close as you can to the copper without having them touch. If the two metals touch inside the fruit, the experiment will NOT work.

Clip your alligator clips to the wires. The red wire goes to the copper wire, and the black wire goes to the magnesium. Record how many volts you have coming from your fruit battery.

Connect the copper to the other side of the diode, and connect the zinc to the side of the diode with the metal strip. (Figure 4)

Predict what will happen next. Record the amount of time it took to light up and the amount of time it was on. Repeat for the other fruit and compare your results.

What happens when you connect the fruit in a series? Attach both the lemon and the kiwi together and see if you can light up the 1.5 volt LED.

Now clip your alligator clips from the battery to the diode. The diode has a small metal strip underneath one of the connection wires; this indicates the negative side of the diode.

Questions

1. Which metal is more reactive, zinc or copper? Why?
2. How many milliamps and volts did your lemon produce?
3. How many milliamps and volts did your kiwi produce?
4. Which fruit produced more milliamps and volts? Why?
5. Did your fruit produce enough voltage and current to power a 1.5 volt mini light bulb? Why or why not?

ORGANIC CHEMISTRY

Have You Ever Wondered?

1. **What is the "petroleum distillate" that I see listed on some product labels?**

2. **Why are benzene-like compounds that have many multiple bonds called "aromatic"?**

3. **Why does fresh fruit smell so good and rotting fruit so bad?**

4. **Why do so many organic compounds have such strong tastes?**

Learning Objectives

> Define *hydrocarbon*, and recognize structural features and properties of alkanes, alkenes, and alkynes. (9.1)

> Identify hydrocarbon molecules as alkanes, alkenes, or alkynes, and name them. (9.1)

> Define *aromatic compound*, and recognize the structural feature such compounds share. (9.2)

> Name simple aromatic hydrocarbons. (9.2)

> Name a halogenated hydrocarbon given its formula, and write the formula for such a compound given its name. (9.3)

> Classify an organic compound according to its functional group(s), and explain why the concept of a functional group is useful in the study of organic chemistry. (9.4)

> Recognize and write the formulas of simple alkyl groups. (9.4)

> Recognize the general structure and properties for an alcohol, a phenol, and an ether. (9.5)

> Name simple alcohols, phenols, and ethers. (9.5)

> Name simple aldehydes and ketones, and list their important properties. (9.6)

> Name simple carboxylic acids and esters, and list their important properties. (9.7)

> Name and write the formulas of simple amines and amides. (9.8)

> Recognize a structure as that of a heterocyclic compounds. (9.8)

> Identify greener solvents, use renewable resources in organic synthesis, and use efficient energy sources for chemical reactions.

ORGANIC CHEMISTRY VERSUS ORGANIC FOODS

Very often, people use the term "organic" to refer to foods that have been grown using "all-natural" methods and without the use of synthetic pesticides or herbicides. Many chemists find this concept ironic because of the modern chemical definition of organic compounds. Most of the materials that "organic" gardeners would never use are chemically described as organic chemical substances. Organic farming and agriculture use techniques that include biological pest-control methods. Ground-cover crops are planted that discourage the growth of weeds. Intercropping methods utilize plants that are naturally repellent to insects and animals to discourage their predation.

The definition of organic chemistry has changed over the years. The changes exemplify the dynamic character of science and exemplify how scientific concepts change in response to experimental evidence. Until the nineteenth century, chemists believed that *organic* chemicals originated only in tissues of living *organisms* and required a "vital force" for their production.

Glyphosate is a common agricultural herbicide, and rotenone is a common agricultural pesticide. Neither would be used by an "organic" farmer because they are synthetic compounds, yet both fit the chemical definition of organic compounds. The overuse of pesticides and herbicides can be a serious environmental problem. Other methods of keeping insects and pests away from crops include using a spray from the oil of chili peppers, or planting garlic, marigolds, or other herbs around the crops. These natural materials are repellent to insects and other pests. Xanthophyll is a natural pesticide produced by Mexican marigolds. Planting crops that have insect-repelling properties in with food crops can extend that protection to the food crops.

Glyphosate

Rotenone

Xanthophyll

All chemicals not manufactured by living tissue were regarded as *inorganic*. Some chemists even believed that organic and inorganic chemicals followed different laws. This all changed in 1828, when Friedrich Wöhler synthesized the organic compound urea (found in urine) from ammonium cyanate, an inorganic compound. This important event led other chemists to attempt synthesis of organic chemicals from inorganic ones and changed the very definition of organic chemicals.

Organic chemistry is now defined as the chemistry of carbon-containing compounds. Most of these compounds do come from living things or from things that were once living, but some do not. Perhaps the most remarkable thing about organic compounds is their sheer number. Of the tens of millions of known chemical compounds, more than 95% are compounds of carbon.

One reason for the huge number of organic compounds is the carbon atom itself. Carbon is unique in that its atoms bond readily to each other and form long chains. (Silicon and a few other elements can form chains, but only short ones.) Organic compounds can have as few as one carbon atom or many thousands of carbon atoms. Carbon chains can also have branches or form rings of various sizes. When we consider that carbon atoms also bond strongly to other elements, particularly nonmetals such as hydrogen, oxygen, and nitrogen, and that these atoms can be arranged in many different ways, it soon becomes obvious why there are so many organic compounds. Almost all organic compounds also contain hydrogen, many contain oxygen and/or nitrogen, and quite a few contain sulfur or halogens. Nearly all the common elements are found in at least a few organic compounds.

In addition to the millions of carbon compounds already known, new ones are being discovered every day. Carbon can form an almost infinite number of molecules of various shapes, sizes, and compositions. We use thousands of carbon compounds every day without even realizing it because they are silently carrying out important chemical reactions within our bodies. Many of these carbon compounds are so vital that we cannot live without them.

9.1 Aliphatic Hydrocarbons

Learning Objectives ❯ Define *hydrocarbon*, and recognize structural features of alkanes, alkenes, and alkynes. ❯ Identify hydrocarbon molecules as alkanes, alkenes, or alkynes, and name them.

Organic compounds can be subdivided into several main classes. All organic compounds could be described as hydrocarbons, but a **hydrocarbon** is usually defined as containing only hydrogen and carbon.

The hydrocarbons can then be subdivided according to the type of bonding between carbon atoms. We divide hydrocarbons into two main classes. The difference is based on the degree of multiple bonding between the atoms. Those discussed in this section are **aliphatic compounds** (the Greek word *aleiphar* means "fat" or "oil"), which have little or no multiple bonding between carbon atoms, and the **aromatic compounds** (aromatic compounds have benzene-type structures), which have extensive multiple bonds between the carbon atoms, as discussed in Section 9.2.

In this first section, we will be considering further subdivisions of the aliphatic compounds. These are the alkanes, cyclic structures, alkenes, and alkynes.

Alkanes

Each carbon atom forms four bonds, and each hydrogen atom forms only one bond, so the simplest hydrocarbon molecule possible is methane, CH_4. Methane is the main component of natural gas. It has the structure

$$
\begin{array}{c}
H \\
| \\
H-C-H \\
| \\
H
\end{array}
$$

Methane is the first member of a group of related compounds called **alkanes**, hydrocarbons that contain only single bonds. (See Figure 9.1.) The next member of the series is ethane

$$
\begin{array}{c}
HH \\
|| \\
H-C-C-H \\
|| \\
HH
\end{array}
$$

Ethane is a minor constituent of natural gas. It is seldom encountered as a pure compound in everyday life, but many common compounds are derived from it.

(a)

(b)

◀ **Figure 9.1** Ball-and-stick (a) and space-filling (b) models of methane (left) and ethane (right).

We saw in Chapter 4 that the methane molecule is tetrahedral, in accord with the VSEPR theory. In fact, the tetrahedral shape results whenever a carbon atom is connected to four other atoms, whether they are hydrogen, carbon, or other elements. Figure 9.1 shows models of methane and ethane. The ball-and-stick models show the bond angles best, but the space-filling models more accurately reflect the

(a)

(b)

▲ **Figure 9.2** Ball-and-stick (a) and space-filling (b) models of propane.

▲ A propane torch. Propane burns in air with a hot flame.

Table 9.1	Stems for Organic Molecule Names
Stem	Number of Carbon Atoms
Meth-	1
Eth-	2
Prop-	3
But-	4
Pent-	5
Hex-	6
Hept-	7
Oct-	8
Non-	9
Dec-	10

shapes of the molecules. Ordinarily, we use simple structural formulas such as the one shown previously for ethane because they are much easier to draw. A **structural formula** shows which atoms are bonded to each other, but it does not attempt to show the actual shape of the molecule.

Alkanes are often called **saturated hydrocarbons** because each carbon atom is *saturated* with hydrogen atoms; that is, each carbon is bonded to the maximum number of hydrogen atoms. In constructing a formula, we connect the carbon atoms to each other through single bonds; then, we add enough hydrogen atoms to give each carbon atom four bonds. All alkanes have two more than twice as many hydrogen atoms as carbon atoms. That is, alkanes can be represented by a general formula C_nH_{2n+2}, in which n is the number of carbon atoms.

The three-carbon alkane is propane. Models of propane are shown in Figure 9.2. To draw its structural formula, we place three carbon atoms in a row.

$$C—C—C$$

Then we add enough hydrogen atoms (eight in this case) to give each carbon atom a total of four bonds. Therefore, the structural formula of propane is

$$H-\underset{\underset{H}{|}}{\overset{\overset{H}{|}}{C}}-\underset{\underset{H}{|}}{\overset{\overset{H}{|}}{C}}-\underset{\underset{H}{|}}{\overset{\overset{H}{|}}{C}}-H$$

Condensed Structural Formulas

The complete structural formulas that we have used so far show all the carbon and hydrogen atoms and how they are attached to one another. But these formulas take up a lot of space, and they can be a bit of trouble to draw. For these reasons, chemists usually prefer to use **condensed structural formulas**. These formulas show how many hydrogen atoms are attached to each carbon atom without showing the bond to each hydrogen atom. For example, the condensed structural formulas for ethane and propane are written $CH_3—CH_3$ and $CH_3—CH_2—CH_3$, respectively. These formulas can be simplified even further by omitting some (or all) of the remaining bond lines, resulting in CH_3CH_3 and $CH_3CH_2CH_3$.

Homologous Series

Note that the given formulas for methane, ethane, and propane form a pattern. We can build alkanes of any length simply by joining carbon atoms together in long chains and adding enough hydrogen atoms to give each carbon atom four bonds. Even the naming of these compounds follows a pattern (Table 9.1), with a stem name indicating the number of carbon atoms. For compounds of five carbon atoms or more, each stem is derived from the Greek or Latin name for the number. The compound names end in *-ane*, signifying that the compounds are saturated and therefore *alkanes*. Table 9.2 on p. 253 gives condensed structural formulas and names for the continuous-chain (straight-chain, or unbranched) alkanes with up to ten carbon atoms.

Notice that the molecular formula for each alkane in Table 9.2 differs from the one preceding it by precisely one carbon atom and two hydrogen atoms—that is, by a CH_2 unit. Such a series of compounds has properties that vary in a regular and predictable manner. This principle, called *homology*, gives order to organic chemistry in much the same way that the periodic table gives organization to the chemistry of the elements. Instead of studying the chemistry of a bewildering array of individual carbon compounds, organic chemists study a few members—called *homologs*—of a **homologous series**, from which they can deduce the properties of other compounds in the series.

We need not stop at ten carbon atoms as Table 9.2 does. Hundreds, thousands, even millions of carbon atoms can be linked together. We can make an infinite number of alkanes simply by lengthening the chain. But lengthening the chain is not the only option. Beginning with alkanes having four carbon atoms, chain branching is also possible.

Name	Molecular Formula	Condensed Structural Formula	Number of Possible Isomers
Methane	CH_4	CH_4	—
Ethane	C_2H_6	CH_3CH_3	—
Propane	C_3H_8	$CH_3CH_2CH_3$	—
Butane	C_4H_{10}	$CH_3CH_2CH_2CH_3$	2
Pentane	C_5H_{12}	$CH_3CH_2CH_2CH_2CH_3$	3
Hexane	C_6H_{14}	$CH_3CH_2CH_2CH_2CH_2CH_3$	5
Heptane	C_7H_{16}	$CH_3CH_2CH_2CH_2CH_2CH_2CH_3$	9
Octane	C_8H_{18}	$CH_3CH_2CH_2CH_2CH_2CH_2CH_2CH_3$	18
Nonane	C_9H_{20}	$CH_3CH_2CH_2CH_2CH_2CH_2CH_2CH_2CH_3$	35
Decane	$C_{10}H_{22}$	$CH_3CH_2CH_2CH_2CH_2CH_2CH_2CH_2CH_2CH_3$	75

Table 9.2 The First Ten Continuous-Chain Alkanes

Isomerism—Branched Molecules

When we extend the carbon chain to four atoms and add enough hydrogen atoms to give each carbon atom four bonds, we get $CH_3CH_2CH_2CH_3$. This formula represents butane, a compound that boils at about 0 °C. A second compound, which has a boiling point of −12 °C, has the same molecular formula, C_4H_{10}, as butane. The structure of this compound, however, is not the same as that of butane. Instead of having four carbon atoms connected in a continuous chain, this compound has a continuous chain of only three carbon atoms. The fourth carbon is branched off the middle carbon of the three-carbon chain. To show the two structures more clearly, let's use complete structural formulas, showing all the bonds to hydrogen atoms.

Compounds that have the same molecular formula but different structural formulas are called **isomers** or **constitutional isomers**. Because it is an isomer of butane, the branched four-carbon alkane is sometimes called *isobutane*. Condensed structural formulas for the two isomeric butanes are written as follows.

$$CH_3CH_2CH_2CH_3 \qquad \underset{\underset{CH_3}{\mid}}{CH_3CHCH_3}$$

Butane   Isobutane

Figure 9.3 shows ball-and-stick models of the two compounds.

The number of isomers increases rapidly with the number of carbon atoms (Table 9.2). There are three pentanes, five hexanes, nine heptanes, and so on. Isomerism is common in carbon compounds and provides another reason for the existence of millions of organic compounds.

Propane and the butanes are familiar fuels. Although they are gases at ordinary temperatures and under normal atmospheric pressure, they are liquefied under pressure and are usually supplied in tanks as liquefied petroleum gas (LPG). Gasoline is a mixture of hydrocarbons, mostly alkanes, with 5–12 carbon atoms.

Not all the possible isomers of the larger molecules have been isolated. Indeed, the task rapidly becomes more and more prohibitive going up the series. There are, for example, 4,111,846,763 possible isomers with the molecular formula $C_{30}H_{62}$.

(a)

(b)

▲ **Figure 9.3** Ball-and-stick models of (a) butane and (b) isobutane.

1. What is the "petroleum distillate" that I see listed on some product labels?

Petroleum distillates are various components of crude oil, most of which are hydrocarbons. Paint thinner, lighter fluid, paraffin wax, petroleum jelly, and asphalt all are petroleum distillates.

Example 9.1	Hydrocarbon Formulas

Without referring to Table 9.2, write the molecular formula, the complete structural formula, and the condensed structural formula for heptane.

Solution

The stem *hept-* means seven carbon atoms, and the ending *-ane* indicates an alkane. For the complete structural formula, we write a string of seven carbon atoms.

$$C—C—C—C—C—C—C$$

Then we attach enough hydrogen atoms to the carbon atoms to give each carbon four bonds. This requires three hydrogens on each end carbon and two hydrogens on each of the other carbons.

$$\begin{array}{c} H \quad H \quad H \quad H \quad H \quad H \quad H \\ | \quad | \quad | \quad | \quad | \quad | \quad | \\ H—C—C—C—C—C—C—C—H \\ | \quad | \quad | \quad | \quad | \quad | \quad | \\ H \quad H \quad H \quad H \quad H \quad H \quad H \end{array}$$

For the condensed form, we simply write each set of hydrogen atoms following the carbon atom to which they are bonded.

$$CH_3CH_2CH_2CH_2CH_2CH_2CH_3$$

For the molecular formula, we can simply count the carbon and hydrogen atoms to arrive at C_7H_{16}. Alternatively, we could use the general formula C_nH_{2n+2}, with $n = 7$, to get C_7H_{16}.

▪ **EXERCISE 9.1**

Write the molecular, complete structural, and condensed structural formulas for **(a)** hexane and **(b)** octane.

Properties of Alkanes

Note in Table 9.3 on the next page that after the first few members of the alkane series, the rest show an increase in boiling point of about 30 °C with each added CH_2

Table 9.3	Physical Properties, Uses, and Occurrences of Selected Alkanes				
Name	Molecular Formula	Melting Point (°C)	Boiling Point (°C)	Density[a] at 20 °C (g/mL)	Use/Occurrence
Methane	CH_4	−183	−162	(Gas)	Natural gas (main component); fuel
Ethane	C_2H_6	−172	−89	(Gas)	Natural gas (minor component); plastics
Propane	C_3H_8	−188	−42	(Gas)	LPG (bottled gas); plastics
Butane	C_4H_{10}	−138	0	(Gas)	LPG; lighter fuel
Pentane	C_5H_{12}	−130	36	0.626	Gasoline component
Hexane	C_6H_{14}	−95	69	0.659	Gasoline component; extraction solvent for food oils
Heptane	C_7H_{16}	−91	98	0.684	Gasoline component
Octane	C_8H_{18}	−57	126	0.703	Gasoline component
Decane	$C_{10}H_{22}$	−30	174	0.730	Gasoline component
Dodecane	$C_{12}H_{26}$	−10	216	0.749	Gasoline component
Tetradecane	$C_{14}H_{30}$	6	254	0.763	Diesel fuel component
Hexadecane	$C_{16}H_{34}$	18	280	0.775	Diesel fuel component
Octadecane	$C_{18}H_{38}$	28	316	(Solid)	Paraffin wax component
Eicosane	$C_{20}H_{42}$	37	343	(Solid)	Paraffin wax and asphalt component

[a]Densities of the gaseous alkanes vary with pressure. Densities of the solids are not available.

group. Note also that at room temperature alkanes that have 1 to 4 carbon atoms per molecule are gases. The molecules with 5 to about 16 carbon atoms per molecule are liquids, and those with more than 16 carbon atoms per molecule are solids.

The densities of liquid and solid alkanes are typically less than that of water. Recall that water has a density of 1.00 g/mL at room temperature. All the alkanes listed in Table 9.3 have densities less than that. Alkanes are nonpolar molecules and are insoluble in water. The combination of these two properties means the alkanes float on top of water. Because these are nonpolar molecules, they will dissolve other organic substances of low polarity—such as fats, oils, and waxes.

Alkanes undergo few chemical reactions, but one important chemical property is that they burn, producing a lot of heat. Alkanes have many uses, but they mainly serve as fuels.

The effects of alkanes on the human body vary. Methane appears to be physiologically inert. We probably could breathe a mixture of 80% methane and 20% oxygen without ill effect. This mixture would be flammable, however, and no fire or spark of any kind could be permitted in such an atmosphere. Breathing an atmosphere of pure methane (the "gas" of a gas-fueled stove) can lead to death—not because of the presence of methane but because of the absence of oxygen, a condition called *asphyxia*.

Light liquid alkanes such as those in gasoline will dissolve and wash away body oils when spilled on the skin. Repeated contact may cause dermatitis. If swallowed, most alkanes do little harm in the stomach. In fact, mineral oil is a mixture of long-chain liquid alkanes and has been used for many years as a laxative.

Heavier liquid alkanes act as emollients (skin softeners). Petroleum jelly (Vaseline™ is one brand) is a semisolid mixture of hydrocarbons that can be applied as an emollient or simply as a protective film. (Skin lotions and creams are discussed in Chapter 21.) However, in the lungs, alkanes cause chemical pneumonia by dissolving fatlike molecules from the cell membranes in the alveoli, allowing the lungs to fill with fluid.

Cyclic Hydrocarbons: Rings and Things

The hydrocarbons we have encountered so far (alkanes) have open-ended chains of carbon atoms. Carbon atoms can also connect to form closed rings. The simplest possible ring-containing hydrocarbon, or **cyclic hydrocarbon**, has the molecular formula C_3H_6 and is called *cyclopropane* (Figure 9.4).

Names of *cycloalkanes* (cyclic hydrocarbons containing only single bonds) are formed by adding the prefix *cyclo-* to the name of the open-chain compound with the same number of carbon atoms as are in the cycloalkane's ring. Note that the formula for the cycloalkanes is different from that for the regular alkane. The cycloalkane would fit a C_nH_{2n} formula, but this would still represent a saturated hydrocarbon as there are only single bonds within the molecule.

Chemists often use geometric shapes to represent cyclic compounds (Figure 9.5). These are sometimes called **skeletal structures**, as the shape represents the carbon skeleton of the molecule. For example, a triangle is used to represent the cyclopropane ring, and a hexagon represents cyclohexane. Each corner of such a shape represents a carbon atom with its associated hydrogen atoms.

Cyclopropane   Cyclohexane   Cyclohexene

SAFETY ALERT

Hydrocarbons and most other organic compounds are flammable or combustible. Volatile ones may form explosive mixtures with air. Hydrocarbons are the main ingredients in gasoline, motor oils, fuel gases (natural gas and bottled gas), and fuel oils. They are also ingredients, identified on labels as "petroleum distillates" and "mineral spirits," of products such as floor cleaners, furniture polishes, paint thinners, wood stains and varnishes, and car waxes and polishes. Some products also contain flammable alcohols, esters, and ketones. Products containing flammable substances can be dangerous but may be used safely with proper precautions. Use only as directed and keep all such products away from open flames.

▲ **Figure 9.4** Ball-and-stick model of cyclopropane. Cyclopropane is a potent, quick-acting anesthetic with few undesirable side effects. It is no longer used in surgery, however, because it forms an explosive mixture with air at nearly all concentrations.

◄ **Figure 9.5** Structural formulas and symbolic representations of some cyclic hydrocarbons.

Example 9.2 | Structural Formulas of Cyclic Hydrocarbons

Write the structural formula for cyclopentane. What geometric figure is used to represent cyclopentane?

Solution
Cyclopentane has five carbon atoms arranged in a ring.

$$\begin{array}{c} C \\ C \qquad C \\ C - C \end{array}$$

Each carbon atom needs two hydrogen atoms to complete its set of four bonds.

$$\begin{array}{c} CH_2 \\ CH_2 \qquad CH_2 \\ CH_2 - CH_2 \end{array}$$

Cyclopentane can also be represented by a pentagon.

■ EXERCISE 9.2A
Write the structural formula for cyclobutane and the geometric shape used to represent it.

■ EXERCISE 9.2B
Explain why the formula for a cycloalkane does not fit that for a regular alkane.

Unsaturated Hydrocarbons: Alkenes and Alkynes

Two carbon atoms can share more than one pair of electrons. In ethylene (C_2H_4), the two carbon atoms share two pairs of electrons and are therefore joined by a double bond (Figure 9.6).

$$\overset{H}{\underset{H}{\cdot \cdot C \cdot \cdot}} \overset{H}{\underset{H}{C \cdot \cdot}} \quad \text{or} \quad \overset{H}{\underset{H}{>}} C = C \overset{H}{\underset{H}{<}} \quad \text{or} \quad CH_2 = CH_2$$

(Ethylene is the common name; the systematic, or IUPAC, name is *ethene*.) Ethylene is the simplest member of the alkene family. An **alkene** is a hydrocarbon that contains one or more carbon-to-carbon double bonds. Alkenes with one double bond have the general formula C_nH_{2n}, where n is the number of carbon atoms.

Ethylene is the most important organic chemical commercially. Annual U.S. production is over 20 billion kg. More than half goes into the manufacture of polyethylene, one of the most familiar plastics. Another 15% or so is converted to ethylene glycol, the major component of many formulations of antifreeze used in automobile radiators.

In acetylene (C_2H_2), the two carbon atoms share three pairs of electrons. The carbon atoms are joined by a triple bond (Figure 9.7).

$$H : C ::: C : H \quad \text{or} \quad H - C \equiv C - H$$

▲ **Figure 9.6** Ball-and-stick (a) and space-filling (b) models of ethylene.

(a)   (b)

▶ **Figure 9.7** Ball-and-stick (a) and space-filling (b) models of acetylene.

Acetylene (IUPAC name, ethyne) is the simplest member of the alkyne family. An **alkyne** is a hydrocarbon that contains one or more carbon-to-carbon triple bonds. Alkynes with one triple bond have the general formula C_nH_{2n-2}, where *n* is the number of carbon atoms.

Acetylene is used in oxyacetylene torches for cutting and welding metals. Such torches can produce very high temperatures. Acetylene is also converted to a variety of other chemical products.

Collectively, alkenes and alkynes are called *unsaturated hydrocarbons*. Recall that a *saturated hydrocarbon* (alkane) has the maximum number of hydrogen atoms attached to each carbon atom; it has no double or triple bonds. An **unsaturated hydrocarbon** can become saturated by having more hydrogen atoms added to it.

Unsaturated
Saturated

Ethylene   Ethane

Unsaturated
Saturated

$H-C{\equiv}C-H$ + 2 H—H ⟶

Acetylene   Ethane

It DOES Matter!

Fats are probably the best-known examples of compounds that can be saturated or unsaturated. In saturated fats, all the carbon–carbon bonds are single bonds. These fats are found mostly in milk, meats, and eggs, and their consumption tends to increase low-density lipoproteins ("bad" cholesterol) in the human bloodstream. Most plant oils are unsaturated fats, with one or more carbon–carbon double bonds. Consumption of unsaturated fats tends to increase high-density lipoproteins ("good" cholesterol) in the blood.

Example 9.3 Molecular Formulas of Unsaturated Hydrocarbons

What is the molecular formula for 1-pentene? (The "1-" is a part of a systematic name that indicates the location of the double bond, which in this case connects the first carbon atom of the chain to the second.)

Solution

The stem *pent-* indicates five carbon atoms, the ending *-ene* tells us that the compound is an alkene. Using the general formula C_nH_{2n} for an alkene, with *n*=5, we see that an alkene with six carbon atoms has the molecular formula C_5H_{12}.

■ **EXERCISE 9.3**

What are the molecular formulas for **(a)** 2-hexene and **(b)** 3-heptyne?

Properties of Alkenes and Alkynes

The physical properties of alkenes and alkynes are much like those of the corresponding alkanes. Unsaturated hydrocarbons with 2 to 4 carbon atoms per molecule are gases at room temperature, those with 5 to 18 carbon atoms are liquids, and most of those with more than 18 carbon atoms are solids. Like alkanes, alkenes and alkynes are insoluble in, and float on, water.

Like alkanes, both alkenes and alkynes burn. However, these unsaturated hydrocarbons undergo many more chemical reactions than alkanes do. An alkene or alkyne can undergo an **addition reaction** to the double or triple bond, in which all the atoms of the reactants are incorporated into a single product. In the preceding reactions, ethylene (C_2H_4) adds hydrogen (H_2) to form ethane (C_2H_6), and acetylene (C_2H_2) adds two moles of hydrogen (2 H_2) to form ethane. Chlorine, bromine, water, and many other kinds of small molecules also add to double and triple bonds.

An unsaturated hydrocarbon tends to burn with a smoky flame, especially if the oxygen supply is limited. Saturated hydrocarbons usually burn with a clean yellow flame. Burning of natural gas, propane, and butane is almost soot-free, but paint thinner, gasoline, and kerosene (all containing unsaturated hydrocarbons) burn with sooty flames.

One of the most unusual features of alkene (and alkyne) molecules is that they can add *to each other* to form large molecules called *polymers*. These interesting molecules are discussed in Chapter 10.

Geometric Isomers (*Cis–Trans* Isomers)

As with the alkanes, there is a series of alkenes. The one with three carbon atoms (C_3H_6) is propylene (IUPAC, propene).

$$CH_2=CHCH_3$$

Propylene is also an important industrial chemical. It is converted to plastics (Chapter 10), isopropyl alcohol (page 266), and a variety of other products. Although there is only one alkene with the formula C_2H_4 (ethene) and only one with the formula C_3H_6 (propene), there are several alkenes with the formula C_4H_8. The compound with a double bond between the first and second carbon atoms is called 1-butene.

$$CH_2=CHCH_2CH_3$$

Now consider the alkene with the formula $CH_3CH=CHCH_3$. We could name it "2-butene," but there are actually two such compounds. The double bond results in geometric (*cis-trans*) isomerism (Figure 9.8). This is due to the double bond of the molecule. We would not have free rotation about the double bond the way we would around the single bonds.

▶ **Figure 9.8** Ball-and-stick models of *cis*-2-butene and *trans*-2-butene.

As you might deduce from the models, the carbon-to-carbon single bonds in alkanes such as butane could function like an axle. The atoms at either end of the single bond should be able to pivot about the shared electrons. In contrast, the structure of alkenes requires that the carbon atoms of a double bond and the two atoms bonded to each carbon all lie in a single plane. This part of the molecule's structure is rigid; rotation about doubly bonded carbon atoms is *not* possible without rupturing the bond. Now look at the two forms of 2-butenes in Figure 9.8. One isomer, called *cis*-2-butene, has both methyl groups on the same side of the molecule. In *trans*-2-butene the methyl groups are on opposite sides of the molecule. Their structural formulas are:

$$
\begin{array}{cc}
\underset{H}{\overset{CH_3}{}}{\diagdown}\!\!\!\!\!\!\!\!C\!\!=\!\!C{\diagup}\!\!\!\!\!\!\!\!\underset{H}{\overset{CH_3}{}} & \underset{H}{\overset{CH_3}{}}{\diagdown}\!\!\!\!\!\!\!\!C\!\!=\!\!C{\diagup}\!\!\!\!\!\!\!\!\underset{CH_3}{\overset{H}{}}
\end{array}
$$

cis-2-butene   trans-2-butene

Note, however, that it is also possible to introduce the structural isomerization that was mentioned for alkanes. A three-carbon alkene chain, with a methyl group attached to the second carbon, would have the same molecular formula as the 2-butene molecule. This molecule might be named 2-methylpropene.

$$
\underset{H}{\overset{H}{}}{\diagdown}\!\!\!\!\!\!\!\!C\!\!=\!\!C{\diagup}\!\!\!\!\!\!\!\!\underset{CH_3}{\overset{CH_3}{}}
$$

2-methylpropene

While this molecule is a structural isomer of the 2-butene molecule, it would not have a geometric isomer. This molecule has two identical groups on at least one of the doubly bonded carbon atoms.

The two requirements for geometric isomerism then are as follows:

1. Rotation must be restricted in the molecule.
2. There must be two nonidentical groups on *each* of the doubly bonded carbon atoms.

Example 9.4 | Geometric Isomers

Which of the following compounds can exist as geometric isomers? Explain.
  a. $CH_3CH{=}CHCH_2CH_3$
  b. $CH_2{=}CBrCH_3$

Solution
Both structures have a double bond and thus meet rule 1 for geometric isomerism.

  a. Structure **(a)** meets rule 2; it has two nonidentical groups on *each* carbon (H and CH_3 on one and H and CH_2CH_3 on the other). It exists as *cis* and *trans* isomers:

  b. Structure **(b)** has two hydrogen atoms on one of its doubly bonded carbon atoms; it fails rule 2 and does not exist as *cis* and *trans* isomers.

▪ **EXERCISE 9.4A**
Are there *cis* and *trans* isomers of 1-butene? Explain.

▪ **EXERCISE 9.4B**
Which of the following compounds can exist as geometric isomers? Draw them.
  a. 1-pentene   b. 2-pentene   c. 3-pentene   d. 2-methyl-1-butene

---

SELF-ASSESSMENT Questions

1. The study of the chemistry of carbon compounds is called
   a. biochemistry
   b. chemical biology
   c. ecology
   d. organic chemistry

2. Which of the following classes of organic compounds has the simplest composition?
   a. alcohols
   b. amino acids
   c. carbohydrates
   d. hydrocarbons

3. Successive members of the alkane series differ from the preceding member by one additional
   a. C atom and one H atom
   b. C atom and two H atoms
   c. C atom and three H atoms
   d. H atom and two C atoms

4. Structural isomers are compounds whose molecules have the same
   a. numbers of C atoms but different numbers of H atoms
   b. numbers of H atoms but different numbers of C atoms
   c. numbers and kinds of atoms but different structures
   d. kinds of atoms but different numbers of these atoms

5. As the molecular mass of the members of the alkane series increases, their boiling points
   a. decrease
   b. increase
   c. remain the same
   d. vary randomly

6. A cyclic compound with 6 C atoms and 12 H atoms is
   a. cyclobutane
   b. cycloheptane
   c. cyclohexane
   d. cyclosexane

7. The family of hydrocarbons whose molecules have a triple bond between carbon atoms is the
   a. alkanes
   b. alkenes
   c. alkynes
   d. aromatic hydrocarbons

8. Addition reactions occur with alkenes but not with alkanes because alkenes have
   a. double bonds
   b. a greater molecular mass
   c. more C atoms per molecule
   d. a tetrahedral arrangement of bonds

9. Geometric isomers are compounds whose molecules have different
   a. numbers of double bonds
   b. arrangements of groups around the double bond
   c. types of atoms attached to each carbon
   d. structures based on the connections between atoms

9.2 Aromatic Compounds: Benzene and Its Relatives

Learning Objectives ❯ Define *aromatic compound*, and recognize the structural features such compounds share. ❯ Name simple aromatic hydrocarbons.

An important and interesting hydrocarbon is benzene. Discovered by Michael Faraday in 1825, benzene has the molecular formula C_6H_6. The structure of benzene puzzled chemists for decades. The formula seems to indicate an unsaturated compound, but benzene does not react as if it contains any double or triple bonds. It does not readily undergo addition reactions the way unsaturated compounds usually do.

Finally, in 1865, August Kekulé proposed a structure with a ring of six carbon atoms, each attached to one hydrogen atom.

The two structures shown appear to contain double bonds, but in fact they do not. Both structures represent the same molecule, and the actual structure of this molecule is a *hybrid* of these two structures. The benzene molecule has six identical carbon-to-carbon bonds that are neither single bonds nor double bonds but something in between. In other words, the three pairs of electrons that would form the three double bonds are not tied down in one location but are spread around the ring (Figure 9.9). Today, we usually represent the benzene ring with a circle inside a hexagon.

The hexagon represents the ring of six carbon atoms, and the inscribed circle represents the six unassigned electrons. Because its ring of electrons resists being disrupted, the benzene molecule is exceptionally stable.

Benzene and similar compounds are called *aromatic hydrocarbons* because quite a few of the first benzene-like substances to be discovered had strong aromas. Even though many compounds derived from benzene have turned out to be odorless, the name has stuck. Today, an **aromatic compound** is any compound that contains a benzene ring or has certain properties like those of benzene. All other compounds are said to be aliphatic (Section 9.1).

Structures of some common aromatic hydrocarbons are shown in Figure 9.10. Benzene, toluene, and the xylenes are all liquids that float on water. They are used mainly as solvents and fuels but are also used to make other benzene derivatives. Because benzene may cause leukemia after long exposure, its use has been restricted. Benzene compounds are therefore classified as *carcinogens*. Naphthalene is a volatile, white, crystalline solid used as an insecticide, especially as a moth repellant.

Monosubstituted benzenes—in which one hydrogen is replaced by another atom or group, called a **substituent**—are often represented by condensed formulas—for example, toluene is $C_6H_5CH_3$ and ethylbenzene is $C_6H_5CH_2CH_3$. Similar designations are sometimes used for disubstituted aromatic rings, indicating the relative positions of substituents with numbers, as in $1,4$-$C_6H_4(CH_3)_2$ for 1,4-dimethylbenzene.

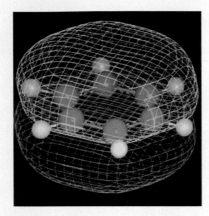

▲ **Figure 9.9** A computer-generated model of the benzene molecule. The six unassigned electrons occupy the yellow and blue areas above and below the plane of the ring of carbon atoms.

2. Why are benzene-like compounds that have many multiple bonds called "aromatic"?

Many of these compounds were named before the details of the structure were known. Some of the first ones known have strong sweet smells and would have been described as "aromatic."

A circle inside a ring indicates that a compound is aromatic. It does not always mean six electrons. The structural formula for naphthalene (Figure 9.10), for example, has a circle in each ring, indicating that it is an aromatic hydrocarbon. The total number of unassigned electrons, however, is ten. Some chemists still prefer to represent naphthalene (and other aromatic compounds) with alternating double and single bonds.

Toluene   Ethylbenzene   Naphthalene

ortho-Xylene
(1,2-Dimethylbenzene)

meta-Xylene
(1,3-Dimethylbenzene)

para-Xylene
(1,4-Dimethylbenzene)

◄ **Figure 9.10** Some aromatic hydrocarbons. Like benzene, toluene and the three xylenes are components of gasoline and also serve as solvents. All these compounds are intermediates in the synthesis of polymers (Chapter 10) and other organic chemicals.

SELF-ASSESSMENT Questions

1. Which of the following *cannot* be the molecular formula for an unsaturated hydrocarbon?
   a. C_4H_{10} **b.** C_5H_{10} **c.** C_7H_{12} **d.** C_8H_{16}

2. Which compound is an aromatic hydrocarbon?
   a. acetylene   **b.** butadiene
   c. chlorobenzene   **d.** cyclohexene

3. A hydrocarbon with a benzene-like structure is called a(n) _____ hydrocarbon.
   a. aliphatic   **b.** aromatic
   c. saturated   **d.** unsaturated

4. Naphthalene is an
   a. alkane   **b.** alkene
   c. alkyne   **d.** aromatic hydrocarbon

5. The reactivity of the benzene ring reflects
   a. its aromatic odor
   b. the presence of carbon–carbon double bonds
   c. its saturated structure
   d. the spreading of six electrons over all six carbon atoms

Answers: 1, a; 2, c; 3, b; 4, d; 5, d

9.3 Halogenated Hydrocarbons: Many Uses, Some Hazards

Learning Objective ❯ Name a halogenated hydrocarbon given its formula, and write the formula for such a compound given its name.

Many other organic compounds are derived from hydrocarbons by replacing one or more hydrogen atoms by another atom or group of atoms. For example, replacement of hydrogen atoms by chlorine atoms gives chlorinated hydrocarbons. When chlorine gas (Cl_2) is mixed with methane gas (CH_4) in the presence of ultraviolet (UV) light, a reaction takes place at a very rapid, even explosive, rate. The result is a mixture of products, some of which may be familiar to you (see Example 9.5 and Exercise 9.5). Several billion kilograms of chlorinated methanes are produced each year for use as solvents and as starting materials for other commercially valuable compounds. We can write an equation for the reaction in which one hydrogen atom of methane is replaced by a chlorine atom to give methyl chloride (chloromethane).

$$CH_4(g) + Cl_2(g) \longrightarrow CH_3Cl(g) + HCl(g)$$

Example 9.5   Formulas of Chlorinated Hydrocarbons

What is the formula for dichloromethane (also known as methylene chloride)?

Solution

The prefix *dichloro*- indicates two chlorine atoms. The rest of the name indicates that the compound is derived from methane (CH_4). We conclude that two hydrogen atoms of methane have been replaced by chlorine atoms; the formula for dichloromethane is therefore CH_2Cl_2.

▪ **EXERCISE 9.5**
What are the formulas for **(a)** trichloromethane (also known as chloroform) and **(b)** tetrachloromethane (carbon tetrachloride)?

Methyl chloride is used mainly in making silicone polymers (Chapter 10). Methylene chloride (dichloromethane) is a solvent used, for example, as a paint remover. Chloroform (trichloromethane), also a solvent, was once used as an anesthetic, but such use is now considered dangerous. The dosage required for effective anesthesia is too close to a lethal dose. Carbon tetrachloride (tetrachloromethane) has been used as a dry-cleaning solvent and in fire extinguishers, but it is no longer recommended for either use. Exposure to carbon tetrachloride or most other chlorinated hydrocarbons can cause severe damage to the liver. The use of a carbon tetrachloride fire extinguisher in conjunction with water to put out a fire can be deadly. Carbon tetrachloride reacts with water at elevated temperatures to form phosgene ($COCl_2$), an extremely poisonous gas that was used against troops during World War I.

A number of chlorinated hydrocarbons are of considerable interest. Vinyl chloride ($CH_2{=}CHCl$) is the starting material for manufacture of polyvinylchloride (Chapter 10).

Many chlorinated hydrocarbons have similar properties. Most are only slightly polar and do not dissolve in (highly polar) water. Instead, they dissolve (and dissolve in) fats, oils, greases, and other substances of low polarity. This is why certain chlorinated hydrocarbons make good dry-cleaning solvents; they remove grease and oily stains from fabrics. This is also why DDT and PCBs cause problems for fish and birds and perhaps for people; these toxic substances are concentrated in fatty animal tissues rather than being easily excreted in (aqueous) urine. DDT (dichlorodiphenyltrichloroethane) and other chlorinated hydrocarbon insecticides are discussed in Chapter 20. In Chapter 10, we will discuss polychlorinated biphenyls (PCBs).

Chlorofluorocarbons and Fluorocarbons

Compounds containing carbon and both fluorine and chlorine are called *chlorofluorocarbons (CFCs)*. CFCs have been used as the dispersing gases in aerosol cans, for making foamed plastics, and as refrigerants. Three common CFCs are best known by their industrial code designations:

$$CFCl_3 \qquad CF_2Cl_2 \qquad CF_2ClCF_2Cl$$
$$\text{CFC 11} \qquad \text{CFC 12} \qquad \text{CFC 114}$$

At room temperature, CFCs are gases or liquids with low boiling points. They are insoluble in water and inert toward most other substances. These properties make them ideal propellants in aerosol cans for deodorant, hair spray, and food products. CFCs are known to participate in chemical reactions that lead to depletion of the ozone layer that protects Earth from harmful UV radiation and so are being phased out. We will look at this problem and some attempts to solve it in Chapter 13.

Fluorinated compounds have found some interesting uses. Some have been used as blood extenders. Oxygen is quite soluble in certain *perfluorocarbons*. (The prefix *per-* means that all hydrogen atoms have been replaced, in this case, by fluorine atoms.) These compounds can therefore serve as temporary substitutes for hemoglobin, the oxygen-carrying protein in blood. Perfluoro compounds have been used to treat premature babies, whose lungs are often underdeveloped.

Polytetrafluoroethylene (PTFE, or Teflon®, discussed in Chapter 10) is a perfluorinated polymer. It has many interesting applications because of its resistance to corrosive chemicals and to high temperatures. It is especially noted for its unusual nonstick properties.

▲ Perfluorinated lubricants are used where highly corrosive or reactive conditions would cause most hydrocarbon greases to burst into flame.

SELF-ASSESSMENT Questions

1. The compound $CHCl_3$ is named
   a. chloroform
   b. methyl chloride
   c. methylene chloride
   d. methyl formate

2. The compound CF_2Cl_2 is
   a. a chlorofluorocarbon
   b. chloroform
   c. methyl chloride
   d. methylene chloride

3. Which of the following is an isomer of 2-chloropropane $(CH_3CHClCH_3)$?
   a. butane
   b. 2-chlorobutane
   c. 1-chloropropane
   d. propane

Answers: 1, b; 2, a; 3, c

9.4 The Functional Group

Learning Objectives ❭ Classify an organic compound according to its functional group(s), and explain why the concept of a functional group is useful in the study of organic chemistry. ❭ Recognize and write the formulas of simple alkyl groups.

While the study of organic chemistry focuses on the compounds containing carbon and hydrogen, we saw in Section 9.1 that these compounds do not undergo extensive chemical reactions. Double and triple carbon–carbon bonds and halogen substituents are examples of **functional groups**, atoms or groups of atoms that give a family of organic compounds its characteristic chemical and physical properties. Table 9.4 lists a number of common functional groups found in organic molecules. Each of these groups is the basis for its own homologous series.

Table 9.4 Selected Organic Functional Groups

Name of Class	Functional Group[a]	General Formula of Class		
Alkane	None	R—H		
Alkene	—C=C—	$R_2C=CR_2$		
Alkyne	—C≡C—	RC≡CR		
Alcohol	—C—OH	R—OH		
Ether	—C—O—C—	R—O—R′		
Aldehyde	—C(=O)—H	R—C(=O)—H		
Ketone	—C(=O)—	R—C(=O)—R′		
Carboxylic acid	—C(=O)—OH	R—C(=O)—O—H		
Ester	—C(=O)—O—C—	R—C(=O)—O—R′		
Amine	—C—N—	R—N(H)—H	R—N(H)—R′	R—N(R′)—R″
Amide	—C(=O)—N—	R—C(=O)—N(H)—H	R—C(=O)—N(H)—R′	R—C(=O)—N(R″)—R′

[a]Neutral functional groups are shown in green, acidic groups in red, and basic groups in blue.

In many simple molecules, a functional group is attached as a substituent to a hydrocarbon stem called an *alkyl group*. An **alkyl group** is derived from an alkane by removing a hydrogen atom. The methyl group (CH_3—), for example, is derived from methane (CH_4), and the ethyl group (CH_3CH_2—) from ethane (CH_3CH_3). Propane yields two different alkyl groups, depending on whether the hydrogen atom is removed from an end or from the middle carbon atom; see Table 9.5. Table 9.5 also lists the four alkyl groups derived from the two butanes.

Often the letter R is used to stand for an alkyl group in general. Thus, ROH is a general formula for an alcohol, and RCl represents any alkyl chloride.

Table 9.5 Common Alkyl Groups

	Name	Structural Formula	Condensed Structural Formula
Derived from Propane	Propyl		$CH_3CH_2CH_2$—
	Isopropyl		CH_3CHCH_3
Derived from Butane	Butyl		$CH_3CH_2CH_2CH_2$—
	Secondary butyl (*sec*-butyl)		$CH_3CHCH_2CH_3$
Derived from Isobutane	Isobutyl		CH_3CHCH_2— with CH_3
	Tertiary butyl (*tert*-butyl)		CH_3—C—CH_3 with CH_3

Self-Assessment Questions

1. A specific structural arrangement of atoms or bonds that imparts characteristic properties to a molecule is called a(n)
   a. catalyst   b. empirical formula
   c. functional group   d. substituent

2. The formula $CH_3CH_2CH_2$— represents
   a. an alkyl group   b. a functional group
   c. propane   d. propylene

3. How many carbon atoms are there in an ethyl group?
   a. 2   b. 3   c. 4   d. 6

4. The formula $CH_3CH_2CH_2CH_2$— represents a(n)
   a. butyl group   b. isobutyl group
   c. isopropyl group   d. propyl group

9.5 Alcohols, Phenols, and Ethers

Learning Objectives ❯ Recognize the general structure for an alcohol, a phenol, and an ether. ❯ Name simple alcohols, phenols, and ethers.

When a hydroxyl group (—OH) is substituted for any hydrogen atom in an alkane (R—H), the molecule becomes an **alcohol** (ROH). Like many organic compounds, alcohols can be called by their common names or by the systematic names of IUPAC. The IUPAC names for alcohols are based on those of alkanes, with the ending changed from -*e* to -*ol*. Methanol, ethanol, and 1-propanol are the first three members of the homologous series of straight-chain alcohols.

For many industries and businesses, the synthesis of alcohols represents the starting point for the production of important chemical products. Lower costs for these starting materials can lead to lower costs for consumers. Likewise, the use of alcohols as gasoline additives can lead to a lesser environmental impact.

A number designates the carbon to which the (—OH) group is attached when more than one location is possible. For example, the 1 in 1-propanol indicates that (—OH) is attached to an end carbon atom of the three-carbon chain The isomeric compound, 2-propanol (also called isopropyl alcohol), has the (—OH) group on the second (middle) carbon atom of the chain.

$$CH_3—OH \qquad CH_3CH_2—OH \qquad CH_3CH_2CH_2—OH \qquad \begin{matrix} CH_3CHCH_3 \\ | \\ OH \end{matrix}$$

Methanol · · · · · · · · · Ethanol · · · · · · · · · · · · · 1–Propanol · · · · · · · · · · · 2–Propanol

Common names for these alcohols are methyl alcohol, ethyl alcohol, and propyl alcohol. The IUPAC names are the ones used in most scientific literature.

Methyl Alcohol (Methanol)

The simplest alcohol is *methanol*, or *methyl alcohol* (Figure 9.11). Methanol is sometimes called *wood alcohol* because it was once made from wood. The modern industrial process makes methanol from carbon monoxide and hydrogen at high temperature and pressure in the presence of a catalyst.

$$CO(g) + 2\ H_2(g) \longrightarrow CH_3OH(l)$$

Methanol is important as a solvent and as a chemical intermediate. It is also a gasoline additive and a potential replacement for gasoline in automobiles.

(a) · (b)

▲ **Figure 9.11** Ball-and-stick (a) and space-filling (b) models of methanol.

Ethyl Alcohol (Ethanol)

The next member of the homologous series of alcohols is *ethyl alcohol* (CH_3CH_2OH), also called ethanol or *grain alcohol* (Figure 9.12). Ethanol is made by fermentation of grain (or other starchy or sugary materials). If the sugar is glucose, the reaction is

(a) · (b)

▲ **Figure 9.12** Ball-and-stick (a) and space-filling (b) models of ethanol.

$$C_6H_{12}O_6(aq) \xrightarrow{\text{yeast}} 2\ CH_3CH_2OH(aq) + 2\ CO_2(g)$$

Ethanol for beverages and for automotive fuel is made in this way. Ethanol for industrial use is made by reacting ethylene with water.

$$CH_2{=}CH_2(g) + H_2O(l) \xrightarrow{H^+} CH_3CH_2OH(l)$$

This industrial alcohol is identical to that made by fermentation and is generally cheaper, but by law, it cannot be used in alcoholic beverages. Because it carries no excise tax, the law requires that noxious substances be added to this alcohol to prevent people from drinking it. The resulting *denatured alcohol* is not fit to drink. This is the kind of alcohol commonly found on the shelves in chemical laboratories.

Gasoline in many parts of the United States contains up to 10% ethanol that is produced by fermentation. Because the United States has a large corn (maize)

The *proof* of an alcoholic beverage is twice the percentage of alcohol by volume. The term originated in a seventeenth-century English method for testing whiskey to ensure that a dealer was not increasing profits by adding water to the booze. A qualitative test was to pour some of the whiskey on gunpowder and ignite it. Ignition of the gunpowder after the alcohol had burned away was considered "proof" that the whiskey did not contain too much water.

surplus, there is a generous government subsidy for gasoline producers who use ethanol made this way. As a result, many factories now make ethanol by fermentation of corn.

Toxicity of Alcohols

Although ethanol is an ingredient in wine, beer, and other alcoholic beverages, alcohols in general are rather toxic. Toxicity depends on the nature of the substance, the amount, and the route by which it is taken into the body. (Toxicity is discussed in detail in Chapter 22.) Methanol, for example, is oxidized in the body to formaldehyde (HCHO). Drinking as little as 1 oz (about 30 mL or 2 tablespoonfuls) can cause blindness and even death. Several poisonings each year result when people mistake methanol for the less toxic ethanol.

Ethanol is not as poisonous as methanol, but it is still toxic. About 50,000 cases of ethanol poisoning are reported each year in the United States, and dozens of people die of acute ethanol poisoning.

Generally, ethanol acts as a mild depressant; it slows down both physical and mental activity. Table 9.6 lists the effects of various doses. Although ethanol generally is a depressant, small amounts of it seem to act as a stimulant, perhaps by relaxing tensions and relieving inhibitions.

Ingesting too much ethanol over a long period of time can alter brain-cell function, cause nerve damage, and shorten life span by contributing to diseases of the liver, cardiovascular system, and practically every other organ of the body. Further, about half of fatal automobile accidents involve at least one drinking driver. Babies born to alcoholic mothers often are small, deformed, and mentally retarded. Some investigators believe that this *fetal alcohol syndrome* can occur even if mothers drink only moderately. Ethanol, by far the most abused drug in the United States, is discussed more fully in Chapter 18.

Table 9.6	**Approximate Relationship among Drinks Consumed, Blood Alcohol Level, and Behavior[a]**	
Number of Drinks[b]	Blood Alcohol Level (percent by volume)	Behavior[c]
2	0.05	Mild sedation; tranquility
4	0.10	Lack of coordination
6	0.15	Obvious intoxication
10	0.30	Unconsciousness
20	0.50	Possible death

[a]Data are for a 70-kg (154-lb) moderate drinker.

[b]Rapidly consumed 30-mL (1-oz) shots of 90-proof whiskey, 360-mL (12-oz) bottles of beer, or 150-mL (5-oz) glasses of wine.

[c]An inexperienced drinker would be affected more strongly, or more quickly, than someone who is ordinarily a moderate drinker. Conversely, an experienced heavy drinker would be affected less.

Rubbing alcohol is a 70% solution of isopropyl alcohol. Because isopropyl alcohol is also more toxic than ethanol, it is not surprising that people become ill, and sometimes die, after drinking rubbing alcohol.

Multifunctional Alcohols

Several alcohols have more than one hydroxyl group. Examples are ethylene glycol, propylene glycol, and glycerol.

Ethylene glycol   Propylene glycol   Glycerol

▲ Warning labels on alcoholic beverages alert consumers to the hazards of consumption.

Ethylene glycol is the main ingredient in many permanent antifreeze mixtures. Its high boiling point keeps it from boiling away in automobile radiators. Ethylene glycol is a syrupy liquid with a sweet taste, but it is quite toxic. It is oxidized in the liver to oxalic acid.

$$\underset{\text{Ethylene glycol}}{\overset{\displaystyle \overset{\text{OH}}{|} \ \overset{\text{OH}}{|}}{\text{CH}_2 - \text{CH}_2}} \xrightarrow{\text{liver enzymes}} \underset{\text{Oxalic acid} \atop \text{(toxic)}}{\text{HO} - \overset{\overset{\text{O}}{\|}}{\text{C}} - \overset{\overset{\text{O}}{\|}}{\text{C}} - \text{OH}}$$

Oxalic acid forms crystals of its calcium salt, calcium oxalate (CaC_2O_4), which can damage the kidneys, leading to kidney failure and death. Propylene glycol, a high-boiling substance that is not poisonous, is now marketed as a safer permanent anti-freeze.

Glycerol (or glycerin) is a sweet, syrupy liquid that is a by-product from fats during soap manufacture (Chapter 21). It is used in lotions to keep the skin soft and as a food additive to keep cakes moist. Its reaction with nitric acid makes nitro-glycerin, the explosive material in dynamite. Nitroglycerin is also important as a vasodilator, a medication taken by heart patients to relieve angina pain.

It DOES Matter!
Antifreeze containing ethylene glycol should always be drained into a container and disposed of properly. Pets have been known to die from licking the sweet, but toxic, ethylene glycol mixture from a driveway or open container.

Example 9.6   Structural Formulas of Alcohols

Write the structural formula for *tert*-butyl alcohol, sometimes used as an octane booster in gasoline.

Solution
An alcohol consists of an alkyl group joined to a hydroxyl group. From Table 9.5, we see that the *tert*-butyl group is

$$\text{CH}_3 - \overset{\overset{\displaystyle \text{CH}_3}{|}}{\underset{\underset{\displaystyle \text{CH}_3}{|}}{\text{C}}} -$$

Connecting this group to an OH group gives *tert*-butyl alcohol.

$$\text{CH}_3 - \overset{\overset{\displaystyle \text{CH}_3}{|}}{\underset{\underset{\displaystyle \text{CH}_3}{|}}{\text{C}}} - \text{OH}$$

▪ **EXERCISE 9.6**
Write the structural formulas for **(a)** butyl alcohol and **(b)** *sec*-butyl alcohol.

Phenols

When a hydroxyl group is attached to a benzene ring, the compound is called a **phenol**. Although a phenol may appear to be an alcohol, it is not. The benzene ring greatly alters the properties of the hydroxyl group. Unlike alcohols, phenol is a weak acid (sometimes called *carbolic acid*), and it is quite poisonous compared to most simple alcohols.

$$\underset{\text{Phenol}}{\text{⬡} - \text{OH}}$$

Phenol was the first antiseptic used in an operating room—by Joseph Lister in 1867. Up until that time, surgery was not antiseptic, and many patients died from infections following surgical operations. Although phenol has a strong germicidal action, it is far from an ideal antiseptic because it causes severe skin burns and kills healthy cells along with harmful microorganisms.

OH

OH
$CH_2CH_2CH_2CH_2CH_2CH_3$
Hexylresorcinol

▲ Phenolic compounds help to ensure antiseptic conditions in hospital operating rooms.

Phenol is still sometimes employed as a disinfectant for floors and furniture, but other phenolic compounds are now used as antiseptics. Hexylresorcinol, for example, is a more powerful germicide than phenol, and it is less damaging to the skin and has fewer other side effects.

Ethers

Compounds with two alkyl or aromatic groups attached to the same oxygen atom are called **ethers**. The general formula is ROR (or ROR′ because the alkyl groups need not be alike). The best-known ether is *diethyl ether* ($CH_3CH_2OCH_2CH_3$), often called simply *ether*.

Diethyl ether dissolves many organic substances that are insoluble in water. It boils at 36 °C, which means that it evaporates readily, making it easy to recover dissolved materials. Although diethyl ether has little chemical reactivity, it is highly flammable. Great care must be taken to avoid sparks or flames when it is in use. Diethyl ether was introduced in 1842 as a general anesthetic for surgery and was once the most widely used anesthetic. It is rarely used for humans today because it has undesirable side effects, such as postanesthetic nausea and vomiting. We will discuss modern anesthesia in Chapter 18.

Another problem with ethers is that they can react slowly with oxygen to form unstable peroxides, which may decompose explosively. Beware of previously opened containers of ether, especially old ones.

The ether produced in the largest amount commercially is a cyclic compound called *ethylene oxide*. Its two carbon atoms and one oxygen atom form a three-membered ring. Like cyclic hydrocarbons, cyclic ethers can be represented by geometric shapes. Each corner of such a shape (except the O) stands for a C atom with enough H atoms attached to give the carbon four bonds. Ethylene oxide is represented as

Ethylene oxide is a toxic gas, used mainly to make ethylene glycol.

| Ethylene oxide | Water | | Ethylene glycol |

Ethylene oxide is also used to sterilize medical instruments and as an intermediate in the synthesis of some detergents (Chapter 21). Most of the ethylene glycol produced is used in making polyester fibers (Chapter 10) and antifreeze.

CONCEPTUAL Example 9.7   Identifying Functional Groups

Classify each of the following as an alcohol, an ether, or a phenol.

(a)   (b)   (c)

(d)   (e)

Solution

a. The compound is an alcohol; the OH is not attached directly to the benzene ring.

b. The OH group is attached to an alkyl group; the compound is an alcohol.

c. The O atom is between two alkyl groups; the compound is an ether.

d. The OH functional group is attached directly to the benzene ring; the compound is a phenol.

e. The compound is an ether; the O atom is between two C atoms.

▪ EXERCISE 9.7

Classify each of the following as an alcohol, an ether, or a phenol.

CH₃CH₂CHOH
|
CH₃

(a)

CH₃O—⬡

(b)

CH₃CH₂CHOCH₃
|
CH₃

(c)

HO—⬡—Br

(d)

(e)

Example 9.8 Formulas for Ethers

What is the formula for isopropyl methyl ether?

Solution

Isopropyl methyl ether has an oxygen atom joined to an isopropyl group (three carbons joined to oxygen by the middle carbon) and a methyl group. The formula is

CH₃CHOCH₃ ◁ Methyl group
Isopropyl group ⟋ |
CH₃

▪ EXERCISE 9.8

Write formulas for **(a)** butyl methyl ether and **(b)** ethyl *tert*-butyl ether.

SELF-ASSESSMENT Questions

1. An organic compound with a hydroxyl (OH) functional group on an aliphatic carbon atom is called a(n)
   a. alcohol   **b.** aldehyde   **c.** amine   **d.** phenol

2. Which of the following formulas represents an alcohol?
   a. $CH_3CHOHCH_2CH_3$ **b.** CH_3COCH_3
   c. CdOH   **d.** CH_3CHO

3. Which of the following alcohols has molecules with more than one hydroxyl group?
   a. 2-butanol   **b.** glycerol
   c. 4-octanol   **d.** 3-pentanol

4. The formula for ethylene glycol is
   a. CH_3CH_2OH **b.** $CH_3CH(OH)_2$
   c. $C_3H_5(OH)_3$ **d.** $HOCH_2CH_2OH$

5. Which of the following alcohols has the lowest boiling point?
   a. 1-butanol   **b.** 2-butanol
   c. 2-pentanol   **d.** 2-propanol

6. The general formula R—O—R' represents a(n)
   a. ester   **b.** ether   **c.** ketone   **d.** phenol

7. The formula $CH_3CH_2OCH_2CH_3$ represents
   a. 2-butanol   **b.** 2-butanone
   c. butyraldehyde   **d.** diethyl ether

8. The formula for butyl ethyl ether is
   a. $CH_3CH_2OCH_2CH_3$
   b. $CH_3OCH_2CH_2CH_3$
   c. $CH_3CH_2CH_2OCH_2CH_3$
   d. $CH_3CH_2OCH_2CH_2CH_2CH_3$

9. The compound $CH_3CHOHCH_2CH_3$ is an isomer of
   a. $CH_3COCH_2CH_2CH_3$ **b.** $CH_3CH_2CH_2COOH$
   c. $CH_3COOCH_2CH_3$ **d.** $CH_3CH_2CH_2CH_2OH$

9.6 Aldehydes and Ketones

Learning Objective ❯ Name simple aldehydes and ketones, and list their important properties.

Two families of organic compounds that share the same functional group are **aldehydes** and **ketones**. Both types of compounds contain the **carbonyl group** ($C{=}O$), but aldehydes have at least one hydrogen atom attached to the carbonyl carbon, whereas ketones have two other carbon atoms joined to the carbonyl carbon.

$$\overset{\displaystyle O}{\underset{\displaystyle \|}{}}{-}C{-} \qquad R{-}\overset{O}{\overset{\|}{C}}{-}H \qquad R{-}\overset{O}{\overset{\|}{C}}{-}R'$$

A carbonyl group   An aldehyde   A ketone

To simplify typing, these structures are often written on one line with the $C{=}O$ bond omitted.

$${-}C({=}O){-} \quad \text{or} \quad {-}CO{-} \qquad R{-}CH({=}O) \ \text{ or } \ R{-}CHO \qquad R{-}C({=}O){-}R' \ \text{ or } \ R{-}CO{-}R'$$

A carbonyl group   An aldehyde   A ketone

Models of three familiar carbonyl compounds are shown in Figure 9.13.

Some Common Aldehydes

The simplest aldehyde is *formaldehyde* (HCHO). It is a gas at room temperature but is readily soluble in water. As a 40% solution called *formalin*, it is used as a preservative for biological specimens and in embalming fluid. Systematic names for aldehydes are based on those of alkanes, with the ending changed from *-e* to *-al*. Thus, by the IUPAC system, formaldehyde is named methanal. IUPAC names are seldom used for simple aldehydes because of possible confusion with the corresponding alcohols. For example, "methanal" is easily confused with "methanol," when spoken or (especially) when handwritten.

Formaldehyde is used in making certain plastics (Chapter 10). It also is used to disinfect homes, ships, and warehouses. Commercially, formaldehyde is made by

(a)

(b)

▶ **Figure 9.13** Ball-and-stick (a) and space-filling (b) models of formaldehyde (left), acetaldehyde (center), and acetone (right).

the oxidation of methanol. The same net reaction occurs in the human body when methanol is ingested and accounts for the high toxicity of that alcohol.

Organic chemists often write equations that show only the organic reactants and products. Inorganic substances are omitted for the sake of simplicity.

$$CH_3OH \xrightarrow{\text{oxidation}} H-\underset{\displaystyle \overset{\displaystyle O}{\|}}{C}-H$$

Methanol   Formaldehyde

The next member of the homologous series of aldehydes is acetaldehyde (ethanal), formed by the oxidation of ethanol.

$$CH_3CH_2OH \xrightarrow{\text{oxidation}} CH_3-\underset{\displaystyle \overset{\displaystyle O}{\|}}{C}-H$$

Ethanol   Acetaldehyde

The next two members of the aldehyde series are propionaldehyde (propanal) and butyraldehyde (butanal). Both have strong, unpleasant odors. Benzaldehyde has an aldehyde group attached to a benzene ring. Also called (synthetic) oil of almond, benzaldehyde is used in perfumery and is the flavoring ingredient in maraschino cherries.

$$CH_3CH_2-\underset{\displaystyle \overset{\displaystyle O}{\|}}{C}-H \qquad CH_3CH_2CH_2-\underset{\displaystyle \overset{\displaystyle O}{\|}}{C}-H$$

Propionaldehyde   Butyraldehyde   Benzaldehyde

Some Common Ketones

The simplest ketone is *acetone*, made by the oxidation of isopropyl alcohol.

$$CH_3-\underset{\displaystyle \overset{\displaystyle OH}{|}}{CH}-CH_3 \xrightarrow{\text{oxidation}} CH_3-\underset{\displaystyle \overset{\displaystyle O}{\|}}{C}-CH_3$$

Isopropyl alcohol   Acetone

Acetone is a common solvent for such organic materials as fats, rubbers, plastics, and varnishes. It is also used in paint and varnish removers and is a major ingredient in some fingernail polish removers. By the IUPAC system, acetone is named propanone. The systematic names for ketones are based on those of alkanes, with the ending changed from *-e* to *-one*. When necessary, a number is used to indicate the location of the carbonyl group. For example, $CH_3CH_2COCH_2CH_2CH_3$ is 3-hexanone.

Two other familiar ketones are ethyl methyl ketone and isobutyl methyl ketone, which, like acetone, are frequently used as solvents.

A ketone is a carbon chain
With a carbonyl inside.
If the carbonyl is on the end,
Then it's an aldehyde.

$$CH_3CH_2-\underset{\displaystyle \overset{\displaystyle O}{\|}}{C}-CH_3 \qquad CH_3\underset{\displaystyle \underset{\displaystyle CH_3}{|}}{CH}CH_2-\underset{\displaystyle \overset{\displaystyle O}{\|}}{C}-CH_3$$

Ethyl methyl ketone   Isobutyl methyl ketone

CONCEPTUAL Example 9.9   Aldehyde or Ketone?

Identify each of the following compounds as an aldehyde or a ketone.

$$CH_3CH_2CH_2CH_2-\underset{\displaystyle \overset{\displaystyle O}{\|}}{C}-H$$

(a)   (b)   (c)

Solution

a. A hydrogen atom is attached to the carbonyl carbon atom; the compound is an aldehyde.

b. The carbonyl group is between two other (ring) carbon atoms; the compound is a ketone.

c. The compound is a ketone. (Remember that the corner of the hexagon stands for a carbon atom.)

▪ EXERCISE 9.9

Identify each of the following compounds as an aldehyde or a ketone.

$$CH_3CH_2CH_2CCH_3$$

(a)   (b)   (c)

SELF-ASSESSMENT Questions

1. The aldehyde functional group has a carbonyl group attached to
   a. an H atom
   b. an N atom
   c. an OH group
   d. two other C atoms

2. The ketone functional group has a carbonyl group attached to
   a. an OH group
   b. an OR group
   c. two other C atoms
   d. two OR groups

3. The general formula R—CO—R′ represents a(n)
   a. ester
   b. ether
   c. ketone
   d. phenol

4. The carbon atom in a carboxyl group is bonded to two oxygen atoms. The bonds are
   a. both single
   b. one single and one double
   c. one single and one triple
   d. both double

5. A name for $CH_3COCH_2CH_3$ is
   a. butanone
   b. butyraldehyde
   c. propanone
   d. propylaldehyde

6. Which alcohol is oxidized to produce formaldehyde?
   a. CH_3OH
   b. CH_3CH_2OH
   c. $CH_3CH_2CH_2OH$
   d. $CH_3CHOHCH_3$

7. Which alcohol is oxidized to produce acetone?
   a. CH_3OH
   b. CH_3CH_2OH
   c. $CH_3CH_2CH_2OH$
   d. $CH_3CHOHCH_3$

Answers: 1, a; 2, c; 3, c; 4, b; 5, a; 6, a; 7, d

9.7 Carboxylic Acids and Esters

Learning Objective ❯ Name simple carboxylic acids and esters, and list their important properties.

Carboxylic Acids

The functional group of organic acids is called the **carboxyl group**, and the acids are called **carboxylic acids**.

A carboxyl group   A carboxylic acid

As with aldehydes and ketones, these formulas are often written on one line:

—C(=O)OH or —COOH   R—C(=O)OH or R—COOH

A carboxyl group   A carboxylic acid

▲ Acetic acid is a familiar weak acid in chemistry laboratories. It is also the principal active ingredient in vinegar.

The simplest carboxylic acid is formic acid (HCOOH). The systematic (IUPAC) names for carboxylic acids are based on those of alkanes, with the ending changed from -*e* to -*oic acid*. For example, the IUPAC name for formic acid is methanoic acid, and $CH_3CH_2CH_2CH_2COOH$ is pentanoic acid.

Formic acid was first obtained by the destructive distillation of ants (the Latin word *formica* means "ant"). It smarts when an ant bites because the ant injects formic acid into the skin. The stings of wasps and bees also contain formic acid (as well as other poisonous compounds).

Acetic acid (ethanoic acid, CH_3COOH) can be made by the aerobic fermentation of a mixture of cider and honey. This produces a solution (vinegar) containing about 4–10% acetic acid plus a number of other compounds that add flavor. Acetic acid is probably the most familiar weak acid used in academic and industrial chemistry laboratories.

The third member of the homologous series of acids, propionic acid (propanoic acid, CH_3CH_2COOH), is seldom encountered in everyday life. The fourth member is more familiar, at least by its odor. If you've ever smelled rancid butter, you know the odor of butyric acid (butanoic acid, $CH_3CH_2CH_2COOH$). It is one of the most foul-smelling substances imaginable. Butyric acid can be isolated from butterfat or synthesized in the laboratory. It is one of the ingredients of body odor, and extremely small quantities of this acid and other chemicals enable bloodhounds to track lost people and fugitives.

The acid with a carboxyl group attached directly to a benzene ring is called *benzoic acid*.

Benzoic acid

Carboxylic acid salts—calcium propionate, sodium benzoate, and others—are widely used as food additives to prevent mold (Chapter 17).

| **Example 9.10** | Structural Formulas of Oxygen-Containing Organic Compounds |

Write the structural formula for each of the following compounds.

  a. propionaldehyde **b.** ethanoic acid   **c.** ethyl methyl ketone

Solution

a. Propionaldehyde has three carbon atoms with an aldehyde function.

$$C-C-\overset{\overset{\textstyle O}{\|}}{C}-H$$

Adding the proper number of hydrogen atoms to the other two carbon atoms gives the structure

or CH_3CH_2CHO

b. Ethanoic acid has two carbon atoms with a carboxylic acid function.

or CH_3COOH

c. Ethyl methyl ketone has a ketone function between an ethyl and a methyl group.

or $CH_3CH_2COCH_3$

3. Why does fresh fruit smell so good and rotting fruit so bad?

Esters are often the main components of fruity flavors. When fruit is broken down by bacteria, the esters are often broken down into their corresponding alcohols and (unpleasant!) carboxylic acids.

■ EXERCISE 9.10

Write the structural formula for each of the following compounds.
a. butyric acid   **b.** acetaldehyde   **c.** diethyl ketone
d. 3-octanone   **e.** heptanal   **f.** hexanoic acid

Esters: The Sweet Smell of RCOOR'

Esters are derived from carboxylic acids and alcohols or phenols. The general reaction involves splitting out a molecule of water.

$$\underset{\text{An acid}}{R-\overset{\overset{\displaystyle O}{\|}}{C}-OH} + \underset{\text{An alcohol}}{R'OH} \overset{H^+}{\rightleftharpoons} \underset{\text{An ester}}{R-\overset{\overset{\displaystyle O}{\|}}{C}-OR'} + HOH$$

The name of an ester ends in *-ate* and is formed by naming the part from the alcohol first and the part from the carboxylic acid last. For example, the ester derived from butyric acid and methyl alcohol is methyl butyrate.

This four-carbon group is derived from butyric acid   This one-carbon group is derived from methyl alcohol

$$CH_3CH_2CH_2COOCH_3$$

Although carboxylic acids often have strongly unpleasant odors, the esters derived from them are usually quite fragrant, especially when dilute. Many esters have fruity odors and tastes. Some examples are given in Table 9.7. Esters are widely used as flavorings in cakes, candies, and other foods and as ingredients in perfumes.

Table 9.7	Ester Flavors and Fragrances	
Ester	Formula	Flavor/Fragrance
Methyl butyrate	$CH_3CH_2CH_2COOCH_3$	Apple
Ethyl butyrate	$CH_3CH_2CH_2COOCH_2CH_3$	Pineapple
Propyl acetate	$CH_3COOCH_2CH_2CH_3$	Pear
Pentyl acetate	$CH_3COOCH_2CH_2CH_2CH_2CH_3$	Banana
Pentyl butyrate	$CH_3CH_2CH_2COOCH_2CH_2CH_2CH_2CH_3$	Apricot
Octyl acetate	$CH_3COOCH_2CH_2CH_2CH_2CH_2CH_2CH_2CH_3$	Orange
Methyl benzoate	$C_6H_5COOCH_3$	Ripe kiwifruit
Ethyl formate	$HCOOCH_2CH_3$	Rum
Methyl salicylate	$o\text{-}HOC_6H_4COOCH_3$	Wintergreen
Benzyl acetate	$CH_3COOCH_2C_6H_5$	Jasmine

SELF-ASSESSMENT Questions

1. Which of the following formulas represents a carboxylic acid?
   a. $CH_3CH_2CH_2OH$ **b.** CH_3COOCH_3
   c. $CH_2CH_2CH_2COOH$ **d.** $CH_3CH_2CH_2CHO$

2. Which of the following is the formula for butanoic acid?
   a. CH_3CH_2COOH **b.** $CH_3CH_2CH_2CH_2OH$
   c. $CH_3CH_2CH_2CHO$ **d.** $CH_3CH_2CH_2COOH$

3. Oxidation of alcohol on the second carbon of a chain forms a(n)
   a. aldehyde   **b.** carboxylic acid   **c.** ester   **d.** ketone

4. Alcohols can be oxidized with hot copper oxide to form carboxylic acids. If the alcohol is ethanol, the carboxylic acid will be
   a. CH_3COOH **b.** CH_3CH_2OH
   c. $CH_3CH_2CH_2OHO$ **d.** CH_3CH_2COOH

5. The general formula for an ester is
   a. ROR'   **b.** RCOR'
   c. RCOOR'   **d.** RCONHR'

6. A name for the compound with the formula $CH_3CH_2CH_2CH_2COOCH_3$ is
   a. ethyl propanoate   **b.** ethyl butanoate
   c. methyl pentanoate **d.** propyl propanoate

7. A name for the compound with the formula $CH_3CH_2COOCH_3$ is
   a. ethyl acetate   **b.** ethyl propanoate
   c. methyl pentanoate   **d.** methyl propanoate

Salicylates: Pain Relievers Based on Salicylic Acid

Salicylic acid is both a carboxylic acid and a phenol. We can use it to illustrate some of the reactions of these two families of compounds.

Salicylic acid

Since ancient times, various peoples around the world have used willow bark to treat fevers. Edward Stone, an English clergyman, reported to the Royal Society in 1763 that an extract of willow bark was useful in reducing fever.

Salicylic acid was first isolated from willow bark in 1838. It was first prepared synthetically in 1860 and soon was used in medicine as an *antipyretic* (fever reducer) and as an *analgesic* (pain reliever). However, it is sour and irritating when taken orally. Chemists sought to use chemical reactions to modify its structure so that these undesirable properties would be reduced while retaining or even enhancing its desirable properties. These reactions are summarized in Figure 9.14. The first such modification was simply to neutralize the acid (Reaction 1 in Figure 9.14). The resulting salt, sodium salicylate, was first used in 1875. It was less unpleasant to swallow than the acid but was still highly irritating to the stomach.

By 1886, chemists had produced another derivative (Reaction 2), the phenyl ester of salicylic acid, called *phenyl salicylate*, or *salol*. Salol was less unpleasant to swallow, and it passed largely unchanged through the stomach. In the small intestine, salol was converted to the desired salicylic acid, but phenol was formed as a by-product. A large dose could produce phenol poisoning.

Acetylsalicylic acid, an ester formed when the phenol group of salicylic acid reacts with acetic acid, was first produced in 1853. It is usually made by reacting salicylic acid with acetic anhydride, the acid anhydride of acetic acid (Reaction 3). The German Bayer Company introduced acetylsalicylic acid as a medicine in 1899 under the trade name Aspirin. It soon became the best-selling drug in the world.

Another derivative, methyl salicylate, is made by reacting the carboxyl group of salicylic acid with methanol, producing a different ester (Reaction 4). Methyl salicylate, called *oil of wintergreen*, is used as a flavoring agent and in rub-on analgesics. When applied to the skin, it causes a mild warming sensation, providing some relief for sore muscles.

Aspirin and its use as a drug are discussed in more detail in Chapter 18.

▲ **Figure 9.14** Some reactions of salicylic acid. In Reactions 1, 2, and 4, salicylic acid reacts as a carboxylic acid; the reactions occur at the carboxyl group. In Reaction 3, salicylic acid reacts as a phenol; the reaction takes place at the hydroxyl group.

Q: *Can you identify and name the functional groups present in (a) salicylic acid, (b) methyl salicylate, (c) acetylsalicylic acid, and (d) phenyl salicylate?*

9.8 Nitrogen-Containing Compounds: Amines and Amides

Learning Objectives > Name and write the formulas for simple amines and amides.
> Recognize a structure as that of a heterocyclic compound.

Many organic substances of interest to us in the chapters that follow contain nitrogen, which is the fourth most common element in organic compounds after carbon, hydro-

4. Why do organic compounds have such strong tastes?

Organic compounds have many different complex structures. The chemoreceptors in the tastebuds and smell receptors have a strong affinity for the various carbon compounds. The aromatics make strong odors, the esters make sweet odors, the carboxylic acids make unpleasant odors, and the amides and amines make fishy or rotten odors.

Biologically, as we are creatures who consume organic compounds, our senses have evolved to recognize the chemical compounds that we either need or should avoid.

gen, and oxygen. The two nitrogen-containing functional groups that we consider in this section, amines and amides, provide a vital background for the material ahead.

Amines

Amines contain the elements carbon, hydrogen, and nitrogen. An **amine** is derived from ammonia by replacing one, two, or three of the hydrogen atoms by one, two, or three alkyl or aromatic groups:

$$H-\underset{\underset{H}{|}}{N}-H \qquad R-\underset{\underset{H}{|}}{N}-H \qquad R-\underset{\underset{R'}{|}}{N}-H \qquad R-\underset{\underset{R'}{|}}{N}-R''$$

Ammonia   Amines

The simplest amine is methylamine (CH_3NH_2). Amines with two or more carbon atoms can be isomers: Both ethylamine ($CH_3CH_2NH_2$) and dimethylamine (CH_3NHCH_3) have the molecular formula C_2H_7N. With three carbon atoms, there are several possibilities, including trimethylamine [$(CH_3)_3N$].

CONCEPTUAL Example 9.11   Amine Isomers: Structures and Names

Write structural formulas and names for the other three-carbon amines.

Solution

Three carbon atoms can be in one alkyl group, and there are two such propyl groups.

$$CH_3CH_2CH_2NH_2 \qquad\qquad CH_3\underset{\underset{NH_2}{|}}{C}HCH_3$$

Propylamine   Isopropylamine

Three carbon atoms can also be split into one methyl group and one ethyl group.

$$CH_3CH_2NHCH_3$$

Ethylmethylamine

■ EXERCISE 9.11

Write structural formulas for the following amines.

  a. butylamine   **b.** diethylamine
  c. methylpropylamine   **d.** isopropylmethylamine

The amine with an $-NH_2$ group (called an **amino group**) attached directly to a benzene ring has the special name *aniline*. Like many other aromatic amines, aniline is used in making dyes. Aromatic amines tend to be toxic, and some are strongly carcinogenic.

Simple amines are similar to ammonia in odor, basicity, and other properties. The larger and aromatic amines are more interesting. Figure 9.15 shows a variety of these.

▲ **Figure 9.15** Some amines of interest. Amphetamine is a stimulant drug (Chapter 18). Cadaverine has the odor of decaying flesh. 1,6-Hexanediamine is used in the synthesis of nylon (Chapter 10). Pyridoxamine is a B vitamin (Chapter 17).

Q: *1,6-Hexanediamine is the IUPAC name for a compound also known by the common name hexamethylenediamine. Cadaverine is a common name. What is the IUPAC name for cadaverine?*

Among the most important kinds of organic molecules are *amino acids*. As the name implies, these compounds have both amine and carboxylic acid functional groups. Amino acids are the building blocks of proteins. The simplest amino acid, H_2NCH_2COOH, is glycine. Amino acids and proteins are considered in detail in Chapter 15.

Amides

Another important nitrogen-containing functional group is the **amide group**, which contains a nitrogen atom attached directly to a carbonyl group.

$$\underset{\text{Amide group}}{\overset{\displaystyle O}{\underset{|}{-\overset{\|}{C}-N-}}} \qquad \underset{}{\overset{\displaystyle O}{R-\overset{\|}{C}-NH_2}} \quad \underset{}{\overset{\displaystyle O}{R-\overset{\|}{C}-NHR'}} \quad \underset{\underset{R''}{|}}{\overset{\displaystyle O}{R-\overset{\|}{C}-N-R'}}$$

Amide group   Amides

Like those of other compounds that have $C{=}O$ groups, the formulas of amides are often written on one line.

$$RCONH_2 \qquad RCONHR' \qquad RCONR'R''$$

Note that urea (H_2NCONH_2), the compound that helped change the understanding of organic chemistry (page 250), is an amide.

Complex amides are of much greater interest than the simple ones considered here. Your body contains many kinds of proteins, all held together by amide linkages (Chapter 15). Nylon, silk, and wool molecules also contain hundreds of amide functional groups.

Names for simple amides are derived from those of the corresponding carboxylic acids. For example, $HCONH_2$ is formamide (IUPAC name, methanamide), and CH_3CONH_2 is acetamide (IUPAC name, ethanamide). Alternatively, we can also view amide names as based on those of alkanes, with the ending changed from *-e* to *-amide*. For example, $CH_3CH_2CH_2CH_2CONH_2$ is pentanamide.

CONCEPTUAL Example 9.12   Amine or Amide?

Which of the following compounds are amides and which are amines? Identify the functional groups.

  a. $CH_3CH_2CH_2NH_2$

  b. CH_3CONH_2

  c. $CH_3CH_2NHCH_3$

  d. $CH_3COCH_2CH_2NH_2$

Solution

  a. An amine: NH_2 is an amine group; there is no $C{=}O$ group.

  b. An amide: $CONH_2$ is the amide functional group.

  c. An amine: NH is an amine functional group.

  d. An amine: NH_2 is an amine functional group; there is a $C{=}O$ group, but the NH_2 is not attached to it.

■ EXERCISE 9.12

Which of the following compounds are amides and which are amines? Identify the functional groups.

  a. CH_3NHCH_3

  b. $CH_3CH_2COCH_2CH_2NHCH_3$

  c. $CH_3CH_2N(CH_3)_2$

  d. $CH_3CH_2CONHCH_2CH_3$

Heterocyclic Compounds: Alkaloids and Others

Cyclic hydrocarbons feature rings of carbon atoms. Now let's look at some compounds that have atoms other than carbon within the ring. These **heterocyclic compounds** usually have one or more nitrogen, oxygen, or sulfur atoms.

CONCEPTUAL Example 9.13 | Heterocyclic Compounds

Which of the following structures represent heterocyclic compounds?

O	S	CH₂	NH
CH₂—CH₂	CH₂—CH₂	CH₂—CH₂	CH₂—CH₂
(a)	(b)	(c)	(d)

Solution

Compounds a, b, and d have an oxygen, a sulfur, and a nitrogen atom, respectively, in a ring structure; these are heterocyclic compounds.

■ EXERCISE 9.13

Which of the following structures represent heterocyclic compounds?

(a)	(b)	(c)	(d)

Many amines, particularly heterocyclic ones, occur naturally in plants. Like other amines, these compounds are basic. They are called **alkaloids**, which means "like alkalis." Among the familiar alkaloids are morphine, caffeine, nicotine, and cocaine. The actions of these compounds as drugs are considered in Chapter 18.

Other important heterocyclic amines are pyrimidine, which has two nitrogen atoms in a six-membered ring, and purine, which has four nitrogen atoms in two rings that share a common side. Compounds related to pyrimidine and purine are constituents of nucleic acids (Chapter 16).

Pyrimidine   Purine

SELF-ASSESSMENT Questions

1. Which of the following is an amine attached to only one carbon group?
   a. dimethylamine
   b. ethyldimethylamine
   c. isopropylamine
   d. methylpropylamine

2. A name for $CH_3CH_2NHCH_3$ is
   a. butylamine
   b. ethylmethylamine
   c. propanamide
   d. propylamine

3. Which of the following amides is formed when ammonia reacts with acetic acid?
   a. CH_3CONH_2
   b. $CH_3CH_2CONH_2$
   c. $CH_3CH_2CH_2CONH_2$
   d. $C_6H_5CONH_2$

4. The amide functional group has a carbonyl group attached to
   a. an H atom
   b. an N atom
   c. an OH group
   d. two other C atoms

5. A cyclic organic compound that contains at least one atom that is not a carbon atom is called a(n)
   a. aromatic compound
   b. cyclic amide
   c. heterocyclic compound
   d. saturated compound

6. A basic organic heterocyclic compound that contains at least one nitrogen atom and is found in plants is called a(n)
   a. alkaloid
   b. amide
   c. cyclic ester
   d. phenol

GREEN CHEMISTRY

Principles **1, 3, 5, 6, 7**

Thomas E. Goodwin, *Hendrix College*

The Art of Organic Synthesis: Green Chemists Find a Better Way

Learning Objective › Identify greener solvents, use renewable resources in organic synthesis, and use efficient energy sources for chemical reactions.

At one time or another, most of us have taken medicines purchased over the counter or obtained by prescription. Many of these are synthetic drugs prepared by an organic chemist at a pharmaceutical company or in a research lab at a college or university, not compounds that occur in nature. These drugs are synthesized via chemical transformations that make more complicated organic compounds from simpler ones. (You will learn more about drugs in Chapter 18.)

Chemical reactions generally proceed faster when there is a higher chance for reacting molecules to collide, such as when they are in heated, homogeneous solutions. In the past, many reactions were carried out in nonrenewable, petroleum-based solvents such as hydrocarbons, chlorinated hydrocarbons, esters, ketones, and ethers (Sections 9.1, 9.3, and 9.5–9.7). These solvents are often flammable, toxic, or both and they present serious disposal problems. Using the Twelve Principles of Green Chemistry (inside front cover), chemists are now replacing these solvents with greener alternatives—or using no solvent at all. They also are seeking to improve the efficiency of reactions by reducing energy, time, and amounts of chemicals.

An increasing number of chemical reactions are run successfully in solvents from renewable resources or even without a solvent (Principle 5). Aqueous media have become popular because water is an ideal green solvent: cheap, abundant, and safe.

Unfortunately, many organic compounds are not very soluble in water. Solutions form readily when intermolecular forces in the solvent and solute are of similar strength (Section 6.4). Most organic compounds have relatively weak dispersion and dipole–dipole intermolecular forces, whereas water molecules are held together by a strong network of hydrogen bonds. Therefore, water molecules tend to associate with one another rather than exchanging some of their hydrogen bonds for weaker attractions to the nonpolar organic solutes.

Homogeneity is not always required, however. K. B. Sharpless (2001 Nobel Laureate) and his colleagues developed procedures in which the reactants are simply floated on the surface of water. In these "on water" reactions, rapid stirring produces suspensions of reactants with large surface contact areas that enhance reaction rates. Green benefits include reduced use of organic solvents, faster reaction times, and simplified isolation of hydrophobic products.

The EPA's Presidential Green Chemistry Challenge Awards recognize individuals, groups, and organizations that have developed chemical technologies that incorporate the principles of green chemistry. For example, the Pfizer pharmaceutical company developed an improved route to the antidepressant sertraline (Zoloft®) (Section 18.7). Four solvents (toluene, tetrahydrofuran, dichloromethane, and hexane) were replaced with ethanol (Section 9.5). In addition, overall solvent use was reduced from 60,000 gallons to 6,000

gallons per ton of sertraline. Another award winner, Life Technologies Corporation, developed the green organic chemistry necessary to synthesize deoxyribonucleotide triphosphates (see an analogous deoxyribonucleotide monophosphate in Example 16.4, Section 16.6). These nucleotide triphosphates are the building blocks that are used in the very important polymerase chain reaction (PCR) (see Section 16.8). Compared to previous syntheses, solvent use was reduced by 95% and other waste was reduced by 65%, resulting in a total savings of 1.5 million pounds of hazardous waste per year.

Green chemistry can also use microwaves to speed up reactions and reduce energy consumption. Microwaves are a form of electromagnetic radiation (Section 3.2) and are more energetic than radio waves but less energetic than X-rays (essay Section 11.1). In kitchen microwave ovens, the targets for microwave energy are the water, sugar, and fat molecules in food. Although home microwave ovens must not be used to carry out chemical reactions due to potential dangers, specially designed microwave ovens are available for laboratory use.

Additional innovations that can enhance organic chemistry reaction rates with greater energy efficiency include sonochemistry and mechanochemistry. Sonochemistry uses ultrasonic waves (ultrasound) to produce cavitation, a process that involves the creation of bubbles that collapse and liberate energy to drive chemical reactions. Mechanochemistry uses mechanical energy to carry out chemical reactions in the absence of a solvent. This can often be carried out on a small scale simply by grinding the solid reactants by hand using a mortar and pestle. The use of specially designed, automated ball mills is more efficient for larger scale or more difficult syntheses. Ball mills typically use stainless steel balls in a rotating cylinder to grind the reactants and enable the chemical reaction. In contrast to the mortar and pestle technique that derives energy from the chemist who does the grinding (that is, originally solar energy), ball mills require electricity. Their advantages, however, include the absence of solvents and, often, faster reactions than those using conventional energy sources.

Organic chemists today are actively designing ways to use greener solvents, renewable starting materials, and more energy-efficient techniques. These green chemistry innovations will provide sustainable solutions for us and for future generations.

▲ Proper application of green chemistry principles in the synthesis of Sertraline reduced the amount of solvents used by almost 90%!

SUMMARY

Section 9.1—**Organic chemistry** is the chemistry of carbon-containing compounds. More than 95% of all known compounds contain carbon. Carbon is unique in its ability to form long chains, rings, and branches. **Hydrocarbons** contain only carbon and hydrogen. One main class of hydrocarbons is **aliphatic compounds**. **Alkanes** are hydrocarbons that contain only single bonds; they have names ending in -ane. Alkanes are **saturated hydrocarbons** because each of their carbon atoms is bonded to the maximum number of hydrogen atoms. A **structural formula** shows which atoms are bonded to one another. A **condensed structural formula** omits the C—H bond lines and is easier to write. A larger straight-chain alkane can be generated by inserting a CH_2 unit into a given straight-chain alkane. A **homologous series** of such compounds has properties that vary in a regular and predictable manner. A member of a homologous series is called a *homolog*.

Alkanes with more than three carbon atoms have **isomers**, compounds with the same molecular formula but different structures. Alkanes are nonpolar and insoluble in water. They undergo few chemical reactions and are used mainly as fuels.

Cyclic hydrocarbons have one or more closed rings. Geometric figures often are used to represent such cyclic compounds: for example, a triangle for cyclopropane and a hexagon for cyclohexane.

An **alkene** is a hydrocarbon with at least one carbon–carbon double bond. Ethylene (CH_2=CH_2) is the simplest alkene and the most important one commercially. It is used to make polyethylene plastic and ethylene glycol. An **alkyne** is a hydrocarbon with at least one carbon-to-carbon triple bond. Acetylene (HC≡CH), the simplest alkyne, is used in welding torches and as a starting material for other chemical products. Alkenes and alkynes are **unsaturated hydrocarbons**, to which more hydrogen atoms can be added. They undergo **addition reactions** in which hydrogen or another small molecule adds to the double or triple bond. They can also add to one another to form polymers. **Geometric isomers** are versions of the molecule that have fixed rotation and result in unique versions of the molecule.

Section 9.2—Benzene (C_6H_6) can be drawn as though it has three double bonds, but its ring of carbon atoms has six pairs of bonding electrons between the carbon atoms, plus six unassigned electrons spread over the ring. Benzene and similar compounds with this type of stable ring structure are called **aromatic compounds**. Substituted benzenes have one or more H atoms replaced by another atom or group called a **substituent**. Aromatic hydrocarbons are used as solvents and fuels and to make other aromatic compounds.

Section 9.3—Chlorinated hydrocarbons are derived from hydrocarbons by replacing one or more hydrogen atoms with chlorine atom(s). Chlorofluorocarbons (CFCs) contain both chlorine and fluorine. Their use has been restricted because of their role in the depletion of the ozone layer. Perfluorinated compounds, in which all hydrogens have been replaced with fluorine, have important uses in plastics manufacture and in medicine.

Section 9.4—A **functional group** is an atom or group of atoms that confers characteristic properties to a family of organic compounds. Compounds with the same functional group undergo similar reactions and have similar properties. A functional group is often attached to an **alkyl group** (R—), an alkane with a hydrogen atom removed.

Section 9.5—A hydroxyl group (—OH) joined to an alkyl group produces an **alcohol (ROH)**. Methanol (CH_3OH), ethanol (CH_3CH_2OH), and 2-propanol [($CH_3)_2CHOH$] are well-known and widely used alcohols. Alcohols with more than one —OH group include ethylene glycol, used in antifreeze, and glycerol, used in skin lotions and as a food additive. A **phenol** is a compound with an —OH group attached to a benzene ring. Phenols are slightly acidic, and some are used as antiseptics.

An **ether** has two alkyl or aromatic groups attached to the same oxygen atom (ROR'). Ethers are used as solvents, and they can react slowly with oxygen to form explosive peroxides. Diethyl ether ($CH_3CH_2OCH_2CH_3$) is a commonly used solvent. Ethylene oxide is a cyclic ether used to make ethylene glycol and to sterilize instruments.

Section 9.6—An **aldehyde** contains a **carbonyl group** (C=O) with a hydrogen atom attached to the carbonyl carbon. A **ketone** has two carbon atoms attached to the carbonyl carbon. Formaldehyde is used in making plastics and as a preservative and a disinfectant. Benzaldehyde is a flavoring ingredient. Acetone, the simplest ketone, is a widely used solvent.

Section 9.7—A **carboxylic acid** has a **carboxyl group** (—COOH) as its functional group. Formic acid (HCOOH) is the acid in ant, bee, and wasp stings. Acetic acid (CH_3COOH) is the acid in vinegar. Butyric acid is the substance that gives rancid butter its odor. Carboxylic acid salts are used as food additives to prevent mold.

The structure of an **ester** (RCOOR') is similar to that of a carboxylic acid, with an alkyl group replacing the hydrogen atom of the carboxyl group. Esters are made by reaction of a carboxylic acid with an alcohol or phenol. They often have fruity or flowery odors and are used as flavorings and in perfumes.

Section 9.8—An **amine** is an organic derivative of ammonia in which one or more hydrogen atoms are replaced by alkyl or aromatic groups. Many amines consist of an alkyl group joined to an **amino group** (—NH_2). Like ammonia, amines are basic and often have strong odors. Amino acids, the building blocks of proteins, contain both amine and carboxylic acid functional groups. An **amide group** consists of a carbonyl group whose carbon atom is attached to a nitrogen atom. Proteins, nylon, silk, and wool contain amide groups.

A **heterocyclic compound** has one or more rings containing one or more nitrogen, sulfur, or oxygen atoms. **Alkaloids** are (usually heterocyclic) amines that occur naturally in plants and include morphine, caffeine, nicotine, and cocaine. Heterocyclic structures are constituents of DNA and RNA.

GREEN CHEMISTRY—Organic chemistry plays an important role in enhancing the quality of human life, such as in the preparation of new life-saving drugs. Organic chemists are designing ways to use greener solvents, renewable starting materials, and more energy-efficient techniques.

Learning Objectives

› Define *hydrocarbon*, and recognize structural features and properties of alkanes, alkenes, and alkynes.	Problems 1, 7, 8, 15, 16, 18, 20, 21, 53, 54
› Identify hydrocarbon molecules as alkanes, alkenes, or alkynes, and name them.	Problems 2, 3, 4, 17–26, 41–45, 46
› Define *aromatic compound*, and recognize the structural feature such compounds share.	Problems 5, 6
› Name simple aromatic hydrocarbons.	Problem 22
› Name a halogenated hydrocarbon given its formula, and write the formula for such a compound given its name.	Problem 52
› Classify an organic compound according to its functional group(s), and explain why the concept of a functional group is useful in the study of organic chemistry.	Problems 47–51, 62
› Recognize and write the formulas of simple alkyl groups.	Problems 25, 26
› Recognize the general structure and properties for an alcohol, a phenol, and an ether.	Problems 10, 11, 13, 30, 48, 56–59, 61, 63
› Name simple alcohols, phenols, and ethers.	Problems 9, 27–32
› Name simple aldehydes and ketones, and list their important properties.	Problems 33, 34, 55
› Name simple carboxylic acids and esters, and list their important properties.	Problems 12, 35–38
› Name and write the formulas of simple amines and amides.	Problems 39, 40
› Recognize a structure as that of a heterocyclic compound.	Problems 14, 49, 50
› Identify greener solvents, use renewable resources in organic synthesis, and use efficient energy sources for chemical reactions.	Problems 66–72

REVIEW QUESTIONS

1. List three characteristics of the carbon atom that make possible the existence of millions of organic compounds.

2. Define or give an example for each of the following terms.
   a. hydrocarbon   **b.** alkyne
   c. alkane   **d.** alkene

3. What are isomers? How are geometric isomers different from constitutional isomers?

4. What is an unsaturated hydrocarbon? Give examples of two types of unsaturated hydrocarbons.

5. What is the meaning of the circle inside the hexagon in the modern representation of the structure of benzene?

6. What is an aromatic hydrocarbon? How can you recognize an aromatic compound from its structure?

7. Which alkanes are gases at room temperature? Which are liquids? Which are solids? State your answers in terms of the number of carbon atoms per molecule.

8. Compare the densities of liquid alkanes with that of water. If you added octane to water in a beaker, what would you expect to observe?

9. What are the systematic names for the alcohols known by the following familiar names?
   a. grain alcohol
   b. rubbing alcohol
   c. wood alcohol

10. What are some of the long-term effects of excessive ethanol consumption?

11. State an important historical use of diethyl ether. What is its main use today?

12. How do carboxylic acids and esters differ in odor? In chemical structure?

13. For what family is each of the following the general formula?
   a. ROH   **b.** RCOR′
   c. RCOOR′   **d.** ROR′
   e. RCOOH   **f.** RCHO

14. What is an alkaloid? Name three common alkaloids.

 # PROBLEMS

Organic and Inorganic Compounds

15. Which of the following compounds are organic?
    a. $CH_3CH_2SCH_2CH_3$ **b.** H_2CrO_4
    c. $HONH_2$ **d.** $CH_3CH_2CCl_3$

16. Which of the following compounds are organic?
    a. $C_6H_{12}O$ **b.** H_2CS
    c. $KMnO_4$ **d.** $Co(NH_3)_6Cl_2$

Names and Formulas of Hydrocarbons

17. How many carbon atoms are there in a molecule of each of the following?
    a. hexane
    b. nonane
    c. cyclopentane
    d. 2-pentene

18. How many hydrogen atoms are there in a molecule of each of the following?
    a. ethane
    b. 1-butyne
    c. propene
    d. cyclooctane

19. The general formula for an alkane is given on page 252. Give the molecular formulas for the alkanes with (a) 8 carbon atoms and (b) 14 carbon atoms.

20. A particular alkyne has one triple bond and five carbon atoms. How many hydrogen atoms does it have?

21. Name the following hydrocarbons.
    a. $CH_3CH_2CH_2CH_3$
    b. $CH_2{=}CHCH_2CH_3$
    c. $HC{\equiv}CH$

22. Name the following hydrocarbons.

     a.   b.   c.

23. Write the molecular formulas and condensed structural formulas for (a) pentane and (b) decane.

24. Write the structural formulas for the four-carbon alkanes (C_4H_{10}). Identify butane and isobutane.

25. Name the following alkyl groups.
    a. $CH_3{-}$

    b. $CH_3CH_2\underset{\underset{\textstyle CH_3}{|}}{CH}{-}$

26. Name the following alkyl groups.
    a. $CH_3{-}\underset{\underset{\textstyle CH_3}{|}}{CH}{-}$

    b. $CH_3{-}\underset{\underset{\textstyle CH_3}{|}}{\overset{\overset{\textstyle CH_3}{|}}{C}}{-}$

Names and Formulas: Alcohols and Phenols

27. Give a structure to match the name or a name to match the structure for each of the following compounds.
    a. CH_3CH_2OH
    b. $CH_3CH_2CH_2OH$
    c. methanol
    d. 2-heptanol

28. Give a structure to match the name or a name to match the structure for each of the following compounds.
    a. $CH_3CH_2\underset{\underset{\textstyle OH}{|}}{CH}CH_3$

    b. $CH_3CH_2CH_2CH_2CH_2OH$
    c. sec-butyl alcohol
    d. isobutyl alcohol

29. Phenols and other aromatic compounds are often named by numbering the carbon atoms of the benzene ring, starting with the carbon atom bounded to the major functional group. (In a phenol, this group is the —OH group.) To

illustrate, the structure in Exercise 9.7d (page 269) is named 3-bromophenol. With this information, write the structures for (a) 2-methylphenol and (b) 4-iodophenol.

30. How do phenols differ from alcohols? How are they similar?

Names and Formulas: Ethers

31. Write the structure for each of the following.
    a. dipropyl ether   b. butyl ethyl ether

32. Write the structure for (a) methyl propyl ether, an anesthetic known as Neothyl, and (b) dimethyl ether, used as a compressed gas to "freeze" warts from the skin. What alcohol is an isomer of dimethyl ether?

Names and Formulas: Aldehydes and Ketones

33. Give a structure to match the name or a name to match the formula of each of the following compounds.
    a. butanone   b. formaldehyde

    c. $CH_3CH_2CH_2\overset{\overset{\textstyle O}{\|}}{C}{-}H$

    d.
    $CH_3CH_2{-}\overset{\overset{\textstyle O}{\|}}{C}{-}CH_2CH_2CH_2CH_3$

34. Give a structure to match the name or a name to match the formula of each of the following compounds.
    a. ethyl methyl ketone   b. propionaldehyde

    c. $CH_3CH_2{-}\overset{\overset{\textstyle O}{\|}}{C}{-}CH_2CH_3$

    d.
    $\underset{\text{(benzene ring)}}{}\overset{\overset{\textstyle O}{\|}}{C}{-}H$

Names and Formulas: Carboxylic Acids

35. Give a structure to match the name or a name to match the structure for each of the following compounds.
    a. CH_3CH_2COOH b. $CH_3CH_2CH_2CH_2COOH$
    c. formic acid   d. benzoic acid

36. Give a structure to match the name or a name to match the structure for each of the following compounds.
    a. CH_3COOH
    b. $CH_3CH_2CH_2CH_2CH_2COOH$
    c. butanoic acid
    d. chloroacetic acid [Hint: To what atom must the chlorine atom (chloro group) be attached?]

Names and Formulas: Esters

37. Give a structure to match the name or a name to match the structure for each of the following.
    a. methyl acetate   b. ethyl butyrate

    c. $CH_3CH_2\overset{\overset{\textstyle O}{\|}}{C}OCH_2CH_3$

38. Give a structure to match the name or a name to match the structure for each of the following.
    a. methyl butyrate   b. ethyl propionate

    c. $H{-}\overset{\overset{\textstyle O}{\|}}{C}{-}OCH_2CH_2CH_2CH_3$

Names and Formulas: Nitrogen-Containing Compounds

39. Give a structural formula to match the name or a name to match the structure for each of the following.
   a. triethylamine
   b. ethylmethylamine
   c. $CH_3CH_2CH_2NH_2$
   d. $CH_3CH_2NHCH_3$

40. Give a structural formula to match the name or a name to match the structure for each of the following.
   a. methylamine
   b. isopropylamine
   c. $CH_3CH_2NHCH_2CH_3$
   d.

Isomers and Homologs

41. Indicate whether the structures in each pair represent the same compound or isomers.
   a. CH_3CH_3 and $\overset{\overset{\textstyle CH_3}{|}}{CH_3}$

   b. $\underset{\overset{|}{CH_3}}{CH_3CH_2}$ and $CH_3CH_2CH_3$

   c. $\underset{\overset{|}{CH_3}}{CH_3CHCH_2CH_2CH_3}$ and $\underset{\overset{|}{CH_3}}{CH_3CH_2CHCH_3}$

42. Indicate whether the structures in each pair represent the same compound or isomers.
   a. $\underset{\overset{|}{CH_3}}{CH_3CHCH_2OH}$ and $\underset{\overset{|}{OH}}{CH_3CHCH_2CH_3}$

   b. $\underset{\overset{|}{NH_2}}{CH_3CHCH_2CH_3}$ and $\underset{\overset{|}{CH_3}}{CH_3CH_2CHNH_2}$

43. Classify the following pairs as homologs, the same compound, isomers, or none of these.
   a. $CH_3CH_2CH_3$ and $CH_3CH_2CH_2CH_3$
   b.
   $\begin{matrix} CH_2-CH_2 \\ | \qquad | \\ CH_2 \quad CH_2 \\ \diagdown \; \diagup \\ CH_2 \end{matrix}$ and $CH_3CH_2CH_2CH_2CH_3$

44. Classify the following pairs as homologs, the same compound, isomers, or none of these.
   a. $\underset{\overset{|}{CH_3}}{CH_3CHCH_2CH_2CH_3}$ and $\overset{\overset{\textstyle CH_3}{|}}{CH_3CH_2CH_2CHCH_3}$

   b. $\underset{\overset{|}{CH_3}}{CH_3CHCH=CH_2}$ and $\begin{matrix} CH_2-CH-CH_3 \\ | \qquad | \\ CH_2-CH_2 \end{matrix}$

Classification of Hydrocarbons

45. Indicate whether each of the following compounds is saturated or unsaturated. Classify each as an alkane, alkene, or alkyne.
   a. $\underset{\overset{|}{CH_3}}{CH_3C=CH_2}$
   b.

46. Indicate whether each of the following compounds is saturated or unsaturated. Classify each as an alkane, alkene, or alkyne.
   a. $CH_3-C\equiv C-CH_3$
   b.

Functional Groups

47. The sour taste of green (unripe) apples comes from malic acid. This acid is also used on salt-and-vinegar chips and in some candy for extreme tartness. What functional groups are present in the malic acid molecule?

48. Angelic acid is found in many plants, especially those of *Angelica* species. What functional groups are present in the angelic acid molecule?

Angelica hendersonii

49. Which of the following represents a heterocyclic compound? Classify each compound as an amine, ether, or cycloalkane.

   a. ⬜—NH

   b. ⬜—NH₂ (NH₂)

50. Which of the following represents a heterocyclic compound? Classify each compound as an amine, ether, or cycloalkane.

   a. ⬜—OCH₃

   b. (⬜—O)

ADDITIONAL PROBLEMS

51. The active constituent of fresh ginger is gingerol. When dried, gingerol is converted to shogaol, which is more pungent than gingerol. What are the molecular formulas for **(a)** gingerol and **(b)** shogaol? What functional groups are present in **(c)** gingerol and **(d)** shogaol? **(e)** What kind of reaction is involved in the conversion of gingerol to shogaol?

Gingerol

Shogaol

52. Noting the following color code for atoms—carbon (black), hydrogen (white), oxygen (red), nitrogen (blue), and chlorine (green)—write the structural and molecular formulas for the compounds whose models are shown here.

a.

b.

c.

d.

e.

53. As noted on page 257, alkenes and alkynes can add hydrogen to form alkanes. These addition reactions, called *hydrogenations*, are carried out using H_2 gas and a catalyst such as nickel or platinum. Write equations, using condensed structural formulas, for the complete hydrogenation of each of the following.

a. $CH_3CH_2C{\equiv}CCH_3$ **b.** $CH_3CH{=}CCH_2CH_2CH_2CH_3$
$\qquad\qquad\qquad\qquad\qquad\qquad\qquad\quad |$
$\qquad\qquad\qquad\qquad\qquad\qquad\qquad CH_3$

54. As exemplified by the reaction of ethylene on page 265, alkenes can add water to form alcohols. These addition reactions, called *hydrations*, are carried out using H_2O and an acid (H^+) as catalyst. Write an equation, using structural formulas, for the hydration of each of the following.

a.   **b.** $CH_3CH{=}CHCH_3$

55. As shown on page 271, alcohols can be oxidized to aldehydes and ketones. Write the structure of the alcohol that can be oxidized to each of the following.
a. $CH_3CH_2CH_2CHO$ **b.** $CH_3CH_2COCH_2CH_3$
c. $CH_3COCH(CH_3)_2$ **d.** C_6H_5CHO

56. Consider the following set of compounds. What concept does the set illustrate?

CH_3OH $\qquad\qquad\qquad$ CH_3CH_2OH
$CH_3CH_2CH_2OH$ $\qquad$ $CH_3CH_2CH_2\,CH_2\,OH$

57. Consider the following set of compounds. What concept does the set illustrate?

$CH_3CH_2CH_2CH_2OH$ $\qquad\qquad$ $CH_3CH_2OCH_2CH_3$
CH_3CHCH_2OH $\qquad\qquad\qquad$ CH_3CHOCH_3
$\quad\; |$ $\qquad\qquad\qquad\qquad\qquad\qquad\quad |$
$\quad CH_3$ $\qquad\qquad\qquad\qquad\qquad\qquad CH_3$

58. Methanol is a possible replacement for gasoline. The complete combustion of methanol forms carbon dioxide and water.
$$CH_3OH + O_2 \longrightarrow CO_2 + H_2O$$
Balance the equation. What mass of carbon dioxide is formed by the complete combustion of 775 g of methanol?

59. Water adds to ethylene to form ethyl alcohol.
$$CH_2{=}CH_2 + H_2O \xrightarrow{\;H^+\;} CH_3CH_2OH$$
Balance the equation. What mass of ethyl alcohol is formed by the addition reaction of water and 445 g of ethylene?

60. Referring to Table 9.7, give the name and condensed structural formula of **(a)** the alcohol and the carboxylic acid that would be needed to make pineapple flavoring and **(b)** the alcohol and the carboxylic acid that would be needed to make apricot flavoring.

61. Refer back to Section 6.3. Describe the type of intermolecular forces that exist **(a)** between dimethyl ether molecules and **(b)** between ethanol molecules. Use this information to explain why ethanol is a liquid at room temperature but dimethyl ether is a gas.

62. Diacetyl (CH_3COCOH_3) is an additive used to impart buttery flavor to popcorn. Popcorn-factory workers exposed to high levels of diacetyl may develop a characteristic lung disease. What functional group is present in diacetyl?

63. Hydroquinone ($HO{-}C_6H_4{-}OH$), a phenol with two hydroxyl groups in the 1 and 4 (or *para*) positions on the ring, is commonly used as a developer in black and white photography. **(a)** Write the structural formula for hydroquinone. (*Hint*: See Figure 9.10.) **(b)** In the developing process, hydroquinone is oxidized to *para*-benzoquinone ($C_6H_4O_2$), a compound that is not aromatic and has two ketone functions. Write the structural formula for *para*-benzoquinone.

64. Using data from Table 9.3, a printed reference such as the *CRC Handbook* or the *Merck Index*, or an online source such as the website of the National Institutes for Standards and Technology (NIST), state which of each pair of isomers boils at a lower temperature.
    a. hexane or 2,3-dimethylbutane
    b. pentane or neopentane (2,2-dimethylpropane)
    c. heptane or 2,4-dimethylpentane
    d. octane or 2,2,4-trimethylpentane

    Use this information to form a generalization about the boiling points of branched-chain versus straight-chain alkanes.

65. Use the ideal gas law to determine the densities in grams per milliliter of the first four alkanes in Table 9.3 at 1.00 atm and 20.0 °C. (*Hint*: Begin with one mole of each gas.) Suggest a more appropriate unit for expressing these densities.

66. Give three reasons why water is often considered to be a green solvent for organic synthesis.

67. Which of the following is a potential drawback to using water as a solvent for organic synthesis?
    a. Water is derived from fossil fuels.
    b. Many organic molecules have limited solubility in water.
    c. The intermolecular forces in water are similar to those in most organic solvents.
    d. Reaction rates are always slower in water.

68. In an "on water" reaction:
    a. Reactants are floated on water.
    b. Rapid stirring leads to large surface contact areas.
    c. Reactions often occur faster than if the reactants were dissolved in an organic solvent.
    d. Insoluble products can be separated easily.
    e. All of the above are true.

69. Identify two aspects of the new synthesis of sertraline that make it greener than the traditional process.

70. Why is the improved synthesis of nucleotide triphosphates more environmentally benign?

71. What advantage does microwave heating provide in carrying out chemical reactions? Why does it have this advantage?

72. Name two advantages that sonochemistry and mechanochemistry have over conventional methods of organic synthesis.

CRITICAL THINKING EXERCISES

Apply knowledge that you have gained in this chapter and one or more of the FLaReS principles (Chapter 1) to evaluate the following statements or claims.

9.1. A television advertisement claims that gasoline with added ethanol burns more cleanly than gasoline without added ethanol.

9.2. A news feature states that herbal remedies are more effective than those produced in the laboratory because they contain fewer harmful chemicals.

9.3. An environmental activist states that all toxic chemicals should be banned from the home.

9.4. An advertisement claims that synthetic amino acid additives in foods are less beneficial than amino acids made by living organisms because they don't contain a life force.

9.5. A Web page claims that acetylsalicylic acid (aspirin), polyester plastics, and polystyrene plastics are all carcinogens (cancer-causing agents). The reason given is that all three contain benzene rings in their structures, and benzene is a carcinogen.

9.6. A television program suggests that life on a distant planet could be based on silicon instead of carbon, because silicon (like carbon) tends to form four bonds. The narrator of the program proposes that long protein molecules and DNA molecules could be based on silicon chains.

COLLABORATIVE GROUP PROJECTS

Prepare a PowerPoint, poster, or other presentation (as directed by your instructor) to share with the class.

1. The theory that organic chemistry was the chemistry of living organisms, which was overturned by Wöhler's discovery in 1828, was known as *vitalism*. Search the Internet for information about this theory. What was the effect of this philosophy on areas outside chemistry?

2. Many organic molecules contain more than one functional group. Look up the structural formula for each of the following in this text (use the index), by searching online, or in a reference work such as the *Merck Index*. Identify and name the functional groups in each.
    a. butesin   b. estrone
    c. tyrosine   d. morphine
    e. eugenol   f. methyl anthranilate

3. Prepare a brief report on one of the alcohols with three or more carbon atoms per molecule. List sources and commercial uses.

4. Prepare a brief report on one of the carboxylic acids with three or more carbon atoms per molecule. List sources and commercial uses.

5. Consider the series of compounds methane (CH_4), chloromethane (CH_3Cl), dichloromethane (CH_2Cl_2), trichloromethane ($CHCl_3$), and tetrachloromethane (CCl_4). Repeat parts (a) through (e) of Problem 49 (Chapter 6) for these compounds. Boiling points may be found in a printed reference such as the *CRC Handbook* or the *Merck Index* or on a Website such as that of the National Institutes for Standards and Technology (NIST). Use intermolecular forces to explain any deviation in the relationship between molar mass and boiling point.

6. Referring to the graph from Problem 49 (Chapter 6), use the molar mass to estimate boiling points for (a) acetic acid (CH_3COOH), (b) acetone (CH_3COCH_3), (c) ethanol (CH_3CH_2OH), (d) hexane ($CH_3CH_2CH_2CH_2CH_2CH_3$) and (e) methyl acetate (CH_3COOCH_3). Compare the values obtained from the graph with the actual boiling points. Is molar mass alone a good predictor of boiling point? Explain.

CHEMISTRY @ HOME Saturate This!

Materials required

- Tincture of iodine, 2% (hint: Do not buy the colorless tincture of iodine. You will need the colored solution.)
- Tablespoon
- Small clear plastic cups
- Shallow pan with warm water
- Safflower oil
- Peanut oil
- Sesame oil (hint: Use the lighter cold-pressed oil rather than toasted sesame oil.)

Why are saturated fats not good for your health? Why do doctors recommend unsaturated fats? How can you tell the difference?

Let's put your knowledge of saturated and unsaturated fats to the test. The terms *saturated and unsaturated* are often used when discussing fats and oils. There are many recommendations to avoid saturated fats because they contribute to "bad" cholesterol that clogs arteries in our bodies. Unsaturated fats are the "healthier" fats that contribute to "good" cholesterol levels. What is the difference?

Fats are made up of triglycerides, which are triesters of glycerol and long-chain fatty acids (hydrocarbon chains with a carboxylic acid on one end). Remember that saturated fatty acids do not have any double bonds and are therefore able to pack together closely with the long hydrocarbon chains, which results in them being solid at room temperature, contributing to "bad" cholesterol. Unsaturated fatty acids have one or more double bonds and do not pack as easily due to the presence of the double bonds, which results in the fats typically being liquid at room temperature. The double bonds create a "kink" in the structure, which disrupts the stacking (figure 1).

saturated

mono-unsaturated

poly-unsaturated

In this experiment, you will determine the degree of unsaturation of the fatty acid hydrocarbon chains by doing a simple experiment with iodine. Carbon–carbon double bonds will react with iodine to produce a diiodide product (figure 2). The iodine is a red-violet color (often looking brown), and the product is colorless. This test is commonly used to determine the degree of unsaturation of a triglyceride and is called the iodine number, which is the grams

colored   colorless

of iodine that will react with 100 grams of the triglyceride. The larger the value, the greater the unsaturation of the triglyceride (and the greater the number of carbon–carbon double bonds). A light color confirms unsaturation.

For this experiment, gather the following vegetable oils that will be used to determine which one has the greatest amount of unsaturation: safflower oil, peanut oil, and sesame oil.

Begin by measuring one tablespoon of each vegetable oil into the small cups (one oil in each) and label appropriately. Place 2–3 drops of the tincture of iodine in each of the oils and gently swirl. Write down any initial observations about the color of each oil solution.

Place the oil solutions in a shallow pan filled with warm tap water to speed up the reaction. The iodine solution will not dissolve in water initially, so be sure to gently swirl the solutions occasionally as you are observing the reaction.

Observe the oil solutions over 10 minutes and note any color changes. What can you conclude about the degree of unsaturation of each oil? Compare the final colors of the oils to the original colors of the oils to observe the overall color change.

Questions

1. Look up the amount of saturated versus unsaturated fats in each of the three oils. Does this help to explain the color differences?

2. What would you expect the degree of unsaturation to be for animal fats in relation to the oils that you tested? (Hint: They are solid at room temperature.)

3. What is the structural difference in *cis* versus *trans* fats? What is it about the structure of *trans* fats that make them contribute to increasing the levels of bad cholesterol in our bodies?

POLYMERS

Have You Ever Wondered?

1. **Are all polymers synthetic?**

2. **Why is it important to recycle plastics?**

3. **Are there polymers in chewing gum?**

4. **Why can silicone be used for flexible baking pans?**

5. **What fabrics are made from natural polymers?**

Learning Objectives

> Define *polymer* and *monomer*. (10.1)

> List several natural polymers including a chemically modified one. (10.1)

> Describe the structure and properties of the two main types of polyethylene. (10.2)

> Use the terms *thermoplastic* and *thermosetting* to explain how polymer structure determines properties. (10.2)

> Identify the monomer(s) of an addition polymer, and write the structural formula for a polymer from its monomer structure(s). (10.3)

> Define *cross-linking* and explain how it changes the properties of a polymer. (10.4)

> Differentiate between addition and condensation polymerization. (10.5)

> Write the structures of the monomers that form polyesters and polyamides. (10.5)

> Understand the concept of the glass transition temperature. (10.6)

> Explain how crystallinity affects the physical properties of polymers. (10.6)

> Describe the environmental problems associated with plastics and plasticizers. (10.7)

> Name two types of sustainable, nonpetroleum-derived polymers and give their sources. (10.7)

> Explain how life-cycle impact analysis can be used to identify the environmental benefits and effects of newly designed products.

GIANTS AMONG MOLECULES Look around you.

Polymers are everywhere. Carpets, curtains, upholstery, towels, sheets, floor tile, books, furniture, most toys and containers (not to mention such things as telephones, toothbrushes, and piano keys), and even your clothes are made of polymers. Your car's dashboard, seats, tires, steering wheel, floor mats, and many parts that you cannot see are made of polymers. Much of the food you eat contains polymers, and many vital molecules in your body are polymers. You couldn't live without them. Some of the polymers that permeate our lives come from nature, but many are synthetic. Like other synthetic chemical compounds, they are made in chemical plants in an attempt to improve on nature in some way.

Plastics—synthetic polymers—are used in most consumer items, including bottles, telephones, calculators, computers, cooking utensils, wire insulation, sunglasses, pens, and most types of packaging. The source of most of these polymers is crude oil, of which there is a limited supply. This means that it is important to recycle these polymers when possible. The bales of plastics shown above are ready to go to the recycling center, where they may be used directly to make toys, pipes, or building materials. Or the recycled material may be converted to shreds or beads of plastic (left) that can be used by molding machines. In this chapter, we examine how polymers are made, review their useful properties, and explain why they have those properties.

▲ Cotton is nearly pure cellulose, a natural polymer of the simple sugar glucose.

1. Are all polymers synthetic?

No. The total weight of natural polymers on Earth's surface far exceeds the weight of synthetic polymers. Starches, proteins, cellulose, latex, DNA, and RNA all are natural polymers.

10.1 Polymerization: Making Big Ones Out of Little Ones

Learning Objectives   ❯ Define *polymer* and *monomer*.   ❯ List several natural polymers, including a chemically modified one.

Polymers make up *macromolecules* (from the Greek *makros*, meaning "large" or "long"). Macromolecules are not very large (in fact, most such "giant" molecules are invisible to the human eye), but compared to other molecules, they are enormous.

A **polymer** (from the Greek *poly*, meaning "many," and *meros*, meaning "part") is made from much smaller molecules called *monomers* (from the Greek *monos*, meaning "one"). Hundreds, even thousands, of monomer units combine to make one polymer molecule. A **monomer** is a small-molecule building block from which a polymer is made. These monomers generally have a functional group, or groups, that allow for multiple reactions that link the units. The process by which monomers are converted to polymers is called *polymerization*. A polymer is as different from its monomer as a long strand of spaghetti is from tiny specks of flour. For example, polyethylene, the familiar waxy material used to make plastic bags, is made from the monomer ethylene, a gas.

Natural Polymers

Polymers have served humanity for centuries in the starches and proteins in our food, in the wood we use for shelter, and in the wool, cotton, and silk we make into clothing. Starch is a polymer made up of glucose ($C_6H_{12}O_6$, a simple sugar) units. Cotton is made of cellulose, also a glucose polymer; and wood is largely cellulose as well. Proteins are polymers made up of amino-acid monomers. Wool and silk are two of the thousands of different kinds of proteins found in nature.

Living things could not exist without polymers. Each plant and animal requires many different specific types of polymers. Probably the most amazing natural polymers are nucleic acids, which carry the coded genetic information that makes each individual unique. The polymers found in nature are discussed in Chapter 15. Some polymers are found in nature. In this chapter text, we focus mainly on macromolecules made in the laboratory.

Celluloid: Billiard Balls and Collars

The earliest synthetic attempt to improve on natural polymers involved chemical modification of a common macromolecule. The semisynthetic material **celluloid** was derived from natural cellulose (from cotton and wood, for example). When cellulose is treated with nitric acid, a derivative called *cellulose nitrate* is formed.

In response to a contest to find a substitute for ivory to use in billiard balls, American inventor John Wesley Hyatt (1837–1920) found a way to soften cellulose nitrate by treating it with ethyl alcohol and camphor. The softened material could be molded into smooth, hard balls. Thus, Hyatt brought the game of billiards within the economic reach of more people—and saved a number of elephants. Celluloid was widely used as a substitute for more expensive substances such as ivory, amber, and tortoiseshell.

The movie industry was once known as the "celluloid industry." Celluloid was used in movie film and also for stiff shirt collars (which didn't require laundering and repeated starching). Unfortunately, the cellulose nitrate material is highly flammable (cellulose nitrate is also used as smokeless gunpowder), and as it becomes older, it starts to decompose, becoming even more likely to explode. The 1988 Italian movie *Cinema Paradiso* shows the evolution of film technology and includes a scene in which the heat from a bulb in the movie projector ignites film that becomes stuck in the projector. Celluloid was removed from the market when safer substitutes became available. Today, movie film is made mainly from polyethylene terephthalate, a polyester (Section 10.5). And high, stiff collars on men's shirts are out of fashion.

It didn't take long for the chemical industry to recognize the potential of synthetic polymers. Scientists found ways to make macromolecules from small molecules rather than simply modifying large ones. The first such truly synthetic polymers were phenol–formaldehyde resins (such as Bakelite), first made in 1909. These complex polymers are discussed in Section 10.5. We'll look at some simpler ones next.

SELF-ASSESSMENT Questions

1. A cellulose is an example of a(n)
   a. fat   **b.** isomer   **c.** monomer   **d.** polymer

2. Which is *not* a polymer?
   a. celluloid   **b.** glucose   **c.** silk   **d.** wool

3. The first semisynthetic polymer was made from a natural polymer. It was
   a. Bakelite, based on bacon grease
   b. celluloid, based on cellulose from cotton
   c. polypropylene, based on isopropyl alcohol
   d. polypantene, based on human hair

4. The first truly synthetic polymer was
   a. Bakelite, made from phenol and formaldehyde
   b. cellulose, made from glucose
   c. polyethylene, made from ethanol
   d. rubber, made from isoprene

Answers: 1, d; 2, b; 3, b; 4, a

10.2 Polyethylene: From the Battle of Britain to Bread Bags

Learning Objectives › Describe the structure and properties of the two main types of polyethylene. › Use the terms *thermoplastic* and *thermosetting* to explain how polymer structure determines properties.

The prevalent plastic *polyethylene* is the simplest and least expensive synthetic polymer. It is familiar to us in the form of plastic bags used for packaging fruit and vegetables, garment bags for dry-cleaned clothing, garbage-can liners, and many other items. Polyethylene is made from ethylene ($CH_2{=}CH_2$), an unsaturated hydrocarbon (Chapter 9). Ethylene is produced in large quantities from the cracking of petroleum, a process by which large hydrocarbon molecules are broken down into simpler hydrocarbons.

With pressure and heat and in the presence of a catalyst, ethylene monomers join together in long chains.

$$\cdots + \underset{\underset{\displaystyle H}{|}}{\overset{\overset{\displaystyle H}{|}}{C}}{=}\underset{\underset{\displaystyle H}{|}}{\overset{\overset{\displaystyle H}{|}}{C} + \cdots \longrightarrow {\sim}\overset{}{C}{-}\overset{}{C}{-}\overset{}{C}{-}\overset{}{C}{-}\overset{}{C}{-}\overset{}{C}{-}\overset{}{C}{-}\overset{}{C}{\sim}}$$

Using condensed formulas, this becomes

$$\cdots + CH_2{=}CH_2 + CH_2{=}CH_2 + CH_2{=}CH_2 + CH_2{=}CH_2 + \cdots \longrightarrow {\sim}CH_2CH_2CH_2CH_2CH_2CH_2CH_2CH_2{\sim}$$

Such equations can be tedious to draw, so we often use abbreviated forms like these:

$$n\,\underset{\underset{\displaystyle H}{|}}{\overset{\overset{\displaystyle H}{|}}{C}}{=}\underset{\underset{\displaystyle H}{|}}{\overset{\overset{\displaystyle H}{|}}{C}} \longrightarrow \left[\!\!\begin{array}{c} \overset{\displaystyle H}{|} \ \ \overset{\displaystyle H}{|} \\ {-}C{-}C{-} \\ \underset{\displaystyle H}{|} \ \ \underset{\displaystyle H}{|} \end{array}\!\!\right]_n$$

or

$$n\,CH_2{=}CH_2 \longrightarrow {+}CH_2CH_2{+}_n$$

The ellipses (. . .) and tildes (~) serve as *et ceteras*; they indicate, respectively, that the number of monomers is greater than the four shown and that the polymer structure extends for many more units in each direction. The molecular fragment within square brackets is called the *repeat unit* of the polymer. In the formula for the polymeric product, the repeat unit is placed within brackets with bonds extending to both sides. The subscript n indicates that this unit is repeated many times (n in the equation above) in the full polymer structure.

The simplicity of the abbreviated formulas facilitates certain comparisons between the monomer and the polymer. Note that the monomer ethylene contains a double bond and polyethylene does not. The double bond of the reactant consists of two shared pairs of electrons. One of these pairs is used to connect one monomer unit to the next in the polymer (indicated by the lines sticking out to the sides in the repeat unit). This leaves only a single pair of electrons—a single bond—between the two carbon atoms of the repeat unit. Note also that each repeat unit in the polymer has the same composition (C_2H_4) as the monomer.

Molecular models provide three-dimensional representations. Figure 10.1 presents models of a tiny part of a very long polyethylene molecule, whose number of carbon atoms can vary from a few hundred to several thousand.

► **Figure 10.1** Ball-and-stick (a) and space-filling (b) models of a short segment of a polyethylene molecule.

(a)

(b)

2. Why is it important to recycle plastics?

Polyethylene and most other polymers are made of petroleum. Since our supply of petroleum is limited, from a sustainability standpoint, we can make the best use of that resource by reusing those polymers. Most plastic items are imprinted with a code number so that they can be sorted for recycling.

Polyethylene was invented shortly before the start of World War II. It proved to be tough and flexible, excellent as an electric insulator, and able to withstand both high and low temperatures. Prior to the use of polyethylene, wires were insulated using a cotton braid weave coated with rubber (both natural polymers). This material was much more susceptible to temperature changes. Polyethylene was used for insulating cables in radar equipment, a top-secret invention that helped British pilots detect enemy aircraft before the aircraft could be spotted visually. Without polyethylene, the British could not have had effective radar, and without radar, the Battle of Britain might have been lost. The invention of this simple plastic helped change the course of history.

Types of Polyethylene

Today, there are three main kinds of polyethylene. *High-density polyethylene* (*HDPE*) has mostly linear molecules that pack closely together and can assume a fairly well-ordered, crystalline structure. HDPEs therefore are rather rigid and have good tensile strength. As the name implies, the densities of HDPEs (0.94–0.96 g/cm^3) are high compared to those of other polyethylenes. HDPEs are used for such items as threaded bottle caps, toys, bottles, and milk jugs.

The Many Forms of Carbon

In many of the smaller molecules that we studied in Chapter 9 and the macromolecules that we encounter here, carbon atoms are bonded to other atoms, especially hydrogen. Carbon atoms alone can form a variety of interesting structures, however, some of which have been known since ancient times. Diamond is pure crystalline carbon, in which each atom is bonded to four other atoms. In graphite, the black material of pencil lead, each carbon atom is bonded to three others. But the most intriguing forms of carbon were discovered only in the last few decades.

Andre Geim and Konstantin Novoselov of the University of Manchester, United Kingdom, used adhesive tape to lift one-atom-thick planar sheets of carbon atoms from graphite. The material, called *graphene*, is like molecular-scale chicken wire made of carbon atoms. Graphene has properties that make it suitable for applications in electronics, sensing devices, and touch screens and for fundamental studies of electron flow in two-dimensional materials. Geim and Novoselov were awarded the 2010 Nobel Prize in Physics for their work on graphene.

Graphite is composed of many stacked graphene layers. A stack of 3 million graphene sheets would be only a millimeter thick. Graphene can also be thought of as an extremely large aromatic molecule, a system of fused benzene rings.

Many other structures are formed exclusively of carbon atoms. The tube-shaped carbon molecule called a *nanotube* can be visualized as a sheet of graphene rolled into a hollow cylinder. Nanotubes have unusual mechanical and electrical properties. They are good conductors of heat, and they are among the strongest and stiffest materials known.

Yet another structure consisting only of carbon is a roughly spherical collection of hexagons and pentagons like the pattern on a soccer ball. This carbon molecule has the formula C_{60}. Because it resembles the geodesic-dome structures pioneered by architect R. Buckminster Fuller, the molecule is called *buckminsterfullerene*. The general name *fullerenes* is used for C_{60} and similar molecules with formulas such as C_{70}, C_{74}, and C_{82}, which are often colloquially referred to as "buckyballs." These materials have enormous potential in basic studies as well as in applied research. In the field of materials science, research is being done on polymers of carbon nanotubes as a type of radiation shielding for aerospace applications.

(a) (b) (c)

(d) (e)

▲ Different forms of carbon have dramatically different properties. (a) Diamond is hard and transparent. (b) Graphite is soft, gray, and conducts electricity. (c) Graphene is a single layer of graphite. (d) Rolling a sheet of graphene into a cylinder makes a carbon nanotube, the strongest material known. (e) Buckminsterfullerene, a C_{60} molecule, resembles a soccer ball.

▲ **Figure 10.2** Two bottles, both made of polyethylene, were heated in the same oven for the same length of time.

Q: *Which of these bottles is made of HDPE and which of LDPE? Explain.*

It DOES Matter!

Polyethylene with a molecular mass from 2 to 6 million, called *ultra-high-molecular-weight polyethylene (UHMWPE)*, is used to make fibers 10 times stronger than steel and around 40% stronger than Kevlar (see Problem 30 on page 312) for use in body armor. Most modern skis are coated with UHMWPE on the bottom surface.

Low-density polyethylene (LDPE), on the other hand, has many side chains branching off the polymer molecules. The branches prevent the molecules from packing closely together and assuming a crystalline structure. LDPEs are waxy, bendable plastics that have lower densities (0.91–0.94 g/cm³) and are lower melting than high-density polyethylenes. Objects made of HDPE hold their shape in boiling water, whereas those made of LDPE are severely deformed (Figure 10.2). LDPEs are used to make plastic bags, plastic film, squeeze bottles, electric wire insulation, and many common household products for which flexibility is important.

The third type of polyethylene, called *linear low-density polyethylene* (LLDPE), is actually a **copolymer**, a polymer formed from two (or more) different monomers. LLDPEs are made by polymerizing ethylene with a branched-chain alkene such as 4-methyl-1-pentene.

$$n\ CH_2{=}CH_2 + m\ CH_2{=}\underset{\displaystyle CH_3-CH-CH_3}{\overset{\displaystyle |}{\underset{|}{CH}}}\underset{CH_2} \longrightarrow \left[CH_2-CH_2\right]_n \left[\underset{CH_3-CH-CH_3}{\overset{|}{\underset{|}{CH_2-CH}}}\right]_m$$

Ethylene   4-Methyl-1-pentene   An LLDPE

LLDPEs are used to make such things as plastic films for use as landfill liners, trash cans, tubing, and automotive parts.

Thermoplastic and Thermosetting Polymers

Polyethylene is one of a variety of thermoplastic polymers. Because its molecules can slide past one another when heat and pressure are applied, a **thermoplastic polymer** can be softened and then reshaped. It can be repeatedly melted down and remolded. Total annual production of thermoplastic polymers in the United States is about 40 billion kg, of which 17 billion kg is polyethylene.

Not all polymers can be readily melted. About 180 billion kg of various plastics and 22 billion kg of rubber are manufactured globally each year. About 12% of U.S. production of polymers consists of *thermosetting polymers*, which harden permanently when formed. They cannot be softened by heat and remolded. Instead, strong heating causes them to discolor and decompose. The permanent hardness of thermosetting plastics is due to cross-linking (side-to-side connection) of the polymer chains, which we'll discuss later in this chapter.

SELF-ASSESSMENT Questions

1. Each building-block molecule that joins to form a polymer is called a
   a. cross-link   **b.** monomer   **c.** polymer   **d.** polypeptide

2. Compared to HDPE, LDPE has a lower melting point because it
   a. is made from fewer polar monomers
   b. is composed of molecules with a much lower molecular mass
   c. has fewer cross-links
   d. has more branches in its molecules, preventing them from packing closely

3. Which of the following is made of polyethylene?
   a. pre-1900 electrical wire insulation
   b. foamed coffee cups
   c. plastic grocery bags
   d. plastic plumbing pipes

4. A copolymer is made
   a. by blending two simple polymers
   b. from cobalt and an alkene
   c. from two identical monomers
   d. from two different monomers

5. A polymer that cannot be melted and reshaped is said to be
   a. highly crystalline   **b.** rubbery
   c. thermoplastic   **d.** thermosetting

6. A buckyball is a
   a. large carbon molecule (C_{60})
   b. carbon nanotube wound up like a ball of string
   c. long polymer molecule wound up like a ball of string
   d. circular ring of carbon atoms

Answers: 1, b; 2, d; 3, c; 4, d; 5, d; 6, a

10.3 Addition Polymerization: One + One + One + ··· Gives One!

Learning Objective > Identify the monomer(s) of an addition polymer, and write the structural formula for a polymer from its monomer structure(s).

There are two general types of polymerization reactions: addition polymerization and condensation polymerization. In **addition polymerization** (also called *chain-reaction polymerization*), the monomer molecules add to one another in such a way that the polymeric product contains all the atoms of the starting monomers. The polymerization of ethylene to form polyethylene is an example. In polyethylene, as we noted in Section 10.2, the two carbon atoms and the four hydrogen atoms of each monomer molecule are incorporated into the polymer structure. In *condensation polymerization* (Section 10.5), some part of each monomer molecule is not incorporated in the final polymer.

Polypropylene

Most of the many familiar addition polymers are made from derivatives of ethylene in which one or more of the hydrogen atoms are replaced by another atom or group. Replacing one of the hydrogen atoms with a methyl group gives the monomer propylene (propene). Polypropylene molecules look much like polyethylene's molecules, except that there is a methyl group ($—CH_3$) attached to every other carbon atom.

$$\sim CH_2-CH-CH_2-CH-CH_2-CH-CH_2-CH\sim \quad \text{or} \quad \left[CH_2-CH\right]_n$$
$$\underset{CH_3}{}\quad\underset{CH_3}{}\quad\underset{CH_3}{}\quad\underset{CH_3}{}\qquad\qquad\underset{CH_3}{}$$

Polypropylene

The chain of carbon atoms is called the polymer *backbone*. Groups attached to the backbone, such as the CH_3 groups of polypropylene, are called *pendant groups*, shown in green.

Polypropylene is a tough plastic material that resists moisture, oils, and solvents. It is molded into hard-shell luggage, battery cases, and various kinds of appliance parts. It is also used to make packaging material, fibers for textiles such as upholstery fabrics and carpets, and ropes that float. Because of polypropylene's high melting point (121 °C), objects made of it can be sterilized with steam.

Polystyrene

Replacing one of the hydrogen atoms in ethylene with a benzene ring gives a monomer called *styrene*, which has the formula $C_6H_5CH=CH_2$, where C_6H_5 represents the benzene ring. Polymerization of styrene produces polystyrene, which has benzene rings as pendant groups, shown in green.

$$CH_2=CH \qquad \sim CH_2CH-CH_2CH-CH_2CH-CH_2CH\sim$$

Styrene   Polystyrene

Polystyrene is the plastic used to make transparent disposable drinking cups. With color and filler added, it is the material of thousands of inexpensive toys and household items. When a gas is blown into polystyrene liquid, it foams and hardens into the familiar material (called Styrofoam®) of ice chests and disposable coffee cups. The polymer can easily be formed into shapes as packing material for shipping instruments and appliances, and it is widely used for home insulation. Unfortunately, it is also one of the materials that most often gets discarded. Americans throw away about 25 billion coffee cups made of polystyrene foam each year.

▲ Styrofoam insulation saves energy by reducing the transfer of heat from the warm interior of a house to the outside in winter and from the hot outside to the cooled interior in summer.

▶ Some furniture, window sashes, house trim, and waterproof clothing are made from PVC. PVC can also be coated onto copper wire for insulation, made into colorful resilient flooring, or formed into many other familiar consumer products.

Vinyl Polymers

Would you like a tough synthetic material that looks like leather at a fraction of the cost? Perhaps a clear, rigid material from which unbreakable bottles could be made? Do you need an attractive, long-lasting floor covering? Or lightweight, rustproof, easy-to-connect plumbing? Polyvinyl chloride (PVC) has all these properties—and more.

Replacing one of the hydrogen atoms of ethylene with a chlorine atom gives vinyl chloride ($CH_2{=}CHCl$), a compound that is a gas at room temperature. Polymerization of vinyl chloride yields the tough thermoplastic material PVC. A segment of the PVC molecule is shown below.

$$\sim CH_2CH-CH_2CH-CH_2CH-CH_2CH\sim$$
$$\qquad | \qquad\quad | \qquad\quad | \qquad\quad |$$
$$\qquad Cl \qquad\quad Cl \qquad\quad Cl \qquad\quad Cl$$

Polyvinyl chloride (PVC)

PVC is readily formed into various shapes. The clear, transparent polymer is used in plastic wrap and clear plastic bottles. Adding color and other ingredients to a vinyl plastic yields artificial leather. Most floor tile and shower curtains are made from vinyl plastics, which are also widely used to simulate wood in home siding panels and window frames. About 40% of the PVC produced is molded into pipes.

Vinyl chloride, the monomer from which vinyl plastics are made, is a carcinogen. Several people who worked closely with this gas later developed a kind of cancer called *angiosarcoma*. (Carcinogens are discussed in Chapter 22.)

PTFE: The Nonstick Coating

In 1938, young Roy Plunkett, a chemist at DuPont, was working with the gas tetrafluoroethylene ($CF_2{=}CF_2$). He opened the valve on a tank of the gas—and nothing came out. Rather than discarding the tank, he decided to investigate. The tank was found to be filled with a waxy, white solid. He attempted to analyze the solid but ran into a problem: It simply wouldn't dissolve, even in hot concentrated acids. Plunkett had discovered polytetrafluoroethylene (PTFE), the polymer of tetrafluoroethylene, best known by its trade name, Teflon®. In this case, the fluorine atoms are pendant groups, and they are shown in green.

$$\sim CF_2-CF_2-CF_2-CF_2-CF_2-CF_2-CF_2-CF_2\sim$$

Teflon

Because its C$-$F bonds are exceptionally strong and resistant to heat and chemicals, PTFE is a tough, unreactive, nonflammable material. It is used to make electric insulation, bearings, and gaskets, as well as to coat surfaces of cookware to eliminate sticking of food.

▲ Frying pans, baking pans, and other cookware often take advantage of the inert, nonstick nature of PTFE.

CONCEPTUAL Example 10.1   Repeat Units in Polymers

What is the repeat unit in polyvinylidene chloride? A segment of the polymer is represented as

$$
\begin{array}{cccccc}
H & Cl & H & Cl & H & Cl \\
| & | & | & | & | & | \\
\sim C & - C & - C & - C & - C & - C \sim \\
| & | & | & | & | & | \\
H & Cl & H & Cl & H & Cl
\end{array}
$$

Solution

Inspection of the segment above reveals that it consists of three repeat units, each with two carbon atoms, two hydrogen atoms, and two chlorine atoms. Placing a double bond between the carbon atoms of one unit, we get

$$\begin{array}{c} H \quad Cl \\ | \quad\; | \\ C{=}C \\ | \quad\; | \\ H \quad Cl \end{array}$$

Joining hundreds of these units would yield a molecule of the polymer.

▲ Granular polymeric resins are the basic stock for many molded plastic goods.

■ **EXERCISE 10.1**

What is the repeat unit in polyacrylonitrile? A segment of the polymer is represented as

$$\sim CH_2CHCH_2CHCH_2CHCH_2CHCH_2CHCH_2CH\sim$$
$$\;\;\;\; | \;\;\;\;\;\; | \;\;\;\;\;\; | \;\;\;\;\;\; | \;\;\;\;\;\; | \;\;\;\;\;\; |$$
$$\;\;\;\; CN \;\; CN \;\; CN \;\; CN \;\; CN \;\; CN$$

Example 10.2   Structure of Polymers

Write the structure of the polymer made from methyl vinyl ketone ($CH_2{=}CHCOCH_3$). Show at least four repeat units.

Solution

The carbon atoms bond to form a chain with only single bonds between carbon atoms. The methyl ketone is a pendant group on the chain. (Two of the electrons in the double bond of the monomer form the bond joining units.) The polymer is

$$\sim CH_2CHCH_2CHCH_2CHCH_2CH\sim$$
$$\;\;\;\; | \;\;\;\;\;\; | \;\;\;\;\;\; | \;\;\;\;\;\; |$$
$$O{=}C \;\; O{=}C \;\; O{=}C \;\; O{=}C$$
$$\;\;\;\; | \;\;\;\;\;\; | \;\;\;\;\;\; | \;\;\;\;\;\; |$$
$$\;\;\;\; CH_3 \;\; CH_3 \;\; CH_3 \;\; CH_3$$

■ **EXERCISE 10.2**

Write the structures of the polymers made from **(a)** vinyl fluoride ($CH_2{=}CHF$) and **(b)** vinyl acetate ($CH_2{=}CHOCOCH_3$). Show at least four repeat units of each polymer.

Conducting Polymers: Polyacetylene

Acetylene ($H{-}C{\equiv}C{-}H$) has a triple bond rather than a double bond, but it can still undergo addition polymerization, forming polyacetylene (Figure 10.3). Notice that, unlike polyethylene, which has a carbon chain containing only single bonds, every other carbon-to-carbon bond in polyacetylene is a double bond.

▲ **Figure 10.3** A ball-and-stick model of polyacetylene.

Q: *Write an equation for the formation of polyacetylene similar to that for polyethylene on page 289, in which the repeat polymer unit is placed within brackets.*

The alternating double and single bonds form a *conjugated* system. Such a system makes it easy for electrons to travel along the chain, so polyacetylene is able to conduct electricity. Most other plastics are electrical insulators. Polyacetylene and similar conjugated polymers can be used as lightweight substitutes for metal. In fact, the plastic even has a silvery luster like metal.

Polyacetylene, the first conducting polymer, was discovered in 1970. Since then, a number of other polymers that conduct electricity have been made. More recently, paints and inks that contain conducting polymers have been made available on the open market. Artists can use the paints and inks as part of their art, incorporating electrical devices like light-emitting diodes (LEDs) and motors into the artwork. Similar uses of these materials in textiles are being investigated. Imagine using a jacket with embedded solar cells to keep your smartphone charged while walking around the city!

▲ Conducting polymers have conjugated systems, as seen in Figure 10.3, and they are used to make electronic sensors, such as the ones shown here. The conductivity of the polymer is affected by impurities on the surface. The change in conductivity varies with the concentration of that impurity.

Processing Polymers

In everyday life, many polymers are called plastics. In chemistry, a *plastic* material is one that can be made to flow under heat and pressure. The material can then be shaped in a mold or in other ways. Plastic products are often made from granular polymeric material. In *compression molding*, heat and pressure are applied directly to such grains in the mold cavity. In *transfer molding*, the polymer is softened by heating before being poured into molds to harden.

There also are several methods of molding molten polymers. In *injection molding*, the plastic is melted in a heating chamber and then forced by a plunger into cold molds to set. In *extrusion molding*, the melted polymer is extruded through a die in continuous form to be cut into lengths or coiled. Bottles and similar hollow objects often are *blow-molded*; a "bubble" of molten polymer is blown up like a balloon inside a hollow mold.

Table 10.1 lists some of the more important addition polymers, along with a few of their uses. The pendant groups are shown in green.

Table 10.1 Some Addition Polymers			
Monomer	Polymer	Polymer Name	Some Uses
$CH_2{=}CH_2$	$\left[\begin{array}{c} H \; H \\ -C-C- \\ H \; H \end{array}\right]_n$	Polyethylene	Bags, bottles, toys, electrical insulation
$CH_2{=}CH{-}CH_3$	$\left[\begin{array}{c} H \; H \\ -C-C- \\ H \; CH_3 \end{array}\right]_n$	Polypropylene	Carpeting, bottles, luggage
$CH_2{=}CH-$⬡	$\left[\begin{array}{c} H \; H \\ -C-C- \\ H \; \text{⬡} \end{array}\right]_n$	Polystyrene	Simulated wood furniture, insulation, cups, toys, packing materials
$CH_2{=}CH{-}Cl$	$\left[\begin{array}{c} H \; H \\ -C-C- \\ H \; Cl \end{array}\right]_n$	Polyvinyl chloride (PVC)	Food wrap, simulated leather, plumbing, garden hoses, floor tile
$CH_2{=}CCl_2$	$\left[\begin{array}{c} H \; Cl \\ -C-C- \\ H \; Cl \end{array}\right]_n$	Polyvinylidene chloride (Saran®)	Food wrap, seat covers
$CF_2{=}CF_2$	$\left[\begin{array}{c} F \; F \\ -C-C- \\ F \; F \end{array}\right]_n$	Polytetrafluoroethylene (Teflon)	Nonstick coating for cooking utensils, electrical insulation
$CH_2{=}CH{-}C{\equiv}N$	$\left[\begin{array}{c} H \; H \\ -C-C- \\ H \; CN \end{array}\right]_n$	Polyacrylonitrile (Acrilan, Creslan, Dynel)	Yarns, wigs, paints
$CH_2{=}CH{-}OCOCH_3$	$\left[\begin{array}{c} H \; H \\ -C-C- \\ H \; O{-}C{-}CH_3 \\ \; \; \; \; \| \\ \; \; \; \; O \end{array}\right]_n$	Polyvinyl acetate	Adhesives, textile coatings, chewing gum resin, paints
$CH_2{=}C(CH_3)COOCH_3$	$\left[\begin{array}{c} H \; CH_3 \\ -C-C- \\ H \; C{-}O{-}CH_3 \\ \; \; \| \\ \; \; O \end{array}\right]_n$	Polymethyl methacrylate (Lucite, Plexiglas)	Glass substitute, bowling balls

SELF-ASSESSMENT Questions

1. When addition polymers form, the monomer units are joined by
   a. delocalized electrons that flow along the polymer chain
   b. dispersion forces
   c. double bonds
   d. new bonds formed by electrons from the double bonds in the monomers

2. The monomer styrene ($C_6H_5CH=CH_2$, where C_6H_5 represents a benzene ring) forms a polymer that has chains with repeating
   a. eight-carbon units in the backbone
   b. six-carbon units in the backbone and two-carbon groups as pendants
   c. CH_2CH units in the backbone and C_6H_5 groups as pendants
   d. $CH_2=CH$ units in the backbone and C_6H_5 groups as pendants

3. Water pipes, bottles, and raincoats are commonly made from
   a. polyethylene
   b. polypropylene
   c. polytetrafluoroethylene
   d. polyvinyl chloride

Answers: 1, d; 2, c; 3, d

10.4 Rubber and Other Elastomers

Learning Objective › Define *cross-linking* and explain how it changes the properties of a polymer.

Although rubber is a natural polymer, it was the basis for much of the development of the synthetic polymer industry. During World War II, Japanese occupation of Southeast Asia cut off most of the Allies' supply of natural rubber. The search for synthetic substitutes resulted in much more than just a replacement for natural rubber. The plastics industry, to a large extent, developed out of the search for synthetic rubber.

Natural rubber can be broken down into a simple hydrocarbon called *isoprene*. Isoprene is a volatile liquid, whereas rubber is a semisolid, elastic material. Chemists can make polyisoprene, a substance identical to natural rubber, except that the isoprene comes from petroleum refineries rather than from the cells of rubber trees.

$$n\ CH_2=C-CH=CH_2 \longrightarrow \left[CH_2-C=CH-CH_2\right]_n$$
$$\qquad\quad\ \ \ | \qquad\qquad\qquad\qquad\qquad | $$
$$\qquad\quad\ \ CH_3 \qquad\qquad\qquad\qquad\ \ CH_3$$

Isoprene   Polyisoprene (rubber)

Chemists have also developed several synthetic rubbers and devised ways to modify these polymers to change their properties.

Vulcanization: Cross-Linking

The long-chain molecules that make up rubber are coiled and twisted and intertwined with one another. When rubber is stretched, its coiled molecules are straightened. Natural rubber is soft and tacky when hot. It can be made harder by reaction with sulfur. In this process, called **vulcanization**, sulfur atoms *cross-link* the hydrocarbon chains side-to-side (Figure 10.4). Charles Goodyear discovered vulcanization and was issued U.S. Patent 3633 in 1844 for the process.

◄ **Figure 10.4** Vulcanized rubber has long hydrocarbon chains (represented here by red lines) cross-linked by short chains of sulfur atoms. The subscript *x* indicates a small, indefinite number of S atoms, usually not more than four.

(a)   (b)   (c)

● = Carbon

● = Sulfur

▲ **Figure 10.5** Vulcanization of rubber cross-links the hydrocarbon chains. (a) In unvulcanized rubber, the chains slip past one another when the rubber is stretched. (b) Vulcanization involves the addition of sulfur cross-links between the chains. (c) When vulcanized rubber is stretched, the sulfur cross-links prevent the chains from slipping past one another. Vulcanized rubber is stronger than unvulcanized rubber.

It DOES Matter!

A polymer related to SBR is poly(styrene-butadiene-styrene), or SBS. Called a *block copolymer*, SBS has molecules made up of three segments: one end is a chain of polystyrene repeat units; the middle is a long chain of polybutadiene repeat units; and the other end is another chain of polystyrene repeat units. SBS is a hard rubber used in items where durability is important, such as shoe soles and tire treads.

▲ Synthetic polymers serve as binders in paints. Pigments provide color and opacity to the paint. Titanium dioxide (TiO_2), a white solid, is the most widely used pigment.

Its cross-linked structure makes vulcanized rubber a harder, stronger substance that is suitable for automobile tires. Surprisingly, cross-linking also improves the elasticity of rubber. With just the right degree of cross-linking, the individual chains are still free to uncoil and stretch somewhat. When stretched vulcanized rubber is released, the cross-links pull the chains back to their original arrangement (Figure 10.5). Rubber bands owe their snap to this sort of molecular structure. Materials that can be extended and will return to their original size are called **elastomers**.

Synthetic Rubber

Natural rubber is a polymer of isoprene, and some synthetic elastomers are closely related to natural rubber. For example, polybutadiene is made from the monomer butadiene (CH_2—CH—CH—CH_2), which differs from isoprene only in that it lacks a methyl group on the second carbon atom. Polybutadiene is made rather easily from this monomer.

$$n\,CH_2{=}CH{-}CH{=}CH_2 \longrightarrow \text{---}CH_2{-}CH{=}CH{-}CH_2\text{---}_n$$

However, this polymer has only fair tensile strength and poor resistance to gasoline and oils. These properties limit its value for automobile tires, the main use of elastomers.

Another synthetic elastomer, polychloroprene (Neoprene), is made from a monomer similar to isoprene but with a chlorine (shown in green) in place of the methyl group on isoprene.

$$n\,CH_2{=}\underset{Cl}{C}{-}CH{=}CH_2 \longrightarrow \text{---}CH_2{-}\underset{Cl}{C}{=}CH{-}CH_2\text{---}_n$$

Neoprene is more resistant to oil and gasoline than other elastomers are. It is used to make gasoline pump hoses and similar items used at automobile service stations.

Styrene–butadiene rubber (SBR) is a copolymer of styrene (about 25%, and shown in green) and butadiene (about 75%). A segment of an SBR molecule might look something like this.

$${\sim}CH_2CH{=}CHCH_2{-}CH_2CH{-}CH_2CH{=}CHCH_2{-}CH_2CH{=}CHCH_2{\sim}$$

| Butadiene unit | Styrene unit | Butadiene unit | Butadiene unit |

SBR is more resistant to oxidation and abrasion than natural rubber, but its mechanical properties are less satisfactory.

Like those of natural rubber, SBR molecules contain double bonds and can be cross-linked by vulcanization. SBR accounts for about a third of the total U.S. production of elastomers and is used mainly for making tires.

Polymers in Paints

A surprising use for elastomers is in paints and other coatings. The substance in a paint that hardens to form a continuous surface coating, often called the *binder*, or resin, is a polymer, usually an elastomer. Paint made with elastomers is resistant to cracking. Various kinds of polymers can be used as binders, depending on the specific qualities desired in the paint. Latex paints, which have polymer particles dispersed in water, and thus avoiding the use of organic solvents, are most common. Brushes and rollers are easily cleaned in soap and water. This replacement of the hazardous organic solvents historically used in paints with water is a good example of green chemistry.

3. Are there polymers in chewing gum?

Chewing gum has always contained polymers. Originally, it was the sap of the sapodilla tree called "chicle." Since World War II, the base of chewing gum has been synthetic rubbers, like polyethylene or polyvinyl acetate.

SELF-ASSESSMENT Questions

1. Natural rubber is a polymer of
   a. butadiene
   b. isobutylene
   c. isoprene
   d. propylene

2. Which of the following is the structure of isoprene?
   a. $CH_2=CH-C\equiv N$
   b. $CH_2=C(CH_3)-CH_3$
   c. $CH_2=CCl-CH-CH_2$
   d. $CH_2=C(CH_3)-CH=CH_2$

3. A cross-linking agent is a(n)
   a. atom or group that bonds polymer chains together
   b. functional group on a polymer chain
   c. repeating unit in a polymer chain
   d. substituent group on a polymer chain

4. Charles Goodyear discovered that natural rubber could be cross-linked by heating it with
   a. a binder
   b. carbon
   c. isoprene
   d. sulfur

5. Styrene–butadiene rubber is an example of a
   a. copolymer
   b. natural elastomer
   c. natural cross-linked polymer
   d. polyamide

6. Polymers, usually elastomers, are used in paints as the
   a. binder
   b. initiator
   c. pigment
   d. solvent

Answers: 1. c; 2. d; 3. a; 4. d; 5. a; 6. a

10.5 Condensation Polymers

Learning Objectives ❯ Differentiate between addition and condensation polymerization. ❯ Write the structures of the monomers that form polyesters and polyamides.

The polymers considered so far are all addition polymers. All the atoms of the monomer molecules are incorporated into the polymer molecules. In a *condensation polymer*, part of the monomer molecule is not incorporated in the final polymer. During **condensation polymerization**, also called *step-reaction polymerization*, a small molecule, usually water (shown in green in the following examples) but sometimes methanol, ammonia, or HCl, is formed as a by-product.

Nylon and Other Polyamides

As an example, let's consider the formation of nylon. The monomer in one type of nylon, called *nylon 6*, is a six-carbon carboxylic acid (magenta) with an amino (blue) group on the sixth carbon atom: 6-aminohexanoic acid ($HOOCCH_2CH_2CH_2$ $CH_2CH_2NH_2$). (There are several different nylons, each prepared from a different monomer or set of monomers, but all share certain common structural features.)

In the polymerization reaction, a carboxyl group of one monomer molecule forms an amide bond with the amine group of another.

$$n \; HO-\overset{\overset{\textstyle O}{\|}}{C}CH_2(CH_2)_3CH_2\overset{\overset{\textstyle H}{|}}{N}-H \; + \; n \; HO-\overset{\overset{\textstyle O}{\|}}{C}CH_2(CH_2)_3CH_2\overset{\overset{\textstyle H}{|}}{N}-H \; \longrightarrow$$

$$\sim\overset{\overset{\textstyle O}{\|}}{C}CH_2(CH_2)_3CH_2\overset{\overset{\textstyle H}{|}}{N}-\overset{\overset{\textstyle O}{\|}}{C}CH_2(CH_2)_3\overset{\overset{\textstyle H}{|}}{N}\sim \; + \; 2n \; H_2O$$

Amide linkage

Water molecules are formed as a by-product. This formation of a nonpolymeric by-product distinguishes condensation polymerization from addition polymerization. Note that the formula of a repeat unit of a condensation polymer is not the same as that of the monomer.

Because the linkages holding the polymer together are amide bonds, nylon 6 is a **polyamide**. Another nylon is made by the condensation of two different monomers: 1,6-hexanediamine ($H_2NCH_2CH_2CH_2CH_2CH_2CH_2NH_2$) and adipic acid ($HOOCCH_2CH_2CH_2CH_2COOH$). Each monomer has six carbon atoms; the polymer is called *nylon 66*.

$$n \text{ H—NCH}_2\text{CH}_2\text{CH}_2\text{CH}_2\text{CH}_2\text{CH}_2\text{N—H} \quad + \quad n \text{ HO—C(CH}_2)_4\text{C—OH} \longrightarrow$$

1,6-Hexanediamine   Adipic acid

$$\text{—NCH}_2\text{CH}_2\text{CH}_2\text{CH}_2\text{CH}_2\text{CH}_2\text{N—CCH}_2\text{CH}_2\text{CH}_2\text{CH}_2\text{C—}_n \quad + \quad 2n \text{ H}_2\text{O}$$

Amide linkage

This was the original nylon polymer discovered in 1937 by DuPont chemist Wallace Carothers. Note that one monomer has two amino groups and the other has two carboxyl groups, but the product is still a polyamide, quite similar to nylon 6. Silk and wool, which are protein fibers, are natural polyamides.

Although nylon can be molded into various shapes, most nylon is made into fibers. Some is spun into fine thread to be woven into silk-like fabrics, and some is made into yarn that is much like wool. Carpeting, which was once made mainly from wool, is now made largely from nylon.

Polyethylene Terephthalate and Other Polyesters

A **polyester** is a condensation polymer made from molecules with alcohol and carboxylic acid functional groups. The most common polyester is made from ethylene glycol and terephthalic acid. It is called *polyethylene terephthalate (PET)*.

$$n \text{ HO—CH}_2\text{CH}_2\text{—OH} \quad + \quad n \text{ HO—C} \bigcirc \text{C—OH} \longrightarrow$$

Ethylene glycol   Terephthalic acid   Ester linkage

$$\text{—O—CH}_2\text{CH}_2\text{—O—C} \bigcirc \text{C—}_n \quad + \quad 2n \text{ H}_2\text{O}$$

Polyethylene terephthalate

The hydroxyl groups in ethylene glycol react with the carboxylic acid groups in terephthalic acid to produce long chains held together by many ester linkages.

PET can be molded into bottles for beverages and other liquids. It can also be formed into a film, which is used to laminate documents and to make tough packaging tape. Polyester finishes are used on premium wood products such as guitars, pianos, and the interiors of vehicles and boats. Polyester fibers are strong, quick-drying, and resistant to mildew, wrinkling, stretching, and shrinking. They are used in home furnishings such as carpets, curtains, sheets and pillowcases, and upholstery. Because polyester fibers do not absorb water, they are ideal for outdoor clothing to be worn in wet and damp environments and for insulation in boots and sleeping bags. For other clothing, they are often blended with cotton for a more natural feel. A familiar use of polyester film (Mylar®) is in the shiny balloons that are filled with helium to celebrate special occasions.

▲ Large plastic items with thin walls, such as the polyethylene terephthalate containers shown here, are often blow-molded. Blow molding is very similar to blowing a soap bubble, except that the bubble is blown inside a mold.

Phenol–Formaldehyde and Related Resins

Let's go back to Bakelite, the original synthetic polymer. Bakelite, a phenol–formaldehyde resin, was first synthesized by Leo Baekeland, who received U.S. Patent 942,699 for the process in 1909. Phenolic resins are no longer important as industrial polymers, but they are used as a substitute for porcelain and in board and tabletop game pieces such as billiard balls, dominoes, and checkers.

Phenol–formaldehyde resins are formed in a condensation reaction that also yields water molecules, the hydrogen atoms coming from the benzene ring of phenol and the oxygen atoms from the aldehyde. The reaction proceeds stepwise, with formaldehyde first adding to the 2 or 4 position of the phenol molecule.

Phenol   Formaldehyde

The substituted phenol molecules then link up as water molecules are formed. (Remember that there are hydrogen atoms at all the unsubstituted corners of a benzene ring.) The hookup of molecules continues until an extensive network is achieved.

Phenol–formaldehyde resin

Water is driven off by heat as the polymer sets. The structure of the polymer is extremely complex, a three-dimensional network somewhat like the framework of a giant building. Note that the phenolic rings are joined together by CH_2 units from the formaldehyde. These network polymers are **thermosetting resins**; they cannot be melted and remolded. Instead, they decompose when heated to high temperatures.

Formaldehyde is also condensed with urea [$H_2N(C{=}O)NH_2$] to make urea–formaldehyde resins and with melamine to form melamine–formaldehyde resins. (Melamine is formed by condensation of three molecules of urea.)

These resins, like phenolic resins, are thermosetting. The polymers are complex three-dimensional networks formed by the condensation reaction of formaldehyde ($H_2C{=}O$) molecules and amino ($-NH_2$) groups (in blue). Urea–formaldehyde resins are used to bind wood chips together in panels of particle board. Melamine–formaldehyde resins are used in plastic (Melmac) dinnerware and laminate countertops.

Melamine

It DOES Matter!

Bisphenol-A (BPA) is an endocrine disruptor in laboratory animals; that is, it can act like a hormone. A tiny amount of BPA leaches out of polycarbonate bottles, especially when they are heated. Concern over long-term, low-dose exposure to BPA led Canada to ban BPA in baby bottles in 2008. Threats of legislation in the United States and elsewhere caused manufacturers of polycarbonate bottles to switch to BPA-free bottles.

Other Condensation Polymers

There are many other kinds of condensation polymers, but we will look at only a few.

Polycarbonates are "clear as glass" polymers tough enough to be used in bulletproof windows. They are also used in protective helmets, safety glasses, clear plastic water bottles, baby bottles, and even dental crowns. One polycarbonate is made from bisphenol-A (BPA) and phosgene ($COCl_2$). The products will have a carbonate group (shown in green).

Phosgene + Bisphenol A ⟶

A polycarbonate + 2 HCl

Polyurethanes are similar to nylon polymers in structure. The repeat unit in one common polyurethane is

Polyurethanes may be elastomeric or tough and rigid, depending on the monomers used. They are common in foamed padding (foam rubber) in cushions, mattresses, and padded furniture. They are also used for skate wheels, in running shoes, and in protective gear for sports activities, as well as for hard lacquer-like coatings for wood.

Epoxies make excellent surface paints and coatings. They are used to protect steel pipes and fittings from corrosion. The insides of metal cans are often coated with an epoxy to prevent rusting, especially in cans for acidic foods like tomatoes. A common epoxy is made from epichlorohydrin and BPA.

An epoxy

Epoxies also make powerful adhesives. These adhesives usually have two components that are mixed just before use. The polymer chains become cross-linked, and the bonding is extremely strong.

Composite Materials

Composite materials are made up of high-strength fibers (of glass, graphite, synthetic polymers, or ceramics) held together by a polymeric matrix, usually a thermosetting condensation polymer. The fiber reinforcement provides the support, and the surrounding plastic keeps the fibers from breaking.

Among the most commonly used composite materials are polyester resins reinforced with glass fibers. These are widely used in boat hulls, molded chairs, automobile panels, and sports gear such as tennis rackets. Some composite materials have the strength and rigidity of steel but with a fraction of the weight of steel.

▲ Composite construction using carbon fiber and epoxies makes bicycle frames strong and light (about 1 kg!). The direction of the carbon fiber allows the maker to tailor the material for maximum strength where needed.

Silicones

Not all polymers are based on chains of carbon atoms. A good example of a different type of polymer is **silicone** (polysiloxane), in which the chains have a series of alternating silicon and oxygen atoms.

$$\sim \underset{\underset{R}{|}}{\overset{\overset{R}{|}}{Si}} - O - \underset{\underset{R}{|}}{\overset{\overset{R}{|}}{Si}} - O - \underset{\underset{R}{|}}{\overset{\overset{R}{|}}{Si}} - O - \underset{\underset{R}{|}}{\overset{\overset{R}{|}}{Si}} - O - \underset{\underset{R}{|}}{\overset{\overset{R}{|}}{Si}} - O - \underset{\underset{R}{|}}{\overset{\overset{R}{|}}{Si}} - O - \underset{\underset{R}{|}}{\overset{\overset{R}{|}}{Si}} \sim$$

(In simple silicones, R represents a hydrocarbon group, such as methyl, ethyl, or butyl.)

Silicones can be linear, cyclic, or cross-linked networks. They are heat-stable and resistant to most chemicals and are excellent waterproofing materials. Depending on chain length and amount of cross-linking, silicones can be oils or greases, rubbery compounds, or solid resins. Silicone oils are used as hydraulic fluids and lubricants. Other silicones are used in such products as sealants, auto polish, shoe polish, and waterproof sheeting. Fabrics for raincoats and umbrellas are frequently treated with silicone.

An interesting silicone product is Silly Putty. It can be molded like clay or rolled up and bounced like a ball. But it is actually a liquid (see page 166) and flows very slowly on standing.

Perhaps the most remarkable silicones are the ones used for synthetic human body parts, ranging from finger joints to eye sockets. Artificial ears and noses are also made from silicone polymers. These can even be specially colored to match the surrounding skin.

Silicon is in the same group (4A) as carbon and, like carbon, is tetravalent and able to form chains. However, carbon can form chains consisting only of carbon atoms (as in polyethylene), whereas the chains of silicone polymers have alternating silicon and oxygen atoms.

4. Why can silicone be used for flexible baking pans?

The silicone material is temperature resistant from the range of −55 to 300 degrees C. It retains its flexibility, shape, and other properties. It is very stable and durable, though it is often reinforced to give it better strength and rigidity.

▲ Cookware made of silicone is colorful, flexible, and nonstick.

Example 10.3	Condensed Structural Formulas for Polymers

Write the condensed structural formula for the polymer formed from dimethylsilanol, $(CH_3)_2Si(OH)_2$.

Solution

Let's start by writing the structural formula of the monomer.

$$HO - \underset{\underset{CH_3}{|}}{\overset{\overset{CH_3}{|}}{Si}} - OH$$

Because there are no double bonds in this molecule, we do not expect it to undergo addition polymerization. Rather, we expect a condensation reaction, in which an OH group of one molecule and an H atom of another combine to form a molecule of water. Moreover, because there are two OH groups per molecule, each monomer can form bonds with two others, on both sides. This is a key requirement for polymerization. We can represent the reaction as follows.

$$HO - \underset{\underset{CH_3}{|}}{\overset{\overset{CH_3}{|}}{Si}} - OH + HO - \underset{\underset{CH_3}{|}}{\overset{\overset{CH_3}{|}}{Si}} - OH + HO - \underset{\underset{CH_3}{|}}{\overset{\overset{CH_3}{|}}{Si}} - OH + \cdots \longrightarrow \left[\underset{\underset{CH_3}{|}}{\overset{\overset{CH_3}{|}}{Si}} - O \right]_n + n\,H_2O$$

■ EXERCISE 10.3

a. Write the structural formula for the polymer formed from glycolic acid (hydroxyacetic acid, $HOCH_2COOH$), showing at least four repeat units.

b. Write a condensed structural formula in which the repeat unit in part **(a)** is shown in brackets.

SELF-ASSESSMENT Questions

1. Condensation polymerization produces a small molecules, usually water, and requires
   a. the presence of a carbon–carbon double bond
   b. the presence of a carbon–oxygen double bond
   c. two monomers with at least two functional groups each
   d. two monomers with only one functional group each

2. Which of the following pairs of molecules can form a polyester?
   a. $HOCH_2CH_2OH$ and $HOCH_2CH_2CH_2CH_2OH$
   b. $H_2NCH_2CH_2CH_2CH_2CH_2NH_2$ and $HOOCCH_2CH_2CH_2CH_2COOH$
   c. $H_2NCH_2CH_2CH_2CH_2CH_2NH_2$ and $HOCH_2CH_2CH_2CH_2CH_2OH$
   d. $HOOCCH_2CH_2CH_2CH_2COOH$ and $HOCH_2CH_2CH_2CH_2OH$

3. Which of the following molecules can serve as the sole monomer for a polyamide?
   a. $H_2NCH_2CH_2CH_2CH_2OH$
   b. $H_2NCH_2CH_2CH_2CH_2NH_2$
   c. $HOOCCH_2CH_2CH_2CH_2CH_2NH_2$
   d. $HOOCCH_2CH_2CH_2CONH_2$

4. Thermosetting polymers
   a. are easily recycled
   b. are always addition polymers
   c. cannot be melted and remolded
   d. usually melt at a lower temperature than do thermoplastic polymers

5. The backbone of a silicone polymer chain is composed of the repeating unit
   a. $\sim OCH_2CH_2OSi\sim$
   b. $\sim OCH_2CH_2Si\sim$
   c. $\sim SiO\sim$
   d. $\sim OSiSi\sim$

10.6 Properties of Polymers

Learning Objectives ❯ Understand the concept of the glass transition temperature.
❯ Explain how crystallinity affects the physical properties of polymers.

Polymers differ from substances consisting of small molecules in three main ways. First, the long chains can be entangled with one another, much like the strands in a dish of spaghetti. It is difficult to untangle the polymer molecules, especially at low temperatures. This property lends strength to many plastics, elastomers, and other materials.

Second, although intermolecular forces affect polymers just as they do small molecules, these forces are greatly multiplied for large molecules. The larger the molecules are, the greater the intermolecular forces between them. Even when ordinarily weak dispersion forces are the only intermolecular forces present, they can strongly bind polymer chains. This property, too, provides strength in polymeric materials. For example, polyethylene is nonpolar, with only dispersion forces between its molecules. As noted on page 292, though, ultra-high-molecular-weight polyethylene forms fibers so strong they can be used in bullet-proof vests.

Third, large polymer molecules move more slowly than small molecules do. A group of small molecules (monomers) can move around more rapidly and more randomly when independent than they can when joined together in a long chain (polymer). The slower molecular speed makes a polymeric material different from one made of small molecules. For example, a polymer dissolved in a solvent will form a solution that is a lot more viscous than the pure solvent.

Crystalline and Amorphous Polymers

Some polymers are highly crystalline; their molecules line up neatly to form long fibers of great strength. Other polymers are largely amorphous, composed of randomly oriented molecules that get tangled up with one another (Figure 10.6). Crystalline polymers tend to make good synthetic fibers, while amorphous polymers are often elastomers.

Sometimes, the same polymer is crystalline in one region and amorphous in another. For example, scientists designed spandex fibers (used in stretch fabrics [Lycra] in ski pants, exercise clothing, and swimsuits) to combine the tensile strength of crystalline fibers with the elasticity of amorphous rubber. Two molecular

(a)

(b)

▲ **Figure 10.6** Organization of polymer molecules. (a) Crystalline arrangement. (b) Amorphous arrangement.

structures are combined in one polymer chain, with crystalline blocks alternating with amorphous blocks. The amorphous blocks are soft and rubbery, while the crystalline parts are quite rigid. The resulting polymer exhibits both sets of properties—flexibility and rigidity.

The Glass Transition Temperature

An important property of most thermoplastic polymers is the **glass transition temperature** (T_g). Above this temperature, the polymer is rubbery and tough. Below it, the polymer is like glass: hard, stiff, and brittle. Each polymer has a characteristic T_g. We want automobile tires to be tough and elastic, so we make them from polymers with low T_g values. On the other hand, we want plastic substitutes for glass to be glassy. Therefore, these polymers have T_g values well above room temperature. We can apply the glass transition temperature in everyday life. For example, we can remove chewing gum from clothing by applying ice to lower the temperature of the polyvinyl acetate resin that gives the gum its "chewiness" below its T_g. The cold, brittle resin then crumbles readily and can be removed.

Fiber Formation

Not all synthetic polymers can be formed into useful fibers, but those that can often yield fibers with properties superior to those of natural fibers. More than half of the 60 billion kg of textile fibers produced each year in the United States are synthetic.

Silk fabrics are beautiful and have a luxurious "feel," but nylon fabrics are also attractive and feel much like silk. Moreover, nylon fabrics wear longer, are easier to care for, and are less expensive than silk.

Polyesters such as PET can substitute for either cotton or silk, but they outperform the natural fibers in many ways. Polyesters are not subject to mildew as cotton is, and many polyester fabrics do not need ironing. Fabrics in which polyester fibers are blended with 35–50% cotton combine the comfort of cotton with the no-iron easy care of polyester.

Acrylic fibers, made from polyacrylonitrile, can be spun into yarns that look like wool. Acrylic sweaters have the beauty and warmth of wool, but they do not shrink in hot water, are not attacked by moths, and do not cause the allergic skin reaction wool causes in some people.

Exceedingly fine fibers—called *microfibers* because they measure less than 10 μm in diameter, half as thick as silk fibers—can be made from almost any fiber-forming polymer, but most are made of polyesters or polyamides or a combination of the two. Varying the size, shape, and composition of the fibers results in products that are water repellent (for apparel) or absorbent (for a mop). Microfibers can be shaped for efficient trapping of dust or for wicking away liquids. These fibers already have many uses and are likely to have many more.

5. What fabrics are made from natural polymers?

Cotton, silk, wool, and linen are all naturally occurring polymers that can be made into fabric. Other materials like rayon, which is made from naturally occurring cellulose, but which is synthetically modified and manufactured into thread, are considered semisynthetic.

▲ Formation of fibers by extrusion through a spinneret. A melted polymer is forced through the tiny holes to make fibers that solidify as they cool.

SELF-ASSESSMENT Questions

1. Crystalline polymers are
   a. elastic
   b. flexible
   c. highly cross-linked
   d. used in fibers ✓

2. The temperature at which a polymer changes from soft and rubbery to glassy and hard is its
   a. T_c
   b. T_f
   c. T_g ✓
   d. T_i

Answers: 1, d; 2, c

10.7 Plastics and the Environment

Learning Objectives ❯ Describe the environmental problems associated with plastics and plasticizers. ❯ Name two types of sustainable, nonpetroleum-derived polymers and give their sources.

An advantage of many plastics is that they are durable and resistant to environmental conditions. Perhaps some of them are too resistant: They last almost forever.

Once plastic objects are dumped, they do not go away. You see them littering our parks, our sidewalks, and our highways, and if you should go out into the middle of the ocean, you would see them there, too. Many small fish have been found dead with their digestive tracts clogged by bits of plastic foam ingested with their food. Scientists estimate that plastic bags and other plastic trash thrown into the ocean kill as many as a million sea creatures each year.

Plastics make up about 12% by mass of solid waste in the United States but about 25% by volume. Their bulk creates a problem because 55% of all solid waste goes into landfills, and it is increasingly difficult to find suitable landfill space. (Solid wastes are discussed in more detail in Chapter 12.) Americans use about 60 million plastic bottles each day, with only about 12% being recycled. To behave in a more responsible and sustainable fashion, recycling of waste plastics is crucial. Recycling one plastic bottle conserves enough energy to burn a 60-W light bulb for six hours. Recycling plastics reduces our dependency on oil and decreases CO_2 emissions due to the use of fossil fuels.

Another way to dispose of discarded plastics is to burn them. Most plastics have a high fuel value. For example, a pound of polyethylene has about the same energy content as a pound of fuel oil. Some communities generate electricity with the heat from garbage incinerators. Some utility companies burn powdered coal mixed with a small proportion of ground-up rubber tires, thereby not only obtaining extra energy from the tires but also helping to solve the problem of tire disposal.

On the other hand, the burning of plastics and rubber can create new problems. For example, PVC produces toxic hydrogen chloride and vinyl chloride gases when it burns, and burning automobile tires give off soot and a stinking smoke. Incinerators are corroded by acidic fumes and clogged by materials that are not readily burned.

Degradable Plastics

About half of the waste plastic generated in the United States is from packaging. One approach to the problem of disposal of plastics is to make plastic packages that are biodegradable or photodegradable (broken down in the presence of bacteria or light). Of course, such packages must remain intact and not start to decompose while still being used. And many people still seem reluctant to pay extra for garbage bags that are designed to fall apart. Recently, though, there has been an increase in degradable, more environmentally friendly plastic items, including plastic tableware, cups, bottles, and delicatessen food containers.

Recycling

Recycling is perhaps the best way to handle waste plastics. The plastics must be collected, sorted, chopped, melted, and then remolded. Collection works well when there is strong community cooperation. The separation step is simplified by code numbers stamped on plastic containers. Once the plastics have been separated, they can be chopped into flakes, melted, and remolded or spun into fibers.

All plastics can be recycled, and steps have been taken to increase the ease of recycling, for example, "single-stream" recycling that allows people to throw most of their recyclables in one container. One of the few exceptions is the disposable plastic bag found at grocery stores. These are recyclable, but they cannot be put into single-stream recycling because they clog up the sorters used for single-stream systems.

Only two kinds of plastics are recycled on a large scale, PET (28% recycled) and HDPE (29%). PET bottles can be made into fibers, mainly for carpets, and HDPE containers can be remolded into detergent bottles. Recycling is green because it keeps plastics out of landfills, and it increases sustainability by lessening the use of petroleum-derived monomers or hazardous chemicals. We have a long way to go: in 2009, only about 7% of the 27 billion kg per year of plastic wastes in the United States were recycled.

Plastics and Fire Hazards

The accidental ignition of fabrics, synthetic or other, has caused untold human misery. The U.S. Department of Health and Human Services estimates that fires

▲ Recycled plastic can be used for many things. The Adirondack chair and the cafe chair are colorful and strong and made from recycled milk jugs.

involving flammable fabrics kill several thousand people annually and injure between 150,000 and 200,000.

Research has led to a variety of flame-retardant fabrics. Many incorporate chlorine and bromine atoms within the polymeric fibers. In particular, federal regulations require that children's sleepwear be made of such flame-retardant materials.

Another synthetic fabric, meta-aramid, or Nomex (from DuPont), has such high heat resistance that it is used for protective clothing for firefighters and race-car drivers. The fibers don't ignite or melt when exposed to flames or high heat. Nomex is also used in electric insulation and for machine parts exposed to high heat.

Burning plastics often produce toxic gases. Hydrogen cyanide is formed in large quantities when polyacrylonitrile and other nitrogen-containing polymers burn. Lethal amounts of cyanide found in the bodies of victims of plane crashes have been traced to burned plastics. Firefighters often refuse to enter burning buildings without gas masks for fear of being overcome by fumes from burning plastics. Smoldering fires also produce lethal quantities of carbon monoxide. To make plastics safer, green chemists are making new kinds of polymers that don't burn or that don't generate toxic chemicals when burned.

Plasticizers and Pollution

Chemicals used in plastics manufacture can also present problems. Plasticizers are an important example. Some plastics, particularly vinyl polymers, are hard and brittle and thus difficult to process. A **plasticizer** can make such a plastic more flexible and less brittle by lowering its glass transition temperature. Unplasticized PVC is rigid and is used for water pipes. Thin sheets of pure PVC crack and break easily, but plasticizers make them soft and pliable. Plastic raincoats, garden hoses, and seat covers for automobiles can be made from plasticized PVC. Plasticizers are liquids of low volatility, but they are generally lost by diffusion and evaporation as a plastic article ages. The plastic becomes brittle and then cracks and breaks.

Once used widely as plasticizers but now banned, polychlorinated biphenyls (PCBs) are derived from biphenyl ($C_{12}H_{10}$), a hydrocarbon that has two benzene rings joined at a corner. In PCBs, some of the hydrogen atoms of biphenyl are replaced with chlorine atoms (Figure 10.7, in green). Note that PCBs are structurally similar to the insecticide DDT.

PCBs were also widely used as insulating materials in electric transformers because their stability and low polarity gave them high electrical resistance and the ability to absorb heat. The same properties that made PCBs so desirable as industrial chemicals cause them to be an environmental hazard. They degrade slowly in nature, and their solubility in nonpolar media—animal fat as well as vinyl plastics—leads to their becoming concentrated in the food chain. PCB residues have been found in fish, birds, water, and sediments. The physiological effect of PCBs is similar to that of DDT. Monsanto Corporation, the only company in the United States that produced PCBs, discontinued production in 1977, but the compounds still remain in the environment.

◄ **Figure 10.7** Biphenyl and some of the PCBs derived from it (only a few of the hundreds of possible PCBs). DDT is also shown for comparison.

Today, the most widely used plasticizers for vinyl plastics are phthalate esters, a group of diesters derived from phthalic acid (1,2-benzenedicarboxylic acid). Phthalate plasticizers (Figure 10.8) have low acute toxicity, and although some studies have suggested possible harm to young children, the FDA has recognized these plasticizers as being generally safe. They pose little threat to the environment because they degrade fairly rapidly. Another approach of green chemists is to make plastics that have the right amount of flexibility and thus do not require any plasticizers when they are manufactured.

Plastics and the Future

Widely used today, synthetic polymers are the materials of the future. New kinds and new uses will be discovered. We already have polymers that conduct electricity, amazing adhesives, and synthetic materials that are stronger than steel but much lighter in weight. Plastics present problems, but they have become such an important part of our daily lives that we would find it difficult to live without them.

In medicine, body replacement parts made from polymers have become common. There are about 200,000 total hip replacements in the United States each year. Artificial lungs and artificial hearts are available, but they are enormously expensive and used for the most part only during recovery from injury or illness or until donor organs are available for transplantation. The cost of these replacements is likely to drop, and their efficacy will probably improve, in the future.

PVC water pipes, siding, window frames, plastic foam insulation, and polymeric surface coatings are used in home construction today. Some homes also contain lumber and wall panels of artificial wood, made from recycled plastics.

Synthetic polymers are used extensively in airplane interiors, and the bodies and wings of some planes are made of lightweight composite materials. Many automobiles have bodies made from plastic composites. Electrically conducting polymers will aid in making lightweight batteries for electric automobiles. The electronics industry will use increasing amounts of electrically conducting thermoplastics in miniaturized circuits.

But here is something to think about: Most synthetic polymers are made from petroleum or natural gas. Both of these natural resources are nonrenewable, and our supplies are limited. We are likely to run out of petroleum during this century. You might suppose that we would be actively conserving this valuable resource, but unfortunately, this is not the case. We are taking petroleum out of the ground at a rapid rate, converting most of it to gasoline and other fuels, and then simply burning it. There are other sources of energy, but is there anything that can replace petroleum as the raw material for making plastics? Yes! Several new types of plastics, such as polylactic acid and polyhydroxybutyrates, are made from renewable resources such as corn, soybeans, and sugarcane. Polymers are an active area of green chemistry research.

▶ **Figure 10.8** Phthalic acid (carboxylic acid groups in magenta) and some esters (ester groups in green) derived from it. Dioctyl phthalate is also called di-2-ethylhexyl phthalate.

Phthalic acid

Dibutyl phthalate (DBP)

Dimethoxyethyl phthalate (DMEP)

Dioctyl phthalate (DOP)

GREEN CHEMISTRY

Eric J. Beckman, *University of Pittsburgh*

Life-Cycle Impact Assessment of New Products

Learning Objective ❯ Explain how life-cycle impact analysis can be used to identify the environmental benefits and effects of newly designed products.

In any proposed design, a key question is, "How do we know that what we've made is an improvement?" The 12 principles of green chemistry provide strategies and outcomes to help chemical professionals create inherently safer products. Yet well-intentioned attempts to create safer products have sometimes led to unintended and undesirable effects. For example, mobile phones allowed developing countries to leapfrog to high-speed communication without grids of wire, which substantially reduced material use and energy. However, these devices rapidly became "disposable" products (average lifetime, 18 months), and they contain toxic and conflict metals including cadmium and tantalum (see Section 12.3). Can green chemistry principles help us avoid unfortunate trade-offs?

New products are assessed against specifications that depend on user requirements, so we can "grade" a new compound or product based on its environmental footprint. One way to do this is life-cycle impact analysis (LCIA), which creates a report card for products in which "grades" are associated with environmental aspects. The first step in an LCIA is to outline a product's full life cycle. If, for example, we examine a polyethylene terephthalate (PET) bottle (see Section 10.5), we would include the manufacturing process that turns PET pellets into bottles, the polymerization process that forms PET from the monomers (ethylene glycol and dimethyl terephthalate), and the synthesis processes used to make the monomers. The outline covers this "chemical family tree" of PET back to the oil well or plant matter that provides the raw materials. Finally, a full life cycle also covers the bottle's end of life – is it sent to a landfill or recycled? Learning about the life cycle provides opportunities to apply green chemistry principles 7 and 10.

Once the life cycle is outlined, the *inventory phase* of the LCIA totals all of the inputs (mass, water, energy) and outputs for each step. Also, because no process is 100% efficient, the waste during each step (emitted to air, land, and water) is tallied, too. The inventory is important when applying green chemistry principles 1, 2, and 6.

In the next phase, inventory is converted to *impact*. Although there are several ways to accomplish this conversion, one method pioneered by the EPA. and widely used in North America is midpoint analysis. In midpoint analysis, the potential for a given chemical to cause harm is calculated for each impact category by comparing the chemical with a compound whose behavior is well studied. For example, the climate-change potential is calculated relative to that of CO_2. As such, a simple bar graph can show the impacts (in 12 categories) of the full life cycle of a given product compared to previous versions. Once the impact is known, green chemistry principles 3 and 4 become relevant.

The report card for previous and "improved" products shows whether or not we've created any unfortunate trade-offs (some impacts declined yet others dramatically increased). For example, when petrochemical-based raw materials and polymers are replaced with those created from soybeans or corn, we often see a significant drop in fossil-fuel use and greenhouse-gas emissions for the agricultural products, but eutrophication impacts increase dramatically (such as damaging algae blooms in estuaries due to high phosphate and nitrogen runoff from fertilizer use).

While LCIA can show which trade-offs have been created during design of an alternative, it cannot make value judgments as to which is better. As in the case of a student's report card, where GPA summarizes performance, the impacts in an LCIA can be averaged to create a total score. While simple, reliance on a single score leads to a loss of detail. Many questions remain about how to conduct an effective LCIA practice. Researchers are trying to resolve how to weight the various measurements, how to include toxicological phenomena like endocrine disruption, and how to include all of a product's often-complex supply chain, among other factors.

Life cycle impact analysis provides a way to explore the question, "Has my use of green design principles led to an alternative with a smaller environmental footprint?" LCIA rarely produces a resounding "*Yes, this new product is greener!*" Yet LCIA leads to insight into the ways that chemical products make an impact on our environment, shows where improvement is needed, and informs the development of green chemistry solutions.

SELF-ASSESSMENT Questions

1. In general, the worst way to dispose of plastics is
  a. composting   **b.** incineration
  c. in landfills   **d.** recycling

2. Many plastics are fire hazards because they burn and produce
  a. CFCs   **b.** nitrogen oxides
  c. solid wastes   **d.** toxic gases

3. Once used as a plasticizer, polychlorinated biphenyls (PCBs) were discontinued because of
  a. their costs
  b. the nonsustainable petroleum source
  c. their environmental effect similar to DDT
  d. the biodegradability of the products

4. Many flame-retardant fabrics incorporate
  a. Br and Cl atoms   **b.** CFCs
  c. PCBs   **d.** phthalate plasticizers

5. Most synthetic polymers are made from
  a. coal   **b.** cotton
  c. petroleum and natural gas **d.** sustainable sources

6. A polymer made from a renewable resource is
  a. LDPE   **b.** polyacrylonitrile
  c. polylactic acid   **d.** styrene–butadiene rubber

Answers: 1, b; 2, d; 3, c; 4, a; 5, c; 6, c

SUMMARY

Section 10.1—A **polymer** is a giant molecule made from smaller molecules. The small molecules that are the building blocks used to make polymers are called **monomers**. There are many natural polymers, including starch, cellulose, nucleic acids, and proteins.

Celluloid was the first semisynthetic polymer, made from natural cellulose treated with nitric acid.

Section 10.2—The simplest, least expensive, and highest-volume synthetic polymer is polyethylene, made from the monomer ethylene. High-density polyethylene molecules can pack closely together to yield a rigid, strong structure. Low-density polyethylene molecules have many side chains, resulting in more flexible plastics. Linear low-density polyethylene is a **copolymer**, formed from two (or more) different monomers.

Polyethylene is one of many **thermoplastic polymers** that can be softened and reshaped with heat and pressure. *Thermosetting* polymers decompose, rather than soften, when heated. They cannot be reshaped.

Section 10.3—In **addition polymerization,** the monomer molecules add to one another; the polymer contains all the atoms of the monomers. Addition polymers, such as polyethylene, polypropylene, polystyrene, and PVC, are made from monomers containing carbon-to-carbon double bonds. Polypropylene is tough and resists moisture, oils, and solvents. Polystyrene is used mainly to make Styrofoam. PVC or polyvinyl chloride is used for plumbing, artificial leather, and flexible tubing. PTFE, or Teflon, is chemically inert and nonflammable; it is widely used in nonstick coatings. Thermoplastic polymers can be molded in many different ways.

Section 10.4—Natural rubber is an **elastomer**, a material that returns to its original shape after being stretched. The monomer of natural rubber, isoprene, can be made artificially and polymerized. Polyisoprene is soft and tacky when hot. In a process called **vulcanization**, polyisoprene is reacted with sulfur. The sulfur atoms cross-link the hydrocarbon chains, making the rubber harder, stronger, and more elastic.

Other elastomers that are similar in structure to polyisoprene include polybutadiene, polychloroprene, and styrene–butadiene rubber (SBR). All of these have molecules that can coil and uncoil. Elastomers are used as binders in paints.

Section 10.5—In **condensation polymerization**, parts of the monomer molecules are not incorporated in the product. Small molecules such as water are formed as by-products. Nylon is a condensation polymer that is a **polyamide**, with amide [—(CO)NH—] linkages joining the monomers.

A **polyester** is a condensation polymer made from monomers with alcohol and carboxylic acid functional groups. Polyethylene terephthalate (PET) is the most common polyester.

Various **thermosetting resins** can be prepared by condensing formaldehyde with urea, melamine, or phenol. Other condensation polymers include polycarbonates (bulletproof windows), polyurethanes (foam rubber), and epoxies (coatings and adhesives). Combining a polymer with high-strength fibers gives a composite material that exploits the best properties of both materials. **Silicones**, which have chains consisting of silicon and oxygen atoms instead of carbon atoms, have varied structures and many uses.

Section 10.6—Properties of polymers differ greatly from those of their monomers. A polymer's strength arises partly because the molecules entangle with one another and partly because the large molecules have strong dispersion forces. Polymers may be crystalline or amorphous. Above the **glass transition temperature** (T_g), a polymer is rubbery and tough; below it, the polymer is brittle. Strong synthetic fibers are made from crystalline polymers because their long molecules align neatly with one another.

Section 10.7—The durability of plastics means that they make up a large fraction of the content of landfills. Proper incineration is one way of disposing of discarded plastics, but it can produce toxic gases. Some polymers are engineered to be degradable. Recycling of plastics requires that they be collected and sorted according to the code numbers. Recycled plastics are being used more and more. Flame-retardant fabrics for clothing are made of polymers that often incorporate chlorine or bromine atoms.

The chemicals used in manufacturing plastics, especially plasticizers, can present problems. A **plasticizer** makes a polymer more flexible. Polychlorinated biphenyls (PCBs) were once used as plasticizers but are now banned. Phthalate esters are the most widely used plasticizers today.

Synthetic polymers will be used even more in the future. However, most synthetic polymers come from petroleum, a limited and nonrenewable resource. This is another important reason for recycling plastics.

GREEN CHEMISTRY—While application of the principles of green chemistry can lead to inherently safer products, it is important to analyze the improvements and understand any unintended and unfortunate impacts of the new products. Life-cycle impact analysis can help measure the environmental footprint and inform the greener design of products.

Learning Objectives

❯ Define *polymer* and *monomer*.	Problems 3, 5, 7
❯ List several natural polymers, including a chemically modified one.	Problems 6, 9, 43, 55
❯ Describe the structure and properties of the two main types of polyethylene.	Problems 1, 13, 14
❯ Use the terms *thermoplastic* and *thermosetting* to explain how polymer structure determines properties.	Problem 8
❯ Identify the monomer(s) of an addition polymer, and write the structural formula for a polymer from its monomer structure(s).	Problems 4, 15–20, 21, 37–39, 41–45, 52, 53
❯ Define *cross-linking*, and explain how it changes the properties of a polymer.	Problems 2, 22–26, 47
❯ Differentiate between addition and condensation polymerization.	Problems 3, 27–32, 35, 36
❯ Write the structures of the monomers that form polyesters and polyamides.	Problems 46, 48–53
❯ Understand the concept of the glass transition temperature.	Problems 33, 40
❯ Explain how crystallinity affects the physical properties of polymers.	Problems 13, 14, 33, 34
❯ Describe the environmental problems associated with plastics and plasticizers.	Problems 10–12
❯ Name two types of sustainable, nonpetroleum-derived polymers and give their sources.	Problem 54
❯ Explain how life-cycle impact analysis can be used to identify the environmental benefits and effects of newly designed products.	Problems 55–57

 ## REVIEW QUESTIONS

1. How does the structure of PVC differ from that of polyethylene? List several uses of polyethylene.

2. Define the following terms.
   a. macromolecule   b. elastomer
   c. copolymer   d. plasticizer

3. What is addition polymerization? What structural feature usually characterizes molecules used as monomers in addition polymerization?

4. What is Teflon? What special property does it have? What are some of its uses?

5. From what monomer are disposable foamed plastic coffee cups made?

6. What plastic is used to make (a) gallon milk jugs and (b) 2-L soft drink bottles?

7. What is celluloid? From what material is it made?

8. What is a thermoplastic polymer? Give an example.

9. Which type of fibers, natural or synthetic, is used most in the United States? Why?

10. What are PCBs? Why are they no longer used as plasticizers?

11. What steps must be taken to recycle plastics?

12. What problems arise when plastics are (a) discarded into the environment, (b) disposed of in landfills, and (c) disposed of by incineration?

 ## PROBLEMS

Polyethylene

13. Describe the structure of low-density polyethylene (LDPE). How does this structure explain the properties of this polymer?

14. Describe the structure of linear low-density polyethylene (LLDPE). How does this structure explain the properties of this polymer?

Addition Polymerization

15. Write the structure of the monomer from which each of the following polymers is made.
    a. polyethylene   b. polystyrene

16. Write the structure of the monomer from which each of the following polymers is made.
    a. polypropylene   b. polyvinyl chloride

17. Write the structure of a chain segment that is at least eight carbon atoms long for the polymer made from each of the following.
    a. polyacrylonitrile
    b. vinylidene fluoride ($H_2C{=}CF_2$)

18. Write the structure of a chain segment that is at least four repeat units long for the polymer formed from each of the following monomers.
    a. tetrafluoroethylene   b. methyl methacrylate

$$CH_2{=}\overset{\overset{\displaystyle CH_3}{|}}{C}COOCH_3$$

19. Write the structure of the polymer made from each of the following. Show at least four repeat units.
    a. 1-pentene ($CH_2{=}CHCH_2CH_2CH_3$)
    b. methyl cyanoacrylate

20. Write the structure of the polymer made from each of the following. Show at least four repeat units.
    a. vinyl acetate [$H_2C{=}CH{-}O(C{=}O)CH_3$]
    b. methyl acrylate [$H_2C{=}CH{-}(C{=}O)OCH_3$]

Rubber and Other Elastomers

21. Draw the structure of the monomer isoprene.

22. Describe the process of vulcanization. How does vulcanization change the properties of rubber?

23. Explain why rubber is elastic, while many other polymers are rigid.

24. How does polybutadiene differ from natural rubber in properties? In structure?

25. How is SBR made? From what monomer(s) is it made?

26. Name three synthetic elastomers and the monomer(s) from which they are made.

Condensation Polymers

27. Nylon 88 is made from the monomers $H_2N(CH_2)_8NH_2$ and $HOOC(CH_2)_6COOH$. Draw the structure of nylon 88, showing at least two repeat units from each monomer.

28. Kodel is a polyester fiber. The monomers used to make it are terephthalic acid (page 300) and 1,4-cyclohexanedimethanol (shown below). Write a condensed structural formula for the repeat unit of the Kodel molecule.

$$HOCH_2{-}\bighexagon{-}CH_2OH$$

1,4-Cyclohexanedimethanol

29. Draw the structure of a polymer made from glycolic acid (hydroxyacetic acid, $HOCH_2COOH$). Show at least four repeat units. (*Hint:* Compare with nylon 6 in Section 10.5.)

30. Kevlar, a polyamide used to make bulletproof vests, is made from terephthalic acid (page 300) and *para*-phenylenediamine (shown below). Write a condensed structural formula for the repeat unit of the Kevlar molecule.

$$H_2N{-}\bigcirc{-}NH_2$$

para-Phenylenediamine

Properties of Polymers

31. Rank the following types of matter from smallest to largest: atom, compound, element, polymer.

32. What does the word *plastic* mean (a) in everyday life and (b) in chemistry?

33. What is the glass transition temperature (T_g) of a polymer? For what uses do we want polymers with a low T_g? With a high T_g?

34. How do plasticizers make polymers less brittle?

ADDITIONAL PROBLEMS

35. In the following equation, identify the parts labeled a, b, and c as monomer, polymer, and repeat unit. What type of polymerization (addition or condensation) is represented?

$$n\;\overbrace{CH_2{=}CHF}^{a}\;\longrightarrow$$

$$\underbrace{{\sim}CH_2{-}\overbrace{CHF{-}CH_2}^{b}{-}CHF{-}CH_2{-}CHF{-}CH_2{-}CHF{\sim}}_{c}$$

36. Is nylon 88 (Problem 27) an addition polymer or a condensation polymer? Explain.

37. One type of Saran has the structure shown below. Write the structures of the two monomers from which it is made.

$${\sim}CH_2CCl_2{-}CH_2CHCl{-}CH_2CCl_2{-}CH_2CHCl{\sim}$$

38. From what monomers could the following copolymer, called poly(styrene-co-acrylonitrile) (SAN), be made?

$$\begin{array}{c}{\sim}CH_2CH{-}CH_2CH{-}CH_2CH{\sim}\\ \quad\;|\qquad\quad\;|\qquad\quad\;|\\ \quad C{\equiv}N\quad\;\bigcirc\quad\; C{\equiv}N\end{array}$$

39. Cyanoacrylates, such as those made from methyl cyanoacrylate (Problem 19b), are used in instant-setting "superglues." However, poly(methyl cyanoacrylate) can irritate tissues. Cyanoacrylates with longer alkyl ester groups are less harsh and can be used in surgery in place of sutures. A good example is poly(octyl cyanoacrylate). Write a polymerization reaction for the formation of poly(octyl cyanoacrylate) from octyl cyanoacrylate, using a condensed structural formula to show the repeat unit of the polymer.

40. What is the first vivid change that occurs **(a)** when a thermoplastic polymer and **(b)** when a thermosetting polymer are heated to increasingly higher temperatures?

41. Isobutylene [CH_2=$C(CH_3)_2$] polymerizes to form polyisobutylene, a sticky polymer used as an adhesive. Draw the structure of polyisobutylene. Show at least four repeat units.

42. Copolymerization of isoprene and isobutylene (Problem 41) forms butyl rubber. Write the structure of butyl rubber. Show at least three isobutylene repeat units and one isoprene repeat unit.

43. The bacteria *Alcaligenes eutrophus* produce a polymer called polyhydroxybutyrate whose structure is shown below. Write the structure of the hydroxy acid from which this polymer is made.

$$\left[O\!-\!\underset{\underset{CH_3}{|}}{CH}\!-\!CH_2\!-\!\overset{\overset{O}{\|}}{C} \right]_n$$

44. DSM Engineering Plastics makes two specialty polymers: Stanyl® nylon 46 and polytetramethylene terephthalamide (PA_4T). (A methylene group is CH_2; tetramethylene consists of four methylene groups: $CH_2CH_2CH_2CH_2$.) Both polymers are made using 1,4-diaminobutane as the diamine. **(a)** What diacid is used for each? Write a condensed structural formula showing the repeat unit of **(b)** Stanyl® nylon 46 and **(c)** PA_4T.

45. A student writes the formula for polypropylene as shown below. Identify the error(s) in the formula.

$$\left[CH_2\!-\!CH\!-\!CH_3 \right]_n$$

46. Based on the condensed structural formula of the repeat unit of poly(ethylene naphthalate) (PEN) shown below, **(a)** write the structure(s) of the monomer(s) and **(b)** state whether the polymer is a polyester or a polyamide.

47. A rubber ball dropped from 100 cm will bounce back up to about 60 cm. Balls made from polybutadiene, called SuperBalls, bounce back up to about 85 cm. Golf balls, made from cross-linked polybutadiene, bounce back up to 89 cm. What type of polymer are all three balls made of? Which kind of ball exhibits the property of this type of polymer to the greatest degree?

48. Draw a structure of a likely product if 2,3-butanediol (shown below) is substituted for ethylene glycol in the reaction with terephthalic acid (page 300).

$$\underset{\underset{OH}{|}}{CH_3CH}\overset{\overset{OH}{|}}{CH}CH_3$$

49. A student is asked to synthesize a polyester from terephthalic acid (page 300) and 1,4-butanediol ($HOCH_2CH_2CH_2CH_2OH$). By mistake, the student uses 2-butanol rather than 1,4-butanediol. What is the likely result of this substitution?

50. A student is asked to synthesize a polyester from terephthalic acid and 1,4-butanediol ($HOCH_2CH_2CH_2OH$). By mistake, the student uses 1,3-butanediol (shown below) rather than the 1,4-butanediol. What is the likely result of this substitution?

$$HOCH_2CH_2\overset{\overset{OH}{|}}{CH}CH_3$$

51. Draw the structure of the silicone polymer formed from the compound shown below, showing four repeating units.

$$(CH_3)CH\!-\!\underset{\underset{OH}{|}}{\overset{\overset{OH}{|}}{Si}}\!-\!CH(CH_3)_2$$

52. The two alkenes shown below are different compounds, but when each undergoes addition polymerization, the same polymer is formed. Explain.

$$CH_3\!-\!\underset{\underset{Cl}{|}}{C}\!=\!\underset{\underset{Br}{|}}{C}\!-\!CH_2CH_3 \qquad CH_3\!-\!\underset{\underset{Cl}{|}}{C}\!=\!\underset{\underset{CH_2CH_3}{|}}{C}\!-\!Br$$

53. The structures of epoxies contain heterocyclic rings, similar to those shown in Example 9.12. Some heterocyclic rings are polymerized by breaking one of the bonds between a carbon atom and the oxygen, nitrogen, or sulfur atom and then undergoing an addition reaction. Draw the structures of the polymers that could result from polymerization of the molecules in parts **(a)** and **(b)** of Example 9.12. Show four repeat units for each polymer.

54. Each *amino acid* shown in Table 16.3 (page 488) has an amino group ($-NH_3^+$) and a carboxylic acid group ($-COO^-$). (In each case, a proton has been donated from the carboxylic group to the amino group.) Proteins are polymers of amino acids. Draw the structure of the protein formed by polymerization of glycine, showing four repeat units.

55. Which of the following processes would be included in the outline of the life cycle of a PET water bottle? Choose all that apply.
  a. Whether the bottle is sent to a landfill or recycled
  b. The PET polymerization process
  c. The source of the water inside the bottle
  d. The synthesis processes to make the monomers
  e. The source of the raw materials for the monomers

56. Give an example of an unintended and undesirable effect that has resulted from an "improved" product or technology.

57. How can LCIA help with the development of green chemistry solutions?
  a. It gives a total score that makes it obvious which product is greener.
  b. It makes sure that people will recycle PET bottles.
  c. It shows which trade-offs have been created during the design of an alternative and enables the comparison of the environmental footprints of products.
  d. It identifies that production of CO_2 is bad for the environment.

CRITICAL THINKING EXERCISES

Apply knowledge that you have gained in this chapter text and one or more of the FLaReS principles (Chapter 1) to evaluate the following statements or claims.

10.1. An environmental activist states that all-natural materials should be used to replace synthetic plastics because they are more sustainable.

10.2. A news report states that incinerators that burn plastics are a major source of chlorine-containing toxic compounds called *dioxins* (Chapter 20).

10.3. Vinyl chloride is a carcinogen. Some people warn that children will get cancer from playing with toys made of PVC.

10.4. The Plastics Division of the American Chemistry Council says that, in comparison to paper bags, "plastic bags are . . . an environmentally responsible choice."

COLLABORATIVE GROUP PROJECTS

Prepare a PowerPoint, poster, or other presentation (as directed by your instructor) to share with the class.

1. Prepare a brief report on possible sources of plastics when Earth's supplies of coal and petroleum become scarce.

2. Prepare a brief report on biobased polymers such as bio-HDPE, nylon 11 (polyundecylamide), biobased PET, and biobased polytrimethylene terephthalate (PTT). Identify the natural source from which each is derived, and describe intermediate steps from source to final product.

3. Evaluate fully the competition between Pepsi and Coca-Cola as to which company is doing more to reduce its environmental impact by using biobased plastic bottles.

4. Do a risk–benefit analysis (Section 1.4) of the use of synthetic polymers for one or more of the following.
   a. grocery bags
   b. building materials
   c. clothing
   d. carpets
   e. food packaging
   f. picnic coolers
   g. automobile tires
   h. artificial hip sockets

5. To what extent is plastic litter a problem in your community? Survey one city block (or other area as directed by your instructor), and inventory the litter found. (You might as well pick it up while you are at it.) What proportion of the litter is plastics? What proportion of it is fast-food containers? To what extent are plastics recycled in your community? What factors limit further recycling?

6. Prepare a brief report on one of the following polymers. List sources and commercial uses.
   a. polybutadiene
   b. ethylene–propylene rubber
   c. polyurethanes
   d. epoxy resins

7. Do some research on Kevlar, which is used in body armor. Report on its other uses, and explain why it is so strong. Describe the Kevlar Survivors' Club, jointly sponsored by the International Chiefs of Police and DuPont.

8. Compare the treatment of the topic of the environmental impact of plastics and other polymers at several websites, such as those of the American Plastics Council, an industry group, and an environmental group such as Greenpeace or the Sierra Club.

CHEMISTRY@HOME   *Polymer Bouncing Ball*

Materials required

- 2 small plastic cups (4 oz.)
- Measuring spoons
- Warm water
- Borax
- 2 wooden craft sticks
- White craft glue
- Cornstarch
- Food coloring (if desired)
- Plastic bag with zip lock (for storage)

Did you know that the earliest balls were made of wood and stone? What are most bouncy balls made of today?

Many bouncing balls are made out of rubber, but they can also be made out of leather or plastic and can be hollow or solid. This experiment will use common, inexpensive ingredients to make a ball that bounces.

Polymers are molecules made up of repeating chemical units. Glue is made up of the polymer polyvinyl acetate (PVA). In this experiment, borax (boric acid) is responsible for hooking the molecules together and cross-linking the molecules, providing the ball with its putty-like and bouncy properties.

To start, label the two cups Borax Solution and Ball Mixture.

–For the Borax Solution, pour 2 tablespoons of warm water and $\frac{1}{2}$ teaspoon of borax powder into the cup. Use a craft stick to stir the mixture to dissolve the borax. Add food coloring, if desired.

–For the Ball Mixture, pour 1 tablespoon of glue into the cup. Add $\frac{1}{2}$ teaspoon of the borax solution you just made and 1 tablespoon of cornstarch. Do not stir. Allow the ingredients to interact on their own for 10–15 seconds. Use the other craft stick to stir them together to fully mix, and once the mixture becomes too thick to stir, take it out of the cup and start molding the ball with your hands.

The ball will start out sticky and messy but will solidify as you knead it. Once the ball is less sticky, go ahead and bounce it! To keep your ball from drying out store your ball in a plastic zip lock bag.

Questions

1. Does your ball bounce? How high?
2. Does making a polymer ball cause a chemical or physical reaction? Explain.
3. Describe how changing the amounts of each ingredient would affect the ball mixture.
4. Is this ball biodegradable? Why or why not?

Learning Objectives

> Identify the sources of the natural radiation to which we are exposed. (11.1)

> List the sources and dangers of ionizing radiation. (11.1)

> Balance nuclear equations. (11.2)

> Identify the types of products formed by various decay processes. (11.2)

> Solve simple half-life problems. (11.3)

> Use the concept of half-life to solve simple radioisotopic dating problems. (11.3)

> Write a nuclear equation for a transmutation, and identify the product element formed. (11.4)

> List some applications of radioisotopes. (11.5)

> Describe the nature of materials needed to block alpha, beta, and gamma radiation. (11.6)

> Explain where nuclear energy comes from. (11.7)

> Describe the difference between fission and fusion. (11.7)

> Describe the goals of the Manhattan Project and how uranium and plutonium bombs were made. (11.8)

> Identify the most hazardous fallout isotopes, and explain why they are particularly dangerous. (11.8)

> List some uses and consequences of nuclear energy. (11.9)

> Explain how applications of Green Chemistry Principles can be applied to handling of radioactive isotopes in spent fuel rods.

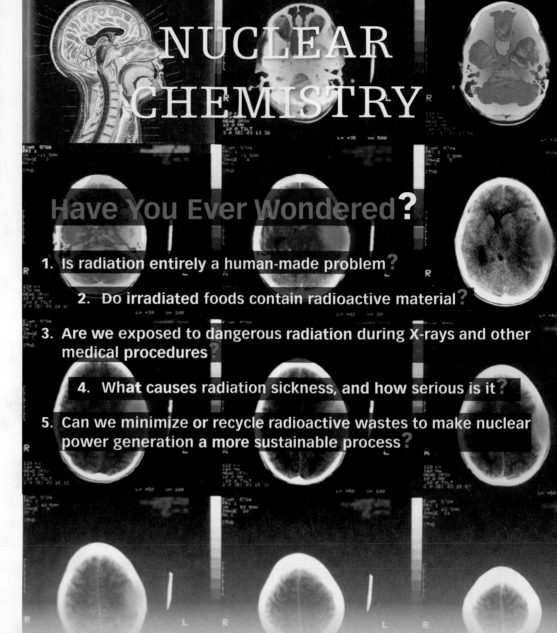

NUCLEAR CHEMISTRY

Have You Ever Wondered?

1. **Is radiation entirely a human-made problem?**

2. **Do irradiated foods contain radioactive material?**

3. **Are we exposed to dangerous radiation during X-rays and other medical procedures?**

4. **What causes radiation sickness, and how serious is it?**

5. **Can we minimize or recycle radioactive wastes to make nuclear power generation a more sustainable process?**

THE HEART OF MATTER Many people associate the term *nuclear energy* with fearsome images of a mighty force: giant mushroom clouds from nuclear explosions that devastated cities and nuclear power plant accidents at Three Mile Island, Pennsylvania, in 1979, Chernobyl, Ukraine, in 1986, and Fukushima, Japan, in 2011 (discussed in Chapter 15). But some amazing stories can also be told about life-giving applications of nuclear energy. Indeed, medical uses of nuclear energy have undoubtedly saved more lives than have been lost as a result of nuclear bombs or accidents.

The photos above show images from MRI (magnetic resonance imaging). At the upper right of this page is an image from PET (positron emission tomography). The picture to the side shows an example of an X-ray, which is used for examining bones and internal organs. All of these diagnostic techniques use radiation or a radioactive isotope. With these techniques, we can now examine tissues and diagnose diseases that previously could only be detected by much more invasive procedures such as biopsy or exploratory surgery. The nuclear age has produced both serious problems and tremendous advantages, which will be examined in this chapter.

The discussion of atomic structure in Chapter 3 focused mainly on the electrons, because the electrons are the particles that determine an element's chemistry. In this chapter, we take a closer look at that tiny speck in the center of the atom—the atomic nucleus.

Atoms undoubtedly are small, but the even-smaller size of the atomic nucleus is almost beyond our imagination. The diameter of an atom is roughly 100,000 times greater than the diameter of its nucleus. If an atom could be magnified to be as large as your classroom, the nucleus would be about as big as the period at the end of this sentence. Yet this very tiny nucleus contains almost all the atom's mass. How dense the atomic nucleus must be! A cubic centimeter of water weighs 1 g, and a cubic centimeter of gold about 19 g. A cubic centimeter of pure atomic nuclei would weigh more than 100 million metric tons!

Even more amazing than the density of the nucleus is the enormous amount of energy contained within it. Some atomic nuclei undergo reactions that can fuel the most powerful bombs ever built or provide electricity for millions of people. Our sun is one huge nuclear power plant, supplying the energy that warms our planet and the light necessary for plant growth. The twinkling light from every star we see in the night sky is produced by powerful nuclear reactions. Radioactive isotopes are used in medicine to save lives every day, through diagnosis and treatment of diseases. Many applications of nuclear chemistry in science and industry have improved the human condition significantly. Nuclear reactions allow us to date archaeological and geological finds, to assess the quality of industrial materials, to provide electricity, and to be alerted to deadly fires. In this chapter, you will learn about the destructive and the healing power of that infinitesimally small and wonderfully dense heart of every atom—the nucleus.

11.1 Natural Radioactivity

Learning Objectives ❯ Identify the sources of the natural radiation to which we are exposed. ❯ List the sources and dangers of ionizing radiation.

Recall from Chapter 3 that most elements occur in nature in several isotopic forms, whose nuclei have the same number of protons but differ in their number of neutrons. Many of these nuclei are unstable and undergo **radioactive decay**. The nuclei that undergo such decay are called **radioisotopes**, and the process of decay produces one or more types of radiation. Stable isotopes have some common characteristics, which are identified on p. 319.

Background Radiation

Humans have always been exposed to radiation. Even as you read this sentence, you are being bombarded by *cosmic rays*, which originate from the sun and outer space. Other radiation reaches us from natural radioactive isotopes in air, water,

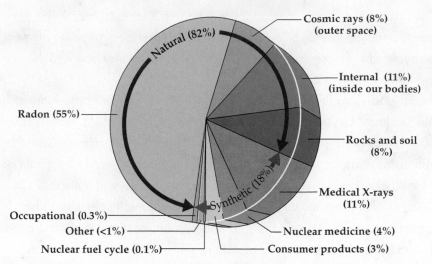

▲ **Figure 11.1** Most of the radiation to which we are exposed comes from natural sources (blue shades). About 18% of this radiation comes from human activities (other colors).

Q: *What natural source of ionizing radiation contributes most to our exposure? What source provides the largest proportion of our exposure due to human activities?*

soil, and rocks. We cannot escape radiation because it is part of many natural processes, including those in our bodies. A naturally occurring radioactive isotope of potassium, ^{40}K, exists in all our cells and in many foods. The average person absorbs about 4000 particles of radiation each second from ^{40}K and another 1200 particles per second from ^{14}C. (This may sound like a lot, but recall how small atoms are and how many atoms exist in even a tiny sample of matter.)

This ever-present natural radiation is called **background radiation**. Figure 11.1 shows that over three-fourths of the average person's radiation exposure comes from background radiation. Most of the remainder comes from medical irradiation such as X-rays. Other sources, such as fallout from testing of nuclear bombs, releases from nuclear industry power plants, and occupational exposure, account for only a minute fraction of the total average exposure.

Harmful effects arise from the interaction of radiation with living tissue. Radiation with enough energy to knock electrons from atoms and molecules, converting them into ions (electrically charged atoms or groups of atoms), is called **ionizing radiation**. Nuclear radiation and X-rays are examples. Because radiation is invisible and because it has such great potential for harm, we are very much concerned about our exposure to it. However, it is worth noting that the total amount of background radiation to which the average person is exposed is less than 0.5% of the amount that can cause symptoms of radiation sickness.

Radiation Damage to Cells

Radiation-caused chemical changes in living cells can be highly disruptive. Ionizing radiation can devastate living cells by interfering with their normal chemical processes. Molecules can be splintered into reactive fragments called *free radicals* (Section 4.10), which can disrupt vital cellular processes. White blood cells, the body's first line of defense against bacterial infection, are particularly vulnerable. High levels of radiation also affect bone marrow, causing a drop in the production of red blood cells which results in anemia. Radiation has also been shown to induce leukemia, a disease of the blood-forming organs.

Ionizing radiation also can cause changes in the molecules of heredity (DNA) in reproductive cells. Such changes can show up as mutations in the offspring of exposed parents. Little is known of the effects of such exposure on humans. However, many of the mutations that occurred during the evolution of present species may have been caused by background radiation.

1. Is radiation entirely a human-made problem?

Many people think that a large proportion of radiation comes from human-made sources. However, Figure 11.1 clearly shows that the majority (82%) of the ionizing radiation to which people are exposed is background radiation that comes from natural sources and only a much smaller proportion of ionizing radiation results from human-made sources.

Cell phone ON   Cell phone OFF

Left   Right

60

0

μmol/100g/min

◀ **Figure 11.2** A brain scan shows slight differences when a cell phone held to the ear is on (left) and off (right).

Ionizing radiation from decaying atomic nuclei is highly energetic and can damage tissue, as discussed above. *Electromagnetic* radiation has many forms—visible light, radio waves, television broadcast waves, microwaves, ultraviolet light, military ULF (ultra-low-frequency), and others. Some types of electromagnetic radiation, such as X-rays and gamma rays, do have enough energy to ionize tissue, and ultraviolet light has been strongly implicated in *melanoma* (skin cancer).

But what about microwaves and radio waves, which don't have nearly as much energy? There is no conclusive evidence that low levels of microwaves pose a significant threat to human health. A 2006 study of nearly half a million Danish citizens failed to show a relationship between cell phone use and cancer. While cell phones *do* give off radiation that affects parts of the brain, as can be seen in Figure 11.2, it is not ionizing radiation and thus does not cause cell damage. However, higher levels of radio frequencies over long periods of time *may* be a different matter. In May 2011, the World Health Organization (WHO) classified heavy cell phone use—30 minutes of talking daily for ten years—as *possibly* posing an increased risk of *glioma*, a type of brain cancer. For low levels of exposure to nonionizing electromagnetic radiation, the hazard appears to be difficult to measure, let alone assess.

Because of these potentially devastating effects on living things, knowledge of radiation, radioactive decay, and nuclear chemistry in general is crucial. Next, we will see how to write balanced nuclear equations and how to identify the various types of radiation that are emitted.

Why Are Isotopes Stable—or Unstable?

Some isotopes are stable, but most are radioactive and not stable. What factors tend to make an atomic nucleus stable? Generally, stable isotopes tend to have:

1. *Even* numbers of either protons or neutrons or (especially) both. Of the 264 stable isotopes, 157 have *even* numbers of both protons and neutrons, and only 4 have odd numbers of both protons and neutrons. Elements with an even Z have more stable isotopes than do those with an odd Z.

2. So-called *magic numbers* of either protons or neutrons. (Magic numbers are 2, 8, 20, 50, 82, and 126.)

3. An atomic number of 83 or less. All isotopes with Z>83 are radioactive.

4. Fewer, or the same number of, protons as neutrons in the nucleus, and a ratio of neutrons to protons close to 1 if the atomic number is 20 or below. As the atomic number gets larger, the stable n/p ratio also increases, up to about 1.5. There is a zone of stability within which the n/p ratio should lie for an atom with a given atomic number.

SELF-ASSESSMENT Questions

1. What percentage of background radiation comes from natural sources?

   a. 5%   **b.** 18%   **c.** 45%   **d.** 82%

2. The largest source of natural background radiation is
   a. cosmic rays   **b.** isotopes in the body
   c. radon   **d.** isotopes in rocks and soil

3. At present levels of exposure, which of the following forms of radiation is most likely to give you cancer?
   a. fallout from the Fukushima nuclear power plant accident
   b. medical X-rays
   c. radiation from operating nuclear power plants
   d. sunlight

11.2 Nuclear Equations

Learning Objectives ❯ Balance nuclear equations. ❯ Identify the types of products formed by various nuclear decay processes.

Writing balanced equations for nuclear processes is relatively simple. Nuclear equations differ in two ways from the chemical equations discussed in Chapter 5. First, while chemical equations must have the same elements on both sides of the arrow, nuclear equations rarely do. Second, while we balance atoms in ordinary chemical equations, we balance the *nucleons* (protons and neutrons) in nuclear equations. What this really means is that we must balance the atomic numbers (number of protons) and nucleon numbers (number of nucleons) of the starting materials and products. For this reason, we must always specify the *isotope* of each element appearing in a nuclear equation. We use nuclear symbols (Section 3.5) when writing nuclear equations because they make the equations easier to balance.

In one example of a nuclear reaction, radon-222 atoms break down spontaneously in a process called **alpha decay**, giving off alpha (α) particles, as shown in Figure 11.3a. Because alpha particles are identical to helium nuclei, this reaction can be summarized by the following equation:

| Mass number of starting material = 222 | Mass numbers of products = 4 + 218 = 222 |

$$^{222}_{86}\text{Rn} \longrightarrow {}^{4}_{2}\text{He} + {}^{218}_{84}\text{Po}$$

| Atomic number of starting material = 86 | Atomic numbers of products = 2 + 84 = 86 |

We use the symbol ${}^{4}_{2}\text{He}$ (rather than α) for the alpha particle because it allows us to check the balancing of mass and atomic numbers more readily. The atomic number, $Z = 84$, identifies the element produced as polonium (Po). In nuclear chemistry, the mass number, A, equates with the number of nucleons in the starting material.

${}^{222}_{86}\text{Rn}$

(a) Alpha decay

${}^{4}_{2}\text{He}$

Alpha particle

${}^{218}_{84}\text{Po}$

${}^{3}_{1}\text{H}$ ${}^{3}_{2}\text{He}$ ${}^{0}_{-1}\text{e}$
                                    Beta particle

(b) Beta decay

▲ **Figure 11.3** Nuclear emission of (a) an alpha particle and (b) a beta particle.

Q: *What changes occur in a nucleus when it emits an alpha particle? A beta particle?*

The number of nucleons in the starting material must equal the total number of the nucleons in the products. The same is true for the atomic numbers. In alpha decay, the atomic number decreases by 2 and the number of nucleons decreases by 4.

The heaviest isotope of hydrogen, hydrogen-3, often called *tritium*, decomposes by a process called **beta decay** (Figure 11.3b). Because a beta (β) particle is identical to an electron, this process can be written as

| Mass number of starting material = 3 | Mass numbers of products = 0 + 3 = 3 |

$$^3_1\text{H} \longrightarrow ^{\ 0}_{-1}\text{e} \quad 1 \quad ^3_2\text{He}$$

| Atomic number of starting material = I | Atomic numbers of products = (−I) + 2 = I |

The atomic number, $Z = 2$, identifies the product isotope as helium.

Beta decay is a little more complicated than indicated by the preceding reaction. In beta decay, a neutron within the nucleus is converted into a proton (which remains in the nucleus) and an electron (which is ejected).

$$^1_0\text{n} \longrightarrow ^1_1\text{p} + ^{\ 0}_{-1}\text{e}$$

With beta decay, the atomic number increases, but the number of nucleons remains the same.

A third kind of radiation may be emitted in a nuclear reaction: gamma (γ) rays. **Gamma decay** is different from alpha and beta decay in that gamma radiation has no charge and no mass. Neither the nucleon number nor the atomic number of the emitting atom is changed; the nucleus simply become less energetic. Table 11.1 compares the properties of alpha, beta, and gamma radiation. Not only do alpha particles have very low penetrating power (Section 11.6), but they also move more slowly than beta particles or gamma rays. In contrast, the penetrating power of gamma rays is extremely high. While a few millimeters of aluminum will stop most β particles, several centimeters of lead are needed to stop γ rays.

Two other types of radioactive decay are *positron emission* and *electron capture*. These two processes have the same effect on the atomic nucleus, but they occur by different pathways. Both result in a decrease of one in atomic number with no change in nucleon number (Figure 11.4).

(a) Positron emission

(b) Electron capture

▲ **Figure 11.4** Nuclear change accompanying (a) positron emission and (b) electron capture.

Q: *What changes occur in a nucleus when it emits a positron? When it undergoes electron capture?*

Table 11.1	Common Types of Radiation in Nuclear Reactions				
Radiation	Mass (u)	Charge	Identity	Velocity[a]	Penetrating Power
Alpha (α)	4	2+	He^{2+}	$0.1c$	Very low
Beta (β)	0.00055	1−	e^-	$<0.9\,c$	Moderate
Gamma (γ)	0	0	High-energy photon	c	Extremely high

[a]c is the speed of light.

The **positron** (β^+) is a particle equal in mass but opposite in charge to the electron. It is represented as $_{+1}^{0}e$. Fluorine-18 decays by positron emission.

$$_{9}^{18}F \longrightarrow {}_{+1}^{0}e + {}_{8}^{18}O$$

We can envision positron emission as the change of a proton in the nucleus into a neutron and a positron, with the positron being emitted from the nucleus.

$$_{1}^{1}p \longrightarrow {}_{0}^{1}n + {}_{+1}^{0}e$$

After a positron is emitted, the original nucleus has one less proton and one more neutron than it had before. The nucleon number of the product nucleus is the same, but its atomic number has been reduced by one. The emitted positron quickly encounters an electron (there are many electrons in all kinds of matter), and both particles are changed into energy—in this case, two gamma rays.

$$_{+1}^{0}e + {}_{-1}^{0}e \longrightarrow 2{}_{0}^{0}\gamma$$

Electron capture (EC) is a process in which a nucleus absorbs an electron from an inner electron shell, usually the first or second. When an electron from a higher shell drops to the level vacated by the captured electron, an X-ray is released. Once inside the nucleus, the captured electron combines with a proton to form a neutron.

$$_{1}^{1}p + {}_{-1}^{0}e \longrightarrow {}_{0}^{1}n$$

Iodine-125, used in medicine to diagnose pancreatic function and intestinal fat absorption, decays by electron capture.

$$_{53}^{125}I + {}_{-1}^{0}e \longrightarrow {}_{52}^{125}Te$$

Note that, unlike alpha, beta, gamma, or positron emission, electron capture has the electron as a reactant (on the left side) and not a product. Conversion of a proton to a neutron (by the absorbed electron) yields a nucleus with the atomic number lowered by 1 but unchanged in atomic mass. Emission of a positron and absorption of an electron have the same effect on an atomic nucleus (lowering the atomic number by 1), except that positron emission is accompanied by gamma radiation and electron capture by X-radiation. Positron-emitting isotopes and those that undergo electron capture have important medical applications (Section 11.5).

The five types of radioactive decay are summarized in Table 11.2.

Table 11.2	Radioactive Decay and Nuclear Change				
Type of Decay	Decay Particle	Particle Mass (u)	Particle Charge	Change in Nucleon Number	Change in Atomic Number
Alpha decay	α	4	2+	Decreases by 4	Decreases by 2
Beta decay	β	0	1−	No change	Increases by 1
Gamma radiation	γ	0	0	No change	No change
Positron emission	β^+	0	1+	No change	Decreases by 1
Electron capture (EC)	e^- absorbed	0	1−	No change	Decreases by 1

Example 11.1 Balancing Nuclear Equations

Write balanced nuclear equations for the following processes. In each case, identify the product element formed.

a. Plutonium-239 emits an alpha particle when it decays.

b. Protactinium-234 undergoes beta decay.

c. Carbon-11 emits a positron when it decays.

d. Carbon-11 undergoes electron capture.

Solution

a. We start by writing the symbol for plutonium-239 and a partial equation showing that one of the products is an alpha particle (helium nucleus).

$$^{239}_{94}\text{Pu} \longrightarrow {}^{4}_{2}\text{He} + ?$$

To balance this equation, the other product must have $A = 239-4 = 235$ and $Z = 94-2 = 92$. The atomic number 92 identifies the element as uranium (U).

$$^{239}_{94}\text{Pu} \longrightarrow {}^{4}_{2}\text{He} + {}^{235}_{92}\text{U}$$

b. We write the symbol for protactinium-234 and a partial equation showing that one of the products is a beta particle (electron).

$$^{234}_{91}\text{Pa} \longrightarrow {}^{0}_{-1}\text{e} + ?$$

The other product must have a nucleon number of 234 and $Z = 92$ to balance the equation. The atomic number identifies this product as another isotope of uranium.

$$^{234}_{91}\text{Pa} \longrightarrow {}^{0}_{-1}\text{e} + {}^{234}_{92}\text{U}$$

c. We write the symbol for carbon-11 and a partial equation showing that one of the products is a positron.

$$^{11}_{6}\text{C} \longrightarrow {}^{0}_{+1}\text{e} + ?$$

To balance the equation, a particle with $A = 11 - 0 = 11$ and $Z = 6-1 = 5$ (boron) is required.

$$^{11}_{6}\text{C} \longrightarrow {}^{0}_{+1}\text{e} + {}^{11}_{5}\text{B}$$

d. We write the symbol for carbon-11 and a partial equation showing it capturing an electron.

$$^{11}_{6}\text{C} + {}^{0}_{-1}\text{e} \longrightarrow ?$$

To balance the equation, the product must have $A = 11+0 = 11$ and $Z = 6+(-1) = 5$ (boron).

$$^{11}_{6}\text{C} + {}^{0}_{-1}\text{e} \longrightarrow {}^{11}_{5}\text{B}$$

As we noted previously, positron emission and electron capture result in identical changes in atomic number and, therefore, affect a given nucleus in the same way, as parts **(c)** and **(d)** illustrate for carbon-11. Also note that carbon-11 (and certain other nuclei) can undergo more than one type of radioactive decay.

■ EXERCISE 11.1

Write balanced nuclear equations for the following processes. In each case, identify the product element formed.

a. Bismuth-214 decays by alpha emission.   **b.** Niobium-94 undergoes beta decay.
c. Gallium-68 decays by positron emission.   **d.** Argon-37 undergoes electron capture.

Table 11.3	Some Differences Between Chemical Reactions and Nuclear Reactions
Chemical Reactions	Nuclear Reactions
Atoms retain their identity.	Atoms usually change their identity—from one element to another.
Reactions involve only electrons and usually only outermost electrons.	Reactions involve mainly protons and neutrons. It does not matter what the valence electrons do.
Reaction rates will be greater at higher temperatures.	Reaction rates are unaffected by temperature.
The energy absorbed or given off in reactions is comparatively small.	Reactions sometimes involve enormous changes in energy.
Mass is conserved. The mass of products equals the mass of starting materials.	Huge changes in energy are accompanied by measurable changes in mass ($E = mc^2$).

Table 11.4   **Symbols for Subatomic Particles**

Particle	Symbol	Nuclear Symbol
Proton	p	$_1^1\text{p}$ or $_1^1\text{H}$
Neutron	n	$_0^1\text{n}$
Electron	e^- or β^-	$_{-1}^0\text{e}$ or $_{-1}^0\beta$
Positron	e^+ or β^+	$_{+1}^0\text{e}$ or $_{+1}^0\beta$
Alpha particle	α	$_2^4\text{He}$ or $_2^4\alpha$
Beta particle	β or β^-	$_{-1}^0\text{e}$ or $_{-1}^0\beta$
Gamma ray	γ	$_0^0\gamma$

We noted earlier that nuclear *equations* differ in two ways from ordinary chemical equations. Nuclear reactions also exhibit many differences from chemical reactions. Some important distinctions are summarized in Table 11.3. Some nuclear reactions also involve processes other than the five simple ones we have discussed here. Nevertheless, all nuclear equations must be balanced for both nucleon (mass) numbers and atomic numbers. When an unknown particle has an atomic number that does not correspond to an atom, that particle may be a subatomic particle. A list of nuclear symbols for subatomic particles is given in Table 11.4.

SELF-ASSESSMENT Questions

1. What are the mass and the charge, respectively, of positron particles?
   a. 0, −1   **b.** 0, 0   **c.** 0, +1   **d.** 4, +2

2. What particle is needed to complete the following nuclear equation?
$$_4^9\text{Be} + ? \longrightarrow _6^{12}\text{C} + _0^1\text{n}$$
   a. alpha particle   **b.** beta particle
   c. neutron   **d.** proton

3. Emission of which of the following will result in an increase of 1 in atomic number?
   a. alpha particle   **b.** beta particle
   c. neutron   **d.** proton

4. Emission of which of the following will result in no change in atomic number or nucleon number?
   a. alpha particle   **b.** beta particle
   c. gamma ray   **d.** neutron

5. For which type of radioactive decay is an electron found on the left side of the equation?
   a. alpha emission   **b.** beta emission
   c. electron capture   **d.** positron emission

6. Which of the following is the largest particle?
   a. alpha particle   **b.** beta particle
   c. neutron   **d.** proton

11.3 Half-Life and Radioisotopic Dating

Learning Objectives   ❯ Solve simple half-life problems.   ❯ Use the concept of half-life to solve simple radioisotope dating problems.

Thus far, we have discussed radioactivity as applied to single atoms. In the laboratory, we generally deal with great numbers of atoms—numbers far larger than the number of all the people on Earth. If we could see the nucleus of an individual atom, we could tell whether or not it would undergo radioactive decay by noting its composition. Certain combinations of protons and neutrons are unstable. However, we would not be able to predict *when* the atom would undergo a change. Radioactivity is a random process, generally independent of outside influences.

Half-Life

With large numbers of atoms, the process of radioactive decay becomes more predictable. We can measure the *half-life*, a property characteristic of each radioisotope. The **half-life** of a radioactive isotope is the time it takes for one-half of the original number of atoms to undergo radioactive decay.

Suppose, for example, we had 16.00 mg of the radioactive isotope iodine-131. The half-life of iodine-131 is 8.0 days. This means that in 8.0 days, half the iodine-131, or 8.00 mg, will have decayed, and there will be 8.00 mg left. In another 8.0 days, half of the remaining 8.00 mg will have decayed. After

▲ **Figure 11.5** The radioactive decay of iodine-131, which has a half-life of 8 days.

Q: *How much of a 32-mg sample of iodine-131 remains after five half-lives have passed?*

two half-lives, or 16.0 days, one-quarter of the original iodine-131, or 4.00 mg, will remain. Note that two half-lives, do not make a whole. The concept of half-life is illustrated by the graph in Figure 11.5. Half-lives of radioisotopes can differ enormously. The half-life of tellurium-128 is 8×10^{24} y, while that of beryllium-13 is 2.7×10^{-21} s.

The rate of decay is inversely related to half-life. An isotope with a long half-life decays slowly; an isotope with a short half-life decays at a high rate. We measure the rate of decay, also referred to as the isotope's **activity**, in disintegrations per second, a unit called a **becquerel (Bq)**. We can calculate the fraction of the original isotope that remains after a given number of half-lives from the relationship

$$\text{Fraction remaining} = \frac{1}{2^n}$$

where n is the number of half-lives.

Example 11.2 Half-Lives

A 4.00-mg sample of cobalt-60, half-life 5.271 y, is to be used for radiation treatment. How much cobalt-60 remains after 15.813 years (three half-lives)?

Solution
The fraction remaining after three half-lives is

$$\frac{1}{2^n} = \frac{1}{2^3} = \frac{1}{2 \times 2 \times 2} = \frac{1}{8}$$

The amount of cobalt-60 remaining is $\frac{1}{8} \times 4.00$ mg $= 0.50$ mg.

■ EXERCISE 11.2A
The half-life of phosphorus-32 is 14.3 days. What percentage of a sample of phosphorus-32 remains after four half-lives?

■ EXERCISE 11.2B
On April 4, 2011, a small fish caught about 50 mi south of the Fukushima nuclear complex had an activity of 4000 Bq of iodine-131 per kilogram. The half-life of iodine-131 is 8.0 d. What was the activity of the isotope **(a)** on April 28, 2011 (three half-lives later)? **(b)** On June 23, 2011 (ten half-lives later)?

CONCEPTUAL Example 11.3 Time and Radioactive Decay

We cannot determine how long it will take for *all* of a radioactive isotope to decay. For many isotopes, it is assumed that the activity is near zero after about ten half-lives. What mass of a 0.0260-mg sample of mercury-190, half-life 20 min, remains after ten half-lives?

Solution
The fraction remaining after ten half-lives is found in the usual manner.

$$\frac{1}{2^n} = \frac{1}{2^{10}} = \frac{1}{2 \times 2 \times 2 \times 2 \times 2 \times 2 \times 2 \times 2 \times 2 \times 2} = \frac{1}{1024}$$

The amount of mercury-190 remaining is $\frac{1}{1024} \times 0.0260$ mg $= 0.000025$ mg.

■ EXERCISE 11.3
The disposal of some radioactive materials is scheduled according to the rule stated in Conceptual Example 11.3. Would the rule work **(a)** for a 1.00-g sample of rubidium-87 with an initial decay rate of 3200 Bq? **(b)** For a 1.00-g sample of cobalt-60, which has an initial activity of 4.1×10^{13} Bq? Explain.

Radioisotopic Dating

The half-lives of certain radioisotopes can be used to estimate the ages of rocks and archaeological artifacts. Uranium-238 decays with a half-life of 4.5 billion years. The initial products of this decay are also radioactive, and they and subsequent products continue to decay until lead-206 is formed. By measuring the relative amounts of uranium-238 and lead-206, chemists can estimate the age of a rock. Some of the older rocks on Earth have been found to be 3.0–4.5 billion years old. Moon rocks and meteorites have been dated at a maximum age of about 4.5 billion years. Thus, the age of Earth (and the solar system itself) is generally estimated to be about 4.5 billion years.

The dating of artifacts derived from plants or animals usually involves radioactive carbon-14. Of the carbon on Earth, about 99% is carbon-12 and 1% is carbon-13, and both of these isotopes are stable. However, in the upper atmosphere, radioactive carbon-14 is formed by the bombardment of ordinary nitrogen by neutrons from cosmic rays.

$$^{14}_{7}N + {}^{1}_{0}n \longrightarrow {}^{14}_{6}C + {}^{1}_{1}H$$

This process results in a tiny but steady concentration of carbon-14 in the CO_2 molecules of Earth's atmosphere. Plants use CO_2, and animals consume plants and other animals; thus, living things constantly incorporate this isotope into their cells. When organisms die, the incorporation of carbon-14 ceases, and the isotope begins to decay—with a half-life of 5730 years—back to nitrogen-14. We can measure the carbon-14 activity remaining in an artifact of plant or animal origin to determine its age, using the technique called **carbon-14 dating**. For instance, a sample that has half the carbon-14 activity of new plant material is 5730 years old; it has been dead for one half-life. Similarly, an artifact with a fourth of the carbon-14 activity of new plant material is 11,460 years old; it has been dead for two half-lives.

We have assumed that the formation of the carbon-14 isotope has been constant over the years, but this is not quite the case. For the last 7000 years or so, carbon-14 dates do correlate with those obtained from the annual growth rings of trees and with documents of known age. Calibration curves have been constructed from which accurate dates can be determined. Generally, carbon-14 is reasonably accurate for dating objects from about 100 to 50,000 years old. Newer objects may not yet have seen measurable decay of carbon-14. Objects older than 50,000 years have too little of the isotope left for accurate measurement.

Charcoal from the fires of ancient peoples, dated by determining the carbon-14 activity, has been used to estimate the age of other artifacts found at the same archaeological sites. For example, carbon dating was used to confirm that ancient Hebrew writing found on a stone tablet unearthed in Israel dates from the ninth century B.C.E. Carbon dating has also been used to date the collection of Dead Sea Scrolls as being written between the third century B.C.E. and the first century C.E.

Tritium, the radioactive isotope of hydrogen, can also be used for dating materials. Its half-life of 12.26 years makes it useful for dating items up to about 100 years old. An interesting application of tritium dating is the dating of brandies. Alcoholic beverages that are 10 to 50 years old can be quite costly. Tritium dating can be used to check the veracity of advertising claims about the ages of the more expensive brandies.

Table 11.5	Several Isotopes Used in Radioactive Dating		
Isotope	Half-Life (years)	Useful Range	Dating Applications
Carbon-14	5730	100 to 50,000 years	Charcoal, organic material
Hydrogen-3 (tritium)	12.26	1 to 100 years	Aged wines and brandies
Lead-210	22	1 to 75 years	Skeletal remains
Potassium-40	1.25×10^9	10,000 years to the oldest Earth samples	Rocks, Earth's crust, the moon's crust
Rhenium-187	4.3×10^{10}	4×10^7 years to the oldest samples in the universe	Meteorites
Uranium-238	4.51×10^9	10^7 years to the oldest Earth samples	Rocks, the Earth's crust

Many other isotopes are useful for estimating the ages of objects and materials. Several of the more important ones are listed in Table 11.5.

It should also be noted that all isotopes of an element react the same way chemically. However, differences in isotopes can be quite important to some investigations. The variance in mass among isotopes can affect their rates of reaction, with lighter isotopes generally moving a bit faster than heavier ones. This difference can lead to a measurable characteristic called an *isotopic signature* in a material. For example, the ratio of carbon-13 to carbon-12 in materials formed by photosynthesis is less than that isotopic ratio in inorganic carbonates.

Water molecules with oxygen-18 atoms are heavier and evaporate less readily than water molecules with oxygen-16 atoms do. This difference is less pronounced at higher temperatures. Oxygen is incorporated into calcium carbonate shells of aquatic organisms, whose fossils provide a chronological record of the temperature of the water in which the organisms lived. The atmospheric oxygen isotope ratio varies with the season and with geographic location and allows scientists to determine the location in which a material originated.

The ratio of nitrogen-14 to nitrogen-15 is different for herbivores and carnivores because organisms higher in the food chain tend to concentrate the nitrogen-15 isotope in their tissues. This allows scientists to learn about the diet of people from ages past.

Example 11.4 Radioisotopic Dating

An old wooden implement shows carbon-14 activity that is one-eighth that of new wood. How old is the artifact? The half-life of carbon-14 is 5730 y.

Solution
Using the relationship

$$\text{Fraction remaining} = \frac{1}{2^n}$$

we see that one-eighth is $\frac{1}{2^n}$, where $n = 3$; that is, the fraction $\frac{1}{8}$ is $\frac{1}{2^3}$. The carbon-14 has gone through three half-lives. The wood is therefore about $3 \times 5730 = 17{,}190$ y old.

▪ EXERCISE 11.4
Calculate the approximate age of each of the following. **(a)** Human remains have been preserved for centuries in the bogs of Northern Europe. How old is a bog body that has carbon-14 activity one-fourth that of living tissue? The half-life of carbon-14 is 5730 y. **(b)** How old is a bottle of brandy that has a tritium activity one-sixteenth that of new brandy? The half-life of tritium (hydrogen-3) is 12.26 years.

SELF-ASSESSMENT Questions

1. A patient is given a 48-mg dose of technetium-99m (half-life 6.0 h) to treat a brain cancer. How much of it will remain in his body after 36 h?
   a. 0.75 mg   **b.** 1.5 mg   **c.** 3.0 mg   **d.** 12 mg

2. What is the half-life of arsenic-74 if a 50.0-g sample decays to 6.25 g in 53.7 d?
   a. 8.9 d   **b.** 17.9 d   **c.** 27.8 d   **d.** 53.7 d

3. Of a 64.0-g sample of strontium-90 (half-life 28.5 y) produced by a nuclear explosion, what mass in grams would remain unchanged after 285 y?
   a. 0.000 g   **b.** 0.000625 g
   c. 0.00625 g   **d.** 0.0625 g

4. Lead-210 (half-life 22.26 y) can be used to date skeletal remains. About how old is a bone that has an activity of 2.0 Bq if new bone has an activity of 16 Bq?
   a. 7.4 y   **b.** 44.5 y   **c.** 67 y   **d.** 89 y

5. About how old is a piece of wood from an aboriginal burial site that has a carbon-14 (half-life 5730 y) activity of 3.9 counts/min per gram of carbon? Assume that the carbon-14 activity of the wood was 15.6 counts per minute per gram of carbon at the time of the burial.
   a. 2865 y   **b.** 11,460 y
   c. 17,190 y   **d.** 22,920 y

11.4 Artificial Transmutation

Learning Objective ❯ Write a nuclear equation for a transmutation, and identify the product element formed.

During the Middle Ages, alchemists tried to turn base metals, such as lead, into gold. However, they were trying to do it chemically and were therefore doomed to failure because chemical reactions involve only the outer electrons of atoms. **Transmutation** (changing one element into another) requires altering the number of protons in the *nucleus*.

Thus far, we have considered only natural forms of radioactivity. Nuclear reactions can also be brought about by bombardment of stable nuclei with alpha particles, neutrons, or other subatomic particles. These particles, given sufficient energy, can penetrate a stable nucleus and result in some kind of radioactive emission. Just as in natural radioactive processes, one element is changed into another. Because the change does not occur naturally, the process is called *artificial transmutation*.

In 1919, a few years after his famous gold-foil experiment (Section 3.4), Ernest Rutherford reported on the bombardment of a variety of light elements with alpha particles. One such experiment, in which he bombarded nitrogen, resulted in the production of protons, as shown in this balanced nuclear equation.

$$^{14}_{7}\text{N} + {}^{4}_{2}\text{He} \longrightarrow {}^{17}_{8}\text{O} + {}^{1}_{1}\text{H}$$

(The hydrogen nucleus is simply a proton, which can be represented by the symbol $^{1}_{1}\text{H}$.) This provided the first empirical verification of the existence of protons in atomic nuclei, which Rutherford had first postulated in 1914.

Recall that Eugen Goldstein had produced protons in his gas-discharge tube experiments in 1886 (Section 3.1). The significance of Rutherford's experiment lay in the fact that he obtained protons from the *nucleus* of an atom other than hydrogen, thus establishing that protons are constituents of nuclei. Rutherford's experiment was the first induced nuclear reaction and the first example of artificial transmutation. His experiment not only produced protons but also changed nitrogen into oxygen!

▲ Ernest Rutherford (1871–1937) carried out the first nuclear bombardment experiment. Element 104 was named rutherfordium (Rf) in his honor.

Example 11.5 | Artificial Transmutation Equations

When potassium-39 is bombarded with neutrons, chlorine-36 is produced. What other particle is emitted?

$$^{39}_{19}\text{K} + {}^{1}_{0}\text{n} \longrightarrow {}^{36}_{17}\text{Cl} + ?$$

Solution

To determine the particle, we need a balanced nuclear equation. To balance the equation, the unknown particle must have $A = 4$ and $Z = 2$. It is an alpha particle.

$$^{39}_{19}\text{K} + {}^{1}_{0}\text{n} \longrightarrow {}^{36}_{17}\text{Cl} + {}^{4}_{2}\text{He}$$

▪ EXERCISE 11.5A

Technetium-97 is produced by bombarding molybdenum-96 with a deuteron (a hydrogen-2 nucleus). What other particle is emitted?

$$^{96}_{42}\text{Mo} + {}^{2}_{1}\text{H} \longrightarrow {}^{97}_{43}\text{Tc} + ?$$

▪ EXERCISE 11.5B

A team of scientists wants to form uranium-235 by bombarding a nucleus of another element with an alpha particle. They expect a neutron to be produced along with the uranium-235 nucleus. What nucleus must be bombarded with the alpha particle?

SELF-ASSESSMENT Questions

1. What isotope is formed in the following artificial transmutation?

$$^{14}_{7}N + ^{1}_{0}n \longrightarrow ^{1}_{1}H + ?$$

   a. carbon-12   **b.** carbon-14
   c. nitrogen-15   **d.** oxygen-15

2. What isotope is formed in the following artificial transmutation?

$$^{9}_{4}Be + ^{1}_{1}H \longrightarrow ^{4}_{2}He + ?$$

   a. boron-9   **b.** boron-10
   c. lithium-6   **d.** lithium-7

3. What isotope is formed in the following artificial transmutation?

$$^{27}_{13}Al + ^{4}_{2}He \longrightarrow ^{1}_{0}n + ?$$

   a. phosphorus-30
   b. phosphorus-31
   c. silicon-29
   d. sulfur-31

11.5 Uses of Radioisotopes

Learning Objective   ❯ List some applications of radioisotopes.

Most of the 3000 known radioisotopes are produced by artificial transmutation of stable isotopes. The value of both naturally occurring and artificial radioisotopes goes far beyond their contributions to our knowledge of chemistry.

Radioisotopes in Industry and Agriculture

Scientists in a wide variety of fields use radioisotopes as **tracers** in physical, chemical, and biological systems. Isotopes of a given element, whether radioactive or not, behave nearly identically in chemical and physical processes. Because radioactive isotopes are easily detected through their decay products, it is relatively easy to trace their movement, even through a complicated system. For example, tracing radioisotopes allows us to do the following:

- **Detect leaks in underground pipes.** Suppose there is a leak in a pipe that is buried beneath a concrete floor. We could locate the leak by digging up extensive areas of the floor, or we could add a small amount of radioactive material to liquid poured into the drain and trace the flow of the liquid with a Geiger counter (an instrument that detects radioactivity). Once we located the leak, only a small area of the floor would have to be dug up to repair it. A compound containing a short-lived isotope (for example, iodine-131, half-life 8.04 days) is usually employed for this purpose.

- **Measure thickness of sheet metal during production.** Radiation from a beta emitter is allowed to pass through sheet metal on the production line. The amount of radiation that passes through a sheet is related to its thickness.

- **Determine frictional wear in piston rings.** The ring is subjected to neutron bombardment, which converts some of the carbon in the steel to carbon-14. Wear in the piston ring is assessed by the rate at which the carbon-14 appears in the engine oil.

- **Determine the uptake of phosphorus and its distribution in plants.** This can be done by incorporating phosphorus-32, a β^- emitter with a half-life of 14.3 d, into phosphate fertilizers fed to plants.

Radioisotopes are also used to study the effectiveness of weed killers, compare the nutritional value of various feeds, determine optimal methods for insect control, and monitor the fate and persistence of pesticides in soil and groundwater.

One of the most successful applications of radioisotopes in agriculture involves inducing heritable genetic alterations known as *mutations*. Exposing seeds or other parts of plants to neutrons or gamma rays increases the likelihood of genetic mutations. At first glance, this technique may not seem very promising. However, genetic variability is vital, not only to improve varieties but also to protect species from extinction. Some hybrid plants, such as seedless watermelons and bananas, are sterile. The lack of genetic variability among these plants may place the entire population at risk.

▲ Scientists can trace the uptake of phosphorus by a green plant by adding a compound containing some phosphorus-32 to the applied fertilizer. When the plant is later placed on photographic film, radiation from the phosphorus isotopes exposes the film, much as light does. This type of exposure, called a *radiograph*, shows the distribution of phosphorus in the plant.

2. Do irradiated foods contain radioactive material?

Irradiated foods have absorbed energy in the form of gamma rays. But the foods themselves do *not* contain any radioactive material, so there is no danger to individuals who ingest irradiated food. Irradiated food must carry labels, but many people are wary of anything that is connected with radiation.

Radioisotopes are also used to irradiate foodstuffs as a method of preservation. The radiation destroys microorganisms and enzymes that cause foods to spoil. Irradiated food shows little change in taste or appearance. Some people are concerned about possible harmful effects of chemical substances produced by the radiation, but there has been no good evidence of harm to laboratory animals fed irradiated food or any known adverse effects in humans living in countries where food irradiation has been used for years. No residual radiation remains in a food after irradiation because gamma rays do not have nearly enough energy to change nuclei.

Radioisotopes in Medicine

Nuclear medicine involves two distinct uses of radioisotopes: therapeutic and diagnostic. In a therapeutic application, an attempt is made to treat or cure disease with radiation. The diagnostic use of radioisotopes is aimed at obtaining information about the state of a patient's health.

Table 11.6 lists some radioisotopes in common use in medicine. The list is necessarily very incomplete, but it should give you an idea of their importance. The claim that nuclear medicine has saved many more lives than nuclear bombs have taken is not an idle one.

Cancer is not one disease but many. Some forms are particularly susceptible to radiation therapy. The aim of **radiation therapy** is to destroy cancerous cells before too much damage is done to healthy tissue. Radiation is most lethal to rapidly reproducing cells, and rapid reproduction is the characteristic of cancer cells that allows radiation therapy to be successful. Radiation is carefully aimed at cancerous tissue while minimizing the exposure of normal cells. If the cancer cells are killed by the destructive effects of the radiation, the malignancy is halted.

Patients undergoing radiation therapy may show signs of radiation sickness during treatment. Nausea and vomiting are the usual early symptoms of radiation sickness, as rapidly growing cells, such as those in the gastrointestinal tract, are affected most. Radiation therapy can also interfere with the replenishment of white blood cells and thus increase patients' susceptibility to infection.

Radioisotopes used for diagnostic purposes provide information about the functioning of some part of the body or about the type or extent of an illness. For example, radioactive iodine-131 is used to determine the size, shape, and activity of the thyroid gland as well as to treat cancers in this gland and to control its hyperactivity. Small doses are used for diagnostic purposes, and large doses for treatment of thyroid cancer. After the patient drinks a solution of potassium iodide incorporating iodine-131, the iodide ions become concentrated in the thyroid. A detector showing the differential uptake of the isotope is used in diagnosis. The resulting *photoscan* can pinpoint the location of tumors or other abnormalities in the thyroid. In cancer treatment, radiation from therapeutic (large) doses of iodine-131 kills the thyroid cells in which the radioisotope has become concentrated.

The radioisotope gadolinium-153 is used to determine bone mineralization. Its widespread use is an indication of the large number of people, mostly women, who suffer from osteoporosis (reduction in bone density) as they grow older. Gadolinium-153 gives off two types of radiation: gamma rays and X-rays. A scanning device compares these types of radiation after they pass through bone. Bone density is then determined from the difference in absorption of the rays.

Technetium-99m is used in a variety of diagnostic tests (Table 11.6). The *m* stands for *metastable*, which means that this isotope gives up some energy when it changes to a more stable version of technetium-99 (which has the same atomic number and the same atomic mass). The energy it gives up is in the form of a gamma ray.

$$^{99m}_{43}\text{Tc} \longrightarrow {}^{99}_{43}\text{Tc} + \gamma$$

It DOES Matter!

The difference between a radioactive isotope and the alpha, beta, gamma, or positron radiation that it produces is very important and often misunderstood. A radioisotope such as iodine-131 or radon-222, when absorbed by the human body, can cause great harm because the radiation continues to be released as the isotope decays. However, matter exposed to ionizing radiation simply absorbs that energy, causing a chemical change. A patient undergoing gamma-radiation treatment does *not* become radioactive.

Note that the decay of technetium-99m produces no alpha or beta particles that could cause unnecessary damage to the body. Technetium-99m also has a short half-life (6.0 h), so the radioactivity does not linger very long in the body after the scan has been completed. With such a short half-life, use of the isotope must be carefully planned. In fact, medical labs do not purchase technetium-99m. Instead they buy molybdenum-99, which decays to form technetium-99m.

$$^{99}_{42}\text{Mo} \longrightarrow ^{99m}_{43}\text{Tc} + ^{0}_{-1}\text{e} + \gamma$$

The decay product, technetium-99m, is "milked" from the container as needed.

Using modern computer technology, *positron emission tomography (PET)* can measure dynamic processes occurring in the body, such as blood flow or the rate at which oxygen or glucose is being metabolized. For example, PET scans have shown that the brain of a schizophrenic metabolizes only about one-fifth as much glucose as a normal brain. These scans can also reveal metabolic changes that occur in the brain during tactile learning (learning by the sense of touch) as well as identify brain damage that triggers severe epileptic seizures.

Compounds incorporating a positron-emitting isotope, such as carbon-11 or oxygen-15, are inhaled or injected before the scan. Before the emitted positron can travel very far in the body, it encounters an electron (numerous in any ordinary matter), and two gamma rays are produced, exiting from the body in exactly opposite directions.

$$^{11}_{6}\text{C} \longrightarrow ^{11}_{5}\text{B} + ^{0}_{+1}\text{e}$$
$$^{0}_{+1}\text{e} + ^{0}_{-1}\text{e} \longrightarrow 2\gamma$$

Detectors, positioned on opposite sides of the patient, record the gamma rays. An image of an area in the body is formed using computerized calculations of the points at which annihilation of positrons and electrons occurs.

Table 11.6	Some Radioisotopes and Their Medical Applications		
Isotope	Name	Half-Life[a]	Use
^{11}C	Carbon-11	20.39 min	Brain scans
^{51}Cr	Chromium-51	27.8 d	Blood volume determination
^{57}Co	Cobalt-57	270 d	Measuring vitamin B_{12} uptake
^{60}Co	Cobalt-60	5.271 y	Radiation cancer therapy
^{153}Gd	Gadolinium-153	242 d	Determining bone density
^{67}Ga	Gallium-67	78.1 h	Scan for lung tumors
^{131}I	Iodine-131	8.040 d	Thyroid diagnoses and therapy
^{192}Ir	Iridium-192	74 d	Breast cancer therapy
^{59}Fe	Iron-59	44.496 d	Detection of anemia
^{32}P	Phosphorus-32	14.3 d	Detection of skin cancer or eye tumors
^{238}Pu	Plutonium-238	86 y	Provision of power in pacemakers
^{226}Ra	Radium-226	1600 y	Radiation therapy for cancer
^{75}Se	Selenium-75	120 d	Pancreas scans
^{24}Na	Sodium-24	14.659 h	Locating obstructions in blood flow
^{99m}Tc	Technetium-99m	6.0 h	Imaging of brain, liver, bone marrow, kidney, lung, or heart
^{201}Tl	Thallium-201	73 h	Detecting heart problems during treadmill stress test
^{3}H	Tritium	12.26 y	Determining total body water
^{133}Xe	Xenon-133	5.27 d	Lung imaging

[a]Abbreviations: y, years; d, days; h, hours; min, minutes.

3. Are we exposed to dangerous radiation during X-rays and other medical procedures?
A number of medical procedures do use ionizing radiation or radioisotopes, but the amount of radiation is kept to a minimum. The hazard of the ionizing radiation is ordinarily much less than the risk due to a lack of diagnosis or treatment!

4. What causes radiation sickness, and how serious is it?
Alpha, beta, and gamma rays, X-rays, and positrons that are absorbed by the body do cause cell damage. By and large, they are *not* energetic enough to create radioactive isotopes. Individuals who undergo radiation treatments often develop radiation sickness and may require some time to recover once treatment ends. However, individuals who are exposed to very large amounts of radiation, which could result from a bomb or a nuclear power plant disaster, will develop very serious radiation sickness or even die from acute radiation exposure.

Example 11.6	Positron Emission Equations

One of the isotopes used to perform PET scans is oxygen-15, a positron emitter. What other isotope is formed when oxygen-15 decays?

Solution
First, we write the nuclear equation

$$^{15}_{8}O \longrightarrow {}^{0}_{+1}e + ?$$

The nucleon number, A, does not change, but the atomic number, Z, does: $8-1 = 7$. The product isotope is nitrogen-15.

$$^{15}_{8}O \longrightarrow {}^{0}_{+1}e + {}^{15}_{7}N$$

▪ **EXERCISE 11.6**
Phosphorus-30 is a positron-emitting radioisotope suitable for doing PET scans. What other isotope is formed when phosphorus-30 decays?

Other Uses of Radioisotopes

Much of what we know about the chemistry of biological systems has been learned by using radioactive tracers in experiments. These include carbon-14, hydrogen-3 (tritium), and phosphorus-32, radioactive isotopes of elements that are found in the four major types of macromolecules in biological systems: carbohydrates, lipids, proteins, and nucleic acids. By adding a labeled compound, it is possible to follow the radioactive atoms through the metabolic pathways of living systems.

Another relatively new use of radioisotopes is in forensics. Nuclear activation analysis (NAA) involves placing a sample in a nuclear reactor and bombarding it with neutrons. The target atoms will then emit a gamma ray that can be detected. For example, NAA has been used to analyze bullet fragments used in the assassination of President John F. Kennedy, and the results support the findings of the Warren Commission that only two bullets were fired.

SELF-ASSESSMENT Questions

1. Iodine-131 is sometimes used for detecting leaks in underground pipes because
   a. it has a short half-life   b. it is highly penetrating
   c. it is nontoxic   d. its radiation is harmless

2. What is used to irradiate foodstuffs to extend shelf life?
   a. alpha particles   b. beta particles
   c. gamma rays   d. microwaves

3. Which of the following isotopes is used in radiation therapy?
   a. cobalt-60   b. gadolinium-153
   c. iodine-131   d. technetium-99m

4. Which of the following isotopes is used in determining bone density?
   a. cobalt-60   b. gadolinium-153
   c. iodine-131   d. technetium-99m

5. Which of the following isotopes is used for detecting heart problems during a treadmill stress test?
   a. cobalt-60   b. gadolinium-153
   c. iodine-131   d. thallium-201

6. Which of the following isotopes is used in thyroid diagnosis and therapy?
   a. cobalt-60   b. gadolinium-153
   c. iodine-131   d. tritium

7. What form of radiation is detected in PET scans?
   a. beta   b. gamma
   c. positron   d. X-rays

Answers: 1, a; 2, c; 3, a; 4, b; 5, d; 6, c; 7, c

11.6 Penetrating Power of Radiation

Learning Objective › Describe the nature of materials needed to block alpha, beta, and gamma radiation.

The danger of radiation to living organisms comes from its potential for damaging cells and tissues. The ability to inflict injury relates to the penetrating power of the radiation. The two aspects of nuclear medicine just discussed (therapeutic and diagnostic) are also dependent on the penetrating power of various types of radiation.

All other things being equal, the more massive the particle, the less its penetrating power. *Alpha particles*, which are helium nuclei with a mass of 4 u, are the least penetrating of the three main types of radiation. *Beta particles*, which are identical to the almost massless electrons, are somewhat more penetrating. *Gamma rays*, like X-rays, have no mass; they are considerably more penetrating than the other two types.

But all other things are not always equal. The faster a particle moves or the more energetic the radiation is, the more penetrating power it has.

It may seem contrary to common sense that the biggest particles make the least headway. But keep in mind that penetrating power reflects the ability of radiation to make its way through a sample of matter. It is as if you were trying to roll some rocks through a field of boulders. The alpha particle acts as if it were a boulder itself. Because of its size, it cannot get very far before it bumps into and is stopped by other boulders. The beta particle acts as if it were a small stone. It can sneak between and perhaps ricochet off boulders until it makes its way farther into the field. The gamma ray can be compared with a grain of sand that can get through the smallest openings.

The danger of a specific type of radiation to human tissue depends on the location of the radiation's source as well as on its penetrating power. If the radioactive substance is outside the body, alpha particles are the least dangerous; they have low penetrating power and are stopped by the outer layer of skin. Beta particles are also usually stopped before they reach vital organs. Gamma rays readily pass through tissues, so an external gamma source can be quite dangerous. People working with radioactive materials can protect themselves through one or both of the following actions:

- Move away from the source. The intensity of radiation decreases with distance from the source.
- Use shielding. A sheet of paper can stop most alpha particles. A block of wood or a thin sheet of aluminum or Plexiglas can stop most beta particles. Yet it takes a meter of concrete or several centimeters of lead to stop most gamma rays (Figure 11.6).

People have used different means of shielding to protect themselves while they were conducting experiments. Researchers using phosphorus-32, which emits beta particles, often wore lead aprons and were quite weary by the end of the day! Plexiglas shields both provided protection and let workers more easily see what they were doing.

◀ **Figure 11.6** The relative penetrating power of alpha, beta, and gamma radiation. Alpha particles are stopped by a sheet of paper (a). Beta particles will not penetrate a sheet of aluminum (b). It takes several centimeters of lead to block gamma rays (c).

When the radioactive source is *inside* the body, as is the case for many medical applications, the situation is reversed. The nonpenetrating alpha particles can do great damage. All such particles are trapped within the body, which must then absorb all of the energy the particles release. Alpha particles inflict all their damage in a tiny area because they do not travel far. Therefore, getting an alpha-emitting therapeutic radioisotope close to the targeted cells is vital.

Beta particles distribute their damage over a somewhat larger area because they travel farther. Tissue may recover from limited damage spread over a large area; it is less likely to survive concentrated damage.

Many diagnostic applications rely on the highly penetrating power of gamma rays. In most cases, the radiation created inside the body must be detected by instruments outside the body, so a minimum of absorption is desirable.

CONCEPTUAL Example 11.7 | Radiation Hazard

Most modern smoke detectors contain a tiny amount of americium-241, a solid element that is an alpha emitter. The americium is in a chamber that includes thin aluminum shielding, and the device is usually mounted on a ceiling. Rate the radiation hazard of this device in normal use as **(a)** high, **(b)** moderate, or **(c)** very low. Explain your choice.

Solution
Alpha particles have very little penetrating ability—they are stopped by a sheet of paper or a layer of skin. The emitted alpha particles cannot exit the detector's chamber because even thin metal is more than sufficient to absorb them. Even if alpha particles could escape, they would likely be stopped by the air after a short distance or by the dead cells of your skin. Therefore, the radiation hazard is rated **(c)**—very low.

▪ **EXERCISE 11.7**
Radon-222 is a gas that can diffuse from the ground into homes. Like americium-241, it is an alpha emitter. Is the radiation hazard from radon-222 likely to be higher or lower than that from a smoke detector? Explain.

SELF-ASSESSMENT Questions

1. Which of the following pairs represent the *least* and *most* (least/most) penetrating types of radiation?
   a. alpha/gamma
   b. beta/gamma
   c. gamma/alpha
   d. X-rays/beta

2. Which form of radiation requires a thin sheet of aluminum to be stopped?
   a. alpha particles
   b. beta particles
   c. gamma rays
   d. all of these

3. A Geiger counter registered 50 Bq of activity from an unknown type of radiation. A piece of paper inserted between the source and the counter caused the reading to drop to about 2 Bq. The radiation was mostly
   a. alpha particles
   b. beta particles
   c. gamma rays
   d. X-rays

11.7 Energy from the Nucleus

Learning Objectives ❯ Explain where nuclear energy comes from. ❯ Describe the difference between fission and fusion.

We have seen that radioactivity—quiet and invisible—can be beneficial or dangerous. A much more dramatic—and equally paradoxical—aspect of nuclear chemistry is the release of nuclear energy by either *fission* (splitting of heavy nuclei into smaller nuclei) or *fusion* (combining of light nuclei to form heavier ones).

Einstein and the Equivalence of Mass and Energy

The potential power in the nucleus was established by Albert Einstein, a famous and most unusual scientist. Whereas most scientists work with glassware and instruments in laboratories, Einstein worked with a pencil and a notepad. By 1905, at the age of 26, he had already worked out his special theory of relativity and developed his famous **mass–energy equation**, in which mass (m) is multiplied by the square of the speed of light (c) to determine the amount of energy (E) released.

$$E = mc^2$$

▲ Albert Einstein (1879–1955). Element 99 was named einsteinium (Es) in his honor.

The equation suggests that mass and energy are equivalent—just two different aspects of the same thing—and that a little bit of mass can yield enormous energy. The atomic bombs that destroyed Hiroshima and Nagasaki (Section 11.8) in World War II converted less than an ounce of matter into energy.

A chemical reaction that gives off heat must also lose mass in the process, but the change in mass is far too small to measure. Reaction energy must be enormous—at the level of the energy given off by nuclear explosions—for the mass loss to be measurable. (If every atom in a 1-kg lump of coal became energy, it could produce 25 billion kWh of electricity—enough to keep a 100-W light bulb going for 29 million years. Burning 1 kg of coal in a conventional power plant produces only enough energy to keep the bulb shining for 67 hours.)

Binding Energy

Nuclear fission releases the tremendous amounts of energy produced by atomic bombs and in nuclear power plants. Where does all this energy come from? It is locked inside the atomic nucleus. When protons and neutrons combine to form atomic nuclei, a small amount of mass is converted to energy. This is the **binding energy** that holds the nucleons together in the nucleus. For example, the helium nucleus contains two protons and two neutrons. The masses of these four particles add up to 2×1.0073 u $+ 2 \times 1.0087$ u $= 4.0320$ u (Figure 11.7). However, the actual mass of the helium nucleus is only 4.0015 u, and the missing mass—called the *mass defect*—amounts to 0.0305 u. Using Einstein's equation $E = mc^2$, we can calculate (see Problem 51) a value of 28.3 million electron volts (28 MeV; 1 MeV $= 1.6022 \times 10^{-13}$ J) for the binding energy of the helium nucleus. This is the amount of energy it would take to separate one helium nucleus into two protons and two neutrons.

When the binding energy per nucleon is calculated for all the elements and plotted against nucleon number, the graph in Figure 11.8 is obtained. The elements with the highest binding energies per nucleon have the most stable nuclei. They include iron and elements with nucleon numbers close to that of iron. When uranium atoms undergo nuclear fission, they split into atoms with higher binding energies. In other words, the fission reaction converts large atoms into smaller ones with greater nuclear stability.

We can also see from Figure 11.8 that even more energy can be obtained by combining small atoms, such as hydrogen or deuterium, to form larger atoms with more

▲ **Figure 11.7** Nuclear binding energy in $_2^4$He. The mass of a helium-4 nucleus is 4.0015 u, which is 0.0305 u less than the masses of two protons and two neutrons. The missing mass is equivalent to the binding energy of the helium-4 nucleus.

◀ **Figure 11.8** Nuclear stability is greatest for iron and elements near iron in the periodic table. Fission of very large nuclei or fusion of very small ones results in greater nuclear stability.

Q: *Which process, fission of uranium nuclei or fusion of hydrogen nuclei, releases more energy?*

▲ Enrico Fermi (1901–1954). Element 100 was named fermium (Fm) in his honor.

▲ Lise Meitner (1878–1968). Element 109 was named meitnerium (Mt) in her honor.

stable nuclei. This kind of reaction is called **nuclear fusion**. It is what happens when a hydrogen bomb explodes, and it is also the source of the sun's energy.

Nuclear Fission

In 1934, the Italian scientists Enrico Fermi and Emilio Segrè (1905–1989) bombarded uranium atoms with neutrons. They were trying to make elements with higher atomic numbers than uranium, which had the highest atomic number then known. To their surprise, they found four radioactive species among the products. One was presumably element 93, formed by the initial conversion of uranium-238 to uranium-239, which then underwent beta decay.

$$^{238}_{92}U + ^{1}_{0}n \longrightarrow ^{239}_{92}U$$

$$^{239}_{92}U \longrightarrow ^{239}_{93}Np + ^{0}_{-1}e$$

They were unable to explain the remaining radioactivity.

German chemists Otto Hahn (1879–1968) and Fritz Strassman (1902–1980) repeated the Fermi–Segrè experiment in 1938 and were perplexed to find isotopes of barium among the many reaction products. Hahn wrote to Lise Meitner, an Austrian physicist who had worked with Hahn in Berlin for many years, to ask what she thought about these strange results. Because she was Jewish, Meitner had fled to Sweden when the Nazis took over Austria in 1938.

On hearing about Hahn's work, she noted that barium atoms were roughly half the size of uranium atoms. Was it possible that the uranium nuclei might be splitting into fragments? She made some calculations that convinced her that the uranium nuclei had indeed been split apart. Her nephew, Otto Frisch (1904–1979), was visiting for the winter holidays, and they discussed this discovery with great excitement. Frisch later coined the term **nuclear fission** (Figure 11.9).

Frisch was working with Niels Bohr at the University of Copenhagen, and when he returned to Denmark, he told Bohr of the fission reaction. Shortly afterward, Bohr left to attend a physics conference in the United States. The discussions in the corridors about this new reaction would be the most important talks to take place at that meeting.

Meanwhile, Enrico Fermi had just received the 1938 Nobel Prize in physics. Fermi's wife, Laura, was Jewish, and the fascist Italian dictator Mussolini was an ally of Hitler. Fermi accepted the award in Stockholm and then immediately traveled to the United States with his wife and children. Thus, by 1939, the United States had received news about the German discovery of nuclear fission and had also acquired from Italy one of the world's foremost nuclear scientists.

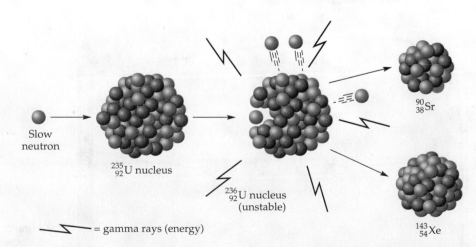

Slow neutron

$^{235}_{92}U$ nucleus

$^{236}_{92}U$ nucleus (unstable)

$^{90}_{38}Sr$

$^{143}_{54}Xe$

⚡ = gamma rays (energy)

▲ **Figure 11.9** One possible way a uranium nucleus can undergo fission. The neutrons produced by the fission reactions can split other uranium nuclei, thus sustaining a chain reaction.

Q: If each of the neutrons emitted by the ^{236}U nucleus caused another ^{235}U nucleus to split in the way shown here, how many more neutrons would be released?

◀ **Figure 11.10** Schematic representation of a nuclear chain reaction. Neutrons released in the fission of one uranium-235 nucleus can strike other uranium-235 nuclei, causing them to split and release more neutrons as well as a variety of other nuclei. For simplicity, some fission fragments are not shown.

Nuclear Chain Reaction

Leo Szilard (1898–1964), another Jewish refugee, had been born in Hungary and had come to the United States in 1937. Szilard was one of the first scientists to realize that neutrons released in the fission of one atom could trigger the fission of other uranium atoms, thus setting off a **chain reaction** (Figure 11.10). Because massive amounts of energy could be obtained from the fission of uranium, such a chain reaction might be used in a bomb with tremendous explosive force.

Aware of the destructive forces that could be produced and concerned that Germany might develop such a bomb, Szilard prevailed on Einstein to sign a letter to President Franklin D. Roosevelt that indicated the importance of the discovery. It was critical that the U.S. government act quickly.

Thermonuclear Reactions

The chapter opening noted that the sun is a nuclear power plant vital to life on Earth. However, the nuclear reactions that take place in the sun are somewhat different from the ones we have discussed so far in this chapter. These **thermonuclear reactions** require enormously high temperatures (millions of degrees) to initiate them. The intense temperatures and pressures in the sun cause nuclei to fuse and thus release enormous amounts of energy. Instead of large nuclei being split into smaller fragments (fission), small nuclei are fused into larger ones (fusion). The main reaction in the sun is thought to be the fusion of four hydrogen nuclei to produce one helium nucleus and two positrons.

$$4\,^1_1\text{H} \longrightarrow \,^4_2\text{He} + 2\,^0_{+1}\text{e}$$

Fusion of 1 g of hydrogen releases an amount of energy equivalent to the burning of nearly 20 tons of coal. Every second, the sun fuses 600 tons of hydrogen, producing millions of times more energy than has been produced on Earth in the entire history of humankind. Much current research is aimed at reproducing such a reaction in the laboratory by using ultrapowerful magnets to contain the intense heat required for ignition. Fusion technology is discussed further in Chapter 15. To date, however, fusion reactions on Earth have been limited to the uncontrolled reactions in explosions of hydrogen (thermonuclear) bombs and to small amounts of energy produced by very expensive experimental fusion reactors.

SELF-ASSESSMENT Questions

Look at the graph in Figure 11.8 to answer questions 1–3.

1. Helium has a particularly high binding energy per nucleon, which means that it
   a. is especially unstable compared to H and Li
   b. is more stable than H and Li
   c. will readily fuse into larger nuclei
   d. will readily split into hydrogen-2 atoms

2. The most stable nuclei are those of
   a. Ba   b. He   c. Fe   d. U

3. Nuclei with nucleon numbers greater than that of iron are
   a. all radioactive
   b. increasingly stable
   c. less stable than iron
   d. easily split into smaller nuclei

4. Which equation explains why the products of fission have less mass than the original substances?
   a. $E = hv/\lambda$ b. $E = hv$
   c. $E = mc^2$ d. $PV = nRT$

5. For a nuclear reaction to become self-sustaining, there must be a release of which particles?
   a. alpha particles   b. beta particles
   c. neutrons   d. protons

6. When uranium-235 absorbs a neutron and undergoes fission, barium-142 and krypton-91 are two possible fission fragments. How many neutrons are released?

$$^{235}_{92}U + {}^{1}_{0}n \longrightarrow {}^{142}_{56}Ba + {}^{91}_{36}Kr + {}^{?}_{0}n$$

   a. 0   b. 1   c. 2   d. 3

7. Combination of two smaller atomic nuclei into one larger nucleus is called
   a. a chain reaction   b. fission
   c. fusion   d. radioactive decay

8. Hydrogen-2 and hydrogen-3 fuse to form helium-4. The other product is a(n)
   a. electron   b. neutron
   c. positron   d. proton

Answers: 1, b; 2, c; 3, c; 4, c; 5, c; 6, d; 7, c; 8, b

11.8 Nuclear Bombs

Learning Objectives ❯ Describe the goals of the Manhattan Project and how uranium and plutonium bombs were made. ❯ Identify the most hazardous fallout isotopes, and explain why they are particularly dangerous.

In 1939, President Franklin D. Roosevelt launched a highly secret research project for the study of atomic energy. Called the *Manhattan Project*, it eventually became a massive research effort involving more scientific brainpower than ever was or has been devoted to a single project. Amazingly, it was conducted under such extreme secrecy that even Vice President Harry Truman did not know of its existence until after Roosevelt's death.

The Manhattan Project included four separate research teams that focused on

- sustaining a nuclear fission chain reaction,
- enriching uranium so that it contained about 90% of the fissionable isotope ^{235}U,
- making plutonium-239 (another fissionable isotope), and
- constructing a bomb based on nuclear fission.

Sustainable Chain Reaction

By 1939, it had been established that neutron bombardment could initiate the fission reaction, but many attributes of this reaction were unknown. Enrico Fermi and his group, working in a lab under the bleachers at Stagg Field on the campus of the University of Chicago, worked on the fission reaction and how to sustain it. They found that the neutrons used to trigger the reaction had to be slowed down to increase the probability that they would actually hit a uranium nucleus. Because graphite slows down neutrons, a large "pile" of graphite was built to house the reaction. Then the amount of uranium "fuel" was gradually increased. The major goal was to determine the **critical mass**—the amount of uranium-235 needed to sustain the fission reaction. There had to be enough fissionable nuclei in the "fuel" for the neutrons released in one fission event to have a good chance of being captured by another fissionable nucleus before escaping from the pile.

On December 2, 1942, Fermi and his group achieved the first sustained nuclear fission reaction. The critical mass of uranium (enriched to about 94% uranium-235) for this reactor turned out to be about 16 kg.

Isotopic Enrichment

Natural uranium is 99.27% uranium-238, which does not undergo fission. Uranium-235, the fissionable isotope, makes up only 0.72% of natural uranium. Because making a bomb required *enriching* the uranium to about 90% uranium-235, it was necessary to find a way to separate the uranium isotopes. This was the job of the Manhattan Project research team in Oak Ridge, Tennessee.

Chemical separation was almost impossible; uranium-235 and uranium-238 are chemically almost identical. The separation method eventually used involved converting uranium to gaseous uranium hexafluoride, UF_6. Molecules of UF_6 containing uranium-235 are slightly lighter and therefore move slightly faster than molecules containing uranium-238. Uranium hexafluoride was allowed to pass through a series of thousands of pinholes, and the molecules containing uranium-235 gradually outdistanced the others. Enough enriched uranium-235 was finally obtained to make a small explosive device.

Synthesis of Plutonium

While the tedious work of separating uranium isotopes was underway at Oak Ridge, another research team, led by Glenn T. Seaborg, approached the problem of obtaining fissionable material by another route. Although uranium-238 would not undergo fission when bombarded by neutrons, this more common isotope of uranium *would* decay to form a new element, named neptunium (Np). This product quickly decayed to another new element, plutonium (Pu).

$$^{238}_{92}U + ^{1}_{0}n \longrightarrow ^{239}_{92}U$$

$$^{239}_{92}U \longrightarrow ^{0}_{-1}e + ^{239}_{93}Np$$

$$^{239}_{93}Np \longrightarrow ^{239}_{94}Pu + ^{0}_{-1}e$$

▲ Glenn T. Seaborg (1912–1999). Element 106 was named seaborgium (Sg) in his honor. Seaborg is the only person to have had an element named for him while still alive. He is shown here pointing to his namesake element on the periodic table of elements.

Plutonium-239 was found to be fissionable and thus was suitable material for the making of a bomb. A group of large reactors was built near Hanford, Washington, to produce plutonium.

Bomb Construction

The actual building of the nuclear bombs was carried out at Los Alamos, New Mexico, under the direction of J. Robert Oppenheimer (1904–1967). In a top-secret laboratory at a remote site, a group of scientists planned and then constructed what would become known as atomic bombs. Two different models were developed, one based on ^{235}U and the other on ^{239}Pu.

The critical mass of uranium-235 could not be exceeded prematurely or the bomb would detonate early, so it was important that no single piece of fissionable material in the bomb be large. The bomb was designed to contain pieces of uranium of subcritical mass plus a neutron source to initiate the fission reaction. Then, at the chosen time, all the pieces would be forced together using an ordinary high explosive, thus triggering a runaway nuclear chain reaction.

The synthesis of plutonium turned out to be easier than the isotopic separation, and by July 1945, enough fissionable material had been made for three bombs to be assembled—two using plutonium and one using uranium. The first atomic bomb (one of the plutonium devices) was tested in the desert near Alamogordo,

▶ **Figure 11.11** An internal schematic of the atomic bomb "Little Boy" dropped on Hiroshima. Each of the cylinders of uranium-235 had less than the critical mass. The high explosive shot the cylindrical "bullet" down the gun barrel and onto the target spike. The result was about two critical masses of uranium-235, and a nuclear explosion occurred about a millisecond later.

High explosive ▪ Hollow uranium "bullet" ▪ Gun barrel ▪ Uranium "target" spike

▲ **Figure 11.12** The mushroom cloud over Nagasaki, following the detonation of "Fat Man" on August 9, 1945.

New Mexico, on July 16, 1945. The heat from the explosion vaporized the 30-m steel tower on which the bomb was placed and melted the sand for several hectares around the site. The light produced was the brightest anyone had ever seen.

Some of the scientists were so awed by the force of the blast that they argued against using the bombs on Japan. A few, led by Leo Szilard, suggested a demonstration of the bombs' power at an uninhabited site. But fear of a well-publicized "dud" and the desire to avoid millions of American casualties during an invasion of Japan led President Harry Truman to order the dropping of the bombs on Japanese cities. The lone uranium bomb, called "Little Boy" (Figure 11.11), was dropped on Hiroshima on August 6, 1945, and caused over 100,000 casualties. Three days later, the other plutonium bomb, called "Fat Man," was dropped on Nagasaki with comparable results (Figure 11.12). World War II ended with the surrender of Japan on August 14, 1945.

Radioactive Fallout

When a nuclear explosion occurs in the open atmosphere, radioactive materials can rain down on parts of Earth thousands of miles away, days and weeks later in what is called **radioactive fallout**. The uranium atom can split in several different ways.

$$^{235}_{92}U + ^{1}_{0}n \longrightarrow ^{90}_{38}Sr + ^{143}_{54}Xe + 3\,^{1}_{0}n$$

$$\longrightarrow ^{102}_{39}Y + ^{131}_{53}I + 3\,^{1}_{0}n$$

$$\longrightarrow ^{95}_{37}Rb + ^{137}_{55}Cs + 4\,^{1}_{0}n$$

The primary (first) fission products are radioactive. These decay to daughter isotopes, many of which are also radioactive. In all, over 200 different fission products are produced, with half-lives that vary from less than a second to more than a billion years. Also, the neutrons produced in the explosion act on molecules in the atmosphere to produce carbon-14, tritium, and other radioisotopes. Fallout is therefore exceedingly complex. We will consider three of the more worrisome isotopes here.

Of all the isotopes released in an atomic explosion, strontium-90 (half-life 28.5 y) presents the greatest hazard to people. Strontium-90 reaches us primarily through dairy products and vegetables. Because of its similarity to calcium (both are group 2A elements), strontium-90 is incorporated into bone. There it remains an internal source of radiation for many years. Strontium-90 has been tied to an increase in bone cancer and leukemia.

Iodine-131 may present a greater threat immediately after a nuclear explosion or reactor meltdown. Its half-life is only 8 days, but it is produced in relatively large amounts. Iodine-131 is readily transferred up the food chain. In the human body, it is concentrated in the thyroid gland, and it is precisely this characteristic that makes a trace of iodine-131 so useful for diagnostic scanning. However, for a healthy individual, larger amounts of radioactive iodine offer only damaging side effects. To minimize the absorption of radioactive iodine, many people in the areas of Chernobyl and Fukushima were given large amounts of potassium iodide, which effectively diluted the amount of radioactive iodine absorbed by their thyroid glands.

Cesium-137 (half-life 30.2 y) is, like strontium-90, capable of long-term effects. Because of its similarity to potassium (both are group 1A elements), it is taken up by living organisms as part of body fluids. It can be obtained from sources in the environment and reconcentrated in living organisms. Elevated levels of cesium-137 were perhaps the greatest health concern following the Fukushima Daiichi disaster.

By the late 1950s, radioactive isotopes from atmospheric testing of nuclear weapons were detected in the environment. Concern over radiation damage from nuclear fallout led to a movement to ban atmospheric testing. Many scientists were leaders in the movement. Linus Pauling, who won the Nobel Prize in Chemistry in 1954 for his bonding theories and for his work in determining the structure of proteins, was a particularly articulate advocate of banning atmospheric tests. In 1963, a nuclear test ban treaty was signed by the major nations—with the exception of France and the People's Republic of China, which continued aboveground tests. Since the signing of the treaty, other countries have joined the nuclear club. Pauling, who had endured being called a communist and a traitor because of his outspoken position, was awarded the Nobel Peace Prize in 1962.

SELF-ASSESSMENT Questions

1. The isotope used in uranium fission reactions is
   a. uranium-232   **b.** uranium-234
   c. uranium-235   **d.** uranium-238

2. What fraction of natural uranium is the fissionable isotope?
   a. < 1%   **b.** 10%   **c.** 50%   **d.** > 99%

3. The uranium isotope from which fissile plutonium-239 is made is
   a. uranium-232   **b.** uranium-234
   c. uranium-235   **d.** uranium-238

4. Strontium-90 substitutes for calcium in bones because Sr and Ca
   a. are in the same group of the periodic table
   b. are in the same period of the periodic table
   c. have identical electron configurations
   d. have identical half-lives

5. Many people in the Chernobyl and Fukushima areas were given large doses of potassium iodide to limit the uptake of iodine-131 and its concentration in the
   a. bones   **b.** kidneys   **c.** lungs   **d.** thyroid

6. Which of the following is *not* one of the isotopes produced by fission that presents the greatest hazard to people?
   a. cesium-137   **b.** iodine-131
   c. iron-59   **d.** strontium-90

7. Which of the following radioisotopes in fallout is dangerous mainly because it becomes concentrated in the thyroid gland?
   a. cesium-137   **b.** iodine-131
   c. strontium-90   **d.** radon-222

Answers: 1. c; 2. a; 3. d; 4. a; 5. d; 6. c; 7. b

Depleted Uranium

Naturally occurring uranium contains 0.720% ^{235}U, the fissile isotope that is used in nuclear reactors. However, nuclear power plants require that the fissile isotope be increased to a concentration of 3.5–5.0% to support a controlled chain reaction. Enrichment to approximately 90% is needed for nuclear weapons.

The enrichment process concentrates the ^{235}U isotope. The remaining uranium ore from which ^{235}U has been removed is known as depleted uranium (DU). After enrichment, the ^{235}U concentration in DU is only ~0.2% of the total.

Depleted uranium has been used to make armor plating and ammunition by the military. A major product has been 30 mm projectiles that can be directed against military vehicles. Uranium's density of 19.1 g/cm³ is much greater than that of most other armored

materials, so a bullet made of depleted uranium rather than lead (with a density of only 11.34 g/cm³) will be heavier but smaller in diameter and will be able to pierce armor plating made from steel, which has a density of only 7.75–8.05 g/cm³. A direct hit will also result in converting some of the uranium into dust particles, which can then be inhaled by people in the area.

There have been myriad studies of the health effects of using depleted uranium. These generally show that the two organs most affected are the lungs and the kidneys. Small particles of uranium that result from impact of DU weapons can be inhaled and settle in the lungs. This can lead to radiation damage or even lung cancer if the concentration is high enough. Other means of exposure are through ingestion of contaminated food and water or from metal shrapnel fragments embedded in the body after impact. The overall toxic effects of DU seem to be less related to the radioactivity in the material than to toxicity to uranium itself. There are numerous reports of increased numbers of birth defects or other health problems in areas where DU has been used.

An additional consideration is that the enrichment process involves separating the uranium-235 from uranium-238 by reacting the uranium to form gaseous UF_6. After the lighter $^{235}UF_6$ has been separated out, much radioactive UF_6 remains and must be dealt with. This material is currently stored in large steel casks, but the containers can undergo corrosion and then leak. How to deal with these wastes has not yet been determined.

11.9 Uses and Consequences of Nuclear Energy

Learning Objective ❯ List some uses and consequences of nuclear energy.

A significant portion of the electricity we use today is generated by nuclear power plants. In the United States, one-fifth of all the electricity produced comes from nuclear power plants. Europeans rely even more on nuclear energy. France, for example, obtains 80% of its electric power from nuclear plants, while Belgium, Spain, Switzerland, and Sweden generate about one-third of their power from nuclear reactors.

Ironically, the same nuclear chain reaction that occurred in the detonation of the bomb dropped on Hiroshima is used extensively today under the familiar concrete containment tower of a nuclear power plant. The key difference is that the power plant employs a *slow, controlled* release of energy from the nuclear chain reaction, rather than an explosion. The slowness of the process is due to the use of uranium fuel that is much less enriched (about 3.0 % ^{235}U rather than the 90% enrichment for weapons-grade uranium).

While the generation of electricity is currently the major use for uranium, nuclear reactors are also used to propel a small number of sea-going vessels. These are mainly military rather than civilian ships. The first of these vessels was the submarine U.S.S. *Nautilus*, which was launched in 1955. Nuclear power enabled the submarine to remain submerged or at sea for long time periods without refueling. The *Nautilus*, for example, was able to reach the North Pole by navigating beneath the Polar Ice Pack. There are currently about 150 marine vessels that carry nuclear reactors, including much larger ships with several reactors, such as the aircraft carrier U.S.S. *Enterprise*.

There are also small reactors that are important in the manufacturing of radioisotopes for medical or other purposes. These include a wide range of isotopes, such as Mo-99 (a precursor to the short-lived Tc-99m, which is used in medical diagnoses), Sr-82, which is used for heart imaging, and Ge-68, which is used to calibrate PET equipment for medical diagnostic procedures.

One of the main problems with the production of nuclear power arises from the products of the nuclear reactions. As in nuclear fallout, most of the daughter nuclei produced by the fission of uranium-235 are also radioactive, some with very long half-lives. We will discuss the problems associated with nuclear waste further in Chapter 15. Another problem is the potential transformation of spent nuclear fuel into weapons-grade material. A third problem occurs when nuclear plants malfunction.

There have been three serious malfunctions at nuclear plants. Three Mile Island involved a partial meltdown of the core. Chernobyl involved a fire and release of radioactivity into the surrounding area. Most recently, Fukushima Daiichi malfunctioned following an earthquake that created tsunami waves that were much higher than the sea walls protecting the facility. The plants were flooded, the cooling system failed, a partial core meltdown occurred, and radioactive material was released.

When power is generated in nuclear plants, important changes occur in the fuel. Neutron bombardment converts uranium-235 to radioactive daughter products. Eventually, the concentration of uranium-235 becomes too low to sustain the nuclear chain reaction. The fuel rods (Figure 11.13) must be replaced about every three years, and the rods then become high-level nuclear waste.

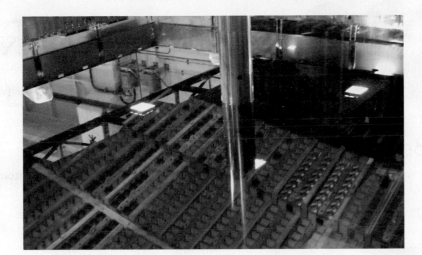

◀ **Figure 11.13** The core of a nuclear reactor contains hollow rods filled with uranium pellets. The heat generated by the fission reaction is used to boil water, which drives turbines to generate electricity in the same way as in a coal-fired or gas-fired generating plant. Because the pellets are only about 3% uranium-235, a nuclear explosion cannot occur, though loss of coolant may lead to a reactor meltdown.

One potential problem that can arise from fuel rods in nuclear reactors is the production of fissile plutonium-239, which could be diverted to use in plutonium bombs. As uranium-235 nuclei undergo fission, the nonfissionable (and very concentrated) uranium-238 nuclei absorb neutrons and are converted to plutonium-239, a transmutation described in Section 11.8. In time, some plutonium-240 is also formed. However, if the fuel rods are removed after only about three months, the fissionable plutonium-239 can be easily separated from the other fission products by chemical means. Plutonium bombs require less sophisticated technology to produce than is needed to make nuclear weapons from uranium. Plutonium is thus of greater concern with respect to weapons proliferation because operation of a nuclear plant can produce materials suitable for use in a bomb. North Korea has nuclear power plants and a plutonium separation facility capable of producing enough plutonium-239 for several weapons each year (Figure 11.14). Iran also has a facility for enriching uranium, which could lead to the production of nuclear bombs. The activities of these and other developing countries raise the fear of a dangerous proliferation of nuclear weapons.

▲ **Figure 11.14** A satellite photograph of the plutonium processing plant at Yongbyon, North Korea.

The amount of nuclear waste from reactors and from isotopic enrichment is huge. Ways to deal with the waste and to minimize the amount of material have not been well developed. In some countries, most notably in Europe, reprocessing used fuel has been carried out for years. Recovery of unused uranium and plutonium can result in 25–30% more energy coming from the original fuels. Recently, interest in recovering actinides with plutonium has grown. This would lower the amount of long-term radioactivity in the waste as well as the risk of having plutonium used for illegal activities. However, the U.S. government has prohibited reprocessing by civilian companies. Much effort and money have been spent on finding a suitable repository for nuclear waste, but development of the most promising site, Yucca Mountain in Nevada, is no longer being funded.

The Nuclear Age

The splitting of the atom made the Chinese curse "May you live in interesting times" seem quite appropriate. The goal of the alchemists, to change one element into another, has been achieved through the application of scientific principles. New elements have been formed, and the periodic table has been extended well beyond uranium ($Z = 92$). This modern alchemy produces plutonium by the ton; neptunium ($Z = 93$), americium ($Z = 95$), and curium ($Z = 96$) by the kilogram; and berkelium ($Z = 97$) and einsteinium ($Z = 99$) by the milligram.

As we have seen, radioactive isotopes have many uses, from killing tiny but deadly cancer cells and harmful microorganisms in food to serving as tracers in a

GREEN CHEMISTRY

Galen Suppes and Sudarshan Loyalka University of Missouri

Can Nuclear Power Be Green?

Learning Objective › Explain how applications of Green Chemistry Principles can be applied to handling of radioactive isotopes in spent fuel rods.

For decades, nuclear power has provided about 20% of the U.S. electricity with a proven performance and safety record (Section 11.9). Building upon this tradition and making the use of nuclear power greener and more sustainable may have economic and environmental benefits.

Like all technologies, nuclear power has advantages and challenges that are not easily compared. Among the advantages advocates of nuclear power claim are (1) reduced CO_2 emissions compared to coal and natural gas; (2) a lower volume of waste; (3) lower fuel cost (~0.7 ¢/kWh of electricity versus ~1.5 to 4 ¢/kWh for coal and natural gas); (4) the best safety history (about one-fifth the annual occupational health deaths per kWh of electrical power versus coal); and (4) reliability (nuclear power plants operate at the industry's highest capacity factors).

Challenges people point to include (1) the need for specialized spent-fuel handling and waste storage; (2) base load mismatch to peak demand; (3) potential for environmental contamination and broad-scale lethal exposure; (4) potential use in weapons proliferation; and (5) high capital costs.

If society is going to use nuclear power, it's probably a good idea to see how green chemistry and improved safety standards can be used to meet these challenges:

Radioactive Waste – Chemists have developed greener approaches to waste processing and storage. Nuclear waste typically contains a small amount of radioactive material that requires handling the entire mixture as radioactive waste. The first pass on handling radioactive waste is to store the waste for several months before attempting to handle. Short half-life isotopes undergo natural and quick degradation to safer materials (Green Chemistry Principle 10) These radioactive parts of the waste can be removed using known chemistry (opportunities for Green Chemistry Principle 3). France and Japan partially concentrate nuclear waste today and produce a reprocessed fuel that can be used to generate energy at a low cost (0.9 ¢/kWh). If all of the nuclear fuel used to date in the United States were fully reprocessed and useful isotopes recycled, the remaining radioactive waste would fit in a building about one third the size of a small house. Also, it is possible to convert that waste into harmless isotopes, and future technology may make that affordable.

Peak Power Demand – Storing excess electrical energy produced at night followed by its use during the day can help make nuclear energy easier to use and more efficient (Green Principle 6). For both safety and economy, nuclear reactors operate continuously and do not change their output in response to electrical demand. However, the need for electricity varies greatly during the day and night. Use of large grid-based batteries and use of plug-in hybrid electric vehicles (being charged at night) are both topics of great interest—solutions to both can be attained through green chemistry.

Safety – Nuclear plants employ multiple safety features and also use the philosophy of "defense in depth" against accidental radioactivity releases (Green Chemistry Principle 12). Yet accidents with large consequences have occurred. The three most costly accidents have been at Three Mile Island, Chernobyl, and Fukushima Daiichi. Chemical processes during accidents include buildup of pressure, formation of hydrogen, combustion of hydrogen with air, and reactions and transport of radioactive fission products and other substances. Use of green adsorbents that will remove these radioactive components from the vented gases is a green chemistry solution.

Security (Weapons Proliferation and Physical Protection) – It is difficult to make a nuclear bomb from low-enriched uranium (used in all power reactors) because the process involves separating uranium isotopes. It is easier to separate plutonium from the spent fuel (mainly uranium-238), because plutonium is a different element with different chemical properties, and hence plutonium should be removed from the spent fuel for recycling or safeguarding. The process used for this separation (known as PUREX) is a first-generation commercial process with ample opportunity to be improved upon with green chemistry. The objective is to remove the plutonium from spent fuel and to use it in new fuel rods thereby minimizing the amount on site—this represents a "recycle to extinction process," which is an example Green Chemistry Principle 1.

High Power-Plant Costs – The high capital cost of nuclear power plants is caused in part by the delays between capital investment and startup due to permitting and licensing processes. The approach taken by the United States to address this concern is the use of small modular nuclear reactors (SMNR), with a $450 million investment announced in 2012. Solutions to higher plant costs are not so much a matter of green chemistry but rather of good practices that improve the economics so that green chemistry can solve the issues related to other topics.

The processing of nuclear waste is performed with chemistry. Chemistry allows recycling of plutonium (weapons proliferation), recycling of unspent fuel, and removal of benign elements from the radioactive elements. Control of chemistry is also the key to preventing the release of radiation to the environment (safety). It is improved and green chemistry that will make nuclear power safer and sustainable for millennium.

► The Sellafield reprocessing plant in England. Some plants in Europe are reprocessing spent fuel from utilities in Europe and Japan. Reprocessing of spent commercial-reactor nuclear fuel is currently not permitted in the United States due to the perceived danger of nuclear proliferation.

variety of biological experiments and imaging technologies and generating fearsome weapons. Figure 11.15 displays a number of other constructive uses of nuclear energy. We live in an age in which the extraordinary forces present in the atom have been unleashed as a true double-edged sword. The threat of nuclear war—and nuclear terrorism—has been a constant specter for some 70 years, yet it is hard to believe that the world would be a better place if we had not discovered the secrets of the atomic nucleus.

▲ **Figure 11.15** Some constructive uses of nuclear energy.

5. Can we minimize or recycle radioactive wastes to make nuclear power generation a more sustainable process?

Processes that involve the production of radioisotopes and processes that use radioisotopes create a large amount of radioactive waste, some of which has very long half-lives. The main strategy so far in the United States has been to store the waste materials until they could be moved to a permanent long-term storage facility, but a suitable site has still not been found. Just the sheer volume of waste is overwhelming. If some of the waste could be reused or if the volume could be reduced by separating out radioactive metals, it would minimize the volume of radioactive waste, increase the U.S. energy supply, and make nuclear power a more sustainable source of energy.

SUMMARY

Section 11.1—Some isotopes of elements are **radioisotopes,** unstable nuclei that undergo changes in nucleon number, atomic number, or energy during the **radioactive decay** process. We are constantly exposed to naturally occurring **background radiation. Ionizing radiation** includes nuclear radiation and X-rays and causes harm by dislodging electrons from living tissue and forming ions. Radiation can disrupt normal chemical processes in cells and can damage DNA.

Section 11.2—Nuclear equations are used to represent nuclear processes. These equations are balanced when the sum of nucleon numbers and the sum of atomic numbers on each side are the same. Four types of radioactive decay are **alpha** ($_2^4\text{He}$) **decay, beta** ($_{-1}^{0}\text{e}$) **decay, gamma** ($_0^0\gamma$) **decay,** and emission of a **positron** ($_{+1}^{0}\text{e}$). **Electron capture (EC)** is a fifth type of decay, in which a nucleus absorbs one of the atom's electrons. There are a number of important differences between nuclear reactions and chemical reactions.

Section 11.3—The unit of radioactive decay is the **becquerel (Bq).**

$$1 \text{ becquerel (Bq)} = 1 \text{ disintegration/s}$$

The **half-life** of a radioactive isotope is the time it takes for half of a sample to decay. The fraction of a radioisotope remaining after n half-lives is given by

$$\text{Fraction remaining} = \frac{1}{2^n}$$

Half-lives of certain isotopes can be used to estimate the ages of various objects. **Carbon-14 dating** is the best-known of the radioisotopic dating techniques.

Section 11.4— **Transmutation,** the conversion of one element into another, cannot be carried out by chemical means but can be accomplished by nuclear processes. Bombarding a stable nucleus with energetic particles can cause artificial transmutation.

Section 11.5—Radioisotopes have many uses. A radioisotope and a stable isotope of an element behave nearly the same chemically, so radioisotopes can be used as **tracers** in physical and biological systems. Radiation can be used to produce useful mutations in agriculture and to irradiate foodstuffs as a method of preservation. **Radiation therapy** to destroy cancer cells depends on the fact that radiation is more damaging to those rapidly reproducing cells than to healthy cells. Radioisotopes are used in the diagnosis of various medical disorders.

Section 11.6—Different types of radiation have different penetrating abilities. *Alpha particles* (helium nuclei) are relatively slow and have low penetrating power. *Beta particles* (electrons) are much faster and more penetrating. *Gamma rays* (high-energy photons) travel at the speed of light and have great penetrating power. How hazardous radiation is depends on the location of the source; alpha particles from a source inside the body are highly damaging.

Section 11.7—Einstein's **mass–energy equation,** $E = mc^2$ shows that mass and energy are related. The total mass of the nucleons in a nucleus is greater than the actual mass of the nucleus. The missing mass, or the mass defect, is equivalent to the **binding energy** holding the nucleons together. Binding energy can be released either by breaking down heavy nuclei into smaller ones, a process called **nuclear fission**, or by joining small nuclei to form larger ones, called **nuclear fusion**.

Bombarding uranium atoms with neutrons produced radioactive species, including lighter nuclei among the products. It was hypothesized that the uranium nuclei had undergone fission and that neutrons released in the fission reaction of one nucleus could initiate a **chain reaction**.

Thermonuclear reactions (fusion reactions) combine small nuclei into larger ones. Fusion is the basis of the hydrogen bomb and the source of the sun's energy and potentially will produce more energy than fission.

Section 11.8—The Manhattan Project had four goals: (1) to achieve sustained nuclear fission and determine the **critical mass** of fissionable material required; (2) to enrich the amount of fissionable uranium-235 from ordinary uranium; (3) to synthesize plutonium-239, another fissionable isotope; and (4) to construct a nuclear fission bomb before the Germans did so. World War II ended shortly after atomic bombs were dropped on Hiroshima and Nagasaki.

In addition to the devastation at the site of a nuclear explosion, much radioactive debris, or **radioactive fallout,** is produced, including strontium-90 and iodine-131, which are particularly hazardous.

Section 11.9—Nuclear power plants use the same nuclear chain reaction as atomic bombs, but fuel rods have a lower concentration of fissionable material and the reaction can be controlled. Disposal of the products of nuclear fission in power plants and the potential conversion of nuclear fuel into weapons are important problems facing us.

GREEN CHEMISTRY—Chemistry is important in nuclear power, and improved application of green chemistry can make nuclear power the safest and most sustainable source of power for humankind. Improved green chemistry can be applied to allowing safe release of pressures that can build up in reactors and to reduce risks associated with spent fuel rods from nuclear reactors.

Learning Objectives

❯ Identify the sources of the natural radiation to which we are exposed.	Problems 1, 2, 18
❯ List the sources and dangers of ionizing radiation.	Problems 19, 20
❯ Balance nuclear equations.	Problems 21–26, 58–59
❯ Identify the types of products formed by various nuclear decay processes.	Problems 5, 6, 27–30, 60–63
❯ Solve simple half-life problems.	Problems 31–35, 37–41, 64–66
❯ Use the concept of half-life to solve simple radioisotopic dating problems.	Problems 36–42, 69–72
❯ Write a nuclear equation for a transmutation, and identify the product element formed.	Problems 10, 43–45
❯ List some applications of radioisotopes.	Problems 11, 46, 67, 68
❯ Describe the nature of materials needed to block alpha, beta, and gamma radiation.	Problems 12, 13, 47, 48
❯ Explain where nuclear energy comes from.	Problems 14, 49–51
❯ Describe the difference between fission and fusion.	Problem 50
❯ Describe the goals of the Manhattan Project and how uranium and plutonium bombs were made.	Problems 15, 16, 52–54
❯ Identify the most hazardous fallout isotopes, and explain why they are particularly dangerous.	Problem 49
❯ List some uses and consequences of nuclear energy.	Problems 17, 55–57, 73
❯ Explain how applications of Green Chemistry Principles can be applied to handling of radioactive isotopes in spent fuel rods.	Problems 76–78

▪▪▪ REVIEW QUESTIONS

1. Which of the following examples of radiation come from naturally occurring sources?
   a. rocks and soil
   b. nuclear medicine
   c. nuclear power plants
   d. radon
   e. cosmic rays

2. Which of the following examples of radiation come from human-made sources?
   a. rocks and soil
   b. nuclear medicine
   c. nuclear power plants
   d. radon
   e. internal radiation from within our bodies

3. Match each description with the type of change.
   i. A new compound is formed.
   ii. A new element is formed.
   iii. Size, shape, appearance, or volume is changed without changing the composition.
   a. nuclear
   b. chemical
   c. physical

4. Define or describe each of the following.
   a. half-life
   b. positron
   c. background radiation
   d. radioisotope

5. What changes occur in the nucleon number and the atomic number of a nucleus during emission of each of the following?
    a. alpha particle   b. gamma ray   c. proton

6. What changes occur in the nucleon number and atomic number of a nucleus during emission of each of the following?
    a. beta particle   b. neutron   c. positron

7. True or False: A half-life is the time it takes for 50% of a radioactive sample to decay, so it takes two half-lives for all of the radioactivity to decay.

8. How many days does it take for 1.00 mg of lead-103 (half-life 17.0 d) to decay to 0.125 mg?

9. Fluorine-20 has a half-life of 11.0 s. If a sample initially contains 5.00 μg of this isotope, how much remains after 33.0 s?

10. How does artificial transmutation differ from naturally occurring transmutation?

11. What are some of the characteristics that make technetium-99m such a useful radioisotope for diagnostic purposes?

12. **(a)** From which type of radiation would a pair of gloves be sufficient to shield the hands: heavy alpha particles or massless gamma rays? **(b)** From which type of radiation would heavy lead shielding be necessary to protect a worker: alpha, beta, or gamma?

13. List two ways in which workers exposed to radioactive materials can protect themselves from radiation hazard.

14. If you add together the masses of all of the particles (protons and neutrons) in a nucleus, the mass will be greater than the actual mass of the nucleus. Explain why this occurs. What happened to the "missing" mass?

15. Identify the four goals of the Manhattan Project.

16. Plutonium is especially hazardous when inhaled or ingested because it emits alpha particles. Why do alpha particles cause more damage to tissue than beta particles when their source is inside the body?

17. Identify three uses of nuclear fission.

PROBLEMS

Natural Radioactivity

18. Radioactivity in the environment
    a. comes only from human activity
    b. comes from many human and natural sources
    c. comes mainly from rocks
    d. is harmless because it is natural

19. Which of the following is not considered to be energetic enough to be ionizing radiation?
    a. gamma rays   b. microwaves
    c. ultraviolet light   d. X-rays

20. All of the following can be a consequence of ionizing radiation except:
    a. production of free radicals   b. changes in DNA
    c. increasing the number of red blood cells
    d. decreasing the number of white blood cells

Nuclear Equations

21. Write a balanced equation for emission of **(a)** an alpha particle by californium-250, **(b)** a beta particle by bismuth-210, and **(c)** a positron by iodine-117.

22. Write a balanced equation for **(a)** alpha decay of gold-173, **(b)** beta decay of iodine-138, and **(c)** capture of an electron by cadmium-104.

23. Complete the following equations.
    a. $^{179}_{79}\text{Au} \longrightarrow {}^{175}_{77}\text{Ir} + ?$ b. $^{12}_{6}\text{C} + {}^{2}_{1}\text{H} \longrightarrow {}^{13}_{6}\text{C} + ?$
    c. $^{154}_{62}\text{Sm} + {}^{1}_{0}\text{n} \longrightarrow ? + 2\,{}^{1}_{0}\text{n}$

24. Radiological laboratories often have a container of molybdenum-99, which decays to form technetium-99m. What other particle is formed? Complete the equation.

    $$^{99}_{42}\text{Mo} \longrightarrow {}^{99\text{m}}_{43}\text{Tc} + ?$$

25. Complete the equation for the decay of technetium-99m to technetium-99.

    $$^{99\text{m}}_{43}\text{Tc} \longrightarrow {}^{99}_{43}\text{Tc} + ?$$

26. When a magnesium-24 nucleus is bombarded with a neutron, a proton is ejected. What element is formed? (*Hint:* Write a balanced nuclear equation.)

27. A radioisotope decays to give an alpha particle and a protactinium-233 nucleus. What was the original nucleus?

28. A radioactive isotope decays to give an alpha particle and a bismuth-211 nucleus. What was the original nucleus?

29. When silver-107 is bombarded with a neutron, a different isotope of silver forms and then undergoes beta decay. What is the final product? (*Hint:* Write two separate nuclear equations.)

30. A nucleus of astatine-210 decays by beta emission, forming nucleus A. Nucleus A also decays by beta emission to nucleus B. Write the nuclear symbol for B.

Half-Life and Isotopic Dating

31. Niobium was first isolated from a rock that was found in a Connecticut farm field and sent to the British Royal Society in 1743 by John Winthrop, the grandson of the first colonial governor of Connecticut and the great-grandson of the first colonial governor of Massachusetts. One isotope, niobium-94, has a half-life of 20,000 years. How long will it take for a 2.00 μg sample of niobium-94 to decay to 0.0625 μg?

32. How long will it take for a 12.0-g sample of iodine-131 to decay to leave a total of 1.5 g of the isotope? The half-life of iodine-131 is 8.07 days.

33. A lab worker reports an activity of 80,000 counts/s for a sample of magnesium-21, whose half-life is 122 ms. Exactly 5.00 min later, another worker records an activity of 10 counts/min on the same sample. What best accounts for this difference? Magnesium-21
    a. gives off only neutrinos
    b. has a very short half-life, so almost every radioactive atom in the sample has decayed
    c. is an alpha emitter   d. is a gamma emitter

34. A patient is injected with a radiopharmaceutical labeled with technetium-99m, half-life of 6.0 h, in preparation for a gamma ray scan to evaluate kidney function. If the original activity of the sample was 48 μCi, what activity (in μCi) remains **(a)** after 24 h and **(b)** after 48 h?

35. In determining the half-life of sulfur-35, students collected the following data, with the time in days and the activity in counts/s.

    Without doing detailed calculations, estimate a value for the half-life.

Time	Activity
0	1000
20	851
40	725
60	616
80	525
100	446
120	380
140	323

36. The ratio of carbon-14 to carbon-12 in a piece of charcoal from an archaeological excavation is found to be one-half the ratio in a sample of modern wood. Approximately how old is the charcoal? How old would it be if the isotopic ratio were 25% of that in a sample of modern wood?

37. Gallium-67 is used in nuclear medicine (Table 11.6). After treatment, a patient's blood shows an activity of 20,000 counts per minute (counts/min). How long will it be before the activity decreases to about 5000 counts/min?

38. How long will it take for a 12.0-g sample of iodine-131 to decay to leave a total of 1.5 g of the isotope? The half-life of iodine-131 is 8.4 days.

39. About 0.0117% of the 600 mg of potassium in a typical banana is radioactive potassium-40. If 1.00 g of potassium-40 has an activity of 2.63×10^5 Bq, what is the activity of the banana?

40. How long will it take a radioactive sample of iodine-131 (half-life 8.07 d) to lose 75% of its original radioactivity?
    a. 8.0 d   **b.** 16 d   **c.** 24 d   **d.** 32 d

41. If it takes 75 days for 10.0 mg of a particular radioactive isotope to decay to 1.25 mg, what is its half-life?

42. Living matter has a carbon-14 activity of about 16 counts/min per gram of carbon. What is the age of an artifact for which the carbon-14 activity is 8 counts/min per gram of carbon?

Artificial Transmutation

43. In 2010, Russian and American scientists produced a few atoms of element 117 by shooting an intense beam of ions of the rare isotope calcium-48 at a target of berkelium-247. Two isotopes of element 117 were formed, one having 176 neutrons and the other 177 neutrons. Write two separate nuclear equations for the formation of the two isotopes. How many neutrons were released in each process?

44. Meitnerium undergoes alpha decay to form element 107, which in turn also emits an alpha particle. What are the atomic number and nucleon number of the isotope formed by these two steps? Write balanced nuclear equations for the two reactions.

45. Scientists have tried to make element 120. Three different combinations of projectile and target were used to try to produce the nucleus $^{302}_{120}$X: (a) nickel-64 and uranium-238, (b) iron-58 and plutonium-244, and (c) chromium-54 and curium-248.

However, after 120 days, no sign of element 120 was found. Write nuclear equations for the three expected reactions.

Uses of Radioisotopes

46. There are several technological applications for the transuranium elements $(Z > 92)$. An important one is in smoke detectors, which can use the decay of a tiny amount of americium-241 to neptunium-237. What subatomic particle is emitted from that decay process?

Penetrating Power of Radiation

47. Barium-140 is a gamma emitter. Bismuth-210 is a beta emitter. Radium-223 is an alpha emitter. Rate these isotopes in order from the most penetrating to least penetrating:
    a. barium-140, bismuth-210, radium-223
    b. bismuth-210, radium-223, barium-140
    c. radium-223, barium-140, bismuth-210
    d. barium-140, radium-223, bismuth-210

48. Alpha emitters are much more likely to cause damage to tissue than gamma emitters are. Why are most alpha emitters less dangerous to living systems than gamma emitters are?

Energy from the Nucleus

49. In the first step of the chain reaction of a nuclear explosion, a ^{235}U nucleus absorbs a neutron. The resulting ^{236}U nucleus is unstable and can fission into ^{92}Kr and ^{141}Ba nuclei as shown in the figure. What are the other products of this reaction? After assessing this reaction, explain how the chain reaction can continue.

50. Compare nuclear fission and nuclear fusion. Why is energy liberated in each case?

51. Einstein's mass–energy equation is $E = mc^2$, where mass is in kilograms and the speed of light is 3.00×10^8 m/s. The unit of energy is the joule (4.184 J = 1 cal; 1000 cal = 1 kcal; 1J = 1 kg·m^2/s^2).
    a. Calculate the energy released, in calories and kilocalories, when 1 g of matter is converted to energy.
    b. A bowl of cornflakes supplies 110 kcal (110 food calories). How many bowls of cornflakes would supply the same amount of energy as you calculated for 1 g of matter in part (a)?

Nuclear Bombs

52. The compounds ^{235}UF$_6$ and ^{238}UF$_6$ are nearly chemically identical. How were they separated to enrich the percentage of ^{235}U?

53. How was plutonium-239 synthesized from uranium-238?

54. Describe the logic behind the designs for the uranium-235 bomb and the plutonium-239 bombs that were built at Los Alamos during World War II.

Uses and Consequences of Nuclear Energy

55. Fuel rods in nuclear power plants are generally replaced after roughly 3 years of use when the amount of ^{235}U remaining falls below the enrichment that is needed to generate electricity efficiently. What happens to the original ^{235}U isotope during nuclear fission?

56. If fuel rods are used and then removed after only three months, why can that lead to the production of nuclear weapons?

57. The same fission reaction is used for power plants that generate electricity and for atomic bombs. Give two differences between the operation of a power plant and the explosion of a bomb.

ADDITIONAL PROBLEMS

58. Complete the following equations.
    a. $^{10}_5B + ^1_0n \longrightarrow ? + ^4_2He$
    b. $^{23}_{10}Ne \longrightarrow ^{23}_{11}Na + ?$
    c. $^{121}_{51}Sb + ? \longrightarrow ^{121}_{52}Te + ^1_0n$

59. In 2006, Soviet dissident Alexander Litvinenko was murdered when Polonium-210 was added to his tea; he died three weeks later. Polonium-210 is an alpha emitter. What other product is formed?

60. A proposed method of making fissionable nuclear fuel is to bombard the relatively abundant isotope thorium-232 with a neutron. The product X of this bombardment decays quickly by beta emission to nucleus Y, and nucleus Y decays quickly to fissionable nucleus Z. Write the nuclear symbol for Z.

61. Radium-223 nuclei usually decay by alpha emission. Once in every billion decays, a radium-223 nucleus emits a carbon-14 nucleus. Write a balanced nuclear equation for each type of emission.

62. A radionuclide undergoes alpha emission, and thorium-234 is produced. What was the original radionuclide?

63. In 1932, James Chadwick discovered a new subatomic particle when he bombarded beryllium-9 with alpha particles. One of the products was carbon-12. What particle did Chadwick discover?

64. Krypton-81m is used for lung ventilation studies. Its half-life is 13 s. How long does it take the activity of this isotope to reach one-quarter of its original value?

65. Radium-223 has a half-life of 11.4 days. Approximately how long would it take for the activity of a sample of ^{223}Ra to decrease to 1% of its initial value?

66. In an experiment with dysprosium-197, half-life of 8.1 h, an activity of 500 counts/min was recorded at 4:00 p.m. on a Friday. What was the approximate activity of this sample at 8:30 a.m. the following Monday morning, when the experiment was resumed?

67. A piece of wood from an Egyptian tomb has a carbon-14 activity of 980 counts/h. A piece of new wood of the same size shows 3920 counts/h. What is the age of the wood from the tomb?

68. You are offered a great price on a case of brandy supposedly bottled during the lifetime of Napoleon (1769–1821). Before buying it, you insist on testing a sample of the brandy and find that its tritium content is 12.5% that of newly produced brandy. How long ago was the brandy bottled? Is it likely to be authentic Napoleon-era brandy?

69. Radioactive copper ($^{64}_{29}Cu$, half-life 12.7 h) is found in quantities exceeding the pollution standard in the sediments of a reservoir during a routine check on Monday, when 56 ppm/m^3 was measured. The standard allows up to 14 ppm/m^3. About when will the level of copper-64 return to 14 ppm/m^3?

70. An unidentified corpse was discovered on April 21 at 7:00 a.m. The pathologist discovered that there were 1.24×10^{17} atoms of $^{32}_{15}P$ remaining in the victim's bones, and so he placed the time of death sometime on March 15. The half-life of $^{32}_{15}P$ is 14.28 days. How much $^{32}_{15}P$ was present in the bones at the time of death?

71. Several different radioisotopes can be used much like carbon-14 for determining the age of rocks and other matter. In the geosciences, the age of rocks may be determined using potassium-40, which decays to argon-40, with a half-life of 1.2 billion years. **(a)** Some rocks brought back from the moon were dated as being 3.6 billion years old. What percentage of the potassium-40 has decayed after that time? **(b)** Give a reason why uranium-238 (half-life of 4.6 billion years) is more useful for confirming this age than is carbon-14.

72. Write balanced nuclear equations for **(a)** the bombardment of $^{121}_{51}Sb$ by alpha particles to produce $^{124}_{53}I$, followed by **(b)** the radioactive decay of $^{124}_{53}I$ by positron emission.

73. A typical smoke detector contains about 0.25 mg of americium-241. The activity of 1 g of ^{241}Am is 1.26×10^{11} Bq. What is the activity of the americium-241 in the smoke detector?

74. A particular uranium alloy has a density of 18.75 g/cm^3. What volume is occupied by a critical mass of 49 kg of this alloy? The critical mass can be decreased to 16 kg if the alloy is surrounded by a layer of natural uranium (which acts as a neutron reflector). What is the volume of the smaller mass? Compare your answers to the approximate volumes of a baseball, a volleyball, and a basketball.

75. Plutonium has a density of 19.1 g/cm^3. What volume is occupied by a critical mass of plutonium-239. If a neutron-reflecting coating (made of beryllium) is used, the critical mass can be lowered to 2.5 kg. Compare the size of this mass to the volume of a baseball, a volleyball, and a basketball.

76. Which of these are fission products, and which is a different type of radioactive product? What is an easy method to distinguish them? What is the name used to refer to the non-fission product?

77. The concentration of an isotope can be calculated as the initial concentration times $(0.5)^{(t/t_{1/2})}$ where $t_{1/2}$ is the half live of the same units as the time. After 10 years of storage, what fraction of the initial concentration of each isotope would remain? What does this indicate about the amount of radiation from each of these isotopes versus the initial amount? Based on this information, how would you recommend handling each isotope to minimize risk of exposure? Which Green Chemistry Principles apply?

78. What other factors have an impact on the amount of radiation and danger of the radiation emitted from each of these?

CRITICAL THINKING EXERCISES

Apply knowledge that you have gained in this chapter and one or more of the FLaReS principles (Chapter 1) to evaluate the following statements or claims.

11.1. Brazil nuts are known to absorb and concentrate the element barium. A nationally known laboratory announces that Brazil nuts contain tiny traces of radium.

11.2. For more than 600 years, it was alleged that the Shroud of Turin was the burial shroud of Jesus. In 1988, several laboratories carried out carbon-14 analyses indicating that the flax from which the shroud was made was grown between 1260 and 1390 C.E. Recently, there have been claims that the 1988 analyses are unreliable because the shroud is contaminated with pollen from plants grown in the fourteenth century, and it is the age of this pollen that was actually measured in 1988. At least one of the scientists has offered to repeat the analysis on a very carefully cleaned sample of the cloth, but further access to the shroud has been refused.

11.3. Carbon-14 analyses of the Shroud of Turin have indicated that the shroud dates back only to 1260–1390 C.E. Some people have claimed that these analyses are flawed, because the shroud was subjected to high temperatures during a fire in Chambery in 1532 and that this affected the carbon-14 samples.

11.4. A scientist reports that he has found an artifact that has been shown to be 80,000 years old by carbon-14 dating.

11.5. The americium in a smoke detector (see Conceptual Example 11.7) is encased in a chamber with aluminum shielding, about as thick as the wall of a soft-drink can. A woman who purchases a smoke detector mounts it at the highest point on the ceiling. She claims that this minimizes her exposure to the radiation.

11.6. A young girl refuses to visit her grandmother who has recently undergone radiation therapy for breast cancer. The teenager is afraid that she will catch radiation sickness from her grandmother.

COLLABORATIVE GROUP PROJECTS

Prepare a PowerPoint, poster, or other presentation (as directed by your instructor) to share with the class.

1. Write a brief report on the impact of nuclear science on one of the following.
   a. war and peace
   b. industrial progress
   c. medicine
   d. agriculture
   e. human, animal, and plant genetics

2. Write an essay on radioisotopic dating using one or more of the isotopes in Table 11.5 other than carbon-14 or tritium.

3. Write a brief biography of one of the following scientists.
   a. Otto Hahn
   b. Enrico Fermi
   c. Glenn T. Seaborg
   d. J. Robert Oppenheimer
   e. Lise Meitner
   f. Albert Einstein

4. The positron is a particle of antimatter. Search the Web for information about antimatter, and the positron in particular.

5. Find a website that is strongly in favor of nuclear power plants and one that is strongly opposed. Note the sites' sponsors, and analyze their viewpoints. Try to find a website with a balanced viewpoint.

6. In 2002 and again in 2006, researchers at Dubna in Russia and at Lawrence Livermore Laboratory in California reported the synthesis of a total of four atoms of element 118. However, in July 1999, researchers at a different California laboratory had also reported creation of element 118, a report that was found to be fraudulent two years later. Report on either (a) the scientific ethical questions raised by the fraudulent report or (b) the difficulties involved in confirming the synthesis of a new human-made element.

7. Find the location of the nuclear power plant closest to where you live. Try to determine the risks and benefits of the plant. To how many houses does it provide power? What are the environmental impacts of the plant under normal operating conditions?

8. Assemble two teams of two to four people each to debate the following resolution: The dropping of the atomic bombs on Hiroshima and Nagasaki was justified. Decide beforehand which team will take the affirmative and which the negative. Each team member is to give a three- to six-minute speech followed by a cross-examination by the opposing team members. Have the rest of the class judge the debate and give written or oral comments.

CHEMISTRY@HOME   The Brief Half-Life of Candy

Materials required

- Milk Chocolate M&M's or Skittles (or similar candy with print on one side)
- resealable plastic bag
- paper and pencil

How do scientists know when an atom will decay? What is the process of radioactive decay? Let's explore and find out more.

Radioactive decay is a random process, much like flipping a coin or a piece of candy. It is not possible to predict the radioactive behavior of one individual atom. One atom can survive for only a single half-life, or it can survive many half-lives. If we are observing not one atom but many, though, we can try to calculate and predict the radioactive decay for the group.

To understand this concept better, we will use candy, such as M&M's or Skittles, to simulate radioactive decay. First, place 100 pieces of candy into a small plastic bag. Shake the bag gently to mix the candy.

Gently pour the candy out on the table. The candies with the printed side up have decayed, while the candies with the printed side down have not. Count and record the number of decayed pieces of candy. Push these aside (or eat them!) and return only the pieces of candy with the print side down to the bag.

Reseal the bag and repeat the pouring, counting, recording, and setting aside of the candy until all of the candy has decayed. Based on your collected data, what is the half-life of the candy? Plot the "radioactive decay" of your candy.

Typical Results

Pour	Trial 1: Number of decayed candies	Trial 2: Number of decayed candies	Average number of non-decayed candies
1	54	49	48.5
2	54 + 20 = 74	49 + 27 = 76	25
3	74 + 10 = 84	76 + 10 = 86	15
4	84 + 10 = 94	86 + 7 = 93	6.5
5	94 + 2 = 96	93 + 2 = 95	4.5
6	96 + 2 = 98	95 + 3 = 98	2
7	98 + 1 = 99	98 + 1 = 99	1
8	99 + 0 = 99	99 + 1 = 100	0.5
9	99 + 1 = 100		0

Radioactive decay plot

Chart: Radioactive decay of the candy (number of non-decayed candies versus number of pours)

Questions

1. If one period of shaking of the bag of candy equals 1,000 years of time, what is the half-life in years of your candy?
2. If you came across a sample of candy containing 85 pieces of "decayed" candy, how "old" would you expect the candy to be? (Again, use 1 period of shaking = 1,000 years.)
3. What would you expect your radioactive decay plot to look like if you started the experiment with 1,000 pieces of candy instead of 100?
4. If you ran this experiment with only one piece of candy, how long would you expect that piece of candy to last? (how many half-lives?)

12

CHEMISTRY OF EARTH

Learning Objectives

> Describe the structure of Earth and the regions of Earth's surface. (12.1)

> List the most abundant elements in Earth's crust. (12.1)

> Describe the arrangement of silicate tetrahedra in common silicate minerals. (12.2)

> Describe how glass differs in structure from other silicates. (12.2)

> List the most important metals with their principal ores, and explain how they are extracted. (12.3)

> Describe some of the environmental costs associated with metal production. (12.3)

> List the main components of solid waste. (12.4)

> Name and describe the three Rs of garbage. (12.4)

> Identify a few elements critical to products used every day by modern society that are not abundant that have to be replaced by earth-abundant materials.

> Describe why recycling and reuse of critical elements is not sustainable.

Have You Ever Wondered?

1. **Why is nuclear waste stored in salt mines?**

2. **How does clumping cat litter work?**

3. **How was medieval red glass made?**

4. **What is the life cycle of an aluminum can?**

5. **Why do scrap metals bring such high prices?**

METALS AND MINERALS This wondrous world of ours is a fertile sphere blanketed in air, with about three-fourths of its surface covered by water. Although Spaceship Earth is about 40,000 km in circumference, with a surface area of 500 million km^2, it is but a tiny, blue-green jewel in the vastness of space.

Spaceship Earth is self-contained and provides, along with the sun, all that is needed for life on it. From the food we eat to the salt we place on the food, to the porcelain plates we eat from, to the metal our utensils are made of · · · The fact that this spaceship is self-contained does mean, however, that its resources are finite and must be managed as such—in other words, sustainably.

Every area of Earth is awash with minerals, many of which are useful to humankind. The otherwise barren Salar de Uyuni in Bolivia contains large amounts of sodium chloride, widely used in both industry and the home. Most sodium chloride is obtained from salt lakes and from the oceans. The water is evaporated, and the solids are heaped in piles as seen at left. After drying, purifying, and packaging, the product finds its way into our kitchens as table salt. Many other minerals make longer journeys to their final destination. We will examine some of them in this chapter.

12.1 Spaceship Earth: Structure and Composition

Learning Objectives > Describe the structure of Earth and the regions of Earth's surface. > List the most abundant elements in Earth's crust.

What kinds of materials do we have aboard this spaceship? Are they sufficient for this enormous load of passengers? Let's begin by looking at the composition of Earth. Earth's solid structure can be broken down into three parts (Figure 12.1).

1. Core: Its diameter is ~3500 km. It has two physical states: solid (inner; ~1300 km in diameter) and liquid (outer; ~2200 km in thickness). The core is composed mainly of Fe and Ni.

2. Mantle: It is ~2900 km thick and consists of a lower (~2000 km thick), transition (~500 km thick), and upper (~360 km thick) mantle. It is composed mainly of high-density Mg and Fe silicates.

3. Crust: This outermost layer is between 8 km (oceans) and 40 km (continents) thick. The crust is composed mainly of oxygenated Si (~60%) and Al (~15%) compounds: silica, quartz, silicates, silicoaluminates, and others (e.g., metal oxides).

The *crust* is the outer solid shell of Earth, often called the *lithosphere*. We will get to the gaseous and watery parts, known as the *atmosphere* and *hydrosphere*, in Chapters 13 and 14, respectively. Based on extensive sampling, the elemental composition of the Earth's surface (including the *atmosphere, hydrosphere,* and *lithosphere*) has been determined and is summarized in Table 12.1.

More than half the atoms in the sample are O atoms, which occur in the atmosphere as molecular oxygen (O_2), in the hydrosphere in combination with hydrogen as water, and in the lithosphere in combination with silicon (pure sand is largely SiO_2) and various other elements. Silicon is the second most abundant element in the sample, and hydrogen is third, with most of the H atoms combined with oxygen

▲ **Figure 12.1** Diagram showing the structural regions of Earth (not to scale).

Q: *Earth is roughly 12,000 km in diameter, and the crust averages 35 km thick. Why is the crust not shown to scale?*

Table 12.1	Elemental Composition of the Earth's Surface	
Element	Atom Percent	Percent by Mass
Oxygen	53.3	49.5
Silicon	15.9	25.7
Hydrogen	15.1	0.9
Aluminum	4.8	7.5
Sodium	1.8	2.6
Iron	1.5	4.7
Calcium	1.5	3.4
Magnesium	1.4	1.9
Potassium	1.0	2.4
All others	3.7	1.4
Total	100.0	100.0

It DOES Matter!

One of the more common rocks on Earth is limestone, which is calcium carbonate ($CaCO_3$). In nature, calcium carbonate is found in many different physical forms, including marble, seashells, eggshells, coral, pearls, and chalk. Striking examples of limestone formations are the stalagmites and stalactites in caves, such as those seen here from the Carlsbad Caverns National Park.

in water. Because hydrogen is the lightest element, it makes up only 0.9% of Earth's crust by mass. Just three elements—oxygen, silicon, and hydrogen—make up 84.3% of the atoms in the sample, and the top nine elements account for 96.3% of the atoms, leaving only 3.7% of the atoms representing all the other elements.

The Lithosphere: Its Importance to Humans

In terms of mass, the lithosphere is almost completely composed of inorganic minerals. However, when discussing the lithosphere's importance to humans and to life on Earth, another view is required. In this view, the lithosphere is composed of three equally important components, namely, inorganic (rocks and minerals), organic (humic materials), and biological (flora and fauna). In this chapter, we will focus mainly on the inorganic components.

The predominant rocks and minerals in the lithosphere are:

- *silicate minerals* (compounds of metals with silicon and oxygen),
- *carbonate minerals* (metals combined with carbon and oxygen),
- *oxide minerals* (metals combined with oxygen only), and
- *sulfide minerals* (metals combined with sulfur only).

Some typical nonsilicate minerals are listed in Table 12.2.

Table 12.2	Some Nonsilicate Minerals of Economic Importance		
Mineral Type	Name	Chemical Formula	Source and/or Use
Oxide	Hematite	Fe_2O_3	Ore of iron; pigment
	Magnetite	Fe_3O_4	Ore of iron
	Corundum	Al_2O_3	Gemstone; abrasive
Sulfide	Galena	PbS	Ore of lead
	Chalcopyrite	$CuFeS_2$	Ore of copper
Carbonate	Calcite	$CaCO_3$	Cement; lime

1. Why is nuclear waste stored in salt mines?

The vast majority of military-grade nuclear waste in the United States is being stored in a salt mine near Carlsbad, New Mexico, at a depth of about 650 m. At the higher temperatures and pressures found at this depth, due to disruption of the ionic interactions (see Chapter 4), salt changes from a crystalline solid to a flowing, plastic-like material. Given time, the salt will encase the nuclear waste and sequester it. This will minimize the potential of the waste to leak out and cause damage. Over time, the radioactive waste will decay to nonradioactive materials (see Chapter 11).

Although much, much smaller in quantity, the *organic* portion of Earth's outer layers includes soil (mostly waste and decomposition products of the *biological* component) and fossilized materials (such as coal, natural gas, petroleum, and oil shale) that were living organisms millions of years ago. This organic material always contains carbon, nearly always hydrogen, and often oxygen, nitrogen, and other elements.

The Lithosphere's Bounty: From Materials to Energy

Early people obtained food by hunting and gathering. After the agricultural revolution (about 10,000 years ago), people no longer were forced to search for food. Domesticated animals and plants supplied their needs for food and clothing. A reasonably assured food supply enabled them to live in villages and created a demand for more sophisticated building materials. People learned to convert natural materials into products with superior properties. For example, adobe bricks, which serve well in arid areas, could be made simply by drying a mixture of clay and straw in the sun.

Fire was one of the earliest agents of chemical change. When people learned to control fire, they learned that cooking improved the flavor and digestibility of meat and grains. People learned that heating adobe bricks made stronger ceramic bricks. Similarly, firing clay at high temperatures produced ceramic pots, making cooking and storage of food much easier. As they became able to produce higher temperatures, people learned to make glass and to extract metals from ores. They made tools from bronze and, later, from iron.

SELF-ASSESSMENT Questions

1. The regions of the Earth, listed in order from the center outward, are
   a. core, crust, mantle, hydrosphere   **b.** core, mantle, crust
   c. core, crust, mantle, hydrosphere   **d.** mantle, crust, core

2. Earth's core is composed mainly of
   a. lead   **b.** iron   **c.** radioactive elements   **d.** sulfur

3. The Earth's lithosphere can be broken down into how many components:

   a. one   **b.** two   **c.** three   **d.** four

4. Which of the following is not a component of Earth's surface?
   a. lithosphere   **b.** hydrosphere   **c.** crust   **d.** mantle

5. Three elements account for more than 80% of the Earth's crust by atom percent. In decreasing order of abundance, they are
   a. H, O, Si   **b.** H, Si, O   **c.** O, H, Si   **d.** O, Si, H

Answers: 1, b; 2, b; 3, c; 4, d; 5, d

12.2 Silicates and the Shapes of Things

Learning Objectives ❯ Describe the arrangement of silicate tetrahedra in common silicate minerals. ❯ Describe how glass differs in structure from other silicates.

We will consider only a few representative minerals of the thousands that occur in the lithosphere. First, let's look at some silicates. The basic unit of silicate structure is the SiO_4 tetrahedron (Figure 12.2). SiO_4 tetrahedron can be connected in a number of ways to make an amazing array of arrangements and unique mineral phases. Some of the possibilities are illustrated in Figure 12.3, with some real mineral phases presented in Table 12.3.

Quartz is pure silicon dioxide, SiO_2. The ratio of silicon to oxygen atoms is 1:2. However, because each silicon atom is surrounded by *four* oxygen atoms, the basic unit of quartz is the SiO_4 tetrahedron. These tetrahedra are arranged in a complex three-dimensional structure. Crystals of pure quartz (rock crystal) are

▲ **Figure 12.2** The silicate tetrahedron has a silicon atom at the center and an oxygen atom at each of the four corners. The shaded area (green) shows how the SiO_4 tetrahedron is typically represented in a mineral structure.

Connecting SiO_4 Tetrahedra

(a) Single-strand silicate chain
$Si_2O_6{}^{4-}$

(b) Two-dimensional silicate sheet
$Si_2O_5{}^{2-}$

Repeating unit

Repeating unit

▲ **Figure 12.3** SiO_4 tetrahedra bridged by oxygen atoms and some resulting minerals (wollastonite, lower left, and muscovite, lower right).

Table 12.3 | **Silicate Tetrahedra in Some Minerals**

Mineral(s)	SiO₄ Arrangement	Formula	Uses
Zirconium silicate	Simple anion (SiO_4^{4-})	$ZrSiO_4$	Ceramics; gemstones (zircon)
Spodumene	Long chains	$LiAl(SiO_3)_2$	Source of lithium and its compounds
Chrysotile asbestos	Double chains	$Mg_3(Si_2O_5)(OH)_4$	Fireproofing (now banned)
Muscovite mica	Sheets	$KAl_2(AlSi_3O_{10})(OH)_4$	Insulation; lustrous paints; packing (vermiculite)
Quartz	Three-dimensional array	SiO_2	Making glass (sand); gemstones (amethyst, agate, citrine)

colorless, but impurities produce a variety of quartz crystals sometimes used as gems (Figure 12.4).

▶ **Figure 12.4** The collection of quartz crystals includes (counterclockwise from upper right) citrine (yellowish quartz), colorless quartz, amethyst (purple quartz), and smoky quartz. The chemical structure of quartz (left) shows that each silicon atom is bonded to four oxygen atoms and each oxygen atom is bonded to two silicon atoms.

⬤ = Oxygen atom
◯ = Silicon atom

Micas are composed of SiO₄ tetrahedra arranged in two-dimensional sheetlike arrays and can be easily cleaved into thin, transparent sheets (Figure 12.5). Micas are used as insulators for electronics and in high-temperature furnaces.

▲ **Figure 12.5** A sample of mica, showing cleavage into thin, transparent sheets. The chemical structure of mica shows sheets of SiO₄ tetrahedra. The sheets are linked by bonds between O atoms and cations, mainly Al^{3+} (not shown). Mica is used as transparent "window" material in industrial furnaces.

Asbestos is a generic term for a variety of fibrous silicates. Perhaps the best known of these is *chrysotile*, a magnesium silicate (Figure 12.6). Chrysotile has double chains of SiO₄ tetrahedra. The oxygen atoms that have only one covalent bond also bear a negative charge. Magnesium ions (Mg^{2+}) balance these negative charges.

▶ **Figure 12.6** A sample of chrysotile, a type of asbestos. The chemical structure of chrysotile shows double chains of SiO₄ tetrahedra. The two chains are joined to each other through O atoms. The double chains are linked by bonds between O atoms and cations, mainly Mg^{2+} (not shown).

Asbestos: Benefits and Risks

Asbestos is an excellent fireproof thermal insulator. It was once used widely to insulate furnaces, heating ducts, and steam pipes.

The health hazards to those who work with asbestos are well known. Asbestos fibers are extremely tiny and have very sharp edges. Inhalation of fibers 5–50 µm long over a period of 10–20 years can cause *asbestosis* and may lead to lung cancer or *mesothelioma*, a rare and incurable cancer of the linings of body cavities.

Long-term occupational exposure to asbestos increases the risk of lung cancer by a factor of two. Cigarette smoking causes a tenfold increase in the risk of lung cancer. We might expect asbestos workers who smoke to have a risk of developing lung cancer that is 20 times that of nonsmokers who do not work with asbestos, but instead, their risk is increased by a factor of 90. Cigarette smoke and asbestos fibers act in such a way that each increases the effect of the other. Such a reinforcing interaction is called a **synergistic effect**.

Aluminum Silicates: From Clays to Ceramics

When two-dimensional sheets of connected SiO_4 tetrahedra are stacked, we have the start of a three-dimensional mineral phase called clay. Use of clay by humans has a long history, dating back to pottery making in 14,000 B.C.E. Today, we use the same basic concept and techniques to manufacture a range of useful items, including clay coffee cups and roofing tiles. Clay owes its usefulness and versatility to the manner in which Al, Si, and O atoms are bonded. There are two major classes of clays, based on how the tetrahedral silicate sheets are assembled with the octahedral, mainly aluminum hydroxide, sheets.

1:1 Clays

In these clays, a tetrahedral silicate sheet and an octahedral aluminum hydroxide sheet are connected by oxygen atoms bound to both the Si atoms of the tetrahedral sheet and the Al atoms of the octahedral sheet, to form a layer. These 1:1 layers are then connected by hydrogen bonding to each other, alternating the silicate and aluminum hydroxide sheets as they pile one on top of the other. It also means that these clays do not expand or swell. A well-known example of this type of clay is a kaolinite.

2:1 Clays

These clays consist of layers composed of one octahedral aluminum hydroxide sheet sandwiched between two tetrahedral silicate sheets, bridged by oxygen atoms. If the space between the 2:1 layers contains H_2O, this type of clay contracts when it is dried and expands when it is wetted. Expanding clays have found applications in drilling muds, clumping cat litter, and in pollutant clean-up, to mention just a few. However, expandability also leads to infrastructure damage of roughly $2 billion a year in the United States alone.

Adding water to clay makes it malleable, and a clay/water mixture can be made into nearly any shape. Once formed, the clay object becomes solid as the excess water is driven away. Bricks, flowerpots, and tiles are made in this manner. When porosity is not desirable—as in cooking pots or water jugs—the clay object can be glazed by adding various salts to the surface. Heat then turns the entire surface into a glass-like matrix. Bricks and pottery are examples of **ceramics**, inorganic materials made by heating clay or other mineral matter to a high temperature at which the particles partially melt and fuse together.

Glass

Up until now, we have focused on the highly ordered manner in which the SiO_4 tetrahedra were connected in sand and clays. However, this high degree of order can

2. How does clumping cat litter work?

The secret to superabsorbent clumping cat litters is that they contain montmorillonite, a 2:1 clay that swells. When urine (mostly water) hits a sodium montmorillonite-based clay, it causes the clay particles to swell, stick together, and, ultimately, create a clump that can easily be scooped out. Importantly, only the soiled portion of litter needs to be removed. This eases day-to-day maintenance of a litter box.

3. How was medieval red glass made?

The medieval glass artisans used salts of gold to manufacture red glass using conditions that would produce gold nanoparticles smaller than 100 nm by reducing the gold (see Chapter 8). Gold nanoparticles interact with light differently from large gold objects. Different hues of red, due to differences in the exact size of gold nanoparticles, could be obtained by slightly varying the conditions used to make the glass. Skilled glass artisans were sought after and could demand high salaries.

● = Oxygen atom
● = Silicon atom

▲ **Figure 12.7** Heat-softened glass can be shaped by blowing or molding. Compare the irregular arrangement of atoms in glass to the regular arrangement of those in quartz (Figure 12.4).

be broken by heating certain silicate minerals, as was discovered about 5000 years ago in northern coastal Syria, Mesopotamia, and Egypt. The resulting material was glass, an early example being decorative glass beads, something manufactured and worn to this day.

In the production of glass, crystalline materials are heated to a temperature at which they start to lose their long-range order (a repeating arrangement of atomic units, such as SiO_4) by the breaking of the bridging interactions within the crystalline matrix. This breaking of some of the bridging interactions leads to an irregular three-dimensional arrangement of the SiO_4 tetrahedra, as seen in Figure 12.7. In this new *phase*, called amorphous, chemical bonds linking the SiO_4 tetrahedra differ in strength. Thus, when glass is heated, the weaker bonds break first and the glass softens gradually. This explains why amorphous substances melt *over a range* of temperatures, instead of *at* one specific temperature.

The basic ingredients in glass can be mixed in different proportions. Ordinary window and container glass has a typical composition of about 75% SiO_2, 15% Na_2O, and 10% CaO. Oxides of various metals can be substituted for some or all of the sand, soda, or limestone. Thus, many special types of glass can be made, including those used in lenses in microscopes, eyeglasses, and even telescopes. The basic ingredients of glass yield an almost colorless glass. Adding extra elements to glass changes its color. Some examples are given in Table 12.4.

Manufacture of ordinary glass uses no vital raw materials, but the furnaces used to melt and shape the glass expend energy. Glass is easily recycled. It can be melted and formed into new objects, using considerably less energy than manufacturing new glass.

Table 12.4 | **Compositions and Properties of Various Glasses**

Type	Special Ingredient(s)	Special Properties and/or Uses
Soda–lime glass	Sodium and calcium silicates	Ordinary glass for windows, bottles, other housewares
Borosilicate glass	Boron oxide (instead of lime)	Heat-resistant, for laboratory ware and ovenware
Lead glass	Lead oxide (instead of lime)	Highly refractive (bends light); optical glass, art glass, table crystal
Colored glass	Selenium compounds	Red (ruby glass)
	Cobalt compounds	Blue (cobalt glass)
	Chromium compounds	Green
	Manganese compounds	Violet
	Carbon and iron oxide	Brown (amber glass)
Photochromic glass	Silver chloride or bromide	Darkens when exposed to light, for sunglasses, hospital windows

Ceramics

The process of heating and then cooling to cause a change in property, just introduced in the formation of glass, is also the basis for the manufacturing of ceramics. Ceramics are inorganic nonmetallic solids that are usually crystalline or partly crystalline. The variety of materials used to make ceramics and variations in heating them means that ceramics can be tailored to specific uses. Many ceramics have been made from kaolinite clays and aluminum oxide. The more advanced ceramics originate from silicon carbide as well as tungsten carbide. Ceramic materials are particularly useful when high temperatures are present.

Cement and Concrete

Cement is a complex mixture of calcium and aluminum silicates. The raw materials for the production of cement are limestone and clay. The materials are finely ground, mixed, and roasted at about 1500 °C in a rotary kiln heated by burning natural gas or powdered coal. The finished product is mixed with sand, gravel, and water to form *concrete*.

Concrete is used widely in construction because it is inexpensive, strong, chemically inert, durable, and tolerant of a wide range of temperatures. However, its production is environmentally damaging in terms of raw material mining, from the destruction of entire mountains to the emission of CO_2, particulate matter and other pollutants, such as sulfur dioxide. On the positive side, tires and toxic organic wastes can be destroyed when they are used as fuel for the kiln. For disposal, concrete can be broken up and used as rock fill.

It DOES Matter!

Optical fibers are hair-thin threads of glass, which carry messages as intermittent bursts of light. Sounds are translated into electric signals, which are converted into pulses of laser light that are transmitted by the glass fibers. At the end of the line, the light pulses are converted back to sound waves. A bundle of optical fibers can carry several hundred times as many messages as a copper cable of the same size, and these fiber bundles have replaced many old telephone lines and computer cables. They are also used in medicine in devices that provide visual access inside the body and that guide surgical instruments.

SELF-ASSESSMENT Questions

1. All silicate minerals contain silicon and
   a. carbon   **b.** hydrogen   **c.** iron   **d.** oxygen

2. The mineral composed of pure silicon dioxide (SiO_2) is
   a. asbestos   **b.** calcite   **c.** quartz   **d.** zircon

3. The silicate tetrahedron consists of one _____ atom at the center and _____ atoms at the corners.
   a. O; 4 Si   **b.** O; 2 Si and 2 Al   **c.** Si; 4 O   **d.** Si; 2 O and 2 Al

   For items 4–9, match each substance with the correct structure.

4. asbestos   **(a)** double chains

5. mica   **(b)** sheets

6. quartz   **(c)** simple anions

7. zircon   **(d)** three-dimensional array

8. clay   **(e)** amorphous

9. glass   **(f)** stacked sheets

10. 2:1 clays are made up of:
    a. tetrahedral/octahedral/tetrahedral sheets
    b. octahedral/tetrahedral/octahedral sheets
    c. tetrahedral/tetrahedral/octahedral sheets
    d. tetrahedral/tetrahedral/tetrahedral sheets

11. The red color in medieval stained glass was due to
    a. blood
    b. iron nanoparticles
    c. iron cations
    d. gold nanoparticles

12. One type of material that is hard and durable but brittle is a
    a. ceramic   **b.** metal
    c. polymer   **d.** semiconductor

It DOES Matter!

Research has led to the development of amazing new ceramic materials. Ceramics have been used to make high-temperature industrial furnaces, rocket nose cones, heat-resistant tiles on the Space Shuttle, automobile engines, jet engine turbine blades, and memory elements in computers. *Superconducting ceramics* exhibit virtually no resistance to the flow of electricity; they make possible high-speed magnetically levitated (maglev) trains like that shown above.

▲ Portland cement is made by roasting a mixture of limestone, clay, and sand. This cement is the "glue" that holds concrete together. About 4 billion tons of Portland cement was produced worldwide in 2012.

13. The main ingredients of ordinary glass are
   a. boron oxide, sand, and limestone
   b. clay and limestone
   c. coke, sand, and limestone
   d. sand, sodium carbonate, and limestone

14. The main ingredients of ordinary cement are
   a. clay and limestone
   b. coke, sand, and limestone
   c. sand and limestone
   d. sand, sodium carbonate, and limestone

Answers: 1, d; 2, c; 3, c; 4, a; 5, b; 6, d; 7, c; 8, f; 9, e; 10, a; 11, a; 12, d; 13, d; 14, a

12.3 Metals and Ores

Learning Objectives ❯ List the most important metals with their principal ores, and explain how they are extracted. ❯ Describe some of the environmental costs associated with metal production.

Human progress through the ages is often described in terms of the materials used for making tools. We speak of the Stone Age, the Bronze Age, and the Iron Age.

Copper and Bronze

Copper is sometimes found in the native state, usually in polycrystalline form, and it was probably also the first metal to be freed from its ore by early smelting techniques. Ancient records from the Middle East show that copper was known as far back as 10,000 years ago. Copper is usually found associated with sulfur, as *chalcopyrite* ($CuFeS_2$) and to a lesser extent as *chalcocite* (Cu_2S). Copper can be isolated from chalcocite by heating, and the two chemical reactions that it takes are:

$$\text{(oxidation of sulfur)}: 2\,Cu_2S + 3\,O_2 \longrightarrow 2\,Cu_2O + 2\,SO_2$$
$$\text{(reduction of copper)}: 2\,Cu_2O \longrightarrow 4\,Cu + O_2$$

Copper gained its historic importance as the main component of bronze. Classic bronze is an alloy (a mixture of two or more elements) of 90% copper and 10% tin. Another form, called mild bronze, contains only 6% tin. Classic bronze is harder and was used for blades, while mild bronze was softer and used for helmets and armor. Bronze alloys are harder than pure copper and, thus, better for a variety of uses, such as weapons as well as boat and ship fittings. Societies that learned bronze technology moved into more dominant roles in the world.

Today, copper is still very valuable due to its excellent electrical conductivity. Most of the electrical wires in buildings around the world are now made of copper. As mentioned in Chapter 8, copper is much sought after as a roofing material due to its thermal conductivity as well as its aesthetic value. It is also a very popular material for plumbing piping.

▲ Soaring prices for scrap metal, largely due to increased demand in China and India, have led to thefts of copper and aluminum from construction sites, empty houses, and other places. Thieves have taken aluminum siding from houses, bleachers from athletic fields, and car wheel rims. Several deaths have resulted from attempts to remove copper wire from live electrical equipment.

Iron and Steel

Iron is barely harder than copper in its natural form. However, when alloyed with carbon to form steel, the result is much different. Steel is much harder than any bronze alloy, and a steel weapon will nearly always be superior to a bronze weapon. Nevertheless, the technology for production of iron and steel lagged far behind that for copper and bronze for two reasons. Iron reacts so readily with oxygen and sulfur that it is not found uncombined in nature. It also melts at a much higher temperature (1536 °C) than does copper (1084 °C) or bronze (600–950 °C). To produce iron from ore (*hematite*), carbon (coke) is employed as the reducing agent (Chapter 8). First, carbon is converted to carbon monoxide.

$$2\,C(s) + O_2(g) \longrightarrow 2\,CO(g)$$

Then, the carbon monoxide reduces the iron oxide in the ore to iron metal.

$$Fe_2O_3(s) + 3\,CO(g) \longrightarrow 2\,Fe(l) + 3\,CO_2(g)$$

The role of carbon in steel production is much more than a simple reducing agent. To fully appreciate the chemistry that takes place in making high-quality steel, let's look at how the best *katanas* (samurai swords) are made. There are three chemically important steps.

The making of the steel

About 25 tons of iron-laden river sediment and charcoal are loaded into a specially designed clay furnace. Charcoal acts as the fuel (raising temperatures up to 2500 °C in the furnace) and as the reducing agent. This process produces about two tons of the desired steel, which is called *tamahagane*. The temperature of the furnace is controlled so that the tamahagane never reaches the molten state. This allows the correct amount of carbon to be dissolved into the iron (between 0.5 and 1.5%). At this point, the carbon and iron are mixed at the atomic scale.

Cleaning the steel

Steel-weakening impurities are removed and the carbon and iron are further homogenized by repeated heating, hammering, and folding of the steel. The swordsmith then determines how much carbon is in the steel. The higher the carbon content is, the harder but less flexible the steel will be. The hardest tamahagane is formed into a blade with a trough in its center. A softer (lower carbon) fragment of the tamahagane is then worked into the trough. As a result, the cutting edge is very sharp and hard, while the center is tough enough to adsorb impact without breaking the blade.

Differential quenching

At this stage, the swordsmith paints a water and clay mixture onto the blade. The coating is thicker at the dull end of the blade and gradually thins out toward the sharp end. The blade is heated to between 750 °C and 1500 °C and then placed in water to rapidly cool (quench) the blade. Different coating thickness results in different quenching rates. Fast cooling causes restricted diffusion of carbon within the steel matrix, creating a supersaturated solution of carbon in iron. To make room for the carbon atoms, the steel crystal stretches in one direction and creates a metastable phase known as martensite. Martensite is highly distorted with high residual stress. It is the distortion that introduces both further strength and hardness to the steel.

As illustrated by the katana-making example, steel is a versatile material with properties that can be fine-tuned through careful manipulation of its chemistry. For instance, mixing in other metals gives the steel special properties, such as hardness, toughness, or corrosion resistance (Table 12.5). The versatility of steel has made it into a material indispensable to society and its advancement. Today, technology perfected during the development of the katana is in daily use, as any chef will attest to, and the majority of uses are peaceful. The abundance and the ability to form so many different alloys make iron the most useful of metals, accounting for about 95% of all metal production worldwide.

Table 12.5 | **Some Alloys of Iron**

Material	Alloying Elements	Properties
Cast iron (pig iron)	2–4% C	Strong, rigid, brittle
Wrought iron	Very low C	Tough, malleable, ductile, easily welded
Stainless steel	12–30% Cr; some Ni	Corrosion resistance
Manganese steel	13% Mn; some C	Hardness; wear resistance
Nickel steel	0.5–6.0% Ni; some C	Strength
Molybdenum steel	10–15% Mo; some C	Wear resistance
Tungsten steel	1–20% W; some C	Strength at high temperatures

Aluminum: Abundant and Light

Aluminum is the most abundant metal in Earth's crust, but much of it is thinly distributed in aluminum-containing clays. The metal is tightly bound in compounds, and considerable energy is required to extract it from its ores. Nevertheless, aluminum has replaced iron for many purposes. Worldwide production of aluminum is second to that of iron, at more than 32 billion kg per year. (Iron production is about 1400 billion kg annually.)

The main ore of aluminum is *bauxite*, impure aluminum oxide (Al_2O_3). The Al_2O_3 is extracted from the impurities by the Bayer process, in which a concentrated NaOH solution at 175 °C and under pressure is used to form sodium aluminate:

$$Al_2O_3 + 2\,NaOH + 3\,H_2O \longrightarrow 2\,NaAl(OH)_4$$

The sodium aluminate is then converted to aluminum hydroxide, $Al(OH)_3$

$$NaAl(OH)_4 \longrightarrow Al(OH)_3 + NaOH$$

The aluminum hydroxide is then heated up to 980 °C and decomposes to Al_2O_3

$$2\,Al(OH)_3 \longrightarrow Al_2O_3 + 3\,H_2O$$

Finally, Al_2O_3 is electrolyzed to form pure aluminum.

$$2\,Al_2O_3 \xrightarrow{\text{electricity}} Al + 3\,O_2$$

To produce 1 ton of aluminum, it takes 2 metric tons (t) (1 t = 1000 kg) of aluminum oxide and 17,000 kilowatt hours (kWh) of electricity. If this electricity is generated from coal, about 16 t of CO_2 would be released into the atmosphere. Further smelting yields aluminum ingots—the starting material for all aluminum products.

Aluminum is both light and strong. An aluminum object weighs two-thirds less than the same-sized steel object. Although it is considerably more reactive than iron, aluminum corrodes much more slowly. Freshly prepared aluminum metal reacts rapidly with oxygen to form a hard, transparent film of aluminum oxide over its surface. This film protects the metal from further oxidation. Iron, on the other hand, forms an oxide coating that is porous and flaky. Instead of protecting the metal, the coating flakes off, allowing further oxidation. Corrosion of metals was already discussed in Chapter 8.

The Environmental Costs of Iron and Aluminum Production

Although steel and aluminum play essential roles in the modern industrial world, both are produced at significant environmental cost.

Both steel mills and aluminum plants produce considerable waste. Environmental damage caused by such wastes was demonstrated when 1 million cubic meters of aluminum waste known as "red mud" was released in 2010 into the surrounding environment of Kolontár, Hungary. The spill led to the death of 10 people and killed all life in the nearby Marcal River. The "red mud" also flowed to the Danube River, causing further damage. Pollution from metal production in developing nations is still a major problem. (See Collaborative Group Project 4.)

Aluminum production from ore is more energy intensive than steel production, but the low density of aluminum means energy savings down the road. An automobile made largely from aluminum is so much lighter than one made mainly from steel that it takes a good deal less energy to operate it.

In addition, aluminum is highly recyclable. Take an aluminum beverage can. Recycling it requires 5% of the energy needed to make a new one. In terms of energy costs, 20 recycled cans are the equivalent to one brand-new can. Thus, recycling is a highly sustainable activity, both environmentally and economically. Clearly, throwing an aluminum can or most other aluminum products in the trash is both environmentally harmful and wasteful. So drink up and recycle!

4. What is the life cycle of an aluminum can?
Once made, an aluminum can has a life cycle of approximately 60 days. Initially, aluminum ingots are rolled into sheets, which are then either rolled to make the can's cylinder or stamped to make the ends. The ends are then attached to the cylinder. The can is then filled, transported to market, purchased, and used. Once used, the can is placed in a recycling bin and transported to the recycling plant, where it is isolated from other materials to be recycled, shredded, and melted back down into aluminum ingots.

Other Important Metals

Many other important metals are essential to modern technology. Some that have high-tech applications are shown in Table 12.6. The United States has depleted most of its high-grade ores and is now dependent on imports of many essential minerals, as shown in Table 12.6. The metal reserves in other countries are also being depleted.

How can we ever run short of a metal? Aren't atoms conserved? Yes, there is as much iron on Earth as there was 100 years ago, but in using it, we scatter the metal throughout the environment. This is why sustainable practices, such as recycling, are important, beyond energy savings.

Table 12.6 Technologically Important Metals

Metal	Source(s)	Typical Use(s)	Annual World Production (t)
Indium	China, Canada	Transparent, conducting coatings on LCD displays and photovoltaic cells	625
Lithium	Chile, Argentina	Batteries for tools, laptops, digital cameras, and cell phones	30,200
Palladium	Russia	Catalytic converters, energy-storing capacitors in electronic devices	225
Platinum	South Africa, Russia	Catalytic converters, computer hard drives, glass for LCD displays, fuel cells	220
Rare earths (lanthanides)	China	Electronics, energy-efficient technologies	117,000
Europium		Red phosphor in CRT displays	
Cerium		Commercial catalysts, glass polishing, self-cleaning ovens	
Neodymium		Ingredient in super magnets and lasers	
Yttrium	China	Fluorescent light bulbs, ceramics, lasers	500
Tantalum	Democratic Republic of the Congo	Electronic capacitors in computers, digital cameras, and cell phones	900

SELF-ASSESSMENT Questions

1. The metal most likely to be found in its native state is
   a. aluminum   **b.** copper   **c.** iron   **d.** sodium

2. When copper is produced from Cu_2S, the by-product is
   a. CuO   **b.** CO_2 **c.** S   **d.** SO_2

3. Bronze is an alloy of Cu and
   a. Fe   **b.** Pb   **c.** Sn   **d.** Zn

4. In steelmaking, carbon acts as
   a. a reducing agent and hardener
   b. an oxidizing agent and a softener
   c. a reducing agent and softener
   d. an oxidizing agent and a hardener

5. Complete the following sentences using the following (a) electrolysis, (b) heat, and (c) carbon. Use each term once:

   An ore of aluminum is reduced by _____.

   An ore of copper is reduced by _____.

   An ore of iron is reduced by _____.

6. Bauxite is impure
   a. Al_2O_3 **b.** Cu_2S **c.** Fe_2O_3 **d.** gold

7. In which of the following reactions does the oxidation number of aluminum change?
   a. $2\ Al(OH)_3 \longrightarrow Al_2O_3 + 3\ H_2O$
   b. $Al_2O_3 + 2\ NaOH + 3\ H_2O \longrightarrow 2\ NaAl(OH)_4$
   c. $NaAl(OH)_4 \longrightarrow Al(OH)_3 + NaOH$
   d. none

8. How much more energy does it take to make a new aluminum can than to recycle one?
   a. 2 times   **b.** 10 times   **c.** 20 times   **d.** 50 times

9. The _____ the tin content of bronze the _____ it is.
   a. lower, harder   **b.** higher, harder
   c. higher, softer   **d.** none of the above

12.4 Earth's Dwindling Resources

Learning Objectives ❯ List the main components of solid waste. ❯ Name and describe the three Rs of garbage.

For decades, international politics has created threats of shortages and high prices for various commodities, including metals and minerals. The United States has exhausted its high-grade ores of metals such as copper and iron. Miners once found nuggets of pure gold and silver, but the "glory holes" of western North America are long gone. Now we mine ores with a fraction of an ounce of gold per ton of ore (see Figure 12.8). There remain very few high-grade deposits of any metal ores that are readily accessible to the industrialized nations.

What's wrong with low-grade ores? Because more material must be mined to obtain the same final amount of metal, there is more environmental disruption (see Figure 12.8), and more energy is required to concentrate the ores. Both environmental cleanup and energy cost money. Consider an analogy. A bag of popcorn is useful. You can pop it and eat it. The same popcorn, scattered all over your room, would be less useful. Of course, you could gather it all up and then pop it, but that would take a lot of energy—perhaps more energy than you would care to expend and perhaps more energy than you would get from eating the corn after popping it.

▲ When the Europeans first came to North America, native copper (shown here) was readily available and was used by Native Americans. In the United States today, ore with less than 0.5% copper is mined.

▶ **Figure 12.8** Miners must move 30 tons of rock to recover 1 oz of gold for a necklace. The crushed rock is leached with cyanide solution to dissolve the gold. The waste cyanide solution is stored in large containment ponds like the one shown here, which is part of a gold mining operation in Khakassia region, Russia.

Land Pollution: Solid Wastes

Productivity and creativity have enabled people in industrialized nations to possess a seemingly endless variety of consumer goods in enormous quantities. These goods are often packaged in paper or plastic. Their wrappers litter the environment and fill our disposal sites. As the goods break, wear out, or merely become obsolete, they add to our disposal problem. The approximate composition of municipal solid wastes (MSWs)—commonly known as trash or garbage—in the United States is given in Figure 12.9. According to the U.S. Environmental Protection Agency (EPA), in 2010 in the United States, 33.8% of MSWs was recovered and recycled or composted, 11.9% was burned at combustion facilities, while 54.3% was disposed of in *sanitary landfills*.

Sanitary landfills have issues with leakage that leads to groundwater contamination and slow decomposition. Newspapers are still readable after being entombed for 20 years. Without water and oxygen, microorganisms are unable to carry out the normal decay processes.

Disposal of solid wastes by *incineration*, when carried out in properly designed incinerators, produces minimal air pollution. However, many incinerators are old or poorly designed and generate much smoke and odor. Building new incinerators tends to be unpopular with local citizens. Nevertheless, some cities burn their combustible solid wastes and also use the heat from the incinerators to warm buildings,

▲ Where will we get metals in the future? The sea is one possible source. Nodules rich in manganese cover vast areas of the ocean floor. These nodules also contain copper, nickel, and cobalt. Questions about who owns them and how they can be mined without major environmental disruption remain to be resolved.

generate power, or both. A kilogram of polyethylene produces about 13 kWh of energy, about the same as a kilogram of no. 2 fuel oil.

Research in solid waste disposal has led to new processes involving the conversion of wastes into gaseous or liquid fuels. Currently, these processes are too expensive to have much of an impact on MSW disposal.

The Three Rs of Garbage: Reduce, Reuse, Recycle

Not all ways of dealing with our garbage are equally desirable. The best approach to the solid waste problem is to *reduce* the amount of throwaway materials produced. This saves resources and energy, and minimizes the disposal problem.

The next best approach is the *reuse* of materials. When possible, items should be made durable enough to withstand repeated use, rather than designed for a single use and disposal. Consider the grocery bag. At stores, we are often asked, "Paper or plastic?" Most studies show that the environmental impact of a plastic bag is somewhat less than that of a paper bag. Nonetheless, paper should be a better choice for several reasons.

- Plastic bags can be recycled, but only about 7% are. Most of the 500 billion to 1 trillion bags used worldwide each year end up in landfills. Many of the rest become litter, hanging from fences and trees, clogging storm drains, and harming wildlife, especially sea creatures that mistake floating bags for food.

- Plastic bags are made from petroleum, a nonrenewable resource, consuming large amounts of oil that could be used for fuel or heating. Paper is made from trees, a renewable resource. However, replacing billions of plastic bags with paper would require an enormous number of trees.

- Paper bags are less of a litter problem because they break down relatively quickly in the environment. Plastic bags last for years; the bags buried in landfills may be there for centuries.

So, which should we use, paper or plastic? Neither! The better answer is reusable shopping bags made of cloth that are not discarded after a single use. All factors must be examined when determining the best solution to a solid waste problem.

The third way to reduce the volume of wastes is to *recycle* them. Recycling requires energy and inevitably results in some loss of material, but it saves materials. Metals such as iron and steel, aluminum, copper, and lead are largely recycled. About 66% of steel cans, 51% of aluminum cans, 28% of plastic soft drink bottles, and 31% of glass containers are recycled. About 60% of paper and cardboard is recycled. Lawn trimmings and food wastes can be composted, converting them to soil. About 60% of yard trimmings are composted. In the future, as raw materials become scarcer, these proportions are likely to increase.

Recycling also saves energy. Using a ton of scrap to make new iron and steel saves 1.5 tons of iron ore and 0.3 ton of coal. It also results in a 74% savings in energy, an 86% reduction in air pollution, and a 76% reduction in water pollution.

By following the three Rs—reduce, reuse, and recycle—we can protect the environment at the same time as we save materials, energy, and money.

How Crowded Is Our Spaceship?

Each day, people die and others are born, but the number born is about 200,000 more than the number who die. Every five days, the world population goes up by a million people, and it reached 7 billion in 2011.

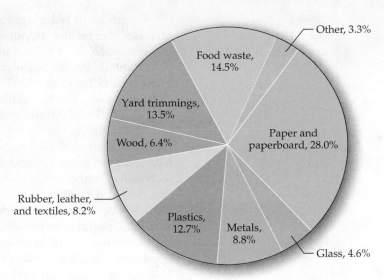

▲ **Figure 12.9** This pie chart shows the percentages of the various materials in municipal solid wastes. Municipal wastes in the United States are largely paper, cardboard, and yard wastes. Paper and cardboard can be recycled. Yard wastes and food wastes can be composted.

Q: *If paper, cardboard, yard wastes, and food wastes were recycled or composted, by about what percentage would municipal solid wastes decrease?*

5. Why do scrap metals bring high prices?

One factor that contributes to the value of scrap metal is the cost of energy needed to extract a metal from its ore. The greater the cost of energy, the more it costs to convert ore to metal. Because scrap metal does not require as much energy to be converted back to useful metal, its value is relatively high.

Figure 12.10 is a graphic picture of population growth. For tens of thousands of years, the human population was never more than a few hundred million. It did not reach the 1 billion mark until about 1800, after which the rate of growth skyrocketed. World population quadrupled during the twentieth century, with growth peaking in the 1960s at about 2.2% a year. The rate of growth in 2011 was 1.09% per year. The Population Division of the United Nations Department of Economic and Social Affairs estimates a world population of 8 billion by 2025 and 9 billion by 2040.

How many people can Spaceship Earth accommodate? Many believe that we have already gone beyond the optimal population for this planet. They predict increasing conflicts over resources and increasing pollution of the environment.

Why did Earth's population start increasing so rapidly after centuries of little change? Population growth depends on both the birth rate and the death rate. If they are equal, population growth is zero. After thousands of years of nearly equal rates, scientific progress in the nineteenth century led to a decline in the death rate in developed countries. Yet the birth rate changed little, and the population grew rapidly. These changes reached the less developed countries in the 1950s, when the death rate fell dramatically but the birth rate remained high—creating a population explosion.

Population growth has slowed considerably in recent years, especially in developed countries. Scientific progress continues to cause a decline in death rates, but birth rates have also declined, especially in Europe and East Asia. The decrease in birth rates in the less developed countries has come more slowly. With more people comes more waste to be processed. We must continue to develop technologies and methods to deal with our ever-increasing wastes.

Population and the food supply are discussed in Chapter 20.

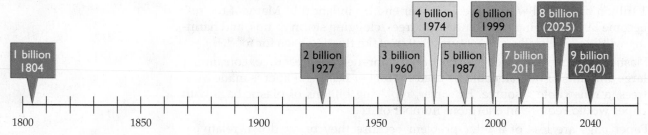

▲ **Figure 12.10** Two thousand years ago, Earth's population was about 300 million—about the same as the population of the United States today. Population changed little over the next thousand years and is estimated to have been only 310 million at the end of the first millennium. It reached 1 billion about 1804. This graph shows the intervals in which an additional billion people were added to Earth's population, with projections to 2040. (*Source:* United Nations, *World Population Prospects: The 2012 Revision.* New York: 2012.)

SELF-ASSESSMENT Questions

1. The three Rs of garbage are
   a. reduce, recycle, and redeploy
   b. reuse, redeploy, and recycle
   c. reuse, reprocess, and recycle
   d. reduce, reuse, and recycle

2. Which kind of material is the largest component of the garbage we put in landfills?
   a. food   b. metals
   c. paper   d. plastic

Answers: 1, d; 2, c

GREEN CHEMISTRY

David Constable

Critical Supply of Key Elements

Learning Objectives ❯ Identify a few elements critical to products used every day by modern society that are not abundant that have to be replaced by earth-abundant materials. ❯ Describe why recycling and reuse of critical elements is not sustainable.

You may not have thought about it this way, but chemists are a lot like people who started out thinking about how to build shelters. Early builders started with what was readily available – sticks, stones, logs, mud, clay – whatever they could use. People who were interested in chemistry began in a similar way. They looked around and started to think about how they could use those same kinds of materials to make different things. They wondered about what the stuff around them, like rocks, was made of and whether or not they could make something of greater value from these materials. Sometimes, they boiled things or put them in water to see what would happen. At one point, they happily discovered that the juice from berries or grapes would sometimes ferment, and when they drank it, it changed the way they felt. From all the things around them – rocks, plants, blood, feathers – they started to experiment.

Fast forward thousands of years, and people are still taking what is at hand and making stuff. Of course, the materials that are made today are a lot more sophisticated than a hundred years ago, but people haven't changed all that much. The holes in the ground have gotten bigger and deeper, the fires are hotter or more efficient, and thankfully, we know how to ferment all kinds of things to get food and chemicals. But we still rely on what we can find on the land, or in the oceans, or in the air. And if you stop for a moment and look around you, you might realize that taking all that stuff and making things can't go on forever in the same way we do it now.

Modern society is heavily dependent on chemicals, and we are rapidly depleting known reserves of many key elements that are used to make the large number and variety of chemicals we use for everyday products. For many elements that are of critical importance to making chemicals and products, we are taking a large amount of mass (think mountains of rock, for example), concentrating the desired elements, and dispersing them into products in forms that are difficult to recover and reuse. As we use up more and more of these materials, it will be harder

and harder to extract the desired elements. At some point, we'll have to figure out how to obtain them from the ocean or from lower-grade ores, which will come at increasing human and environmental costs.

Let's go through a few examples where critical elements are used. There are several in catalytic converters used on automobiles, including platinum, rhodium, and palladium. While a large portion of these valuable elements is recycled when a car is scrapped, some of these metals are lost through the exhaust pipes of automobiles. As long as we drive cars that use gasoline and employ these metals in catalytic converters to ensure better air quality, the growing number of automobiles means that more metals are lost to the environment. We will have to develop catalytic converters that rely on earth-abundant elements like iron or nickel, or we will have to figure out another way to transport ourselves and our products that does not rely on an internal combustion or diesel engine.

Another example is indium. Why should you care about indium, you ask? Surely, you have a cell phone, or perhaps a tablet, laptop, or some other electronic device that has a visual display. Or perhaps you've driven by a field of solar panels. All of these contain indium. Now multiply your devices by a few billion and add yearly replacements on the order of 500 million. Even if only a small amount of indium is in these devices, it adds up to metric tons of indium per year. We currently don't recycle indium, and doing so would be a major challenge. Eventually, getting indium is going to be harder than it is already. So what do we do?

This is where green chemistry comes in. In the case of visual displays, we can move toward the use of things like organic light-emitting diodes to replace the current displays. That is what the world needs to start thinking about. How can we move from the chemicals we currently use to new kinds of chemicals that don't have all the problems we have now? It's possible, but we need to get moving on this sooner rather than later.

SUMMARY

Section 12.1—Earth is divided into the core, the mantle, and the crust. The core is thought to be mainly iron. The crust consists of the solid lithosphere, the liquid (water) hydrosphere, and the gaseous atmosphere. Nine elements make up 96% of the atoms in the crust. The lithosphere is made up largely of rocks and minerals, including silicates, carbonates, oxides, and sulfides. The lithosphere is composed of an inorganic component as well as organic and biological components.

Section 12.2—Silicates contain SiO_4 tetrahedra in various arrangements. **Quartz** is a crystalline silicate that consists of a three-dimensional network of these tetrahedra. Sand is mainly quartz. The **micas** consist of sheets of SiO_4 tetrahedra. **Asbestos** is a fibrous silicate mineral made of chains of SiO_4 tetrahedra. Asbestos exposure has a **synergistic effect** with smoking; that is, the two together produce a higher risk of lung cancer than their simple combination indicates. Clays are aluminum silicates made up of tetrahedral silica and octahedral aluminum sheets. They come in two types: the 1:1 and 2:1 clays, with the 2:1 type being potentially water expandable. Ceramics, glass, and cement are modified silicates. **Glass** is a noncrystalline solid having no fixed melting point. Most glass is made from sand, with additives to impart desired properties such as heat resistance, color, and light sensitivity. Glass does not degrade in the environment, but it is easy to recycle. **Ceramics** are made by heating clay and other minerals to fuse them. **Cement** is a complex mixture of calcium and aluminum silicates made from limestone and clay. Producing the energy needed in the cement-baking step has a negative environmental impact.

Section 12.3—Copper was one of the first metals to be obtained from its ore (chalcopyrite or chalcocite), but it is too soft to be used for tools. **Bronze** is an **alloy**—a mixture of a metal and one or more other elements. Bronze contains copper and tin. The more tin bronze contains, the harder it is. Bronze is harder than copper, and tools made of it were used for thousands of years. Iron-making technology was developed much later. Iron is produced in a furnace from iron ore (hematite) and carbon (coke). **Steel** is an alloy of iron and carbon, and is the form in which iron is normally used. The higher the carbon content, the harder the steel is. Aluminum is less dense than steel and does not rust. Aluminum is isolated from its ore, bauxite, by a reduction process that uses electricity. Both the energy required and the waste produced in metal extraction have a heavy environmental impact. Recycling reduces this impact.

Section 12.4—We face potential shortages of many metals and minerals because most of the high-grade ores have been used up. The United States now imports some metals and ores that it used to mine. It takes much less energy to recycle most metals than it does to produce them from ores.

The United States produces large amounts of waste, most of which is paper, cardboard, and yard waste. Municipal solid waste now is either buried in sanitary landfills, burned, or otherwise processed. Some wastes can be converted to fuels. The three Rs of garbage are as follows: *Reduce* the amount of throwaway materials produced; *reuse* items when possible; *recycle* as many materials as possible. Steel, aluminum, plastic, and paper are easily recycled, and yard waste can be composted.

Although birth rates have declined somewhat, Earth is crowded and is going to become more so in years to come. We must develop technologies and methods to deal with ever-increasing wastes.

GREEN CHEMISTRY—Green chemistry helps us to think about ways we might make the things we need without using rare elements. It helps us to think about recycling, new kinds of materials, or using more materials from waste and turning them into useful products.

Learning Objectives

❯ Describe the structure of Earth and the regions of Earth's surface.	Problems 13, 18, 22
❯ List the most abundant elements in Earth's crust.	Problems 18–22
❯ Describe the arrangement of silicate tetrahedra in common silicate minerals.	Problems 26–34
❯ Describe how glass differs in structure from other silicates.	Problems 35–38
❯ List the most important metals with their principal ores, and explain how they are extracted.	Problems 6, 9, 44, 47, 48, 53
❯ Describe some of the environmental costs associated with metal production.	Problems 10, 52, 54, 63
❯ List the main components of solid waste.	Problems 67, 68
❯ Name and describe the three Rs of garbage.	Problem 11, 69
❯ Identify a few elements critical to products used every day by modern society that are not abundant that have to be replaced by earth-abundant materials.	Problems 71–72
❯ Describe why recycling and reuse of critical elements is not sustainable.	Problems 73–75

REVIEW QUESTIONS

1. What is a synergistic effect? Give an example.
2. What are two main classes of clay?
3. Why is montmorillonite added to cat litter?
4. How can you make red glass?
5. What environmental problems are associated with the manufacture of cement?
6. Why was copper one of the first metals used?
7. Why did the Bronze Age precede the Iron Age in most places?
8. What is steel? How does it differ from pure iron in composition and in properties?

9. Aluminum is the most abundant metal in Earth's crust, yet aluminum ores are not very plentiful. Explain.
10. What are the environmental costs and benefits of aluminum?
11. List three methods of solid waste disposal. Give the advantages and disadvantages of each.
12. If matter is conserved, how can we ever run out of a metal?
13. Explain why metals can be recycled fairly easily. What factors limit the recycling of metals?

PROBLEMS

Composition of Earth

14. Which statement about Earth's structure is incorrect?
    a. The crust is between 8 and 40 km thick.
    b. The mantle is composed mainly of silica.
    c. The inner core is liquid.
    d. The outer core is liquid.
15. The Earth's surface consists of:
    a. the atmosphere   b. the hydrosphere
    c. the lithosphere   d. all of the above
16. Define *lithosphere*, *hydrosphere*, and *atmosphere*.
17. Name the three equally important components that the lithosphere is composed of.
18. Name four kinds of minerals found in Earth's crust, and give an example of each.
19. Rank the following elements in terms of their abundance on the Earth's surface by atom percent: calcium, hydrogen, silicon, magnesium, potassium, iron, and sodium.
20. Rank the following elements in terms of their abundance on the Earth's surface by percentage by mass: calcium, hydrogen, silicon, magnesium, potassium, iron, and sodium.
21. Why are the rankings in Problems 19 and 20 different?
22. What materials make up the organic portion of the lithosphere?
23. What is the oxidation number of iron (Fe) in hematite and magnetite? (*Hint:* Refer to Table 12.2.)
24. Referring to Table 12.2, write a balanced equation for the dissolving of galena in hydrochloric acid. The products are hydrogen sulfide gas and lead(II) chloride.
25. How did the discovery of how to control fire change the types of materials humans could use?

Silicate Minerals

26. What is the chemical composition of quartz? How are the basic structural units of quartz arranged?
27. In silica, four O atoms surround each Si atom, yet the formula for silica is SiO_2. Explain how this can be.

28. How are the SiO_4 tetrahedra connected? How does this compare to how carbon atoms are connected in diamond?
29. Draw the Lewis dot formula for SiO_4^{4-}, and then draw the Lewis dot formulas for two connected SiO_4 tetrahedra. (Hint: Look at it as $O_3Si-O-SiO_3^{6-}$.)
30. Using the answers to Problems 28 and 29 discuss how chains and sheets of SiO_4 in wollastonite and muscovite, respectively, are formed. (Hint: Refer to Figure 12.3.)
31. Why does mica occur in sheets? How are the basic structural units of mica arranged?
32. Why does asbestos occur as fibers? How are the basic structural units of chrysotile asbestos arranged?
33. In clays, silica is found only in the:
    a. tetrahedral sheet
    b. octahedral sheet
    c. in both tetrahedral and octahedral sheets
    d. in sheets other than tetrahedral or octahedral
34. Which of the following clays would be expandable, and how?
    a. a 1:1 clay
    b. a 2:1 clay with no water between 2:1 layers
    c. a 2:1 clay with water between 2:1 layers
    d. there are no expandable clays

Modified Silicates

35. Which of the following elements is the most abundant in a typical glass window, by atom percent? Does this change when the percentage by mass is used?
    a. Si   b. O   c. Ca   d. Na
36. How does heating destroy long-range order in crystalline materials?
37. Focusing on the bonds, explain how glass becomes softer when heated.
38. Compare an amorphous substance to a crystalline substance.

39. How is the basic recipe for glass modified to make glasses with special properties?

40. What are most modern advanced ceramic materials made of?

41. How is the manufacturing of ceramics similar to that of glass?

42. What are the two basic raw materials required for making cement?

43. What is the difference between cement and concrete?

Metals and Ores

44. What are the main ores from which aluminum, copper, and iron are extracted?

45. For each of the following chemical reactions, discuss the change in oxidation number of the metal atom:
    a. $2\,Cu_2O \longrightarrow 4\,Cu + O_2$
    b. $Fe_2O_3 + 3\,CO \longrightarrow 2\,Fe + 3\,CO_2$
    c. $2\,Al_2O_3 \longrightarrow 4\,Al + 3\,O_2$

46. How many electrons are involved in each of the reactions in Problem 45?

47. By what kind of chemical process (see Chapter 8) is a metal obtained from its ore? Give an example.

48. By what chemical process does a metal corrode? Give an example.

49. a. What is the advantage of adding tin to copper?
    b. What alloy is formed?
    c. Which copper tin alloy is harder, one with 6% or 10% of tin content?

50. Explain why carbon is used in the production of steel and what happens to carbon when very hot steel (between 750 and 1500 °C) is quickly quenched.

51. What modern-day uses do copper and iron have?

52. What is "red mud," where does it come from, and what is its environmental impact?

53. Of Al, Cu, and Fe, which metal requires the most energy to extract and purify, and why?

54. Compare the energy cost of production of new aluminum from bauxite extraction to that from recycled aluminum.

55. Discuss at least two chemical reasons as to why a katana is such a quality weapon.

Oxidation and Reduction

For Problems 56–59, first write (if it is not given) or complete and balance the equation for the reaction. Next, answer the following. **(a)** *What substance is reduced?* **(b)** *What is the reducing agent?* **(c)** *What substance is oxidized?* **(d)** *What is the oxidizing agent? (These questions require some knowledge of material in Chapter 8.)*

56. Vanadium metal can be prepared by reacting vanadium(V) oxide with calcium; the other product is calcium oxide.

57. Erbium metal (Er) can be prepared by reacting erbium(III) fluoride with magnesium; the other product is magnesium fluoride.

58. The Toth Aluminum Company produces aluminum from kaolin (rocks that are rich in kaolinite). One step converts aluminum oxide to aluminum chloride by the following reaction.

$$? + C + Cl_2 \longrightarrow AlCl_3 + CO$$

59. Europium (Eu) was used in older television screens to give a red color. The metal can be prepared by electrolysis of molten europium(III) chloride; chlorine gas is a by-product.

Mass Relationships

Problems 60 and 61 require some knowledge of material in Chapter 5.

60. Neodymium metal, a vital component of the magnets used in gasoline–electric hybrid automobiles, is prepared by reduction of neodymium(III) fluoride with calcium metal.

$$2\,NdF_3 + 3\,Ca \longrightarrow 2\,Nd + 3\,CaF_2$$

What mass of neodymium is obtained from 143 g of NdF_3?

61. Indium is a vital component of the electrically conducting transparent coatings on LCD screens. Indium metal can be prepared by electrolysis of salts such as indium(III) chloride. What mass in grams of indium(III) chloride is required to produce 33.2 g of indium?

$$2\,InCl_3 \longrightarrow 2\,In + 3\,Cl_2$$

ADDITIONAL PROBLEMS

62. An aluminum plant produces 72 million kg of aluminum per year. How much aluminum oxide is required? How much bauxite is required? (It takes 2.1 kg of crude bauxite to produce 1.0 kg of aluminum oxide.)

63. It takes 17 kWh of electricity to produce 1.0 kg of aluminum. How much electricity does the plant in Problem 62 use for aluminum production in 1 year?

64. The amount of trash produced per person per day in the United States is about 4.5 lb. If the trash has an average density of 85 lb/ft³, how many cubic feet of trash are produced each year by a small town of 14,000 people? If a sanitary landfill is constructed that is 100 ft wide by 100 ft long, how deep must it be to contain this trash?

65. The equation for the reaction by which a sodium cyanide solution dissolves gold from its ore is

$$4\,Au + 8\,NaCN + 2\,H_2O + O_2 \longrightarrow$$
$$4\,NaAu(CN)_2 + 4\,NaOH$$

What is the minimum mass of NaCN required to dissolve the 10 g of Au in a ton of gold ore?

66. Why is coal heated in the absence of air to make coke? What would happen if the coal were heated in air? Write the equation.

67. Based on Figure 12.9, about what percentage of municipal waste might be burned as fuel?

68. Look again at Figure 12.9. If everyone recycled all paper and cardboard, composted yard waste and food scraps, and recycled all plastics and metals, how would the answer to Problem 64 change?

69. What do the three Rs of garbage stand for?

70. One pound of plastic bags is about 67 bags. **(a)** What is the mass in kilograms of 500 billion bags? An Australian study concluded that 8.7 plastic bags equal the fuel consumed by driving a car 1 km. How many kilometers could a car travel on the fuel equivalent of **(b)** 1 lb of bags and **(c)** 500 billion bags?

71. Find out what minerals contain indium and where these are mined.
    a. What is the process used to get pure indium?
    b. What are some of the environmental problems from mining indium?

72. Describe the process of obtaining platinum.
    a. Chemists like to use platinum in chemical processes. Describe one form of platinum they use.
    b. Why do chemists like to use platinum and what might some alternatives be?

73. Explain why platinum, palladium, and rhodium might be easier to recycle than indium.

74. What makes recycling an element like indium so difficult?

75. Give an example of a different approach to electiric lighting that wouldn't use a rare element like indium.

CRITICAL THINKING EXERCISES

Apply knowledge that you have gained in this chapter and one or more of the FLaReS principles (Chapter 1) to evaluate the following statements or claims.

12.1. An economist has said that we need not worry about running out of copper because it can be made from other metals.

12.2. A citizen testifies against establishing a landfill near his home, claiming that the landfill will leak substances into the groundwater and contaminate his well water.

12.3. A citizen lobbies against establishing an incinerator near her home, claiming that plastics burned in the incinerator will release hydrogen chloride into the air.

12.4. An environmental activist claims that we could recycle all goods, leaving no need for the use of raw materials to make new ones.

12.5. A katana sword is available for sale on the Internet. The seller advertises this sword as superior by being made only from martensite steel.

12.6. A salesperson tells you that ceramics is just a fancy word for glass.

COLLABORATIVE GROUP PROJECTS

Prepare a PowerPoint, poster, or other presentation (as directed by your instructor) to share with the class.

1. Prepare a brief report on one of the metals listed in Table 12.6. List the main ores, and describe how the metal is obtained from one of those ores. Describe some of the uses of the metal, and explain how its properties make it suitable for those uses.

2. Prepare a brief report on recycling one of the following types of municipal solid waste. List the advantages of recycling, and identify problems involved in the process.
    a. glass
    b. plastics
    c. yard waste
    d. paper
    e. lead
    f. aluminum

3. Compare disposal in landfills, incineration, and recycling as methods of dealing with each of the types of municipal solid waste listed in Figure 12.9. List advantages and disadvantages of each method for each type of waste.

4. Search the Internet for material on recent mine waste disasters or long-term mine waste problems. Prepare a brief report on one of the events or situations.

5. Discuss the environmental effects **(a)** of use of cleaning cloths, mop heads, and sponges that can be cleaned and reused versus use of similar disposable products and **(b)** of use of cloth diapers that need to be washed versus use of disposable diapers.

6. Search the Internet to find the current estimated population of the United States and of the world. What is the current rate of population growth, as a percentage per year, in **(a)** France, **(b)** Bolivia, **(c)** Uganda, **(d)** United States, and **(e)** the world?

CHEMISTRY@HOME   Fizzy Flintstones, Crumbling Calcium Carbonate

Materials required

- Vinegar
- Lemon juice
- Water
- Clear plastic cups
- Dropper
- Several different rock types (limestone, chalk, quartz, granite, or others)

Why do stone statues dissolve over time? Which rock types are sensitive to acids?

Limestone statues are common in our society. Many are found in parks, such as those in the Gettysburg National Battlefield and in parks in New York City.

Unfortunately, these statues are suffering damage due to acid rain. What is happening is that the limestone ($CaCO_3$) is water insoluble (normally, limestone won't dissolve), but it will dissolve if it is in an acidic environment. Acids in rain such as sulfuric acid (H_2SO_4) contribute to the dissolving of the limestone. Sulfuric acid will dissolve the calcium carbonate to make a moderately soluble form of calcium, $CaSO_4$ (called gypsum), along with carbon dioxide and water. The equation is listed below.

$$CaCO_3 + H_2SO_4 \longrightarrow CaSO_4 + CO_2 + H_2O$$

In this experiment, you will collect at least 3 rocks of 3 different types. Limestone, chalk, and granite are available outdoors in some regions, or at your hardware store in others areas. You will use lemon juice and vinegar to test the presence of carbonate in rocks.

Prepare 3 sets of clear plastic cups, three cups for each of the rock types. Label appropriately.

- Put 5–10 drops of lemon juice on one piece of each of the 3 rock types. What happens when you put lemon juice on each rock?
- Put 5–10 drops of vinegar on the other piece of each of the 3 rock types. What happens when you put vinegar on each rock?
- Put 5–10 drops of water on the third piece of each of the 3 rock types. What happens when you put water on each rock?

Look and listen carefully each time you add the lemon juice, vinegar, and water to the rocks.

Questions

1. Did the lemon juice and vinegar act the same way on each rock?
2. Why did some of the rocks react differently?
3. What does this experiment have to do with weathering?
4. Write the chemical equation for acetic acid ($C_2H_4O_2$) and limestone ($CaCO_3$).

AIR

Have You Ever Wondered?

1. Is air less polluted today than it was in the past?

2. Is it practical to collect automobile emissions and convert them back to gasoline?

3. How do greenhouse gases keep the Earth warm?

4. Is global warming caused by the ozone hole?

5. What does smog testing of vehicles actually test?

Learning Objectives

> List and describe the layers of the atmosphere. (13.1)

> Give the proportions of N_2, O_2, Ar, and CO_2 in Earth's atmosphere. (13.1)

> Describe the nitrogen and oxygen cycles. (13.2)

> Describe the origin and effects of temperature inversions. (13.2)

> List some natural sources of air pollution. (13.3)

> List the main pollutants formed by burning coal, and describe some technologies used to clean up these pollutants. (13.3)

> List the main gases in automobile emissions, and describe how catalytic converters reduce these gaseous pollutants. (13.4)

> Explain how carbon monoxide acts as a poison. (13.4)

> Distinguish the origin of photochemical smog from the origin of sulfurous smog. (13.5)

> Describe the technologies used to alleviate photochemical smog. (13.5)

> Name the air pollutants that contribute to acid rain. (13.6)

> List the major industrial and consumer sources of acid-rain-producing pollutants. (13.6)

> List the main indoor air pollutants and their sources. (13.7)

> Explain where radon comes from and why it is hazardous. (13.7)

> Explain the link between CFCs and depletion of the ozone layer. (13.8)

> Describe the consequences of stratospheric ozone depletion. (13.8)

> List the important greenhouse gases, and describe the mechanism and significance of the greenhouse effect. (13.9)

> Describe some strategies for reducing the amount of CO_2 released into the atmosphere. (13.9)

THE BREATH OF LIFE We could live about 4 weeks without food. We could live for 4 days without water. But without air we cannot live even 4 minutes. Most of us cannot hold our breath for very long, even if we had to do so in an emergency. The photograph gives an idea of the atmosphere that is above us all. Although the atmosphere has no definitive boundary, 99% of its gas is less than 30 km from the surface of Earth. Compared to Earth's diameter, the atmosphere is thinner than the skin of an apple is to the rest of the fruit.

Sally Ride, the first American woman in space, said the following after her experience: "I saw the blackness of space, and then the bright blue Earth. And then it looked as if someone had taken a royal blue crayon and traced along Earth's horizon. And then I realized that blue line, that really thin royal blue line, was Earth's atmosphere, and that was all there was of it. And it's so clear from that perspective how fragile our existence is."

The concept of living today in such a way that does not compromise the lives of future generations is one way of viewing sustainability. How humans interact with our atmosphere is clearly a determining factor in the sustainability of the Earth. If large parts of our planet do not have air that is healthy to breathe, or if the condition of the overall atmosphere causes too much of the sun's energy to be retained with negative consequences, we have not fulfilled our obligation to those who come after us. As you read about the topics related to air in this chapter, keep in mind the concept of sustainability as a measuring tool that can indicate the need for action.

A community may run short of food or fresh water, but we cannot run out of air given the size of Earth's atmosphere. On the other hand, we *can* pollute the air so badly that it becomes unpleasant or even unhealthy to breathe. In some areas, the air is already of such poor quality that people become sick from breathing it, even to the point of dying in some cases. The World Health Organization (WHO) estimates that in 2012 a total of 7 million people died as a result of air pollution. This corresponds to one of eight deaths worldwide. Most of these deaths occur in developing countries.

This chapter first discusses the natural chemistry of the atmosphere and then presents some of the effects human intervention is having on the natural balance in the components of our air. Some possible ways to reduce these negative effects are also considered.

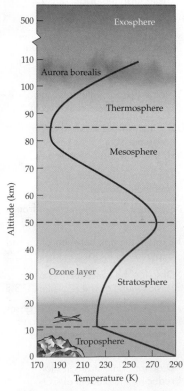

▲ **Figure 13.1** Approximate altitudes and temperature variations of the layers of the atmosphere.

13.1 Earth's Atmosphere: Divisions and Composition

Learning Objectives ❯ List and describe the layers of the atmosphere. ❯ Give the approximate proportions of N_2, O_2, Ar, and CO_2 in Earth's atmosphere.

We passengers on Spaceship Earth live under a thin blanket of air called the **atmosphere**. We divide the atmosphere into four main layers based on the properties of the gases in those regions (Figure 13.1). The temperature in each layer varies with altitude. The layer nearest Earth, called the *troposphere* contains nearly all living things and nearly all human activity. Although other planets in our solar system have atmospheres, Earth's atmosphere is unique in its ability to support higher forms of life, such as us humans. Many people suppose that atmospheric temperature decreases as the altitude increases, but this is mainly true only for the troposphere and *mesosphere.* In the *stratosphere* and *thermosphere,* the temperature increases as you go higher.

The composition of dry air is summarized in Table 13.1. The amount of water in the air varies markedly from almost none up to about 4%. The atmosphere has a number of minor constituents, the most important of which is CO_2. The concentration of carbon dioxide in the atmosphere increased from about 280 parts per million (ppm) in the preindustrial world to 402 ppm in 2014, and it continues to rise at 2–3 ppm each year.

Table 13.1	Approximate Composition of Clean Dry Air near Sea Level	
Component	Percent by Volume
Nitrogen (N_2)	78.08
Oxygen (O_2)	20.94
Argon (Ar)	0.93
Carbon dioxide (CO_2)	0.04
Trace gases[a]	<0.01

[a]Neon (Ne), helium (He), methane (CH_4), krypton (Kr), hydrogen (H_2), dinitrogen monoxide (N_2O), xenon (Xe), ozone (O_3), sulfur dioxide (SO_2), nitrogen dioxide (NO_2), ammonia (NH_3), carbon monoxide (CO), and iodine (I_2), plus some others.

SELF-ASSESSMENT Questions

1. Nearly all human activity occurs in the
   a. mesosphere   b. stratosphere   c. thermosphere   d. troposphere

2. The ozone layer is found in the
   a. mesosphere   b. stratosphere   c. thermosphere   d. troposphere

3. Earth's atmosphere
   a. blends into outer space   b. ends abruptly at 30 km altitude
   c. ends abruptly at 50 km altitude   d. ends abruptly at the moon

4. The approximate percentage of nitrogen in the atmosphere is
   a. 18%   b. 28%   c. 48%   d. 78%

5. After nitrogen and oxygen and ignoring water vapor concentration, the most abundant gas in the Earth's atmosphere is
   a. argon   b. carbon dioxide   c. hydrogen   d. methane

6. The present carbon dioxide concentration in the Earth's atmosphere is about
   a. 280 ppm   b. 400 ppm   c. 1%   d. 4%

7. The stratosphere occurs in what range of altitude?
   a. 0–11 km   b. 11–20 km   c. 11–50 km   d. 50–85 km

Answers: 1, d; 2, b; 3, a; 4, d; 5, a; 6, b; 7, c

It DOES Matter!

Although the increase in atmospheric CO_2 over the last two centuries—from 0.028% to 0.040%—appears to be small in absolute terms, that increase of almost a factor of 1.5 represents a significant change with major consequences. This change has been for the entire volume of the atmosphere above every part of the Earth, which should give us pause to consider the impact of humans on this grand scale. Most of the increased CO_2 comes from carbon that was stored in fossil fuels for tens of millions of years but has recently been burned in air. About 30 billion tons of CO_2 are emitted into our atmosphere each year from this burning.

13.2 Chemistry of the Atmosphere

Learning Objectives   ❯ Describe the nitrogen and oxygen cycles.   ❯ Describe the origin and effects of temperature inversions.

Under ordinary conditions, nitrogen and oxygen gases coexist in the atmosphere as a simple mixture, with little or no reaction between them. Under certain circumstances, however, the two elements can combine in a reaction that has consequences for life itself.

Nitrogen makes up 78% of the atmosphere in the form of diatomic N_2 molecules. The element nitrogen is essential to living things, but most animals and plants cannot incorporate N_2 directly. How then has nitrogen become a component of so many vital compounds, such as the proteins and nucleic acids of living organisms? The answer is that organisms first combine nitrogen with another element, a process called **nitrogen fixation**. This process does not occur readily because the nitrogen atoms in N_2 are held together by a strong triple bond ($N\equiv N$), which must be broken for fixation to take place.

The Nitrogen Cycle

Several natural phenomena convert nitrogen gas to more usable forms. Energy from lightning and from the heat of autos as well as industrial engines fixes nitrogen by causing it to combine with oxygen, forming first nitrogen monoxide (NO), commonly called nitric oxide, and then nitrogen dioxide (NO_2).

$$N_2 + O_2 \xrightarrow{\text{energy}} 2\,NO$$

$$2\,NO + O_2 \longrightarrow 2\,NO_2$$

(These oxides of nitrogen, NO and NO_2, are collectively designated as NO_x.) Nitrogen dioxide reacts with water to form nitric acid (HNO_3) and nitrogen monoxide.

$$3\,NO_2 + H_2O \longrightarrow 2\,HNO_3 + NO$$

Nitric acid in rainwater falls on Earth's surface, adding to the supply of available nitrates in the oceans and the soil.

Nitrogen is fixed industrially by combining nitrogen with hydrogen to form ammonia, a procedure called the *Haber–Bosch process* (described in Chapter 20), which is facilitated with a catalyst.

$$N_2 + 3\,H_2 \longrightarrow 2\,NH_3$$

This technology has greatly increased our food supply because the availability of fixed nitrogen is often the limiting factor in the production of food. Not all consequences of this intervention have been favorable, however. Excessive runoff of nitrogen fertilizer has led to serious water pollution problems in some areas (which we discuss in Chapter 14).

In an amount comparable to the production from the Haber–Bosch process, nitrogen fixation is performed by bacteria in the roots of legumes (peas, beans, clover, and the like). Certain types of bacteria reduce N_2 to ammonia (NH_3). Other bacteria oxidize ammonia to nitrites (NO_2^-), and still others oxidize nitrites to nitrates (NO_3^-). Plants are then able to take up the nitrates and ammonia from the soil. Animals in turn can get their required nitrogen compounds from eating plants, both directly and by eating animals that consume plants. The **nitrogen cycle** (Figure 13.2) is completed by the action of other types of microbes, which can use nitrate ions as their oxygen source for the decomposition of organic matter and release N_2 gas back to the atmosphere in a process called denitrification.

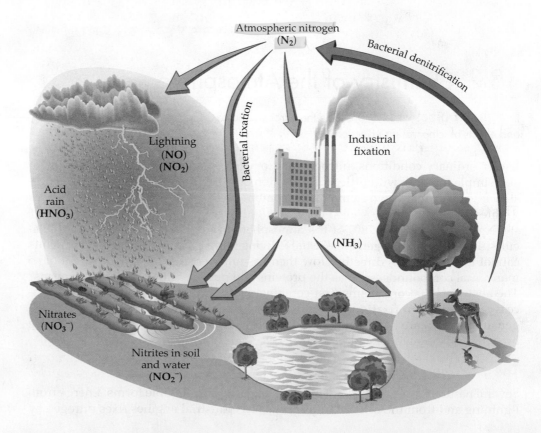

▶ **Figure 13.2** The nitrogen cycle. Atmospheric nitrogen is *fixed*, or converted to water-soluble forms, both naturally and industrially. Animal wastes and dead plants and animals are converted back to atmospheric nitrogen by certain bacteria.

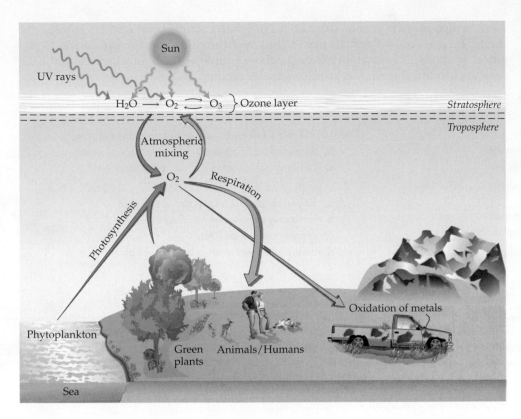

◀ **Figure 13.3** The oxygen cycle. Animals and people use oxygen gas and produce carbon dioxide. Plants, in turn, consume the carbon dioxide, converting it to oxygen gas and glucose for food. In the stratosphere, atmospheric oxygen is involved in ozone production.

The Oxygen Cycle

Oxygen makes up 21% of Earth's atmosphere. As with nitrogen, a balance is maintained between consumption and production of oxygen in the troposphere. Both plants and animals use oxygen in the metabolism of the food that they eat. The decay and combustion of plant and animal materials consume oxygen and produce carbon dioxide, as does the burning of fossil fuels such as coal, oil, and natural gas. The rusting of metals and the weathering of rocks also consume oxygen. A simplified **oxygen cycle**, illustrated in Figure 13.3, shows the influence of green plants, including one-celled organisms (phytoplankton) in the sea, which consume carbon dioxide in photosynthesis and, in the process, replenish the oxygen supply.

$$6 CO_2 + 6 H_2O \longrightarrow C_6H_{12}O_6 + 6 O_2$$

Another vital balancing act occurs in the stratosphere far above the Earth's surface. There, oxygen is formed by the action of ultraviolet (UV) radiation on water molecules. Perhaps more important, some oxygen is converted to ozone (Section 13.8).

$$3 O_2(g) + energy (UV radiation) \longrightarrow 2 O_3(g)$$

This ozone absorbs high-energy UV radiation that if it reached the surface might otherwise make higher forms of life on Earth impossible. We discuss the atmosphere in more detail in subsequent sections, paying particular attention to changes wrought by human activities.

Temperature Inversions

Normally, air is warmest near the ground due to the heat released by land and gets cooler at moderate altitudes. On clear nights, the ground cools rapidly, but the wind usually mixes the cooler air near the ground with the warmer air above it. If the air is still, and the lower layer of cold air becomes trapped by the layer of warm air above it, a meteorological condition known as a **temperature inversion** (or *thermal inversion*) happens. Pollutants in the cooler air are trapped near the ground, and the air can become quite seriously polluted in a short period of time (Figure 13.4).

▲ **Figure 13.4** Ordinarily, the air is colder at increasing altitudes (a). During a temperature (thermal) inversion (b), a cooler layer is trapped near the surface, remains beneath a warmer layer, and can readily be polluted.

A temperature inversion can also occur when a warm front collides with a cold front. The less dense warm air mass slides over the cold air mass, producing a condition of atmospheric stability. Because there is little vertical air movement, the air near the ground stagnates and air pollutants accumulate.

SELF-ASSESSMENT Questions

1. Lightning can convert atmospheric N_2 to
   a. nitroglycerin
   b. ammonia
   c. nitrogen oxides
   d. bacteria

2. Conversion of atmospheric N_2 to biologically useful forms is called nitrogen
   a. addition
   b. fixation
   c. reduction
   d. dinitrification

3. The starting materials in the industrial process for making ammonia are
   a. N_2 and H_2
   b. N_2 and O_2
   c. NO_3^- and H_2
   d. NO_3^- and O_2

4. Which of the following processes removes carbon dioxide from the atmosphere?
   a. photosynthesis
   b. respiration
   c. temperature inversions
   d. burning of fossil fuels

5. Which of the following processes consumes oxygen?
   a. breakdown of ozone
   b. corrosion of metals
   c. Haber–Bosch process
   d. photosynthesis

6. A temperature inversion is a meteorological condition that
   a. makes people put on thermal underwear
   b. commonly occurs over flat countryside
   c. concentrates air pollutants
   d. occurs when warm air is below cold air

Answers: 1. c; 2. b; 3. a; 4. a; 5. b; 6. c

13.3 Pollution through the Ages

Learning Objectives ❯ List some natural sources of air pollution. ❯ List the main pollutants formed by burning coal, and describe some technologies used to clean up these pollutants.

Air pollution has always been with us. Wildfires, windblown dust, and volcanic eruptions added pollutants to the atmosphere long before humans existed and continue to do so. Volcanoes spew ash and poisonous gases into the atmosphere. The 1995 and subsequent eruptions of the Soufriere Hills volcano on Montserrat covered much of the Caribbean island with ash, destroying the capital city, Plymouth, and forcing the evacuation of two-thirds of the population. Kilauea volcano in Hawaii emits 1000–2000 t of sulfur dioxide per day, producing acid rain downwind that has helped create a barren region called the Kau Desert.

Dust storms, especially in arid regions, add massive amounts of particulate matter to the atmosphere. Dust from the Sahara Desert often reaches the Caribbean and South America. Dust and pollution from China blanket Japan and even reach western North America. Nature isn't always benign.

The Air Our Ancestors Breathed

People have always altered their environment. The discovery of tools and the use of fire forever changed the balance between people and their environment. The problem of air pollution probably first occurred when fires were built in poorly ventilated caves or other dwellings. People cleared land, leading to larger dust storms. They built cities, and the soot from their hearths and the stench from their wastes filled the air. The Roman author Seneca wrote in C.E. 61 of the stink, soot, and "heavy air" of the imperial city. The first laws to regulate the burning of coal in cities in England were enacted in the thirteenth century. The Industrial Revolution brought even more air pollution, as coal was burned in large amounts to power factories. Soot, smoke, and sulfur dioxide filled the air. The good old days? Not in factory towns. But there were large rural areas that were less affected by air pollution.

Air pollution today is much more complex than that affecting our ancestors. When society changes its activities, the nature of its waste materials changes, including the ones it dumps into the atmosphere. The phenomenon is not new, but today's rapid rate of change is unprecedented. Our environment may not be able to absorb the changes without irreversible damage to living systems.

Pollution Goes Global

Winds and precipitation act to purify the air to a degree, but we pour more pollutants into the atmosphere than it can readily handle. This clearly runs counter to the concept of sustainability when the emissions are high enough that natural processes cannot correct for them. Air pollution knows no political boundaries. Pollution from Midwestern power plants leads to acid rain in the Northeast. Pollution originating in the United States contributes to acid rain in Canada. Contaminants from England and Germany pollute the snow in Norway. Within the United States, Los Angeles smog drifts to Colorado and beyond. There is evidence that the shift of manufacturing from the eastern United States to Asia has led to cleaner New England air but the arrival of more pollutants on the West Coast.

As the number of people increases, more of the world's population lives in cities. Especially in developing countries, industrialization takes precedence over the environment. Cities in China, Iran, Mexico, Indonesia, and many other countries have experienced frightening episodes of air pollution. Large metropolitan areas are troubled the most by air pollution, but rural areas are affected, too. Neighborhoods around smoky factories have seen evidence of increased rates of miscarriage and decreased wool quality in sheep, decreased egg production and high mortality in chickens, and increased feed and care requirements for cattle. Plants are stunted, deformed, and even killed. Our agricultural operations for plants and animals are a key part of the need for sustainability, so it is important that we consider impacts to this industry.

What is a **pollutant**? It is too much of any substance in the wrong place or at the wrong time. A chemical may be a pollutant in one place and helpful in another. For example, ozone is a natural and important constituent of the stratosphere, where it shields Earth from life-destroying UV radiation. In the troposphere, however, ozone is a dangerous pollutant (Section 13.4).

Coal + Fire ⟶ Industrial (Sulfurous) Smog

The word *smog* is a blend of the words *smoke* and *fog*. There are two basic types of smog (Table 13.2). Polluted air associated with industrial activities is often called **industrial smog**. It is characterized by the presence of smoke, fog, sulfur dioxide, and particulate matter such as ash and soot. The burning of coal, especially high-sulfur coal such as that found in the eastern United States, China, and Eastern Europe, causes most industrial smog. (Photochemical smog is discussed in Section 13.5.)

The chemistry of industrial smog is fairly simple. Coal is a complex combination of organic materials and inorganic materials. The organic materials are mainly carbon and burn when the coal is combusted. The inorganic materials—minerals—wind up

It DOES Matter!

A vast plume of polluted air called the *Asian brown cloud (ABC)* drapes over South Asia and the Indian Ocean during the winter. It is so huge that it may cool the area as much as or more than the greenhouse gases warm it. The cloud is composed of soot and ash, sulfates, nitrates, and mineral dust. Burning of biomass in forest fires and cooking and heating are responsible for half or more of the pollution. Motor vehicles and factories also contribute.

1. Is air less polluted today than it was in the past?

The answer depends on when and where. As noted in the text, air quality varies markedly by location such as urban areas compared to rural areas. The Industrial Revolution caused major degradation of air quality, but in the latter half of the twentieth century, many governments enforced environmental laws, which led to a significant improvement in the air in many locations. For some parts of the world, the air in 2000 was much cleaner than it was in 1900, but in many places in the developing world, the negative trend has not been reversed. Some cities in China and India have recently reached record levels of air pollutants.

Table 13.2	Types of Smog	
	Industrial Smog	Photochemical Smog
Alternative names	Winter smog, sulfurous smog, London smog	Summer smog, Los Angeles smog
Main initial components	SO_2, particulates	NO_x, hydrocarbons
Secondary components	SO_3, H_2SO_4	O_3, aldehydes, peroxyacetyl nitrate (PAN)
Main source(s)	Electric power plants, factories	Automobiles
Typical weather	Cold, damp, foggy	Warm, sunny, dry

as ash. Some coal can contain 10% sulfur or more. When burned, the carbon in coal is oxidized to carbon dioxide and heat is given off.

$$C(s) + O_2(g) \longrightarrow CO_2(g) + heat$$

Not all of the carbon is completely oxidized, however; some winds up as carbon monoxide.

$$2\,C(s) + O_2(g) \longrightarrow 2\,CO(g)$$

And some carbon, unburned, ends up as soot.

The sulfur in coal also burns, forming sulfur dioxide, a choking, acrid gas that gives rise to the term *sulfurous pollution*.

$$S(s) + O_2(g) \longrightarrow SO_2(g)$$

Sulfur dioxide is readily absorbed in the respiratory system. It is a powerful irritant known to aggravate the symptoms of people who suffer from asthma, bronchitis, emphysema, and other lung diseases.

The next step in this chemistry makes the situation even worse. Some of the sulfur dioxide reacts further with oxygen in the air to form sulfur trioxide.

$$2\,SO_2(g) + O_2(g) \longrightarrow 2\,SO_3(g)$$

Sulfur trioxide then reacts with water to form sulfuric acid.

$$SO_3(g) + H_2O(l) \longrightarrow H_2SO_4(l)$$

Collectively, the two oxides of sulfur are often designated as SO_x.

In air, sulfuric acid forms an *aerosol*, a dispersion of tiny particles (solid) or droplets (liquid) in a gas. This aerosol is corrosive and even more irritating to the respiratory tract than sulfur dioxide.

Usually, industrial smog also has high levels of **particulate matter (PM)**, solid and liquid particles of greater than molecular size. The largest particles are often visible in the air as dust and smoke. PM consists mainly of soot and the mineral matter that occurs in coal.

Minerals do not burn, even in the roaring fire of a huge factory or power plant boiler, because they mainly are very stable, ionically bonded species. Some mineral

▲ Burning of coal in electric power plants and other facilities is the main source of industrial smog, which is characterized by high levels of sulfur dioxide and particulate matter. Industrial smog can be reduced by the use of electrostatic precipitators, scrubbers, and other devices.

Air Pollution in China

As China becomes a major industrial power, its citizens pay a heavy price in terms of increased pollution. Three-fourths of China's commercial energy is generated from burning coal. The high sulfur content of the coal and the inadequate emission controls result in levels of sulfur dioxide and particulate matter (ash, soot, and dust) that are among the highest in the world.

Over two-thirds of major Chinese cities have SO_2 or NO_x levels above the maximums identified by WHO guidelines. The WHO-recommended maximum of small particulates is 25 micrograms per cubic meter. In early 2014, Beijing's air reached 505 on this scale. Many other cities also exceed the WHO maximums for particulates. It has been found that these particulates interfere with photosynthesis by plants, so there can be an impact on the growing of food. Of 443 Chinese cities monitored, 189 suffered harm from acid rain. The World Bank predicts that, in the first two decades of the twenty-first century, about 590,000 people a year will die prematurely in China as a result of urban air pollution.

Private ownership of motor vehicles was almost unknown in China until the 1980s. Now, according to the Chinese Ministry of Communications, the number of cars on the roads is predicted to grow from 20 million in 2005 to 1 billion by 2050.

China is attacking the air quality problem by closing heavily polluting factories in some larger metropolitan areas, investing in natural gas, and replacing raw coal with cleaner-burning briquettes for domestic cooking and heating. China is also emerging as a world leader in clean energy, producing compact fluorescent lightbulbs, solar water heaters, solar photovoltaic cells, and wind turbines. The leaders of China, many of whom are technically trained, are realizing the severe negative impacts of pollution, including increased carbon dioxide, so they are stressing sustainable development, but the large supply of coal has been a competing factor in their decisions.

matter is left behind as *bottom ash*, but much of it is carried aloft in the tremendous draft created by the fire. This *fly ash* settles over the surrounding area, covering everything with dust. It is also inhaled, contributing to respiratory problems in animals and humans.

Small particulates—less than 10 μm in diameter, called PM10—are believed to be especially harmful. They contribute to respiratory and heart disease. The U.S. Environmental Protection Agency (EPA) also monitors even finer particulates, called PM2.5. EPA studies indicate that tens of thousands of premature deaths a year are linked to PM and that 20,000 of them are due to PM2.5. Particulate concentrations have been lowered significantly since nationwide monitoring began in 1999. In 2010, three out of ten people in the United States lived in counties with particulate pollution levels above the EPA's standards for PM2.5, PM10, or both.

Health and Environmental Effects of Industrial Smog

Minute droplets of liquid sulfuric acid, as well as PM10 and smaller solids, are easily trapped in the lungs. Interaction can considerably magnify the harmful effects of pollutants. A certain level of sulfur dioxide, without the presence of PM, might be reasonably safe. A particular level of PM might be fairly harmless without sulfur dioxide around, but the effect of both together can be deadly. PMs can be very effective carriers of other pollutants into the lungs. *Synergistic effects* such as this are quite common whenever chemicals act together. Two examples are the synergistic effects of asbestos and cigarette smoke (discussed in Chapter 12), and the synergistic effects of some drugs (discussed in Chapter 18).

When the pollutants in industrial smog come into contact with the alveoli of the lungs, the alveoli lose their resilience, making it difficult for them to expel carbon dioxide. Such lung damage contributes to pulmonary emphysema, a condition characterized by increasing shortness of breath.

Sulfuric acid and SO_x pollutants also damage plants. Leaves become bleached and splotchy when exposed to SO_x. The yield and quality of farm crops can be severely affected. These compounds are also major culprits in the production of acid rain.

What to Do about Industrial Smog

An aspect of sustainability is the effort to prevent and alleviate industrial smog. We do need to have industries to provide needed products to support our life, but how these plants operate is a significant factor in the impact they have on our atmosphere and therefore on humans as well as other animals and plants.

PM can be removed from smokestack gases by means of several devices.

- An **electrostatic precipitator** (Figure 13.5) induces electric charges on the particles, which are then attracted to oppositely charged plates and deposited.
- *Bag filtration* works much like the bag in a vacuum cleaner. Particle-laden gases pass through filters in a bag house. These filters can be cleaned by shaking and by periodically blowing air through them in the opposite direction.
- A *cyclone separator* causes the stack gases to spiral upward through it in a circular motion. The particles hit the outer walls, settle out, and are collected at the bottom.
- A **wet scrubber** removes PM by passing the stack gases through a fine mist of water. After use, the wastewater must be treated to remove the particulates, which adds to the cost of this method.

The choice of device depends on the type of coal being burned, the size of the plant, and other factors. All require energy—electrostatic precipitators use about 10% of the plant's output—and the collected ash has to be disposed somewhere. Some of the ash is used to make concrete, as a substitute for aggregate in road base, as a soil modifier, and for backfilling mines. The rest has to be stored. Most of it goes into ponds, and the rest into landfills.

Sulfur and SO_x are harder to get rid of than PM is. Sulfur can be removed by processing coal before burning, but both the flotation method and the gasification

▲ False-color scanning electron micrograph of PM from a coal-burning power plant.

▲ Industrial smog was once so common a problem in London that it was called *London smog*. A notorious smog episode began in London on Thursday, December 4, 1952, lasted 5 days, and may have killed more than 4000 people.

Fly ash particle

50,000 volts

Stack gas flow

▲ **Figure 13.5** A cross section of a cylindrical electrostatic precipitator for removing particulate matter from smokestack gases. Electrons from the negatively charged discharge electrode (in the center) become attached to the particles of fly ash, giving them a negative charge. These charged particles are then attracted to and deposited on the outer, positively charged collector plate, which permits their removal.

or liquefaction process (Chapter 15) are expensive. Another way to get rid of sulfur is to scrub sulfur dioxide out of stack gases after the coal has been burned.

The most common scrubber uses the limestone–dolomite process. Limestone ($CaCO_3$) and dolomite (a mixed calcium–magnesium carbonate) are pulverized and heated. Heat drives off carbon dioxide to form calcium oxide (lime), a basic oxide that reacts with sulfur dioxide to form solid calcium sulfite ($CaSO_3$).

$$CaCO_3(s) + heat \longrightarrow CaO(s) + CO_2(g)$$
$$CaO(s) + SO_2(g) \longrightarrow CaSO_3(s)$$

This by-product presents a sizable disposal problem. Removal of 1 t of sulfur dioxide produces almost 2 t of solids. Some modified scrubbers oxidize the calcium sulfite to calcium sulfate ($CaSO_4$).

$$2 CaSO_3(s) + O_2(g) \longrightarrow 2 CaSO_4(s)$$

Calcium sulfate is much more useful than calcium sulfite; the sulfate is used to make commercial products such as plasterboard. In nature, calcium sulfate occurs as gypsum ($CaSO_4 \cdot 2H_2O$), which has the same composition as hardened plaster. It should be noted that the first step in this process produces additional amounts of CO_2, which creates problems of its own in terms of affecting the Earth's climate (Section 13.9).

SELF-ASSESSMENT Questions

1. The air in cities in thirteenth-century England
   a. smelled of the sea
   b. smelled of roses
   c. was smoky from coal burning
   d. was pristine

2. Which of the following is *not* usually released from burning fossil fuels?
   a. N_2 b. NO_x c. CO_2 d. SO_2

3. The pollutant usually described by size rather than composition is
   a. acid rain
   b. CFCs
   c. particulates
   d. photochemicals

4. Which of the following pairs of pollutant act synergistically in causing lung damage?
   a. O_3 and soot
   b. O_3 and PM
   c. SO_2 and NO_x
   d. SO_2 and PM

5. A device that cleans stack gases by means of electric charges is called a(n)
   a. catalytic converter
   b. electric generator
   c. electrostatic precipitator
   d. particle accelerator

6. Which pollutant is removed from stack gases by scrubbers that use lime?
   a. CO_2 b. CO   c. NO_x d. SO_2

7. A common by-product of sulfur dioxide removal from stack gases is
   a. CaO   b. $CaSO_4$ c. $CaCO_3$ d. solid S

Answers: 1. c; 2. a; 3. c; 4. d; 5. c; 6. d; 7. b

13.4 Automobile Emissions

Learning Objectives ❭ List the main gases in automobile emissions, and describe how catalytic converters reduce these gaseous pollutants. ❭ Explain how carbon monoxide acts as a poison.

When a hydrocarbon burns in sufficient oxygen, the products are carbon dioxide and water. For example, consider the combustion of octane, one of the hundreds of hydrocarbons that make up the mixture we call gasoline:

$$2 C_8H_{18}(l) + 25 O_2(g) \longrightarrow 18 H_2O(g) + 16 CO_2(g)$$

Thus, the main components of automotive exhaust are water vapor, carbon dioxide, and unreacted nitrogen and oxygen gas from the atmosphere. Water vapor and nitrogen are innocuous, but CO_2 contributes to global warming. Furthermore, the combustion process is never quite complete, and side reactions also occur. These factors give rise to smaller quantities of more harmful products.

▪ Carbon monoxide (CO) is a colorless, odorless, poisonous gas formed by incomplete combustion of fuels that contain carbon.

- Nitrogen oxides (NO_x) contribute to smog and acid rain and also cause irritation to human mucous membranes. Sunlight breaks down NO_2 to form NO and O atoms, both of which are reactive.

- Volatile organic compounds (VOCs) come mainly from unburned fuel or fuel that evaporates before being burned. They react with O atoms to form ground-level ozone (O_3), aldehydes (RCHO), and PAN ($RCOOONO_2$, page 385).

Carbon Monoxide: The Quiet Killer

When insufficient oxygen is present during combustion, carbon monoxide (CO) is formed. In the United States, CO makes up more than 60% (by mass) of all air pollutants entering the atmosphere, with more than half of all CO emissions coming from transportation sources. Total emissions of CO in the United States decreased by almost 50% over a period of 20 years but have plateaued since 2009.

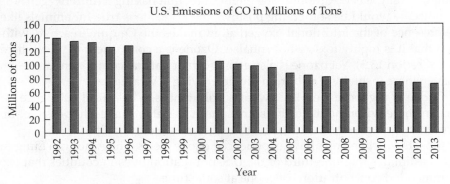

U.S. Emissions of CO in Millions of Tons

▲ Annual emissions of carbon monoxide in the United States.

In urban areas, the proportion of CO pollution coming from motor vehicles can be as high as 95%. Other sources of CO include industrial activities such as metal processing, residential wood burning, and natural sources such as forest fires. The EPA has set danger levels for CO at 9 ppm (average) over 8 h and 35 ppm (average) over 1 h. On city streets, these danger levels are exceeded much of the time. Even in off-street urban areas, levels often average 7–8 ppm. Such levels do not cause immediate death, but exposure over a long period can cause physical and mental impairment.

Because it is colorless and odorless, we can't tell that carbon monoxide is present except by using CO detectors or test reagents. (Automobile exhaust gets its odor from unburned hydrocarbons, not carbon monoxide.) Drowsiness, usually the only early symptom, is not always unpleasant.

Carbon monoxide acts by tying up the hemoglobin in the blood. Normally, hemoglobin transports oxygen throughout our body (Figure 13.6), but CO binds to hemoglobin much more strongly than oxygen does, which prevents the binding of oxygen. The symptoms of carbon monoxide poisoning are therefore those of oxygen deprivation. All except the most severe cases of acute carbon monoxide poisoning are reversible, but prolonged hospital stays with oxygen therapy are sometimes necessary. Carbon monoxide poisoning is discussed further in Chapter 22.

Nitrogen Oxides: Some Chemistry of Amber Air

Nitrogen oxides are formed when N_2 reacts with O_2 at high temperatures. Because air contains both nitrogen and oxygen, NO_x can be formed during the combustion of any fuel regardless of whether nitrogen is present in the fuel. Automobile exhaust and power plants that burn fossil fuels are major sources of NO_x. The main product of the reaction of nitrogen and oxygen is nitrogen monoxide (NO, also called nitric oxide).

$$N_2(g) + O_2(g) \longrightarrow 2\,NO(g)$$

Nitric oxide is then oxidized by atmospheric oxygen to nitrogen dioxide, an amber-colored gas that causes eye irritation and creates a brownish haze.

$$2\,NO_2(g) + O_2(g) \longrightarrow 2\,NO_2(g)$$

The two nitrogen oxides play a vital but nasty role in atmospheric chemistry.

2. Is it practical to collect automobile emissions and convert them back to gasoline?

This is hypothetically possible, though it would be difficult and require much energy to accomplish. The main combustion products from engines are CO_2 and H_2O. Both are very low in energy because a considerable amount of energy was released in their formation from gasoline and oxygen.

▲ **Figure 13.6** Schematic representations of a portion of the hemoglobin molecule (see Figure 16.15). Carbon monoxide bonds much more tightly than oxygen, as indicated by the heavier bond line.

At typical atmospheric levels, nitrogen oxides don't seem particularly dangerous in themselves. Nitric oxide at high concentrations reacts with hemoglobin. As in carbon monoxide poisoning, this leads to oxygen deprivation. Such high levels seldom, if ever, result from ordinary air pollution, but they might be reached in areas close to industrial sources.

The most serious environmental effect of nitrogen oxides is their role in smog formation. These gases also contribute to the fading and discoloration of fabrics and to acid rain when they form nitric acid (Section 13.6).

Ozone as an Air Pollutant

The ordinary oxygen in the air we breathe is made up of O_2 molecules. As was noted earlier, ozone is a form of oxygen that consists of O_3 molecules. Ozone and oxygen are **allotropes**, different forms of the same element. Properties of allotropes, though, differ greatly. Although one might think that having a third oxygen atom in the molecule would be something positive, the opposite is true for animals like us. The presence of the additional oxygen atom makes the O_3 quite reactive, with the result that it is highly toxic when inhaled. Ozone is a constituent of photochemical smog (Section 13.5). Yet ozone is also an important natural component of the stratosphere, where it shields Earth from life-destroying UV radiation.

Ozone is a good example of what a pollutant is, a chemical substance out of place in the environment. In the stratosphere, it helps make life possible. In the lower troposphere—the part we breathe—it makes life difficult.

Most U.S. urban areas have experienced ozone alerts. The American Lung Association estimates that one-third of the U.S. population lives in counties that exceed recommended concentrations of ozone at some time.

Ozone is a powerful oxidizing agent and is highly reactive. This makes it a severe irritant to the respiratory system. Episodes of high ozone levels correlate with increased hospital admissions and emergency room visits for respiratory problems. At low levels, it causes eye irritation. Repeated exposure can make people more susceptible to respiratory infection, cause lung inflammation, aggravate asthma, decrease lung function, and increase chest pain and coughing.

Ozone is particularly damaging to children. The WHO estimates that 80% of all deaths attributed to air pollution occur among children.

Ozone causes economic damage beyond its adverse effect on health. It is a strong oxidizing agent that causes rubber to harden and crack, shortening the life of automobile tires and other rubber items. Ozone also causes extensive damage to crops, especially cotton, peanuts, and soybeans.

Volatile Organic Compounds

Volatile organic compounds (VOCs) are organic substances that vaporize significantly at ordinary temperatures and pressures. They are major contributors to smog formation. There are many sources of VOCs, including trees, gasoline vapors and spills, incomplete combustion of fuels, and consumer products such as paints and aerosol sprays. Many VOCs are hydrocarbons.

Hydrocarbons are released from a variety of natural sources, such as the decay of plant matter in swamps. Only about 15% of all hydrocarbons found in the atmosphere are put there by people. In most urban areas, however, the processing and use of gasoline are the major sources of air-polluting hydrocarbons. Gasoline can evaporate anywhere it is used, contributing substantially to the total amount of hydrocarbons in urban air. This is why it is important to have a good seal on the cap to your gas tank and to not overfill and spill the liquid. Hydrocarbons from automobiles come largely from those vehicles with no pollution control devices or those with devices that are not operating properly. The automobile's internal combustion engine also contributes by exhausting unburned and partially burned hydrocarbons.

Hydrocarbons can act as pollutants even when they aren't burned. Certain hydrocarbons, particularly alkenes (Section 9.1), combine with oxygen atoms or ozone molecules to form aldehydes. Many aldehydes have foul, irritating odors.

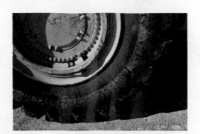

▲ Ozone causes rubber to harden and crack. Tire manufacturers incorporate paraffin wax into the rubber to protect tires from ozone. The alkanes that make up the wax are among the few substances that are resistant to attack by ozone. As the wax wears off, more migrates to the surface to replace it.

Another series of reactions involving hydrocarbons, oxygen, and nitrogen dioxide leads to the formation of peroxyacetyl nitrate (PAN).

$$CH_3\overset{\displaystyle O}{\overset{\|}{C}}-O-ONO_2$$

PAN

Ozone, aldehydes, and PAN are responsible for much of the destruction wrought by smog. They make breathing difficult and cause the eyes to smart and itch. People who already have respiratory ailments may be severely affected. The very young and the very old are particularly vulnerable.

The incidence of asthma has increased dramatically in recent years. Although it is unlikely that air pollution is the direct cause of the increase, medical studies show that pollutants at moderate levels can exert a small but measurable effect on the lung function and level of symptoms of asthmatic individuals. It seems more likely that pollutants and allergens interact to enhance the severity of asthma attacks rather than cause attacks.

A broad question to ask is how many individual automobiles can be used sustainably in a country or region. The efficiency of the auto is a factor in this discussion. Changes in the U.S. standards for average mileage for cars were made in 2013. These include a fleet average of 35.5 mpg in 2016, which will increase to 54.5 mpg in 2025. Consider these data in the context of the number of vehicles, which is 797 per 1000 people in the United States, but only 519 in the United Kingdom and just 183 for China, although this last number is rapidly increasing. Related to this is use of public transportation, which is much lower in the United States than many other countries. Buses and trains do produce the emissions discussed in this section, but the amount per person or per mile is usually much less.

SELF-ASSESSMENT Questions

1. Which of these is the largest source of carbon monoxide?
   a. transportation vehicles   b. volcanoes
   c. coal-burning power plants   d. home furnaces

2. Which of the following is *not* a problem caused by NO_x emissions?
   a. addiction
   b. formation of nitric acid, leading to acid rain
   c. formation of smog   d. eye irritation

3. Many volatile organic compounds (VOCs) have molecules composed of
   a. C and H only   b. C and N only
   c. N and H only   d. N and O only

4. Except in urban atmospheres, volatile organic compounds (VOCs) come mainly from
   a. automobiles   b. dry cleaning plants
   c. electric power plants   d. natural sources

5. Alkenes react with oxygen atoms to form
   a. alcohols   b. aldehydes   c. alkanes   d. ozone

6. Carbon monoxide is formed as a product of
   a. animal respiration
   b. removing SO_x from flue gas
   c. combustion of fossil fuels with excess O_2
   d. partial combustion of fossil fuels

7. Automobiles emit
   a. CFCs that cause ozone depletion
   b. O_3 directly
   c. CO_2 which reacts with hydrocarbons in sunlight to produce ozone
   d. NO_x and VOCs that react in sunlight to produce ozone

8. Which pollutant is likely to make breathing problems worse?
   a. CO   b. CO_2 c. NO   d. CH_4

9. Between 2003–2013, by approximately what percent have CO emissions decreased?
   a. 1%   b. 5%   c. 10%   d. 25%

Answers: 1. a; 2. a; 3. a; 4. d; 5. b; 6. d; 7. d; 8. a; 9. d

13.5 Photochemical Smog: Making Haze While the Sun Shines

Learning Objectives ⟩ Distinguish the origin of photochemical smog from the origin of sulfurous smog. ⟩ Describe the technologies used to alleviate photochemical smog.

Individually, hydrocarbons and nitrogen oxides are worrisome and have dramatic environmental impacts, including acid rain. Collectively, in the presence of sunlight, these pollutants can undergo a complex series of reactions that produces a very significant pollutant, **photochemical smog**, which is visible as a brownish haze.

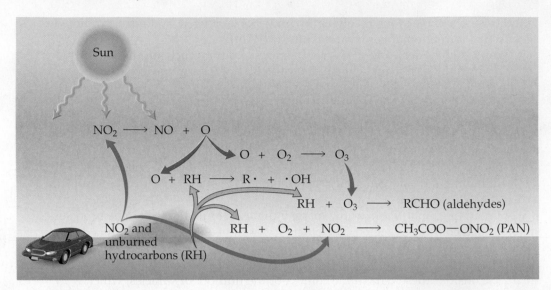

▲ **Figure 13.7** Some chemical processes involved in the formation of photochemical smog. Many other reactive intermediates have been omitted from this simplified scheme.

▲ Photochemical smog results from the action of sunlight on nitrogen oxides emitted from automobiles and other high-temperature combustion sources. A brownish haze like that shown here over the Los Angeles harbor characterizes this type of smog.

Unlike sulfurous smog, which accompanies cold, damp air, photochemical smog usually occurs during dry, sunny weather. The warm, sunny climate that has drawn so many people to the Los Angeles area is also the perfect setting for photochemical smog at any time of year. The principal culprits are unburned hydrocarbons and nitrogen oxides from automobiles. The chemistry of photochemical smog is exceedingly complex (Figure 13.7).

The development of air pollutants over time on a typical sunny summer day is shown in Figure 13.8. As traffic builds up in the early morning, NO enters the air in auto exhaust and begins to react with O_2 in the air to form NO_2. Hydrocarbons enter the air in exhaust as unburned components of fuel and from fueling leaks and spills. Sunlight splits the NO_2 into NO and O atoms. The very reactive O atoms combine with O_2 to form O_3, ozone. Ozone levels continue to rise all day and then decrease after the sun sets because there are fewer reactant gases and little solar energy.

Solutions to Photochemical Smog

Photochemical smog requires the action of sunlight on nitrogen oxides and hydrocarbons. Reducing the quantity of any of these would diminish the amount of smog. It isn't likely that we would want to reduce the amount of sunlight, so let's focus on the other two.

▶ **Figure 13.8** Concentrations of several urban air pollutants at different times during a typical sunny day. Hydrocarbons and NO are produced first. As they interact with sunlight, NO_2 and then ozone form.

Hydrocarbons (commonly called HC in air pollution reports) have many important uses as solvents. But if we could reduce the quantity of hydrocarbons entering the atmosphere, the amounts of aldehydes and PAN formed would also be reduced. Improved design of storage and dispensing systems has decreased HC emissions from gasoline stations. Modified gas tanks and crankcase ventilation systems have reduced evaporative emissions from automobiles. Most of the reduction, however,

Catalytic Converters and Nanotechnology

For maximum effectiveness, the catalysts inside a catalytic converter must have a large surface area because the reactions take place on the solid surface. To achieve this, the catalysts are thinly coated on a collection of small ceramic beads or a honeycomb matrix. One gram of ceramic pellets can have over 25 m^2 of surface area! The surface area of either structure is coated with a precious metal such as palladium, rhodium, or platinum. (These metals really are precious; they cost hundreds or thousands of dollars per gram.)

Catalytic converters have used nanotechnology for several decades. A converter uses only about 4–5 g of precious metal to coat the honeycomb structure or pellets. This technology exposes the exhaust stream of the vehicle to a catalyst area equal to that of several football fields.

Researchers continue to try to improve catalytic converters. Catalysts vary in particle size and composition and the support material on which the precious metals are deposited. For example, scientists at the University of California, Davis, are studying iridium (Ir) catalyst particles consisting of just four atoms. These researchers found that the catalytic nanoclusters are chemically bonded to the ceramic support; previously, the support material was thought to be inert. By modifying the support material under the nanoparticles, the researchers increased the efficiency of the catalyst by a factor of ten, possibly opening the way for a new class of nanosized catalysts.

At Brookhaven National Laboratory, cerium(IV) oxide nanoparticles were impregnated with zirconium (Zr) or gold (Au). The zirconium-doped nanoparticles store or release oxygen, depending on the engine conditions, thus making the catalyst more efficient in converting CO and NO to CO$_2$ and N$_2$.

Other experiments have shown that gold-doped nanoparticles act as active catalysts in helping CO combine with O$_2$ to make CO$_2$. Gold is not catalytic in its bulk form, but in the form of particles less than 6 nm in diameter, it is a very effective catalyst. Nanoscale catalysts open the way for many innovations that will make various chemical processes more efficient and thus save resources.

has resulted from the use of **catalytic converters** to lower hydrocarbon and carbon monoxide emissions in automotive exhausts in two stages:

- The first stage employs a *reduction catalyst* made of platinum and rhodium to reduce NO$_x$ emissions. Some of the carbon monoxide is used to reduce nitric oxide to N$_2$.

$$2\,NO(g) + 2\,CO(g) \longrightarrow N_2(g) + 2\,CO_2(g)$$

- The second stage in the catalytic converter employs an *oxidation catalyst*. It uses some of the remaining oxygen in the exhaust gas to oxidize the unburned HC and CO over a platinum and palladium catalyst to produce water and carbon dioxide.

Lowering the operating temperature of an engine also helps to reduce the quantity of nitrogen oxides emitted, but the engine then becomes less efficient in producing energy to propel the car. Running an engine on a richer (more fuel, less air) mixture lowers NO_x emissions but tends to raise CO and hydrocarbon emissions. A control system is needed to monitor the exhaust stream for optimum operation.

Catalytic converters convert more than 90% of HC, CO, and NO_x into less harmful CO_2, N_2 and water vapor. Over the past 30 years, their use has prevented more than 12 billion tons of harmful exhaust gases from entering Earth's atmosphere.

Many people now drive *hybrid vehicles* to save gasoline and to benefit the environment. A hybrid vehicle uses both an electric motor and a gasoline engine. The small gasoline engine drives the vehicle most of the time and recharges the batteries that run the electric motor. The electric motor provides additional power when it is needed (for example, when climbing a hill). Hybrid vehicles are much more efficient than conventional gasoline vehicles. Although these vehicles do provide a reduction in air pollution, a complete evaluation of their environmental impact has to include the production, replacement, and recycling of the batteries. Researchers are working to develop more compact, more efficient batteries that generate less pollution in manufacture.

There are a few electric-only vehicles in production. At present, their usefulness is somewhat limited. Electric vehicles have less range before recharging, take hours to recharge, and have poorer acceleration than gasoline-powered vehicles. To attain widespread use, electric cars will have to have improved batteries to provide a longer range before needing to be charged and faster recharging. More recharging stations and more power plants to provide the electricity will also be required. A sustainability factor for electric vehicles is the source of energy used to produce the electricity. For states such as California, which has a high percentage of renewal energy, the electric vehicle produces much less carbon dioxide than an internal combustion vehicle. For states with high use of coal, such as Ohio, there is still an advantage for electric vehicles, but the difference is small. For electric vehicles to be a net positive in terms of emissions, electricity produced by renewable methods must increase significantly.

SELF-ASSESSMENT Questions

1. Nitrogen oxides and hydrocarbons combine in the presence of sunlight to cause
   a. acid rain
   b. global warming
   c. an ozone hole
   d. photochemical smog

2. An amber haze over a city indicates the presence of
   a. HNO_3 **b.** NO   **c.** NO_2 **d.** SO_2

3. Photochemical smog occurs mainly in
   a. cold, wet weather
   b. dry, sunny weather
   c. flat, dry areas
   d. snowy, mountainous areas

4. The main source of photochemical smog in most areas is
   a. automobiles
   b. electric power plants
   c. chemical factories
   d. solid waste burning

5. Removing NO_x from automobile exhaust requires a(n)
   a. bag filter
   b. electrostatic precipitator
   c. reduction catalyst
   d. wet scrubber

6. How long does it take for ozone concentrations to drop to one-half of their maximum value according to the time progression in Figure 13.8?
   a. 2.5 hours
   b. 4 hours
   c. 6 hours
   d. 18 hours

Answers: 1, d; 2, c; 3, b; 4, a; 5, c; 6, a

13.6 Acid Rain: Air Pollution ⟶ Water Pollution

Learning Objectives   ❯ Name the air pollutants that contribute to acid rain.   ❯ List the major industrial and consumer sources of acid-rain-producing pollutants.

We have seen how sulfur oxides are converted to sulfuric acid (Section 13.3) and nitrogen oxides to nitric acid (Section 13.2). If they are in the atmosphere, these acids fall on Earth as acid rain or acid snow or are deposited from acid fog or adsorbed on particulates. **Acid rain** is defined as any form of precipitation having a pH less than 5.6. Rain with a pH as low as 2.1 and fog with a pH of 1.8 have been reported (Figure 13.9). These values are lower than the pH of vinegar or lemon juice.

▲ **Figure 13.9** The pH of acid rain in relation to that of other familiar substances. Normal rainwater, if saturated with dissolved CO_2, has a pH of 5.6 because carbon dioxide reacts with water to make it acidic and not neutral. During thunderstorms, the pH of rainwater can be much lower because of nitric acid formed by lightning. Recall (from Chapter 7) that a solution with a pH value one unit lower than that of another is ten times more acidic. A decrease in pH from 5.6 to 4.6, for example, means an increase in acidity by a factor of 10. Two pH units lower means 100 times more acidic, and three pH units lower means 1000 times more acidic.

Acid rain is mainly due to sulfur oxides emitted from power plants and smelters and nitrogen oxides discharged from power plants and automobiles. These substances form acids that are often carried great distances before falling as rain or snow (Figure 13.10).

Acids corrode metals and can even erode stone buildings and statues. Sulfuric acid dissolves metals to form soluble salts and hydrogen gas.

$$Fe(s) + H_2SO_4(aq) \longrightarrow FeSO_4(aq) + H_2(g)$$

Iron (in steel)

A soluble salt

The reaction shown here is oversimplified. For example, in the presence of water and oxygen (air), the iron is converted to rust (Fe_2O_3). One effect of these reactions is the increased concentration of metal ions in natural waters. This can lead to additional environmental problems when these ions are taken up by plants. The U.S. Environmental Protection Agency has a website with "Quick Finder" links that

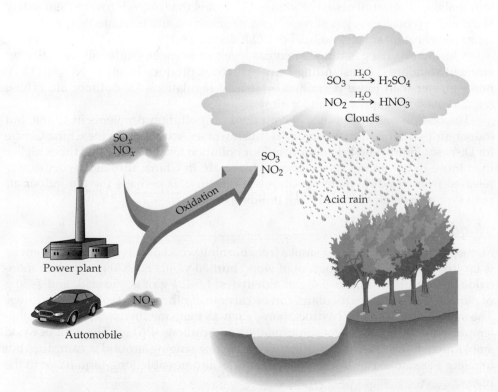

◀ **Figure 13.10** Acid rain. The two main substances responsible for acid rain are sulfur dioxide (SO_2) from power plants and nitric oxide (NO) from power plants and automobiles. These oxides are converted to SO_3 and NO_2, respectively, which then react with water to form H_2SO_4 and HNO_3. The acids then fall in rain, often hundreds of kilometers from their sources.

▲ Statues can be slowly eroded by the action of acid rain on limestone (calcium carbonate).

will lead you to more information on topics such as acid rain, air, the Clean Air Act, climate change, ozone, and radon.

Marble or limestone buildings and statues disintegrate through a similar reaction with sulfuric acid that forms calcium sulfate, a slightly soluble, crumbly compound.

$$CaCO_3(s) + H_2SO_4(aq) \longrightarrow CaSO_4(aq) + H_2O(l) + CO_2(g)$$

Marble or limestone

SELF-ASSESSMENT Questions

1. Acid rain is defined as precipitation with a pH
   a. above 7.4
   b. above 7.0
   c. below 5.6
   d. below 7.0

2. Which of these reactions leads to acid rain?
   a. $C + O_2 \longrightarrow CO_2$
   b. $Cl_2 + H_2 \longrightarrow 2HCl$
   c. $N_2 + 3H_2 \longrightarrow 2NH_3$
   d. $S + O_2 \longrightarrow SO_2$

Answers: 1, c; 2, d

13.7 The Inside Story: Indoor Air Pollution

Learning Objectives ❯ List the main indoor air pollutants and their sources. ❯ Explain where radon comes from and why it is hazardous.

Indoor air pollution can pose a major health concern. It can be serious in the United States but is often much worse in developing countries where people use wood, charcoal, coal, or dried dung as fuel for heating and cooking.

EPA studies on human exposure to air pollutants indicate that indoor air levels of many pollutants may be 2–5 times higher, and on occasion more than 100 times higher, than outdoor levels. Near high-traffic areas, the air indoors has the same carbon monoxide level as the air outside. In some areas, office buildings, airport terminals, and apartments have indoor CO levels that exceed government safety standards. Woodstoves, gas stoves, cigarette smokers, and unvented gas and kerosene space heaters are also sources of CO indoors.

A kitchen with a gas range often has levels of nitrogen oxides above U.S. government standards. Freestanding kerosene stoves produce levels of NO_x up to 20 times greater than those permitted by federal regulations for outdoor air. (These regulations do not apply to indoor air.)

The box on page 380 noted the outdoor air pollution problems in China, but indoor air pollution in that country is much worse. According to the China Centre for Disease Control and Prevention, indoor pollution levels can be 5–10 times higher than those in the nation's very poor outdoor air. In China, formaldehyde, slowly released from building materials and new furniture, is perhaps the top indoor air pollutant, as a result of the ongoing building boom.

Wood Smoke

Many people like the smell of smoke from burning wood or leaves, but wood smoke is far from benign. Each kilogram of wood burned yields 80–370 g of carbon monoxide, 7–27 g of VOCs, 0.6–5.4 g of aldehydes, 1.8–2.4 g of acetic acid, and 7–30 g of particulates. These particulates can be carriers of other pollutants into the lungs. The smoke also contains hydrocarbons, such as methane, benzene, and naphthalene, and carcinogenic polycyclic aromatic hydrocarbons (PAHs). The odor of wood smoke may evoke memories of autumns past or singing around a campfire, but inhaling the smoke can lead to asthma attacks and possible long-term harm to the lungs.

Cigarette Smoke

Another indoor polluter is tobacco smoke. Only about 15% of cigarette smoke is inhaled by the smoker; the rest remains in the air for others to breathe. More than 40 carcinogens have been identified among the 4000 or so chemical compounds found in cigarette smoke. The EPA even classifies secondhand smoke as a Class A carcinogen, a substance known to cause cancer in humans. The carcinogens (Chapter 22) in tobacco smoke are some of the same ones found in wood smoke. Tobacco smoke has PAHs, aromatic amines, nitrosamines, and radioactive polonium-210.

The health effects of smoking on the smoker are well known (and discussed in more detail in Chapter 19). Reports released by the Surgeon General of the United States have dealt with the effects of tobacco smoke as an air pollutant. Air quality in smoke-filled rooms is poor. Smoke from just one burning cigarette can raise the level of particulates above government standards.

The risk to nonsmokers from cigarette smoke is also well established. Medical research has shown that nonsmokers who regularly breathe secondhand smoke suffer many of the same diseases as active smokers, including lung cancer and heart disease. Women who have never smoked but live with a smoker have a 91% greater risk of heart disease and twice the risk of dying from lung cancer. Women who are exposed to secondhand smoke during pregnancy have a higher rate of miscarriages and stillbirths. Their children have decreased lung function and a greater risk of sudden infant death syndrome (SIDS). Children exposed to secondhand smoke are more likely to experience middle ear and sinus infections. They also show an increased frequency of asthma, colds, bronchitis, pneumonia, and other lung diseases. These health problems and others have caused many states and municipalities to ban smoking in many public places.

Radon and Its Dirty Daughters

A most enigmatic indoor air pollutant is radon. A noble gas, radon is colorless, odorless, tasteless, and unreactive chemically. Radon is, however, radioactive. The decay products of the radon nucleus, called **daughter isotopes**, are the major problem. Radon-222 decays by alpha emission (Section 11.2) with a half-life of 3.8 days.

$$^{222}_{86}\text{Rn} \longrightarrow ^{218}_{84}\text{Po} + ^{4}_{2}\text{He}$$

When radon is inhaled, polonium-218 and other daughter isotopes, including lead-214 and bismuth-214, are trapped in the lungs, where their decay damages the tissues.

Radon is released naturally from soils and rocks, particularly granite and shale, and from minerals such as phosphate ores and pitchblende. The ultimate source is uranium atoms found in these materials. Radon is only one of several radioactive materials formed during the multistep decay of uranium. However, radon is unique in that it is a gas and escapes into the atmosphere. The other decay products are solids and remain in the soil or rock.

Outdoors, radon dissipates and presents no problems. However, a house built on a solid concrete slab or over a basement can trap the gas inside. Radon levels build up, sometimes reaching several times the maximum safe level established by the EPA (0.15 Bq per liter of air). At five times this level, the hazard is thought to equal that of smoking two packs of cigarettes a day. Although the hazard has not been precisely determined, scientists at the National Cancer Institute estimate that radon may cause 20,000 lung cancer deaths a year. The "safe level" was set for people who work in uranium mines. These workers have high rates of lung cancer, but they also breathe radioactive dust and many smoke cigarettes. These risk factors may be synergistic and so are difficult to evaluate separately.

Other Indoor Pollutants

Some people use kerosene heaters or unvented natural gas heaters to help reduce heating costs in the winter. Heating only the occupied areas of a home seems like a good idea. However, when such heaters are not properly adjusted, carbon monoxide can be generated. Carbon monoxide from gas stoves, gas furnaces, and gasoline generators or even from automobile exhaust in attached garages can also contribute to the high levels of CO found in some houses. The EPA recommends a maximum level of 9 ppm CO over an eight-hour period. Carbon monoxide levels from a poorly adjusted gas heater can exceed 30 ppm—continuously. Commercial carbon monoxide detectors are readily available, reliable, and easy to install. Proper ventilation is key to preventing high levels of carbon monoxide.

Mold is an often-ignored pollutant in many homes. Leaky pipes or cool areas where water vapor condenses can lead to moisture problems, and mold will grow where there is moisture. Mold spores are a form of PM that can worsen asthma, bronchitis, and other lung diseases. Generally, mold is controlled by controlling moisture.

Electronic air cleaners are widely advertised. These seem a convenient solution to indoor air pollution: Just plug in a cleaner and let it remove all the bad pollutants. Unfortunately, some of these cleaners *produce* pollution. In particular, some of them generate ozone. As we shall see in the next section, ozone is quite reactive and can indeed reduce the levels of some pollutants by reacting with them. But, in doing so, it can generate other pollutants, such as formaldehyde. The EPA advises the public "to use proven methods of controlling indoor air pollution. These methods include eliminating or controlling pollutant sources, increasing outdoor air ventilation, and using proven methods of air cleaning."

SELF-ASSESSMENT Questions

1. Even properly operated gas ranges in kitchens are a source of the indoor air pollutant
   a. CO   **b.** NO_x **c.** PAHs   **d.** VOCs

2. What pollutant can be generated by advertised indoor air electronic air cleaners?
   a. CO   **b.** ozone   **c.** VOCs   **d.** radon

3. Radon in homes comes from
   a. gas cooking ranges   **b.** smoke detectors
   c. leaking heater exhausts   **d.** soil and rocks

4. Which of the following is a radioactive radon daughter?
   a. cobalt-60   **b.** helium-4
   c. polonium-218   **d.** uranium-238

Answers: 1, b; 2, b; 3, d; 4, c

13.8 Stratospheric Ozone: Earth's Vital Shield

Learning Objectives ❯ Explain the link between CFCs and depletion of the ozone layer. ❯ Describe the consequences of stratospheric ozone depletion.

In the mesosphere (Figure 13.1), some ordinary oxygen molecules are split into oxygen atoms by short-wavelength, high-energy UV radiation.

$$O_2(g) + \text{energy (UV radiation)} \longrightarrow 2\,O(g)$$

Some of these highly reactive atoms diffuse down to the stratosphere, where they react with O_2 molecules to form ozone molecules.

$$O_2(g) + O(g) \longrightarrow O_3(g)$$

The ozone in turn absorbs longer-wavelength, but still lethal, UV radiation, thus shielding us from this harmful radiation. In absorbing these photons, the ozone molecules are converted back to oxygen molecules and oxygen atoms in a reversal of the previous reaction.

$$O_3(g) + \text{energy (UV radiation)} \longrightarrow O_2(g) + O(g)$$

Undisturbed, the concentration of ozone in the stratosphere remains fairly constant due to this cyclic process. Over 300 billion tons of ozone are destroyed and created every day in this way in a very diffuse layer of the stratosphere about 20 km thick. However, because of the reduced pressure and the low concentration of ozone in this layer, the actual number of ozone molecules is not that large. If they were compressed to normal sea-level pressure, the layer would be only 3 mm thick! This delicate barrier protects all living things from harmful UV radiation. In recent decades, human activity has upset the balance and caused a decrease of the protective qualities of the ozone layer in some areas of the world.

UV light is sometimes used to sterilize tools in hair salons and safety glasses in laboratories to prevent the transfer of infectious microorganisms from one person to another. We do not want the entire planet rendered sterile, however, for we are part of the life that would be harmed, so it is important to protect the integrity of the ozone shield.

Chlorofluorocarbons and the Ozone Hole

The less ozone there is in the stratosphere, the more harmful UV radiation reaches Earth's surface. For humans, increased exposure to UV radiation can lead to skin cancer, cataracts, and impaired immune systems. The U.S. National Research Council predicts a 2–5% increase in skin cancer for each 1% depletion of the ozone layer. Even a 1% increase in UV radiation can lead to a 5% increase in melanoma, a deadly form of skin cancer. Increased UV also causes lower yields of many crops. Depletion of stratospheric ozone can also decrease the population of phytoplankton in the oceans, disrupting the web of sea life and the oxygen cycle (Figure 13.3).

The thickness of the ozone layer changes with latitude and also with the seasons. The cycling of ozone concentration over the course of the year is most prevalent over Antarctica, in part because the chemical reactions responsible for ozone destruction occur much more rapidly on the surfaces of ice crystals. During the extreme cold of Antarctic winter (June–August), more clouds containing ice crystals are formed and the levels of ozone decrease. The lowest levels of ozone over the Antarctic typically occur in September when the increasing sunlight of the southern spring causes the decomposition reaction on the ice crystals. In the early 1970s, serious concerns were raised because the ozone layer was not recovering properly during the warm months. In 1974, Mario Molina and F. Sherwood Rowland described a mechanism for the enhanced ozone depletion that implicated the presence of chlorofluorocarbons (CFCs) in the stratosphere. Their work was awarded the Nobel Prize in Chemistry in 1995.

CFCs are not found in nature but were developed to be used as the dispersing gases in aerosol cans, as foaming agents for plastics, and as refrigerants. At room temperature, CFCs are either gases or liquids with low boiling points. They are almost completely insoluble in water and inert toward most other substances. These properties make them ideal for many uses. However, once CFCs are released into the atmosphere, their lack of reactivity allows them to persist and diffuse to the higher regions of the stratosphere. There, above the protective ozone layer, energetic UV radiation cleaves one of the C—Cl bonds and initiates a series of reactions that results in the net decomposition of ozone molecules.

This is a simplified version of the chemistry that occurs:

$$CF_2Cl_2 + \text{energy (UV light)} \longrightarrow CF_2Cl\cdot\ + Cl\cdot$$

$$Cl\cdot\ + O_3 \longrightarrow ClO\cdot\ + O_2$$

$$ClO\cdot\ + O \longrightarrow Cl\cdot\ + O_2$$

Both products of the initial reaction are highly reactive free radicals (Section 4.10), species with an unpaired electron (indicated here by a dot). The chlorine atoms then react with ozone molecules to produce molecular oxygen. Note that the third reaction results in the formation of another chlorine atom, which can break down another molecule of ozone. The second and third steps are repeated many times. The decomposition of one CFC molecule in this catalytic *chain reaction* can result in the destruction of *thousands* of molecules of ozone (see Section 7.8).

▲ In 1986, Susan Solomon, a chemist at the Oceanic and Atmospheric Administration in Boulder, Colorado, proposed a mechanism that explained the reason for greater ozone depletion over the poles by CFCs. Later experiments confirmed her mechanism and led to an international ban on the use of CFCs. Solomon was awarded a 1999 National Medal of Science for her work.

September 2013

▲ **Figure 13.11** The ozone hole (purple) over Antarctica is at its largest in September. This is an image from the hole's largest value in 2013, which occurred on September 16. The area is approximately equal to that of North America. This is 20% smaller than the record low from 2000 but still far from pre-CFC days.

International Cooperation

The United Nations has addressed the problem of ozone depletion through the 1987 Montreal Protocol, an international agreement enforcing the reduction and eventual elimination of the production and use of ozone-depleting substances. As a result, CFCs have been banned in the United States and many other countries, and the search for effective substitutes has been successful.

CFCs and other chlorine- and bromine-containing compounds that might diffuse into the stratosphere have been replaced for the most part by more benign substances. Hydrofluorocarbons (HFCs), such as CH_2FCF_3, and hydrochlorofluorocarbons (HCFCs), such as $CHCl_2CF_3$, are some of these alternatives. The C—H bonds in these compounds are more susceptible to reactive species such as hydroxyl radicals, so the molecules generally break down before reaching the stratosphere. For every solution, it seems there is a new problem; CFCs, HFCs, and HCFCs are all greenhouse gases (Section 13.9). Also, HFCs and HCFCs are more reactive than CFCs and can break down while in use, corroding components such as compressors and refrigeration coils.

Due to the Montreal Protocol, the concentration of CFCs in the stratosphere has peaked. Chlorine concentrations leveled off in 1998 and will likely continue to decline slowly for decades but still remain high enough to be at a saturation level and cause significant ozone destruction until 2025 or later. The size of the ozone hole over Antarctica (Figure 13.11) varies from year to year with temperature and other meteorological factors, which are the primary determinants of the annual variation at present. A complete recovery from CFC-caused damage is not expected for decades.

SELF-ASSESSMENT Questions

1. In the stratosphere, some O_2 is converted to
   a. acid rain   **b.** ammonia   **c.** ozone   **d.** water

2. Ozone is an allotrope of
   a. carbon   **b.** chlorine   **c.** nitrogen   **d.** oxygen

3. The pollutant that is harmful at Earth's surface yet protects life when in the stratosphere is
   a. carbon monoxide   **b.** chlorine
   c. oxygen   **d.** ozone

4. In the mesosphere, oxygen atoms are produced by
   a. breakdown of O_3 molecules
   b. breakdown of H_2O molecules
   c. breakdown of H_2O_2 molecules
   d. splitting of O_2 molecules

5. Which portion of the sun's radiation spectrum is absorbed by ozone?
   a. blue   **b.** infrared
   c. violet   **d.** ultraviolet

6. Chlorofluorocarbons harm the ozone layer by
   a. adding more ozone
   b. blocking UV radiation
   c. destroying oxygen molecules
   d. destroying ozone molecules

Answers: 1. c; 2. d; 3. d; 4. d; 5. d; 6. d

13.9 Carbon Dioxide and Climate Change

Learning Objectives ❭ List the important greenhouse gases, and describe the mechanism and significance of the greenhouse effect. ❭ Describe some strategies for reducing the amount of CO_2 released into the atmosphere.

No matter how clean an engine or a factory is, if it burns coal or petroleum products, it produces carbon dioxide. The analysis of air bubbles trapped in ice cores, which date back 800,000 years, indicated that the concentration of carbon dioxide in the atmosphere did not exceed 300 ppm in that time period. Values in the early twentieth century rose above 300 ppm and reached 402 in 2014. Careful analysis indicates that the main cause is the burning of fossil fuels. In effect, we are turning solid and liquid carbon that has been stored in the Earth for millions of years into a gaseous form with significant consequences.

Carbon dioxide is a natural component of the environment and is not considered toxic. In fact, we exhale this gas with every breath. But its effect on humans, other animals, and plants is starting to become significant, and projections of the future are cause for great concern. In 2007, the U.S. Supreme Court decided that carbon dioxide should be considered an air pollutant for the purposes of environmental regulations.

The sun radiates many different types of radiation, of which visible, infrared, and ultraviolet are most prominent. About half of this energy is either reflected or absorbed by the atmosphere. The light that gets through (mostly visible) acts to heat the surface of Earth.

The three main constituents of the atmosphere—oxygen, nitrogen, and argon— are small, nonpolar molecules that do not absorb infrared energy. However, carbon dioxide and some other gases, including water, produce a **greenhouse effect** (Figure 13.12). These gases do not absorb visible light—they are transparent. So visible light from the sun passes through the atmosphere to warm the surface of the Earth. This warming causes the production of infrared photons, which we perceive as heat. This infrared energy radiates toward space, but greenhouse gases in the atmosphere absorb and re-emit these photons, which results in a containment of some of the energy near the surface. This makes the air, water, and land warmer than they would be without these gases.

Some greenhouse effect is necessary to life. Without an atmosphere, all of the radiated heat would be lost to outer space, and the Earth would be much colder than it is. In fact, based on the distance from the sun, it is estimated that the Earth's average temperature would be a cold $-18°C$. which means that ice would cover much of the surface.

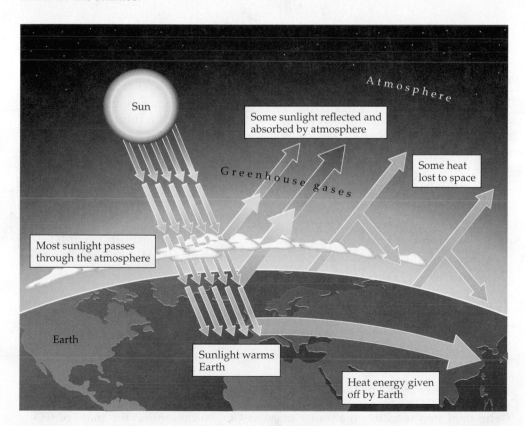

◀ **Figure 13.12** The greenhouse effect. Sunlight passing through the atmosphere is absorbed by the surface of the Earth, causing it to warm. The warm surface reemits energy as infrared radiation. Some of this radiation is absorbed by CO_2, H_2O, CH_4, and other gases and therefore retained in the atmosphere.

Example 13.1 | CO_2 Stoichiometry

Many reports on emissions of carbon dioxide quantify the amount of the emissions in gigatons of carbon. This value does not include the mass of oxygen included in the emitted gas.

If 4.0×10^{10} g of carbon (molar mass = 12.0 g/mol) from all sources are released by human actions in a year, how many grams of carbon dioxide (molar mass = 44.0 g/mol) are produced assuming complete combustion?

$$C(s) + O_2(g) \longrightarrow CO_2(g)$$

Solution

We have the mass of carbon and want to determine the mass of carbon dioxide produced from this amount of carbon, assuming complete reaction, so this is a stoichiometry problem (see Section 5.4).

We must convert the mass of carbon to moles.

$$4.0 \times 10^{10} \text{ g C} \times \frac{1 \text{ mole C}}{12.0 \text{ g C}} = 3.3 \times 10^9 \text{ mol C}$$

For the reaction, the mole relationship is 1 mol of C is equivalent to 1 mol of CO_2.

$$3.3 \times 10^9 \text{ mol C} \times \frac{1 \text{ mole } CO_2}{1 \text{ mole C}} = 3.3 \times 10^9 \text{ mol } CO_2$$

Finally we use the molar mass of CO_2 to determine the mass of CO_2 produced.

$$3.3 \times 10^9 \text{ mol } CO_2 \times \frac{44 \text{ g } CO_2}{1 \text{ mol } CO_2} = 1.5 \times 10^{11} \text{ g } CO_2$$

The final mass of CO_2 is several times the mass of C that was emitted, which is reasonable since the product now includes oxygen, which adds to the mass.

Example 13.2   CO₂ Emissions from a Car

This example provides a perspective for the emissions from driving a car. What mass of carbon dioxide (molar mass = 44.0 g/mol) is produced by burning 2670 g (1 gal) of gasoline? Gasoline may be represented by the formula C_8H_{18} (molar mass = 114.0 g/mol).

$$2 C_8H_{18}(l) + 25 O_2(g) \longrightarrow 18 H_2O(g) + 16 CO_2(g)$$

Solution

The problem gives us a mass of a reactant, and we are to find the mass of a product, so this is a second stoichiometry problem but with a few more aspects to consider.

We begin by converting the mass of the given substance, C_8H_{18}, to moles.

$$2670 \text{ g } C_8H_{18} \times \frac{1 \text{ mol } C_8H_{18}}{114.0 \text{ g } C_8H_{18}} = 23.4 \text{ mol } C_8H_{18}$$

Now we use a relationship from the balanced equation, that 2 mol of C_8H_{18} are equivalent to 16 mol of CO_2, to find the number of moles of CO_2 produced.

$$23.4 \text{ mol } C_8H_{18} \times \frac{16 \text{ mol } CO_2}{2 \text{ mol } C_8H_{18}} = 187 \text{ mol } CO_2$$

The final step is to use the molar mass of CO_2 to determine the mass of CO_2 produced.

$$187 \text{ mol } CO_2 \times \frac{44.0 \text{ g } CO_2}{1 \text{ mol } CO_2} = 8240 \text{ g } CO_2$$

The mass of CO_2 is greater than the mass of gasoline consumed because the carbon of the gasoline combines with oxygen from the air.

▪ **EXERCISE 13.1A**

Calculate the mass in grams of water vapor produced from burning 2670 g (1 gal) of gasoline.

▪ **EXERCISE 13.1B**

Calculate the mass in kilograms of carbon dioxide produced by a class of 60 students in one week if each student burns 10 gal of gasoline in a week.

Greenhouse Gases and Global Warming

The present problem is an *enhanced* greenhouse effect caused by rapidly increasing concentrations of carbon dioxide and other greenhouse gases in the atmosphere. This enhancement is leading to a rise in Earth's average temperature, an effect called **global warming** (Figure 13.13). Indeed, periods of high CO_2 concentration in Earth's past have correlated with increased global temperatures.

◀ **Figure 13.13** Carbon dioxide content of the atmosphere and surface temperature variations, which are clearly correlated as seen in this figure. The significant increase in carbon dioxide corresponds with the impact of the Industrial Revolution. Ice cores indicate that the atmospheric concentration of carbon dioxide did not exceed 300 ppm for at least 800,000 years.

About 35 billion t of carbon dioxide were emitted into the atmosphere in 2011, which was 54% higher than in 1990. Most of these emissions come from the burning of fossil fuels as determined by the isotopic analysis of the carbon. About 57% of this CO_2 is removed, mostly by plants and soil (29%) and the oceans (28%). But this leaves 43% of emissions, which cause a net increase in the atmospheric level of about 2 ppm per year.

Methane also contributes to the greenhouse effect. The concentration of methane in the atmosphere increased from about 0.7 ppm in 1750 to about 1.8 ppm. Most atmospheric methane comes from natural wetlands, where methane-producing bacteria decompose organic material. Decomposition of organic materials in landfills is the largest human-related source of methane in the United States. Other sources include cattle and termites, which produce methane as part of microbial fermentation during their normal digestive processes. Recently, the process of fracking has produced large quantities of methane. One effect has been a decrease in the price of this gas used to heat many homes. However, there is concern that the drilling process causes some leaks of this gas to the atmosphere.

Molecules that are polar or are easily polarized (having moderate to strong dispersion forces) are very effective as greenhouse gases. Although present in much smaller amounts than carbon dioxide, trace gases such as methane, CFCs, and HCFCs are much more efficient at trapping heat. Methane is 20 times, CFCs 5000–14,000 times, and HCFCs 140–11,700 times as effective as carbon dioxide at holding heat in Earth's atmosphere. Water is only about one-tenth as efficient at trapping the heat, but when water is present in significant amounts, it has a noticeable effect.

3. How do greenhouse gases keep the Earth warm?

Some polar molecules (recall Section 4.12) act as greenhouse gases because they strongly absorb infrared radiation (IR). Most of the radiation absorbed from the sun is in the form of visible light, and most of the radiation emitted by the Earth is IR. The more polar the molecule, the more readily it can absorb IR and cause warming of the Earth. This allows our planet to have a temperature that is reasonable for living systems.

For instance, cloudy winter nights tend to be warmer than clear winter nights due to the presence of significant amounts of water in the clouds, which act to trap the heat close to the Earth's surface.

Predictions and Consequences

A massive study by the United Nations' Intergovernmental Panel on Climate Change (*Fifth Assessment Report: Climate Change 2013–4*) provided a comprehensive review of past changes and predictions of future changes. The global average surface temperature increased about 0.85 °C from 1880 to 2012.

Some areas, such as Russia and other northern countries, may well benefit from a warmer climate. However, many of the regions facing the greatest risks are among the world's poorest nations.

Climate Change and Weather

We can look out the window and see weather—the conditions of the atmosphere over a short period of time. Weather forecasts are seldom accurate for more than a few days. Climate is an average of daily and seasonal weather events over a long period of time—30 years is typically used as a minimum. Even over a decade or so, short-term natural variability can mask long-term trends. *Climate change* means changes in long-term averages of daily weather—temperatures, rainfall, wind speeds, snow depths, and so on.

The IPCC panel predicted a variety of effects of global warming, some of which are regarded as more certain than others. Climate change is expected to bring more severe droughts to many areas, as well as harsher heat waves, stronger storms, more ferocious floods, more outbreaks of agricultural pests, and increased affliction by infectious diseases, such as malaria, which is already widespread in parts of Africa.

The potential impact on food output is a serious concern. Semiarid regions, where water is already scarce and cropland overused, could experience further devastation from climate change. The humanitarian crisis in the Darfur region of the Sudan is thought to be caused in part by the effect of global warming on crops and pastureland. Although one might think that more carbon dioxide would be good for plants that take up this gas,

anyone who has experienced the negative effects of overwatering a plant knows that too much of a good thing can be a bad thing. The growing of crops has been optimized for present amounts of carbon dioxide and water. When there are significant changes in these amounts in a relatively short period of time, nature cannot respond.

The rise in sea level can bring flooding that endangers low-lying islands and crowded river deltas such as those in southern Asian areas. Tens of millions of inhabitants of Bangladesh live at elevations that are less than 1 meter above sea level. A rise of this amount by 2100 is quite possible, so these people will be displaced from their homes. Approximately half of the U.S. population lives in a county that has an ocean coastline. Recent hurricanes have shown the vulnerability of the New Orleans, Florida, and New York areas.

As carbon dioxide levels in the atmosphere increase, more CO_2 will dissolve in the oceans, making the seawater more acidic. This acidification will lead to dissolving the shells of marine animals whose shells are made out of calcium carbonate. This effect has already started to damage the coral reefs, which are vital to ocean ecosystems. Small floating animals that are a vital part of the oceanic food chain are also at risk as increased acidity weakens their shells and makes them more brittle.

Estimated deaths attributed to climate change in the year 2000, by subregion*

- ☐ 0 – 2
- ☐ 2 – 4
- ☐ 4 – 70
- ☐ 70 – 120
- ☐ No data

◀ This map shows the areas where human health is most affected by global warming.

*Change in climate compared to baseline 1961–1990 climate

Data source:
McMichael, JJ, Campbell-Lendrum D, Kovats RS, et al. Global Climate. In comparative quantification of health risks: global and regional burden of disease due to selected major risk factors. M Ezzati, Lopez, AD, Rodgers A., Murray CJL. Geneva, World Health Organization, 2004

The large number of interrelated natural variables (clouds, volcanoes, El Niño weather patterns, and so forth) as well as the varying estimates of future greenhouse gas emissions complicate predicting the magnitude of future warming, but the IPCC study predicts that the temperature in 2100 will be 1–6 °C higher compared to the preindustrial level. That temperature rise may not seem like much, but the ramifications of such warming can be severe because so many of our physical and biological systems are attuned to early twentieth-century conditions. This includes the location of populations, which tend to congregate near bodies of water, as well as plants and animals, which have life cycles that are acutely sensitive to environmental factors such as temperature.

Another important factor is that the increases will not be uniform around the Earth. For example, in just the last 30 years, the temperature of states in the U.S. Northeast has increased by 1.4 °C, while some states in the Southwest have experienced temperature changes of as much as 1.9 °C.

So far, some predictions made by models have underestimated the actual changes, particularly at high latitudes. Losses from the ice sheets of Greenland and Antarctica have exceeded expectations. Satellite imagery in September 2012 showed the lowest extent of Arctic ice ever seen. If the overall trend continues, the Arctic Ocean may be ice free in summers by 2030.

Sea-level rise is a consequence of the warming of ocean waters and therefore an expansion of the volume, which has caused about 40% of the change. The remaining increase has resulted from the melting of land-based ice on Greenland, Antarctica, and glaciers. However, the melting of Arctic Sea ice is not a factor in sea-level rise.

You can do your own experiment to simulate melting of the floating Arctic ice cap. Place some water and two ice cubes in a glass. Mark the water level. Has the level changed after the ice has melted? To simulate melting of the Antarctic or Greenland glaciers, place some rocks in a glass and fill the glass with water to about a cm above the top of the rocks. Place two ice cubes on top of the rocks and mark the water level. Has the water level in the glass changed after the ice has melted?

An important effect of less Arctic ice is the reduced reflection of sunlight back into space. Arctic waters absorb more solar energy than ice, which causes warming. This in turn leads to more ice melting and creates what is called a positive feedback effect.

The polar ice caps need not melt completely for global warming to create problems. The oceans have risen 19 cm since 1901 at an average rate of 0.17 cm/year. Again, this rise may seem trivial, but even slight rises in ocean level increase tides and result in higher, more damaging storm surges. The annual rate of change in sea level is now 0.32 cm/year, which is almost double the long-term average. The IPCC report predicts an additional rise of 26–98 cm by 2100, increasing perhaps as much as 1 m. The IPCC earned a share of the 2007 Nobel Peace Prize for its work on climate change.

Mitigation of Global Warming

Scientists know in broad outline what we need to do to alleviate global warming: Technologically advanced countries must make quick and dramatic cuts in emissions. They also have to transfer technology to China, India, and the rest of the developing world so that those countries can continue to develop their economies without heavy use of coal-fired power plants. The problems involved in implementing these ideas are also well known: Can we make such rapid cuts? Are governments and individuals willing to tackle these issues?

We discuss a variety of alternatives to fossil fuels for energy production in Chapter 15. However, most scientists realize that no single alternative technology, whether it be solar power, nuclear power, biofuels, or wind power, will solve the problem of increasing CO_2 emissions. We will no doubt have to pursue several strategies, especially conservation, which pays for itself in lower costs.

More energy-efficient cars, appliances, and home heating and cooling systems will help somewhat, along with general energy conservation. In fact, perhaps as much as one-third of the needed reductions in emissions can come from such measures. Large-scale plans to capture CO_2 from smokestacks and sequester it underground are

4. Is global warming caused by the ozone hole?

The loss of some ozone in the stratosphere has an overall cooling effect on the Earth, but the amount is quite small. Most global warming is due to the recent large increases in greenhouse gas emissions.

under development, but they are quite costly and require energy to operate. **Carbon sequestration** is the removal of CO_2 from the atmosphere by collecting and transporting CO_2 from large emission sources, such as power plants and factories, and storing it in underground reservoirs. Sequestration also involves removal of CO_2 from the atmosphere by forestry and agricultural practices such as planting trees and stopping deforestation. All these alternatives are more difficult than simply burning coal or petroleum. But without effective carbon sequestration measures it will be almost impossible to keep CO_2 levels at values necessary to avoid major negative impacts.

A few nations have moved forward in reducing or capping CO_2 emissions, but overall there has been little or no progress. China is building coal-fired power plants at a breakneck rate—in fact, since 2008, China has become the largest emitter, replacing the United States. But to make a realistic comparison, if one looks at carbon dioxide emissions per person, the United States emits at a rate 2.5 times that of China.

One promising factor has been the greater availability and reduced cost of methane. That gas can produce electricity approximately 50% more efficiently than coal in terms of energy per amount of carbon dioxide. Methane also burns much cleaner than coal. The greater availability of methane is primarily due to fracking, which does have limitations in terms of leaks and some local reports of increase in earthquakes.

To consider perhaps the most important consequences of climate change, the WHO estimates that Earth's warming climate contributes to more than 150,000 deaths and 5 million illnesses each year and predicts that this toll could double by 2030. According to data published in the journal *Nature,* a warmer climate is driving up rates of malaria, malnutrition, and diarrhea. These health effects are in addition to other emissions, such as particulates and mercury, that come from burning coal.

SELF-ASSESSMENT Questions

1. What type of radiation is trapped on Earth's surface by the greenhouse effect?
   a. gamma   b. infrared
   c. ultraviolet   d. visible

2. During the twentieth century, the global average air temperature near the Earth's surface increased about
   a. 0.5 °C   b. 0.85 °C
   c. 1.25 °C   d. 2.25 °C

3. The main cause of recent increased global temperatures is
   a. CO_2 from factories, power plants, and automobiles
   b. Earth's orbital eccentricities
   c. variations in the sun's output
   d. water vapor

4. When CO_2 dissolves in the oceans, it
   a. decreases the acidity of the seawater
   b. forms an acid that dissolves shells of sea creatures
   c. raises the temperature of the ocean
   d. reacts with Ca^{2+} ions to form $CaCO_3$

5. To combat global warming, people should
   a. drain wetlands
   b. heat with charcoal
   c. pave dirt roads
   d. reduce the use of fossil fuels

6. If there were no greenhouse gases in our atmosphere, the average temperature of the Earth would be
   a. below the freezing point of water
   b. between the freezing point and the boiling point of water
   c. above the boiling point of water

7. In addition to CO_2 and methane, which gas is also an important greenhouse gas?
   a. Ar   b. NO   c. N_2O d. HCl

8. Atmospheric carbon dioxide concentrations increased by approximately what percent in the twentieth century?
   a. 1%   b. 10%   c. 33%   d. 50%

13.10 Who Pollutes? Who Pays?

Learning Objective ❯ List the EPA's criteria pollutants and the major air pollutants that come mainly from automobiles and mostly from industry.

The EPA lists six *criteria pollutants,* so called because scientific criteria are employed to determine their health effects. Since the first Earth Day in 1970, nationwide emissions of the six criteria pollutants have declined dramatically (Table 13.3). These improvements in air quality have occurred even though the U.S. population increased by one-third and both gross domestic product and vehicle miles traveled tripled.

Table 13.3	Ambient Air Quality Standards for Six Criteria Air Pollutants	
Pollutant		Limit
Carbon monoxide		
8-h average		9 ppm
1-h average		35 ppm
Nitrogen dioxide		
Annual average		0.053 ppm
Ozone[a]		
8-h average		0.075 ppm
Particulate matter		
PM10, 24-h average		150 μ/m^3
PM2.5, 24-h average		35
Sulfur dioxide		
3-h average		0.50 ppm
1-h average		0.075 ppm
Lead		
3-month average		0.15

[a] Formed from precursor volatile organic compounds (VOCs) and NO_x.

5. What does smog testing of vehicles actually test?

Tests vary depending on the location, but most measure unburned hydrocarbons and carbon monoxide emissions concentrations. Unburned hydrocarbons may come from the tailpipe or may arise from evaporation or leakage elsewhere in the fuel system. Some states and cities also test for nitrogen oxides or particulates.

Table 13.4 lists the main sources of seven major air pollutants along with their health and environmental effects. Note that motor vehicles are responsible for several of the major air pollutants; indeed, they are the source of nearly one-half (by mass) of all air pollutants. Our transportation system accounts for about 85% of urban carbon monoxide emissions, 40% of hydrocarbon emissions, and 40% of nitrogen oxide emissions. From the early twentieth century through the mid-1970s, cars were also a major source of lead in the air in the United States. The compound *tetraethyllead* was added to premium gasoline during those years. In 1976, the United States began phasing out the use of tetraethyllead in automobile fuels. Now the major sources of lead in the air are industrial processes and nonroad equipment.

Table 13.4	Seven Major Air Pollutants				
Pollutant	Formula or Symbol	Major Sources	Health Effects	Environmental Effects
Carbon monoxide	CO	Motor vehicles	Interferes with oxygen transport; contributes to heart disease	Slight
Hydrocarbons	C_nH_m	Motor vehicles, industry, solvents	Narcotic at high concentrations; some aromatics are carcinogens	Precursors of aldehydes, PAN
Sulfur oxides	SO_x	Power plants, smelters	Irritate respiratory system; aggravate lung and heart diseases	Reduce crop yields; precursors of acid rain, SO_4^{2-} particulates
Nitrogen oxides	NO_x	Power plants, motor vehicles	Irritate respiratory system	Reduce crop yields; precursors of ozone and acid rain; produce brownish haze
Particulate matter	PM	Industry, power plants, dust from farms and construction sites, mold spores, pollen	Irritates respiratory system; synergistic with SO_2; contains adsorbed carcinogens and toxic metals	Impairs visibility
Ozone	O_3	Secondary pollutant from NO_2	Irritates respiratory system; aggravates lung and heart diseases	Reduces crop yields; kills trees (synergistic with SO_2); destroys rubber and paint
Lead	Pb	Motor vehicles, smelters	Toxic to nervous system and blood-forming system	Toxic to all living things

Nonetheless, because most transportation in the United States is by private automobile, cars are a major source of air pollution.

On the other hand, most PM comes from power plants (about 40%) and industrial processes (about 45%). Similarly, more than 80% of sulfur oxide emissions come from power plants, with an additional 15% coming from other industries. Power plants alone contribute about 55% of nitrogen oxide emissions. Who uses electricity from power plants? We all do. A coal-fired plant must burn 275 kg of coal to light an ordinary 100-W bulb for one year.

What is the worst pollutant? Carbon monoxide is produced in huge amounts and is quite toxic. However, it is deadly only in concentrations approaching 4000 ppm. Its contribution to cardiovascular disease, by increasing stress on the heart, is difficult to measure. The WHO rates sulfur oxides as the worst pollutants. They are powerful irritants, and, according to WHO, people with respiratory illnesses are more likely to die from exposure to SO_x than from exposure to any other kind of pollutant. Sulfur oxides and sulfuric acid formed from them have been linked to more than 50,000 deaths per year in the United States.

We all share the responsibility for pollution. In the words of Walt Kelly's comic-strip character Pogo, "We have met the enemy, and he is us." But we can all be part of the solution by conserving fuel and electricity. Many utility companies now offer suggestions and incentives for saving energy. Some even give free analyses of home energy use.

Paying the Price

Air pollution costs us tens of billions of dollars each year. It wrecks our health by causing or aggravating bronchitis, asthma, emphysema, and lung cancer. It destroys crops and sickens and kills livestock. It corrodes machines and blights buildings. Replacing these items takes more energy and produces more pollution—along with carbon dioxide emissions that have climate-change effects.

Elimination of air pollution will be neither cheap nor easy. It is especially difficult to remove the last fractions of pollutants. Cost curves are exponential, soaring toward infinity as pollutants approach zero. For example, if it costs $200 per car to reduce emissions by 50%, it usually costs about $400 to reduce them by 75%, $800 to reduce them by 87.5%, and so on. It would be extremely expensive to reduce emissions by 99%. We can have cleaner air, but how clean depends on how much we are willing to pay.

What would we gain by getting rid of air pollution? How much is it worth to see the clear blue sky or to see the stars at night? How much is it worth to breathe clean, fresh air?

SELF-ASSESSMENT Questions

1. The U.S. agency responsible for gathering and analyzing air pollution data is the
   a. EPA   **b.** FAA   **c.** FCC   **d.** FDA

2. Air pollutants have decreased significantly since 1970 because
   a. there are fewer electric power plants
   b. there are fewer people
   c. there are more pollution controls
   d. we are planting more trees

3. The largest source of carbon monoxide pollution is
   a. electric power plants   **b.** coal mining
   c. motor vehicles   **d.** oil refineries

4. Electric power plants are the largest source of
   a. CO pollution   **b.** ozone   **c.** SO_2 pollution   **d.** VOCs

5. According to the World Health Organization, the worst pollutant in terms of health effects is
   a. CO   **b.** ozone   **c.** NO_x **d.** SO_x

6. The largest sources of NO_x pollution are
   a. electric power plants and motor vehicles
   b. electric power plants and industry
   c. industry and motor vehicles
   d. smelters and motor vehicles

7. The largest sources of particulate pollutants are
   a. electric power plants and motor vehicles
   b. electric power plants and industry
   c. industry and motor vehicles
   d. smelters and motor vehicles

Answers: 1. a; 2. c; 3. c; 4. c; 5. d; 6. a; 7. b

GREEN CHEMISTRY

Philip Jessop and Jeremy Durelle, *Queen's University*

It's Not Easy Being Green

Learning Objective ❯ Describe how to use waste CO_2 to lessen the environmental impact of industrial processes.

The alarming rate of carbon dioxide (CO_2) emission into the atmosphere is causing the average temperature of the oceans, and even the air, to steadily increase. Because humans have burned roughly 550 billion tons of carbon since the Industrial Revolution, the concentration of atmospheric CO_2 is 100 parts per million (ppm) higher than it was 200 years ago. Despite this, energy demand is on the rise, which means we are burning more carbon faster. While CO_2 isn't the only greenhouse gas produced when burning carbon, it gets the most attention because it is responsible for 60% of the greenhouse effect (see Section 13.9).

To minimize CO_2 emissions, power plants can separate the CO_2 from the waste gas before it is released into the atmosphere. This is known as scrubbing and involves cooling the gas and treating it with a liquid solvent that binds to CO_2 (such as aqueous solutions of ammonia or ethanolamine). As you can imagine, scrubbing the world's power plants would produce a lot of waste CO_2. While most of that CO_2 would have to be sequestered somewhere, such as in depleted oil or gas reservoirs, could some of it be used to benefit society and the environment? While waste CO_2 is already used for making products such as urea or carbonated beverages, could some of it be used to make industrial processes greener?

As it turns out, we can use waste CO_2 to make a number of processes more environmentally friendly. For example, a very new kind of solvent, called switchable-hydrophilicity solvents (SHS), can exist in either of two forms that can be interconverted by the addition of CO_2. SHS are amines. In the absence of CO_2, they are hydrophobic solvents, meaning that, like hexane, they won't mix with water. However, in the presence of CO_2, SHS become hydrophilic, meaning that, like methanol, they do mix with water. (Equation 1 shows how this interconversion happens.)

SHS can be used, for example, to extract oily materials from insoluble solids such as removing oil from oil sands (a naturally occurring mixture of sand, clay, and heavy oil), extracting vegetable oil from soybeans, and separating and recycling the oil and plastic in used bottles of motor oil. Most extractions of oily materials are done with a conventional (non-switchable) organic solvent. The mixture to be extracted (such as soybeans) is soaked in the conventional solvent. After the solids are removed by filtration, you are left with a solution of oil in solvent. The solvent is then removed by distillation. Unfortunately, that last step will only work if the solvent is volatile, which means it is also likely to be flammable, smog-forming, and an inhalation risk to workers. Switchable-hydrophilicity solvents, because they can be removed from product and recycled without distillation, do not need to be volatile; they therefore offer a potentially safer alternative (Figure 1). The mixture to be extracted is soaked in the SHS. After the solids are removed by filtration, the SHS is extracted from the product by carbonated water. Removing the CO_2 from the water causes the SHS to come out of the water, so it can be recovered and reused.

While use of CO_2 isn't a solution to global warming, the utilization of waste CO_2 enables us to modify industrial processes in unconventional ways that can decrease environmental impact. That is, after all, the purpose of green chemistry.

$$NR_3 + H_2O + CO_2 \rightleftharpoons [NR_3H^2][HCO_3^-]$$

Hydrophobic   Hydrophilic
form of SHS   form of SHS

▲ **Equation 1.** This chemical reaction interconverts the hydrophobic and hydrophilic forms of the SHS. Adding CO_2 shifts the equilibrium to the hydrophilic form, while removing CO_2 shifts the equilibrium to the hydrophobic form.

▲ **Figure 1.** The extraction of product (non-switchable oil) from a product-solid mixture using an SHS. Waste carbon dioxide from power plants can be used to make industrial processes such as product extraction from a product-solid mixture greener.

SUMMARY

Section 13.1—The thin blanket of air that is Earth's **atmosphere** is made up of layers: the troposphere (nearest Earth), the stratosphere (which includes the ozone layer), the mesosphere, and the thermosphere. Dry air is a mixture of about 78% nitrogen, 21% oxygen, and 1% argon by volume, plus small amounts of carbon dioxide and trace gases. Moist air can contain up to 4% water vapor.

Section 13.2—Animals and most plants cannot use atmospheric nitrogen unless it has undergone **nitrogen fixation** (combination with other elements). Nitrogen goes from the air into plants and animals and eventually back to the air via the **nitrogen cycle**. Oxygen from the air is involved in oxidation (of plant and animal materials) and is eventually returned to the air via the **oxygen cycle**. In the stratosphere diatomic oxygen, O_2, is converted to ozone, O_3, and then changed back to diatomic oxygen. In this process, the ozone absorbs UV radiation that might otherwise make life on Earth impossible. A **temperature inversion** occurs when a layer of cooler air is trapped under a layer of warmer air. The cooler air can become quite polluted in a short time.

Section 13.3—A **pollutant** is a substance that is in the wrong place or time and causes problems. Air pollution has existed for millions of years. Natural air pollution includes dust storms, noxious gases from swamps, and ash and sulfur dioxide from erupting volcanoes. Today air pollution is more complex than in the past. Air pollution is a global problem because pollutants from one geographic area often migrate to another. The main air pollutants introduced by human activity are the smoke and gases produced by the burning of fuels and the fumes and particulates emitted by factories. **Industrial smog** is the kind of smog produced in cold, damp air by excessive burning of fossil fuels. It consists of a combination of smoke and fog with sulfur dioxide, sulfuric acid, and **particulate matter (PM)**, which consists of solid or liquid particles of greater than molecular size. Soot and fly ash from coal combustion are forms of PM. The pollutants that make up industrial smog can act synergistically to cause severe damage to living tissue. PM can be removed from smokestack gases using an **electrostatic precipitator**, which charges the particles, or with a **wet scrubber**, which passes the gases through water that contains chemicals to trap or destroy the pollutants. Sulfur dioxide can be scrubbed from stack gasses using limestone to form calcium sulfite, which can then be oxidized to useful calcium sulfate.

Section 13.4—Complete combustion of gasoline produces carbon dioxide and water, but combustion is always incomplete. Carbon monoxide is one product of incomplete combustion, and three-fourths of the carbon monoxide produced results from transportation. Carbon monoxide is a poisonous gas that ties up hemoglobin in the blood so that it cannot transport oxygen to the cells. Nitrogen oxides are present in automobile exhaust gases and in emissions from power plants that burn fossil fuels. The greatest problem with nitrogen oxides is their contribution to smog. The amber color of nitrogen dioxide causes the brownish haze often seen over certain large cities. Ozone, O_3, an allotrope of oxygen, is formed in a complex reaction in the troposphere. It is very hazardous to breathing and is a significant

component of urban pollution. **Volatile organic compounds (VOCs)** are major contributors to smog. VOCs come from evaporation of gasoline, incomplete combustion of fuels, and some consumer products. Hydrocarbons can be pollutants in themselves and can react to form other pollutants such as aldehydes and peroxyacetyl nitrate (PAN), both of which are very irritating to tissues.

Section 13.5—**Photochemical smog** results when hydrocarbons and nitrogen oxides are exposed to bright sunlight. A complex series of reactions produces a variety of pollutants, including ozone. **Catalytic converters** in automobiles act to reduce photochemical smog by oxidizing unburned hydrocarbons and decreasing the emission of nitrogen oxides. Hybrid vehicles are more efficient than conventional vehicles and emit fewer pollutants.

Section 13.6—Nitrogen oxides (mainly from automobiles and power plants as well as the action of lightning) and sulfur oxides (mainly from power plants) can dissolve in atmospheric moisture, forming **acid rain**. Acid rain often falls far from the original sources of the acids, and it can corrode metals and erode marble or limestone buildings and statues.

Section 13.7—Indoor pollution can be as bad as, or worse than, outdoor pollution. Cigarette smoke can raise both levels of PM and carbon monoxide above the allowed EPA safety standards. Because of the effects of secondhand smoke, most cities and states restrict tobacco smoking in public places. The radioactive gas radon can accumulate indoors in some cases, and inhaled radon produces **daughter isotopes** that are also radioactive and can accumulate in the lungs. Inhaled radon can produce a significant risk of lung cancer.

Section 13.8—While ozone is harmful in the troposphere, it forms a protective layer in the stratosphere that shields Earth against UV radiation from the sun. Chlorofluorocarbons (CFCs) have been linked to the destruction of ozone, termed a "hole" in the ozone layer, and are now widely banned. This ban should stop the expansion of the ozone hole, but it will take many years for complete recovery.

Section 13.9—Carbon dioxide and other gases contribute to the **greenhouse effect**, which occurs when infrared radiation emitted from the Earth's surface cannot escape the atmosphere. The result is **global warming**, an increase in the Earth's average temperature, which is predicted to cause undesirable climate change.

Section 13.10—The EPA has listed six criteria pollutants, which have all been reduced in concentration in the atmosphere during recent years. Motor vehicles are a prominent source of carbon monoxide, hydrocarbons, and nitrogen oxides, while most PM and sulfur oxides come from industrial processes. Carbon monoxide and sulfur oxides are the most problematic pollutants. We all share responsibility for pollution—and the responsibility for reducing it.

GREEN CHEMISTRY—We can recycle the waste greenhouse gas, CO_2, and help our environment at the same time. Applying CO_2 technology to industrial processes can reduce the waste emitted from plants and factories and lead to greener applications.

Learning Objectives

Objective	Problems
❯ List and describe the layers of the atmosphere.	Problems 13, 14, 16
❯ Give the approximate proportion of N_2, O_2, Ar, and CO_2 in Earth's atmosphere.	Problem 12
❯ Describe the nitrogen and oxygen cycles.	Problems 10, 15
❯ Describe the origin and effects of temperature inversions.	Problems 17, 70
❯ List some natural sources of air pollution.	Problems 7, 18, 59
❯ List the main pollutants formed by burning coal, and describe some technologies used to clean up these pollutants.	Problems 3, 4, 8, 20, 23, 35
❯ List the main gases in automobile emissions, and describe how catalytic converters reduce these gaseous pollutants.	Problems 8, 28, 32, 36
❯ Explain how carbon monoxide acts as a poison.	Problem 31
❯ Distinguish the origin of photochemical smog from the origin of sulfurous smog.	Problems 9, 25, 26
❯ Describe the technologies used to alleviate photochemical smog.	Problem 28
❯ Name the air pollutants that contribute to acid rain.	Problems 43, 44, 46
❯ List the major industrial and consumer sources of acid-rain-producing pollutants.	Problems 43, 45
❯ List the main indoor air pollutants and their sources.	Problems 47, 51, 52
❯ Explain where radon comes from and why it is hazardous.	Problems 49, 51
❯ Explain the link between CFCs and depletion of the ozone layer.	Problems 1, 2, 39, 40
❯ Describe the consequences of stratospheric ozone depletion.	Problems 7, 10, 41, 42
❯ List the important greenhouse gases, and describe the mechanism and significance of the greenhouse effect.	Problems 5, 6, 53, 54, 55, 57, 63
❯ Describe some strategies for reducing the amount of CO_2 released into the atmosphere.	Problems 56, 58, 68, 69
❯ List the EPA's criteria pollutants and the major air pollutants that come mainly from automobiles and mostly from industry.	Problem 66
❯ Describe how to use waste CO_2 to lessen the environmental impact of industrial processes.	Problems 72, 73, 74

REVIEW QUESTIONS

1. List two (former) uses of CFCs.

2. Name one replacement for CFCs. What problems are associated with the replacements?

3. What is bottom ash? What is fly ash? Give two uses for fly ash.

4. Describe how (a) a bag filter and (b) a cyclone separator remove particulates from stack gases.

5. Describe the action of a greenhouse gas in terms of how it interacts with sunlight. Give three examples of such gases. What molecular feature of the gas is responsible for this effect?

6. What are the main sources of the three major greenhouse gases that have increased significantly over the past 100 years?

7. What are the health effects of (a) ground-level ozone as an air pollutant and (b) depletion of stratospheric ozone?

8. What is smog?

9. What makes photochemical smog different from industrial smog?

10. A student says that the hole in the ozone layer is the primary reason for warming of the Earth because it allows more energy to enter the lower atmosphere. Explain why this is incorrect.

PROBLEMS

The Atmosphere: Composition and Cycles

11. What is nitrogen fixation? Why is it important?

12. What are the approximate proportions of the four main components of dry air?

13. Look again of Figure 13.1. The X-15 was an experimental aircraft tested from 1959 to 1968. One test flew to an altitude of 67 miles. What layer of the atmosphere did the X-15 reach?

14. Referring to Figure 13.1, consider a small airplane flying at an altitude of 12,000 ft. In what layer of the atmosphere is the plane flying?

15. Figure 13.3 shows oxidation of metals as one aspect of the oxygen cycle. Write the balanced equations for (a) the oxidation of iron metal by atmospheric oxygen to form iron(III) oxide and (b) the oxidation of chromium metal to form chromium(III) oxide.

16. Trace gases in the atmosphere tend to be concentrated at different levels according to molar mass, with the heavier gases closer to the surface and the lighter gases at higher altitudes. Refer to Figure 13.1 and Table 13.1, and answer the following. (a) Which of the trace gases listed in Table 13.1 are likely to be found at altitudes above about 40 km? (b) Which ones are likely to be found below about 20 km? (c) Which gas is most likely to be found in the troposphere? [*Hint:* Consider the location of the ozone layer to answer parts (a) and (b).]

Industrial Smog

17. What weather conditions are associated with industrial smog?

18. Name two elements that are reactants in the production of industrial smog.

For Problems 19–22, write the balanced equation for the reaction described.

19. Sulfur is oxidized to sulfur dioxide by atmospheric oxygen.

20. Sulfur dioxide is oxidized to sulfur trioxide by atmospheric oxygen.

21. Sulfur dioxide reacts with hydrogen sulfide to form elemental sulfur and water.

22. Calcium sulfite is oxidized to calcium sulfate by atmospheric oxygen.

23. Describe how a limestone scrubber removes sulfur dioxide from stack gases. Write the equation(s) for the chemical reaction(s) involved.

24. Suggest a reason for the fact that PM2.5 is more hazardous to health than PM10.

Photochemical Smog

25. Under what conditions do nitrogen and oxygen combine? Give the equation for the reaction.

26. What is the formula for the oxide of nitrogen that initiates the formation of photochemical smog?

27. What is PAN? From what is it formed? What are its health effects?

28. Describe two ways in which the level of nitrogen oxide emissions from an automobile can be reduced.

29. Which of the following could be sources of VOCs?
    a. leftover oil-based paint
    b. a truckload of plastic milk jugs
    c. a cracked pipeline carrying crude oil from Alaska

30. An electrostatic precipitator could be useful for reducing soot emitted from a shoe factory but not for reducing noxious vapors from adhesives used in that factory. Explain.

Automobile Emissions and Carbon Monoxide

31. Which of the following is a free radical? CO, SO_2, O_3, NO?

32. A fellow student claims that carbon monoxide has an odor and is colored, because he can easily see and smell automobile exhaust, especially in the winter. How might you correct his misconception?

33. How can exposure to carbon monoxide contribute to heart disease?

34. Write the equation for the reaction by which carbon monoxide reduces nitric oxide to nitrogen gas.

35. Describe the change in CO emissions over time in the United States. Give a plausible explanation for this pattern.

36. Which pollutants are reduced in concentration by a catalytic converter?

The Ozone Layer

37. Oxygen and ozone are the same element in two different forms. What term describes this phenomenon?

38. Seawater contains roughly 30 g of dissolved sodium chloride per liter. Suggest a reason why seawater is not a potent source of ozone-depleting chlorine atoms.

39. What environmental problem arises from the use of CFC substitutes?

40. How are free radicals related to the ozone layer?

41. Give the pollutants that are primarily responsible for tropospheric ozone increases and stratospheric ozone decreases, and distinguish why each of them causes the specified effect.

42. Give a medical condition that becomes more prevalent with a decreased ozone layer.

Acid Rain

43. What two acids are mainly responsible for acid rain?

44. Write the equations for the reaction of each acid in Problem 42 with marble.

45. Write the equation for the reaction of nitric acid (from acid rain) with iron to form iron(III) nitrate and a gaseous product.

46. Acid rain can be formed by the reaction of water with sulfur dioxide to form *sulfurous* acid. Write the equation for this reaction.

Indoor Air Pollution

47. Name an indoor air pollutant that is also an outdoor pollutant. What is the major source of that pollutant in each environment?

48. List three risks associated with secondhand cigarette smoke.

49. Explain why a house built over a crawl space is likely to have less of a radon problem than a house built on a concrete slab.

50. How does better insulation of buildings make indoor air pollution worse?

51. What is the physical state of radon, and why does its physical state make it especially hazardous?

52. What kind of particulate matter is often found inside homes?

Carbon Dioxide and Climate

53. What is the greenhouse effect?

54. Give the major greenhouse gases in the atmosphere.

55. How much does the exhaling of humans affect the carbon dioxide levels of the atmosphere? Think about the source of the carbon in the exhaled gas and how it was produced for human consumption.

56. If your neighbor asks how she can reduce her greenhouse gas emissions, what suggestions would you give to her?

57. By approximately what percent has the concentration of atmospheric carbon dioxide increased over the past 130 years?

58. What substance can contain carbon dioxide from the atmosphere for the longest period of time?

 # ADDITIONAL PROBLEMS

59. Why is zero pollution not possible?

60. The atmosphere contains about 5.2×10^{15} t of air. What mass in metric tons of carbon dioxide is in the atmosphere if the concentration of CO_2 is 402 ppm?

61. A person who exercises vigorously several hours a day might take in about 22 m^3 of air per day. What mass in milligrams of particulates would the person inhale in a day if the particulate level averages 312 $\mu g/m^3$?

62. A tree 33 m tall and 0.55 m in diameter at its base produces about 84,000 L of oxygen per year. How many trees are needed to provide oxygen to 1000 people breathing as described in question 61?

63. Water vapor is a greenhouse gas that is present in significant concentrations in the Earth's atmosphere. Water is also a product of the combustion of fossil fuels. Why is there little concern about increasing atmospheric water vapor and its contribution to global warming? There is a correlation with water temperature and water vapor concentration, so how does this change affect your analysis?

64. Evaluate the claim, "There are more molecules in one breath of air than there are breaths in Earth's entire atmosphere." Use the following information. The total mass of the atmosphere is about 5.2×10^{21} g. The average molecular mass of air is about 29 u. An average breath has a volume of about 0.50 L and a density of about 1.3 g/L.

65. Evaluate the claim, "The breath that you just took contains at least one molecule of air that was in the last breath of the Buddha, Siddhartha Gautama, who died about 400 B.C.E." See Problem 64 and assume complete mixing of Earth's atmosphere over 2400 years.

66. What is a criteria pollutant? Which of the pollutants in Table 13.3 come mainly from automobiles, and which come mostly from industry?

67. The reaction for formation of nitric acid is more complex than that shown in Figure 13.10. In the first step, three molecules of nitrogen dioxide react with a water molecule to form nitric acid and nitrogen oxide. In the second step, the nitrogen oxide is oxidized by atmospheric oxygen to nitrogen dioxide, and then the cycle continues. Write balanced equations representing these two steps.

68. Although carbon dioxide is the actual greenhouse gas, emissions from the burning of fossil fuels are often reported as gigatons (Gt) of carbon. In 2011, China emitted 2.7 Gt of carbon while the Unites States released 1.6 Gt of carbon. To what mass in gigatons of CO_2 do these amounts of carbon correspond?

69. Given the information in Problem 68 and an estimate of population, compare the tons of carbon dioxide released per person in China to that figure for the United States. Comment on this fact in terms of how you might approach U.S. citizens to convince them to reduce their emissions even though China's total emissions are greater than those of the United States.

70. Explain why a thermal inversion causes pollution problems.

71. The specific heat of a substance is the amount of heat required to raise the temperature of 1 g of the substance by 1 °C. The specific heat of air varies with temperature and humidity, but for ordinary calculations a value of 1.0 kJ/(kg K) (1.0 kJ/kg °C) is sufficient. The average temperature of Earth according to NASA figures is 15 °C, and the mass of Earth's atmosphere is 5.1×10^{18} kg. **(a)** How much heat, in kilojoules, is added to the atmosphere for a 1.0 °C increase in temperature? How does this value compare to **(b)** the total world annual energy consumption of about 5.0×10^{20} J? **(c)** a hurricane that releases about 2×10^{20} J?

72. Why is it necessary for solvents to be volatile in conventional separation processes? Why isn't it necessary when employing CO_2-switching technology?

73. List 3 disadvantages of volatile solvents. Do switchable-hydrophilicity solvents (SHS) also have these problems?

74. Which of the following components is not recycled and used in multiple extractions using SHS technology: water, amine solvent, or CO_2?

CRITICAL THINKING EXERCISES

Apply knowledge that you have gained in this chapter and one or more of the FLaReS principles (Chapter 1) to evaluate the following statements or claims.

13.1. A councilmember claims that the air pollution problem in the Los Angeles area could be solved by allowing only zero-emission vehicles to be sold and licensed there.

13.2. Ozone in aerosol cans was once used as a room deodorizer. An inventor proposes that such preparations be reintroduced because any ozone entering the environment would help to restore the protective ozone layer in the stratosphere.

13.3. Some people claim that aerosols will cool the planet, offsetting the enhanced greenhouse effect.

13.4. Some experts believe that global warming is mostly due to methane produced by such natural sources as plant decay in swamps and cattle flatulence. They say that industrial activities that produce carbon dioxide raise the standard of living and should be allowed to continue without interference because they are not the only sources of greenhouse gases.

13.5. An activist claims that if catalytic converters can remove 90% of pollutants from automobile exhaust, it would be easy to remove the other 10%.

13.6. A scientist claims that the increase in the atmosphere concentration of carbon dioxide from 0.02% to 0.04% is not important in terms of global warming. His reasoning is that water vapor makes up about 2–3% of the atmosphere and water vapor is only about one-tenth as effective as CO_2 as a greenhouse gas; thus, the 0.02% increase in CO_2 is equivalent to a trivial 0.2% increase in water vapor.

COLLABORATIVE GROUP PROJECTS

Prepare a PowerPoint, poster, or other presentation (as directed by your instructor) to share with the class.

1. What are the average and peak concentrations of each of the following in your community or in a nearby large city? How can you find out?
   a. carbon monoxide   **b.** ozone
   c. nitrogen oxides   **d.** sulfur dioxide
   e. particulate matter

2. The American Lung Association publishes a list of metropolitan areas with the worst ozone air pollution each year. Look up that list and others with other worst air problems. Find a list of areas with the best air quality.

3. The box on page 380 reports on air pollution in China. Prepare a similar short essay on India or another country as assigned by your instructor.

4. Using the Internet or reference books, compare the amount of sulfur dioxide produced by Mount Kilauea in Hawaii with that from all U.S. industry. (Remember to use the same time span for both.)

5. Write a brief essay comparing the atmospheres of Venus and Mars to Earth's atmosphere and explaining the differences.

6. Air quality standards are maximum allowable amounts of various pollutants. The federal government and some state governments issue these standards. Using the Internet, find the current standards from by the EPA. Does your state issue such standards? (*Hint*: Try the EPA site and your own state's environmental protection site.)

7. Divide your class into several teams, each taking a different view of global warming. Possible positions are (1) we must act now, (2) we need more study before we act, (3) there is no global warming, and (4) human activity is a minor contributor to global warming. Research your position, and be prepared to state your case with data to support your arguments. Hold a debate with the other groups in your class, paying close attention to the information presented by the other groups. Are their arguments persuasive? Are their sources reliable? Are yours?

8. Do a historical search for change in air quality environmental regulations over time. Have these standards become more or less strict since the passage of environmental laws in the 1970s? Discuss why you think these changes were made. Be on the lookout for changes in both directions depending on the pollutant and the time period.

CHEMISTRY@HOME   Let the Sun Shine

Materials required

- UV-sensitive color changing beads (40)
- 4 small plastic zipper bags
- Permanent marker
- Baking sheet or tray
- Spray sunscreens with three different SPFs: 4, 15, and 30 (or 50)

Have you ever wondered how well your sunscreen really works? And is there a difference between SPF 4 and 50? Does one really protect more than the other from harmful UV rays?

As we all hear news about the depletion of the ozone layer and the resulting increase of UV light reaching the Earth's surface, sunscreen is becoming increasingly important to protect against skin cancer. The highest rates of skin cancer have been recorded in Australia, where approximately 1,200 people die from skin cancer each year. Australia has higher UV levels than other parts of the world because it is very close to the ozone hole over the Antarctic. Australia also gets closer to the sun than other countries do in the summer.

Sunscreens are provided in different SPFs, or skin protection factor ratings. SPF 15 sunscreen provides 15 times longer protection than unprotected skin and blocks harmful UV rays. In this experiment, you will be using UV-sensitive color changing beads as indicators so that you can visually determine what SPF sunscreen is most effective at protecting your skin. The first part of the experiment is done indoors, away from open windows or areas with strong sunlight, while the second part of the experiment is performed outside in direct sunlight.

First, while indoors, place 12–15 UV sensitive beads in each of the 4 plastic bags and seal. (Hint: Use the same distribution of colors of beads in each bag for easy comparison.) Label one bag of beads as "control" and place on the tray.

Next, spray each bag of beads with your three different SPF sunscreens with one brief spray (1 to 2 seconds). As you spray, keep the nozzle at a distance of about 4–5 inches from the bag. Also try to keep the length of each spray the same for consistency between the sets of beads. Label each bag with the appropriate SPF value and place the bags on the tray. Allow the sunscreen to dry for about 5 minutes.

Finally, bring your samples outdoors into the sun and immediately observe any color changes. What do you notice about the colors of the different sets of beads? Leave the samples in the sun for only about 1 minute, and then bring them back indoors to look at the changes more closely. What do you notice when you bring the beads back indoors?

Questions

1. What trends did you see in your observations? What does this tell you about the different SPF values of sunscreens (if anything)?
2. What SPF sunscreen do you typically use? Do you think this protects you from harmful UV rays?
3. What do you think would happen if you were to rinse the sunscreen off the bags?

14

WATER

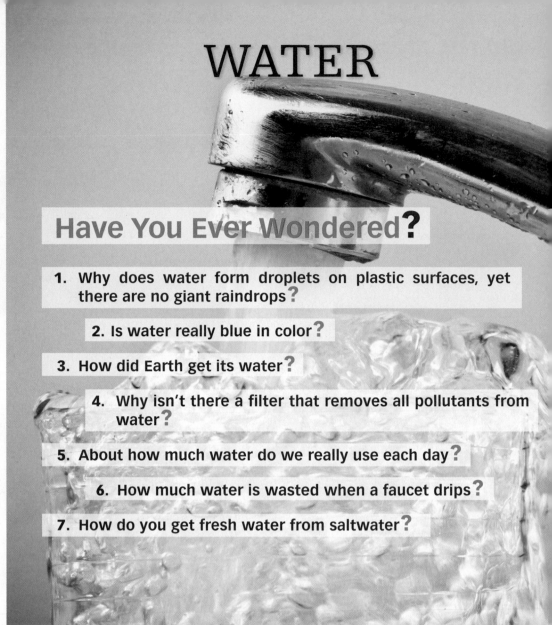

Learning Objectives

> Relate water's unique properties to polarity of the water molecule and to hydrogen bonding. (14.1)

> Explain how water on the surface of Earth acts to moderate daily temperature variations. (14.1)

> Explain why humans can only make use of less than 1% of all the water on Earth. (14.2)

> Explain the water cycle on Earth. (14.2)

> Describe how human activities affect water quality. (14.3)

> Give an example of a biological water contaminant. (14.3)

> List some groundwater contaminants. (14.4)

> Identify the sources of nitrates in groundwater. (14.4)

> List the major uses of water. (14.5)

> Describe how water is purified for drinking and other household uses. (14.6)

> Describe primary, secondary, and tertiary treatment of wastewater. (14.7)

> Connect the properties of chemicals to their fate in the environment.

> Describe how chemicals migrate between environmental compartments, including how chemicals' effects can magnify as they travel through food webs.

Have You Ever Wondered?

1. **Why does water form droplets on plastic surfaces, yet there are no giant raindrops?**

2. **Is water really blue in color?**

3. **How did Earth get its water?**

4. **Why isn't there a filter that removes all pollutants from water?**

5. **About how much water do we really use each day?**

6. **How much water is wasted when a faucet drips?**

7. **How do you get fresh water from saltwater?**

RIVERS OF LIFE, SEAS OF SORROWS
Earth is a water world. Most of its surface is covered with oceans and seas, lakes, and rivers. People contain a lot of water, too. About two-thirds of our body weight is water, and water makes up 60–90% of a typical cell. The water in our blood is much like ocean water, containing a variety of dissolved ions. You might even say that we are walking sacks of seawater.

The presence of large quantities of water makes our planet unique in the solar system, the only planet capable of supporting higher forms of life.

Water is the only substance on Earth that commonly exists in large amounts in all three physical states. Go outside on a snowy day and

Water is truly a unique substance. It is the most familiar substance that commonly exhibits all three physical states. The most common state, and the one that is most important to life, is the liquid state. Water is also known as the "universal solvent." This solvent power allows water to dissolve many of the substances plants and animals need for proper functioning. Unfortunately, the solvent power also makes water easy to contaminate and difficult to purify. In this chapter, we will look at the nature of water, its many uses, and the methods currently used for purifying water.

you are likely to experience all three forms at once. Gaseous water vapor is invisible (and is all around us), but tiny droplets of liquid water form clouds. Solid water falls to the ground as snow and melts into puddles of liquid water.

The early Greek philosopher Thales (ca. sixth century B.C.E)—whom some consider the first scientist—held water in the highest regard, believing that it was the "primordial substance" from which all other things were made. Little wonder that a man from a nation with many islands would think so. Water's unique nature makes it essential to life, and life as we know it is dependent on water.

The properties that make water able to support life also make it easy to pollute and therefore potentially hazardous. Water, with its polar molecules, is a good solvent. Many substances are easily dispersed throughout the environment because they are soluble in water. Once dissolved, it is not easy to remove substances from water. Furthermore, many strains of bacteria and other microorganisms that are harmful to humans thrive in water.

We start this chapter by discussing some of the unusual properties of water. Then we look at water pollution and water treatment. We should neither underestimate the importance of clean drinking water nor take it for granted. We could live for several weeks without food, but without water, we would last a few days at most.

14.1 Water: Some Unique Properties

Learning Objectives > Relate water's unique properties to polarity of the water molecule and to hydrogen bonding. > Explain how water on the surface of Earth acts to moderate daily temperature variations.

The bent geometry of a water molecule (recall Chapter 4) and the large difference in electronegativities between oxygen and hydrogen together result in water being highly polar. The central oxygen atom in water also has two sets of nonbonding (lone) electron pairs. These lone pairs, in combination with the positive and negative partial charges on the hydrogen and oxygen atoms, respectively, favor hydrogen bonding among water molecules (Chapter 6), giving water a number of unique properties.

High Density of Water

Think about the weight of a container filled with gasoline versus what it would be if it were filled with water. Also, envision a container filled with part water and part oil and think about oil floating on top of water during oil spills. A single water molecule can interact with four other water molecules through hydrogen bonding (utilizing two lone pairs and two hydrogen atoms), which allows water molecules to be held together more tightly than molecules of other substances in their pure liquid state. Since there are more molecules occupying a certain volume and the molecules of water are small in size, water is very dense. Further, the hyperdense hydrogen bonding network gives water another of its unique properties—liquid water is denser than its solid form. You have surely seen ice cubes (solid water) floating on top of liquid water and other water-based drinks!

As shown in Figure 14.1, when water freezes, each water molecule interacts with its four nearest neighbors solely through hydrogen bonding. This leads to an open and highly ordered tetrahedral structure of water molecules in ice.

(a)

(b)

▲ **Figure 14.1** Hydrogen bonds in ice. (a) Oxygen atoms are stacked in layers of distorted hexagonal rings. Hydrogen atoms lie between pairs of oxygen atoms, closer to one (covalent bond) than to the other. The yellow dashed lines indicate hydrogen bonds. The structure has large "holes." (b) The hexagonal arrangement of water molecules in the crystal structure of ice is revealed at the macroscopic level in the hexagonal shapes of snowflakes.

When ice melts, the hydrogen bonding network is perturbed and weakened, making water molecules more mobile. It also allows packing more water molecules per unit volume, giving rise to the higher density of liquid water versus that of ice.

The fact that ice is less dense than liquid water is essential to life on Earth. If the opposite were true, lakes and rivers in colder climates would completely freeze as ice sank until there was no more liquid water to freeze. If this were to happen, all life in the lakes and rivers would be eliminated. The same would be the case during the ice ages our planet has gone through. In short, if ice did not float, all life on this planet would have become extinct a long time ago, and humans would never have lived.

However, the same property of water can also be life threatening. The majority of cells in our bodies can be viewed as water-filled balloons (the balloon being the outer cell membrane). When water expands—by as much as 10% when it becomes frozen—the balloon or cell membrane may burst. Amorphous ice, which does not have these drawbacks, is currently at the center of a large amount of research, ranging from the frozen food industry to cryonics (the low-temperature preservation of humans for future medical treatment).

Solvation Ability of Water

The main reason for water being an extremely good solvent is, once again, its hydrogen bonding network. For instance, $NaCl$ readily dissolves in water; in fact, 1 L of water dissolves 359 g of $NaCl$, but 1 L of methanol only dissolves 14.9 g of $NaCl$. Why is this so? When $NaCl$ dissolves in water, each Cl^- ion interacts with four water molecules through the hydrogen atoms in these water molecules. (This interaction is, in fact, a very special case of hydrogen bonding and is only possible due to the full 1− charge of the chloride ion.) At the same time, oxygen atoms of four to five water molecules surround each Na^+ ion (using ion–dipole forces described in Section 6.4).

Also, the Cl^- and Na^+ ions fit well within the free spaces among water molecules. This means that dissolving $NaCl$ does not significantly disturb the hydrogen bonding network in water, and hence, little energy is required to solvate $NaCl$. Yet size does matter! KBr, consisting of the larger potassium and bromide ions, is somewhat less soluble (119 g/L) in water.

Water's ability to hydrogen-bond also explains why water is such a good solvent for organic molecules with functional groups capable of hydrogen bonding, such as alcohols, carboxylic acids, and amides (refer to Section 9.4). An example of this can be seen if we compare the solubility of benzene (no functional groups) with that of phenol (a single alcohol functional group on the benzene ring) which, in water, are 1.8 g/L and 83 g/L, respectively.

The Amphoteric Nature of Water

Water is amphoteric, meaning that it can act as both an acid and a base. Chemically, this can be expressed as follows:

$$H_2O + H_2O \rightleftharpoons H_3O^+ + OH^-$$

Due to the hydrogen bonding network in water, the H_3O^+ and OH^- move (diffuse) very rapidly as only the transfer of protons, either to or from water molecules, is required. For all other ions, such as Na^+ or Cl^-, which tend to be associated with a number of water molecules while in solution, diffusion in water means both breaking and reestablishing interactions with new water molecules. The unique rapid diffusion of H_3O^+ and OH^- ions in water is essential to the acid–base chemistry of water.

High Specific Heat Capacity of Water

Specific heat capacity is the quantity of heat required to raise the temperature of 1 g of a substance by 1 °C. Water's hyperdense hydrogen bonding network allows water to absorb and store a large amount of energy. Compared to other substances, water can absorb a relatively large amount of heat energy before its temperature

▲ Crude oil coats the surface in the Gulf of Mexico after the *Deepwater Horizon* oil rig sank following an explosion. The leak was a mile below the surface, making it difficult to estimate the size of the spill. One liter of oil can create a slick with an area of 2.5 hectares (6.3 acres). This and similar spills provide a reminder that hydrocarbons and water don't mix.

Table 14.1 **Specific Heat Capacities of Some Familiar Substances at 25 °C**

Substance	Specific Heat	
	(cal/g °C)	(J/g K)
Aluminum (Al)	0.216	0.902
Copper (Cu)	0.0920	0.385
Ethanol (CH_3CH_2OH)	0.588	2.46
Iron (Fe)	0.107	0.449
Ethylene glycol ($HOCH_2CH_2OH$)	0.561	2.35
Magnesium (Mg)	0.245	1.025
Mercury (Hg)	0.0332	0.139
Lead (Pb)	0.0306	0.128
Silver (Ag)	0.0562	0.235
Sulfur (S)	0.169	0.706
Water (liquid)	1.00[a]	4.184

[a]Note that in cal/g °C, the specific heat capacity of water is 1.00. As the metric system was established, the properties of liquid water were often taken as the standard.

increases by 1 °C. Conversely, water must release a relatively large amount of heat energy before its temperature drops by 1 °C. Table 14.1 gives the specific heat capacities of several familiar substances in the old units—calories per gram per degree (cal/g °C)—and in the SI units—joules per gram per kelvin (J/g K).

The definition of a calorie dictates that the specific heat capacity of water is 1.00 cal/(g °C), while in SI units, it is 4.184 J/(g K). Note that metals have much lower values of the specific heat capacity than does water. It takes almost ten times as much heat to raise the temperature of 1 g of water by 1 °C as to raise the temperature of 1 g of iron by the same amount. Imagine heating two iron kettles on the stove, one empty and one filled with water. It takes much longer (and much more energy) to heat the water-filled kettle. Because water stores heat so well, the water-filled kettle will stay hot a lot longer than the empty kettle when the stove is turned off. The vast amounts of water on the surface of Earth thus act as a giant heat reservoir to moderate daily temperature variations. The extreme temperature changes on the surface of the waterless moon, ranging from 100 °C at noon to −173 °C at night, dramatically illustrate this important property of water.

We can use the following equation, in which ΔT is the change in temperature (in either °C or kelvins), to calculate the quantity of heat absorbed or released by a system.

$$\text{Heat absorbed or released} = \text{mass} \times \text{specific heat capacity} \times \Delta T$$

Example 14.1 Heat Absorbed

How much heat, in calories, kilocalories, and kilojoules, does it take to raise the temperature of 225 g of water from 25.0 °C to 100.0 °C?

SOLUTION

Let's list the quantities we need for the calculations.
Specific heat capacity of water = 1.00 cal/(g °C)
Then we use the equation

$$\text{Heat absorbed} = \text{mass} \times \text{specific heat capacity} \times \Delta T$$

$$= 225\,\text{g} \times 1.00\,\text{cal}/(\text{g °C}) \times 75.0\,\text{°C}$$

$$= 16{,}900\,\text{cal}$$

We can then convert the unit cal to the units kcal and kJ.

$$16{,}900\,\text{cal} \times \frac{1\,\text{kcal}}{1000\,\text{cal}} = 16.9\,\text{kcal}$$

1. Why does water form droplets on plastic surfaces, yet there are no giant raindrops?

Plastic surfaces are hydrophobic (water hating). Water tends to minimize its interactions with the plastic surface and maximize its interactions within itself by exploiting the hydrogen bonding to the maximum. Water molecules at the surface are unable to fully engage in hydrogen bonding with other water molecules and their number is, therefore, minimized. The geometric shape with the lowest surface-to-volume ratio is a sphere. So, why don't we see raindrops the size of a beach ball? Enter gravity. Gravity overcomes the strength of the hydrogen bonding network in a water droplet, which breaks into smaller, though still spherical, droplets.

2. Is water really blue in color?

The simple answer is yes, and it is yet another unusual property of water. Why blue? As in other substances, molecules in water constantly vibrate, with the vibrational overtone of water being just in the visible rather than infrared part of the electromagnetic spectrum. This means that water slightly absorbs red light and, in turn, appears pale blue. This is the same reason why the deeper one digs into snow, the bluer the snow appears.

$$16.9 \text{ kcal} \times \frac{4.184 \text{ kJ}}{1 \text{ kcal}} = 70.7 \text{ kJ}$$

▪ **EXERCISE 14.1A**

How much heat, in calories, kilocalories, and kilojoules, is released by 975 g of water as it cools from 100.0 °C to 18.0 °C?

▪ **EXERCISE 14.1B**

Using information from Table 14.1, identify the substance if 148 J of heat energy are needed to heat 32.0 g of it by 12 K.

High Heat of Vaporization of Water

Heat of vaporization is the amount of heat required to evaporate a substance. A large amount of heat needed to evaporate even a small amount of water goes toward breaking all of the existing intermolecular forces, among which hydrogen bonding is the strongest. This fact is of enormous importance to us because large amounts of body heat can be dissipated by the evaporation of small amounts of water (perspiration) from the skin.

The high heat of vaporization of water (40.8 kJ/mol) also accounts in part for the climate-modifying property of lakes and oceans. A large portion of the heat that would otherwise raise the temperature of the air and land instead vaporizes water from the surface of lakes or seas. Thus, in summer, it is cooler near a large body of water than in interior land areas.

All these fascinating properties of water depend on the unique structure of the highly polar water molecule and its unique hyperdense hydrogen bonding network.

SELF-ASSESSMENT Questions

1. Which of the following is *not* a unique property of water?
   a. solid water floats on liquid water
   b. water can act as both a base and an acid
   c. water has three states (phases): solid, liquid, and gas
   d. water has a hyperdense hydrogen bonding network

2. In ice and water, each water molecule forms hydrogen bonds with how many water molecules?
   a. one   b. three   c. four   d. five

3. Water's unique properties arise because water molecules
   a. have hydrogen atoms that do not have a stable electron configuration
   b. associate through hydrogen bonds
   c. can form covalent bonds with ionic substances
   d. can form covalent bonds with nonpolar substances

4. In a collection of water molecules, hydrogen bonds form between
   a. an H atom in one H_2O molecule and the O atom in another H_2O molecule
   b. the O atoms in different H_2O molecules
   c. the two H atoms in a single H_2O molecule
   d. two H atoms in different H_2O molecules

5. Frozen water has an open structure with
   a. an amorphous molecular arrangement
   b. large hexagonal holes
   c. molecules that are in constant motion
   d. molecules that tend to repel each other

6. How much heat (in cal) is required to raise the temperature of 50.0 g of water from 20.0 °C to 50.0 °C?
   a. 30.0 cal   b. 50.0 cal   c. 1500 cal   d. 2500 cal

7. How much heat (in kJ) is required to raise the temperature of 131 g of iron from 15.0 °C to 95.0 °C?
   a. 0.058 kJ   b. 1.11 kJ   c. 4.71 kJ   d. 4710 kJ

Answers: 1. c; 2. c; 3. b; 4. a; 5. b; 6. c; 7. c

14.2 Water in Nature

Learning Objectives ❯ Explain why humans can only make use of less than 1% of all the water on Earth. ❯ Explain the water cycle on Earth.

Three-fourths of the surface of Earth is covered with water, but nearly 98% of it is salty seawater—unfit for drinking and not suitable for most industrial purposes. Much of the fresh water is frozen in ice caps, leaving less than 1% of all Earth's

▲ **Figure 14.2** Where is Earth's water?

water available for human use. Of that, most is underground. Lakes and streams account for only 0.01% of the fresh water on the planet. While rain falls onto the Earth in enormous amounts, most of it falls into the sea or on inaccessible land areas. A more detailed breakdown of the water distribution on planet Earth is presented in Figure 14.2.

If you consider how important fresh water is to you and how little of it there is, you must think of using water sustainably, especially given the ever-increasing human population. In fact, a large part of our planet already suffers from water scarcity. About 875 million people do not have access to adequate quantities of fresh water, and 2.7 billion people live without basic sanitation. About 3.6 million people—most of whom are children—die each year because they drink water contaminated with bacteria, viruses, or parasites. According to the Pacific Institute in Oakland, California, more than 76 million people will die from water-related diseases by 2020 unless major prevention efforts are undertaken. Water resources around the globe are threatened by pollution, misuse, and climate change. Some believe that water shortage will be the norm in the future, resulting in regional conflicts. It ranks as #1 (second only to climate change) in terms of overall threat to humans on planet Earth.

In the United States several cities risk running short of fresh water: Los Angeles and the San Francisco Bay Area in California; Houston, San Antonio, and Fort Worth in Texas; Phoenix and Tucson in Arizona; Las Vegas, Nevada; Atlanta, Georgia; and Orlando, Florida.

The Water Cycle and Natural Contaminants

Water is constantly cycled on planet Earth through its evaporation (powered by the sun), precipitation, and flow (due to gravity). As a whole, the planet's water cycle is at a steady state (Figure 14.3), meaning that the percentages of water apportioned to the oceans, the ice caps, and the freshwater rivers, lakes, and streams remain fairly constant. Water constantly evaporates from both water and land surfaces, and water vapor condenses into clouds and returns to Earth as rain, sleet, and snow. This fresh water becomes part of the ice caps, runs off in streams and rivers, and fills both lakes and underground pools of water in rocks and sand called *aquifers*.

Gases

Atmospheric CO_2 dissolves and subsequently reacts with water to form carbonic acid (H_2CO_3):

$$CO_2(g) + H_2O(l) \longrightarrow H_2CO_3(aq)$$

3. How did Earth get its water?

Scientists have put forth several hypotheses, but none have yet been fully accepted. One idea, long favored by many, was that water was carried to Earth by comets, many of which are little more than balls of ice. This hypothesis was recently disproved by isotope signatures (Section 11.3). Comet water has a deuterium-to-protium ratio ($^2H/^1H$) twice that of Earth's waters.

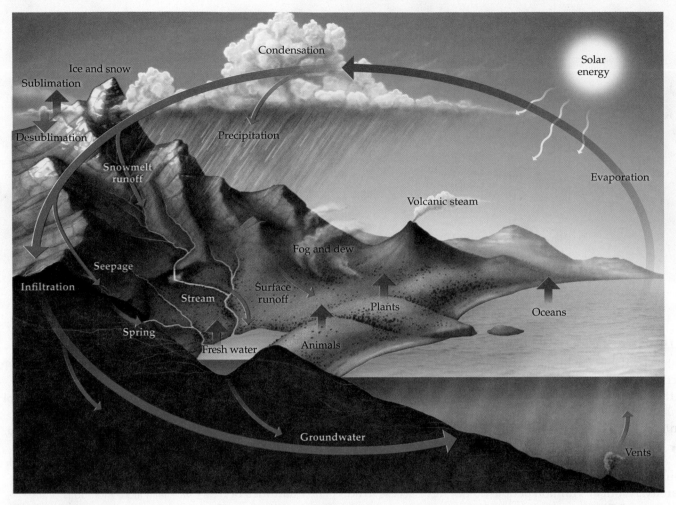

▲ **Figure 14.3** The water (hydrologic) cycle. Powered by the sun, evaporation of water from oceans, lakes, and land occurs. As moist air rises, it cools, and the water vapor condenses to form clouds. Water returns to the surface as precipitation. Some of this water becomes groundwater and recharges aquifers. Some of it enters rivers and streams and is carried back to the oceans. Evapotranspiration is water discharged to the atmosphere from soils and transpiration by plants.

This chemistry would yield "pristine" rainwater with a pH of ~5.65. Lightning can also make rainwater acidic by causing nitrogen, oxygen, and water vapor to combine into nitric acid. Further, there can be a number of other constituents within rainwater. In fact, rainwater is far from being pure due to both natural processes and human activities. Human inputs have led to acid rain (as well as acid fog, smog, and snow). Rainwater in a polluted atmosphere typically contains acids (HCl, HNO_3, H_2SO_4), bases (NH_3, $CaCO_3$, and $MgCO_3$), and dust ($CaSO_4$, SiO_2, Al-silicates, $NaCl$, and KCl), resulting in pH of around 4.3. Acid rain has caused the destruction of a large number of statues and other architectural treasures around the world. It has corroded metals and even ruined the finishes on automobiles. In extreme cases, acid rain has even led to death, as was the case with the Great Smog of 1952 in London, generated by inefficient combustion engines.

Groundwater also contains the naturally occurring gas radon (Section 13.7), but thanks to its very low concentrations, the emission of damaging radiation is not a concern.

Dissolved Minerals

As stated above, water is a wonderful solvent. It moves along or beneath the surface of Earth, dissolving minerals from rocks and soils, as demonstrated by the formation of the Grand Canyon. Recall that minerals (salts) are ionic and that ions are either positively charged (cations) or negatively charged (anions). Table 14.2 lists the substances typically found in natural waters. The main cations in natural water,

Table 14.2　**Some Substances Found in Natural Waters**

Substance	Formula	Source
Carbon dioxide	CO_2	Atmosphere
Dust	—	Atmosphere
Nitrogen	N_2	Atmosphere
Oxygen	O_2	Atmosphere
Nitric acid	HNO_3	Atmosphere (thunderstorms)
Sand and soil particles	—	Soil and rocks
Sodium ions	Na^+	Soil and rocks
Potassium ions	K^+	Soil, rocks, and fertilizer
Calcium ions	Ca^{2+}	Limestone rocks
Magnesium ions	Mg^{2+}	Dolomite rocks
Iron(II) ions	Fe^{2+}	Soil and rocks
Chloride ions	Cl^-	Soil, rocks, and fertilizer
Sulfate ions	SO_4^{2-}	Soil, rocks, and fertilizer
Bicarbonate ions	HCO_3^-	Soil and rocks
Radon	Rn	Radioactive decay

shown in red in Table 14.2, are ions of sodium, potassium, calcium, magnesium, and sometimes iron (as Fe^{2+} or Fe^{3+}). The anions (shown in blue) are usually sulfate, bicarbonate, and chloride ions.

Water for domestic use is usually classified as either soft (containing mostly Na^+ and K^+) or hard (containing high concentrations of Ca^{2+}, Mg^{2+}, and $Fe^{2+/3+}$ ions). When soap is added to hard water, it forms a white solid (soap scum, which causes bathroom fixtures to look dingy; see Chapter 21) due to formation of calcium stearate:

$$2\ C_{17}H_{35}COO^-(aq)\ +\ Ca^{2+}(aq) \longrightarrow Ca(C_{17}H_{35}COO)_2(s)$$

As Figure 14.3 shows, the water cycle replenishes our supply of fresh water. When water evaporates from the sea, salts are left behind. When water moves through the ground, impurities are filtered out and trapped in the rock, gravel, sand, and clay. This capacity to purify is not infinite. Yet, globally, the water cycle cleans and purifies over 16 million liters of water a second, and it does so for free!

Organic Matter

Rainwater dissolves matter from decaying plants and animals. As part of the natural cycle in a forest, small quantities of this organic matter enrich the soil. As you will see in the next section, not all organic inputs are good for the environment. Lubricants, fuels, some fertilizers, and pesticides, all contaminate water. Bacteria, other microorganisms, and animal wastes are all potential water contaminants.

SELF-ASSESSMENT Questions

1. Energy to power the water cycle comes from
   a. electric power plants
   b. hurricanes
   c. the sun
   d. thunderstorms

2. Most of the Earth's water is in
   a. groundwater
   b. ice and permafrost
   c. lakes and rivers
   d. oceans

3. Rainwater is naturally acidic because water reacts with
   a. CO_2　　b. N_2　　c. O_2　　d. SO_2

4. Which of the following is not commonly found in rainwater?
   a. HNO_3
   b. SiO_2
   c. H_2CO_3
   d. Rn (radon)

5. The main cations in water are
   a. Na^+, Al^{3+}, Ca^{2+}, and Mg^{2+}
   b. Na^+, K^+, Ca^{2+}, and Li^+
   c. Na^+, K^+, Ca^{2+}, and Mg^{2+}
   d. Ra^{2+}, Sr^{2+}, Ca^{2+}, and Mg^{2+}

6. Hard water may be characterized by the presence of all of the following ions *except*
   a. Ca^{2+}　　b. Fe^{2+}　　c. K^+　　d. Mg^{2+}

4. Why isn't there a filter that removes all pollutants from water?
Some water pollutants are present at extremely low levels, and the removal techniques available to us just aren't efficient enough to remove those pollutants. Also, water's polarity gives it a very strong attraction for many pollutants.

▲ The eutrophication of a lake is a natural process, but the process can be greatly accelerated by human wastes, phosphates from detergents, and the runoff of fertilizers from farms, lawns, and golf courses.

▲ *Cryptosporidium*, shown here in a fluorescent image, sickened 400,000 people and killed about 100 in the Milwaukee area in 1993. Since then, water utilities have generally improved their treatment systems.

14.3 Chemical and Biological Contamination

Learning Objectives ❯ Describe how human activities affect water quality. ❯ Give an example of a biological water contaminant.

Humans, especially in large metropolitan areas, produce much organic waste, which must be disposed of. Historically, the most logical manner of disposal was to apply it to land or release it into the nearest body of water. These forms of disposal led to environmentally damaging effects, some deadly.

Too Much Organic Matter Means Too Little Oxygen

Organic matter from human and farm-animal waste is still very rich in nutrients. When this organic matter is introduced into the environment, a number of micro-organisms, including bacteria, break it down further, as they themselves grow, multiply, and increase the biomass. If oxygen is required for this breakdown, it is called *aerobic* (as opposed to *anaerobic*). When this process takes place in a body of water, **dissolved oxygen (DO)** is being depleted. A measure of the amount of oxygen needed for the degradation to occur is the **biochemical oxygen demand (BOD)**. If too much organic matter is present, too much oxygen will be removed from the water. When this happens, there is not enough oxygen in the water for the more advanced organisms, such as fish, potentially causing death by suffocation.

Streams and rivers can regenerate themselves by reintroducing oxygen from the atmosphere. Those with rapids soon come alive again as the swirling water helps with this process. Lakes with little or no flow can remain dead for years. Small human-made ponds may be oxygenated by percolating air through them using special pumping equipment.

Human or animal waste also introduces nitrates and phosphates to water, which may serve as nutrients for the growth of algae. When this extra biomass dies and becomes organic matter itself, the cycle resumes, amplified by the biomass added due to the newly incorporated CO_2, further increasing the BOD. This process is called **eutrophication**. The eutrophication of a lake is a natural process, but the action can be greatly accelerated by human waste, phosphates from detergents, and the runoff of fertilizers from farms and lawns, all of which stimulate algal bloom and die-off. Streams and lakes die because nature cannot purify them nearly as quickly as we can pollute them. A high-profile example of the ecological consequences of eutrophication and the contributions of fertilizers and other agricultural activities is the **dead zone** in the northern Gulf of Mexico.

When too much organic matter—whether from sewage, dying algae, or other sources—depletes the dissolved oxygen in a body of water, **anaerobic decay** processes take over. Instead of oxidizing the organic matter, anaerobic bacteria reduce it. Methane (CH_4) is formed. Sulfur is converted to hydrogen sulfide (H_2S) and other foul-smelling organic compounds. Nitrogen is reduced to ammonia and odorous amines (Section 9.8). The foul odors are a good indication that the water is overloaded with organic wastes. Only anaerobic microorganisms can survive in such water.

Chemical Pollution from Waste

Discharge of human and animal waste into the environment raises several concerns. The first of these issues is the release of hormonally active and endocrine-disrupting chemicals. These chemicals interfere with the delicate balance of hormones in most mammals, birds, and fish. Endocrine disruption can result in birth defects and damage to the reproductive cycle of the affected individual or its offspring. One of the most efficient ways of inducing extinction is to make sure that the species cannot breed, which is precisely what the hormonally active and endocrine-disrupting chemicals can do.

A second concern stems from antibiotics introduced to the environment in human and animal waste. Antibiotics have been overprescribed to humans, especially in a number of developed nations. Also, antibiotics have been overused in farming to prevent livestock illnesses. A large amount of antibiotics taken by humans and livestock passes through and enters the environment unmodified. The constant exposure to the antibiotics has an unintended and serious drawback. Many harmful organisms are now known to have developed resistance to the antibiotics that were designed to fight diseases caused by them. This happens because a small fraction of organisms that are not killed by an antibiotic mutate into stronger individuals, which multiply into new generations of drug-resistant *super bugs*.

Our waters have been tainted by a number of other chemical pollutants. The production of crops (and golf-course greens) has resulted in the release of large quantities of pesticides and fertilizers into waterways. Industries, such as tanneries, wood treatment plants, pharmaceutical manufacturing, petrochemical plants, and transportation, have also introduced a long list of chemical pollutants into the environment. Household chemicals and cosmetics also contribute to water pollution. Overall, our consumer society has polluted natural waters with pesticides, radioisotopes, detergents, drugs, toxic metals, and industrial chemicals.

Waterborne Diseases

Contamination of water supplies by *pathogenic* (disease-causing) microorganisms from human wastes was a severe problem throughout the world until about 100 years ago. In 1900, for example, there were more than 35,000 deaths from typhoid in the United States. Waterborne diseases are still quite common in much of the developing world. At any given time, about half the world's hospital beds are occupied by people who have waterborne diseases.

Today, as a result of chemical treatment, municipal water supplies in developed nations are generally safe. Municipal water utilities are constantly improving their treatment systems to deal with biological contamination. However, millions of people in the United States are still at risk because of bacterial contamination of drinking water. Ongoing threats include *Cryptosporidium* and *Giardia*, protozoans excreted in human and animal feces that resist standard chemical disinfection. Biological contamination also lessens the recreational value of water when it makes swimming, fishing, and other recreational activities hazardous.

▲ Contaminated beaches are closed to swimming and other recreational activities.

Acidic Waters

Despite the reduction of SO_x emissions (Section 13.6) in recent years, and the subsequent decrease of the severity and frequency of acid rain, thousands of bodies of water in eastern North America remain acidified. Acids often flow into these water bodies from abandoned mines.

Acidic water is neutralized when limestone, $CaCO_3$, is present:

$$\underset{\text{Limestone}}{CaCO_3(s)} + 2\,\underset{\text{Acid}}{H^+(aq)} \longrightarrow Ca^{2+}(aq) + CO_2(g) + H_2O(l)$$

Without the abundance of limestone—as is the case where rock is mainly granite—the acidic water is detrimental to aquatic life by causing the release of aluminum from the aluminum-silicate minerals (Chapter 12). Even at very low concentrations, aluminum ions are deadly to juvenile fish. Ironically, lakes destroyed by excess acidity are often quite beautiful—clear and sparkling due to lack of life.

Acidic waters have also been linked to declining crop yields and the destruction of forests and their inhabitants. In fact, acid rain has been linked to lower maple syrup production. Not a sweet situation.

▲ Acidic water draining from an old mine.

SELF-ASSESSMENT Questions

1. It is estimated that half of the world's hospital beds are occupied by people with waterborne diseases. The main causes of these are
   a. microorganisms
   b. DDT and dioxins
   c. lead and mercury
   d. pesticides

2. Water in a lake made acidic by acid rain or mine drainage is often
   a. clear
   b. eutrophic
   c. rich in game fish
   d. rich in lime

3. The biochemical oxygen demand (BOD) of a water sample indicates the
   a. dissolved oxygen level
   b. organic matter level
   c. pH level
   d. salt levels (salinity)

4. How are dissolved oxygen and BOD related?
   a. BOD has no impact on dissolved oxygen.
   b. High BOD means a high level of dissolved oxygen.
   c. High BOD reduces dissolved oxygen as the organic matter decays.
   d. Low BOD means a low level of dissolved oxygen.

5. Anaerobic reduction produces
   a. CO_2, H_2O, and inorganic ions
   b. CO, NH_3, and H_2O
   c. CH_4, NH_3, and H_2S
   d. sewage sludge

6. Excess nitrates or phosphates in a lake or river cause
   a. aerobic decay
   b. eutrophication
   c. an increase in game fish
   d. nitrogen fixation

7. Which of the following is released into water by human and animal waste?
   a. fertilizers
   b. pesticides
   c. detergents
   d. antibiotics

8. Lakes situated in areas rich in limestone do not suffer from excessive acidity because limestone
   a. neutralizes acids
   b. prevents acid rain from falling
   c. serves as food for fish
   d. causes nitrogen fixation

9. Which of the following is most likely a source of safe drinking water?
   a. filtered pond water
   b. a municipal water supply
   c. a mountain lake
   d. a wilderness stream

Answers: 1, a; 2, a; 3, b; 4, c; 5, c; 6, b; 7, d; 8, a; 9, b

14.4 Groundwater Contamination ⟶ Tainted Tap Water

Learning Objectives ❯ List some groundwater contaminants. ❯ Identify the sources of nitrates in groundwater.

Surface water in the United States supplies about half the drinking water, and the other half is supplied by groundwater. In rural areas in particular, 97% of people drink groundwater.

Due to differences in the physical nature of various rocks, water does not move within all rock in the same way. An aquifer forms when water-bearing rock readily transmits water to wells and springs. Wells are drilled into an aquifer, and water is pumped out. Precipitation recharges the aquifer. In many instances, water is being pumped out of the aquifer much faster than it can be recharged, causing the water table to drop. In such areas, deeper and deeper wells have to be drilled. Clearly, this situation is not sustainable. Using an already depleted aquifer to irrigate crops today will cause crop losses tomorrow. Consequently, both thirst and hunger will become major concerns if the current practices continue.

In addition to withdrawing groundwater faster than it can be recharged, human activity is also actively polluting it. For example:

- Many wells throughout the United States are contaminated with the gasoline additive methyl *tert*-butyl ether (MTBE) (Section 15.6), making the water undrinkable by imparting an offensive taste and odor.
- Wells around the Rocky Mountain Arsenal, near Denver, are contaminated by wastes from the production of pesticides.
- Wells in many areas are contaminated with perfluorooctanoic acid [PFOA, $CF_3(CF_2)_6COOH$] and related compounds. PFOA is an industrial surfactant used for processing polytetrafluoroethylene (PTFE). These compounds persist in the environment where they accumulate in living organisms.
- Some community water supplies in New Jersey have been shut down because of contamination by industrial wastes.

Let's now examine a few other common forms of groundwater pollution.

▲ Half of Chinese cities have significantly polluted groundwater, and some cities are facing a water crisis. More than 400 Chinese cities are threatened with water shortages, with 136 of them experiencing severe shortages. Here, a water company worker takes a sample from the Songhua River in Songyuan in Jilin Province.

Nitrates

In many agricultural areas, well water is contaminated with nitrate ions (NO_3^-). Nitrates in the groundwater (Figure 14.4) come from fertilizers used on farms and lawns, from the decomposition of organic wastes during sewage treatment, and from runoff from animal feedlots. Nitrate-containing substances are highly soluble, making them difficult and expensive to remove from water. One consequence of nitrate ion contamination is *methemoglobinemia*, or blue baby syndrome. In an infant's delicate digestive tract, nitrate ions are reduced to nitrite ions. If not treated, methemoglobinemia can be fatal. This is a serious issue, and in such farming areas as California's Imperial Valley, parents sometimes have to buy bottled water for their babies.

Volatile Organic Chemicals

In addition to being air pollutants (Section 13.4), VOCs are also water pollutants. They add undesirable odor to water, and many are suspected carcinogens. VOCs are used as solvents, cleaners, and fuels, and they are components of gasoline, spot removers, oil-based paints, inks, thinners, and some drain cleaners. Common VOCs are hydrocarbon solvents such as benzene (C_6H_6) and toluene (C_6H_5—CH_3), chlorinated hydrocarbons, such as trichloroethylene (CCl_2=$CHCl$), widely used in the past as a dry-cleaning solvent and a degreasing compound, as well as carbon tetrachloride (CCl_4), chloroform ($CHCl_3$), and methylene chloride (CH_2Cl_2).

When spilled or discarded, VOCs enter the soil and, eventually, the groundwater. One well-documented case is the Love Canal site in Niagara Falls, New York, where people built schools and houses on or near old dump sites. (See Collaborative Group Project 8.) A more recent environmental and health concern in regards to VOCs comes from **induced hydraulic fracturing (fracking)** techniques used to extract fossil fuels, such as shale gas. VOCs are generally only slightly soluble in water, with solubilities in the parts-per-million or parts-per-billion range. These trace amounts are found in groundwater. Many VOCs degrade so slowly that they are likely to be around for a long time.

It DOES Matter!

Homes and a school were built on the site of an old chemical dump in the Love Canal section of Niagara Falls, New York. A contaminated area around the old dump was fenced off to keep people out. Over 250 different industrial contaminants were found on the site. Cleanup was completed in the 1990s, and the evacuated neighborhood was repopulated and renamed Black Creek Village.

Probability of Nitrate Contamination of Shallow Groundwater

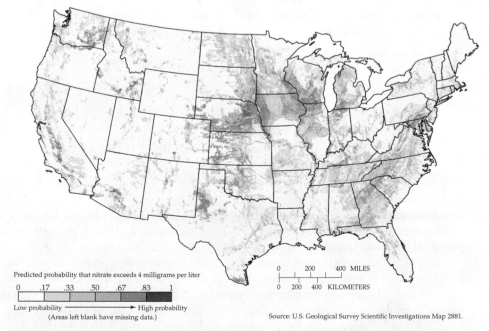

Predicted probability that nitrate exceeds 4 milligrams per liter

| 0 | .17 | .33 | .50 | .67 | .83 | 1 |

Low probability ⟶ High probability
(Areas left blank have missing data.)

0   200   400   MILES
0   200   400   KILOMETERS

Source: U.S. Geological Survey Scientific Investigations Map 2881.

▲ **Figure 14.4** Areas of the contiguous United States where groundwater is likely to be contaminated by nitrates.

Q: *Why do you think that eastern Nebraska and western Iowa have high probabilities of nitrate contamination? Is your water supply threatened?*

Leaking Storage Tanks

A major source of groundwater contamination is underground storage tanks (USTs), such as those at gas stations, that contain petroleum or hazardous chemicals. These buried steel tanks last an average of about 15 years before they rust through and begin to leak. In the 1980s, the EPA estimated that there were about 2.5 million such tanks. About 500,000 leaks from USTs have been detected, and 80% of those have been cleaned up. About 1,750,000 of all known tank sites have been cleaned up, and the frequency and severity of leaks from USTs have been reduced greatly. However, as of 2010, there were still 600,000 sites that had not been cleaned up.

Aboveground storage tanks are not immune to leakage either. In January 2014, 28,000 L of crude 4-methylcyclohexanemethanol (MCHM) leaked from a small hole in a tank capable of storing 150,000 L of the chemical. In spite of the existence of a containment area, the spill reached the groundwater and eventually contaminated the Elk River, which supplies water to the city of Charleston, West Virginia, and the surrounding areas. The "do-not-use" advisory for drinking water affected about 300,000 residents for several days. The long-term effects of the Elk River spill may not be known for some time.

Groundwater contamination is particularly alarming because, once contaminated, an underground aquifer may remain unusable for decades or longer. There is no easy way to remove the contaminants. Pumping out the water and purifying it could take years and cost billions of dollars.

SELF-ASSESSMENT Questions

1. Which ion, from fertilizer runoff and wastewater discharges, can lead to methemoglobinemia in young children?
   a. Ca^{2+} **b.** K^+ **c.** NO_3^- **d.** PO_4^{3-}

2. Which of the following relationships between the withdrawal from and recharge of an aquifer is of concern?
   a. withdrawal $>$ recharge   **b.** withdrawal $<$ recharge   **c.** withdrawal $=$ recharge

3. "V" in VOC stands for
   a. volcano   **b.** volatile   **c.** venomous   **d.** virulent

4. Which of the following is a VOC that contaminates groundwater?
   a. acetaldehyde from polluted air   **b.** acetic acid from fermenting fruit
   c. PAN from polluted air   **d.** toluene, a gasoline component

5. What is a possible source of VOCs?
   a. concrete   **b.** fracking liquid   **c.** glass bottles   **d.** rust

Answers: 1, c; 2, a; 3, b; 4, d; 5, b

14.5 Water: Who Uses It and How Much?

Learning Objective   ❯ List the major uses of water.

The total *direct* daily use of water is about 400 L per person in the United States. While only about 2 L are needed for drinking, such activities as cooking food, personal hygiene, laundry, and car washing consume the rest.

A typical automobile takes several hundred kilograms of steel to produce. To make a metric ton (t) of steel requires about 100 t of water. About 4 t of water are lost through evaporation. The remainder is contaminated with acids, grease and oil, lime, and iron salts. Given the environmental and economic costs of producing elastomers for tires, fabrics for upholstery, glass for windows, and so on, it is easy to see that the private automobile is an ecological problem even before it hits the road. It takes 800 L of water to produce 1 kg of vegetables and 13,000 L of water to produce a steak. We also use water for recreation (for example, swimming, boating, and fishing). For most of these purposes, we need water that is free of bacteria, viruses, and parasitic organisms.

It DOES Matter!

Traditional paper production from virgin wood fibers uses enormous quantities of water. Worldwide water use for producing paper is about 315 billion kg each year, or about 100 lb of water for a single ream of paper. Wood is about half cellulose, but the cellulose fibers are held together by lignin, a resinous material that must be removed to make paper. According to the EPA, recycling can reduce water use in paper production by nearly 60% and energy consumption by 40%. The EPA also says that recycling causes 35% less water pollution and 74% less air pollution. An even more effective measure is to reduce paper use: Print only what you must!

Most other industries and activities also contribute to water pollution. About 70% of the world's freshwater supply is used in agriculture, almost all of it for irrigation.

Table 14.3 lists the quantities of water required for the production of a variety of industrial and consumer products. Much of this water is cleaned up and recycled, but the need for clean water is still enormous. Industries in the United States have substantially reduced their contribution to water pollution. Most are in compliance with the Water Pollution Control Act, which requires that they use the best practicable technology.

Table 14.3 **Typical Quantities of Water Required[a] to Produce Various Materials**

Industrial Products	Water Required[b] (t)	Consumer Products	Water Required (L)
Steel	100	Laptop computer	10,600
Paper	20	1 hamburger	2400
Copper	400	1 bowl rice	525
Rayon	800	1 kg bananas	860
Aluminum	1280	1 cup coffee	140
Synthetic rubber	2400	1 pair blue jeans	11,000

[a]Includes irrigation water, rainwater, water consumed directly, and water used in processing, cleaning, and waste disposal.

[b]Per metric ton of product.

Significantly, more water is used *indirectly* in agriculture and industry (Table 14.4) to produce food and other materials.

Table 14.4 **Use of Water in the United States**

Use	Percentage of Total Usage
Coolant for electric power plants	48
Irrigation	34
Public water supplies	11
Industrial	5
Miscellaneous[a]	2

[a]Includes mining, livestock, aquaculture, and other uses.

SELF-ASSESSMENT Questions

1. The human activity that uses the most water is
   a. energy production   b. manufacturing electronics
   c. making elastomers   d. producing paper

2. Most of the water used by the steel industry is
   a. discharged untreated
   b. lost through evaporation
   c. recycled
   d. included in the final product

3. Most of the water used in agriculture is used for
   a. cooling   b. irrigation
   c. drinking   d. clean up

4. How much water does each person in the United States use each day (for all direct uses)?
   a. 70 L   b. 100 L   c. 200 L   d. 400 L

Answers: 1, a; 2, c; 3, b; 4, d

5. About how much water do we really use each day?

The direct average daily water use per person in the United States is about 400 L, of which about 7 L is used for drinking and cooking, with the remainder being used for personal hygiene, laundry, flushing toilets, washing dishes and cars, and other tasks. However, Table 14.4 shows that the indirect use of water is even more significant, most of it going toward energy production and agriculture.

14.6 Making Water Fit to Drink

Learning Objective ❯ Describe how water is purified for drinking and other household uses.

The per capita direct and indirect use of water in the United States is about 2.8 million L per year, slightly less than the volume of an Olympic pool. This value is more than twice the per capita consumption in Europe. Although we often take drinking water for granted, significant energy and resources are spent every year to ensure the safety and quality of drinking water supplied by the 155,000 public water systems in the United States.

Safe Drinking Water Act

The U.S. Safe Drinking Water Act was passed in 1974 and amended in 1986 and 1996. The act gives the EPA power to set, monitor, and enforce national health-based standards for a variety of contaminants in municipal water supplies. As our ability to identify smaller and smaller concentrations of potentially harmful substances improves, the number of regulated substances with *maximum contaminant levels (MCLs)* increased from 22 in 1976 to 90 in 2004. The 1996 amendments have MCLs for 7 types of bacteria or viruses, 7 disinfectants—such as chlorine—or disinfectant products—such as bromate compounds, 16 inorganic compounds, 54 organic compounds, and 4 radioactive isotopes. Table 14.5 lists the MCLs for some of these contaminants.

Calculations of Parts per Million and Parts per Billion

We discussed solution concentrations in Section 5.5. For solutions that are extremely dilute, we often express concentrations in parts per million (ppm), parts per billion (ppb), or even parts per trillion (ppt). For example, in fluoridated drinking water, the fluoride ion (F^-) concentration is maintained at about 1 ppm. A typical level of the contaminant chloroform ($CHCl_3$) in municipal drinking water taken from the lower Mississippi River is 8 ppb.

Table 14.5	U.S. Environmental Protection Agency Drinking Water Standards for Selected Substances[a]
Substance	Maximum Contaminant Level (mg/L)
Primary standards: inorganic	
Arsenic	0.010
Barium	2
Copper	1.3
Cyanide ion	0.2
Fluoride ion	4.0
Lead	0.015
Nitrate ion	10[b]
Primary standards: organic	
Atrazine	0.003
Benzene	0.005
p-Dichlorobenzene	0.075
Dichloromethane	0.005
Heptachlor	0.0004
Lindane	0.0002
Toluene	1
Trichloroethylene	0.005
Secondary standards (nonenforceable)	
Chloride ion	250
Iron	0.3
Manganese	0.05
Silver	0.10
Sulfate ion	250
Total dissolved solids	500
Zinc	5

[a]A more extensive list and a more detailed explanation of the rules can be found on the EPA website.

[b]Measured as N. When measured as nitrate ion, the level is 45 mg/L.

For aqueous solutions, ppm, ppb, and ppt are generally based on mass. Thus, 1 ppm of solute in a solution is the same as 1 g of solute per 1×10^6 g (1 million g) of solution, and 1 ppb is 1 g of solute per 10^9 g (1 billion g) of solution. In other words,

$$1 \text{ ppm} = \frac{1 \text{ g solute}}{10^6 \text{ g solution}} \qquad 1 \text{ ppb} = \frac{1 \text{ g solute}}{10^9 \text{ g solution}}$$

Calculations of these concentration levels are much like those for finding percent by mass (Section 5.4). Example 14.2 introduces a useful relationship for aqueous solutions.

Example 14.2 | Contaminant Concentrations

According to standards, the EPA maximum allowable level of fluoride ion in drinking water is 4 mg F^- per liter. What is this level expressed in ppm?

Solution
The density of water, even if it contains traces of dissolved substances, is essentially 1.00 g/mL. One liter of water has a mass of 1000 g. So, we can express the allowable fluoride level as the ratio

$$\frac{4 \text{ mg } F^-}{1000 \text{ g water}}$$

To convert this fluoride level to ppm, we have to have the numerator and denominator in the same units. Using milligrams makes the denominator 1 million mg. The numerator then expresses the ppm solute, that is, ppm F^-.

$$\frac{4 \text{ mg } F^-}{1000 \text{ g water}} \times \frac{1 \text{ g water}}{1000 \text{ mg water}} = \frac{4 \text{ mg } F^-}{1{,}000{,}000 \text{ mg water}} = 4 \text{ ppm } F^-$$

▪ EXERCISE 14.2A

What is the concentration in **(a)** ppb and **(b)** ppt that is equivalent to a maximum allowable level in water of 0.1 μg/L of the gasoline additive MTBE (methyl *tert*-butyl ether)?

▪ EXERCISE 14.2B

What is the molarity of the MTBE solution in Exercise 14.2A?

But Not a Drop to Drink

▲ A village well in Bangladesh.

Clean drinking water is scarce in Bangladesh and the Indian state of West Bengal, one of the poorest regions in the world. This area is also often ravaged by floods. The surface waters that supplied drinking water for most of the region until the late 1970s were often contaminated by disease-causing microorganisms. During the 1970s, UNICEF and the World Bank provided funds for the construction of thousands of wells to provide a consistent supply of clean drinking water within 100 m of every family. The project halved the infant mortality rate during the 1980s.

However, the wells brought a new risk: chronic arsenic poisoning. Arsenic occurs naturally in the mineral formations of the region, contaminating well waters. Arsenic poisoning threatens over 100 million people in Bangladesh and West Bengal, perhaps as much as half the area's population. Long-term exposure to arsenic poses a number of health concerns, from skin discoloration to liver and kidney deficiencies to cancer.

While deeper, more expensive wells that reach water below the arsenic-containing formations can alleviate the problem, a simple, inexpensive filter with layers of cast iron turnings, river sand, wood charcoal, and wet brick chips can remove most of the arsenic. However, with nearly one-third of Bangladesh's population living in acute poverty, even these cheap devices are beyond their reach.

Water Treatment

Since both surface and groundwater are subject to contamination, most cities in developed nations treat their water supply before it flows into homes (Figure 14.5).

▲ **Figure 14.5** Diagram of a municipal water purification plant. The plant takes water from a river, lake, or waterway and removes suspended matter, kills microorganisms, and adds dissolved air before piping the water to consumers.

Q: *Why are aluminum sulfate and calcium hydroxide added before the water enters the settling basin?*

The water to be purified is usually placed in a settling basin where it is treated with slaked lime (calcium hydroxide) and a **flocculent** (a substance that causes particles to clump together), such as alum (aluminum sulfate). These materials react to form a gelatinous mass of aluminum hydroxide.

$$3 \, Ca(OH)_2(aq) \; + \; Al_2(SO_4)_3(aq) \; \longrightarrow \; 2 \, Al(OH)_3(s) \; + \; 3 \, CaSO_4(aq)$$

The aluminum hydroxide carries down dirt particles and bacteria. The water is then filtered through sand and gravel, and sometimes through charcoal to remove colored and odorous compounds. The filtered water is usually further treated by *aeration*. It is sprayed into the air to remove odors and improve its taste. Water without dissolved air tastes flat.

Chemical Disinfection

In the final step of water treatment, chlorine is added to kill any remaining bacteria. In some communities that use river water, a lot of chlorine is needed to kill all the bacteria, and you can taste the chlorine in the water. Some people question the use of chlorine because it converts dissolved organic compounds into chlorinated hydrocarbons, including trihalomethanes such as chloroform ($CHCl_3$).

Analyses of the drinking water of several cities that take their water from rivers have found chlorinated hydrocarbons, including such known carcinogens as chloroform and carbon tetrachloride. The concentrations are in the parts-per-billion range, probably posing only a small threat, but worrisome nonetheless. (The presence of chlorinated hydrocarbons is not nearly as worrisome as the waterborne diseases that prevail in much of the world where adequate water treatment is not available.)

Increasingly, ozone (O_3) is being used to disinfect drinking water. Adding ozone is more expensive than adding chlorine, but less of it is needed. Ozonation, however, kills viruses, on which chlorine has little, if any, effect. For example, ozone is 100 times more effective than chlorine in killing polioviruses.

Ozone acts by transferring its "extra" oxygen atom to the contaminant. Oxygenated contaminants are generally less toxic than chlorinated ones. In addition, ozone imparts no chemical taste to water. Unlike chlorine, however, ozone does not provide residual protection against microorganisms. Some systems therefore use a combination of disinfectants: ozone for initial treatment and subsequent addition of chlorine to provide residual protection.

Heating water to a full, rolling boil for at least 1 minute often provides a quick and effective method of ridding water of pathogens.

UV Irradiation

Water contaminated with a variety of microorganisms can be purified by irradiation with ultraviolet (UV) light. UV works rapidly, and it can be cost effective in small-scale applications. For instance, pouring clear water that has been previously filtered of solid impurities into a clear plastic bottle and exposing it to direct sunlight for at least 6 hours can purify a small amount of drinking water in an emergency. No generation, storage, or handling of chemicals is required. UV is effective against *Cryptosporidium*, and no by-products are formed at levels that cause concern. The disadvantages include no residual protection for drinking water and no taste and odor control. UV has limited effectiveness in turbid water and generally costs more than chlorine treatment.

Fluorides

Dental caries (tooth decay) was once considered the leading chronic disease of childhood. That this is no longer true is attributed mainly to fluoride toothpastes (Chapter 21) and the addition of fluoride to municipal water supplies. The hardness of tooth enamel can be correlated with the amount of fluoride present. Tooth enamel is a complex calcium phosphate called *hydroxyapatite*. Fluoride ions replace some of the hydroxide ions, forming a harder mineral called *fluorapatite*.

Hydroxyapatite		Fluorapatite

$$Ca_5(PO_4)_3OH(s) + F^-(aq) \longrightarrow Ca_5(PO_4)_3F(s) + OH^-(aq)$$

The fluoride concentration in the drinking water of many communities has been adjusted to 0.7–1.0 ppm (by mass) by adding fluoride, usually as H_2SiF_6 or Na_2SiF_6. Early studies showed reductions in the incidence of dental caries by 50–70%. More recent studies show a much smaller effect, perhaps because of the widespread use of fluoride toothpastes and the presence of fluoride in food products prepared with fluoridated water.

Some people object to water fluoridation. Fluoride salts are acute poisons in moderate to high concentrations. Indeed, sodium fluoride (NaF) is used as a poison for roaches and rats. Small amounts of fluoride ion, however, seem to contribute to our well-being through strengthening bones and teeth. There is some concern about the cumulative effects of consuming fluorides in drinking water, in the diet, in toothpaste, and from other sources. Excessive fluoride consumption during early childhood can cause mottling of tooth enamel. The enamel becomes brittle in certain areas and gradually discolors. Fluorides in high doses also interfere with calcium metabolism, kidney action, thyroid function, and the actions of other glands and organs.

▲ Excessive fluoride consumption in early childhood can cause mottling of tooth enamel. The severe case shown here was caused by continuous consumption during childhood of water from a supply that had an excessive natural concentration of fluoride.

SELF-ASSESSMENT Questions

1. About how many substances are regulated under EPA drinking water standards?
   a. 25   **b.** 45   **c.** 90   **d.** 180

2. A value of 3 ppm of dissolved oxygen means
   a. 3 mg O_2/L H_2O **b.** 3 mg O_2/mL H_2O
   c. 3 g O_2/mL H_2O **d.** 3 g O_2/L H_2O

3. Which of the following corresponds to the *lowest* concentration?
   a. 1 ppt   **b.** 1 ppm   **c.** 1 ppb

4. Public water supplies are aerated to
   a. improve the taste   **b.** kill bacteria
   c. remove suspended matter   **d.** remove trihalomethanes

5. Chlorine is added to public water supplies to
   a. improve the taste   **b.** kill bacteria
   c. remove suspended matter   **d.** remove trihalomethanes

6. What advantage does treatment of water with O_3 have over chlorination?
   a. O_3 is cheaper than Cl_2.
   b. O_3 provides residual protection; Cl_2 does not.
   c. Oxygenated by-products are generally less toxic than chlorinated by-products.
   d. Sedimentation is eliminated.

7. The chemical reaction responsible for the disinfecting properties of ozone is
   a. flocculation   **b.** precipitation
   c. reduction   **d.** oxidation

8. Fluoridation of drinking water strengthens tooth enamel by converting hydroxyapatite to
   a. $CaCO_3$ **b.** CaF_2 **c.** fluorapatite   **d.** fluorotartrate

Answers: 1. c; 2. a; 3. a; 4. a; 5. b; 6. c; 7. d; 8. c

The Soft Drink in Vogue: Bottled Water

Bottled water is an extremely profitable segment of the beverage industry. Though not their exclusive source of water, more than half of all Americans drink bottled water, even though it costs 240–10,000 times as much per liter as tap water. In 2007, bottled water consumption per capita was 110 L. The sales of bottled water decreased slightly in 2008 (108 L) and then again in 2009 (104)—a possible result of the economic downturn or the bisphenol A (BPA) scare. However, by 2011, the bottled water industry had more than recovered.

In the United States in general, both bottled water and tap water are quite safe. Yet some people will continue to buy bottled water for its convenience, taste, and assumed (but not necessarily real) health benefits. When surveyed, residents of Washington, D.C., report the largest percentage (36%) of water consumption as bottled water.

Because bottled water is considered as food, it is regulated by the Food and Drug Administration (FDA) rather than the EPA. Even though the FDA has adopted the EPA standards for tap water as the standards for bottled water, testing of the latter is typically less rigorous than testing of municipal water. Most people are unaware that about 25% of bottled water sold in the United States comes from municipal water supplies. And just because water comes in a bottle with a glacier or a mountain spring on the label does not mean that it is "more pure." Mineral water is, in fact, likely to have *more dissolved ions* (typically Ca^{2+} and Mg^{2+}) than normal tap water.

Consider the environmental impact of bottled water. It takes about 17 million barrels of oil to make the polyethylene terephthalate (PET) water bottles that Americans use each year, enough to fuel 1,000,000 cars for a year. Only about 13% of those bottles are recycled. Add the fuel used for transporting bottled water to stores, and its environmental cost is even higher.

6. How much water is wasted when a faucet drips?

When an average kitchen or bathroom faucet drips at an average rate of 15 drips a minute and an average faucet drop has a volume of 0.25 mL, over the span of one year, nearly 2000 L of water go straight down a drain. If in a medium-size city (200,000 homes), there is one such faucet per household, each day homeowners pay a utility company for over 1 million liters of water going to waste.

14.7 Wastewater Treatment

Learning Objective ❭ Describe primary, secondary, and tertiary treatment of wastewater.

The wastes generated by nearly two-thirds of the U.S. population are gathered in sewer systems and carried to treatment plants by more than 50 billion L of water each day. Much of the drinking water used by the U.S. population has been used by other municipalities upstream. Cities have to treat the used water before discharging it back into the environment, yet about 10% of it passes untreated into streams or the ocean. Treatment and purification of wastewater render it suitable for return to the water cycle.

Sewage Treatment Methods

For decades, most communities treated sewage simply by holding it in settling ponds for a while before discharging the resulting *effluent* into a stream, lake, or ocean, a process now called **primary sewage treatment** (Figure 14.6). Primary treatment removes 40–60% of suspended solids as *sludge* and about 30% of organic matter. The effluent still has a BOD level two-thirds of the original level and nearly all its nitrates and phosphates. All the dissolved oxygen in the pond may be used up, and anaerobic decomposition—with its resulting odors—takes over.

In **secondary sewage treatment**, the effluent from primary treatment is passed through sand and gravel filters. There is some aeration in this step, and aerobic bacteria convert much of the organic matter to inorganic materials. In the **activated sludge method** (Figure 14.7), a combination of primary and secondary treatment methods, the sewage is placed in tanks and aerated with large blowers. This causes the formation of large, porous biological clumps called *flocs*, which filter and absorb contaminants. Aerobic bacteria further convert the organic material to sludge. Part of the sludge is recycled to keep the process going, but huge quantities must be removed for disposal. This sludge is stored on land (where it requires large areas), dumped at sea (where it pollutes the ocean), or burned in incinerators (which requires energy—such as natural gas—and can contribute to air pollution). Some of the sludge is used as fertilizer.

Secondary treatment of wastewater lowers the BOD by about 90% but often does not adequately reduce nitrates and phosphates. Increasingly, federal mandates require **advanced treatment** (sometimes called *tertiary treatment*). Several advanced processes are in use, and most are quite costly.

- In **charcoal filtration**, charcoal adsorbs certain organic molecules, including trihalomethanes such as chloroform ($CHCl_3$), that are difficult to remove by any other method. The organic molecules are adsorbed on the surface of the charcoal and thus removed from the water. After a period of time, the charcoal becomes saturated and is no longer effective. It can be regenerated by heating it to drive off the adsorbed substances.

- In **reverse osmosis**, pressure forces the wastewater through a semipermeable membrane, leaving contaminants behind.

- **Phytoremediation** involves passage of the effluent into large natural or constructed lagoons for storage, allowing plants, such as reeds, to remove metals and other contaminants.

Finding the money to finance adequate sewage treatment will be a major political problem for years to come.

The effluent from sewage plants is usually treated with chlorine to kill any remaining pathogenic microorganisms before it is returned to a waterway. Chlorination has been quite effective in preventing the spread of waterborne infectious diseases such as typhoid fever. Further, some chlorine remains in the water, providing residual protection against pathogenic bacteria. However, as mentioned before, chlorination is not effective against some viruses such as those that cause hepatitis.

Water Pollution and the Future

For most of human history, our bodily wastes were an integral part of Earth's natural recycling system. The wastes provided food for

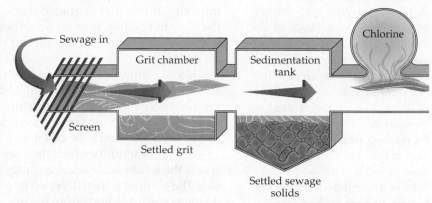

▲ **Figure 14.6** Diagram of a primary sewage treatment plant. Such treatment minimizes the harmful effect of wastewater on waterways.

Q: *Why isn't primary treatment alone sufficient for wastewater purification?*

▲ **Figure 14.7** Diagram of a secondary sewage treatment plant that uses the activated sludge method.

Q: *After organic matter is converted to sludge, why is some of the sludge recycled to the aeration tank?*

7. How do you get fresh water from saltwater?

With more than 97% of our planet's water being saltwater, desalination holds much promise. There are several ways of doing so. Water can be evaporated (to separate it from the salt) and the resulting steam condensed back to liquid form. In reverse osmosis, water is allowed to pass through a membrane leaving salt behind. Another method uses the difference in conductivity of saline versus fresh water to concentrate salt and isolate the salt-depleted water. Finally, careful freezing and thawing of saltwater may capture salt-depleted ice from saltwater with higher salt concentration, which will melt first. Desalination can be energy costly, as at least 1 kWh/m^3 is required to desalinate water. It takes only 0.2 kWh/m^3 or less to process fresh water.

microorganisms that degraded them, returning nutrients to soil and water. But with the growth of cities, human waste became disconnected from the cycle. In an effort to keep water clean and safe for our use, we also rid it of nutrients that could fertilize the land.

Many communities dry and sterilize sludge and then transport it to farmlands for return of nutrients to the soil. Others pump wet, suspended sludge directly to the fields. The water in the mixture irrigates the crops, and the sludge provides nutrients and humus. One concern is that the sludge is often contaminated with toxic metals that could be taken up by plants and eventually end up in our food.

A few communities treat their sewage by first holding it in sedimentation tanks, where the solids settle out as a sludge that is removed and processed for use as fertilizer. The effluent is then diverted into a marshy area where the marsh plants filter the water and use nutrients from the sewage as fertilizer. Some plants even remove toxic metals. Effluent from the marsh is often as clean as the water in municipal reservoirs.

Other solutions are possible. Septic tanks have been used for home sewage treatment for decades, but their use is generally limited to rural and some suburban areas. They also require significant upkeep to remain effective. Toilets have been developed that compost wastes and use no energy or water. The mild heat of composting drives off water from the wastes. The system is ventilated to keep the process aerobic, and no odors enter the house from a properly installed system. Dried waste is removed about once a year. The initial cost is much higher than that of a flush toilet.

Each person in the United States flushes about 35,000 L of drinking-quality water each year. While newer toilet models use an average of 6 L of water, many households still use toilets that require about 15 L to flush.

We're the Solution to Water Pollution

We generally take our drinking water for granted. Perhaps we shouldn't. There are between 4,000 and 40,000 cases of waterborne illnesses in the United States each year. Twenty million people have no running water at all, and many more obtain water from suspect sources: 10% of public water supplies do not meet one or more of the EPA standards. Another 30 million tap individual wells or springs whose water is often of unknown quality. Much remains to be done before we can all be assured of safe drinking water.

The Clean Water Act has drastically reduced water pollution from industrial sources. However, complete elimination of pollution is not possible—to use water is to pollute it. All of us can do our share by conserving water and by minimizing our use of products that require vast amounts of water to make. As our population grows, it will cost a lot just to maintain present water quality. To clean up our water, and then keep it clean, will cost more. However, the costs of unclean water are even higher—discomfort, loss of recreation, illness, and even death.

SELF-ASSESSMENT Questions

1. At what stage in sewage treatment do bacteria consume dissolved organic matter?
   a. aeration
   b. primary
   c. secondary
   d. screening and sand removal

2. Trihalomethanes, such as chloroform, are formed when chlorine reacts with
   a. bacteria
   b. dissolved organic compounds
   c. ethanol
   d. phenols

3. Trihalomethanes, such as chloroform, can be removed from water by
   a. charcoal filtration
   b. chlorination
   c. flocculation
   d. sand filtration

4. Reverse osmosis is a way to purify water by using pressure to force the water through a
   a. charcoal filter
   b. sand filter
   c. semipermeable membrane
   d. trickling filter

5. Phytoremediation utilizes _____ to remove metals and other contaminants from wastewater.
   a. plants
   b. UV irradiation
   c. charcoal
   d. ozone

6. A wastewater treatment plant treats 500,000 gal of sewage per day, using 16 lb of chlorine per day. Assume that 1 gal of sewage weighs about 8 lb. The chlorine concentration, in parts per million, of the wastewater is about
   a. 1 ppm
   b. 4 ppm
   c. 8 ppm
   d. 16 ppm

7. Approximately, how much water is wasted when a bathtub faucet drips for 24 hours at the rate of 10 times a minute? Assume the volume of a drip to be 0.25 mL.
   a. 1 L
   b. 3 L
   c. 4 L
   d. 15 L

Answers: 1. c; 2. b; 3. a; 4. c; 5. a; 6. b; 7. c

GREEN CHEMISTRY

Alex S. Mayer, Michigan Technological University

Fate of Chemicals in the Water Environment

Learning Objectives › Connect the properties of chemicals to their fate in the environment. › Describe how chemicals migrate between environmental compartments, including how chemicals' effects can magnify as they travel through food webs.

A key part of green chemistry is understanding how chemicals move and change when they enter the environment. Important questions include how chemicals move, how and why they react in the environment, and how these chemicals affect organisms in the environment like fish, animals, plants, and people. Here, we focus on the movement of organic chemicals in water—lakes, rivers, and oceans—but the principles we are presenting also apply to other classes of chemicals and where they end up in the environment.

To make things easier, scientists and engineers like to track chemicals by dividing the larger environment into smaller parts or compartments such as air, water, and solids. Solids include sediments (found at the bottom of rivers, lakes, and oceans) and soils or other materials, such as layers of sand or rock that occur below the earth's surface. Once a chemical enters the environment, it can move into these different compartments through a process known as partitioning. Partitioning is best understood as the amount of a chemical that ends up in each compartment.

One way to think about partitioning is to think about salad dressing made of oil and vinegar. You may have seen how oil and vinegar will separate into distinct layers unless you vigorously mix them together. When you do mix them, most of the oil and vinegar will once again settle into different layers, but a little bit of the oil will dissolve or partition into the vinegar and a little bit of the vinegar will dissolve in the oil. The same phenomenon happens when a chemical in water comes into contact with air or sediment; some of the chemical will stay in the water, but some will partition into the sediment or into the air. (See Section 14.6 on groundwater contamination.)

How much of the chemical remains in the water and how much goes into the solid depends on the properties of the water and the solid and on the properties of the chemical. To understand this process better, scientists use water and oil as a model system for predicting how much of a chemical will remain in water, and how much will go into a solid. For example, a pesticide like DDT is about 10 million times more likely to go from water into oil (or fats, sediments, or soils) than a solvent like acetone. Why? DDT is very soluble in oil and is a nonpolar compound, whereas acetone (Section 9.6) is very soluble in water (less soluble in oil) and polar. Compounds like DDT tend to "hate" water, which is the most polar compound on earth (Section 4.12). Therefore, compounds such as DDT are usually found in smaller amounts in water than in other environmental compartments. More polar compounds, such as acetone, "prefer" to stay in the water compartment.

You might think that, in terms of environmental impact, it is better to have chemicals that like to stay in the solid (or in the oil) because less of the chemical will be found in water. However, chemicals that partition more strongly into solids tend to stay in the environment for a longer time. Once they go into or onto the solids, only minute quantities are released into surrounding water over time, although potentially at toxic levels. Therefore, we can say that DDT is 10 million times more persistent than acetone. (See Section 1.1 and the work of Rachel Carson on pesticides, especially DDT.) Understanding the properties of chemicals can help us prevent pollution and use and design safer products through green chemistry (Principles 1, 4, and 5).

Organisms exposed to organic chemicals in the environment may break down or change the chemicals in some way before they excrete them. Green chemistry can help to design chemicals that degrade into benign products (Principle 10). However, sometimes organisms absorb or retain the chemicals. Many organic chemicals tend to be absorbed into fatty deposits or tissues in organisms. As discussed above, some chemicals like DDT tend to be more highly absorbed in the fatty tissues. These chemicals can lead to toxic effects including neurological damage and birth defects if present at high enough levels.

Chemical absorption in animals usually leads to the progressive increase in the concentration of some organic chemicals in animals that eat other animals. This progressive increase in concentration is known as *biomagnification* (Section 20.2). For example, if the smallest fish species in a food chain is exposed to a chemical, then absorbs and stores the chemical, a larger fish that eats many of those fish will store a much larger amount of the chemical. This phenomenon is bad news for animals at the top of the food web, such as predatory birds or humans.

Principles like the one we just described help scientists understand that the properties of chemicals determine where they end up in the environment. Thus, as we make new chemicals that are supposed to benefit humans, we should apply green chemistry principles and design these chemicals so that they are less persistent in the environment with less likelihood to absorb solids and biomagnify (Principles 4, 5, and 10). Furthermore, it makes sense to synthesize chemicals so that when their useful lives are over, they will break down quickly in the environment or

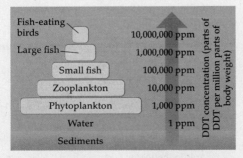

we have an easy way to recover and reuse them. Testing chemicals before they are introduced is critical so we can avoid unintended consequences like biomagnification. Finally, we should minimize the generation of waste chemicals that are likely to persist in the environment.

431

SUMMARY

Section 14.1—Water has unusual properties: It is the only common liquid on Earth; its solid form is less dense than the liquid; and it is more dense than most other common liquids. **Specific heat capacity** is the amount of heat needed to raise the temperature of 1 g of a substance by 1 °C (or 1 K). For liquid water, it is quite high: 1 cal/g °C (or 4.18 J/g K). Water also has a high **heat of vaporization**, the amount of heat required to vaporize a fixed amount of a liquid. These properties arise because of the strong hyperdense hydrogen bonding network that exists among water molecules. Water is also an excellent solvent, especially for many other polar and ionic solutes.

Section 14.2—Water covers 75% of Earth's surface, but less than 1% of it is available as fresh water for human use. Water dissolves many ionic substances, which is why the oceans are salty. Potable water is readily available in most parts of the United States, but many other countries do not have enough fresh water. In the water (hydrologic) cycle, water evaporates from oceans and lakes, condenses into clouds, and returns to Earth as rain or snow. During this cycle, water can be contaminated by various chemicals and microorganisms from both natural sources and human activities. **Hard water** is formed when minerals (salts of calcium, magnesium, and/or iron) dissolve in groundwater.

Section 14.3—Waterborne diseases were a severe problem until about 100 years ago and are still common in many parts of the world. Acid rain created by the release of sulfur oxides and nitrogen oxides when coal and other fuels are burned has caused acidification of thousands of bodies of water. Besides corrosive effects, acid rain is detrimental to both plant and animal life. When sewage is dumped into waterways, the organic matter is biodegraded by microorganisms. **Aerobic oxidation** occurs in the presence of **dissolved oxygen**, and the **biochemical oxygen demand (BOD)** is a measure of the amount of oxygen needed. Sewage increases the BOD. If the BOD is high enough, only **anaerobic decay**, or decay in the absence of oxygen, can occur. High levels of nitrates and phosphates can accelerate **eutrophication**, in which algae grow and die, thereby increasing the BOD of the water. Other new substances introduced into the water cycle may cause new problems.

Section 14.4—About half of the U.S. population drinks surface water, and half drinks groundwater. Use of groundwater is especially common in rural areas. The aquifers into which wells are drilled are being consumed faster than they are being recharged by precipitation, and deeper wells are now required in many places. Well water may be contaminated with various chemicals, including nitrates and VOCs.

Section 14.5—Producing industrial and consumer products uses a great deal of water, which is polluted in the process and must be cleaned up and recycled. We need only about 1.5–2.0 L of water per day for drinking, but in the United States, each person directly uses a total of about 400 L per day, which includes various household uses. Indirect water use is much higher.

Section 14.6—The U.S. Safe Water Drinking Act sets and enforces standards for water quality. In many cases, concentrations of contaminants must be expressed in tiny units, such as parts per million (ppm) or parts per billion (ppb). Treatment of water to make it safe to drink usually includes settling, treatment with a **flocculent** (to cause particles to clump together and settle out), filtration, aeration, and chemical disinfection with chlorine or ozone. Fluorides may also be added to prevent tooth decay.

Section 14.7—Treatment of wastewater (used water) begins with **primary sewage treatment**, allowing the wastes to settle and removing sludge before discharging the water into the environment. In **secondary sewage treatment**, the effluent is filtered through sand and gravel. The **activated sludge method**, in which the sewage is aerated and the biological sludge is removed, may be used instead. **Advanced treatment** (tertiary treatment) may involve **charcoal filtration** to adsorb organic compounds, **reverse osmosis** to remove contaminants by forcing the wastewater through a semipermeable membrane, or **phytoremediation**, to allow plants to remove metals and other contaminants by storing the wastewater in lagoons. These advanced processes are expensive. Maintaining water quality is expensive and will become more so, but not maintaining it will cost much more in terms of our health and comfort.

GREEN CHEMISTRY—Chemicals can be released into the environment and have toxic effects on humans and other species. The properties of chemicals determine where and for how long they stay in the environment. It makes sense to design chemicals that will persist for shorter periods and occur in smaller amounts in organisms and to minimize the release of chemicals that are persistent and tend to magnify in the food web.

Learning Objectives

› Relate water's unique properties to polarity of the water molecule and to hydrogen bonding.	Problems 1, 2, 12–19, 21, 57
› Explain how water on the surface of Earth acts to moderate daily temperature variations.	Problem 20
› Explain why humans can only make use of less than 1% of all the water on Earth.	Problems 22, 59
› Explain the water cycle on Earth.	Problems 23, 58
› Describe how human activities affect water quality.	Problems 3, 23–32, 61,
› Give an example of a biological water contaminant.	Problems 3–6, 26, 66
› List some groundwater contaminants.	Problems 23, 24, 64, 65

❯ Identify the sources of nitrates in groundwater.	Problems 36, 62, 68
❯ List the major uses of water.	Problems 37–39, 67
❯ Describe how water is purified for drinking and other household uses.	Problems 33–35, 40, 60
❯ Describe primary, secondary, and tertiary treatment of wastewater.	Problems 41–46, 63
❯ Connect the properties of chemicals to their fate in the environment.	Problem 69
❯ Describe how chemicals migrate between environmental compartments, including how chemicals' effects can magnify as they travel through food webs.	Problems 70–71

REVIEW QUESTIONS

1. A tanker filled with light crude oil sinks and breaks open. Will the oil dissolve in the water? Will it float or sink?

2. Why should foods be frozen swiftly rather than slowly?

3. Name several major sources of nutrients that enter waterways.

4. How do fertilizers contribute to the formation of a dead zone?

5. What are pathogenic microorganisms?

6. List some waterborne diseases. Why are these diseases no longer common in developed countries?

7. List some ways in which groundwater is contaminated.

8. Discuss how sewage is related to biological oxygen demand (BOD), dissolved oxygen (DO), and eutrophication.

9. Give examples of how an individual can help prevent the pollution of water sources.

10. What problems do leaking underground storage tanks cause?

11. Why do chlorinated hydrocarbons remain in groundwater for such a long time?

PROBLEMS

Properties of Water

12. Why is ice less dense than liquid water? Use the concept of hyperdense hydrogen bonding in your explanation.

13. What consequences does the lower density of ice compared to liquid water have for life in northern lakes?

14. Define *specific heat capacity*. Why is the high specific heat of water important to Earth?

15. Refer to Table 14.1. How much heat, in calories, does it take to warm 750 g of water from 12.0 °C to 45.0 °C?

16. How much heat, in calories, does it take to warm 750 g of iron from 12.0 °C to 45.0 °C? How does this compare to the heat required to warm an equal quantity of water to the same extent? (See Problem 15.)

17. Specific heat capacity of solid water is roughly half of that for liquid water. What does this mean?

18. Define heat of vaporization. Explain why it is exceptionally high for water.

19. Why is the high heat of vaporization of water important to our bodily functions?

20. Why is it cooler near a lake than inland during the summer?

21. Why does your skin feel cool when you step out of a swimming pool into a breeze?

22. Why are oceans salty? Are they getting saltier?

Natural Waters

23. What impurities are present in rainwater?

24. What are the products of the breakdown of organic matter by anaerobic decay?

25. What is the difference between aerobic and anaerobic bacteria?

26. Eutrophication is amplified by
    a. heavy metals from landfills
    b. plant nutrients from fertilizer runoff and wastewater
    c. radioactive waste from nuclear power plants
    d. toxic chemicals from factories

27. Water containing more than 3.0 g of dissolved solids per gallon is considered to be hard [1 grain (gr) = 64.8 mg]. What is this "hardness limit" in milligrams of dissolved solids per liter?

28. Refer to Problem 27. A kettle contains 18 gal of tap water, which is allowed to evaporate. The calcium- and magnesium-containing solid material left behind has a mass of 2.1 g. Can the tap water be considered as being hard?

Acidic Waters

29. List two ways in which lakes and streams become acidified.

30. Surface water is most likely to be acidified by acid rain in areas underlain by
    a. dolomite   b. granite
    c. limestone   d. magnesite ($MgCO_3$)

31. Acidic water that is neutralized by natural rock often becomes hard water. Explain.

32. Why is acidic water especially harmful to fish?

Municipal Water Supplies

33. What is the optimal level of fluoride in drinking water?

34. What are some health effects of too much fluoride in the diet?

35. Can water be disinfected without adding chemicals? Explain.

36. What is methemoglobinemia? How is it caused?

37. How much water does a person need per day for drinking?

38. Explain why it takes many times as much water to produce a single serving of steak as it takes to produce a single serving of rice.

39. What are the pros and cons of using bottled water?

40. Which federal agency regulates drinking water standards from municipal water supplies? Which federal agency regulates bottled water?

Wastewater Treatment

41. Describe primary sewage treatment. What impurities does it remove?

42. Describe secondary sewage treatment. What impurities does it remove?

43. What substances remain in wastewater after effective secondary treatment?

44. Describe the activated sludge method of sewage treatment.

45. Identify each of the following as a primary, secondary, or tertiary method of wastewater treatment.
    a. charcoal filtration   b. settling pond
    c. sand and gravel filters

46. What are the advantages and disadvantages of spreading sewage sludge on farmland?

Chemical Equations

47. Write the balanced equation for the neutralization of acid rain (assume HNO_3 is dissolved in water) by limestone (calcium carbonate).

48. Write the balanced equation for the reaction of slaked lime (calcium hydroxide) with alum (aluminum sulfate) to form aluminum hydroxide used in wastewater treatment.

49. Write the balanced equation for the reaction in which fluoride ions replace hydroxide ions in tooth enamel.

50. Write the balanced equation for the reaction that shows why natural water has an acidic pH.

Parts per Million and Parts per Billion

51. Express each aqueous concentration in the unit indicated.
    a. 11 μg of benzene per liter of water, as ppb benzene
    b. 0.014% $BaCO_3$, by mass, as ppm $BaCO_3$

52. Express each aqueous concentration in the unit indicated.
    a. 25 μg of trichloroethylene in 9.5 L of water, as ppb trichloroethylene
    b. 38 g Cl_2 in 1.00×10^4 L 1.00×10^4 L of water, as ppm Cl_2

53. A 2.0-L sample of drinking water is found to contain 18 μg of copper and 16 mg of nitrate ion. Does either of these concentrations exceed the standards in Table 14.5?

54. A 0.50-L sample of drinking water is found to contain 4.0 μg of toluene. Does this exceed the standard in Table 14.5?

55. Using Table 14.5, determine 1 mg of which substance must be more toxic.
    a. arsenic   b. cyanide
    c. benzene   d. heptachlor

56. Which sample of fluoride ions is more concentrated?
    a. 4 ppm   b. 3×10^{-4} mol/L

 ADDITIONAL PROBLEMS

57. How is charge distributed in a molecule of water?
    a. Evenly; the molecule is nonpolar.
    b. There is a negative partial charge on the H atoms and a positive partial charge on the O atom.
    c. There is a negative partial charge on one H atom and a positive partial charge on the other.
    d. There is a positive partial charge on the H atoms and a negative partial charge on the O atom.

58. Which of the following processes is *not* a part of the water cycle?
    a. biomagnification   b. condensation
    c. evaporation   d. precipitation

59. Most of the fresh water on Earth is
    a. above in the atmosphere
    b. frozen in the polar ice caps
    c. in motion in rivers, lakes, and streams
    d. underground in aquifers

60. Which of the following processes is *not* used in a conventional method of water treatment?
    a. aeration   b. coagulation
    c. filtration   d. percolation

61. Thermal pollution is harmful to aquatic environments because it
    a. decreases nutrient levels
    b. increases the level of pathogens
    c. increases the level of radioactivity
    d. reduces the amount of dissolved oxygen

62. Express each aqueous concentration in the unit indicated.
    a. 3.1 ppm F^-, as molarity of fluoride ion
    b. 27 ppm NO_3^- as molarity of nitrate ion
    c. Why do some scientists prefer to express concentrations of water contaminants in the units parts per million and parts per billion rather than molarity?

63. Wastewater disinfected with chlorine must be dechlorinated before it is returned to sensitive bodies of water. The dechlorinating agent is often sulfur dioxide. The reaction is
    $$Cl_2 + SO_2 + 2 H_2O \longrightarrow 2 Cl^- + SO_4^{2-} + 4 H^+$$
    Is the chlorine oxidized or reduced? Identify the oxidizing agent and reducing agent in the reaction.

64. Look back at the molecular formulas for volatile organic compounds (VOCs) on page 421. Write structural formulas for the following compounds.
    a. benzene   b. toluene   c. chloroform
    d. methylene chloride   e. trichloroethylene

65. The text indicates that radioactive radon gas is slightly soluble in water. What are the intermolecular forces responsible for the solubility?

66. BOD measures the levels of _____ in water.
    a. acids   b. bases   c. nitrates   d. sewage

67. A typical gas-fired home water heater holds 50 gal of water and has the thermostat set to 60 °C.
    a. If the inlet water supply is at 10 °C, how much heat, in kilocalories, is needed to bring the contents of the water heater to the set temperature? (1 gal = 3.8 L)

b. Burning 1.00 mol of methane (CH_4), the major component of natural gas, produces 890 kJ of energy. What mass (in grams) of methane must be burned to produce the amount of heat determined in part **(a)**?

c. What volume in cubic feet (at STP) of methane does the mass from part **(b)** correspond to? (1 ft^3 = 28.3 L)

d. A *therm* of natural gas is about 100 ft^3 and costs about $1.22 once delivered to residential customers (average U.S. price in 2013). Use the results from parts **(a)–(c)** to calculate how much it costs to take a 10-minute shower at a usage rate of 3.0 gal of hot water per minute.

68. How much calcium nitrate has to be added to 1000 L of solution to provide 180 ppm Ca^{2+} if the water supply contains 40 ppm Ca^{2+}? How much NO_3^-, in parts per million, does this quantity of calcium nitrate add to the solution?

69. An experiment is conducted with two chemicals, X and Y, where equal masses of chemicals are exposed to a sample of water mixed with soil. At the end of the experiment, chemical X is found at a concentration in the soil of 1/100th that of chemical Y. Which chemical is more polar?

70. The Michivannia State Department of Public Health is setting fish advisories for two different fish, red fish and blue fish, that may be exposed to toxic organic chemicals. Red fish and blue fish have fat contents of 5% and 15%, respectively. Red fish is typically consumed by blue fish. Which fish would you recommend can be eaten more often than the other?

71. If a chemist were charged with developing a new pesticide and was concerned with the fate of the pesticide in the environment should the new pesticide be more polar or more nonpolar?

CRITICAL THINKING EXERCISES

Apply knowledge that you have gained in this chapter and one or more of the FLaReS principles (Chapter 1) to evaluate the following statements or claims.

14.1. A friend states that ice cubes made of saltwater or heavy water will float on normal "light" water.

14.2. A company states that its special sports water, through a secret molecular process utilizing advanced laser technology, contains 500 mg of NaCl per 1 g of water.

14.3. A mother discovers that tests have found 1.0 ppb of trichloroethylene in the well water her family uses for drinking, bathing, cooking, and so on. The family has used the well for 2 years. The mother decides that the whole family should be tested for cancer.

14.4. A group of citizens wants to ban fluoridation of a community water supply because fluorides are toxic.

14.5. A company claims that its "superoxygenated water can boost athletic performance." (Note that, under pressure, the water can contain at most 0.3 g O_2/L H_2O, the amount in a 1-L breath.)

14.6. A company claims that its "oxygenated and structured water has smaller molecules that penetrate more quickly into the cells, and therefore hydrate your body faster and more efficiently."

14.7. A friend states, "The water we drink in the present day may be some of the same water that flowed in the time of dinosaurs."

COLLABORATIVE GROUP PROJECTS

Prepare a PowerPoint, poster, or other presentation (as directed by your instructor) to share with the class.

1. Consult online or print references, and prepare a report on the desalination of seawater by one of the following methods.
   a. distillation   **b.** freezing   **c.** electrodialysis
   d. reverse osmosis   **e.** ion exchange

2. Discuss how sustainable is the practice of withdrawing underground water from an aquifer to irrigate crops aboveground.

3. Where does your drinking water come from? What steps are used in purifying it?

4. Call your local water utility's office or consult its website and obtain a chemical analysis of your drinking water. What substances are monitored? Are any of these substances considered problems? (If you use water from a private well, has the water been analyzed? If so, what were the results?)

5. The website of the EPA's Office of Wastewater Management (OWM) has a menu of numerous water-related topics.

Choose one, and write a few paragraphs about that aspect of wastewater management. Is wastewater treatment used in your community adequate?

6. Poll your class on consumption of bottled water. About how many bottles do they drink each year? Why do your classmates use it? Are there concerns regarding its purity?

7. Using the USGS Water Science School website (**http://water.usgs.gov/edu/sq3.html**), estimate your group's daily indoor water use.

8. The EPA's website identifies Superfund sites with a National Priorities List and a list by regions. These sites are uncontrolled or abandoned places where hazardous waste is located. If not cleaned up, these wastes can affect nearby people and ecosystems. Prepare a report on a site in your region, listing, if possible, the toxic materials involved.

9. Using the website of the Natural Resources Defense Council (NRDC) or another environmental group, investigate pollution from urban stormwater runoff, which some say rivals sewage plants and factories as a source of water contamination. Write a brief report on your findings.

CHEMISTRY@HOME   Disappearing Dilution

Materials required

- 6 plastic cups
- Measuring cup
- Water
- Dropper
- Spoon
- Colored powdered drink mix
- Sugar

Is dilution the solution to pollution? Let's use powered drink mix and sugar as our contaminants to experiment with. How dilute does our mixture have to be before we can no longer see or taste them? Does that mean that our mixture is no longer polluted?

During the Industrial Revolution and up until the 1970s, it was common practice to dilute known hazardous substances in water. Environmental health research discovered that even small concentrations of certain chemicals can and do have very damaging effects on the environment. While our ecosystems have natural defense systems against many chemicals that enter our water supply, dilution is not a reliable method of preventing pollution. It is far better to reduce or eliminate the use of hazardous chemicals in the first place than to try to clean up or remediate afterward.

During this experiment, you will compare pollution amounts using powdered drink mix and sugar as your "contaminants." Begin the experiment by labeling cups 1 through 6. Then, create a chart to record your observations for each cup.

Mix the powdered drink mix using the recommended amount of sugar. Measure $\frac{1}{2}$ cup of this prepared drink with sugar into cup 1 and $\frac{1}{4}$ cup of water into cups 2—6. Taste the drink in cup 1 using a teaspoon. Now cup 1 is contaminated.

Place $\frac{1}{4}$ cup of the "polluted water" from cup 1 into cup 2 using the measuring cup. Make observations and notes.

Is this water less polluted than water in cup 1? What color differences do you notice? What is the difference in sweetness? Remember to record descriptions in your chart. Predict how dark the color will be and how it will taste in cups 3—6.

Slowly add ¼ of the "polluted water" from cup 2 to cup 3. Mix and record observations. Repeat this procedure for cups 4—6. When these observations are recorded, compare cup 1 to cup 3, and then compare it to cup 6. Place a white sheet of paper underneath each cup to emphasize the color differences. Note the differences in taste.

Questions

1. Was there evidence that pollution still remained in the water even when the solution was diluted?
2. How many more times do you think the polluted water would have to be diluted before color or taste changes ceased?
3. Do you think dilution is a good solution for pollution? Why or why not?
4. Does pollution always remain in the water? If not, where does it go?

ENERGY

Have You Ever Wondered?

1. **How can you measure energy?**

2. **How can molecules give off heat?**

3. **Do we really have an energy shortage?**

4. **What is "frac sand," and how is it different from ordinary beach sand?**

5. **Why don't we use more alternative fuels for automobiles?**

6. **Is solar power, wind power, or the fuel cell the answer to the energy crisis?**

Learning Objectives

> Perform power and energy calculations. (15.1)

> Classify chemical reactions and physical processes as exothermic or endothermic. (15.2)

> Explain how the heat of a reaction is calculated using bond energies. (15.2)

> List factors that affect the rates of chemical reactions. (15.3)

> State the first and second laws of thermodynamics, and discuss their implications for energy production and use. (15.4)

> List the common fossil fuels, and describe how modern society is based on their use. (15.5)

> List the origins, advantages, and disadvantages of coal as a fuel. (15.6)

> List the characteristics, advantages, and disadvantages of natural gas and petroleum. (15.7)

> Explain why gaseous and liquid fuels are more convenient to use than solid fuels. (15.8)

> List the advantages and disadvantages of nuclear energy. (15.9)

> Describe how a nuclear power plant generates electricity. (15.9)

> List important characteristics, advantages, "sources," and disadvantages of various kinds of renewable energy sources. (15.10)

> Explain how applying the green chemistry principles can help identify improved methods for energy generation.

A FUEL'S PARADISE
We were tempted to call this chapter "Fire" so that the titles of Chapters 12, 13, 14, and 15 would be "Earth," "Air," "Water," and "Fire"—the four elements of the ancient Greeks.

Indeed, "Fire" is an appropriate title for this chapter. We obtain most of our energy by burning fuels, which certainly involves fire. Many sources of energy do not involve burning anything, however, and we will depend more heavily on these other sources as our reserves of fossil fuels are depleted.

Nearly all Earth's energy comes indirectly from the sun, a nuclear fusion reactor about 150 million km away. The wind that drives wind turbines is a result of solar heating. Biofuels such as biodiesel and biomass come from plants, which use sunlight as their source of energy. Even fossil fuels are derived from the sun. An increasingly popular method of directly harnessing solar energy is the use of solar cells that convert sunlight to electricity. Today, it is possible to buy enough solar cells to run an entire house, but at considerable expense. In this chapter, we will look at the general nature and properties of energy and at various ways of generating energy or converting it from one form to another. Only tiny fractions of the energy we use come from Earth's internal heat, visible in geysers and tapped as geothermal energy,

Everything that we consume or use—our food and clothes, our homes and their contents, our cars and roads—requires energy to produce, package, distribute, operate, and discard. The United States, with less than 5% of the world's population, uses one-fifth of all the energy generated on the planet. Abundant energy provides people in the United States with a high standard of living. But much of this energy is wasted. Australia, Switzerland, France, and the Scandinavian countries achieve higher standards of living with lower per capita use of energy. Our high energy consumption has enormous costs: to our health, to the environment, and to our national security. It affects our foreign debt and the stability of other countries. It pollutes the air we breathe and the water we drink.

Industry uses about 30% of all energy produced in the United States. This energy is used to convert raw materials to the many products our society needs and wants. Transportation uses about 29%, powering automobiles, trucks, trains, airplanes, and buses. Private homes and commercial spaces consume most of the rest. Utilities use about 38% of the nation's energy production, mainly to generate electricity for use in homes, businesses, transportation, and industry.

Energy lights our homes, heats and cools our living spaces, and makes us the most mobile society in the history of the human race. It powers the factories that provide us with abundant material goods. Indeed, energy is the basis of modern civilization.

It DOES Matter!
Consumers often have misconceptions about energy usage in the home. Appliances that generate or transfer heat usually consume a lot of energy. The two major energy "sinks" in most homes are the heating and cooling system and the water heater. Refrigerators, stoves, toasters, and similar appliances are also energy hogs. Lighting is often responsible for a surprisingly small fraction of the monthly energy bill. An ordinary toaster oven heating a slice of pizza for 10 minutes consumes as much energy as a 20-W fluorescent light bulb uses in 10 hours.

15.1 Our Sun, a Giant Nuclear Power Plant

Learning Objective ❯ Perform power and energy calculations.

All living things on Earth—including us—depend on nuclear energy for survival. Most of the energy available to us on this planet comes from the giant nuclear reactor we call the sun. Although the sun is about 150 million km away, it has supplied Earth with most of its energy for billions of years, and is likely to continue to do so for billions more (Table 15.1).

Recall from Chapter 11 that the sun is a nuclear fusion reactor that steadily converts hydrogen to helium. The sun has a power output of 4×10^{26} W. (W is the symbol for watt.) Earth receives only about 1 part in 50 billion of this energy. Even so, this tiny fraction is equivalent to over 100 million nuclear power plants. In three days, Earth receives energy from the sun equivalent to all our fossil fuel reserves!

We measure energy, in SI units, in joules (J), which is related to calories (see Section 1.11). One *watt* (W), the SI unit of power, is 1 joule per second (J/s).

$$1\,W = 1\,\frac{J}{s}$$

A unit of more convenient size is the kilowatt: 1 kw = 100 W. To express energy consumption, the watt is combined with a unit of time. For example, electricity use is usually measured (and billed for) in terms of the *kilowatt hour* (kWh), the quantity of energy used by a 1-kW device in 1 h. There are 3600 seconds in an hour, so 1 k Wh = 3600 kJ. Power is the *rate* at which energy is used (just as speed is the *rate* at which distance is covered).

Table 15.1	Earth's Energy Ledger	
Item	Energy (TW)[a]	Approximate Percent
Energy in		
Solar radiation	174,000	99.97
Internal heat	46	0.025
Tides	3	0.002
Waste heat[b]	13	0.007
Energy out		
Direct reflection	52,000	30
Direct heating[c]	81,000	47
Water cycle[c]	40,000	23
Winds[c]	370	0.2
Photosynthesis[c]	40	0.02

[a]TW (terawatt) $= 10^{12}$ W.
[b]From fossil fuel use.
[c]This energy is eventually returned to space by means of long-wave radiation (heat).

1. How can you measure energy?

Temperature, a measure of the average kinetic energy of molecules, is measured in degrees C, with a thermometer. Energy is not so simple. It is measured in terms of how much "work" it can accomplish, such as move a piano, provide light from a light bulb, or bake a cake. It is measured in units of calories or joules. Heat is thermal energy that is transferred from one object to another. The rate of consumption of energy is the watt, and your electric bill reflects the length of time you used energy at a certain rate.

Example 15.1 Power and Energy Conversion

How much electrical energy, in joules, is consumed by a 75-W bulb burning for 1.0 h?

Solution
One watt is 1 J/s, so we know that 75 W = 75 J/s. The bulb burns for 1 h so

$$1 \text{ h} \times \frac{60 \text{ min}}{1 \text{ h}} \times \frac{60 \text{ s}}{1 \text{ min}} = 3600 \text{ s}$$

$$3600 \text{ s} \times \frac{75 \text{ J}}{1 \text{ s}} = 270,000 \text{ J}$$

▪ EXERCISE 15.1A
How much electrical energy, in joules, does a 650-W microwave oven consume in heating a cup of coffee for 1.0 min?

▪ EXERCISE 15.1B
Compute the energy consumed by a 13-W compact fluorescent bulb burning for 1.0 h, and compare it to the energy consumed by a 60-W bulb that produces the same amount of light energy. What percent savings would this amount to, per hour?

▪ EXERCISE 15.1C
At 11.0 cents/kWh, how much would use of that 13-W compact fluorescent bulb save you in costs for a month in which you burned that bulb for 240 hours, compared to a regular 60-W bulb used for 240 hours? Both are supposed to provide the same intensity of light.

Kinetic and Potential Energy

Energy exists in two main forms. Energy due to position or arrangement is called potential energy. The water at the top of a dam has potential energy due to gravitational attraction. When the water is allowed to flow through a turbine to a lower level, the potential energy is converted to kinetic energy (energy of motion). As the water falls, it moves faster. Its kinetic energy increases as its potential energy decreases. The turbine can convert part of the kinetic energy of the water into electrical energy. The electricity thus produced can be carried by wires to homes and factories, where it can be converted to light energy, to heat, or to mechanical energy.

Energy and the Life-Support System

The *biosphere* is the thin (about 15 km thick) film of air, water, and soil in which all life exists. Only a small fraction of the energy that the biosphere receives is used to support life. About 30% of the incident solar radiation is immediately reflected back into space as ultraviolet and visible light. Nearly half is converted to heat, making our planet a warm and habitable place. About 23% of solar radiation powers the water cycle (Section 14.2), evaporating water from land and seas. The radiant energy of the sun is converted to the potential energy of water vapor, water droplets, and ice crystals in the atmosphere. This potential energy is converted to the kinetic energy of falling rain and snow and of flowing rivers.

A tiny but most important fraction—less than 0.02%—of solar energy is absorbed by green plants, which use it to power **photosynthesis**. In the presence of chlorophyll and a series of enzymes, the energy converts carbon dioxide and water to glucose, a simple sugar rich in energy.

$$6\,CO_2 \ + \ 6\,H_2O \ + \ \text{energy} \ \xrightarrow{\text{chlorophyll}} \ C_6H_{12}O_6 \ + \ 6\,O_2$$

Sunlight

Glucose (a simple sugar)

Photosynthesis also replenishes oxygen in the atmosphere. Glucose can be stored, or it can be converted to more complex foods and structural materials. All animals depend on the stored energy of green plants for survival.

SELF-ASSESSMENT Questions

1. The rate of using or producing energy, in units of J/second, is the
   a. energy   **b.** watt
   c. kilowatt-hour   **d.** volt

2. What sector of the U.S. economy uses the largest fraction of the nation's energy?
   a. residential   **b.** commercial
   c. industrial   **d.** transportation

3. About how much of the world's energy is used by the United States?
   a. 3%   **b.** 5%   **c.** 10%   **d.** 20%

4. An eagle in flight has
   a. force energy   **b.** kinetic energy
   c. potential energy   **d.** rotational energy

5. About a third of Earth's incident solar radiation
   a. powers the water cycle   **b.** is converted to heat
   c. powers photosynthesis   **d.** is reflected back to space

6. About what percentage of Earth's incident solar radiation is used in photosynthesis?
   a. 0.02%   **b.** 2%   **c.** 5%   **d.** 10%

Answers: 1. b; 2. c; 3. c; 4. b; 5. d; 6. a

15.2 Energy and Chemical Reactions

Learning Objectives ❯ Classify chemical reactions and physical processes as exothermic or endothermic. ❯ Explain how the heat of a reaction is calculated using bond energies.

We usually discuss energy changes in terms of an object or region losing energy and another object or region gaining it. When we warm our cold hands over a campfire, the burning wood gives off energy (as heat) and our hands gain energy, raising their temperature. In science, we define the **system** as the part of the universe under consideration. In the case of the campfire, the system is the burning wood. The **surroundings** are everything else—the rest of the universe (in theory)—but we usually limit the surroundings to those parts of the universe that exchange energy or matter or both with the system. In the case of the campfire, the surroundings are your hands and the air near the campfire.

Chemical reactions (or physical processes) that result in the release of heat from the system to the surroundings are **exothermic**. The molecules producing the heat are the "system," and other things near those molecules are the "surroundings."

The burning of methane, gasoline, and coal (Figure 15.1) are all exothermic reactions. In each case, chemical energy is converted to heat energy, which is lost by the burning molecules but is absorbed by the surroundings. If heat is released, the amount is written in the reaction on the right, as a "product" of the reaction, as in the reaction for the burning of methane, the main component of "natural gas," the fuel that is used in most "gas" furnaces in people's homes:

$$CH_4(g) + 2\ O_2(g) \longrightarrow CO_2(g) + 2\ H_2O(g) + 803\ kJ$$

In other reactions, such as the decomposition of water, energy must be supplied to the reactants from the surroundings; it is an **endothermic** process (Figure 15.2). We can write the amount of heat required for this process as a reactant in the chemical equation, since it must be absorbed by the "system" molecules, as in

$$2\ H_2O(g) + 573\ kJ \longrightarrow 2\ H_2(g) + O_2(g)$$

Physical processes can also be either exothermic or endothermic. Table 15.2 lists several examples of physical and chemical processes and classifies them as exothermic or endothermic.

Table 15.2	Some Exothermic and Endothermic Processes	
Exothermic Processes	Endothermic Processes
Freezing of water	Melting of ice
Condensation of water vapor	Evaporation of water
Metabolism in animals	Photosynthesis in plants
Forming chemical bonds	Breaking chemical bonds
Discharging a battery	Charging a battery

For chemical processes, an important thing to remember is that the "heat of reaction" is the energy output (or input) for the number of moles of reactants in the balanced chemical reaction. Obviously, much more heat would be emitted by burning a ton of coal compared to burning one charcoal briquet. Consider Example 15.2.

▲ **Figure 15.1** Coal burns in a highly exothermic reaction. The heat released can convert water to steam that can turn a turbine to generate electricity.

▲ **Figure 15.2** A striking endothermic reaction occurs when barium hydroxide octahydrate reacts with ammonium thiocyanate to produce barium thiocyanate, ammonia gas, and water.

Heat + Ba(OH)$_2$ + 8 H$_2$O(s) + 2 NH$_4$SCN(s) $\longrightarrow$ Ba(SCN$_2$)(s) + 2 NH$_3$(g) + 10 H$_2$O(l)

Here the reaction is carried out in a flask placed on a wet block of wood. The temperature drops well below the freezing point of water, freezing the flask to the block.

Example 15.2   Energy Release in Chemical Reactions

Experiments show that burning 1.00 mol (16.0 g) methane to form carbon dioxide and water releases 803 kJ (192 kcal) energy as heat. How much heat is given off if we burn 2.00 mol methane?

Solution

$$2.00\ mol \times \frac{803\ kJ}{1\ mol} = 1606\ kJ\ of\ heat\ released$$

Example 15.3   Energy Changes in Chemical Reactions

How much energy, in kilojoules, is released when 225 g propane is burned? The heat of reaction for burning propane is 2201 kJ/mol propane, considerably larger than for methane.

$$C_3H_8(g) + 5\ O_2(g) \longrightarrow 3\ CO_2(g) + 4\ H_2O(g) + 2201\ kJ$$

Solution

For this problem, we are given grams, not moles. The formula mass of propane, whose molecule consists of 3 C atoms and 8 H atoms, is

$$(3 \times 12.0\ u) + (8 \times 1.0) = 36.0\ u + 8.0\ u = 44.0\ u$$

2. How can molecules give off heat?

In reality, energy must be put into molecules first to break the bonds in the molecules. When the fragments recombine in a different arrangement, energy is released. It is the net result of those energy interactions that makes the overall process either give off heat or require heat to occur.

The molar mass is therefore 44.0 g. Next, we use the molar mass to convert grams of propane to moles of propane.

$$225 \text{ g } C_3H_8 \times \frac{1 \text{ mol } C_3H_8}{44.0 \text{ g } C_3H_8} = 5.11 \text{ mol } C_3H_8$$

Now we need the heat of combustion, 2201 kJ/mol, to complete our computation:

$$5.11 \text{ mol } C_3H_8 \times \frac{2201 \text{ kJ}}{1 \text{ mol } C_3H_8} = 11{,}300 \text{ kJ}$$

■ EXERCISE 15.3

How much energy in kilojoules is absorbed when 10.1 mol N_2 reacts with O_2 to form NO? The reaction of nitrogen and oxygen to form nitrogen monoxide requires an input of energy, so we write the energy as a reactant on the left.

$$N_2(g) + O_2(g) + 18.07 \text{ kJ} \longrightarrow 2 \text{ NO}(g)$$

Bond Energies

Why do some processes, either physical or chemical, require heat to happen and other processes emit heat during the process? What is happening with the molecules? It's fairly simple: First, all the bonds between atoms must break, which requires energy input, and then new bonds form from the molecular fragments, making new molecules, releasing energy to the surroundings. The net result is the amount of heat released to the surroundings, or the amount of heat that has been absorbed into the new molecules. The energy inherent in every atom-to-atom bond can be measured and is called the bond energy. The units are kJ/mol.

A simple example of how we determine if a chemical process is exothermic or endothermic is forming hydrogen chloride molecules from hydrogen molecules and chlorine molecules:

$$H_2(g) + Cl_2(g) \longrightarrow 2 \text{ HCl}(g)$$

For that reaction to happen, the bonds between the two hydrogen atoms in H_2 must first be broken, and then the bonds between the two chlorine atoms in Cl_2 must be broken. The free H atoms (each with one electron) and the free chlorine atoms (each with 7 electrons) now bond together, forming single covalent bonds, so the octet rule can be satisfied. Note that two HCl molecules are formed.

To calculate the heat of this reaction, we first find the bond energies from a reference book. We find that it takes 432 kJ to split up one mole of H—H bonds in the hydrogen molecules and 243 kJ of energy to split up 1 mole of Cl—Cl bonds in the chlorine molecules. We also find that 427 kJ of energy is released when 1 mole of HCl molecules is formed. Once we have the bond energies, we can compute the "enthalpy change" (the amount of heat released in this case) of the reaction:

enthalpy change =
sum of energy to break all the bonds − sum of energy released in forming bonds.

For this reaction, the energy of the reaction is

$$(1 \text{ mol H—H bonds} \times 432 \text{ kJ/mol} + 1 \text{ mol Cl—Cl bonds} \times 243 \text{ kJ/mol})$$

$$-(2 \text{ mol H—Cl bonds} \times 427 \text{ kJ/mol}) = -179 \text{ kJ/mol}$$

The negative sign of the answer means that more energy was released to the surroundings than was put into the molecules to break them apart. This reaction is exothermic, and heat can be considered a "product" of the reaction.

We can now write a thermochemical reaction as

$$H_2(g) + Cl_2(g) \longrightarrow 2 \text{ HCl}(g) + 179 \text{ kJ}$$

Writing it this way reminds us that 179 kJ of heat are given off if one starts with 1 mol of hydrogen and 1 mol of chlorine. In the event the sum of the bond energies is greater than the sum of the heat evolved in creating bonds, the resultant kJ are written on the left side of the equation and the reaction is endothermic.

In calculating the heat of reaction, it is usually best to draw all the Lewis structures for every molecule in the reaction, considering the stoichiometric coefficients in the balanced chemical equation. In this way, you can easily count the number and type of bonds that need to be broken and formed. Then find the bond energies and perform the calculation.

SELF-ASSESSMENT Questions

1. Which of the following is an exothermic process?
   a. $H_2O(g) \longrightarrow H_2O(l)$
   b. $H_2O(s) \longrightarrow H_2O(g)$
   c. $SiO_2(g) + 3\ C(s) + 624.7\ kJ \longrightarrow SiC(s) + 2\ CO(g)$
   d. $H_2O(l) \longrightarrow H_2O(g)$

2. Consider a burning candle. Which of the following is a correct statement?
   a. The entire room in which the candle is burning is considered the "system."
   b. The burning process is endothermic.
   c. Energy is needed to break bonds in the wax, but more energy than that is released when carbon dioxide and water vapor molecules are formed.
   d. The numerical value of the heat of reaction must be positive.

3. Melting an ice cube:
   a. is an exothermic process
   b. releases heat to the air
   c. cannot happen below the freezing point of water
   d. is an endothermic process

4. 400 g of propane are burned. Which of the following is true?
   a. About 2000 kJ of heat are released
   b. About 2000 kJ of heat are needed
   c. About 18000 kJ of heat are released
   d. About 800000 kJ of heat are needed

Answers: 1, a; 2, c; 3, d; 4, c

15.3 Reaction Rates

Learning Objective ➤ List factors that affect the rates of chemical reactions.

Chemical kinetics is concerned with the rates at which chemical reactions occur. Reaction rates depend on several factors, including temperature, concentrations of reactants, and the presence or absence of catalysts. Because reaction rates are related to temperature, they are closely related to energy, the focus of this chapter.

Reactions generally proceed faster at higher temperatures because molecules move faster and collide more frequently at higher temperatures, increasing the chance that they will react. For example, at room temperature, coal (carbon) reacts so slowly with oxygen (from the air) that the change is imperceptible. However, if coal is heated to several hundred degrees, it reacts rapidly. The heat evolved in the reaction keeps the coal burning smoothly. The increase in temperature also supplies more energy to break chemical bonds.

The kinetics of reactions is important both in everyday life and in industrial processes. In manufacturing a medicinal product, for example, we usually want the chemical synthesis to happen rather quickly rather than take hours or days on the production line. We heat water to boiling to cook noodles in a few minutes rather than let them sit in water a few hours. Sometimes we want to slow down reactions, not speed them up. Refrigeration slows down spoilage reactions in foods.

The concentrations of reactants affect the rate of most reactions because when we crowd more molecules into a given volume of space, the molecules collide more often. More collisions each second means more reactions each second. For example, if you light a wood splint and then blow out the flame, the splint continues to glow as the wood reacts slowly with oxygen in the air. If the glowing splint is placed in pure oxygen—five times more concentrated than O_2 in air—the splint bursts into flame because of the increase in reaction rate.

It DOES Matter!

We use the effect of temperature on chemical reactions in our daily lives. For example, we refrigerate milk or freeze vegetables to retard the chemical reactions that lead to spoilage. When we want to stir-fry meat or vegetables faster, we turn up the temperature under the frying pan.

Catalysts also affect the rates of chemical reactions. A carefully selected catalyst can increase the rate of a reaction that otherwise would be so slow as to be impractical. For example, the platinum in your automobile's catalytic converter causes the rapid breakdown of NO pollutant molecules coming from the engine and changes them back to nitrogen and oxygen molecules. Those oxygen molecules further oxidize carbon monoxide to carbon dioxide. This means that less CO and NO are emitted into our atmosphere. Catalysts are of great importance in the chemical industry and in biology, where they are usually termed enzymes. Catalysts may provide an alternative method, called a pathway, to form the same products, or lower the *activation energy*, the initial energy needed to get the reaction started in the first place.

SELF-ASSESSMENT Questions

1. The rate of a chemical reaction usually decreases when
   a. a catalyst is added
   b. a chemist is watching
   c. the concentration of one of the reactants is decreased
   d. the temperature is increased

2. If a chemical process that is occurring in aqueous solution in a vessel of some sort seems to be proceeding far too rapidly, what practical thing can be done to slow the process and bring the reaction under control?
   a. add water to the container to dilute the contents
   b. turn up the heat
   c. nothing, just let the reaction continue until the reactants are used up

3. A catalyst speeds up the rate of a chemical reaction by
   a. decreasing the favorability of product formation
   b. increasing the pressure of reactants and thus favoring product formation
   c. lowering the activation energy required for the reaction
   d. raising the temperature at which the reaction occurs

4. Hydrogen peroxide breaks down over time into water and oxygen gas. Manganese dioxide will increase that decomposition rate by at least a factor of 100. Manganese dioxide is a(n)
   a. catalyst
   b. inhibitor
   c. reactant
   d. supplement

Answers: 1, c; 2, a; 3, c; 4, a

It DOES Matter!

The tendency of energy to disperse helps to explain why it is relatively easy to pollute air or water and hard to clean up such pollution. For example, it would take little energy to dump a ton of a chlorofluorocarbon (CFC) into the air. The rapidly moving CFC molecules would quickly disperse among the nitrogen, oxygen, and other molecules in the air. Once the CFC molecules were scattered, the entire atmosphere would have to be processed to separate them from the air. Cleaning up pollution is good, but prevention of pollution is a far better alternative.

15.4 The Laws of Thermodynamics

Learning Objective ❯ State the first and second laws of thermodynamics, and discuss their implications for energy production and use.

We will take a look at our present energy sources and our future energy prospects shortly. To do so scientifically, we first examine some natural laws. Recall that natural laws merely summarize the results of many experiments. We won't recount all those experiments here. We will merely state the laws and some of their consequences.

Energy and the Laws of Thermodynamics

The **first law of thermodynamics** (*thermo* refers to heat; *dynamics* to motion) states that energy can be neither created nor destroyed. Energy can be changed from one form to another, however. This law (also called the **law of conservation of energy**) has been restated in several ways, including "You can't get something for nothing" and "There is no such thing as a free lunch." Energy cannot be made from nothing, which means that a machine cannot be made that produces more energy than it takes in. Energy does not just appear or disappear.

From the first law alone, we might conclude that we can't possibly run out of energy because energy is conserved. This is true enough, but it doesn't mean that we don't have problems. One problem is that energy transformation may be into a form that we cannot "harness" for useful work. Recall from the first chapter that energy is the "ability to do work." There is another long-armed law from which we cannot escape, as well.

Energy and the Second Law: You CAN'T Break Even

Despite innumerable attempts (and even the granting of several patents), no one has ever built a successful perpetual-motion machine. You can't make a machine that runs indefinitely without consuming energy. Even if an engine isn't doing any work, it loses energy (as heat) because of the friction of its moving parts. In fact, in any real engine, it is impossible to get as much useful energy out as you put in. In other words, you can't break even.

If energy is neither created nor destroyed, why do we always need more? Won't the energy we have now last forever? The answer lies in these facts:

- Energy can be changed from one form to another.
- Not all forms are equally useful.
- More useful forms of energy are constantly being degraded into less useful forms or distributed in a way that makes it impossible to recover.

Consider a cup of hot coffee sitting on the kitchen table. The hot cup of coffee tends to cool off, dissipating its thermal energy to molecules in the air, the ceramic cup into which it was poured, and every other object in the kitchen. Thus, there is a tendency toward an even distribution of energy. If all the thermal energy from that hot coffee is spread out among the molecules in the air, and the objects in the kitchen, and the walls, that thermal energy no longer is useful.

The second law of thermodynamics can be stated in many ways. One of them is "Heat always flows from a hot object to a cooler one" (Figure 15.3). The reverse does not occur spontaneously. (The hot coffee does not get hotter and the air around it get cooler.) Another way to state that law is "The forms of energy available for *useful* work are continually decreasing; energy spontaneously tends to distribute itself among the objects in the universe." Mechanical energy (machinery) is eventually changed into heat energy by friction and loss of energy to the surroundings. The energy still exists, but we cannot easily use it.

It is true that we can make energy flow from a cold region to a hot one— refrigerators and freezers do so—but we cannot do so without an input of energy and without producing changes elsewhere. We can reverse a spontaneous process only at a price. The price, in the case of a refrigerator, is the consumption of electricity; that is, you must use energy to cause energy flow from a cold space to a warmer one.

When we change energy from one form to another, we can't concentrate all the energy in a particular source to do the job we want it to do. For example, we use the energy in a fuel to push a piston in a car engine, or we use water rushing down from the top of a dam to run dynamos to generate electricity. In either case—indeed in all cases—some of the energy is converted to heat and thus is not available to do *useful* work.

Entropy

Yet another way to look at the second law is in terms of *entropy*. Scientists use **entropy** as a measure of the dispersal of energy in a system. The more the energy is spread out, the higher the entropy of the system and the less likely it is that this energy can be harnessed to do useful work. Spontaneous processes tend toward greater entropy or are exothermic, or both. The total entropy always increases for an isolated system.

As was noted in Chapter 6, molecules move about constantly. Their motion in solids is limited to rapid but tiny back-and-forth movements much like vibrations about a nearly fixed point. The molecules in liquids move more freely but still over only short distances. Those in gases move still more freely and over much greater distances.

In Chapter 3, we saw that the energy of light occurs in little packets called *photons*. Similarly, the energy of molecular motion is described using a concept called *microstates*. If you could take a snapshot capturing the positions of all molecules in a sample of matter at a given instant, you would have captured an image of a microstate. The number of microstates in which a given sample of matter can exist differs depending on whether it is in the solid, liquid, or gaseous state. The number of possible energy microstates will be lowest for a solid because the molecules in a solid are limited mainly to vibrational motion. Because molecules in the liquid state

▲ **Figure 15.3** Energy always flows spontaneously from a hot object to a cold one, never the reverse. It flows from a hot fire to the cooler marshmallow. (A spontaneous event is one that occurs without outside influence.)

The energy to run an engine usually comes from the concentrated chemical energy inside molecules of oil or coal. In biochemistry, food molecules are the concentrated energy source. In either case, energy is spread out during the process. The spread-out energy in the product gases—CO_2 and H_2O, in each case—is less useful. A car won't run on exhaust gases, nor can organisms obtain energy for life processes from respiratory products.

can move more freely, the number of possible energy microstates is much larger for liquids than for solids. When converted to a gas, the molecules can move still more freely and for much greater distances, so even more microstates are available to molecules in the gaseous state.

As any form of matter is heated, the energy in it is spread out among more accessible microstates (see Figure 15.4). Technically, entropy is the dispersal of energy among these microstates. In practice, entropy is often thought of as being analogous to "molecular disorder." Of course, we can often reverse the tendency toward greater entropy—but only through an input of energy.

▶ **Figure 15.4** The photograph depicts the vaporization of water; a sample of liquid water [$H_2O(l)$] at room temperature spontaneously changes to $H_2O(g)$ through the process of evaporation. At the macroscopic level, nothing appears to be taking place. However, in the molecular view, we see that the molecules are in motion and are much more widely spaced in the gaseous state than in the liquid state. Vaporization is spontaneous because the gas has greater *entropy* than the liquid. Molecules in the gas can be "arranged" in many more ways in their spread-out spacing than can molecules of the liquid. We can make liquid water from water vapor but only by compressing the gas and/or lowering its temperature.

SELF-ASSESSMENT Questions

1. The first law of thermodynamics is also called the law of
   a. conservation of energy
   b. conservation of mass
   c. entropy
   d. perpetual motion

2. That energy always goes spontaneously from more useful forms to less useful forms is a statement of the
   a. first law of thermodynamics
   b. law of unintended consequences
   c. second law of thermodynamics
   d. standard law of energy conversion

3. According to the second law of thermodynamics, the
   a. entropy of a system always decreases
   b. entropy of a system always increases
   c. total entropy always decreases for an isolated system
   d. total entropy always increases for an isolated system

4. In the process represented by the equation $H_2O(l) \longrightarrow H_2O(g)$, the entropy
   a. decreases
   b. depends on the catalyst used
   c. increases
   d. remains the same

5. If you place a cool hand on a warm cup of tea,
   a. heat spontaneously is transferred from the hand to the cup
   b. heat spontaneously is transferred from the cup to the hand
   c. both are in thermal equilibrium and no energy is transferred, because of the first law of thermodynamics
   d. the first law is relevant here but not the second

Answers: 1. a; 2. c; 3. d; 4. c; 5. b

15.5 Power: People, Horses, and Fossils

Learning Objective › List the common fossil fuels, and describe how modern society is based on their use.

Early people obtained their energy (food and fuel) by collecting wild plants and hunting wild animals. They expended this energy in hunting and gathering. Domestication of horses and oxen increased the availability of energy only slightly. The raw materials used by these work animals were natural, replaceable plant materials.

A **fuel** is a substance that burns readily with the release of significant amounts of energy. Plant materials were also the first fuels. These combustible materials kept early fires burning. As late as 1760, wood was almost the only fuel in use. Wood, dried dung, and crop residues still remain the main sources of heat for about one-third of the world's people.

One of the first mechanical devices used to convert energy to useful work was the waterwheel. The Egyptians first used waterpower about 2000 years ago, mainly for grinding grain. Later, waterpower was used for sawmills, textile mills, and other small factories. Windmills were introduced into western Europe during the Middle Ages, mainly for pumping water and grinding grain. In the 1800s, small windmills were seen on every small farm in the Midwest. More recently, large-scale wind power has been used to generate electricity.

Windmills and waterwheels are fairly simple devices for converting the kinetic energy of blowing wind and flowing water to mechanical energy. They were sufficient to power the early part of the Industrial Revolution. The development of the steam engine allowed factories to be located away from waterways. Since 1850, turbines turned by water, steam, and gas, the internal-combustion engine, and a variety of other energy-conversion devices have boosted the energy available for society's use by an estimated factor of 10,000.

The Industrial Revolution was fueled, in effect, by fossils—the buried remains of living organisms. Combustion of this material initiated modern industrial civilization. Today, more than 85% of the energy used to support our way of life comes from **fossil fuels**—coal, petroleum, and natural gas that formed during Earth's Carboniferous period around 300 million years ago. In the following sections, we consider the origin and chemical nature of these fuels that release the energy captured by ancient plants from rays of sunlight.

Fuels are *reduced* forms of matter, and the burning process is an oxidation (Chapter 8). If an atom already has its maximum number of bonds to oxygen atoms (or to other electronegative atoms such as chlorine or bromine), the substance cannot serve as a fuel. Indeed, some such substances can be used to put out fires. Figure 15.5 shows some representative fuels and nonfuels.

▲ Waterwheels at Hama, Syria, are 2000 years old. Some are more than 20 m high. Several are still used to lift water into aqueducts.

3. Do we really have an energy shortage?

There is no shortage of energy itself, but not energy is equally useful to us. The supply of materials like fossil fuels that provide convenient, *useful* energy is dwindling.

◀ **Figure 15.5** (a) Some fuels. Fuels are reduced forms of matter that release relatively large quantities of heat when burned. (b) Some nonfuels. These compounds are oxidized forms of matter.

(a) H—H Hydrogen

H—C—H (with H above and below) Methane (in natural gas)

C Carbon (in coal)

$C_6H_{12}O_6$ Glucose

C_8H_{18} Octane (in gasoline)

Fuels (reduced substances)

O_2 →

Cl_2 →

(b) O=C=O Carbon dioxide

O—H (with H below) Water

Cl—C—Cl (with Cl above and below) Carbon tetrachloride

H—Cl

Nonfuels (oxidized substances)

Reserves and Consumption Rates of Fossil Fuels

Earth has a limited supply of fossil fuels. Estimated U.S. and world reserves and annual U.S. and world consumption are given in Table 15.3. Estimates of reserves

Table 15.3	**Estimated U.S. and World Reserves of Economically Recoverable Fuels and Annual Consumption of Fossil Fuels**			
	Reserves		Consumption	
Fuel	United States	World	United States	World
Coal, billion tons	259	1038	0.890	8.40
Petroleum, billion barrels	33.4	1526	6.7	32.6
Natural gas, trillion cubic feet	323	6845	24.5	120

Source: U.S. Energy Information Administration, April 2014 report;
Data are as of January 1, 2013, for the year ending December 31, 2012.

Energy *production* refers to conversion of some form of energy into a more useful form. For example, production of petroleum means pumping, transporting, and refining it. Energy *consumption* involves using it in a way that changes it to a less useful form. In either case, energy is neither created nor destroyed.

vary greatly, depending on the assumptions made, and the numbers in the table imply far greater certainty than there is in reality. Even the most optimistic estimates, however, lead to the conclusion that these nonrenewable energy resources are being depleted rapidly. Indeed, in just a century, we will have used up more than half the fossil fuels that were formed over millions of years. In only a few hundred more years, we will have removed from Earth and burned virtually all the remaining recoverable fossil fuels. Of all that ever existed, about 90% will have been used in a period of 300 years.

Within the lifetime of today's 18-year-olds, natural gas and petroleum will likely become so scarce and so expensive that they won't be used much as fuels. At the current rate of production, U.S. reserves of petroleum and natural gas will be substantially depleted sometime during this century. Coal reserves should last perhaps 300 years. However, the rate of use of all fossil fuels is increasing, especially in developing nations.

Presumably, fossil fuels are still being formed in nature, a process that is perhaps most evident in peat bogs. The rate of formation is extremely slow, estimated to be only one fifty-thousandth of the rate at which fuels are being used.

SELF-ASSESSMENT Questions

1. Coal, petroleum, and natural gas are called fossil fuels because they
   a. are burned to release energy
   b. are nonrenewable and will run out
   c. cause air pollution
   d. were formed over millennia from the remains of ancient plants and animals

2. Which fossil fuel will likely last the longest, based on current rate of consumption?
   a. natural gas   b. crude oil   c. coal   d. peat

3. Which of the following is not a fuel?
   a. C   b. $CH_3CH_2CH_3$ c. CH_3CH_2OH d. CO_2

4. All fuels are
   a. carbon compounds   b. hydrocarbons
   c. oxidized forms of matter   d. reduced forms of matter

5. What fraction of the world's coal reserves is found in the United States?
   a. 2%   b. 10.7%   c. 31%   d. 25%

Answers: 1, d; 2, c; 3, d; 4, d; 5, d

15.6 Coal: The Carbon Rock of Ages

Learning Objective ⟩ List the origins, advantages, and disadvantages of coal as a fuel.

People probably have used small amounts of coal since prehistoric times. After the steam engine came into widespread use (by about 1850), the Industrial Revolution was powered largely by coal. By 1900, about 95% of the world's energy production came from the burning of coal. Today, coal supplies about 27% of worldwide energy production.

Coal is a fossil fuel. Giant ferns, reeds, and grasses that grew during the Carboniferous period around 300 million years ago were buried and converted over the ages to the coal we burn today. Coal is a complex combination of organic materials that burn and inorganic materials that produce ash. Coal consists primarily of carbon, plus water and other inorganic materials. The quality of coal is based on carbon content and those other elements.

Complete combustion of carbon produces carbon dioxide.

Carbon (from coal)   Oxygen (from air)

$$C(s) + O_2(g) \longrightarrow CO_2(g)$$

When combustion occurs in limited quantities of air, however, carbon monoxide and soot are formed.

$$2\,C(s) + O_2(g) \longrightarrow 2\,CO(g)$$

Soot is mostly unburned carbon.

Table 15.4	Major Components of Various Types of Coal (Minor Components Include Volatile Materials and Sulfur)		
Fuel Type	Carbon	Water	Ash (Minerals)
Lignite	25 to 35%	35 to 66%	6 to 20%
Sub-bituminous	35 to 65%	13 to 30%	10 to 15%
Bituminous	65 to 85%	5 to 10%	3 to 12%
Anthracite	85 to 95%	< 5%	2 to 8%

Source: Diessel, F. K. *Coal-Bearing Depositional Systems*. New York: Springer-Verlag, 1992.

Coal is ranked by carbon content, from low-grade peat and lignite to high-grade anthracite (Table 15.4). The energy obtained from coal is roughly proportional to its carbon content. Soft (bituminous) coal is much more plentiful than hard coal (anthracite). Lignite and peat have become increasingly important as the supplies of higher grades of coal have been depleted.

Coal deposits that exist today are less than 600 million years old. For millions of years, Earth was much warmer than it is now, and plant life flourished. Most plants lived, died, and decayed—playing their normal role in the carbon cycle (Figure 15.6). But some plant material became buried under mud and water. There,

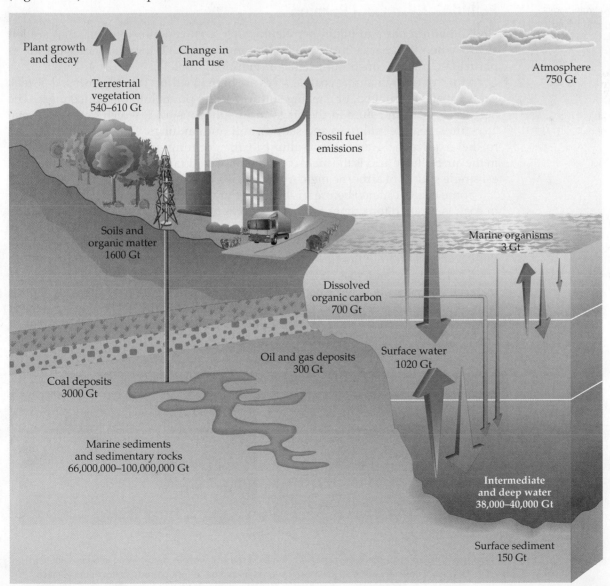

▲ **Figure 15.6** The carbon cycle. The numbers indicate the quantity of carbon, in gigatons (1Gt = 10^9 t). in each location. The arrows indicate the general direction of travel of carbon during its cycle.

▲ **It DOES Matter!**
This aerial view shows how over 4 million gallons of coal fly-ash slurry, the material removed from the flue gases of a coal-burning plant in Kingston, Tennessee, spread over 300 acres in 2008, damaging homes, washing out a road, rupturing a gas line and a water main, blocking a rail line, and felling trees.

in the absence of oxygen, it decayed only partially. The structural material of plants is largely cellulose $[(C_6H_{10}O_5)_n]$. Under increasing pressure, as the material was buried more deeply, the cellulose molecules broke down. Small molecules rich in hydrogen and oxygen escaped, leaving behind a material increasingly rich in carbon.

Thus, peat is an immature coal, only partly converted, with plant stems and leaves clearly visible. Anthracite, on the other hand, has been almost completely carbonized. Most coal has a measurable water content, though.

Abundant but Inconvenient Fuel

Coal is by far the most plentiful fossil fuel. The United States has about a quarter of the world's reserves. Electric utilities in the United States burn 1.0 billion metric tons of coal each year, generating 3.78 trillion kWh of electricity (45% of the total).

Coal, a solid, is an inconvenient fuel to use and dangerous to obtain. Coal mining is one of the most dangerous occupations in the world, accounting for over 100,000 deaths in the United States in the twentieth century alone, including accidents and black lung disease. Strip mining, though efficient, can devastate large areas. Coal is hauled in trains, barges, and trucks. We continue to pay great costs to extract coal from the ground and to transport it to the power plants and factories where it is used.

Pollution from Coal Burning

Unlike natural gas and liquid petroleum, solid coal contains minerals that are left as ash when the coal is burned. As noted in Chapter 13, minerals enter the air as particulate matter, constituting a major pollution problem.

Much of our remaining coal reserves are high in sulfur. When it burns, the stack gases must be scrubbed, or choking sulfur dioxide pours into the atmosphere. The SO_2 reacts with moisture in the air to form sulfurous acid, which damages metal structures, marble buildings and statues, and human lungs. The sulfur dioxide can further oxidize in the air to form sulfur trioxide, forming sulfuric acid with moisture in the air. Sulfuric acid is the main component of acid rain. Coal is currently the largest single source of airborne mercury emissions in the United States.

Some coal is cleaned before it is burned. Pyrite, (FeS_2), the major source of sulfur in coal, is three to four times more dense than the coal itself, so a flotation method is used to separate the heavier minerals from the coal. Coal can also be converted to more convenient gaseous and liquid fuels, again leaving the minerals behind. All these processes add to the cost of the coal.

Coal is more than just a fuel. When it is heated in the absence of air, volatile material is driven off, leaving behind a product—mostly carbon—called *coke*, which is used in the production of iron and steel. The more volatile material is condensed to liquid coal oil and a sticky mixture called *coal tar*, both of which are sources of organic chemicals for medical and industrial use.

(a)

(b)

▲ Strip mining bares vast areas of vegetation. The exposed soil washes away, filling streams with mud and silt. U.S. laws now require the (expensive) restoration of most stripped areas. Unfortunately, much damage was done before these laws were passed, and many consider the present laws inadequate. These photographs show the site of a strip mine in Morgan County, Tennessee: (a) the abandoned mine in 1963 and (b) the area after it was reclaimed in a demonstration project in 1971.

SELF-ASSESSMENT Questions

1. Coal comes from
   a. microscopic ocean creatures
   b. compressed minerals under oceans
   c. decomposed plants
   d. other minerals

2. Coal is mainly carbon because
   a. plants have carbon dioxide in their cells
   b. plants are mainly cellulose, a compound of C, H, and O
   c. plants are mainly proteins
   d. all living things have carbon in them

3. Analysis of a solid fuel shows it to be 87% carbon. It is most likely
   a. anthracite coal
   b. bituminous coal
   c. peat
   d. wood

4. When coal is burned, the inorganic constituents end up as
   a. flue gases
   b. solid sulfur compounds
   c. ashes
   d. organic matter

5. Which fossil fuel contributes the most to atmospheric sulfur oxides that are major air pollutions?
   a. coal
   b. natural gas
   c. petroleum
   d. propane

6. On what physical property is the flotation method of coal cleaning based?
   a. density
   b. electrostatic precipitation
   c. melting point
   d. temperature

Answers: 1, c; 2, b; 3, b; 4, c; 5, a; 6, a

15.7 Natural Gas and Petroleum

Learning Objective ❯ List the characteristics, advantages, and disadvantages of natural gas and petroleum.

Both natural gas and petroleum consist of hydrocarbons formed by the anaerobic decomposition of remains of living microorganisms. These remains settled to the bottom of the sea millions of years ago. The organic matter was buried under layers of mud and converted over the ages by high temperature and pressure to gaseous and liquid hydrocarbons.

Natural Gas

Natural gas, composed principally of methane, is the cleanest of the fossil fuels. Minor components of this gaseous fossil fuel vary greatly. In North America, a pipeline natural gas supply might contain 83–95% methane, 2–6% ethane, 1–2% propane, and smaller amounts of butanes and pentanes. Natural gas burns with a relatively clean flame, and the products are mainly carbon dioxide and water.

$$CH_4(g) + 2\,O_2(g) \longrightarrow CO_2(g) + 2\,H_2O(g) + heat$$

The gas, as it comes from the ground, often contains nitrogen (N_2), sulfur compounds, and other substances as impurities. As in any combustion in air, some nitrogen oxides are formed. When natural gas is burned in insufficient air, carbon monoxide and soot can be major products.

$$2\,CH_4(g) + 3\,O_2(g) \longrightarrow 2\,CO(g) + 4\,H_2O(g)$$

$$CH_4(g) + O_2(g) \longrightarrow C(s) + 2\,H_2O(g)$$

Natural gas is trapped in geological formations capped by impermeable rock. It is removed through wells drilled into the gas-bearing formations. About 90% of today's natural gas in the United States is obtained by hydraulic fracturing, or fracking, of shale formations up to 5000 feet below ground. Up until recently, fracking has mainly involved forcing chemically treated water under high pressure into the layers of rock. The fractured rock releases the gas.

A recently developed method for propping open the cracks in the shale formations is using silica sand (often called "frac sand") so that fluids (both liquid and gaseous) can easily flow out of the cracks. One major oil or natural gas well can require a few thousand tons of sand, so mining the specialized sand has become a major industry in recent years in several midwestern states. Between 2008 and 2013, the amount of "frac" sand used by the petroleum industry has more than tripled. This industrial boom has brought with it much controversy in small-town America, where energy industries seek to establish large mining operations (see Figure 15.6).

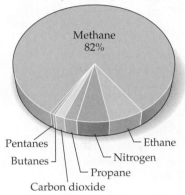

▲ A rough guide to the composition of typical natural gas. Natural gas is mostly methane, with small amounts of other hydrocarbons, nitrogen, and a few other gases.

▲ Natural gas burns with a relatively clean flame.

4. What is "frac sand," and how is it different from ordinary beach sand?

All sand is not the same! Usually sand is a mixture of small particles of varying color, size, and composition. "Frac sand" is 95% silicon dioxide (quartz), with rounded particles about 0.4 to 0.8 mm in diameter.

▶ Ordinary sand and fracking sand. The sand on the left consists of ordinary, multivariant particles, but the frac sand on the right consists of small, rounded quartz particles, found extensively in North Dakota, Minnesota, Wisconsin, and Iowa. Grains in this image are about 0.50 mm in size.

Most natural gas is used as fuel, supplying about 23% of worldwide energy consumption, but it is also an important raw material. In North America, a portion of the two- to four-carbon alkanes is separated from the rest of the natural gas. Ethane and propane are *cracked*—decomposed by heating with a catalyst—to form ethylene and propylene. These alkenes are intermediates in the synthesis of plastics (Chapter 10) and many other useful commodities. Natural gas is also the raw material from which methanol and many other organic compounds are made. Like other fossil fuels, the supply of natural gas is limited (refer to Table 15.3).

Petroleum: Liquid Hydrocarbons

Natural gas and petroleum, often called "crude oil," are frequently found close together in nature. With the development of the internal combustion engine, petroleum became increasingly important and by 1950 had replaced coal as the principal fuel. Modern culture was forever changed by the invention of the automobile.

Petroleum is an extremely complex, black, viscous liquid mixture of organic compounds—as many as 17,000 compounds were separated from a sample of Brazilian crude oil. Most are hydrocarbons: alkanes, cycloalkanes, and aromatic compounds. As with natural gas, complete combustion of these substances yields mainly carbon dioxide and water. A representative reaction is that of an octane.

$$2 \, C_8H_{18}(l) + 25 \, O_2(g) \longrightarrow 16 \, CO_2(g) + 18 \, H_2O(g)$$

Combustion of petroleum in air also produces nitrogen oxides. Incomplete burning yields carbon monoxide and soot. Petroleum usually contains small amounts of sulfur compounds, as well, that produce sulfur dioxide when burned.

Petroleum is thought to be formed mainly from the fats of ocean-dwelling, microscopic organisms because it is nearly always found in rocks of oceanic origin. Fats are made up mainly of compounds containing carbon, hydrogen, and a little oxygen (for example, $C_{57}H_{110}O_6$). Removal of some oxygen and a slight rearrangement or even splitting bonds in these fats form typical petroleum hydrocarbon molecules.

Crude oil can be separated into a wide variety of substances, including fuel oil, which is used to heat homes and to produce electricity, and gasoline, which is the major fraction of petroleum used to power automobiles. Because internal combustion engines are both numerous and rather inefficient, the combustion of gasoline contributes greatly to air pollution (Chapter 13). Petroleum-derived fuels are generally dirtier than natural gas because they contain more impurities. However, both types of fuel are major sources of CO_2 emissions that are causing global climate change.

Air pollution isn't the only problem: Burning up our petroleum reserves will leave us without a ready source of many familiar materials. Most industrial organic chemicals come from petroleum (others are derived from coal and natural gas). These chemicals yield plastics, synthetic fibers, solvents, and many other consumer products.

Worldwide, petroleum still appears to be quite abundant (see Table 15.3). However, U.S. petroleum reserves have been declining since 1972. Further tapping of offshore deposits and deeper drilling would produce only a few years' supply and would require a great deal more energy (and money) than drilling on land.

The developed countries of North America, western Europe, and Japan depend heavily on oil imports from politically unstable developing nations, making the industrial nations economically and politically vulnerable. U.S. dependence on imported oil leads to economic and political problems. Political events in the oil-rich Middle East have caused huge oil price increases several times. Continued military involvement in the Middle East, disastrous hurricanes in the Gulf of Mexico, and increased demand in developing countries, especially China, caused crude oil prices to hit record highs in 2008, with only small price drops afterward.

Obtaining and Refining Petroleum

Crude oil is liquid, a convenient form for transportation. Petroleum is pumped easily through pipelines or hauled across the oceans in giant tankers. Pumping petroleum from the ground requires little energy. As domestic supplies diminish, however, we will have to expend an increasing fraction of the energy content of petroleum to transport it to where it is needed. Also, as petroleum is pumped out of the ground, the remaining oil becomes increasingly difficult to extract. The oil that is left behind is more scattered, and more energy is required to collect it.

As it comes from the ground, crude oil is of limited use. To make it better suited to our needs, we separate it into fractions by heating it in a fractional distillation column (Figure 15.7). Petroleum deposits nearly always have associated natural gas, part or all of which also goes through a separation process. The lighter hydrocarbon molecules come off at the top of the column, and the heavier ones at the bottom (Table 15.5 on the next page).

▲ **Figure 15.7** The fractional distillation of petroleum. Crude oil is vaporized, and the column separates the components according to their boiling points. The lower-boiling constituents reach the top of the column, and the higher-boiling components come off lower in the column. A nonvolatile residue collects at the bottom.

Table 15.5	Typical Petroleum Fractions		
Fraction	Typical Size Range of Hydrocarbons	Approximate Range of Boiling Points (°C)	Typical Uses
Gas	CH_4 to C_4H_{10}	Less than 40	Fuel, starting materials for plastics
Gasoline	C_5H_{12} to $C_{12}H_{26}$	40–200	Fuel, solvents
Kerosene	$C_{12}H_{26}$ to $C_{16}H_{34}$	175–275	Diesel fuel, jet fuel, home heating, cracking to gasoline
Heating oil	$C_{15}H_{32}$ to $C_{16}H_{34}$	250–400	Industrial heating, cracking to gasoline
Lubricating oil	$C_{17}H_{36}$ and up	Above 300	Lubricants
Residue	$C_{20}H_{42}$ and up	Above 350 (some decomposition)	Paraffin, asphalt

Gasoline is usually the fraction of petroleum most in demand, and fractions that boil at higher temperatures are often converted to gasoline by cracking. This process, with $C_{14}H_{30}$ as an example, is illustrated in Figure 15.8. Cracking not only converts some of the large molecules to those in the gasoline range (C_5H_{12} through $C_{12}H_{26}$) but also produces a variety of useful by-products. The unsaturated hydrocarbons are starting materials for the manufacture of a host of petrochemicals.

The cracking process illustrates the way chemists modify nature's materials to meet human needs and desires. Starting with petroleum or coal tar, chemists can create a dazzling array of substances with a wide variety of properties, including plastics, pesticides, herbicides, perfumes, preservatives, painkillers, antibiotics, stimulants, depressants, dyes, and detergents.

The ability to modify hydrocarbon molecules enables the petroleum industry to shift production to whatever fraction is desired. The industry can, on demand, increase the proportion of gasoline in summer, or of fuel oil in winter, from a given supply of petroleum. It can even make gasoline from coal, a more difficult process. However, fossil fuels and other products from them are not sustainable. Scientists are seeking new sources of energy that do not depend on petroleum. Perhaps we can soon reduce this profligate waste of resources. Spaceship Earth has aboard it all the supplies it will have in the foreseeable future. We must use them wisely.

Gasoline

Gasoline, like the petroleum from which it is derived, is mainly a mixture of hydrocarbons. Commercial gasoline typically contains more than 150 different compounds, but up to 1000 have been identified in some blends. Among the hydrocarbons, a typical gasoline sample might include straight-chain alkanes, branched-chain alkanes, alkenes, cyclic hydrocarbons, and 20% or more aromatic hydrocarbons. Gasoline also contains a variety of additives, including antiknock agents, antioxidants, antirust agents, anti-icing agents, upper-cylinder lubricants, detergents, and dyes. Typical alkanes in gasoline range from C_5H_{12} to $C_{12}H_{26}$. There are also small amounts of some sulfur- and nitrogen-containing compounds.

The gasoline fraction of petroleum as it comes from a distillation column is called *straight-run gasoline*. It doesn't burn very well in modern high-compression automobile engines, but chemists are able to modify it to make it burn more smoothly.

$$CH_3CH_2CH_2CH_2CH_2CH_2CH_2CH_2CH_2CH_2CH_2CH_2CH_2CH_3 \xrightarrow[\text{catalyst}]{\text{heat}}$$

$$CH_3CH_2CH_2CH_2CH_2CH_2CH_2CH_2CH_2CH_2CH_2CH_3 \ + \ CH_2{=}CH_2$$

and

$$CH_3CH_2CH_2CH_2CH_2CH_2CH_2CH_2CH_2CH_2CH_3 \ + \ CH_3CH{=}CH_2$$

and

$$CH_3CH_2CH_2CH_2CH_2CH_2CH_2CH_3 \ + \ CH_3CH_2CH_2CH_2CH{=}CH_2$$

and so on

▶ **Figure 15.8** Formulas of a few of the possible products formed when $C_{14}H_{30}$, a typical molecule in kerosene, is cracked. In practice, a wide variety of hydrocarbons (most of which have fewer than 15 carbon atoms), hydrogen gas, and char (mostly elemental carbon) are formed. Cyclic and branched-chain hydrocarbons are also produced.

The Octane Ratings of Gasolines

In an internal combustion engine, the gasoline–air mixture sometimes ignites before the spark plug "fires." This is called *knocking* and can damage the engine. Early on, scientists learned that some types of hydrocarbons, especially those with branched structures, burned more evenly and were less likely to cause knocking than others. An arbitrary performance standard, called the **octane rating**, was established in 1927. Isooctane was assigned an octane rating of 100. An unbranched-chain compound, heptane, was given an octane rating of 0. A gasoline rated 90 octane was one that performed the same as a mixture that was 90% isooctane and 10% heptane.

$$
\begin{array}{cc}
\underset{\substack{| \\ CH_3}}{CH_3-\overset{\overset{CH_3}{|}}{C}-CH_2-\overset{\overset{CH_3}{|}}{CH}-CH_3} & CH_3CH_2CH_2CH_2CH_2CH_2CH_3 \\
\\
\text{Isooctane} & \text{Heptane} \\
\text{(Octane rating 100)} & \text{(Octane rating 0)}
\end{array}
$$

During the 1930s, chemists discovered that the octane rating of gasoline could be improved by heating it in the presence of a catalyst such as sulfuric acid (H_2SO_4) or aluminum chloride ($AlCl_3$). This *isomerizes* some of the unbranched molecules to highly branched molecules. For example, heptane molecules can be isomerized so that they have branched structures. Chemists also can combine small hydrocarbon molecules (below the size range of gasoline) into larger ones more suitable for use as fuel. This process is called *alkylation*. In a typical alkylation reaction, isobutylene is reacted with propane. The product molecules are in the right size range for gasoline, and the highly branched molecules are high in octane number. Scientists have found other ways to get high octane ratings for unleaded fuels. For example, petroleum refineries use **catalytic reforming** to convert low-octane alkanes to high-octane aromatic compounds. Hexane (with an octane number of 25) can be converted to benzene (octane number 106).

Certain additives substantially improve the antiknock quality of gasoline. Tetraethyllead [$Pb(CH_2CH_3)_4$] was found to be especially effective. As little as 1 mL of tetraethyllead per liter of gasoline (1 part per 1000) increases the octane rating by 10 or more. Lead, unfortunately, fouls the catalytic converters used in modern automobiles. More important, lead is especially toxic to the brain. Even small amounts can lead to learning disabilities in children. In the United States, unleaded gasoline became available in 1974, and leaded gasoline has been phased out as automotive fuel. Yet in many other countries, in Central America and Africa, and in Mexico, leaded gas is still an option at many gas stations.

Octane boosters that have replaced tetraethyllead include ethanol, methanol, *tert*-butyl alcohol, and methyl *tert*-butyl ether (MTBE). None of these is nearly as effective as tetraethyllead in boosting the octane rating. They must therefore be used in fairly large proportions. MTBE, like ethers in general (Chapter 9), is rather unreactive chemically, but it is soluble in water to the extent of 4.8 g per 100 g of water. When gasoline spills or leaks from storage tanks, MTBE enters the groundwater, leading to widespread contamination. MTBE is listed as a hazardous substance under the federal Superfund Act and is considered a potential human carcinogen by the EPA. The exact threat to human health is far from clear, but use of MTBE in gasoline has been banned in many areas.

Ethanol has become a common and important gasoline additive. The EPA allows up to 15% ethanol in gasoline (E15 fuel) for cars built in 2001 or later. Some states require all gasoline to contain 10% ethanol. Most ethanol comes from corn, so the use of ethanol in gasoline is controversial, because much of the corn grown in the central part of the United States is used to feed cattle rather than to be made into ethanol to be burned in car engines, a competing use. Diversion of corn to ethanol production apparently leads to increased food prices.

Unlike gasoline, which is made up of hydrocarbons, the alcohols used as octane boosters all contain oxygen and therefore are sometimes called *oxygenates*. Not only do these additives improve the octane rating, but they also decrease the amount of

5. Why don't we use more alternative fuels for automobiles?

Use of alternative fuels is increasing, but the cost (EROEI) of those fuels is very high compared to that of fossil fuels. Agriculture is a major contributor to modern life and economics. Farmers prefer to keep corn as feed for animals, not to grow it to make E-85 fuel. Also, the current infrastructure is set up to use fossil fuels, and it is very costly to build new infrastructure (such as hydrogen filling stations).

carbon monoxide in auto exhaust gas. A disadvantage of oxygenates is that they are partially oxidized. That makes their energy content lower than that of pure hydrocarbon fuels, so the distance a car can travel per tankful is somewhat shorter.

Alternative Fuels

An automobile engine can be made to run on nearly any liquid or gaseous fuel. There are cars on the road today powered by natural gas, by propane, by diesel fuel, by fuel cells, and even by used fast-food restaurant grease. There are electric cars that can be plugged into the power grid and hybrid cars that can switch from electricity to gasoline as needed.

Diesel fuel for automobiles overlaps the kerosene fraction of petroleum (refer to Table 15.5); it consists mainly of C_9 to C_{20} hydrocarbons. Diesel fuel has a greater proportion of straight-chain alkanes than gasoline does. The standard for performance, called the *cetane number*, is based on hexadecane ($C_{16}H_{34}$), once known as cetane. A renewable fuel called *biodiesel* can be used in some unmodified diesel engines. Biodiesel is made by reacting ethanol with vegetable oils and animal fats.

Brazil makes extensive use of ethanol, made by fermentation of sucrose from sugarcane. In the United States, flexible fuel vehicles (FFVs) are designed to run on E85 gasoline, a fuel that is 85% ethanol and 15% gasoline. Ethanol alone or blended with gasoline is not likely to be an answer to our energy problems. Most ethanol is made from corn, and widespread use would require conversion of huge tracts of farmland to corn production.

Energy Return on Energy Invested

When evaluating an energy source, we must consider the *energy return on energy invested* (EROEI) of exploiting the source. EROEIs are difficult to evaluate, and the results often have a high degree of uncertainty. However, these ratings can be quite important because if the EROEI of a source is 1 or less, it becomes an energy sink rather than a source.

In the early days of the petroleum industry, the EROEI for Texas crude oil may have been as much as 100:1; investing the equivalent of 1 barrel of oil could produce 100 barrels. The EROEI for oil from the Middle East is still about 10:1, and that of oil produced today in the United States is about 3:1. Oil from ever more remote places or ever deeper offshore wells will have ever lower EROEIs.

The EROEIs of alternative energy sources are currently quite low. Canada has vast deposits of tar sands, but the EROEI is only about 1.5:1. Colorado has huge deposits of oil shale, but the EROEI is likely to be quite low.

The EROEI for ethanol is the subject of much debate, with proposed values ranging from a low of 0.78:1 to the highest estimate for ethanol from corn of 1.67:1. There are two reasons for the low EROEI for ethanol: Much energy is needed to distill or evaporate the ethanol after fermentation; and ethanol has a lower energy content than petroleum fuels.

The EROEI of wind energy in good locations is about 20:1, and that for silicon-based solar panels is about 12:1. Hydrogen has an EROEI of less than 1:1 because it cannot be simply extracted from the ground. Hydrogen can be generated by electricity from water or by chemical reactions such as metals with acids. For now, those measures require more energy than the hydrogen produces when burned.

In addition to the EROEI, we have to consider the environmental consequences of exploiting an energy source. For example, getting oil from tar sands or oil shale is a messy process. Thus, our quest for plentiful energy will be costly and controversial.

SELF-ASSESSMENT Questions

1. The main constituent in natural gas is
   a. CH_4 **b.** $CH_3CH_2CH_3$ **c.** C_6H_6 **d.** CH_3OH

2. Which of the fossil fuels is the cleanest and simplest in composition?
   a. coal
   b. it depends on the source
   c. petroleum
   d. natural gas

3. In the United States, oil production
   a. peaked in 1970   **b.** peaked in 1999
   c. peaked in 2010   **d.** will peak in 2030

4. Cracking is used to
   a. convert heavier fractions to lighter ones
   b. improve the octane rating
   c. remove sulfur
   d. separate various fractions

5. Energy return on energy investment (EROEI):
   a. is a larger number where the infrastructure for extraction of energy sources is already in place, such as the Middle East
   b. is a small number where it is economically reasonable to pursue
   c. is high in the United States but low in areas with significant energy reserves
   d. is higher for alternative fuels than for traditional fuels

6. An alkylation unit
   a. converts lighter fractions to heavier ones
   b. improves the asphalt yield
   c. removes sulfur
   d. separates various fractions

7. Isomerization is used to convert
   a. alcohols to ethers
   b. branched alkane molecules to straight-chain ones
   c. hexane to isooctane
   d. straight-chain molecules to branched ones

8. Catalytic reforming converts
   a. branched molecules to straight-chain ones
   b. branched molecules to aromatic ones
   c. straight-chain molecules to aromatic ones
   d. straight-chain molecules to branched ones

9. The octane rating for gasoline is related to the fuel's
   a. concentration of octane (C_8H_{16})
   b. energy content in kilocalories
   c. power rating
   d. tendency to cause knocking

10. Most gasoline stations offer, or are required to sell, automobile fuel that is
    a. 15% ethanol, 85% gasoline
    b. 10% ethanol, 90% gasoline
    c. 90% isooctane, 10% ethanol
    d. 10% ether, 90% octane

11. Hydraulic fracturing technology, including the use of fracking sand, has caused at least a 40% increase in reserves in the last eight years of
    a. coal
    b. biomass
    c. gasoline
    d. natural gas

Answers: 1, a; 2, d; 3, a; 4, a; 5, a; 6, a; 7, d; 8, c; 9, d; 10, b; 11, d

15.8 Convenient Energy

Learning Objective ❯ Explain why gaseous and liquid fuels are more convenient to use than solid fuels.

The convenience of a fuel depends on its physical state: Gases and liquids are convenient, while solids are much less so. Perhaps the most convenient form of energy is electricity (Table 15.6). We can use electricity to provide light and hot water and to run motors of all sorts. We can use it to heat and cool our homes and workplaces. When looking at future energy sources, then, we look to a large degree at ways of generating electricity. But what is the advantage to electricity if we make it by burning coal? There is no simple answer.

Table 15.6 **Convenience of Fuels in Various Physical States**

Physical State	Extraction	Transportation to Cities	Distribution within a City	In Use Convenience	Cleanliness
Solids (coal, wood)	Shovels, borers, blasting	Trucks, trains, barges (slurry with water in pipe)	Trucks, buckets	Least	Dirtiest
Liquids (gasoline, fuel oil)	Pumps	Pipelines, tankers, barges, trucks	Trucks		
Gases (natural gas)	Pumps, fracking sand	Pipeline	Pipes		
Electricity[a] (electron flow)	—	Wires	Wires	Most	

[a] Produced by burning any of the primary fuels and included for comparison.

CO_2, NO_x, SO_x

To smokestack

Steam
turbine

Generator

Steam

Pulverized
coal

Transmission
lines

Hot
air

Water

Boiler   Warm   Condenser   Cold
          water   water

River

▲ **Figure 15.9** A diagram showing how a coal-burning power plant generates electricity.

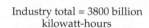

Industry total = 3800 billion
kilowatt-hours

Coal
45%

Other
0.3%

Other renewables 4%

Hydroelectric 7%

Petroleum 1%

Gas
23%

Nuclear
20%

▲ **Figure 15.10** Percentages of electric power generation in the United States from various energy sources in 2009.

Any fuel can be burned to boil water, and the steam produced can turn a turbine to generate electricity. Figure 15.9 shows a coal-fired steam power plant. At present, about 45% of U.S. electric energy comes from coal-burning plants (Figure 15.10). Such facilities are at best only about 40% efficient. Thus, about 60% of the energy of the fossil fuel is wasted as heat, though some power installations use waste heat to warm buildings.

Coal Gasification and Liquefaction

Coal can be converted to gas or oil. When we run short of gas and petroleum, why not make them from coal? The technology has been around for years. Gasification and liquefaction do have some advantages: Gases and liquids are easy to transport, and the process of conversion leaves much of the sulfur and minerals behind, thus overcoming a serious disadvantage of coal as a fuel.

The basic process for converting coal to a synthetic gaseous fuel involves reduction of carbon by hydrogen. Passing steam over hot charcoal produces **synthesis gas**, a mixture of hydrogen and carbon monoxide.

$$C(s) + H_2O(g) \longrightarrow CO(g) + H_2$$

The hydrogen can be used to change the carbon in coal or other substances to methane. Coal can also be converted to methanol by way of synthesis gas, a multistep process that requires catalysts at every step.

Both gasification and liquefaction of coal require a lot of energy; up to one-third of the energy content of the coal is lost in the conversion. Liquid fuels from coal are high in unsaturated hydrocarbons and sulfur, nitrogen, and arsenic compounds. Their combustion products require large amounts of water, yet the large coal deposits that would be used are in arid regions. Furthermore, these processes are messy. Without stringent safeguards, conversion plants would seriously pollute both air and water. Coal conversion also produces a lot of particulate matter.

Other processes that have been used to make liquid fuels from coal are the Bergius and Fischer–Tropsch methods. In the Bergius method, coal is reacted with hydrogen. In the Fischer–Tropsch method, coal is reacted with steam to make a mixture of carbon monoxide and hydrogen, which is then reacted over an iron catalyst to produce a mixture of hydrocarbons. Both processes were used in Germany during World War II. Since 1955, the Sasol Company has used a variation of the Fischer–Tropsch method to provide a significant portion of liquid fuels for South Africa.

SELF-ASSESSMENT Questions

1. About what percentage of the electricity produced in the United States comes from coal-burning plants?
   a. 25%   **b.** 35%   **c.** 45%   **d.** 80%

2. Natural gas is transported mainly by
   a. ocean-going tanker   **b.** pipelines
   c. railroad car   **d.** truck

3. About what percent of the energy from coal burned in a power plant reaches customers as electricity?
   a. 20   **b.** 40   **c.** 60   **d.** 80

4. Coal gasification produces mainly
   a. coke   **b.** H_2 **c.** CH_4 **d.** $CH_3CH_2CH_3$

5. The convenience of a fuel depends on its
   a. carbon content   **b.** density
   c. odor   **d.** physical state

▲ **Figure 15.11** A diagram showing how a nuclear power plant generates electricity. Fission of uranium heats the water in the reactor, which generates steam that drives the turbines, producing electricity. Control rods absorb neutrons to slow the fission reaction as needed. Nuclear reactors are housed in containment buildings made of steel and reinforced concrete, designed to withstand nuclear accidents and prevent the release of radioactive substances into the environment.

15.9 Nuclear Energy

Learning Objectives ❭ List the advantages and disadvantages of nuclear energy. ❭ Describe how a nuclear power plant generates electricity.

In Chapter 11, we explored nuclear reactions, radioactive decay, medical uses for radioactive isotopes for both diagnosis and therapy, and both nuclear fission and fusion. So far, nuclear fusion reactions cannot be controlled for producing energy here on Earth, only in the stars, including our own sun. Nuclear fission reactions, however, can be controlled in a **nuclear reactor**. The energy released during fission can be used to generate steam, which can turn a turbine to generate electricity (Figure 15.11).

At the dawn of the nuclear age, some people envisioned nuclear power as likely to fulfill the biblical prophecy of a fiery end to our world. Others saw it as a source of unlimited energy. During the late 1940s, some claimed that electricity from nuclear power plants would become so cheap that it eventually would not have to be metered. Nuclear power has not yet brought either paradise or perdition, but it is highly controversial. Our great demand for energy indicates that the controversy will continue for years to come.

At present, about 20% of U.S. electricity comes from nuclear power plants. The eastern seaboard and upper midwestern states, many of which have minimal fossil fuel reserves, are heavily dependent on nuclear power for electricity.

The United States could do as other nations do and rely more on nuclear power (Table 15.7), but the public is quite fearful of nuclear power plants. This apprehension was exacerbated in 2011 by the accident at Fukushima, Japan. The United States has 104 operating nuclear reactors, but only one new plant has been ordered since 1978. It takes about 10 years to build a nuclear power plant. There will have to be a dramatic change in public attitude if nuclear power is to play a big role in our energy future.

Table 15.7	**Electricity Generation Using Nuclear Power Plants (Selected Countries)**		
Country	Total Electricity from Nuclear Power Plants (%)	Number of Operating Nuclear power Plants	Number of Nuclear Power Plants under Construction
Canada	16.0%	19	0
China	2.1%	20	28
France	73.3%	58	1
India	3.5%	21	6
Japan	1.7%	50	2
Korea	27.6%	23	5
Russia	17.5%	33	10
Sweden	42.7%	10	0
Ukraine	43.6%	15	2
United Kingdom	18.3%	16	0
United States	19.4%	104	5
Other countries	NA	72	13
World total	NA	441	72

Nuclear Power Plants

There are several types of nuclear power plants, but we won't discuss the different designs. The one illustrated in Figure 15.11 is a pressurized water reactor. Earlier models were mainly boiling water reactors, in which the steam from the reactor was used to power the turbine directly.

Nuclear power plants use the same fission reactions employed in nuclear bombs (see Chapter 11) but nuclear power plants cannot blow up like bombs. The uranium used in power plants is enriched to only 3–4% uranium-235. A bomb requires about 90% uranium-235.

In a nuclear power plant, a *moderator* is used to slow down the neutrons produced by the fission reaction so that they can be absorbed by uranium-235 atoms. Ordinary water serves as the moderator in 75% of reactors worldwide, graphite is used in 20% of reactors, and heavy water (^2H_2O or D_2O) in 5% of reactors. The fission reaction is controlled by the insertion of boron steel or cadmium *control rods*. Boron and cadmium absorb neutrons readily, preventing them from participating in the chain reaction. These rods are installed when the reactor is built. Removing them partway starts the chain reaction; pushing them in all the way stops the reaction.

The Nuclear Advantage: Minimal Air Pollution

The main advantage of nuclear power plants over those that burn fossil fuels is in what they do not do. Unlike power plants that burn fossil fuels, nuclear power plants produce no carbon dioxide to add to the greenhouse effect, and they add no sulfur oxides, nitrogen oxides, soot, or fly ash to the atmosphere. They contribute almost nothing to global warming, air pollution, or acid rain. They reduce our dependence on foreign oil and lower our trade deficit. If the 104 nuclear plants in the United States were replaced by coal-burning plants, airborne pollutants would increase by 18,000 tons per day!

Problems with Nuclear Power

Nuclear power plants have some disadvantages. Elaborate and expensive safety precautions must be taken to protect plant workers and the inhabitants of surrounding areas from radiation. The reactor must be heavily shielded and housed inside a containment building of metal and reinforced concrete. Because loss of coolant water can result in a meltdown of the reactor core, backup emergency cooling systems are required.

Despite what proponents call utmost precautions, some opponents of nuclear power still fear a runaway nuclear reaction in which a containment building is breached and massive amounts of radioactivity escape into the environment. The chance of such an accident is very small, but one did happen at Fukushima, Japan. Yet the benefit of nuclear power—abundant electric energy—is clear, so the small probability of a serious accident causes scientists and others to endlessly debate its desirability.

Another problem is that the fission products are highly radioactive and must be isolated from the environment for centuries. Again, scientists disagree about the feasibility of disposal of nuclear waste. Proponents of nuclear power say that such wastes can be safely stored in old salt mines or other geologic formations. Opponents fear that the wastes may rise from their "graves" and eventually contaminate the groundwater. It is impossible to do a million-year experiment in a few years to determine who is right. Federal funding for an underground repository at Yucca Mountain, Nevada, was terminated in 2011 after billions of dollars were spent on the project. This leaves the United States with no long-term storage site for high-level radioactive waste. These wastes are currently stored at 126 sites around the country. It is important to note that high-level waste from nuclear power plant operations in the United States totals about 3000 tons per year. Compare this number to the coal ash produced in the United States—over 100 million tons per year! It is important to realize that

▲ Mildly radioactive tailings are a by-product of the processing of uranium ores.

most of the nuclear wastes awaiting disposal is from nuclear weapons production, not energy production.

Mining and processing of uranium ore produce wastes called *tailings*. Over 200 million tons of tailings now afflict 10 western states. These tailings are mildly radioactive, giving off radon gas and gamma radiation. Dust from the mounds of tailings is dispersed to surrounding areas.

Any power plant has another problem that is unavoidable—thermal pollution. As the energy from any material is converted to heat to generate electricity, some of the energy is released into the environment as waste heat. Nuclear power plants generate more thermal pollution than plants that burn fossil fuels, but this provides an opportunity for engineers to design a mechanism to use the hot wastewater in some sustainable way.

Nuclear Accidents

In 1979, a loss-of-coolant accident at the Three Mile Island nuclear power plant near Harrisburg, Pennsylvania, released a tiny amount of radioactivity into the environment. Although no one was killed or seriously injured, the accident heightened public fear of nuclear power.

A 1986 accident at Chernobyl, Ukraine, was much more frightening. There, a reactor core meltdown killed several people outright. Others died from radiation sickness in the following weeks and months, and 135,000 people were evacuated. The Ukraine Radiological Institute estimates that the accident caused more than 2500 deaths overall. A large area will remain contaminated for decades. Radioactive fallout spread across much of Europe. The thyroid cancer rate among Ukrainians increased tenfold, and the overall risk of cancer rose because of exposure to radiation. At Three Mile Island, a containment building kept nearly all the radioactive material inside. The Chernobyl plant had no such protective structure.

In 2011, a tsunami caused by an earthquake destroyed the external power supply to a nuclear power plant at Fukushima, Japan. Thousands of people were killed by the tsunami, and large areas were rendered uninhabitable by released radiation, perhaps for centuries. The lack of power led to partial core meltdowns in three reactors, with widespread release of radiation. The Fukushima accident is rated as the second worst in history, after Chernobyl. Thousands were killed by the tsunami, but so far only a few by radiation.

There is considerable controversy over most aspects of nuclear power. Although scientists may be able to agree on the results of laboratory experiments, they don't always agree on what is best for society.

Breeder Reactors: Making More Fuel Than They Burn

The supply of the fissionable uranium-235 isotope is limited, as it makes up less than 1% of naturally occurring uranium. Separation of uranium-235 leaves behind large quantities of uranium-238, which is not fissionable. However, uranium-238 can be converted to fissionable plutonium-239 by bombardment with neutrons. Unstable uranium-239 is formed initially, but it rapidly decays to neptunium-239, which then decays to plutonium.

$$^{238}_{92}\text{U} + ^{1}_{0}\text{n} \longrightarrow ^{239}_{92}\text{U} \longrightarrow ^{239}_{93}\text{Np} + ^{0}_{-1}\text{e}$$

$$^{239}_{93}\text{Np} \longrightarrow ^{239}_{94}\text{Pu} + ^{0}_{-1}\text{e}$$

If a reactor is built with a core of fissionable plutonium surrounded by uranium-238, neutrons from the fission of plutonium convert the uranium-238 shield to more plutonium. In this way, the reactor, called a breeder reactor, produces more fuel than it consumes. There is enough uranium-238 to last a few centuries, so one of the disadvantages of nuclear plants could be overcome by the use of breeder reactors.

Breeder reactors have some problems of their own, however. Plutonium is fairly low melting (640 °C), and a plant is therefore limited to fairly cool, inefficient operation. Failure of the cooling system could cause the reactor's core to melt. Water is not adequate as a coolant, so molten sodium metal is used in the primary loop. These reactors are often called *liquid-metal fast breeder reactors*. If an accident occurred in such a breeder, the sodium could react violently with both the water and the air.

Plutonium is highly toxic and has a half-life of about 24,000 years. It emits alpha particles, making it especially dangerous if ingested. An estimated 1 μg in the lungs of a human is enough to induce lung cancer. Yet another problem is that plutonium is chemically different from uranium-238. That makes it much easier than uranium-235 to separate from uranium-238, for use in illicit nuclear weapons.

Another type of breeder reaction converts thorium-232 into fissionable uranium-233.

$$^{232}_{90}\text{Th} + {}^{1}_{0}\text{n} \longrightarrow {}^{233}_{90}\text{Th} \longrightarrow {}^{233}_{91}\text{Pa} + {}^{0}_{-1}\text{e}$$
$$^{233}_{91}\text{Pa} \longrightarrow {}^{233}_{92}\text{U} + {}^{0}_{-1}\text{e}$$

Thorium-232 is especially attractive for use in breeder reactors because it is quite abundant. There is about as much thorium in the Earth's crust as there is lead.

Uranium-233 is like plutonium in that it emits damaging alpha particles, but it is thought to be rather difficult to make bombs from reactor-grade uranium-233.

Only 11 breeder reactors with a production capacity of more than 100 MW have ever been built, none in the United States. Only one commercial breeder reactor is still operating in Russia, and it has never been fueled with plutonium.

Nuclear Fusion: The Sun in a Magnetic Bottle

Chapter 11 discussed the thermonuclear reactions that power the sun and that occur in the explosion of hydrogen bombs. Control of these fusion reactions to produce electricity would give us nearly unlimited power. To date, fusion reactions have been useful only for making bombs, but research on the control of nuclear fusion is progressing (Figure 15.12).

| Hydrogen-2 (deuterium) | Hydrogen-3 (tritium) | Helium-4 (stable) | | Energy |

$$^{2}_{1}\text{H} + {}^{3}_{1}\text{H} \longrightarrow {}^{4}_{2}\text{He} + {}^{1}_{0}\text{n}$$

▲ **Figure 15.12** A promising fusion reaction is the deuterium–tritium reaction. A hydrogen-2 (deuterium) nucleus fuses with a hydrogen-3 (tritium) nucleus to form a helium-4 nucleus. A neutron is released, along with a considerable quantity of energy.

▲ **Figure 15.13** A giant, doughnut-shaped electromagnet called a tokamak is designed to confine plasma at the extremely high temperatures and pressures required for nuclear fusion.

Great technical difficulties have to be overcome before a controlled fusion reaction can be used to produce energy. A sustainable fusion reaction would require attainment of a critical ignition temperature between 100 million °C and 200 million °C, a confinement time of 1–2 s, and an ion density of between 2×10^{20} and 3×10^{20} ions per cubic meter. No molecule could hold together at the fusion temperature. No material on Earth can withstand more than a few thousand degrees. Even atoms are unstable under these conditions. Atoms are stripped of their electrons, and the nuclei and free electrons form a mixture called a *plasma*. The plasma, made of charged particles (nuclei and electrons), can be contained by a strong magnetic field (Figure 15.13).

Controlled fusion would have several advantages over nuclear fission as an energy source. The main fuel, deuterium ($^{2}_{1}\text{H}$), is plentiful and is obtained from fractional electrolysis (splitting apart by means of electricity) of water. The problem of radioactive wastes would be minimized. The end product, helium, is stable and biologically inert. Escape of tritium (^3_1H) might be a problem because this hydrogen isotope would be readily incorporated into organisms. Also, neutrons are emitted in most fusion reactions, and neutrons can convert stable isotopes into radioactive ones. Finally, we would still be concerned with thermal pollution—the unavoidable loss of part of the energy as heat.

Nuclear fusion may well be our best hope for producing relatively clean, abundant energy in the future, but much work remains to be done. Once controlled fusion is achieved in a laboratory, it will still be decades before it becomes a practical source of energy.

SELF-ASSESSMENT Questions

1. In a nuclear fission reactor,
   a. carbon-14 decays to nitrogen-14
   b. hydrogen nuclei fuse to form helium
   c. uranium-235 absorbs a neutron and splits into two smaller nuclei
   d. uranium-238 decays to plutonium-238

2. The control rods in a nuclear reactor
   a. absorb neutrons, allowing them to initiate fission
   b. absorb neutrons, preventing them from causing fission
   c. slow the neutrons down so the moderator can stop them
   d. speed the neutrons up so they will initiate fission

3. What percentage of the electricity used in the United States is produced by nuclear power plants?
   a. 5%
   b. 10%
   c. 20%
   d. 50%

4. Nuclear reactors that produce more nuclear fuel than they consume
   a. are called breeder reactors
   b. are called fusion reactors
   c. are called transuranic reactors
   d. violate the law of conservation of energy

5. Approximately how many nuclear power plants are in operation in the United States?
   a. 50   b. 100   c. 200   d. 400

6. Which of the following is a disadvantage of nuclear power plants?
   a. They produce greenhouse gases
   b. They produce more radioactive waste than wastes left from nuclear weapons development
   c. It is difficult to build safe reactors
   d. They produce thermal pollution of nearby water sources

7. What is the missing product in the following nuclear reaction?
   $$^2_1H + ^3_1H \longrightarrow ^1_0n + \text{?}$$
   a. ^5_2He b. ^3_2He c. ^4_2He d. ^3_1H

8. Fission, not fusion, is used in nuclear power plants because fusion
   a. uses expensive transuranium elements as fuel
   b. requires temperatures of millions of degrees, making the reaction difficult to contain
   c. produces less heat than fission
   d. produces waste products that are radioactive for centuries

9. Which country has more nuclear power plants?
   a. France
   b. United States
   c. England
   d. Germany

15.10 Renewable Energy Sources

Learning Objective ❯ List important characteristics, advantages, and disadvantages of various kinds of renewable energy sources.

Burning fossil fuels leads to air pollution and to the depletion of vital resources. Using nuclear power also presents problems. Nuclear fuel is not unlimited, and the problem of waste disposal remains unsolved. We are turning to renewable energy sources, which account for about 8–11% of the energy production in the United States. This section discusses these sustainable energy sources.

Section 15.1 noted that most of the energy available on Earth comes from the sun. With all that energy from our celestial power plant, why are we currently dependent on fossil fuels or nuclear power? The answer lies in the fact that solar energy is thinly spread out and difficult to capture directly.

▲ **Figure 15.14 (a)** Energy in sunlight is absorbed by solar collectors and used to heat water. The hot water can be used directly or circulated to partially heat a building. This diagram shows how a solar collector furnishes hot water and warm air for heating a building. **(b)** A variety of collectors can be used to absorb solar energy.

Solar Heating

Of all the solar energy that arrives on the surface of the Earth, 30% is reflected back into space and is thus unavailable for our use. About half of that solar energy is converted into heat. We can increase the efficiency of this conversion rather easily. A black surface absorbs heat better than a light-colored one. To make a simple solar collector, we only have to cover a black surface with a glass plate. The glass is transparent to the incoming solar radiation, but it partially prevents the heat from escaping back into space. The hot surface is used to heat water or other liquids, and the hot liquids are usually stored in an insulated reservoir.

Water heated this way can be used directly for bathing, dish washing, and laundry, or it can be used to heat a building. Air is passed around the warm reservoir, and the warmed air is then circulated through the building (Figure 15.14). Even in cold northern climates, solar collectors could meet about 50% of home heating requirements. These installations are expensive but can pay for themselves, through fuel savings, in a few years.

Solar Cells: Electricity from Sunlight

Sunlight also can be converted directly to electricity by devices called **photovoltaic cells**, or *solar cells*. These devices can be made from a variety of substances, but most are made from elemental silicon. In a crystal of pure silicon, each silicon atom has four valence electrons and is covalently bonded to four other silicon atoms (Figure 15.15). To make a solar cell, extremely pure silicon is "doped" with small amounts of specific impurities and formed into crystals.

▶ **Figure 15.15** Models of silicon crystals. Crystals doped with impurities such as arsenic and boron are more conductive than pure silicon and are used in solar cells.

Crystal of pure silicon

Silicon doped with arsenic (*n*-type)

Silicon doped with boron (*p*-type)

One type of silicon crystal has about 1 ppm of arsenic added. Arsenic atoms have five valence electrons, four of which are used to form bonds to silicon atoms. The fifth electron is relatively free to move around. Because this material has extra electrons, and electrons are negatively charged, it is called an *n-type* (negative) *semiconductor*. Adding about 1 ppm of boron to silicon forms a different type of material. Boron has three valence electrons, producing a shortage of one electron and leaving a *positive hole* in the crystal. This boron-doped silicon is called a *p-type semiconductor.*

Joining the two types of crystals (*n*-type and *p*-type) forms a photovoltaic cell (Figure 15.16). Electrons flow from the *n*-type region, which has a high concentration of them, to the *p*-type region. However, the holes near the junction are quickly filled by nearby mobile electrons, and the flow ceases.

When sunlight hits the photovoltaic cell, an electric current is generated. The energetic photons knock electrons out of the Si—Si bonds, creating more mobile electrons and more positive holes. Because of the barrier at the junction between the two semiconductors, electrons cannot move through the interface. When an external circuit connects the two crystals, electrons flow from the *n*-type region around the circuit to the *p*-type region and that current can be used directly.

An array of solar cells, combined to form a solar battery, can produce about 100 W/m^2 of surface. That is, it takes 1 m^2 of cells to power one 100-W light bulb. Consider how much area in solar cells would be needed to provide the electrical energy needed to power devices in a single home! This makes solar cells on rooftops rather impractical. Solar batteries have been used, however, for years to power artificial Earth satellites. They are now widely used to power small devices such as electronic calculators. They are also used to provide electricity for weather instruments in remote areas.

Current solar cells are not very efficient, converting about 12–18% of incident sunlight into electricity, though experimental systems using mirrors have achieved efficiencies of more than 40%. Much of the sunlight striking them is reflected back into space or converted to heat. The generation of enough energy to meet a significant portion of our demands would require covering vast areas of desert land with solar cells. It would require about 20 km^2 (or 5000 acres) of cloud-free desert land to produce as much energy as one nuclear power plant. However, research has led to more efficient solar cells, and their cost is decreasing.

Using solar energy requires storing the energy for use at night and on cloudy days. The technology is now widely available for using solar energy for space heating and for providing hot water. Several companies sell home-sized solar electric systems that can be connected to the normal supply line and can reduce electric bills to nearly zero. However, these systems are quite expensive. Solar power currently provides less than 1% of U.S. energy needs. Though use of solar energy is increasing, widespread use is still some years away.

Biomass: Photosynthesis for Fuel

Why bother with solar collectors and photovoltaic cells to capture energy from the sun when green plants do it every day? Indeed, dry plant material, called **biomass** when used as a fuel, burns quite well—consider a campfire that produces plenty of heat. The problem is that a lot of smoke and ash is produced when plant matter is burned. It could possibly be used to fuel a power plant for the generation of electricity. The emissions are water vapor and the carbon dioxide the plants took from the air in the first place, plus smoke and ash. "Energy plantations" could grow plants for use as fuel. Biomass is a renewable resource whose production is powered by the sun.

Unfortunately, there are several disadvantages to this energy source, too. Most available land is needed for the production of food. Even where productive land is available, plants have to be planted, harvested, and transported to the power plant. Often, the land is far from where the energy is needed. However, some hybrid species of trees grow quickly and densely, reducing the needed growing area. The overall efficiency of biomass as an energy source is even less than that of solar

▲ **Figure 15.16** Schematic diagram of the operation of a solar cell. Electrons flow from the *n*-type region (lower layer) to the *p*-type region (upper layer) through the external circuit.

6. Is solar power, wind power, or fuel cells the answer to the energy crisis?

Solar cells and fuel cells have made great progress but much work remains. Today's solar cells are far more expensive than fossil-fuel electricity and are too inefficient to provide a complete solution to our energy needs. Wind power is also expensive and has a high start-up cost but does pay for itself after time. None of those sources can directly power buses or cars.

▲ These willow trees are grown specifically as fuel. The biomass is harvested by cutting the trees near ground level, which stimulates regrowth. Willow is especially suitable for biomass because of its rapid growth.

cells—only about 3% at best. Nevertheless, there is considerable research activity focused on biomass because nature "constructs" plants much more easily and more quickly than we can construct industrial plants.

Also, we don't have to burn plant material directly.

- Starches and sugars from plants can be fermented to form ethanol. Wood can be distilled in the absence of air to produce methanol. Both alcohols are liquids and thus convenient to transport, and both are excellent fuels that burn quite cleanly.
- Bacterial breakdown of plant material produces methane. Under proper conditions, this process can be controlled to produce a clean-burning fuel similar to natural gas.
- Oils and fats can be converted to a fuel called *biodiesel*. The triacylglycerols are converted into the methyl esters of the constituent fatty acids. A typical biodiesel molecule from palm oil is methyl palmitate, $CH_3(CH_2)_{14}COOCH_3$. Biodiesel from waste, algae, or nonfood plants can have a reasonably high EROEI and can be profitable.

All these conversions, however, result in the loss of a portion of the useful energy. The laws of thermodynamics tell us that we can get the most energy by burning the biomass directly rather than converting it to a more convenient liquid or gaseous fuel.

Biomass and biofuels currently provide about half of the renewable energy used in the United States, or about 5% of the country's overall energy needs. We could make greater use of these sources by converting appropriate materials to biodiesel, fermenting some agricultural wastes to ethanol, and fermenting human and animal wastes to produce methane. The technology for all these processes is available now and can be further improved.

Hydrogen: Light and Powerful

Natural gas is sent through pipes to wherever it is needed, and other gaseous fuels could be sent through the same pipes. One such gas is hydrogen.

When hydrogen burns, it produces water and gives off energy.

$$2\ H_2(g) + O_2(g) \longrightarrow 2\ H_2O(l) + 572\ kJ$$

Gram for gram, hydrogen yields more energy than any other chemical fuel. It is also a clean fuel, yielding only water as a chemical product. Although hydrogen is the most abundant element in the universe, elemental hydrogen (H_2) is almost nonexistent on Earth. There is a lot of hydrogen on Earth, but it is tied up in chemical compounds, mainly water, and releasing it requires more energy than the hydrogen produces when it is burned. Hydrogen can be made from seawater, so the supply is almost inexhaustible, but the production process is costly.

Fuel Cells

A **fuel cell** is a device in which fuel is oxidized in an electrochemical cell (Section 8.3) so as to produce electricity directly. Fuel cells differ from the usual electrochemical cell in two ways:

- The fuel and oxygen are fed into the cell continuously. As long as fuel is supplied, current is generated.
- The electrodes are made of an inert material such as platinum that does not react during the process.
- Most of today's fuel cells use hydrogen and oxygen (Figure 15.17). At the platinum anode, H_2 is oxidized to yield hydrogen ions and electrons.

$$2\ H_2(g) \longrightarrow 4\ H^+ + 4e^-$$

▲ **Figure 15.17** A hydrogen–oxygen fuel cell. The fuel cell continues to provide electricity as long as reactants are supplied.

The electrons produced at the anode travel through the external circuit and arrive at the cathode, where they combine with the hydrogen ions and oxygen molecules to form water.

$$4\ e^- + O_2(g) + 4\ H^+ \longrightarrow 2\ H_2O(g)$$

The overall reaction (below) is identical to direct combustion of hydrogen, but not all the chemical energy is converted to heat. About 40–55% of the chemical energy is converted directly to electricity, making fuel cells much more efficient than internal combustion engines.

$$2\ H_2(g) + O_2(g) \longrightarrow 2\ H_2O(l)$$

Fuel cells are often used on spacecraft to produce electricity, mainly because they have a weight advantage over storage batteries—an important consideration when launching a spaceship—and the water produced can be used for drinking. Because they have no moving parts, fuel cells are usually tough and reliable.

On Earth, research is under way to reduce costs and design long-lasting cells. Perhaps fuel cells will someday provide electricity to meet peak needs in large power plants, or run most of our vehicles. Unlike huge boilers and nuclear reactors, they can be started and stopped simply by turning the fuel on or off. Electric vehicles may be the car of the future, but as of yet most can travel no more than about 100 miles before they need recharging. Most are quite expensive, and the very heavy lithium batteries may be able to be recharged only a finite number of times. Replacement is a daunting cost, equivalent to the cost of a modest new car.

Some people are afraid of using hydrogen as fuel for home heating because of the possibility of explosion, but natural gas leaks can also lead to serious explosions. Hydrogen escapes more readily than natural gas or gasoline because of its smaller molecular size, but it also dissipates more readily, rather than forming a flammable low-lying vapor as gasoline sometimes does.

Other Renewable Energy Sources

Modern civilization requires tremendous amounts of energy and will require more and more in the coming years. We are depleting our reserves of fossil fuels, and many see significant disadvantages to nuclear power. Using the sun's energy seems to be a good idea, but it would be difficult to meet all our needs with solar energy.

The sun, by heating Earth, causes winds to blow and water to evaporate and rise into the air, later to fall as rain. The kinetic energy of blowing wind and flowing water can be used as sources of energy—as they have been for centuries.

Why not use wind power and waterpower to help solve the energy crisis? We do. Waterpower provides almost 7% of current electricity production in the United States, most of it in the mountainous West. In a modern hydroelectric plant, water is held behind huge dams. Some of it is released through penstocks against the blades of water turbines. The potential energy of the stored water is converted to the kinetic energy of flowing water. The moving water imparts mechanical energy to the turbine, which drives a generator that converts mechanical energy to electrical energy.

Hydroelectric plants are relatively clean, but most of the good dam sites in the United States are already in use. To obtain more hydroelectric energy, we would have to dam up scenic rivers and flood valuable cropland and recreational areas. Reservoirs silt up over the years, and sometimes dams break, causing catastrophic floods. Dams block the migration of fish upstream to spawning beds. Declining fish populations have led to closure of salmon fishing in waters off California and Oregon and removal of dams from a few rivers where salmon spawn.

Worldwide, hydroelectric plants provide about 20% of the electricity used, and more plants are being built in many developing countries. As a major example, China's huge Three Gorges project on the Yangtze River, completed in 2009, includes a 22,500-MW hydroelectric plant. It provides more than 10% of China's electricity. Unfortunately, the project displaced 1.3 million people and may cause significant environmental damage. Water quality in the Yangtze's tributaries is already dete-

▲ Hoover Dam, on the Colorado River, was completed in 1936. It generates 4 billion kWh a year—enough to supply 1.3 million people.

Hydrogen in Your Future Car?

Hydrogen can be used as a fuel for cars, either directly or in fuel cells. Among the advantages of hydrogen as a fuel are the following:

- The exhaust is almost entirely water vapor, which cuts down on urban air pollution and the production of the greenhouse gas CO_2.
- It can be produced from renewable sources.
- It could reduce U.S. reliance on foreign oil and the associated economic and political costs.

There are, however, significant obstacles to making the transition to hydrogen, so the roads will not be filled with hydrogen cars anytime soon. Among the problems are the following:

- Hydrogen is not a source of energy; there are no hydrogen "mines" or "reservoirs."
- The hydrogen-powered cars now available are expensive novelties, costing $100,000 or more.
- There is no widespread distribution system of hydrogen fueling stations; most exist in southern California.
- Hydrogen is a low-density gas that liquefies at −253 °C (20 K). Use of the gas requires large, heavy tanks. Liquid hydrogen must be maintained at a temperature only a few degrees above absolute zero. Therefore, storage, transportation, and dispensing of the fuel are problematic.

Some progress has been made, mostly with fleets of vehicles that operate in a limited area. Fuel cell technology is becoming more efficient and costs are coming down, but there is still the problem of producing hydrogen gas economically. Hydrogen has to be made using another energy source: fossil fuels, nuclear power, or—preferably—some renewable source such as solar energy or wind power.

Even liquid H_2, with a density of 0.07 g/cm^3, requires a large fuel tank, and the tank must be well insulated. It may be possible to store hydrogen in other ways: Scientists have found that various metals can absorb up to a thousand times their own volume of hydrogen gas. Special forms of carbon, such as ultra-thin carbon nanotubes, may also hold large quantities of the gas.

The cost of establishing pipelines and filling stations to handle hydrogen will be immense. It takes many years for revolutionary technologies to come to the marketplace. The increased emphasis on research into hydrogen fuel cells appears to be a step in the right direction. Most of the main manufacturers of vehicles are introducing hydrogen fuel cell vehicles in 2014.

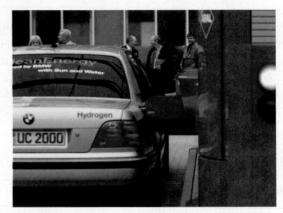

▲ The BMW Hydrogen-7 is claimed to be the first production-ready hydrogen vehicle. It was designed to run on either hydrogen or gasoline. The hydrogen is stored as a liquid in a large vacuum-insulated tank. In 2007, 100 of these vehicles were leased to drivers.

▲ Wind turbines, such as these in an off-coast wind farm, supply about 20% of Denmark's electricity. By the end of 2010, windmills with a generating capacity of almost 200,000 MW were operating worldwide, producing about 2.5% of the world's electricity.

riorating rapidly because the dammed river disperses pollutants less effectively and algae blooms flourish. The rising water caused extensive soil erosion, riverbank collapses, and landslides. Even renewable hydroelectric power has its problems.

We could use more wind power. The kinetic energy of moving air is readily converted to mechanical energy to pump water, grind grain, or turn turbines and generate electricity. One large wind turbine can provide 1.65 megawatts of electrical energy. Wind power currently supplies only about 2% of U.S. energy production, but it is the fastest-growing energy source, increasing at an annual rate of 20–30%. Some regions of the country are fueled by many square miles of wind turbines, such as the Fox River Valley in central Wisconsin. The upfront cost is enormous, but they pay for themselves in time.

Wind is clean, free, and abundant. However, it does not blow constantly, and some means of energy storage or an alternative source of energy is needed. Not all regions have enough wind to make wind power feasible. Some environmentalists oppose wind power because the rotating blades kill thousands of birds each year, but so do domestic cats and collisions with television and microwave towers. The amount of land required for windmills might become a problem if wind power were used widely, but the land under windmills could be used for farming or grazing.

◀ **Figure 15.18** Geothermal energy contributes to energy supplies in some areas. A geothermal field at Wairakei, New Zealand.

Geothermal Energy

The interior of Earth is heated by immense gravitational forces and by natural radioactivity. This heat comes to the surface in some areas through geysers and volcanoes. **Geothermal energy** has long been used in Iceland, New Zealand, Japan, and Italy. It has some potential in the United States—it is being used now in California (Figure 15.18)—but generally this potential can be realized in areas where steam or hot water is at or near the surface.

Even in areas where steam or hot water is NOT near the surface, installation of a geothermal heating system for a home is now possible. Though expensive upfront, the system may pay for itself in 10 to 12 years, even in northern climates. Natural gas, the most commonly used fuel for home heating, may become much more expensive in the next few decades, so choosing this home heating method for new home construction may be a viable option (see Figure 15.19). Four to six feet below the surface of the earth, the temperature is fairly constant, year round. A geothermal heating (and cooling system) consists of an indoor handling unit and a buried system of pipes, called an "earth loop," and a pump. In the winter the warmed water warms the house, and in the summer it cools the house.

▲ **Figure 15.19** Geothermal system for heating a home. The earth loop of pipes buried underground brings water into the house. Electrical energy is used to operate the unit's fan, compressor, and pump.

Oceans of Energy

The oceans that cover three-fourths of Earth's surface are an enormous reservoir of potential energy. The use of *ocean thermal energy* was first proposed in 1881 and was shown to be workable in the 1930s. The difference in temperature between the surface and the depths is 20 °C or more, enough to evaporate a liquid and use the vapor to drive a turbine. The liquid is then condensed by the cold from the ocean depths, and the cycle is repeated.

Other ways of using ocean energy have been tested. In some areas of the world, the daily rise and fall of the tide can be harnessed, in much the same way as the energy of a river is harnessed by a hydroelectric plant. At high tide, water fills a reservoir or bay. At low tide, the water escapes through a turbine to generate electricity. Even the energy of the waves crashing to shore can be used with the appropriate technology.

Energy: How Much Is Too Much?

Our energy future is quite uncertain. World petroleum production will peak soon—some claim this has already occurred. Developing nations will increasingly compete for fuels on the world market. Science and technology will have to be applied to provide an ever-growing supply of energy. The Energy Information Administration of the U.S. Department of Energy projected that world energy use will increase by 50% from 2007 to 2035, with much of the new demand from developing countries.

Table 15.8	Total Primary Energy Consumption Per Capita, (quadrillion BTU's in 2011)
Country	Consumption/ Capita
United States	97.5
Canada	12.9
Mexico	8.0
Germany	13.5
France	10.8
China	103.7
India	23.5
Thailand	4.6
Russia	30.0
Brazil	12.1
Guatemala	0.2
Saudi Arabia	9.0
Zimbabwe	0.2
Nigeria	0.8

Source: US Energy Information Administration

Each of the energy sources discussed in this chapter has advantages and disadvantages. How do we choose the best way to deal with energy problems? Wise choices require informed citizens who examine the process from beginning to end. We must realize what is involved in the construction of power plants, the production of fuels, and the ultimate use of energy in our homes and factories. We must recognize that energy is wasted (as heat) at every step in the process.

Will our profligate consumption of energy affect Earth's climate? Our activities have already modified the climate in and around metropolitan areas. The worldwide effects of our expanding energy consumption are harder to estimate.

What can we do as individuals? We can conserve. We can walk more and use cars less. We can reduce our wasteful use of electricity. We can buy more efficient appliances, and we can reduce our use of energy-intensive products (leaf blowers, lawn tractors, and larger automobiles).

Over the past three decades, we have made significant progress in energy conservation. Appliances are more energy efficient. New furnaces have efficiencies of 90–95%, as compared with the 60% efficiency of 20-year-old furnaces. New refrigerators and air conditioners use about 35% less energy than earlier models. Incandescent lamps are being replaced by compact fluorescent lamps, which are at least four times more energy efficient. Overall, U.S. industry has reduced its energy consumption per product by almost 30%.

We could significantly reduce energy consumption in the United States by greater use of public transportation. In Europe, where there is much wider use of public transit, per capita energy use is considerably less (Table 15.8), partly because the average price for gasoline is usually more than twice that in the United States. So far, few people used to the convenience of personal cars seem eager to start using buses and trains. As the price of gasoline in the United States continues to rise, perhaps public transportation will seem more attractive.

The simple facts are that our population on Spaceship Earth is increasing and our fuel resources are decreasing. People in developing countries want to raise their standard of living, and that will require more energy. We need to conserve energy and to look for new energy sources.

SELF-ASSESSMENT Questions

1. Which of the following is an *n*-type semiconductor?
   a. arsenic doped with silicon
   b. arsenic doped with germanium
   c. silicon doped with arsenic
   d. silicon doped with boron

2. *p*-Type semiconductors feature crystal sites with
   a. photons
   b. positrons
   c. positive holes
   d. protons

3. Which of the following is *not* a renewable energy source?
   a. biomass
   b. solar power
   c. hydropower
   d. petroleum

4. Biodiesel cannot be made from
   a. sugar
   b. olive oil
   c. soybean oil
   d. waste cooking fat

5. The major product from burning hydrogen gas as a fuel is
   a. CO_2 b. H_2 c. H_2O d. O_2

6. Which of the following fuels has the lowest EROEI?
   a. biodiesel
   b. hydrogen
   c. natural gas
   d. petroleum

7. Which of the following energy technologies does not use energy that originated in the sun?
   a. biomass
   b. hydroelectric
   c. nuclear
   d. wind

8. The fuel used by almost all current fuel cells is
   a. electricity
   b. hydrogen
   c. natural gas
   d. propane

9. A disadvantage of wind turbines is
   a. high maintenance costs
   b. production of greenhouse gases
   c. high upfront costs
   d. competition from other energy sources

10. The renewable energy source that provides the most electrical energy in the United States today is
    a. geothermal
    b. hydroelectric
    c. solar
    d. wind

11. The energy that comes from the internal heat of the Earth is
    a. bioenergy
    b. geothermal energy
    c. hydroelectric
    d. solar energy

12. Problems to overcome in the development of electric vehicles include all the following except
    a. more miles before recharging
    b. the excessive cost of replacing batteries
    c. lack of enough recharging stations
    d. designing engines to run at highway speeds

Answers: 1, c; 2, c; 3, d; 4, a; 5, c; 6, b; 7, c; 8, b; 9, c; 10, b; 11, b; 12, d

GREEN CHEMISTRY

Michael Heben, *University of Toledo*

Where Will We Get the Energy?

Learning Objective > Explain how applying the green chemistry principles can help identify improved methods for energy generation.

Energy permeates every aspect of our existence. Think about your heart pumping blood through your body, the power of a rocket lifting explorers to Mars, a family drive to Grandma's house for Thanksgiving, a plant absorbing CO_2 and sunlight to make food, an actor, musician, artist, or athlete doing their thing, or a company making chemical compounds for industrial or pharmaceutical use. Energy is required anytime anything does something.

Is there anything that we do that does not require energy? No – and even thinking about the question can be exhausting – because thinking requires energy!

Chapter 15 considers sources of energy that power our world. Yet what we commonly consider to be energy sources, such as natural gas, coal, and oil, are not really energy sources at all. Rather, these are fuels. They contain stored energy in carbon-carbon and carbon-hydrogen chemical bonds. As we learned, these bonds react with oxygen during combustion. The released energy can provide heat to homes or industrial processes or can be used to power a mechanical engine to do work or generate electricity.

Today's fossil fuels are the remains of ancient plant and animal matter that were produced by the energy from our own star, the Sun. Though fossil fuels have been built up over hundreds of millions of years by photosynthesis, our society is consuming the easily obtained portion very quickly. It's like putting a small amount of money in the bank each week for a long time and then spending it all at once.

Besides the limitations on the amount of stored energy still available in fossil fuels, we have to recognize broader concerns. Green chemistry principles help us to do so. by explicitly including the impacts of waste generation, toxic substances, transportation costs, feedstocks, and overall energy efficiency. Consider the figure below, which shows the inputs and outputs for a generic process. To generate energy efficiently, we minimize the inputs and maximize the energy output. As principle 1 reminds us, clearly, waste must be reduced, and the process should produce other products only if needed.

As demonstrated by principle 6, processes should not limit the main product – in this case, energy – but should reduce negative environmental and economic impacts. It is only within the past 50 years that environmental pollution – undesired outputs from energy production – has become a big concern. The Clean Air Act of 1970, signed by President Nixon, has helped reduce dangerous smog in our cities and improve the health and economic vitality of our country. Recently, the U.S. Supreme Court upheld a regulation that treated CO_2 as a pollutant. Unfortunately, the combustion of oil, coal, and natural gas produce CO_2 as a byproduct, and CO_2 is the big player in the world's urgent climate-change problem.

From a green chemistry point of view and particularly relating to principles 1, 5, and 12, hydraulic fracturing for production of natural gas makes an interesting case. Once considered a non-conventional method, "fracking" uses fluids to move the natural gas more easily from the ground to the surface and now accounts for 50% of U.S. natural gas production. The benefit of this process is that it allows access to natural-gas resources that were previously not available, but many chemicals, some of which are carcinogens, may be added to the fracture fluids. These and other species released by fracturing (including naturally occurring radioactive species) may reach aquifers or be diverted to municipal water treatment facilities. Clearly, a great deal of waste is not accounted for in the process. Also, besides CO_2 emissions associated with combustion, considerable amounts of CH_4, which is 25 times more active as a greenhouse gas than CO_2, leak into the atmosphere during production.

Difficulties obtaining fuels from the dwindling supply of stored fossil energy and the impacts these fuels have on the Earth itself mean that we need to create a balance between energy supply and consumption by using the energy from the Sun. Direct methods include technologies like photovoltaics, wind power, and bioenergy. Luckily, there's more than enough solar energy available. For example, if we covered ~0.1% of the land area in the contiguous 48 U.S states with solar panels that are 15% efficient, all of our country's energy needs could be met. For comparison, the land needed is less than a fourth of the area covered by roads.

The biggest hurdle to developing clean, renewable energy has to do with cost. If we do the complete accounting and measure all inputs and outputs and impacts of a given process correctly, the true costs to society will guide us in making good choices. New science and technology and new mindsets, including those based on green chemistry, will be required. Perhaps you will want to help in this grand challenge?

▲ Color use? What do the colors mean?

SUMMARY

Section 15.1—Energy is the ability to do work. The United States has about 5% of the world's population but uses about one-fifth of all the energy generated. Most of the energy used on Earth comes from the sun. The SI unit of energy is the joule (J), and the unit of power is the watt (W), which is 1 joule per second. Energy can be classified as **potential energy** (energy of position) or **kinetic energy** (energy of motion). In the process called **photosynthesis**, solar energy is absorbed by plants and used to produce glucose, and oxygen is generated.

Section 15.2—The study of energy changes that occur during chemical reactions and physical processes is called **thermochemistry**. In a chemical reaction, all the chemical bonds must be broken in the reactants; then the fragments combine in a different way to form the products. The first process requires an input of energy, and the second process releases energy. The net result of both is the heat of reaction. A chemical reaction or a physical process may be either **exothermic** (giving off energy to the surroundings) or **endothermic** (requiring energy from the surroundings). Reactions involving burning of fuels are all exothermic.

Section 15.3—The rate of a chemical reaction is affected by temperature, by concentrations of the reactants, and by the presence of catalysts. The rate increases if the temperature is increased or the concentrations of solutions are increased. Catalysts speed up reactions.

Section 15.4—The **first law of thermodynamics (law of conservation of energy)** says that energy can be neither created nor destroyed. The **second law of thermodynamics** states that in a spontaneous process, energy is degraded from more useful forms to less useful forms. **Entropy** is a measure of the dispersal of energy among the possible states of a system. There is a tendency for a system to increase in entropy.

Section 15.5—Ancient societies used human and animal power to do work. The main fuel was wood. A **fuel** is a substance that will burn readily with the release of significant energy. The first mechanical devices for doing work were the water-wheel and the windmill. Energy from water, steam, gas, the internal combustion engine, and other sources fueled the Industrial Revolution. **Fossil fuels are** natural fuels derived from once-living plants and animals. They include coal, petroleum, and natural gas.

Section 15.6—**Coal** is a solid fuel that is also a source of chemicals. The main element in coal is carbon. The quality of coal is determined mostly by its carbon and energy content, with anthracite being highest in rank and peat lowest. Coal is the most plentiful fossil fuel but is inconvenient to use and produces more pollution than other fuels.

Section 15.7—**Natural gas** is mainly methane and burns relatively cleanly. It is important both as a fuel and a raw material for synthesis of plastics and other products. **Petroleum**, or crude oil, is a thick liquid mixture of organic compounds, mainly hydrocarbons. Petroleum products can be burned fairly cleanly, but inefficient combustion produces pollution. Petroleum is refined by separating it, by distillation, into different fractions. **Gasoline** is the fraction consisting of hydrocarbons from about C_5 to C_{12}. Branched-chain hydrocarbons such as isooctane burn more smoothly than straight-chain hydrocarbons. The **octane rating** of gasoline compares its antiknock performance to that of pure isooctane. To raise the octane rating of gasoline, refineries use isomerization (to increase branching), **catalytic**

reforming (to convert straight-chain hydrocarbons to aromatic hydrocarbons), and alkylation (to convert small hydrocarbons to larger branched molecules). Octane boosters such as methanol, ethanol, MTBE, and *tert*-butyl alcohol are added as well. Tetraethyllead was used to improve octane rating for more than 50 years but has been discontinued in the United States. It is still used in many other countries, however.

Section 15.8—Electricity is the most convenient form of energy. About half of the electricity in the United States is generated from coal-burning steam power plants. Coal can be converted to more convenient gaseous or liquid fuels, but at an energy cost.

Section 15.9—Nuclear fission reactions can be controlled in a **nuclear reactor**, which uses a low concentration (3–5%) of uranium-235. The reactions are controlled with rods of cadmium or boron steel. The energy released generates steam that turns a turbine to generate electricity. Approximately 20% of the United States' electricity comes from nuclear fission reactors. A nuclear power plant cannot explode like a nuclear bomb, it produces minimal air pollution, and its wastes are collected rather than dispersed. But elaborate safety precautions are needed to prevent escape of radioactive material, the needed fuel is limited in availability, and ultimate disposal of radioactive waste is an ongoing problem. A **breeder reactor** converts other isotopes to useful nuclear fuel and can make more fuel than it consumes. Nuclear fusion cannot yet be controlled, as there are great technical difficulties. Temperatures in the millions of degrees are needed to generate a **plasma** consisting of free electrons and nuclei, for controlled fusion. But fusion has very important potential advantages over most other energy sources.

Section 15.10—Solar energy is diffuse and difficult to collect. Simple solar collectors can produce hot water for heating. Solar cells, or **photovoltaic cells**, produce electricity directly from sunlight, using *n*-type and *p*-type semiconductors. The cells are becoming less expensive and more efficient, and photovoltaic systems require storage systems or connection to the local electricity grid. **Biomass** such as wood can be burned directly or converted to liquid or gaseous fuels, but it requires much land area to produce and has a very low overall efficiency. Hydrogen is an energy storage and transport method rather than an energy source. It burns cleanly but requires more energy to make than it produces. One advantage of hydrogen is that it can be used in **fuel cells**, which consume fuel and oxygen continuously to generate electricity efficiently. Other renewable energy sources include wind power and hydroelectric power, which can be harnessed only in certain locations. Both sources have high initial costs. Heat energy from the interior of Earth is **geothermal energy**. We can also make use of the temperature difference between the ocean's surface and deep waters, tidal energy, and the energy of the waves. Renewable energy sources produced more than 10% of the electricity generated in the United States in 2012. Each energy source has advantages, limitations, and consequences. We can all conserve energy by using more efficient appliances and simply by using less energy.

GREEN CHEMISTRY—Energy is needed for everything we do, and there are many ways we can get it. An accounting of all inputs, outputs, and impacts of an energy-generating technology should use green chemistry principles to assess its true value.

Learning Objectives

❯ Perform power and energy calculations.	Problems 17–22, 58, 60, 69–71
❯ Classify chemical reactions and physical processes as exothermic or endothermic.	Problems 66–68
❯ Explain how to calculate the heat of a reaction using bond energies.	Problems 15, 16, 72
❯ List factors that affect the rates of chemical reactions.	Problems 13, 14
❯ State the first and second laws of thermodynamics, and discuss their implications for energy production and use.	Problems 23–29
❯ List the common fossil fuels, and describe how modern society is based on their use.	Problems 5–7, 9, 11, 12, 31–35, 76, 77
❯ List the origins, advantages, and disadvantages of coal as a fuel.	Problems 2, 8, 10, 30, 75
❯ List the characteristics, advantages, and disadvantages of natural gas and petroleum.	Problems 3, 36–42
❯ Explain why gaseous and liquid fuels are more convenient to use than solid fuels.	Problem 74
❯ List advantages and disadvantages of nuclear energy.	Problems 1, 43–48, 50, 51, 54–56
❯ Describe how a nuclear power plant generates electricity.	Problems 49, 52
❯ Explain how applying the green chemistry principles can help identify improved methods for energy generation.	Problems 78–80

REVIEW QUESTIONS

1. What kind of reaction powers the sun?

2. What was the main fuel used in the United States before 1800?

3. What was the main fuel used in the United States from about 1850 to 1950? What has been the main fuel since 1950?

4. List some advantages and disadvantages of hydrogen as a fuel for vehicles.

PROBLEMS

Fuels and Combustion

5. Write a balanced chemical reaction for the complete combustion of the following hydrocarbons in oxygen gas:
   a. propane, C_3H_8 **b.** butane, C_4H_{10}

6. For each substance in Problem 5, write a balanced equation for its incomplete combustion in oxygen gas (O_2) to form carbon monoxide gas as one of the products.

7. Write a balanced chemical reaction for the complete combustion of tridecane, ($C_{13}H_{28}$), in oxygen.

8. Write the equation for the complete combustion of coal, assuming that the coal is simply carbon.

9. Write a generalized word equation for the complete combustion of any hydrocarbon.

10. Write the equation for the incomplete combustion of coal to form carbon monoxide, assuming that the coal is simply carbon.

11. Write the equation for the complete combustion of methane.

12. Write the equation for the incomplete combustion of methane to form carbon monoxide and water vapor.

Energy and Chemical Reactions

13. How does temperature affect the rate of a chemical reaction?

14. Why does wood burn more rapidly in pure oxygen than in air?

15. Using bond energies, calculate the amount of energy, in kilojoules, that are released when 1.0 mol of methane is burned in plenty of oxygen gas, using the following steps:

a. Draw the Lewis structures of all the molecules involved in the reaction (remember the balancing numbers):
$$CH_4 + 2 O_2 \longrightarrow CO_2 + 2 H_2O$$
b. If the bond energy for the C—H bond is 413 kJ/mol, how much energy is needed to break all the bonds in 1 mol of methane molecules?
c. If the bond energy for the O=O bond is 498 kJ/mol, how much energy is needed to break all the bonds in 2 mol oxygen gas?
d. If the bond energy for the C=O bond is 798 kJ/mol, how much energy is released when 1 mol carbon dioxide gas is formed?
e. If the bond energy for the O—H bond is 467 kJ/mol, how much energy is released when 2 mol water molecules are formed?
f. What is the net result of energy needed to break the bonds, less the energy released when new bonds are formed? How do you interpret the sign of the answer?

16. Calculate the amount of energy, in kilojoules, that is involved when 1 mol of nitrogen gas is reacted with 3 mol hydrogen gas to form 2 mol ammonia gas, using the following steps:
a. Draw the Lewis structures of all the molecules involved in the reaction:
$$N_2(g) + 3 H_2 (g) \longrightarrow 2 NH_3(g)$$
b. If the bond energy for the N≡N bond is 946 kJ/mol, how much energy is needed to break all the bonds in 1 mol nitrogen molecules?

c. If the bond energy for the H—H bond is 432 kJ/mol, how much energy is needed to break all the bonds in 3 mol hydrogen gas?

d. If the bond energy for the N—H bond is 391 kJ/mol, how much energy is released when 1 mol ammonia is formed?

e. What is the net result of energy needed to break the bonds, less the energy released when new bonds are formed? How do you interpret the sign of that answer?

17. Burning 1.00 mol of methane releases 803 kJ of energy. How much energy is released by burning 24.5 mol of methane?

$$CH_4(g) + 2\ O_2(g) \longrightarrow CO_2(g) + 2\ H_2O(g) + 803\ kJ$$

18. It takes 572 kJ of energy to decompose 2.00 mol of liquid water. How much energy does it take to decompose 30.0 mol of water?

$$2\ H_2O(l) + 572\ kJ \longrightarrow 2\ H_2(g) + O_2(g)$$

19. When burned, 1.00 g of gasoline yields 1060 cal. What is this quantity in kilojoules?

20. How much heat, in kilojoules, is released when 15.8 g $H_2(g)$ reacts with plenty of $O_2(g)$ to form steam [$H_2O(g)$] according to the following equation?

$$2\ H_2(g) + O_2(g) \longrightarrow 2\ H_2O(g) + 483.6\ kJ$$

21. Refer to Problem 17, and determine how much energy, in kilojoules, must be supplied to convert 1.00 mol $CO_2(g)$ and 2.00 mol $H_2O(g)$ into $CH_4(g)$ and $O_2(g)$.

22. Refer to Problem 20, and determine how much energy, in kilojoules, must be supplied to convert 1 mol of water vapor into hydrogen gas and oxygen gas.

Energy and the Laws of Thermodynamics

23. State the first law of thermodynamics.

24. State the second law of thermodynamics in terms of energy flow and in terms of degradation or distribution of energy.

25. What is entropy? Does entropy increase or decrease when a fossil fuel is burned?

26. Which has higher entropy, nitrogen in the atmosphere or nitrogen in solid ammonium nitrate?

27. Which has higher entropy, potassium in solid potassium metal or potassium in KCl, in commercial fertilizer?

28. How does the statement "You can't even break even" relate to the second law of thermodynamics?

29. Explain why ice cream melts in a bowl at room temperature, in terms of energy transfer and the second law of thermodynamics.

Fossil Fuels

30. What are the advantages and disadvantages of coal as a fuel?

31. Why did the United States shift from coal to petroleum and natural gas when we have much larger reserves of coal than we do of the other two fuels?

Estimates in Problems 32–35 are from the U.S. Energy Information Administration 2014; see data in Table 15.3.

32. The estimated proven world oil reserves in 2013 were 1526 billion barrels. The world annual rate of use was 32.6 billion barrels. How long will these reserves last if this rate of use continues? (The rate of use is actually likely to increase.)

33. The estimated proven U.S. oil reserves in 2013 were 33.4 billion barrels. **(a)** How long will these reserves last if there are no imports or exports and if the U.S. annual rate of use of 6.7 billion barrels continues? **(b)** Taking the mean projection for oil reserves in the Arctic National Wildlife Refuge—10.4 billion barrels—how long would exploiting that resource extend our reserves at the current U.S. annual rate of use?

34. The estimated world natural gas reserves in 2013 were 6845 trillion cubic feet. The world annual rate of use was 120. trillion cubic feet. How long will these reserves last if this rate of use continues?

35. The U.S. proven natural gas reserves in 2013 were 323 trillion ft^3. How long will these reserves last if there are no imports or exports and if the U.S. annual rate of use of 24.5 trillion ft^3 continues?

36. What is thought to be the origin of petroleum? Compare the origins of petroleum to the origins of coal.

37. What are the advantages and disadvantages of petroleum as a source of fuels?

38. Describe the process of fractional distillation and how it is able to separate the various "fractions".

39. What does the term *octane rating* mean?

40. What are the advantages and disadvantages of tetraethyllead as an octane booster?

41. Consult Table 15.6, then suggest a reason why asphalt is a relatively inexpensive way to pave highways and driveways (compared to concrete, for example).

42. Which should have a higher octane rating, octane ($CH_3CH_2CH_2CH_2CH_2CH_2CH_2CH_3$) or 2,3,3-trimethylpentane [$CH_3CH(CH_3)C(CH_3)_2CH_2CH_3$]?

Nuclear Power

43. What proportion of U.S. electricity is generated by nuclear power plants?

44. What proportion of electricity in France is generated by nuclear power plants?

45. Explain why a nuclear power plant cannot explode like a nuclear bomb.

46. Write nuclear equations showing how uranium-238 is converted to fissionable plutonium-239.

47. Can a nuclear bomb be made from reactor-grade uranium? Explain.

48. Compare the amount of radioactive nuclear waste from power plants with that from nuclear weapons development.

49. How does a breeder reactor produce more fuel than it consumes? Does doing so violate the law of conservation of energy?

50. What are some of the advantages and disadvantages of breeder reactors?

51. List some possible advantages of a nuclear fusion reactor over a fission reactor. What is plasma?

52. What are the main challenges in the development of nuclear fusion reactors?

53. Write nuclear equations showing how thorium-232 is converted to fissionable uranium-233.

54. Write the nuclear equation that shows how deuterium and tritium fuse to form helium and a neutron.

55. The fission of 1 mol of uranium-235 can be represented by

$$^{235}_{92}U + {}^{1}_{0}n \longrightarrow 2{}^{1}_{0}n + {}^{139}_{54}Xe + {}^{95}_{38}Sr + 1.8 \times 10^{10} \text{ kJ}$$

See the equation in Problem 17 for the combustion of methane. How many moles of methane must be burned to generate the energy produced by fission of 1.00 mol (235 g) of uranium-235? What is the mass of this amount of methane, in metric tons (1 t = 1000 kg)?

56. Coal is mostly carbon. Burning 1 mol (12.0 g) of carbon to form carbon dioxide releases 393 kJ of energy. Refer to Problem 55, and determine how many moles of carbon must be burned to generate the energy produced by fission of 1.00 mol (235 g) of uranium-235. What is the mass of this amount of carbon, in metric tons?

Renewable Energy Sources

57. What is a photovoltaic cell?

58. What are some problems associated with the use of solar cells, for providing electrical energy both for whole cities and for a single home?

59. The average power demand of an American household that uses gas for heating, cooking, and the water heater is 1.3 kW. Solar cells can produce about 100 W/m². What area of solar cells is needed to meet this demand? What are the limits of this source of energy?

60. Large wind turbines can produce 1.5 MW of electrical power. How many of the homes described in Problem 59 could be powered by one big wind turbine? What are the disadvantages of dependence on this source of energy?

61. What is biomass? What are the problems and advantages of biomass as an energy source?

62. List two ways in which fuel cells differ from electrochemical cells.

63. List the advantages, disadvantages, and limitations of each of the following as an energy source.
    a. wind power   b. geothermal power
    c. biodiesel   d. hydroelectric power
    e. geothermal home heating system

Synthetic and Converted Fuels

64. Write the chemical equations for the basic processes by which coal (carbon) is converted to (a) methane and (b) carbon monoxide and hydrogen.

65. Write the chemical equations for (a) the conversion of carbon monoxide and hydrogen to methanol and (b) the reaction that occurs in a hydrogen–oxygen fuel cell.

ADDITIONAL PROBLEMS

66. A cold pack works by dissolving ammonium nitrate in water. Cold packs are carried by athletic trainers when transporting ice is not possible. Is this process endothermic or exothermic? Explain.

67. One type of hot-pack hand warmer contains a supersaturated and unstable solution of sodium acetate. It is activated by compressing a metal piece in the solution, which stimulates the crystallization. Hot packs are used by hunters and other outdoor sportsmen and workers in places where access to heaters or fires is not possible. Is this process endothermic or exothermic? Explain.

68. Decide if the following are exothermic or endothermic processes:
    a. striking a match
    b. freezing water in an ice-cube tray
    c. boiling potatoes   d. vaporizing water

69. The average human expends about 2100 kcal of energy per day.
    a. What is this output in watts?
    b. How does one human power compare to one horsepower? (See Problem 70.)

70. With the invention of the steam engine, inventors tried to compare the output of steam engines to that of the horses the engines would replace. Over a day of sustained work, an average workhorse expends energy at a rate of—you guessed it—one horsepower (hp), originally defined as 550 foot pounds/second. This means that the average horse could pull 550 pounds a distance of one foot, in one second. In modern units, one hp = 745 W. A modern race car with a 2.4-L V8 engine can develop about 740 hp, or the power output of 740 horses. What is the power output of the race car in units of kilowatts?

71. Both a banana and a hand grenade have about 170 kcal of energy. (a) What is the power output in watts of a banana if its energy is expended over 2.0 h by lying on a couch watching television? (b) What is the power output in watts of a hand grenade if its energy is expended in 0.0012 s? How do the banana and hand grenade compare in energy and in power?

72. Heats of combustion of two gaseous fuels, in kilojoules per mole, are given below. Which yields more energy (a) per kilogram and (b) per liter when the volume is measured under the same conditions of temperature and pressure?

    Hydrogen (H_2), 286.6 kJ

    Isobutane $CH_3CH(CH_3)_2$], 2868 kJ

73. The United States leads the major developed countries in per capita emission of $CO_2(g)$ with a rate of 19.0 t per person per year (1 t = 1000 kg). What mass, in metric tons of methane would yield this quantity of CO_2?

74. Explain why and for what applications gaseous and liquid fuels are more convenient than solid fuels.

75. (a) Write the chemical reaction for the burning of sulfur in coal to form sulfur dioxide. (b) A large coal-burning power plant burns 2600 tons of coal per day. The coal contains 0.65% S by mass. Assume that all the sulfur is converted to SO_2. What mass of SO_2 is formed? If a thermal inversion traps all this SO_2 in a volume of air that is 45 km by 60 km by 0.40 km, will the level of SO_2 in the air exceed the primary national air quality standard of 365 μg SO_2/m^3 air?

76. The contribution of the combustion of various fuels to the buildup of CO_2 in the atmosphere can be assessed in different ways. One way relates the mass of CO_2 formed to the mass of fuel burned; another relates the mass of CO_2 to the quantity

of heat evolved in the combustion. Which of the three fuels, C(graphite), $CH_4(g)$, or $C_4H_{10}(g)$, produces the smallest mass of CO_2 **(a)** per gram of fuel and **(b)** per kilojoule of heat evolved? The heat released per mole of each substance is C(graphite), 393.5 kJ; $CH_4(g)$, 803 kJ; and $C_4H_{10}(g)$, 2877 kJ.

77. Estimates of recoverable energy are notoriously uncertain, but some scientists think that a total of only 9.92×10^6 terawatt-hours (TWh) of recoverable energy is stored in the Earth (in the form of oil, coal, natural gas, and uranium). Worldwide use is about 1.32×10^5 TWh per year. **(a)** If demand for energy remains the same as today, approximately how many years will it be before all the energy stored in the Earth is gone? **(b)** Per capita consumption in the United States (population of about 313,000,000) is about four times that of the rest of the world (population of about 7.0 billion). If all the countries throughout the world consumed energy at the same per capita rate as the United States, approximately how many years would it be before all the energy stored in the Earth is used up? **(c)** Evaluate your answers to parts **(a)** and **(b)**.

78. If 5% of the energy that a PV system will generate over a 30-year lifetime is needed to build the system, what is the energy payback time (the time at which the energy investment is recovered) for the system?

79. Production of gasoline from tar sands requires natural gas. If the ratio between the energy needed to generate the gasoline and the energy content of the gasoline itself is very low, why is this production method pursued?

80. Use the green chemistry principles to suggest ways of making hydraulic fracturing a greener process.

CRITICAL THINKING EXERCISES

Apply knowledge that you have gained in this chapter and one or more of the FLaReS principles (Chapter 1) to evaluate the following statements or claims.

15.1. A futurist and inventor predict that advances in nanotechnology will result in solar energy powering the world in just 16 years.

15.2. In 1996, Indian inventor Ramar Pillai claimed to have discovered a secret herbal formula that converted water to a hydrocarbon fuel.

15.3. An inventor claims to have discovered a catalyst that speeds the conversion of linear alkanes, such as hexane, to branched-chain isomers.

15.4. While watching TV during the summer, you hear someone proclaim that a way to cool your kitchen is to keep the refrigerator door open.

15.5. A fuel cell in every house can give each household energy independence.

15.6. A company claims that it can use a metal such as magnesium as a fuel for automobiles. A coil of the metal would be fed into a chamber where it would react with superheated steam to produce hydrogen gas, which would power a fuel cell that would run the car.

COLLABORATIVE GROUP PROJECTS

Prepare a PowerPoint, poster, or other presentation (as directed by your instructor) to share with your class.

1. Find appliances such as a water heater, television set, computer monitor, or electric frying pan and determine the wattage of the appliance. Examine your electric bill to determine the cost in your area per kilowatt hour for electrical energy. Determine the cost for running that device for one hour. Determine the cost for 40 hours.

2. Which would you rather have in your neighborhood, a nuclear or a coal-burning power plant? Why? Explain.

3. What characteristics should an ideal energy source have? Which of these characteristics do the different sources of energy discussed in this chapter have?

4. Social-cost pricing takes into account all the costs of a product or activity that are not part of market costs. For example, one of the social costs of gasoline-based transportation is air pollution. Select three sources of energy, and list the possible social costs that should be considered.

5. Compare the quantity of electricity used for two appliances that are alike except for different efficiencies. Extend this comparison to CO_2 emissions from the appliances, assuming that the electricity is generated by burning coal.

6. Compare qualitatively the efficiency of heating a home with natural gas versus heating it with electricity produced from burning natural gas at a power plant.

7. All of the following are used for heating homes. What problems with supply, use, and waste products are involved in each case?
   a. natural gas
   b. electricity
   c. biomass/wood
   d. coal
   e. fuel oil
   f. geothermal energy

8. There was an accident at nuclear power plants at Fukushima, Japan, following an earthquake and tsunami on March 11, 2011. Using your favorite search engine, find out what happened and compare this accident with the ones at Chernobyl and Three Mile Island. How could these accidents have been avoided? Do these incidents prove that nuclear power plants should be phased out? Why or why not?

9. Use Internet sources to find directions and construct **(a)** a simple solar heater or **(b)** a solar oven. These devices are important in underdeveloped nations, particularly in areas with sunny climates such as much of Africa.

CHEMISTRY @ HOME   Some Like It Hot and Some Like It Cool!

Materials required

- 2 small clear plastic cups
- 1 tablespoon water
- 1 tablespoon hydrogen peroxide 3% solution
- 3 grams powdered yeast
- Wooden splint (wooden coffee stirrer)
- Matches
- 3 grams Pixy Stix or Fun Dip (candies containing citric acid)
- Kitchen scale
- Spoon
- Thermometer

How do you determine if a physical or a chemical change has occurred? What are the key differences between an exothermic and an endothermic reaction?

Many industrial chemical processes involve exothermic reactions. Understanding the hazards of the chemicals used in the lab is one way of reducing the overall risk associated with the reactions. Green chemistry focuses on reducing risks by reducing or eliminating the use of hazardous chemicals and processes whenever possible. For this experiment, you will preform two different chemical reactions using safe materials and conditions. One will be an exothermic reaction that results in the release of heat from the system to the surrounding area. The other will be an endothermic reaction that results in energy being absorbed as heat.

Measure 1 tablespoon of water. Pour the water into a cup and label it. Be sure to record the initial starting temperature with the thermometer. Create a data table to record the starting temperature and the temperature at 10-second intervals for 60 seconds. Weigh out 3 grams of Pixy Stix granules using the kitchen scale. Quickly add all of the candy to the water and stir using spoon. (The candy does not need to fully dissolve in the water.) Collect temperature data for 60 seconds.

What happens to the temperature of the water? What type of reaction occurred? (Figure 1).

► **Figure 1**

Measure 1 tablespoon of hydrogen peroxide. Pour the hydrogen peroxide into a cup and label it. Record the starting temperature in your data table. Create a data table to record at 10-second intervals for 60 seconds. Weigh out 3 grams of yeast using the kitchen scale. Add the yeast to the hydrogen peroxide and stir using the spoon. What happens when you add the yeast? Collect temperature data for 60 seconds. Figure 2:

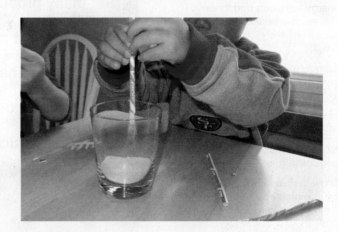

▲ **Figure 2**

Use matches to light the end of the wooden coffee stir stick, and let it burn for a moment. Then blow out the flame. You'll want it to remain glowing red but not flaming. Carefully bring the glowing end of the splint up to the larger bubbles in the foam. What happens next?

Questions

1. Were both reactions chemical or physical changes? Explain.
2. Which reaction caused an endothermic reaction? Why?
3. Which reaction caused an exothermic reaction? Why?
4. What gas was produced in the yeast and hydrogen peroxide experiment?
5. If you were to repeat the candy and water experiment, would you be able to relight the wooden splint? Why or why not?

16

Learning Objectives

> List the major parts of a cell, and describe the function of each part. (16.1)

> Name the primary source of energy for plants and three classes of substances that are the sources of energy for animals. (16.1)

> Compare and contrast starch, glycogen, and cellulose. (16.2)

> Describe the fundamental structure of a fatty acid and of a fat. (16.3)

> Classify fats as saturated, monounsaturated, or polyunsaturated. (16.3)

> Draw the fundamental structure of an amino acid, and show how amino acids combine to make proteins. (16.4)

> Describe the four levels of protein structure, and give an example of each. (16.5)

> Describe how enzymes work as catalysts. (16.5)

> Name the two types of nucleic acids, and describe the function of each type. (16.6)

> Explain complementary base pairing, and describe how a copy of DNA is synthesized. (16.6)

> Explain how mRNA is synthesized from DNA and how a protein is synthesized from mRNA. (16.7)

> List important characteristics of the genetic code. (16.7)

> Describe recombinant DNA technology, and explain how it is used. (16.8)

> Name some advantages of using biochemistry to create useful molecules.

> Give examples of the use of biochemistry for energy production and other applications.

BIOCHEMISTRY

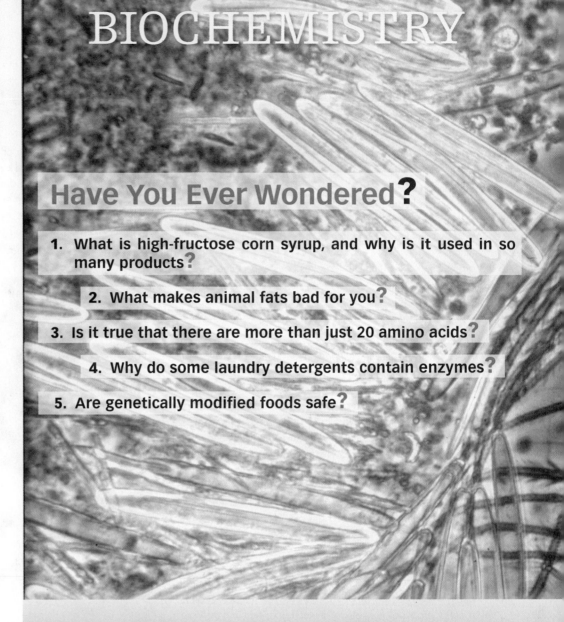

Have You Ever Wondered?

1. **What is high-fructose corn syrup, and why is it used in so many products?**

2. **What makes animal fats bad for you?**

3. **Is it true that there are more than just 20 amino acids?**

4. **Why do some laundry detergents contain enzymes?**

5. **Are genetically modified foods safe?**

A MOLECULAR VIEW OF LIFE The human body is an incredible chemical factory, far more complex than any industrial plant. To stay in good condition and perform its varied tasks, it needs many specific chemical compounds—most of which it manufactures in an exquisitely organized network of chemical production lines.

Every minute of every day, thousands of chemical reactions take place within each of the 100 trillion tiny cells in your body. The study of these reactions and the chemicals they produce is called *biochemistry*.

Every form of life is chemical in nature. The substances and reactions that occur in living organisms are often more complex than the ones we have already studied. Nonetheless, basic chemical concepts such as acid–base reactions, intermolecular forces, and the reactivity of organic functional groups all apply to living organisms.

Many organisms in nature exist in a very complex relationship with their environment. A specific example is the relationship between the clownfish and the sea anemone. Sea anemones are sessile organisms that sting organisms that might try to prey on them. They then digest those predators. Clownfish, however, live in a symbiotic relationship with the anemones. The clownfish consume small predators and parasites that might threaten the anemone, as well as helping with the metabolism of the anemone. The sea anemone provides a safe environment for the clownfish by stinging larger fish that might prey on them. The clownfish appear to be immune to the toxins in the nematocysts (stinging organs that are shown in the photograph at right) of the anemone. It seems that the clownfish have a different kind of mucous membrane than other fish, which offers protection and camouflage. Digestion, the development of toxins, and the unusual adaptation of clownfish are just three aspects of biochemistry in action.

In this chapter, we will examine acid–base reactions that govern the behavior of proteins in our bodies. We will look at intermolecular forces that influence the properties and behavior of DNA and RNA. And we will see that the functional groups on fats are the same as those on other organic compounds we have studied.

16.1 Energy and the Living Cell

Learning Objectives ❭ List the major parts of a cell, and describe the function of each part. ❭ Name the primary source of energy for plants and three classes of substances that are the sources of energy for animals.

Biochemistry is the chemistry of living things and life processes. The structural unit of all living things is the *cell*. Every cell is enclosed in a *cell membrane*, a double layer of lipid molecules through which it gains nutrients and gets rid of wastes. Plant cells (Figure 16.1 on the next page) also have walls made of cellulose. Animal cells (see Figure 16.2 on the bottom of the next page) do not have cell walls. Cells have a variety of interior structures that serve a multiplicity of functions. We can consider only a few of them here.

The largest interior structure of a cell is usually the *nucleus*, which contains the DNA molecules. These molecular materials control heredity. Protein synthesis takes place in the *ribosomes*. The *mitochondria* are the cell's "batteries," where energy is produced. Plant cells (but not animal cells) also contain *chloroplasts*, in which energy from the sun is converted to chemical energy, which is stored in the plant in the form of carbohydrates.

Energy in Biological Systems

Life requires energy. Living cells are inherently unstable, and only a continued input of energy keeps them from falling apart. Living organisms are restricted to using certain forms of energy. Supplying a plant with heat energy by holding it in a flame will do little to prolong its life. On the other hand, a green plant is uniquely able to use sunlight, the richest source of energy on Earth. Chloroplasts in green plant cells capture the radiant energy of the sun and convert it to chemical energy, which is then stored in carbohydrate molecules. The photosynthesis of glucose is represented by the equation

$$6\,CO_2(g) + 6\,H_2O(l) \longrightarrow C_6H_{12}O_6(aq) + 6\,O_2(g)$$

▶ **Figure 16.1** The general form of a plant cell. Not all the structures shown here occur in every type of plant cell.

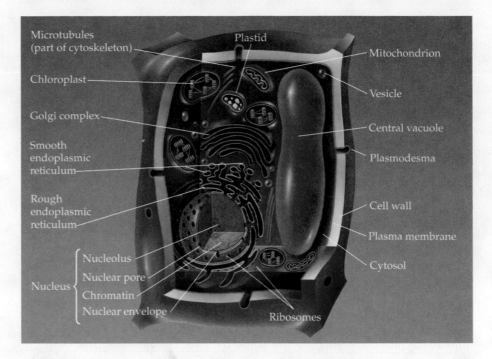

Plant cells can also convert the carbohydrate molecules to fat molecules and, given the proper inorganic nutrients, to protein molecules.

Animals cannot directly use the energy of sunlight. They must get their energy by eating plants or by eating other animals that eat plants. Animals obtain energy from three major types of substances: carbohydrates, fats, and proteins. Carbohydrates, fats, and proteins as foods are discussed in Chapter 17. In this chapter, we deal mainly with the synthesis and structure of these vital materials.

▶ **Figure 16.2** An animal cell. The entire range of structures shown here seldom occurs in a single cell, and only a few of them are discussed in this text. Each kind of plant or animal tissue has cells specific to the function of that tissue. Muscle cells differ from nerve cells, nerve cells differ from red blood cells, and so on.

Once digested and transported to a cell, a food molecule can be used as a building block to make new cell parts or to repair old ones, or it can be "burned" for energy. The entire series of coordinated chemical reactions that keep cells alive is called **metabolism**. In general, metabolic reactions are divided into two classes: The degrading of molecules to provide energy is called **catabolism**, and the process of building up, or synthesizing, the molecules of living systems is termed **anabolism**.

SELF-ASSESSMENT Questions

1. The three major types of substances from which we obtain energy are
   a. amino acids, proteins, and carbohydrates
   b. burgers, pizza, and soft drinks
   c. proteins, nucleic acids, and oils
   d. carbohydrates, fats, and proteins

2. The process of synthesizing the molecules to make cell structures within a living cell is called
   a. anabolism
   b. catabolism
   c. metabolism
   d. transcription

3. The overall set of chemical reactions that keep cells alive is called
   a. anabolism
   b. metabolism
   c. enzymology
   d. proteolysis

Answers: 1, d; 2, a; 3, b

16.2 Carbohydrates: A Storehouse of Energy

Learning Objective ❭ Compare and contrast starch, glycogen, and cellulose.

It is difficult to give a simple formal definition of *carbohydrates*. Chemically, **carbohydrates** are polyhydroxy aldehydes or ketones or compounds that can be hydrolyzed (split by water) to form such aldehydes and ketones. Composed of the elements carbon, hydrogen, and oxygen, carbohydrates include sugars, starches, and cellulose. Usually, the atoms of these elements are present in a ratio expressed by the formula $C_x(H_2O)_y$, which means that the compounds could be described as a combination of carbon and water. Glucose, a simple sugar, has the formula $C_6H_{12}O_6$, which we can write as $C_6(H_2O)_6$. The term *carbohydrate* is derived from formulas written in this way, but keep in mind that carbohydrates are not in fact hydrates of carbon.

Some Simple Sugars

Sugars are sweet-tasting carbohydrates. The simplest sugars are **monosaccharides**, carbohydrates that cannot be further hydrolyzed. Three familiar dietary monosaccharides are shown in Figure 16.3. They are *glucose* (also called *dextrose*), *galactose* (a component of lactose, the sugar in milk), and *fructose* (fruit sugar). Glucose and galactose are **aldoses**, monosaccharides with an aldehyde functional group (the functional groups were presented in Table 9.4). Fructose is a **ketose**, a monosaccharide with a ketone functional group. Pure fructose is about 25% sweeter than table sugar (sucrose, shown in Figure 16.5). Glucose is about 25% less sweet than table sugar.

▲ **Figure 16.3** Three common monosaccharides. All have hydroxyl groups. Glucose and galactose have aldehyde functional groups, and fructose has a ketone group. Glucose and galactose differ only in the arrangement of the H and OH on the fourth carbon (green) from the top. Living cells use glucose as a source of energy. Fructose is fruit sugar, and galactose is a component of milk sugar.

Q: *What is the molecular formula of each of the three monosaccharides? How are the three compounds related?*

1. What is high-fructose corn syrup, and why is it used in so many products?

High-fructose corn syrup (HFCS) has had some of its glucose enzymatically converted to fructose. This makes it significantly sweeter than ordinary corn syrup, because fructose is sweeter than glucose. HFCS is quite cheap in the United States. Unfortunately, like table sugar, it provides little more than empty calories.

Example 16.1	Classification of Monosaccharides

Shown below are structures of (left to right) erythrulose, used in some sunless tanning lotions; mannose, a sugar found in some fruits, including cranberries; and ribose, a component of ribonucleic acid (RNA; Section 16.7).

$$
\begin{array}{ccc}
 & \text{CHO} & \\
 & \text{HO}-\text{C}-\text{H} & \\
\text{CH}_2\text{OH} & \text{HO}-\text{C}-\text{H} & \text{CHO} \\
\text{C}=\text{O} & \text{H}-\text{C}-\text{OH} & \text{H}-\text{C}-\text{OH} \\
\text{HO}-\text{C}-\text{H} & \text{H}-\text{C}-\text{OH} & \text{H}-\text{C}-\text{OH} \\
\text{CH}_2\text{OH} & \text{CH}_2\text{OH} & \text{H}-\text{C}-\text{OH} \\
 & & \text{CH}_2\text{OH} \\
\text{Erythrulose} & \text{Mannose} & \text{Ribose}
\end{array}
$$

Classify erythrulose and ribose as an aldose or a ketose.

Solution

Erythrulose is a ketose. The carbonyl (C=O) group is on the second C atom from the top; it is between two other C atoms, an arrangement that defines a ketone. Ribose is an aldose. The carbonyl group includes a chain-ending carbon atom, as in all aldehydes.

▪ EXERCISE 16.1

How does the structure of mannose (shown above) differ from that of galactose?

The monosaccharides glucose, galactose, and fructose are represented in Figure 16.3 as open-chain compounds to show the aldehyde or ketone functional groups. However, these sugars exist in solution mainly as cyclic molecules (see Figure 16.4).

▶ **Figure 16.4** Cyclic structures for glucose, galactose, and fructose. A corner with no letter represents a carbon atom. Glucose and galactose differ only in the arrangement of the H and OH (green) on the fourth carbon. Some sugars exist in more than one cyclic form, but, for simplicity, only one form of each is shown here.

Glucose   Galactose   Fructose

Sucrose and lactose are examples of **disaccharides**, carbohydrates whose molecules can be hydrolyzed to yield two monosaccharide units (Figure 16.5).

▲ Although we have represented the cyclic monosaccharides as flat hexagons, they are three-dimensional. Most assume a conformation (shape) called a *chair conformation* because it somewhat resembles a reclining chair.

Sucrose   Lactose

▲ **Figure 16.5** Sucrose and lactose are disaccharides. On hydrolysis, sucrose yields glucose and fructose, whereas lactose yields glucose and galactose. Sucrose is cane or beet sugar, and lactose is milk sugar.

Q: *What is the molecular formula of each of these disaccharides? How are the two compounds related? Label the two monosaccharide units in each as fructose, galactose, or glucose.*

Sucrose is split into glucose and fructose. Hydrolysis of lactose yields glucose and galactose.

$$\text{Sucrose} + H_2O \longrightarrow \text{Glucose} + \text{Fructose}$$

$$\text{Lactose} + H_2O \longrightarrow \text{Glucose} + \text{Galactose}$$

Polysaccharides: Starch and Cellulose

Polysaccharides are composed of large molecules that yield many monosaccharide units on hydrolysis. Polysaccharides include starches and cellulose. These comprise the main energy-storage system of many plants and the structural material of plants. Figure 16.6 shows short segments of starch and cellulose molecules. Notice that both are polymers of glucose. Starch molecules generally have from 100 to about 6000 glucose units. Cellulose molecules are composed of 1800–3000 or more glucose units.

(a) Segment of a starch molecule

(b) Segment of a cellulose molecule

▲ **Figure 16.6** Both starch and cellulose are polymers of glucose. They differ in that the glucose units are joined by alpha linkages (blue) in starch and by beta linkages (red) in cellulose.

Q: *The formulas for most polymers can be written in condensed form (page 289). Write a condensed formula for starch. How would the condensed formula for cellulose differ from that of starch?*

Another difference between starch and cellulose is the way that the glucose units are hooked together. In starch, with the —CH₂OH group at the top as a reference, the oxygen atom joining the glucose units is pointed *down*. This arrangement is called an *alpha linkage*. In cellulose, the oxygen atom connecting the glucose units is pointed *up*, an arrangement called a *beta linkage*.

This subtle but important difference in linkage determines whether or not the material can be digested by humans (Chapter 17). The different linkages also result in different three-dimensional forms for cellulose and starch. For example, cellulose in the cell walls of plants is arranged in *fibrils*, bundles of parallel chains. As shown in Figure 16.7a, these fibrils lie parallel to each other in each

(a)

(b)

▲ **Figure 16.7** Cellulose molecules form fibers, whereas starch molecules (glycogen) form granules. Electron micrographs of (a) the cell wall of an alga, made up of successive layers of cellulose fibers in parallel arrangement, and (b) glycogen granules in a liver cell of a rat.

► **Figure 16.8** Schematic representations of amylose, amylopectin, and glycogen. Amylose is unbranched. Amylopectin has a branch approximately every 25 glucose units. Glycogen branches about every 10 glucose units.

Amylose
(found in plants)

Amylopectin

Glycogen
(found in animals)

layer of the cell wall. In alternate layers, the fibrils are perpendicular, an arrangement that imparts great strength to the cell wall.

There are two kinds of starches found in plants. One, called *amylose*, has glucose units joined in a continuous chain like beads on a string. The other kind, *amylopectin*, has branched chains of glucose units. These starches are perhaps best represented schematically, as in Figure 16.8, where each glucose unit is represented by open circles.

Animal starch is called *glycogen*. Like amylopectin, it is composed of branched chains of glucose units. In contrast to cellulose, we see in Figure 16.7b that glycogen in muscle and liver tissue is arranged in granules, clusters of small particles. Plant starch, on the other hand, forms large granules. When cornstarch is heated at about 400 °F for an hour, the starch polymers are broken down into shorter chains to form a product called *dextrin*, which has properties intermediate between those of sugars and starches. Mixed with water, dextrin makes a slightly thick, sticky mixture. Starch and dextrin adhesives account for about 58% of the U.S. packaging market.

Granules of plant starch rupture in boiling water to form a paste, which gels when it cools. Potatoes and cereal grains form this type of starchy broth. All forms of starch are hydrolyzed to glucose during digestion.

SELF-ASSESSMENT Questions

1. A monosaccharide with a ketone group is called
   a. a ketol
   b. a ketal
   c. ketose
   d. ketosis

2. An aldose is a monosaccharide
   a. diet aid
   b. that forms polyhydroxy cellulose
   c. that forms aldosterols
   d. with an aldehyde group

3. When most monosaccharides dissolve in water, they form
   a. branched polysaccharides
   b. disaccharides
   c. ring structures
   d. polysaccharides

4. The two monosaccharide units that make up a lactose molecule are
   a. both glucose
   b. fructose and galactose
   c. glucose and fructose
   d. glucose and galactose

5. Which of these polysaccharide molecules consists of branched chains of glucose units?
   a. amylose and amylopectin
   b. amylose and cellulose
   c. amylose and glycogen
   d. amylopectin and glycogen

6. Carbohydrates are stored in the liver and muscle tissue as
   a. amylose
   b. amylopectin
   c. cellulose
   d. glycogen

Answers: 1. c; 2, d; 3, c; 4, d; 5, d; 6, d

16.3 Fats and Other Lipids

Learning Objectives ❯ Describe the fundamental structure of a fatty acid and of a fat.
❯ Classify fats as saturated, monounsaturated, or polyunsaturated.

Fats are the predominant forms of a class of compounds called *lipids*. These substances are not defined by a functional group, as are most organic compounds. Rather, lipids have common solubility properties. A **lipid** is a cellular component that is insoluble in water but soluble in organic solvents of low polarity, such as hexane, diethyl ether, and chloroform. In addition to fats, the lipid family includes **fatty acids** (long-chain carboxylic acids), steroids such as cholesterol and sex hormones (Chapter 18), fat-soluble vitamins (Chapter 17), and other substances. Figure 16.9 shows three representations of palmitic acid, a typical fatty acid.

A **fat** is an ester of fatty acids and the trihydroxy alcohol glycerol (Figure 16.10). A fat has three fatty acid chains joined to glycerol through ester linkages (which is why fats are often called *triglycerides*, or triacylglycerols). Related compounds are classified according to the number of fatty acid chains they contain: A *monoglyceride* has one fatty acid chain joined to glycerol, and a *diglyceride* has two.

$$CH_3CH_2CH_2CH_2CH_2CH_2CH_2CH_2CH_2CH_2CH_2CH_2CH_2CH_2CH_2COOH$$
(a)

$$\text{COOH}$$
(b)

(c)

▲ **Figure 16.9** Three representations of palmitic acid: (a) Condensed structural formula. (b) Line-angle formula, in which the lines denote bonds and each intersection of lines or end of a line represents a carbon atom. (c) Space-filling model.

Naturally occurring fatty acids typically have an even number of carbon atoms. Representative ones are listed in Table 16.1 on the next page. Animal fats are generally rich in saturated fatty acids (fatty acids with no carbon-to-carbon double bonds) and have a smaller proportion of unsaturated fatty acids. At room temperature, most animal fats are solids. Liquid fats, called *oils*, are obtained mainly from vegetable sources. Oils typically have a higher proportion of unsaturated fatty acid units than do fats. Fats and oils feel greasy. They are less dense than water and float on it.

Fats are often classified according to the degree of unsaturation of the fatty acids they incorporate. A *saturated fatty acid* contains no carbon-to-carbon double bonds, a *monounsaturated fatty acid* has one carbon-to-carbon double bond per molecule, and a *polyunsaturated fatty acid* has two or more carbon-to-carbon double bonds. A *saturated fat* contains a high proportion of saturated fatty acids; these fat molecules have relatively few carbon-to-carbon double bonds. A *polyunsaturated fat* (oil) incorporates mainly unsaturated fatty acids; these fat molecules have many double bonds.

The iodine number is a measure of the degree of unsaturation of a fat or oil. The **iodine number** is the mass in grams of iodine that is consumed by 100 g of fat or oil. Iodine, like other halogens, adds to a carbon-to-carbon double bond.

$$\underset{/}{\overset{\backslash}{C}}{=}\underset{\backslash}{\overset{/}{C}} + I_2 \longrightarrow -\overset{|}{\underset{I}{C}}-\overset{|}{\underset{I}{C}}-$$

2. What makes animal fats bad for you?

The saturated fats found in most animal fats can pack closely together to form artery-clogging plaque, which contributes to heart disease. The structures of unsaturated fats do not stack neatly and do not form this plaque.

$$\begin{array}{c}
\overset{\text{O}}{\overset{\|}{\text{HOCCH}_2(\text{CH}_2)_{11}\text{CH}_3}} \\
\begin{array}{l}
\text{CH}_2\text{OH} \\
| \\
\text{CHOH} \\
| \\
\text{CH}_2\text{OH}
\end{array}
\quad + \quad
\begin{array}{c}
\overset{\text{O}}{\overset{\|}{\text{HOCCH}_2(\text{CH}_2)_{11}\text{CH}_3}} \\
\overset{\text{O}}{\overset{\|}{\text{HOCCH}_2(\text{CH}_2)_{15}\text{CH}_3}}
\end{array}
\quad \longrightarrow \quad
\begin{array}{l}
\overset{\text{O}}{\overset{\|}{\text{CH}_2-\text{OCCH}_2(\text{CH}_2)_{11}\text{CH}_3}} \\
\overset{\text{O}}{\overset{\|}{\text{CH}-\text{OCCH}_2(\text{CH}_2)_{11}\text{CH}_3}} \\
\overset{\text{O}}{\overset{\|}{\text{CH}_2-\text{OCCH}_2(\text{CH}_2)_{15}\text{CH}_3}}
\end{array}
\quad + \quad 3\,\text{H}_2\text{O}
\end{array}$$

Glycerol   Fatty acids   A triglyceride

(a)

(b)

◄ **Figure 16.10** Triglycerides (triacylglycerols) are esters in which the trihydroxy (having three OH groups) alcohol glycerol is esterified with three fatty acid groups. (a) The equation for the formation of a triglyceride. (b) Space-filling model of a triglyceride.

Table 16.1 Some Fatty Acids in Natural Fats

Number of Carbon Atoms	Condensed Structural Formula	Name	Source
4	$CH_3CH_2CH_2COOH$	Butyric acid	Butter
6	$CH_3(CH_2)_4COOH$	Caproic acid	Butter
8	$CH_3(CH_2)_6COOH$	Caprylic acid	Coconut oil
10	$CH_3(CH_2)_8COOH$	Capric acid	Coconut oil
12	$CH_3(CH_2)_{10}COOH$	Lauric acid	Palm kernel oil
14	$CH_3(CH_2)_{12}COOH$	Myristic acid	Oil of nutmeg
16	$CH_3(CH_2)_{14}COOH$	Palmitic acid	Palm oil
18	$CH_3(CH_2)_{16}COOH$	Stearic acid	Beef tallow
18	$CH_3(CH_2)_7CH{=}CH(CH_2)_7COOH$	Oleic acid	Olive oil
18	$CH_3(CH_2)_4CH{=}CHCH_2CH{=}CH(CH_2)_7COOH$	Linoleic acid	Soybean oil
18	$CH_3CH_2(CH{=}CHCH_2)_3(CH_2)_6COOH$	Linolenic acid	Fish oils
20	$CH_3(CH_2)_4(CH{=}CHCH_2)_4CH_2CH_2COOH$	Arachidonic acid	Liver

The more double bonds a fat contains, the more iodine is required for the addition reaction. Thus, a high iodine number means a high degree of unsaturation. Representative iodine numbers are listed in Table 16.2. Note the generally lower values for animal fats (butter, tallow, and lard) compared with those for vegetable oils. Coconut oil, which is highly saturated, and fish oils, which are relatively unsaturated, are notable exceptions to the general rule.

Table 16.2 Typical Iodine Numbers for Some Fats and Oils[a]

Fat or Oil	Iodine Number	Fat or Oil	Iodine Number
Coconut oil	8–10	Cottonseed oil	100–117
Butter	25–40	Corn oil	115–130
Beef tallow	30–45	Fish oils	120–180
Palm oil	37–54	Canola oil	125–135
Lard	45–70	Soybean oil	125–140
Olive oil	75–95	Safflower oil	130–140
Peanut oil	85–100	Sunflower oil	130–145

[a]Oils shown in blue are from plant sources.

▲ Many salad dressings are made of an oil and vinegar. In the bottle shown here, olive oil is floating on wine vinegar, an aqueous solution of acetic acid.

SELF-ASSESSMENT Questions

1. Fats are defined by their
   a. chemical reactivity
   b. functional group
   c. function in the body
   d. degree of unsaturation

Questions 2–6 refer to the structures S, T, U, and V.

S: $CH_3(CH_2)_{10}COOH$ 　　　　 T: $CH_3(CH_2)_{16}COOH$

U: $CH_3(CH_2)_7CH{=}CH(CH_2)_7COOH$

V: $CH_3CH_2(CH{=}CHCH_2)_3(CH_2)_6COOH$

2. Which are saturated fatty acids?
   a. S and T
   b. S and U
   c. T and U
   d. U and V

3. Which is a monounsaturated fatty acid?
   a. S　　b. T　　c. U　　d. V

4. Which is a polyunsaturated fatty acid?
   a. S　　b. T　　c. U　　d. V

5. Saturated fats often have a high proportion of
   a. S and T
   b. S and U
   c. T and U
   d. U and V

6. Polyunsaturated fats (oils) often have a high proportion of
   a. S　　b. T　　c. U　　d. V

7. The iodine number of a fat or oil expresses its
   a. calories per gram
   b. degree of acidity
   c. degree of unsaturation
   d. digestibility

8. In general, animal fats differ from vegetable oils in that the oil molecules
   a. are higher in calories
   b. are shorter
   c. have fewer C=C bonds
   d. have more C=C bonds

Answers: 1. d; 2. a; 3. c; 4. d; 5. a; 6. d; 7. c; 8. d

16.4 Proteins: Polymers of Amino Acids

Learning Objective › Draw the fundamental structure of an amino acid, and show how amino acids combine to make proteins.

Proteins are vital components of all life. No living part of the human body—or of any other organism—is completely without protein. There is protein in blood, muscles, brain, and even tooth enamel. The smallest cellular organisms—bacteria—contain protein. Viruses, so small that they make bacteria look like giants, are little more than proteins and nucleic acids, a combination that is the stuff of life itself.

Each type of cell makes its own kinds of proteins. Proteins serve as the structural materials of animals, much as cellulose does in plants. Muscle tissue is largely protein, and so are skin and hair. Silk, wool, nails, claws, feathers, horns, and hooves are proteins. All proteins contain the elements carbon, hydrogen, oxygen, and nitrogen, and most also contain sulfur. The structure of a short segment of a typical protein molecule is shown in Figure 16.11.

Like starch and cellulose, *proteins* are polymers. They differ from other polymers that we have studied in that the monomer units are about 20 different amino acids (Table 16.3, on the next page). The amino acids differ in their side chains (shown in green). An **amino acid** has two functional groups, an amino group ($-NH_2$) and a carboxyl group ($-COOH$), attached to the same carbon atom (called the *alpha carbon*).

(a)   (b)

▲ **Figure 16.11** Space-filling model (a) and structural formula (b) of a short segment of a protein molecule. In the structural formula, hydrocarbon side chains (green), an acidic side chain (red), a basic side chain (blue), and a sulfur-containing side chain (amber shading) are highlighted. The dashed lines crossing the formula indicate where two amino-acid units join (see Section 16.5).

Q: *The formulas for most polymers can be written in condensed form (page 289). Those for natural proteins cannot. Explain.*

Table 16.3	**The 20 Amino Acids Specified by the Human Genetic Code**	

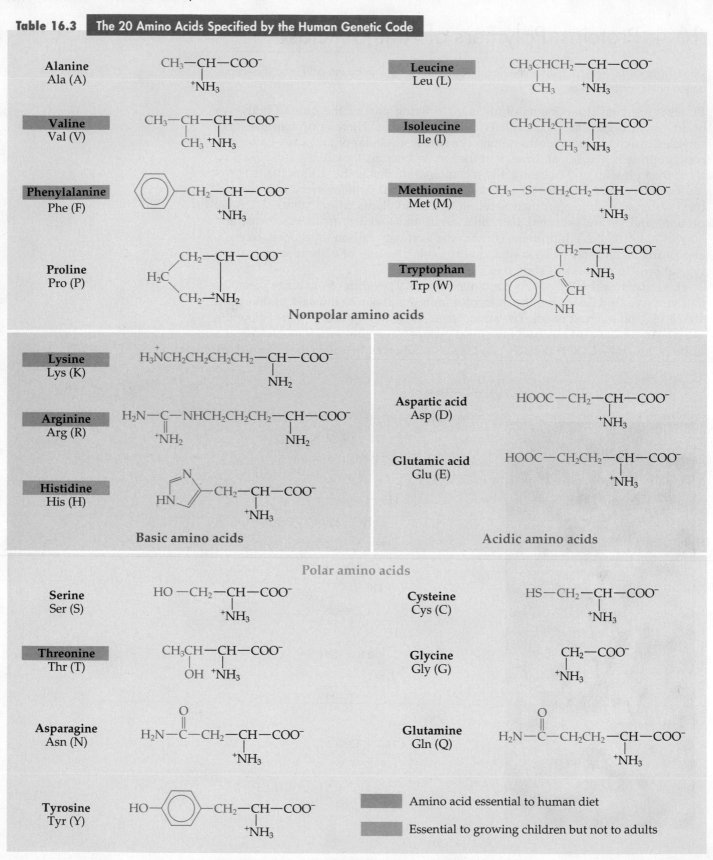

Nonpolar amino acids

Basic amino acids

Acidic amino acids

Polar amino acids

Amino acid essential to human diet

Essential to growing children but not to adults

In this formula, the R can be a hydrogen atom (as it is in glycine, the simplest amino acid) or any of the groups shown in green in Table 16.3. The formula shows the proper placement of the groups, but it is not really correct. Acids react with bases to form salts. The carboxyl group is acidic, and the amino group is basic. The two functional groups interact, the acid transferring a proton to the base. The resulting product is an inner salt, or **zwitterion**, a compound in which the negative charge and the positive charge are on different parts of the same molecule.

$$H_3N^+ \!-\! \overset{\overset{\displaystyle R}{|}}{\underset{\underset{\displaystyle H}{|}}{C}} \!-\! COO^-$$

A zwitterion

Plants can synthesize amino acids and proteins from carbon dioxide, water, and minerals such as nitrates (NO_3^-) and sulfates (SO_4^{2-}). Animals need to consume proteins in their foods. Humans can only synthesize some of the amino acids in Table 16.3. Others must be part of the proteins consumed in a normal diet. The latter are called *essential amino acids*.

The Peptide Bond: Peptides and Proteins

The human body contains tens of thousands of different proteins. Each of us has a tailor-made set. Proteins are polyamides. The amide linkage is called a **peptide bond** (shaded part of the structure below) when it joins two amino-acid units.

$$H_2N \!-\! \overset{\overset{\displaystyle R_1}{|}}{\underset{\underset{\displaystyle H}{|}}{C}} \!-\! \overset{\overset{\displaystyle H}{|}}{\underset{\underset{\displaystyle O}{||}}{C}} \!-\! \overset{\overset{\displaystyle H}{|}}{N} \!-\! \overset{\overset{\displaystyle H}{|}}{\underset{\underset{\displaystyle R_2}{|}}{C}} \!-\! COOH$$

Note that this molecule still has a reactive amino group on the left and a carboxyl group on the right. These groups can react with other amino-acid units. This process can continue until thousands of units have joined to form a giant molecule—a polymer called a *protein*. We will examine the structure of proteins in the next section, but first let's look at some molecules called *peptides* that have only a few amino-acid units.

When only two amino acids are joined, the product is a *dipeptide*.

Glycylphenylalanine
(a dipeptide)

Three amino acids combine to form a *tripeptide*.

Serylalanylcysteine
(a tripeptide)

In describing peptides and proteins, scientists find it simpler to identify the amino acids in a chain by using the abbreviations given in Table 16.3. The three-letter abbreviations are more common, but the single-letter ones are also used. Thus, glycylphenylalanine can be abbreviated as either Gly-Phe or G-F, and serylalanyl-cysteine as either Ser-Ala-Cys or S-A-C. Example 16.2 further illustrates peptide names and their abbreviations.

Example 16.2 | Names of Peptides

Give the **(a)** designation using one-letter abbreviations and **(b)** full name of the pentapeptide Met-Gly-Phe-Ala-Cys. You may use Table 16.3.

Solution

a. M-G-F-A-C

b. The endings of the names for all except the last amino acid are changed from *-ine* to *-yl*. The name is therefore methionylglycylphenylalanylalanylcysteine.

▪ EXERCISE 16.2A

Give the **(a)** designation using one-letter abbreviations and **(b)** full name of the tetrapeptide His-Pro-Asn-Ala.

▪ EXERCISE 16.2B

Use **(a)** three-letter abbreviations and **(b)** one-letter abbreviations to identify all the amino acids in the peptide threonylglycylalanylalanylleucine.

3. Is it true that there are more than just 20 amino acids?

Besides the 20 common amino acids, two others have been found. They are the 21st, selenocysteine, and the 22nd, pyrrolysine. Selenocysteine, a selenium-containing analog of cysteine, is found in selenoproteins in all kingdoms of life. Pyrrolysine is found in methanogenic archaea and other bacteria, and it seems to be part of the enzyme that allows them to produce methane.

A molecule with more than 10 amino-acid units is often simply called a **polypeptide**. Some protein molecules are enormous, with molecular weights in the tens of thousands. The molecular formula for hemoglobin, the oxygen-carrying protein in red blood cells, is $C_{3032}H_{4816}O_{780}N_{780}S_8Fe_4$, corresponding to a molar mass of 64,450 g/mol. Although they are huge compared with ordinary molecules, a billion average-sized protein molecules could still fit on the head of a pin. When the molecular weight of a polypeptide exceeds about 10,000, it is called a **protein**. These distinctions are arbitrary and not always precisely applied.

The Sequence of Amino Acids

For peptides and proteins to function properly, it is not enough that they incorporate certain *amounts* of specific amino acids. The order, or *sequence*, in which the amino acids are connected is also of critical importance. The sequence is written starting at the free amino group ($-NH_3^+$), called the *N-terminal end*, and continuing to the free carboxyl group ($-COO^-$), called the *C-terminal end*.

N-terminal end   C-terminal end

Glycylalanine (Gly-Ala) is therefore different from alanylglycine (Ala-Gly). Although the difference seems minor, the structures are different, and the two substances behave differently in the body.

Glycylalanine   Alanylglycine

As the length of a peptide chain increases, the number of possible sequential variations becomes enormous. Just as millions of different words can be made from the 26 letters of the English alphabet, millions of different proteins can be made from the 20 amino acids. And just as we can write gibberish with the English alphabet, nonfunctioning proteins can be formed by putting together the wrong sequence of amino acids.

Example 16.3 | Numbers of Peptides

How many different tripeptides can be made from one unit each of the three amino acids methionine, valine, and phenylalanine? Write the sequences of these tripeptides, using the three-letter abbreviations in Table 16.3.

Solution

We write the various possibilities. Two begin with Met, two start with Val, and two with Phe:

Met-Val-Phe	Val-Met-Phe	Phe-Val-Met
Met-Phe-Val	Val-Phe-Met	Phe-Met-Val

There are six possible tripeptides.

■ EXERCISE 16.3A

How many different tripeptides can be made from two methionine units and one phenylalanine unit?

■ EXERCISE 16.3B

How many different tetrapeptides can be made from one unit each of the four amino acids methionine, valine, tyrosine, and glycine?

Although the correct sequence is ordinarily of utmost importance, it is not always absolutely required. Just as you can sometimes make sense of incorrectly spelled English words, a protein with a small percentage of "incorrect" amino acids may function, but just not as well. And sometimes a seemingly minor difference can have a disastrous effect. Some people have hemoglobin with one incorrect amino-acid unit out of about 300. That "minor" error is responsible for sickle cell anemia, an inherited condition that often proves fatal.

SELF-ASSESSMENT Questions

1. Peptides are polymers of
   a. amino acids
   b. fatty acids
   c. monoacylglycerides
   d. monosaccharides

2. The 20 common amino acids that make up proteins differ mainly in their
   a. alpha carbon atoms
   b. amino groups
   c. carboxyl groups
   d. side chains

3. Which of the following is *not* an alpha amino acid?
   a. $CH_3C(CH_3)(NH_2)COOH$
   b. $(CH_3)_2CHCH(NH_2)COOH$
   c. H_2NCH_2COOH
   d. $H_2NCH_2CH_2CH_2COOH$

4. Which of the following is a zwitterion?
   a. $H_2NCH_2COO^-$
   b. $^-NHCH_2COO^-$
   c. $H_3N^+CH_2COOH$
   d. $^+H_3NCH_2COO^-$

5. In a dipeptide, two amino acids are joined through a(n)
   a. amide linkage
   b. dipolar interaction
   c. ionic bond
   d. hydrogen bond

6. The N-terminal amino acid and the C-terminal amino acid of the peptide Met-Ile-Val-Glu-Cys-Tyr-Gln-Trp-Ile are, respectively,
   a. Ile and Met
   b. Met and Asp
   c. Met and Ile
   d. Trp and Asp

7. How many different tripeptides can be formed from alanine, valine, and lysine, when each appears only once in each product?
   a. 1   b. 3   c. 6   d. 9

8. The tripeptides represented as Ala-Val-Lys and Lys-Val-Ala are
   a. different only in name
   b. different in molar mass
   c. exactly the same
   d. two different peptides

16.5 Structure and Function of Proteins

Learning Objectives ❯ Describe the four levels of protein structure, and give an example of each. ❯ Describe how enzymes work as catalysts.

The structures of proteins have four organizational levels:

- **Primary structure**. Amino acids are linked by peptide bonds to form polypeptide chains. The primary structure of a protein molecule is simply the order of its amino acids. By convention, this order is written from the amino (N-terminal end) to the carboxyl (C-terminal end).
- **Secondary structure**. Polypeptide chains can fold into regular structures such as the alpha helix and the beta pleated sheet (described in this section).

▲ The protein strands in an alpha helix are often represented as coiled ribbons.

▲ The protein strands in a pleated sheet are often represented as ribbons.

▶ **Figure 16.12** Beta pleated-sheet structure consisting of protein chains. (a) Ball-and-stick model. (b) Model emphasizing the pleats. The side chains extend above or below the sheet and alternate along the chain. The protein chains are held together by interchain hydrogen bonds.

■ **Tertiary structure**. Protein folding creates spatial relationships between amino-acid units that are relatively far apart in the protein chain.

■ **Quaternary structure**. Two or more polypeptide chains can assemble into multiunit structures.

To specify the primary structure, we write out the sequence of amino acids. For even a small protein molecule, this sequence can be quite long. For example, it takes about two pages, using the one-letter abbreviations, to give the sequence of the 1927 amino-acid units in lactase, the enzyme that catalyzes the hydrolysis of the disaccharide lactose into galactose and glucose. The primary structure of angiotensin II, a peptide that causes powerful constriction of blood vessels and is produced in the kidneys, is

Asp-Arg-Val-Tyr-Ile-His-Pro-Phe

This sequence specifies an octapeptide with aspartic acid at the N-terminal end, followed by arginine, valine, tyrosine, isoleucine, histidine, proline, and then phenylalanine at the C-terminal end.

(a)

(b)

The secondary structure of a protein refers to the arrangement of chains about an axis. The two main types of secondary structure are a *pleated sheet*, as in silk, and a *helix*, as in wool.

In the pleated-sheet conformation (Figure 16.12), protein chains are arranged in an extended zigzag arrangement, with hydrogen bonds holding adjacent chains together. The appearance gives this type of secondary structure its name, the **beta (β) pleated sheet**. This structure, with its multitude of hydrogen bonds, makes silk strong and flexible.

The protein molecules in wool, hair, and muscle contain large segments arranged in the form of a right-handed helix, or **alpha (α) helix** (Figure 16.13). Each turn of the helix requires 3.6 amino-acid units. The

(a)

(b)

◀ **Figure 16.13** Two representations of the α-helical conformation of a protein chain. (a) Intrachain hydrogen bonding between turns of the helix is shown in the ball-and-stick model. (b) The skeletal representation better shows the helix.

N—H group at one turn forms a hydrogen bond to a carbonyl (C=O) group at another turn. These helices wrap around one another in threes or sevens like strands of a rope. Unlike silk, wool can be stretched, much like stretching a spring by pulling the coils apart.

The tertiary structure of a protein refers to folding that affects the spatial relationships between amino-acid units that are relatively far apart in the chain. An example is the protein chain in a **globular protein**. Figure 16.14 shows the tertiary structure of myoglobin, which is folded into a compact, spherical shape.

Quaternary structure exists only if there are two or more polypeptide chains, which can form an aggregate of subunits. Hemoglobin is the most familiar example. A single hemoglobin molecule contains four polypeptide units, and each unit is roughly comparable to a myoglobin molecule. The four units are arranged in a specific pattern (Figure 16.15). The quaternary structure of hemoglobin is this arrangement of the four units.

Four Ways to Link Protein Chains

As we noted earlier, the primary structure of a protein is the order of the amino acids, which are held together by peptide bonds. What forces determine the secondary, tertiary, and quaternary structures? Four kinds of forces operate between protein chains: hydrogen bonds, ionic bonds, disulfide linkages, and dispersion forces. Hydrogen bonds and dispersion forces, introduced in Chapter 6 as intermolecular forces, can also be intramolecular, as occurs in proteins. These forces are illustrated in Figure 16.16 on page 494.

The most important hydrogen bonding in a protein involves an interaction between the atoms of one peptide bond and those of another. The amide hydrogen (N—H) of one peptide bond can form a hydrogen bond to a carbonyl (C=O) oxygen located **(a)** some distance away on the same chain, an arrangement that occurs in the secondary structure of wool (alpha helix), or **(b)** on an entirely different chain, as in the secondary structure of silk (beta pleated sheet). In either case, there is usually a pattern of such interactions. Because peptide bonds are regularly spaced along the chain, the hydrogen bonds also occur in a regular pattern, both intramolecularly (in wool) and intermolecularly (in silk). Other types of hydrogen bonding can occur (between side chains of amino acids, for example) but are less important.

Ionic bonds occur when an amino acid with a basic side chain is located near one with an acidic side chain. Proton transfer results in opposite charges, which then attract one another. These interactions can occur between groups that ordinarily are relatively distant that happen to come in contact because of folding or coiling of a single chain. They also occur between groups on adjacent chains.

A **disulfide linkage** is formed when two cysteine units (whether on the same chain or on two different chains) are oxidized. A disulfide linkage is a covalent bond, and thus much stronger than a hydrogen bond. Although far less numerous than hydrogen bonds, disulfide linkages are critically important in determining the shape of some proteins (for example, many of the proteins that act as enzymes) and the strength of others (such as the fibrous proteins in connective tissue and hair).

▲ **Figure 16.14** The tertiary structure of myoglobin. The protein chain is folded to form a globular structure, much as a string can be wound into a ball. The disk shape represents the heme group, which binds the oxygen carried by myoglobin (or hemoglobin).

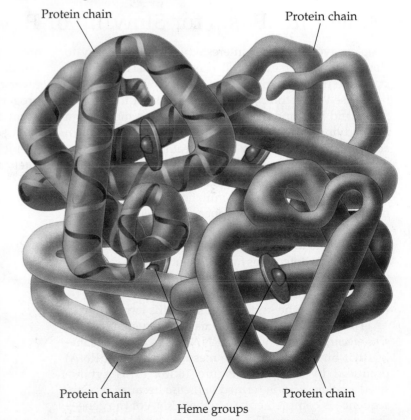

▲ **Figure 16.15** The quaternary structure of hemoglobin has four coiled protein chains, each analogous to myoglobin (Figure 16.14), grouped in a nearly tetrahedral arrangement.

▶ **Figure 16.16** The tertiary structure of proteins is maintained by four different types of forces.

Hydrogen bonding

Ionic bond (salt bridge)

Disulfide linkage (covalent)

Dispersion forces

▲ **Figure 16.17** A protein chain often folds with its nonpolar groups on the inside, where they are held together by dispersion forces. The outside has polar groups, visible in this space-filling model of a myoglobin molecule as oxygen atoms (red) and nitrogen atoms (blue). The carbon atoms (black) are mainly on the inside.

Dispersion forces are the only kind of forces that exist between nonpolar side chains. Recall (Section 6.3) that dispersion forces are relatively weak. These interactions can be important, however, when other types of forces are missing or are minimized. Dispersion forces are increased by the cohesiveness of the water molecules surrounding the protein. Nonpolar side chains minimize their exposure to water by clustering together on the inside folds of the protein in close contact with one another (Figure 16.17). Dispersion forces become fairly significant in structures such as that of silk, in which a high proportion of amino acids in the protein have nonpolar side chains.

Enzymes: Exquisite Precision Machines

Enzymes, highly specialized classes of proteins, are biological catalysts produced by cells. They have enormous catalytic power and are ordinarily highly specific, catalyzing only one reaction or a closely related group of reactions. Nearly all known enzymes are proteins.

Enzymes enable reactions to occur at much more rapid rates and lower temperatures than they otherwise would. They do this by changing the reaction path. The reacting substance, called the **substrate**, attaches to an area on the enzyme called the **active site**, to form an enzyme–substrate complex. Biochemists often use the model

Molecular Basis for Slowing or Reversing Aging

People have long been interested in finding a way to slow or even reverse aging. To do so, we must first understand the mechanism of aging so that some means can be devised to accomplish this. Scientists in the United States and in France have identified such a mechanism by studying progeria, a rare genetic disease in which accelerated aging usually brings death by old age when the person is only about 13 years old. A point mutation responsible for quickened aging in progeric patients was identified in 2003. This mutation, in which cytosine is replaced with thymine, appears in a gene that codes for the nuclear membrane protein LMNA—or lamin A—and leads to a defective protein called progerin.

After this defect was found, scientists at the National Cancer Institute (NCI) showed that much of the cellular damage accompanying normal old age is caused by irregular use of the same defect site in the lamin A gene.

The genetic defect can be masked by using an *antisense agent*, a strand of DNA, RNA, or a nucleic acid analog that binds tightly to the messenger RNA (mRNA) produced by the gene (Figure 16.18). (This synthesized nucleic acid is termed *antisense* because its base sequence is complementary to the mRNA of the gene—the *sense* sequence.) The antisense molecule physically obstructs the translation machinery, effectively turning the gene off. Analogs with altered backbone linkages

are used. This makes the agent resistant to digestion by nuclease enzymes. Such an agent has been shown to reverse age-related defects in cultured cells taken from progeric patients and also in cultured cells taken from normal persons of advanced age.

Use of antisense drugs is currently limited by a lack of efficient delivery into defective tissues and cells and by safety aspects such as general immune system activation. If these problems can be overcome, antisense technology may help us to attain the long-sought fountain of youth.

(a) Segment of normal DNA (b) Antisense analog

▲ **Figure 16.18** (a) Segment of normal DNA, and (b) antisense analog.

pictured in Figure 16.19, called the *induced-fit* model, to explain enzyme action. In this model, the shapes of the substrate and the active site are not perfectly complementary, but the active site adapts to fit the substrate, much as a glove molds to fit the hand that is inserted into it. The enzyme–substrate complex decomposes to form products, and the enzyme is regenerated. We can represent the process as follows.

Enzyme + Substrate $\longrightarrow$ Enzyme–substrate complex $\Longleftrightarrow$ Enzyme + Products

An enzyme–substrate complex is held together by electrical attraction. Certain charged groups on the enzyme complement certain charged or partially charged groups on the substrate. The formation of new bonds between enzyme and substrate weakens bonds within the substrate, and these weakened bonds can then be more easily broken to form products.

Portions of the enzyme molecule other than the active site may be involved in the catalytic process. Some interaction at a position remote from the active site can change the shape of the enzyme and thus change its effectiveness as a catalyst. In this way, it is possible to slow or stop the catalytic action. Figure 16.20 illustrates a model for the inhibition of enzyme catalysis. An inhibitor molecule attaches to the enzyme at a position (called the *allosteric site*) away from the active site where the substrate is bound. The enzyme changes shape as it accommodates the inhibitor, and the substrate is no longer able to bind to the enzyme. This is one of the mechanisms by which cells "turn off" enzymes when their work is done.

Some enzymes consist entirely of protein chains. In others, another chemical component, called a **cofactor**, is necessary for proper function of the enzyme. This cofactor may be a metal ion such as zinc (Zn^{2+}), manganese (Mn^{2+}), magnesium (Mg^{2+}), iron(II) (Fe^{2+}), or copper(II) (Cu^{2+}). An organic cofactor is called a **coenzyme**. By definition, coenzymes are nonprotein. The pure protein part of an enzyme is called the **apoenzyme**. Both the coenzyme and the apoenzyme must be present for enzymatic activity to take place.

Coenzyme + Apoenzyme $\longrightarrow$ Enzyme

Many coenzymes are vitamins or are derived from vitamin molecules. Enzymes are essential to the function of every living cell.

▲ **Figure 16.19** The induced-fit model of enzyme action. In this case, a single substrate molecule is broken into two product molecules.

Enzymes as Green Catalysts

Scientists are hard at work trying to find enzymes to carry out all kinds of chemical conversions. Enzymes are often more efficient than the usual chemical catalysts, and they are more specific in that they produce more of the desired product and fewer by-products that have to be disposed of. Further, processes involving enzymes do not require toxic solvents and thus produce less waste.

Companies have spent hundreds of millions of dollars studying the special characteristics of the enzymes inside *extremophiles*, microorganisms that live in harsh environments that would kill other creatures. Scientists hope to replace ordinary enzymes with enzymes from extremophiles. They are already finding uses for these enzymes in specialty chemicals and new drugs. Many industrial processes can only be carried out at high temperatures and pressures. Enzymes make it possible to carry out some of these processes at fairly low temperatures and atmospheric pressure, thus reducing the energy used and the need for expensive equipment.

Another area of enzyme use is in cleaning up pollution. For example, polychlorinated biphenyls (PCBs), notoriously persistent pollutants, are usually destroyed by incineration over 1200 °C. Microorganisms have been isolated that can degrade PCBs and thus have the potential to destroy these toxic pollutants. However, much research is still needed to make them cost-effective.

▲ **Figure 16.20** A model for the inhibition of an enzyme. (a) The enzyme and its substrate fit exactly. (The allosteric site is where the inhibitor binds.) (b) With the inhibitor bound to the enzyme, the active site of the enzyme is distorted, and the enzyme cannot bind to its substrate.

It DOES Matter!

You can demonstrate protein hydrolysis. Mix a gelatin-dessert powder according to directions. Divide into two parts. Add fresh pineapple, kiwi, or papaya to one portion. Add cooked fruit or none at all to the other. The portion with the fresh fruit will not gel! These fruits contain a protease enzyme that breaks down proteins (gelatin is a protein). The enzyme is inactivated by cooking, so canned pineapple is perfectly fine in gelatin. (Why do you think cooking ham with pineapple tenderizes the ham, and eating too much raw pineapple can "burn" the lips?)

4. Why do some laundry detergents contain enzymes?

Enzymes in laundry detergents catalytically break down proteins that used to be difficult for detergents and bleaches to remove. Years ago, grass stains in children's clothing were almost impossible to remove, because the proteins of grass have a strong attraction for cotton and other cloth. Enzymes have alleviated that problem.

Applications of Enzymes

Enzymes find many uses in medicine, industry, and everyday life. One widespread use is in the test strips used by diabetics. Each strip contains *glucose oxidase*, an enzyme that catalyzes the oxidation of glucose at an electrode. The reaction generates an electrical current that is proportional to the amount of glucose in the blood that has reacted with the enzyme. The result is displayed directly on an external meter.

Clinical analysis for enzymes in body fluids or tissues is a common diagnostic technique in medicine. For example, enzymes normally found only in the liver may leak into the bloodstream from a diseased or damaged liver. The presence of these enzymes in blood confirms liver damage.

Enzymes are used to break up blood clots after a heart attack. If these medicines are given immediately after an attack, the patients' survival rate increases significantly. Other enzymes are used to do just the opposite: Blood-clotting factors are used to treat hemophilia, a disease in which the blood fails to clot normally.

Enzymes are widely used in a variety of industries, from baby foods to beer. Enzymes in intact microorganisms have long been used to make bread, beer, wine, yogurt, and cheese. Now the use of enzymes has been broadened to include such things as the following:

- Enzymes that act on proteins (called *proteases*) are used in the manufacture of baby foods to predigest complex proteins and make them easier for infants to digest.
- Enzymes that act on starches (*carbohydrases*) are used to convert corn starch to corn syrup (mainly glucose) for use as a sweetener.
- Enzymes called *isomerases* are used to convert the glucose in corn syrup into fructose, which is sweeter than glucose and can be used in smaller amounts to give the same sweetness. (Glucose and fructose are isomers, both having the molecular formula $C_6H_{12}O_6$.)
- Protease enzymes are used to make beer and fruit juices clear by breaking down the proteins that cause cloudiness.
- Enzymes that degrade cellulose (*cellulases*) are used in stonewashing blue jeans. These enzymes break down the cellulose polymers of cotton fibers. By carefully controlling their activity, manufacturers can get the desired effect without destroying the cotton material. Varying the cellulase enzymes creates different effects to make true "designer jeans."
- Proteases and carbohydrases are added to animal feed to make nutrients more easily absorbed and improve the animals' digestion.

Enzymes are important components in some detergents. Enzymes called *lipases* attack the fats and grease that make up many stains. Proteases attack the proteins in certain types of stains, such as those from blood, meat juice, and dairy products, breaking them down into smaller, water-soluble molecules. Total worldwide production of enzymes is worth more than $1 billion per year.

SELF-ASSESSMENT Questions

1. Hydrogen bonds form between the N—H group of one amino acid and the C=O group of another, giving a protein molecule the form of an alpha helix or a beta pleated sheet. What level of protein structure do those forms represent?
   - **a.** primary
   - **b.** quaternary
   - **c.** secondary
   - **d.** tertiary

2. Which level of protein structure is maintained in part by dispersion forces?
   - **a.** primary structure
   - **b.** quaternary structure
   - **c.** secondary structure
   - **d.** tertiary structure

3. The arrangement of several protein subunits into a specific pattern, as in hemoglobin, is an example of
   - **a.** primary structure
   - **b.** quaternary structure
   - **c.** secondary structure
   - **d.** tertiary structure

4. Which level of protein structure is maintained in part by dispersion forces?
   - **a.** dispersion linkages
   - **b.** disulfide linkages
   - **c.** hydrogen bonds
   - **d.** salt bridges

5. An acidic side chain of an amino-acid unit on a protein chain reacts with the basic side chain of an amino-acid unit on another chain or at some distance away on the same chain to form a
   - **a.** dispersion linkage
   - **b.** disulfide linkage
   - **c.** hydrogen bond
   - **d.** salt bridge

6. When nonpolar side chains of amino-acid units in a protein chain interact with other nonpolar side chains of amino-acid units on another chain or at some distance away on the same chain, the interactions are
   - **a.** dispersion forces
   - **b.** a disulfide linkage
   - **c.** a hydrogen bond
   - **d.** a salt bridge

7. The molecule on which an enzyme acts is called the enzyme's
   a. catalyst   **b.** coenzyme   **c.** cofactor   **d.** substrate

8. According to the induced-fit model of enzyme action, the
   a. action of an enzyme is enhanced by an inhibitor
   b. active site is the same as the allosteric site
   c. shapes of active sites are rigid and only fit substrates with exact complementary shapes
   d. shape of the active site can change somewhat to fit a substrate

9. An inorganic metal ion working with an enzyme molecule is called a(n)
   a. cofactor   **b.** apoenzyme   **c.** coenzyme   **d.** stimulator

10. An enzyme is a catalyst, or substance that
    a. binds to other molecules
    b. breaks down other molecules
    c. is made from smaller molecules
    d. increases reaction rate

11. The pure protein part of an enzyme is called a(n)
    a. apoenzyme   **b.** coenzyme
    c. holoenzyme   **d.** ribozyme

Answers: 1, c; 2, d; 3, b; 4, b; 5, d; 6, d; 7, d; 8, d; 9, a; 10, d; 11, a

16.6 Nucleic Acids: Parts, Structure, and Function

Learning Objectives ❯ Name the two types of nucleic acids, and describe the function of each type. ❯ Explain complementary base pairing, and describe how a copy of DNA is synthesized.

Life on Earth has a fantastic range of forms, but all life arises from the same molecular ingredients: five nucleotides that serve as the building blocks for nucleic acids, and 20 common amino acids (Section 16.4) that are the building blocks for proteins. These components limit the chemical reactions that can occur in cells and thus determine what Earth's living things are like.

Nucleic acids serve as the information and control centers of the cell. There are two kinds of nucleic acids: *Deoxyribonucleic acid* (*DNA*) provides a mechanism for heredity and serves as the blueprint for all the proteins of an organism. *Ribonucleic acid* (*RNA*) carries out protein assembly. DNA is a coiled threadlike molecule found mainly in the cell nucleus. RNA is found in all parts of the cell, where different forms do different jobs. Both DNA and RNA are chains of repeating units called **nucleotides**. Each nucleotide in turn consists of three parts (Figure 16.21, on the next page): a pentose (five-carbon sugar), a phosphate unit, and a heterocyclic amine (Section 9.8) base. The sugar is either ribose (in RNA) or deoxyribose (in DNA). Looking at the sugar in the nucleotide, note that the hydroxyl group on the first carbon atom is replaced by one of five bases. The bases with two fused rings, adenine and guanine, are classified as **purines**. The **pyrimidines**, cytosine, thymine, and uracil, have only one ring.

The hydroxyl group on the fifth carbon of the sugar unit is converted to a phosphate ester group. Adenosine monophosphate (AMP) is a representative nucleotide. In AMP, the base (blue) is adenine and the sugar (black) is ribose.

Adenosine monophosphate

Nucleotides can be represented schematically as shown in the margin, where P_i is the biochemists' designation for "inorganic phosphate." A general representation is shown on the left and a specific schematic for AMP on the right.

DNA only **DNA & RNA** **RNA only**

Thymine   Adenine   Guanine   Cytosine   Uracil

2-Deoxyribose   Phosphate (P_i)   Ribose

▲ **Figure 16.21** The components of nucleic acids. The sugars are 2-deoxyribose (in DNA) and ribose (in RNA). Note that deoxyribose differs from ribose in that it lacks an oxygen atom on the second carbon atom. *Deoxy* indicates that an oxygen atom is "missing." Phosphate units are often abbreviated as P_i ("inorganic phosphate"). Heterocyclic bases in nucleic acids are adenine, guanine, and cytosine in both DNA and RNA. Thymine occurs only in DNA, and uracil only in RNA. Note that thymine has a methyl group (red) that is lacking in uracil.

Nucleotides are joined to one another through the phosphate group to form nucleic acid chains. The phosphate unit on one nucleotide forms an ester linkage with the hydroxyl group on the third carbon atom of the sugar unit in a second nucleotide. This unit is in turn joined to another nucleotide, and the process is repeated to build up a long nucleic acid chain (Figure 16.21). The backbone of the chain consists of alternating phosphate and sugar units, and the heterocyclic bases are branches off this backbone.

~sugar-P_i-sugar-P_i-sugar-P_i-sugar-P_i-sugar-P_i-sugar-P_i~

base   base   base   base   base   base

The numbers in Figure 16.22 refer to positions on the pentose sugar ring (look again at Figure 16.21). The 3′ end has a hydroxyl group and the 5′ end has a phosphate group. If the above diagram represents DNA, the sugar is deoxyribose and the bases are adenine, guanine, cytosine, and thymine. In RNA, the sugar is ribose and the bases are adenine, guanine, cytosine, and uracil.

▲ **Figure 16.22** A DNA molecule. Each repeating unit is composed of a sugar, a phosphate unit, and a base. The sugar and phosphate units form backbones on the outside. The bases are attached to the sugar units. Pairs of bases make "steps" on the inside of the spiral staircase.

Example 16.4	Nucleotides

Consider the following nucleotide. Identify the sugar and the base. State whether it is found in DNA or RNA.

Solution

The sugar has two H atoms on the second C atom and therefore is deoxyribose, found in DNA. The base is a pyrimidine (one ring). The amino group (—NH₂) helps identify it as cytosine.

■ **EXERCISE 16.4A**

Consider the following nucleotide. Identify the sugar and the base. State whether it is found in DNA or RNA.

■ **EXERCISE 16.4B**

A nucleotide is composed of a phosphate unit, deoxyribose, and uracil. Is it found in DNA, RNA, or neither? Explain.

▲ Francis H. C. Crick (1916–2004) (seated) and James D. Watson (b. 1928) used data obtained by British chemist Rosalind Franklin (1920–1958) to propose a double-helix model of DNA in 1953. Franklin used a technique called X-ray diffraction, which showed DNA's helical structure. Without her permission, Franklin's colleague Maurice Wilkins shared her work with Watson and Crick. The data helped Watson and Crick decipher DNA's structure. Wilkins, Watson, and Crick were awarded the Nobel Prize for this discovery in 1962, a prize Franklin might have shared had she lived.

The vast amount of genetic information needed to build living organisms is stored in a primary structure, the *sequence* of the four bases along the nucleic acid strand. Not surprisingly, these molecules are huge, with molecular masses ranging into the billions for mammalian DNA. Along these chains, the four bases can be arranged in almost infinite variations. We will examine this aspect of nucleic acid chemistry shortly, after considering another important feature of nucleic acid structure.

The Double Helix

The three-dimensional, or secondary, structure of DNA was the subject of an intensive research effort in the late 1940s and early 1950s. Experiments showed that the molar amount of adenine (A) in DNA corresponds to the molar amount of thymine (T). Similarly, the molar amount of guanine (G) is the same as that of cytosine (C). To maintain this balance, researchers concluded that the bases in DNA must be paired, A to T and G to C. But how?

At the midpoint of the twentieth century, it was clear that whoever answered this question would win a Nobel Prize. Many illustrious scientists worked on the problem, but two who were relatively unknown announced in 1953 that they had worked out the structure of DNA. Using data that involved quite sophisticated chemistry, physics, and mathematics, and working with models not unlike a child's construction set, James D. Watson and Francis H. C. Crick determined that DNA must be composed of two helices wound about one another. James D. Watson gave a personal account of the discovery of the structure of DNA in his book *The Double Helix*. The two strands are antiparallel; they run in opposite directions. The phosphate and sugar backbones of the polymer chains form the outside of the structure, which is rather like a spiral staircase. The heterocyclic amines are paired on the inside—with guanine always opposite cytosine and adenine always opposite thymine. In the spiral staircase analogy, these base pairs are the steps (Figure 16.23).

Why do the bases pair in this precise pattern, always A to T and T to A and always G to C and C to G? The answers: hydrogen bonding and a truly elegant molecular arrangement. Figure 16.24, on the next page, shows the two sets of base pairs. You should notice two things. First, a pyrimidine is paired with a purine in each case, and the long dimensions of both pairs are identical (1.085 nm).

Second, notice the hydrogen bonding between the bases in each pair. When guanine is paired with cytosine, three hydrogen bonds can be formed between

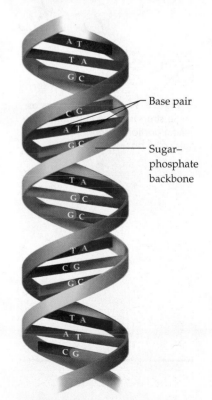

Base pair

Sugar–phosphate backbone

▲ **Figure 16.23** A model of a portion of a DNA double helix is shown in Figure 16.21. This schematic representation of the double helix shows the sugar–phosphate backbones as ribbons and the complementary base pairs as steps on the spiral staircase.

▶ **Figure 16.24** Pairing of the complementary bases thymine and adenine (a) and cytosine and guanine (b). The pairing involves hydrogen bonding.

(a)   (b)

▲ **Figure 16.25** RNA occurs as single strands that can form double-helical portions through internal pairing of bases.

the bases. No other pyrimidine–purine pairing permits such extensive interaction. Indeed, in the combinations shown in the figure, each pair of bases fits like a lock and a key.

Other scientists around the world quickly accepted the Watson–Crick structure because it answered so many crucial questions: how cells are able to divide and go on functioning, how genetic data are passed on to new generations, and even how proteins are built to required specifications. All of these processes depend on the base pairing.

Structure of RNA

Most RNA molecules consist of a single strand of nucleic acids. Some internal (intramolecular) base pairing can occur in sections where the molecule folds back on itself. Portions of some RNA molecules exist in double-helical form (Figure 16.25).

DNA: Self-Replication

Dogs have puppies that grow up to be dogs. Chickens lay eggs that hatch and grow up to be chickens. How is it that each species reproduces its own kind? How does a fertilized egg "know" that it should develop into a kangaroo and not a koala?

The physical basis of heredity has been known for a long time. Higher organisms reproduce sexually. A sperm cell from the male unites with an egg cell from the female. The fertilized egg that results must carry all the information needed to make the various cells, tissues, and organs necessary for the functioning of a new individual. Further, if the species is to survive, information must be passed along in the germ cells—both sperm and egg—for the production of new individuals.

The hereditary material is found in the nuclei of all cells, concentrated in elongated, threadlike bodies called *chromosomes*. Chromosomes form compressed X-shaped structures when strands of DNA coil up tightly just before a cell divides. The number of chromosomes varies with the species. In sexual reproduction, chromosomes come in pairs, with one member of each pair provided by each parent. Each human inherits 23 pairs and so has 46 chromosomes in his or her body's cells. Thus, the entire complement of chromosomes is achieved only when the egg's 23 chromosomes combine with a like number from the sperm.

Chromosomes are made of DNA and proteins. Arranged along the chromosomes are the basic units of heredity, the genes. Structurally, a **gene** is a section of the DNA molecule, although some viral genes contain only RNA. Genes control the synthesis of proteins, which tell cells, organs, and organisms how to function in their surroundings. The environment helps determine which genes become active at a particular time. The complete set of genes of an organism is called its *genome*. When cell division occurs, each chromosome produces an exact duplicate of itself. Transmission of genetic information therefore requires the **replication** (copying or duplication) of DNA molecules.

The double helix provides a precise model for replication. If the two chains of the double helix are pulled apart, each chain can direct the synthesis of a new DNA chain using nucleotides from the cellular fluid surrounding the DNA. Each of the separating chains serves as a template, or pattern, for the formation of a new complementary chain. The two DNA strands are *antiparallel*. Synthesis begins with a base on a nucleotide pairing with its complementary base on the DNA strand—adenine with thymine and guanine with cytosine (Figure 16.26). Each base unit in the separated strand can only pick up a base unit identical to the one with which it was paired before.

As the nucleotides align, enzymes connect them to form the new chain. In this way, each strand of the original DNA molecule forms a duplicate of its former partner. Whatever information was encoded in the original DNA double helix is now contained in each of the replications. When the cell divides, each daughter cell gets one of the DNA molecules and thus has all the information that was available to the parent cell.

How is information stored in DNA? The code for the directions for building all the proteins that comprise an organism and enable it to function resides in the *sequence* of bases along the DNA chain. Just as *cat* means one thing in English and *act* means another, the sequence of bases CGT means one amino acid and GCT means another. Although there are only four "letters"—the four bases—in the genetic code of DNA, their sequence along the long strands can vary so widely that unlimited information storage is available. Each cell carries in its DNA all the information that determines its hereditary characteristics.

Why is a code that must specify 20 different amino acids based on a triplet of bases? Four "letters" can be arranged in $4 \times 4 \times 4 = 64$ possible three-letter "words." A "doublet" code of four letters would have only $4 \times 4 = 16$ different words, and a "quadruplet" code of four letters can be arranged in $4 \times 4 \times 4 \times 4 = 256$ different ways. A triplet code specifies 20 different amino acids with some redundancy, a doublet code is inadequate, and a quadruplet code would provide too much redundancy.

▲ Before cell division, human chromosomes have a distinctive X-shape.

OLD

NEW

DNA polymerase

DNA nucleotide

◄ **Figure 16.26** A simplified schematic diagram of DNA replication. The original double helix is "unzipped," and new nucleotides (as triphosphate derivatives) are brought into position by the enzyme DNA polymerase. Phosphate bridges are formed, restoring the original double-helix configuration. Each newly formed double helix consists of one old strand and one new strand.

Key

▪ Adenine

▪ Thymine

▪ Guanine

▪ Cytosine

SELF-ASSESSMENT Questions

1. The monomer units of nucleic acids are
   a. amino acids
   b. monosaccharides
   c. nucleosomes
   d. nucleotides

2. An RNA nucleotide could not contain
   a. A, P_i, and ribose
   b. G, P_i, and glucose
   c. T, P_i, and deoxyribose
   d. U, P_i, and deoxyribose

3. A possible base pair in DNA is
   a. A-G
   b. A-T
   c. A-U
   d. T-G

4. A possible base pair in RNA is
   a. A-G
   b. A-T
   c. A-U
   d. T-G

5. Nucleic acid base pairs are joined by
   a. amide bonds
   b. ester bonds
   c. glucosidic bonds
   d. hydrogen bonds

6. Replication of a DNA molecule involves breaking bonds between the
   a. base pairs
   b. pentose sugars
   c. phosphate units
   d. bases and pentoses

7. The second step of DNA replication involves
   a. bonding of free nucleotides in the correct sequence
   b. formation of a single-stranded RNA molecule
   c. linking of a phosphate group to an amino acid
   d. unzipping of the DNA molecule when the hydrogen bonds break

Answers: 1, d; 2, a; 3, b; 4, c; 5, d; 6, a; 7, a

Table 16.4	DNA Bases and Their Complementary RNA Bases
DNA Base	**Complementary RNA Base**
Adenine (A)	Uracil (U)
Thymine (T)	Adenine (A)
Cytosine (C)	Guanine (G)
Guanine (G)	Cytosine (C)

▲ **Figure 16.27** A transfer RNA (tRNA) molecule doubles back on itself, forming three loops with intermolecular hydrogen bonding between complementary bases. The anticodon triplet at the head of the molecule joins with a complementary codon triplet on mRNA. Here the base triplet CAU in the anticodon specifies the amino acid valine.

16.7 RNA: Protein Synthesis and the Genetic Code

Learning Objectives ❯ Explain how mRNA is synthesized from DNA and how a protein is synthesized from mRNA. ❯ List important characteristics of the genetic code.

DNA carries a message that must somehow be transmitted and then acted on in a cell. Because DNA does not leave the cell nucleus, its information, or "blueprint," must be transported by something else, and it is. In the first step, called **transcription**, a segment of DNA called the *template strand* transfers its information to a special RNA molecule called *messenger RNA (mRNA)*. The base sequence of DNA specifies the base sequence of mRNA. Thymine in DNA calls for adenine in mRNA, cytosine specifies guanine, guanine calls for cytosine, and adenine requires uracil (Table 16.4). Remember that in RNA molecules, uracil appears in place of DNA's thymine. Notice the similarity in the structure of these two bases (revisit Figure 16.20). When transcription is completed, the RNA is released, and the DNA helix re-forms.

The next step in creating a protein involves deciphering the code copied by mRNA, followed by **translation** of that code into a specific protein structure. The decoding occurs when the mRNA travels from the nucleus and attaches itself to a ribosome in the cytoplasm of the cell. Ribosomes are constructed of about 65% RNA and 35% proteins.

Genes have functional regions called *exons* interspersed with inactive portions called *introns*. During protein synthesis, introns are snipped out and not translated. Some genes, called *housekeeping genes*, are expressed in all cells at all times and are essential for the most basic cellular functions. Other genes are expressed only in specific types of cells or at certain stages of development. For example, the genes that encode brain nerve cells are expressed only in brain cells, not in the liver.

Another type of RNA molecule, called *transfer RNA (tRNA)*, carries amino acids from the cell fluid to the ribosomes. A tRNA molecule has the looped structure shown in Figure 16.27. At the head of the molecule is a set of three base units, a *base triplet* called the *anticodon*, that pairs with a set of three complementary bases on mRNA, called the **codon**. The codon triplet determines which amino acid is carried at the tail of the tRNA. In Figure 16.27, for example, the codon GUA on the segment of mRNA pairs with the anticodon base triplet CAU on the tRNA molecule. All tRNA molecules with the base triplet CAU always carry the amino acid valine. Once the tRNA has paired with the base triplet of mRNA, it releases its amino acid and returns to the cell fluid to pick up another amino-acid molecule.

Table 16.5	The Genetic Code			

		SECOND BASE				
		U	**C**	**A**	**G**	
FIRST BASE	**U**	UUU=Phe UUC=Phe UUA=Leu UUG=Leu	UCU=Ser UCC=Ser UCA=Ser UCG=Ser	UAU=Tyr UAC=Tyr UAA=Termination UAG=Termination	UGU=Cys UGC=Cys UGA=Termination UGG=Trp	U C A G
	C	CUU=Leu CUC=Leu CUA=Leu CUG=Leu	CCU=Pro CCC=Pro CCA=Pro CCG=Pro	CAU=His CAC=His CAA=Gln CAG=Gln	CGU=Arg CGC=Arg CGA=Arg CGG=Arg	U C A G
	A	AUU=Ile AUC=Ile AUA=Ile AUG=Met	ACU=Thr ACC=Thr ACA=Thr ACG=Thr	AAU=Asn AAC=Asn AAA=Lys AAG=Lys	AGU=Ser AGC=Ser AGA=Arg AGG=Arg	U C A G
	G	GUU=Val GUC=Val GUA=Val GUG=Val	GCU=Ala GCC=Ala GCA=Ala GCG=Ala	GAU=Asp GAC=Asp GAA=Glu GAG=Glu	GGU=Gly GGC=Gly GGA=Gly GGG=Gly	U C A G

(THIRD BASE)

Errors can occur at each step in the replication–transcription–translation process. In replication alone, each time a human cell divides, 4 billion bases are copied to make a new strand of DNA, and there may be up to 2000 errors. Most such errors are corrected, and others are unimportant, but some have terrible consequences: genetic disease or even death may result.

Each of the 61 different tRNA molecules carries a specific amino acid into place on a growing peptide chain. The protein chain gradually built up in this way is released from the tRNA as it is formed. A complete dictionary of the genetic code has been compiled (Table 16.5). It shows which amino acids are specified by all the possible mRNA base triplets. There are 64 possible triplets and only 20 amino acids, so there is some redundancy in the code. Three amino acids (serine, arginine, and leucine) are each specified by six different codons. Two others (tryptophan and methionine) have only one codon each. Three base triplets on mRNA are "stop" signals that call for termination of the protein chain. The codon AUG signals "start" as well as specifying methionine in the chain. Figure 16.28 provides an overall summary of protein synthesis.

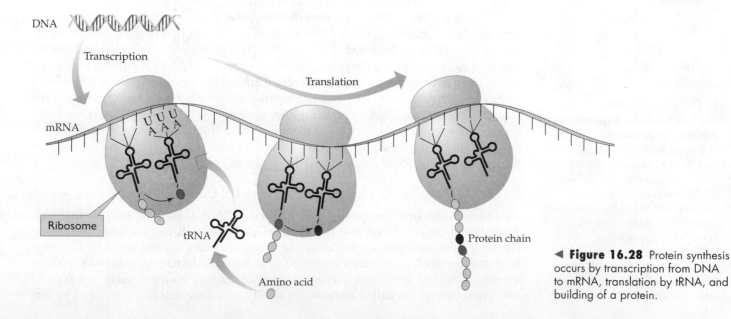

DNA

Transcription

Translation

mRNA

Ribosome

tRNA

Amino acid

Protein chain

◀ **Figure 16.28** Protein synthesis occurs by transcription from DNA to mRNA, translation by tRNA, and building of a protein.

SELF-ASSESSMENT Questions

1. The conversion of mRNA to a sequence of amino acids in a protein is called
   a. transaction
   b. transcription
   c. transition
   d. translation

2. The anticodon base triplet is found on the
   a. original DNA
   b. ribosome
   c. mRNA
   d. tRNA

3. How many amino acids and how many codons are involved in the genetic code?
   a. 20 amino acids, 20 codons
   b. 20 amino acids, 64 codons
   c. 64 amino acids, 20 codons
   d. 64 amino acids, 64 codons

4. Each amino acid except tryptophan and methionine is coded for by more than one codon, indicating that the genetic code has
   a. evolved
   b. redundancy
   c. sequence assurance
   d. translation equability

5. Refer to Table 16.5; the codon UGA
   a. codes for Leu and signals "start"
   b. codes for Leu and signals "stop"
   c. signals "stop" only
   d. codes for Leu only

16.8 The Human Genome

Learning Objective ❯ Describe recombinant DNA technology, and explain how it is used.

In 1990, scientists set out to determine the sequence of all 3 billion base pairs in the human genome. The Human Genome Project was completed in 2003 at a cost of about $2.7 billion. We can now read the complete genetic blueprint for a human. This project has driven a worldwide revolution in biotechnology—and today a genome can be sequenced in a few days at a cost of a few hundred dollars.

Many human diseases have clear genetic components. Some are directly caused by one defective gene, and others arise through involvement of several genes. The Human Genome Project has already led to the discovery of 2000 or more genes related to disease, allowing the development of more than 2000 genetic tests for human disorders. These tests enable patients to learn their genetic risk for certain diseases and also help healthcare professionals to diagnose these diseases. Humans were long thought to have 80,000 or more active genes. When scientists completed the Human Genome Project in 2003, they had found only about 20,000 to 25,000 genes in the human genome.

A gene suspected of causing an inherited disease can be located on the human genome map in a few days, instead of the years it took before the genome sequence was known. Once the genes are identified, the ability to use this information to diagnose and cure genetic diseases will revolutionize medicine.

DNA is sequenced by using enzymes to cleave it into segments of a few to several hundred nucleotides each. These fragments differ in length from each other by a single base that is identified in a later step. The pieces are duplicated and amplified by a technique called the *polymerase chain reaction (PCR)*. PCR employs enzymes called *DNA polymerases* to amplify the small amount of DNA by making millions of copies of each fragment. This builds a minuscule sample into a far larger quantity, which is needed for DNA sequencing. An electric current is used to sort the DNA segments by length, and the base at the end of each fragment is identified. Computers are then used to compile the short sequences into longer segments that recreate the original sequence of bases for the short pieces generated in the first step.

Recombinant DNA: Using Organisms as Chemical Factories

All living organisms (except some viruses) have DNA as their hereditary material. *Recombinant DNA* is DNA that has been created artificially. DNA from two different sources is incorporated into a single *recombinant* DNA molecule. The first step is to cut the DNA to extract a fragment of it, which scientists accomplish with an enzyme obtained from bacteria called an *endonuclease*. Endonuclease is a type of *restriction enzyme*, so called because its ability to cleave DNA is restricted to cer-

It DOES Matter!

Blue eyes result from a genetic mutation that involved the change of a single base in the code, from A to G. This change is thought to have occurred between 6000 and 10,000 years ago; before that time, no humans had blue eyes. The mutation turned off a gene involved in the production of melanin, the pigment that gives color to hair, eyes, and skin. Only people who inherit this gene from both parents have blue eyes.

DNA Profiling

About 99.9% of DNA sequences are the same in every human, yet the 0.1% difference is enough to distinguish one person from another (except for identical twins). DNA profiling does not require sequencing of an entire genome. Rather, it uses *short tandem repeats*, or *STRs*, at 13 particular locations on the human genome. An STR is typically from two to five base units long and is repeated several times. An example is ACGT-ACGT-ACGT. The number of such repeats at the key points differs from one person to another. This is the key to a DNA fingerprint. When all 13 points are considered, each person has a different profile.

DNA fingerprinting is used to screen newborn babies for inherited disorders such as cystic fibrosis, sickle cell anemia, Huntington's disease, hemophilia, and many others. Early detection of such disorders enables doctors and parents to choose and initiate proper treatment of the child.

Because children inherit half their DNA from each parent, DNA fingerprinting is also used to establish parentage when there is a question about paternity. The odds of identifying the father through DNA fin-gerprinting are at least 99.99%, and they are 100% for excluding a man as a possible father.

British scientist Alec Jeffreys invented DNA finger-printing in 1985 and gave it its name. Like fingerprints, each person's DNA is unique. Any cells—skin, blood, semen, saliva, and so on—can supply the necessary DNA sample.

DNA fingerprinting was a major advance in criminal investigation, allowing thousands of criminal cases to be solved. DNA samples from evidence found at a crime scene are amplified by PCR and compared with DNA obtained from suspects and other people known to have been at the scene.

This technique has led to many criminal convictions, but perhaps more important, it can readily prove someone innocent. If the DNA does not match, the suspect could not have left the biological sample. More than 300 people have been shown to be innocent and freed, some after spending years in prison, including 18 who had been condemned to death. The technique is a major advance in the search for justice.

tain short sequences of DNA called *restriction sites*. This enzyme cuts two DNA molecules at the same site. There are three different methods by which recombinant DNA is made. We will consider just one of them here.

After scientists determine the base sequence of the gene that codes for a particular protein, they can isolate it and amplify it by PCR. The gene can then be spliced into a special kind of bacterial DNA called a *plasmid*. The recombined plasmid is then inserted into the host organism, the bacteria from which the plasmids came (Figure 16.29, on the next page). Once inside the host bacteria, the plasmids replicate, making multiple exact copies of themselves, a process called *cloning*. As the engineered bacteria multiply, they become effective factories for producing the desired protein.

What kinds of proteins might scientists wish to produce using biotechnology? Insulin, a protein coded by DNA, is required for the proper use of glucose by cells. People with diabetes, an insulin-deficiency disease, formerly had to use insulin from pigs or cattle. Now human insulin is made using recombinant DNA technology. Scientists take the human gene for insulin production and paste it into the DNA of *Escherichia coli*, a bacterium commonly found in the human digestive tract. Expression factors, signals that provide instructions for transcription and translation of the gene by the cell, are also added. The bacterial cells multiply rapidly, making billions of copies of themselves, and each new *E. coli* cell carries in its DNA a replica of the gene for human insulin. The hope for the future is that a functioning gene for insulin can be incorporated directly into the cells of insulin-dependent diabetics.

Besides insulin, many other valuable materials that are used in human therapy and are difficult to obtain in any other way can now be made using recombinant DNA technology. Some examples are

- *human growth hormone* (HGH), which replaced cadaver-harvested HGH for treating children who fail to grow properly;
- *erythropoietin* (EPO) for treating anemia resulting from chronic kidney disease and from treatment for cancer;
- *factor VIII* (formerly harvested from blood), a clotting agent for treating males with hemophilia;

▲ This DNA test included samples from the mother (top), the child (middle), and the alleged father (bottom). The maternal marker 6 has been passed to the child. This means that marker 7 of the child must have come from the father, and the alleged father does indeed have a marker 7.

▶ **Figure 16.29** Recombinant DNA: cloning a human gene into a bacterial plasmid. The bacteria multiply and, in doing so, make multiple copies of the recombinant gene. The gene can be one that codes for insulin, human growth hormone, or another valuable protein. Potentially, a gene from any organism—microbe, plant, or animal—can be incorporated into any other organism.

- *tissue plasminogen activator* (TPA) for dissolving blood clots associated with diseases such as heart attack and stroke;
- *interferons*, which assist the immune response and induce the resistance of host cells to viral infection and are promising anticancer agents; and
- *recombinant vaccines*, such as that for hepatitis B.

Gene Therapy

In gene therapy, a functioning gene is introduced into a person's cells to correct the action of a defective gene. Viruses are commonly used to carry DNA into cells. Current gene therapy is experimental, and human gene transplants so far have had only modest success.

- In 1999, ten children with severe combined immunodeficiency disease (SCID) were injected with working copies of a gene that helps the immune system develop. Almost all the children improved and most are healthy today, but in 2002, two of them developed leukemia.

- Four severely blind young adults had a curative gene injected into their eyes. They can now see more light and have enough vision to walk without help. Two of them can read several lines of an eye chart.

- Genetically altered cells injected into the brain of patients with Alzheimer's disease appear to nourish ailing neurons and may slow cognitive decline in these people.

- In 2006, researchers at the National Cancer Institute (NCI) successfully reengineered immune cells to attack cancer cells in patients with advanced melanoma, the first successful use of gene therapy to treat cancer in humans.

- Researchers have genetically engineered the formation of new beta cells in the liver of mice. They also added a gene that inhibits activity of the T cells around the new beta cells in the liver and not in the rest of the body. (The T cells would otherwise destroy the new beta cells.) If this works in humans, diabetics could produce their own insulin.

Many problems remain, including getting the gene in the right place and targeting it so that it inserts itself only into the cells where it is needed. The stakes in gene therapy are huge. We all carry some defective genes. About one in ten people either has or will develop an inherited genetic disorder. Gene therapy could become an efficient way of curing many diseases.

5. Are genetically modified foods safe?

There are potential problems with today's genetically modified foods, but in practice, we have been using genetically modified foods for over a century—ever since Mendel discovered the concept of genetics. Most of today's foods are hybrids, the result of genetic modification by cross-breeding. Of course, sometimes a hybrid tomato isn't tasty or is too small. Likewise, some genetically modified plants aren't exactly what we'd like.

Genetically Modified Organisms: Controversy and Promise

Genes can be transferred from nearly any organism to any other. New animals can be cloned from cells in adult animals. Genetically modified (GM) organisms are in widespread—and often controversial—use. For example, by 2010 in the United States, 93% of the soybeans, 93% of the cotton, and 86% of the maize (corn) planted were GM varieties.

- Genes for herbicide resistance are now incorporated into soybeans so that herbicide application will kill weeds without killing the soybean plants. People worry that these genes will escape into wild plants (weeds), making them resistant to herbicides.

- Genes from the bacteria *Bacillus thuringiensis* (Bt) are incorporated into corn and cotton plants. The genes cause the plants to produce a protein toxin that kills caterpillars that would otherwise feed on the plants. People worry that insects will quickly become resistant to the toxin and that butterflies and other desirable insects will also be killed by it.

GM foods are made from GM organisms with altered DNA. GM foods first entered the market in the early 1990s. The most common modified foods—soybeans, corn, canola oil, and cottonseed oil—are derived from GM plants. People worry that GM foods will have proteins that will cause allergic reactions in some people. To protect against such developments, strict guidelines for recombinant DNA research have been instituted. Some people think that these guidelines are not strict enough.

Molecular genetics has already resulted in some impressive achievements. Its possibilities are mind-boggling—elimination of genetic defects, a cure for cancer, and who knows what else? Knowledge gives power, but it does not necessarily give wisdom. Who will decide what sort of creature the human species should be? The greatest problem we are likely to face in our use of bioengineering is choosing who is to play God with the new "secret of life."

SELF-ASSESSMENT Questions

1. Recombinant DNA cloning involves
   a. combining DNA from two different organisms to make a single new organism
   b. creating a genetically identical organism from a skin cell
   c. isolation of a genetically pure colony of cells
   d. splitting of a fertilized egg into two cells to generate identical twins

2. In producing recombinant DNA, the DNA from the two sources is cut with
   a. DNA ligase
   b. phages
   c. restriction enzymes
   d. vectors

3. Gene therapy is a process where scientists
   a. create new species of animals
   b. insert a functioning gene in place of a defective one
   c. increase the frequency of mutations
   d. use a DNA profile to identify an organism

4. Some geneticists suggest transferring some genes that direct photosynthesis from an efficient crop plant to a less efficient one, thus producing a more productive plant variety. This project would most likely involve
   a. genetic profiling
   b. genetic engineering
   c. genetic screening
   d. transcription

Answers: 1, a; 2, c; 3, b; 4, b

GREEN CHEMISTRY

David A. Vosburg, *Harvey Mudd College*

Green Chemistry and Biochemistry

Learning Objectives ❯ Name some advantages of using biochemistry to create useful molecules. ❯ Give examples of the use of biochemistry for energy production and other applications.

Chemistry has gone on constantly for millions of years in plants, animals, and bacteria. These living systems perform many chemical reactions, and plants have evolved to harness energy from the sun using photosynthesis. Living things store energy in the form of carbohydrates (like glucose, sucrose, and cellulose; Section 16.2) and lipids (fats and oils; Section 16.3). These renewable feedstocks (Principle 7) hold great potential for supplying human energy needs in the future.

Chemists are devising ways of converting these natural energy reservoirs into substitutes for nonrenewable petroleum fuels, and biochemists are engineering existing biochemical pathways in various microorganisms to directly produce usable fuels. In 2009 and 2010, three Presidential Green Chemistry Challenge Awards were given for work in this area to Virent Energy Systems, James Liao, and LS9. Virent's process transforms plant carbohydrates into gasoline (see graphic below), which could reduce dependence on fossil fuels. Liao and coworkers (UCLA and Easel Biotechnologies) have engineered bacteria to turn carbohydrates and carbon dioxide into alcohols that can be used as fuels. The LS9 company developed microorganisms that directly produce hydrocarbon fuels. All of these achievements use the products or processes of biochemistry to address the energy needs of tomorrow.

Using biochemistry to make molecules has several distinct advantages over traditional chemical synthesis and invokes many of the green chemistry principles. The reactions normally occur in water, a ubiquitous, nontoxic, and nonflammable solvent (Principle 5). When reaction products are nonpolar, they can often be separated easily from the more polar water. In contrast to many current industrial reactions that are performed at very high temperatures and pressures, most biochemical reactions are extremely rapid and occur at mild temperatures and atmospheric pressure. These reactions reduce both energy costs and potential hazards (Principles 6 and 12). The atom economy of biochemical reactions is very high, as protecting groups and auxiliaries are not necessary (Principles 2 and 8), and toxic reagents and products also can be avoided in most cases (Principles 3 and 4). Biological reactions are frequently catalytic, using a single enzyme (Section 16.5) for thousands or millions of repeated reactions that selectively generate products with very little waste produced (Principles 1 and 9). Furthermore, the products formed (and the biological catalysts themselves) are generally biodegradable and innocuous (Principle 10). When compounds are not themselves biodegradable, other biochemical pathways may be employed to degrade molecules that otherwise would persist in the environment. This bioremediation of environmental waste by cleaning up toxins and purifying water is a very important advantage of using biochemistry.

Biochemical reactions can reduce waste and simplify processes, in part due to their impressive selectivity. Buckman International found enzymes that can strengthen paper fibers, which reduces the amount of wood pulp used and saves energy, money, and trees. Yi Tang (at UCLA) and Codexis developed an enzymatic route to the cholesterol-lowering drug Zocor that eliminated several synthetic steps and reduced waste. Both of these achievements were recognized with Presidential Green Chemistry Challenge Awards in 2012. Codexis also had received a Presidential Green Chemistry Challenge Award in 2010, with Merck, for their enzymatic production of the diabetes drug Januvia. All of these biochemical innovations benefit companies, customers, the environment, and society at large.

The self-replicating nature of the cell and its DNA and the self-assembling (folding) properties of proteins (Section 16.5) make biological systems ideal candidates for the discovery and implementation of novel chemical processes. One of the greatest strengths of biochemical reactions is also the greatest challenge: specificity. Biological catalysts have evolved to have exquisite selectivity for their natural substrate(s), so adapting these catalysts to have more general functions for a wider range of (potentially unnatural) substrates is difficult. Yet this is precisely what Merck and Codexis did for the synthesis of Januvia, so there is hope that similar approaches could lead to other successes.

▲ Genetic engineering of bacteria may transform natural energy sources into materials that will be energy-rich for human use. *Synechococcus elongatus*, shown here, may be particularly useful because of its small genome and its aptitude for photosynthesis.

SUMMARY

Section 16.1—**Biochemistry** is the chemistry of life processes. Life requires chemical energy. **Metabolism** is the set of chemical reactions that keep cells alive. Metabolism includes many processes of both **anabolism** (building up of molecules) and **catabolism** (breaking down of molecules). Substances that provide animals with energy are carbohydrates, fats, and proteins.

Section 16.2—A **carbohydrate** is a compound whose formula can be written as a hydrate of carbon. Sugars, starches, and cellulose are carbohydrates. The simplest sugars are **monosaccharides**, carbohydrates that cannot be further hydrolyzed. A monosaccharide is either an **aldose** (having an aldehyde functional group) or a **ketose** (having a ketone functional group). A **disaccharide** can be hydrolyzed to yield two monosaccharide units. **Polysaccharides** contain many monosaccharide units linked together.

Section 16.3—A **lipid** is a cellular component that is insoluble in water and soluble in solvents of low polarity. Lipids include solid fats and liquid oils; both are triglycerides (esters of fatty acids with glycerol). Lipids also include steroids, hormones, and **fatty acids** (long-chain carboxylic acids). A **fat** is an ester of fatty acids and glycerol. Fats may be saturated (all carbon-to-carbon bonds in the fatty acid are single bonds), monounsaturated (one $C=C$), or polyunsaturated (more than one $C=C$). The **iodine number** of a fat or oil is the mass in grams of iodine that reacts with 100 g of the fat or oil.

Section 16.4—An **amino acid** contains an amino ($-NH_2$) group and a carboxyl ($-COOH$) group. An amino acid exists as a **zwitterion** in which a proton from the carboxyl group has been transferred to the amino group. Proteins are polymers of amino acids, with 20 amino acids forming millions of different proteins.

The bond that joins two amino-acid units in a protein is called a **peptide bond**. Two amino acids form a dipeptide, three form a tripeptide, and more than 10 form a **polypeptide**. When the molecular weight of a polypeptide exceeds about 10,000, it is called a **protein**. The sequence of the amino acids in a protein is of great importance to its function.

Section 16.5—Protein structure has four levels. The **primary structure** of a protein is simply the sequence of its amino acids. The **secondary structure** is the arrangement of polypeptide chains about an axis. Two such arrangements are the **beta pleated sheet**, in which the arrays of chains form zigzag sheets, and the **alpha helix**, in which protein chains coil around one another. The **tertiary structure** of a protein is its folding pattern; **globular proteins** such as myoglobin are folded into compact shapes. Some proteins have a **quaternary structure** consisting of an aggregate of subunits arranged in a specific pattern.

There are four types of forces that determine the secondary, tertiary, and quaternary structures of proteins: (a) hydrogen bonds; (b) ionic bonds formed between acidic and basic side chains; (c) **disulfide linkages**, which are S—S bonds formed between cysteine groups; and (d) dispersion forces arising between nonpolar side chains.

Enzymes are biological catalysts. In operation, the reacting substance, or **substrate**, attaches to the **active site** of the enzyme to form a complex, which then decomposes to the products. An enzyme is often made up of an **apoenzyme** (a protein) and a **cofactor** that is necessary for proper function and that may be a metal ion. An organic cofactor (such as a vitamin) is called a **coenzyme**.

Section 16.6—**Nucleic acids** are the information and control centers of a cell. DNA (deoxyribonucleic acid) and RNA (ribonucleic acid) are polymers of **nucleotides**. Each nucleotide contains a pentose sugar unit, a phosphate unit, and one of four amine bases. Bases with one ring are called **pyrimidines**, and those with two fused rings are **purines**. In DNA, the sugar is deoxyribose and the bases are adenine, thymine, guanine, and cytosine. In RNA, the sugar is ribose and the bases are the same as those in DNA, except that uracil replaces thymine. In DNA, the bases thymine and adenine are always paired, as are the bases cytosine and guanine. Pairing occurs via hydrogen bonding between the bases and gives rise to the double-helix structure of DNA. RNA consists of single strands of nucleic acids, some parts of which may hydrogen-bond to form double helixes. Chromosomes are made of DNA and proteins. A **gene** is a section of DNA. Genetic information is stored in the base sequence; a three-base sequence codes for a particular amino acid. Transmission of genetic information requires **replication**, or copying, of the DNA molecules.

Section 16.7—In **transcription**, a segment of DNA transfers its information to messenger RNA (mRNA). The next step is the **translation** of the code into a specific protein structure. Transfer RNA (tRNA) delivers amino acids to the growing protein chain. Each base triplet on a tRNA pairs with a set of three complementary bases on mRNA, called the **codon**, which codes for a specific amino acid.

Section 16.8—Many diseases have genetic components. In genetic testing, DNA is cleaved and duplicated. The patterns of DNA fragments are examined and compared to those of individuals with genetic diseases in order to identify and predict the occurrence of such diseases. A similar technique is used to compare DNA from different sources in DNA fingerprinting. In recombinant DNA technology, the base sequence for the gene that codes for a desired protein is determined and amplified; the gene is then spliced into a plasmid. The recombined plasmid is inserted into a host organism, which generates the protein as it reproduces.

GREEN CHEMISTRY—Biochemistry has important applications in renewable energy and offers several advantages over traditional chemical synthesis, including the use of water as the solvent and the low levels of waste and energy use. Drugs and fuels are examples of products that may be made using biochemical methods.

Learning Objectives

❯ List the major parts of a cell, and describe the function of each part.	Problem 2
❯ Name the primary source of energy for plants and three classes of substances that are the sources of energy for animals.	Problems 1, 4, 8
❯ Compare and contrast starch, glycogen, and cellulose.	Problems 17–30
❯ Describe the fundamental structure of a fatty acid and of a fat.	Problems 31, 32, 35, 36
❯ Classify fats as saturated, monounsaturated, or polyunsaturated.	Problems 33, 34
❯ Draw the fundamental structure of an amino acid, and show how amino acids combine to make proteins.	Problems 7, 39, 40, 42–48, 70
❯ Describe the four levels of protein structure, and give an example of each.	Problems 3, 5, 6, 69
❯ Describe how enzymes work as catalysts.	Problem 50
❯ Name the two types of nucleic acids, and describe the function of each type.	Problems 51, 52
❯ Explain complementary base pairing, and describe how a copy of DNA is synthesized.	Problems 9, 53–58, 71–74
❯ Explain how mRNA is synthesized from DNA and how a protein is synthesized from mRNA.	Problems 10, 11, 59–68, 75–78
❯ List important characteristics of the genetic code.	Problems 12, 14, 59
❯ Describe recombinant DNA technology, and explain how it is used.	Problems 13, 15, 16
❯ Name some advantages of using biochemistry to create useful molecules.	Problems 79, 82
❯ Give examples of the use of biochemistry for energy production and other applications.	Problems 80, 81

REVIEW QUESTIONS

1. What is the importance of photosynthesis to plants and animals?

2. Briefly identify and state a function of each of the following parts of a cell.
   a. cell membrane   b. cell nucleus
   c. chloroplasts   d. mitochondria
   e. ribosomes

3. In what parts of the body are proteins found? What tissues are largely proteins?

4. How does the elemental composition of proteins differ from that of carbohydrates and fats?

5. What is the chemical nature of proteins?

6. Amino-acid units in a protein are linked by peptide bonds. What is another name for this kind of bond?

7. What is the difference between a polypeptide and a protein?

8. What provides most of the energy for plants? Write the equation for the reaction that is driven by that energy.

9. What kind of intermolecular force is involved in base pairing?

10. Describe how replication and transcription are similar and how they differ.

11. How do DNA and RNA differ in structure?

12. What is the relationship among the cell parts called chromosomes, the units of heredity called genes, and the nucleic acid DNA?

13. What is the polymerase chain reaction (PCR)?

14. Explain what is meant by redundancy in the genetic code. Does redundancy exist for every amino acid?

15. List the steps in recombinant DNA technology.

16. How can a virus be used to replace a defective gene in a human being?

PROBLEMS

Carbohydrates

17. Which of the following compounds are carbohydrates?

   a.
   H—C=O
   HO—C—H
   CH₂OH

   b.
   CH₂OH
   H—C—OH
   CH₂OH

   c.
   CH₂OH
   C=O
   CH₂OH

   d.
   CH₃
   C=O
   CH₂OH

18. What is a disaccharide? Name three common ones.

19. What is glycogen? How does it differ from amylose? From amylopectin?

20. In what way are amylose and cellulose similar? What is the main structural difference between starch and cellulose?

21. Which of the following are monosaccharides?
   a. amylose   b. cellulose
   c. mannose   d. glucose

22. Which of the following are monosaccharides?
   a. sucrose   b. galactose
   c. fructose   d. lactose

23. Which of the carbohydrates in Problems 21 and 22 are disaccharides?

24. Which of the carbohydrates in Problems 21 and 22 are polysaccharides?

25. What are the hydrolysis products of each of the following?
    a. amylose   b. glycogen

26. What are the hydrolysis products of each of the following?
    a. amylopectin   b. cellulose

27. What functional groups are present in the formula for the open-chain form of lactose?

28. When an aqueous solution of arabinose is heated, no other molecules are produced. Is arabinose a monosaccharide, a disaccharide, or a polysaccharide?

29. When a 0.10 M aqueous solution of trehalose is heated, a 0.20 M solution of glucose is formed. Is trehalose a monosaccharide, a disaccharide, or a polysaccharide?

30. Mannose differs from glucose only in having the positions of the H and OH on the second carbon atom reversed. Write the formula for the open-chain form of mannose. What functional groups are present?

Lipids: Fats and Oils

31. How do fats and oils differ in structure? In properties?

32. A triacylglycerol contains fatty acids and
    a. glucose   b. glycerol
    c. glycogen   d. trehalose

33. Which of the following fatty acids are saturated? Which are unsaturated?
    a. palmitic acid   b. linoleic acid
    c. oleic acid   d. stearic acid

34. Which of the fatty acids in Problem 33 are monounsaturated? Which are polyunsaturated?

35. How many carbon atoms are in a molecule of each of the following fatty acids?
    a. linolenic acid   b. palmitic acid   c. stearic acid

36. How many carbon atoms are in a molecule of each of the following fatty acids?
    a. lauric acid   b. oleic acid   c. butyric acid

37. Which of the two foodstuffs shown below would you expect to have a higher iodine number? Explain your reasoning.

38. Which of the two fats shown below is likely to have a lower iodine number? Explain your reasoning.

Proteins

39. Amino acids are the building blocks of
    a. carbohydrates   b. fats
    c. nucleic acids   d. proteins

40. What is a dipeptide? A tripeptide? A polypeptide?

41. Of the amino acids aspartic acid, lysine, serine, methionine, and glycine, which are essential to the human diet?

42. Examine Table 16.3, and write the condensed structural formula for the part of each structure that is identical for 19 of the 20 amino acids. Which amino acid does not have this particular structural feature?

43. Write structural formulas for the following amino acids.
    a. threonine   b. phenylalanine

44. Identify the following amino acids.

$$HOOC-CH_2CH_2-\underset{\underset{\textstyle ^+NH_3}{|}}{CH}-COO^- \qquad HS-CH_2-\underset{\underset{\textstyle ^+NH_3}{|}}{CH}-COO^-$$

(a)   (b)

45. Write structural formulas for the following dipeptides.
    a. glycylarginine   b. alanylcysteine

46. Identify the following dipeptides.

$$\overset{\textstyle HO-CH_2}{\underset{\textstyle ^+NH_3-CH-CONH-}{|}}\overset{\textstyle CH_2CH(CH_3)_2}{\underset{\textstyle CH-COO^-}{|}}$$

(a)

$$\overset{\textstyle HS-CH_2}{\underset{\textstyle ^+NH_3-CH_2-CONH-}{|}}\overset{}{\underset{\textstyle CH-COO^-}{|}}$$

(b)

47. The sweetener *aspartame* has the structure shown below, in which a CH_3O- group (at right) is attached to a dipeptide. Identify the dipeptide.

$$H_2N-\underset{\underset{\textstyle COOH}{\underset{\textstyle |}{CH_2}}}{\overset{\textstyle |}{CH}}-\overset{\textstyle O}{\overset{\|}{C}}-NH-\underset{\underset{\textstyle \bigcirc}{\underset{\textstyle |}{CH_2}}}{\overset{\textstyle |}{CH}}-\overset{\textstyle O}{\overset{\|}{C}}-OCH_3$$

48. Refer to Problem 47, and draw the structure of the other dipeptide that contains the same amino acids as aspartame.

49. List the four different forces that link protein chains.

50. Describe (a) the induced-fit model of enzyme action and (b) how an inhibitor deactivates an enzyme.

Nucleic Acids: Parts and Structure

51. Which of the following nucleotides can be found in DNA, which in RNA, and which in neither?

    $$\underset{\textstyle a.\ deoxyribose-P_i}{\overset{\textstyle thymine}{|}} \qquad \underset{\textstyle b.\ ribose-P_i}{\overset{\textstyle adenine}{|}}$$

    $$\underset{\textstyle c.\ ribose-P_i}{\overset{\textstyle cytosine}{|}}$$

52. Which of the following nucleotides can be found in DNA, which in RNA, and which in neither?

a.
uracil
|
ribose — P_i

b.
adenine
|
deoxyribose — P_i

c.
cytosine
|
deoxyribose — P_i

53. Identify the sugar and the base in the following nucleotide.

54. Identify the sugar and the base in the following nucleotide.

55. In DNA, which base would be paired with the base listed?
a. cytosine   **b.** adenine
c. guanine   **d.** thymine

56. In RNA, which base would be paired with the base listed?
a. adenine   **b.** guanine
c. uracil   **d.** cytosine

DNA: Self-Replication

57. In replication, a DNA molecule produces two daughter molecules. What is the fate of each strand of the original double helix?

58. DNA controls protein synthesis, yet most DNA resides within the cell nucleus and protein synthesis occurs outside the nucleus. How does DNA exercise its control?

RNA: Protein Synthesis and the Genetic Code

59. Which nucleic acid(s) is(are) involved in **(a)** the process referred to as transcription and **(b)** the process referred to as translation?

60. Explain the role of **(a)** mRNA and **(b)** tRNA in protein synthesis.

61. The process in which DNA unzips and makes a strand of mRNA is
a. pairing   **b.** replication
c. transcription   **d.** translation

62. Which of the following point mutations in DNA would be most likely to affect protein function? You may consult Table 16.5.
a. AGG to AGA   **b.** CAA to TAA
c. CTT to CTC   **d.** TAA to TGA

63. mRNA leaves the nucleus and binds to
a. chromatin   **b.** hemoglobin
c. a mitochondrion   **d.** a ribosome

64. What entities do tRNA carry to the mRNA?
a. amino acids   **b.** codons
c. genes   **d.** nucleic acids

65. Which of the following is *not* found in RNA?
a. adenine   **b.** guanine
c. thymine   **d.** uracil

66. What anticodon on tRNA would pair with each of the following mRNA codons?
a. UUU   **b.** CAU

67. What codon on mRNA would pair with each of the following tRNA anticodons?
a. UUG   **b.** CAC

68. Cystic fibrosis (CF) is an inherited disorder. It is characterized by abnormal transport of chloride ions and sodium ions across an epithelial membrane, leading to thick, viscous secretions that build up in the lungs and block airways. The most common mutation causing CF is a CTT deletion. What amino acid is deleted? You may consult Table 16.5.

 ADDITIONAL PROBLEMS

69. Human insulin molecules are made up of two chains with the following sequences.

Chain A: G-I-V-E-Q-C-C-T-S-I-C-S-L-Y-Q-L-E-N-Y-C-N

Chain B: F-V-N-Q-H-L-C-G-D-H-L-V-E-A-L-Y-L-V-C-G-E-R-G-F-F-Y-T-P-K-T

Chain A has a loop formed by a disulfide linkage between the sixth and eleventh amino acids (designated A-6 to A-11) and is joined to chain B by two disulfide linkages (A-7 to B-7 and A-20 to B-19). What level of protein structure is described by **(a)** the chain sequence of one-letter abbreviations and **(b)** the description of the loop and chain linkages?

70. Synthetic polymers can be formed from amino-acid units of a single kind. Write the formula for a segment of **(a)** polyglycine and **(b)** polycysteine. Show at least four repeating units of each.

71. Identify the base in the structure in **(a)** Problem 53 and **(b)** Problem 54 as a purine or a pyrimidine.

72. Answer the following questions for the molecule shown.
a. Is the base a purine or a pyrimidine?
b. Would the compound be incorporated in DNA or in RNA?

73. Answer the questions posed in Problem 72 for the following compound.

74. Use Table 16.5 to determine the amino acid specified by the DNA triplet CTC. What amino acid is specified if a mutation changes the DNA triplet to CTT? To CTA? To CAC?

75. Many laundry detergents have enzymes to aid removal of stains of biological origin, such as those from food or blood. The enzyme subtilisin, produced by *Bacillus subtilis*, is one of these. The natural enzyme was not very effective because it was largely deactivated by the harsh detergent environment. A genetically modified form, in which the base sequence ACCAGCAUGGCG is replaced by ACCAGC-GCGGCG, is much more effective because it is more stable. What is the amino-acid sequence specified by the bases in this segment in (a) the original enzyme and (b) the genetically modified enzyme? You may consult Table 16.5.

76. In the novel *Jurassic Park* by Michael Crichton, the cloned dinosaurs were genetically engineered so as to be unable to survive outside the island park because they were unable to synthesize the amino acid lysine. This was supposed to make the dinosaurs dependent on their makers to feed them a source of lysine. Examine Table 16.3, and suggest a reason why this genetic engineering would not keep the dinosaurs from surviving elsewhere.

77. With what mRNA codon would the tRNA in the diagram form a codon–anticodon pair?

78. Write the abbreviated versions of the following structural formula using (a) the three-letter abbreviations and (b) the one-letter abbreviations.

79. What solvent is typically used for biochemical reactions?

80. What types of molecules are used to store energy in biological systems?
    a. hydrocarbons
    b. carbohydrates and lipids
    c. amino acids
    d. water and carbon dioxide

81. Which is an example of a way to produce a renewable fuel using biochemical processes or products?
    a. turn carbohydrates into fuels
    b. use bacteria to convert carbohydrates or CO_2 into biofuels
    c. engineer microbes to make gasoline
    d. all of the above

82. Which of the following is NOT an advantage of using biochemical methods compared to traditional chemical synthesis?
    a. Water is often used as a solvent.
    b. Separation of products is difficult.
    c. Reaction conditions are mild.
    d. Reactions are usually catalytic.

CRITICAL THINKING EXERCISES

Apply knowledge that you have gained in this chapter and one or more of the FLaReS principles (Chapter 1) to evaluate the following statements or claims.

16.1. The label on an energy drink claims, in large print, "Contains no artificial amino acids!"

16.2. DNA is an essential component of every living cell. An advertisement claims that DNA is a useful diet supplement.

16.3. A restaurant menu states, "Other restaurants use saturated beef fat for frying. We use only pure vegetable oil to fry our fish and french fries, for healthier eating."

16.4. An agricultural company claims that none of the plants or animals used in its products has ever been genetically modified.

16.5. A dietician states that a recommendation of 60 g of protein per day for an adult is somewhat misleading. She claims that the right kinds of proteins, with the proper amino acids in them, must be consumed; otherwise, even a much larger amount of protein per day may be insufficient to maintain health.

16.6. A man convicted of rape claims that he is innocent because DNA fingerprinting of a semen sample taken from the rape victim showed that it contains DNA from another man.

COLLABORATIVE GROUP PROJECTS

Prepare a PowerPoint, poster, or other presentation (as directed by your instructor), to share with the class.

1. Prepare a brief report on **(a)** a carbohydrate such as fructose, glycogen, lactose, maltose, sucrose, or starch or **(b)** a lipid such as beef tallow, corn oil, lard, oleic acid, or palmitic acid. List principal sources and uses of the material.

2. Prepare a brief report on enzyme action, including a comparison of the induced-fit model of action with the older lock-and-key model.

3. Prepare a brief report on one of the following products of genetic engineering. List some advantages and disadvantages of the product.
   a. golden rice
   b. herbicide-resistant transgenic soybeans
   c. transgenic cotton that produces Bt toxin
   d. transgenic tobacco that produces human serum albumin

e. transgenic tomatoes that have improved resistance to viruses

f. transgenic *E. coli* that produce human interleukin-2, a protein that stimulates the production of T-lymphocytes that play a role in fighting selected cancers

4. Genetic testing carries both promise and peril, and its use is an important topic in bioethics today. After some online research, write a brief essay on one of the following—or on a similar question assigned by your instructor.
   a. In what cases might a person not want to be tested for a disease his or her parent had?
   b. When is genetic testing most valuable? What privacy issues must be addressed in this area?
   c. Does testing negative for the breast cancer genes mean that a woman doesn't have to have mammograms?

CHEMISTRY@HOME DNA Dessert

Materials required

- 1 resealable plastic bag
- Strawberries (fresh or frozen)
- 2 teaspoons dish detergent
- 1 teaspoon salt
- 1 cup of water
- 2 clear plastic cups (One cup will be used for the filtering apparatus below)
- Filtering apparatus: coffee filter and plastic cup
- Ice cold 90 percent rubbing alcohol
- 1 wooden popsicle stick or plastic coffee stirrer

Ever wonder how scientists extract DNA from a cell? How many scientific fields use human DNA samples in their research?

Cells are the basic unit of life and make up all plants, animals, and bacteria. Deoxyribonucleic acid, or DNA, is the molecule that controls everything that happens in the cell. DNA contains instructions that direct the activities of cells and, ultimately, the body. To get the DNA from a cell, scientists typically rely on one of many DNA extraction kits available from biotechnology companies. During a DNA extraction, a detergent will cause the cell to pop open, or lyse, so that the DNA is released into solution. Then alcohol added to the solution causes the DNA to precipitate out.

In this activity, strawberries will be used because each strawberry cell has eight copies of the genome (an octoploid genome), giving them a lot of DNA per cell. Most organisms only have one genome copy per cell.

Begin by pulling off any green leaves on the strawberry that have not been removed yet. Put the strawberry into the plastic bag, seal it and gently smash it for about two minutes. Completely crush the strawberry. This starts to break open the cells and release the DNA.

In a plastic cup, make your DNA extraction liquid: mix together 2 teaspoons of detergent, 1 teaspoon of salt, and 1 cup of water. Pour 2 teaspoons of the DNA extraction liquid into the bag with the strawberry. This will further break open the cells. Reseal the bag and gently smash for another minute. Avoid making too many soap bubbles.

Place the coffee filter inside the other plastic cup. Open the bag and pour the strawberry liquid into the filter.

Pouring into a coffee filter.

You can twist the filter just above the liquid and gently squeeze the remaining liquid into the cup. Next, pour down the side of the cup an amount of cold rubbing alcohol equal to the strawberry liquid. Do not mix or stir.

You have just isolated the DNA from the rest of the material contained in the cells of the strawberry. What happens to the mixture? Within a few seconds, watch for the development of a white cloudy substance (DNA) in the top layer above the strawberry-extract layer.

The pulp in a glass with DNA floating on it.

Tilt the cup and pick up the DNA using a plastic coffee stirrer or wooden stick. Can you spool it onto the stick?

Questions

1. Were you able to see the DNA clearly?
2. Were you able to pick up clumps of the DNA?
3. How do DNA samples help detectives solve crimes?
4. Why was the discovery of the structure of DNA so important?

17

Learning Objectives

> Identify dietary carbohydrates, and state their sources and function. (17.1)

> Identify dietary lipids, and state their function. (17.2)

> List the essential amino acids, and explain why we need proteins. (17.3)

> Describe some protein deficiency diseases and their causes. (17.3)

> Identify the vitamins and the bulk dietary minerals, and state their functions. (17.4)

> Describe the effects of starvation, fasting, and malnutrition. (17.5)

> List commonly used flavorings in food. (17.6)

> Describe the historic impact of our desire for a variety of flavors and aromas, and of our search for sugar substitutes. (17.6)

> Identify the beneficial additives in foods and those that are somewhat controversial. (17.7)

> Define the GRAS list and food additives allowed under its provisions. (17.7)

> Identify and describe some of the main problems with harmful substances in our food. (17.8)

> Explain how food supply chain waste can be used as a resource in the chemical industry.

> Identify the advantages of using food supply chain waste instead of fossil fuels as a source of chemicals, materials, and fuels

FOOD

Have You Ever Wondered?

1. **Since fruits are sweet, do they cause tooth decay like candy?**

2. **Is high blood cholesterol mainly a problem for older people?**

3. **How much fat in the diet is "too much"?**

4. **The doctor said my mother should cut her salt intake. Why?**

5. **Are large doses of vitamins beneficial?**

6. **What's the difference between natural and artificial sweeteners?**

FOOD—FEASTS TO FAMINE To give in to the temptation of a luscious piece of chocolate cake ... or not to give in—that is the question! How many of us choose the healthier, crunchy apple? From holiday feasts to late-night snacks, many of life's joys involve food. Yet the primary purpose of food is not to give pleasure; it is to sustain life. Food supplies all the molecular building blocks from which our bodies are made, enables children to grow, and provides all the energy for our life activities. That energy comes ultimately from the sun through photosynthesis.

In many places on Earth, some people never have enough food. According to *The Hunger Project*, about 1 billion people (one in seven) are always hungry. Wars make the news, but ten times as many people die of chronic malnutrition than die in war. In October 2011, the world's population hit seven billion. Feeding a growing world population is a challenging task, especially in countries that are experiencing the highest birthrates and the deepest poverty. These two factors combine to foreshadow major challenges in feeding those growing populations. The population of Niger, for example, is growing at a rate of more than 3% per year; most of the population lives in the direst poverty with little food to support them.

While millions starve, other locales have a surplus. Most of us in the Western world have an overabundance of food and often eat too much. Yet even in developed nations, many people experience hunger, frequently skipping meals or eating too little. These people often have lower-quality diets or must resort to seeking food from emergency sources.

Many of us also frequently eat the wrong kinds of food. Our diet, often too rich in saturated fats, sugar, and alcohol, has been linked in part to at least five of the ten leading causes of death in the United States: heart disease, cancer, stroke, diabetes, and kidney disease. The U.S. Centers for Disease Control and Prevention (CDC) found that 68% of the adults in the United States are overweight, which contributes to poor health, increased risk of diabetes, heart attacks, strokes, and some forms of cancer. It also leads to increased susceptibility to other diseases.

In this chapter, we discuss food, what it's made of and the substances added to it—by accident or design. For proper nutrition, our diet should include balanced proportions of carbohydrates, fats, and proteins as well as water, vitamins, minerals, and fiber. In Chapter 19 we will discuss the role of foods in health and fitness.

17.1 Carbohydrates in the Diet

Learning Objective > Identify dietary carbohydrates, and state their sources and function.

Dietary carbohydrates include sugars and starches (Figure 17.1). Sugars are mainly monosaccharides and disaccharides; starches are polysaccharides. (See Chapter 1 for the structures of these molecules.)

Sugars have been used since ancient times to make food sweeter and more pleasant tasting. Besides the unique flavors and aromas of fruits, the underlying sweetness of fruits is due to the presence of fructose, from the Latin word for fruit, which is *fructus*. The most ancient sweetener is honey, consisting mainly of a mixture of fructose and glucose, both of which are monosaccharides. Common table sugar is sucrose, a disaccharide usually obtained from sugarcane or sugar beets. Ordinary corn syrup, a viscous liquid, consists mainly of glucose made by splitting long cornstarch chains. *High-fructose corn syrup (HFCS)* is made by treating corn syrup with enzymes to convert much of the glucose to fructose. Foods sweetened to the same degree with fructose have somewhat fewer calories than those sweetened with sucrose.

Most sugars are consumed in soft drinks, presweetened cereals, candy, and other highly processed foods with little or no nutritive value besides calories. Sugars in sweetened foods also contribute to tooth decay and obesity. From the 1960s

▲ **Figure 17.1** The main sugars in our diet are sucrose (cane or beet sugar), glucose (corn syrup), and fructose (fruit sugar, often in the form of high-fructose corn syrup).

Q: *What is the molecular formula for glucose? For fructose? How are the two compounds related? How is sucrose related to glucose and fructose? (Hint: You may refer to Chapter 16, if necessary.)*

▲ Sugarcane is a major agricultural crop in tropical regions. It is the source of about 45% of the refined sugar used in the United States.

▲ **Figure 17.2** Infants born with galactosemia can thrive on a milk-free substitute formula.

1. Since fruits are sweet, do they cause tooth decay like candy?

No. The main bacteria in the mouth that cause decay of tooth enamel, *Streptococcus mutans*, feed primarily on sucrose, the disaccharide that is found in candy and table sugar; they cannot attack free glucose or fructose.

You can do your own carbohydrate digestion experiment. Chew an unsalted saltine cracker for several minutes, and you will notice a slight sweet taste. Your saliva contains enzymes that begin the digestion process. Explain the sweet taste.

through 2008, per-capita consumption of sugars skyrocketed but over the last six years has slightly fallen. "Diet" soft drinks, with artificial sweeteners instead of the HFCS usually added to regular soft drinks, are becoming quite popular, which may account for the slight decrease in total sugar consumption among the general public in the last few years. A typical can of ordinary soda pop contains about 40 g of sugar, in the form of HFCS, but diet soft drinks contain none.

Digestion and Metabolism of Carbohydrates

Glucose and fructose are absorbed directly into the bloodstream from the digestive tract. Sucrose is hydrolyzed (split by water) during digestion to glucose and fructose.

$$\text{Sucrose} + H_2O \longrightarrow \text{Glucose} + \text{Fructose}$$

The disaccharide lactose occurs in milk. During digestion, it is hydrolyzed to two simpler sugars, glucose and galactose.

$$\text{Lactose} + H_2O \longrightarrow \text{Glucose} + \text{Galactose}$$

Nearly all human babies have the enzyme necessary to accomplish this breakdown, but many adults do not. People who lack the enzyme get digestive upsets from drinking milk, a condition called *lactose intolerance*. When milk is cooked or fermented, the lactose is at least partially hydrolyzed. People with lactose intolerance may be able to enjoy cheese, yogurt, or cooked foods containing milk with little or no discomfort. Lactose-free milk, made by treating milk with an enzyme that hydrolyzes lactose, is available in most grocery stores. Lactose intolerance is particularly common among Asians and Africans, and much less common among those of European descent.

Although it has long been thought that all monosaccharides are converted to glucose during metabolism, research shows that fructose may remain in the liver, stimulating the formation of triglycerides (fats). Hence the current controversy over the extensive use of HFCS. Glucose is the sugar used by the cells of our bodies for energy. Because it is the sugar that circulates in the bloodstream, it is often called **blood sugar**. Some babies are born with *galactosemia*, a deficiency of the enzyme that catalyzes the conversion of galactose to glucose. For proper nutrition, they must be fed a synthetic formula (Figure 17.2) in place of milk.

Complex Carbohydrates: Starch and Cellulose

Starch and cellulose are both polymers of glucose, but the connecting links between the glucose units are different (Figure 16.6). Humans can digest starch but not cellulose. Digestive enzymes are able to easily split **starch**, a polymer of glucose in which the units are joined by alpha linkages, resulting in a slinky-like shape. On the other hand, human digestive enzymes cannot easily split apart **cellulose** because the beta linkages result in a straight chain of glucose units. Starch is an important part of the diet (Figure 17.3) and should provide most of your caloric intake. Cellulose is an important component of dietary fiber.

▲ **Figure 17.3** Bread, flour, cereals, and pasta are rich in starches and form the basis of the U.S. diet. On the Left, various grains for sale in Oshakati, Namibia, show the range of carbohydrates eaten throughout the world.

When digested, starch is hydrolyzed to glucose, as represented by the following equation:

$$(C_6H_{10}O_5)_n + n\ H_2O \xrightarrow{\text{Carbohydrates}} n\ C_6H_{12}O_6$$

$$\text{Starch} \qquad\qquad\qquad\qquad \text{Glucose}$$

The body then metabolizes the glucose, using it as a source of energy. Glucose is broken down in a complex set of more than 50 chemical reactions that produce carbon dioxide and water, with the release of energy.

$$C_6H_{12}O_6 + 6\ O_2 \longrightarrow 6\ CO_2 + 6\ H_2O + \text{Energy}$$

This net reaction is the reverse of photosynthesis. In this way, animals are able to make use of the energy from the sun that was captured by plants using the process of photosynthesis.

Carbohydrates, which supply about 4 kcal of energy per gram, are our bodies' preferred fuels. When we eat more than our bodies can use, small amounts of carbohydrates can be stored in the liver and in muscle tissue as **glycogen** (animal starch), a highly branched polymer of α-glucose. Large excesses of carbohydrates are converted to fat for storage. Most health authorities recommend obtaining carbohydrates from a diet rich in whole grains, fruits, vegetables, and legumes (beans). We should minimize our intake of the simple sugars and refined starches found in many prepared foods.

Cellulose is the most abundant carbohydrate in nature. It is present in all plants, forming their cell walls and other structural features such as stems, bark, leaves, and seeds. Wood is about 50% cellulose, and cotton is almost pure cellulose. Unlike starch, cellulose cannot be digested by humans and many other animals. Cellulose does, however, play an important role in human digestion, providing *dietary fiber* that absorbs water and helps move food through the digestive tract (Section 17.4).

We get no caloric value from dietary cellulose because its glucose units are joined by beta linkages, and most animals lack the enzymes needed to break this kind of bond. Certain bacteria that live in the gut of termites and in the digestive tract of grazing animals such as cows or deer produce these enzymes, so that these animals can convert cellulose to glucose.

It DOES Matter!

With today's emphasis on low-carbohydrate foods, labels on some diet foods give the mass in grams of carbohydrate that can be readily digested. "Only 1 carb" means that a serving contains 1 g of readily digestible carbohydrate. It is important to read the labels of such foods carefully. They may contain a large amount of fat, including saturated fat. They may also contain relatively large amounts of additives (such as glycerin or xylitol) that are digested as carbohydrate—though much more slowly than sugars or even starches.

SELF-ASSESSMENT Questions

1. About _____ people in the world are hungry today.
   a. 1 in 4   **b.** 1 in 7   **c.** 1 in 12   **d.** 1 in 20

2. The monomer units that make up cellulose and starch, respectively, are
   a. glucose and fructose
   b. α-glucose and β-glucose
   c. β-glucose and α-glucose
   d. fructose and sucrose

3. Examples of monosaccharides are
   a. lactose and fructose
   b. galactose and sucrose
   c. glucose and fructose
   d. lactose and sucrose

4. People who have lactose intolerance are deficient in the
   a. enzyme that catalyzes the hydrolysis of lactose to galactose and glucose
   b. enzyme that catalyzes the conversion of galactose to glucose
   c. enzymes that catalyze the oxidation of lactose to CO_2 and H_2O
   d. taste receptors for lactose, leaving a bitter taste

5. Ordinary corn syrup
   a. consists of glucose and fructose
   b. consists mainly of glucose
   c. is mainly sucrose, just like table sugar
   d. is just the same as high-fructose corn syrup

6. Small quantities of carbohydrates are stored in liver and muscle tissue as
   a. amylose
   b. cellulose
   c. glucose
   d. glycogen

7. Humans cannot digest cellulose because they lack enzymes for the hydrolysis of
   a. α-amino acid linkages
   b. α-glucose linkages
   c. β-glucose linkages
   d. sucrose

Answers: 1, b; 2, c; 3, c; 4, a; 5, b; 6, d; 7, c

17.2 Fats and Cholesterol

Learning Objective ❯ Identify dietary lipids, and state their function.

Fats—esters of fatty acids and glycerol—are high-energy foods, yielding about 9 kcal of energy per gram, more than twice as much as carbohydrates. Some fats are "burned" as fuel for our activities. Others are used to build and maintain important constituents of our cells, such as cell membranes. Fats help produce prostaglandins, which function as temperature regulators, inflammation mediators, and many other functions in the body. Fats can store vitamins and make many foods more palatable. The fat in our diet comes from many sources, some of which are shown in Figure 17.4.

Digestion and Metabolism of Fats

Dietary fats are mainly *triacylglycerols*, commonly called **triglycerides**. Fats are digested by enzymes called *lipases* and are ultimately broken down into fatty acids and glycerol (Figure 17.5). Some fat molecules are hydrolyzed to a monoglyceride (*monoacylglycerol*; glycerol combined with only one fatty acid) or a diglyceride (*diacylglycerol*; ester of two fatty acids and glycerol). Once absorbed, these products of fat digestion are reassembled into triglycerides, which are attached to proteins for transportation through the bloodstream.

▲ **Figure 17.4** Cream, butter, margarine, cooking oils, and foods fried in fat are rich in fats. The average American diet contains too much fat. Americans get 37% of their calories from fat, while the recommendation of the FDA is 20–30% fat calories.

$$HO-CH_2$$
$$HO-CH$$
$$CH_3(CH_2)_{14}COOCH_2$$

A monoglyceride

$$CH_3(CH_2)_7CH=CH(CH_2)_7COOCH_2$$
$$HO-CH$$
$$CH_3(CH_2)_{14}COOCH_2$$

A diglyceride

Fats are stored throughout the body, principally in **adipose tissue**, in locations called **fat depots**. Fat depots around vital organs, such as the heart, kidneys, and spleen, cushion and help prevent injury to these organs. Fat is also stored under the skin, where it helps to insulate against temperature changes.

When fat reserves are called on for energy, fat molecules are hydrolyzed back to glycerol and fatty acids. The glycerol can be burned for energy or converted to glucose. The fatty acids enter a process called the *fatty acid spiral* that removes carbon atoms two at a time. The two-carbon fragments can be used for energy or for the synthesis of new fatty acids.

$$CH_3(CH_2)_7CH=CH(CH_2)_7COOCH_2$$
$$CH_3(CH_2)_7CH=CH(CH_2)_7COOCH$$
$$CH_3(CH_2)_{14}COOCH_2$$
Fat (triglyceride)

$$\xrightarrow[\text{lipase}]{\text{water}}$$

$$2\ CH_3(CH_2)_7CH=CH(CH_2)_7COOH$$
Oleic acid
+
$$CH_3(CH_2)_{14}COOH$$
Palmitic acid

+

$$HO-CH_2$$
$$HO-CH$$
$$HO-CH_2$$
Glycerol

▲ **Figure 17.5** In the digestion of fats, a triglyceride is hydrolyzed to fatty acids and glycerol in a reaction catalyzed by the enzyme lipase.

Q: *What diglyceride is formed by removal of the palmitic acid part of the triglyceride? What monoglyceride is formed by removal of both oleic acid parts? (Hint: You may refer to Chapter 16, if necessary.)*

Fats, Cholesterol, and Human Health

Dietary *saturated fats* and cholesterol have been implicated in *arteriosclerosis* ("hardening of the arteries"). Recall from Section 16.3 that saturated fats are those containing a large proportion of saturated fatty acids, such as palmitic and stearic acids. Incidence of cardiovascular disease is strongly correlated with diets rich in saturated fats. As the disease develops, deposits form on the inner walls of arteries. Eventually these deposits harden, and the vessels lose their elasticity (Figure 17.6). Blood clots tend to lodge in the narrowed arteries, leading to a heart attack (if the blocked artery is in heart muscle) or a stroke (if the blockage occurs in an artery that supplies the brain).

The plaque in clogged arteries is rich in cholesterol, a fat-like steroid alcohol found in animal tissues and various foods. Cholesterol is normally synthesized by the liver and is important as a constituent of cell membranes and a precursor to steroid hormones. High blood levels of cholesterol, like those of triglycerides, correlate closely with the risk of cardiovascular disease. Like fats, cholesterol is insoluble in water, as we can determine from its molecular formula ($C_{27}H_{45}OH$) and structure (shown in the margin). Cholesterol is transported in blood by water-soluble proteins. The cholesterol–protein combination is an example of a **lipoprotein**, any of a group of proteins combined with a lipid, such as cholesterol or a triglyceride.

Lipoproteins are usually classified according to their density (Table 17.1). Very-low-density lipoproteins (VLDLs) serve mainly to transport triglycerides, whereas low-density lipoproteins (LDLs) are the main carriers of cholesterol. LDLs carry cholesterol to the cells for use, and these lipoproteins are the ones that deposit cholesterol in arteries, leading to cardiovascular disease. High-density lipoproteins (HDLs) also carry cholesterol, but they carry it to the liver for processing and excretion. Exercise is thought to increase the levels of HDLs, the lipoproteins sometimes called "good" cholesterol. High levels of LDLs, called "bad" cholesterol, increase the risk of heart attack and stroke. The American Heart Association recommends a maximum of 300 mg/day of cholesterol for the general population and 200 mg/day for people with heart disease or at risk for it.

▲ **Figure 17.6** Photomicrographs of cross sections of a normal artery (left) and a "hardened" artery (right), which shows deposits of plaque that contain cholesterol.

Table 17.1	Lipoproteins in the Blood			
Class	Abbreviation	Protein (%)	Density (g/mL)	Main Function
Very low density	VLDL	5	1.006–1.019	Transport triglycerides
Low density	LDL	25	1.019–1.063	Transport cholesterol to the cells for use
High density	HDL	50	1.063–1.210	Transport cholesterol to the liver for processing and excretion

▲ Molecular model and structural formula of cholesterol.

Fats differ in their effect on blood-cholesterol levels. Many nutritionists advise us to use olive oil and canola oil as our major sources of dietary lipids because they contain a high percentage of monounsaturated fatty acids, which have been shown to lower LDL cholesterol. There is also statistical evidence that fish oils can prevent heart disease. For example, Greenlanders who eat a lot of fish have a low risk of heart disease despite a diet that is high in total fat and cholesterol. The probable effective agents are polyunsaturated fatty acids such as eicosapentaenoic acid (EPA) and docosahexaenoic acid (DHA):

$$CH_3(CH_2CH{=}CH)_5(CH_2)_3COOH \qquad CH_3(CH_2CH{=}CH)_6(CH_2)_2COOH$$
$$\text{EPA} \qquad\qquad\qquad\qquad \text{DHA}$$

These fatty acids are known as *omega-3 fatty acids* because they have a carbon-to-carbon double bond that begins at the *third* carbon from the end opposite the COOH group—the *omega* end. Studies have shown that adding omega-3 fatty acids to the diet leads to lower cholesterol and triglyceride levels in the blood.

Fats and oils containing carbon-to-carbon double bonds can undergo hydrogenation, addition of an H_2 molecule to each double bond. Hydrogenation of

2. Is high blood cholesterol mainly a problem for older people?

The effects of high blood cholesterol are seen mainly in older people because the buildup of plaque in the blood vessels takes time. But those effects are often the result of years of an unhealthy diet and high levels of LDLs. To minimize the long-term effects of high cholesterol, you should consider early preventive measures. Reducing saturated fat in your diet is a good start.

▲ It DOES Matter!

Half of the total fat, three-fourths of the saturated fat, and all the cholesterol in a typical human diet come from animal products such as meat, milk, cheese, and eggs. Advertising that a vegetable oil (for example) contains no cholesterol is silly. No vegetable product contains cholesterol.

vegetable oils to produce semisolid fats is an important process in the food industry. The chemistry of this conversion process is identical to the hydrogenation reaction of alkenes described in Section 9.1.

$$CH_3(CH_2)_7CH \!-\! CH(CH_2)_7COOH \xrightarrow[\text{Ni}]{H_2} CH_3(CH_2)_7CH_2CH_2(CH_2)_7COOH$$

Oleic acid (monounsaturated)   Stearic acid (saturated)

By properly controlling the reaction conditions, inexpensive vegetable oils (cottonseed, corn, and soybean) can be partially hydrogenated to yield soft, spreadable fats suitable for use in margarine or fully hydrogenated to produce harder fats like shortening. The consumer would get much higher unsaturation by using the oils directly, but most people would rather spread margarine than pour oil on their toast.

Concern about the role of saturated fats in raising blood cholesterol and clogging arteries caused many consumers to switch from butter to margarine. However, some of the unsaturated fats that remain after partial hydrogenation of vegetable oils have structures similar to saturated fats. These unsaturated fats raise cholesterol levels and increase the risk of coronary heart disease.

Remember that a fat is a triglyceride, three carbons in a row (with the appropriate number of hydrogen atoms), each of which has a fatty acid chain attached to it. Figure 17.7 presents molecular models of three types of fatty acids. Saturated fatty acids have all single bonds connecting the row of carbon atoms (they are "saturated" with hydrogen atoms). The unsaturated fatty acids have at least one double bond somewhere in the string of carbon atoms. Most naturally occurring unsaturated fatty acids have a *cis* arrangement about the double bond. For example, oleic acid has the structure given by Figure 17.7c. Recall from Chapter 9 that a *cis* arrangement about double-bonded carbon atoms has both hydrogen atoms on the same side of the double bond. During hydrogenation, the arrangement in some of the molecules is changed so that the hydrogen atoms of the double-bonded carbon atoms are on opposite sides of the double bond, a *trans* arrangement, shown in Figure 17.7b. If we draw a straight line passing through the double-bonded carbon atoms and if the hydrogen atoms on those carbon atoms are on the same side of the line, the molecule represents a *cis* fatty acid. If they are on opposite sides, it is a *trans* fatty acid.

Note in Figures 17.7a and 17.7b that both saturated fatty acids (such as stearic acid) and *trans* fatty acids are more or less straight and can stack neatly like logs. This maximizes the intermolecular attractive forces, making saturated and *trans* fatty acids more likely to be solids than *cis* fatty acids.

Emulsions

When oil and water are vigorously shaken together, the oil is broken up into tiny, microscopic droplets and dispersed throughout the water, a mixture called an *emulsion*. Unless a third substance has been added, the emulsion usually breaks down rapidly, as the oil droplets recombine and float to the surface of the water.

Emulsions can be stabilized by adding a type of gum, a soap, or a protein that can form a protective coating around the oil droplets and prevent them from coming together. Lecithin in egg yolks keeps mayonnaise from separating, while casein in milk keeps fat droplets suspended. Compounds called *bile salts* keep tiny fat droplets suspended in aqueous media during human digestion. This greatly aids the digestive process. The tiny emulsified droplets provide a much greater surface area on which the water-soluble lipase enzymes can break down the triacylglycerides to glycerol and fatty acids.

▲ Many foods are emulsions. Milk is an emulsion of butterfat in water. The stabilizing agent is a protein called *casein*. Mayonnaise is an emulsion of vegetable oil in water, stabilized by egg yolk.

◀ **Figure 17.7** The structures of (a) stearic acid (a saturated fatty acid) and (b) the *trans* isomer of oleic acid (a *trans* unsaturated fatty acid) are similar in shape, and these acids behave similarly in the body; (c) oleic acid (a *cis* unsaturated fatty acid) has a very different shape.

trans configuration

cis configuration

On the other hand, *cis* fatty acids (Figure 17.7c) have a bend in their structure, fixed in position by the double bond. They have weaker intermolecular forces and are more likely to be liquids. Because *trans* fatty acids also resemble saturated fatty acids in their tendency to raise blood levels of LDL cholesterol, the FDA requires manufacturers to provide the *trans* fat content of foods on labels and is considering banning *trans* fats from prepared foods. Many fast-food establishments have eliminated the use of *trans* fats due to public pressure.

Many Americans eat too much fat, especially saturated and *trans* fats. Health experts generally advise us to limit our overall intake of fats and of saturated and *trans* fats in particular. Many health professionals recommend that fats should not exceed 30% of total calories, and no more than one-third of the fat should be saturated fat.

3. How much fat in the diet is "too much"?
Not more than about 30% of total daily calories should come from fat, and not more than 10% should come from saturated fat. For a 2000-kcal daily allowance, this means less than 600 kcal from fat and less than 200 kcal from saturated fat.

Example 17.1 Nutrient Calculations

A single-serving pepperoni pan pizza has 38 g of fat and 780 total calories. (Recall that a food calorie is a kilocalorie.) Estimate the percentage of the total calories from fat. (Further calculations of this sort are found in Chapter 19.)

Solution
First, we calculate the calories from fat. Fat furnishes about 9 kcal/g, so 38 g of fat furnishes

$$38 \text{ g fat} \times \frac{9 \text{ kcal}}{1 \text{ g fat}} = 340 \text{ kcal}$$

Now, we divide the calories from fat by the total calories. Then multiply by 100% to get the percentage (parts per 100).

$$\text{Percentage of calories from fat} = \frac{340 \text{ kcal}}{780 \text{ kcal}} \times 100\% = 44\%$$

This answer is only an estimate for two reasons: The value of 9 kcal/g is approximate, and the 38 g of fat is known only to the nearest gram. A proper answer is <u>about</u> 44%.

■ **EXERCISE 17.1A**
A serving of french fries has 12 g of fat and furnishes 240 kcal. What percentage of the total calories comes from fat?

What percent of one's recommended maximum intake of fats is provided by that single-serving pepperoni pizza and the serving of french fries from the example and exercise above? How many additional grams of fat could one ingest on that day, to remain within those guidelines? Do you think that would be an easy or a difficult goal?

Example 17.2 Fatty Acids

Following are line-angle structures of three fatty acids (see Section 9.1). Each corner and each end of a line is a carbon atom, and each carbon atom is attached to enough hydrogen atoms to give each carbon atom four bonds. **(a)** Which is a saturated fatty acid? **(b)** Which is a monounsaturated fatty acid? **(c)** Which is an omega-3 fatty acid?

I.

II.

III.

Solution

a. Fatty acid II has no carbon-to-carbon double bonds; it is a saturated fatty acid.

b. Fatty acid III has one carbon-to-carbon double bond; it is a monounsaturated fatty acid.

c. Fatty acid I has one of its carbon-to-carbon double bonds three carbons removed from the end farthest from the carboxyl group (the omega end); it is an omega-3 fatty acid.

▪ EXERCISE 17.2A
Which of the fatty acids in Example 17.2 is polyunsaturated?

▪ EXERCISE 17.2B
Is fatty acid III likely to be more similar physiologically to fatty acid II or to fatty acid I? Explain.

SELF-ASSESSMENT Questions

1. Fats are
   a. mixtures of fatty acids
   b. esters of glycerol and fatty acids
   c. esters of cholesterol and fatty acids
   d. polymers of amino acids

2. Among lipoproteins, LDLs are
   a. bad because they can block arteries
   b. the form that carries cholesterol to the liver for processing and excretion
   c. the good form because they can clear arteries
   d. the kind increased by exercise

Questions 3–5 refer to the following structures.
   a. $CH_3(CH_2)_{16}COOH$
   b. $CH_3(CH_2)_5CH\!=\!CH(CH_2)_7COOH$
   c. $CH_3(CH_2)_3(CH_2CH\!=\!CH)_2(CH_2)_7COOH$
   d. $CH_3(CH_2CH\!=\!CH)_3(CH_2)_7COOH$

3. Which is a monounsaturated fatty acid?

4. Which is an omega-3 fatty acid?

5. Which is a saturated fatty acid?

6. The general shape of *trans* fatty acid molecules is similar to
   a. cholesterol
   b. disaccharides
   c. omega-3 fatty acids
   d. saturated fatty acids

7. According to most health professionals, what percentages of total calories should the total daily intake of fat and of saturated fat, respectively, not exceed?
   a. 30, 15   b. 10, 30
   c. 30, 10   d. 60, 20

17.3 Proteins: Muscle and Much More

Learning Objectives ❯ List the essential amino acids, and explain why we need proteins. ❯ Describe some protein deficiency diseases and their causes.

As we saw in Chapter 16, proteins are copolymers of amino acids. A gene carries the blueprint for a specific protein, and each protein serves a particular purpose. We require protein in our diet to provide the amino acids needed to make muscles, hair, enzymes, and many other cellular components vital to life. Proteins are mainly found in meats, poultry, fish, and eggs, as well as in moderate amounts in all types of grains, nuts, and beans. Fruits and vegetables contain little protein.

Protein Metabolism: Essential Amino Acids

Proteins are broken down in the digestive tract into their component amino acids.

$$\text{Proteins} + n\ H_2O \xrightarrow{\text{Proteases}} \text{Amino acids}$$

From these amino acids, our bodies synthesize proteins for growth and repair of tissues. When a diet contains more protein than is needed for the body's growth and repair, the excess protein is used as a source of energy, providing about 4 kcal per gram.

The adult human body can synthesize all but nine of the amino acids needed for making proteins. These nine are called **essential amino acids**—isoleucine, lysine, phenylalanine, tryptophan, leucine, methionine, threonine, arginine, and valine (see Table 16.3 for structures)—and must be included in our diet. Each of the

Vegetarian Diets

Green plants trap a small fraction of the energy that reaches them from the sun. They use some of this energy to convert carbon dioxide, water, and mineral nutrients (including nitrates, phosphates, and sulfates) to proteins. Cattle eat plant protein, digest it, and convert a small portion of it to animal protein. It takes 100 g of protein feed to produce 4.7 g of edible beef or veal protein, an efficiency of only 4.7%. People eat this animal protein, digest it, and reassemble some of the amino acids into human protein.

Some of the energy originally transformed by green plants is lost as heat at every step. If people ate the plant protein directly, one highly inefficient step would be skipped. A vegetarian diet conserves energy. Pork production, at a protein conversion efficiency of 12.1%, and chicken or turkey production (at 18.2%) are more efficient than beef production. Milk production (22.7%) and egg production (23.3%) are still more efficient but do not compare well with eating plant protein directly.

Vegetarians generally are less likely than meat eaters to have high blood pressure. Vegetarian diets that are low in saturated fat can help us avoid or even reverse coronary artery disease. These diets also offer protection from some other diseases. However, although complete proteins can be obtained by eating a carefully selected mixture of vegetable foods, total (*vegan*) vegetarianism can be dangerous, especially for young children. Even when the diet includes a wide variety of plant materials, an all-vegetable diet is usually short in several nutrients, including vitamin B_{12} (a nutrient not found in plants), calcium, iron, riboflavin, and vitamin D (required by children not exposed to sunlight). A modified vegetarian (*lacto-ovo*) diet that includes eggs, milk, and milk products without red meat can provide excellent nutrition.

A variety of traditional dishes supply relatively good protein by combining foods from plant sources, usually a cereal grain with a legume (beans, peas, peanuts, and so on). The grain is deficient in tryptophan and lysine, but it has sufficient methionine. The legume is deficient in methionine, but it has enough tryptophan and lysine. A few such combinations are listed in Table 17.2. Peanut butter sandwiches are a popular American example of a legume–cereal grain combination.

Table 17.2 Traditional Foods That Combine a Cereal Grain with a Legume

Group	Food (Cereal listed first)
Mexican	Corn tortillas and beans
Japanese	Rice and soybean curd (tofu)
English working class	Toasted bread with baked beans
Native American	Corn and beans (succotash)
Western African	Rice and peanuts (groundnuts)
Cajun (Louisiana)	Rice and red beans
Middle Eastern	Pita bread and hummus

essential amino acids is a **limiting reactant** in protein synthesis. When the body is deficient in one of them, it can't make proper proteins.

An *adequate* (or *complete*) *protein* supplies all the essential amino acids in the quantities needed for the growth and repair of body tissues. Most proteins from animal sources contain all the essential amino acids in adequate amounts. Lean meat, milk, fish, eggs, and cheese supply adequate protein. Gelatin, a component of jellied candies and desserts, is one of the few inadequate animal proteins. It contains almost no tryptophan and has only small amounts of threonine, methionine, and isoleucine.

In contrast, most plant proteins are deficient in one or more amino acids. Corn has insufficient lysine and tryptophan, and people who subsist chiefly on corn may suffer from malnutrition, even though they get adequate calories. Pearl millet, a food staple for many who live in India and sub-Saharan Africa, has an excellent amino acid profile, with more lysine than corn. Even soy protein, one of the best nonanimal proteins, is deficient in the essential amino acid methionine. Quinoa, consumed mainly in South America, but becoming more popular in the United States, is the only grain that contains complete protein. Quinoa has no gluten and is an alternative to wheat for those who require a gluten-free diet.

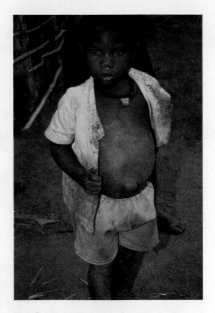

▲ **Figure 17.8** An extreme lack of proteins and vitamins causes a deficiency disease called *kwashiorkor*. The symptoms include retarded growth, discoloration of skin and hair, bloating, a swollen belly, and mental apathy.

Protein Deficiency in Young and Old

Our daily requirement for protein is about 0.8 g per kilogram of body weight. Diets with inadequate protein are common in some parts of the world. A protein-deficiency disease called *kwashiorkor* (Figure 17.8) is rare in developed countries but is common during times of famine in areas of the world where grains with incomplete protein are the only food staple available. In the United States, protein deficiency occurs mainly among elderly persons in nursing homes.

Nutrition is especially important during a child's early years. This is readily apparent from the fact that the human brain reaches nearly full size by the age of two. Early protein deficiency leads to both physical and mental retardation.

SELF-ASSESSMENT Questions

1. Gram for gram, protein foods provide the same number of kilocalories as
   a. fats
   b. vitamins
   c. fatty acids
   d. carbohydrates

2. Proteins are copolymers of
   a. amino acids
   b. fatty acids
   c. monosaccharides
   d. peptides

3. An essential amino acid is one that
   a. has more calories than other amino acids
   b. is needed in greater quantities than some others
   c. is synthesized in the body
   d. must be included in the diet

4. Which of the following foods do NOT furnish complete protein?
   a. brown rice and beans
   b. eggs
   c. peanuts
   d. quinoa

5. The daily protein requirement for a 65-kg female is
   a. 0.8 g
   b. 52 g
   c. 65 g
   d. 100 g

6. One can get complete protein by eating whole-wheat bread with
   a. butter
   b. jelly
   c. peanut butter
   d. corn chips

7. Strict vegetarian diets are often deficient in
   a. B vitamins and vitamin C
   b. magnesium and folic acid
   c. vitamin B_{12} and iron
   d. vitamin B_{12} and folic acid

Answers: 1, d; 2, a; 3, d; 4, c; 5, b; 6, c; 7, c

17.4 Minerals, Vitamins, and Other Essentials

Learning Objective ⟩ Identify the vitamins and the bulk dietary minerals, and state their functions.

In addition to the three major foodstuffs—carbohydrates, fats, and proteins—humans require a variety of minerals and vitamins for good nutrition. We also need dietary fiber and adequate water. According to the World Health Organization (WHO), one of every three people in developing countries is affected by mineral and vitamin deficiencies. Let's consider some of the most important minerals and vitamins.

Dietary Minerals

Thirty elements, listed in Table 17.3, are known to be essential to one or more living organisms. Among these are six elements found in organic compounds such as carbohydrates, fats, and proteins, as well as water, which is about two-thirds the weight of the human body. The other elements in the table, called **dietary minerals**, are vital to life. They exist primarily in the form of charged particles (ions), not as solid, neutral metallic elements. Minerals represent about 4% of the weight of the human body, the main ones being calcium and phosphorus. The 19 trace elements include iron, copper, zinc, and 16 others called *ultratrace elements*.

Minerals serve a variety of functions; that of iodine is quite dramatic. According to WHO, 740 million people suffer from iodine deficiency, and 50 million of them have some degree of mental impairment. A small amount of iodine is necessary for proper thyroid function; 0.15 mg of iodine is recommended for adults per day. Greater deficiencies have dire effects, of which goiter is perhaps the best known (Figure 17.9). Pregnant women deficient in iodine can experience stillbirths or spontaneous abortions or have babies with congenital abnormalities. Iodine is available naturally in seafood, but to guard against iodine deficiency, a small amount of potassium iodide (KI) is often added to table salt. "Iodized" salt was first put on the market in the United States in 1924. Many countries have put forth effort to increase the consumption of iodine among their populations.

Iron(II) ions (Fe^{2+}) are necessary for proper functioning of the oxygen-transporting compound hemoglobin. Without sufficient iron, the oxygen supply to body tissues is reduced, and anemia, a general weakening of the body, results. According to WHO, more than 30% of people worldwide, but especially in developing countries, suffer from anemia, which is often made worse by malaria and parasitic

▲ **Figure 17.9** A person with goiter. The swollen thyroid gland in the neck results from a dietary deficiency of the trace element iodine.

Table 17.3	Elements Essential to Life				
Element	Symbol	Form Used	Element	Symbol	Form Used
Bulk Structural Elements			**Ultratrace Elements**		
Hydrogen	H	Covalent	Manganese	Mn	Mn^{2+}
Carbon	C	Covalent	Molybdenum	Mo	Mo^{2+}
Oxygen	O	Covalent	Chromium	Cr	?
Nitrogen	N	Covalent	Cobalt	Co	Co^{2+}
Phosphorus[a]	P	Covalent	Vanadium	V	?
Sulfur[a]	S	Covalent	Nickel	Ni	Ni^{2+}
			Cadmium	Cd	Cd^{2+}
Macrominerals			Tin	Sn	Sn^{2+}
Sodium	Na	Na^+	Lead	Pb	Pb^{2+}
Potassium	K	K^+	Lithium	Li	Li^+
Calcium	Ca	Ca^{2+}	Fluorine	F	F^-
Magnesium	Mg	Mg^{2+}	Iodine	I	I^-
Chlorine	Cl	Cl^-	Selenium	Se	SeO_4^{2-}?
Phosphorus[a]	P	$H_2PO_4^-$	Silicon	Si	?
Sulfur[a]	S	SO_4^{2-}	Arsenic	As	?
			Boron	B	H_3BO_3
Trace Elements					
Iron	Fe	Fe^{2+}			
Copper	Cu	Cu^{2+}			
Zinc	Zn	Zn^{2+}			

[a]Note that phosphorus and sulfur each appear twice; they are structural elements and are also components of the macrominerals phosphate and sulfate.

↑ It DOES Matter!

Iron is an example of a substance that can be both essential and toxic. The National Institutes of Health recommend a daily intake of 8 mg for adult males and 18 mg for adult females but also point out that a 200-mg dose of iron in children can cause death.

4. The doctor said my mother should cut her salt intake. Why?

A low-sodium diet (no more than 1500 mg per day) is often recommended for anyone suffering from high blood pressure and for people whose family history includes early heart attack or stroke. Your mother may be at risk for kidney stones, and lowering sodium intake may avoid the use of prescription medication. In brief, it is better healthwise to cut salt.

5. Are large doses of vitamins beneficial?

Although there is some evidence that large doses of antioxidants such as vitamin C may have beneficial effects, "megadoses" of most vitamins have not generally been shown to have any significant benefit. In fact, some of the fat-soluble vitamins are toxic in large amounts. There are well-documented examples of polar explorers who suffered poisoning from eating the livers of polar bears or seals, which contain extremely high levels of vitamin A.

worm infections. Foods especially rich in iron compounds include red meat and liver. It appears that most adult males need very little dietary iron because iron is retained by the body, but most women need higher amounts because of loss of blood monthly. Iron "dust" is added to many dry cereals so that the body can digest it more efficiently, compared to iron compounds found in iron supplements.

Calcium and phosphorus are necessary for the proper development of bones and teeth. Growing children need about 1.5 g of each of these minerals each day, which they can get from milk or milk products. The calcium and phosphorus needs of adults are less precisely known but are as real. For example, calcium ions are necessary for the coagulation of blood (to stop bleeding) and for maintenance of the rhythm of the heartbeat. Phosphorus occurs in phosphate units in adenosine triphosphate (ATP), the "energy currency" of the body. Phosphorus is necessary for the body to obtain, store, and use energy from foods. In phosphate units, phosphorus is also an important part of the backbone of the DNA and RNA chains (Section 16.6). Osteoporosis is an increasing problem among older women, who should continue to consume milk products throughout their lifetime.

Sodium ions and chloride ions make up sodium chloride (salt). In moderate amounts, salt is essential to life. The sodium ions are important to the exchange of fluids between cells and plasma, so excess salt increases water retention. A high volume of retained fluids can cause swelling (called "edema") and high blood pressure (hypertension). About 65 million people in the United States suffer from hypertension, the leading risk factor for stroke, heart attack, kidney failure, and heart failure. Antihypertensives are among the most widely prescribed drugs in the United States, one reason being that we consume too much salt.

Most Americans eat far more than the recommended 1500 mg of salt per day, and it is not from the salt shaker on everyone's kitchen table. Convenience foods often contain an astonishingly high concentration of sodium. Canned soups, vegetables, and pasta dishes, as well as rice mixtures and instant noodles, all contain a large amount of salt. Most recently, sodium has been implicated in the creation of kidney stones, since it is involved in the sodium/calcium "pump" in the kidneys. Too much sodium results in the retention of too much calcium in the kidneys, which can form kidney stones. Fortunately many convenience food manufacturers are now offering "no salt added" options for the consumer.

Iron, copper, zinc, cobalt, manganese, molybdenum, calcium, and magnesium are *cofactors* (Section 16.5) essential to the proper functioning of many life-sustaining enzymes. Copper, for example, is involved in the production of melanin, the pigment in skin and hair. Cobalt is in the center of the large vitamin B-12 molecule, nicknamed "cobalamine" because of the presence of that metal ion in the vitamin. A great deal remains to be learned about the role of inorganic chemicals in our bodies. Bioinorganic chemistry is a flourishing area of research.

The Vitamins: Vital, but Not All Are Amines

Why were British sailors called "limeys"? And what does this term have to do with food? Sailors on long voyages had been plagued since early times by *scurvy*. In 1747, Scottish navy surgeon James Lind showed that this disease could be prevented by including fresh fruit and vegetables in the diet. Fresh fruits that could conveniently be carried on long voyages were limes, lemons, and oranges. British ships put to sea with barrels of limes aboard, and sailors ate a lime or two every day.

In 1897, the Dutch scientist Christiaan Eijkman showed that polished rice lacked something found in the hull of whole-grain rice. Lack of that substance caused the disease *beriberi*, which was a serious problem in the Dutch East Indies (modern Indonesia) at that time. A British scientist, F. G. Hopkins, found that rats fed a synthetic diet of carbohydrates, fats, proteins, and minerals were unable to sustain healthy growth. Again, something was missing.

In 1912, Casimir Funk, a Polish biochemist, coined the word *vitamines* (from the Latin word *vita*, meaning "life") for these missing factors. Funk thought all these factors contained an amine group. In the United States, the final *e* was dropped after it was found that not all the factors were amines. The generic term became *vitamin*. Eijkman and Hopkins shared the 1929 Nobel Prize in Physiology or Medicine for their discoveries relating to vitamins.

Vitamins are specific organic compounds that are required in the diet (in addition to the usual proteins, fats, carbohydrates, and minerals) to prevent specific diseases. Some vitamins, along with their sources and deficiency symptoms, are listed in Table 17.4. The role of vitamins in the prevention of deficiency diseases, such as those shown in Figure 17.10, has been well established.

Vitamins do not share a common chemical structure. They can, however, be divided into two broad categories: *fat-soluble vitamins* (A, D, E, and K) and *water-soluble vitamins* (B vitamins and vitamin C). The fat-soluble vitamins incorporate a high proportion of hydrocarbon parts. They contain one or two oxygen atoms but are only slightly polar as a whole.

(a)

Retinol

Vitamin D₂ (calciferol)

Fat-soluble vitamins

Fat-soluble vitamins dissolve in the fatty tissue of the body, where reserves can be stored for future use. An adult can store months' or even years' supply of vitamin A. If the diet becomes deficient in vitamin A, these reserves are mobilized, and the adult remains free of the deficiency disease for quite a while. However, a small child who has not built up a store of the vitamin soon exhibits deficiency symptoms. WHO estimates that more than 100 million children in developing countries are deficient in vitamin A, and a quarter million to a half million become blind each year. Half the blinded children die within a year.

Because they are efficiently stored in the body, overdoses of fat-soluble vitamins can have adverse effects, although these are rarely encountered. Large excesses of vitamin A cause irritability, dry skin, and a feeling of pressure inside the head. Too much vitamin D can cause pain in the bones, hard deposits in the joints, nausea, diarrhea, and weight loss. Vitamins E and K are also fat soluble, but they are metabolized and excreted. They are not stored to the extent that vitamins A and D are, and excess intake seldom causes problems.

The body has a limited capacity to store water-soluble vitamins (the B-complex and vitamin C, ascorbic acid), since the human body will excrete anything over the amount that can be used immediately. Water-soluble vitamins are needed frequently, every day or so. Some foods lose their vitamin content when they are cooked in water and then drained. The water-soluble vitamins go down the drain with the water.

(b)

▲ **Figure 17.10** (a) Softened bones characterize rickets, caused by vitamin D deficiency. (b) Inflammation and abnormal pigmentation characterize pellagra, caused by niacin deficiency.

Ascorbic acid

Nicotinic acid

Nicotinamide

Water-soluble vitamins (sites for hydrogen bonding in color)

Many skin creams and lotions contain added vitamin C or vitamin E. Vitamin E has been demonstrated to accelerate healing of wounds and surgical incisions, as well as very dry and inflamed skin. The addition of vitamin C has not been proved to be beneficial in skin creams, but vitamin C seems to help the body fight off infections and may help prevent cataracts.

Table 17.4 | Some of the Vitamins

Vitamin[a]	Name	Sources	Deficiency disease or conditions
Fat-Soluble Vitamins			
A	Retinol	Fish, liver, eggs, butter, cheese; also (as β-carotene, a vitamin precursor) in carrots and other orange or red vegetables	Blindness in children; night blindness in adults
D_2	Calciferol	Cod liver oil, mushrooms, irradiated ergosterol (milk supplement)	Soft bones: Rickets (children), osteomalacia (adults)
E	α-Tocopherol	Wheat germ oil, green vegetables, egg yolks, meat	Sterility, muscular dystrophy
K_1	Phylloquinone	Spinach, other green leafy vegetables	Hemorrhage
Water-Soluble Vitamins			
B_1	Thiamine	Germ of cereal grains, legumes, nuts, milk, and brewer's yeast	Beriberi—polyneuritis resulting in muscle paralysis, enlargement of heart, and ultimately heart failure
B_2	Riboflavin	Milk, red meat, liver, egg white, green vegetables, whole wheat flour (or fortified white flour), and fish	Dermatitis, glossitis (tongue inflammation)
B_3	Niacin	Red meat, liver, collards, turnip greens, yeast, and tomato juice	Pellagra—skin lesions, swollen and discolored tongue, loss of appetite, diarrhea, and various mental disorders (Figure 17.10)
B_6	Pyridoxine	Eggs, liver, yeast, peas, beans, and milk	Dermatitis, apathy, irritability, and increased susceptibility to infections; convulsions in infants
B_9	Folic acid	Liver, kidney, mushrooms, yeast, and green leafy vegetables	Anemias (folic acid is used to treat megaloblastic anemia, a condition characterized by giant red blood cells); neural tube defects in fetuses of deficient mothers
B_{12}	Cyanocobalamin	Liver, meat, eggs, and fish (not found in plants)	Pernicious anemia
C	Ascorbic acid	Citrus fruits, tomatoes, green peppers, broccoli, strawberries	Scurvy

[a]Some vitamins exist in more than one chemical form. We name a common form of each here.

Other Essentials: Fiber and Water

We need carbohydrates, proteins, fats, minerals, and vitamins in our diets, but some other items are also important. One is *fiber*; another is *water*.

Dietary fiber may be soluble or insoluble. Insoluble fiber is usually cellulose; soluble fiber generally consists of sticky materials called *gums* and *pectins*, often used for gelling, thickening, and stabilizing foods such as jams, jellies, and dairy products such as yogurt. High-fiber diets prevent constipation and are an aid to dieters. Fiber has no calories because the body doesn't absorb it. Therefore, high-fiber foods such as fruits and vegetables are low in fat and often low in calories. Fiber takes up space in the stomach, making us feel full and, therefore, eat less food. Soluble fiber lowers cholesterol levels, perhaps by removing bile acids that digest fat. It may also help control blood sugar by delaying the emptying of the stomach, thus slowing sugar absorption after a meal. This may reduce the amount of insulin needed by a diabetic. These properties make dietary fiber beneficial to people with high blood pressure, diabetes, heart disease, and diverticulitis.

Many of the foods we eat are mainly water. It should come as no surprise that tomatoes are 90% water or that melons, oranges, and grapes are largely water. But water is one of the main ingredients in practically all foods, from roast beef and seafood to potatoes and onions.

In addition to the water we get in our food, we need to drink about 1.0–1.5 L of water each day. Some urologists recommend drinking 2.0 L of water per day. We could satisfy this need by drinking plain water, but we often choose other beverages—milk, coffee, tea, and soft drinks. One problem with counting coffee and soft drinks as part of your water intake is that caffeine is a diuretic when consumed in large amounts. Studies have shown that only one cup of coffee or one soft drink has little effect on urination volumes. Bottled water containing added vitamins and minerals is becoming quite popular, but should not be a substitute for fresh fruits and vegetables.

Many people also drink beverages that contain ethanol, made by fermenting grains or fruit juices. Beer is usually made from malted barley, and wine from grape juice. Even these alcoholic beverages are mainly water, but they should not be considered "nutrients." Fruit juices and plain water are better alternatives. Water as an essential part of what we consume on a daily basis is discussed further in Chapter 19.

It's a Drug! No, It's a Food! No, It's … a Dietary Supplement!

Almost every day, we see advertisements for products that claim to promote rapid weight loss, improve stamina, aid memory, or provide other seemingly miraculous benefits. (There are thousands of such products; see Collaborative Group Project 5 for some examples.) Although these products may appear to act as drugs, many are not classified as such. Legally, they are *dietary supplements*.

The Dietary Supplement Health and Education Act, enacted by the U.S. Congress in 1994, changed the law so that dietary supplements became regulated as foods, not as drugs. Manufacturers are permitted to describe some specific benefits that may be attributed to use of a supplement. However, they must also include a disclaimer, such as: "This statement has not been evaluated by the Food and Drug Administration. This product is not intended to diagnose, treat, cure, or prevent any disease."

Some supplements are simply combinations of various vitamins. Others contain minerals, amino acids, other nutrients, herbs or other plant materials, or extracts of animal or plant origin. Should you take a particular supplement? Maybe, maybe not. A supplement containing omega-3 oils might well aid in reducing LDL cholesterol. But a tablespoon a day of a special preparation of vitamins and minerals is not likely to reverse the effects of aging, no matter how brightly colored the bottle, or how attractive the person in the advertisement. In considering the use of a dietary supplement, using the FLaReS principles to evaluate the manufacturer's claims is certainly recommended.

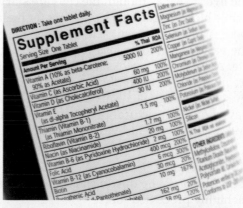

▲ Most dietary supplements do not go through the rigorous testing that is required by law for all prescription drugs and over-the-counter drugs.

SELF-ASSESSMENT Questions

1. About what percentage of our body weight is minerals?
   a. 1%   **b.** 4%   **c.** 10%   **d.** 20%

2. Vitamins are
   a. a class of compounds with an amine group in the structure
   b. most effective when taken as supplements
   c. specific organic compounds required in the diet to prevent diseases
   d. vital (essential) amines

3. A deficiency of iodine may be remedied by
   a. including a greater percentage of seafood in the diet
   b. consuming less salt
   c. eating more fruits and vegetables
   d. using a vitamin supplement

4. Iron in red blood cells is part of the
   a. cytochromes   **b.** hemoglobin
   c. myoglobin   **d.** plasma

5. Iron is swiftly depleted from the body by
   a. weight loss   **b.** energetic exercise
   c. inactivity   **d.** blood loss

6. Most of the calcium and phosphorus in the body is in the
   a. blood   **b.** bones and teeth
   c. liver   **d.** muscle tissue

7. People with high blood pressure are usually told to restrict intake of
   a. Ca^{2+} **b.** Mg^{2+} **c.** Na^+ **d.** SO_4^{2-}

8. The fat-soluble vitamins are vitamins A, D, E and
   a. B_{12} **b.** folic acid
   c. ascorbic acid   **d.** vitamin K

9. Eating foods high in fiber
   a. can cause constipation   **b.** helps build muscle
   c. helps to fill you up   **d.** provides quick energy

Answers: 1. b; 2. c; 3. a; 4. b; 5. d; 6. b; 7. c; 8. d; 9. c

17.5 Starvation, Fasting, and Malnutrition

Learning Objective ＞ Describe the effects of starvation, fasting, and malnutrition.

Weight loss through diet and exercise is discussed in Chapter 19.

When totally deprived of food, whether voluntarily or involuntarily, the human body suffers **starvation**. Involuntary starvation is a serious problem in much of the world. Although starvation is seldom the sole cause of death, those weakened by malnutrition succumb readily to disease. Even a seemingly minor disease, such as measles, can become life threatening.

Metabolic changes like those that accompany starvation also occur during fasting. During total fasting, the body's glycogen stores are depleted in less than a day and the body calls on its fat reserves. Fat is first taken from around the kidneys and the heart. Then it is removed from other parts of the body, eventually even from the bone marrow.

Increased dependence on stored fats as an energy source leads to *ketosis,* a condition characterized by the appearance of compounds called *ketone bodies* in the blood and urine (Figure 17.11). Ketosis rapidly develops into *acidosis;* the blood pH drops, and oxygen transport is hindered. Oxygen deprivation leads to depression and lethargy.

Acidosis is also associated with the insulin-deficiency disease diabetes. Insulin enables the body's cells to take up glucose from the bloodstream. A lack of insulin causes the liver to act as though the cells are starving, and they start burning fat for energy while blood sugar levels rise. This fat metabolism leads to the production of ketone bodies and subsequent acidosis. (See the essay on diabetes in Section 18.5.)

In the early stages of a *total* fast, body protein is metabolized at a relatively rapid rate. After several weeks, the rate of protein breakdown slows considerably as the brain adjusts to using the breakdown products of fatty acid metabolism for its energy source. When fat reserves are substantially depleted, the body must again draw heavily on its structural proteins for its energy requirements. The emaciated appearance of a starving individual is due to the depletion of muscle proteins.

Processed Food: Less Nutrition

Malnutrition need not be due to starvation or dieting. It can be the result of eating too much highly processed food.

Whole wheat is an excellent source of vitamin B_1 and other vitamins. To make white flour, the wheat germ and bran are removed from the grain. This greatly increases the storage life of the flour, but the remaining material has few minerals

$$CH_3-\overset{\overset{\displaystyle O}{\|}}{C}-CH_3$$
Acetone

$$CH_3-\overset{\overset{\displaystyle O}{\|}}{C}-CH_2-\overset{\overset{\displaystyle O}{\|}}{C}-OH$$
Acetoacetic acid

$$CH_3-\overset{\overset{\displaystyle OH}{|}}{CH}-CH_2-\overset{\overset{\displaystyle O}{\|}}{C}-OH$$
β-Hydroxybutyric acid

▲ **Figure 17.11** The three ketone bodies produced in fat metabolism.

Q: *Identify the functional groups in each of the compounds. Which ketone body is not a ketone?*

or vitamins and little fiber. We eat the starch and use much of the germ and bran for animal food. Cattle and hogs often get better nutrition than we do. Similarly, polished rice has had most of its protein and minerals removed, and it has almost no vitamins. The disease beriberi became prevalent when polished rice was introduced into Southeast Asia.

When many fruits and vegetables are peeled, they lose most of their vitamins, minerals, and fiber. The heat used to cook food also destroys some vitamins. If water is used in cooking, some of the water-soluble vitamins (vitamin C and B vitamins) and some of the minerals are often drained off and discarded with the water.

It is estimated that 90% of the food budget of an average family in the United States goes to buy processed foods. A diet of hamburgers, potato chips, and soft drinks is lacking in many essential nutrients. Highly processed convenience foods are making many people in developed nations obese but poorly nourished despite their abundance of food.

SELF-ASSESSMENT Questions

1. During fasting or starvation, glycogen stores are depleted in about
   a. 1 hour **b.** 1 day **c.** 1 week **d.** 1 month

2. After glycogen stores are depleted, the body draws on its reserves of
   a. amino acids **b.** fat **c.** glycogen **d.** protein

3. When fat reserves have been used up, the body uses for its energy source
   a. adipose tissue **b.** amino acid reserves
   c. glycogen stores **d.** structural proteins

4. The average family in the United States spends what portion of its food budget on fresh fruits and vegetables, meats, and dairy products?
   a. 10% **b.** 25%
   c. 50% **d.** 90%

Answers: 1, b; 2, b; 3, d; 4, a

17.6 Flavorings: Spicy and Sweet

Learning Objective ❭ Appreciate the historic impact of our desire for a variety of flavors and aromas, and of our search for sugar substitutes.

The search for new flavors to enhance food has changed human history. One well-known example is that Christopher Columbus was sent west with three small ships at considerable expense by the Queen of Spain over five hundred years ago in an attempt to find a shorter route to East Asia to enhance the spice trade.

Spices, Herbs, and Flavorings

Spice cake, soft drinks, gingerbread, sausage, and many other foods depend on spices and other additives for most of their flavor. Cloves, for example, contain a unique molecule called eugenol that contributes to the captivating smell of a roast ham. Cinnamon, used on toast and in apple pie, contains an ester called, appropriately, cinnamaldehyde. Ginger, turmeric, and nutmeg are examples of natural spices that come from the seeds, roots, or bark of those plants. Basil, marjoram, thyme, and rosemary are widely used herbs. Natural flavors are also extracted from fruits and other plant materials.

Some compounds that serve as flavors are listed in Table 9.7. Other flavor compounds are shown in Figure 17.12. Chemists can analyze natural flavors and then synthesize components and make mixtures that resemble those flavors. Major components of natural and artificial flavors are often identical. For example, both vanilla extract and imitation vanilla owe their flavor mainly to a compound called vanillin. The natural flavor is often more complex because vanilla extract contains a wider variety of chemicals than imitation vanilla does. Flavor additives, whether natural or synthetic, probably present little hazard when used in moderation, and they contribute considerably to our enjoyment of food.

Methyl anthranilate
(Grape flavoring)

Diallyl disulfide
(Oil of garlic)
$CH_2=CHCH_2SSCH_2CH=CH_2$

Benzaldehyde
(Oil of bitter almond)

Vanillin
(Vanilla)

Eugenol
(Oil of cloves)

Menthol   Menthone

Oil of peppermint

Cinnamaldehyde
(Oil of cinnamon)

▲ **Figure 17.12** Some molecular flavorings. See Table 9.7 for others.

Q: *Which of the compounds shown here have aldehyde functional groups? Which are phenols? Ethers? Alkenes? Which is an ester? A ketone? An alcohol?*

6. What's the difference between natural and artificial sweeteners?

Except for sucralose, which structurally looks very much like sucrose, but with chlorine atoms substituted for some OH groups, the molecules that are commonly used as artificial sweeteners are completely different from natural sugars. Why they seem to taste "sweet" is somewhat of a mystery. Many people say that some artificial sweeteners have a bitter aftertaste, which may be due to the -NH$_2$ groups on the molecule. We do know that artificial sweeteners have almost no calories.

Table 17.5	Relative Sweetness Sweetness of Some of Some Compounds
Compound	Sweetness[a]
Lactose	0.16
Maltose	0.33
Glucose	0.74
Sucrose	1.00
Fructose	1.73
Steviol glycoside	30
Cyclamate	45
Aspartame	180
Acesulfame K	200
Saccharin	300
Sucralose	600
Neotame	13,000

[a]Sweetness is relative to sucrose at a value of 1.

Other Natural and Artificial Sweeteners

Obesity is a major problem in most developed countries. Presumably, people could reduce their intake of calories by replacing sugars with noncaloric sweeteners, but there is little evidence that artificial sweeteners are of value in controlling obesity, since people tend to eat more of other foods when consuming "diet" soft drinks.

A natural product of note is *stevia*, a South American herb long used as a sweetener by the Guarani Indians of Paraguay. Leaves of this herb (*Stevia rebaudiana*) contain glycosides that provide a sweetness at least 30 times that of sucrose. Stevia, an approved food additive in Japan and South America, is available in the United States in small paper packets (usually green) in grocery stores.

For many years, the major artificial sweeteners were saccharin and cyclamates. Cyclamates were banned in the United States in 1970 after studies showed that they caused cancer in laboratory animals. (Subsequent studies have failed to confirm these findings, but the FDA has not lifted the ban.)

In 1977, saccharin was shown to cause bladder cancer in laboratory animals. However, the move by the FDA to ban it was blocked by Congress because at that time saccharin was the only approved artificial sweetener. Its ban would have meant the end of diet soft drinks and other low-calorie products. Repeated studies did not show the same results as in 1977, so in 2000, warnings disappeared from saccharin packets or products containing saccharin.

There are now five FDA-approved artificial sweeteners (Figure 17.13). *Aspartame* (the methyl ester of the dipeptide aspartylphenylalanine) was approved in 1981. A closely related compound, called *neotame*, has a 3,3-dimethylbutyl group $CH_3C(CH_3)_2CH_2CH_2—$ on the nitrogen atom of the aspartyl unit of the dipeptide. There are anecdotal reports of problems with aspartame, but repeated studies have shown it to be generally safe, except for people with phenylketonuria, an inherited condition in which phenylalanine cannot be metabolized properly. Other artificial sweeteners approved for use in the United States include acesulfame K (Sunette®). and sucralose (Splenda®); these sweeteners can survive the high temperatures of cooking processes, whereas aspartame is broken down by heat. Table 17.5 compares the sweetness of a variety of substances.

What makes a compound sweet? There is little structural similarity among the compounds that taste sweet, so the question remains unanswered. Most bear little resemblance to sugars. Recall from Chapter 16 that sugars are polyhydroxy

Sodium saccharin

Calcium cyclamate

Aspartame

Acesulfame K

Steviol

Sucralose

Neotame

▲ **Figure 17.13** Seven artificial sweeteners. Note that sucralose (Splenda®) is a chlorinated derivative of sucrose. It is the only artificial sweetener actually made from sucrose.

compounds. Like sugars, many compounds with hydroxyl groups on adjacent carbon atoms are sweet. Ethylene glycol ($HOCH_2CH_2OH$) is sweet, although it is quite toxic. Glycerol, obtained from the hydrolysis of fats (Section 17.2), is also sweet and is approved as a food additive. It is used principally as a **humectant** (moistening agent), however, and only incidentally as a sweetener.

Other polyhydroxy alcohols (polyols) used as sweeteners are *sorbitol*, made by the reduction of glucose, and *xylitol*, which has five carbon atoms with a hydroxyl group on each. These compounds occur naturally in foods such as fruits and berries. They are used as sweeteners in sugar-free chewing gums and candies. Unlike sugars, polyols do not cause sudden increases in blood sugar, and thus they can be used in moderation by diabetics. Large amounts—more than about 10 g—can cause gastrointestinal distress.

Several thousand sweet-tasting compounds have been discovered. They belong to more than 150 chemical classes. We now know that all the sweet substances act on a single taste receptor. (In contrast, we have more than 30 receptors for bitter substances.) Unlike other taste receptors, the sweet receptor has more than one area that can be activated by various molecules. The different areas have varying affinities for certain molecules. For example, sucralose fits the receptor more tightly than sucrose does, partly because its chlorine atoms carry more negative charge than the oxygen atoms in the OH groups they replace. Neotame fits the receptor so tightly that it keeps the receptor firing repeatedly.

Flavor Enhancers

Some chemical substances, though not particularly flavorful themselves, are used to enhance other flavors. Common table salt (sodium chloride) is a familiar example. In addition to being a necessary nutrient, salt seems to increase sweetness and helps to mask bitterness and sourness.

Another popular flavor enhancer is monosodium glutamate (MSG). MSG is the sodium salt of glutamic acid, one of the 20 amino acids that occur naturally in proteins. It is used in many convenience foods. Although glutamates are found naturally in proteins, there is evidence that huge excesses can be harmful. MSG can numb portions of the brains of laboratory animals. It may also be *teratogenic*, causing birth defects when eaten in large amounts by women who are pregnant. MSG has been suspected as a cause of headaches in some individuals.

Sorbitol   Xylitol

▲ Polyhydroxy alcohols (polyols) are used to sweeten sugar-free products such as chewing gum. These products aid in control of dental caries because the polyols are metabolized slowly if at all in dental plaque.

Besides the well-known tastes of sweet, sour, and salty, "umami" is a protein-like taste. It is said that MSG stimulates the umami taste sensors in our mouths.

$$HOOC-CH_2CH_2CH-\overset{\overset{\displaystyle O}{\|}}{C}-O^-$$
$$\underset{{}^+NH_3}{}$$

Glutamic acid

$$HOOC-CH_2CH_2CH-\overset{\overset{\displaystyle O}{\|}}{C}-O^-\,Na^+$$
$$\underset{NH_2}{}$$

MSG

SELF-ASSESSMENT Questions

1. Compounds that taste sweet to most people include all the following except:
   a. xylitol   **b.** neotame   **c.** saccharin   **d.** MSG

2. Artificial vanilla
   a. contains exactly the same vanillin molecule as in natural vanilla
   b. contains a molecule different from vanillin but tastes similar to it
   c. contains every type of molecule found in natural vanilla
   d. is enhanced by sugars added to it

3. Organic molecules called esters are
   a. found in every spice
   b. sour or bitter flavorings in foods
   c. unique molecules found in highly aromatic and unique plant seeds or bark
   d. often found in vitamin supplements

4. Artificial sweeteners include all the following except
   a. sucralose
   b. stevia
   c. cyclamate
   d. saccharin

5. MSG
   a. is safe to consume in an amount
   b. is the sodium salt of an amino acid
   c. is a sweetener with a structure similar to sucrose
   d. is safe to consume by those who wish to lower their blood pressure

Answers: 1, d; 2, a; 3, c; 4, b; 5, b

17.7 Other Food Additives: Beneficial or Dangerous?

Learning Objective ⟩ Identify the beneficial additives in foods and those that are somewhat controversial.

More than 3000 substances appear on the FDA's website in a list called "Everything Added to Food in the United States (EAFUS)." Most of the substances listed on a label are **food additives**, substances other than basic foodstuffs that are put into food for various reasons related to production, processing, packaging, or storage. Other substances are added to enhance color and flavor, to retard spoilage, to provide texture, to sanitize, to bleach, to ripen or prevent ripening, to control moisture levels, or to control foaming. Sugar, salt, and corn syrup are used in the greatest amounts. These three, plus citric acid, baking soda, vegetable colors, mustard, and pepper, make up more than 98% (by weight) of all additives.

In the United States, food additives are regulated by the Food and Drug Administration (FDA). The original Food, Drug, and Cosmetic Act was passed by Congress in 1938. Under this act, the FDA had to prove that an additive was unsafe before its use could be prevented. The Food Additives Amendment of 1958 shifted the burden of proof to the food industry. A company that wishes to use a food additive must first furnish proof to the FDA that the additive is safe for the intended use. The FDA can also regulate the quantity of additives that can be used.

Additives to Improve Nutrition

The first nutrient supplement approved by the Bureau of Chemistry (which later became the FDA) of the U.S. Department of Agriculture was potassium iodide (KI), added to table salt in 1924 to reduce the incidence of goiter (recall Figure 17.9).

Several other chemicals are added to foods to prevent deficiency diseases. Addition of vitamin B$_1$ (thiamine) to polished rice is essential in the Far East, where

The GRAS List

Some food additives have been used for many years without apparent harmful effects. In 1958, the U.S. Congress established a list of additives *generally recognized as safe* (GRAS). Many of the substances on the **GRAS** list are familiar spices, flavors, and nutrients. Some of the substances placed on the 1958 list have since been removed, including cyclamate sweeteners and some food colors. Some other substances have been added to the original list. About 7000 substances are now given GRAS status.

Some deficiencies have come to light in the original testing procedures. The FDA has since reevaluated several of them based on new research findings—and greater consumer awareness. Improved instruments and better experimental designs have revealed the possibility of harm, though slight, from some additives previously thought safe. Most of the newer experiments involve feeding massive doses of additives to small laboratory animals, and these studies have been criticized for that reason.

beriberi is still a problem. The replacement of the B vitamins thiamine, riboflavin, folic acid, and niacin (which are removed in processing) and the addition of iron, usually ferrous carbonate ($FeCO_3$), to flour are referred to as **enrichment**. Enriched bread or pasta made from this flour still isn't as nutritious as bread or pasta made from whole wheat. It lacks vitamin B_6, pantothenic acid, zinc, magnesium, and fiber, nutrients usually provided by whole-grain flour. Despite these shortcomings, the enrichment of bread, corn meal, and cereals has almost eliminated pellagra, a disease that once plagued the southern United States.

Vitamin C (ascorbic acid) is frequently added to fruit juices, flavored drinks, and other beverages. Although our diets generally contain enough ascorbic acid to prevent scurvy, some scientists recommend a much larger intake than minimum daily requirements. Vitamin D is added to milk in developed countries, and consumption of fortified milk has led to the almost total elimination of rickets. Similarly, beta-carotene, which changes to vitamin A in the body, is added to margarine so that the substitute more nearly matches butter in nutritional quality since vitamin A occurs naturally in butter.

If we were to eat a balanced diet of fresh foods, we probably wouldn't need nutritional supplements. But many people choose to eat mainly processed foods and convenience foods. If their usual diet is composed mainly of highly processed foods, people may need the nutrients provided by vitamin and mineral food additives.

Additives That Retard Spoilage

Food spoilage can result from the growth of molds, yeasts, or bacteria. Substances that prevent such growth are often called *antimicrobials*, and they include certain carboxylic acids and their salts. Propionic acid and its sodium and calcium salts are used to inhibit molding of bread and cheese. Sorbic acid, benzoic acid, and their salts are also used (Figure 17.14) in some soft drinks and a wide variety of other prepared foods.

Some inorganic compounds can also be added to inhibit spoilage. Sodium nitrite ($NaNO_2$) is used to cure meat and to maintain the pink color of smoked hams, frankfurters, and bologna. It also contributes to the tangy flavor of processed meat products. Nitrites are particularly effective as inhibitors of *Clostridium botulinum*, the bacterium that produces botulism poisoning. However, only about 10% of the amount used to keep meat pink is needed to prevent botulism. Nitrites have been investigated as possible causes of cancer of the stomach. In the presence of the hydrochloric acid (HCl) in the stomach, nitrites are converted to nitrous acid.

$$NaNO_2 + HCl \longrightarrow HNO_2 + NaCl$$

This acid may then react with secondary amines (amines with two alkyl groups on nitrogen) to form *nitroso* compounds.

$$\underset{\text{Nitrous acid}}{H-O-N{=}O} + \underset{\substack{\text{A secondary} \\ \text{amine}}}{R-\overset{\displaystyle R}{\overset{|}{N}}-H} \longrightarrow \underset{\substack{\text{A nitroso} \\ \text{compound}}}{R-\overset{\displaystyle R}{\overset{|}{N}}-N{=}O} + H_2O$$

CH_3CH_2COOH

Propionic acid

$CH_3CH_2COO^- Na^+$

Sodium propionate

$CH_3CH{=}CHCH{=}CHCOOH$

Sorbic acid

$CH_3CH{=}CHCH{=}CHCOO^- K^+$

Potassium sorbate

⬡—COOH

Benzoic acid

⬡—COO⁻ Na⁺

Sodium benzoate

▲ **Figure 17.14** Most spoilage inhibitors are carboxylic acids or salts of carboxylic acids.

The R groups of nitroso compounds can be alkyl groups such as methyl (CH_3—), or ethyl (CH_3CH_2—), or they can be more complex. In any case, these compounds are among the most potent carcinogens known. The rate of stomach cancer is higher in countries where people use prepared meats than in developing nations, where people eat little or no cured meat. However, the incidence of stomach cancer is *decreasing* in the United States, perhaps because ascorbic acid (vitamin C) inhibits the reaction between nitrous acid and amines to form nitrosamines, and many people have orange juice with their breakfast bacon or sausage. Nevertheless, possible problems with nitrites have led the FDA to approve sodium hypophosphite (NaH_2PO_2) as a meat preservative.

Other inorganic food preservatives include sulfur dioxide and sulfite salts. A gas at room temperature, sulfur dioxide (SO_2) serves as a disinfectant and preservative, particularly for dried fruits such as peaches, apricots, and raisins. It is also used as a bleach to prevent the browning of wines, corn syrup, jellies, dehydrated potatoes, and other foods. Sulfur dioxide seems safe for most people when ingested with food, but it is a powerful irritant when inhaled and is a damaging ingredient of polluted air in some areas (Chapter 13). Sulfur dioxide and sulfite salts cause severe allergic reactions in some people. The FDA requires food labels to indicate the presence of these compounds in a food.

Antioxidants: BHA and BHT

One class of preservatives is composed of **antioxidants**, which inhibit the chemical spoilage of food that occurs in the presence of oxygen. A good example of chemical spoilage is a cut apple turning brown within a short time when exposed to air. Antioxidants are added to foods (or their packaging) to prevent fats and oils from forming rancid products that make foods unpalatable. Antioxidants also minimize the destruction of some essential amino acids and vitamins. Packaged foods that contain fats or oils (such as bread, potato chips, sausage, and breakfast cereal) often have antioxidants added. Compounds commonly used as antioxidants include butylated hydroxytoluene (BHT), butylated hydroxyanisole (BHA), propyl gallate, and *tert*-butylhydroquinone (Figure 17.15).

Fats turn rancid, in part as a result of oxidation, a process that occurs through the formation of molecular fragments called **free radicals**, which have an unpaired electron as a distinguishing feature. (Recall from Section 4.6 that covalent bonds are shared *pairs* of electrons.) Without specifying the structures of radicals, we can summarize the process. First, a fat molecule reacts with oxygen to form a free radical.

$$\text{Fat} + O_2 \longrightarrow \text{Free radical}$$

The radical then reacts with another fat molecule to form a new free radical that can repeat the process. A reaction such as this, in which intermediates are formed that keep the reaction going, is called a **chain reaction**. One molecule of oxygen can lead to the decomposition of many fat molecules.

To preserve foods containing fats, processors package the products to exclude air. However, it cannot be excluded completely, so chemical antioxidants such as BHT are used to stop the chain reaction by reacting with the free radicals.

▲ **Figure 17.15** Four common antioxidants. BHA is a mixture of two isomers.

Q: *What functional group is common to all four compounds? What other functional group is present in BHA? In propyl gallate?*

$$Rad\cdot \; + \; H\!:\!O\!-\!\langle\text{ring}\rangle\!-\!CH_3 \; \longrightarrow \; Rad\!:\!H \; + \; \cdot O\!-\!\langle\text{ring}\rangle\!-\!CH_3$$

(ring substituents: $C(CH_3)_3$ top and bottom on both structures)

BHT

The new radical formed from BHT is rather stable. The unpaired electron doesn't have to stay on the oxygen atom but can move around in the electron cloud of the benzene ring. The BHT radical doesn't react with fat molecules, and the chain is broken.

Why are the butyl groups important? Without them, two phenol molecules (Section 9.5) would simply couple when exposed to an oxidizing agent.

$$2 \;\langle\text{phenol}\rangle \xrightarrow{\text{oxidation}} \langle\text{coupled biphenyl}\rangle$$

With the bulky butyl groups attached, the rings can't get close enough together for coupling. They are free, then, to trap free radicals formed by the oxidation of fats.

Many food additives have been criticized as being harmful, and BHA and BHT are no exceptions. They have been reported to cause allergic reactions in some people. In one study, pregnant mice fed diets containing 0.5% BHA or BHT gave birth to offspring with brain abnormalities. On the other hand, when relatively large amounts of BHT were fed to rats daily, their life spans were increased by a human equivalent of 20 years. One theory about aging is that it is caused in part by the formation of free radicals. BHT retards this chemical breakdown in cells in the same way that it retards spoilage in foods.

BHA and BHT are synthetic chemicals, but antioxidants such as vitamin E and vitamin C occur naturally. Vitamin E (like BHT) is a phenol, with several substituents on the benzene ring. Presumably, its action as an antioxidant is quite similar to that of BHT. However, one recent study suggests that large doses of vitamin E may also be somewhat harmful.

Color Additives

Some foods are naturally colored, especially fruits and vegetables. For example, the yellow compound β-carotene occurs in carrots and is used as a color additive in foods such as butter and margarine. Our bodies convert β-carotene to vitamin A by cutting the molecule in half at the center double bond. Thus, it is a vitamin additive as well as a color additive, especially in margarines.

β-Carotene

Other natural food colors include beet juice, grape-hull extract, and saffron (from autumn-flowering crocus flowers).

We expect many foods to have characteristic colors. To increase the attractiveness and acceptability of its products, the food industry has used synthetic food colors for decades. Since the Food and Drug Act of 1906, the FDA has regulated the use of these chemicals and set limits on their concentrations. But the FDA is not infallible. Some colors once on the approved list were later shown to be harmful and were removed from the list. In 1950, Food, Drug, and Cosmetic (FD&C) Orange No. 1 in pumpkin-colored Halloween candy caused gastrointestinal upsets in several children and was then banned by the FDA.

FD&C blue #1 ("brilliant blue")

FD&C red #40 ("allura red")

FD&C yellow #5 ("tartrazine")

FD&C yellow #6 ("sunset yellow")

FD&C blue #2 ("indigo carmine")

FD&C red #3 ("erythrosine")

FD&C green #3 ("fast green")

▲ **Figure 17.16** Food colorants accepted for use in foods.

In following years, other dyes were banned. FD&C Yellow No. 3 and No. 4 were found to contain small amounts of β-naphthylamine, a carcinogen that causes bladder cancer in laboratory animals. Furthermore, they reacted with stomach acids to produce more β-naphthylamine. FD&C Red No. 2 was also shown to be a weak carcinogen in laboratory animals.

Currently, six artificial colorants are commonly found in foods, including candies, prepared foods such as "mac and cheese," gelatin and pudding mixes, and a surprising number of prepared foods and beverages, such as "orange" flavored soft drinks. The most common colorants include FD&C Red No. 40, Blue No. 1, and Yellow No. 5. Some candies also contain Red No. 3 (pink), Blue No. 2, and Yellow No. 6 (orange). Green No. 3, though approved, is rarely found in foods; some mouthwash products contain that color. The structures of those 7 dyes are shown in Figure 17.16.

Food colors, even those that have been banned, present little risk. They have been used for years with apparent safety and are normally used in tiny amounts. Although the risk is low, the benefit is largely aesthetic. Kids like colorful candies! Any foods that contain artificial colors must say so on the label, so you can avoid them if you want to. If you see the word "lake" on a candy label, it means that the dye is entrapped in an aluminum oxide matrix, so the dyes will not rub off onto skin or clothing as easily.

SELF-ASSESSMENT Questions

1. To use a new food additive, a company must
   a. notify the FDA that it plans to use the additive
   b. pay the FDA to test the additive for safety
   c. provide the FDA with evidence that the additive is safe for the intended use
   d. submit an application to the FDA, but does not have to prove it safe and effective

2. The food additive that inhibits reproduction of botulism-causing bacteria in processed meats, such as bologna, ham, and bacon, is
   a. sodium benzoate
   b. sodium ascorbate
   c. sodium sorbate
   d. sodium nitrite

3. Calcium propionate is added to bread to
   a. act as an antioxidant
   b. enhance the flavor
   c. inhibit mold growth
   d. replace Ca^{2+} removed in processing

4. Antioxidants
   a. aid in lipid transport
   b. aid in oxygen transport
   c. prevent color fading
   d. trap free radicals

5. Which of the following is an antioxidant used to prevent rancidity?
   a. ascorbic acid
   b. BHT
   c. sodium sulfite
   d. sugar

6. The number of colors that have been accepted as safe to use in foods is
   a. 4
   b. 7
   c. 40
   d. well over 100

7. Vitamin C, vitamin E, BHA, BHT, and propyl gallate are
   a. antimicrobial
   b. antioxidants
   c. flavor enhancers
   d. unintentional additives

Answers: 1, c; 2, d; 3, c; 4, d; 5, b; 6, b; 7, b

17.8 Problems with Our Food

Learning Objective > Identify and describe some of the main problems with harmful substances in our food.

People have been trying to deal with poisons in their food for millennia. Early foragers learned—by the painful process of trial and error—that some plants and animals were poisonous. Rhubarb leaves contain toxic oxalic acid. Bruised celery produces *psoralens*, compounds that are powerful mutagens and carcinogens. The Japanese relish a variety of puffer fish that contains deadly poison in its ovaries and liver. Fifty or so Japanese people die each year from improperly prepared puffers.

One of the most toxic substances known is the toxin botulin that is produced by the bacterium *Clostridium botulinum*. This organism grows in improperly canned food. If the food isn't properly sterilized before it is sealed in jars or cans, the microorganism flourishes under anaerobic (without air) conditions. Botulin is so toxic that 1 g of it could kill more than a million people. The point is that a food is not inherently good simply because it is natural. Neither is it necessarily bad because a synthetic chemical substance has been added to it.

Carcinogens

There is little chance that we will suffer acute poisoning from approved food additives. But what about cancer? Could all these chemicals in our food increase our risk of developing cancer? The possibility exists, though the risk is low.

Carcinogens occur naturally in food. A charcoal-broiled steak contains 3,4-benzpyrene, a carcinogen also found in cigarette smoke and automobile exhaust fumes. Cinnamon and nutmeg contain *safrole*, a carcinogen that has been banned as a flavoring in root beer.

3,4-Benzpyrene   Safrole

Oxalic acid

▲ Poisonous oxalic acid is found in rhubarb leaves.

Aflatoxin B₁

Among the most potent carcinogens are **aflatoxins**, compounds produced by molds growing on stored peanuts and grains (Figure 17.17). Aflatoxin B$_1$ is estimated to be 10 million times as potent a carcinogen as saccharin, and there is no way to keep it completely out of our food. The FDA sets a limit of 20 ppb for the maximum level of aflatoxins.

Scientists estimate that our consumption of natural carcinogens is 10,000 times our consumption of synthetic carcinogens. Should we ban steaks, spices, peanuts, and grains because they contain naturally occurring carcinogens? Probably not. The risk is slight, and more serious risks face us in everyday life. Should we ban additives that have been shown to be carcinogenic? Certainly we should carefully weigh the risks against any benefits the additives might provide.

Food Contaminants

Food contamination can come from many sources and can occur at any step between producer and consumer. Pesticide residues, insect parts, hair from food workers, glass from broken containers, and antibiotics added to animal feeds are examples of contaminants. Antibiotics in animal feed are a troubling example of food contamination because they often show up in the meat we eat. Antibiotics are added in low-level dosages to animal feed to promote weight gain. In fact, in 2009, 13.1 million kg of antibiotics were sold for use in animals in the United States. Residues of these antibiotics in meat may result in the sensitization of individuals who eat the meat, thus hastening the development of allergies. Scientists also fear that the use of antibiotics in animal feeds will accelerate the process by which bacteria become drug resistant (Section 18.3).

Today's food contamination problems are usually biological, not chemical. For example, bacteria such as the O157:H7 strain of *Escherichia coli* (*E. coli*), a fecal contaminant sometimes found in raw meat or dairy products and occasionally in raw fruits and vegetables, can cause serious food poisoning. *E. coli* contamination has been responsible for many costly food recalls in recent years. *Salmonella* contamination of poultry, eggs, unprocessed milk, meat, or water can cause cramping, fever, dehydration, and diarrhea. *Salmonella* is also carried by pet turtles and birds. *Listeria monocytogenes* causes listeriosis, a food-borne illness marked by fever, muscle aches, nausea, and diarrhea.

Viruses such as hepatitis A, which causes a serious contagious disease of the liver, and the Norwalk virus, which causes about 50% of all outbreaks of food-borne gastroenteritis in the United States, can be spread when infected workers handle food products.

Parasites such as the roundworms *Trichinella spiralis*, which causes trichinosis, and *Anisakis simplex*, which causes anisakiasis, are relatively rare problems in

GREEN CHEMISTRY

Katie Privett, *Green Chemistry Centre of Excellence, York, United Kingdom*

The Future of Food Waste – A Green Chemistry Perspective

Learning Objectives > Explain how food supply chain waste can be used as a resource in the chemical industry. > Identify the advantages of using food supply chain waste instead of fossil fuels as a source of chemicals, materials, and fuels.

A study by the United Nations Food and Agriculture Organization discovered that, globally, we generate 1.3 billion metric tons (t) (1 t = 1000 kg) of food waste every year – one-third of all the food we grow. Much of this waste can be avoided by improving the storage and processing of food before it reaches the shelves and by better educating shoppers to minimize post-consumer waste. However, some food waste within the supply chain is simply unavoidable – straw from farms, seafood shells, and citrus peels all are by-products that were never intended for human consumption.

▲ A simple food-waste bin in use.

In most cases, these food supply chain wastes (FSCW) currently go to landfills, where their decomposition affects soil quality, pollutes local water supplies, and releases the potent greenhouse gas methane. With the cost of disposal rising and the social acceptability of landfill sites decreasing, we have to find new ways to deal with this waste.

This is where green chemistry steps in. Green Chemistry Principle 7 states that resources should be renewable whenever technically and economically practicable. FSCW is a great example of an economically viable renewable material – instead of paying landfill taxes and fees to dispose of it as waste, the material can be used as a cheap feedstock for chemical processes. A relatively simple approach to gaining value out of FSCW is to turn it into a fuel. Anaerobic digestion is a technique that allows mixed biomass waste to be converted through microbial processes into a fuel and a fertilizer. Both of these products can replace alternatives derived from fossil fuels. However, these are relatively low-value products, and the efficiency of the process has to be very high to match the prices offered by the well-developed fossil-fuel industry.

When particular types of supply chain wastes are concentrated, such as agricultural wastes at large farms, citrus peels at juicing plants, and spent grains at breweries, it can become technically practicable to collect and process them at large scales. Such concentrated wastes contain many higher-value chemical compounds that have industrial uses and that can be extracted economically.

One example of an industry that would benefit from utilizing its supply chain waste is orange juice. During juicing, half of the orange goes to waste, mostly as peel. Over 45 million t of oranges are juiced annually, so 22 million t of peel become waste. The usual disposal process is to bury the peels far underground because some of the components are toxic to vital soil microbes. Yet citrus peels contain a vast array of useful chemicals including limonene, a fragrant molecule used in detergents and personal care products, and pectin, used as a thickening agent in foods such as jam. These components are complex chemicals that nature has spent time and energy to make. It is a waste to break these chemicals down to a hydrocarbon mixture and try to rebuild similar compounds using synthetic organic techniques. Instead, by using mild, selective extraction techniques, these chemicals can be taken straight from the peel.

Innovative green chemistry also can be used to make bio-based material from FSCW for safer consumer products. Chemists have used waste straw from agricultural processes to make a bioboard that can replace traditional woodchip boards in furniture. The straw replaces the wood within the board, and the binder that holds the material together is made from waste biomass ash. This silicate binder replaces widely used and toxic chemical binders and makes the bioboards carbon neutral and nontoxic.

By using FSCW as a feedstock for chemical processes, we can avoid using fossil-based resources, minimize chemical processing, and reduce pollution. Green chemistry is a key to a bio-based economy that treats waste as a resource.

▲ **Figure 1** Valuable chemicals from orange peel

developed countries but are fairly common in developing parts of the world. The few cases of trichinosis that occur in the United States result mainly from eating undercooked game meat or pork from home-raised pigs. Trichinosis is characterized by symptoms such as nausea, heartburn, and diarrhea. Anisakiasis results from eating raw or undercooked fish in dishes such as sushi and sashimi (Japan), cod livers (Scandinavia), fermented herrings (Netherlands), or ceviche, a citrus-marinated, raw seafood that is popular in Latin America.

Proper cooking and food handling procedures reduce the chance of contracting most food-borne diseases.

A World without Food Additives

Could we get along without food additives? Some of us could. But food spoilage might drastically reduce the food supply in some parts of an already hungry world, and diseases due to vitamin and mineral deficiencies might increase. Foods might cost more and be less nutritious. Food additives seem to be a necessary part of modern society. Use of some food additives poses potential hazards, but the major problem with our food supply is still contamination by harmful microorganisms, rodents, and insects. Indeed, according to the CDC, about 48 million illnesses and 3000 deaths result each year in the United States from food poisoning caused by bacteria, viruses, and parasites. Few, if any, deaths associated with the use of intentional food additives have been documented.

What should we do about food additives? We should be sure that the FDA is staffed with qualified personnel who can perform adequate testing of proposed food additives. People trained in chemistry are necessary for the control and monitoring of food additives and the detection of contaminants. Research on the analytical techniques necessary for the detection of trace quantities is vital to adequate consumer protection. We should demand laws to prevent the unnecessary and excessive use of pesticides and other agricultural chemicals that might contaminate our food. Above all, we should be alert and informed about these problems that are so vital to our health and well-being.

SELF-ASSESSMENT Questions

1. Aflatoxins are
   a. antioxidants
   b. carcinogens
   c. on the GRAS list
   d. found only in peanuts

2. About how many people die from food poisoning in the United States each year?
   a. 100   b. 300   c. 3000   d. 30,000

3. The major problem with the food supply is contamination by
   a. aflatoxins
   b. food additives
   c. microorganisms
   d. pesticides

Answers: 1, b; 2, c; 3, c

⬛ SUMMARY

Section 17.1—The three main classes of substances in foods are carbohydrates, fats, and proteins. We also need vitamins, minerals, fiber, and water in our diets. Carbohydrates include sugars, starches, and cellulose. Glucose, also called **blood sugar**, is the sugar used directly by cells for energy. Other sugars include fructose, sucrose (table sugar), and lactose. Sucrose and lactose are broken down during digestion. **Starch** is a polymer of α-glucose, and **cellulose** is a β-glucose polymer. Human beings can hydrolyze starch to glucose but cannot hydrolyze cellulose, which instead serves as dietary fiber. The liver and muscles store small amounts of carbohydrates as **glycogen**.

Section 17.2—Dietary fats are esters called **triglycerides**, which are broken down by enzymes to form fatty acids and glycerol. Fats are stored in **adipose tissue** located in

fat depots and are hydrolyzed back to glycerol and fatty acids when needed. A **lipoprotein** is a cholesterol–protein combination transported in the blood. Low-density lipoproteins (LDLs) carry cholesterol to the cells for use and increase the risk of heart disease, while high-density lipoproteins (HDLs) carry it to the liver for excretion. Polyunsaturated fats (mostly from plants), *cis* fatty acids, and omega-3 fatty acids tend to lower LDL levels. Saturated fats (mostly from animals) and *trans* fatty acids made by hydrogenation of polyunsaturated fats have been implicated in cardiovascular disease.

Section 17.3—Proteins, polymers of amino acids, are broken down to amino acids during digestion. The **essential amino acids** must be included in the diet. Each essential amino acid is a **limiting reactant** in protein synthesis; a deficiency leads to an inability to make the proper proteins. Most animal proteins have these essential amino acids; plant proteins usually are deficient and must be combined with other plant proteins for complete nutrition. Protein deficiency is common in developing nations.

Section 17.4—**Dietary minerals** are inorganic substances vital to life. Bulk structural elements include carbon, hydrogen, and oxygen. Macrominerals include sodium, potassium, and calcium. We also need trace elements such as iron and ultratrace elements such as manganese, chromium, and vanadium. Minerals serve a variety of functions: Iodine is needed by the thyroid; iron is part of hemoglobin; and calcium and phosphorus are vital to the bones and teeth.

Vitamins are organic compounds that are required in the diet to prevent certain diseases. The B vitamins and vitamin C are water soluble and are needed frequently, whereas vitamins A, D, E, and K are all fat soluble and can be stored.

Dietary fiber may be soluble (gums and pectins) or insoluble (cellulose). It prevents digestion problems such as constipation. Drinking enough water is important, but it need not be plain water. Most drinks are mainly water.

Section 17.5—**Starvation** is deprivation of food that causes metabolic changes. The body first depletes its glycogen and then metabolizes fat and muscle tissue. Malnutrition can result from starvation, dieting, or eating too much highly processed food.

Section 17.6—Spices and herbs come from plants, and make food more interesting, aromatic, and flavorful. Synthetic flavorings, such as vanilla, contain the same primary molecule as the original plants but are less expensive. A variety of artificial sweeteners has been developed to reduce sugar intake but does not appear to aid in controlling obesity. Glycerol is a sweet-tasting compound that is used mainly as a **humectant** or moistening agent. Salt and MSG are flavor enhancers.

Section 17.7—**Food additives** are substances other than basic foodstuffs that are added to food to aid nutrition, inhibit spoilage, enhance color and flavor, provide texture, and so on. There are thousands of additives. The FDA regulates which additives, and how much of them, can be used.

The list of additives generally recognized as safe is the **GRAS list**, which is periodically reevaluated. Some additives have been found to be harmful; additives are usually banned if they are shown to cause cancer in laboratory animals.

Enrichment includes the replacement of B vitamins and the addition of iron to flour. Vitamin C is added to many beverages, and vitamin D to milk.

Propionate, sorbate, benzoate and nitrite salts inhibit and spoilage and bacterial growth. Fats may turn rancid partly from formation of **free radicals** with unpaired electrons. One free radical can cause a **chain reaction** that leads to decomposition of many fat molecules. BHT and BHA are **antioxidants** that react with free radicals and prevent rancidity.

Natural food colorings, such as β-carotene, and synthetic food colorings improve the appearance of food. Seven artificial colorants have been approved for use in foods, but only six of them are easily found in foods.

Section 17.8—Toxic substances occur naturally in foods, but occasionally are added in the form of pesticide residues or animal feed additives. Charcoal-broiled steak, cinnamon, and nutmeg contain carcinogens. **Aflatoxins** are produced by molds on peanuts and grain and are potent carcinogens. We may consume about 10,000 times as much of natural carcinogens as synthetic carcinogens. Most food contaminants are not chemicals but rather organisms such as bacteria, viruses, and parasites.

Without food additives, spoilage and disease would be likely to cause serious problems worldwide. Additives continue to be carefully scrutinized and regulated.

GREEN CHEMISTRY—Food supply chain waste (FSCW) can be used as a renewable source of valuable chemicals, materials, and fuels. Diverting food waste from other polluting endpoints such as landfills and incinerators reduces its environmental impact. More importantly, economically and technically practicable green chemistry routes to the creation of higher-value products from FSCW are being developed. Therefore, bio-based materials made from food waste can replace fossil-fuel-derived alternatives and facilitate the movement toward a bio-based economy.

Learning Objectives

❯ Identify dietary carbohydrates, and state their sources and function.	Problems 1, 17–20, 49, 50, 52, 55–59, 61
❯ Identify dietary lipids, and state their function.	Problems 2, 21–24, 55, 56, 51, 53–56, 65
❯ List the essential amino acids, and explain why we need proteins.	Problems 4, 25–27, 29, 30, 60
❯ Describe some protein deficiency diseases and their causes.	Problem 28
❯ Identify the vitamins and the bulk dietary minerals, and state their functions.	Problems 3, 5, 11, 31–40, 63, 65
❯ Describe the effects of starvation, fasting, and malnutrition.	Problem 6
❯ List some common food flavorings in food.	Problems 7–9, 12, 13, 15, 16, 41, 42, 44, 46–48, 64, 67
❯ Describe the historic impact of our desire for a variety of flavors and aromas, and of our search for sugar substitutes.	Problems 12, 13, 42, 68
❯ Identify the beneficial additives in foods, and those that are somewhat controversial.	Problems 7–10, 14, 15, 40, 41, 43–48 69, 71
❯ Define the GRAS list and food additives allowed under its provision.	Problem 16
❯ Explain how food supply chain waste can be used as a resource in the chemical industry.	Problem 70–71
❯ Identify the advantages of using food supply chain waste instead of fossil fuels as a source of chemicals, materials, and fuels.	Problem 72

REVIEW QUESTIONS

1. What is the role of carbohydrates in the diet?

2. What functions do fats serve?

3. Which vitamins and minerals are organic, and which are inorganic?

4. What is the role of proteins in the diet?

5. Is an excess of a water-soluble vitamin or an excess of a fat-soluble vitamin more likely to be dangerous? Why?

6. What is starvation?

7. What is a food additive?

8. What are the two major categories of food additives? Give an example of each.

9. What is MSG?

10. What is botulism? What are aflatoxins?

11. What fat-soluble vitamin serves as an antioxidant? What water-soluble vitamin serves as an antioxidant?

12. Name three artificial sweeteners. Which are approved for current use in the United States?

13. What is the chemical nature of aspartame?

14. List some contaminants that have been found in foods.

15. List five functions of food additives.

16. What U.S. government agency regulates the use of food additives? What must be done before a company can use a new food additive?

PROBLEMS

Carbohydrates

17. The two monosaccharide units of a disaccharide are joined through a
    a. C-to-O-to-C linkage   b. C-to-O-to-H linkage
    c. C-to-O-to-O linkage   d. H-to-O-to-H linkage

18. What are the chemical names of the following sugars?
    a. blood sugar   b. table sugar
    c. fruit sugar

19. What type of chemical reaction is involved in the digestion of starch?

20. What sugar is formed when starch is digested?

Fats

21. What type of chemical reaction is involved in the digestion of fats? What products are formed?

22. The average energy yield per gram of carbohydrate and of fat is
    a. 4 kcal each
    b. 9 kcal each
    c. 4 kcal and 9 kcal, respectively
    d. 9 kcal and 4 kcal, respectively

23. How do animal fats differ from vegetable oils?

24. What is a *trans* fat? How are *trans* fats made?

Proteins

25. What is an adequate protein? List some foods that contain adequate proteins.

26. What is the limiting reactant in any protein synthesis?

27. Which essential amino acids are likely to be lacking in corn? In beans?

28. What is kwashiorkor? What age group in developed countries suffers a similar condition?

29. Ezekiel 4:9 describes a bread made from "wheat, and barley, and beans, and lentils, and millet, and spelt . . . ." Would the bread supply complete protein?

30. How do dietary proteins differ from dietary carbohydrates and fats in elemental composition?

Minerals

31. Name the mineral ion that matches the biological function.
    a. thyroid (regulating metabolism)
    b. oxygen transport in the blood
    c. bones and teeth, heartbeat rhythm
    d. water regulation in the cells

32. Of the minerals Ca, Cl, Co, Mo, Na, P, and Zn, which is likely to be found in relatively large amounts in the human body? Explain.

Vitamins

33. Classify the following vitamins as water soluble or fat soluble.

Pantothenic acid

Phylloquinone

Biotin

34. Coenzyme Q_{10} (CoQ_{10}; shown below) is claimed by some to have vitamin-like activity: It prevents oxidation of LDLs and may act as an antihypertensive, perhaps reducing the risk of cardiovascular disease. CoQ_{10} belongs to a family of substances called *ubiquinones* and is synthesized in the body. **(a)** Is CoQ_{10} a vitamin? **(b)** Is it fat soluble or water soluble?

CoQ$_{10}$

35. Match the compound with its designation as a vitamin.

Compound	Designation
ascorbic acid	vitamin A
calciferol	vitamin B$_{12}$
cyanocobalamin	vitamin C
retinol	vitamin D
tocopherol	vitamin E

36. Which of the following are B vitamins?
a. niacin
b. phylloquinone
c. pyridoxine
d. calciferol
e. ascorbic acid

37. Name a vitamin that prevents the deficiency disease
a. scurvy
b. pellagra
c. beriberi
d. pernicious anemia

38. Identify each of the following vitamins as water soluble or fat soluble.
a. vitamin A
b. vitamin B$_6$
c. vitamin B$_{12}$
d. vitamin C

39. Identify each of the following vitamins as water soluble or fat soluble.
a. calciferol
b. niacin
c. riboflavin
d. tocopherol

Food Additives

40. Coffee, tea, and cola drinks all contain the stimulant
a. amphetamine
b. caffeine
c. fructose
d. cocaine

41. BHA and BHT help preserve the quality of packaged food by
a. enabling radiation to sterilize the food
b. killing pathogenic bacteria
c. preventing the food from turning brown
d. scavenging free radicals, consequently stopping fats from becoming rancid

42. Which of the following sugar substitutes are banned in the United States but available elsewhere?
a. aspartame
b. cyclamate
c. stevia
d. sucralose

43. What is the purpose of each of the following food additives?
a. BHA
b. FD&C Blue #2
c. saccharin

44. What is the purpose of each of the following food additives?
a. aspartame
b. vitamin D
c. sodium hypophosphite
d. calcium propionate

45. Which of the following is true about a dietary supplement labeled "natural"? It is **(a)** mild acting; **(b)** without risk of side effects; **(c)** always safe to use with medications; or **(d)** none of the above.

46. Propyl gallate is made by esterification of gallic acid, which is obtained by the hydrolysis of tannins from pods of the tara tree. Is propyl gallate a natural antioxidant?

47. What are antioxidants? Name a natural antioxidant and two synthetic antioxidants.

48. What is a chain reaction? What is the action of an antioxidant on a chain reaction?

Calorie and Nutrient Calculations

49. The label on a can of "Healthy Request" chicken noodle soup indicates that each 1-cup portion supplies 110 kcal and has 7 g of protein, 14 g of carbohydrate, and 2.5 g of fat. Calculate the percentages of calories that come from carbohydrate, fat, and protein.

50. The label on a can of New Orleans-style navy beans indicates that each $\frac{1}{2}$-cup serving supplies 130 kcal and has 8 g of protein, 23 g of carbohydrate, and 1.5 g of fat. Calculate the percentages of calories that come from carbohydrate, fat, and protein.

51. A $\frac{1}{4}$-cup serving of Martha Rose Shulman's asparagus-and-herb lasagna provides 5 g of fat, 6 g of carbohydrate, and 3 g of protein. About how many kilocalories does a serving of lasagna provide? What percentage of the calories comes from fat?

52. A 3-oz grilled lamb chop provides about 170 kcal, 23.5 g protein, and 6 g fat. How much carbohydrate does the lamb provide?

53. An adult female goes on a diet that provides 1200 kcal per day with no more than 25% from fat and no more than 30% of that fat being saturated fat. How much saturated fat, in grams, is permitted in this diet?

54. A very active male teenager needs about 3000 kcal per day. If the guideline of 30% or less of total calories from fat is followed, how much fat, in grams, is permitted?

ADDITIONAL PROBLEMS

55. Omega-6 fatty acids are unsaturated fatty acids in which the double bond closest to the methyl (omega) end of the molecule occurs at the sixth carbon from that end. Which of the following are omega-6 fatty acids? Refer to Table 16.1 for structures not given here.
a. palmitoleic acid, $CH_3(CH_2)_5CH{=}CH(CH_2)_7CO_2H$
b. oleic acid
c. linoleic acid
d. linolenic acid
e. arachidonic acid

56. Below are line-angle formulas for two fats. **(a)** Which is a saturated fat and which is a polyunsaturated fat? **(b)** Identify the fatty acid units in each.

(a)

(b)

Use the nutritional labels shown below to answer Problems 57–61.

57. What percentage of the energy of whole milk comes from fat?

58. Based on a 2200-kcal diet, what percentage of the maximum daily amount of cholesterol does a cup of whole milk provide?

59. Based on a 2200-kcal diet, what percentage of the maximum daily amount of saturated fat does a cup of whole milk provide?

60. A student drinks 3 cups of fat-free milk in a day and wants to consume 60 g per day of protein. What percentage of that protein is obtained from the milk?

61. What percentage of the calories in fat-free milk comes **(a)** from sugars and **(b)** from protein? What sugar is in milk?

62. Shown below are three substances sold as nutritional supplements. Pangamic acid (I) has not been shown to be required in the human diet. Dietary deficiency in pangamic acid is not associated with any disease. Carnitine (II) is synthesized in the body from the amino acids lysine and methionine. It is required for the transport of fatty acids from

the cellular fluid into the mitochondria during the breakdown of fats. Orotic acid (III) is manufactured in the body by intestinal microorganisms. For each substance: **(a)** Is it likely to be water soluble or fat soluble? **(b)** Is it a vitamin?

(I)

(II)

(III)

63. Of the vitamins calciferol, riboflavin, retinol, and cyanocobalamin, which are most likely to be needed on a daily basis? Explain.

64. Sodium saccharin and sucralose (Figure 17.13) are both readily soluble in water, but for somewhat different reasons. Explain.

65. Pioneers in the United States made heavy use of butter, beef tallow, and lard for their long treks across the country. One reason for this was the ready availability of these fats. But even if canola oil, soybean oil, and similar oils had been available, they probably would not have been used much. Consult Table 16.2 and suggest a chemical reason that is related to storage.

66. A diet that includes a lot of meat makes less efficient use of the energy originally captured by plants through photosynthesis than a vegetarian diet does. Explain.

67. What is one advantage of using beta-carotene as a yellow colorant in foods?

68. What structural differences are there between sucrose (Figure 16.5) and sucralose (Figure 17.13)?

69. Match each natural product with the food(s) in which it can be found.

a. lycopene	1. algae and green vegetables
b. ascorbic acid	2. carrots and squash
c. vitamin A	3. lemons and grapefruits
d. chlorophyll	4. tomatoes

70. Match each source of food waste along the supply chain with an example usable product.
    a. Agricultural waste
    b. Processing waste
    c. Post-consumer waste
        1. Orange peel
        2. Canteen leftovers
        3. Straw

71. Name three chemicals that can be derived from citrus peel and give a potential use for each.

72. Describe how each of the following benefits of using FSCW instead of fossil fuels can be realized.
    a. Reduced dependence on fossil fuels
    b. Minimized energy use and derivative use
    c. Saved money
    d. Improved business opportunities

CRITICAL THINKING EXERCISES

Apply knowledge that you have gained in this chapter and one or more of the FLaReS principles (Chapter 1) to evaluate the following statements or claims.

17.1. A website states that natural vitamins may be worth the extra cost because those vitamins occur within a family of "things like trace elements, enzymes, cofactors and other unknown factors that help them absorb into the human body and function to their full potential," whereas "synthetic vitamins are usually isolated into that one pure chemical, thereby leaving out some of the additional benefits that nature intended."

17.2. A friend states that he is going to use the "no-carb" diet to lose weight. He eats plenty of fruits and vegetables because he says they don't contain carbohydrates. His protein intake is high, since he eats meat at every meal, usually fried in butter or other fats. What is erroneous in this thinking?

17.3. An opponent of genetically modified (GM) foods suggests that the outcry against genetic modification occurred because the "public didn't want to eat food with 'genes' in it."

17.4. A website states that a chemical in marijuana, delta 1-tetrahydrocannabinol (delta 1-THC), is a fat-soluble vitamin called "vitamin M." The site claims that vitamin status is justified "because many of the properties of delta 1-THC are similar to those of the fat-soluble vitamins."

17.5. 7-Day Detox is a unique detoxification supplement whose label states that it contains 34 different ingredients intended to flush toxins and fat out of your system.

17.6. A woman's doctor orders her to follow a strict low-fat diet. She makes a bowl of fat-free popcorn and then sprays it with a "flavor spray." The label of the spray lists the ingredients as canola oil, butter, and lecithin. It also indicates that a serving size of 1 spray (0.5 g) has 5 calories and 0 g of fat. (The FDA allows less than 0.5 g to be rounded to zero.) She sprays the popcorn about 40 times to give it a lot of flavor, pointing out that at zero grams of fat per spray, she is still adhering to the low-fat diet.

COLLABORATIVE GROUP PROJECTS

Prepare a PowerPoint, poster, or other presentation (as directed by your instructor) to share with the class.

1. Prepare a short report on Olestra, a fat substitute, including the history of its preparation and studies as to its efficacy and problems with its use.

2. Prepare a brief report on the history of NaCl, where it is found in nature, important uses for sodium chloride throughout history, and dangers of overuse. Examine the labels on three convenience foods (a rice or spaghetti dish, soup), and compare the sodium content.

3. Prepare a brief report on one of the vitamins listed in Table 17.4. Identify the principal dietary sources and uses of the vitamin, as well as the history of its discovery, dangers (if any) of excessive ingestion, and physiological results of lack or low ingestion of that vitamin.

4. Examine the label on each of the following. Make a list of the food additives in each. Try to determine the function of each additive. Do all the labels provide this information?
    a. a can of soft drink
    b. a can of beer
    c. a box of dried soup mix
    d. a can of soup
    e. a can of fruit drink
    f. a cake mix box

5. Prepare a brief report on one of the following dietary supplements. What is the presumed function of each?
    a. acidophilus
    b. androstenedione Q_{10}
    c. coenzyme
    d. diindolylmethane
    e. glucosamine
    f. L-arginine
    g. St. John's wort
    h. valerian

6. Challenge: Can you eat on a $4.00 a day budget for food? Go to a local grocery store and investigate the costs of a variety of foods that you (theoretically) would buy to supply you with three meals a day for a week, assuming that you have only $28 and some change in your pocket. Those foods should supply you with at least 1800 kcal per day, provide minerals, vitamins, and enough protein and carbohydrates for a balanced diet, and leave you feeling reasonably "full." Assume that you have condiments, spices, and some margarine, cooking oil, or butter in your cupboard or refrigerator, plus plenty of potable water or bottled water. Create a detailed list of what you would buy and the cost, together with a list of what you would eat at each meal and the amount. Don't forget healthy beverages. We don't care how boring the menu is—for example, a large bowl of fortified cereal, milk, and a banana for breakfast.

CHEMISTRY@HOME   How Sweet It Is to Be Fermented by You!

Materials required

- Yeast (jar)
- Large measuring cup: 2 cup or larger capacity
- Measuring spoons (teaspoon and tablespoon)
- 6 resealable plastic bags
- 1 tablespoon of sugar
- 1 tablespoon of sweetener (Equal®, Sweet'N Low®)
- 1 tablespoon of flour
- 2 breakfast cereal samples (each with sugar listed as ingredient)
- Lukewarm water
- Paper towels (for clean-up)

What does yeast need to survive and thrive? Can yeast also digest artificial sweeteners and flour?

Yeast is most commonly used in the kitchen to make dough rise. Have you ever watched pizza crust or a loaf of bread swell in the oven? Yeast makes the dough expand. But what is yeast exactly and how does it work? Yeast strains are made up of living eukaryotic microbes, meaning that they contain cells with nuclei and are classified as fungi. In this experiment, we will watch yeast come to life as it breaks down sugar, also known as sucrose, through a process called fermentation.

To begin, create a data table for your experiment results. The data table should include columns for 6 bags, their contents, and your observations. Label bags 1 through 6.

Bag 1 will be your control.

–To bag 2, add 1 tablespoon of sugar.

–To bag 3, add 1 tablespoon of sweetener (Sweet'N Low® or Equal®).

–To bag 4, add 1 tablespoon of flour.

–To bag 5, add 1 tablespoon of breakfast cereal A, crushed.

–To bag 6, add 1 tablespoon of breakfast cereal B, crushed.

Next add $\frac{1}{4}$ cup of lukewarm water and 2 teaspoons of yeast to each bag.

▲ **Figure 1**

▶ **Figure 2**

Carefully, without spilling any of the contents, squeeze out as much air as possible and seal each bag. Put the bags in a warm place for 20 minutes. (Either a window or a large bowl with warm water works well.) Observe the bags periodically. After 20 minutes, remove the bags from the warm place and observe them.

▶ **Figure 3**

What changes have occurred? Which bag has grown in size the most?

To measure the volume of the bags, fill the large measuring cup with 1 cup water and lower the bag into the large measuring cup. To find the estimated volume, you will use displacement measurement. Record the volume of the water with the bag in it and subtract the initial starting volume of 1 cup of water to obtain your volume. (Don't forget to account for any volume change of your control bag.)

▶ **Figure 4**

Questions

1. Which ingredients help yeast grow best?
2. Write a balanced equation for the reaction of sugar, water, and yeast.
3. Estimate how much sugar was in each cereal sample.

DRUGS

Have You Ever Wondered?

1. **Why is aspirin not recommended for children?**

2. **What are the dangers of acetaminophen (Tylenol®)?**

3. **Why must I continue taking an antibiotic even after I am feeling better?**

4. **What kinds of drugs work for colds or the flu?**

5. **How should I dispose of old medicines?**

6. **What is the difference between a name-brand drug and a generic drug?**

CHEMICAL CURES, COMFORTS, AND CAUTIONS

The word *drug* originally referred to a dried plant (or plant part) used as a medicine, either directly or after extracting active ingredients as a tea. Today, a drug is defined as a chemical substance that affects the functioning of living things. Drugs are used to relieve pain, to treat illnesses, and to improve one's health or well-being. Many people literally owe their lives to drugs. Drugs can kill bacteria, lower blood pressure, prevent seizures, relieve allergies, and do many other remarkable things. In this chapter, we will look at natural and synthetic drugs that are intended to combat a wide range of ills, as well as those that see illicit use.

Willow bark and the herb meadowsweet (shown in the main image above) contain salicylates, which became the basis for aspirin, the most widely used drug in the world. French chemist Charles Frédéric Gerhardt made crude acetylsalicylic acid (o-$CH_3COOC_6H_4COOH$) by reacting sodium salicylate (o-HOC_6H_4COONa) with acetyl chloride (CH_3COCl). *Aspirin*, Bayer's brand name, came from *acetylated Spirsäure*, the German name for salicylic acid, with the typical drug-naming ending *-in* added.

Learning Objectives

> Identify common drugs as natural, semisynthetic, or synthetic. (18.1)

> Define *chemotherapy*, and explain its origin. (18.1)

> List common over-the-counter analgesics, antipyretics, and anti-inflammatory drugs, and describe how each works. (18.2)

> Name several common narcotics, describe how each functions, and state its potential for addiction. (18.2)

> List the common antibacterial drugs, and describe the action of each. (18.3)

> Name the common categories of antiviral drugs, and describe the action of each. (18.3)

> Describe the action of the common types of anticancer drugs. (18.4)

> Define the terms *hormone*, *prostaglandin*, and *steroid*, and explain the function of each. (18.5)

> List the three types of sex hormones, and explain how each acts and how birth control drugs work. (18.5)

> Describe the action of four types of drugs used to treat heart disease. (18.6)

> Explain how the brain amines norepinephrine and serotonin affect the mind and how various drugs change their action. (18.7)

> Identify some stimulant drugs, depressant drugs, and psychotropic drugs, and describe how they affect the mind. (18.7)

> Differentiate between drug abuse and drug misuse. (18.8)

> Describe how a new drug is developed and brought to market. (18.8)

> Identify green chemistry principles that can improve the E-factor of chemical syntheses.

> Explain how prodrugs can be important for drug delivery and green chemistry.

551

▲ Opium poppy.

▲ Madagascar periwinkle.

▲ Pacific yew tree *(Taxus brevifolia).*

▲ Cone snail *(Conus textile).*

We still obtain many drugs from natural sources. The following are a few examples of drugs that have been obtained from plants.

- Quinine, the antimalarial drug, from the bark of *Cinchona* species
- Morphine, the analgesic, from the opium poppy
- Digoxin, for heart disorders, from *Digitalis purpurea*
- Vinblastine and vincristine, anticancer agents from the Madagascar periwinkle *(Catharanthus roseus)*
- The anticancer drug paclitaxel (Taxol), first obtained from the bark of the Pacific yew tree *(Taxus brevifolia)*
- Tubocurarine, the muscle relaxant, from *Chondrodendron tomentosum*, used by Amazon natives in the arrow poison curare

Many other drugs are obtained from microorganisms, including the following important ones.

- Antibacterial agents (penicillins) and cholesterol-lowering agents (statins) from *Penicillium* species
- Immunosuppressants, such as cyclosporins, from *Streptomyces* species

A potentially vast resource for new drugs is marine organisms. The following are examples of a few drugs from the sea.

- The anticancer drug dolastatin-10 from a sea hare
- An anti-inflammatory agent manoalide from the sponge *Luffariella variabilis*
- Ziconotide, a drug for treatment of severe pain, derived from cone snail venom

A diminishing source for naturally occurring drugs is tropical rainforests, warm, moist, and fertile areas that contain more different kinds of plants and animals than anyplace else on Earth. These forests are living chemical factories full of valuable and irreplaceable natural resources. Unfortunately, the world's rainforests are rapidly disappearing, as people clear the trees and convert the land to agricultural uses.

18.1 Scientific Drug Design

Learning Objectives ＞ Identify common drugs as natural, semisynthetic, or synthetic.
＞ Define *chemotherapy*, and explain its origin.

Some drugs are made from molecules that come from natural sources. While there is no legal definition for *natural,* the word is commonly used to describe materials that are extracted directly from plant or animal sources by physical processes as opposed to materials formed by chemical reactions.

Other drugs are made by modifying molecules derived from natural sources to improve the substances' properties. These drugs are said to be *semisynthetic.* Many of the earliest science-based drugs were semisynthetic. Examples include the following.

- Salicylic acid (first obtained from willow bark) was converted to acetylsalicylic acid (aspirin).
- Morphine (from opium poppies) was converted to heroin.
- Lysergic acid (from ergot fungus) was converted to LSD.

There are now many completely synthetic drugs on the market. These substances are represented in nearly all categories, from antibacterial drugs to sleeping pills to narcotics such as methadone and fentanyl.

Drugs are used to treat, diagnose, and prevent diseases. People use drugs for many reasons—to relieve pain, to fight infections, to stay awake, to sleep, to calm anxiety, to prevent conception, and to treat various conditions from arthritis to heart disease to pneumonia to cancer. Many types of drugs can, however, do more harm than good, especially if used in the wrong amounts or for the wrong reasons.

Humans have used drugs since prehistoric times, and drug use occurs in all cultures. Most societies have used alcohol, and the use of marijuana goes back to at least 3000 B.C.E. The narcotic effect of the opium poppy was known to the ancients. As early as 1400 B.C.E., the Egyptians grew poppies and the Minoans on Crete had terracotta statues of a Poppy Goddess. The Indians of the Andes Mountains have long chewed leaves of the coca plant for the stimulating effect of the cocaine.

In 1904, Paul Ehrlich (1854–1915), a German chemist, found that certain dyes used to stain bacteria to make them more visible under a microscope could also be used to kill the bacteria. He used dyes to combat the organism that causes African sleeping sickness. He also prepared an arsenic compound that proved somewhat effective against the organism that causes syphilis. Ehrlich realized that certain chemicals were more toxic to disease organisms than to human cells and could therefore be used to control or cure infectious diseases. He coined the term **chemotherapy** (from "chemical therapy"). Ehrlich was awarded the Nobel Prize in Physiology or Medicine in 1908.

The use of drugs is not new, but never before has there been such a vast array of them. There are dozens of pharmaceutical companies producing thousands of drugs. Their research laboratories spend huge sums to develop new drugs each year. According to a recent study, it costs an estimated $4.5 billion to develop and bring a new drug to market. (The cost varies substantially depending on the kind of drug.) That great cost means that companies must often charge high prices for the products they develop, at least for a while, making them unaffordable for many of the people who need them. After the patent rights expire, other companies can make generic versions of the same products and sell them at lower prices because they have incurred no research costs. Generic drugs must act identically to the original products.

Because many drugs are sold under generic names and several different brand names, there are thousands of prescription medicines on the market. Several hundred other medicines are available over-the-counter (OTC) under thousands of brand names and in many combinations. Some of these drugs are vital to the health of the people who take them. Drug-industry sales worldwide in 2013 are estimated to be more than $1 trillion. In 2013, Americans had 3.9 billion prescriptions filled, including refills, an average of about 13 per person, and spent about $329 billion for prescription drugs.

SELF-ASSESSMENT Questions

For questions 1–3, state whether the drug is

    a. natural

    b. semisynthetic

    c. synthetic

1. Quinine
2. Cyclosporins
3. Aspirin
4. Chemotherapy is

    a. improving one's health by avoiding chemicals

    b. improving one's mind by studying chemistry

    c. treating cancer with radiation

    d. treating a disease with chemicals

18.2 Pain Relievers: From Aspirin to Oxycodone

Learning Objectives ❯ List common over-the-counter analgesics, antipyretics, and anti-inflammatory drugs, and describe how each works. ❯ Name several common narcotics, describe how each functions, and state its potential for addiction.

Acetylsalicylic acid, commonly called *aspirin* in the United States, is widely used around the world. About 40 million kg are consumed annually—enough to make 100 billion standard tablets. Its history goes back at least 2400 years to the time of Hippocrates in ancient Greece, who knew that sick people could ease their pain and lower their fever by chewing willow leaves.

It was not until 1835 that chemists isolated the active ingredient, salicylic acid, an effective **analgesic** (pain reliever), **antipyretic** (fever reducer), and **anti-inflammatory** that, unfortunately, also caused considerable stomach distress and bleeding. Acetylsalicylic acid is a modified version of salicylic acid that had the desired medicinal properties but was gentler to the stomach. It was introduced in 1893 by the Bayer Company in Germany.

Aspirin tablets are sold under a variety of trade names and store brands. A standard aspirin tablet contains 325 mg of acetylsalicylic acid held together with an inert binder such as starch. "Extra strength" formulations usually contain 500 mg.

▲ Acetylsalicylic acid (aspirin).

Nonsteroidal Anti-Inflammatory Drugs (NSAIDs)

Aspirin is one of several substances called **nonsteroidal anti-inflammatory drugs (NSAIDs)**, a designation that distinguishes these drugs from the more potent steroidal anti-inflammatory drugs such as cortisone and prednisone (Section 18.5). Other NSAIDs include ibuprofen (Advil®, Motrin®), and naproxen (Aleve®) (Figure 18.1). Acetaminophen, like aspirin, relieves minor aches and reduces fever but is not anti-inflammatory and is therefore not an NSAID.

▶ **Figure 18.1** Two NSAIDs. Ibuprofen and naproxen are derivatives of propionic acid (CH_3CH_2COOH).

Ibuprofen

Naproxen

NSAIDs act to relieve pain and reduce inflammation by inhibiting the production of **prostaglandins**, hormone-like lipids that are derived from a fatty acid and are involved in sending pain messages to the brain (Section 18.5). Inflammation is caused by an overproduction of prostaglandin derivatives, and inhibiting prostaglandin synthesis reduces the inflammatory effect.

Regrettably, for those who take NSAIDs regularly, prostaglandins also affect the blood platelets, the kidneys, and the stomach lining, leading to side effects most often associated with taking NSAIDs: excessive bleeding and stomach pains. The **anticoagulant** effect (inhibition of the clotting of blood) of NSAIDs often leads to complications in patients taking NSAIDs for treatment of arthritis. About 1.5% of patients with rheumatoid arthritis taking NSAIDs for a year have a serious stomach complication. This is a small proportion, but it translates to a large number of people because of the vast number of patients taking NSAIDs.

Because NSAIDs act as anticoagulants, small daily doses also seem to lower the risk of heart attack and stroke, presumably by the same anticoagulant action that causes bleeding in the stomach. Adult low-strength (usually 81 mg) aspirin tablets are now routinely used by people at risk for heart attack and stroke. NSAIDs should not be used by people facing surgery, childbirth, or some other hazard involving the possible loss of blood for at least a week before the event.

It DOES Matter!

Almost every single-ingredient analgesic product sold today uses one of four active ingredients: acetaminophen, aspirin, ibuprofen, or naproxen. These drugs are available in generic forms, under dozens of brand names, and in many combinations, including cough/cold and allergy/sinus products. You can search the Internet for brand names, using the generic names as key words.

NSAIDs also reduce body temperature. Fevers are induced by substances called *pyrogens*, compounds produced by and released from leukocytes (white blood cells) and other circulating cells. Pyrogens usually use prostaglandins as secondary mediators. Fevers therefore can be reduced by aspirin and other prostaglandin inhibitors. Pyrogens that do not work through prostaglandins are not affected by NSAIDs.

The body tries to fight off infection by elevating its temperature. Mild fevers in adults (those below 39 °C, or 102 °F) are usually best left untreated. High fevers, however, can cause brain damage and require immediate treatment.

How NSAIDs Work

Prostaglandins are produced in the body from a cell-membrane component called *arachidonic acid* (Section 18.5). Scientists have identified enzymes called *cyclooxygenases* (COX) that catalyze the conversion. Two of these are COX-1, found in stomach and kidney tissues where NSAID side effects occur, and COX-2, found in tissues where inflammation occurs. The older NSAIDs, such as aspirin, ibuprofen, and naproxen, inhibit both COX-1 and COX-2, providing relief from pain and inflammation but also producing undesirable side effects. Newer NSAIDs preferentially inhibit COX-2. Three COX-2 inhibitors came onto the market as anti-inflammatory agents but two were quickly removed from the market because they led to a higher risk of stroke and heart attacks.

Celecoxib (Celebrex®) (Figure 18.2) remains on the market, but the U.S. Food and Drug Administration (FDA) now requires labels on all prescription NSAIDs to include a boxed warning highlighting the potential for increased risk of heart problems, as well as information regarding allergic reactions and internal bleeding.

Acetaminophen: A COX-3 Inhibitor

Acetaminophen, perhaps best known by the brand name Tylenol®, is the most widely used analgesic in the United States. It provides relief of pain and reduction of fever comparable to that of aspirin. The total world market for acetaminophen (called *paracetamol* in many countries) is about 110 million kg/year. Acetaminophen acts on a third variant of cyclooxygenase enzyme, COX-3. Inhibition of COX-3 may represent a mechanism by which acetaminophen decreases pain and fever. Unlike NSAIDs, it is not an anticoagulant, so people allergic to aspirin or susceptible to bleeding can safely take acetaminophen. However, COX-3 appears to play no role in controlling inflammation, so it is of limited use to people with arthritis. Acetaminophen is often used to relieve the pain that follows minor surgery. Regular acetaminophen tablets contain 325 mg, and extra-strength forms have 500 mg.

Acetaminophen

Combination Pain Relievers

Many analgesic products are a combination of one or more NSAIDs, acetaminophen, caffeine, antihistamines, or other drugs. Acetaminophen, for example, is found in more than 70 combination products for pain relief, allergy symptoms, and cold and flu treatment. These combinations are available under various brand names and as store brands. Familiar brands include Excedrin and Anacin, each of which is available in several different combinations and formulations.

Many other combination pain relievers are available. Most claim to be better than regular aspirin. However, such advantages are marginal at best. For occasional use by most people, plain aspirin may be the cheapest, safest, and most effective product.

1. Why is aspirin not recommended for children? The use of aspirin in children suffering from viral infections, such as the flu or chickenpox, is associated with *Reye's syndrome*, a potentially fatal illness. For this reason, aspirin products carry a warning that they should not be used to treat children with fevers.

Celecoxib (Celebrex®)

▲ **Figure 18.2** Celecoxib is the only COX-2 inhibiting prescription NSAID that remains on the market.

2. What are the dangers of acetaminophen (Tylenol®)? Although the normal dose of acetaminophen is safe, larger doses are toxic, causing liver damage. This effect is synergistic with alcohol. As little as 4 g (eight extra-strength tablets) in 24 hours, coupled with recent alcohol use, can cause severe liver toxicity. Every year over 33,000 people are hospitalized because of acetaminophen toxicity, and over 150 deaths are recorded. Accidental overdose of acetaminophen is far too common, and it often occurs because people do not realize that acetaminophen is an ingredient in many OTC medicines for treatment of cold symptoms, allergies, insomnia, and other maladies. A careful review of the active ingredients in such medications can save a life!

Chemistry, Allergies, and the Common Cold

Store shelves are stocked with a variety of cold and allergy medicines, which contain antihistamines, cough suppressants, expectorants, bronchodilators, or nasal decongestants. None cures the common cold, which is caused by as many as 200 related viruses. In fact, no drug provides a cures and most cold remedies just treat the symptoms. An FDA advisory panel reviews these substances periodically for safety and effectiveness.

Many cold medicines contain an **antihistamine**, such as diphenhydramine or cetirizine (Figure 18.3). Antihistamines temporarily relieve the symptoms of allergies: sneezing, itchy eyes, and runny nose.

When an **allergen** (a substance that triggers an allergic reaction) binds to the surfaces of certain cells, it triggers the release of *histamine*, which causes the redness, swelling, and itching associated with allergies. An antihistamine inhibits the release of histamine. Many cough and cold products contain more than one ingredient (see Collaborative Group Project 1).

Other OTC cold medicines include *antitussives* (cough suppressants) and *expectorants* (substances that

help bring up mucus from the bronchial passages). Ordinarily, a cough is functional; the respiratory tract uses the coughing mechanism to rid itself of congestion. However, when a cough is dry or interferes with needed rest, temporary cough suppression may be advisable. Only one expectorant, glyceryl guaiacolate (guaifenesin), is rated as safe and effective, and its effectiveness is not well documented.

Nasal *decongestants*, such as naphazoline, phenylephrine, oxymetazoline, and xylometazoline, seem to be safe and effective for occasional use, although repeated use leads to a *rebound effect* in which the nasal passages swell and make congestion seem worse.

How should you treat a common cold? First, you should drink plenty of liquids and get lots of rest. When you are in good physical condition and have a strong immune system, colds seem to strike less often. Frequent hand washing, especially when colds are prevalent, can dramatically reduce transmission of the virus. And many people still swear by chicken soup!

(a) Histamine (b) Diphenhydramine (c) Cetirizine

▲ **Figure 18.3** Histamine (a) and two antihistamines: (b) diphenhydramine (Benadryl®) and (c) cetirizine (Zyrtec®). Diphenhydramine is also used as a cough suppressant.

Q: *To what family of organic compounds do these three substances belong?*

Narcotics

When pain is too great to be relieved by OTC analgesics, stronger prescription drugs are available. Most such drugs are classified as **narcotics**, drugs that produce narcosis (stupor or general anesthesia) and analgesia (relief of pain). Many drugs produce these effects, but in the United States only those that are also *addictive* are legally classified as narcotics.

Several narcotics are products of opium, the dried, resinous juice of the unripe seeds of the opium poppy (*Papaver somniferum*) (Figure 18.4). Opium is a complex mixture of 20 or so alkaloids, plus sugars, resins, waxes, and water. The principal alkaloid, morphine, makes up about 10% of the weight of raw opium. Opium was used in many patent medicines during the nineteenth century. Laudanum, a solution of opium in alcohol, contained about 10 mg of morphine per mL of solution and was widely used during the Victorian era for everything from toothaches to tuberculosis. It was even used to quiet colicky babies. Paregoric, a much weaker solution that contained only 0.4 mg of morphine per mL, was also widely used, especially for diarrhea, and was readily available until 1970.

Morphine was first isolated in 1805 by Friedrich Sertürner, a German pharmacist. With the invention of the hypodermic syringe in the 1850s, a new method

▲ Some cults in ancient Greece associated opium with several divinities. This Greek coin from that period shows an opium poppy capsule to the left of the head of a goddess.

of administration became available. Injection of morphine directly into the bloodstream was more effective for the relief of pain, but this method also seriously escalated the problem of addiction.

Morphine was used widely during the American Civil War (1861–1865) for relief of pain due to battle wounds. One side effect of morphine use is constipation. Noting this, soldiers came to use morphine as a treatment for another common malady of men on the battlefront—dysentery. More than 100,000 soldiers became addicted to morphine while serving in the war. The affliction was so common among veterans that it came to be known as "soldier's disease."

Morphine and other narcotics were placed under control of the federal government by the Harrison Act of 1914. Morphine is still prescribed for the relief of severe pain. It induces lethargy, drowsiness, confusion, euphoria, chronic constipation, and depression of the respiratory system. Morphine is addictive, which becomes a problem when it is administered in amounts greater than the prescribed dose or for a period longer than the prescribed time.

Changes in the morphine molecule alter its physiological properties. Replacement of the phenolic hydroxyl group ($-OH$) by a methoxy group ($-OCH_3$) produces codeine (see Additional Problem 89). Codeine is present in opium at about 0.7–2.5%, but it is usually synthesized by methylating the more abundant morphine molecules. Codeine resembles morphine in its action, but it is less potent, has less tendency to induce sleep, and is less addictive. For relief of moderate pain, codeine is often combined with acetaminophen (for example, in Tylenol 2 and Tylenol 3) or with aspirin (in Empirin Codeine). For cough suppression, codeine is given in liquid preparations that are regulated less stringently than stronger narcotics.

Conversion of both $-OH$ groups of the morphine molecule to acetate ester groups produces heroin (see Additional Problem 90). This semisynthetic morphine derivative was first prepared by chemists at the Bayer Company in Germany in 1874. It received little attention until 1890, when it was proposed as an antidote for morphine addiction. Shortly thereafter, Bayer advertised heroin widely as a sedative for coughs, often in the same ads describing aspirin. However, it was soon found that heroin induced addiction more quickly than morphine and that heroin addiction was harder to cure.

The physiological action of heroin resembles that of morphine. Heroin is less polar than morphine, so it enters the fatty tissues of the brain more rapidly, and it seems to produce a stronger feeling of euphoria than morphine. Heroin is not legal in the United States, even by prescription. It has, however, been advocated for use in the relief of pain in terminal cancer patients and is used in Britain for that purpose.

Addiction probably has three components: psychological dependence, physical dependence, and tolerance. Psychological dependence is evident in the uncontrollable desire for the drug. Physical dependence is shown by acute withdrawal symptoms such as convulsions. Tolerance for the drug is evidenced by the fact that increasing dosages are required to produce the same degree of narcosis and analgesia.

Deaths from heroin and other narcotics are usually attributed to overdoses, but the situation is not always clear. The problem is often a matter of quality control. Street drugs vary considerably in potency, and a particular dose can be much higher in potency than expected.

Much research has gone into developing a drug that would be as effective as morphine for the relief of pain but would not be addictive. Several synthetic narcotics are available. Some common ones are listed in Table 18.1 on page 558. Structures of some of these and other narcotics are given in Figure 18.5 on page 558.

Oxycodone is a semisynthetic opioid related to codeine (see Additional Problem 91). It is used for relief of moderate to severe pain. It is available alone and in combinations with acetaminophen, ibuprofen, or aspirin. A sustained-release form of oxycodone is called OxyContin®. Abused for its euphoric effects, OxyContin and its generic equivalents are widely available illegally.

▲ **Figure 18.4** Opium poppy seed pod. The slits on the seed pod are exuding resinous juice, which is dried to form opium. About 10% of the weight of raw opium is morphine.

▲ Heroin was regarded as a safe medicine in 1900 and was widely used as a cough suppressant. It was also thought to be a nonaddictive substitute for morphine.

Table 18.1 **Some Synthetic Narcotics**

Substance	Duration of Action (h)	Approximate Oral Dose (mg) Equivalent to 30 mg of Morphine
Meperidine (Demerol®)	2–4	300
Hydrocodone	4–8	20
Fentanyl	1–2[a]	<1
Oxycodone	4–6[b]	20
Hydromorphone (Demerol®)	4–5	7.5
Methadone	4–6[c]	Not applicable

[a]Used in transdermal patches for chronic pain.
[b]Often dispensed in a time-release form (OxyContin®) that allows 12 h between doses.
[c]Used for treatment of heroin addiction; not usually given for pain relief.

▶ **Figure 18.5** Structural formulas of some synthetic narcotics: (a) meperidine (Demerol®), (b) methadone, (c) pentazocine (Talwin®), and (d) naloxone.

(a) Meperidine (Demerol®)

(b) Methadone

(c) Pentazocine (Talwin®)

(d) Naloxone

Hydrocodone

Anionic site binds N

Cavity binds carbon atoms

Flat hole binds benzene ring

▲ Diagram of a morphine receptor.

Hydrocodone, another synthetic narcotic, is always combined with acetaminophen or another medication. Sold as HYCD/APAP (hydrocodone/acetaminophen), this combination was the most prescribed drug in the United States in 2010, with 131.2 million new and refilled prescriptions.

The synthetic narcotic methadone is widely used to treat heroin addiction. Like heroin, methadone is highly addictive. However, when taken orally, it does not induce the sleepy stupor characteristic of heroin intoxication, so a person on methadone maintenance is usually able to hold a productive job. If an addict who has been taking methadone reverts to heroin, the methadone in his or her system effectively blocks the euphoric rush normally produced by heroin and so reduces the addict's temptation to use heroin.

Morphine Agonists and Antagonists

Chemists have synthesized many morphine analogs, but few have shown significant analgesic activity, and most of those are addictive. Morphine acts by binding to receptors in the brain. A morphine receptor has a flat hole that binds to the benzene ring, a cavity that binds two carbon atoms, and an anionic site that binds the nitrogen atom. A molecule that has morphine-like action is called a morphine **agonist**. A morphine **antagonist** inhibits the action of morphine by blocking

Natural Opiates: Endorphins and Enkephalins

Morphine acts by binding to specific receptor sites in the brain. Why should the human brain have receptors for a plant-derived drug such as morphine? Scientists concluded that the body must produce its own substances that fit these receptors. Actually, it produces several morphine-like substances, called **endorphins** (from "endogenous morphines"). Each endorphin is a short peptide chain composed of amino-acid units. Those with five amino-acid units are called *enkephalins*. There are two enkephalins, which differ only in the amino acid at the end of the chain. *Leu*-enkephalin has the sequence Tyr-Gly-Gly-Phe-Leu, and *Met*-enkephalin has the sequence Tyr-Gly-Gly-Phe-Met. Other endorphins have chains of 30 or more amino acids.

Some enkephalins have been synthesized and shown to be potent pain relievers. Their use in medicine is quite limited, however, because they are rapidly broken down in the body by the enzymes that hydrolyze proteins. Researchers have sought to make analogs that are more resistant to hydrolysis and can be employed as morphine substitutes for the relief of pain. Unfortunately, both natural enkephalins and their analogs, such as morphine, seem to be addictive.

It appears that endorphins are released during strenuous exercise and in response to pain. Some evidence indicates that acupuncture causes the release of brain "opiates" that relieve pain. The long needles stimulate deep sensory nerves, which release peptides that then block pain signals for a brief time.

Endorphin release has also been used to explain other phenomena once thought to be largely psychological. A soldier who has been wounded in battle may feel no pain until the skirmish is over. His body has secreted its own painkiller.

morphine receptors. Some molecules have both agonist and antagonist effects. An example is pentazocine, Figure 18.5c, which is less addictive than morphine and is effective for the relief of pain.

Pure antagonists such as naloxone, Figure 18.5d, can be used to treat opiate addicts. An addict who has overdosed can be brought back from death's door by an injection of naloxone.

SELF-ASSESSMENT Questions

1. Which of the following types of compounds works as a fever reducer?
   a. analgesic
   b. anticoagulant
   c. antihistamine
   d. antipyretic

2. NSAIDs act by inhibiting the production of
   a. endorphins
   b. ketone bodies
   c. norepinephrine
   d. prostaglandins

3. Which of the following is not an anticoagulant?
   a. acetaminophen
   b. aspirin
   c. ibuprofen
   d. naproxen

4. Allergens trigger the release of
   a. endorphins
   b. histamines
   c. prostaglandins
   d. pyrogens

5. Which of the following cures the common cold?
   a. antibiotics
   b. antihistamines
   c. nothing yet discovered
   d. vitamin C

6. An active ingredient in opium that is less abundant and less powerful than morphine is
   a. caffeine
   b. codeine
   c. methadone
   d. pentazocine

7. A semisynthetic opiate produced by adding acetyl groups to morphine molecules is
   a. heroin
   b. MDMA
   c. meperidine
   d. methadone

8. Which of the following has been used to treat heroin addiction?
   a. endorphins
   b. methadone
   c. morphine
   d. opium

9. Compounds that mimic the effects of opiates and produce a "high" following strenuous exercise are
   a. endorphins
   b. histamines
   c. pyrogens
   d. thyroxins

Answers: 1, d; 2, d; 3, a; 4, b; 5, c; 6, b; 7, a; 8, b; 9, a

18.3 Drugs and Infectious Diseases

Learning Objectives ❯ List the common antibacterial drugs, and describe the action of each. ❯ Name the common categories of antiviral drugs, and describe the action of each.

A century ago, infectious diseases were the main cause of death in the United States (Figure 18.6, page 560). At the time of the American Civil War, thousands of wounded soldiers required amputations of arms or legs, and nearly 80% of the patients died after coming to a hospital, mostly from infections. Today, infectious

▶ **Figure 18.6** (a) In 1900, five of the ten leading causes of death—responsible for three-fifths of all deaths—in the United States were infectious diseases. (b) The leading causes of death in 2011 were so-called lifestyle diseases: heart disease, stroke, and diabetes, related in part to our diets; cancer and lung diseases, to cigarette smoking; and accidents, often to excessive consumption of alcohol.

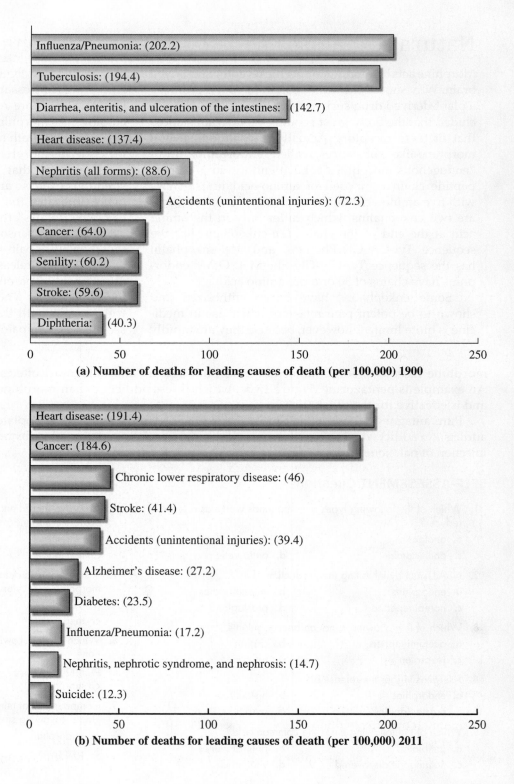

(a) Number of deaths for leading causes of death (per 100,000) 1900

(b) Number of deaths for leading causes of death (per 100,000) 2011

disease categories have moved toward the bottom of the list of the top 10 leading causes of death. (These 10 causes account for more than three-quarters of all deaths in the United States.) Many diseases have been brought under control through the use of *antibacterial drugs*.

Antibacterial Drugs

The first antibacterial drugs were *sulfa drugs*, whose prototype was discovered in 1935 by the German chemist Gerhard Domagk (1895–1964). Sulfa drugs were used extensively during World War II to prevent wound infections. Many soldiers who would have died in earlier wars survived.

Sulfanilamide, the simplest sulfa drug, was one of the first to have its action understood at the molecular level. Its effectiveness is based on a case of mistaken identity. Bacteria need *para*-aminobenzoic acid (PABA) to make folic acid, which is essential for the formation of certain compounds the bacteria require for proper growth. But bacterial enzymes can't tell the difference between sulfanilamide and PABA because their molecules are so similar.

Sulfanilamide   *para*-Aminobenzoic acid

When sulfanilamide is applied to an infection in large amounts, bacteria incorporate it into pseudo–folic acid molecules that cannot act normally and the bacteria cease to grow. Of the thousands of sulfanilamide analogs that have been developed and tested, only a few are used today. Two common ones are sulfathiazole and sulfaguanidine. Some sulfa drugs tend to cause kidney damage or other problems.

The next important discovery was that of penicillin, an antibiotic. An **antibiotic** is a soluble substance that is derived from molds or bacteria and inhibits the growth of other microorganisms. Penicillin was first discovered in 1928 but was not tried on humans until 1941. Alexander Fleming (1881–1955), a Scottish microbiologist then working at the University of London, first observed the antibacterial action of a mold, *Penicillium notatum*. Fleming was studying an infectious bacterium, *Staphylococcus aureus*, and one of his cultures became contaminated with a blue mold, but Fleming astutely noted that bacterial colonies had been destroyed in the vicinity of the mold.

Fleming was able to make crude extracts of the active substance. This material, later called *penicillin*, was further purified and improved by Howard Florey (1898–1968), an Australian, and Ernst Boris Chain (1906–1979), a refugee from Nazi Germany, both working at Oxford University in England. Fleming, Florey, and Chain shared the 1945 Nobel Prize in Physiology or Medicine for their work on penicillin.

Penicillin is not a single substance but a group of related compounds (Figure 18.7). By designing molecules with different structures, chemists can change the properties of the drug, producing penicillins that vary in effectiveness. Some can be taken orally; others must be injected. Bacteria resistant to one penicillin may be killed by another. Amoxicillin has a broad spectrum of activity against many types of microorganisms. It is among the top 10 prescribed drugs with more than 52.3 million prescriptions in 2010, including refills, in the United States and sales of more than $2.41 billion worldwide in 2011. Overall, penicillins account for about half of all antimicrobial prescriptions.

Penicillin works by inhibiting enzymes that the bacteria use to make their cell walls. The bacterial cell walls are made up of *mucoproteins*, polymers in which amino

Sulfathiazole

Sulfaguanidine

(a) General formula   (b) Penicillin G   (c) Amoxicillin

▲ **Figure 18.7** Penicillins. (a) A general formula where R is a variable side chain. (b) Penicillin G is generally considered the most effective penicillin but can only be given by injection. (c) Amoxicillin can be administered orally.

sugars are combined with protein molecules. (An amino sugar contains an $-NH_2$ group in place of an $-OH$ group.) Penicillin prevents cross-linking between these large molecules. This leaves holes in the cell walls, and the bacteria swell and rupture. Cells of higher animals have only external membranes, not mucoprotein walls, and are not affected by penicillin. Thus, penicillin can destroy bacteria without harming human cells. However, some people are allergic to penicillin.

In their early days, antibiotics were known as miracle drugs. The number of deaths from blood poisoning (septicemia), pneumonia, and other infectious diseases was reduced substantially by the use of antibiotics. Before 1941, a person with a major bacterial infection almost always died. Today, such deaths are rare except for those ill with other conditions such as AIDS. Six decades ago, pneumonia was a dreaded killer of people of all ages. Today, it kills mainly the elderly and those with AIDS.

Antibiotics have indeed worked miracles in our time, but even miracle drugs are not without problems. It wasn't long after antibiotics were first introduced that disease organisms began to develop strains resistant to them. One strain can spread antibiotic resistance to another by sharing genes, and the emergence of more and more resistant strains of bacteria is a serious threat to world health. For example, tuberculosis had been almost completely wiped out in developed countries, but a drug-resistant strain has become rampant in Russia and among AIDS patients everywhere.

Another example of the development of resistance involves erythromycin, an antibiotic obtained from *Streptomyces erythreus*. As long as it had only limited use, erythromycin could handle all strains of staphylococci. After it was put into extensive use, resistant strains of these bacteria began to appear. Staph infections are now a serious problem in hospitals. People who are admitted to a hospital for treatment sometimes develop serious bacterial infections. Some even die of these staph infections. The CDC estimated in 2007 that staph infections cause more than 94,000 serious illnesses and about 19,000 deaths each year. Later studies have shown a decline in staph infections, but no more precise data are available.

In a race to stay ahead of resistant strains of bacteria, scientists continue to seek new antibiotics. Penicillins have been partially displaced by related compounds called *cephalosporins* such as cephalexin (Keflex®). Unfortunately, some strains of bacteria are now resistant to cephalosporins.

3. Why must I continue taking an antibiotic even after I am feeling better?

Antibiotics inhibit the growth of bacteria. A prescription will be written for the time it will take to completely kill off all of the bacteria. A large percentage of bacteria will be killed fairly early during treatment, so a person will feel much better. However, some individual bacteria may take longer to be killed. It is important to take all of the prescription to make sure that there are no remaining bacteria that can grow and start the infection again. Any bacteria not killed have a greater potential to develop resistance to the drug.

Cephalexin

Another important development in the field of antibiotics was the discovery of a group of compounds called *tetracyclines*. The first of these four-ring compounds, chlortetracycline (Aureomycin®), was isolated by Benjamin Duggor (1872–1956) in 1948 from *Streptomyces aureofaciens*. Scientists at Pfizer Laboratories isolated oxytetracycline (Terramycin®) from *Streptomyces rimosus* in 1950, and both drugs were later found to be derivatives of tetracycline, a compound now obtained from *Streptomyces viridifaciens*. All three compounds (Figure 18.8) are **broad-spectrum antibiotics**, so called because they are effective against a wide variety of bacteria.

▼ **Figure 18.8** Three tetracycline antibiotics. Subtle structural differences are highlighted by color.

Tetracycline

Aureomycin®
(chlortetracycline)

Terramycin®
(oxytetracycline)

Tetracyclines bind to bacterial ribosomes, inhibiting bacterial protein synthesis and blocking growth of the bacteria. Tetracyclines do not bind to mammalian ribosomes and thus do not affect protein synthesis in host cells. Several disease-causing organisms have developed strains resistant to tetracyclines.

When given to young children, tetracyclines can cause the discoloration of permanent teeth, even though the teeth may not appear until several years later. Women are told to avoid tetracyclines during pregnancy for the same reason. This probably results from the interaction of tetracyclines with calcium during the period of tooth development. Calcium ions in milk and other foods combine with hydroxyl groups on tetracycline molecules.

Fluoroquinolone antibiotics were first introduced in 1986 and now represent about one-third of the $42 billion global antibiotics market. They act against a broad spectrum of bacteria and seemingly have few side effects. A major use is against bacteria with penicillin resistance. Fluoroquinolones act by inhibiting DNA replication in bacteria through interference with the action of an enzyme called DNA gyrase. Humans do not have this enzyme, so fluoroquinolones do not harm human cells. Because their mechanism of action differs from that of other antibiotics, it was hoped that resistance to fluoroquinolones would be slow to emerge. However, such resistance has already been observed.

The fluoroquinolones are also of particular interest to chemists and pharmacologists because they have a number of structural features that can be correlated with their activity. This provides a rational and logical approach to designing and synthesizing new drugs in this class. The basic skeletal structure for a fluoroquinolone is

The fluorine atom at position 6 is essential for broad antimicrobial activity when taken orally. Effectiveness also depends on the carboxyl group at position 3 and the carbonyl oxygen at position 4, which are responsible for binding to the bacterial DNA complex. A nitrogen-containing ring structure at position 7 or a methoxy group at position 8 broadens the range of bacteria affected. If position 7 has a bulky substituent, the drug has fewer side effects on the nervous system. Several of these features can be seen in Ciprofloxacin (Cipro®) in the margin.

Ciprofloxacin (Cipro®)

Viruses and Antiviral Drugs

For most of us, antibiotics have eliminated the terror of bacterial infections such as pneumonia and diphtheria. We worry about resistant strains of bacteria, but for most people these problems are not insurmountable. However, viral diseases cannot be cured by antibiotics, and viral infections, from colds and influenza to herpes and **acquired immune deficiency syndrome (AIDS)**, still plague us. Some viral infections—such as poliomyelitis, mumps, measles, and smallpox—can be prevented by vaccination. Influenza vaccines are quite effective against common recurrent strains of flu viruses, but there are many different strains of these viruses, and new ones appear periodically.

DNA Viruses and RNA Viruses

Viruses are composed of nucleic acids and proteins (Figure 18.9). They have an external coat that shows a repetitive pattern of protein molecules. Some coats also include a lipid membrane, and others have sugar–protein combinations called *glycoproteins*. The genetic material of a virus is either DNA or RNA. A *DNA virus* moves to the location in a host cell where the DNA is replicated, and it directs the host cell to produce viral proteins.

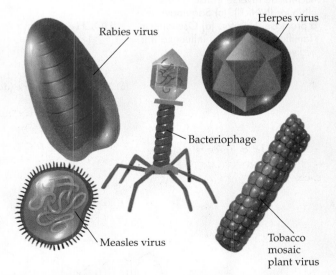

▲ **Figure 18.9** Viruses come in a variety of shapes, which are determined by their protein coats.

The viral proteins and viral DNA assemble into new viruses that are released by the host cell. These new viruses can then invade other cells and continue the process.

Most *RNA viruses* use their nucleic acids in much the same way. The virus penetrates to where the RNA strands of a host cell are replicated and induces the synthesis of viral proteins. The new RNA strands and viral proteins are then assembled into new viruses. Some RNA viruses, called **retroviruses**, synthesize *DNA* in the host cell. This process is the opposite of the transcription of DNA into RNA (Section 16.7) that normally occurs in cells (the term *retro* implies working backward). The synthesis of DNA from an RNA template is catalyzed by an enzyme called *reverse transcriptase*. The human immunodeficiency virus (HIV) that causes AIDS is a retrovirus. HIV invades and eventually destroys *T cells*, white blood cells that normally help protect the body from infections. Once the T cells are destroyed, the AIDS victim often succumbs to pneumonia or some other infection.

Worldwide, 35.3 million people were living with AIDS in 2012. More than 36 million have already died from AIDS, and 1.7 million more died in 2011. Some 2.5 million people became infected with HIV in 2011. In the United States, more than 1.0 million persons are living with HIV/AIDS, and about 40,000 new HIV infections occur each year.

Antiviral Drugs

Scientists have developed a variety of drugs that are effective against some viruses, but none of them provides cures. Structures of some common antiviral agents are given in Figure 18.10. Another antiviral agent, acyclovir (Zovirax®), is used to treat chickenpox, shingles, cold sores, and the symptoms of genital herpes.

Antiretroviral drugs prevent the reproduction of retroviruses such as HIV and are used against AIDS. The following are three important kinds of antiretrovirals.

- *Nucleoside analogs*, or nucleoside reverse transcriptase inhibitors (NRTIs), include didanosine (ddI, Videx®), lamivudine (3TC, Epivir®), stavudine (d4T, Zerit®), zalcitabine (ddC, Hivid®), zidovudine (AZT, Retrovir®), and tenofovir

▶ **Figure 18.10** Some antiviral drugs. (a) Didanosine (ddI) is a nucleoside analog, or nucleoside reverse transcriptase inhibitor (NRTI). (b) Delavirdine is a non-nucleoside reverse transcriptase inhibitor (NNRTI). (c) Saquinavir is a protease inhibitor. (d) Oseltamivir (Tamiflu®) can prevent influenza if it is given in early stages.

(a) 2′,3′-Dideoxyinosine (ddI)

(b) Delaviridine

(c) Saquinavir

(d) Oseltamivir

(part of the combination drug Atripla®). Substitution of an analog for a nucleoside in viral DNA cripples the retrovirus, slowing down its replication.

- *Nonnucleoside reverse transcriptase inhibitors (NNRTIs)* stop the reverse transcriptase from working properly to make more of the retrovirus. NNRTIs include delavirdine (Rescriptor®), efavirenz, rilpivirine, and nevirapine (Viramune®).

- *Protease inhibitors* block the enzyme protease so that new copies of the retrovirus can't infect new cells. Protease inhibitors include ritonavir (Norvir®), darunavir, atazanavir, and saquinavir (Invirase®).

Combinations of AIDS drugs seem to be more effective than any one of them alone. For example, Atripla® contains efavirenz, emtricitabine, and tenofovir. It provides a once daily single-pill treatment that can control HIV for long periods of time.

Basic Research and Drug Development

Scientists had to understand the normal biochemistry of cells before they could develop drugs to treat diseases caused by viruses. Gertrude Elion and George Hitchings of Burroughs Wellcome Research Laboratories in North Carolina and James Black of Kings College in London did much of the basic biochemical research that led to the development of antiviral drugs and many anticancer drugs (Section 18.4). They determined the shapes of cell membrane receptors and learned how normal cells work. They and other scientists were then able to design drugs to block receptors in infected cells. Elion, Hitchings, and Black shared the 1988 Nobel Prize in Physiology or Medicine for their work.

Drug design in its early days was often a hit-or-miss procedure. Today, scientists use powerful computers to design molecules to fit receptors, making drug design a more precise science.

Prevention of Viral Diseases with Vaccination

For many viral diseases, there are no effective drugs. However, these diseases can often be prevented by vaccination, which causes the body to develop immunity to the virus or microorganism. Examples include poliomyelitis (polio) and smallpox, as well as formerly common childhood diseases such as measles, mumps, and whooping cough.

Polio had been a major public health problem throughout the world, including among its victims President Franklin Roosevelt. In a 1952 epidemic, more than 50,000 victims were reported in the United States, with roughly half of them suffering paralysis. Jonas Salk developed a vaccine that was introduced in 1955 and administered widely. Albert Sabin developed an oral vaccine in the early 1960s. Introduction of these vaccines ended outbreaks of polio in the United States and almost all of the rest of the world.

Smallpox vaccination has been practiced for a much longer time, with the best-known vaccine being developed by Edward Jenner in 1796. Smallpox vaccination was discontinued in the United States in 1972, when the tiny statistical risk from the vaccine was judged to be greater than the risk of acquiring the disease.

The MMR (measles, mumps, rubella) vaccine was developed in the 1970s and ordinarily is given to children before they enter kindergarten. Although some of these diseases can be treated after onset, preventing them is much preferred.

Unfortunately, many parents have recently decided not to have their children vaccinated, based on a 1998 study by Andrew Wakefield that purported to link MMR vaccination to autism. This work has since been declared fraudulent and Wakefield has been barred from practicing medicine, but some well-known public figures have continued to support his work. Uninformed parents, fearful of autism, have elected not to have their children vaccinated. The antivaccination movement has resulted in epidemics in several states. For example, in 2010, there were over 9000 confirmed cases of whooping cough and 10 infant deaths from the disease in California—the worst outbreak in 60 years—and another whooping cough outbreak occurred in California in 2014. There have also been large increases in other preventable diseases in recent years.

4. What kinds of drugs work for colds or the flu? Colds and the flu are the result of viral infection. Antibiotics work against bacteria, but viruses have proved to be much more difficult to treat, in part because viruses mutate quite rapidly. There are some prescription drugs, such as oseltamivir (Tamiflu®), which can minimize the effects of the flu when taken within 1 to 2 days of onset. However, there still is no effective treatment for colds, which can be triggered by any of some 200 rhinoviruses. Treatments to help alleviate the symptoms rather than the cause are widely used.

SELF-ASSESSMENT Questions

1. Which of the following works by inhibiting the normal growth of bacteria?
   a. sulfa drugs
   b. reverse transcriptase inhibitors
   c. analgesics
   d. NSAIDs

2. Penicillins act by inhibiting the synthesis of
   a. bacterial cell walls
   b. folic acid
   c. β-lactams
   d. viral RNA

3. A compound that is derived from bacteria or molds and inhibits the growth of other microorganisms is a(n)
   a. antibiotic
   b. antiviral
   c. anticarcinogen
   d. retroviral

4. Taking antibiotics for a stomach virus will
   a. cure the illness
   b. increase the chance that drug-resistant bacteria will develop
   c. lessen the symptoms
   d. shorten the duration of the illness

5. Viruses consist of a protein coat surrounding a core of
   a. lipids
   b. nucleic acids
   c. polysaccharides
   d. proteins

6. Most RNA viruses replicate in host cells by replicating RNA strands and synthesizing
   a. host-cell lipids
   b. host-cell proteins
   c. viral polysaccharides
   d. viral proteins

7. Retroviruses replicate in host cells by
   a. replicating RNA strands and synthesizing viral proteins
   b. replicating RNA strands and synthesizing host-cell proteins
   c. synthesizing DNA and forming new viruses
   d. synthesizing DNA and replicating host cells

8. All of the following are major types of antiretroviral drugs except
   a. protease inhibitors
   b. nonnucleoside reverse transcriptase inhibitors (NNRTIs)
   c. sulfa drugs
   d. nucleoside analogs (NRTI)

9. What is the best way of dealing with viral diseases such as diphtheria, mumps, and smallpox is
   a. antibacterial drugs
   b. antiviral drugs
   c. tetracyclines
   d. vaccinations

Answers: 1. a; 2. a; 3. a; 4. b; 5. b; 6. d; 7. c; 8. c; 9. d

18.4 Chemicals against Cancer

Learning Objective ❯ Describe the action of the common types of anticancer drugs.

Despite decades of "war" on cancer, it remains a dread disease. Each year in the United States, more than 1.6 million new cases are diagnosed and cancer kills about 580,000 people. Scientists have made progress, but much more remains to be done. A major problem is that the drugs that kill cancer cells also damage normal cells, especially rapidly growing cells such as those that line the digestive tract or produce hair. Side effects of chemotherapy therefore include nausea and loss of hair. Thus, a main aim of cancer research is to find a way to kill cancerous tissue without killing too many normal cells.

Treatment with drugs, radiation, and/or surgery yields a high rate of cure for some kinds of cancer. For example, with treatment, early-stage prostate cancer has an overall five-year survival rate of nearly 100%. For other types, such as lung and bronchus cancer, the overall five-year survival rate is only 15%, mainly because lung cancer is often advanced at the time of diagnosis. The five-year survival rate for all cancers is about 68%.

Several categories of anticancer drugs are used widely, and we look at some of them here.

Antimetabolites: Inhibition of Nucleic Acid Synthesis

An **antimetabolite** is a compound that closely resembles a substance essential to normal body metabolism, which allows it to interfere with physiological reactions involving that substance. Rapidly dividing cells, characteristic of cancer, require an abundance of DNA. Cancer antimetabolites block DNA synthesis and therefore block the increase in the number of cancer cells. Because cancer cells are undergoing rapid growth and cell division, they are generally affected to a greater extent than normal cells. Research over the last two decades has led to refinements in how antimetabolites are administered, increasing their effectiveness.

Gertrude Elion and George Hitchings patented 6-mercaptopurine (6-MP) in 1954. This compound can substitute for adenine in nucleotides, the phosphate–sugar–base units of both DNA and RNA (Section 16.6), and the pseudonucleotides then inhibit the synthesis of nucleotides incorporating adenine and guanine. This slows DNA synthesis and cell division, thus inhibiting the multiplication of cancer cells. Before the use of 6-MP, half of all children with acute leukemia died within a few months. Combined with other medications, 6-MP was able to cure approximately 80% of child leukemia patients.

Another prominent antimetabolite is 5-fluorouracil (5-FU), which blocks synthesis of the thymine-containing nucleotide thymidine, an essential component for DNA replication. 5-FU is employed against a variety of cancers, especially those of the breast and the digestive tract.

6-Mercaptopurine

Adenine

5-Fluorouracil   Uracil

The antimetabolite methotrexate acts somewhat differently. It is a folic acid antagonist that interferes with cellular reproduction. Note the similarity between its structure and that of folic acid. Like the pseudo-folic acid formed from sulfanilamide, methotrexate competes successfully with folic acid for an essential enzyme but cannot perform the growth-enhancing function of folic acid. Again, cell division is slowed and cancer growth is retarded. Methotrexate is used frequently against leukemia. It is also used in the treatment of psoriasis and certain inflammatory diseases such as rheumatoid arthritis.

Methotrexate   Folic acid

Alkylating Agents: Turning Old Weapons into Anticancer Drugs

Alkylating agents are highly reactive compounds that can transfer alkyl groups to compounds of biological importance. These added alkyl groups then block the usual action of the biological molecules. Some alkylating agents are used against cancer, including nitrogen mustards.

Interestingly enough, these compounds grew out of research for chemical warfare agents. More than 30 chemical agents were employed during World War I, killing 91,000 and wounding 1.2 million (disabling many of them for life).

The use of chemical warfare agents was largely avoided during World War II. However, they have since been used in smaller wars—for example, by Iraq against Iran in the 1980s and by the Iraqi government against Kurdish rebels. Most recently sarin has been used in Syria. Chemical warfare agents are considered to be one of the *weapons of mass destruction (WMDs)* that can kill huge numbers of people and might be used by a rogue nation or a terrorist group. (The other WMDs are nuclear devices and biological agents such as anthrax and botulism.)

The original mustard gas was a sulfur-containing blister agent used during World War I. Contact with either the liquid or the vapor causes blisters that are painful and slow to heal. It is easily detected, however, by its garlic or horseradish odor. Mustard gas is denoted by the military symbol H.

$$Cl-CH_2CH_2-S-CH_2CH_2-Cl$$

Mustard gas (H)

Nitrogen mustards (symbol HN) were developed in about 1935. Though not quite as effective overall as mustard gas, nitrogen mustards produce greater eye damage and don't have an obvious odor. Structurally, nitrogen mustards are chlorinated amines.

$$CH_3CH_2—N\begin{array}{c}CH_2CH_2—Cl\\CH_2CH_2—Cl\end{array}$$

$$CH_3—N\begin{array}{c}CH_2CH_2—Cl\\CH_2CH_2—Cl\end{array}$$

$$Cl—CH_2CH_2—N\begin{array}{c}CH_2CH_2—Cl\\CH_2CH_2—Cl\end{array}$$

HN₁   HN₂   HN₃

In cancer treatment, nitrogen mustards, which are bifunctional alkylating agents (that is, agents with two functional groups), act by cross-linking two DNA strands. Cross-linking prevents or hinders replication and thus impedes growth of cancer cells. Knowledge gained through science is neither good nor evil. The same knowledge—in this case, the ability to make nitrogen mustards—can be used either for our benefit or for our destruction.

The nitrogen mustard often used for cancer therapy is a compound called cyclophosphamide (Cytoxan®). It is used to treat Hodgkin's disease, lymphomas, leukemias, and other cancers.

Alkylating agents can cause cancer as well as cure it. For example, the nitrogen mustard HN₂ causes lung, mammary, and liver tumors when injected into mice, yet it can be used with some success in the management of certain human tumors. There is still a lot of mystery—and seeming contradiction—regarding the causes and cures of cancer.

The platinum-containing compound cisplatin [PtCl₂(NH₃)₂] is a prominent anticancer drug. Even though cisplatin was first synthesized in 1844, its biological effect was discovered by accident in 1965 by Barnett Rosenberg at Michigan State University, who was looking at the effect of electrical currents on cell division. He found that *E. coli* were growing in length but failing to divide, sometimes reaching 300 times their normal length. Upon further study, Rosenberg and his team found that the electric current had caused a chemical reaction between the platinum in the electrodes and nutrients in the solution containing the bacteria, producing a new compound, cisplatin. Because the compound inhibited cell division, Rosenberg reasoned that it might be effective as an anticancer drug. It is. Cisplatin, an alkylating agent, binds to DNA and blocks its replication. It is widely used to treat cancers of the ovaries, testes, uterus, head, neck, breast, and lungs and advanced bladder cancers.

Cyclophosphamide

Cisplatin

Other Anticancer Agents

Many other anticancer agents are in use today. Alkaloids from vinca plants have been shown to be effective against leukemia and Hodgkin's disease. Paclitaxel (Taxol®), first obtained from the Pacific yew tree, is effective against cancers of the breast, ovary, and cervix.

Imatinib (Gleevec®) is a synthetic drug that is particularly effective against chronic myeloid leukemia. Cell growth is controlled by substances called *growth factors*, which act by attaching to receptor proteins on the surface of certain types of cells. People with chronic myeloid leukemia produce cells with damaged receptors that send grow-and-divide signals to the cells even with no growth factor present. Imatinib inhibits the faulty receptors, preventing them from stimulating the cells to grow and divide; the cancer cells cannot multiply.

Several antibiotics have been found to kill cancer cells as well as bacteria. Actinomycin, obtained from the molds *Streptomyces antibioticus* and *S. parvus*, is used against Hodgkin's disease and other types of cancer. It is quite effective but extremely toxic. Actinomycin acts by binding to the double helix of DNA, thus blocking the replication of RNA on the DNA template. Protein synthesis is inhibited.

Chemotherapy is only part of the treatment for cancer. Surgical removal of tumors and radiation treatment remain major tools. It is unlikely that research will discover a single agent that can cure all cancers. Active research is under way

Imatinib

on the mechanisms of carcinogenesis, and a better understanding will lead to better cures. Prevention of cancer is a greater hope. Deaths from smoking-related cancers account for at least 30% of all cancer deaths. Reducing cigarette smoking can significantly reduce cancer deaths.

SELF-ASSESSMENT Questions

1. Which of the following is an antimetabolite?
   a. alkylating agents   **b.** cyclophosphamide
   c. cisplatin   **d.** nitrogen mustard

2. 6-Mercaptopurine mimics the base adenine, forming a pseudonucleotide and thus slowing
   a. cell-mediated immune reactions
   b. DNA synthesis
   c. RNA transport
   d. viral replication

3. Methotrexate is a folic-acid antagonist that slows
   a. cell division
   b. cell-mediated immune reactions
   c. transport of nutrients to the cancer cell
   d. viral replication

4. Cisplatin inhibits cell division by
   a. being incorporated in RNA
   b. binding to DNA and blocking its replication
   c. halting viral replication
   d. substituting for cytosine in a nucleotide

5. Which of the following acts as an alkylating agent?
   a. 6-mercaptopurine   **b.** cyclophosphamide
   c. cisplatin   **d.** methotrexate

6. Cyclophosphamide acts by
   a. being incorporated in RNA
   b. cross-linking two DNA strands and blocking replication
   c. halting viral replication
   d. substituting for cytosine in a nucleotide

Answers: 1, a; 2, b; 3, a; 4, b; 5, b; 6, b

18.5 Hormones: The Regulators

Learning Objectives ❯ Define the terms *hormone*, *prostaglandin*, and *steroid*, and explain the function of each. ❯ List the three types of sex hormones, and explain how each acts and how birth control drugs work.

Before we discuss the next group of drugs, we need to take a brief look at the human endocrine system and some of the chemical compounds, called *hormones*, that this system manufactures. A **hormone** is a chemical messenger produced in the endocrine glands (Figure 18.11). Hormones released in one part of the body send signals for profound physiological changes in other parts of the body. By causing reactions to speed up or slow down, hormones control growth, metabolism, reproduction, and many other functions of body and mind. Some of the important human hormones and their physiological effects are listed in Table 18.2 on the next page. Still other hormones are formed in tissues of the heart, liver, kidney, gut, and placenta. Most hormones are proteins, peptides, or amino-acid derivatives, although hormones produced by the adrenal gland and the gonads are steroids.

Prostaglandins: Hormone Mediators

A *prostaglandin* is a hormone-like lipid derived from a fatty acid. Each prostaglandin molecule has 20 carbon atoms, including a 5-carbon ring. Prostaglandins function similarly to hormones in that they act on target cells. However, they differ from hormones in that they (1) act near the site where they are produced, (2) can have different effects in different tissues, and (3) are rapidly metabolized. Prostaglandins are synthesized in the body from arachidonic acid (Figure 18.12 is on page 571). There are several primary prostaglandins, which are widely distributed throughout the body. Extremely small doses of these potent biological

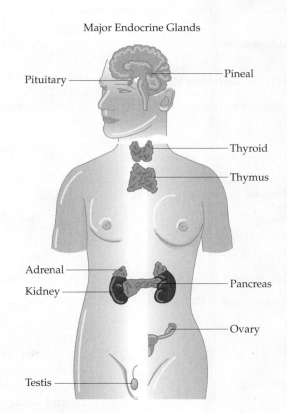

▲ **Figure 18.11** The approximate locations of the eight major endocrine glands in the human body.

Table 18.2 Some Human Hormones and Their Physiological Effects		
Name	Chemical Nature	Function(s)
Pituitary Hormones		
Vasopressin (antidiuretic hormone)	Nonapeptide	Stimulates contractions of smooth muscle; regulates water retention and blood pressure
Oxytocin	Nonapeptide	Stimulates contraction of the smooth muscle of the uterus; stimulates secretion of milk
Growth hormone (GH) (or somatotropin)	Protein	Stimulates body growth and bone growth
Thyroid-stimulating hormone (TSH)	Protein	Stimulates growth of the thyroid gland and production of thyroid hormones
Adrenocorticotrophic hormone (ACTH)	Protein	Stimulates growth of the adrenal cortex and production of cortical hormones
Follicle-stimulating hormone (FSH)	Protein	Stimulates maturation of egg follicles in ovaries of females and of sperm cells in testes of males
Luteinizing hormone (LH)	Protein	Stimulates female ovulation and male secretion of testosterone
Prolactin	Protein	Maintains the production of estrogens and progesterone; stimulates the formation of milk
Thyroid Hormone		
Thyroxine	Amino-acid derivative	Increases rate of cellular metabolism
Pancreatic Hormones		
Insulin	Protein	Increases cellular usage of glucose; increases glycogen storage
Glucagon	Protein	Stimulates conversion of liver glycogen to glucose
Adrenal Cortical Hormones		
Cortisol	Steroid	Stimulates conversion of proteins to carbohydrates
Aldosterone	Steroid	Regulates salt metabolism; stimulates kidneys to retain Na^+ and excrete K^+
Adrenal Medullary Hormones		
Epinephrine (adrenaline)	Amino-acid derivative	Stimulates a variety of mechanisms to prepare the body for emergency action, including the conversion of glycogen to glucose
Norepinephrine (noradrenaline)	Amino-acid derivative	Stimulates sympathetic nervous system; constricts blood vessels; stimulates other glands
Gonadal Hormones		
Estradiol	Steroid	Stimulates development of female sex characteristics; regulates changes during menstrual cycle
Progesterone	Steroid	Regulates menstrual cycle; maintains pregnancy
Testosterone	Steroid	Stimulates development of and maintains male sex characteristics

chemicals can elicit marked changes. Besides the primary prostaglandins, many others have been identified.

Prostaglandins act as mediators of hormone action. They regulate such things as blood pressure, blood clotting, pain sensation, smooth muscle activity, and secretion of substances related to reproduction. A single prostaglandin can have different, or even opposite, effects in different tissues. This range of physiological activity has led to the synthesis of hundreds of prostaglandins

▲ **Figure 18.12** Prostaglandins are derived from arachidonic acid, an unsaturated carboxylic acid with 20 carbon atoms (a). Two representative prostaglandins are shown here: (b) prostaglandin E_2 and (c) prostaglandin $F_{2\alpha}$.

and analogs. Prostaglandin E_2 (PGE_2), also known as dinoprostone (Cervidil®), is used to induce labor. PGE_1 can lower blood pressure. A PGE_1 analog called misoprostol is used to help prevent peptic ulcers, a common side effect of large doses of NSAIDs. Other prostaglandins can be used clinically to relieve nasal congestion, to provide relief from asthma, to treat glaucoma, to treat pulmonary hypertension, and to prevent formation of blood clots associated with heart attacks and strokes.

$PGE_{2\alpha}$ is used in cattle to synchronize breeding. It is also used in the artificial insemination of prize cows. Injection of $PGE_{2\alpha}$ along with a hormone into a prize cow will induce the release of many ova, which are then fertilized with sperm from a champion bull. The developing embryos are implanted in less valuable cows, enabling a farmer to get several calves a year from one outstanding cow.

Steroids

A **steroid** is a compound with a four-ring skeletal structure. Steroids occur widely in living organisms, but not all steroids are hormones (Figure 18.13). Cholesterol, for example, is a steroid component of all animal tissues and is the starting material for the synthesis of all other naturally occurring steroids. About 10% of the brain is cholesterol; it is a vital part of the membranes of nerve cells. Cholesterol is also found in deposits in hardened arteries and is a major component of certain types of gallstones. Cortisol, another natural steroid, is an adrenal hormone (Table 18.2). Prednisone is a synthetic steroid used to reduce inflammation in arthritis sufferers and to treat injuries.

▲ Skeletal structure of steroids.

(a) Cholesterol (b) Cortisol

(c) Prednisone (d) Methandrostenolone

◀ **Figure 18.13** Structural formulas of four steroids. (a) Cholesterol is an essential component of all animal cells. (b) Cortisol is a hormone secreted by the adrenal glands in response to physical or psychological stress. (c) Prednisone is a synthetic anti-inflammatory substance. (d) Methandrostenolone (Dianabol®) is an anabolic steroid (Chapter 19). Note that all have the same basic four-ring structure.

Diabetes

The pancreas produces the hormone *insulin*, which increases cellular usage of glucose. *Diabetes* arises when the pancreas does not produce enough insulin (type 1) or when the insulin is not properly used by the body (type 2). In both cases, elevated blood glucose levels are the result. Over 90% of Americans diagnosed with diabetes suffer from type 2, which has both a strong genetic component as well as a close tie to lifestyle. Poor diet, obesity, and lack of exercise all appear to be contributing factors to type 2. Gestational diabetes is a form of type 2 that occurs in 2 to 10% of pregnant women with no history of the disease. This form generally disappears after delivery but does persist in some women permanently. Paralleling the increase in obesity, type 2 diabetes has become increasingly common, even among children and adolescents.

People who suffer from type 1 diabetes ordinarily must take insulin, which has to be injected because insulin taken orally is broken down by the body's digestive system before it can reach the bloodstream. Type 2 diabetics may be able to control their disease with careful diet, exercise, and loss of weight. When these measures aren't enough, a biguanide such as metformin (Glucophage®) is often prescribed. Metformin works by reducing the production of glucose in the liver. It is one of the most widely prescribed medications, with over 48 million new and refilled prescriptions dispensed in the United States in 2010. Sulfonylureas, which increase the production of insulin from the pancreas, are also used to treat type 2 diabetes. Sometimes these oral drugs are not enough to maintain glucose levels in individuals with type 2 diabetes, and insulin must be administered. The economic cost of diabetes in the United States was estimated to be $245 billion in 2012.

$$CH_3-N-C-NH-C-NH_2$$

Metformin

Diabetes can cause a number of complications, including blindness, cardiovascular disease, kidney disease, and nerve damage. Thus, diagnosis and control of diabetes is very important. Over 32 million Americans have the disease—but almost a quarter of them aren't aware of it.

Many drugs, both natural and synthetic, are based on steroids, including the notorious anabolic steroids (Chapter 19) that are abused by athletes and body builders. Some steroid drugs are anti-inflammatories used to treat arthritis, bronchial asthma, dermatitis, and eye infections. Some are sex hormones that are active ingredients in birth control pills.

Serendipity often plays a role in the discovery of new drugs. Percy Julian, a grandson of slaves, was a chemist at the Glidden Paint Company doing research on soybeans when his work led to the development of new steroid-based drugs. It often happens that new drugs are discovered by chemists who are working on something entirely different.

Sex Hormones

Sex hormones are steroids (Figure 18.14) on page 573. Note that male sex hormones differ only slightly in structure from female sex hormones. In fact, the female hormone progesterone can be converted to the male hormone testosterone by a simple biochemical reaction. The physiological actions of these structurally similar compounds, however, are markedly different.

An **androgen** is any compound that stimulates the development or controls the maintenance of masculine characteristics. These male sex hormones are secreted by the testes. In males, the pituitary hormones FSH and LH (Table 18.2) are required for the continued production of sperm and of androgens. These hormones are responsible for development of the sex organs and for secondary sexual characteristics, such as voice and hair distribution. The most important androgen is testosterone.

An **estrogen** is a compound that controls female sexual functions, such as the menstrual cycle, breast development, and other secondary sexual characteristics. The two important estrogens are estradiol and estrone. These female sex hormones are produced mainly in the ovaries. Another female sex hormone is progesterone, which prepares the uterus for pregnancy and prevents the further release of eggs

▲ Percy Lavon Julian (1899–1975) was involved in the synthesis of a variety of steroids, including physostigmine, a drug used to treat glaucoma, which can cause blindness. Julian is shown here on a 1992 U.S. postage stamp.

(a) Testosterone

(b) Estrone

(c) Estradiol

(d) Progesterone

◀ **Figure 18.14** Structural formulas of the principal sex hormones. Testosterone (a) is the main male sex hormone (an androgen). Estrone (b) and estradiol (c) are female sex hormones (estrogens). Progesterone (d), also produced by females, is essential to the maintenance of pregnancy.

from the ovaries during pregnancy. A related type of compound, called a **progestin**, is any steroid hormone that has the effect of progesterone. In females, the pituitary hormones FSH and LH (Table 18.2) are required for the production of ova and of estrogens and progesterone.

Sex hormones—both natural and synthetic—are sometimes used therapeutically. For example, a woman who has passed menopause may be given hormones to compensate for those no longer being produced by her ovaries. Hormone replacement therapy was used quite widely, but its use has largely been discontinued because of concerns that the increased health risks it posed outweighed the benefits.

Chemistry and Social Revolution: The Pill

When administered by injection, progesterone serves as an effective birth control drug. It fools the body into acting as if it were already pregnant. The structure of progesterone was determined in 1934 by Adolf Butenandt (1903–1995), who received the Nobel Prize in Chemistry in 1939. Other chemists began to try to design a contraceptive that would be effective when taken orally.

In 1938, Hans Inhoffen (1906–1992) synthesized the first oral contraceptive, ethisterone, by incorporating an ethynyl group ($—C\equiv CH$). (The ethynyl group is derived from ethyne, $HC\equiv CH$, also called acetylene.) However, ethisterone had to be taken in large doses to be effective and was not widely used.

In 1951, Carl Djerassi synthesized 19-norprogesterone, which is simply progesterone with one of its methyl groups missing. It was four to eight times as effective as progesterone as a birth control agent, but it had to be given by injection, an undesirable property. Djerassi then combined the two improvements: removal of a methyl group to make the drug more effective, and addition of an ethynyl group to allow oral administration to synthesize norethindrone (Norlutin®), which proved effective when taken in small doses (Figure 18.15), and patented it in 1956. Working at about the same time, Frank Colton synthesized norethynodrel, another progestin, for which G. D. Searle was awarded patents in 1954 and 1955. Norethynodrel, a progestin, was used in Enovid, the first birth control pill approved by the FDA (1960).

The progestins—norethynodrel, norethindrone, and related compounds—mimic the action of progesterone. Mestranol, a synthetic estrogen, regulates the menstrual cycle and the progestin establishes a state of false pregnancy. A woman does not ovulate or conceive when she is pregnant or in a state of false pregnancy established by a progestin.

▶ **Figure 18.15** Formulas of some synthetic sex hormones: ethisterone (a), norethindrone b), norethynodrel (c), and mestranol (d). In 1960, G. D. S earle's Enovid, which contained 9.85 mg of norethynodrel and 150 mg of mestranol, became the first birth control pill approved by the FDA. Djerassi's norethindrone and Colton's norethynodrel differ only in the position of a double bond.

(a)   Ethisterone

(b)   Norethindrone (Norlutin®)

(c)   Norethynodrel

(d)   Mestranol

Levonorgestrel

Ulipristal acetate

▲ The Copper T 380A IUD (ParaGard®).

Emergency Contraceptives

Products called *emergency contraceptive pills (ECPs)* can be used to prevent pregnancy after unprotected intercourse. Two common products are Plan B One-Step® and ella®. Plan B One-Step contains only a progestin, levonorgestrel, but in higher doses than regular birth control pills. It is available over the counter without a prescription. Plan B, like progestins in general, acts by tricking the body into thinking it's already pregnant, halting development of the uterine lining and inhibiting ovulation and fertilization. Ella, a non-hormonal pill available only by prescription, contains ulipristal acetate, a progesterone antagonist. This delays ovulation for up to five days, by which time sperm will have died.

An intrauterine device (IUD), the Copper T 380A IUD (ParaGard®), is also used for emergency contraception. IUD insertion reduces the incidence of pregnancy by 99.9% if done within three to five days of unprotected intercourse. Copper(II) ions in the IUD interfere with sperm transport and fertilization. The copper IUD probably causes an inflammation that makes the endometrium unsuitable for implantation.

ECPs act differently from mifepristone (Mifeprex® or RU-486), which causes the uterus to expel an implanted egg and end the pregnancy. Thus, ECPs prevent pregnancy after sexual intercourse, while mifepristone ends an unwanted pregnancy at an early stage.

Mifepristone

People who believe that human life begins when the ovum is fertilized by the sperm equate the use of mifepristone with abortion and oppose the use of the drug. Others consider the drug another method of birth control and see its use as being safer than a surgical abortion.

Risks of Taking Birth Control Pills

Oral contraceptives are currently used by more than 100 million women world-wide and by about 12 million women in the United States. Most women report no side effects. Of the side effects that are reported, almost all are minor. Some women experience hypertension, acne, or abnormal bleeding. These pills increase the risk of blood clotting in some women, but so does pregnancy. Blood clots can clog arteries and cause death by stroke or heart attack. The death rate associated with birth control pills is about 3 in 100,000, only one-tenth of the death rate associated with childbirth. For smokers, however, the risks are much higher. For women over 40 who smoke 15 cigarettes per day and take an oral contraceptive, the risk of death from stroke or heart attack is 1 in 5000. The FDA advises all women who smoke, especially those over 40, to use some other method of contraception.

The Minipill

Because most of the side effects of oral contraceptives are associated with the estrogen component, the amount of estrogen in birth control pills has been greatly reduced over the years. Today's pills contain only a fraction of a milligram of estrogen. "Minipills" are now available that contain only small amounts of progestin and no estrogen at all. Minipills are not quite as effective as the combination pills, but they have fewer side effects.

A Pill for Males?

Why should females have to bear all the responsibility for contraception? Why not a pill for males? Many men are willing to share the risks and the responsibility of contraception, but condoms and vasectomies are the only effective forms of contraception available to them. There are biological reasons for females to bear the burden. Women are the ones who get pregnant when contraception fails, and in females contraception has to interfere with only one monthly event: ovulation. Males produce sperm continuously.

In males, the pituitary hormones FSH and LH (Table 18.2) are required for the continued production of sperm and of the male hormone testosterone. Several research groups have developed what may be a safe, effective, and reversible contraceptive for males. The pill has a progestin—the same key ingredient as is used in pills for women—combined with the male sex hormone testosterone. The progestin seems to function much as it does in the women's pill: It suppresses the rate of sperm production and the quantity of sperm produced. When will such male birth control pills be available to the public? Optimistic projections estimate a wait of several years.

SELF-ASSESSMENT Questions

1. Which organ system consists of hormone-secreting glands?
   a. endocrine
   b. lymphatic
   c. respiratory
   d. urinary

2. Prostaglandins are synthesized in the body from
   a. arachidonic acid
   b. ascorbic acid
   c. cholesterol
   d. progesterone

3. How many contraceptives have been approved by the FDA for use by males?
   a. none
   b. one
   c. three
   d. five

4. The gonads are stimulated to produce sex hormones and eggs or sperm by
   a. ACTH and LH
   b. FSH and LH
   c. LH and CRF
   d. TRF and GH

5. The hormone that maintains pregnancy is
   a. estradiol
   b. estrone
   c. progesterone
   d. prolactin

6. The functional group that makes a birth control drug effective orally is
   a. CH_3CH_2-
   b. $CH_2{=}CH_2-$
   c. $HC{\equiv}C-$
   d. CH_3CO-

18.6 Drugs for the Heart

Learning Objective ❯ Describe the action of four types of drugs used to treat heart disease.

The heart is a muscle that beats virtually every second of every day for as long as we live. Diseases of the cardiovascular system are responsible for one-third of deaths in the United States and more than one-fifth of deaths worldwide. Four of the top 10 prescription drugs worldwide are for treating cardiovascular disease. These drugs prolong life and improve its quality.

Major diseases of the heart and blood vessels include

- ischemic ("lacking oxygen") coronary artery disease,
- heart arrhythmias (abnormal heartbeat),
- hypertension (high blood pressure), and
- congestive heart failure.

Atherosclerosis (buildup of fatty deposits in the lining of the arteries) is the primary cause of coronary artery disease, which in turn causes myocardial infarction (heart attack). Thus, most drug treatments for the heart aim to increase its supply of blood (and oxygen), to normalize its rhythm, to lower blood pressure, or to prevent accumulation of lipid plaque deposits in blood vessels.

Lowering Blood Pressure

Hypertension, or high blood pressure, is defined as pressure, in millimeters of mercury (mmHg), above 140/90. Normal blood pressure is defined as less than 120/80. Hypertension is the most common cardiovascular disease, affecting more than one in four adults in the United States. Because it seldom produces symptoms, many people have hypertension without realizing it. There are four major categories of drugs for lowering blood pressure.

- *Diuretics* (for example, hydrochlorothiazide [HCT]) cause the kidneys to excrete more water and thus lower the blood volume.
- *Beta blockers,* (for example, propranolol and metoprolol; see Section 18.7) slow the heart rate and reduce the force of the heartbeat.
- *Calcium channel blockers* (for example, amlodipine) are powerful vasodilators, inducing muscles around the blood vessels to relax.
- *Angiotensin-converting enzyme (ACE) inhibitors* (for example, lisinopril) inhibit the action of an enzyme that causes blood vessels to contract.

Studies show that diuretics, the oldest, simplest, and cheapest of the blood-pressure–lowering drugs, may also be the most effective for treating hypertension in most people. However, both a diuretic and one of the other medications are often prescribed.

Normalizing Heart Rhythm

An *arrhythmia* is an abnormal heartbeat. Some arrhythmias exhibit no symptoms and are discovered only during a physical examination, but others can be life threatening. The electrical properties of nerves and muscles arise from the flow of ions across cell membranes, and drugs for arrhythmia alter this flow. There are several types of such drugs, with different mechanisms of action, but all of them tend to have a narrow margin between the therapeutic dose and a harmful amount. A change in the heart's rhythm can have serious consequences. Tachycardia (too rapid heartbeat) and abnormal heart rhythms are quite common. Atrial fibrillation, a type of irregular heartbeat, is so common that defibrillator devices are now available on many airplanes and in various other public places.

NO—A Messenger Molecule

The simple nitrogen monoxide molecule (NO), notorious as an air pollutant that contributes to smog (Chapter 13), was found in 1986 to act as a *messenger molecule* that carries signals between cells in the body. All previously known messenger molecules are more complex substances, such as norepinephrine and serotonin (Section 18.7) that act by fitting specific receptors in cell membranes. Commonly called nitric oxide, NO is essential to maintaining blood pressure and establishing long-term memory. It also aids in the immune response to foreign invaders in the body and mediates the relaxation phase of intestinal contractions in the digestion of food.

NO is formed in cells from arginine, a nitrogen-rich amino acid (Section 16.4), in an enzyme-catalyzed reaction. NO kills invading microorganisms, probably by deactivating iron-containing enzymes in much the same way as carbon monoxide destroys the oxygen-carrying capacity of hemoglobin (Section 13.4).

Louis Ignarro, Robert F. Furchgott, and Ferid Murad, who discovered the physiological role of NO, were awarded a 1998 Nobel Prize in Physiology or Medicine. This award has a fortuitous link to Alfred Nobel, whose invention of dynamite made him wealthy and provided the financial basis of the Nobel prizes. Nitroglycerin, the explosive ingredient of dynamite, relieves the chest pain of heart disease. In his later years, Nobel refused to take nitroglycerin for his heart disease because it causes headaches, and he did not think it would relieve his chest pain. Murad showed that nitroglycerin acts by releasing NO.

NO also dilates the blood vessels that allow blood flow into the penis to cause an erection. Research on this role of NO led to the development of the anti-impotence drug sildenafil (Viagra®). One of the physiological effects of sildenafil is the production of small quantities of NO in the bloodstream. Related research has led to drugs for treating shock and a drug for treating high blood nitric oxide pressure in newborn babies.

Treating Coronary Artery Disease

A common symptom of coronary artery disease is chest pain, called *angina pectoris*. This pain is caused by an insufficient supply of oxygen to the heart, usually due to partial blockage of the coronary arteries by lipid-containing plaque (arteriosclerosis). When the blockage is complete, a heart attack occurs, and some of the heart muscle dies. Medical treatment for coronary artery disease usually involves dilation (widening) of the blood vessels to the heart to increase the blood flow and slowing of the heart rate to decrease its workload and its demand for oxygen. Some of the drugs used are the same as those used to lower high blood pressure, such as beta blockers.

In addition, several organic nitro compounds, especially nitroglycerin and amyl nitrite ($CH_3CH_2CH_2CH_2CH_2ONO$), have a long history in the treatment of angina pectoris. These compounds act by releasing nitric oxide (NO), which relaxes the constricted vessels that are reducing the supply of blood and oxygen to the heart.

$$H_2C-O-NO_2$$
$$HC-O-NO_2$$
$$H_2C-O-NO_2$$

Nitroglycerin

Although many new drugs are being used to treat heart failure, one that has been used for centuries still plays an important role. The foxglove plant was used by the ancient Egyptians and Romans. The plant contains a mixture of glycosides that yield carbohydrates and steroids on hydrolysis. Hydrolysis of digoxin (one of those glycosides) yields the steroid digitoxigenin, which affects the rhythm and strength of heart muscle contractions. Digoxin is still used to treat patients with heart failure.

SELF-ASSESSMENT Questions

1. All of the following types of drugs are used to lower blood pressure except
   a. amphetamines
   b. calcium channel blockers
   c. diuretics
   d. angiotensin-converting enzymes

2. Most types of drug treatment for the heart focus on the following goals except
   a. regulating heart rate
   b. increasing blood flow to the heart
   c. lowering blood pressure
   d. increasing the deposition of lipid plaque in blood vessels

3. Drugs such as amyl nitrite and nitroglycerin act by releasing a substance that relaxes the smooth muscles in blood vessels. That substance is
   a. an amino acid
   b. digitalis
   c. nitric oxide
   d. a steroid

Answers: 1, a; 2, d; 3, c

18.7 Drugs and the Mind

Learning Objectives ❯ Explain how the brain amines norepinephrine and serotonin affect the mind and how various drugs change their action. ❯ Identify some stimulant drugs, depressant drugs, and psychotropic drugs, and describe how they affect the mind.

A **psychotropic drug** is one that affects the human mind. The first drugs used probably were mind-altering substances. Alcoholic beverages, marijuana, opium, coca leaves, peyote, and other plant materials have been used for their psychotropic effects for thousands of years. Generally, only one or two of these were used in any given society. Today, thousands of psychotropic drugs are readily available. Some still come from plants, but many are synthetic.

There is no clear distinction between drugs that affect the mind and those that affect the body. Most drugs probably affect both mind and body. It can still be helpful, however, to distinguish between drugs that act mainly on the body and drugs that primarily affect the mind.

Psychotropic drugs are divided into three classes.

- A **stimulant drug**, such as cocaine or an amphetamine, increases alertness, speeds mental processes, and generally elevates the mood.

- A **depressant drug**, such as alcohol, almost any anesthetic, an opiate, a barbiturate, or any of certain tranquilizers, reduces the level of consciousness and the intensity of reactions to environmental stimuli. In general, depressants dull emotional responses.

- A **hallucinogenic drug**, such as lysergic acid diethylamide (LSD) or mescaline, alters qualitatively the perception of one's surroundings.

We will examine some of the major drugs in each category, but first we need to look at some chemistry of the nervous system.

Chemistry of the Nervous System

The nervous system is made up of about 12 billion **neurons** (nerve cells) with 10^{13} connections between them. The brain has the capacity to handle about 10 trillion bits of information. Nerve cells vary a great deal in shape and size. One type is shown in Figure 18.16. The essential parts of each cell are the cell body, the axon, and the dendrites. We discuss here only the nerves that make up the involuntary (autonomic) nervous system. These nerves carry messages between organs and glands that act involuntarily (such as the heart, the digestive organs, and the lungs) and the brain and spinal column.

The axon on a nerve cell may be up to 60 cm long, but there is no continuous pathway from an organ to the central nervous system. Messages must be transmitted across tiny, fluid-filled gaps, or **synapses** (Figure 18.17). When an electrical signal from a nerve cell in the brain reaches the end of an axon of a presynaptic nerve cell, chemicals called **neurotransmitters** are released from tiny vesicles (small fluid-filled sacs) into the synapse. Receptors on the postsynaptic cell bind the neurotransmitter, causing changes in that receiving cell. After a brief interval, the neurotransmitters are released from the receptor site and carried back to the presynaptic cell by substances called *transporters.*

There are many neurotransmitters. Substances that act as neurotransmitters include amino acids, peptides, and monosubstituted amines (monoamines). For example, glutamate, the carboxylate anion of the amino acid glutamic acid, is the most common neurotransmitter in the brain. More than 50 peptides function as neurotransmitters. Messages are carried to other nerve cells, to muscles, and to endocrine glands (such as the adrenal glands). Each neurotransmitter fits one or more receptor sites on the receptor cell. For example, when nerve impulses trigger the release of glutamate from the presynaptic cell, the glutamate receptors in the postsynaptic cell bind glutamate and are activated. Neurotransmitters

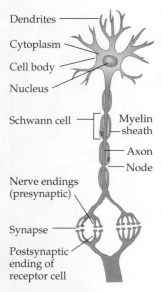

Dendrites
Cytoplasm
Cell body
Nucleus
Schwann cell
Myelin sheath
Axon
Node
Nerve endings (presynaptic)
Synapse
Postsynaptic ending of receptor cell

▲ **Figure 18.16** Diagram of a human nerve cell.

determine to a large degree how you think, feel, and move about. If there are problems with their synthesis or uptake, things can go quite wrong. Many drugs (and some poisons) act by mimicking the action of a neurotransmitter. Others act by blocking the receptor sites and preventing neurotransmitter molecules from acting on them.

Biochemical Theories of Brain Diseases

Like other organs, the brain can suffer from disease. Normal brain activity involves many chemical substances. Problems arise when an imbalance of these substances develops. We all have ups and downs in our lives. These moods probably result from multiple causes, but it is likely that a variety of compounds formed in the brain are involved. Before we consider these ups and downs, however, let's take a look at epinephrine, an amine formed in the adrenal glands and in some central nervous system cells (Figure 18.18).

Epinephrine is secreted by the adrenal glands—and is thus often called *adrenaline*—when a person is under stress or is frightened. A tiny amount of epinephrine causes a large increase in blood pressure, and its flow prepares the body for fight or flight. Because culturally imposed inhibitions prevent fighting or fleeing in most modern situations, the adrenaline-induced supercharge is often not used. This sort of frustration has been implicated in some forms of mental illness.

Biochemical theories of mental illness usually involve chemical imbalances of brain amines, which can be improved with medication. One such brain amine is norepinephrine (NE), a relative of epinephrine. NE is a neurotransmitter formed in the brain (Figure 18.18). When produced in excess, NE causes euphoria. In large excess, NE induces a manic state.

NE and related compounds fall into several general categories. NE *agonists* (drugs that enhance or mimic the action of NE) are stimulants. NE *antagonists* (drugs that block the action of NE) slow down various processes. For example, beta blockers (Figure 18.19) reduce the stimulant action of epinephrine and NE on various kinds of cells. Propranolol (Inderal®) is used to treat cardiac arrhythmias, angina, and hypertension by slightly lessening the force of the heartbeat. Unfortunately, it also causes lethargy and depression. Metoprolol (Lopressor®) acts selectively on the cells of the heart. It can be used by hypertensive patients who have asthma because it does not act on receptors in the bronchi.

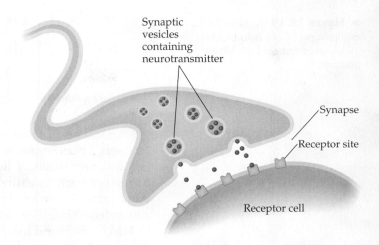

▲ **Figure 18.17** Diagram of a synapse. When an electrical signal reaches the presynaptic nerve ending, neurotransmitter molecules are released from the vesicles. They migrate across the synapse to the postsynaptic nerve cell, where they fit specific receptor sites.

Tyrosine → Dopa → Dopamine →

Norepinephrine → Epinephrine (adrenaline)

▲ **Figure 18.18** The biosynthesis of epinephrine and norepinephrine from tyrosine. L-Dopa, the left-handed form of the compound, is used to treat Parkinson's disease, which results from inadequate dopamine production. Dopamine cannot be used directly to treat the disease because it is not absorbed into the brain. Schizophrenia has been attributed to an overabundance of dopamine in nerve cells.

▶ **Figure 18.19** Propranolol and metoprolol are beta blockers, widely used to treat high blood pressure.

Propranolol   Metoprolol

Another brain amine is the neurotransmitter *serotonin*. Serotonin is involved in sleep, appetite, memory, learning, sensory perception, mood, sexual behavior, and regulation of body temperature. This brain amine is also involved in behaviors such as eating, sleeping, and aggression. Serotonin inhibits the nervous system in ways that calm, soothe, and generate feelings of contentment and satisfaction. The main metabolite of serotonin, 5-hydroxyindoleacetic acid (5-HIAA), is found in unusually low levels in the cerebrospinal fluid of severely depressed patients with a history of suicide attempts; this finding indicates that abnormal metabolism of serotonin plays a role in depression. Some research suggests that a reduced flow of serotonin through the synapses in the frontal lobe of the brain causes depression. Cerebrospinal fluid levels of 5-HIAA are also low in murderers and other violent offenders. However, they are higher than normal in people with obsessive–compulsive disorder, sociopaths, and people with guilt complexes.

Serotonin agonists are used to treat depression, anxiety, and obsessive–compulsive disorder. Serotonin antagonists are used to treat migraine headaches and to relieve the nausea caused by cancer chemotherapy.

Brain Amines and Diet: You Feel What You Eat

Richard Wurtman of the Massachusetts Institute of Technology has demonstrated a relationship between diet and serotonin levels in the brain. As shown in Figure 18.20, serotonin is produced in the body from the amino acid tryptophan. Wurtman found that diets high in carbohydrates lead to high levels of serotonin. High levels of protein lower the serotonin concentration.

Norepinephrine is synthesized in the body from the amino acid tyrosine. As noted in Figure 18.18, the synthesis is complex and proceeds through several intermediates. Because tyrosine is also a component of our diets, it may well be that our mental state depends to a fair degree on what we eat.

Nearly 1 out of every 10 people in the United States suffers from some form of mental illness. More than half the patients in hospitals are there because of mental problems. When the biochemistry of the brain is more fully understood, mental

▶ **Figure 18.20** Serotonin is produced in the brain from the amino acid tryptophan. The synthesis involves several steps; some are omitted here for simplicity. 5-HIAA is a metabolite of serotonin.

Right-Handed and Left-Handed Molecules

Like people, molecules can be either right-handed or left-handed. Ball-and-stick models of two structures for the amino acid alanine [$CH_3CH(NH_2)COOH$] are shown in Figure 18.21. These structures are **stereoisomers**, isomers having the same structural formula but differing in the arrangement of atoms or groups of atoms in three-dimensional space. Models of the two stereoisomers of alanine are as alike—and as different—as a pair of gloves. If you place one of the models in front of a mirror, the image in the mirror will be identical to the other model. Molecules that are nonsuperimposable (nonidentical) mirror images of each other are stereoisomers of a specific type called **enantiomers** (Greek *enantios,* "opposite").

Enantiomers have a **chiral carbon**, a carbon atom to which four different groups are attached. For example, the central carbon of alanine has four groups (H, CH_3, COOH, and NH_2) joined to it. If a molecule contains one or more chiral carbons, it is likely to exist as two or more stereoisomers. In contrast, propane ($CH_3CH_2CH_3$), for example, does not contain a chiral carbon and thus does not exist as a pair of stereoisomers.

Stereoisomerism is quite common in organic chemicals of biological importance. The simple sugars (Section 16.2) are all right-handed. While 19 of the 20 amino acids that make up proteins are left-handed, the other, glycine (H_2NCH_2COOH), has no handedness.

A right-hand glove doesn't fit on a left hand, or vice versa. Similarly, enantiomers fit enzymes differently, and they have different effects. Mixtures of compounds that have equal amounts of each enantiomer are called racemates. Many older drugs were sold as racemic mixtures, even though we now know that only one enantiomer is effective and the other either does nothing or, worse yet, is toxic. As an example, consider atorvastatin (Lipitor®), the best-selling drug in the world in 2010, with U.S. sales of $7.2 billion, which is used to lower blood cholesterol. Initial research on this drug in 1989 was promising but not outstanding. Later it was found that only the left-handed isomer is active; thus, it is much more effective when separated from its right-handed form. The development of drugs that consist of only one enantiomer is becoming increasingly important in the pharmaceutical industry.

Patent rights for new drugs exist only for a limited period. In recent years, as patents expire on racemic drugs, many pharmaceutical companies have engaged in *chiral switching* and brought forth single enantiomer drugs, often claiming greater effectiveness or safety. The FDA is now requiring information on each enantiomer in new racemic mixtures.

▲ **Figure 18.21** Ball-and-stick models and structural formulas of D- and L-alanine. The molecules are *enantiomers,* mirror images of one another. Like right and left hands, enantiomers cannot be superimposed on one another.

illness may be cured (or at least alleviated) by the administration of drugs—or by adjusting the diet.

Anesthetics

An **anesthetic** is a substance that causes lack of feeling or awareness. A **general anesthetic** acts on the brain to produce unconsciousness and a general insensitivity to pain. A local anesthetic causes loss of feeling in a part of the body. Diethyl ether ($CH_3CH_2OCH_2CH_3$), the first general anesthetic, was introduced into surgical practice in the 1840s. Inhalation of ether vapor produces unconsciousness by depressing the activity of the central nervous system. Ether is relatively safe because there is a fairly wide gap between the dose that produces an effective level of anesthesia and the lethal dose. Its disadvantages are high flammability and an undesirable side effect, nausea.

Nitrous oxide (N_2O, laughing gas) was discovered by Joseph Priestley in 1772, and its narcotic effect was soon noted. Mixed with oxygen, nitrous oxide is used in modern anesthesia. It is quick acting but not very potent. Concentrations of 50% or greater must be used for it to be effective. When nitrous oxide is mixed with

Table 18.3 | Inhaled Anesthetic Agents

Generic or Chemical Name	Formula	Commercial Name	Year Introduced	Currently in Use?
Diethyl ether	$CH_3CH_2OCH_2CH_3$	Ether	1842	No
Nitrous oxide	N_2O	Nitrous oxide	1844	Yes
Chloroform	$CHCl_3$	Chloroform	1847	No
Isoflurane	$CHF_2OCHClCF_3$	Forane®	1980	Yes
Desflurane	$CHF_2OCHFCF_3$	Suprane®	1992	Yes
Sevoflurane	$CH_2FOCH(CF_3)_2$	Ultane®	1995	Yes

ordinary air instead of oxygen, not enough oxygen gets into the patient's blood, and permanent brain damage can result.

Chloroform ($CHCl_3$) was introduced as a general anesthetic in 1847. It quickly became popular after Queen Victoria gave birth to her eighth child in 1853 while anesthetized by chloroform. Chloroform was used widely for years. It is nonflammable and produces effective anesthesia, but it has serious drawbacks. For one, it has a narrow safety margin; the effective dose is close to the lethal dose. It also causes liver damage, is a suspected carcinogen, and must be protected from oxygen during storage to prevent the formation of deadly phosgene gas.

Modern inhalant anesthetics include fluorine-containing compounds (Table 18.3). These compounds are nonflammable and relatively safe for patients. Their safety for operating room personnel, however, has been questioned. For example, female operating room workers suffer a higher rate of miscarriages than women in the general population.

Modern surgical practice usually makes use of a variety of drugs. Generally, a patient is given

- a tranquilizer such as a benzodiazepine (Valium® or Versed®) to decrease anxiety,
- an intravenous anesthetic such as thiopental to produce unconsciousness quickly,
- a narcotic pain medication such as fentanyl to block pain,
- an inhalant anesthetic to provide insensitivity to pain and to keep the patient unconscious, often combined with oxygen and nitrous oxide to support life, and
- a relaxant such as pancuronim bromide to relax the muscles and make it easier to insert the breathing tube.

General anesthetics reduce nerve transmission at the synapses by inhibiting the excitatory effect of certain neurotransmitters on central nervous system receptors. However, the anesthetics bind only weakly, and it is difficult to determine their exact mode of action.

Local Anesthetics

Local anesthetics are used to render a part of the body insensitive to pain. They block nerve conduction by reducing the permeability of the nerve cell membrane to sodium ions. The patient remains conscious during dental work or minor surgery.

The first local anesthetic to be used successfully was cocaine, a drug first isolated in 1860 from the leaves of the coca plant (Figure 18.22). Its structure was determined by Richard Willstätter in 1898. Scientists have made many attempts to develop synthetic compounds with similar properties. Cocaine is a powerful stimulant whose abuse is discussed on page 588.

Because local anesthetics are weak bases (amines), they are usually used in the form of hydrochloride salts, which are water-soluble. Some local anesthetics (Figure 18.23) are amine–esters (cocaine, procaine, and chloroprocaine), and others are amine–amides (lidocaine, mepivacaine, prilocaine, bupivacaine, and

▲ **Figure 18.22** Coca leaves contain the alkaloid cocaine, a local anesthetic and stimulant.

para-Aminobenzoic acid

Butyl para-aminobenzoate (Butesin®)

Lidocaine (Xylocaine®)

Ethyl para-aminobenzoate (Benzocaine®)

Procaine (Novocaine®)

Mepivacaine

▲ **Figure 18.23** Some local anesthetics. They are often used in the form of a hydrochloride or picrate salt, which is more soluble in water than the free base.

Q: *Which of these are derived from para-aminobenzoic acid? Which have amide functional groups? Which are esters?*

etidocaine). The amine–esters cause allergic reactions in some people; the amine–amides do not. The ethyl and butyl esters of *para*-aminobenzoic acid (PABA) are topical anesthetics, usually used in the form of picrate salts in ointments that are applied to the skin to relieve the pain of burns and open wounds.

Introduction of a second nitrogen atom in the alkyl group of the ester produces a more powerful anesthetic (Table 18.4). Perhaps the best known of these is procaine (Novocaine®), first synthesized in 1905 by Alfred Einhorn (1865–1917), who had worked with Willstätter on the structure of cocaine. Procaine takes a fairly long time to take effect, wears off very quickly, and causes allergic reactions. It is no longer used in dentistry, having been replaced largely by the amine–amide anesthetics.

Lidocaine was introduced in the 1940s and is still the most widely used local anesthetic. It takes effect quickly. When combined with a small quantity of epinephrine, it acts for an hour or more. (See Collaborative Group Project 12.)

Table 18.4	Substances Commonly Used as Local Anesthetics
Substance	**Duration of Action**
Procaine (Novocain®)	Short
Lidocaine (Xylocaine®)	Medium (30–60 min)
Mepivacaine (Carbocaine®)	Fast (6–10 min)
Bupivacaine (Marcaine®)	Moderate (8–12 min)
Prilocaine (Citanest®)	Medium (30–90 min)
Chloroprocaine (Nesacaine®)	Short (15–30 min)
Cocaine	Medium
Etidocaine (Duranest®)	Long (120–180 min)

Dissociative Anesthetics: Ketamine and PCP

Ketamine, an intravenous anesthetic, is called a *dissociative anesthetic* because it disconnects a person's perceptions from his or her sensations. It reduces or blocks signals to the conscious mind from parts of the brain that are associated with the senses. Ketamine induces hallucinations like those reported by people who have had near-death experiences. They seem to remember observing their rescuers from a vantage point above the scene or moving through a dark tunnel toward a bright light.

Ketamine acts as an NMDA-receptor antagonist. N-methyl-D-aspartate, or NMDA, is an amino-acid derivative that mimics the action of the neurotransmitter glutamate. Because ketamine acts by binding to receptors in the body, it is assumed that the body produces its own chemicals that fit these receptors. These compounds may be synthesized or released only in extreme circumstances—such as in near-death experiences.

Ketamine is used widely in veterinary medicine. Because it suppresses breathing much less than most other available anesthetics, ketamine is sometimes used as an anesthetic for humans with unknown medical histories and for children and persons of poor health.

Phencyclidine, commonly known as PCP, is closely related to ketamine. PCP was formerly used as an animal tranquilizer and for a brief time as a general anesthetic for humans. It is now fairly common on the illegal drug scene. PCP, which is soluble in fat and has no appreciable water solubility, is stored in fatty tissue and released when the fat is metabolized, accounting for the "flashbacks" commonly experienced by users. Many users experience bad "trips" with PCP, and about 1 in 1000 develops a severe form of schizophrenia. High doses cause illusions and hallucinations and can also cause seizures, coma, and death. However, death of PCP users more often results from an accident or suicide during a "trip."

Depressant Drugs

We start our exploration of depressant drugs by reconsidering ethyl alcohol, discussed in some detail in Chapter 9, because it is by far the most used and abused depressant drug in the world.

In nature, sugars in fruit are often fermented into alcohol by airborne yeasts, but purposeful production of ethanol probably did not begin until people began to farm. As early as 3700 B.C.E., the Egyptians fermented fruit to make wine and the Babylonians made beer from barley. People have been fermenting fruits and grains ever since, but relatively pure ethanol was first produced by Muslim alchemists who invented distillation in the eighth or ninth century.

People often think they are stimulated ("get high") when they drink, but ethanol is a depressant. It slows down both physical and mental activity. Nearly two-thirds of adults in the United States drink alcohol, and nearly one-third have five or more drinks on at least one day each year. There are at least 15 million alcoholics in the United States, and alcoholism costs over $200 billion a year. Approximately 30% of current drinkers in the United States drink to excess. According to the CDC, excessive drinking of alcohol kills about 85,000 people each year in the United States, and underage drinking causes about 5000 deaths of people under 21 each year. For 15- to 24-year-olds, the three leading causes of death are automobile accidents, homicides, and suicides, and alcohol is a leading factor in all three.

For some, there is a small positive side to drinking alcohol. Longevity studies indicate that those who use alcohol moderately (no more than a drink or two a day) live longer than nondrinkers. This may result from alcohol's relaxing effect. Heavier drinking, however, can cause many health problems. Alcoholism shortens the life span of alcoholics by 10 to 12 years.

Alcoholic beverages are generally high in calories. Pure ethanol furnishes about 7 kcal/g. Ethanol is metabolized by oxidation to acetaldehyde at a rate of about 1 oz (about 30 mL) per hour, and the buildup of ethanol concentration in the blood caused by drinking at a rate faster than this results in intoxication.

Oxidation of ethanol uses up a substance called NAD^+, the oxidized form of nicotinamide adenine dinucleotide; the reduced form is represented as NADH, where H is a hydrogen atom:

$$CH_3CH_2OH + NAD^+ \longrightarrow CH_3CHO + NADH + H^+$$

Ethanol   Acetaldehyde

Ketamine

Phencyclidine
(PCP)

Because NAD^+ is usually employed in the oxidation of fats, drinking too much alcohol causes fat to be deposited—mainly in the abdomen—rather than metabolized. This results in the familiar "beer belly" of many heavy drinkers.

Just how ethanol intoxicates is still somewhat of a mystery. Researchers have found that ethanol disrupts receptors for two neurotransmitters: *gamma*-aminobutyric acid (GABA), which inhibits impulsiveness, and glutamate, which excites certain nerve cells. Long-term drinking changes the balance of GABA and glutamate, disrupting the brain's control over muscle activity and causing the drinker to stagger and fall. Ethanol also raises dopamine levels in the brain; dopamine is associated with the pleasurable aspects of alcohol and other drugs. One recent explanation for disruption of the receptors is that ethanol can replace some water molecules involved in maintaining a protein's three-dimensional structure, thus affecting the receptor's function.

Excessive drinking over time changes the levels of some of the brain chemicals, causing a craving for ethanol in order to bring back good feelings or to avoid bad feelings. Studies on twins raised separately show that there is undoubtedly a genetic component to alcoholism. There are also emotional, psychological, social, and cultural factors. We still have much to learn about this ancient drug.

Barbiturates

A family of depressants, the barbiturates display a wide range of properties. They can be employed to produce mild sedation, deep sleep, or even death. Barbiturates are cyclic amides that act on GABA receptors. The mechanism of their action is similar in some respects to that of alcohol. More than 2500 barbiturates have been synthesized over the years, but only a few have found widespread use in medicine (Figure 18.24).

- Pentobarbital is employed as a short-acting hypnotic drug. Before the discovery of modern tranquilizers, it was used widely to calm anxiety.
- Phenobarbital is a long-acting drug. It is employed as an anticonvulsant for people suffering from seizure disorders such as epilepsy.
- Thiopental, which differs from pentobarbital only in having a sulfur atom on the ring in place of one of the oxygen atoms, is used as an anesthetic.

Barbiturates were once used in small doses (a few milligrams) as sedatives. In larger doses (about 100 mg), barbiturates induce sleep. They were also widely prescribed as sleeping pills but have now been replaced by drugs such as benzodiazepines, which have less potential for abuse and are less likely to be lethal.

Barbiturates are especially dangerous when ingested along with ethyl alcohol. This combination produces an effect perhaps 10 times greater than the sum of the effects of the two depressants. In the past, many people died by accident or through suicide by ingesting this combination.

The phenomenon, in which two chemicals bring about an effect greater than that from each individual chemical, is called a **synergistic effect** (Section 12.2). Synergistic effects can be deadly, and they are not limited to alcohol–barbiturate combinations. Two drugs should never be taken at the same time without competent medical supervision.

Barbiturates, like ethanol, are intoxicating, and they are strongly addictive. Habitual use leads to the development of a tolerance, meaning that ever-larger doses are required to produce the same degree of intoxication. The side effects of

(a)　　　　　　　(b)　　　　　　　(c)

◀ **Figure 18.24** Formulas of some barbiturate drugs. (a) Pentobarbital (Nembutal®), (b) phenobarbital (Luminal®), and (c) thiopental (Pentothal®). These drugs, derived from barbituric acid, are often used in the form of their sodium salts; for example, thiopental is used as sodium pentothal.

barbiturates are similar to those of alcohol: hangovers, drowsiness, dizziness, and headaches. Withdrawal symptoms are often severe, including convulsions and delirium, and withdrawal can cause death.

Antianxiety Agents

The hectic pace of life in the modern world causes some people to seek rest and relaxation in chemicals. Many turn to ethyl alcohol. The drink before dinner—to "unwind" from the tensions of the day—is a part of the way of life for many people. This search for relief from stress and anxiety has made antidepressant drugs highly popular. According to the CDC, antidepressants are now the most commonly prescribed drugs, with 254 million prescriptions, including refills, in the United States in 2010.

One class of antianxiety drugs (anxiolytics) is the *benzodiazepines*, compounds that feature seven-member heterocyclic rings (Figure 18.25). Three common ones are diazepam (Valium®), a classic antianxiety agent; clonazepam, an anticonvulsant as well as antianxiety drug; and lorazepam, used to treat insomnia. Antianxiety agents—sometimes called *minor tranquilizers*—make people feel better simply by making them feel dull and insensitive, but they do not solve any of the underlying problems that cause anxiety. They are thought to act on GABA receptors, dampening neuron activity in parts of the brain associated with cognitive functioning.

The first antipsychotic drugs—sometimes referred to as *major tranquilizers*—were compounds called *phenothiazines*. In 1952, chlorpromazine (Thorazine®) was administered as a tranquilizer to psychotic patients in the United States. The drug had been tested in France as an antihistamine, and medical workers there had noted that it calmed mentally ill patients being treated for allergies. Found to be helpful in controlling the symptoms of schizophrenia, chlorpromazine revolutionized therapy for mental illness. Chlorpromazine is one of several phenothiazines used as antipsychotics.

Phenothiazines act in part as dopamine antagonists. They block postsynaptic receptors for dopamine, a neurotransmitter important in the control of detailed motion (such as grasping small objects), in memory and emotions, and in exciting the cells of the brain. Some researchers think schizophrenic patients produce too much dopamine, whereas others think that they have too many dopamine receptors. In either case, blocking the action of dopamine relieves the symptoms of schizophrenia.

A second generation of antipsychotics, called *atypical antipsychotics*, includes aripiprazole (Abilify®), risperidone (Risperdal®), clozapine (Clozaril®), and olanzapine (Zyprexa®). These drugs are thought to act on a type of serotonin receptor that loosens the binding of dopamine receptors, allowing more dopamine to reach the neurons. Aripiprazole is used to treat schizophrenia, acute manic episodes of bipolar disorder, and depression. Risperidone is also used to treat schizophrenia. Clozapine, the first of the atypical antipsychotics to be developed, has been shown to be the most effective drug for treating schizophrenia, but its severe side effects—such as destruction of white blood cells—cause it to be used only if other antipsychotic drugs have failed. Olanzapine is used to treat psychotic disorders, such as schizophrenia and acute manic episodes, and to stabilize bipolar disorder.

Chlorpromazine
(Thorazine®)

Olanzapine (Zyprexa®)

▶ **Figure 18.25** Three benzodiazepines: diazepam (Valium®), clonazepam (Klonopin®), and lorazepam (Ativan®).

Diazepam

Clonazepam

Lorazepam

◀ **Figure 18.26** Three selective serotonin reuptake inhibitors (SSRIs): fluoxetine (Prozac®), paroxetine (Paxil®), and sertraline (Zoloft®).

Fluoxetine   Paroxetine   Sertraline

Antipsychotic drugs have served to reduce greatly the number of patients confined to mental hospitals. They do not cure schizophrenia, but they control its symptoms well enough that 95% of all schizophrenics no longer need hospitalization. Patients who stop taking these medications relapse.

The oldest class of antidepressant drugs, the tricyclic (three-ring) antidepressants, such as amitriptyline, block the reabsorption ("reuptake") of neurotransmitters such as norepinephrine and serotonin into the presynaptic neuron. These antidepressants have serious side effects and have been largely replaced by newer drugs.

Antidepressants commonly prescribed today include drugs called *selective serotonin-reuptake inhibitors* (SSRIs). Three major ones are shown in Figure 18.26. Doctors prescribe these drugs to help people cope with a wide variety of psychological disorders, including anxiety syndromes such as panic disorder, obsessive-compulsive disorders (including gambling problems and overeating), and premenstrual syndrome (PMS). The drugs enhance the effect of serotonin, blocking its reuptake by nerve cells. They seem to be safer than tricyclic antidepressants and more easily tolerated.

Amitriptyline

Stimulant Drugs

Among the more widely known stimulant drugs are a variety of synthetic amines related to β-phenylethylamine (Figure 18.27). These drugs, called **amphetamines**, are similar in structure to epinephrine and norepinephrine (Figure 18.18). They seem to act by increasing levels of norepinephrine, serotonin, and dopamine in the brain.

Amphetamine and methamphetamine are inexpensive and have been widely abused. Amphetamine was once used as a diet drug, but it had little long-term effect. Amphetamine induces excitability, restlessness, tremors, insomnia, dilated pupils, increased pulse rate and blood pressure, hallucinations, and psychoses.

Methamphetamine has a more pronounced psychological effect than amphetamine. Methamphetamine is made readily from an antihistamine and household chemicals. Illegal "meth labs" have operated in all parts of the United States. Like other amine drugs, amphetamines are often distributed as hydrochloride salts.

(a)   (b)   (c)

(d)   (e)

◀ **Figure 18.27** β-Phenylethylamine (a) and related compounds. (b) Amphetamine, (c) methamphetamine, (d) methylphenidate, and (e) phenylpropanolamine.

The free-base form (the basic amine form that has not been neutralized by an acid) of methamphetamine is smoked because it vaporizes more readily than the salts. Long-term effects of methamphetamine use include severe mental problems, loss of memory, impotence, and serious dental problems.

Either methylphenidate (Ritalin®) or a mixture of amphetamines is used to treat attention-deficit/hyperactivity disorder (ADHD) in children. Although they are stimulants, these drugs seem to calm children who otherwise can't sit still. This use has received criticism that it "leads to drug abuse" and "solves the teacher's problem, not the kid's."

Like many other drugs, amphetamine exists as mirror-image isomers (enantiomers). Benzedrine® is a mixture of the two isomers in equal amounts. The dextro (right-handed) isomer is a stronger stimulant than the levo (left-handed) isomer. The pure dextro isomer is sold under the trade name Dexedrine®.

▶ Benzedrine® is a mixture of Dexedrine® and its enantiomer, levoamphetamine. As is often the case, the two isomers differ greatly in their biological activity.

Levoamphetamine   Dextroamphetamine (Dexedrine®)

Amphetamine (Benzedrine®)

Cocaine, Caffeine, and Nicotine

Three plant alkaloids have long been used as stimulants. Cocaine, first used as a local anesthetic, is also a powerful stimulant. The drug is obtained from the leaves of a shrub that grows almost exclusively on the eastern slopes of the Andes Mountains. Many of the Indians living in and around the area of cultivation chew coca leaves—mixed with lime and ashes—to experience the stimulant effect. Cocaine used to arrive in the United States as the salt cocaine hydrochloride, but now much of it comes in the form of broken lumps of the free base, a form called *crack cocaine.*

Cocaine hydrochloride is readily absorbed through the mucous membrane of the nose, and this is the form used by those who "snort" cocaine. Those who smoke cocaine use crack, which readily vaporizes at the temperature of a burning cigarette. When smoked, cocaine reaches the brain in 15 seconds. It acts by preventing the reuptake of dopamine after it is released by nerve cells, leaving high levels of dopamine to stimulate the pleasure centers of the brain. After the binge, dopamine is depleted in less than an hour, leaving the user in a pleasureless state and (often) craving more cocaine. The use of cocaine increases stamina and reduces fatigue, but the effect is short lived. Stimulation is followed by depression.

Coffee, tea, and cola soft drinks naturally contain the mild stimulant caffeine. Caffeine is also added to many other soft drinks (Table 18.5) and is the source of the "lift" provided by many so-called energy drinks. An effective dose of caffeine is about 200 mg. This is about the amount in one 10-oz cup of strong drip coffee or three to five cups of tea and about half the dose in many energy drinks.

Is caffeine addictive? The "morning grouch" syndrome suggests that it is mildly so. Well-known effects of excessive caffeine consumption include nervousness, headache, and sleeping problems. Overall, the hazards of moderate caffeine ingestion seem to be slight.

Another common stimulant is nicotine. This drug is taken by smoking or chewing tobacco. Nicotine is highly toxic to animals and has been used in agriculture as a contact insecticide. It is especially deadly when injected. The lethal dose for a

Cocaine

Caffeine

human is estimated to be about 50 mg. Nicotine seems to have a rather transient effect as a stimulant, with the initial response followed by depression. Most smokers keep a near-constant level of nicotine in their bloodstreams by indulging often.

Nicotine is powerfully addictive. Consider the 1972 memorandum from a Philip Morris scientist who noted that "no one has ever become a cigarette smoker by smoking cigarettes without nicotine." He suggested that the company "think of the cigarette as a dispenser for a dose unit of nicotine."

Nicotine

Hallucinogenic Drugs

Hallucinogenic drugs are consciousness-altering substances that induce changes in sensory perception, qualitatively altering the way users perceive things. Common hallucinogenic drugs include natural products from psilocybin mushrooms and peyote cactus, synthetic chemicals such as MDMA ("Ecstasy"), dimethyltryptamine (DMT), PCP, ketamine, and semisynthetic drugs such as LSD and mescaline. Marijuana is sometimes considered a mild hallucinogen.

Lysergic acid diethylamide (LSD), a semisynthetic drug, is a powerful hallucinogen. Its physiological properties were discovered accidentally by Swiss chemist Albert Hofmann (1906–2008) in 1943 when he unintentionally ingested some LSD. He later took 250 mg, which he considered a small dose, to verify that LSD had caused the symptoms he had experienced. Hofmann had a rough time for the next few hours, experiencing such symptoms as visual disturbances and schizophrenic behavior.

LSD can create a feeling of lack of self-control and sometimes of extreme terror. The exact mechanism by which LSD exerts its effects is still unknown, but it is thought to act on dopamine receptors and to excite by increasing the release of glutamate.

Lysergic acid is obtained from ergot, a fungus that grows on rye. This carboxylic acid is converted to its diethylamide derivative.

Table 18.5	Caffeine in Soft Drinks
Brand	Caffeine[a]
5-Hour Energy (2 oz)	138
Red Bull (8.2 oz)	80
Sun Drop	63
Mountain Dew	55
Mello Yello	53
Diet Coke	46
Dr Pepper	41
Diet Sunkist Orange	41
Pepsi-Cola	38
Diet Pepsi	36

[a]Milligrams per 12-oz serving.
Sources: National Soft Drink Association, FDA.

Lysergic acid diethylamide
(LSD)

The potency of LSD is indicated by the small amount required for a person to experience its extraordinary effects. The usual dose is probably about 10–100 µg (no wonder Hofmann had a bad time after taking 250 mg). To give you an idea of how small this is, a portion of LSD the size of an aspirin tablet could provide up to 30,000 doses.

Many kinds of plants or fungi produce hallucinogenic compounds. The following are two examples.

▪ Psilocybin, a hallucinogenic alkaloid of the tryptamine family, is found in several species of mushrooms, including *Psilocybe cubensis*. Its effects resemble those of LSD but are not as long lasting.

▪ Mescaline (3,4,5-trimethoxyphenylethylamine) is a hallucinogenic drug related to phenylethylamine (see Figure 18.27). It is found in the peyote cactus, *Lophophora williamsii*, which is used in the religious ceremonies of some Indian tribes, and in other species. Mescaline is also made synthetically. The effects last up to 12 hours.

Mescaline

Marijuana

The plant *Cannabis sativa*, commonly known as marijuana, has long been useful. The plant stems yield tough fibers (hemp) for making ropes. *Cannabis* has been used as a drug in tribal religious rituals and also has a long history as a medicine, particularly

Tetrahydrocannabinol
(THC)

Club Drugs: Raves and Rapes

Club drugs are substances used by teenagers and young adults at all-night dance parties called "raves." These drugs include 3,4-methylenedioxymethamphetamine (MDMA, or Ecstasy), *gamma*-hydroxybutyrate ($HOCH_2CH_2CH_2COOH$; GHB), Rohypnol® (flunitrazepam), ketamine, methamphetamine, and LSD. Use of such drugs can cause serious health problems, especially in combination with alcohol.

Especially troubling are substances known as *date rape drugs*: Rohypnol, ketamine, and GHB have been used to facilitate sexual assault because they render the victim incapable of resisting. Events that happen while a person is under the influence of these drugs often cannot be remembered. The GHB analogs 1,4-butanediol ($HOCH_2CH_2CH_2CH_2OH$) and *gamma*-butyrolactone (GBL) have similar effects. (See Additional Problems 93 and 94.)

Flunitrazepam (Rohypnol®)

MDMA (Ecstasy)

gamma-Butyrolactone (GBL)

in India. In the United States, marijuana is the most commonly used illegal drug.

The term **marijuana** refers to a mixture made by gathering the leaves and flower buds of the plant (Figure 18.28), which are generally dried and smoked. There are several active cannabinoids in marijuana. The main one is *tetrahydrocannabinol (THC)*.

Marijuana plants vary considerably in THC potency, depending on their genetic variety. Wild plants native to the United States have a low THC content, usually about 0.1%, but some marijuana sold in North America has a THC content approaching 6%.

The effects of marijuana are difficult to measure, partly because of the variable amount of THC in different samples. Smoking marijuana increases the pulse rate, distorts the sense of time, and impairs some complex motor functions. Other possible effects include a euphoric floating sensation, a feeling of anxiety, a heightened enjoyment of food, and a false impression of brilliance. Although studies have shown no mind-expanding effects, users sometimes experience hallucinations. Because it is fat-soluble, THC is stored in the body. Stress and dieting can produce a positive THC test long after the drug was last used.

The long-term effects of marijuana, such as causing psychotic symptoms that persist beyond temporary intoxication, are unclear. There is some evidence of increased risk of psychotic problems in people who have used marijuana, with the greatest increase (50–200%) observed in people who used the drug most frequently. People who use marijuana heavily often appear to be lazy, passive, and mentally sluggish, but it is difficult to prove that marijuana is the cause. Even if it is, the damage is less extensive than that caused by heavy use of alcohol.

When a person smokes marijuana, THC rapidly passes from the lungs into the bloodstream and is carried to the brain, where it binds to specific sites on nerve cells called *cannabinoid receptors*. Some regions of the brain have many such receptors; other areas have few or none. The parts of the brain that influence pleasure, memory, thought, concentration, judgment, and sensory and time perception and that regulate movement are rich in these receptors. As THC enters the brain, it activates the brain's reward system in the same way that food and drink do. Like nearly all drugs of abuse, THC causes a euphoric feeling by stimulating the release of dopamine.

▲ **Figure 18.28** Prepared marijuana.

The location of receptors in movement control centers in the brain explains the loss of coordination seen in those intoxicated by the drug. The presence of receptors in memory and cognition areas of the brain explains why marijuana users do poorly on tests. That few receptors are present in the brainstem, where breathing and heartbeat are controlled, is probably why it is hard to get a lethal dose of pure marijuana.

The brain also produces *anandamide*, a THC-like substance that binds to cannabinoid receptors in the brain. This substance is derived from arachidonic acid, which is the precursor for prostaglandin synthesis.

Anandamide

Marijuana has some legitimate medical uses. It reduces eye pressure in people who have glaucoma. If not treated, this increasing pressure eventually causes blindness. Marijuana also relieves the nausea that afflicts cancer patients undergoing radiation treatment and chemotherapy. The use of marijuana has been on the ballot in a number of states. Some states, such as Washington and Colorado, have now legalized the sale of recreational marijuana, while voters in many other states and cities have approved the medical use of marijuana. In some cases, the sale of medical marijuana is restricted to pill form.

SELF-ASSESSMENT Questions

1. All of the following are true of neurotransmitters except that they
   a. are released from vesicles in postsynaptic cells
   b. fit into receptors on postsynaptic cells
   c. are steroids
   d. may be an amino acid

2. Norepinephrine and epinephrine are produced in the body from the amino acid
   a. cysteine
   b. serine
   c. tryptophan
   d. tyrosine

3. Depression may result from abnormal metabolism of
   a. acetylcholine
   b. GABA
   c. nitric oxide
   d. serotonin

4. A hazard of the use of nitrous oxide as an anesthetic is that it
   a. can cause brain damage if not combined with O_2
   b. has too long a recovery time
   c. induces anesthesia that is too deep
   d. is flammable

5. Which of the following is the most used and abused depressant drug in the world?
   a. amphetamines
   b. cocaine
   c. ethyl alcohol
   d. marijuana

6. Which of the following classes of drugs is commonly used to treat anxiety?
   a. amphetamines
   b. benzodiazepines
   c. opiates
   d. steroids

7. Several stimulant drugs are derivatives of
   a. *para*-aminobenzoic acid
   b. caffeine
   c. ketamine
   d. b-phenylethylamine

8. Dextroamphetamine is composed of molecules that
   a. differ from amphetamine by a —CH_3 group
   b. are a mixture of left- and right-handed isomers
   c. are all the left-handed isomer
   d. are all the right-handed isomer

9. LSD acts on the receptors for the neurotransmitter
   a. acetylcholine
   b. dopamine
   c. GABA
   d. serotonin

10. How do antagonists and agonists for a drug work?
    a. Agonists mimic the action of the drug, but antagonists block the action of the drug.
    b. Both agonists and antagonists mimic the action of the drug.
    c. Both agonists and antagonists block the action of the drug.
    d. Antagonists mimic the action of the drug, but agonists block the action of the drug.

Answers: 1, a; 2, d; 3, d; 4, a; 5, c; 6, b; 7, d; 8, d; 9, d; 10, a

18.8 Drugs and Society

Learning Objectives > Differentiate between drug abuse and drug misuse. > Describe how a new drug is developed and brought to market.

5. How should I dispose of old medicines?

The Substance Abuse and Mental Health Services Administration recommends that old medicine be mixed with coffee grounds, cat litter, or some similar material, then bagged and disposed of in the trash. This minimizes the possibility of abuse (especially if used cat litter is employed!). Alternatively, some communities now provide periodic disposal services. There are environmental concerns about flushing most medications down the sink or toilet. Some medications may affect fish and wildlife even in very low doses.

Illegal drugs cause enormous problems. The market is covert, with sellers failing to report their income or pay taxes on it, making the illicit drug business enormously lucrative. Annual revenues for drug dealers amount to at least $400 billion, about half of which comes from the United States. Worldwide, people spend more money for illegal drugs than for food. The large amounts of money involved make illegal drugs a dangerous business in which crimes are frequent, murders are common, and corrupt politicians abound. **Drug abuse** (using drugs for their intoxicating effects) is a serious problem not only for the abusers but for society in general.

The illegal drug user is the biggest loser. Street drugs are expensive, and most are addictive. Many addicted users steal to pay for drugs and eventually end up in jail. One study found that 16% of convicted jail inmates admitted that they committed their offense to get money for drugs. In the workplace, 50–80% of all accidents and personal injuries are drug related. Drug users are absent from work over twice as often as nonusers, and they are five times as likely to file claims for worker's compensation. They are a drain on their employers' income, and they often have trouble keeping a job.

Illegal drugs are not always what their sellers claim they are. Buyers simply have to trust the information sellers give them about the identity and quality of the products they buy. In fact, crime labs have generally found that nearly two-thirds of all drugs (other than marijuana) brought in for analysis are something other than what the dealers said they were.

There can be difficulties even with legal drugs that have been approved and tested. According to the CDC, drug overdoses killed more than 38,000 people in 2010. Contrary to popular belief, most were not caused by cocaine or heroin, but by OxyContin and other painkillers diverted into the illegal drug trade. More than 15 million Americans admitted to using prescription drugs for nonmedical reasons.

Other problems with legal drugs range from faulty prescriptions written by physicians to pharmacies' errors in filling prescriptions to patients' mistakes in taking medications. Some drugs have undesirable side effects that are worse than the condition being treated. Some drugs (both prescription and over the counter) have such similar names that they are easily confused. **Drug misuse**—for example, using penicillin, which has no effect on viruses, to treat a viral infection—is all too common. Such overuse of penicillin has led to strains of bacteria that are now immune to penicillin.

Design and Approval of New Drugs

The process of developing and bringing a new drug to market is both costly and lengthy. As noted earlier, there are several approaches to designing and synthesizing new drugs. One is to modify an already existing drug with the goal of improving its effectiveness or its ability to reach the target organ or molecules. Initially, most modifications were somewhat haphazard, but more recently drug design has incorporated knowing what structural features are involved in the mechanism of the drug's action, as is the case with the fluoroquinolones.

Another relatively new approach is combinatorial chemistry, in which several starting chemicals are reacted in all possible ways to give a large number of compounds. These products are tested for their biological activity, and then the process of testing the more promising compounds for safety and effectiveness begins, in anticipation of receiving FDA approval.

Preliminary testing of a drug is not carried out on humans but is instead conducted with other systems, often in bacteria, tissue culture, or animal models. The drug is examined for a number of attributes: how effective it is in treating the malady, its ability to reach the site of action and, of course, its safety. If initial tests in laboratory or animal models are positive, then clinical trials will be undertaken to determine its effects in humans. Phase 1 trials involve a small number of healthy volunteers to determine whether there are side effects and to optimize the dosage and means of administration. Phase 2 trials include a somewhat larger number of people and focus on whether the drug is effective against the disease. If a drug appears to be effective, Phase 3 trials will be conducted on a larger group. In Phase 2 and 3 trials, the new drug will be compared to placebo or other treatments for the disease. A safe and effective drug that receives FDA approval will be monitored for safety and side effects even after its release to the market.

A common way to evaluate a new drug is to administer it to one group of patients and to give a placebo to a similar "control" group. A placebo is an inactive substance given in the form of medication to a patient. In a double-blind study, which is the type most accepted by the medical community, neither the patients nor the doctors know who is receiving the real drug and who is receiving the placebo.

An interesting phenomenon associated with the testing of drugs is the **placebo effect**. Sometimes people who think they are receiving a certain drug expect positive results and may actually experience such results, even though they have not been given the actual drug. The psychological effect of a placebo can be very powerful. The placebo effect confers health benefits from a treatment that should have no effect.

There are also a number of diseases that are quite rare and affect relatively small numbers of individuals. (Many of these involve genetic defects.) As a result, they have been classified as orphan diseases, and various ways of encouraging development of **orphan drugs** to treat them have been pursued. Governments sometimes intervene to encourage research on orphan drugs, offering tax incentives, enhancing patent protection, or even developing a government-run entity to pursue research in this area. Such drugs still have to meet safety and effectiveness standards, but variations in testing procedure have included smaller test groups for clinical trials on very rare diseases. Before passage of the Orphan Drug Act in 1983, fewer than 40 drugs had been approved for treatment of orphan diseases in the United States. In the roughly three decades following its passage, more than 350 drugs have received marketing approval, and many others are being developed or tested.

Many drugs have supplied enormous benefits to society, including longer, healthier lives and relief from pain. Sometimes drugs can create problems, such as addiction, dangerous side effects, and even death. We must use them wisely.

6. What is the difference between a generic drug and a brand-name drug?
When a new drug is developed, the manufacturer has patent rights to produce it for a given period of time. This enables the pharmaceutical company to recoup the high costs of developing and testing the drug. Once patent rights expire, other companies can market a generic version of the drug, but they must show that the same amount of the active ingredient is absorbed into the bloodstream and that it has the same activity as the brand-name drug. There may be differences in inactive ingredients. Generic drugs cost much less than name-brand drugs do.

SELF-ASSESSMENT Questions

1. Using an antibiotic to treat a cold is an example of
   a. appropriate therapy
   b. drug abuse
   c. drug misuse
   d. a placebo effect

2. Using the narcotic OxyContin for its intoxicating effect is an example of
   a. appropriate recreation
   b. drug abuse
   c. drug misuse
   d. legal intoxication

3. A placebo is
   a. an alcohol solution of an active drug
   b. an inactive substance that looks like real medication
   c. a PCB
   d. a platinum/cesium/boron drug

4. In a double-blind study, some patients are given the drug being tested and others are given
   a. acupuncture
   b. a homeopathic formulation
   c. morphine
   d. a placebo

5. An orphan drug is
   a. derived from an unknown source
   b. used to treat diseases for which vaccines exist
   c. a drug whose use has been abandoned
   d. used against rare diseases

Answers: 1, c; 2, b; 3, b; 4, d; 5, d

Joseph M. Fortunak

Green Pharmaceutical Production

Learning Objectives › Identify green chemistry principles that can improve the E-factor of chemical syntheses. › Explain how prodrugs can be important for drug delivery and green chemistry.

This chapter discusses principles for finding new medicines. First, we investigate the pathway of a disease, select a molecular target for treatment, and then identify drugs that affect the molecular target and provide benefit. Because drugs must be selective and safe, newer drugs tend to be structurally complex and require lengthy syntheses. Companies spend about twice the amount of money on manufacture as on new drug research, so there is a powerful incentive to implement green chemistry to reduce waste and cost. Green chemistry essays in Chapters 4 and 9 discuss organic synthesis and drug manufacture. Now that you have learned how drugs target things like bacterial infections, cancer, and pain, we'll discuss how green chemistry principles apply.

In 1992, Roger Sheldon at Delft University of Technology, Netherlands, coined the term *E-factor* (environmental factor) for chemical production (see Chapter 8 essay). The E-factor is the mass of generated waste for each kilogram of manufactured product. Drug synthesis often uses large amounts of solvents and complex reagents. Drug manufacturers commonly generate more than 100 kg of waste for every kilogram of drug—an E-factor greater than 100. Syntheses in water, enzymatic processes, catalysts that mimic biological processes, and processes without hazardous reagents are increasingly used to make drug production more efficient and green (Principles 5 and 9).

"The Holý Trinity" is a pun on the name of Dr. Antonín Holý (1936–2012, Prague) and his collaborations with Drs. John C. Martin (Gilead Sciences, U.S.A.) and Erik De Clercq (Rega Institute for Medical Research, Belgium). These scientists pioneered a new class of drugs to treat viral infections including tenofovir disoproxil fumarate (TDF) and tenofovir alafenamide fumarate (TAF). TDF is heavily used worldwide to treat HIV/AIDS. In 2013, over 6 million people, mainly in low- and middle-income countries (LMICs) where most HIV/AIDS infections occur, took TDF.

The synthesis and use of TDF and TAF demonstrate several principles (1–5 and 8–9) of green chemistry. The HIV reverse transcriptase enzyme mistakenly incorporates tenofovir as a raw material for synthesizing viral DNA. When tenofovir is incorporated into viral DNA particles, viral replication stops.

Tenofovir is synthesized from adenine and (R)-propylene carbonate (RPC) as shown.

Tenofovir is the active drug, but tenofovir has a hard time crossing lipophilic (fat-loving) cell membranes to enter HIV-infected cells because it is very hydrophilic (water-loving). Because of this, tenofovir is delivered in a lipophilic "prodrug" form known as TDF. A prodrug is

Tenofovir diisopoxil fumarate (TDF)

Tenofovir alafenamide fumarate (TAF)

Tenofovir

Adenine   catalytic KOH, RPC   →   2 steps →   Tenofovir

⚜ REVIEW QUESTIONS

1. What is the difference between a natural drug, a semisynthetic drug, and a synthetic drug?

2. What is the difference between an antihistamine, an antitussive, and an expectorant?

3. What is an antibiotic?

4. What is a hormone?

5. What is cortisol? Prednisone?

6. How do birth control pills work?

7. What are prostaglandins? How do prostaglandins differ from hormones?

8. Describe two medical uses of barbiturates, and state the relative doses for these purposes. What are the hazards of long-term barbiturate use?

9. Name two dissociative anesthetics.

10. Describe a synergistic effect involving drugs.

11. What is a narcotic?

12. Classify the following drugs as natural, semisynthetic, or synthetic: paclitaxel, heroin, morphine, penicillin, cisplatin.

13. How may a person's mental state be related to his or her diet?

14. What are psychotropic drugs?

15. Are tranquilizers a cure for schizophrenia?

16. What are the effects of a hallucinogenic drug?

⚜ PROBLEMS

Scientific Drug Design

17. Give an example of a natural drug, a semisynthetic drug, and a synthetic drug.

18. Classify the following drugs as natural, semisynthetic, or synthetic: codeine, fluoroquinolone, quinine, vinblastine, Taxol, 6-mercaptopurine.

19. What is chemotherapy?

20. Give four possible reasons that people use drugs.

Pain Relievers

21. What is the chemical name for aspirin?

22. In what ways do aspirin and acetaminophen act similarly? Why is aspirin preferred over acetaminophen for the treatment of arthritis?

23. Why is acetaminophen used instead of aspirin for the relief of pain associated with surgical procedures?

24. What is a COX-2 inhibitor?

25. What two functional groups are present in the acetaminophen molecule?

26. What two functional groups are present in the aspirin (acetylsalicylic acid) molecule?

27. Which of the following was originally marketed as a cough suppressant?
    a. acetaminophen   b. aspirin
    c. heroin   d. methadone

28. Which of the following compounds is most similar in structure to a DNA base?
    a. aspirin   b. caffeine
    c. ibuprofen   d. morphine

29. Which of the following is not considered to be an NSAID?
    a. acetaminophen   b. aspirin
    c. ibuprofen   d. naproxen

30. How does heroin differ from morphine in its physiological effects? In what ways are their physiological effects similar?

31. How does codeine differ from morphine in its physiological effects? In what ways are their physiological effects similar?

32. How are endorphins related to **(a)** the anesthetic effect of acupuncture and **(b)** the absence of pain in a wounded soldier?

Antibacterial and Antiviral Drugs

33. Look at the molecular models of sulfanilamide and *para*-aminobenzoic acid on page 561 and write structural formulas for the two compounds.

34. What are penicillins? How do they kill bacteria?

35. Tetracyclines are broad-spectrum antibiotics. What does this mean?

36. What are fluoroquinolones? How do they kill bacteria?

37. Quinolone antibiotics are
    a. antimetabolites
    b. broad-spectrum
    c. *beta*-lactams
    d. very specific narrow-spectrum

38. Do antiviral drugs cure viral diseases? What is the best way to deal with viral diseases?

39. What are the three classes of antiretroviral drugs? How does each work?

40. Why should antibiotics not be prescribed for treatment of a viral disease?

Anticancer Drugs

41. All of the following are antimetabolites except
    a. 6-mercaptopurine   b. cyclophosphamide
    c. 5-fluorouracil   d. methotrexate

42. List two major classes of anticancer drugs.

43. Do anticancer drugs sometimes cause cancer? Explain.

44. How does cisplatin work?

45. What compound does the following formula represent? To which class of anticancer drugs does it belong?

46. What compound does the following formula represent? To which class of anticancer drugs does it belong?

47. Give three differences between hormones and prostaglandins.

48. Show the steroid ring structure.

49. Identify the three functional groups in the progesterone molecule (Figure 18.14).

50. What is an estrogen? What is an androgen?

51. How does mifepristone (RU-486) work?

52. What molecular structural feature makes a contraceptive steroid effective orally?

53. What are emergency contraceptives? How do they work?

54. Which of the following is *not* a steroid?
    a. estradiol   b. enkephalin
    c. progesterin   d. testosterone

Drugs for the Heart

55. Diuretics work to lower blood pressure by
    a. causing the kidneys to excrete more water and thus lower the blood volume.
    b. slowing the heart rate.
    c. acting as vasodilators, causing the muscles around blood vessels to relax.
    d. inhibiting an enzyme that causes blood vessels to contract.

56. Calcium channel blockers work to lower blood pressure by
    a. causing the kidneys to excrete more water and thus lower the blood volume.
    b. slowing the heart rate.
    c. acting as vasodilators, causing the muscles around blood vessels to relax.
    d. inhibiting an enzyme that causes blood vessels to contract.

57. Which of the following small molecules acts as a messenger molecule that allows the dilation of blood vessels, thereby relieving chest pain and alleviating the symptoms of erectile dysfunction?
    a. carbon dioxide, CO_2
    b. ammonia, NH_3
    c. nitric oxide, NO
    d. sulfur dioxide, SO_2

58. Which of the following is often treated with organic nitro compounds?
    a. angina pectoris   b. erectile dysfunction
    c. heart arrhythmias   d. hypertension

Drugs and the Mind

59. What is a psychotropic drug?

60. What is a hallucinogenic drug?

61. Which of the following is not considered to be a class of psychotropic drugs?
    a. antimetabolite   b. depressant
    c. hallucinogenic   d. stimulant

62. Beta blockers work by
    a. decreasing the stimulant action of serotonin.
    b. limiting the action of a drug so that only one enantiomer is active.
    c. acting as an anesthetic.
    d. decreasing the stimulant action of epinephrine and norepinephrine.

63. Which of the following has been used as a local anesthetic?
    a. ketamine   b. lidocaine
    c. nitrous oxide   d. thiopental

64. A compound that causes lack of feeling or awareness is a(n)
    a. anesthetic   b. antidepressant
    c. placebo   d. stimulant

65. Which of the following plant alkaloids has *not* been used as a stimulant?
    a. caffeine   b. cocaine
    c. coniine   d. nicotine

66. Which of these anesthetics is dangerous because of flammability?
    a. diethyl ether   b. halothane
    c. chloroform   d. isoflurane

67. For each of the following anesthetics, identify a disadvantage other than flammability that is associated with its use.
    a. nitrous oxide   b. halothane
    c. diethyl ether

68. What is an agonist? What is an antagonist?

Drugs and Society

69. For a drug to receive FDA approval for further testing, all of the following requirements must be satisfied except
    a. safety for human use
    b. low cost
    c. effectiveness
    d. ability to reach the site of action

70. Which of the following statements about illegal drug use is *not* true?
    a. Buyers have no good way of knowing what the actual content or concentration of the drug is.
    b. Many users steal to obtain money to pay for drugs.
    c. Illegal drug use affects only the users.
    d. Many accidents and personal injuries are drug-related.

71. Tests on a new investigative drug include using a double-blind test procedure. In a double-blind study,
    a. all test subjects receive the drug
    b. some test subjects receive the drug and others receive a placebo
    c. the doctor administering the drug knows who is receiving the drug or the placebo
    d. the patient knows if he/she is receiving the drug.

72. What is the difference between drug abuse and drug misuse?

✿ ADDITIONAL PROBLEMS

73. Review the information on structure and function for fluoroquinolone drugs. Draw the structure of a fluoroquinolone drug, which is similar to ciprofloxacin in action but does not have the large nitrogen-containing ring at position 7.

74. Why is acetaminophen not classified as an NSAID?

75. A 140-lb patient was treated with the antibiotic ampicillin for a urinary tract infection. The daily dose was 40 mg/kg divided into three doses per day. **(a)** What was the daily dose, in grams, for the patient? **(b)** Each ampicillin capsule contains 500 mg of active ingredient. How many capsules did the patient have to take every 8 hours?

76. What kind of disease is a diuretic used to treat? How does it work?

77. What structural feature is shared by all steroids?

78. Ephedrine hydrochloride has the chemical formula $C_{10}H_{16}NO^+Cl^-$. Is it water soluble or fat soluble? Explain.

79. Diphenhydramine (Benadryl®) has the chemical formula $C_{17}H_{21}NO$. Is Benadryl water soluble or fat soluble? Explain.

80. What structural feature is common to all barbiturate molecules? How is this structure modified to change the properties of individual barbiturate drugs?

81. The dissociative anesthetics ketamine and PCP are classified as derivatives of cyclohexylamine. Write the structural formula for cyclohexylamine.

82. Some psychotropic drugs can cause flashbacks long after the drug was originally used. Identify two such drugs and explain why they can cause flashbacks.

83. Alcohol can interact with other drugs and greatly increase their potency and even result in death. Identify two such drugs.

Problems 84–87 use the concept of an LD_{50} value, which is discussed more fully in Chapter 22. The LD_{50} of a substance is the dose (in mg substance per kg body mass) that would be lethal to 50% of a population of test animals.

84. When administered orally to rats, ibuprofen and naproxen have LD_{50} values of 1000 mg/kg and 534 mg/kg, respectively. Which is more toxic? Explain.

85. When administered subcutaneously to rats, the LD_{50} values of the toxins of the Southern copperhead snake and the timber rattlesnake are 25.6 mg/kg and 3.1 mg/kg, respectively. Which is more toxic? Explain.

86. When administered orally to rats, aspirin has an LD_{50} value of 1500 mg/kg of body weight. If the toxicity is the same for humans, how many 325-mg tablets would likely kill a typical 10.0-kg child?

87. When administered intravenously to rats, the LD_{50} of procaine is 50 mg/kg, and that of nicotine is 1.0 mg/kg. Which drug is more toxic? What is the approximate lethal dose of each that would likely kill a 50-kg human?

88. If the minimum lethal dose (MLD) of amphetamine is 5 mg/kg, what is the MLD for a 70-kg person? Can toxicity studies on animals always be extrapolated to humans?

89. As noted in Section 18.2, replacement of the phenolic —OH group of the morphine molecule by a methoxy ($-OCH_3$) group produces codeine. Draw the structure of the codeine molecule.

90. As noted in Section 18.2, conversion of both —OH groups of the morphine molecule to acetate esters produces heroin. Draw the structure of the heroin molecule.

91. As noted in Section 18.2, oxycodone is related to codeine, differing only in that the hydroxyl group of codeine has been oxidized to a carbonyl group (as in ketone synthesis, Chapter 9). Draw the structure of the oxycodone molecule.

92. Nalorphine, a morphine antagonist, is related to morphine in that the methyl group on the N atom of morphine is replaced by a propenyl group ($-CH_2CH=CH_2$). Draw the structure of the nalorphine molecule.

Problems 93 and 94 are based on the boxed feature "Club Drugs." You may need to review some topics in Chapter 9.

93. What kind of compound is the GHB analog *gamma-butyrolactone* (GBL)? What kind of reaction would convert GBL to GHB?

94. What kind of compound is the GHB analog 1,4-butanediol? What kind of reaction would convert 1,4-butanediol to GHB?

95. Rank the following from lowest to highest risk of death:
    a. pregnancy and childbirth
    b. taking birth control pills
    c. smokers who take birth control pills

96. Which of the following compounds are classified as steroids?
    a. cholesterol
    b. prednisone
    c. progesterone
    d. prostaglandin E_2

97. How do NSAIDs work to counter the effects of prostaglandins in inflammation?

98. How would removal of the *para*-hydroxyl group from the molecule represented below affect its solubility in **(a)** water and **(b)** fat?

99. Which NSAID does the following formula represent? To what aromatic hydrocarbon is it related? Name the two oxygen-containing functional groups.

100. Chloramphenicol (Section 1.3, Exercise 1.1A) is a broad-spectrum antibiotic that acts by inhibiting bacterial protein synthesis. It is soluble in water to the extent of 2.5 mg/mL. How would conversion of chloramphenicol (R = —H) to **(a)** its palmitate ester [R = —CO(CH$_2$)$_{14}$CH$_3$] and **(b)** its sodium succinate (R = —COCH$_2$CH$_2$COONa) derivative affect its solubility? Explain.

101. What type of drug does the following formula represent? Name the three types of oxygen-containing functional groups present.

102. What type of drug is megestrol acetate (shown below), which is used for the treatment of some cancers?

  a. phencyclidine
  b. prostaglandin
  c. steroid
  d. tetracycline

103. If the E-factor for synthesizing TDF is about 70 and the E-factor for synthesizing TAF is about 85, what is the difference in waste generated per year during drug manufacturing of TAF versus TDF for 6 million patients?

104. What are the green chemistry principles exercised in the enzymatic synthesis of (R)-propylene carbonate (RPC) versus a chemical synthesis in organic solvents?

CRITICAL THINKING EXERCISES

Apply knowledge that you have gained in this chapter and one or more of the FLaReS principles (Chapter 1) to evaluate the following statements or claims.

18.1. A television advertisement featured Dr. Robert Jarvik, inventor of the artificial heart, encouraging consumers to "talk to their doctor" about using the cholesterol-lowering drug Lipitor. (The advertisement was pulled from the air in February 2008.)

18.2. Researchers at the Centre for Complementary Medicine in Munich, Germany, reviewed 29 studies of patients with depression that compared treatment with St. John's wort (*Hypericum perforatum*) with treatment with a placebo or with standard antidepressant medications. They concluded, "Overall ... the St. John's wort extracts ... were superior to placebos and as effective as standard antidepressants, with fewer side effects." They also noted that studies in German-speaking countries, where the herbal remedy has long been used, were more favorable to St. John's wort than were studies from other countries and that products on the market vary in composition and can sometimes compromise the effects of other medications.

18.3. A nurse claims to be able to help patients by "therapeutic touch," a technique that she says allows her to sense a patient's energy fields by moving her hands above the patient's body.

18.4. A television advertisement shows an actor taking a medicine that inhibits the production of stomach acid, then eating a large meal of rich, spicy food.

18.5. A television advertisement shows an actor taking an antihistamine and then joyously walking through a grassy, flower-filled meadow without experiencing the usual allergy symptoms.

18.6. A website recommends S-adenosylmethionine (SAMe) for treatment of depression, arthritis, and liver disease.

18.7. Many people believe that the MMR vaccine is responsible for autism and cite a study on 12 children by Andrew Wakefield. However, autism is generally diagnosed at approximately the same age that children usually receive the vaccine, and the study did not compare autism rates of vaccinated and unvaccinated children.

18.8. A website claims that red wine is good for your heart.

COLLABORATIVE GROUP PROJECTS

Prepare a PowerPoint, poster, or other presentation (as directed by your instructor) to share with the class. For Projects 1–7, give the chemical structure, medical use, toxicity, and (if possible) side effects of each substance.

1. Prepare a brief report, including a list of the ingredients and their amounts, on a combination product such as Advil® Cold & Sinus, Aleve® Cold & Sinus, Dimetapp® Cold & Flu, Theraflu®, Excedrin PM®, Alka-Seltzer® Plus, DayQuil®, or NyQuil.

2. Prepare a brief report on an antihistamine, such as azatadine, fexofenadine, cyproheptadine, cetirizine, dexchlorpheniramine, loratadine, promethazine, or tripelennamine.

3. Prepare a brief report on one of the narcotics listed in Table 18.1.

4. Prepare a brief report on an antibiotic, such as vancomycin, gramicidin, erythromycin, ciprofloxacin, trimethoprim, cefoxitin, cefoperazone, or azithromycin.

5. Prepare a brief report on an anticancer drug, such as bleomycin, fludarabine, hydroxyurea, procarbazine, tamoxifen, or vinblastine.

6. Prepare a brief report on an antiviral drug, such as ganciclovir, indinavir, ribavirin, rimantadine, ritonavir, or valacyclovir.

7. Prepare a brief report on an antidepressant, such as sertraline, paroxetine, citalopram, desipramine, isocarboxazid, phenelzine, fluvoxamine, or nortriptyline.

8. Four major drug categories for lowering blood pressure are listed on page 576. Give the chemical structure, toxicity, and side effects for a drug in each of the categories listed.

9. Do a cost analysis of five brands of plain aspirin, calculating the cost per gram of each. Compare the cost per gram of an extra-strength aspirin formulation with that of plain aspirin.

10. Search the Internet to learn about drug trials, and answer the following questions. **(a)** Why might a person who is gravely ill not want to participate in a placebo-controlled drug study? **(b)** What are the advantages and disadvantages of participating in such a drug study? **(c)** Why is it important that studies use placebos as well as the test drug? **(d)** Sometimes the control group receives the standard treatment for the disease instead of a placebo. Why does this happen?

11. Search the Internet for information on new drugs for treating one of the following diseases.
    a. pneumonia   **b.** arthritis
    c. cancer   **d.** diabetes

12. Use *The Merck Index* or a similar reference work to look up the toxicities of cocaine, procaine, lidocaine, mepivacaine, and bupivacaine. Is it always accurate to compare toxicities in different animals and extrapolate those animal toxicities to humans? Does the method of administration have an effect on the observed toxicity?

13. Prepare a brief report on a neurotransmitter. Describe its function and site of action.

14. Prepare a brief report on thalidomide—its structure, original intended use, problems that arose, and proposed new uses. Identify the chiral carbon atom(s) in thalidomide that were the source of the problems.

CHEMISTRY@HOME   Heal My Heartburn

Materials required

- 3 different kinds of commercial chewable antacids (Hint: Use white tablets, not colored tablets, and look for brands with different active ingredients)
- 4 small clear plastic cups
- Mortar and pestle, rolling pin. or kitchen mallet (to crush the pills)
- Cabbage juice indicator (see preparation instructions below)
- Vinegar
- Measuring spoons (a tablespoon and a teaspoon)

Why do doctors recommend particular medicines over others? How do over-the-counter medicines differ in effectiveness? In this experiment, you will analyze three different brands of chewable antacids to determine which active ingredient is the most effective.

Medicines and drugs are seldom given to patients in pure form. Typically, the active ingredient is combined with other (inactive) ingredients so that the drug can be delivered in a pill form or intravenously, for example. The inactive ingredients help to control the timing and method of delivery of a particular dose of the drug. The active ingredient is the molecule that functions biologically to provide a cure or remedy an adverse symptom. Usually, several different active ingredients can be used to cure an ailment.

For this experiment, we will be using commercial chewable antacid tablets to analyze the effectiveness of the different active ingredients. Antacids are taken to help relieve the symptoms of heartburn, and almost all of the active ingredients function by neutralizing the excess acid in the stomach with weak bases. The most common bases used are magnesium, aluminum, and calcium hydroxides and carbonates.

First, gather three different brands of antacids that have three different active ingredients. Many antacids will have more than one active ingredient and will be combinations of different hydroxides and carbonates.

Prepare four small clear plastic cups by labeling them with the three different names of the antacids and labeling one as "control." Prepare the control solution by adding 1 tablespoon of vinegar and 1 teaspoon of cabbage juice indicator to the plastic cup. You can use this control solution to compare the colors of the reactions.

Next, take two tablets of the first brand of antacid and crush them using a mortar and pestle, kitchen mallet, or another kitchen device. Add the crushed tablets to the appropriately labeled plastic cup. Do the same for the other two brands of antacids.

Then, measure one tablespoon of vinegar, followed immediately by 1 teaspoon of the cabbage juice indicator to each plastic cup. Note the time that you added the vinegar and indicator. Gently swirl each mixture and observe the reactions for 5–10 minutes. What do you notice about the color of each solution? What does the color change indicate? According to your results, rank the antacid brands in order of most effective to least effective.

How to make cabbage juice indicator: To prepare the cabbage juice indicator, first peel off six leaves from a head of red cabbage and chop them into fine pieces. Bring 8 cups of water to boil and add the chopped cabbage leaves to the boiling water. Lower the heat and allow the cabbage mixture to simmer for 30 minutes. Pour the mixture through a strainer into a large container and let the juice cool to room temperature. This juice will be your indicator solution.

Typical results

Questions

1. Write out the chemical reactions for each brand of the active ingredients. Remember to balance your equations.
2. Do you think that the conditions of this experiment mimic that of the stomach? What differences might exist between the conditions of this experiment and those of the stomach (and the conditions associated with heartburn)?
3. What other factors associated with the antacid tablets might affect this experiment? For example, do the different brands have the same inactive ingredients?

FITNESS AND HEALTH

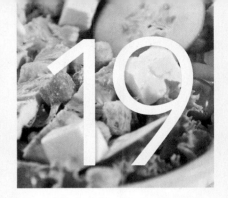

Have You Ever Wondered**?**

1. Do large doses of vitamins improve a person's health**?**

2. Does vitamin C help to cure cancer**?**

3. If I stop exercising, will the muscle I've developed turn to fat**?**

4. What is the difference between being overweight and being obese**?**

Learning Objectives

- List the recommendations (sources and percentages) for calories from fats and other sources in the American diet. (19.1)

- Describe the special dietary requirements of athletes. (19.1)

- Describe the dietary requirements for vitamins, minerals, and water. (19.2)

- Explain how weight is lost through diet and exercise. (19.3)

- Calculate weight loss due to calorie reduction and to exercise. (19.3)

- Describe several ways to measure fitness. (19.4)

- Calculate BMI values. (19.4)

- Differentiate between aerobic exercise and anaerobic exercise, and describe the chemistry that occurs during each. (19.5)

- Describe how muscles are built and how they work. (19.5)

- Describe the physiological effects of restorative drugs, stimulant drugs, and anabolic steroids. (19.6)

- Explain how endorphins, neurotrophins, and tobacco can affect the brain and body. (19.6)

- Explain how green chemistry principles can help us make transportation choices.

- Describe the relationship between walking or biking and personal health, especially the implications for weight loss.

THE CHEMISTRY OF WELLNESS

For much of human history, the main concern of most people was obtaining enough food to stay alive. How the world has changed! Especially in developed countries, people now have scores of labor-saving devices and abundant food. Most people earn their daily bread with little physical exertion. So much food is available, and so little physical effort is required to obtain it, that many people eat more than they should and get much less exercise than they need.

Obesity has become a major epidemic. According to the Centers for Disease Control and Prevention (CDC), 68% of American adults are either overweight or obese; half of those are considered obese. The

Exercise and a proper diet as parts of a healthy lifestyle are essential to good health, reducing the risk of diseases of the mind and body. Through chemistry, we gain a better understanding of the effects of diet and exercise on our bodies and minds.

International Obesity Task Force estimates that 1.5 billion people worldwide are overweight, with 500 million of those being obese.

How do we stay healthy and physically fit? By some special diet or kind of exercise? In this chapter, we examine nutrition, electrolyte balance, muscle action, drugs, and other topics related to well-being and physical fitness.

19.1 Calories: Quantity and Quality

Learning Objectives ❯ List the recommendations (sources and percentages) for calories from fats and other sources in the American diet. ❯ Describe the special dietary requirements of athletes.

Although obesity is rampant in the developed world, many people still struggle daily just to obtain enough food to survive. Research actually shows that undereating is healthier than overeating. Large studies have shown that mice given 40% less food than a control group live longer and have fewer tumors.

Total calorie intake is important, but the distribution of calories is even more important. The *2010 Dietary Guidelines for Americans* from the U.S. Departments of Agriculture (USDA) and Health and Human Services (HHS) include some recommendations, presented as a food plate in Figure 19.1. HHS and USDA jointly publish *Dietary Guidelines for Americans* every 5 years. You can find this document on the Internet using the title as key words.

A food plan based on these general recommendations should be tailored to the individual. For the average 2000-calorie-a-day diet, the guidelines make the following suggestions:

- Enjoy your food, but eat less.
- Avoid oversized portions.
- Make half of your plate fruits and vegetables.
- Whole grains should be at least half of total grains.
- Switch to fat-free or low-fat (1%) milk.
- Compare the sodium content of foods like soup, bread, and frozen meals, and choose the foods with lower amounts.
- Drink water instead of sugary drinks.

The 2000-calorie-per-day diet is an average. You should follow a diet that takes into account your weight, age, and level of activity. Then you should adjust it to include fewer calories if you want to lose weight or more calories if you want to gain weight. Calorie-intake calculators available on the Internet might be of some help.

An important point to remember when considering caloric intake is that the Calorie listed on a food item is not the same as a calorie calculated in chemical energy. The food Calorie is 1000 times larger than an energy calorie, and the food Calorie is often expressed as a kcal (kilocalorie). This means that the average 2000-calorie-a-day recommendation would actually be 2000 kilocalories, or 2 million calories. This chapter refers mainly to food Calories and uses the kcal notation when referring to food Calories as energy calories.

A key recommendation for adults is to keep fat intake between 20% and 35% of all calories. Most fats should be made up of polyunsaturated and monounsaturated fatty acids. Only 7–10% of calories should come from saturated fats, and intake

▲ **Figure 19.1** A daily food guide presented as a plate of food. More detailed recommendations in *Dietary Guidelines for Americans* are based on an individual's age, sex, activity level, and general health.

of synthetic *trans* fatty acids should be kept to a minimum. Also, the diet should contain less than 300 mg/day of cholesterol.

The "good" fats come from sources such as fish, nuts, and vegetable oils. Olive oil and canola oil are rich in monounsaturated fatty acids, and fish oils contain beneficial omega-3 fatty acids. A study of people living on the Greek island of Crete showed that they had an amazingly low incidence of cardiovascular disease, in spite of their diet, which averaged about 40% fat. This result is thought to be due to the high percentage of olive oil in their diet.

More than half the fats in the typical American diet are animal fats, and 70% of saturated fat comes from animal products. Saturated fats and cholesterol are implicated in the clogging of arteries. They are found in animal products such as butter, lard, red meats, and fast-food hamburgers. We should choose meat, poultry, milk, and milk products that are lean, low in fat, or fat free.

Trans fats, produced when vegetable oils are hydrogenated (for example, to produce margarine), are high in *trans* fatty acids (Section 17.2). As the name implies, *trans* fatty acids contain carbon-to-carbon double bonds with the *trans* configuration, so that they behave more like saturated fatty acids (Figure 17.7). Unless margarine has been specially treated to remove the *trans* fat, it has about the same health effects as butter.

The *percentage* of fat in the American diet has dropped from 40% in 1990 to about 34% today, but the absolute quantity of fat consumed has increased because Americans are eating more total calories. Also, 34% is an average figure; for some people, the percentage is as high as 45%.

A healthy diet can help us avoid disease. Harvard Medical School studies indicate that correct dietary choices, regular exercise, and avoidance of smoking would prevent about 82% of heart attacks, about 70% of strokes, over 90% of type 2 diabetes, and over 70% of colon cancer. In contrast, the most effective drugs against cholesterol buildup, called *statins*, only reduce heart attacks by about 20–30%.

Nutrition and the Athlete

The recommended ranges for energy nutrients for most people are 20–35% of calories from fat, 45–65% of calories from carbohydrates, and 10–35% of calories from protein. (Recall from Chapter 17 that each gram of carbohydrate or protein provides about 4 kcal; a gram of fat provides about 9 kcal.) Athletes generally need more calories because they expend more energy than the average sedentary individual. Those extra calories should come mainly from carbohydrates. Foods rich in carbohydrates, especially starches, are the preferred source of energy for the healthy body.

Fatty and protein-rich foods also supply calories, but protein metabolism produces more toxic wastes that tax the liver and kidneys. The pregame steak dinner consumed by some athletes in the past was based on a myth that protein builds muscle. It doesn't. Although athletes do need the **Dietary Reference Intake (DRI)**, quantity of protein (0.8 g protein/kg body weight), with few exceptions, they do not need an excess. DRIs are nutrient-based reference values established by the Food and Nutrition Board of the U.S. National Academy of Sciences for use in planning and assessing diets. They have replaced the Recommended Dietary Allowances (RDAs) that were published since 1941 by the National Academy of Sciences. Protein consumed in amounts greater than that needed for synthesis and repair of tissue only makes an athlete fatter (as a result of excessive calorie intake)—not more muscular.

Muscles are built through exercise, not through eating excess protein. When a muscle contracts against a resistance, an organic acid called *creatine* is released. Creatine stimulates production of the protein myosin, thus building more muscle tissue. If the exercise stops, the muscle begins to shrink after about two days. After about two months without exercise, muscle built through an exercise program is almost completely gone.

$$NH_2 - \underset{\underset{NH}{\|}}{C} - \underset{\underset{CH_3}{|}}{N} - CH_2COOH$$

Creatine

SELF-ASSESSMENT Questions

1. The two major requirements for good health and fitness are
   a. food and entertainment   b. food and medicine
   c. good nutrition and exercise   d. nutrition and steroids

2. Which of the following has been shown to extend the life span of mice?
   a. amino acid supplements   b. low-fat diets
   c. undereating   d. vitamin supplements

3. Which of the following is not a source of "good" fats?
   a. fish   b. peanuts   c. olives   d. lard

4. What is the maximum amount of fat that a diet providing 2200 kcal per day should include?
   a. 22 g   b. 86 g   c. 198 g   d. 220 g

5. What is the maximum amount of saturated fat that a diet providing 2000 kcal per day should include?
   a. 11 g   b. 22 g   c. 50 g   d. 200 g

6. *Statins* are a class of drugs that are designed to
   a. burn calories   b. reduce cholesterol buildup
   c. build muscle   d. metabolize sugar

7. Dietary Reference Intakes (DRIs) are nutrient-based reference values that are
   a. appropriate for undernourished and ill people
   b. guarantees of good health for everyone
   c. useful for planning and assessing diets
   d. minimum daily requirements

8. About how much protein does a 66-kg athlete require per day?
   a. 6.6 g   b. 8.3 g   c. 53 g   d. 2.5 kg

Answers: 1. c; 2. c; 3. d; 4. b; 5. b; 6. b; 7. c; 8. c

19.2 Vitamins, Minerals, Fluids, and Electrolytes

Learning Objective ❯ Describe the dietary requirements for vitamins, minerals, and water.

Good nutrition requires sufficient carbohydrates, fats, and proteins; proper proportions of essential minerals and vitamins; and adequate water. *Vitamins* are organic substances that the human body needs but cannot manufacture in sufficient quantities. Unlike hormones and enzymes, which the body can synthesize, vitamins must be included in the diet. *Minerals*, inorganic elements that the body needs, must also be present in the diet. Table 19.1 lists DRIs of vitamins and minerals for young adult women and men. A more complete list for various ages and with a number of qualifications is available from the Food and Nutrition Board. Vitamins and minerals are discussed in Chapter 17. See Table 17.3 for a list of essential minerals and trace minerals. Table 17.4 lists most vitamins along with food sources and deficiency symptoms.

Many medical professionals say that vitamin and mineral supplements are unnecessary when the diet is well balanced and includes the DRI for each nutrient. However, for those who choose to take such supplements, reasonable doses of vitamins and minerals from tablets and capsules are not likely to cause harm and can be beneficial in some cases. For example, the body has an increased demand for vitamins and minerals during periods of rapid growth, during pregnancy and lactation, and during periods of trauma and recovery from disease. A study of people aged 65 years and older showed that a daily dose of 18 vitamins and minerals seems to strengthen the immune system. The number of infections in the study group was 50% less than that in a control group, which received no supplements.

The DRI values for vitamins and minerals set by the Food and Nutrition Board are quite modest, and they are readily supplied by any well-balanced diet. The DRI values for vitamins are the amounts that will prevent deficiency diseases such as beriberi, pellagra, and scurvy. Some scientists believe that *optimum* intakes of some vitamins are somewhat higher than the DRI values. For example, they think that the current DRIs for vitamins C, D, and E are too low. If you eat a well-balanced diet and you are in good health, you probably do not need vitamin supplements. Small doses of vitamins are not toxic; some of the fat-soluble vitamins (A and D) are toxic in large doses, however, so caution is warranted.

Vitamin A is essential for good vision, bone development, and skin maintenance. There is some evidence that it may confer resistance to certain kinds of cancer. This may help to explain the anticancer activity that has been noted for

Table 19.1	Dietary Reference Intakes of Vitamins and Minerals for Young Adults	
Nutrient	Females	Males
Vitamins		
Vitamin A	700 μg[a]	900 μg[a]
Vitamin C	75 mg[b]	90 mg[b]
Vitamin D	200 IU[c]	200 IU[c]
Vitamin E	30 IU	30 IU
Thiamine (B$_1$)	1.1 mg	1.2 mg
Riboflavin (B$_2$)	1.1 mg	1.3 mg
Niacin	14 mg	16 mg
Pyridoxine (B$_6$)	1.5 mg	1.7 mg
Cyanocobalamin (B$_{12}$)	3 μg	3 μg
Folacin (folic acid)	400 μg	400 μg
Pantothenic acid	5 mg	5 mg
Biotin	100–200 μg	100–200 μg
Minerals		
Calcium	1200 mg	1200 mg
Phosphorus	700 mg	700 mg
Magnesium	320 mg	420 mg
Iron	15 mg	10 mg
Zinc	12 mg	15 mg
Iodine	150 μg	150 μg
Fluoride	3 mg	4 mg
Selenium	55 μg	70 μg
Potassium	2 g	2 g

[a]To the extent that the vitamin A requirement is met by β-carotene, multiply these by 6.
[b]Smokers should add 35 mg.
[c]IU (for "international unit") is a measure of the biological activity of many vitamins, hormones, and drugs.

cruciferous vegetables such as broccoli, cauliflower, Brussels sprouts, and cabbage. Most cruciferous vegetables are rich in β-carotene, which is converted to vitamin A in the body.

Vitamin A is a fat-soluble vitamin stored in the fatty tissues of the body and especially in the liver. Large doses can be toxic. The recommended upper limit for intake of vitamin A is 3000 μg/day. Studies in affluent countries have shown that ingesting vitamin A from supplements and in fortified foods at levels even slightly above the DRI leads to an increased risk of bone fractures later in life.

Larger quantities of β-carotene can be taken safely because excess β-carotene is not converted to vitamin A. It may have important functions other than as a precursor of vitamin A. Some nutritionists argue that β-carotene is needed in quantities greater than those needed to meet the vitamin A requirement. However, a single ½-cup serving of carrots is sufficient to provide the DRI of vitamin A from β-carotene. Consuming foods that contain β-carotene is probably the safest way to obtain the proper quantity of vitamin A.

1. Do large doses of vitamins improve a person's health?

Vitamins should not be thought of as fuel like food or water or oxygen. Although a daily vitamin tablet may be good insurance for many people, vitamin doses in large excess of the DRIs have not been found to have any special health benefit. There is some evidence that larger doses of some vitamins can strengthen the immune system, but care must be taken.

▲ Dorothy Crowfoot Hodgkin (1910–1994) used X-rays to determine the structures of several important organic compounds, including vitamin B_{12}, penicillin, and cholesterol.

An international unit (IU) measures the biological activity of many vitamins, hormones, and drugs. For each substance to which the IU applies, an international agreement specifies the biological effect expected from a dose of 1 IU. The IU is used to measure comparative potency of a substance such as a vitamin because the vitamin may exist in more than one form. For example, 1 IU of vitamin A is the biological equivalent of 0.3 μg retinol or 0.6 μg β-carotene.

The B family of vitamins has eight members. Because they are all water soluble, excess intake is excreted in the urine. Little or no toxicity is connected with B vitamins, with the possible exceptions of vitamin B_6 and folic acid, both of which apparently can cause neurological damage in some people if taken in extremely large daily doses. Several B vitamins serve as coenzymes (Section 16.5). Besides preventing the skin lesions of pellagra, niacin (vitamin B_3) offers some relief from arthritis and helps in lowering the blood cholesterol level.

Vitamin B_6 (pyridoxine) has been found to help people with arthritis by shrinking the connective tissue membranes that line the joints. Vitamin B_6 is a coenzyme for more than 100 different enzymes.

Vitamin B_{12} (cyanocobalamin) is not found in plants, and vegetarians are apt to be deficient in this vitamin. That deficiency can lead to pernicious anemia. The molecular formula of vitamin B_{12} is $C_{63}H_{88}CoN_{14}O_{14}P$, giving it a molecular mass of 1355.38. Its very complicated structure was determined by Dorothy Hodgkin of Oxford University in 1956 using X-ray crystallography, a technique in which an X-ray beam is used to bombard a crystal. The beam is scattered in a definite pattern determined by the crystal structure. No one had ever attempted to establish the structure of a molecule of this size and complexity before. Hodgkin received the 1964 Nobel Prize in Chemistry for this work.

Another B vitamin, folic acid, is critical in the development of the nervous system of a fetus. Its presence in a pregnant woman's diet prevents spina bifida in her baby. Folic acid also helps prevent cardiovascular disease. An upper limit of 1000 μg has been set; more than that can cause nerve damage.

Vitamin C is ascorbic acid, the component in citrus fruits that combats scurvy. About 60–80 mg daily will prevent scurvy, but vitamin C does more. It promotes the healing of wounds, burns, and lesions such as gastric ulcers. It also seems to play an important role in maintaining collagen, the body's major structural protein. Like vitamin E, it is an antioxidant, and these two vitamins, along with β-carotene, are included in many antioxidant formulations. Antioxidants may act as anticarcinogens. About 200 mg of vitamin C per day is probably optimal, and an upper limit of 2000 mg/day has been set.

Vitamin C seems to be essential for efficient functioning of the immune system. *Interferons*, large molecules formed by the action of viruses on their host cells, are agents in the immune system. By producing an interferon, one virus can interfere with the growth of another. An increased level of vitamin C has been shown to increase the body's production of interferons. People with low levels of vitamin C are more likely to develop cataracts and glaucoma, as well as gingivitis and periodontal disease. Some suggest that very large doses of vitamin C may cure or prevent colds, but there is little evidence for this.

Vitamin D is a steroid hormone that protects children against rickets. Vitamin D is not strictly an essential dietary vitamin because most mammals produce enough of it when they are exposed to sunlight. It promotes the absorption of calcium and phosphorus from foods to produce and maintain healthy bones. Too much vitamin D can lead to excessive calcium and phosphorus absorption, with subsequent formation of calcium deposits in various soft body tissues, including those of the heart. The DRI for vitamin D increases with age, from 200 international units (IU) for adults aged 20–50 to reaching 600 IU for those over 70. The recommended upper limit is 2000 IU. Since the primary source of vitamin D is from our exposure to sunlight, it should be noted that use of sunscreens may limit the capacity of the body to synthesize vitamin D. It also suggests that exercise in the outdoors has specific benefits for vitamin D production, though the amount of vitamin D that the body can produce is self-limiting to avoid toxic levels of the vitamin. Foods that supplement the availability of vitamin D can prevent problems associated with vitamin D deficiency.

2. Does vitamin C help to cure cancer?

A 2008 study by the National Institutes of Health found that *injected* vitamin C does appear to slow brain, ovarian, and pancreatic tumor growth in mice. However, these studies have not yet been extended to human beings. Also, the body precisely regulates the amount of vitamin C in the blood when it is taken orally, so oral doses of the vitamin do not provide these benefits.

Vitamin E is a mixture of *tocopherols*, phenols with hydrocarbon side chains. Its antioxidant activity may have value in maintaining the cardiovascular system, and it has been used to treat coronary heart disease, angina, rheumatic heart disease, high blood pressure, arteriosclerosis, varicose veins, and a number of other cardiovascular problems. As an antioxidant, vitamin E can inactivate free radicals. It is generally believed that much of the physiological damage from aging is a result of the production of free radicals. Indeed, vitamin E has been called the "antiaging vitamin." However, studies of these effects are often contradictory and far from conclusive. Vitamin E is also an anticoagulant that has been useful in preventing blood clots after surgery.

Rats deprived of vitamin E become sterile. Vitamin E deficiency can also lead to muscular dystrophy, a disease of the skeletal muscles. A lack of vitamin E can lead to a deficiency in vitamin A. This occurs because vitamin A can be oxidized to an inactive form when vitamin E is not present to act as an antioxidant. Vitamin E also collaborates with vitamin C in protecting blood vessels and other tissues against oxidation. Vitamin E is the fat-soluble antioxidant vitamin, and vitamin C the water-soluble one. Oxidation of unsaturated fatty acids in cell membranes can be prevented or reversed by vitamin E, which is itself oxidized in the process. Vitamin C can then restore vitamin E to its unoxidized form. The upper limit for vitamin E is 800 IU/day or 400 IU/day, depending on side effects. And, according to a study published in October 2011, even 400 IU/day may increase the risk of prostate cancer in men. LDL cholesterol is oxidized before it is deposited in arteries, and vitamin E prevents the oxidation of cholesterol. Some think this is the mechanism by which vitamin E helps to protect against cardiovascular disease.

Body Fluids and Electrolytes

Another aspect of the relationship of chemistry and nutrition is the balance between fluid intake and electrolyte intake. An **electrolyte** is a substance that conducts electricity when dissolved in water. In the body, electrolytes are ions required by cells to maintain their internal and external electric charge and thus control the flow of water molecules across the cell membrane. The main electrolytes are sodium ions (Na^+), potassium ions (K^+), and chloride ions (Cl^-). Others include calcium ions (Ca^{2+}), magnesium ions (Mg^{2+}), sulfate ions (SO_4^2), hydrogen phosphate ions (HPO_4^{2-}), and bicarbonate ions (HCO_3^-).

Water is an essential nutrient, a fact obvious to anyone who has been deprived of it. Many people seem to prefer to meet the body's need for water by consuming soft drinks, coffee, beer, fruit juice, energy drinks, and other beverages. Some of these beverages impair the body's use of the water that they contain. Alcoholic drinks promote water loss by blocking the action of *antidiuretic hormone* (*ADH*), also known as *vasopressin*. Caffeine has a diuretic effect on the kidneys, promoting urine formation and consequent water loss.

The best way to replace water lost through respiration, sweat, tears, and urination is to drink water. Unfortunately, thirst is often a *delayed* response to water loss, and it may be masked by such symptoms of dehydration as exhaustion, confusion, headache, and nausea. Sweat is about 99% water, but a liter of sweat typically contains 1.15 g Na^+, 1.48 g Cl^-, 0.02 g Ca^{2+}, 0.23 g K^+, 0.05 g Mg^{2+}, and minute amounts of urea, lactic acid, and body oils. Most people consume too much sodium chloride (Na^+ and Cl^-), and only traces of the other electrolytes are lost. Thus, it makes the most sense to replace the water component of lost sweat with plain water.

Commercial beverages such as sports drinks, energy drinks, vitamin waters, protein waters, and fitness waters usually contain one or more ingredients that are more effective as advertising gimmicks than as aids to athletic performance. Sports drinks usually contain sweeteners and electrolytes. Energy drinks usually have sugars and often contain caffeine as a mild stimulant. The ingredients in vitamin waters and protein waters are obvious, but there are far better and less expensive sources of both. Although these drinks are quite popular with both serious and weekend athletes, they are so concentrated (a hazard that can lead to diarrhea) that they are of marginal value except for endurance athletes (Figure 19.2).

▲ **Figure 19.2** The best replacement for fluids lost during exercise generally is plain water. Sports drinks help little, except for those athletes engaging in endurance activities lasting for 2 h or more. At that point, carbohydrates in the drinks delay the onset of exhaustion by a few minutes.

Table 19.2	Effects of Varying Degrees of Dehydration
Percentage of Body Weight Lost as Sweat	Physiological Effect
2%	Performance impaired
4%	Muscular work capacity declines
5%	Heat exhaustion
7%	Hallucinations
10%	Circulatory collapse and heat stroke

How do you know if you are drinking enough water and are in a proper state of hydration? The urine is a good indicator of hydration. When you are properly hydrated, your urine is clear and almost colorless. When you are dehydrated, your urine gets cloudy or dark because your kidneys are trying to conserve water so as to keep the blood volume from shrinking and to prevent shock.

Dehydration can be quite serious, even deadly. We become thirsty when total body fluid volume decreases by 0.5–1.0%. Beyond that, things get worse (Table 19.2). Muscles tire and cramp. Dizziness and fainting may follow, and brain cells shrink, resulting in mental confusion. Finally, the heat regulatory system fails, causing *heat stroke*, which can be fatal without prompt medical attention.

Improving Athletic Performance through Chemistry

Chemistry has transformed athletic performance in recent decades. New materials have been used to make protective gear such as plastic helmets and foam padding for football, ice hockey, skateboarding, and other sports. Improved equipment has changed the nature of most sports events. Baseball, football, and other sports are quite different when played on artificial turf or under a dome than when played outdoors on grass. Traction changes, the ball bounces differently, and so on. Skateboards of the 1950s consisted of metal roller-skate wheels on a flat wooden board. Today's skateboards have wide urethane wheels, specially shaped composite-construction boards, and shock-absorbing wheel mounts that make incredible stunts almost commonplace. Several decades ago, running shoes had thin leather soles and little or no foot support. Now these shoes have thick, shock-absorbing soles and built-in support for arches and ankles.

Biochemistry has brought a better understanding of the human body and the way it works. Chemistry has helped to provide better nutrition. Today's athletes are bigger, faster, and stronger than their predecessors. More than 25 new world records were set at the 2012 Olympic Games in London.

▲ Sometimes technology can be *too* beneficial. Specially designed full-length swimsuits dramatically reduce drag. So many swimming world records were set in 2008 that the suits were banned in 2010.

SELF-ASSESSMENT Questions

1. Which of the following cannot be synthesized by the body and therefore must be included in the diet?
   a. enzymes   b. hormones
   c. unsaturated fats   d. vitamins

2. Which of the following is a precursor of vitamin A?
   a. β-carotene   b. cholesterol
   c. pyridoxine   d. tryptophan

3. For which of the following are large doses most likely to be harmful?
   a. β-carotene   b. niacin
   c. vitamin A   d. vitamin C

4. Which of the following vitamins provides the most benefit to bone health and development?
   a. vitamin D   b. vitamin B
   c. vitamin C   d. vitamin E

5. Vitamin E is a(n)
   a. antimetabolite   b. fat-soluble antioxidant
   c. oxidizing agent   d. water-soluble antioxidant

6. The major electrolytes in body fluids are
   a. Ca^{2+}, Fe^{2+}, and Cl^- b. Ca^{2+}, Na^+, and HSO_4^-
   c. Na^+, K^+, and Cl^- d. Na^+, K^+, and HCO_3^-

7. The best replacement for water lost except in prolonged exercise is

a. beer   **b.** non-fat milk

c. plain water   **d.** soft drinks

8. What is the minimal percentage of body weight lost in fluids that can cause heat exhaustion?

a. 2%   **b.** 4%   **c.** 5%   **d.** 10%

Answers: 1, d; 2, a; 3, c; 4, c; 5, b; 6, c; 7, c; 8, c

19.3 Weight Loss: Diets and Exercise

Learning Objectives ❭ Explain how weight is lost through diet and exercise.
❭ Calculate weight loss due to calorie reduction and to exercise.

With obesity an epidemic and so many people overweight, dieting is a major U.S. industry. It is possible to lose weight through dieting alone, but it isn't easy. One pound of adipose (fatty) tissue stores about 3500 kcal of energy. If you reduce your intake by 100 kcal/day and keep your activity level constant, you will burn off a pound of fat in 35 days. Unfortunately, people are seldom patient enough, and they resort to more stringent diets. To achieve their goals more rapidly, they exclude certain foods and reduce the amounts of others. Such diets can be harmful. Diets with fewer than 1200 kcal/day are likely to be deficient in necessary nutrients, particularly in B vitamins and iron. Further, dieting slows down metabolism. Weight lost through dieting is quickly regained when the dieter resumes old eating habits.

Example 19.1   Weight Loss through Dieting

If you ordinarily expend 1800 kcal/day and you go on a diet limited to 1500 kcal/day, about how long will it take to lose 1.0 lb of fat?

Solution
You will use 1800−1500 = 300 kcal/day more than you consume. There are about 3500 kcal in 1.0 lb of fat, so it will take

$$3500 \text{ kcal} \times \frac{1 \text{ day}}{300 \text{ kcal}} = 11.66 \text{ or about 12 days}$$

Keep in mind, however, that your weight loss will not be all fat. You will probably lose more than 1 lb, but it will be mostly water with some protein and a little glycogen.

▪ **EXERCISE 19.1A**
A person who expends 2000 kcal/day goes on a diet limited to 1200 kcal/day without a change in activities. Estimate how much fat she will lose if she stays on this diet for 3 weeks.

▪ **EXERCISE 19.1B**
A person who expends 2200 kcal/day goes on a diet limited to 1800 kcal/day and adds exercise activities that use 220 kcal/day. Estimate how much fat he will lose if he stays on this program for 6 weeks.

Biochemistry of Hunger

Scientists are just beginning to understand the complex biochemistry of hunger mechanisms. Several molecules that regulate body weight have been identified. Some determine whether we want to eat now or stop eating. Others control long-term fat balance. Much of what we now know is disappointing for people who want to lose weight: The hunger mechanisms protect against weight loss and favor weight gain.

Two peptide hormones, known as *ghrelin* and *peptide YY* (*PYY*), are produced by the digestive tract and are linked to short-term eating behaviors. Ghrelin, a modified peptide, is an appetite stimulant produced by the stomach. PYY acts as an appetite suppressant. Studies at Imperial College, London, found that people ate about 30% less after they were given a dose of PYY. The research also found that obese people had lower natural levels of PYY, which may explain why these people feel hungrier and overeat.

The hormone insulin and a substance called *leptin*, which is produced by fat cells, determine longer-term weight balance. When insulin levels go up, glucose levels go down, and we experience hunger. Conversely, when glucose levels are high, the activity of brain cells sensitive to glucose is lessened, and we feel satiated.

Leptin, a protein consisting of 146 amino-acid units, is produced by fat cells. It causes weight loss in mice by decreasing their appetite and increasing their metabolic rates. Levels of leptin tell the hypothalamus (a regulatory center in the brain) how much fat is in the body. Humans also produce leptin, and scientists hoped it would be the route to a cure for the ever-growing obesity problem. That hope is largely unrealized. Only a few cases of severe human obesity, caused by defects in leptin production, have been helped by leptin treatment. As it turns out, most obese humans have *higher* than normal blood levels of leptin and are resistant to its actions. Leptin's main role seems to be to protect against weight loss in times of scarcity rather than against weight gain in times of plentiful food.

Other substances involved in weight control include *cholecystokinin (CCK)*, a peptide formed in the intestine that signals that we have eaten enough food, and a class of compounds called *melanocortins*, which act on the brain to regulate food intake.

It remains to be seen whether this new knowledge about the body's weight-control systems will pay off in better obesity treatments. A complication is that many social factors are also involved in eating behavior. Some people are motivated by environmental cues to eat. A family gathering, the sight or smell of food, and a stressful situation can all trigger the hunger mechanism.

Crash Diets: Quick = Quack

Any weight-loss program that promises a loss of more than a pound or two a week is likely to be dangerous quackery. Most quick-weight-loss diets depend on factors other than fat metabolism to hook prospective customers. The diets often include a **diuretic**, such as caffeine, to increase the output of urine. Weight loss is water loss, and that weight is regained when the body is rehydrated.

Other quick-weight-loss diets depend on depleting the body's stores of glycogen. On a low-carbohydrate diet, the body draws on its glycogen reserves, depleting them in about 24 hours. Recall that glycogen is a polymer of glucose (Section 16.2). Glycogen molecules have lots of hydroxyl (—OH) groups that can form hydrogen bonds to water molecules. We can store at most about 1 lb of glycogen. Each pound of glycogen carries about 3 lb of water held to it by these hydrogen bonds. Depleting the pound of glycogen results in a weight loss of about 4 lb (1 lb glycogen + 3 lb water). No fat is lost, and the weight is quickly regained when the dieter resumes eating carbohydrates.

If your normal energy expenditure is 2400 kcal/day, the most fat you can lose by *total fasting* for a day is 0.69 lb (2400 kcal/day divided by 3500 kcal/lb of adipose tissue). This assumes that your body burns nothing but fat—which does not occur. The brain runs on glucose, and if that glucose isn't supplied in the diet, it is obtained from protein. Any diet that restricts carbohydrate intake results in a loss of muscle mass as well as fat. When you gain the weight back (as 90% of all dieters do), you gain mostly fat. People who diet without exercising will replace metabolically active tissue (muscle) with inactive fat when they gain back the lost weight. Weight loss becomes harder with each subsequent attempted diet.

There is little evidence that commercial weight-loss programs are effective in helping people drop excess pounds and keep off. Almost no rigorous studies of the programs have been carried out, and U.S. Federal Trade Commission officials say that companies are unwilling to conduct such studies. Many crash diets are also deficient in minerals such as iron, calcium, and potassium. A deficiency of these minerals can disrupt nerve-impulse transmissions to muscles, which impairs athletic performance. Nerve-impulse transmission to vital organs may also be impaired in cases of severe restriction, and death can result from cardiac arrest.

Exercise for Weight Loss

Studies consistently show that people who exercise regularly live longer. They are sick less often and have fewer signs of depression. They can move faster, and they have stronger bones and muscles. Although there are dozens of good reasons for regular exercise, many people begin exercise programs for one simple reason: They want to lose weight.

People who do not increase their food intake when they begin an exercise program lose weight. Contrary to a common myth, exercise (for up to an hour a day) does not cause an increase in appetite. Most of the weight loss from exercise results from an increase in metabolic rate during the activity, but the increased metabolic rate continues for several hours after completion of the exercise. Exercise helps us maintain both fitness and proper body weight. On a weight-loss diet (without exercise), about 65% of the weight lost is fat and about 11% is protein (muscle tissue). The rest is water and a little glycogen.

3. If I stop exercising, will the muscle I've developed turn to fat?
Muscle does not turn into fat, although without regular exercise muscles become flabby and will lose mass.

Example 19.2	Weight Loss through Exercise

A 135-lb person doing high-impact aerobics burns about 6.9 kcal/min. How long does a person have to do such exercise to lose 1.0 lb of adipose (fat) tissue?

Solution

One pound of adipose tissue stores 3500 kcal of energy. To burn it at 6.9 kcal/min requires

$$3500 \text{ kcal} \times \frac{1 \text{ min}}{6.9 \text{ kcal}} = 500 \text{ min}$$

It takes about 500 min (more than 8 h) to burn 1 lb of fat, even doing high-impact aerobics.

■ EXERCISE 19.2A
Walking a mile uses about 100 kcal. About how far do you have to walk to burn 2.0 lb of fat?

■ EXERCISE 19.2B
A moderately active person can calculate the calories needed each day to maintain a desired weight by multiplying the desired weight (in pounds) by 15 kcal/lb. How many calories per day does such a person need to maintain a weight of 180 lb?

Fad Diets

Weight-loss diets are often lacking in balanced nutrition and can be harmful to one's health. In the more extreme low-carbohydrate diets, ketosis (Section 17.5) is deliberately induced, and possible side effects include depression and lethargy. In the early stages of a diet deficient in carbohydrates, the body converts amino acids to glucose that the brain requires. If there are enough adequate proteins in the diet, tissue proteins are spared.

Even low-carbohydrate diets high in adequate proteins are hard on the body, which must rid itself of the nitrogen compounds—ammonia and urea—formed by the breakdown of proteins. This puts an increased stress on the liver, where the waste products are formed, and on the kidneys, where they are excreted.

Contrary to a popular notion, fasting does not "cleanse" the body. Indeed, quite the reverse occurs. A shift to fat metabolism produces ketone bodies (Section 17.5), and protein breakdown produces ammonia, urea, and other wastes. You can lose weight by fasting, but the process should be carefully monitored by a physician.

The most sensible approach to weight loss is to adhere to a balanced low-calorie diet that meets the DRI for essential nutrients and to engage in a reasonable, consistent, individualized exercise program. This approach applies the principles of weight loss by decreasing intake and increasing output.

Weight loss or gain is based on the law of conservation of energy (Section 15.3). When we take in more calories than we use up, the excess calories are stored as fat. When we take in fewer calories than we need for our activities, our bodies burn some of the stored fat to make up for the deficit. One pound of adipose tissue requires 200 mi of blood capillaries to serve its cells. Excess fat therefore puts extra strain on the heart.

SELF-ASSESSMENT Questions

1. How many kilocalories of energy are stored in 1.0 lb of adipose tissue?
   a. 454 kcal
   b. 1000 kcal
   c. 3500 kcal
   d. 10,000 kcal

2. To lose 1.0 lb per week, how many more kilocalories must you burn each day than you take in?
   a. 100
   b. 300
   c. 500
   d. 1000

3. Which of the following hormones acts as an appetite suppressant?
   a. ADH
   b. ghrelin
   c. leptin
   d. PYY

4. Blood glucose levels are lowered by the hormone
   a. cholecystokinin
   b. glucagon
   c. insulin
   d. oxytocin

5. Which of the following seems to prevent weight loss in humans during times when the body cannot get food?
   a. cholecystokinin (CCK)
   b. ghrelin
   c. leptin
   d. oxytocin

6. About how much glycogen can the adult body store?
   a. 100 g
   b. 1 lb
   c. 4 lb
   d. an almost unlimited quantity

7. Crash diets
   a. are a good way to lose weight and keep it off
   b. depend on glycogen depletion for quick weight loss
   c. result in a decrease in the number of fat cells
   d. lead to a depletion of adipose tissue

Answers: 1. c; 2. c; 3. d; 4. c; 5. c; 6. b; 7. b

19.4 Measuring Fitness

Learning Objectives › Describe several ways to measure fitness. › Calculate BMI values.

Measuring fitness is roughly the same as measuring fatness. How much fat is enough? The male body requires about 3% body fat, and the average female body needs 10–12%. It is not easy to measure percent body fat accurately. Weight alone does not indicate degree of fitness. A tall 200-lb man may be much more fit than a 160-lb man with a smaller frame. Skinfold calipers are sometimes used, but they are quite inaccurate and measure water retention as well as fat.

One way to estimate body fat is by measuring a person's density. Mass is determined by weighing, and volume is calculated with the help of a dunk tank like the one shown in Figure 19.3. The difference between a person's weight in air and when submerged in water corresponds to the *mass* of the displaced water. When this mass is divided by the density of water and then corrected for air in the lungs, it gives a reasonable value for the person's volume. Mass divided by volume yields the person's density, although results can vary with the amount of air in the lungs. Fat is less dense (0.903 g/mL) than the water (1.00 g/mL) that makes up most of the body's mass. The higher the proportion of body fat a person has, the lower the density and the more buoyant that person is in water.

A simpler way to estimate degree of fatness is by measuring the waist and the hips. The waist should be measured at the narrowest point and the hips should be measured where the circumference is the largest. The waist measurement should then be divided by the hip measurement. This ratio should be less than 1 for men and should be 0.8 or less for women. (Because the units cancel out, the measurements can be made in inches or centimeters, as long as the same units are used for both.)

Some modern scales provide a measure of body fat content, using *bioelectric impedance analysis*. The person stands on the scale in bare feet, and a small electric

▲ **Figure 19.3** When submerged in water, a body displaces its own volume of water. The difference between a person's weight in air and when submerged in water corresponds to the *mass* of the displaced water. Because the density of water is 1.00 g/mL, the mass of water displaced (in grams) equals the person's volume (in milliliters).

Q: *What is the volume, in liters, of a person who displaces 48.5 kg of water?*

current is sent through the body. Fat has greater impedance (resistance to varying current) than does muscle. By measuring the impedance of the body, the percentage of body fat can be calculated based on height and weight. However, there are many other variables, such as bone density, water content, and location of fat. Although such scales are not very accurate, they may be useful for monitoring *changes* in body fat content.

Body Mass Index

Body mass index (BMI) is a commonly used measure of fatness. It is defined as weight (in kilograms) divided by the square of the height (in meters). For a person who is 1.6 m tall and weighs 62 kg, the body mass index is $62/(1.6)^2 = 24$. A BMI below 18.5 indicates that a person is underweight. A BMI from 25 to 29.9 indicates that a person is overweight, and a BMI of 30 or more indicates obesity. When measurements are in pounds and inches, the equation is

$$\text{BMI} = \frac{705 \times \text{body weight (lb)}}{[\text{height (in.)}]^2}$$

In other words, a person who is 5 ft 10 in. tall (70 in.) and weighs 140 lb has a BMI of

$$\frac{705 \times 140}{70 \times 70} = 20$$

which is within the ideal range.

It DOES Matter!
In Europe during the Middle Ages—and even later—people accused of crimes were often tried by some kind of ordeal. In trial by water, the innocent sank and the guilty floated. Suspected witches were tied hand to foot and thrown into the water. The guilty floated, were fished out, dried off, and executed. In those days, body density was *really* important!

Example 19.3 | Body Mass Index

What is the BMI for a person who is 6 ft 3 in. tall and weighs 350 lb?

Solution

The person's height is $(6 \times 12) + 3 = 72 + 3 = 75$ in.

$$\text{BMI} = \frac{705 \times 350}{75 \times 75} = 43.9$$

The body mass index is 44.

▪ **EXERCISE 19.3A**
What is the BMI for a person who is 6.0 ft tall and weighs 120 lb?

▪ **EXERCISE 19.3B**
What is the maximum weight, in pounds, that a person who is 5 ft 10 in. tall can maintain and have a BMI that does not exceed 25.0?

V_{O_2} max: A Measure of Fitness

As we increase exercise intensity, our uptake of oxygen must also increase. For example, the faster we run, the more oxygen we need to sustain the pace. However, the body reaches a point at which it simply cannot increase the amount of oxygen it consumes even if the intensity of exercise increases. The V_{O_2} max is the maximum amount (in milliliters per kilogram of body weight) of oxygen that a person can use in 1 minute.

V_{O_2} max is therefore a measure of fitness. The higher the V_{O_2} max, the greater is an athlete's fitness. A person with a high V_{O_2} max can exercise more intensely than those who are less fit. The V_{O_2} max can be increased by working out at an intensity that raises the heart rate to 65–85% of its maximum for at least 20 minutes three to five times a week. Limitations on V_{O_2} max include the ability of muscle cells to use oxygen in metabolizing fuels and the ability of the cardiovascular system and lungs to transport oxygen to the muscles.

Direct testing of V_{O_2} max requires expensive equipment, including a gas analyzer to measure O_2 taken in and exhaled. Percent V_{O_2} max can be estimated

4. What is the difference between being overweight and being obese?
While the human body needs some minimal fat stores to function normally, any amount more than the optimum is considered unhealthy. Anyone with a body mass index (BMI) of 25 kg/m² is considered overweight. A BMI of 30 kg/m² is defined as being obese. Being overweight can lead to increased health risks, but being obese dramatically increases the likelihood of type 2 diabetes, heart disease, osteoarthritis, obstructive sleep apnea, and certain types of cancer.

indirectly from percent maximum heart rate (%MHR), where MHR is the highest number of beats the heart makes in a minute of exercising.

$$MHR = (0.64 \times \%V_{O_2} \text{ max}) + 37$$

The relationship holds quite well for both males and females of all ages and activity levels. For example, 80% MHR corresponds to a $\%V_{O_2}$ max of

$$80 = (0.64 \times \%V_{O_2} \text{ max}) + 37$$

$$\%V_{O_2} \text{ max} = 67$$

Equations for determining MHR values and tables for evaluating fitness levels can be found in exercise physiology textbooks and on the Internet (see Collaborative Group Project 2).

SELF-ASSESSMENT Questions

1. Body mass index (BMI) is calculated as
   a. percentage of body fat × waist circumference (in.)
   b. (height ÷ weight) × 100
   c. [705 × weight (lb)] ÷ [height (in.)]
   d. weight (kg) ÷ [height (m)]^2

2. A person with a BMI of 22 is
   a. obese
   b. overweight but not obese
   c. quite fit
   d. underweight

3. The maximum amount of oxygen used in a minute of exercise is the
   a. aerobic threshold
   b. lactate threshold
   c. oxygen debt
   d. V_{O_2} max

Answers: 1. d; 2. c; 3. d

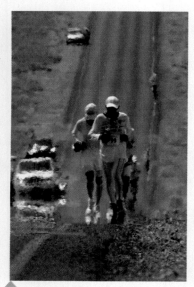

It DOES Matter!

Extreme-endurance athletes, such as triathletes and ultramarathoners, may need a bit more protein than the DRI. However, nearly all Americans eat 50% more protein than they need, so even these athletes seldom need protein supplements. Weightlifters and bodybuilders need no extra protein.

19.5 Some Muscular Chemistry

Learning Objectives ❯ Differentiate between aerobic exercise and anaerobic exercise, and describe the chemistry that occurs during each. ❯ Describe how muscles are built and how they work.

The human body has about 600 muscles. Exercise makes these muscles larger, more flexible, and more efficient in their use of oxygen. Exercise strengthens the heart because the heart is an organ comprised mainly of muscle. With regular exercise, resting pulse and blood pressure usually decline. A person who exercises regularly is able to do more physical work with less strain. Exercise is an art, but it is also increasingly a science—a science in which chemistry plays a vital role.

Energy for Muscle Contraction: ATP

When cells metabolize glucose or fatty acids, only part of the chemical energy in these substances is converted to heat. Some of the energy is stored in the high-energy phosphate bonds of adenosine triphosphate (ATP) molecules.

Adenosine triphosphate

Stimulation of muscles causes them to contract. This contraction is *work*, and it requires energy that the muscles get from the molecules of ATP. The energy stored in ATP powers the physical movement of muscle tissue. Two proteins, actin and myosin, play important roles in this process. Together they form a loose complex called *actomyosin*, the contractile protein that makes up muscles (Figure 19.4).

When ATP is added to actomyosin in the laboratory, the protein fibers contract. Myosins turn the chemical energy of ATP into motion. Myosin molecules "walk" along the actin filaments. It takes about 2×10^{12} myosin molecules acting in unison in the arm to lift a 40-g spoonful of sugar. Besides serving as part of the structural complex in muscles, myosin also acts as an enzyme for the removal of a phosphate group from ATP. Thus, it is directly involved in liberating the energy required for muscle contraction.

In a resting person, muscle activity (including that of the heart muscle) accounts for only about 15–30% of the body's energy requirements. Other activities, such as cell repair, transmission of nerve impulses, and maintenance of body temperature, account for the remaining energy needs. During intense physical activity, the energy requirements of muscle may be more than 200 times the resting level.

Aerobic Exercise: Plenty of Oxygen

The ATP in muscle tissue is sufficient for activities lasting at most a few seconds. Fortunately, muscles have a more extensive energy supply in the form of glycogen, a starchlike form of dietary carbohydrate that has been ingested, digested to glucose, absorbed, and stored.

When muscle contraction begins, glycogen is converted to pyruvic acid by muscle cells, in a series of steps.

$$(C_6H_{10}O_5)_n \longrightarrow 2n\ CH_3\overset{\overset{\displaystyle O}{\|}}{C}-\overset{\overset{\displaystyle O}{\|}}{C}OH$$

Glycogen   Pyruvic acid

Then, if sufficient oxygen is readily available, the pyruvic acid is oxidized to carbon dioxide and water in another series of steps. Because acids in biological systems are usually ionized at the pH of cellular fluids, biochemists usually refer to them by the names of their anions. For example, lactic acid becomes lactate, and pyruvic acid becomes pyruvate.

$$2\ CH_3\overset{\overset{\displaystyle O}{\|}}{C}-\overset{\overset{\displaystyle O}{\|}}{C}OH + 5\ O_2 \longrightarrow 6\ CO_2 + 4\ H_2O$$

Muscle contractions that occur under these circumstances—that is, in the presence of oxygen—constitute **aerobic exercise** (Figure 19.5).

Anaerobic Exercise and Oxygen Debt

When sufficient oxygen is not available, pyruvic acid is reduced to lactic acid.

$$CH_3COCOOH + [2\ H] \longrightarrow CH_3CHOHCOOH$$

[2 H] represents hydrogen ions (H^+) from one of several biochemical reducing agents.

If **anaerobic exercise** (muscle activity with insufficient oxygen) persists, an excess of lactic acid builds up in the muscle cells. This lactic acid ionizes, forming lactate ions and hydronium ions.

$$CH_3CHOHCOOH + H_2O \longrightarrow CH_3CHOHCOO^- + H_3O^+$$

Muscle fatigue correlates well with lactate levels, which were long thought to be its cause. However, studies have shown that muscle tiredness is related to calcium ion flow. Ordinarily, muscle contractions are managed by the ebb and flow of Ca^{2+} ions. As muscles grow tired, tiny channels in muscle cells start leaking Ca^{2+}, which weakens contractions. At the same time, the leaked Ca^{2+} ions stimulate an enzyme that breaks down muscle fibers, further contributing to the muscle fatigue.

(a)

Actin   Myosin

Extended muscle fibers

Resting fibers

Partially contracted fibers

(b)

▲ **Figure 19.4** Skeletal muscle tissue has a banded, or *striated*, appearance, shown here in a micrograph at 180 × magnification (a). The diagram of the actomyosin complex in muscle (b) shows extended muscle fibers (top), resting fibers (middle), and partially contracted fibers (bottom).

▲ **Figure 19.5** Aerobic exercise is performed at a pace that allows us to get enough oxygen to our muscle cells to oxidize pyruvic acid to carbon dioxide and water. Aerobic dance is a popular form of aerobic exercise.

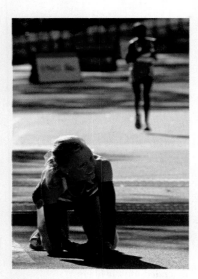

▲ **Figure 19.6** After a race, the metabolism that fueled the effort continues. The athlete gulps air to repay her oxygen debt.

Levels of several other products of muscle metabolism, including phosphocreatine (the phosphorylated form of creatine, page 605), ATP, and ions such as Na^+, K^+, and $H_2PO_4^-$, change during fatigue. These changes may also contribute to muscle tiredness.

$$H_2O_3PNH-C-N-CH_2COOH$$
$$\underset{NH}{\parallel}\ \underset{CH_3}{\mid}$$

Phosphocreatine

Well-trained athletes can continue for a while after muscle fatigue sets in, but most people quit. At this point, the **oxygen debt** starts to be repaid (Figure 19.6). After exercise ends, the cells' demand for oxygen decreases, making more oxygen available to oxidize the lactic acid resulting from anaerobic metabolism back to pyruvic acid. This acid is then converted to carbon dioxide, water, and energy.

Most athletes emphasize one type of exercise (anaerobic or aerobic) over the other. For example, an athlete training for a 60-m dash does mainly anaerobic exercising, but one planning to run a 10-km race does mainly aerobic exercising. Sprinting and weightlifting are largely anaerobic activities. A marathon run (42 km) is largely aerobic. During a marathon, athletes must set a pace to run for more than 2 hours. Their muscle cells depend on slow, steady aerobic conversion of carbohydrates to energy. During anaerobic activities, however, muscle cells use almost no oxygen. Rather, they depend on the quick energy provided by anaerobic metabolism.

After glycogen stores are depleted, muscle cells can switch over to fat metabolism. Fats are the main source of energy for sustained activity of low or moderate intensity, such as the last part of a marathon run.

Muscle Fibers: Twitch Kind Do You Have?

Muscles are tools with which we do work. The quality and type of muscle fibers that an athlete has affect his or her athletic performance, just as the quality of machinery influences how work is done. For example, we can remove snow from a driveway in more than one way. We can do it in 10 min with a snowblower, or we can spend 50 min shoveling. Muscles are classified according to the speed and effort required to accomplish this work. The two classes of muscle fibers (Figure 19.7) are **fast-twitch fibers** (which are stronger and larger and most suited for anaerobic activity) and **slow-twitch fibers** (which are best for aerobic work). Table 19.3 lists some characteristics of these two types of muscle fibers.

Type I (slow-twitch) fibers are called on during activity of light or moderate intensity. The respiratory capacity of these fibers is high, which means that they can provide a large amount of energy via aerobic pathways. The myoglobin level is also high. Myoglobin is a red, heme-containing protein in muscle that stores oxygen (similar to the way hemoglobin stores and transports oxygen in the blood). Aerobic oxidation requires oxygen, and muscle tissue rich in slow-twitch fibers is supplied with high levels of oxygen.

▲ **Figure 19.7** Slow-twitch muscle fibers have more mitochondria (elongated violet dots) than fast-twitch fibers do.

Table 19.3	A Comparison of Two Types of Muscle Fibers	
Characteristic	Type I	Type IIB[a]
Category	Slow twitch	Fast twitch
Color	Red	White
Respiratory capacity	High	Low
Myoglobin level	High	Low
Catalytic activity of actomyosin	Low	High
Capacity for glycogen use	Low	High

[a]There is a type IIA fiber (not considered here) that resembles type I in some respects and type IIB in others.

Type I muscle fibers have a low capacity to use glycogen and thus are not geared to anaerobic generation of energy. Their action does not require the hydrolysis of glycogen. The catalytic activity of the actomyosin complex is low. Remember that actomyosin not only is the structural unit in muscle that undergoes contraction but also is responsible for catalyzing the hydrolysis of ATP to provide energy for the contraction. Low catalytic activity means that the energy is parceled out more slowly. Slow energy output is not good if you want to lift 200 kg, but it is great for a 15-km run.

Type IIB (fast-twitch) fibers have characteristics opposite those of type I fibers. Low respiratory capacity and low myoglobin levels do not bode well for aerobic oxidation. A high capacity for glycogen use and a high catalytic activity of actomyosin allow tissue rich in fast-twitch fibers to generate ATP rapidly and also to hydrolyze this ATP rapidly during intense muscle activity. Thus, this type of muscle tissue has the capacity to do short bursts of vigorous work but fatigues rather quickly. A period of recovery, during which lactic acid is cleared from the muscle, is required between the brief periods of activity.

▲ **Figure 19.8** The New York City Marathon attracts more than 30,000 runners each year.

Q: *What is the main muscle type in the elite runners in this race? Do their muscles have high or low aerobic capacity?*

Building Muscles

Endurance exercise increases myoglobin levels in skeletal muscles. The increased myoglobin provides faster oxygen transport and increased respiratory capacity (Figure 19.8), and these changes usually are apparent within 2 weeks. Endurance training does not necessarily increase the size of muscles.

If you want larger muscles, try weightlifting. Weight training (Figure 19.9) develops fast-twitch muscle fibers. These fibers increase in size and strength with repeated anaerobic exercise. Weight training does *not* increase respiratory capacity.

Some bodybuilders use supplements to try to increase muscle mass. Creatine is an organic acid that is naturally produced in the liver and kidneys (Section 19.1). As such, it is not an essential nutrient. Creatine is also acquired through the consumption of meat. A normal diet including protein can provide an adequate amount of creatine. An athlete or body builder, though, might switch to a high-protein diet to increase muscle mass. Creatine when used as a supplement for those seeking to build muscle mass is often 2 or 3 times the amount available from a high-protein diet.

Muscle-fiber type seems to be inherited. Research shows that world-class marathon runners may possess as high as 80–90% slow-twitch fibers, while championship sprinters may have up to 70% fast-twitch muscle fibers. Some exceptions have been noted, however, and factors such as training and body composition are important in athletics, as are nutrition, fluid and electrolyte balance, and drug use or misuse.

▲ **Figure 19.9** Weightlifting is a popular activity in many gyms and fitness centers.

Q: *What is the predominant muscle type in elite weightlifters? Do their muscles have high or low aerobic capacity?*

SELF-ASSESSMENT Questions

1. Which of the following is a molecule used by the cells to energize the ATP molecule?
   a. an amino acid **b.** actomycin
   c. glycogen **d.** glucose

2. When muscle contraction begins, glycogen is converted to
   a. creatine **b.** creatinine
   c. lactic acid **d.** pyruvic acid

3. During aerobic exercise, pyruvic acid is converted to
   a. CO_2 and H_2O **b.** glycogen
   c. lactic acid **d.** phosphocreatine

4. During anaerobic exercise, pyruvic acid is converted to
   a. CO_2 and H_2O **b.** glycogen
   c. lactic acid **d.** phosphocreatine

5. When produced during exercise, which of the following results in oxygen debt?
   a. ATP **b.** glycogen
   c. lactic acid **d.** pyruvic acid

6. Slow-twitch muscle fiber is classified as
   a. type I **b.** type IIA
   c. type IIB **d.** type III

7. The reddish color of slow-twitch muscle fibers is due to the presence of
   a. actomyosin **b.** creatine
   c. myoglobin **d.** pyruvic acid

Answers: 1, d; 2, d; 3, a; 4, c; 5, c; 6, a; 7, c

19.6 Drugs, Athletic Performance, and the Brain

Learning Objectives ❯ Describe the physiological effects of restorative drugs, stimulant drugs, and anabolic steroids. ❯ Explain how endorphins, neurotrophins, and tobacco can affect the brain and body.

Muscle chemistry and metabolism, aerobic and anaerobic exercise, and nutrition and fluid balance all rely on normal internal processes. It would seem that hard work and proper nutrition are the best answers to improved performance. However, many athletes turn instead to drugs, such as the stimulants amphetamine and cocaine, to improve performance and to anabolic steroids to build muscles.

Like most other people, athletes use drugs to alleviate pain or soreness that results from overuse and to treat injuries. These **restorative drugs** include analgesics (painkillers), such as aspirin and acetaminophen (Section 18.2), and anti-inflammatory drugs, such as aspirin, ibuprofen, ketoprofen, and cortisone. Cortisone derivatives are often injected to reduce swelling in damaged joints and tissues. Relief is often transitory, however, and side effects can be severe. Prolonged use of cortisone derivatives can cause fluid retention, hypertension, ulcers, disturbance of the sex-hormone balance, and other problems.

Other substances that can be bought over the counter and applied externally include oil of wintergreen (methyl salicylate) and capsaicin (the active ingredient in hot peppers). These substances are usually one ingredient of an ointment or cream. When applied to the skin, they cause a mild burning sensation, thus serving as a counterirritant for sore muscles. Methyl salicylate is also an aspirin derivative and also acts as an analgesic.

Stimulant Drugs

Some athletes use *stimulant drugs* (Section 18.7) to try to improve performance. The caffeine in a strong cup of coffee may be of some benefit. Caffeine triggers the release of fatty acids. Metabolism of these compounds may conserve glycogen, but any such effect is small. Caffeine also increases the heart rate, speeds metabolism, and increases urine output. The latter effect could lead to dehydration.

Other athletes resort to stronger stimulants, including amphetamines and cocaine. These drugs stimulate the central nervous system, increasing alertness, respiration, blood pressure, muscle tension, and heart rate. They also mask symptoms of fatigue and give an athlete a sense of increased stamina.

Anabolic Steroids

Many strenuous athletic performances depend on well-developed muscles. Muscle mass depends on the level of the male hormone *testosterone* (Section 18.5). When boys reach puberty, testosterone levels rise, and the boys become more muscular if they exercise. Men generally have larger muscles than women because they have more testosterone.

Testosterone and some of its semisynthetic derivatives are taken by athletes in an attempt to build muscle mass quickly. Steroid hormones used to increase muscle mass are called **anabolic steroids**. These chemicals aid in the building (anabolism) of body proteins (Section 16.4) and thus of muscle tissue.

There are no reputable controlled studies demonstrating the effectiveness of anabolic steroids. They do seem to work—at least for some people—but the side effects are many. In males, side effects include testicular atrophy and loss of function, impotence, acne, liver damage that may lead to cancer, edema (swelling), elevated cholesterol levels, and growth of breasts.

Anabolic steroids act as male hormones (androgens), making women more masculine. They help women build larger muscles, but they also result in balding, extra body hair, a deep voice, and menstrual irregularities. What price will athletes pay for improved performance?

Drugs, Athletic Performance, and Drug Screening

The use of drugs to increase athletic performance not only is illegal and physically dangerous but also can be psychologically damaging. Stimulant drugs give users a false sense of confidence by affecting their ego, giving the delusion of invincibility. Such a feeling of "greatness" often ends as the competition begins, however, because the stimulant effect is short lived (it lasts only half an hour to an hour for cocaine). Exhaustion and extreme depression usually follow. More stimulants are needed to combat these "down" feelings, and the user then runs the risk of addiction or overdose.

Because drug use for the enhancement or improvement of performance is illegal, chemists play an important role in sports: screening blood and urine samples for illegal drugs. Using sophisticated instruments, chemists can detect minute amounts of illegal drugs. Drug testing has been used at the Olympic Games since 1968, and it is rapidly becoming standard practice for athletes in college and professional sports.

Drugs are used at great risk of health (and legal!) problems. The use of illegal drugs violates the spirit of fair athletic competition. Let's work toward a world in which events and medals are won by drug-free athletes who are highly motivated, well-nourished, and well-trained.

Exercise and the Brain

Hard, consistent training improves athletic performance. Few drugs help, but athletes' own bodies manufacture a variety of substances that aid performance. Examples are the pain-relieving **endorphins** (Section 18.2).

After vigorous activity, athletes have an increased level of endorphins in their blood. Stimulated by exercise, deep sensory nerves release endorphins to block the pain message. Exercise extended over a long period of time, such as distance running, sometimes causes in an athlete many of the same symptoms experienced by opiate users. Athletes get a euphoric high during or after a hard run. Unfortunately, both natural endorphins and their analogs, such as morphine, seem to be addictive. Athletes, especially runners, tend to suffer from withdrawal: They feel bad when they don't get the vigorous exercise of a long, hard run. This can be positive because exercise is important to the maintenance of good health. It can be negative if the person exercises when injured or to the exclusion of family or work obligations. Athletes also seem to develop a tolerance to their own endorphins. They have to run farther and farther to get that euphoric feeling.

Exercise also directly affects the brain by increasing its blood supply and by producing **neurotrophins**, substances that enhance the growth of brain cells. Exercises that involve complex motions, such as dance movements, lead to an increase in the connections between brain cells. Both our muscles and our brains work better when we exercise regularly.

No Smoking

If you want to stay healthy and fit, one thing you certainly should *not* do is use tobacco. Tobacco use and smoking are dangerous addictions that cause a wide variety of diseases, including cancer, heart disease, and emphysema, and often result in death. More than 400,000 children become regular smokers each year. Almost a third will eventually die from smoking.

Cigarette smoking is the chief preventable cause of premature death in the United States. One in five deaths in the United States is smoking related. According to the CDC, cigarette smoking is associated with death from 24 different diseases, including heart disease, stroke, and lung diseases such as cancer, emphysema, and pneumonia. Smoking causes diseases of the gums and mouth, chronic hoarseness, vocal cord polyps, and premature aging and wrinkling of the skin. Lung cancer is not the only malignancy caused by cigarette smoking. Cancers of the pancreas, bladder, breast, kidney, mouth and throat, stomach, larynx, and cervix are also associated with smoking. In fact, smoking kills more people than AIDS, alcohol, illegal drugs, car accidents, murders, and suicides combined.

GREEN CHEMISTRY

Doris Lewis, *Suffolk University*

Your Fitness Benefits the Planet

Learning Objectives ❯ Explain how green chemistry principles can help us make better transportation choices. ❯ Explain some health benefits of walking and biking, including implications for weight loss.

How do you get to class each day? Do you walk, bike, drive, or take public transportation? You might be surprised to learn that green chemistry principles can apply to your personal transportation.

According to green chemistry ideals, we should limit the use of the fossil fuels that support most transport, such as gasoline, because they are nonrenewable resources (Principle 7). Further, burning of these materials produces greenhouse gases including CO_2. As shown in the equation in Section 13.4, the combustion of 1 mol of octane, a component of gasoline, releases 8 mol of CO_2. Principle 3 suggests that use of fossil fuels should be reduced because this process releases harmful substances to the environment, including gases that have been linked to destructive climate change.

Although the chemical reactions that power your body when you walk or bike produce CO_2, they are based on renewable fuels – the carbohydrates in your food (Section 17.1). The reaction of carbohydrates with oxygen powers your body and leads to CO_2 as a byproduct. The plants that produced the carbohydrates you eat incorporated CO_2 from the atmosphere through photosynthesis (Section 15.1) and this process decreased the amount of this greenhouse gas. Your energy source, then, is carbon-neutral because the carbon dioxide that you produce is balanced by the carbon dioxide used up to make the carbohydrate fuel for your body. Because the plants you consume use the energy of the sun to power photosynthesis, it is fair to say that you, too, are powered by renewable solar energy. Although the carbon compounds in fossil fuels came originally from plants, those plants died millions of years ago, so their removal of CO_2 does not help our atmosphere today.

Unlike internal combustion engines that burn at high temperatures, your body is able to fuel your motion at the temperature of 98.6 °F, or 37 °C. Therefore, walking or biking is consistent with Principle 6, design for energy efficiency. How does your body perform this feat? Its energy reactions involve enzymes, or selective biochemical catalysts, as prescribed by Principle 9.

Walking and biking are healthier for the planet and also for you. Exercise like walking and biking has been shown to provide protection from heart attack, stroke, and diabetes. It also triggers the release of endorphins, the body's stress-relieving and mood-lifting chemicals (Section 19.6), so that you arrive at work refreshed and less stressed. Studies have shown that an average of two or more walking trips a week results in a yearly projected weight loss of 0.9-1.8 pounds- approximately the yearly weight gain of the average American. A 150-pound person walking only 20 minutes at 4 miles per hour burns 114 calories that would be deposited as fat if that person were sitting in a car for that mount of time (Section 19.3).

Prefer biking to walking? Although five times as many people walk to work as those who bike, the popularity of biking is rising quickly. The number of bike commuters rose 61.6% between 2000 and 2011. Riding a bicycle instead of driving a car saves an average of $8000 per year, and biking 10 miles a day burns 110,000 calories in a year. This choice can keep off more than 30 pounds of fat and prevent a whopping 3500 pounds of greenhouse gas emissions each year even as the biking commuter saves money.

Bike riders have banded together to promote commuting by bike, safer bike routes, and bike-to-work days in many cities. Hundreds of thousands of people participate in the San Francisco Bay area Bike to Work Day, and universities in Boston sponsor "Hub on Wheels," a city-wide bike ride and festival. Suffolk University created a "SuffolkBikes" YouTube video as a service project to promote biking. Does your college encourage biking? Are student groups involved?

On Earth Day 2010, the U.S. Department of Transportation released a study that recommends improvement of walking, biking, and transport networks as a way of reducing greenhouse gas emissions. Doing so could reduce greenhouse gases generated by transport 2 to 5 percent by 2030. These recommendations are being implemented in cities all over the United States. The City of Atlanta approved $2.5 million for bike projects in 2013, and New York, Philadelphia, Boston, and San Francisco are among the cities with action plans to make bike riding easier and safer. Easily accessible rental or shared bikes with access points all over the city are becoming commonplace, so it is no longer even necessary to own a bike or to return it to the same place where it was picked up. Although bikers may not realize it, they are saving money and improving their own health and the health of the planet through the principles of green chemistry.

◀ Bicycling to work or school is an all-win proposition. Even an elaborate bicycle is much less expensive than a car. Bicycling provides healthy exercise, it does not generate pollution, and operating cost is nil.

We fear cancer, but heart attack and stroke are the major causes of disability and death of smokers. Cigarette smokers have a 70% higher risk of heart attack than nonsmokers. When they are also overweight, with high blood pressure and high cholesterol, their risk is 200% higher. At every age, the death rate is higher among smokers than among nonsmokers. A study of military veterans, conducted at Harvard University, concluded that smokers are 4.3 times as likely as nonsmokers to develop Alzheimer's disease. Heavy smokers get Alzheimer's 2.3 years sooner, on average, than nonsmokers.

Women who smoke during pregnancy have more stillborn babies, more premature babies, and more babies who die before they are a month old. Women who take birth control pills and also smoke have an abnormally high risk of stroke. Women who smoke are advised to use some other method of birth control.

One of the gases in cigarette smoke is carbon monoxide, which ties up about 8% of the hemoglobin in the blood. Smokers therefore breathe less efficiently. They work harder to breathe, but less oxygen reaches their cells. It is no wonder that fatigue is a common problem for smokers. According to the Centers for Disease Control and Prevention, more than 7000 chemicals have been identified in cigarette smoke, including many that are quite poisonous and about 70 that are known or suspected carcinogens.

In the linings of the lungs are *cilia* (tiny, hairlike processes) that help to sweep out particulate matter breathed into the lungs. In smokers, the tar from cigarette smoke forms a sticky coating that keeps the cilia from moving freely. The reduced action of the cilia may explain the smoker's cough. Pathologists claim that during an autopsy it is usually easy to tell if the body was that of a smoker. Lungs are normally pink. A smoker's lungs are black.

Unfortunately, cigarette smoke also harms nonsmokers. Secondhand smoke causes an estimated 3000 premature deaths each year in the United States and causes up to 300,000 children to suffer from lower respiratory tract infections. Children of

Chemistry of Sports Materials

The athlete's world is shaped by chemicals. The ability to perform reflects biochemistry within the athlete. Chemicals taken by athletes may hinder or enhance their performance. Yet another chemical dimension to the sports world is that chemicals are used to enhance athletic clothing and equipment.

Athletic clothing depends on chemicals for its shape and protective qualities. Swimsuits, ski pants, and elastic support clothing stretch because of synthetic fibers. Undergarments made of polypropylene or polyester fibers wick perspiration away from the skin and keep the athlete dry even during vigorous exercise.

Athletes of all sorts are aided by equipment made of materials developed by the chemical industry. Football, hockey, and baseball players are protected by polycarbonate helmets and protective pads of synthetic foamed rubbers. Brightly dyed nylon uniforms with synthetic colors add to the glamour of amateur and professional teams.

The dramatic effect of new materials is perhaps best illustrated in pole vaulting (Figure 19.10). The sport probably originated with the use of

▲ **Figure 19.10** U.S. silver medalist Jennifer Stuczynski Suhr in the women's pole vault final during the Beijing 2008 Olympic Games.

wooden poles to vault over streams or other obstacles. It became a sport in the early nineteenth century when the Germans introduced the vertical vault form of competition. The record using a wooden pole was set at 3.48 m in 1887. Bamboo poles were introduced in 1879 and were popular for decades, with the record set at 4.77 m in 1942. Metal poles came into use in the 1950s with records set in 1957 at 4.78 m using an aluminum pole and in 1960 at 4.80 m with a steel pole. Fiberglass poles were introduced in 1952, but it took several years for athletes to learn how to use these highly flexible poles effectively. The first world record using a fiberglass pole was 4.83 m, set in 1961. Carbon fiber, stronger for its weight than glass fiber, was introduced in 1990. Modern poles are constructed from composites of either fiberglass or carbon fiber and fiberglass in several layers. Today, the world-record pole vault is 6.16 m.

From the soles of sports shoes and the wax used on cross-country skis to titanium golf clubs and tennis sweaters that stretch and yet retain their shape, the sports world (like the world itself) is thoroughly reliant on chemicals for its existence.

smokers miss twice as much school time because of respiratory infections as do children of nonsmokers.

Efforts to lessen indoor pollution caused by smoking have led many restaurants, bars, and public buildings to be declared nonsmoking areas. About half of the U.S. population now lives under a ban on smoking covering all workplaces, restaurants, and bars.

In 2007, electronic or e-cigarettes were introduced into the United States from China. Generally considered safer than tobacco cigarettes because they produce fewer harmful gases, these devices are inhalers that vaporize nicotine solutions. While some traditional cigarette smokers use these devices as part of a regimen to quit smoking, some evidence exists that teenagers who use these devices may eventually become smokers. Another health concern arises because many of these devices use flavored nicotine solutions that taste like candy or fruit and young children may consume the refill solution. The nicotine is itself poisonous, and the concentrated solutions contain potentially lethal levels of nicotine. Also, other harmful chemicals have been found in the solutions used in e-cigarettes like diethylene glycol. The long-term effects of nicotine inhalation are not yet known, but many health experts recommend avoiding exposure.

SELF-ASSESSMENT Questions

1. Which of the following, as used by athletes, is used to reduce swelling in joints?
   a. creatine
   b. caffeine
   c. cortisone
   d. testosterone

2. Caffeine is thought to aid endurance athletes by
   a. conserving creatine
   b. conserving stored O_2
   c. stimulating the release of free amino acids
   d. stimulating the release of fatty acids

3. Anabolic steroids
   a. build muscles without exercise
   b. increase sexual drive
   c. help build larger muscles
   d. make female athletes more feminine

4. Endorphins are
   a. chemicals produced by the body that are similar to morphine
   b. chemicals produced by the body that carry pain messages
   c. chemicals produced by the body that stimulate muscle growth
   d. synthetic drugs similar to morphine

5. Exercise is thought to help the brain work better by
   a. acting as a stimulant
   b. increasing aerobic capacity
   c. increasing levels of neurotrophins
   d. inhibiting production of endorphins

6. The chemical in cigarette smoke that makes breathing less efficient is
   a. CO
   b. CO_2
   c. nicotine
   d. NO

7. What is the addictive substance inhaled by those who use e-cigarettes?
   a. carbon dioxide
   b. diethylene glycol
   c. carbon monoxide
   d. nicotine

Answers: 1, c; 2, d; 3, c; 4, a; 5, c; 6, a; 7, d

SUMMARY

Section 19.1—Good health and fitness require a nutritious diet and regular exercise. Today's dietary guidelines emphasize nutrient-dense foods and a balanced eating program. A balanced diet consists largely of fruits, vegetables, whole grains, and dairy products in the proper proportions. Total fats intake should not exceed 35% of calories; saturated fats (mostly of animal origin) should account for less than 10% of calories. Athletes generally need more calories, which should come mostly from carbohydrates—especially starches. Exercise, not extra protein, builds muscle tissue. The **Dietary Reference Intakes (DRIs)** for protein and other nutrients are established by the U.S. National Academy of Sciences for planning and assessing diets.

Section 19.2—Organic substances (vitamins) and inorganic substances (minerals) that the body cannot produce must be supplied by the diet. Vitamin and mineral supplements may not be necessary with a well-balanced diet, but they do no harm and may be beneficial. Vitamin A is essential for vision and skin maintenance. There are several B vitamins; B_3 and B_6 may help arthritis patients; B_{12} is not found in plants, and a lack can cause anemia. Vitamin C prevents scurvy, promotes healing, is needed for the immune system, and is an antioxidant. Vitamin D promotes absorption of calcium and phosphorus. Vitamin E is an antioxidant and an anticoagulant, and a deficiency can lead to muscular dystrophy. An **electrolyte** is a substance that conducts electricity in a water solution. The main electrolytes in the body are ions of sodium, potassium, chlorine, calcium, and magnesium, as well as sulfate, hydrogen phosphate, and bicarbonate ions. Water is an essential nutrient.

Section 19.3—Drastic diets are unlikely to be permanently successful, and the weight lost is usually regained. One pound of adipose tissue stores about 3500 kcal of energy. A variety of chemical substances that are produced in the body are regulators of body weight. Quick-weight-loss diets often include a **diuretic** to increase urine output, which results in temporary weight loss. Low-carbohydrate diets cause quick weight loss by depleting glycogen and water.

Exercise aids in weight loss, because the increase in metabolic rate that it causes continues after it ends. The most sensible approach to weight loss involves a balanced low-calorie diet and a consistent exercise program.

Section 19.4—The male body requires about 3% body fat; the female body, 10–12%. The percentage of body fat can be estimated by several methods. Density measurement is probably the most accurate. Body mass index (BMI) indicates fatness, and V_{O_2} max is a measure of fitness.

Section 19.5—Exercise makes muscles larger, more flexible, and more efficient. Energy for muscular work comes from ATP. A protein complex called *actomyosin* contracts when ATP is added to it. ATP provides energy for just a few seconds, after which glycogen is metabolized. If metabolism occurs with plenty of oxygen—during **aerobic exercise**—CO_2 and H_2O are formed. With insufficient oxygen—during **anaerobic exercise**—lactic acid is formed and muscle fatigue occurs. When exercise ends, the **oxygen debt** is repaid; the cells oxygen demand decreases, and the lactic acid can be oxidized to CO_2 and H_2O. There are two classes of muscle fibers. **Fast-twitch fibers** are larger and stronger and good for short bursts of vigorous exercise, while **slow-twitch fibers** are geared for steady exercise of long endurance. Weight training develops fast-twitch muscles but does not increase respiratory capacity. Long-distance running develops slow-twitch muscles and increases respiratory capacity.

Section 19.6—Athletes sometimes use **restorative drugs**, such as aspirin, ibuprofen, or cortisone, to alleviate pain and treat injuries. They may use stimulant drugs such as caffeine and cocaine. **Anabolic steroids** appear to increase muscle mass but have many bad effects, including impotence and liver cancer.

The body can manufacture pain-relieving **endorphins** that may help performance, but it appears that some athletes can become addicted to them. Exercise also directly affects the brain by producing **neurotrophins**, substances that enhance the growth of brain cells. Smoking reduces athletic performance, causes diseases, and leads to earlier death, and athletes should avoid it.

GREEN CHEMISTRY—Walking or biking instead of driving follows green chemistry principles and is healthy and enjoyable. Your body's energy comes from renewable plant carbohydrate sources rather than nonrenewable fossil fuels. Photosynthesis reactions of the plants contribute to balancing carbon dioxide in the atmosphere rather than creating harmful greenhouse gases like most transportation options.

Learning Objectives

› List the recommendations (sources and percentages) for calories from fats and other sources in the American diet.	Problems 1, 2, 12
› Describe the special dietary requirements of athletes.	Problems 6, 11, 45
› Describe the dietary requirements for vitamins, minerals, and water.	Problems 13–22
› Explain how weight is lost through diet and exercise.	Problems 3, 4, 9, 23, 24, 31, 32, 60
› Calculate weight loss due to calorie reduction and exercise.	Problems 25–30, 58
› Describe several ways to measure fitness.	Problems 7, 56, 59
› Calculate BMI values.	Problems 8, 33, 34, 57, 59, 61
› Differentiate between aerobic exercise and anaerobic exercise, and describe the chemistry that occurs during each.	Problems 5, 38, 39, 41–44
› Describe how muscles are built and how they work.	Problems 35–46, 62
› Describe the physiological effects of restorative drugs, stimulant drugs, and anabolic steroids.	Problems 10, 47, 48, 51
› Describe how endorphins, neurotrophins, and tobacco can affect the brain and body.	Problems 31, 32, 49, 50, 53, 54
› Explain how green chemistry principles can help us make better transportation choices.	Problems 64, 67
› Explain some health benefits of walking and biking, including implications for weight loss.	Problems 65, 66

REVIEW QUESTIONS

1. What kinds of foods are the main dietary source of saturated fats?

2. Why are the federal dietary guidelines (Figure 19.1) not the same for everyone?

3. How might you lose 5 lb in just 1 week? Would it be a useful way to lose weight and keep it off?

4. Do you think it is likely that obesity is inherited?

5. List three ways in which chemistry has had an impact on sports.

6. How do the nutritional needs of an athlete differ from those of a sedentary individual? How is this extra need best met?

7. List two ways to determine percent body fat. Describe a limitation of each method.

8. What are the common diseases or health problems associated with obesity?

9. List some problems that result from high-fat diets.

10. What are the effects of anabolic steroids on females?

PROBLEMS

Nutrition

11. What are the common dietary needs for athletes? Explain how athletes' needs differ from the typical diet.

12. What are two good reasons for not going on a high-protein diet?

Vitamins and Minerals

13. What benefit is derived from vitamin B_{12}?

14. What is scurvy, and what vitamin prevents it?

15. Which of the B vitamins seem to have an effect on arthritis?

16. What is the safest way to supplement your vitamin A intake?

17. What are the benefits of vitamin D? Is taking a daily megadose of vitamin D a good idea?

18. Vitamins C and E are antioxidants. What does this mean?

Electrolytes

19. What is a diuretic? Describe the function of antidiuretic hormone (ADH).

20. How is the appearance of urine related to dehydration?

21. Is thirst a good indicator of dehydration? Are you always thirsty when dehydrated?

22. Are sports drinks the best way to rehydrate? Why or why not?

Diet and Exercise

23. What are some popular diets, and in what ways do they stimulate quick weight loss? Why are the effects sometimes short lasting?

24. Why does a diet that restricts carbohydrate intake lead to loss of muscle mass as well as fat?

25. A quarter-pound burger provides 420 kcal of energy. How long would a 180-lb person have to walk to burn those calories if 1 h of walking uses about 210 kcal?

26. One kilogram of fat tissue stores about 7700 kcal of energy. An average person burns about 40 kcal while walking 1 km. If such a person walks 6 km each day, how much fat will be burned in 1 year?

27. The DRI for protein is about 0.8 g/kg body weight. How much protein is required each day by a 220-lb football player?

28. How much protein is required each day by a 110-lb gymnast? (See Problem 27.)

29. A 70-kg man can store about 2000 kcal as glycogen. How far could such a man run on this stored starch if he expends 100 kcal/km while running and the glycogen is his only source of energy?

30. A 70-kg man can store about 100,000 kcal of energy as fat. How far could such a man run on this stored fat if he expends 100 kcal/km while running and the fat is his only source of energy?

31. Describe the role of each of the following substances involved in the control of body weight.
    a. leptin   b. ghrelin

32. Describe the role of each of the following substances involved in the control of body weight.
    a. melanocortins   b. PYY

Body Mass Index

33. What is the body mass index (BMI) for a 5-ft 10-in. baseball player who weighs 186 lb?

34. What is the BMI for a 6-ft 2-in. football player who weighs 300 lb?

Muscles

35. When exercising, what is the process that increases muscle mass? Do you create new muscles?

36. What two proteins make up the actomyosin complex?

37. Muscles are made of protein. Does eating more protein result in larger muscles?

38. What is aerobic exercise? What is anaerobic exercise?

39. Which type of metabolism (aerobic or anaerobic) is primarily responsible for providing energy for (a) intense bursts of vigorous activity and (b) prolonged low levels of activity?

40. What are the two functions of the actomyosin protein complex?

41. Explain why high levels of myoglobin are appropriate for muscle tissue geared to aerobic oxidation.

42. Categorize type I and type IIB muscle fibers as suited to aerobic oxidation or to anaerobic use of glycogen.

43. Why does the high catalytic activity of actomyosin in type IIB fibers suggest that these are the muscle fibers engaged in brief, intense physical activity?

44. Describe the differences between fast-twitch and slow-twitch muscle fibers. Can you change which type you develop?

45. Muscle is protein. Does an athlete need extra protein (above the DRI) to build muscles? What is the best way to build muscles?

46. Describe the biochemical process by which muscles are built.

Drugs

47. How are cortisone derivatives used in sports medicine? What are some of the side effects of their use?

48. What are anabolic steroids? List some side effects of the use of anabolic steroids (a) in males and (b) in females.

49. Give a biochemical explanation of the "runner's high."

50. What evidence indicates that long-distance running is addictive? Give a biochemical explanation of addiction to long-distance running.

51. Describe how regular exercise can also improve brain function.

52. What is the role of chemists in the control of drug use by athletes?

Smoking and Health

53. What are some of the health problems related to smoking?

54. Why is it important for pregnant women not to smoke?

ADDITIONAL PROBLEMS

55. If you are moderately active and want to maintain a weight of 160 lb, about how many calories do you need each day?

56. An athlete can run a 400-m race in 45 s. Her maximum oxygen intake is 4 L/min, but working muscles at their maximum exertion requires about 0.2 L of oxygen per minute for each kilogram of body weight. If the athlete weighs 50 kg, what oxygen debt will she incur?

57. Fat tissue has a density of about 0.90 g/mL, and lean tissue a density of about 1.1 g/mL. Calculate the density of a person who has a body volume of 110 L and weighs 90 kg. Is the person fat or lean?

58. The British measure body weight by the stone (1 stone = 14 lb). By how many kilocalories would you have to overeat each day to gain 1.0 stone over the course of a year?

59. Following is a table of data used to determine an individual's percentage of body fat. Make a graph of the data.
    a. Estimate the percent body fat for person A, who has a body density of 1.037 g/cm^3.
    b. Estimate the percent body fat for person B, who weighs 165 lb in air and 14 lb when submerged in water.
    c. Which person is more likely to be a well-trained athlete?
    d. A 20-year-old male weighs 89.34 kg on land and 5.30 kg underwater. The water has a density of 0.9951 kg/L. The male's residual lung volume is 1.57 L, and his maximum lung volume is 6.51 L. Calculate his body density. Why does a person float in spite of the fact that his or her body density is greater than that of water?

Body Density (g/cm^3)	Body Fat (%)
1.010	38.3
1.030	29.5
1.050	21.0
1.070	12.9
1.090	5.07

60. An athlete gains 40 lb after retiring. What is the likely explanation?

61. What is the body mass index (BMI) for **(a)** the tallest man in medical history, who was 8 ft 11 in. tall and weighed 199 kg, and **(b)** one of the heaviest men in history, who weighed 486 kg and stood 184 cm tall?

62. Birds use large, well-developed breast muscles for flying. Pheasants can fly at 80 km/h, but only for short distances. Great blue herons can fly at about 35 km/h but can cruise great distances. What kind of fibers predominate in the breast muscles of each?

63. A 100-mL sample of blood contains 15 g of hemoglobin (Hb). Each gram of Hb can combine with 1.34 mL of O_2(g) at body temperature and pressure. How much O_2 is in **(a)** 100 mL of blood and **(b)** the approximately 6.0 L of blood in an average adult?

64. Give two examples of green chemistry principles that support healthy choices about transportation.

65. If a 155-lb man bicycles at a moderate rate of 12 to 13.9 mph, he burns about 45 calories per mile. If he lives 1.4 miles from campus and commutes round trip eighty days per semester, how many pounds lighter will he be at the end of the semester than if he had driven to class? (3500 calories of energy are in one pound of fat.)

66. Enzymes are
    a. toxic auto emissions
    b. mood-enhancing chemicals
    c. renewable fuels
    d. biochemical catalysts

67. Carbon dioxide is an undesirable by-product because
    a. it is not found in nature
    b. it inhibits plant growth
    c. it contributes to climate change
    d. it is a fossil fuel

CRITICAL THINKING EXERCISES

Apply knowledge that you have gained in this chapter and one or more of the FLaReS principles (Chapter 1) to evaluate the following statements or claims.

19.1. An advertisement in an American sports magazine claims that an amino-acid supplement helps build muscle mass.

19.2. Proponents of the Paleolithic diet suggest that we would be healthier if we only ate foods like those consumed by primitive pre-agricultural peoples, mainly fats and proteins, with few carbohydrates.

19.3. Consuming large doses of vitamins and minerals will lead to significant increases in health and fitness.

19.4. The various ways by which performance can be improved are called *ergogenic aids*. These include mechanical, physiological, psychological, pharmacological, and nutritional aids. Unfortunately, many of the claims for these aids have not been substantiated by rigorous scientific trials. Here are several claims:

a. A creatine supplement "makes muscles much less prone to fatigue and the capacity to undertake strenuous exercise is increased."

b. Sodium bicarbonate reduces the acidity of the blood and "may be able to draw more of the acid produced within the muscle cells out into the blood and thus reduce the level of acidity within the muscle cells themselves. This could delay the onset of fatigue."

c. Two factors that limit prolonged exercise are depletion of the body's carbohydrate stores and dehydration. Consuming sports drinks containing carbohydrates and electrolytes before, during, and after exercise will help prevent blood glucose levels from falling too low, help maintain the body's glycogen stores, and replace electrolytes lost through perspiration.

19.5. An online advertisement says, "I cut down 47 lb of stomach fat in a month by obeying this one old rule."

19.6. An advertisement for a weight-loss pill claims that the substance in the pill "melts fat from your body."

 # COLLABORATIVE GROUP PROJECTS

Prepare a PowerPoint, poster, or other presentation (as directed by your instructor) to share with the class.

1. Popular diets are often based on books, such as the following:

   YOU: On a Diet: The Owner's Manual for Waist Management by Michael F. Roizen and Mehmet Oz

   The Fat Smash Diet: The Last Diet You'll Ever Need by Ian Smith

   The Sonoma Diet: Trimmer Waist, Better Health in Just 10 Days! by Connie Guttersen

   The South Beach Diet: The Delicious, Doctor-Designed, Foolproof Plan for Fast and Healthy Weight Loss by Arthur Agatston

   The Good Mood Diet: Feel Great While You Lose Weight by Susan M. Kleiner

   The Paleo Diet Revised: Lose Weight and Get Healthy by Eating the Foods You Were Designed to Eat by Loren Cordain

   Search the Internet or print publications such as *Consumer Reports* for characteristics and views of each diet. Prepare a brief report, pro or con, on one of the diets.

2. Equations for determining maximum heart rate (MHR) and tables for evaluating fitness levels can be found in exercise physiology textbooks and online. Use these resources to calculate your V_{O_2} max. How does your fitness level compare with that of your classmates? With that of each of the following athletes: **(a)** endurance runner or bicyclist, 75 mL/kg/min; **(b)** volleyball (female), 50 mL/kg/min; **(c)** football (male), 60–65 mL/kg/min; and **(d)** baseball (male), 50 mL/kg/min?

3. Acrylonitrile, benzene, toluidene, butadiene, and nitropropane are all known or potential carcinogens. Use a reference such as The Merck Index to determine the formula and properties of the substances

4. Only four Nobel Prizes in Chemistry have been awarded to women: Marie Curie (1911), her daughter Irène Joliot-Curie (1935), Dorothy Crowfoot Hodgkin (1964), and Ada E. Yonath (2009). Write a brief essay about Hodgkin or Yonath based on information from the library or the Internet.

5. Search the Internet or sources from the library for information about drugs that athletes use to enhance their performance. Use a reference such as *The Merck Index* to determine the formula and function of one or more of these drugs.

CHEMISTRY@HOME   Pumping Iron for Breakfast

Materials required

- Box of iron-fortified breakfast cereal (Total works well.)
- Box of breakfast cereal not fortified with iron (Hint: Check that trace iron is not listed among ingredients.)
- Measuring cup
- Super-strong magnet
- Quart-size resealable bags (2)
- Water

Are you getting enough iron in your diet? Does your breakfast cereal contain iron? Do you taste any difference between cereals fortified with iron and not? Can you see the difference?

A well-balanced diet of vegetables, fruits, grains, protein, and dairy along with adequate water intake provides average young adults with the necessary vitamins and minerals. There are slight variations in the amounts of vitamins and minerals needed by men and women.

Recommendations for iron, in particular, vary by 10 mg per day. The recommendation is 18 mg of iron for women yet only 8 mg of iron for men. Iron(II) ions are needed for the proper functioning of the oxygen transport of hemoglobin. Women are more susceptible to anemia, a condition that can result in fatigue and reduced resistance to diseases. Many breakfast cereals are fortified with food-grade iron particles (metallic iron) as a mineral supplement. Generally, this form of iron cannot be seen or tasted.

Start by tasting each of the two cereals in a side-by-side test, one iron-fortified and other not. Does the iron-fortified cereal taste metallic? It shouldn't. Otherwise, people probably would not eat it for breakfast.

Continuing your experiment, prepare two batches of cereal "soup." One bag will be filled with your iron-fortified cereal and the other non-iron-fortified cereal. Measure 1 cup of cereal into a quart-size resealable bag. Fill the bag half full with warm water. Carefully seal the bag, leaving an air pocket inside.

Mix the cereal and the water by squeezing the bag until the contents become a brown, soupy mixture. Allow the mixture to sit for at least 20 minutes.

Begin by placing your super-strong magnet on your palm. See figure 1:

▲ **Figure 1**

Place the non-iron-fortified cereal soup bag on top of the super-strong magnet. Sandwich the bag and the magnet between your two hands as in figure 2:

▶ **Figure 2**

Slowly shake the contents of the bag, using a circular motion, for 15 or 20 seconds. The idea is to attract any free moving bits of metallic iron in the cereal to the magnet.

Use both hands again and flip the bag and magnet over so the magnet is on top. Gently squeeze the bag to lift the magnet a little above the cereal soup. Don't move the magnet just yet. Look closely at the edges of the magnet where it's touching the bag. What do you see?

Repeat with the iron-fortified cereal soup. Now what do you see? What happens when you keep the magnet touching the bag and move it in circles? Figure 3:

▶ **Figure 3**

Questions

1. Were you able to detect any iron filings in the cereal not fortified with iron?
2. Why are there iron filings in your cereal?
3. Where else can you get iron in your diet? List at least three foods that are high in iron.

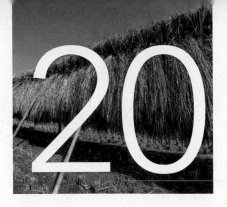

20

CHEMISTRY DOWN ON THE FARM

...AND IN THE GARDEN AND ON THE LAWN

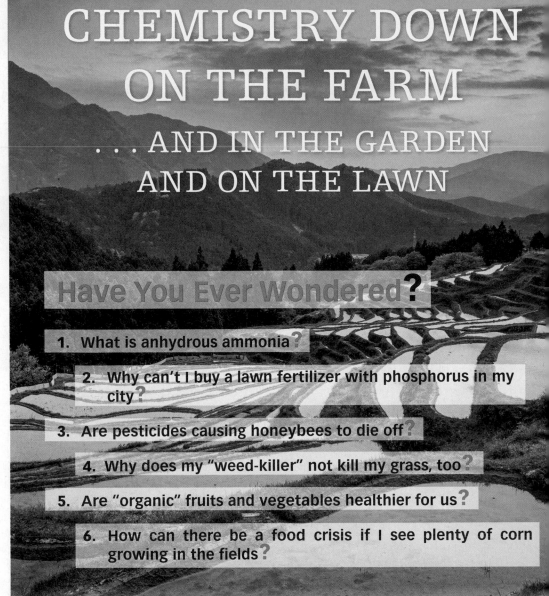

Learning Objectives

> List the three primary plant nutrients as well as several secondary nutrients and micronutrients, and describe the function of each. (20.1)

> Differentiate between organic fertilizers and conventional fertilizers. (20.1)

> Name and describe the action of the main kinds of pesticides. (20.2)

> List several biological pest controls, and explain how they work. (20.2)

> Name and describe the action of the major herbicides and defoliants. (20.3)

> Describe sustainable agriculture and organic farming. (20.4)

> Assess the challenges of feeding an increasing human population. (20.5)

> Identify the benefits of pesticides to humans and the challenges in their use.

> Give examples of how pesticides can be designed to reduce hazard to humans and the environment.

Modern agriculture produces abundant food for much of Earth's growing population, but it has led to many problems, both economic and environmental. Many people are turning to sustainable practices.

Have You Ever Wondered?

1. What is anhydrous ammonia?

2. Why can't I buy a lawn fertilizer with phosphorus in my city?

3. Are pesticides causing honeybees to die off?

4. Why does my "weed-killer" not kill my grass, too?

5. Are "organic" fruits and vegetables healthier for us?

6. How can there be a food crisis if I see plenty of corn growing in the fields?

The earliest humans obtained their food by hunting and gathering. The dawn of the agricultural revolution about 10,000 years ago led to a rapid increase in population, which in turn created a need for more organized ways to obtain food and sparked the development of modern agriculture, with all of its benefits and drawbacks. The most dramatic changes in agricultural chemistry have happened over the last century. In this chapter, we examine chemical aspects of past, present, and potential future agricultural practice.

Our food comes ultimately from green plants. All organisms can transform one type of food into another, but green plants can use the energy from sunlight and the chlorophyll in the plant cells to convert carbon dioxide and water to the sugars that directly or indirectly fuel all living things.

$$6\,CO_2 + 6\,H_2O \xrightarrow{\text{sunlight}} C_6H_{12}O_6 + 6\,O_2$$

This simplified reaction also replenishes the oxygen in the atmosphere and removes carbon dioxide (Section 13.2). Using other nutrients, particularly compounds of nitrogen and phosphorus, plants can convert the sugars produced by photosynthesis to proteins, fats, and other chemicals that we use as food.

The main chemical elements in plants—carbon, hydrogen, and oxygen—are found in cellulose, the primary compound in their stems, leaves, and roots; those elements come from air and water. Other plant nutrients are taken from the soil, and energy is supplied by the sun. In early agricultural societies, people grew plants for food and obtained energy from the food. Much of this energy was reinvested in the production of food, although a portion went into making clothing and building shelter. Figure 20.1 shows a simplified diagram of the energy flow in such a society. A real society is much more complicated than indicated here. Some plants, for example, might be fed to animals, and some human energy would then be obtained from animal flesh or animal products such as milk and eggs.

In early societies, nearly all the energy came from renewable resources. One unit of human work energy, supplemented liberally by energy from the Sun, might produce ten units of food energy. The surplus energy could be used to grow crops for cloth to make clothing and to provide shelter. It also might be used in games or cultural activities.

The flow of nutrients is also rather simple. Unused portions of plants as well as human and animal wastes are returned to the soil. These are broken down by microorganisms to provide nutrients for the growth of new plants (Figure 20.2) and to maintain the humus content of the soil. Properly practiced, this kind of agriculture could be continued for centuries without seriously depleting the soil, but farming at this level supports relatively few people. By making use of fertilizers, pesticides, and energy from fossil fuels, modern high-production farming has greatly expanded crop yields. Many people living in urban areas use materials and methods similar to those of modern farming to maintain green lawns and sustain productive vegetable and flower gardens.

▶ Soil consists of rock broken down by weathering, plus various types of decaying plant and animal matter. To build even a few millimeters of soil from rock takes many years. The United States loses 5 billion tons of soil each year to erosion. Developing countries often suffer far greater soil losses as more land is cleared for farming in an attempt to feed an increasing population.

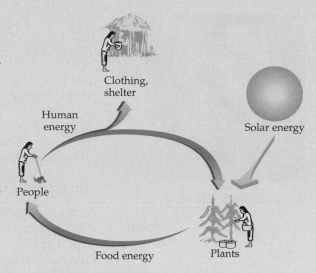

▲ **Figure 20.1** Energy flow in an early agricultural society.

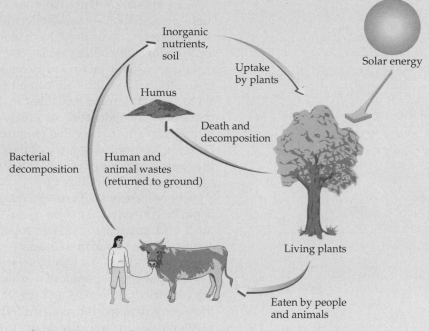

▲ **Figure 20.2** Flow of nutrients in a simple system.

▲ **Figure 20.3** Bacteria in nodules on the roots of legumes fix atmospheric nitrogen by converting it to soluble compounds that plants can use as nutrients.

20.1 Farming with Chemicals: Fertilizers

Learning Objectives ❯ List the three primary plant nutrients as well as several secondary nutrients and micronutrients, and describe the function of each. ❯ Differentiate between organic fertilizers and conventional fertilizers.

To replace nutrients lost from the soil and to increase crop production, modern farmers use a variety of chemical fertilizers. The three **primary plant nutrients** are nitrogen, phosphorus, and potassium. Let's consider nitrogen first.

Nitrogen Fertilizers

Nitrogen, although present in air in the elemental form (N_2), is not generally available to plants. Some bacteria are able to *fix* nitrogen—that is, to convert it to water-soluble nitrogen-containing compounds. Colonies of bacteria that can perform this vital function grow in nodules on the roots of legumes (plants such as clovers and peas) (Figure 20.3). Thus, farmers are able to restore fertility to the soil by crop rotation. A nitrogen-fixing crop (such as clover) can be alternated with a nitrogen-consuming crop (such as corn).

Legumes are still used to some extent to supply nitrogen to the soil. But modern high-yield methods of production demand chemical fertilizers. With the application of fertilizers, farmers don't have to alternate crops to restore soil fertility. Why raise a corn crop every other year if you can raise one every year?

Plants usually take up nitrogen in the form of nitrate ions, NO_3^-, or ammonium ions, NH_4^+. These ions are combined with carbon compounds from photosynthesis to form the amino acids that make up proteins, compounds essential to all life processes. For thousands of years, farmers were dependent on manure as a soil fertilizer. We now know that manure does contain nitrates, but it is also full of *E. coli* bacteria. After the discovery of deposits of sodium nitrate (called *Chile saltpeter*) in the deserts of northern Chile, this substance ($NaNO_3$) was widely used as a source of nitrogen as soil fertilizer.

The atmosphere offers a seemingly inexhaustible supply of nitrogen—if only it could be converted to a form useful to humans. Every flash of lightning forms some nitric acid in the air, which is brought to the ground by rain. Lightning contributes about a billion tons of fixed nitrogen each year to soil—more than is provided by nitrogen-fixing bacteria. But lightning is random rather than frequent and dependable.

A rapid rise in population growth during the late nineteenth and early twentieth centuries put increasing pressure on the available food supply, which led to an increasing demand for nitrogen fertilizers. The first real breakthrough in nitrogen fixation came in Germany on the eve of World War I. A process developed by Fritz Haber, transformed into a large-scale method using a catalyst and high pressure by Carl Bosch, made possible the combination of nitrogen and hydrogen to make ammonia.

$$3\,H_2 + N_2 \longrightarrow 2\,NH_3$$

By 1913, one nitrogen-fixation plant was in production, and several more were under construction. The Germans were interested in ammonium nitrate mainly as an explosive, but it turned out to be a valuable nitrogen fertilizer as well. The Germans were able to make ammonium nitrate (NH_4NO_3), by oxidizing some ammonia to nitric acid

$$NH_3 + 2\,O_2 \longrightarrow HNO_3 + H_2O$$

The nitric acid was then reacted with more ammonia to produce ammonium nitrate.

$$HNO_3 + NH_3 \longrightarrow NH_4NO_3$$

A gas at room temperature, ammonia is easily compressed into a liquid that can be stored and transported in tanks. It is applied directly to the soil as fertilizer

(Figure 20.4). This form of ammonia [$NH_3(l)$] is not the same as household ammonia [$NH_3(aq)$], which usually contains detergents and other ingredients as well as NH_3.

Some ammonia is reacted with carbon dioxide to form urea, an organic compound that releases nitrogen into the soil slowly (rather than all at once as inorganic forms do). Urea is a natural component of urine. Human urine can be used as a fertilizer if it is kept separate from feces, diluted with five times its weight in water 5:1, and used fresh.

▲ **Figure 20.4** A farmer applies anhydrous ammonia, a source of the plant nutrient nitrogen, to his fields.

$$2\,NH_3 + CO_2 \longrightarrow NH_2{-}\overset{\displaystyle O}{\overset{\|}{C}}{-}NH_2 + H_2O$$
Urea

Some solids made from ammonia for application as fertilizers are listed in Table 20.1. These products can be applied separately or combined with other plant nutrients to make a more complete fertilizer.

The atmosphere has vast amounts of nitrogen, but current industrial methods of fixing it require a lot of energy and use nonrenewable resources. (The hydrogen needed for the synthesis of ammonia is made from natural gas.) Genes for nitrogen fixation have been transferred from bacteria into nonlegume plants. Perhaps someday soon we will see the development of transgenic corn and cotton capable of producing their own nitrogen fertilizer the way clovers and peas do.

The use of fertilizers containing nitrogen has negative impacts on those living on farms. Waters from wells on farms will likely be high in nitrates because of fertilizer runoff and runoff of manure from livestock. The use of well water to mix powdered baby formula can be disastrous to infants (see Section 15.5 and Chapter 22). Commonly called "blue baby syndrome," methemoglobinemia led to deaths of numerous babies until use of well water with high nitrate content was determined to be the cause in the 1970s. Use of purchased distilled water to mix powdered baby formula is now recommended for anyone having well water as the family's water supply.

1. What is anhydrous ammonia?

"Anhydrous" means "without water." The ammonia solution used in laboratories and household cleaning products is ammonia gas dissolved in water. Agricultural vehicles transporting "anhydrous ammonia" contain ammonia that has been compressed until it liquefies. Anhydrous ammonia is an effective nitrogen-containing fertilizer, partly because strong hydrogen bonds form between ammonia and water in the soil.

Table 20.1	Various Nitrogen Fertilizers Made from Ammonia	
Reacted with:	Product Fertilizer	Formula
None	Anhydrous ammonia	NH_3
Carbon dioxide	Urea	NH_2CONH_2
Sulfuric acid	Ammonium sulfate	$(NH_4)_2SO_4$
Nitric acid	Ammonium nitrate	NH_4NO_3
Phosphoric acid	Ammonium hydrogen phosphate	$(NH_4)_2HPO_4$

Phosphorus Fertilizers

The limiting factor in plant growth is often the availability of phosphorus, usually in the form of phosphate ions, PO_4^{3-}. Plants incorporate phosphates into DNA and RNA (Chapter 16) and other compounds essential to plant growth. Phosphates have probably been used as fertilizers since ancient times because those ions are found in bone, guano (bird droppings), and fish meal. However, phosphates as such were not recognized as plant nutrients until about 1800. Following this discovery, the great battlefields of Europe were dug up and bones were shipped to chemical plants for processing into fertilizer.

2. Why can't I buy a lawn fertilizer with phosphorus in my city?

Some large cities, such as Minneapolis, Minnesota, banned the use of lawn fertilizers containing phosphorus in the early 2000s because the soil there has enough phosphorus. Excess fertilizer runoff had caused rapid algae growth in the cities' lakes, which was not only an aesthetic but an economic problem.

▲ **Figure 20.5** The widespread use of phosphate fertilizers often leads to rampant growth of blue-green algae and other water plants. More is not better, though. Eventually, these plants deprive the body of water of oxygen.

Animal bones are rich in phosphorus, but most phosphates are poorly soluble in water, so the phosphorus is not readily available to plants. In the 1840s, chemists learned how to treat animal bones with sulfuric acid to convert them to a mixture of calcium sulfate and calcium dihydrogen phosphate, which is sometimes nicknamed *superphosphate*. By the 1860s, the same treatment was being applied to phosphate rock to produce thousands of tons a year. The crucial reaction for forming superphosphate is

$$Ca_3(PO_4)_2 + 2\ H_2SO_4 \longrightarrow \underbrace{Ca(H_2PO_4)_2 + 2\ CaSO_4}$$

Phosphate rock   Superphosphate
or bone (insoluble)   (more soluble)

Modern phosphate fertilizers are often produced by treating phosphate rock with phosphoric acid to make water-soluble calcium dihydrogen phosphate.

$$Ca_3(PO_4)_2 + 4\ H_3PO_4 \longrightarrow 3\ Ca(H_2PO_4)_2$$

More commonly used today is ammonium monohydrogen phosphate [$(NH_4)_2HPO_4$], which supplies both nitrogen and phosphorus.

Phosphates are common in the soil but often at concentrations too low for adequate support of plant growth. Fortunately, there are more concentrated deposits. The presence of bones and teeth from early fish and other animals in these ore deposits indicates that they are largely the skeletal remains of sea creatures of ages past. Unfortunately, fluorides are often associated with phosphate ores, and they can cause a serious pollution problem during the production of phosphate fertilizers.

About 90% of all phosphates produced are used in agriculture. China is the leading producer and user, with the United States second. The rich phosphate deposits in the United States may be depleted within 30 years. Worldwide, Morocco has about one-third of the reserves. Our use of phosphates scatters them irretrievably throughout the environment.

A major problem with fertilizer runoff is the increased amount of phosphates that enters lakes, ponds, and rivers. Since phosphates are plant nutrients, it makes sense that excess phosphates would cause rapid growth of blue-green algae and other aquatic plants in waterways as well. This process is called *eutrophication*, and eutrophication (Figure 20.5) has become a major concern to environmentalists, residents, and governments of cities with lakes and ponds, as well as to the general public (see Chapters 14 and 21).

▲ **Figure 20.6** When a root tip takes up K^+ ions from the soil, H_3O^+ ions are transferred to the soil. The uptake of potassium ions therefore tends to make soil acidic.

Potassium Fertilizers

The third major element necessary for plant growth is potassium. Plants use it in the form of the simple ion K^+. Generally, potassium is abundant, and there are no problems with solubility. Potassium ions, along with Na^+ ions, are essential to the fluid balance of cells. They also seem to be involved in the formation and transport of carbohydrates and may be necessary for the assembly of proteins from amino acids. Uptake of potassium ions from the soil leaves the soil acidic. Each time a positive potassium ion enters the root tip, a positive hydronium ion must leave for the plant to maintain electrical neutrality (Figure 20.6).

The usual chemical form of potassium in commercial fertilizers is potassium chloride (KCl). Vast deposits of this salt occur in and around Stassfurt, Germany, and for years this source supplied nearly all the world's potassium fertilizer. With the coming of World War I, the United States sought supplies within its own borders. Deposits at Searles Lake, California, and Carlsbad, New Mexico, now supply most U.S. needs. Canada has vast deposits in Saskatchewan and Alberta. Beds of potassium chloride up to 200 m thick lie about 1.5 km below the Canadian prairies. Although the reserves are large, potassium salts are a nonrenewable resource that we should use wisely.

Other Essential Elements

In addition to the three major nutrients (nitrogen, phosphorus, and potassium), several other elements are necessary for proper plant growth. Three **secondary plant nutrients**—magnesium, calcium, and sulfur—are needed in moderate amounts. Calcium, in the form of lime (calcium oxide), is used to neutralize acidic soils.

$$CaO(s) + 2\,H^+(aq) \longrightarrow Ca^{2+}(aq) + H_2O(l)$$

Calcium ions are also necessary plant nutrients. Magnesium ions (Mg^{2+}) are incorporated into chlorophyll molecules and therefore are necessary for photosynthesis. Sulfur is a constituent of several amino acids and is necessary for protein synthesis.

Plants need eight other elements, called **micronutrients**, in small amounts. These elements are summarized in Table 20.2. Many soils contain these trace elements in sufficient quantities. Some soils are deficient in one or more, and their productivity can be markedly increased by adding small amounts of the needed elements.

Plants may also require other elements, including sodium, silicon, vanadium, chromium, selenium, cobalt, fluorine, and arsenic. Most of these elements are present in soil, but it is not known if they are necessary for plant growth.

Fertilizers: A Mixed Bag

Farmers and gardeners often buy *complete fertilizers*, which, despite the name, usually contain only the three main nutrients. The three numbers—for example, 5-10-5—on fertilizer bags (Figure 20.7) indicate the proportions of nitrogen, phosphorus, and potassium (NPK). The first number represents the percentage of nitrogen (N); the second, the percentage of phosphorus (calculated as P_2O_5); and the third, the percentage of potassium (calculated as K_2O). So, 5-10-5 means that a fertilizer contains the equivalent of 5% N, 10% P_2O_5, and 5% K_2O; the rest is inert material.

Organic Fertilizers

Most of the fertilizers we have discussed so far are "inorganic" in the chemical sense, because they are not carbon-based molecules. They are simple molecules, such as the NH_3 of anhydrous ammonia, or ionic compounds such as NH_4NO_3, $Ca(H_2PO_4)_2$, and KCl.

Recall from Chapter 9 that the word *organic* has several meanings. Urea is organic in the chemical sense: It is a carbon-based compound with the chemical

▲ **Figure 20.7** The numbers on this container of fertilizer indicate that the fertilizer is 18% N, 18% P_2O_5, and 21% K_2O. Actually, there is no K_2O or P_2O_5 in fertilizer. Those formulas are used merely as a basis for calculation. The actual form of potassium in fertilizers is nearly always KCl, although any potassium salt can furnish the needed K^+ ions such as KNO_3. Phosphorus is supplied as one of several salts with soluble phosphates.

Table 20.2	Eight Micronutrients Necessary for Proper Plant Growth		
Element	Form Used by Plants	Function	Symptoms of Deficiency
Boron	H_3BO_3	Required for protein synthesis; essential for reproduction and for carbohydrate metabolism	Death of growing points of stems, poor growth of roots, poor flower and seed production
Chlorine	Cl^-	Increases water content of plant tissue; involved in carbohydrate metabolism	Shriveling
Copper	Cu^{2+}	Constituent of enzymes; essential for reproduction and for chlorophyll production	Twig dieback, yellowing of newer leaves
Iron	Fe^{2+}	Constituent of enzymes; essential for chlorophyll production	Yellowing of leaves, particularly between veins
Manganese	Mn^{2+}	Essential for redox reactions and for the transformation of carbohydrates	Yellowing of leaves, brown streaks of dead tissue
Molybdenum	MoO_4^{2-}	Essential to nitrogen fixation by legumes and to reduction of nitrates for protein synthesis	Stunting, pale-green or yellow leaves
Nickel	Ni^{2+}	Required for iron absorption; constituent of enzymes	Failure of seeds to germinate
Zinc	Zn^{2+}	Essential for early growth and maturing	Stunting, reduced seed and grain yields

▲ **Figure 20.8** In 1912, American farmers produced an average of 26 bushels of corn per acre. In 2013, the yield per acre was 159 bushels. This sixfold increase is mainly due to the increased use of fertilizers. The yield per acre in 2014 was projected to be more than 165 bushels per acre.

It DOES Matter!

Some soil additives are used for purposes other than fertilization. Calcium hydroxide [$Ca(OH)_2$, slaked lime] brings the acidity of soil to a better range for most plants. Vermiculite (above) is made from mica, in a process similar to that used in making puffed rice cereal. It lightens the soil and increases its ability to hold moisture. The backyard farmer may obtain vermiculite from packages in which it is used as cushioning material.

formula CH_4N_2O, or the abbreviated structural formula NH_2CONH_2. People engaged in organic farming and gardening use the word *organic* not to refer to carbon-containing compounds but to imply the use of natural plant and animal products as fertilizers, such as cottonseed meal, blood meal, fish emulsion or fish meal, manure, compost, and sewage sludge. Rock phosphate is sold as an "organic" fertilizer even though it is clearly inorganic in the chemical sense.

Organic fertilizers generally must be broken down by soil organisms to release the nutrients that the plants use. Whether from cow manure or a chemical factory, nitrogen is taken up by plants as NO_3^- and NH_4^+ ions. Your garden plants don't care if the nitrogen they need came from a compost pile or a chemical factory. Nutrient release from organic fertilizers generally takes some time. Usually, slow release over a long growing period is desirable, but organic materials may not release sufficient nutrients when needed by the plants.

Organic materials also have the advantage in that they provide humus, a dark-colored substance consisting of partially decayed plant or animal matter. Humus improves the texture of soils, thus improving water retention, reducing the loss of nutrients through leaching, and helping to resist erosion. It also provides a better environment for beneficial soil organisms such as earthworms.

If sold as fertilizers, organic products have an NPK ratio on the package label, just as synthetic fertilizers do. However, some organic materials, such as composted manure and sewage sludge, are sold as soil "conditioners." These products have no claim as to nutrient content on the package, although they do furnish some nutrients.

Fresh human manure should not be used to fertilize fruits and vegetables to avoid the possibility of transmitting human pathogens, such as *E. coli*, a common fecal bacterium. The variant *E. coli* O157:H7 causes a food-borne illness that has increasingly been linked to contaminated vegetables. In Germany in 2011, bean sprouts contaminated with *E. coli* killed 22 people and infected over 2400 more. The illness can cause severe problems in susceptible people, particularly children and the elderly. Pig, dog, and cat feces should not be used as fertilizers as they can carry internal parasitic worms from those animals to humans.

Organic fertilizers are often inexpensive or even free, if you can find the right source. [For example, the NPK ratio of urine (page 633) is about 18:2:5.] In contrast, manufactured nitrogen fertilizers are usually made using natural gas and require a high energy input. Intelligent use of organic fertilizers can save money and be environmentally friendly. Unwise use can be expensive or even disastrous (Figure 20.8).

Example 20.1 | Fertilizer Production Equations

Write an equation to show the formation of ammonium sulfate (Table 20.1) from ammonia. What other compound is needed?

Solution

We have seen that ammonium nitrate is made by reacting ammonia with nitric acid. Ammonium sulfate should therefore be formed by reacting ammonia with sulfuric acid. We write the equation.

$$NH_3 + H_2SO_4 \longrightarrow (NH_4)_2SO_4 \text{ (not balanced)}$$

Balancing the equation requires the coefficient 2 for NH_3.

$$2\,NH_3 + H_2SO_4 \longrightarrow (NH_4)_2SO_4$$

▪ **EXERCISE 20.1A**

Write an equation to show the formation of ammonium monohydrogen phosphate (Table 20.1) from ammonia. What other compound is needed?

▪ **EXERCISE 20.1B**

The micronutrient zinc is often applied in the form of zinc sulfate. Write the equation for the formation of zinc sulfate from zinc oxide. What other compound is needed?

SELF-ASSESSMENT Questions

1. The three primary plant nutrients are nitrogen,
   a. phosphorus and kaolin   **b.** potassium and plutonium
   c. potash and phosphorus   **d.** potassium and phosphorus

2. Nitrogen is taken up by plants in the form of
   a. N_2 **b.** NO_2 **c.** NO_2^- **d.** NO_3^-

3. The second number in 24-5-10 on a fertilizer label represents 5%
   a. active ingredients   **b.** inert ingredients
   c. K_2O **d.** P_2O_5

4. Which of the following compounds furnishes two primary plant nutrients?
   a. NH_4NO_3 **b.** $(NH_4)_2HPO_4$
   c. $(NH_4)_2SO_4$ **d.** NH_2CONH_2

5. Potassium uptake in plants leaves the soil
   a. more acidic   **b.** more basic
   c. neutral   **d.** less contaminated with toxins

6. To make phosphates more available to plants, phosphate rock is treated with
   a. CO_2 **b.** H_2O **c.** H_2SO_4 **d.** NH_3

7. The secondary plant nutrients are
   a. C, H, and O   **b.** Ca, Mg, and S
   c. N, P, and K   **d.** Zn, Cu, and Fe

8. The plant nutrient essential to the function of chlorophyll is
   a. Ca^{2+} **b.** Co^{2+} **c.** Fe^{2+} **d.** Mg^{2+}

9. What is the percent nitrogen in a bag of 8-0-24 fertilizer?
   a. 8%   **b.** 0%   **c.** 24%   **d.** 32%

10. The main difference between organic fertilizer and synthetic fertilizer is that organic fertilizers
    a. are more soluble   **b.** are risk free
    c. provide better soil quality   **d.** smell better

11. What substance is added to make soil less acidic AND provide calcium for plants?
    a. 20-10-5 fertilizer   **b.** 5-10-5 fertilizer
    c. lime   **d.** vermiculite

12. Iron is added to some fertilizers to
    a. accelerate growth   **b.** adjust the soil pH
    c. produce larger flowers   **d.** prevent yellowing of leaves

13. About how many elements are known to be important to a plant's growth and survival?
    a. 3   **b.** 6   **c.** 14   **d.** 26

Answers: 1. d; 2. d; 3. d; 4. b; 5. a; 6. c; 7. b; 8. d; 9. a; 10. c; 11. c; 12. d; 13. c

20.2 The War against Pests

Learning Objectives ❯ Name and describe the action of the main kinds of pesticides.
❯ List several biological pest controls, and explain how they work.

Insects are critical to life on Earth. Honeybees, butterflies, and other insects pollinate flowering plants, including trees that provide shade, oxygen production, and fruits. Thousands of species of birds and many amphibians are insectivores. Insects are extremely important for the survival of nearly every ecosystem on our planet, and they are critical for fruit and flower production and maintenance of many animal species.

However, people have always been plagued by insect pests. Three of the ten plagues of Egypt (described in the book of *Exodus*) were insect plagues—lice, flies, and locusts. The decline of Roman civilization has been attributed in part to malaria, a disease that is carried by mosquitoes and that destroys vigor and vitality when it does not kill. Bubonic plague, carried by fleas from rats to humans, swept through the Western world repeatedly during the Middle Ages. One such plague during the 1660s is estimated to have killed 25 million people, 25% of the population of Europe at that time. The first attempt (by the French during the 1880s) to dig a canal across Panama was defeated by outbreaks of yellow fever and malaria. During the Dust Bowl era in the central United States in the 1930s, swarms of locusts plagued Kansas and Oklahoma farmers who were already suffering from drought, massive black clouds of lost topsoil and dust, and nearly complete crop failure, resulting in economic disaster.

Only a few species—of the millions of insect species that exist—are harmful. Yet we have to exercise some control of insects that destroy specific crops or cause human diseases. The use of modern chemical **pesticides** (substances that kill organisms that we consider pests) may be all that stands between us and some of these plagues. Note that the term *pesticides* includes insecticides specifically targeted to insects and rodenticides specifically targeted to rats, mice, and other rodents. Pesticides prevent the loss of a major portion of our food supply that would otherwise

It DOES Matter!

Locust plagues have devastated crops throughout history. Desert locusts (*Schistocerca gregaria*) are usually solitary insects, but under certain environmental conditions, they change to a swarm-forming "gregarious" phase and can devastate crops. A neurochemical mechanism underlies this change, which also includes a change in body color from green to yellow. The key is the neurotransmitter serotonin, which in humans modulates anger, body temperature, mood, sleep, appetite, and metabolism (Section 18.7). In locusts, serotonin is synthesized in response to increased numbers and increased social contacts, and perhaps other factors.

be eaten by insects and other pests. Pesticides are also used extensively in urban areas to control annoying insects such as backyard mosquitoes, box elder bugs, ants, or other flying or crawling insects. Mosquito and insect repellants do not kill those insects; they only keep them away.

Up until the last few decades, people tried to control insect pests by draining swamps, pouring oil on ponds to kill mosquito larvae, and applying arsenic compounds to areas where rodents were a problem. Lead arsenate [$Pb_3(AsO_4)_2$] is a particularly effective poison because of both the lead and the arsenic in it. Yet it was banned in the United States about 25 years ago, because it can kill other wildlife and pets, instead of the rats or other rodents that were targeted by its use.

A few pesticides, such as pyrethrum (used in mosquito control) and nicotine sulfate (Black Leaf 40), have been obtained from plant matter. To protect themselves from being eaten, some plants produce their own pesticides, which often make up 5–10% of their dry weight. Nicotine protects tobacco plants. Pyrethrins are also plant-produced pesticides. Physostigmine is a naturally occurring carbamate.

Most poisons are indiscriminate. They kill all insects, not just those we consider pests. Many of those poisons are also toxic to humans and other animals. Some say we should call such poisons *biocides* (because they kill living things) rather than **insecticides** (substances that kill insects). Table 20.3 lists the acute toxicities (from short-term exposures) of some insecticides. Effects of long-term exposure are more difficult to measure. Toxic substances in general are discussed in Chapter 22.

Table 20.3 lists the milligrams of specific pesticides that will kill 50% of a test population of rats, when ingested orally. Ingestion by humans could occur if pesticides were accidentally left on the hands or skin, not effectively washed off, and then food or drink was handled by a home gardener, farmer, or lawn-maintenance personnel. Also, accidents have occurred when children or pets inadvertently found a container of pesticide in a garage or garden shed and ate it or drank it. Pesticides such as lindane, found in some head lice shampoos, are not meant to be ingested, but accidental swallowing can occur.

Table 20.3 Approximate Acute Toxicity of Insecticidal Preparations Administered Orally to Rats

Pesticide	LD$_{50}$[a]	Category of Acute Toxicity	Selected Uses
Pyrethrins[b]	200–2600	Slightly toxic	Food crops; pest control (flea, tick, fly)
Malathion	1000 (1375)	Slightly toxic	Crops (alfalfa, lettuce)
Lead arsenate	825	Slightly toxic	Banned in 1988
Diazinon	285 (250)	Moderately toxic	Crops (lettuce, almonds, broccoli)
Carbaryl	250	Moderately toxic	Crops (apples, pecans, grapes, citrus fruits)
Nicotine[c]	230	Moderately toxic	Restricted to use by certified applicators
DDT[d]	118 (113)	Moderately toxic	Most uses banned; malaria-carrying mosquito control
Lindane	91 (88)	Moderately toxic	Crops (cotton); head lice shampoos
Methyl parathion	14 (24)	Highly toxic	Crops (cotton, rice, fruit trees)
Parathion	3.6 (13)	Highly toxic	Crops (alfalfa, barley, corn, cotton)
Carbofuran[e]	2	Highly toxic	Field crops, some fruits and vegetables
Aldicarb	1	Highly toxic	Crops (cotton)

[a]Dose in milligrams per kilogram of body weight that will kill 50% of a test population. Values in parentheses are for male rats. (LD$_{50}$ is discussed in more detail in Chapter 22.)
[b]Active ingredients of pyrethrum; LD$_{50}$ depends on variability of concentration of active components in the formulation.
[c]Oral in mice. Nicotine is much more toxic by injection.
[d]Estimated LD50 for humans is 500 mg/kg.
[e]In mice.

Sources: O'Neill, Maryadele J., Patricia E. Heckelman, Cherie B. Koch, Kristin J. Roman, and Catherine M. Kenny, *The Merck Index*, 14th ed. (Whitehouse Station, NJ: Merck & Co., 2006), and the Extension Toxicology Network.

DDT: The Dream Insecticide—or Nightmare?

Shortly before World War II, Swiss scientist Paul Müller (1899–1965) found that DDT (dichlorodiphenyltrichloroethane), a chlorinated hydrocarbon, is a potent insecticide. DDT was soon used effectively against grapevine pests and against a particularly severe potato beetle infestation. DDT is easily synthesized from cheap, readily available chemicals. Like other chlorinated hydrocarbons, it is almost insoluble in water.

When the war began, supplies of pyrethrum, a major insecticide of the time, were cut off by the Japanese occupation of Southeast Asia and the Dutch East Indies (now Indonesia). Lead, arsenic, and copper that were used in insecticides were diverted for armaments and other military purposes. The Allies, desperately needing an insecticide to protect soldiers from disease-bearing lice, ticks, and mosquitoes, obtained a small quantity of DDT and quickly tested it. Combined with talcum, DDT was an effective delousing powder. Clothing was impregnated with DDT, and it seemed to have no harmful effects even on those exposed to large doses. Allied soldiers were nearly free of lice, but German troops were heavily infested and many were sick with typhus, a disease carried by lice. (In earlier wars, more soldiers probably died from typhus than from bullets.)

A cheap insecticide that is effective against a variety of insect pests, DDT came into widespread use after the war, mainly applied by "crop-dusters," small planes spraying large areas (Figure 20.9). Other chlorinated hydrocarbons were synthesized, tested, and used against insects. Although invaluable to farmers in the production of food and fiber, chlorinated hydrocarbons won their most dramatic victories in the field of public health. According to the World Health Organization (WHO), approximately 25 million lives have been saved and hundreds of millions of illnesses prevented by the use of DDT and related pesticides, particularly in tropical areas such as Central and South America and in Africa.

DDT seemed to be a dream come true. It would at last free the world from insect-borne diseases. It would protect crops from the ravages of insects and thus increase food production. In recognition of his discovery, Müller was awarded the Nobel Prize in Physiology and Medicine in 1948.

Even before Müller received his prize, however, there were warnings that all was not well. Houseflies resistant to DDT were reported as early as 1946, and DDT's toxicity to fish was documented by 1947. Such early warnings were largely ignored, and it was also assumed that the toxicity would disappear soon after the chemical was discharged into the environment. DDT was used extensively to protect crops and control mosquitoes and to try to prevent Dutch elm disease. By 1962, the year Rachel Carson's book *Silent Spring* (Section 1.1) appeared, U.S. production of DDT had reached 76 million kg/year.

Chlorinated hydrocarbons generally are fairly stable, which was a major advantage of DDT. Sprayed on a crop, DDT stayed there and killed insects for weeks. This *pesticide persistence* also turned out to be a major disadvantage: The substance did not break down readily in the environment, and persists at least a decade after application.

Biological Magnification: Concentration in Fatty Tissues

DDT's lack of reactivity to oxygen, water, and components of the soil led to its buildup in the environment, where it threatened fish, birds, and other wildlife. Although not very toxic to humans and other warm-blooded creatures, DDT is highly toxic to cold-blooded organisms, which include insects, of course, and fish. Chlorinated hydrocarbons are fat-soluble, so chlorinated hydrocarbons tend to become concentrated in animals higher on the food chain.

This *biological magnification* or *biomagnification* was graphically demonstrated in California in 1957. Clear Lake, about 100 miles north of San Francisco, was sprayed with DDT in an effort to control gnats. After spraying, the water contained only 0.02 ppm of DDT, but the microscopic plant and animal life contained 5 ppm—250 times as much. Fish feeding on these microorganisms contained up to 2000 ppm. Grebes, the diving birds that ate the fish, died by the hundreds (Figure 20.10) on page 640. Even a few parts per billion of DDT interfere with the growth of plankton and the reproduction of crustaceans such as shrimp.

▲ **Figure 20.9** Insecticides are often applied by aerial spraying. Winds can spread the pesticide over a wide area.

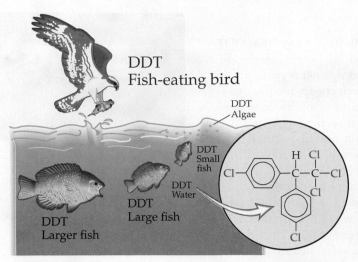

DDT
Fish-eating bird

▲ **Figure 20.10** Biomagnification: Concentration of DDT going up a food chain. Starting with algae that incorporate DDT in ponds from contaminated groundwater, and up through the food chain to ospreys, fish-eating birds, the concentrations of pesticide increase. The larger the fish, the more DDT in the fatty membranes of cells. The wedge-shaped DDT molecules open channels in the membranes, causing them to leak.

DDT interferes with calcium metabolism essential to the formation of healthy bones and teeth. Although harm to humans has never been conclusively demonstrated, the disruption of calcium metabolism in birds was disastrous for some species. The shells of their eggs, composed mainly of calcium compounds, were thin and poorly formed. The bald eagle, peregrine falcon, brown pelican, and other species became endangered but have made dramatic recoveries since DDT was banned in the United States and other industrialized countries in the 1970s.

DDT is still used in some countries where malaria and typhus are great health problems. It is applied mainly on the inside walls of houses, so the environmental impact is much less than that of the earlier widespread use of DDT in agriculture. Malaria infects between 300 million and 500 million people and kills 1 million every year. About 90% of the deaths occur in Africa, and most of the victims are children under 5.

Today, in developed countries, DDT is known mostly for its harmful environmental effects. In developing nations, its use is praised as a relatively cheap way to control malaria-carrying mosquitoes, thus saving lives. The question, "What is more important, birds or people?" implies that DDT is the only option. Perhaps there are alternatives other than DDT for control of malaria-bearing insects.

In 2000, more than 120 countries signed a treaty to phase out persistent organic pollutants (POPs), a group of chemicals, many of them chlorinated hydrocarbons, that includes DDT. This treaty has the goal of reducing and ultimately eliminating the use of DDT, but individual countries may continue to use it for controlling malaria. As bad as DDT may sound, it may have saved the lives of more people than any other chemical substance.

Development of Insect Resistance

In the six decades or so in which pesticides have been widely used, hundreds of insect species have become resistant to one or more of these poisons. Resistance has resulted in increases in crop losses and in insect-transmitted diseases. Some insect species such as the cotton bollworm, Colorado potato beetle, malaria-transmitting Anopheles mosquitoes, and German cockroach exhibit resistance to all commercially available pest control agents. But what would crop losses have been without any insecticides? Probably much higher.

Insects develop resistance to a pesticide by natural selection. A genetic mutation for resistance can spread quickly: For example, if a farmer uses a new pesticide on a field with 10.0 billion pest insects, perhaps 9.9 billion are killed. Resistant insects survive and pass the gene for resistance to the next generation. The resistant insect group becomes a larger percentage of the whole. Through repetition of this process over several generations, the resistant insects become the main form and the pesticide is no longer effective.

Organophosphorus Compounds

Bans and restrictions on chlorinated hydrocarbon insecticides have led to increased use of *organophosphorus* compounds (containing carbon and phosphorus) such as malathion, diazinon, and parathion (Figure 20.11) on page 641. More than two dozen of these insecticides are available commercially. They have been extensively studied and evaluated

Malathion

Parathion

Diazinon

Chlorpyrifos

▲ **Figure 20.11** Four organic phosphorus compounds used as insecticides.

for effectiveness against insects and for toxicity to people, laboratory animals, and farm animals.

Organophosphorus compounds are nerve poisons (Chapter 22); they interfere with the conduction of nerve signals in insects. At high levels of exposure, they do the same in humans. Most are more toxic to mammals than chlorinated hydrocarbons (Table 20.3). Malathion is a notable exception; it is less toxic than DDT. Like chlorinated hydrocarbons, organophosphorus pesticides concentrate in fatty tissues. However, the phosphorus compounds are less persistent in the environment. They break down in days or weeks, whereas chlorinated hydrocarbons often persist for years. Residues of organophosphorus compounds are seldom found in food.

Carbamates: Targeting the Pest

Another widely used family of insecticides is the carbamates. Examples are carbaryl (Sevin®), carbofuran (Furadan®), and aldicarb (Temik®) (Figure 20.12). Like the phosphorus compounds, carbamates are nerve poisons, but they act over a shorter span of time. Most carbamates are *narrow-spectrum insecticides* directed specifically at one, or a few, insect pests. In contrast, chlorinated hydrocarbons and organophosphorus compounds kill many kinds of insects and are called *broad-spectrum insecticides*. Carbaryl has a low toxicity to mammals, but carbofuran and aldicarb have toxicities similar to that of parathion. Carbaryl is particularly effective against wasps but unfortunately is also quite toxic to honeybees. Honeybees are important pollinators, and their declining numbers could affect some crop yields by 30% or more in years to come.

Carbamates are characterized by the presence of the carbamate group:

$$\underset{|}{\overset{\displaystyle O}{\underset{|}{\overset{\|}{O-C-N-}}}}$$

Many variations can be obtained by changing the groups attached to the O and the N. Generally, carbamates break down fairly rapidly in the environment and do not accumulate in fatty tissue, which gives these insecticides an advantage over chlorinated hydrocarbons and organic phosphorus compounds.

▲ **Figure 20.12** Three carbamate insecticides.

Organic Pesticides

The United States produces about 500 million kg of pesticides annually. About a quarter of this total is used in houses, yards, parks, and golf courses. More than 1000 active ingredients are found in over 16,000 pesticide products marketed in the United States. Many people seek safer ways to get rid of pests.

Most of the pesticides we have discussed so far are organic in the chemical sense of being carbon-containing compounds. As mentioned earlier, organic farmers and gardeners use *organic* to imply the use of materials derived from natural sources rather than made synthetically. Organic pesticides include the following.

- Insecticidal soap acts by breaking down the insect's cuticle (outer covering). The cuticle is mainly chitin, a polysaccharide. The soap only acts while wet and in direct contact with the insect. It is not toxic to animals, and it leaves no harmful residue. This method is usually used by gardeners, who must spray the diluted soap directly on the insects, then "wash" the plants with water two to three hours after applying. Repetition may be needed four to seven days later. It is impractical for commercial farms.

3. Are pesticides causing honeybees to die off?

Bees not only fly significant distances from hives, but are often transported to new fields by beekeepers, and thus are exposed to a wide variety of agricultural pesticides. According to the USDA, many studies have shown that pesticides are contributing factors to *colony collapse disorder* that first appeared in 2006, but viruses and mites have been found in higher concentrations in hives experiencing significant loss as well, indicating more than one contributing factor. One of the suspect pesticides is the one used to kill varroa mites in hives.

- Pyrethrins are obtained from the perennial plant pyrethrum (*Chrysanthemum cinerariaefolium*). Pyrethrins are low in toxicity to mammals because they are quickly broken down into inactive forms by mammalian liver enzymes. Some are moderately toxic to mammals and quite toxic to fish and tadpoles. Insects, which have no liver, are much more susceptible to pyrethrins.
- Rotenone is a natural product obtained from the roots and stems of several tropical and subtropical plant species. It is slightly toxic to mammals, but extremely toxic to insects and fish.
- Boric acid (H_3BO_3), usually applied as a bait, dust, or powder, is mainly used for control of ants and cockroaches. It acts as a stomach poison and as a desiccant by abrading the wax from the insect's cuticle. Boric acid is moderately toxic to humans.
- Cryolite (Na_3AlF_6) is used on food crops and ornamental plants. It blocks caterpillars and other grazing insects from feeding. Toxicological hazards, if any, are very slight.
- Diatomaceous earth is the fossilized remains of diatoms, a type of algae whose shells consist largely of silica. The shells are ground to a fine powder with sharp-edged particles that cut the insects' cuticles and absorb oils, causing the insects to dehydrate and die. If ingested, the particles cause the same sort of damage to the digestive system. Diatomaceous earth is harmless to people.
- Ryania is a botanical insecticide obtained from *Ryania speciosa*, a tropical plant. The active principle is an alkaloid called *ryanodine*. Ryania is highly toxic to the caterpillars of fruit moths, codling moths, and corn earworms. It has a very low toxicity to mammals but is very toxic to fish.

Just because a product is considered organic doesn't mean it is safe. Some organic pesticides are as toxic as or more so than some synthetic pesticides. They can also be quite toxic to beneficial insects, such as honeybees. To use these products most effectively, you should obtain detailed directions from a university cooperative extension office, located in most counties.

Biological Insect Controls

The use of natural enemies is another method for controlling pests. These biological controls include predatory insects, mites, and mollusks; parasitic insects; and microbial controls, which are insect pathogens such as bacteria, viruses, fungi, and nematodes. The following are a few examples.

- Predatory insects such as praying mantises and ladybugs will destroy garden pests and are sold commercially.
- Parasitic insects such as *Trichogramma* wasps are used to control moth larvae such as tomato hornworm, corn earworm, cabbage looper, codling moth, cutworm, and armyworm.
- *Bacillus thuringiensis (Bt)*, sold under trade names such as Dipel®, is widely used by home gardeners against cabbage loopers, hornworms, and other moth caterpillars. Bt is also used against Colorado potato beetles, mosquito larvae, black flies, European corn borers, grape leaf rollers, and gypsy moths.
- Microbial controls such as Bt are host-specific; they don't harm organisms other than the targeted ones.
- Naturally occurring nuclear polyhedrosis virus (NPV) is present at low levels in many insect populations. These viruses can be grown in culture and applied to crops. NPV is highly selective, affecting only *Heliothis* caterpillars. Natural viral pesticides appear to be harmless to humans, wildlife, and beneficial insects. They are completely biodegradable but are generally quite expensive to produce.

Genetically Engineered Insect Resistance

A highly successful biological approach is the breeding of insect- and fungus-resistant plants. This field of biotechnology, sometimes called genetic engineering, is a very active field of current research worldwide. Researchers in Thailand, China, and other parts of Asia are working on rice; those in the Western world are focusing on corn, soybeans, and wheat. Yields of corn (maize), wheat, rice, and other grains have already been increased substantially in this manner. The gene for the toxin produced by Bt (*Bacillus thuringiensis*) has been inserted into cotton, corn, potato, and other plants. These genetically modified (GM) cotton plants are protected from damage by cotton bollworms. Corn has been genetically modified to resist corn root worms and corn borers.

Statistics show that the use of insecticides and pesticides has decreased significantly due mainly to the introduction of genetically modified plants. In the United States, insecticide use fell from 25% of corn crops treated in 2005 to 9% of cornfields treated in 2010. Unfortunately, by 2013 corn root worms increased again, so pesticide use for corn is on the upswing.

No scientific development is without controversy. Some people fear that the introduced genes will spread to wild relatives of the cultivated species, leading to the development of "super weeds." People also fear that proteins produced in GM plants will cause allergic reactions in susceptible individuals. For example, introduction of a gene for a peanut protein into another food plant could cause a dangerous reaction in people allergic to peanuts. Plant breeders produced a potato that is insect resistant, but it had to be taken off the market because it is also toxic to people. Public fears about foods from genetically modified plants have slowed developments, particularly in Europe. A main argument against GM plants is that more herbicides need to be applied. The question remains: Is the fact that more herbicides are now required than even ten years ago the result of GM technology, or is it the result of weeds developing a resistance to herbicides that have been used for some time, just as insects develop a resistance to insecticides over time?

Sterile Insect Technique

A *sterile insect technique (SIT)* is a method of insect control that involves rearing large numbers of males, sterilizing them with radiation or chemicals or by cross-breeding, and then releasing them in areas of infestation. These sterile males, which far outnumber the local fertile males, mate with wild females. If a female mates with a sterile male, no offspring are produced, thus reducing the reproductive potential of the insect population and controlling its growth.

Successful SIT programs have been conducted against screwworm, a pest that seriously affects cattle in the southern United States, Mexico, and Central America, as well as in Libya. SIT programs have also been employed against the Mediterranean fruit fly (medfly) in Latin America and against the codling moth in Canada. The great expense and limited applicability of SIT probably mean that it will not become a major method of insect control.

Pheromones: The Sex Trap

Substances called *pheromones* are increasingly important in insect control. A **pheromone** is a chemical that is secreted externally by an insect to mark a trail, send an alarm, or attract a mate. Insect **sex attractants** are usually secreted by females to attract males (Figure 20.13).

Chemical research has identified pheromones of hundreds of insect species. Most are blends of two or more chemicals that must be present in exactly the right proportions to be biologically active. Chemists can synthesize these compounds, and workers can use them to lure male insects into traps, allowing a determination of which pests are present and the level of infestation. The workers can then undertake measures, including the use of conventional pesticides, to minimize damage to the crops.

If the attractant is exceptionally powerful and the insect population level is very low, a pheromone trap technique called "attract and kill" may achieve sufficient control. Otherwise, the attractant can be used in quantities sufficient to confuse and disorient males, who detect a female in every direction but can't find one to mate

▲ **Figure 20.13** A male gypsy moth uses its large antennae to detect pheromones from a female.

▲ Dandelions, introduced into North America from Europe because of their attractive flowers and their uses as a salad vegetable and a folk medicine, are now generally considered a lawn weed. About half of all homeowners treat their lawns with herbicides such as 2,4-D (Weed-B-Gon®) and glyphosate (Roundup®). More than 10 million pounds of 2,4-D are used on lawns in the United States each year.

with. Mating disruption has been used successfully in controlling some insect pests. Many grape growers in Germany and Switzerland use this technique, allowing them to produce wine without using conventional insecticides.

Some sex attractants have relatively simple structures. The sex attractant for the codling moth, which infests apples, is an alcohol with a straight chain of 12 carbon atoms and two double bonds.

However, most sex attractants have complicated structures, and all are secreted in extremely tiny amounts. This can make research on these attractants difficult and tedious. For example, a team of U.S. Department of Agriculture researchers had to use the tips of the abdomens of 87,000 female gypsy moths to isolate a minute amount of a powerful sex attractant.

Yet pheromones are effective at extremely low levels. A male silkworm moth can detect as few as 40 molecules per second. If a female releases as little as 0.01 mg, she can attract every male within 1 km. Gypsy moth larvae have defoliated great areas of forest, mainly in the northeastern United States, and have now spread over much of the country. The gypsy moth pheromone has been used mainly in traps to monitor insect populations.

Pheromones are usually too expensive to play a huge role in insect control, though the use of recombinant DNA methods (Section 16.8) to synthesize them holds promise for future work. For now, the cost is high, and research is painstaking and time consuming. Workers must be careful not to get the attractants on their clothes. Who wants to be attacked on a warm summer night by a million sex-crazed gypsy moths?

Juvenile Hormones

Some insects can be controlled by the use of *juvenile hormones*. Hormones are the chemical messengers that control many life functions in plants and animals, and minute quantities produce profound physiological changes. In the insect world, a **juvenile hormone** controls the rate of development of the young. Normally, production of the hormone is shut off at the appropriate time to allow proper maturation to the adult stage.

Chemists have been able to isolate insect juvenile hormones and determine their structures. With knowledge of the structure, they can synthesize a hormone or one of its analogs. The application of juvenile hormones to ponds where mosquitoes breed keeps the mosquitoes in the harmless pre-adult stage. Because only adult insects can reproduce, juvenile hormones appear to be a nearly perfect method of mosquito control.

A natural juvenile hormone

Methoprene, a juvenile hormone analog, is approved by the EPA for use against mosquitoes and fleas.

Methoprene

The synthesis of juvenile hormones is difficult and expensive, and they can only be used against insects that are pests at the adult stage. Little would be gained by keeping a moth or a butterfly in the caterpillar stage for a longer period of time. Caterpillars have voracious appetites and do a lot of damage to crops.

SELF-ASSESSMENT Questions

1. A pesticide is a product that kills
   a. insects and weeds only
   b. insects or other animals that are considered to be pests
   c. ants or mosquitoes only
   d. ticks and fleas but not mice

2. How has the use of genetically modified crops changed the use of pesticides on farms? Use has
   a. decreased on many crops b. gone up dramatically
   c. gone up on some crops d. not changed noticeably

3. If pesticides get into a lake, which organism will show the highest level in its fat tissues?
   a. fish b. microscopic animals
   c. microscopic plants d. great blue heron (fish eater)

4. Spraying of pesticides on crops
   a. affects only the sprayed crops
   b. has no effect on the food chain
   c. is necessary if farmers are to grow crops
   d. may result in pesticides ending up in rivers and lakes

5. Compared to DDT, organic phosphorus compounds are generally
   a. less persistent and less toxic
   b. less persistent and more toxic
   c. more persistent and less toxic
   d. more persistent and more toxic

6. "Organic" pesticides include all the following except
   a. carbamates b. pyrethrins
   c. rotenone d. insecticidal soaps

7. The sterile insect technique method of insect control works best when
   a. there is a large target insect population
   b. the females mate repeatedly
   c. the males of the pest species can be reared in mass
   d. the males mate with related species

8. A substance produced by an organism to influence the behavior of another member of the same species is a(n)
   a. agonist b. inducer
   c. marker d. pheromone

9. The use of ladybugs and praying mantises to control insect pests is an example of
   a. biocidal control b. biological control
   c. abiotic control d. exploitation of insect pests

Answers: 1. b; 2. a; 3. d; 4. d; 5. b; 6. d; 7. c; 8. d; 9. b

20.3 Herbicides and Defoliants

Learning Objective › Name and describe the action of the major herbicides and defoliants.

Ralph Waldo Emerson once wrote that a weed is "a plant whose virtues have not yet been discovered." Unfortunately, most of the plants defined as weeds in the nineteenth century are still defined as weeds today, and they appear to have few virtues. Colloquially, a weed is a rapidly growing plant that is hard to get rid of and tends to choke out plants that we seek to grow. A dictionary might define a weed as a wild plant growing where it is not wanted and in competition with cultivated plants.

The United States produces about 225 million kg of herbicides annually. **Herbicides**, four of which are shown in Figure 20.14, are chemicals used to kill weeds. Some herbicides are **defoliants**, which cause leaves to fall off plants.

2,4-Dichlorophenoxyacetic acid
(2,4-D)

2,4,5-Trichlorophenoxyacetic acid
(2,4,5-T)

Atrazine

Glyphosate

▲ **Figure 20.14** Four common herbicides: 2,4-dichlorophenoxyacetic acid (2,4-D), 2,4,5-trichlorophenoxyacetic acid (2,4,5-T), atrazine, and glyphosate.

Q: *What are the alkyl groups on the atrazine molecule?*

2,4-D and 2,4,5-T

Crop plants that have no competition from weeds produce more abundant harvests. Weeds cause crop losses of billions of dollars a year in the United States. Removing weeds by hand or hoe is tedious, backbreaking work, so chemical herbicides are used to kill unwanted plants in large-scale agricultural operations. Many small-scale gardeners prefer to dig or pull weeds rather than use chemical herbicides.

Early herbicides included solutions of copper salts, sulfuric acid, and sodium chlorate ($NaClO_3$). It wasn't until the introduction of 2,4-D (2,4-dichlorophenoxyacetic acid) in 1945 that the use of herbicides became common. 2,4-D and its derivatives are growth-regulator herbicides, which are especially effective against newly emerged, rapidly growing broad-leaved plants. One derivative of 2,4-D is 2,4,5-T (2,4,5-trichlorophenoxyacetic acid), which is especially effective against woody plants and works by defoliation.

2,3,7,8-Tetrachlorodibenzo-*para*-dioxin
(a dioxin)

Combined in a formulation called **Agent Orange**, 2,4-D and 2,4,5-T were used extensively in Vietnam to remove enemy cover and to destroy crops that maintained enemy armies. Agent Orange caused vast ecological damage and is suspected of causing birth defects in children born to both American soldiers and Vietnamese exposed to the herbicides. Laboratory studies show that 2,4-D and 2,4,5-T, when pure, do not cause abnormalities in fetuses of laboratory animals. Extensive birth defects are caused, however, by **dioxins**, contaminants of 2,4,5-T frequently found in the herbicide. The most toxic dioxin is 2,3,7,8-tetrachlorodibenzo-*para*-dioxin, abbreviated 2,3,7,8-TCDD, or just TCDD. Continuing concern about dioxin contamination led the EPA to ban 2,4,5-T in 1985.

Almost all "selective" herbicides (that kill only certain types of plants, not every plant with which it comes in contact), contain 2,4-D or a related compound abbreviated as MCPA (2-methyl, 4-chlorophenoxyacetic acid). Nonselective herbicides will kill all plants.

Atrazine and Glyphosate

The most widely used nonselective herbicides in the United States are atrazine and glyphosate. Atrazine binds to a protein in the chloroplasts of plant cells, shutting off the electron-transfer reactions of photosynthesis. Atrazine is often used on corn (maize). Corn plants deactivate atrazine by removing the chlorine atom. Weeds cannot deactivate the compound and are killed. Some studies indicate that atrazine interferes with the hormone system, disrupting estrogen function. Atrazine has been linked to sexual abnormalities in frogs. Atrazine is the second most commonly used herbicide in the United States in agriculture, although its use has been banned in the European Union.

Glyphosate, sold under several trade names, including Roundup®, is the most commonly used herbicide in the United States. It is a derivative of the amino acid glycine and a nonselective herbicide that kills all vegetation by inhibiting the function of a certain plant enzyme. Glyphosate can be used to treat the soil before a crop is planted and will effectively kill weeds before they emerge through the soil. When used in this way, glyphosate is called a "pre-emergent" herbicide. Fortunately, it is metabolized by bacteria in the soil, so that other plants can be sown or transplanted into treated areas shortly after spraying the area with glyphosate. Glyphosate can also be applied to plants that have already emerged from the soil, but it will kill almost every plant it contacts.

Genetically modified soybeans, corn, alfalfa, and other plants that are resistant to glyphosate have been developed. When glyphosate is applied to a field, the weeds are killed but the crop plants remain unharmed. However, widespread use of glyphosate has resulted in many glyphosate-resistant weeds.

4. Why does my "weed-killer" not kill my grass, too?

Most garden and lawn weeds are classified as "broad-leaf plants" and include dandelions, henbit, and plantain, to name a few. Lawn grass is not classified as a broad-leaf plant, so is unaffected by the application of a selective herbicide, such as Weed-B-Gon™. Read the labels carefully. If an ingredient is glyphosate, it will kill your entire lawn if applied to all the grass, because glyphosate is a nonselective herbicide.

Paraquat: A Preemergent Herbicide—and More

Paraquat, an ionic compound that is toxic to most plants but is rapidly broken down in the soil, is a notable example of a preemergent herbicide. Paraquat inhibits photosynthesis by accepting the electrons that otherwise would reduce carbon dioxide.

$$CH_3-{}^+N \bigcirc \bigcirc N^+-CH_3$$
$$Cl^- \qquad\qquad Cl^-$$

Paraquat

Paraquat can also be used to destroy the leaves of almost any plant. Sugarcane, an important crop used for the production of white sugar, brown sugar, molasses, and rum, has large leaves with sharp edges on top of the sugar-containing stems, which are traditionally burned before the sugarcane is harvested. The use of paraquat, applied just before the sugarcane is harvested to quickly destroy the leaves, is becoming popular in sugar-producing countries. The large leaves at the top of the cane stems are destroyed, but not the stems, so harvesting is then easier.

Paraquat is one of the most potent toxins used in agriculture. It not only has astonishingly rapid herbicidal effects when applied directly to plants, killing them within minutes, but it has insecticidal and pesticidal effects as well. It is also a dangerous herbicide for workers to apply. If inhaled or even if tiny amounts somehow enter the mouth, paraquat quickly affects the lungs, liver, and kidneys, and has the potential to kill. Farm workers exposed to crops that have had paraquat applied, either as a preemergent herbicide or postemergent, have a greater probability to develop Parkinson's disease or other health problems.

Organic Herbicides

Weeds can be killed by methods other than synthetic herbicides. The manual labor of hoeing and other cultivation practices such as mulching have been used for millennia. These practices are readily applied to small areas such as lawns and gardens. There are also herbicides made from natural ingredients. The following are some examples.

- Oil of cloves (in which eugenol is the active ingredient) helps control young broadleaf weeds.
- Acetic acid, often combined with citric acid, helps kill young grasses. (Some preparations contain both oil of cloves and acetic acid, making them useful against a broad assortment of weeds.)
- Soap-based herbicides cause clogging of plants' *stomata*, the respiratory organs of the leaves.
- Gluten meal, a by-product of the wet-milling process for corn, acts as a preemergent herbicide by inhibiting the root formation of germinating plant seeds.

These types of organic herbicides do not work as rapidly or as well as synthetic herbicides. For instance, corn gluten meal often requires four years of repeated applications to achieve good weed control. And some organic herbicides are effective only at fairly high concentrations, making them quite expensive for widespread use.

Genetically Engineered Herbicide Resistance

Because weeds tend to choke out planted crops, herbicides often are applied to crops and lawns. However, some of those herbicides, as we have discussed, are so potent that they may negatively affect the very crops and plants we wish to grow. Biotechnology research has developed genetically modified organisms (GMOs) that are herbicide tolerant. Herbicide-resistant corn and soybeans have been developed so far. The use of glyphosate now appears to be increasing, probably due to the natural process of plants evolving further herbicide resistance, much like the development of insect resistance in plants. Those who argue against GMO crops will cite the increase in use of herbicides, yet often fail to recognize the general decrease in use of insecticides with such crops.

▲ Many pesticides are used in homes against insect infestations and on gardens and lawns to prevent plant damage and to kill weeds. But less toxic alternatives are available. For example, diatomaceous earth is effective against snails and slugs.

Human Risks

The EPA estimates that physicians diagnose 10,000–20,000 pesticide poisonings each year among agricultural workers. Many agricultural poisoning cases are never reported, and many other incidents affect people who have used pesticides in their home, lawn, or garden. The WHO estimates that pesticide poisonings kill some 300,000 agricultural workers yearly worldwide and adversely affect the health of 2 million to 5 million more.

Many homeowners routinely hire lawncare companies to spray weed-killers and fertilizers in order to create the perfectly green lawn, and use insect sprays to kill mosquitoes and other flying insects in order to enjoy a pleasant backyard get-together. But there are potential adverse effects from inhaling airborne sprays; even homeowners would be wise to read labels carefully before use, and consider avoiding such products as much as possible.

SELF-ASSESSMENT Questions

1. Agent Orange, a mixture of 2,4-D and 2,4,5-T used as a defoliant by the U.S. military during the Vietnam War, was harmful to humans mainly due to
   a. 2,4-D
   b. 2,4,5-T
   c. an impurity in 2,4-D
   d. dioxin impurity in 2,4,5-T

2. One of the most potent toxins used as an herbicide is
   a. paraquat   b. atrazine   c. 2,4-D   d. eugenol

3. The herbicide atrazine acts by inhibiting
   a. amino-acid synthesis
   b. cell division
   c. lipid synthesis
   d. photosynthesis

4. Glyphosate
   a. is a selective herbicide
   b. is quite long-lasting in the soil
   c. does not kill crop plants
   d. can be used as a preemergent herbicide

5. The most common compound found in selective herbicides is
   a. atrazine
   b. 2,4-D
   c. glyphosate
   d. paraquat

Answers: 1. d; 2. a; 3. d; 4. d; 5. b

Household storage and preparation (31.7%)

Agricultural production (21.4%)

Processing industry (16.4%)

Transportation (13.6%)

Commercial food service (6.6%)

Packaging material (6.6%)

Food retail (3.7%)

Energy Consumed

▲ **Figure 20.15** Energy use in modern agriculture and food production. (Data from the University of Michigan Center for Sustainable Systems.)

20.4 Sustainable Agriculture

Learning Objective > Describe sustainable agriculture and organic farming.

Agriculture changed dramatically in the twentieth century. Mechanization and increased use of pesticides, synthetic fertilizers, and fossil fuel energy led to vastly increased production. With reduced labor demands, fewer and fewer farmers could produce more and more food and fiber.

These changes also brought problems that have led to calls for alternatives to conventional farming. Most prominent among these alternatives is **sustainable agriculture**, which is the ability of a farm to produce food and fiber indefinitely, without causing irreparable damage to the ecosystem. Sustainable agriculture has three main goals: a healthy environment, farm profitability, and social and economic equity. Much of sustainable agriculture is similar to the practices that organic farmers and gardeners have followed for generations.

Modern agriculture is energy intensive. Nonrenewable petroleum energy is required for the production of fertilizers, pesticides, and farm machinery. Energy is also required to run the machinery needed to till, harvest, dry, and transport the crops, to process and package the food, and to preserve and prepare the food in consumers' households. A breakdown of the energy used in agriculture and food production is presented in Figure 20.15.

A 21-year Swiss study compared conventional plots that used synthetic fertilizers and synthetic pesticides to organic plots that were fertilized with manure and treated only occasionally with a copper fungicide. Crops of potatoes, winter wheat, grass clover, barley, and beets were grown under otherwise identical conditions. The organic method appeared to be more efficient, with yields only 20% less, even though the nutrient input had been reduced by 50%. The organic method was said to use 20–56% less energy than the conventional approach when the energy required for production of fertilizers and pesticides was taken into account.

Organic farming is carried out without the use of synthetic fertilizers or pesticides. As was mentioned earlier, organic farmers (and gardeners) use manure from farm animals for fertilizer, and they rotate other crops with legumes to restore nitrogen to the soil. They control insects by planting a variety of crops, alternating the use of fields. (A corn pest has a hard time surviving during the year that its home field is planted in soybeans.) Organic farming is also less energy intensive. According to a study by the Center for the Biology of Natural Systems at Washington University, comparable conventional farms used 2.3 times as much energy as organic farms. Production on organic farms was 10% lower, but costs were comparably lower. Organic farms require 12% more labor than conventional ones. Human labor is a renewable resource though, whereas petroleum is not. Compared with conventional methods, organic farming uses less energy and leads to healthier soils.

In addition to organic practices, sustainable agriculture involves buying local products and using local services when possible, thus avoiding the cost of transportation while getting fresher food and strengthening the economy of the local community. Transportation's share of food costs soars as fuel prices rise. Half the cost of broccoli in New York City may well be freight costs.

Sustainable agriculture promotes independent farmers and ranchers producing good food and making a good living while protecting the environment. Conventional agriculture can result in severe soil erosion and is the source of considerable water pollution. No doubt we should practice organic farming to the limit of our ability to do so. But we should not delude ourselves. Abrupt banning of synthetic fertilizers and pesticides would likely lead to a drastic drop in food production.

As far as human energy is concerned, U.S. agriculture is enormously efficient. Each farm worker produces enough food for about 80 people. But this productivity is based on fossil fuels. About 10 units of petroleum energy are required to produce 1 unit of food energy. In terms of production per hectare, modern farming is marvelously efficient. But in terms of the energy used in relation to the energy produced, it is remarkably inefficient. It should be noted, however, that in energy-efficient early agricultural societies, nearly all human energy went into food production. In modern societies, only about 10% of human energy is devoted to producing food. The other 90% is used to provide the materials and services that are so much a part of our civilization. We should try to make our food production more energy-efficient, but it is unlikely that we will want to return to an outmoded way of life.

5. Are organic fruits and vegetables healthier for us?

Organically grown fruits and vegetables do not contain the pesticides and fertilizer residues found in foods grown by conventional methods, but they can contain natural toxins or contaminants such as *E. coli* from organic fertilizer. It is worth noting that most applied pesticides are concentrated on the surfaces of fruits or vegetables. Organic bananas, oranges, and grapefruit may be no better than the conventionally grown fruits because their peels are not eaten.

SELF-ASSESSMENT Questions

1. Farming that meets human needs without degrading the environment or depleting resources is called
   a. corporate farming
   b. industrial farming
   c. local farming
   d. sustainable agriculture

2. Organic farming differs from conventional agriculture in that organic farmers use no
   a. animal manure
   b. crop rotation
   c. legumes
   d. synthetic pesticides

3. Comparing modern agriculture to organic farming, which is not true?
   a. Modern farming uses far less human energy and much more mechanical energy.
   b. Each modern farm worker provides food for about 80 people, many more than organic farmers do.
   c. Organic farmers use far more petroleum-based energy overall than farmers who use commercially available fertilizers and herbicides.
   d. Organic farmers use fewer inorganic fertilizers and more carbon-based fertilizers.

Answers: 1, d; 2, d; 3, c

20.5 Looking to the Future: Feeding a Growing, Hungry World

Learning Objective ⟩ Assess the challenges of feeding an increasing human population.

In 1830, Thomas Robert Malthus, an English clergyman and political economist, made the statement that the world's population would increase faster than the world's food supply. Unless the birthrate was controlled, he said, poverty and war would have to serve as restrictions on the increase in population. That was a startling statement!

Malthus's prediction was based on simple mathematics: Population grows geometrically, while the food supply increases arithmetically. In **arithmetic growth**, a constant amount is added during each growth period. As an example, consider a child who starts to save money in a piggy bank. The first week, the child puts in 25¢. Each week thereafter, she adds 25¢. The growth of her savings is *arithmetic*, and it increases by a constant amount (25¢) each week. At the end of five weeks she will have $1.25 saved.

In **geometric growth**, the increment increases in size for each growth period. Again, let's use a child's bank as an example. The first week she puts in 25¢. The second week she puts in 50¢ to double the amount deposited, for a total of 75¢ saved. After five weeks, she has $20.25 deposited. Before long, she will have to start robbing banks to keep up her geometrically growing deposits! Population growth rates obviously are not doubled weekly, but an overview of population growth shows an approximately geometric increase (see Table 20.4).

For a world population growing geometrically, we can estimate the **doubling time** using the *rule of 72*. Simply divide 72 by the percentage of annual growth.

Table 20.4	World Population Milestones.		
World Population		Year	Time to Add 1 Billion
1 billion people		1804	
2 billion		1927	123 years
3 billion		1960	33 years
4 billion		1974	14 years
5 billion		1987	13 years
6 billion		1999	12 years
7 billion		2011	12 years
8 billion		?	

Example 20.2 Population Doubling Time

Earth's population was 7.0 billion in 2011 and growing by 1.092% per year. If it continues to grow at this rate, how long will it (theoretically) take to double to 14 billion?

Solution

$$\frac{72}{1.092\%} = 66 \text{ years from 2011, or in 2077}$$

Be cautious. The world's population growth rate is not steady at 1.092% per year!

▪ EXERCISE 20.2A
Consult Table 20.4. What was the average population growth rate from 1927 to 1974, when the world population doubled from 2 billion to 4 billion?

▪ EXERCISE 20.2B
What was the average population growth rate from 1804 to 1927, when the world population doubled from 1 billion to 2 billion? Compare your answer to Exercise 20.2A.

The calculations using the rule of 72 are only speculative. World population growth, individual country growth, and even small region growth rates vary significantly. In 2011, for example, the U.S. growth rate was 0.963% per year. For many years, China enforced a rule of one child per family in urban areas, but now appears to be softening that rule. India's growth rate is such that it may within a decade surpass China as the most populous country on Earth. Some areas of Africa are growing at a rapid rate, which, unfortunately, often mirrors the poverty rate. It is simply more difficult to feed larger families with diminishing economic resources. So the rule of 72 is, at best, an approximation. Many factors will affect the growth rate. An epidemic or other catastrophe might also change the death rate.

Earth's population has nonetheless grown enormously since the time of Malthus, reaching 7 billion in 2011. Famine has brought suffering and death to millions in war-ravaged areas around the world (Figure 20.16), while modern farming often produces surpluses in developed countries. Some developing nations have made great progress in food production, with many of them becoming self-sufficient. Despite surpluses in some parts of the world, an estimated 800 million people are seriously malnourished. Half are children under five years old, who will carry the physical and mental scars of this deprivation for the rest of their lives. Scientific developments, such as those outlined in this chapter, have brought abundance to many, but millions still go hungry.

Can We Feed a Hungry World?

The United Nations Population Division projects that Earth's population will reach 9 billion in 2045. It could be sooner. It could be later. Can we feed all those people?

An alliance between science and agriculture has increased food supplies beyond the imagination of people of a few generations ago, as a result of irrigation, synthetic fertilizers, pesticides, and improved genetic varieties of plants and animals. Food production can be further increased through genetic engineering. Scientists are designing plants that produce more food, that are resistant to disease and insect pests, and that grow well in hostile environments. They can design animals that grow larger and produce more meat or milk. Such efforts may someday provide us with food in unimaginable abundance. But the hungry are with us now, and 75 million more people come to dinner each year. One challenge is that many people oppose the genetic modification of food crops, which may hamper the use of this approach.

Even quadrupling current food production would meet our needs for only a few decades. Virtually all of the world's available arable land is now under cultivation, about 38.6% of ice-free land available on our planet. About 46.5% of land on Earth is desert, high mountains, tundra, or deep forest, and so not really amenable to expansion of agriculture. About 14.9% of land has been human-modified, as cities and towns, highways, mines, and logged areas. We lose farmland every day to housing, roads, erosion, encroaching deserts, and the increasing salt content of irrigated soils.

Regional climate swings, such as severe droughts in parts of Africa or monsoons in Asia, affect the ability of nations to grow food. Distribution of food to famine-ravaged areas is not a simple task, due to political and transportation challenges. It does appear that keeping food production ahead of the rate of population growth, particularly in developing countries, will be increasingly difficult.

An interesting aspect of the world's food crisis is the percent of "food" produced that is used for human food and the percent that is used to feed livestock or for other uses. In developing nations, the vast majority of food grown is used for human food, including rice and quinoa, for example. In developed nations, for example in the U.S. Midwest, 83% of the corn and soybean crops are used for animal food (beef, pork, and poultry) and for the production of ethanol, a gasoline additive, and only 17% for human food.

It has been suggested that one solution to the food crisis is changing our choices in food to a diet higher in grains and lower in meat and dairy products. A challenge for that solution is that it appears that developed nations seem to have a larger appetite for meat products compared to developing nations where rice, corn, and other grains are the main food staples. As developing nations become developed nations, with increased prosperity may come an increased appetite for meats. But raising beef cattle requires pasture and corn.

Despite a growing movement toward sustainable agriculture, we are still greatly dependent on a high-energy form of agriculture that uses synthetic fertilizers, pesticides, and herbicides and depends on machinery that burns fossil fuels.

▲ **Figure 20.16** In developed countries, science has thwarted the Malthusian prediction of hunger. But starvation is still a fact of life for many people in developing countries. In 2008, according to the United Nations, more than 2 million people faced death from starvation and disease in the Darfur region of Sudan. Since then, the southern part of the country has become independent as South Sudan, which has suffered political turmoil and violence.

6. How can there be a food crisis if I see plenty of corn growing in the fields?

Surprisingly, the vast majority of that corn is used to feed farm animals, including chickens and beef cattle, not to make cornflakes and corn meal for people. Much is used to make ethanol, most likely 10% of the fuel for your car.

GREEN CHEMISTRY

Amy S. Cannon, *Beyond Benign*

Safer Pesticides through Biomimicry and Green Chemistry

Learning Objectives ❯ Identify the benefits of pesticides to humans and the challenges in their use. ❯ Give examples of how pesticides can be designed to reduce hazard to humans and the environment.

The practice of agriculture has been largely responsible for the growth of human civilization, allowing humans to settle in societies and raise food to sustain the community. Population growth brought the challenge of producing enough food, in a sustainable manner, to feed the world's populations. This challenge today is one of the toughest that humans have faced in history. The solution involves global issues such as clean water, population growth, land use, energy use, genetic modification, and pesticide and fertilizer use.

From a scientific perspective, the chemistry we use on the farm and in the garden can have a drastic impact on the output of our food production and the sustainability of agricultural practices. Pesticide use in agriculture has led to a drastic reduction in crop failure and increased crop yields, but pesticides often are toxic toward other than the target organisms. For example, the use of neonicotinoids, a class of neuro-active pesticides, has been found to contribute to honeybee colony collapse disorder and the decline of honeybee populations worldwide. The European Commission issued a ban on three neonicotinoids that went into effect in December 2013 to further protect honeybee populations. How do we address the issue of creating pesticides that target pest organisms and not beneficial ones, such as honeybees?

Green chemists are addressing the need for more highly targeted pesticides. Green chemistry principle 4 encourages the design of safer, more benign products and processes without compromising on efficacy or cost. This is perhaps the most important application of green chemistry in the production and use of pesticides. Generally, a safer pesticide means higher selectivity toward the pest organism and fewer effects on the surrounding environment and beneficial organisms.

One place to look for inspiration when making safer pesticides is nature. There are many examples of organisms in nature that naturally and selectively ward off pests. A recent example is that of a pesticide based on spider venom. Years ago, Glenn King, from the University of Queensland in Australia, identified a peptide from the venom of the Blue Mountains funnel-web spider. The venom of the spider was found to be toxic to insects but nontoxic to mammals. This selectivity inspired additional researchers to investigate this unique venom. A recent publication reports the development of a biopesticide that is inspired by the spider-venom peptide. The biopesticide is found to target pest organisms but has no adverse effect on honeybees.

In creating more targeted pesticides, scientists focus on structure–function relationships to find specific modes of action that are unique to the target pest. New research is tapping into naturally inspired, or biomimetic, methods for repelling or mitigating pests, such as the biopesticide inspired by spider venom. These pesticides represent a growing trend in the field of green chemistry: that of looking to nature for inspiration. Biomimicry, derived from the two terms *bios* (life) and *mimic* (to copy or emulate), is the imitation of the models, systems, and elements of nature for the purpose of solving complex human problems. By looking to nature, we can find inspiration for solving the challenges our society faces, such as pesticides and crop protection.

Through green chemistry we can make greener pesticides and also reduce the environmental impact of processes for making the pesticides. We can design less hazardous chemical synthesis (Principle 3), use catalytic reagents (Principle 9), improve the energy efficiency of processes (Principle 6), rely on safer solvents (Principle 5), and design the pesticides to be biodegradable (Principle 10). Biomimicry and the application of the green chemistry may be the key to providing food for our people and protecting our environment at the same time.

▲ Australian funnel web spider *Hadronyche versuta*.

Ultimately, the only solution to the problem is to stabilize population. Obviously, that will come someday. The only questions are when and how. Population control could be accomplished through decreasing the birthrate, which is happening in almost all developed countries and in many developing ones. A few nations still have populations growing at explosive rates that far outstrip their food supplies. Birth control isn't the only way to limit population growth. Another possibility is an increase in the death rate—through catastrophic war, famine, pestilence, or the poisoning of the environment by the wastes of an ever-expanding population. The ghost of Thomas Malthus haunts us yet.

SELF-ASSESSMENT Questions

1. Factors that will have to be considered in addressing the world's food crisis include all the following except
   a. the production levels of corn and soybeans, irrespective of their food and non-food use
   b. variations in population increases
   c. loss of farmland to urban sprawl
   d. efficiency of crop production

2. The rapid population growth that occurred in the late nineteenth and early twentieth centuries was due in large part to
   a. conservation of natural resources
   b. global peace
   c. use of scientific agricultural practices
   d. equitable distribution of wealth

3. Uganda's estimated population in 2013 was 35.9 million, and it is growing at a rate of 3.32% per year. If that growth rate continues, the population will have doubled in about
   a. 10 y   b. 20 y
   c. 40 y   d. 80 y

4. By 2025, what country is estimated to have the highest population?
   a. China   b. India
   c. USA   d. Nigeria

Answers: 1, a; 2, c; 3, b; 4, b

■ SUMMARY

Section 20.1—The three **primary plant nutrients** are nitrogen, phosphorus, and potassium. Atmospheric nitrogen is fixed naturally by soil bacteria and by lightning. Artificial fixation of nitrogen produces ammonia and nitrates that can be added to the soil. Phosphorus can be made available by treating phosphate rock. Potassium, as potassium chloride, is usually mined. The **secondary plant nutrients** are calcium, magnesium, and sulfur. Eight other **micronutrients** are needed in small amounts. The three numbers on commercial fertilizers indicate the percentages of N, percentages of P_2O_5, and percentages of K_2O in the fertilizer. Organic fertilizers include composted manure and sewage sludge.

Section 20.2—Pests can cause plagues and ruin food supplies. **Pesticides** are used to kill organisms that we consider harmful, including many insects. Most **insecticides** kill all insects they come in contact with, not just the harmful ones. The insecticide DDT saved millions of lives during and after World War II, yet its persistence in the environment caused problems. Widely banned, DDT continues to be used in some developing countries for malaria control. Organic phosphorus compounds are nerve poisons. Although they accumulate in fatty tissues, they are less persistent in the environment than chlorinated compounds like DDT. Carbamates are mostly narrow-spectrum insecticides, harmful to just a few insect pests. They neither accumulate in fatty tissue nor persist in the environment. Organic pesticides include pyrethrins, permethrins, rotenone, boric acid, and diatomaceous earth. Some pests can be controlled biologically, using praying mantises, ladybugs, and pest-specific bacteria and viruses. Some insects can be controlled by SIT, or sterilization and release of males. A **pheromone** is

a chemical secreted by an insect to mark a trail, send an alarm, or, in the case of a **sex attractant**, attract a mate. **Juvenile hormones** can be used to keep insect pests in an immature stage, in which they cannot reproduce. Pheromones and juvenile hormones have proved useful to some extent in monitoring and control of insect pests but are difficult to produce and expensive to use.

Section 20.3—**Herbicides** kill weeds, and **defoliants** cause leaves to fall off plants. The herbicide 2,4-D and the defoliant 2,4,5-T were combined in **Agent Orange**, used to remove ground cover in Vietnam. Highly toxic **dioxins** that were contaminants in this mixture caused birth defects, resulting in a ban on 2,4,5-T. Atrazine and glyphosate are the most widely used herbicides in the United States. Paraquat is a **preemergent herbicide** that kills weed plants before crop seedlings emerge, but can be used to quickly kill emergent weeds. Organic herbicides include oil of cloves, acetic acid, and gluten meal.

Section 20.4—Sustainable agriculture is the ability of a farm to produce food and fiber indefinitely, without causing irreparable damage to the ecosystem. **Organic farming** avoids the use of synthetic fertilizers and pesticides. It is less energy intensive and less productive than conventional farming but costs less and uses renewable resources.

Section 20.5—According to Malthus, food production shows a steady increase called **arithmetic growth**. Because population increase historically has occurred as **geometric growth**, with the rate of increase itself increasing, food production cannot keep up with population. The **rule of 72** predicts the **doubling time** for population predictions, but cultural and political conditions and changes make such predictions speculative. Additional scientific and technical advances may help increase food production or control population in years to come, but Malthus's prediction still hangs over us.

GREEN CHEMISTRY—Through inspiration from nature and the application of green chemistry principles in the design of new pesticides, scientists can create effective pest control products that target only the pest and not the surrounding environment or beneficial organisms. These new pesticides can be designed using more benign reagents and processes that require less energy. The pesticides can also be designed so that they biodegrade, leaving behind no harmful residues.

Learning Objectives

› List the three primary plant nutrients as well as several secondary nutrients and micronutrients, and describe the function of each.	Problems 7, 8, 31, 37
› Differentiate between organic fertilizers and conventional fertilizers.	Problems 9–14, 32, 35–36, 39
› Name and describe the action of the main kinds of pesticides.	Problems 15–18, 33
› List several biological pest controls, and explain how they work.	Problems 19–21, 37
› Name and describe the action of the major herbicides and defoliants.	Review question 3 Problems 22, 23, 34, 38, 40
› Describe sustainable agriculture and organic farming.	Review questions 2, 4 Problems 40, 41, 44
› Assess the challenges of feeding an increasing human population.	Review questions 5, 6 Problems 24–30, 43
› Identify the benefits of pesticides to humans and the challenges in their use.	Problems 47–48
› Give examples of how pesticides can be designed to reduce hazard to humans and the environment.	Problem 49

REVIEW QUESTIONS

1. Where does most of the matter of a growing plant come from?

2. List the three main goals of sustainable agriculture.

3. What is a preemergent herbicide?

4. Compare organic farming with conventional farming. Consider energy requirements, labor, profitability, and crop yields.

5. What did Thomas Malthus predict in his famous 1830 statement?

6. What are the primary challenges in feeding an increasing human population?

PROBLEMS

Fertilizers

7. List the three chemical elements that form the structural parts of plants.

8. What are the three elements, other than those used to make roots, stems and leaves, that are needed by plants?

9. List several ways that nitrogen can be fixed.

10. How is ammonia made?

11. What is the difference between an ammonia solution and anhydrous ammonia?

12. What is the source of phosphate fertilizers? What is the role of phosphorus in plant nutrition?

13. Why does soil become acidic when potassium ions are absorbed by plants?

14. What is eutrophication? What ions are primarily responsible for this problem in ponds and lakes?

Pesticides and Herbicides

15. List the advantages and disadvantages of DDT as an insecticide.

16. Why is DDT especially harmful to birds?

17. Describe how chlorinated hydrocarbons become increasingly concentrated in a food chain.

18. Define and give an example of (a) a narrow-spectrum insecticide and (b) a broad-spectrum insecticide.

19. How are pheromones used in insect control? Give an example.

20. How are juvenile hormones used against insect pests?

21. Describe SIT as a method for controlling insects. Why is it not more widely used?

22. List the two most commonly used compounds in weed-killers, and differentiate between them in terms of the types of plants that are killed by each.

Toxicity

23. How much DDT would it take to kill a person weighing 70 kg if the lethal dose is 0.50 g per kilogram of body weight?

24. Refer to the toxicity of carbofuran in Table 20.3. If the toxicity in mice approximates that in humans, what is the lethal dose in a 12 kg child?

25. In the Green Chemistry essay in Chapter 22, diquat dibromide is indicated as a less toxic substitute for paraquat (page 647). The lethal doses, in milligrams per kilogram of body weight when administered orally, are: diquat dibromide, 600, and paraquat, 150. How much of each would it take to kill a person weighing 56 kg?

Growth, Population Changes, and the Food Crisis

26. You start a savings account, planning to add $125 each month. How many months will it take you to save $1000? Do your savings grow arithmetically or geometrically?

27. You decide to raise gerbils. Starting with two, you have four at the end of 6 weeks, eight at the end of 12 weeks, and so on. The gerbil population doubles every 6 weeks. How many gerbils will you have at the end of 24 weeks? Is the gerbil population growing arithmetically or geometrically? Note that the gerbil litters range from 2 to 5, and the gestation period is only about 3 1/2 weeks.

28. The population of India was estimated to be 1.24 billion in 2012 and was growing at the rate of 1.35% a year. At this rate, how many years will it take for the population to double to 2.48 billion? What factors are likely to change this rate of growth?

29. The population of China was estimated to be 1.364 billion in 2014 and was growing at an annual rate of 0.493%. At this rate, how many years will it take for the population to double to 2.728 billion? What factors are likely to change this rate of growth?

30. If there are about 7.7 billion acres of ice-free land on Earth, how many billion acres of land are currently used for agriculture? (See Section 20.5 for more information.)

31. How many billion acres of land on Earth are currently used for urban areas, roads and mines? (See question 28 and Section 20.5 for further information).

32. If the percent of corn produced that is used to make ethanol was 7% in 2000, and about 40% in 2014, what percent increase is that? What are some impacts of that trend?

ADDITIONAL PROBLEMS

33. Give the balanced overall chemical equation for photosynthesis.

34. Give the chemical equation for the synthesis of ammonia.

35. Indicate whether each of the following pesticides is organic (a) in the chemical sense only, (b) in the sense used in organic farming only, (c) in both senses, or (d) in no way at all.
    a. boric acid
    b. diatomaceous earth
    c. lead arsenate
    d. malathion
    e. rotenone

36. Indicate whether each of the following herbicides is organic (a) in the chemical sense only, (b) in the sense used in organic farming only, (c) in both senses, or (d) in no way at all.
    a. acetic acid
    b. atrazine
    c. 2,4-D
    d. gluten meal
    e. glyphosate

37. The compound potassium nitrate may be used as a fertilizer. Write the correct formula for potassium nitrate, and list what plant nutrients that compound would supply.

38. The compound ammonium monohydrogen phosphate is frequently used as a fertilizer. (a) Write the chemical formula for that compound. (b) What two plant nutrients does it supply? (c) Write the equation for the formation of this compound from ammonia and the appropriate acid.

39. The micronutrient copper is often applied in the form of copper(II) sulfate. Write the equation for the formation of copper(II) sulfate from copper(II) oxide and the appropriate acid.

40. Examine the chemical formula for paraquat in Section 20.3. What are the functional groups found in that molecule?

41. What is lime, and what is its chemical formula? Why is it commonly added to gardens and farm soil?

42. Oil of cloves, used as an organic herbicide, has eugenol as its principal active component. Name the functional groups in the eugenol molecule.

Eugenol

43. Potassium bicarbonate, usually combined with horticultural oil (a highly refined petroleum product), is often sold as an organic pesticide. To make potassium bicarbonate, we start with potassium hydroxide and then react it with carbon dioxide to form potassium carbonate and water. The potassium carbonate is reacted with more carbon dioxide and water to form the potassium bicarbonate. Write balanced equations for the two reactions. Is potassium bicarbonate an organic pesticide? Explain.

44. The herbicide dicamba (Banvel®), widely used to control broadleaf weeds, has the systematic name 2-methoxy-3,6-dichlorobenzoic acid. The methoxy group is —OCH$_3$. Draw the structure of dicamba.

45. The average woman in Uganda has 5.9 children. The population of Uganda, which, by some estimates, is growing faster than that of any other country in the world, was estimated to be 37.5 million in 2012, compared to 34.5 million in 2011. (a) What is the annual rate of increase in population during that year time span? (b) At this rate, how many years will it take for the population to double to 75.0 million? (c) What factors are likely to change this rate of growth?

46. Why is the use of insecticidal soaps not practical for large-scale agriculture?

47. Which of the following are benefits of using pesticides on food crops? Choose all that apply.
    a. increased yield of food production
    b. reduced crop failure
    c. identification of new pests
    d. improved taste of foods

48. Give two potential drawbacks of using pesticides on food crops.

49. What are some potential benefits of applying green chemistry principles during the design of pesticides?
    a. safer, less toxic pesticides that are more selective for the pest organism and are harmless to other organisms
    b. pesticides that biodegrade after their useful lifetime and leave behind no toxic residues
    c. reductions in waste, energy use, and exposure to harmful reagents during the synthesis of pesticides
    d. all of the above

CRITICAL THINKING EXERCISES

Apply knowledge that you have gained in this chapter and one or more of the FLaReS principles (Chapter 1) to evaluate the following statements or claims.

20.1. An advertisement claims that a certain cereal made from organically grown grains provides a "life energy" that cannot be obtained from ordinary processed cereals.

20.2. An advertisement implies that rotenone is safer than synthetic pesticides because it is obtained from natural sources.

20.3. A newspaper claims that certain genetically modified crops may become weeds if not properly controlled.

20.4. Many people claim that vegetables grown in backyard gardens are safer to eat than those grown on commercial farms, because no commercial fertilizer or weed-killers have been used.

20.5. A website states that nitrate ions from synthetic fertilizers such as ammonium nitrate are less effective as plant nutrients than nitrate ions from the breakdown of organic fertilizers by soil bacteria, and thus nonorganic foods are less nutritious.

20.6. A newspaper article suggests, "Try out tobacco 'sun tea' as a nontoxic pesticide." In the article is this claim: "This special tea can help you eliminate most garden pests without any unwanted toxicity."

COLLABORATIVE GROUP PROJECTS

Prepare a PowerPoint, poster, or other presentation (as directed by your instructor) to share with the class.

1. Compare labels for several brands of commercially available spray insecticides targeting the same type of insect. Look for the active ingredients, note their concentrations, and note safety precautions on the label for its use. Find commonalities and differences. Focus on one type of targeted pest:
    a. ant killers
    b. box elder bugs
    c. wasps or hornets
    d. mosquitoes or flies

2. Prepare a brief report on one of the insecticides listed in Table 20.3. List its principal advantages and disadvantages.

3. Prepare a brief report on one of the following alternative methods of insect control. List its principal advantages and disadvantages.
    a. Bt
    b. a viral agent
    c. SIT
    d. sex attractants
    e. a juvenile hormone

4. Go to a garden supply center and find several fertilizers for use with houseplants or garden flowers. Compare the percents of N, P, and K for different targeted plants, such as roses, or indoor plants.

5. Examine the label on a package of garden pesticide. List its trade name and active ingredients.

6. Prepare a brief report on one of the following scientists.
    a. Fritz Haber
    b. F. G. Hopkins
    c. Justus von Liebig
    d. Ellen Swallow Richards

7. Look for several websites with different viewpoints on the use of fertilizers and pesticides. Defend one side of an issue involving the use of these substances.

8. Look for several websites with different perspectives on factory farms, also called *confined animal feeding operations (CAFOs)*. Choose one perspective and defend it.

CHEMISTRY@HOME   Wash Away the Weeds

Materials required

- 6 cups of vinegar
- 2 tablespoons of dish detergent
- $\frac{1}{8}$ cup of table salt
- Measuring cup
- Measuring spoons
- 3 spray bottles (each holding a quart of liquid)
- 4 pots of plants (weeds or inexpensive annuals)
- Permanent marker

Note: *(double vinegar, detergent and salt if you preform both the indoor and outdoor experiments)*

How do you get rid of unwanted weeds in your garden? Are there any homemade recipes that are just as effective but less expensive and less hazardous than commercially manufactured herbicides?

Get outside! This experiment works best if you can get outdoors and test this homemade herbicide on weeds in your yard. (Your friends' or neighbors' yard would work, too.)

By definition. herbicides are plant killers. Weed killers, both homemade and commercial products, start by killing the aboveground foliage. Systemic weed killers, like Roundup, are designed to cause injury to the entire plant including the root system so it will not grow back. The use of synthetic weed killers is known to be a health hazard to the environment. These herbicides leach into ground water and causes contamination of the water table. Ponds and rivers become contaminated and endanger the lives of organisms.

In this experiment, you will be comparing three different homemade herbicide recipes. Begin by making your weed killers. Measure out the ingredients and label the spray bottles.

- Weed Killer 1: 2 cups vinegar
- Weed Killer 2: 2 cups vinegar + 1 tbsp liquid dish soap
- Weed Killer 3: 2 cups vinegar + 1 tbsp liquid dish soap + $\frac{1}{8}$ c sallt

Outdoors experiment with recipes 1 and 2: (3 days)

The homemade herbicides you will be experimenting with are not selective; they can potentially harm plants you wish to keep. If you are able to do this experiment outside, be careful to spray the weed killer directly onto the weeds so there is no floating mist. The objective is to thoroughly coat the visible foliage. Only test weed killer 1 and 2 outside (the salt in weed killer 3 could also contaminate ground water). It's best to do this in a walkway or area where you do not want plants at all.

Expected Results for Weed Killer with Vinegar

Indoors experiment with all three recipes:

You will want to prepare 4 potted plants using either weeds or inexpensive leafy annuals from a gardening store. One will be your control and the others will be labeled weed killer 1–3.

Place your plants in conditions that are the same for all 4 plants. A sunny windowsill works well. For the next 4 days, consistently spray the weed killers over the weeds in the corresponding pots saturating the leaves. Spray at the same time each day, and monitor the conditions of the weeds. What happened to the weeds? Are there any color changes in the weeds? Record your results?

Expected Results for Indoor Weed Killer Experiment

Day 1:

Day 2:

Day 3:

Day 4:

Questions

1. Which weed killer was the most effective indoors? Why?
2. Which weed killer was most effective outdoors? Why?
3. Which weed killer was the least effective indoors? Why?
4. Which weed killer was least effective outdoors? Why?
5. Will you consider making your own herbicide rather than buying a synthetic weed killer?

▲ **Figure 1** Day 1 Outdoors

21

HOUSEHOLD CHEMICALS

Learning Objectives

> Describe the structure of soap, and explain how it is made and how it works to remove greasy dirt. (21.1)

> Explain the advantages and disadvantages of soap. (21.1)

> List the structures, advantages, and disadvantages of synthetic detergents. (21.2)

> Classify surfactants as amphoteric, anionic, cationic, and nonionic, and describe how they are used in various detergent formulations. (21.2)

> Identify a fabric softener from its structure, and describe its action. (21.3)

> Name two types of laundry bleaches, and describe how they work. (21.3)

> List the major ingredient(s) (and their purposes) of some all-purpose cleaning products and some special-purpose cleaning products. (21.4)

> Identify compounds used in solvents and paints, and explain their purposes. (21.5)

> Identify waxes by their structure. (21.5)

> Describe the chemical nature of skin, hair, and teeth. (21.6)

> Identify the principal ingredients in various cosmetic products and their purposes. (21.6)

> Identify how green chemistry principles can be applied when selecting greener household products.

Have You Ever Wondered?

1. **How does soap remove that grease from my shirt and hands?**

2. **Why can't hand dishwashing liquid be used in a dishwasher?**

3. **Does putting more fabric softener in the washer make fabrics even softer?**

4. **Should I worry about lead-based paint if I purchase a classic home built in the 1950s?**

5. **Does a thicker shampoo work better to clean my hair?**

6. **Why must I leave a hair coloring preparation on my hair for the full time suggested on the bottle if I want to become a blonde?**

HELPS AND HAZARDS

If someone offered you a job in a place where poisonous chemicals were used every day, where toxic vapors and harmful dusts and molds were common, where corrosive acids and alkalis were often used, and where highly flammable liquids and vapors posed a fire hazard, would you take the job? You probably have, many times. This is a description of a typical American home.

People tend to be careful in a chemistry laboratory because they know it can be dangerous there. They often are much less cautious in their homes, even though some of the chemicals on the shelves can be just as toxic and hazardous as those in a laboratory—and many are exactly the same substances.

The household chemicals sold in greatest volume are cleaning products—soaps, detergents, and various special-purpose and all-purpose cleaners. In this chapter, we examine a variety of familiar products and discuss how they work.

Perhaps half a million chemical products are available for use in the American home, including waxes, paints, paint removers, bleaches, insecticides, rodenticides, spot removers, solvents, disinfectants, detergents, toothpastes, shampoos, perfumes, lotions, shaving creams, deodorants, hair sprays, and hair dyes (Figure 21.1). Some of these products are harmless, but others contain corrosive or toxic chemicals or present fire hazards. Some cause environmental problems when they are used or discarded.

Extensive use of chemicals in the home has resulted in many accidents. Studies show that chemicals are often used without regard to the directions or precautions given on their labels. Frequently, the labels aren't read at all, and *misuse* of household chemicals can sometimes end in tragedy.

We discussed the chemical composition of food and the chemicals that are used in producing it in Chapter 17. Some agricultural chemicals are also used around the home, especially in the yard and garden (Chapter 20). We discussed polymers used in our clothing and home furnishings in Chapter 10 and the fuels burned in our furnaces and automobiles in Chapter 15. We discussed the chemistry of our bodies in Chapter 16. In this chapter, we will look at other chemicals around the house—cleaning products, personal care supplies, and paint, to name just a few. Let's begin with cleaning agents, which make up the largest volume of household chemicals.

▲ **Figure 21.1** A modern home is stocked with a variety of chemical products.

21.1 Cleaning with Soap

Learning Objectives ❯ Describe the structure of soap, and explain how it is made and how it works to remove greasy dirt. ❯ Explain the advantages and disadvantages of soap.

Personal Cleanliness

The use of soap and the attitudes of various cultures on cleanliness have a fascinating history. In developing societies, clothes were cleaned by beating them with rocks in the nearest stream. Sometimes plants, such as the soapworts of Europe or the soapberries of tropical America, were used as cleansing agents. The leaves of soapworts and soapberries contain *saponins*, chemical compounds that produce a soapy lather.

Ashes of burned plants contain potassium carbonate (K_2CO_3) and sodium carbonate (Na_2CO_3). The carbonate ion present in both these compounds reacts with water to form an alkaline solution that can attack grease and oil. The word "alkali" comes from an Arabic word meaning "the ashes." The Babylonians used these alkaline plant ashes to make cleansing agents at least 4000 years ago.

The Romans, with their great public baths, probably did not use any sort of soap. They covered their bodies with oil, worked up a sweat in a steam bath, and then scraped off the oil. A dip in a pool of fresh water completed the cleansing.

During the Middle Ages, bodily cleanliness was prized in some cultures but not in others. For example, twelfth-century Paris, with a population of about 100,000, had many public bathhouses. In contrast, the Renaissance, which was the revival of learning and art that lasted from the fourteenth to the seventeenth centuries, was not noted for cleanliness. Queen Elizabeth I of England (1533–1603) bathed once a month, a habit that caused many to think her overly fastidious. A common remedy for unpleasant body odor back then was the liberal use of perfume.

▲ Queen Isabella of Castile (1451–1504), who supported the voyage of Columbus to the New World in 1492, is reported to have bathed only twice in her life.

And today? Perhaps we have gone too far in the other direction. With soap, detergent, body wash, shampoo, conditioner, deodorant, antiperspirant, aftershave, cologne, and perfume, we may add more during and after a shower than we remove in the shower.

Although soap has been known for hundreds of years, it was first used mainly as a medicine. Even today, particularly in Asia and Africa, soaps made from plants such as the neem tree (*Azadirachta indica*) are used for skin treatments. In India, 80% of neem oil is used to make soap that treats skin rashes, psoriasis, eczema, acne, and chicken pox. The discovery of disease-causing microorganisms increased interest in cleanliness and improved public health practices during the eighteenth century. By the middle of the nineteenth century, soap was in common use as a cleansing agent.

Soap-Making: Fat Plus Lye Forms a Soap Plus Glycerol

The first written record of soap-making is found in the writings of Pliny the Elder (C.E. 23–79), a Roman scholar who described the Phoenicians' synthesis of soap using goat tallow and ashes. What substance was in ashes that could change a fat into a soap? A base! By the second century C.E., sodium hydroxide (lye) was created from sodium carbonate and calcium hydroxide by a multistep process. Seashells or pieces of limestone were crushed and heated strongly to drive off carbon dioxide to form calcium oxide (lime).

$$CaCO_3(s) \longrightarrow CaO(s) + CO_2(g)$$

The calcium oxide was then mixed with water to form calcium hydroxide, which was heated with sodium carbonate (obtained by evaporating alkaline water) to produce sodium hydroxide and calcium carbonate via the reaction:

$$Na_2CO_3 + Ca(OH)_2 \longrightarrow 2\,NaOH + CaCO_3$$

The sodium hydroxide was heated with animal fats or vegetable oils to produce soap and glycerol (sometimes called glycerin on labels of commercial products) as shown in Figure 21.2. The glycerol by-product is a useful, oily liquid found in many hand creams and lotions (see Section 21.6).

Note that a **soap** is a salt of a long-chain carboxylic acid (Chapter 9). An example is sodium tetradecanoate (commonly called sodium myristate), $CH_3CH_2CH_2CH_2CH_2CH_2CH_2CH_2CH_2CH_2CH_2CH_2CH_2COO^-Na^+$. To save space, the CH_2 groups can be lumped together within parentheses to give a shorter formula, $CH_3(CH_2)_{12}COO^-Na^+$.

American pioneers made soap in a process similar to that used by ancient people. They did not have sodium hydroxide, so instead filled a large pot with wood ashes and allowed water to trickle down through the ashes, dissolving the basic compounds in the ashes. These compounds were mostly potassium carbonate and

▶ **Figure 21.2** Soap can be made by reacting animal fat or vegetable oil with sodium hydroxide. Vegetable oils, with unsaturated carbon chains, generally produce softer soaps. Coconut oil, with shorter carbon chains, yields soap that is more soluble in water.

Q: Write the structure of triolein, the oil in which all three fatty acid residues are from oleic acid.

Typical fat

3 NaOH

Soap (fatty acid salts)

Glycerol

potassium hydroxide. Using a pot of ash gave rise to the term *potash* for the mixture of these compounds. The potash solution was added to animal fat in a huge iron kettle, and the mixture was cooked over a wood fire for several hours. The soap rose to the surface and, on cooling, solidified. The glycerol remained as a liquid on the bottom of the pot. Both the glycerol and the soap often contained unreacted alkali, which was a strong irritant on the skin since its pH was often over 10. The harshness of Grandma's lye soap is not just a myth.

In modern commercial soap-making, fats and oils are often hydrolyzed to fatty acids and glycerol with superheated steam. The fatty acids are then neutralized to make soap. Hand soaps usually contain additives such as dyes, perfumes, creams, oils, or even compounds with deodorizing properties. Scouring soaps contain abrasives such as silica and pumice. Some soaps have air blown in before they solidify to lower their density so that they float.

Potassium soaps are softer than sodium soaps and produce a finer lather. They are used alone, or in combination with sodium soaps, in some liquid soaps and shaving creams. However, beware that most liquids for hand cleaning contain synthetic detergents, despite the labels, which may read "liquid hand soap."

How Soap Works

Dirt and grime usually adhere to skin, clothing, and other surfaces because they are combined with greases and oils—body oils, cooking fats, lubricating greases, and other similar substances—that act a little like sticky glues. Because oils are not miscible with water, washing with water alone does little good.

A soap molecule has a dual nature. One end is ionic and, therefore, **hydrophilic** (water attracting). The rest of the molecule is a hydrocarbon chain and therefore nonpolar and **hydrophobic** (water repelling). Figure 21.3 shows a typical soap. The hydrophilic "head" dissolves in water, while the hydrophobic "tail" dissolves in nonpolar substances, such as oils.

The cleansing action of soap is illustrated in Figure 21.4. A spherical collection of molecules like that shown in the figure is called a **micelle**. The hydrocarbon tails stick in the oil, with their ionic heads remaining in the aqueous phase. The formation of micelles breaks the oil into tiny droplets and disperses them throughout the

(a) $CH_3CH_2CH_2CH_2CH_2CH_2CH_2CH_2CH_2CH_2CH_2CH_2CH_2CH_2CH_2COO^- Na^+$

        Hydrocarbon tail   Ionic head

(b)

(c)

(d)

◀ **Figure 21.3** Representations of sodium palmitate, a soap. (a) Condensed formula. (b) Structural formula. (c) Space-filling model. (d) Schematic representation of the palmitate anion.

1. How does soap remove that grease from my shirt and hands?

Soap molecules have a long hydrocarbon end that is nonpolar so it attracts nonpolar molecules, such as grease. The other end of the molecule is ionic (usually negatively charged), so it is attracted to the positive "poles" of polar water molecules. Large, spherical masses, called *micelles*, consisting of many soap molecules surrounding a nonpolar one, are pulled down the drain by the myriad water molecules.

solution. The droplets don't coalesce because of the repulsion of the charged groups (the carboxyl anions) on their surfaces. The oil and water form an *emulsion*, with soap acting as the *emulsifying agent*. Because the oil no longer is "glued" to hair, skin, or any other "dirty" surface, the dirt can be removed easily. Any agent, including

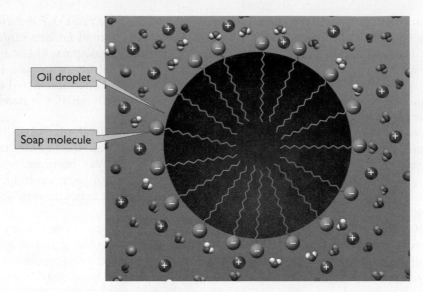

▲ **Figure 21.4** The cleansing action of soap is visualized in this diagram of a soap micelle. A tiny oil droplet is suspended in water because the hydrophobic hydrocarbon tails of soap molecules are immersed in the oil, while their hydrophilic ionic heads extend into the water. Attraction between the water and the ionic ends of the soap molecules carries the oil droplet into the water.

soap, that stabilizes the suspension of nonpolar substances in water—such as oil and grease— is called a **surface-active agent** (or **surfactant**).

Disadvantages and Advantages of Soap

The major disadvantage of soap is that it doesn't work well in hard water. Hard water contains calcium, magnesium, and iron ions. Soap anions react with these metal ions to form greasy, insoluble curds (Figure 21.5). With calcium ions, the reaction is

$$2\ CH_3CH_2CH_2CH_2CH_2CH_2CH_2CH_2CH_2CH_2CH_2CH_2CH_2CH_2CH_2COO^-Na^+(aq) + Ca^{2+}(aq) \longrightarrow$$
A sodium soap (soluble)
$$(CH_3CH_2CH_2CH_2CH_2CH_2CH_2CH_2CH_2CH_2CH_2CH_2CH_2CH_2CH_2COO^-)_2Ca^{2+}(s) + 2\ Na^+(aq)$$
A calcium soap (insoluble)

▶ **Figure 21.5** Sudsing quality of hard water versus soft water. *From left*: Detergent in hard water, soap in hard water, detergent in soft water, and soap in soft water. Note that the sudsing of the detergent is about the same in both hard and soft water. Note also that there is little sudsing and that insoluble material is formed when soap is used in hard water.

Q: *In acidic solutions, soaps are converted to free fatty acids, which have no detergent action and are also insoluble in water and separate as a greasy scum. Write the equation for this reaction, using sodium stearate as the soap.*

Detergent in hard water
Detergent works in hard or soft water

Detergent in soft water
Detergent works in hard or soft water

Soap curd in hard water

Soap works well only in soft water

These deposits make up the familiar ring around the bathtub. Decades ago, freshly washed hair was left sticky, and soap-laundered clothing took on a "tattletale gray." For cleaning clothes and hair, soap has been largely replaced by synthetic detergents.

Soap does have some advantages. It is an excellent cleanser in soft water, it is relatively nontoxic, it is derived from renewable resources (animal fats and vegetable oils), and it is biodegradable.

Water Softeners

To alleviate the problem of sticky precipitates in bathtubs and to improve the sudsing action of soaps, a variety of water-softening agents and devices may be used. Water softeners are used to remove ions of calcium, magnesium, and iron, the ions that make water hard. An effective water softener is washing soda, sodium carbonate ($Na_2CO_3 \cdot 10\,H_2O$). Carbonate ions react with water molecules to raise the pH and thus prevent the precipitation of fatty acids.

$$CO_3^{2-}(aq) + H_2O(l) \longleftrightarrow HCO_3^-(aq) + OH^-(aq)$$

The carbonate ions also react with the ions that cause hard water and remove them as insoluble salts.

$$Mg^{2+}(aq) + CO_3^{2-}(aq) \longrightarrow MgCO_3(s)$$
$$Ca^{2+}(aq) + CO_3^{2-}(aq) \longrightarrow CaCO_3(s)$$

Sodium phosphate (Na_3PO_4, commonly called *trisodium phosphate*, or *TSP*) is another water-softening agent. The phosphate ions form precipitates with hard water ions such as magnesium ions, shown below.

$$2\,PO_4^{3-}(aq) + 3\,Mg^{2+}(aq) \longrightarrow Mg_3(PO_4)_2(s)$$

Water-softening tanks are widely used in homes and businesses. These tanks contain an insoluble polymeric resin that usually consists of complex sodium aluminosilicates called *zeolites*. The resin attracts and holds calcium, magnesium, and iron ions to its surface, releasing sodium ions into the water and thus softening it (Figure 21.6).

Na⁺
Ca²⁺
Fe²⁺
Mg²⁺

◀ **Figure 21.6** Water softeners work by *ion exchange*. Hard water going into the softener contains doubly charged cations—Ca^{2+}, Mg^{2+}, and Fe^{2+}. Those ions attach to the ion-exchange resin, and Na^+ (violet) ions are released. The water leaving the softener contains mostly Na^+ ions.

Q: If one mole each of Ca^{2+}, Mg^{2+}, and Fe^{2+} is present in hard water, how many moles of Na^+ will be released from the ion-exchange resin?

This process is called *ion exchange*:

$$Ca^{2+}(aq) + Na_2Al_2Si_2O_8(s) \longrightarrow 2\,Na^+(aq) + CaAl_2Si_2O_8(s)$$

After a period of use, the resin becomes saturated with hard-water ions and must be regenerated by adding salt (NaCl) to replace its sodium ions. Note that water filters such as Brita® that attach to a faucet usually contain activated carbon, which absorbs dissolved organic substances that give water an off taste; most do not remove hard-water ions.

SELF-ASSESSMENT Questions

1. Which of the following is NOT a soap?
   a. sodium stearate
   b. sodium palmitate
   c. sodium myristate
   d. sodium phosphate —

2. Which of the following is a soap formula?
   a. $CH_3(CH_2)_{12}CH_2OH$
   b. $CH_3(CH_2)_{12}COOH$
   c. $CH_3(CH_2)_{14}COONa$ —
   d. $CH_3(CH_2)_{10}SO_3Na$

3. Which of the following does NOT function as a water softener?
   a. sodium carbonate
   b. sodium chloride —
   c. sodium phosphate
   d. sodium zeolite

4. The hydrocarbon part of a soap molecule
   a. is attracted to nonpolar oil —
   b. is repelled by nonpolar oil
   c. is attracted to polar water
   d. is repelled by polar oil

5. The ionic end of a soap molecule is
   a. hydrophobic
   b. hydrophilic —
   c. polar covalent
   d. acidic

6. Soap removes oily dirt by forming
   a. an acidic solution
   b. curds
   c. fat globules
   d. micelles —

7. In the cleansing action of soap, the hydrocarbon tail
   a. intermingles with the oily dirt, while the ionic head interacts with the water —
   b. intermingles with the water, while the ionic head interacts with the oily dirt
   c. remains inert and takes no part in the process
   d. separates from the ionic head and dissolves in the oily dirt

8. Which of the following ions does not contribute to making water hard?
   a. Ca^{2+}
   b. Fe^{2+}
   c. Mg^{2+}
   d. Na^+ —

9. In hard water, metal ions combine with soap anions, and the soap
   a. cleans about as well as in soft water
   b. dissolves completely but doesn't clean
   c. forms suds but doesn't clean
   d. precipitates and doesn't clean —

Answers: 1, d; 2, c; 3, b; 4, a; 5, b; 6, d; 7, a; 8, d; 9, d

21.2 Synthetic Detergents

Learning Objectives › List the structures, advantages, and disadvantages of synthetic detergents. › Classify surfactants as amphoteric, anionic, cationic, and nonionic, and describe how they are used in various detergent formulations.

A technological approach to the problems associated with soap was the development of new synthetic detergents. Molecules of synthetic detergents are enough like those of soap to have the same cleaning action but different enough to resist the effects of acids and hard water. The raw materials for soap manufacture were scarce and expensive during and immediately after World War II. The synthetic detergent industry developed rapidly in the postwar period.

ABS Detergents: Nonbiodegradable

Within a few years of the war's end, cheap synthetic detergents, made from petroleum products, were widely available. Alkylbenzenesulfonate (ABS) detergents were made from propylene ($CH_2{=}CHCH_3$), benzene (C_6H_6), and sulfuric acid (H_2SO_4). The resulting sulfonic acid (RSO_3H) was neutralized with a base, usually sodium carbonate, to yield the final product.

Note that the detergent molecule is much like a soap molecule. It, too, has a long hydrocarbon tail and an ionic head, but in this case, it is $-SO_3^-$, not $-CO_2^-$. Micelles still form around nonpolar grease droplets, and the ionic ends are attracted to polar water molecules (Figure 21.4). The significant difference is that the sulfonate

(a) (b)

◄ **Figure 21.7** ABS detergents degrade very slowly in nature. Their use led to foam on rivers such as that on the Bogotá River in Colombia (a). They also caused contaminated water from a ground-water source to foam as it came from the tap (b).

detergents would not form insoluble precipitates in hard water. As Figure 21.5 shows, the cleansing action of a synthetic detergent is little affected by hard water. Detergents work well in acidic water as well.

Sales of ABS detergents soared. For a decade or more, nearly everyone was happy, but suds began to accumulate in sewage treatment plants. Foam piled high in rivers, and in some areas, a head of foam even appeared on drinking water (Figure 21.7). The new problem was that the branched-chain structure of ABS molecules was not readily broken down by the microorganisms in sewage treatment plants, and the groundwater supply was threatened. Public outcries caused laws to be passed and industries to change their processes. Biodegradable detergents were quickly put on the market, and nonbiodegradable detergents were banned.

LAS Detergents: Biodegradable

Biodegradable detergents called *linear alkylsulfonates (LASs)* have a linear chain of carbon atoms, rather than the branched chains of the ABS detergents.

$$\text{\raisebox{0pt}{$\diagdown$}}-\!\!\!\!\bigcirc\!\!\!\!-SO_3^-\,Na^+$$

Microorganisms can break down LAS molecules by producing enzymes that degrade the molecule two (and only two) carbon atoms at a time (Figure 21.8). The branched chain of ABS molecules blocked this enzyme action, preventing their degradation. Thus, technology solved the problem of foaming rivers.

Surfactants are used in thousands of products, not just in cleaning products. A small amount of lecithin, an edible surfactant, is often added to chocolate in the manufacturing process. The lecithin helps the chocolate disperse on the tongue more easily. The chocolate tastes "more chocolatey."

$$CH_3CH_2CH_2CH_2CH_2CH_2CH_2CH_2CH_2CH_2CH\!-\!\!\bigcirc\!\!-SO_3^-\,Na^+$$
$$|$$
$$CH_3$$

$$CH_3CHCH_2CHCH_2CHCH_2CH\!-\!\!\bigcirc\!\!-SO_3^-\,Na^+$$
$$\quad|\qquad|\qquad|\qquad|$$
$$\quad CH_3\;\;CH_3\;\;CH_3\;\;CH_3$$

(a) (b)

▲ **Figure 21.8** Microorganisms such as *Escherichia coli*, shown in (a) magnified 42,500 times by scanning electron microscopy, are able to degrade LAS detergents. They can readily metabolize these detergents (b), removing two carbon atoms at a time from each molecule. It takes them much longer to break down the branched chains of the ABS molecules.

Laundry Detergent Formulations

Detergent products used in homes and commercial laundries usually contain a variety of ingredients. The main component is a surfactant, but other additives include builders, brighteners, fabric softeners, and other substances that lessen the redeposition of dirt.

Surfactants are generally classified according to the ionic charge, if any, at one end of the long molecule. Soaps and ABS and LAS detergents are all **anionic surfactants**; they have a negative charge on one end of the molecule. Other common categories of anionic surfactants are the alkyl sulfates, such as sodium dodecyl sulfate (often called sodium lauryl sulfate on commercial product labels), and the alcohol ethoxysulfates (AESs). An ionic detergent is always associated with a small ion of opposite charge, called a *counter ion*. The counter ion for most anionic surfactants is Na^+.

$$CH_3(CH_2)_nOSO_3^-Na^+$$
An alkyl sulfate
$n = 11$ to 13

$$CH_3(CH_2)_mO(CH_2CH_2O)_nSO_3^-Na^+$$
An alcohol ethoxysulfate
$m = 6$ to 13, $n = 7$ to 13

Anionic surfactants are used in laundry and hand dishwashing detergents, household cleaners, and personal cleansing products, such as shampoo. They have excellent cleaning properties and generally make a lot of suds.

As the name indicates, **nonionic surfactants** have no electrical charge. They are low sudsing and not affected by water hardness. They work well on most soils and are typically used in laundry and automatic dishwasher formulations. The most widely used nonionic surfactants are the *alcohol ethoxylates*.

$$CH_3(CH_2)_mO(CH_2CH_2O)_nH$$
An alcohol ethoxylate
$m = 6$ to 13, $n = 7$ to 13

Cationic surfactants have a positive charge on the active part. These surfactants are not particularly good detergents, but they have a germicidal action. They are therefore used as cleansers and disinfectants in the food and dairy industries and as the sanitizing ingredient in some household cleaners. The most common cationic surfactants are *quaternary ammonium salts* (or quats), so called because they have four hydrocarbon groups attached to a nitrogen atom that bears a positive charge.

$$CH_3(CH_2)_nCH_2N^+(CH_3)_3Cl^-$$
A quaternary ammonium salt
$n = 10$ to 16

Sometimes, cationic surfactants are used along with nonionic surfactants. Cationic surfactants are seldom used with anionic ones because the ions of opposite charge tend to clump together and precipitate from solution, destroying the detergent action of both.

Amphoteric surfactants carry both a positive and a negative charge. They react with both acids and bases and are noted for their mildness, sudsing, and stability. They are used in personal cleansing products such as shampoos for babies and in household cleaning products such as liquid handwashing soaps. Typical amphoteric surfactants are compounds called *betaines*.

$$CH_3(CH_2)_nCH_2NH_2^+CH_2COO^-$$
A betaine
$n = 10$ to 16

CONCEPTUAL Example 21.1   Classification of Surfactants

Classify each of the following surfactants as anionic, cationic, nonionic, or amphoteric.

  a. $CH_3(CH_2)_{14}CH_2N^+(CH_3)_3\,Cl^-$
  b. $CH_3(CH_2)_{13}O(CH_2CH_2O)_7SO_3^-Na^+$
  c. $CH_3(CH_2)_{12}CH_2NH_2^+CH_2COO^-$
  d. $CH_3(CH_2)_{12}CON(CH_2CH_2OH)_2$

Solution

a. The N atom of the active part bears a positive charge, making this a cationic surfactant. (The counter ion is Cl^-.)

b. There is a negative charge on the $-SO_3$ group of the active part, making this an anionic surfactant. (The counter ion is Na^+.)

c. This substance has both a positive charge (on the N atom) and a negative charge (on the $-COO^-$ group), making this an amphoteric surfactant.

d. This substance has neither a positive charge nor a negative charge, so it is a nonionic surfactant.

■ **EXERCISE 21.1**

Classify each of the following surfactants as anionic, cationic, nonionic, or amphoteric.

a. $CH_3(CH_2)_8-C_6H_4-O(CH_2CH_2O)_9H$

b. $CH_3(CH_2)_{12}CH_2N^+(CH_3)_3Cl^-$

c. $CH_3(CH_2)_9-C_6H_4-SO_3^-\ Na^+$

d. $CH_3(CH_2)_{14}COO^-\ K^+$

Any substance added to a surfactant to increase its detergency is called a **builder**. Most builders are water softeners that reduce water hardness. Sodium citrate ($Na_3C_6H_5O_7$) and complex phosphates such as sodium tripolyphosphate ($Na_5P_3O_{10}$) and sodium hexametaphosphate [$(NaPO_3)_6)$] tie up Ca^{2+} and Mg^{2+} ions in soluble complexes, a process called *sequestration*. Sometimes, mixtures of builders enhance cleaning more than either component alone. A major problem with builders is the eutrophication of lakes by phosphates (Chapter 14). Several state and local governments have banned the sale of detergents containing phosphates.

Sodium carbonate acts by reacting with hard-water ions to form an insoluble substance (Section 21.1). However, washing machines can be harmed by the $CaCO_3$ and $MgCO_3$ precipitates. These builders also produce a mild alkalinity, which assists cleaning, especially of acidic soils and stains. Zeolites (see Section 21.1 regarding water softeners) also may be used as builders, but in this case the calcium and magnesium ions are held in suspension by the zeolites rather than being precipitated (Figure 21.9).

Almost all detergent formulations include fluorescent dyes called **optical brighteners**. After white clothing is worn quite a few times, it often looks yellowish and drab. Optical brighteners absorb ultraviolet rays in sunlight and reemit that energy primarily as blue light. This blue light both camouflages the yellowish color and increases the amount of visible light reaching the eye, giving the garment the appearance of being "whiter than white". Brighteners are also used in cosmetics, paper, soap, plastics, and other products.

Optical brighteners may cause skin rashes in some people. Their effect on lakes and streams is largely unknown, despite the large amounts entering our waterways. The only benefit of these compounds is visual.

Early laundry detergent preparations were powders, but liquid laundry detergent formulations now command most of the market. Laundry detergent formulations two or three times more concentrated than in the past are often called "ultra" detergents. Liquid products may also have a solvent such as ethanol, isopropyl alcohol, or propylene glycol to help prevent separation of the other components and to help dissolve greasy soils. Some liquid laundry detergents use sodium citrate, sodium silicate, sodium carbonate, or zeolites as builders, or they may include bleaches and colorants.

Some formulations are *unbuilt*—high in surfactants but containing no builders. Linear alkylbenzene sulfonate (LAS) surfactants are the cheapest surfactants used in liquid laundry detergents. In unbuilt formulations, they usually are in the form of the sodium salt or the triethanolamine [$N(CH_2CH_2OH)_3$] salt.

$$CH_3(CH_2)_9CH(CH_3)-C_6H_4-SO_3^-\ HN^+(CH_2CH_2OH)_3$$

Triethanolamine salt of an LAS

It DOES Matter!

Using more than the recommended amount of dishwasher detergent generally does not result in cleaner dishes. Moreover, the higher pH leads to faster etching of the glass in the dishwasher.

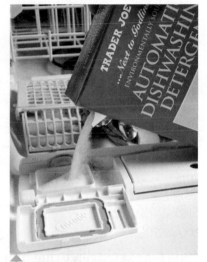

▲ **Figure 21.9** Zeolites used in detergent formulations trap positive ions such as Ca^{2+} and Mg^{2+} in their cagelike structures and hold the ions in suspension in the wash water.

In built varieties, LAS surfactants are often present as the potassium salt.

Other popular surfactants for liquid formulations are alcohol ethoxysulfonates (AESs). Alcohol ethoxylates have the unusual property of being more soluble in cold water than in hot, which makes them particularly suitable for cold-water laundering.

Some detergent formulations include *lipases* (enzymes that work on lipids) to help remove fats and oils, *amylases* (enzymes that work on starches) to help remove starchy stains such as pasta, and *proteases* (enzymes that work on proteins) to aid in the removal of protein stains such as blood.

Dishwashing Detergents

2. Why can't hand dishwashing liquid be used in a dishwasher?
The surfactants in hand dishwashing liquids generally form lots of suds. In a dishwasher, those suds would fill the chamber and inhibit the sprays of water that do much of the cleaning. Removal of suds from glassware and plastic or ceramic plates would require much more water in the rinse cycles. Use a product specifically designed for an automatic dishwasher.

Although colloquially called "dish soap," liquid cleaning formulations for washing dishes by hand generally contain at least one LAS detergent as the main active ingredient. Some use nonionic surfactants such as cocamido DEA, an amide made from a fatty acid and diethanolamine [$HN(CH_2CH_2OH)_2$]. Dishwashing liquids may also contain enzymes to help remove greases and protein stains, fragrances, preservatives, solvents, bleaches, and colorants.

$$CH_3(CH_2)_nCON(CH_2CH_2OH)_2$$

Cocamido DEA

$$n = 8 \text{ to } 12$$

Detergents for automatic dishwashers are quite different from dishwashing liquids. They are strongly alkaline and should never be used for hand dishwashing. They contain sodium tripolyphosphate ($Na_5P_3O_{10}$), sodium carbonate, sodium metasilicate (Na_2SiO_3), sodium sulfate, a chlorine or oxygen bleach, and only a small amount of surfactant, usually a nonionic type. Some contain sodium hydroxide, a strong base that attacks skin. They depend mainly on their strong alkalis, heat, and the vigorous agitation of the machine for cleaning. Dishes that are washed repeatedly in an automatic dishwasher may be permanently etched by these strong alkalis, which is why delicate crystal stemware is often washed by hand.

SELF-ASSESSMENT Questions

1. The critical parts of a molecule used to mimic the function of a soap are:
   a. a benzene ring in a long hydrocarbon chain and a non-polar end
   b. a long hydrocarbon chain with —OH at the one end
   c. a long hydrocarbon chain with an anionic end
   d. a long hydrocarbon chain with a hydrophilic end

2. Which of the following are not biodegradable?
   a. LAS detergents
   b. ABS detergents
   c. sodium lauryl sulfate
   d. quaternary ammonium salts

3. Which of the following is an LAS detergent?
   a. $CH_3(CH_2)_{10}CH_2N^+(CH_3)_3Cl^-$
   b. $CH_3(CH_2)_{11}OSO_3^-Na^+$
   c. $CH_3(CH_2)_9CH(CH_3)C_6H_4SO_3^-Na^+$
   d. $CH_3(CH_2)_8O(OCH_2CH_2)_9H$

4. Hard-water ions react with carbonate ions to form products such as
   a. $CaCO_3(s)$
   b. $Ca(OH)_2(s)$
   c. $Na_2CO_3(s)$
   d. soap curds

5. When it softens water, an ion-exchange resin retains
   a. magnesium ions
   b. chloride ions
   c. hydroxide ions
   d. sodium ions

6. An optical brightener converts ultraviolet light to
   a. black light
   b. blue light
   c. heat
   d. yellow light

7. What kind of surfactant is cocamido DEA, $CH_3(CH_2)_{10}CON(CH_2CH_2OH)_2$, which is used in hand dishwashing detergents?
   a. amphoteric   b. anionic
   c. cationic   d. nonionic

8. Which of the following is the most likely to irritate the skin?
   a. detergent for automatic dishwashers
   b. liquid handwashing soap
   c. liquid dishwashing detergent
   d. powdered laundry detergent

9. Which of the following cleaning agents is likely to have the highest pH?
   a. a liquid dish detergent for hand washing
   b. a liquid laundry detergent
   c. an automatic dishwasher detergent
   d. an LAS detergent

Answers: 1, d; 2, b; 3, b; 4, a; 5, a; 6, b; 7, d; 8, a; 9, c

21.3 Laundry Auxiliaries: Softeners and Bleaches

Learning Objectives ❭ Identify a fabric softener from its structure, and describe its action. ❭ Name two types of laundry bleaches, and describe how they work.

Section 21.2 discussed cationic surfactants, whose active part is a positive ion and which are often quaternary ammonium salts. The cations have four hydrocarbon groups attached to a nitrogen atom that bears a positive charge. One of the hydrocarbon groups is a long chain with 12 to 18 carbon atoms. The other three are small, usually methyl groups. An example of such a cationic surfactant is octadecyltrimethylammonium chloride. The chloride counter ion is not shown.

$$CH_3CH_2CH_2CH_2CH_2CH_2CH_2CH_2CH_2CH_2CH_2CH_2CH_2CH_2CH_2CH_2CH_2CH_2\overset{\overset{\displaystyle CH_3}{|}}{\underset{\underset{\displaystyle CH_3}{|}}{N^+}}-CH_3$$

Fabric Softeners

Another kind of quaternary salt with *two* long carbon chains and two smaller groups on a nitrogen atom is used as a fabric softener. An example is dioctadecyldimethylammonium chloride. This compound is strongly adsorbed by the fabric, forming a film one molecule thick on the surface. The long hydrocarbon chains lubricate the fibers, imparting increased flexibility and softness to the fabric.

$$CH_3CH_2CH_2CH_2CH_2CH_2CH_2CH_2CH_2CH_2CH_2CH_2CH_2CH_2CH_2CH_2CH_2CH_2-\overset{\overset{\displaystyle CH_3}{|}}{N^+}-CH_3$$
$$CH_3CH_2CH_2CH_2CH_2CH_2CH_2CH_2CH_2CH_2CH_2CH_2CH_2CH_2CH_2CH_2CH_2CH_2$$

Laundry Bleaches: Whiter Whites

Bleaches are oxidizing agents (Chapter 8) that remove colored stains from fabrics. Two main types of laundry bleaches are chlorine bleaches and oxygen bleaches. Most familiar liquid chlorine laundry bleaches (such as Clorox® and Purex®) are dilute solutions (usually about 6%) of sodium hypochlorite (NaOCl) that differ mainly in price. Hypochlorite bleaches release chlorine rapidly, and high concentrations of chlorine can damage fabrics. These bleaches work best on cotton clothing or towels. They do not work well on polyester fabrics, often causing yellowing rather than the desired whitening.

Other chlorine-based bleaches are available as a solid powder that releases chlorine slowly in water to minimize damage to fabrics. Trichloroisocyanuric acid, also known as trichlor or symclosene, is an example of a cyanurate-type bleach.

Oxygen bleaches usually contain sodium percarbonate ($2\,Na_2CO_3 \cdot 3\,H_2O_2$) or sodium perborate ($NaBO_2 \cdot H_2O_2$). As indicated by the formulas, these compounds are complexes of Na_2CO_3 or $NaBO_2$ and hydrogen peroxide (H_2O_2). In hot water, the hydrogen peroxide is liberated and acts as a strong oxidizing agent.

Borates are somewhat toxic. Perborate bleaches are less active than chlorine bleaches and require higher temperatures, higher alkalinity, and higher concentrations to do an equivalent job. They are used mainly for bleaching white, resin-treated, polyester–cotton fabrics, which last much longer with oxygen bleaching than with chlorine bleaching. Less toxic than the perborate bleaches, percarbonate bleaches are rapidly becoming the predominant type of oxygen bleach. Properly used, oxygen bleaches make fabrics whiter than do chlorine bleaches.

Bleaches work by acting on certain light-absorbing chemical groups, called *chromophores*, that cause a substance to be colored; most have a number of carbon-to-carbon double bonds that are attacked by the bleach. The oxidation of a chromophore can be written as:

3. Does putting more fabric softener in the washer make the fabrics even softer?

A very small amount of fabric softener gives a soft feeling to the laundry. Too much produces a coating that can make the laundry feel damp or waxy.

Symclosene

$$-CH=CH-\overset{\overset{\displaystyle O}{\|}}{C}-CH_2- \xrightarrow{[O]} -\overset{\overset{\displaystyle O}{\|}}{C}-OH + HO-\overset{\overset{\displaystyle O}{\|}}{C}-\overset{\overset{\displaystyle O}{\|}}{C}-CH_2-$$

Chromophore	Fragments
(colored)	(colorless)

Thus, the bleach does not actually remove the stain, but merely changes it to a colorless form. Sometimes not all of the stain is oxidized, and a very faint ghost of the original stain can be seen.

SELF-ASSESSMENT Questions

1. Which of the following could serve as a fabric softener?
   a. $CH_3(CH_2)_{10}CON(CH_2CH_2OH)_2$
   b. $CH_3(CH_2)_{10}CH_2N^+(CH_3)_3Cl^-$
   c. $CH_3(CH_2)_{16}CH_2N^+(CH_3)_3Cl^-$
   d. $CH_3(CH_2)_{16}CH_2N^+(CH_3)_2CH_2(CH_2)_{16}CH_3Cl^-$

2. To what class of compounds do most fabric softeners belong?
   a. amphoteric detergents
   b. anionic detergents
   c. nonionic detergents
   d. quaternary ammonium salts

3. Oxygen bleaches
   a. release hydrogen peroxide when placed in hot water
   b. release oxygen molecules to act as an oxidizing agent
   c. include borates and hypochlorites
   d. are mild, nontoxic chemicals

4. The main component (other than water) of a chlorine-based household bleach is
   a. NaOH   b. Cl_2 c. NH_4Cl d. NaOCl

5. Bleaches act by
   a. enhancing surfactant action
   b. opening active sites
   c. sequestering hard-water ions
   d. oxidizing chromophores

6. Which is not a disadvantage of powdered perborate bleaches?
   a. work best in concentrated solutions only
   b. don't work well with cotton fabrics
   c. are less active than chlorine bleaches
   d. require higher temperatures

Answers: 1, d; 2, d; 3, a; 4, d; 5, d; 6, b

21.4 All-Purpose and Special-Purpose Cleaning Products

Learning Objective ❯ List the major ingredient(s) (and their purposes) of some all-purpose cleaning products and some special-purpose cleaning products.

All-Purpose Cleaners

Various all-purpose cleaning products are available for use on walls, floors, countertops, appliances, and other tough, durable surfaces. Those for use in water solution may contain surfactants, sodium carbonate, ammonia, solvent-type grease cutters, disinfectants, bleaches, deodorants, and other ingredients. Some are great for certain jobs but not as good for others. They damage some surfaces but work especially well on others. Most important, they may be harmful when used improperly. Reading the labels is important.

Household ammonia solutions, straight from the bottle, are effective for loosening baked-on grease or burned-on food. Diluted with water, these solutions clean mirrors, windows, and other glass surfaces well. Mixed with detergent, ammonia rapidly removes wax from vinyl floor coverings. Ammonia vapors are highly irritating, so this cleanser should not be used in a closed room. Ammonia should not be used on asphalt tile, wood surfaces, or aluminum because it may stain, pit, or erode these materials.

Baking soda (sodium bicarbonate, $NaHCO_3$) straight from the box is a mild abrasive cleanser. It absorbs food odors to some extent, making it good for cleaning the inside of a refrigerator.

Vinegar (acetic acid) cuts grease film. Vinegar should not be used on marble, though, because it reacts with and dissolves the marble, pitting the surface.

The physical and chemical processes that clean a surface take some time. An often overlooked technique in cleaning is allowing the surface to soak. Plain water or dilute soap solution is an amazingly effective, cheap, and nonpolluting cleaner when it is simply sprayed on a surface and allowed to stand for a few minutes.

▲ Vinegar reacts with marble, pitting the surface. Carbon dioxide gas is given off, forming bubbles.

$$CaCO_3(s) + 2\ CH_3COOH(aq) \longrightarrow Ca^{2+}(aq) + 2\ CH_3COO^-(aq) + CO_2(g) + H_2O(l)$$

Marble   Vinegar

Hazards of Mixing Cleaners

Mixing bleach with other household chemicals can be quite dangerous. For example, mixing a hypochlorite bleach with hydrochloric acid produces poisonous chlorine gas.

$$2\,HCl(aq) + ClO^-(aq) \longrightarrow Cl^-(aq) + H_2O(l) + Cl_2(g)$$

Mixing bleach with toilet bowl cleaners that contain HCl is especially dangerous. Most bathrooms are small and poorly ventilated, so generating chlorine in such a limited space is hazardous. Chlorine can do enormous damage to the throat and the entire respiratory tract. If the concentration of chlorine in the air is high enough, it can kill.

Mixing bleach with ammonia is also extremely hazardous. Two of the gases produced are chloramine (NH_2Cl) and hydrazine (NH_2NH_2), both of which are quite toxic. *Never* mix bleach with other chemicals without specific directions to do so. In fact, it is a good rule not to mix any chemicals unless you know exactly what you are doing.

Special-Purpose Cleaners

Many highly specialized cleaning products are on the market. For metals, there are chrome cleaners, brass cleaners, copper cleaners, and silver cleaners. There are lime removers, rust removers, and grease removers, cleaners specifically for wood surfaces, for vinyl floor coverings, and for ceramic tile. Let's look at just a few of the special-purpose cleaners found in almost any home.

Toilet bowl cleaners are acids that dissolve the "lime" buildup that forms in toilet bowls. The residue is mainly calcium carbonate ($CaCO_3$), deposited from hard water and often discolored by iron compounds and fungal growth. Calcium carbonate is readily dissolved by acid. The solid crystalline cleaners usually contain sodium bisulfate ($NaHSO_4$), and the liquid cleaners include hydrochloric acid (HCl), citric acid, or some other acidic material.

If rust is the main discoloration, a product specifically meant for rust removal may be the best, which will usually contain oxalate $(C_2O_4)^{2-}$ ions to make a complex of the iron ions.

Most scouring powder cleansers contain an abrasive such as sodium carbonate, calcium carbonate, or silica (SiO_2) that scrapes soil from hard surfaces and a surfactant to dissolve grease. Some include a bleach. Scouring powders are mainly intended for removing stains from porcelain tubs and sinks. Such abrasive cleansers may scratch the finish on appliances, countertops, and metal utensils. They may even scratch the surfaces of sinks, toilet bowls, and bathtubs. Dirt gets into the scratches and makes cleaning even more difficult.

Glass cleaners are volatile liquids that evaporate without leaving a residue. A common glass cleaner is simply isopropyl alcohol (rubbing alcohol) diluted with water. Most commercial glass cleaners contain ammonia or vinegar for greater cleaning power.

When a kitchen drain becomes clogged, it is usually because the pipe has been blocked by grease. Drain cleaners often contain sodium hydroxide, either in the solid form or as a concentrated liquid. The sodium hydroxide reacts with the water in the pipe to generate heat, which melts much of the grease. The sodium hydroxide then reacts with some of the grease, converting it to soap, which is easier to remove than the grease. Some products also contain bits of aluminum metal that react with the sodium hydroxide solution to form hydrogen gas, which bubbles out of the clogged area of the drain, creating a stirring action.

Bathtub or shower drains are often clogged with hair, so the sodium hydroxide in the drain cleaner, like all bases, attacks the protein-based hair and breaks it apart. Many liquid drain cleaners contain bleach (NaOCl) as well. The best drain cleaner is prevention: Don't pour grease down the kitchen sink, and try to keep hair out of the

$$H_2C-COOH$$
$$HO-\underset{|}{\overset{|}{C}}-COOH$$
$$H_2C-COOH$$

Citric acid

You can make your own glass cleaner. Put about 1.6 L of cold water into a 1-gal bucket. Carefully add 60 mL of sudsy ammonia solution and 240 mL of isopropyl (rubbing) alcohol. Mix well and pour the solution into clean spray bottles. Add 1 or 2 drops of blue food coloring if you want your cleaner to look like a popular name-brand window cleaner. (Adapted from *How to Clean and Care for Practically Anything*, Yonkers, NY: Consumer Reports Special Publications, 2002.)

bathtub drain. If a drain does get plugged, a mechanical device such as a plumber's snake is often a better choice than a chemical drain cleaner.

The active ingredient in most oven cleaners is sodium hydroxide. Several popular products are dispensed as an aerosol foam. The greasy deposits on oven walls are converted to soaps when they react with the sodium hydroxide. The resulting mixture can then be washed off with a wet sponge. (Wear rubber gloves, because sodium hydroxide is extremely caustic and damaging to the skin. Wearing safety goggles to protect the eyes from spray is also recommended.)

A hand sanitizer is useful when there is no water available for hand washing. Most hand sanitizers contain a high concentration of alcohol, which kills bacteria and evaporates rapidly during use, leaving the hands clean and dry. However, alcohol is flammable, so care should be taken around flames. A surfactant, often a quaternary ammonium salt, provides additional germicidal properties, and a thickening agent makes the sanitizer easier to spread over the hands. Triclosan is the active germicide in some products. Hand sanitizers protect for a limited time. They must be applied several times during the day to continue to kill bacteria. Nonetheless, using a hand sanitizer is a convenient way to minimize exposure during flu season.

Do-it-yourselfers and garage mechanics often use a waterless hand cleaner to remove grease and grime from their hands. Like hand sanitizers, these hand cleaners do not need water to work. In fact, they work best if applied without water at first. Most waterless hand cleaners contain lanolin (Section 21.5), plus an oil such as oil of lemons or oranges and a surfactant that thickens the mixture into a creamy emulsion. Pumice (powdered volcanic ash) is often added to help loosen the dirt from the creases and folds of the skin. The oil acts as a solvent for the grease on the hands, and the surfactant keeps the oil and grease suspended so that it can be wiped off with a towel.

"Green" and "Natural" Cleaners

Many cleaning products marketed for home use are claimed to be "natural" or "green" and thus "safer to use" than traditional products. Consumer choices are hampered by lack of a standard definition or federal oversight of green cleaners. Manufacturers do not have to list all the ingredients because doing so could disclose trade secrets. There are 84,000 chemical compounds in the EPA's inventory, and the EPA requires manufacturers to provide only a caution of toxicity. Products claiming to be green can contain harmful substances. For example, a solvent made with a natural compound called *limonene*, derived from orange peels, is combustible and can irritate the skin and eyes.

In general, green products have more ingredients derived from plants. If scented, they usually employ a natural scent such as citrus or lavender. Green substances derived from corn or soy are common. One useful example is the ester ethyl lactate ($CH_3CHOHCOOCH_2CH_3$); both the alcohol (ethanol) and the carboxylic acid (lactic acid) from which the ester is made can be produced from corn. Ethyl lactate dissolves many different substances and has a low volatility, thus contributing little to air pollution. It also degrades readily in the environment.

You can evaluate green cleaners yourself; see Collaborative Group Project 6.

SELF-ASSESSMENT Questions

1. The most dangerous mixture of cleaning agents, because of the release of a toxic gas, is
   a. rubbing alcohol and ammonia
   b. rubbing alcohol and vinegar
   c. acidic toilet cleaner and bleach
   d. bleach and rubbing alcohol

2. Household ammonia can be used safely for all of the following *except*
   a. cleaning aluminum
   b. loosening baked-on grease
   c. polishing mirrors
   d. wax removal

3. Vinegar can be used safely for all of the following *except*
   a. cutting grease
   b. dissolving mineral deposits
   c. polishing marble surfaces
   d. removing soap scum

4. Baking soda (sodium bicarbonate) can be used safely for all of the following *except*
   a. deodorizing a carpet
   b. deodorizing a refrigerator
   c. neutralizing acids
   d. neutralizing bleach

5. If you mix ammonia solution with vinegar, the products are
   a. a better toilet cleaner   b. a salt solution ←
   c. a good solution for cleaning metals
   d. a surfactant effective on lime deposits

6. Mixing hypochlorite bleach and ammonia produces
   a. ammonium hypochlorite   b. a more effective cleaner
   c. a surfactant   d. toxic gases ←

7. Lime (CaCO₃) deposits in toilet bowls can be removed by treatment with
   a. NaOCl   b. NaCl   c. HCl ←   d. NaOH

8. The most effective way to keep drains open is to
   a. avoid letting grease and hair get in them ←
   b. convert grease to soap before putting it down a drain
   c. treat them once a week with NaOCl
   d. treat them twice a month with NaOH

Answers: 1. c; 2. a; 3. c; 4. d; 5. b; 6. d; 7. c; 8. a

21.5 Solvents, Paints, and Waxes

Learning Objectives ❯ Identify compounds used in solvents and paints, and explain their purposes. ❯ Identify waxes by their structure.

Of the thousands of chemicals available for use in the home, three common categories are solvents, paints, and waxes.

Solvents

Solvents are used in the home to remove paint, varnish, adhesives, waxes, and other materials, from surfaces or even from skin, if paint is spilled on skin. "Turpentine" is a mixture of liquids obtained from pine trees. Petroleum solvents, called petroleum distillates or "spirits" on labels, are also added to some all-purpose cleansers as grease cutters (Figure 21.10). They dissolve grease readily but, like gasoline, are highly flammable and deadly when swallowed. The lungs become saturated with hydrocarbon vapors, fill with fluid, and fail to function.

Most organic solvents used around the home are volatile and flammable. Many have toxic fumes, and nearly all are narcotic at high concentrations. Such solvents should be used only with adequate ventilation and never around a flame. Be sure to read—and heed—all precautions before you use any solvent. Gasoline should not be used for cleaning. It is too hazardous in too many ways.

A troubling problem connected with household solvents is the practice of inhaling fumes to get "high." The popularity of solvent sniffing seems to be related mainly to peer pressure, especially among young teenagers. Long-term sniffing can cause permanent damage to vital organs, especially the lungs. There can be irreversible brain damage, and some individuals have died of heart failure while sniffing solvents.

Paints

Paint is a broad term used to cover a wide variety of products—lacquers, enamels, varnishes, oil-base coatings, and a number of different acrylic- or latex-base finishes. Any or all of these materials can be found in any home. A paint contains three basic ingredients: a pigment, a binder, and a solvent. A pigment is a solid substance that is insoluble in water; it may be white or colored.

The history of paint dates back to the beginnings of human civilization. In 2011, grinding tools and some ground red ochre pigment were discovered in abalone shells in Blombos Cave in South Africa and dated to 100,000 B.C.E. Cave paintings have been found in Europe and Africa that depict animals and cultural activities of prehistoric peoples. Since the Middle Ages, artists have used crushed minerals as pigments mixed with natural plant oils to create paintings. Until fairly recently, relatively few pigments were available as colorants. Many were oxides or hydroxides of iron, which were called "ochres" or "umbers," including yellow and red ochre, or burnt and raw umber. Green pigments were made of chromium oxides or copper compounds. Blues were more difficult to find; ground lapis lazuli was the best but rarest source of blue pigment. A red pigment called alizarin was obtained from the roots of a plant called madder or from crushed cochineal insects. Even today, most of these colored pigments are available in art stores.

▲ **Figure 21.10** Cleansers that contain petroleum distillates have labels warning of their combustibility and of the hazard of swallowing them.

4. Should I worry about lead-based paint if I purchase a classic home built in the 1950s?
Yes and no. Flaking paint in older homes can be inadvertently inhaled or ingested by small children or even adults, with serious health results. However, federal laws require an analysis of the paint in homes built before 1978 to determine if any lead-based paint was used. When you purchase a home, you should receive an analysis of the paint used in the home to be sure it is lead-free.

For purposes of painting walls or other surfaces, "white lead" [basic lead carbonate, $2\,PbCO_3 \cdot Pb(OH)_2$] was the white pigment of choice for most paints until the 1970s. Its use was banned in 1977, and it has been replaced by titanium dioxide (TiO_2). Titanium dioxide is a brilliant white nontoxic pigment with great stability and excellent hiding power. All ordinary paints are pigmented with titanium dioxide. For colored paint, small amounts of manufactured colored pigments or dyes are added to the white base mixture to create an almost unlimited number of tints.

The binder, or film former, is the substance that binds the pigment particles together and holds them on the painted surface. The most ancient binder consisted of egg yolks mixed with water. In oil paints, the binder is usually tung oil or linseed oil; cleanup requires mineral spirits or turpentine. In water-based paints, the binder is a latex-based polymer. Most interior paints have polyvinyl acetate as the binder, and spills can be washed off with water. Artists' watercolor binders usually contain gum arabic, obtained from acacia trees. Exterior water-based paints use viscous acrylic polymers, called *resins*, as binders. Acrylic latex paints are much more resistant to rain and sunlight.

The solvent in paint keeps the paint fluid until it is applied to a surface. The solvent might be an alcohol, a hydrocarbon, an ester, a ketone (or some mixture thereof), or water.

Paint may also contain additives such as a drier (or activator) to make the paint dry faster, a fungicide to resist mold growth, a thickener to increase the paint's viscosity, an anti-skinning agent to keep the paint from forming a skin inside the can, and a surfactant to stabilize the mixture and keep the pigment particles separated.

Paint, whether it is enamel, oil-based, or latex, hardens in different ways. Oil-based paints commonly use linseed oil that oxidizes to form a hard surface. Lacquer contains a polymer in a solvent, and it hardens by evaporation of the solvent.

Waxes

Chemically, a **wax** is an ester of a long-chain organic acid (fatty acid) with a long-chain alcohol. Waxes are produced by plants and animals mainly as protective coatings. These compounds are not to be confused with paraffin wax, which is made up of hydrocarbons and used for birthday candles.

Three typical waxes are shown in Figure 21.11. Beeswax is the material with which bees build honeycombs and is used in such household products as candles

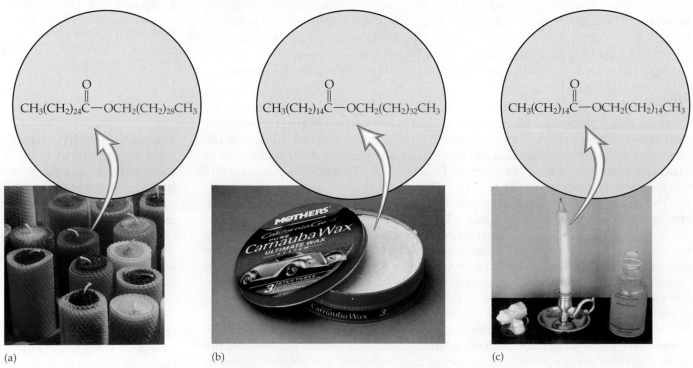

(a) (b) (c)

▲ **Figure 21.11** The molecular views show the esters that are typical components of (a) beeswax, (b) carnauba wax, and (c) spermaceti.

and shoe polish. Carnauba wax is a coating that forms on the leaves of certain palm trees found in Brazil. It is a mixture of esters similar to those in beeswax and is used in making automobile wax, floor wax, and furniture polish, as well as lip balms such as Chapstick™. Spermaceti wax, which is extracted from the head of a sperm whale, is largely cetyl palmitate. Once widely used in making cosmetics and other products, spermaceti wax is now in short supply because the sperm whale was hunted almost to extinction and is now protected by international treaties.

Lanolin, the grease in sheep's wool, is also a wax. Because it forms stable emulsions with water, it is used in various skin creams and lotions.

Many natural waxes have been replaced by synthetic polymers such as silicones (Section 10.5), which are often cheaper and more effective.

SELF-ASSESSMENT Questions

1. Which is *not* a property of organic solvents in household and commercial products?
   a. They are generally good for removing varnishes and adhesives.
   b. They are usually flammable.
   c. They are volatile, and the vapors, when inhaled, affect breathing and function of the heart and brain.
   d. They have a rather low toxicity if ingested.

2. The three basic components of a paint are a pigment, a solvent, and a
   a. builder   b. preservative   c. binder   d. wax

3. Which of the following is a wax?
   a. $CH_3(CH_2)_{14}COOCH_3$
   b. $CH_3(CH_2)_{28}CH_2OH$
   c. $CH_3(CH_2)_{28}COOCH_3$
   d. $CH_3(CH_2)_{14}COOCH_2(CH_2)_{28}CH_3$

4. Waxes are
   a. long-chain fatty acids
   b. long-chain alcohols
   c. esters with two long chains
   d. proteins

5. Modern paint pigments
   a. use PbS for black
   b. use copper compounds for blues
   c. substitute TiO_2 for $PbCO_3$
   d. use no more inorganic components

Answers: 1, d; 2, c; 3, d; 4, c; 5, c

21.6 Cosmetics: Personal-Care Chemicals

Learning Objectives ❯ Describe the chemical nature of skin, hair, and teeth. ❯ Identify the principal ingredients in various cosmetic products and their purposes.

Ages ago, people used materials from nature for cleansing, beautifying, and otherwise altering their appearance. Evidence indicates that 7000 years ago Egyptians used powdered antimony and the green copper ore *malachite* as eye shadow. Egyptian pharaohs used perfumed hair oils as far back as 3500 B.C.E. Galen, a Greek physician of the second century C.E., is said to have invented cold cream. Fashion-conscious gentlemen of seventeenth-century Europe used cosmetics lavishly, often to cover the fact that they seldom bathed. Ladies of eighteenth-century Europe as well as Japanese women whitened their faces with lead carbonate ($PbCO_3$), and many died from lead poisoning.

The use of cosmetics has a long and interesting history, but past usage doesn't even come close to the amounts and varieties of cosmetics used by people in the modern industrial world. Each year, we spend billions of dollars on everything from hair sprays to nail polishes, from mouthwashes to foot powders. Combined sales of the world's 100 largest cosmetics companies are more than $170 billion annually.

What is a cosmetic? The U.S. Food, Drug, and Cosmetic Act of 1938 defined **cosmetics** as "articles intended to be rubbed, poured, sprinkled or sprayed on, introduced into, or otherwise applied to the human body or any part thereof, for cleansing, beautifying, promoting attractiveness or altering the appearance." Soap, though obviously used for cleansing, is specifically excluded from coverage by the law. Also excluded are substances that affect the body's structure or functions. Antiperspirants, products that reduce perspiration, are legally classified as drugs, as are antidandruff shampoos.

▶ **Figure 21.12** Cross section of skin. Skin has two main layers: Each square inch of the dermis contains about 1 m of blood vessels, 4 m of nerves, 100 sweat glands, several oil glands, more than 3 million cells, and the active part of hair follicles. The epidermis, lying over the dermis, consists of a thin layer of cells that divide continuously. These cells move upward to the corneal layer, dying as they do so. Cosmetics generally affect only the outer corneal layer.

▲ **Figure 21.13** A lotion is an emulsion of oil in water (a). A cream is an emulsion of water in oil (b). A lotion feels cool because evaporating water removes heat from the skin. A cream feels greasy.

The main difference between drugs and cosmetics is that drugs must be proven safe and effective before they are marketed, while cosmetics generally do not have to be tested before being marketed. The Food, Drug, and Cosmetic Act states that if a product has drug properties, it must be approved as a drug. Nevertheless, the cosmetics industry uses the term *cosmeceutical* to refer to cosmetic products that allegedly have medicinal or druglike benefit.

More than 8000 different chemical compounds are used in cosmetics, sold in tens of thousands of different combinations. Most brands of a given type of cosmetic contain the same (or quite similar) active ingredients. Thus, advertising is usually geared toward selling a name, a container, or a fragrance rather than the product itself.

Skin Creams and Lotions

Skin is the body's largest organ, with an area of about 18 ft^2. It encloses the body, forming a barrier to keep harmful substances out and moisture and nutrients in (Figure 21.12). The outer layer of skin, the *epidermis*, is divided into two parts: dead cells on the outside (the corneal layer) and living cells on the inside, continually replacing corneal cells, which are then sloughed off.

The corneal layer is composed mainly of a tough, fibrous protein called **keratin**. Keratin has a moisture content of about 10%. Below 10% moisture, the human skin is dry and flaky. Above 10%, conditions are ideal for the growth of harmful microorganisms. Skin is protected from loss of moisture by **sebum**, an oily secretion of the sebaceous glands. Exposure to sun and wind can leave the skin dry and scaly, and too frequent washing removes natural skin oils.

Cosmetics are applied to the dead cells of the corneal layer. Most of the preparations applied to the skin are in the form of lotions or creams. A **lotion** is an emulsion of tiny oil droplets dispersed in water. A **cream** is the opposite, having tiny water droplets dispersed in oil (Figure 21.13), and generally has a much higher viscosity than a lotion. The essential ingredients of either creams or lotions are water, an oily substance that forms a protective film, and an emulsifier that binds the polar water to the nonpolar oily component, usually glyceryl stearate. A **moisturizer** contains all three.

Typical substances used as the oily component are glycerol or mixtures of alkanes from crude oil, including mineral oil and petroleum jelly. Others are natural fats and oils, such as lanolin obtained from sheep's wool, aloe vera gel, and olive or palm oil.

Creams and lotions protect the skin by coating and softening it. Such skin softeners are called **emollients**. Petroleum jelly (such as Vaseline®) or mineral oil (baby oil) works well for most people. It may seem strange that gasoline, a mixture of alkanes, dries out the skin but that higher alkanes in mineral oil and petroleum jelly soften it. Keep in mind, however, that gasoline is a thin, free-flowing liquid. It dissolves natural skin oils and carries them away. Higher alkanes are viscous, staying right on the skin and serving as emollients.

As in other industries, cosmetic companies are moving toward greener products. Sales of natural cosmetics were about $30 billion worldwide in 2013. Made from renewable plant, animal, and mineral products, these cosmetics may be better for the environment, but there is little evidence that they work better than traditional cosmetics. In fact, natural components may be more likely to cause allergic reactions than the synthetic ingredients. Natural is not necessarily better: Think of poison ivy as an extreme example.

Some creams have been formulated with hormones, vitamins, and other unusual ingredients. Some cosmetics contain *humectants* such as glycerol, lactic acid, or urea. Glycerol, with its three hydroxyl groups, holds water by hydrogen bonding. Urea binds water below the surface of the epidermis, right down to the skin-building cells. Urea and lactic acid also act as *exfoliants*, causing the dead cells to fall off more rapidly, leaving new, fresher-looking skin exposed.

Shaving Creams

Shaving creams consist of a soap or soap-like compound such as stearic acid, glycerol, water, plus fragrances, preservatives, and possibly a foaming agent such as cocamide. Stearic acid, a long-chain saturated fatty acid (see Chapter 17), acts like a soap, forming a smooth, slippery surface on the skin and hair. Glycerol is attracted to water by hydrogen bonding and acts as a humectant. It hydrates the beard, easing hair removal. It also increases the viscosity of the product.

Sunscreens

Ultraviolet rays in sunlight turn light skin darker by triggering production of **melanins**. The dark melanin protects the deeper layers of the skin from damage. Excessive exposure to ultraviolet radiation causes premature aging of the skin and leads to skin cancer. Our quest for tanned skin has resulted in an epidemic of skin cancer. Shorter-wavelength ultraviolet rays (UV-B) are more energetic and are especially harmful.

Sunscreens offer either physical or chemical protection from UV rays. Physical sunscreens, or sunblocks, are opaque films that prevent UV rays from reaching the skin, thus protecting against both UV-A and UV-B. Most contain white zinc oxide (ZnO) or titanium dioxide TiO_2 pigments to reflect the sun's rays. Chemical sunscreens absorb UV rays before they can cause any damage. Typical ingredients include avobenzone or oxybenzone, which protect against UV-A.

For many years, the active ingredient in many sunscreen lotions was *para*-aminobenzoic acid (PABA) or one of its esters, but they are seldom used today because they caused rashes and swelling in rare cases. Octyl methoxycinnamate (OMC) is used as a UV-B absorber in many sunscreen lotions, replacing PABA.

Anti-aging Creams and Lotions

Some cosmetics are claimed to reduce wrinkles, spots, and other signs of aging skin, and consumers spend billions of dollars each year for such products. Many contain alpha hydroxy acids (AHAs), derived from fruit and milk sugars. An alpha hydroxy acid is a carboxylic acid that has a hydroxyl group on the carbon atom next to the carboxyl carbon. Glycolic acid and lactic acid are typical examples. AHAs and related substances act as exfoliants. They seem relatively safe, but they may cause redness, swelling, burning, blistering, bleeding, rash, itching, and skin discoloration in some people. People who use AHA-containing products have greater sensitivity to sun, perhaps putting them at greater risk of skin cancer. The best treatment for wrinkling of the skin is prevention, by avoiding excessive exposure to the sun and by not smoking cigarettes. Cigarette smoking leads to premature aging of the skin. Nicotine causes constriction of the tiny blood vessels that feed the skin. Repeated constriction over the years causes the skin to lose its elasticity and become wrinkled.

Avobenzone

Oxybenzone

$$CH_3O—\bigcirc—CH=CHCOOCH_2CH(CH_2CH_3)CH_2CH_2CH_2CH_3$$

Octyl methoxycinnamate (OMC)
(2-ethylhexyl-4'-methoxycinnamate)

The **skin protection factor (SPF)** is a rating that indicates the effectiveness of a product's UV-absorbing ability in terms of length of time. SPF values range from 2 to 45 or more. An SPF of 15, for example, indicates that the product should allow you to stay in the sun without burning 15 times longer than you could with unprotected skin. Consumers should be aware, however, that the required amount applied for such protection is usually much greater than what people apply and that the creams can easily be rubbed off. Reapplying often is recommended no matter what the SPF rating.

Lipsticks and Lip Balms

Lipsticks and lip balms are quite similar to skin creams in composition and function. They are made of an oil and a wax, with a higher proportion of wax to provide solidity. Because the lips have little in the way of protective oils, they often dry out, leading to chapped lips. Lipsticks and lip balms prevent moisture loss as well as soften and brighten the lips. The oil in these products is frequently castor oil, sesame oil, or mineral oil. Waxes often employed are beeswax, carnauba wax, and candelilla wax. Dyes and pigments provide color to lipsticks. Perfumes are added to cover up the unpleasant fatty odor of the oil, and antioxidants are used to retard rancidity. Bromo acid dyes such as tetrabromofluorescein, a bluish-red compound, are responsible for the color of many lipsticks

Tetrabromofluorescein

Eye Makeup

A thick, black, slightly oily mixture called kohl has been used around the eyes for thousands of years. Egyptian queens and noblewomen used such mixtures to enhance the look of the eyes. Even today, kohl is widely used to decorate the face and eyes in southern Asia, especially in India, in the Middle East, western Africa, and the Horn of Africa in social and religious ceremonies, particularly Islamic festivals, for traditional dances and for medicinal reasons. Many believe that kohl protects eyesight and has a cooling and healing effect on eyes. Certainly, black substances absorb much of the sun's radiation, including harmful UV light. Even twenty-first-century football players who use black streaks under the eyes on game days take advantage of this property.

So what is kohl? In the Western world, carbon is the main ingredient, but traditional kohl in other cultures has consisted of finely ground lead(II) sulfide (galena) or, less commonly, antimony sulfide. Naturally, there is a concern about the use of lead compounds on the skin and near the eyes, especially with children. In the United States, it is illegal to import or sell foreign-made kohl; it is not on the list of color additives approved by the FDA.

Commercially available mascara and eyeliners have a base of soap, oils, fats, and waxes. Mascara is colored brown by iron(III) oxide pigments, and black by carbon (lampblack). A typical composition is 40% wax, 50% soap, 5% lanolin, and 5% coloring matter. Eyebrow pencils have roughly the same ingredients.

Eye-shadow creams have a base of petroleum jelly with the usual fats, oils, and waxes. Powdered eye shadows have talc [a hydrated magnesium silicate, $Mg_3Si_4O_{10}(OH)_2$] or corn silk as a base. Eye shadows are colored green by chromium(III) oxide (Cr_2O_3), blue by ultramarine (a silicate that contains some sulfide ions), or made white with zinc oxide or titanium dioxide pigments.

Some people have allergic reactions to ingredients in eye makeup. A more serious problem is eye infection caused by bacterial contamination. It is recommended that eye makeup be discarded after 3 months. Mascara is of special concern because of the wand applicator, which can easily scratch the cornea.

Deodorants and Antiperspirants

Many commercially available products are called "deodorants" by most people, who think that "antiperspirant" is a more sophisticated term for the same thing. In reality, a **deodorant** and an antiperspirant have different functions. Most commercial products contain both of those components, plus ingredients to create the correct consistency, plus perfumes.

A chemical deodorant is a germicide to kill odor-causing bacteria. Bacteria act on perspiration residue and sebum (natural body oil) to produce malodorous compounds such as short-chain fatty acids and amines. The germicide is usually a long-chain quaternary ammonium salt (Section 21.2) or triclosan. Powdered deodorants for the feet also contain germicides.

Antiperspirants retard perspiration. Active antiperspirant ingredients include complexes of chlorides and hydroxides of aluminum and zirconium. Aluminum chlorohydrate $[Al_2(OH)_5Cl \cdot 2\,H_2O]$ or an aluminum-zirconium complex are the two typical compounds found in many antiperspirants. These compounds function as **astringents**, which constrict the openings of the sweat glands and thus restrict the amount of perspiration that can escape.

Commercial products for underarm use can be formulated into creams or lotions, or they can be dissolved in alcohol and applied as sprays. The roll-on mechanism was invented in the 1960s, but deodorant "sticks" have now taken over the market share. Products targeted at men typically contain a higher percentage of both major active components compared to products meant for women. Sweating is a natural, healthy body process, and to stop it routinely may not be wise. Regular bathing and changing of clothes make antiperspirants unnecessary for most people, but modern culture seems to require its use.

Triclosan

Toothpaste: Soap with Grit and Flavor

Centuries ago people used small sticks, crushed charcoal, bird feathers, or porcupine quills to clean the teeth. People still buy toothpicks for removing food particles stuck between teeth, though dental floss is by far the norm in twenty-first-century culture. Tooth powders were invented in the nineteenth century and used commonly until at least the mid-twentieth century. Toothpastes and gels are a more recent development, and now, one may choose among a vast variety of flavors and additives.

The only essential components of toothpaste are a detergent and an abrasive. Abrasives may account for at least 50% of a typical toothpaste formulation. The ideal abrasive should be hard enough to clean teeth but not hard enough to damage tooth enamel. Most toothpastes do not feel gritty when rubbed between fingers or in the mouth because the particles are so small. Abrasives frequently used in toothpaste are listed in Table 21.1.

The typical detergent found in toothpaste is sodium dodecyl sulfate [sodium lauryl sulfate, $CH_3(CH_2)_{11}OSO_3^-Na^+$], which is surprisingly the same detergent

▲ Toothpastes are available under many brand names and in various formulations. Some contain baking soda (sodium bicarbonate) and/or hydrogen peroxide as ingredients, but there is only marginal evidence of their effectiveness. The only essential ingredients in a toothpaste are a detergent and an abrasive.

Table 21.1	Abrasives Commonly Used in Toothpastes
Name	Chemical Formula
Precipitated calcium carbonate	$CaCO_3$
Insoluble sodium metaphosphate	$(NaPO_3)_n$
Calcium hydrogen phosphate	$CaHPO_4$
Tricalcium phosphate	$Ca_3(PO_4)_2$
Calcium pyrophosphate	$Ca_2P_2O_7$
Hydrated alumina	$Al_2O_3 \cdot nH_2O$
Hydrated silica	$SiO_2 \cdot nH_2O$

Methyl *para*-hydroxybenzoate
(Methylparaben)

You can make your own toothpaste. Stir together 180 mL (about $2/3$ cup) of sodium bicarbonate (baking soda) and 60 mL (about $1/4$ cup) of sodium chloride (table salt). To this dry mixture, add 15 mL (about 1 tablespoon) of glycerol. Stir in just enough water to make a thick paste. Add a few drops of peppermint flavoring to improve the taste. Store in a closed container.

found in most hair shampoos (see below). Toothpastes have a variety of flavors, colors, and sweeteners such as sorbitol, glycerol, or saccharin (Section 17.6). The classic flavors include spearmint, wintergreen, and peppermint but more recent additions to the flavor options include ginger, cinnamon, bubble gum (especially for children), lemon, orange, and vanilla. Most toothpastes are colored or even striped with food dyes or contain fine mica to make it sparkly. Thickeners such as cellulose gum and polyethylene glycols and preservatives such as methyl *para*-hydroxybenzoate are important in toothpaste formulations. Titanium dioxide often accounts for a significant percentage of a toothpaste formulation, functioning mainly as a white pigment, but also as a mild abrasive.

Fluorine compounds are added to most modern toothpastes, even the least expensive generic products, to reduce tooth decay. Sodium fluoride, NaF, and sodium monofluorophosphate, Na_2PO_3F, are the most common fluorine-containing compounds used, though tin(II) fluoride (stannous fluoride) is still found in some products. The enamel of teeth is composed mainly of hydroxyapatite $[Ca_5(PO_4)_3OH]$. Fluoride from toothpaste (or drinking water) converts part of the enamel to fluoroapatite $[Ca_5(PO_4)_3F]$, which is stronger and more resistant to decay than hydroxyapatite.

Tooth decay is caused mainly by bacteria that convert sugars to *plaque*, a biofilm that is composed of thousands of bacteria, small particles, proteins, and mucus and is deposited on the teeth when they are not cleaned adequately. These bacteria convert sugars to acids such as lactic acid ($CH_3CHOHCOOH$). Acids dissolve tooth enamel. If not removed, plaque can harden into *calculus*, also known as *tartar*. Brushing and flossing remove plaque and thus prevent decay. Decay can be minimized by eating sugars only at meals rather than in snacks and by brushing immediately after eating. Acids such as lactic acid in beer and phosphoric acid (H_3PO_4) in soft drinks may also erode the tooth enamel of people who consume these beverages in large amounts.

Specialized toothpastes for highly sensitive teeth may contain potassium nitrate or strontium chloride. Tartar-control products and whitening toothpastes contain a higher percentage of abrasives or hydrogen peroxide. Toothpaste formulations with baking soda ($NaHCO_3$) and hydrogen peroxide (H_2O_2) as ingredients are purported to prevent gum disease, the main cause of tooth loss in adults, but there seems to be little evidence that they do.

Popular teeth whiteners often include hydrogen peroxide as a bleaching agent. The peroxide works on colored compounds in teeth in much the same way as bleaches work on stained clothing. However, the action of the H_2O_2 is slow. In toothpaste, the peroxide is not in contact with the teeth long enough to have a significant effect. Most of the successful teeth whiteners require application for 30 minutes or more. Dentists' preparations often use higher concentrations of peroxide along with ultraviolet light, which speeds the reaction. Caution is advised concerning teeth-whitening preparations. If used too often, they can cause teeth to become brittle.

Perfumes, Colognes, and Aftershaves

Perfumes are among the most ancient and widely used cosmetics. Originally, all perfumes were extracted from natural sources such as fragrant plants. Their chemistry is exceedingly complex, but chemists have identified many of the components of perfumes and synthesized them in the laboratory, allowing the production of many synthetic perfumes. The best perfumes are probably still made from natural materials because chemists have so far been unable to identify all the many important, but minor, ingredients.

A good perfume may have a hundred or more constituents. The components are divided into three categories, called *notes*, based on differences in volatility. The most volatile fraction (the one that vaporizes most readily) is called the **top note**. This fraction, made up of relatively small molecules, is responsible for the odor when a perfume is first applied. Common top notes include citrus and ginger scents and chemical compounds such as phenylacetaldehyde (Table 21.2), which has a lilac or hyacinth odor. Note that fragrance molecules in Table 21.2 are fat soluble. They dissolve in skin oils and can be retained for hours.

Table 21.2	Compounds with Flowery and Fruity Odors Used in Perfumes		
Name	Structure[a]	Odor	Molecular Formula
Citral		Lemon	$C_{10}H_{16}O$
Irone		Orris root, iris	$C_{14}H_{22}O$
Jasmone		Jasmine	$C_{11}H_{16}O$
Phenylacetaldehyde		Lilac, hyacinth	C_8H_8O
2-Phenylethanol		Rose	$C_8H_{10}O$

[a.] Note that each compound has only 1 oxygen atom and 10 or more carbon atoms.

The **middle note** (*or heart note*) is intermediate in volatility. This fraction is responsible for the lingering aroma after most of the top-note compounds have vaporized. Typical middle notes include lavender and rose scents and chemical compounds such as 2-phenylethanol, which has the aroma of roses. The **end note** (*or base note*) is the low-volatility fraction and is made up of compounds with large molecules, often with musky odors. Essential oils—volatile oily compounds from plants with pleasant aromas—such as those from sandalwood and patchouli are typically used to supply base notes.

Odors vary with dilution. A concentrated solution of a compound may have an unpleasant odor, yet a dilute solution of it will have a pleasant aroma. Such compounds include musks (Table 21.3), which are often added to perfumes to moderate the odors

Table 21.3	Unpleasant Compounds Used to Fix Delicate Odors in Perfumes			
Compound	Structure	Natural Source	Molecular Formula	Molecular Mass (u)
Civetone		Civet	$C_{17}H_{30}O$	250.42
Muscone		Musk deer	$C_{16}H_{30}O$	238.41
Indole		Feces	C_8H_7N	117.15

Aromatherapy

Aromatherapy is the practice of using essential oils as a purported way to promote health and well-being. Certainly olfactory sensations are very important in everyday life. Aromatherapy includes the use of soap, bath additives, shower gels, candles, room fragrances, oil burners, and cosmetic products containing essential oils.

Commonly used essential oils are those from marigold, lemon, orange, grapefruit, geranium, lavender, jasmine, and bergamot. The essential oils are diluted by carrier oils, which are vegetable oils such as sweet almond oil, apricot kernel oil, and grapeseed oil, before being applied to the skin.

The U.S. aromatherapy market is valued at $800 million a year and accounts for most of worldwide sales. Home fragrance products account for nearly half the aromatherapy sales in the United States. It is difficult to evaluate the claims of aromatherapy's proponents. The pleasant aromas from these oils are supposed to have a positive effect on the nervous system or, minimally, have a positive psychological effect on people. It may be as simple as a pleasant feeling caused when a scent recalls a pleasant experience. The chemical effects of the molecules found in the essential oils on the nervous system need further study, and the sensitivity of the human nose is more complex than we may realize.

α-Androstenol

Menthol

▲ Shampoos are available in many forms and under many brand names. The only essential ingredient in any shampoo is a detergent.

of flowery or fruity top and middle notes. The civet, from which the compound civetone is obtained, is a skunklike animal. Its secretion, like that of the skunk, is a defensive weapon. The secretion from musk deer is probably a pheromone (Chapter 18) that serves as a sex attractant for the deer. Synthetic civetone and muscone have been produced, but many upscale perfume makers still prefer natural civetone. Almost all muscone used in perfumes today is synthetic.

Are there sex attractants for humans? The evidence is scanty, but some perfume makers add α-androstenol to their products. α-Androstenol is a steroid that occurs naturally in human hair and urine. Some studies hint that it may act as a sex attractant for human females, but this seems more likely to be just an advertising ploy. Even if there are human sex attractants, it is doubtful that they have much influence on human behavior because we probably have overriding cultural constraints. Anyway, we seem to prefer the sex attractant of the musk deer.

A perfume usually consists of 10–25% fragrant compounds and fixatives dissolved in ethyl alcohol. **Colognes** are perfumes diluted with ethyl alcohol or an alcohol–water mixture. They are only about one-tenth as strong as perfumes, usually containing only 1–2% perfume essence.

Aftershave lotions are similar to colognes. Most are about 50–70% ethanol, the remainder being water, perfume, and food coloring. Some have menthol or eucalyptol added for a cooling effect on the skin. Others contain an emollient to soothe chapped skin.

Perfumes are the source of many allergic reactions associated with cosmetics and other consumer products. **Hypoallergenic cosmetics** are those that purport to cause fewer allergic reactions than regular products. The term has no legal meaning, but most of these cosmetics do not contain perfume.

Hairy Chemistry

Like skin, hair is composed mainly of the fibrous protein keratin. Recall (Chapter 16) that protein molecules are made up of amino-acid chains held together by four types of forces: hydrogen bonds, salt bridges, disulfide linkages, and dispersion forces. Of these, hydrogen bonds and salt bridges are important to understanding the actions of shampoos and conditioners. Hydrogen bonds between protein chains are disrupted by water (Figure 21.14); salt bridges are destroyed by changes in pH (Figure 21.15). Disulfide linkages are broken and restored when hair is permanently waved or straightened.

Shampoo

The keratin of hair has five or six times as many disulfide linkages as the keratin of skin. When hair is washed, the keratin absorbs water and is softened and made more elastic. The water disrupts hydrogen bonds and some of the salt bridges. Acids and bases are particularly disruptive to salt bridges, making control of pH important in hair care. The number of salt bridges is maximized at a pH of 4.1.

(a)   (b)

▲ **Figure 21.14** In a strand of hair, adjacent protein chains are held together by hydrogen bonds that link the carbonyl group of one chain to the amide group of another (a). When hair is wet, these groups can hydrogen-bond with water rather than with each other (b), disrupting the hydrogen bonds between chains.

The visible portion of hair is dead. Only the root is alive. The hair shaft is lubricated by sebum. Washing the hair removes this oil and any dirt adhering to it.

Before World War II, the cleansing agent in shampoos was a soap, which worked well in soft water but left a dulling film on hair in hard water. People often removed the film by using a rinse containing vinegar or lemon juice. Such rinses are not needed with today's products.

Modern shampoos use a synthetic detergent as a cleansing agent, which is the only essential ingredient, usually 20 to 25% of the formulation. In adult shampoos, the detergent is often an anionic type such as sodium dodecyl sulfate, ammonium lauryl sulfate, or sodium laureth sulfate, or a mixture of detergents. In shampoos used for babies and children, the detergent is often an amphoteric surfactant (Section 21.2) that is less irritating to the eyes.

Why is there such a significant difference in cost between the least expensive and the most expensive shampoos? Most of the difference is traced to additives.

You can buy shampoos that are fruit or herb scented, protein enriched, or made especially for oily, dry, or color-treated hair. Shampoos for oily, normal, and dry hair seem to differ mainly in the concentration of the detergent. Shampoo for oily hair is more concentrated; shampoo for dry hair is more dilute. Shampoos meant for color-treated hair contain sunscreen, since UV radiation destroys the molecules used to darken gray or blonde hair. Whether or not the sunscreen stays on the hair after the hair is rinsed is questionable.

Because hair is protein, a protein-enriched shampoo does give it more body. The protein (usually keratin or collagen) coats the hair and literally glues split ends

5. Does a thicker shampoo work better to clean my hair? Shampoo is thickened with fine silica or a polymer. A thicker shampoo simply has more of the thickening agent added, rather than more detergent. Consumers seem to want thicker shampoo for greater convenience in the shower: A thinner shampoo would dribble through the fingers. It is not a better cleaning agent for your hair.

Strong attraction   Weak attraction   Weak attraction
(opposite charges)

—COO⁻   H₃N⁺—   —COOH   H₃N⁺—   —COO⁻   H₂N—

(a)   (b)   (c)

▲ **Figure 21.15** Strong electrostatic forces between an ionized carboxyl group on one protein chain and an ionized amino function on another hold the chains together (a). A change in pH can disrupt this salt bridge. If the pH drops, the carboxyl group takes on a proton and loses its charge (b). If the pH rises, a proton is removed from the amino group and it is left uncharged (c). In either case, the forces between the protein chains are weakened considerably.

6. Why must I leave a hair coloring preparation on my hair for the full time suggested on the bottle, if I want to become a blonde?

The eumelanin in your hair, which is black or dark brown, is fairly easily oxidized to a nearly colorless compound. Any pheomelanin (reddish) that may exist in your hair is oxidized with difficulty. If you do not leave a bleaching hair colorant on your hair for the full time, you may end up being a "strawberry" blonde with definite reddish tints instead of the pale blonde you intended.

It DOES Matter!

Why does the type of melanin in your skin matter? It is not just cosmetic. People with dark skin are perhaps a hundred times less likely to get melanoma or other skin cancers. Melanin is a good sunblock. How easily someone gets sunburn or how hard it is for some people to get a tan depends on the amount and kind of melanin in their skin. Having predominantly pheomelanin is a major risk factor for most forms of skin cancer.

together. Protein is often added to conditioners, too. Conditioners are mainly long-chain alcohols or long-chain quaternary ammonium salts, which are similar to the compounds used in fabric softeners (Section 21.3) and work in much the same way to coat hair fibers.

Because there are acidic and basic groups on the protein chains in hair, the acidity or basicity of a shampoo affects hair. Hair and skin are both slightly acidic. Highly basic (high-pH) or strongly acidic (low-pH) shampoos would damage hair. Most shampoos have pH values between 4 and 7, close to neutral or very slightly acidic.

What about all those fragrances? Ample evidence indicates that such "natural" ingredients as honey, strawberries, herbs, cucumbers, and lemons add nothing to the usefulness of shampoos or other cosmetics. Why are they there? Smells sell, and such ingredients also appeal to those interested in a more natural lifestyle. There is one hazard in the use of such fragrances: Bees, mosquitoes, and other insects like certain fruit and flower odors, too. Using such products before going on a picnic or a hike could lead to a bee in your bonnet.

Hair Coloring

Melanin is a broad term that refers to colorants in skin and hair. The color of hair and skin is determined by the relative amounts of two pigments: *eumelanin*, a brownish-black pigment, and *pheomelanin*, a reddish pigment that colors the hair of redheads and is the main colorant in freckles. Brunettes have mostly eumelanin in the hair, but blondes have little of either pigment.

Brunettes who would like to become blondes can do so by oxidizing the colored pigments in their hair to colorless compounds. Hydrogen peroxide is the oxidizing agent usually used to bleach hair. (The same substance that bleaches darker hair blonde turns it gray. With increasing age, the hydrogen peroxide concentration in hair follicles builds up, ultimately inhibiting the production of melanin.)

Dyeing hair to create darker hair or restore graying hair to the original brown or black coloration is more complicated than bleaching, because colorants have to be added to the hair. The color may be temporary, from water-soluble dyes that can be washed out or more permanent dyes that penetrate the hair and remain. Such dyes are often used in the form of a water-soluble, often colorless, precursor that soaks into the hair and then is oxidized by hydrogen peroxide to a colored compound. Permanent dyes affect only the dead outer portion of the hair shaft. New hair, as it grows from the scalp, has its natural color.

Permanent dyes are often derivatives of an aromatic amine called *para*-phenylenediamine (Figure 21.16). Variations in color can be obtained by placing substituents on this molecule. The *para*-phenylenediamine molecule produces a black color, and the derivative *para*-aminodiphenylaminesulfonic acid is used in blonde formulations. Intermediate colors can be obtained by the use of other derivatives. One derivative, *para*-methoxy-*meta*-phenylenediamine (MMPD), has been shown to be carcinogenic when fed to rats and mice, but the hazard to those who use it as hair dye is not yet known. It is interesting to note that one substitute for MMPD was its homolog, *para*-ethoxy-*meta*-phenylenediamine (EMPD). Screening revealed that EMPD causes mutations in bacteria. Such mutagens are often also carcinogens.

para-Phenylenediamine
(a)

para-Aminodiphenylaminesulfonic acid
(b)

MMPD
(c)

EMPD
(d)

▲ **Figure 21.16** Most hair dyes are derivatives of *para*-phenylenediamine (a). These include *para*-aminodiphenylaminesulfonic acid (b), *para*-methoxy-*meta*-phenylenediamine (MMPD) (c), and *para*-ethoxy-*meta*-phenylenediamine (EMPD) (d).

Hair treatments that develop color gradually, such as Grecian Formula®, use rather simple chemistry. A solution containing colorless lead acetate [Pb(CH$_3$COO)$_2$] is rubbed on the hair. As it penetrates the hair shaft, Pb^{2+} ions react with sulfur atoms in the hair to form black lead(II) sulfide (PbS). Repeated applications produce darker colors as more lead sulfide is formed. The use of lead compounds in contact with skin has been questioned as to its safety.

Permanent Waving: Chemistry to Curl Your Hair

The chemistry of curly hair is interesting. Hair is protein, and adjacent protein chains are held together by disulfide linkages. Permanent wave lotion contains a reducing agent such as thioglycolic acid (HSCH$_2$COOH), which ruptures the disulfide linkages (Figure 21.17), allowing the protein chains to be pulled apart as the hair is held in a curled position on rollers. The hair is then treated with a mild oxidizing agent such as hydrogen peroxide. Disulfide linkages are formed in new positions to give shape to the hair.

The same chemical process can be used to straighten naturally curly hair. The change in curliness depends only on how the hair is arranged after the disulfide bonds have been reduced and before the linkages have been restored.

Hair Sprays

Hair can be held in place by **resins**, solid or semisolid organic materials that form a sticky film on the hair. Common resins used on hair are polyvinylpyrrolidone (PVP) and its copolymers.

The resin is dissolved in a solvent, and the mixture is sprayed on the hair, where the solvent evaporates. The propellants in hair sprays are usually volatile hydrocarbons, such as butane, which are flammable.

Holding resins are also available as mousses. A **mousse** is simply a foam or froth. The active ingredients, like those of hair sprays, are resins such as PVP. Coloring agents and conditioners are also available as mousses.

Hair Removers

Chemicals that remove unwanted hair are called **depilatories**. Most of them contain a soluble sulfur compound, such as sodium sulfide or calcium thioglycolate [Ca(OOCCH$_2$SH)$_2$], formulated into a cream or lotion. These strongly basic mixtures destroy some of the peptide bonds in the hair so that it can be washed off. Remember that skin is made of protein, too, so any chemical that attacks the hair can also damage the skin.

Hair Restorers

For years, men have been searching for a way to make hair grow on bald spots. Women suffer from baldness, too, but seem to consider wigs more acceptable than men do.

Minoxidil was first introduced as a drug for treating high blood pressure. It acts by dilating the blood vessels. When people who were taking the drug started growing hair on various parts of their bodies, it was applied to the scalps of people who were becoming bald. Minoxidil can produce a growth of fine hair anyplace on the skin where there are hair follicles. It is sold under the trade name Rogaine®, although generic versions are now available. To be effective, it must be used continuously, and the cost can be several hundred dollars a year or more.

The Well-Informed Consumer

This chapter cannot even attempt to tell you everything about the many chemical products you have in your home. Books have been written about some of them, and there are

Natural hair

Wave lotion containing HSCH$_2$COOH

Neutralizer containing H$_2$O$_2$

Waved hair

▲ **Figure 21.17** Permanent waving of hair is accomplished by breaking disulfide bonds between protein chains and then re-forming them in new positions.

GREEN CHEMISTRY

Marty Mulvihill, *University of California–Berkeley*

Practicing Green Chemistry at Home

Learning Objective ❯ Identify how green chemistry principles can be applied when selecting greener household products.

The Twelve Principles of Green Chemistry help chemists design and use chemicals safely and more efficiently. These principles can also guide the use of chemical products in our own homes. While we don't often get the opportunity to design the products found in our homes, we do control which ones we buy and how we use them. You will see how we can become greener consumers by combining these principles with an understanding of the chemistry found in this chapter. The guidelines below are an example of the way that the twelve principles of green chemistry can be used to inspire greener consumer habits.

1 **Buy and use only what you need.** Principles 1, 2, 8, and 9 all help a chemist avoid unnecessary waste. You can avoid waste at home by only buying and using the products that you need.

2 **Choose safer products.** Principles 3, 4, and 5 all remind chemists to choose the safest ingredients possible that still provide the desired function. The same is true at home. Consult expert resources to determine which products are the safest.

3 **Choose products that minimize resources depletion.** Principle 7 encourages the chemist to use renewable feedstock chemicals and Principle 6 promotes energy efficiency. We can minimize depletion of resources by choosing products that are energy efficient or made from renewable resources.

4 **Choose reusable, recyclable, or readily degradable materials.** Principle 10 tells the chemist to design chemicals that degrade in the environment. Look for products that readily degrade in the environment. Buy items in packaging that can be reused or recycled.

5 **Stay informed.** Principle 11 encourages chemists to monitor reactions in real time so that they can avoid hazards and waste. As consumers, we can monitor new developments in product safety and regulations so that we can choose the best products.

6 **Prevent accidents.** Principle 12 reminds chemists that they should strive to prevent accidents by using inherently safer chemistry. Accidents are prevented by reading product labels, using proper protective gear, maximizing ventilation, and choosing the safest products.

This chapter introduces many of the chemical ingredients found in household products and helps you understand what functions they perform. You should identify the function of as many ingredients as you can in the products that you buy. Avoid items with many extra ingredients. This is how chemists think about buying and using only what we need. For example, we learned that soap improves hygiene and health by damaging microorganisms (Section 21.1). This means that all soap is antibacterial and that adding antibacterial agents may be unnecessary.

Training yourself to identify and understand product ingredients will also help you choose safer products. For example, we learned that paints contain more than pigment (Section 21.5). They also have solvents that allow them to spread before drying. Traditional solvents were volatile hydrocarbons, often called VOCs (Section 13.4). These chemicals have low boiling points and high vapor pressures. Many VOCs can irritate the respiratory tract and cause health problems. Greener products found at a paint store replace some or all of the hydrocarbon solvent with water. These usually have labels that say "low-VOC or VOC-free."

We can ensure a healthier environment by minimizing resource depletion. For example, new concentrated detergents can be used in cold water to improve energy efficiency by removing the need to heat wash water. Products made from renewable resources reduce the need for petroleum and may also be better for the environment. For example, many of the fragrances discussed in this chapter are naturally occurring chemicals. There are also examples of biologically derived plastics and fuels that reduce the amount of CO_2 emitted.

Products made from plant materials help transition away from petroleum and are often more degradable. Degradability is controlled by chemical structure. Molecules that are linear and contain only carbon, hydrogen, and oxygen degrade more quickly than complicated molecules that contain many rings, branching points, and halogen atoms. Molecules that degrade quickly are less likely to cause harm when they are released into the environment.

Understanding basic chemistry and the importance of green chemistry helps us become greener, better informed consumers and can prevent accidents. We can apply our chemistry knowledge every day and make decisions based on the ingredients in the household products that we buy. In this way, we can use our purchasing power to lead to a more sustainable world.

many volumes in the library that can help you if you want to know more. There is also much information available on the Internet, but much of it is little more than advertising hype; read it with caution! We hope that the knowledge you have gained here and the information you read on product labels will make you a better-informed consumer.

When you are faced with many different brands of a product at the supermarket or drugstore, remember that the most expensive one is not necessarily better than the others. Consider the soap and detergent industry, which does a lot of advertising. Each laundry powder and shampoo is claimed to be superior to all its competitors, but most brands are much alike. Advertising is expensive, so the brands that are the most widely advertised probably cost the most. Sometimes, the better product might be the less expensive one.

If you are unhappy with a product you have bought, tell the company that made it. The cosmetic industry gets thousands of complaints from customers every year. You can also complain to the FDA. Many reports are presented each year to the FDA regarding adverse effects of cosmetic products. The FDA cannot ban a cosmetic without proof of harm, and testing a product for carcinogenicity (Chapter 22) is an involved process, takes several years, and costs a minimum of half a million dollars.

Most cosmetics are made from inexpensive ingredients, yet many highly advertised cosmetics have extremely high price tags. Are they worth it? This is a judgment that lies beyond the realm of chemistry. The $100 product inside that fancy little bottle with the famous label may have cost the manufacturer less than $5 to produce. On the other hand, if the product makes you look better or feel better, perhaps the price is not important. Only you can decide.

SELF-ASSESSMENT Questions

1. Skin creams and lotions may contain all the following except
   a. proteins
   b. mineral oil
   c. glycerin
   d. an emulsifying agent

2. To market a new cosmetic, a manufacturer
   a. does not have to prove that it is safe and effective for its intended use
   b. must pay the FDA to test it for safety
   c. must provide the FDA with evidence that the ingredients are safe for the intended use
   d. must submit an application to the FDA showing that the product is not a cosmeceutical

3. Which type of ultraviolet radiation is most responsible for sunburn?
   a. UV-A   **b.** UV-B   **c.** UV-C   **d.** UV-X

4. Why does hair get "dirty"?
   a. Our hands pick up oils, and they get into the air by touching the hair.
   b. Dirt and dust are naturally in the air and settle on the hair.
   c. Hair, being a protein, attracts greasy dirt.
   d. Sebaceous glands near the hair roots secrete oils that pick up airborne dirt.

5. Sucrose contributes to tooth decay by
   a. being converted by bacteria into acid that erodes tooth enamel
   b. directly attacking tooth enamel
   c. mechanically abrading tooth enamel
   d. triggering the release of stomach acid

6. Which of the fractions of a perfume is made up of the smallest molecules?
   a. end note   **b.** middle note   **c.** base note   **d.** top note

7. Aftershave lotions contain all the following except
   a. ethanol   **b.** menthol   **c.** water   **d.** protein

8. If a cosmetic is labeled as hypoallergenic, it
   a. is all natural
   b. is dermatologist tested
   c. probably has no perfume in it
   d. still may contain substances that can cause allergic reactions

9. When hair is wetted, what type of force is disrupted?
   a. hydrogen bonds   **b.** disulfide linkages
   c. salt bridges   **d.** peptide bonds

10. Kohl is
    a. simply crushed coal
    b. used in face decorating in many cultures
    c. a good reflector of UV and visible radiation from the sun
    d. is effective at protecting the eyes from disease

11. The essential ingredient in a shampoo is
    a. a conditioner   **b.** a fragrance
    c. a detergent   **d.** protein

12. What chemical forces are disrupted during home permanents?
    a. hydrogen bonds   **b.** disulfide linkages
    c. salt bridges   **d.** peptide bonds

13. People who have little melanin in the skin
    a. are more susceptible to sunburn and skin cancer
    b. usually are naturally dark haired
    c. have hair that turns gray early in life
    d. seldom have to use sunscreen

Answers: 1. a; 2. a; 3. b; 4. d; 5. a; 6. d; 7. d; 8. c; 9. a; 10. b; 11. c; 12. b; 13. a

SUMMARY

Section 21.1—Some plants contain saponins, which produce lather. Plant ashes contain K_2CO_3 and Na_2CO_3, which are alkaline because they react with water to form hydroxide ions. A **soap** is a salt of a long-chain carboxylic acid, traditionally made from fat and lye (NaOH). A soap molecule has a **hydrophobic** hydrocarbon tail (soluble in oil or grease) and a **hydrophilic** ionic head (soluble in water) usually COO^-. Soap molecules disperse oil or grease in water by forming **micelles**, tiny spherical oil droplets in which the hydrocarbon tails of soap molecules are embedded. Agents that stabilize suspensions in this way are called **surface-active agents (surfactants)**. Soaps do not work well in hard water (water containing Ca^{2+}, Fe^{2+}, or Mg^{2+} ions) because they form insoluble salts.

Section 21.2—A synthetic detergent usually has a long hydrocarbon tail and a polar or ionic head, usually with SO_3^- in the structure. ABS detergents have branched-chain structures and are not easily biodegraded. LAS detergents have a linear chain of carbon atoms that can be broken down by microorganisms. Soaps, ABS detergents, and LAS detergents are **anionic surfactants** that have a negative charge on the active part. A **nonionic surfactant** has no charge. A **cationic surfactant** such as a quaternary ammonium salt (quat) has a positive charge. An **amphoteric surfactant** carries both a positive and a negative charge. Detergent formulations often include **builders** such as complex phosphates to increase detergency. **Optical brighteners**, which are fluorescent dyes, are often added to detergents to make whites appear "whiter." Bleaches, fragrances, and fabric softeners may be in laundry detergents. Liquid dishwashing detergents contain mainly LAS surfactants as the active ingredients. Detergents for automatic dishwashers are strongly alkaline and should not be used for hand dishwashing.

Section 21.3—Cationic surfactants include quaternary ammonium salts, and those with two long hydrocarbon chains are used as fabric softeners. **Bleaches** are oxidizing agents. Hypochlorite bleaches release chlorine. Oxygen bleaches usually contain perborates or percarbonates. Bleaches act by oxidizing colored chromophores to colorless fragments.

Section 21.4—All-purpose cleaners may contain surfactants, ammonia, and disinfectants. Reading the label is imperative, so that a cleaner may be used properly and safely. Household ammonia, sodium bicarbonate (baking soda), and vinegar are good cleaners for many purposes. Special-purpose cleaners include toilet bowl cleaners that contain an acid, scouring powders that contain an abrasive, and glass cleaners that contain ammonia. Drain cleaners contain NaOH and sometimes bleach. The active ingredient in oven cleaners is NaOH.

Section 21.5—Solvents are used to remove paint and other materials. Many organic solvents are volatile and flammable. **Paint** contains a pigment, a binder, and a solvent. Titanium dioxide is the most common pigment. Water-based paints contain a polymer as the binder; oil-based paints use tung oil or linseed oil. A **wax** is an ester of a fatty acid with a long-chain alcohol. Beeswax and carnauba wax are commonly used waxes. **Lanolin,** from sheep's wool, is also a wax, used in skin creams and lotions.

Section 21.6—A **cosmetic** is something applied to the body for cleansing, promoting attractiveness, or a similar purpose, but cosmetics do not have to be proven safe and effective like drugs. Skin has an outer layer made of a tough, fibrous protein called **keratin. Sebum**, an oily secretion, protects skin from loss of moisture. A **lotion** is an emulsion of oil droplets in water; a **cream** is an emulsion of water droplets in oil. Each of these is a **moisturizer** that forms a protective physical barrier over the skin to hold in moisture. Creams and lotions also soften skin; such skin softeners are called **emollients**. Humectants such as glycerol hydrogen-bond to water and hold it to the skin. Ultraviolet rays trigger the production of the pigment **melanin**, which darkens the skin. **Sunscreens** block or absorb ultraviolet (UV) radiation, of which UV-B rays are more harmful than UV-A rays. The **skin protection factor (SPF)** indicates how effective a sunscreen's UV-absorbing substances are. Eye makeup and lipstick are mainly blends of oil, waxes, and pigments. Some traditional makeup components are dangerous. **Deodorants** mask body odor and kill odor-causing bacteria. **Antiperspirants** retard perspiration, acting as **astringents**, constricting the openings of the sweat glands. Toothpaste contains a detergent and an abrasive, as well as a thickener, flavoring, and an added fluoride compound. The fragrance of a **perfume** is due to three fractions: the **top note** (the most volatile), the **middle note** (of intermediate volatility), and the **end note** (of lowest volatility). **Colognes** are diluted perfumes. **Hypoallergenic cosmetics** purport to cause fewer allergic reactions than regular products, but the term has no legal meaning. Shampoos are synthetic detergents blended with water, thickening agents, and fragrances. Dark hair contains the pigment eumelanin, red hair contains pheomelanin, and blonde hair contains very little of either pigment. Many hair dyes are based on *para*-phenylenediamine. Bleaching hair uses hydrogen peroxide. Permanent waving or straightening of the hair uses a reducing agent to break the disulfide linkages between protein chains and then an oxidizing neutralizer to re-form the linkages in different positions. Hair sprays contain **resins**, organic materials that form a sticky film on the hair. Such resins are also available in foam form as **mousses**. Chemicals that remove hair are called **depilatories**, and most such chemicals can also damage the skin.

GREEN CHEMISTRY—The principles of green chemistry can be interpreted to help us make greener choices. Understanding chemical properties can lead to the selection of greener products.

Learning Objectives

❯ Describe the structure of soap, and explain how it is made and how it works to remove greasy dirt.	Problems 3, 9, 12–16, 69, 85
❯ Explain the advantages and disadvantages of soap.	Problems 1, 3, 10, 17–22, 74
❯ List the structures, advantages, and disadvantages of synthetic detergents.	Problems 2, 23–26, 31–33, 78, 83, 85
❯ Classify surfactants as amphoteric, anionic, cationic, and nonionic, and describe how they are used in various detergent formulations.	Problems 4, 27–30, 35, 70, 72, 76
❯ Identify a fabric softener from its structure, and describe its action.	Problems 37–38
❯ Name two types of laundry bleaches, and describe how they work.	Problems 3, 39–42, 85
❯ List the major ingredient(s) (and their purposes) of some all-purpose cleaning products and some special-purpose cleaning products.	Problems 3–7, 11, 34, 36, 77, 81
❯ Identify compounds used in solvents and paints, and explain their purposes.	Problems 43–46, 82
❯ Identify waxes by their structure.	Problems 79, 80, 85
❯ Identify the principal ingredients in various cosmetic products and their purposes.	Problems 8, 47–58, 59–62, 63–68, 71, 73, 75, 84
❯ Identify how green chemistry principles can be applied when selecting greener household products.	Problems 83, 84, 85, 86

REVIEW QUESTIONS

1. What are some advantages and disadvantages of soaps?

2. What are some advantages and disadvantages of synthetic detergents?

3. Match the formula in the left column with the description or use in the right column.

   (1) CH_3COOH (a) ingredient in vinegar
   (2) $Na_2Al_2Si_2O_8$ (b) mild abrasive cleaner
   (3) $NaHCO_3$ (c) used as bleach
   (4) $NaOCl$ (d) used to make soap
   (5) $NaOH$ (e) water softener
   (6) Na_3PO_4 (f) zeolite

4. What ingredients are used in liquid dishwashing detergents (for hand dishwashing)? How do detergents for automatic dishwashers differ from those used for hand dishwashing?

5. List some uses of diluted household ammonia. What safety precautions should be followed when using ammonia?

6. What are some properties of ammonia solution that make it useful? What are some drawbacks?

7. List two properties of baking soda that make it useful as a cleaning agent.

8. What is the legal definition of a cosmetic? Is soap a cosmetic?

PROBLEMS

Soaps

9. How does a potassium soap differ from a sodium soap? Write the formulas for sodium dodecyl sulfate and potassium dodecyl sulfate.

10. Why does soap fail to work in hard water?

11. What ingredient is added to scouring soaps? What property of that additive makes it useful for scouring?

12. How does soap (or detergent) clean a dirty surface on the molecular level? Use a detailed diagram.

13. Write a generalized word equation for the formation of soap from lye and a fat.

14. Write a word equation that describes the reaction of tripalmitin with lye (sodium hydroxide).

15. Give the structural formula for each of the following.
    a. potassium stearate
    b. sodium palmitate

16. Give the structures of the products formed in the following reaction.

$$CH_2O-\overset{\overset{O}{\|}}{C}(CH_2)_{10}CH_3$$
$$CH-O-\overset{\overset{O}{\|}}{C}(CH_2)_{10}CH_3 \quad + \quad 3\,NaOH \longrightarrow$$
$$CH_2O-\overset{\overset{O}{\|}}{C}(CH_2)_{10}CH_3$$

Water Softeners

17. Describe how trisodium phosphate softens water.

18. How does a water-softening tank work?

19. What ions make water "hard"?

20. Write the equation that shows how carbonate ions react with magnesium ions in hard water to form an insoluble precipitate.

21. Write the equation that shows how phosphate ions react with calcium ions in hard water to form an insoluble precipitate.

22. Write a word equation that shows how a water softener using sodium zeolite removes calcium ions from the water.

Builders

23. What is a (detergent) builder?

24. How does sodium tripolyphosphate aid the cleansing action of a detergent?

25. How do zeolites aid the cleansing action of a detergent?

26. What advantage do zeolites have over carbonates as builders?

Detergents: Structures and Properties

27. What is an amphoteric surfactant?

28. Classify each of the following surfactants as anionic, cationic, nonionic, or amphoteric.
    a. $CH_3(CH_2)_9CH_2CH_2OSO_3^- \ Na^+$
    b. $CH_3—C_6H_4—(CH)_{10}N^+(CH_3)_3 \ Cl^-$

29. Cationic surfactants are often used with nonionic surfactants but are seldom used with anionic surfactants. Why not?

30. What is the structural difference between an ABS and an LAS detergent? What are the similarities?

Problems 31 through 34 refer to compounds I, II, and III below; C_6H_4 represents a 1, 4-disubstituted benzene ring.

    I. $CH_3(CH_2)_9CH(CH_3)—C_6H_4—SO_3^-Na^+$

    II. $CH_3(CH_2)_{11}OSO_3^-Na^+$

    III. $CH_3(CH_2)_{15}N^+(CH_3)_3Br^-$

31. Which is a linear alkyl sulfonate (LAS)?

32. Which is an alkyl sulfate ?

33. Which is/are not biodegradable?

34. Which is a quaternary ammonium salt?

35. Which is/are anionic surfactants? Which is a cationic surfactant?

36. What sorts of surfaces should not be cleaned with ammonia? Why? What sorts of surfaces should not be cleaned with vinegar? Why?

Fabric Softeners

37. Give an example of a compound that acts as a fabric softener.

38. How do fabric softeners work?

Bleaches

39. Give the names of two important compounds found in powdered bleaches.

40. List some advantages and disadvantages of perborate and chlorine bleaches.

41. How do sodium percarbonate and sodium perborate work as bleaches?

42. What is the name and chemical formula of the compound found in all liquid bleaches?

Solvents and Paint

43. What are the main hazards of using solvents in the home?

44. List two hazards of cleansers that contain petroleum distillates.

45. Should gasoline be used as a cleaning solvent? Why or why not?

46. What are the name and chemical formula for the white base pigment found in most paints?

Skin Treatments

47. What is an emollient?

48. List the three main components of a skin lotion.

49. Name one advantage of OMC over PABA in sunscreen lotions.

50. Name two compounds and one element used in some types of eye makeup.

51. What is the dangerous ingredient in kohl, used in many cultures for religious, social, and supposedly medicinal purposes?

52. How does ZnO function differently from OMS in a sunscreen formulation?

Lipsticks and Lip Balms

53. What are the main ingredients in lip balms and lipsticks?

54. What materials are used to color lipsticks?

Toothpastes

55. What is the principal cause of tooth decay? What are the best ways to prevent tooth decay?

56. What is the chemical formula of sodium monofluorophosphate? What is its purpose in toothpaste?

57. What is the purpose of **(a)** glycerol, **(b)** sodium fluoride, **(c)** sodium dodecyl sulfate, **(d)** potassium nitrate, **(e)** hydrogen peroxide and **(f)** hydrated silica in toothpaste?

58. How do fluorides strengthen tooth enamel?

Perfumes and Colognes

59. What is a perfume? What is a cologne?

60. What is a musk? Why are musks added to perfumes?

61. What is the function of menthol in some aftershave lotions?

62. Give the name of **(a)** a compound that functions as an antiperspirant and tell how it functions and **(b)** the name of a compound that functions as a deodorant and tell how it functions

Hair and Hair Care

63. What is the difference between a temporary and a permanent hair dye? Why is a permanent dye not really permanent?

64. What are resins? How are resins used in hair care?

65. Briefly describe the two processes involved in curling straight or straightening curly hair, with respect to the disulfide linkages in the hair.

66. What is the most important chemical component of hair shampoo? Write the name and chemical formula for a commonly used compound.

67. Describe the difference between hair coloring that allows one to go from dark to light-haired, compared to changing gray hair to a darker color.

68. What is the difference between a temporary, semipermanent, and permanent hair dye in terms of how they work?

ADDITIONAL PROBLEMS

Problems 69 through 72 refer to structures I through IV below.

    I. $CH_3(CH_2)_{15}N^+H_2CH_2COO^-$

    II. $CH_3(CH_2)_{10}COO^-$

    III. $CH_3(CH_2)_9CH(CH_3)-C_6H_4-SO_3^-\ Na^+$

    IV. $CH_3(CH_2)_{11}-C_6H_4-N^+(CH_3)_3\ Cl^-$

69. Which are soaps?

70. Which are synthetic detergents?

71. Which is a principal ingredient in baby shampoo?

72. Which is an amphoteric surfactant?

73. Write the structure for isopropyl palmitate, an ingredient in skin creams.

74. The hardness of water is reported as milligrams of calcium carbonate per liter of water. Calculate the quantity of sodium carbonate needed to soften 10.0 L of water with a hardness of 295 mg/L. (*Hint:* How much Ca^{2+} is present in the water?)

75. Phenylacetaldehyde and 2-phenylethanol have similar molecular masses, but phenylacetaldehyde is a top-note component and 2-phenylethanol is a middle-note component of perfumes. Referring to Table 21.2, explain why this is so.

76. When you search the Internet for information about the composition of a particular industrial detergent mixture, you find that it contains quats. What is the full name of this type of detergent (not the nickname)? What type of surfactant are these ingredients?

77. Sodium hydroxide performs several functions in a drain cleaner. Name two of these functions.

78. Optical brighteners make fabric appear to reflect more light (energy) than strikes the fabric. Do optical brighteners violate the law of conservation of energy? Explain.

79. Referring to Figure 21.11, describe how the esters of carnauba wax and spermaceti are similar and how they are different.

80. Review Figure 21.11a and Section 9.7. Draw the condensed structure of **(a)** the carboxylic acid and **(b)** the alcohol that is formed when the ester in beeswax undergoes hydrolysis.

81. Write equations for the dissolution of the calcium carbonate buildup in a toilet bowl by each of the following toilet bowl cleaners.
    a. hydrochloric acid
    b. sodium bisulfate
    c. citric acid $(HC_6H_7O_7)$

82. If a sunscreen label states "SPF 30," and you have skin that will burn in about 15 minutes when exposed to direct, bright sun, how long could you theoretically stay in the sun before reapplying the cream? What are some reasons you should reapply sooner than your calculation?

83. Which of the following molecules would not be considered a volatile organic compound?
    a. hexane
    b. ether
    c. formaldehyde
    d. water
    e. acetone

84. Which of the following molecules do you expect to be degraded most quickly by microorganisms in the environment?

85. Identify the purpose for each of the following ingredients.
    a. NaOCl
    b. $CH_3(CH_2)_{14}COONa$
    c. $(Na_5P_3O_{10})$
    d. $CH_3(CH_2)_{14}COOCH_2(CH_2)_{28}CH_3$

86. Calculate how much energy we can save by using cold (unheated tap water) compared to hot water (65 °C) per load of laundry. A typical modern high-efficiency washer uses between 50–100 L of water per load (older top loading washers used as much as 170 L). Complete your calculation assuming that tap water is 10 °C and that your washer uses 75 L of water.

CRITICAL THINKING EXERCISES

Apply knowledge that you have gained in this chapter and one or more of the FLaReS principles (Chapter 1) to evaluate the following advertising claims.

21.1. A laundry detergent "leaves clothes 50% brighter, 50% whiter [and is] 100% new & improved."

21.2. A product is claimed to be an odor-removing spray.

21.3. A brand of toothpaste claims to be "all natural" and contains silica and SLS [sodium lauryl sulfate].

21.4. A cosmetics advertisement states, "Most mineral-based cosmetics have synthetic preservatives such as parabens, dyes, and fillers which may be harmful. Our brand uses bismuth oxychloride, a natural ingredient."

21.5. A new skin cream "reduces wrinkles and prevents or reverses damage caused by aging and sun exposure."

21.6. A vitamin in a skin cream "nourishes the skin."

21.7. "Products that contain artificial ingredients do not provide true aromatherapy benefits."

21.8. "Laundry balls contain no chemicals [and yet are] reusable indefinitely [in the washing machine to] clean, deodorize, sterilize, bleach and soften clothes."

21.9. An advertisement for a deodorant claims to be "pH balanced for a woman's tender skin"; its proof is showing that a wet piece of litmus paper placed on her wrist does not change color.

COLLABORATIVE GROUP PROJECTS

Prepare a PowerPoint, poster, or other presentation (as directed by your instructor) for presentation to the class.

1. Research the kinds of pigments used by Renaissance artists and the Dutch Masters, how they were obtained and prepared, and some of the dangers of those pigments.

2. Read the poem, "Watching the Mayan Women," by Luisa Villani, in *Hayden's Ferry Review*, issue 26 (Spring/Summer 2000, Arizona State University, Tempe, AZ; http://www.loc.gov/poetry/180/067.html). Relate its content to the material in this chapter.

3. Examine the label on several brands of one or more of the following household or personal care products. Identify the essential ingredients in each type of product. Use a reference such as *The Merck Index* to determine the formula and function of each ingredient.
   a. scouring cleaner
   b. window cleaner
   c. oven cleaner
   d. toilet bowl cleaner
   e. liquid drain cleaner
   f. solid drain cleaner

4. Consult an industry-sponsored website about soaps and detergents. Then find a site sponsored by an environmental organization that presents information on how these materials affect the environment. Compare and contrast the two viewpoints.

5. Research the use of henna and its importance in South Asian and other cultures.

6. Compare facial makeup in three different cultures and/or historical periods, including the social significance and the chemical components.

7. Go to a local grocery store or discount store, find ten different variations of one or more of the following personal care products, and compare the ingredients, finding the commonalities and the unique ingredients. Compare the cost per ounce.
   a. toothpaste or tooth gel
   b. shampoos
   c. deodorants/antiperspirants
   d. hand creams and lotions

8. A website lists the following as green cleaners (see the essay on page 686). In what sense is each one green? Are any of them not green? If so, in what sense? Consider whether each substance is natural or synthetic, whether it comes from a renewable or nonrenewable source, its toxicity, and its effect on the environment.
   a. baking soda
   b. borax
   c. cat litter
   d. cornstarch
   e. hydrogen peroxide
   f. isopropyl alcohol
   g. lemon
   h. lemon juice
   i. olive oil
   j. vinegar (acetic acid)

CHEMISTRY @ HOME   Happy Hands

Materials required

- $^2/_3$ cup 99% rubbing alcohol (70%–90% isopropyl alcohol)
- $^1/_3$ cup plain aloe vera gel (the fewer additives, the better)
- 8–10 drops essential oil (such as lavender, thyme, clove, cinnamon leaf, peppermint, chamomile), optional
- Soap (without triclosan)
- Mixing bowl
- Spatula/wooden spoon
- Funnel
- Plastic bottle with pump or squirt top
- Glo Germ Mini Kit (to visualize bacteria)
- Friend

How clean are your hands? Do hand sanitizers kill more bacteria than washing with soap and water?

It is important to wash your hands several times a day to prevent the spread of disease and germs. What if you found out that your antibacterial soap and hand sanitizer were killing the "good" bacteria and were suspected of having harmful effects on the endocrine system?

For this experiment, you will make your own hand sanitizer and use soap that does not contain triclosan, a chemical found in most antibacterial soaps and cleaners. The Minnesota legislature just passed a ban on triclosan to take effect in 2017, and the chemical is still under investigation by the EPA and FDA.

This experiment investigates how washing your hands and using hand sanitizer can clean your hands without the need of an additive like triclosan present.

Part 1: Homemade Hand Sanitizer

Start by acquiring your supplies and making homemade hand sanitizer. You will pour $^2/_3$ cup of rubbing alcohol (70–90% isopropyl) into a small mixing bowl.

Next, you will measure out $^1/_3$ cup of aloe vera. To lessen the alcohol scent, you have the option of adding 8–10 drops of an essential oil. Mix the ingredients using a spatula or wooden spoon. Pour your solution into a container with a pump or squirt top using a funnel to prevent spills, and label your hand sanitizer as in Figure 1.

▲ **Figure 1**

Part 2: Hand Cleaning Effectiveness Experiment

Teaming up with a partner for this experiment will work best. Start by applying a nickel-sized amount of the Glo Germ gel on the palms of your hands. Rub it on your hands as you would lotion, completely covering hands, fingernails, and between your fingers.

Once the Glo Germ gel has been applied, have your partner shine the UV pen light on your hands. Doing this in a darkened room or closet makes it easier to see. What do you see? Is there any evidence of germs? (See Figure 2.)

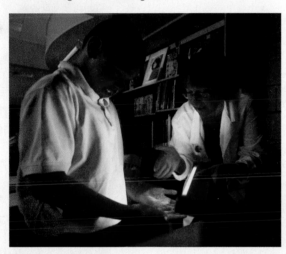

▲ **Figure 2**

Wash your hands with soap and water. Now return to the darkened room to shine the UV pen light on your hands again as in Figure 2.

What do you see? Was there a change in the number or size of spots highlighted under the UV light?

Switch roles and have your partner apply the Glo Germ gel. Follow the steps as you did above, but this time have your partner wash his or her hands using the hand sanitizer. Did you notice a difference? Were you able to control as many variables as you could? Did you both spend 20 seconds rubbing the soap and hand sanitizer into your hands?

Questions

1. Whose hands appeared to have less area with glowing germs?
2. Not all soaps and hand sanitizers are created equal. What other variables could you include to expand this experiment?
3. How are the mechanisms of soap and hand sanitizer different?

22

Learning Objectives

> Name some natural poisons and their sources. (22.1)

> Distinguish among corrosive poisons, metabolic poisons, and heavy metal poisons, and explain how each type acts. (22.2)

> Identify antidotes for some common metabolic poisons and heavy metal poisons. (22.2)

> Define *neurotransmitter*, and describe how various substances interfere with the action of neurotransmitters. (22.3)

> Explain the concept of an LD_{50} value, and list some of its limitations as a measure of toxicity. (22.4)

> Calculate lethal doses from LD_{50} values and body weights. (22.4)

> Describe how the liver is able to detoxify some substances. (22.5)

> Describe how cancers develop. (22.6)

> Name and describe three ways to test for carcinogens. (22.6)

> Define *hazardous waste*, and list and give an example of the four types of such wastes. (22.7)

> Explain how the structure of a chemical can lead to both hazardous properties and commercial effectiveness.

> Trace the process for designing safer chemical structures.

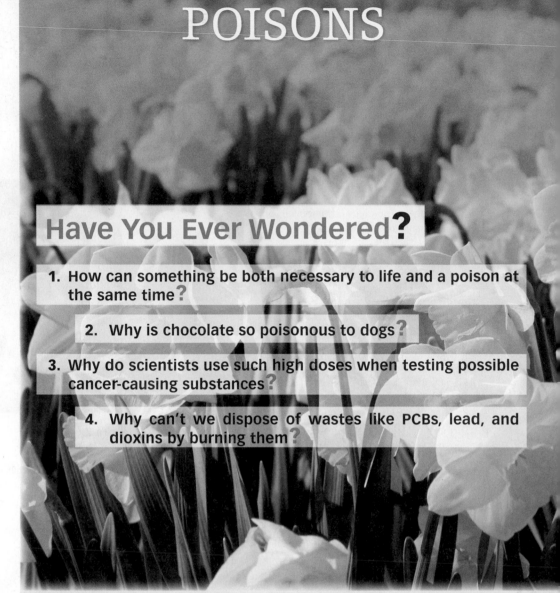

POISONS

Have You Ever Wondered?

1. **How can something be both necessary to life and a poison at the same time?**

2. **Why is chocolate so poisonous to dogs?**

3. **Why do scientists use such high doses when testing possible cancer-causing substances?**

4. **Why can't we dispose of wastes like PCBs, lead, and dioxins by burning them?**

TOXICOLOGY: WHAT MAKES A POISON?

What is a poison? Perhaps a better question is: How much is a poison? A substance may be harmless in one amount but injurious—or even deadly—in another. It was probably Paracelsus who around 1500 C.E. first suggested that "the dose makes the poison." Even a common substance such as table salt or sugar can be poisonous if eaten in abnormally large amounts.

A **poison** is a substance that causes injury, illness, or death of a living organism. We usually think of a substance as poisonous if it can kill or injure at a low dosage. The toxic dose need not be the same for everyone. An amount

We tend not to think of *poisons* and *natural* in the same context. But when it comes to poisons, nature has outperformed human beings for millennia. Even today, the most toxic substances come from nature, not scientific laboratories. The bulbs and main bodies of the common daffodil and other members of the amaryllis family are quite poisonous. All of the *Narcissus* species contain an alkaloid poison called lycorine. Symptoms of lycorine toxicity are vomiting, diarrhea, and convulsions. Its toxicity can cause touch dermatitis called "daffodil itch." The bulb's similarity to a common onion has led to incidents of accidental poisoning.

of salt that is safe for an adult could be deadly for a tiny infant. An amount of sugar that is all right for a healthy teenager might be quite harmful to her diabetic father.

Of course, some compounds are much more toxic than others. It would take a massive dose of salt to kill a healthy adult, whereas a few nanograms of botulin could be fatal. How the substance is administered also matters. Nicotine given intravenously is more than 50 times as toxic as when taken orally. Pure fresh water that is delightful to drink can be deadly if imbibed in large quantity. Recall from Chapter 17 that vitamin A is essential to health but that it can build to toxic levels in the body's fatty tissues.

In this chapter we take a look at poisons—both natural and human-made. We will learn what those poisons do to the body and how various poisonings are treated. **Toxicology** is the study of the effects of poisons, their detection and identification, and their antidotes. This chapter covers only a few of the many toxic substances that are known, giving priority to those that are more likely to be encountered in everyday life.

1. How can something be both necessary to life and a poison at the same time? There are many substances that, at low doses, carry out a needed function in the body. At high doses, the same substances cause a detrimental biochemical reaction. For example, iron ions are needed to make red blood cells. But an excess of iron can be absorbed by other cells, causing cellular death. Iron can also interfere with liver function.

22.1 Natural Poisons

Learning Objective ❯ Name some natural poisons and their sources.

When Socrates was accused of corrupting the youth of Athens in 399 B.C.E., he was given the choice of exile or death. He chose death by drinking a cup of hemlock. A **toxin** is a poison that is naturally produced by a plant or animal. Toxins were well known in the ancient world. Poisoning was an official means of execution in many ancient societies. Hemlock was the official Athenian poison. Snake and insect venoms as well as plant alkaloids were widely used.

Today, many aboriginal tribes still use various natural poisons for hunting and warfare. Curare, used by certain South American tribes to poison their arrows, is a notorious example.

Within the past 150 years, we have learned much more about these natural poisons. The hemlock taken by Socrates was probably prepared from the unripe fruit of *Conium maculatum* (poison hemlock), dried and brewed into a tea (Figure 22.1). That fruit contains coniine, which causes, nausea, weakness, paralysis, and—as in the case of Socrates—death.

◀ **Figure 22.1** Poison hemlock (*Conium maculatum*), the plant whose unripe fruit was probably the source of the hemlock taken by Socrates. The main alkaloid in poison hemlock is coniine.

▲ Oleander blossoms are beautiful—but all parts of the plant are poisonous.

▲ Rosary peas are often used to make necklaces and have been used for rosaries.

Alkaloids are heterocyclic amines (Section 9.8) that occur naturally in plants. In addition to coniine and the toxins in curare, alkaloids include caffeine, nicotine, morphine, and cocaine (Section 18.7). One of the most poisonous alkaloids is strychnine, which occurs in the seeds of several varieties of trees in the species *Strychnos*. A dose of only 30 mg can be fatal.

Toxins are produced by animals—snakes, lizards, frogs, and others—as well as by plants. Many insects and microorganisms also produce poisons. For example, each year about 20,000 Americans get *E. coli* infections, and approximately 1% of them die. Most *E. coli* bacteria are harmless, but some are particularly virulent and some produce verotoxin. Perhaps the most poisonous bacterial toxin of all is *botulin*, the nerve poison that causes botulism (Section 22.3).

Poisonous Plants in the Garden and Home

Because many natural poisons are alkaloids that occur in plants, it is not surprising that poisons are found in gardens and on farms or ranches. In addition to the toxic pesticides that might be found on a shelf (Chapter 20), some of the plants themselves are toxic. For example, oleander (*Nerium oleander*), a beautiful shrub, contains several types of poison, including the potent cardiac glycosides *oleandrin* and *neriine*. (Cardiac glycosides are compounds that have a steroid part and a sugar part and that increase the heart's force of contraction.) Oleander's poisons are so strong that a person can be poisoned by eating the honey made by bees that have fed on oleander nectar.

Iris, azaleas, and hydrangeas all are poisonous. So are holly berries, wisteria seeds, and the leaves and berries of privet hedges. Indoor plants can also be poisonous. Philodendron, one of the most popular, is quite toxic. The rosary pea (*Abrus precatorius*) has beautiful seeds that are often used to make jewelry. However, the seeds contain *abrin*. Abrin is composed of two peptide chains that act together to inhibit protein synthesis by shutting down ribosomes. The amount of poison in one pea seed, about 3 μg, is enough to kill a person. Fortunately, the seeds present little danger when swallowed whole. However, if the coating is broken, the toxin is released.

SELF-ASSESSMENT Questions

1. The study of poisons is called
   a. oncology
   b. pharmacology
   c. proctology
   d. toxicology

2. A poison is
   a. any alkaloid
   b. any chemical
   c. best defined by dose
   d. a synthetic chemical

3. Which of the following is not an alkaloid?
   a. caffeine
   b. botulin
   c. nicotine
   d. cocaine

4. The active ingredient in the poison that Socrates took was
   a. arsenic
   b. an alkaloid
   c. botulin
   d. ricin

Answers: 1, d; 2, c; 3, b; 4, b

22.2 Poisons and How They Act

Learning Objectives ❯ Distinguish among corrosive poisons, metabolic poisons, and heavy metal poisons, and explain how each acts. ❯ Identify antidotes for some common metabolic poisons and heavy metal poisons.

Poisons act in many ways. We examine the action of a few prominent poisons here. Recall from Chapter 7 that strong acids and strong bases have corrosive effects on human tissue. These substances indiscriminately destroy living cells. Corrosive chemicals in lesser concentrations can exhibit more subtle effects.

Strong Acids and Bases as Poisons

Both acids and bases catalyze the hydrolysis of amides, including proteins (polyamides).

Intact protein molecule + H₂O $\xrightarrow{\text{H}^+ \text{ or OH}^-}$ Fragments

Shape is vital to the function of a protein, and the hydrolysis products cannot carry out the functions of the original protein. For example, if the protein is an enzyme, it is deactivated by hydrolysis. In cases of severe exposure, fragmentation continues until the tissue is completely destroyed.

Acids in the lungs are particularly destructive. In Chapter 13, we saw how sulfuric acid is formed when sulfur-containing coal is burned. Acids are also formed when certain plastics and other wastes are burned. These acid air pollutants cause the breakdown of lung tissue.

Oxidizing Agents as Poisons

Other air pollutants also damage living cells. Ozone, peroxyacetyl nitrate (PAN), and the other oxidizing components of photochemical smog probably do their main damage through the deactivation of enzymes. The active sites of enzymes often incorporate the sulfur-containing amino acids cysteine and methionine. Cysteine is readily oxidized by ozone to cysteic acid.

Cysteine → Cysteic acid

Methionine is oxidized to methionine sulfoxide.

Methionine → Methionine sulfoxide

Tryptophan also reacts with ozone. This amino acid does not contain sulfur, but it undergoes a ring-opening oxidation at the double bond.

Tryptophan → Oxidation product

No doubt oxidizing agents can break bonds in many other chemical substances in a cell. Such powerful agents as ozone are more likely to make an indiscriminate attack than to react in a highly specific way.

Metabolic Poisons

Certain chemical substances prevent cellular oxidation of metabolites by blocking the transport of oxygen in the bloodstream or by interfering with oxidative processes in the cells. These chemicals act on the iron atoms in complex protein molecules. Probably the best known of these metabolic poisons is carbon monoxide. Recall (Section 13.4) that CO blocks the transport of oxygen by binding tightly to the iron atom in hemoglobin. Hemoglobin is bright red and is responsible for the red color of blood. Hemoglobin contains Fe^{2+}. During cooking, red meat turns brown because hemoglobin is oxidized to *methemoglobin*. Methemoglobin, which contains Fe^{3+}, is brown. Dried bloodstains turn brown for the same reason.

Nitrate ions, found in dangerous amounts in the groundwater in some agricultural areas (Section 14.5), also diminish the ability of hemoglobin to carry oxygen. Microorganisms in the digestive tract reduce nitrates to nitrites. We can write the process as a reduction half-reaction (Section 8.3).

$$2\,H^+(aq) + \underset{\text{Nitrate ion}}{NO_3^-(aq)} + 2\,e^- \longrightarrow \underset{\text{Nitrite ion}}{NO_2^-(aq)} + H_2O$$

The nitrite ions oxidize the Fe^{2+} in hemoglobin to Fe^{3+}, forming methemoglobin, which is incapable of carrying oxygen. The resulting oxygen-deficiency disease is called *methemoglobinemia*, known when it affects infants as "blue-baby syndrome." A compound called *methylene blue* is capable of reducing the methemoglobin back to hemoglobin.

Cyanides, compounds that contain a $C{\equiv}N$ group, are among the most notorious poisons in both fact and fiction. They include salts such as sodium cyanide (NaCN) and the covalent compound hydrogen cyanide ($H-C{\equiv}N$). Cyanides act quickly and are powerful. It takes only about 50 mg of HCN or 200–300 mg of a cyanide salt to kill. Cyanide exposure occurs frequently in victims of smoke inhalation from house fires. Experts use HCN gas to exterminate pests in ships, warehouses, and railway cars, and on citrus and other fruit trees. Sodium cyanide (NaCN) is employed to extract gold and silver from ores and in electroplating baths.

Worldwide, about 1.1 billion kg of hydrogen cyanide is produced annually. About 150 million kg is used to produce sodium cyanide for gold processing. The rest is used industrially in the production of plastics, adhesives, fire retardants, cosmetics, pharmaceuticals, and other materials.

Deaths that occur in house fires are often actually caused by toxic gases. Smoldering fires produce carbon monoxide, but hydrogen cyanide (formed by burning plastics and fabrics; Chapter 10) is also important. Some fire department rescue crews carry spring-loaded hypodermic syringes filled with sodium thiosulfate solution for emergency treatment of victims of smoke inhalation. In the Nazi death camps during World War II, both carbon monoxide and hydrogen cyanide were used to murder 6 million Jews, gypsies, Poles, and others. Treblinka, Belzec, and Sobibor used CO from internal combustion engines in closed chambers. Auschwitz/Birkenau, Stutthof, and other camps used HCN in the form of *Zyklon-B* (HCN absorbed in a carrier, typically wood pulp or diatomaceous earth).

Cyanides act by blocking the oxidation of glucose inside cells; cyanide ions form a stable complex with iron(III) ions in oxidative enzymes called *cytochrome oxidases*. These enzymes normally act by providing electrons for the reduction of oxygen in the cell. Cyanide blocks this action and brings an abrupt end to cellular respiration, causing death in minutes. Cyanides are sometimes used to commit suicide, particularly by health care and laboratory workers.

Any antidote for cyanide poisoning must be administered quickly. Providing 100% oxygen to support respiration can sometimes help. Sodium nitrite is often given intravenously to oxidize the iron atoms in the enzymes back to the inactive Fe^{3+} form. The resultant methemoglobin strongly binds the cyanide anion, which frees the cytochrome oxidase. As before, the methemoglobin must be removed. Sodium thiosulfate ($Na_2S_2O_3$) is then used if time permits. The thiosulfate ion transfers a sulfur atom to the cyanide ion, converting it to the relatively innocuous thiocyanate ion.

$$\underset{\text{Cyanide ion}}{CN^-(aq)} + \underset{\text{Thiosulfate ion}}{S_2O_3^{2-}(aq)} \longrightarrow \underset{\text{Thiocyanate ion}}{SCN^-(aq)} + \underset{\text{Sulfite ion}}{SO_3^{2-}(aq)}$$

Unfortunately, few victims of cyanide poisoning survive long enough to be treated.

CH₂—COOH
|
HO—C—COOH
|
CH₂—COOH

Citric acid

F—CH—COOH
|
HO—C—COOH
|
CH₂—COOH

Fluorocitric acid

Make Your Own Poison: Fluoroacetic Acid

The body generally acts to detoxify poisons (Section 22.5), but it can also convert an essentially harmless chemical to a deadly poison. Fluoroacetic acid (FCH_2COOH) is one such compound. Our cells use acetic acid to produce citric acid, which is then broken down in a series of steps, most of which release energy. When fluoroacetic acid is ingested, it is incorporated into fluorocitric acid. The latter effectively blocks the citric acid cycle by tying up the enzyme that acts on citric acid. Thus, the energy-producing mechanism of the cell is shut off, and death comes quickly.

Sodium fluoroacetate (FCH_2COONa), a salt of fluoroacetic acid and also known as *Compound 1080*, is used to poison rodents and predatory animals. It is not selective, making it dangerous to humans, pets, and other animals.

Fluoroacetic acid occurs in nature in an extremely poisonous South African plant called *gifblaar*. Natives have used this plant to poison the tips of their arrows.

Heavy Metal Poisons

Metals with densities at least five times that of water are called *heavy metals*. Many heavy metals are toxic, but lead, mercury, and cadmium are especially notable. Of course, metals need not be dense to be toxic. One especially toxic metal is beryllium, a very light metal. All beryllium compounds are poisonous and can cause a painful and usually fatal disease known as *berylliosis*.

People have long used a variety of metals in industry and agriculture and around the home. Most metals and their compounds show some toxicity when ingested in large amounts. Even essential mineral nutrients can be toxic when taken in excessive amounts. In many cases, too little of a metal ion (a deficiency) can be as dangerous as too much (toxicity). This effect is illustrated in Figure 22.2.

Some metal ions are critical to human health—in the right amounts. The average adult requires 10–18 mg of iron every day. When less is taken in, the person suffers from anemia. Yet an overdose can cause vomiting, diarrhea, shock, coma, and even death. As few as 10–15 tablets, each containing 325 mg of $FeSO_4$ (65 mg Fe per tablet) have been fatal to children. Large excesses of Fe^{2+} can damage the intestinal lining. Iron poisoning occurs when the concentration of circulating Fe^{2+} is more than the iron-binding proteins in the blood can take up.

Other heavy metals exert their action primarily by inactivating enzymes. In simple laboratory chemical reactions, heavy metal ions react with hydrogen sulfide to form insoluble sulfides.

$$Pb^{2+}(aq) + H_2S(g) \longrightarrow PbS(s) + 2 H^+(aq)$$
$$Hg^{2+}(aq) + H_2S(g) \longrightarrow HgS(s) + 2 H^+(aq)$$

Most enzymes have amino acids with sulfhydryl (—SH) groups. These groups bind with heavy metal ions in the same way that H_2S does, rendering the enzymes inactive (Figure 22.3).

Mercury (Hg) is a most unusual metal. It is the only common metal that is a liquid at room temperature. People have long been fascinated by this bright, silvery, dense liquid, once known as *quicksilver*. Children sometimes play with the mercury from a broken thermometer.

Mercury metal has many uses. It is used in thermometers and barometers. Dentists use it to make amalgams for filling teeth. It is used as a liquid metal electrical contact in switches. These uses are now restricted in many areas.

In the United States, about 140,000 kg of mercury is released each year into the air, about 40% from coal-fired power plants. (Although mercury occurs in only trace amounts in coal, we burn a billion metric tons of coal a year.) Other sources of mercury are waste incinerators and factories that produce chlorine and sodium hydroxide (chlor-alkali plants). The mercury returns to the land and water.

Mercury presents a hazard to those who work with it because its vapor is toxic. Mercury vapor is quite hazardous when inhaled, particularly when exposure takes

▲ **Figure 22.2** The effect of copper ions on the height of oat seedlings. From left to right, the concentrations of Cu^{2+} are 0, 3, 6, 10, 20, 100, 500, 2000, and 3000 $\mu g/L$. The plants on the left show varying degrees of deficiency; those on the right show copper ion toxicity. The optimum level of Cu^{2+} for oat seedlings is therefore about 100 $\mu g/L$.

▲ **Figure 22.3** Mercury poisoning. Enzymes catalyze reactions by binding a reactant molecule at the active site (Section 16.5). Mercury ions react with sulfhydryl groups to change the shape of the enzyme and destroy the active site.

place over a long period of time. An open container of mercury or a spill on the floor can release enough mercury vapor into the air to exceed the established maximum safe level by a factor of 200.

Hazardous chronic exposure usually occurs with regular occupational use of the metal, such as in mining or extraction. The body converts the inhaled mercury to Hg^{2+} ions. Because mercury is a cumulative poison (it takes the body about 70 days to rid itself of *half* of a given dose), chronic poisoning is a threat to those continually exposed.

In aquatic systems, mercury vapor is converted by anaerobic organisms to highly toxic methylmercury ions (CH_3Hg^+). Fish tend to concentrate CH_3Hg^+ in their bodies. Federal and state environmental agencies have warned people to limit consumption of certain species of fish—particularly swordfish and shark—or to avoid them entirely.

Fortunately, there are antidotes for mercury poisoning. While searching for an antidote for the arsenic-containing war gas lewisite (see the accompanying box, Arsenic Poisoning), British scientists came up with a compound for treating heavy metal poisoning as well. The compound, a derivative of glycerol, is called *British antilewisite (BAL)*. It acts by *chelating* (from the Greek *chela* meaning "claw") Hg^{2+} ions, surrounding the ions so that they are tied up and cannot attack vital enzymes.

$$\begin{array}{c} CH_2-CH-CH_2 \\ | \quad\quad | \quad\quad | \\ OH \quad SH \quad SH \end{array}$$

BAL

Mercury atom chelated by two BAL molecules

The bad news is that the effects of mercury poisoning may not show up for several weeks. By the time the symptoms—loss of equilibrium, sight, feeling, and hearing—are recognizable, extensive damage has already been done to the brain and nervous system. Such damage is largely irreversible. BAL and similar antidotes are effective only when a person knows that he or she has been poisoned and seeks treatment right away.

All compounds of mercury, except those that are virtually insoluble in water, are poisonous no matter how they are administered. However, metallic mercury does not seem to be very toxic when ingested (swallowed). Most of it passes through the system unchanged. Indeed, there are numerous reports of mercury being given orally in the eighteenth and nineteenth centuries as a remedy for obstruction of the bowels. Doses varied from a few ounces to a pound or more!

Lead is widespread in the environment, reflecting the many uses we have for this soft, dense, corrosion-resistant metal and its compounds. Lead (as Pb^{2+} ions) is present in many foods, generally in concentrations of less than 0.3 ppm. Lead ions also get into our drinking water (up to 0.1 ppm) from lead-sealed pipes. Lead compounds were once widely used in house paints, and tetraethyllead was used in most gasolines. Since those two uses were banned, exposure to lead has decreased dramatically, from about 15 $\mu g/dL$ in the 1970s to less than 2 $\mu g/dL$ today. The CDC sets a blood lead level above 10 $\mu g/dL$ as an unacceptable health risk, but adverse health effects can occur at lower concentrations. Effects include lower intelligence and poor school performance.

Lead and its compounds are quite toxic. Metallic lead is generally converted to Pb^{2+} in the body. Lead can damage the brain, liver, and kidneys. Extreme cases can be fatal.

Lead poisoning is especially harmful to children. Some children develop a craving that causes them to eat unusual things, and children with this syndrome (called *pica*) eat chips of peeling lead-based paints. These children probably also pick up lead compounds from the streets, where they were deposited by automobile exhausts. They also ingest lead from food and even from toys coated with

▲ In 2007, Fisher-Price voluntarily recalled almost a million children's toys because the paint may have contained excessive levels of lead. Less extensive children's toy recalls in 2011 affected particular varieties of memory testing cards, toy garden rakes, sketchbooks, and ESI-R Screening Materials.

Arsenic Poisoning

Arsenic is not a metal, but it has some metallic properties. In commercial poisons, arsenic is usually found as arsenate (AsO_4^{3-}) or arsenite (AsO_3^{3-}) ions. Like heavy metal ions, these ions render enzymes inactive by tying up sulfhydryl groups.

Arsenite ion   Enzyme   Enzyme (inactive)

There are numerous organic compounds containing arsenic. One such compound, *arsphenamine*, was the first antibacterial agent and was once used widely in the treatment of syphilis.

Arsphenamine

Another arsenic compound, *lewisite*, first synthesized by (and named for) W. Lee Lewis, was developed as a blister agent for use in chemical warfare. The United States started large-scale production of lewisite in 1918, but fortunately World War I came to an end before this gas could be employed.

Lewisite

lead-containing paint. Large amounts of Pb^{2+} in a child's blood can cause mental retardation, behavior problems, anemia, hearing loss, developmental delays, and other physical and mental problems.

Adults can excrete about 2 mg of lead per day. Most people take in less than that from air, food, and water, and thus generally do not accumulate toxic levels. If intake exceeds excretion, however, lead builds up in the body and chronic irreversible lead poisoning can result.

Lead poisoning is usually treated with a combination of BAL and another chelating agent called *ethylenediaminetetraacetic acid* (*EDTA*).

EDTA

Lead–EDTA complex

The calcium salt of EDTA is administered intravenously. In the body, calcium ions are displaced by lead ions, to which EDTA binds more tightly.

$$CaEDTA^{2-} + Pb^{2+} \longrightarrow PbEDTA^{2-} + Ca^{2+}$$

The lead–EDTA complex is then excreted.

As with mercury poisoning, the neurological damage caused by lead compounds is irreversible. Treatment must begin early to be effective.

Cadmium is another useful but troublesome heavy metal. It is used in alloys, in the electronics industry, in nickel–cadmium rechargeable batteries, and in many other applications. Cadmium (as Cd^{2+} ions) is quite toxic. Cadmium poisoning leads to loss of calcium ions (Ca^{2+}) from the bones, leaving them brittle and easily broken. It also causes severe abdominal pain, vomiting, diarrhea, and a choking sensation.

The most notable cases of cadmium poisoning occurred along the upper Jinzū River in Japan, where cadmium ions entered the water in milling wastes from a mine. Downstream, farm families used the water to irrigate their rice fields and for drinking, cooking, and other household purposes. Many of these people soon began to suffer from a strange, painful malady that became known as *itai-itai*, the "it hurts, it hurts" disease. Over 200 people died, and thousands were disabled.

▲ After importation of Chinese-made toys was restricted because they contained lead, some overseas manufacturers substituted cadmium. Unfortunately, cadmium ions are even more toxic than lead ions.

SELF-ASSESSMENT Questions

1. Which of the following is *not* a corrosive poison?
   a. HCN   **b.** HNO_3 **c.** O_3 **d.** NaOH

2. What type of poisons are carbon monoxide and cyanides?
   a. catalytic   **b.** heavy metal
   c. hemolytic   **d.** metabolic

3. Nitrites poison by
   a. blocking the action of cytochrome oxidase
   b. blocking the action of acetylcholinesterase
   c. displacing O_2 from oxyhemoglobin
   d. oxidizing Fe^{2+} in hemoglobin

4. Cyanides block normal respiration by acting as a(n)
   a. coenzyme   **b.** enzyme
   c. enzyme activator   **d.** enzyme inhibitor

5. The most important toxic heavy metals are
   a. gold, platinum, and silver
   b. iron, calcium, and mercury
   c. lead, silver, and gold
   d. lead, mercury, and cadmium

6. Which of the following is more likely to be deadly to a young child? An overdose of a multivitamin that contains
   a. ascorbic acid   **b.** biotin
   c. iron   **d.** lycopene

7. One reason for the dramatic decrease in lead found in the environment is the banning of
   a. leaded gasoline   **b.** lead in pencils
   c. lead solder for copper pipes   **d.** lead alloys

8. Lead poisoning can be treated with
   a. a chelating agent   **b.** an oxidizing agent
   c. a reducing agent   **d.** a strong acid

9. Cadmium compounds
   a. are used in some dental fillings
   b. act as blister agents in warfare
   c. cause "it hurts-it hurts" disease
   d. are found in high concentrations in fish

Answers: 1, a; 2, d; 3, d; 4, d; 5, d; 6, c; 7, a; 8, a; 9, c

22.3 More Chemistry of the Nervous System

Learning Objective ❯ Define *neurotransmitter*, and describe how various substances interfere with the action of neurotransmitters.

Some of the most toxic substances known act on the nervous system. Signals are shuttled across synapses between nerve cells by chemical messengers called *neurotransmitters* (Section 18.7). Neurotoxins can disrupt the action of a neurotransmitter in several ways: by interfering with its synthesis or transport, by occupying its receptor site, or by blocking its degradation.

One such chemical messenger is *acetylcholine (ACh)*. It activates the postsynaptic nerve cell by fitting into a specific receptor and thus changing the permeability of the cell membrane to certain ions. Once ACh has carried the impulse across the synapse, it is rapidly hydrolyzed to acetic acid and relatively inactive choline in a reaction catalyzed by an enzyme, acetylcholinesterase.

Acetylcholine   Acetic acid   Choline

The postsynaptic cell releases the hydrolysis products and is then ready to receive further impulses. Other enzymes, such as acetylase, convert the acetic acid and choline back to acetylcholine, completing the cycle (Figure 22.4).

▶ **Figure 22.4** The acetylcholine cycle.

People with Alzheimer's disease are deficient in the enzyme acetylase. They produce too little acetylcholine for proper brain function. Drugs to treat the disease, such as donepezil (Aricept®), inhibit the action of acetylcholinesterase, thus helping to prevent the decline of ACh levels. These drugs are only moderately effective.

Nerve Poisons and the Acetylcholine Cycle

Various substances can disrupt the acetylcholine cycle at one of three different points, as illustrated by the following examples.

Atropine

- Botulin, the deadly toxin produced by *Clostridium botulinum* (an anaerobic bacterium) found in improperly processed canned food, has a powerful effect on ACh; it blocks the synthesis of ACh. When no messengers are formed, no messages are carried. Paralysis sets in and death occurs, usually from respiratory failure.
- Curare, atropine, and some local anesthetics act by blocking ACh receptor sites. In this case, the message is sent but not received. Local anesthetics use this mechanism to provide pain relief in a limited area, but these drugs, too, can be lethal in sufficient quantity.
- Anticholinesterase poisons act by inhibiting the enzyme cholinesterase.

Organophosphorus Compounds as Insecticides and Weapons of War

Organic phosphorus insecticides (Section 20.2) are well-known nerve poisons. The phosphorus–oxygen linkage is thought to bond tightly to acetylcholinesterase, blocking the breakdown of acetylcholine (Figure 22.5). Acetylcholine therefore builds up, causing postsynaptic nerve cells to fire repeatedly. This overstimulates the muscles, glands, and organs. The heart beats wildly and irregularly, and the victim goes into convulsions and dies quickly.

(a) Normal catalysis of acetylcholine

(b) Catalysis inhibited by organophosphate toxin

▲ **Figure 22.5** (a) Acetylcholinesterase catalyzes the hydrolysis of acetylcholine to acetic acid and choline. (b) An organophosphate ties up acetylcholinesterase, preventing it from breaking down acetylcholine.

Q: *What functional group is split in the hydrolysis of acetylcholine?*

CH_3—N——$\overset{\overset{\displaystyle O}{\|}}{P}$—$OCH_2CH_3$
| |
CH_3 C≡N

Tabun
(agent GA)

CH_3—$\overset{\overset{\displaystyle O}{\|}}{\underset{F}{P}}$—$OCH$—$CH_3$
|
CH_3

Sarin
(agent GB)

CH_3—$\overset{\overset{\displaystyle O}{\|}}{\underset{F}{P}}$—$OCH$—$\overset{\overset{\displaystyle CH_3}{|}}{\underset{CH_3}{C}}$—$CH_3$

Soman
(agent GD)

CH_3—CH—CH_3
|
CH_3—CH—N—CH_2CH_2S—$\overset{\overset{\displaystyle O}{\|}}{\underset{CH_2CH_3}{P}}$—$OCH_3$
|
CH_3

VX

▲ **Figure 22.6** Four organo-phosphorus compounds used as nerve poisons in chemical warfare. Compare these structures with those of the insecticides malathion and parathion (Figure 20.12).

While doing research on organophosphorus compounds for use as insecticides during World War II, German scientists discovered some extremely toxic compounds with frightening potential for use in warfare. The Russians captured a German plant that manufactured a compound called *tabun* (referred to as *agent GA* by the U.S. Army), a compound with a fruity odor. The Soviets dismantled the factory and moved it to Russia. The U.S. Army, though, captured some of the stock.

The United States has developed other nerve poisons (Figure 22.6). One, called *sarin* (*agent GB*), is four times as toxic as tabun. It also has the "advantage" of being odorless. Another organophosphorus nerve poison is *soman* (or *agent GD*). It is moderately persistent, whereas tabun and sarin are generally nonpersistent. Yet another nerve poison is referred to as *VX*. It is only slightly more toxic than sarin, but it is more persistent in the environment. Note the variation in structure among these compounds. The approach to developing chemical warfare agents is much the same as that for developing drugs—find one that works, then synthesize and test structural variations.

These nerve poisons are among the most toxic synthetic chemicals known (although still not nearly as toxic as the natural toxin botulin). They are inhaled or absorbed through the skin, causing a complete loss of muscular coordination and subsequent death by cessation of breathing through paralysis, as described previously. The usual antidote consists of atropine injection, which blocks the acetylcholine receptor sites preventing the paralysis by the nerve agent, and artificial respiration. Care must be taken, because atropine in too large a dose is itself a poison. Without an antidote, death usually occurs in 2–10 min, depending on the dose absorbed.

The phosphorus-based insecticides malathion and parathion (Section 20.2) are similar to the nerve poisons used as chemical warfare agents but are far less toxic. Nonetheless, they and other insecticides like them should be used with great caution.

Nerve poisons have helped us gain an understanding of the chemistry of the nervous system. This knowledge enables scientists to design antidotes for nerve poisons, to better understand diseases of the nervous system, and to develop new drugs to treat pain and diseases such as Alzheimer's disease and Parkinson's disease.

SELF-ASSESSMENT Questions

1. Receptor sites for the neurotransmitter acetylcholine (ACh) are blocked by
   a. atropine   b. choline
   c. opiates   d. naloxone

2. Acetylcholinesterase is a(n)
   a. enzyme that breaks down acetylcholine
   b. hormone
   c. neurotransmitter
   d. stimulant drug

3. Curare blocks the acetylcholine receptors on muscle tissue, resulting in
   a. contraction of the muscle fiber
   b. excessive contractions and convulsions

   c. inability of the muscle to respond to motor nerve stimulus
   d. increased stimulation of the muscle fiber

4. Which of the following nerve poisons is much less toxic than the others?
   a. malathion   b. sarin
   c. soman   d. tabun

5. The most hazardous nerve poisons are
   a. alkaloids such as cocaine
   b. chlorinated hydrocarbons such as DDT
   c. hydrocarbons such as gasoline
   d. organophosphorus compounds

Answers: 1, a; 2, a; 3, c; 4, a; 5, d

22.4 The Lethal Dose

Learning Objectives ❯ Explain the concept of an LD_{50} value, and list some of its limitations as a measure of toxicity. ❯ Calculate lethal doses from LD_{50} values and body weights.

Some substances are much more poisonous than others. To quantify toxicity, scientists use the **LD_{50}** (lethal dose for 50%) value, which specifies the dosage that kills

50% of a population of test animals. This statistic is used because animals vary in strength and in their susceptibility to toxins. The dose that kills 50% is the average lethal dose.

Usually, LD_{50} values are given in terms of mass of poison per unit of body weight of the test animal (for example, milligrams of poison per kilogram of animal). Tested substances are most often given orally. (Values for intravenous administration can differ greatly from those for oral ingestion.) Although LD_{50} values are useful in comparing the relative toxicities of various substances, the values for test animals are not necessarily the same values that would be measured for humans. Clearly, it is unethical to test such toxins on human subjects, though data can be gathered through the testing of toxic substances on human cell cultures.

Table 22.1 lists LD_{50} values for a variety of substances. The larger the LD_{50} value, the less toxic the substance. In general, substances with oral LD_{50} values greater than 15,000 mg/kg are considered nearly nontoxic. Substances with LD_{50} values from 7500 to 15,000 mg/kg are considered to be of low toxicity; those with values from 500 to 7500 mg/kg, moderately toxic; and those with values less than 500 mg/kg, highly toxic.

Table 22.1 **Approximate LD_{50} Values for Selected Substances**

Substance	Test Animal	Route	LD_{50} (mg/kg)	Use or Occurrence
Sucrose	Rat	Oral	29,700	Table sugar
Sodium chloride	Rat	Oral	3000	Table salt
Ethyl alcohol	Rat	Oral	2080	Beverage alcohol
Aspirin	Rat	Oral	1500	Analgesic
Acetaminophen	Mouse	Oral	340	Analgesic
Nicotine	Mouse	Oral (intravenous)	230 (0.3)	Tobacco component, insecticide
Caffeine	Rat	Oral	192	Coffee and cola ingredient
Rotenone	Rat	Oral (intravenous)	132 (6)	Insecticide
Sodium cyanide	Rat	Oral	15	Gold extraction
Arsenic trioxide	Rat	Oral	15	Manufacture of insecticides and drugs
Ethylene glycol	Rat	Oral	6.86	Antifreeze
Ketamine	Rat	Oral	0.229	Veterinary anesthetic
Sarin	Human	Skin contact	0.01	Chemical warfare agent
Agent VX	Human	Skin contact	0.01	Chemical warfare agent
Tetanus toxin	Human	Puncture wound	0.0000025	In soil
Ricin	Mouse	Oral	0.000005	Castor beans
Botulin toxin	Human	Inhalation	0.000003	Possible biological warfare agent
		Oral	0.0000002	Food poisoning

The Botox Enigma

Botulin is the most toxic substance known, with a median lethal dose of only about 0.2 ng/kg of body weight. (Recall that 1 nanogram is one-billionth of a gram.) Yet botulin, in a commercial formulation called Botox®, is used medically to treat intractable muscle spasms and is widely used in cosmetic surgery to remove wrinkles. When a muscle contracts over a long period of time without relaxing, it can cause severe pain. Tiny amounts of Botox can be injected into the muscle, where it binds to receptors on nerve endings. This stops the release of acetylcholine, and the signal for the muscle to contract is blocked. The muscle fibers that were pulling too hard are paralyzed, providing relief from the spasm.

Botox is also used to treat afflictions such as uncontrollable blinking, crossed eyes, and Parkinson's disease. In the case of crossed eyes, for example, the optic

▶ Botox is a purified and extremely dilute preparation of the botulin toxin that causes the food poisoning known as *botulism*. When Botox is injected into specific muscles, it blocks the signals that cause muscles to contract. Because the muscles can't constrict, the skin levels out and can appear less wrinkled.

muscles cause the eyeballs to be drawn to focus inward. Treatment with botulin prevents the muscles from doing so, and repeated treatments correct the problem.

Botox curbs migraine headache pain in some people, probably by blocking nerves that carry pain messages to the brain and by relaxing muscles, making them less sensitive to pain. It is also used to treat excessive sweating, most likely by blocking the release of acetylcholine, the chemical that stimulates the sweat glands. Botox injections are used to treat bladder problems in which the patients are suffering from involuntary contractions of the bladder muscles. These contractions can cause incontinence or make it impossible to completely empty the bladder. Botox blocks the contractions.

In cosmetic surgery, small, carefully delivered amounts of Botox inactivate small facial muscles, markedly reducing "surprise wrinkles" in the forehead, frown lines between the eyebrows, and crow's feet at the corners of the eyes. These Botox treatments wear off in a few months.

SELF-ASSESSMENT Questions

1. Toxicity is often reported in terms of an LD_{50} value, which is the
   a. dose that kills half of a tested population
   b. lowest dose that kills an average 50-year-old person
   c. lowest dose likely to kill a 50-month-old child
   d. portion of the tested population killed by a 50-mg dose

2. According to Table 22.1, which of the following substances is least toxic?
   a. antifreeze
   b. nicotine
   c. ketamine
   d. sodium cyanide

Answers: 1, a; 2, b

2. Why is chocolate so poisonous to dogs? Chocolate contains several compounds related to caffeine, including the alkaloid *theobromine*. Dogs metabolize theobromine much more slowly than humans, so its toxic effects of hyperactivity, high blood pressure, rapid heart rate, and seizures last longer. This can lead to respiratory failure and cardiac arrest.

Theobromine

22.5 The Liver as a Detox Facility

Learning Objective ❯ Describe how the liver is able to detoxify some substances.

The human body can handle moderate amounts of some poisons. The liver is able to detoxify some compounds by oxidation or reduction or by coupling them with amino acids or other normal body chemicals.

Perhaps the most common route is oxidation. Ethanol (Section 9.5) is detoxified by oxidation to acetaldehyde, which in turn is oxidized to acetic acid and then to carbon dioxide and water.

$$CH_3CH_2OH \longrightarrow CH_3CHO \longrightarrow CH_3COOH \longrightarrow CO_2 + H_2O$$

A traditional antidote for methanol or ethylene glycol poisoning is ethanol, administered intravenously. This "loads up" the liver enzymes with ethanol, blocking oxidation of methanol until the compound can be excreted. A safer antidote, the drug fomepizole, inhibits the liver enzyme that catalyzes the oxidation of alcohols.

Highly toxic nicotine from tobacco is detoxified by oxidation to cotinine.

Nicotine → (liver enzymes) → Cotinine

Cotinine is less toxic than nicotine, and the added oxygen atom makes it more water soluble, and thus more readily excreted in the urine, than nicotine.

The liver has a system of iron-containing enzymes called *P-450* enzymes. The iron atoms are able to transfer oxygen to compounds that are otherwise highly resistant to oxidation. The P-450 enzymes catalyze the oxidation of fat-soluble substances (which are otherwise likely to be retained in the body) into water-soluble ones that are readily excreted. These enzymes also conjugate compounds with amino acids. For example, toluene is virtually insoluble in water. P-450 enzymes oxidize toluene to the more soluble benzoic acid, and then couple the benzoic acid with the amino acid glycine to form hippuric acid, which is even more soluble and is readily excreted.

It DOES Matter!

Before prescribing certain drugs such as statins, doctors will often perform a blood test for liver enzymes. The liver must function properly for these drugs to work; if the liver is damaged, some of these drugs can worsen the damage. "Leakage" of liver enzymes into the bloodstream indicates a problem that must be rectified before the drug is administered.

Toluene → oxidation → Benzoic acid → (H_2N-CH_2-COOH, Glycine) → Hippuric acid

Note that liver enzymes simply oxidize, reduce, or conjugate. The end product is not always less toxic. For example, as was noted in Section 9.5, methanol is oxidized to more toxic formaldehyde, which then reacts with proteins in the cells to cause blindness, convulsions, respiratory failure, and death.

The liver enzymes that oxidize alcohols also deactivate the male hormone testosterone. Buildup of these enzymes in a chronic alcoholic leads to a more rapid destruction of testosterone. This is the mechanism underlying alcoholic impotence, one of the well-known characteristics of the disease.

Benzene, because of its general inertness in the body, does not react until it reaches the liver. There it is slowly oxidized to an epoxide.

Benzene → (oxidation in the liver) → An epoxide (carcinogen)

The epoxide is a highly reactive molecule that can attack certain key proteins. The damage done by this epoxide sometimes results in leukemia.

Carbon tetrachloride (CCl_4) is also quite inert in the body. But when it reaches the liver, it is converted to the reactive trichloromethyl free radical ($Cl_3C \cdot$), which in turn attacks the unsaturated fatty acids in the body. This action can trigger cancer.

Getting Rid of "Toxins"

Two thousand years ago, Greek physicians applied the theory of the four *humors*—blood, phlegm, black bile, and yellow bile—to diagnose illnesses. They held that people in good health had a balance of these fluids and that too much or too little of one or more of them caused disease. A person who is positive and happy is still said to be "in a good humor." For a patient short of a humor, treatment included bed rest, a change in diet, or medicines. For those with too much of a humor, treatment included sweating, purging, and bloodletting. Today, some people believe that sweating gets rid of "toxins." And there is a rather large business built on the idea that laxatives and other "colon cleansers" somehow purify the body. Erroneous beliefs often persist for centuries.

▲ In the Middle Ages, bloodletting was often the treatment for inflammation from infection.

SELF-ASSESSMENT Questions

1. In the human body, which of the following statements is *not* true?
   a. Benzene is inert and thus nontoxic.
   b. Mercury vapor is converted to Hg^{2+}.
   c. Some nontoxic substances can be converted to toxic forms.
   d. Some poisons can be converted to nontoxic forms.

2. What substance is oxidized to formaldehyde in the liver?
   a. benzene
   b. methanol
   c. nicotine
   d. toluene

Answers: 1, a; 2, b

22.6 Carcinogens and Teratogens

Learning Objectives ❯ Describe how cancers develop. ❯ Name and describe three ways to test for carcinogens.

A **carcinogen** is something that causes the growth of tumors. A *tumor* is an abnormal growth of tissue and can be either benign or malignant. *Benign tumors* do not invade neighboring tissues. They often regress spontaneously, and they are characterized by slow growth. *Malignant tumors*, often called *cancers*, can invade and destroy neighboring tissues. Their growth can be slow or rapid, but the growth is unrestricted.

Cancer is not a single disease. Rather, the term is a catchall for about 200 different afflictions, many of them not even closely related to each other. We worry about carcinogens because half of the men and one-third of the women in the United States will develop cancer at some point in their lives.

What Causes Cancer?

Most people seem to believe that synthetic chemicals are a major cause of cancer, but the facts indicate otherwise. Like deaths in general (Section 18.3), most cancers are caused by lifestyle factors. Nearly two-thirds of all cancer deaths in the United States are linked to diet, tobacco, or a lack of exercise (Figure 22.7).

The U.S. Occupational Safety and Health Administration (OSHA) has a National Toxicology Program (NTP) that compiles ongoing lists of carcinogens in two categories. The 2013 list titled "Known Human Carcinogens" has 56 entries. For these, the NTP thinks there is sufficient evidence of carcinogenicity from studies in humans to establish a causal relationship between exposure to the agent, substance, or mixture, and human cancer. Another 187 entries are included in the list titled "Reasonably Anticipated to Be Human Carcinogens." These suspected carcinogens often are structurally related to substances that are known to be carcinogens, or there is limited evidence of their carcinogenicity from studies in humans or in experimental animals.

Some carcinogens, such as sunlight, radon, and safrole in sassafras, occur naturally. Some scientists estimate that 99.99% of all carcinogens that we ingest are natural ones. Plants produce compounds to protect themselves from fungi, insects, and higher animals, including humans. Some carcinogenic compounds are found in mushrooms, basil, celery, figs, mustard, pepper, fennel, parsnips, and citrus oils—

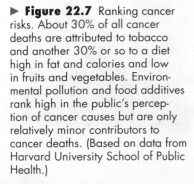

▶ **Figure 22.7** Ranking cancer risks. About 30% of all cancer deaths are attributed to tobacco and another 30% or so to a diet high in fat and calories and low in fruits and vegetables. Environmental pollution and food additives rank high in the public's perception of cancer causes but are only relatively minor contributors to cancer deaths. (Based on data from Harvard University School of Public Health.)

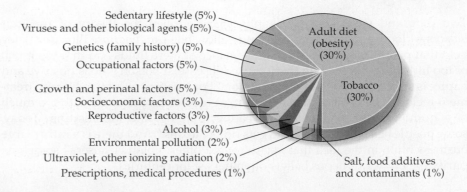

Sedentary lifestyle (5%)
Viruses and other biological agents (5%)
Genetics (family history) (5%)
Occupational factors (5%)
Growth and perinatal factors (5%)
Socioeconomic factors (3%)
Reproductive factors (3%)
Alcohol (3%)
Environmental pollution (2%)
Ultraviolet, other ionizing radiation (2%)
Prescriptions, medical procedures (1%)
Adult diet (obesity) (30%)
Tobacco (30%)
Salt, food additives and contaminants (1%)

How Cigarette Smoking Causes Cancer

The association between cigarette smoking and cancer has been known for decades, but the precise mechanism was not determined until 1996. The research scientists who found the link focused on a tumor-suppressor gene called *P53*, a gene that is mutated in about 60% of all lung cancers, and on a metabolite of benzpyrene, a carcinogen found in tobacco smoke.

In the body, benzpyrene is oxidized to an active carcinogen (an epoxide) that binds to specific nucleotides in the gene—sites called "hot spots"—where mutations frequently occur. It seems quite likely that the benzpyrene metabolite causes many of the mutations.

almost every place that a curious chemist looks. Carcinogens are also produced during cooking and as products of normal metabolism. Because carcinogens are so widespread, we must have some way of protecting ourselves from them.

How Cancers Develop

How do chemicals and physical factors cause cancer? Their mechanisms of action are probably quite varied. Some carcinogens chemically modify DNA, thus scrambling the code for its replication and for the synthesis of proteins. For example, aflatoxin B, produced by molds on foods, is known to bind to guanine residues in DNA. Just how this initiates cancer, however, has not yet been determined.

Genetics plays a role in the development of many forms of cancer. Certain genes, called *oncogenes*, seem to trigger or sustain the processes that convert normal cells to cancerous ones. There are about 100 known oncogenes, which develop from ordinary genes that regulate cell growth and cell division. Chemical carcinogens, radiation, or perhaps some viruses can activate oncogenes. It seems that more than one oncogene must be turned on, perhaps at different stages of the process, before a cancer develops. There are also *suppressor genes* that ordinarily prevent the development of cancers. These genes must be inactivated before a cancer develops. Suppressor gene inactivation can occur through mutation, alteration, or loss. In all, several mutations may be required in a cell before it turns cancerous. A hereditary form of breast cancer that usually develops before age 50 results from a mutation in a tumor-suppressor gene called *BRCA1*. Women who have a mutant form of *BRCA1* have an 82% risk of developing breast cancer, compared with most women in the United States, who have about a 10% risk.

Chemical Carcinogens

A variety of widely different chemical compounds are carcinogenic. We will concentrate on only a few major classes here.

Polycyclic aromatic hydrocarbons (PAHs), of which 3,4-benzpyrene (Section 13.7) is perhaps the best known, are among the more notorious carcinogens. These hydrocarbons are formed during the incomplete burning of nearly any organic material. They have been found in charcoal-grilled meats, cigarette smoke, automobile exhausts, coffee, burnt sugar, and many other materials. Not all polycyclic aromatic hydrocarbons are carcinogenic. There are strong correlations between carcinogenicity and certain molecular sizes and shapes.

Aromatic amines make up another important class of carcinogens. Two prominent ones are β-naphthylamine (Section 17.6) and benzidine. Once widely used in the dye industry, these compounds were responsible for a high incidence of bladder cancer among workers whose jobs brought them into prolonged contact with them.

Not all carcinogens are aromatic compounds. Two prominent aliphatic (nonaromatic) ones are dimethylnitrosamine (Section 17.6) and vinyl chloride (Section 10.3). Other nonaromatic carcinogens include three- and four-membered heterocyclic rings containing nitrogen or oxygen, such as epoxides and derivatives of ethyleneimine, as well as cyclic esters called *lactones* (Figure 22.8) on the facing page.

This list of carcinogens is far from all-inclusive. Its purpose is to give you an idea of some of the kinds of compounds that have tumor-inducing properties.

H_2N—⬡—⬡—NH_2

Benzidine

CH₂—CH—CH—CH₂

Bis(epoxy)butane

N-Laurylethyleneimine

β-Propiolactone

▲ **Figure 22.8** Three small-ring heterocyclic carcinogens.

Q: *To what family of compounds does each compound belong?*

Anticarcinogens

If the food we eat has many natural carcinogens, why don't we all get cancer? Probably because other substances in our food act as **anticarcinogens**. Antioxidant vitamins are believed to protect against some forms of cancer, and the food additive butylated hydroxytoluene (BHT) may give protection against stomach cancer. Certain vitamins have also been shown to have anticarcinogenic effects.

Antioxidant vitamins include vitamin C, vitamin E, and β-carotene, a precursor of vitamin A. A diet rich in cruciferous vegetables (cabbage, broccoli, Brussels sprouts, kale, and cauliflower) has been shown to reduce the incidence of cancer both in animals and in human population groups. The evidence for the anticarcinogenicity of the vitamins taken as supplements is less conclusive and, in the case of β-carotene, even contradictory. Yellow, red, or blue plant pigments called *flavonoids* are thought to be anticarcinogens. Good sources of flavonoids are citrus fruits, berries, red onions, green tea, and dark chocolate.

There are probably many other anticarcinogens in our food that have not yet been identified.

Three Ways to Test for Carcinogens

How do we know that a chemical causes cancer? Obviously, we can't experiment on humans to see what happens. That leaves us with no way to prove absolutely whether a chemical causes cancer in humans. Three ways to gain evidence against a substance are bacterial screening for mutagenesis, animal tests, and epidemiological studies.

The quickest and cheapest way to find out whether or not a substance may be carcinogenic is to use a screening test such as that developed by Bruce N. Ames of the University of California at Berkeley. The **Ames test** is a simple laboratory procedure that can be carried out in a petri dish (Figure 22.9). It assumes that most carcinogens are also mutagens, altering genes in some way. This usually seems to be the case. About 90% of the chemicals that appear on a list of either mutagens or carcinogens are found on the other list as well.

The Ames test uses a special strain of *Salmonella* bacteria that have been modified so that they cannot produce histidine, which must then be consumed. The bacteria are placed in an agar medium containing all nutrients except histidine. Incubating the mixture in the presence of a mutagenic chemical causes the bacteria to mutate so that they no longer require external histidine and can grow like normal bacteria. Cancer is an uncontrolled growth of cells, so growth of bacterial colonies in a petri dish means that the chemical added was a mutagen and, probably, also a carcinogen.

Chemicals suspected of being carcinogens can be tested on animals. Tests involving low dosages and millions of rats would cost too much, so tests are usually done by using large doses and a few dozen rats. An equal number of rats serve as controls; these are exposed to the same diet and environment but not given the suspected carcinogen. A higher incidence of cancer in the experimental animals than in the controls indicates that the compound is carcinogenic.

Animal tests are not conclusive. Humans are not usually exposed to comparable doses; there may be a threshold below which a compound is not carcinogenic. Further, human metabolism is somewhat different from that of the test animals. A substance might be carcinogenic in rats but not in humans (or vice versa). There is

Mutant induced revertants

Spontaneous revertants

▲ **Figure 22.9** The Ames test. Both petri dishes contain a modified strain of *Salmonella* bacteria. A chemical added to the upper petri dish has caused the *Salmonella* to revert back to their unmodified form, indicating that mutations have occurred and the chemical is a mutagen. The bottom dish is a control that shows only a few spontaneous mutations and little reversion.

3. Why do scientists use such high doses when testing possible cancer-causing substances? The validity of some animal tests is sometimes questioned in the media. However, it has been observed repeatedly that a substance that is not a carcinogen will not cause cancer even in high doses. The high doses often used in animal testing simply make positive results appear sooner.

only a 70% correlation between the carcinogenesis of a chemical in rats and that in mice. The correlation between carcinogenesis in either rodent and that in humans is probably less.

Animal studies are expensive. In cancer studies, animal tests of a single substance may take 4–8 years and cost hundreds of thousands of dollars. Further, animal testing is controversial. Supporters and opponents argue over both the ethics and the value of the tests.

Epidemiological studies use case series studies to provide evidence that a substance causes cancer in humans. A population that has a higher than normal rate for a particular kind of cancer is studied for common factors in the individuals' backgrounds. Studies of this sort showed that cigarette smoking causes lung cancer, that vinyl chloride causes a rare form of liver cancer, and that asbestos causes cancer of the lining of the pleural cavity (the body cavity containing the lungs). These studies sometimes require sophisticated mathematical analyses, and there is always the chance that some other (unknown) factor is involved in the carcinogenesis.

More recently, epidemiological studies were carried out to determine whether or not electromagnetic fields, such as those surrounding high-voltage power lines, certain electric appliances, and cellular phones could cause cancer. The results so far indicate that if there is such an effect, it is exceedingly small.

Birth Defects: Teratogens

A **teratogen** is a substance that causes birth defects. Perhaps the most notorious teratogen is the tranquilizer *thalidomide*. Fifty years ago, thalidomide was considered so safe, based on laboratory studies, that it was often prescribed for pregnant women. In Germany, it was available without a prescription. It took several years for the human population to provide evidence that laboratory animals had not provided.

Thalidomide

▲ Structure of thalidomide.

The drug had a disastrous effect on developing human embryos. About 12,000 women who had taken the drug during the first 12 weeks of pregnancy had babies who suffered from *phocomelia*, a condition characterized by shortened or absent arms and legs and other physical defects. The drug was used widely in Germany and Great Britain, and these two countries bore the brunt of the tragedy. The United States escaped relatively unscathed because Frances O. Kelsey of the FDA believed that there was evidence to doubt the drug's safety and therefore did not approve it for use in the United States. Kelsey received the Distinguished Federal Civilian Service Award from President John F. Kennedy in 1962.

Thalidomide is now being used for treating certain conditions, with strict restrictions in place to prevent its use by pregnant women. It has a unique anti-inflammatory action against a debilitating skin condition that often occurs with leprosy. Thalidomide is also being studied for use in the treatment of *wasting*, the severe weight-loss condition that often accompanies AIDS. Scientists are also studying thalidomide derivatives, hoping to enhance the beneficial effects while reducing the harmful properties.

Other chemicals that act as teratogens include isotretinoin (Accutane®), a prescription medication approved for use in treating severe acne. When taken by women during the first trimester of pregnancy, it can cause multiple major malformations. Educational materials provided to physicians and to patients have prevented all but a few tragedies associated with the use of isotretinoin.

▲ Frances O. Kelsey (left front) of the FDA receives a Distinguished Federal Civilian Service Award from President John Kennedy for her refusal to approve thalidomide for use in the United States.

Isotretinoin
(13-*cis*-retinoic acid)

By far the most hazardous teratogen, in terms of the number of babies born with birth defects, is ethyl alcohol, which causes fetal alcohol syndrome.

SELF-ASSESSMENT Questions

1. Some genes that are involved in cancer development when they are switched on are called
   a. DNA repair genes
   b. oncogenes
   c. P53
   d. suppressor genes

2. Some genes are involved in preventing the development of cancers. These genes, when switched off, allow cancerous cells to grow. They are called
   a. DNA repair genes
   b. oncogenes
   c. BRCA1 genes
   d. suppressor genes

3. Which of the following is not an aromatic carcinogen?
   a. β-naphthylamine
   b. ethyleneimine
   c. benzidine
   d. they are all aromatic

4. Many polycyclic aromatic hydrocarbons (PAHs) are known carcinogens. Sources of PAHs include
   a. artificial flavorings
   b. automobile exhausts
   c. pesticides
   d. plastics

5. A prominent aliphatic carcinogen is
   a. arachidonic acid
   b. butane
   c. valine
   d. vinyl chloride

6. Which of the following has not been seen to function as an anticarcinogen?
   a. flavonoids
   b. bis(epoxy)butane
   c. butylated hydroxytoluene
   d. vitamin E

7. The fastest way to determine whether a substance is likely to be a carcinogen is to use
   a. the Ames test
   b. animal tests
   c. epidemiological studies
   d. metabolic testing

8. The Ames test is a(n)
   a. evaluation of new compounds for hepatotoxicity
   b. immunological test for melanoma
   c. standardized final exam for introductory chemistry courses
   d. test for mutagenicity used as a screen for potential carcinogens

9. A teratogen is a substance that causes
   a. birth defects
   b. skin, eye, and respiratory irritation
   c. panic attacks
   d. tetanus

10. The teratogen that caused phocomelia—missing or shortened limbs—as a birth defect is
    a. ethanol
    b. isotretinoin
    c. malathion
    d. thalidomide

Answers: 1, b; 2, d; 3, b; 4, b; 5, d; 6, b; 7, a; 8, d; 9, a; 10, d

22.7 Hazardous Wastes

Learning Objective ❯ Define *hazardous* waste, and list and give an example of the four types of such wastes.

The public has become increasingly concerned in recent years about hazardous wastes in the environment. Problems created by chemical dumps made household words out of Love Canal in New York and Valley of the Drums in Kentucky. Although often overblown in the news media, serious problems do exist. Hazardous wastes can cause fires or explosions. They can pollute the air, and they can contaminate our food and water. Occasionally, they poison by direct contact. As long as we want the products that industries produce, however, we will have to deal with the problems of hazardous wastes (Table 22.2).

The first step in dealing with any problem is to understand the problem. A **hazardous waste** is one that can cause or contribute to death or illness or that

Table 22.2	Industrial Products and Hazardous Waste By-Products
Product	Associated Waste
Plastics	Organic chlorine compounds
Pesticides	Organic chlorine compounds, organophosphate compounds
Medicines	Organic solvents and residues, heavy metals (for example, mercury and zinc)
Paints	Heavy metals, pigments, solvents, organic residues
Oil, gasoline	Oil, phenols and other organic compounds, heavy metals, ammonium salts, acids, strong bases
Metals	Heavy metals, fluorides, cyanides, acid and alkaline cleaners, solvents, pigments, abrasives, plating salts, oils, phenols
Leather	Heavy metals, organic solvents
Textiles	Heavy metals, dyes, organic chlorine compounds, solvents

threatens human health or the environment when improperly managed. For convenience, hazardous wastes are divided into four types: reactive, flammable, toxic, and corrosive.

A **reactive waste** tends to react spontaneously or to react vigorously with air or water. Such wastes can generate toxic gases, such as hydrogen cyanide (HCN) or hydrogen sulfide (H_2S), or explode when exposed to shock or heat. Explosives such as trinitrotoluene (TNT) and nitroglycerin obviously are reactive wastes. Examples of household wastes that can explode include improperly handled propane tanks and aerosol cans. Another example of a reactive waste is sodium metal. It reacts with water to form hydrogen gas, which can then explode when ignited in air.

$$2\,Na(s) + 2\,H_2O(l) \longrightarrow 2\,NaOH(aq) + H_2(g)$$
$$2\,H_2(g) + O_2(g) \longrightarrow 2\,H_2O(g)$$

Reactive wastes can usually be deactivated before disposal. Propane tanks and aerosol cans can be thoroughly emptied and properly discarded. Sodium can be treated with isopropyl alcohol, with which it reacts slowly, rather than being dumped without treatment.

A **flammable waste** is one that burns readily on ignition, presenting a fire hazard. An example is hexane, a hydrocarbon solvent. Hexane (presumably dumped accidentally by Ralston-Purina) was ignited in the sewers of Louisville, Kentucky, in 1981, causing explosions that blew up several blocks of streets.

$$2\,C_6H_{14}(l) + 19\,O_2(g) \longrightarrow 12\,CO_2(g) + 14\,H_2O(g)$$

Examples of flammable household wastes include gasoline, lighter fluid, many solvents, and nail polish.

A **toxic waste** contains or releases toxic substances in quantities sufficient to pose a hazard to human health or to the environment. Most of the toxic substances discussed in this chapter would qualify as toxic wastes if they were improperly dumped in the environment. Some toxic wastes can be incinerated safely. For example, polychlorinated biphenyls (PCBs; Section 10.7) are burned at high temperatures to form carbon dioxide, water, and hydrogen chloride. If the hydrogen chloride is removed by scrubbing or is safely diluted and dispersed, this is a satisfactory way to dispose of PCBs. Some toxic wastes cannot be incinerated, however, and must be contained and monitored for years. Examples of household toxic wastes include paint, pesticides, motor oil, medicines, and cleansers.

A **corrosive waste** is one that requires a special container because it corrodes conventional container materials. Acids cannot be stored in steel drums because they react with and dissolve the iron.

$$Fe(s) + 2\,H^+(aq) \longrightarrow Fe^{2+}(aq) + H_2(aq)$$

Acid wastes can be neutralized (Chapter 7) before disposal, and lime (CaO) is an inexpensive base for this neutralization.

$$2\,H^+(aq) + CaO(s) \longrightarrow Ca^{2+}(aq) + H_2O(l)$$

Examples of household corrosive wastes include battery acid, drain cleaners, and oven cleaners.

The best way to handle hazardous wastes is not to produce them in the first place. This is a major focus of green chemistry. Many industries have modified manufacturing processes to prevent wastes (green chemistry principle 1) and maximize atom economy (principle 2), and some wastes can be reprocessed to recover energy or materials. Hydrocarbon solvents such as hexane can be purified and reused or burned as fuels. Often the waste from one industry can become raw material for another industry. For example, waste nitric acid from the metals industry can be converted to fertilizer.

If a hazardous waste cannot be used or incinerated or treated to render it less hazardous, it must be stored in a secure landfill. Unfortunately, landfills often leak, contaminating the groundwater. We clean up one toxic waste dump and move the materials to another, playing a rather macabre shell game. The best current technology for treating organic wastes, including chlorinated compounds, is incineration

GREEN CHEMISTRY

Richard Williams

Designing Safer Chemicals with Green Chemistry

Learning Objectives › Explain how the structure of a chemical can lead to both hazardous properties and commercial effectiveness. › Trace the process for designing safer chemical structures.

The chemical industry makes a large number of products that improve the quality of life for humans. However, uncertainty about the safety of many human-made chemicals has proved to be a concern. A good question is, "How can chemical developers identify and respond to hazards early in the research and development process?" Green chemists can address this challenge by understanding what makes a chemical toxic and using this information to design products that are both effective and safe.

The public and the regulators they influence are generally becoming much more concerned about risk, as shown by the European Union's Registration, Evaluation, Authorisation, and Restriction of Chemicals (REACH) legislation and proposed changes to the Toxic Substances Control Act in the United States. REACH requires companies to submit human health and environmental safety test data and an assessment of risks before manufacturing or importing chemicals. Although these are a step in the right direction, most chemical testing is typically done near the end of the research-and-development process. At that point, the product might have consumed many years and millions of dollars, and changes to a chemical product can be hard to make at that time.

Green chemistry offers the opportunity to optimize the commercial effectiveness of a chemical during R&D while minimizing the hazard and risk (Principle 4). Risk is a function of both a molecule's inherent hazard and exposure–contact between a chemical and an organism. As you learned in Section 22.2, hazard, the capability to cause harm, is an inherent characteristic of a molecule. Likewise, the commercial function is dependent on the molecule's content and three-dimensional arrangement of atoms. Hazards may be either physical (such as combustion or explosion) or toxicological (such as acute or chronic poisoning, carcinogens, reproductive toxins, or irritants). Risk often is reduced by the use of protective equipment that prevents exposure, but green chemistry provides a better idea.

Designing safer chemicals relies on understanding what makes a molecule hazardous. For example, halogen atoms are often used to make molecules stable, but that stability also prevents biodegradation and can increase the concentration of these materials in the environment. Polychlorinated biphenyls (PCBs) have become a health hazard because they build up in fish that live in polluted waters. The dose to a human who eats the fish can therefore be much higher than is healthy (Section 22.4). Design of molecules to include fewer chlorine atoms on aromatic rings can promote degradation (Principle 10) and eliminate significant exposure and risk. Current innovative design strategies specifically target unique physiological features of

the organisms of concern using chemicals with only the degree of stability needed to achieve the commercial function.

Understanding how molecular features are linked to the presence or lack of risks is critical. Stating that the nonselective contact herbicide paraquat is toxic to mammals provides little insight to a design chemist. But by knowing that paraquat accumulates and causes damage to the lung because of its charge, shape, and number of carbon atoms between the charged nitrogen atoms, chemists were able to design diquat. Diquat is equally effective but much less toxic because its structure lowers its ability to get into lung cells and reduces cellular damage (Principle 3).

Paraquat, $C_{12}H_{14}Cl_2N_2$ Diquat, $C_{12}H_{12}Br_2N_2$

▲ Paraquat accumulates and causes damage to the lung because of its charge, shape, and number of carbon atoms between the charged nitrogens. Diquat is equally effective but much less toxic because its structure lowers its ability to get into lung cells, thus reducing cellular damage.

Scientific advances are being sought to more effectively identify hazards based on structure during chemical design because traditional current testing methods are slow and expensive, rely on the use of lots of test animals, and do not provide information about how molecules are toxic. What we do have at this point are approaches including rules of thumb that link structural features to hazards, computational methods, databases of known hazards, models, and short-term assays. Green chemistry supports these ways of helping design chemists, who make thousands of new chemicals annually, to design safer molecules. These approaches can save money and time if they are introduced early in the design process.

For the future, researchers are trying to develop chemical design tools that can quickly screen large groups of structurally similar or diverse chemicals and build the knowledge base to support the design of safer and commercially successful chemicals. The innovation challenges are significant, but incorporating safety early in the chemical design process holds great promise.

Furnace

Gases

Gases vented
to atmosphere

Mechanism
for inserting
sample

Vessel containing
waste sample

Heated
air

High-temperature
furnace where
gases are incinerated

Sampling system
to determine any
residual compounds
not destroyed

▲ **Figure 22.10** A schematic diagram of an incinerator for hazardous wastes.

Q: *PCBs are burned in air at high temperatures, forming carbon dioxide, water, and hydrogen chloride. Write the equation for the incineration of the PCB component $C_6H_2Cl_3$—$C_6H_3Cl_2$.*

(Figure 22.10). At 1260 °C, greater than 99.9999% destruction is achieved. Often an issue with incineration is finding a place to build the incinerator. No one wants a hazardous waste incinerator nearby.

Biodegradation is another method that shows great promise. Scientists have identified microorganisms that degrade hydrocarbons such as those in gasoline. Other bacteria, when provided with proper nutrients, can degrade chlorinated hydrocarbons. Certain bacteria in the soil can even break down TNT and nitroglycerin. Through genetic engineering, scientists are developing new strains of bacteria that can decompose a great variety of wastes.

At What Price Poisons?

We use so many poisons in and around our homes and workplaces that accidents are bound to happen. Poison control centers have been established in many cities to help physicians deal with emergency poisonings. Are insecticides, medicines, cleansers, and other chemicals worth the price we pay in accidental poisonings? That is for you to decide. Generally, it is misuse of these chemicals that leads to tragedy.

Perhaps it is easy to be negative about chemists and chemistry when you think of such horrors as nerve gases, carcinogens, and teratogens. But keep in mind that many toxic chemicals are of enormous benefit to us and that they can be used safely despite their hazardous nature. The plastics industry was able to control vinyl chloride emissions once the hazard was known. We are still able to have valuable vinyl plastics, even though the vinyl chloride from which they are made causes cancer.

We have to decide whether the benefits we gain from hazardous substances are worth the risks we assume by using them. Many issues involving toxic chemicals are emotional. Most of the decisions regarding them are political. Yet possible solutions to such problems lie mainly in the field of chemistry.

We hope that the chemistry you have learned here will help you make wise decisions. Most of all, we hope that you continue to learn more about chemistry throughout your life, because chemistry affects nearly everything you do. We wish you success and happiness, and may the joy of learning go with you always.

4. Why can't we dispose of wastes like PCBs, lead, and dioxins by burning them?
PCBs, nerve gases, and other organic materials usually can be disposed of by incineration (Figure 22.10) because they are oxidized to simple compounds like CO_2 and H_2O. However, toxins such as lead, mercury, and arsenic are elements. If a waste containing lead compounds is incinerated, the lead will still be present in some form, such as PbO or elemental Pb, after incineration.

SELF-ASSESSMENT Questions

For items 1–4, match the waste described or named in the left column with the category in the right column.

1. tends to react vigorously with water
2. common strong acids and bases
3. discarded unused pesticides
4. charcoal lighter fluid

(a) corrosive
(b) flammable
(c) reactive
(d) toxic

5. The best way to deal with hazardous wastes is to
   a. burn them in an incinerator
   b. bury them in a landfill
   c. compost them
   d. minimize or eliminate their use

SUMMARY

A **poison** is a substance that causes injury, illness, or death. **Toxicology** is the branch of pharmacology that deals with poisons.

Section 22.1—A **toxin** is a poison that is naturally produced by a plant or animal. Many natural poisons exist, including curare, strychnine, and botulin. Many plants, including hemlock, holly berries, iris, azalea, and hydrangea, are toxic.

Section 22.2—Poisons act in different ways. Strong acids and strong bases are toxic because they are corrosive. They cause hydrolysis of proteins. Strong oxidizing agents such as ozone and PAN damage largely by deactivating enzymes. Carbon monoxide and nitrite ions are toxic because they interfere with the transport of oxygen by the blood. Cyanide is a poison because it shuts down cell respiration. Several substances, including fluoroacetic acid, are not highly toxic themselves, but in the body they form substances that are toxic. Heavy metal poisons such as lead and mercury inactivate enzymes by tying up their —SH groups. Cadmium leads to loss of calcium ions from bones. Heavy metal poisoning can be treated with chelating agents that tie up the metal ions so that they can be excreted.

Section 22.3—Nerve poisons, such as organophosphorus compounds, interfere with the acetylcholine cycle. Nerve poisons are among the most toxic synthetic chemicals known.

Section 22.4—An **LD$_{50}$** value indicates a dosage that kills 50% of a population of test animals. Many substances not ordinarily thought of as poisons do have some toxicity, indicated by a high LD$_{50}$ value. Botulism toxin has the lowest LD$_{50}$ value and is the most toxic substance known.

Section 22.5—The liver can detoxify substances by oxidizing or reducing them or by coupling them with other chemicals normally found in the body. The liver's P-450 enzymes carry out many such detoxifying reactions. Sometimes liver enzymes convert a less toxic substance, such as benzene or CCl$_4$, into one that is more toxic.

Section 22.6—A **carcinogen** causes the growth of tumors. A benign tumor grows slowly and does not invade neighboring tissues. A malignant tumor, or cancer, can invade and destroy neighboring tissues. Some carcinogens are natural, but most cancer deaths are linked to tobacco, diet, and obesity. Oncogenes appear to trigger processes that convert normal cells to cancer, and suppressor genes act to prevent the development of cancers. Some substances in our food, including antioxidant vitamins, act as **anticarcinogens**.

The **Ames test** screens substances for carcinogenicity by observing bacterial growth. Animal testing is often necessary but is not conclusive. Epidemiological studies appear to be most useful for identifying carcinogens.

A **teratogen** is a substance that causes birth defects.

Section 22.7—**Hazardous wastes** can be classified as **reactive waste**, which tends to react spontaneously or to react vigorously with air or water; **flammable waste**, which burns readily on ignition; **toxic waste**, which contains or releases toxic substances; and **corrosive waste**, which destroys conventional container materials. The best way to handle hazardous wastes is not to produce them in the first place. Wastes may be stored in a landfill or incinerated, and biodegradation shows promise for disposing of some wastes.

GREEN CHEMISTRY—Advances in chemistry can enable the identification and control or elimination of the hazards and risks that a new chemical might contain. Designing to eliminate non-preferred features can be pursued early in the development of new chemicals to achieve commercial effectiveness and maximize safety.

Learning Objectives

› Name some natural poisons and their sources.	Problems 45, 47
› Distinguish among corrosive poisons, metabolic poisons, and heavy metal poisons, and explain how each type acts.	Problems 4, 5, 9–15, 17–19, 22
› Identify antidotes for some common metabolic poisons and heavy metal poisons.	Problems 16, 20, 21
› Define *neurotransmitter*, and describe how various substances interfere with the action of neurotransmitters.	Problems 23–26
› Explain the concept of an LD$_{50}$, and list some of its limitations as a measure of toxicity.	Problems 7, 33, 34, 45–48
› Calculate lethal doses from LD$_{50}$ values and body weights.	Problems 1–3, 33, 34, 45–48, 52–54, 57
› Describe how the liver is able to detoxify some substances.	Problems 27–32, 55, 56
› Describe how cancers develop.	Problems 7, 8, 35, 36, 38, 41, 55
› Name and describe three ways to test for carcinogens.	Problems 39, 40, 42, 49
› Define *hazardous waste*, and list and give an example of the four types of such wastes.	Problems 43, 44
› Explain how the structure of a chemical can lead to both hazardous properties and commercial effectiveness.	Problems 60, 61
› Trace the process for designing safer chemical structures.	Problem 62

REVIEW QUESTIONS

1. Is ethyl alcohol (drinking alcohol) poisonous? Explain.
2. How can a substance be more harmful to one person than to another? Give an example.
3. How does the toxicity of a substance depend on the route of administration?
4. How does fluoroacetic acid exert its toxic effect?
5. List some sources of mercury poisoning and of lead poisoning.
6. What are the two leading causes of cancer?
7. Name several natural carcinogens.
8. How does cigarette smoking cause cancer?

PROBLEMS

Corrosive Poisons

9. Which of the following are corrosive poisons?
   a. sulfuric acid
   b. sodium hydroxide
   c. trinitrotoluene
   d. hexane
10. How do dilute solutions of acids and bases damage living cells?
11. Describe how hydrolysis affects the function of proteins.
12. How does ozone damage living cells?

Poisons Affecting Oxygen Transport and Oxidative Processes

13. What is a metabolic poison? List two such poisons.
14. What is methemoglobin? How does methylene blue affect it?
15. How do nitrates exert their toxic effect?
16. How does sodium thiosulfate act as an antidote for cyanide poisoning?

Heavy Metal Poisons

17. Which of the following are heavy metals?
   a. beryllium   **b.** lithium
   c. molybdenum   **d.** tellurium
18. Iron (as Fe^{2+}) is a necessary nutrient. What are the effects of too little Fe^{2+}? Of too much?
19. How does the toxic effect from eating certain fish compare to ordinary mercury poisoning?
20. How does BAL act as an antidote for mercury poisoning?
21. How does EDTA act as an antidote for lead poisoning?
22. How does cadmium (as Cd^{2+}) exert its toxic effect? What is *itai-itai*?

Chemistry of the Nervous System

23. List three nerve poisons developed for use in warfare.
24. Why was *tabun* considered to be less effective as a nerve poison?
25. What are the acetylcholine blocking poisons? How do they act on the acetylcholine cycle?
26. Describe some uses of botulin in medicine.

Detoxification

27. How does the liver detoxify nicotine?
28. What is the P-450 system? What is its function?
29. Do the P-450 enzymes always detoxify foreign substances? Explain.
30. List two steps in the detoxification of ingested toluene. What is the effect of these steps?
31. Why does chronic alcoholism also lead to decreases in testosterone?
32. Why is fomepizole a better antidote for methanol poisoning?

Lethal Dose

33. The LD_{50} value for methyl isocyanate (orally in rats), the substance that caused the Bhopal tragedy, is 140 mg/kg. Estimate the lethal dose for a 125-lb human.
34. The LD_{50} value for carbaryl (Sevin®), given orally to rats, is 307 mg/kg. If this value could be extrapolated to humans, what would be the lethal dose for an 18-kg child?

Carcinogens and Teratogens

35. A mutagen is a generic term for a mutation-causing agent. Some mutagens are also carcinogens, meaning that they cause cancer. How would a scientist determine if a substance is a mutagen?
36. What are teratogens? Why can teratogens be particularly difficult to detect?
37. List some conditions under which polycyclic hydrocarbons are formed.
38. Name **(a)** two aromatic amines and **(b)** two aliphatic compounds that are carcinogens.
39. List some of the limitations involved in testing compounds for carcinogenicity by using laboratory animals.
40. What is an epidemiological study? Can such a study prove absolutely that a substance causes cancer?
41. What is an oncogene? How do they compare to suppressor genes?
42. Describe the Ames test for mutagenicity. What are its limitations as a screening test for carcinogens?

Hazardous Wastes

43. Define and give an example of a toxic waste.
44. Which of the following are corrosive wastes?
   a. sodium hydroxide, which is used as a drain cleaner
   b. Sr metal, which reacts with water to form flammable H_2 gas
   c. trinitrotoluene, an explosive
   d. phosphoric acid, which dissolves steel drums

ADDITIONAL PROBLEMS

45. Botulin toxin has an estimated LD_{50} value of 200 pg/kg of body weight and an estimated molar mass of 150,000 g/mol. About how many molecules would likely comprise a lethal dose for a 66-kg human?

46. Refer to Problem 45. How much botulin would it take to likely kill **(a)** a 60-kg person and **(b)** all 7.0 billion people on Earth, assuming an average body weight of 60 kg?

47. Absinthe, a wormwood-flavored liqueur that was highly popular in France from about 1880 to 1914, contains thujone, a neurotoxin with an LD_{50} value (orally in mice) of 87.5 mg/kg. Absinthe was the subject of famous artworks by Degas, Van Gogh, and others. Banned in 1912 in the United States, the liqueur became legal again in 2007, with levels in the commercially distilled product limited to 10 mg/L or less. **(a)** Determine the molecular formula of thujone from the structure below. **(b)** Estimate the likely lethal dose for a 55-kg person. **(c)** What is the maximum mass of thujone that a 0.50-L bottle of absinthe can contain?

$$CH_3$$
$$O$$
$$H_3C \quad CH_3$$
Thujone

48. Phosphorus comes in two forms, or *allotropes*. Red phosphorus is used in manufacture of matches and is only mildly toxic. White phosphorus, a waxy yellow solid, is highly toxic, with an orally ingested lethal dose of just 70 mg for a 55-kg person. **(a)** What is the LD_{50} (in milligrams per kilogram) for white phosphorus? **(b)** Where does white phosphorus fall in Table 22.1?

49. A British study more than 50 years ago involved 1357 people with lung cancer. Of these, 1350 were smokers and 7 were nonsmokers. A control group without cancer, matched in age and other characteristics, consisted of 1296 smokers and 61 nonsmokers. **(a)** Calculate the percentage of cancer sufferers who smoked and the percentage of controls who smoked. What can you infer from these proportions? **(b)** Calculate the odds of smoking for the cancer sufferers and the odds of smoking for the controls. **(c)** Calculate the odds ratio. Interpret this result.

50. Which of the nutrients listed in Table 17.3 are heavy metals?

51. How is the statement "The dose makes the poison" related to Table 22.1?

52. Plutonium is an extremely hazardous heavy metal, mainly because it is radioactive. In one set of experiments, the LD_{50} value for plutonium (injected into rats) was found to be somewhat more than 200 μg per/kg. Where in Table 22.1 should plutonium be placed?

53. Refer to Problem 52, and determine whether either of the following doses of plutonium would likely be considered lethal for a 55-kg female: **(a)** a 1.5-mg dose and **(b)** a 20-mg dose.

54. Referring to Table 22.1, determine whether the following would be likely to be lethal to a 60-kg male: **(a)** a 10-mg dose of arsenic trioxide and **(b)** a 25-mg dose of ketamine.

55. Justify the following statement: "Benzene itself is not toxic; the body makes it toxic."

56. Why does the added oxygen atom in cotinine make it more soluble in water? Why is this important?

57. The LD_{50} value for ethyl alcohol given orally to rats is 10.3 g/kg. **(a)** What volume in milliliters of 100 proof vodka (50% v/v ethanol) would be likely to kill a typical 395-g rat? **(b)** Assuming that the rat's mass is 67% water, what would its blood alcohol level be, in milligrams per milliliter? (Density of 100 proof vodka is 0.92 g/mL and the density of pure ethanol is 0.79 g/mL.)

58. Can a chemical be classified as toxic if it causes injury to cells only at high concentrations? Explain.

59. What is the current "gold standard" for chemical toxicity testing?
  a. cultured cell testing
  b. rodent testing
  c. human testing
  d. nanotechnology testing

60. Which of these is an example of how green chemistry can contribute to the design of safer chemicals?
  a. A consumer chooses a safer product that does not work as well as the original version of the product.
  b. A chemist identifies structural features of a chemical that are responsible for hazardous properties and replaces those portions of the molecule with safer alternatives.
  c. Legislators pass a law that bans the use of any chemical that contains chlorine.
  d. A chemist suggests that protective equipment be worn during the use of a toxic chemical.

61. How can green chemistry lead to the design of safer chemicals?
  a. Testing chemicals at the end of the R&D process will make sure they are safe.
  b. By linking specific structural features to hazards, chemists can design those features out of new chemicals.
  c. Risk can be reduced by the use of protective equipment.
  d. Chemists can make molecules less biodegradable so that they are not introduced to the environment.

62. Explain why it would be greener to replace paraquat with diquat as an herbicide.

CRITICAL THINKING EXERCISES

Apply knowledge that you have gained in this chapter and one or more of the FLaReS principles (Chapter 1) to evaluate the following statements or claims.

22.1. An online advertisement implies that echinacea is non-toxic because it is natural.

22.2. A book claims that all aromatic compounds are carcinogens and should be banned.

22.3. A natural foods enthusiast contends that no food that contains a carcinogen should be allowed on the market.

22.4. An advertisement promotes "Organic Natural Chemical-Free Mattresses." The company claims its products contain "no toxins, formaldehyde, VOCs, pesticides, or synthetic or chemical foams."

22.5. An advertisement implies that a supplement containing β-carotene should be taken in megadoses because it is an antioxidant and can therefore prevent cancer.

 COLLABORATIVE GROUP PROJECTS

Prepare a PowerPoint, poster, or other presentation (as directed by your instructor) to be shared with the class.

1. Prepare a brief report on one of the following pesticides. Include chemical formula, uses, toxicity, and possible carcinogenicity.
   a. alachlor
   b. fenoxycarb
   c. propoxur
   d. propachlor
   e. tribufos
   f. trichlorfon

2. Propose a disposal method for each of the following wastes. Be as specific as possible, and justify your choice.
   a. hydrochloric acid contaminated with iron salts
   b. picric acid (an explosive)
   c. soybean oil contaminated with PCBs

3. Choose one of the following arguments, and be prepared to support either side (for or against).

   a. Carcinogens that occur naturally in foods should be subjected to the same tests used to evaluate synthetic pesticides.
   b. Substances should be tested for toxicity or carcinogenicity on laboratory animals.
   c. Nerve gases are less humane than bullets in warfare.

4. Search the Internet for information on brownfields. What are they? What is being done about them? Are there any near you?

5. Many tooth fillings consist of amalgams containing mercury, and the safety of these amalgams is a recurring controversy. Using your favorite search methods, find some websites dealing with this issue and write a brief analysis of the opposing points of view.

6. Search the Internet for information on the effects of cadmium in the environment and do a risk–benefit analysis (Chapter 1) of cadmium use.

CHEMISTRY@HOME Salty Seeds

Materials requried

- Table salt (NaCl)
- 6 small plastic bags
- 5 small clear plastic cups
- Kitchen scale
- Dropper
- Teaspoon
- Lettuce seeds
- Paper towels
- Measuring cup
- Distilled water

Who doesn't like salt on their popcorn, French fries, or buttered corn on the cob? Table salt is safe for humans to consume in small amounts but what about plants? How sensitive are certain plants to saltwater? How much salt is toxic to lettuce seeds?

We all have sodium in our diets. But where else do we use sodium chloride? It is a common chemical in many industrial processes. Sodium chloride (rock salt) is a common de-icer, but more and more places are using alternatives since it damages concrete, contaminates soil, and harms plants and animals. The goal of green chemistry is the design of materials and processes that are inherently safer for human health and the environment. It is important that chemists be trained to consider the effects of the materials they use on human health and the environment. Understanding ecotoxicity is essential to designing safer chemicals and processes.

This is an ecotoxicity experiment that uses different concentrations of table salt (sodium chloride, NaCl) on samples of lettuce seed. In this experiment, you will determine at what concentrations NaCl is toxic to lettuce seeds.

Start by making a 10% by weight NaCl stock solution. Weigh out 10 g of NaCl and fill the measuring cup with water just short of the $1/2$ cup line.

Next you will perform a serial dilution complete $1/10$ dilution for each solution. Label 5 cups with 10%, 1%, 0.1%, 0.01%, and 0.001% NaCl.

Take one $1/4$ teaspoon of the 10% solution and dilute with nine $1/4$ teaspoon portions of distilled water to make the 1% solution. Then take one $1/4$ teaspoon of the 1% solution with nine $1/4$ teaspoon portions of distilled water to make the next, and so on.

Label six plastic bags control and 10%, 1%, 0.1%, 0.01%, and 0.001% NaCl. Place a folded paper towel in each plastic bag.

Pour 1 teaspoon of distilled water into the control and the other bags.

Carefully add six lettuce seeds to each of the bags, spacing the seeds evenly on the wet paper towel inside the bag. Figure 1 shows each bag aligned with the cup of the solution it contains.

▲**Figure 1**

Carefully trickle the different concentration NaCl solutions into the corresponding bags. Check to make sure the seeds are still on the paper towel after adding the solutions. Seal the bags to retain moisture and place in a well-lit location but out of direct sunlight. Figure 2 shows the control.

▲**Figure 2**

Check the seeds each day. Record how many seeds have germinated in each bag. How many seeds sprouted in each bag? Wait five days to allow the seeds to germinate.

After germination is complete, use the figure below as a model to measure growth of the radical (length is indicated in Figure 3).

▲**Figure 3**

Questions

1. Did the seeds in the control bag sprout faster than the others?
2. Which concentration is sufficiently toxic that the seeds do not germinate at all?
3. Can you determine which concentration impedes seed germination?
4. What do your results tell you about the effects of salt toxicity on lettuce seeds?

APPENDIX REVIEW OF MEASUREMENT AND MATHEMATICS

Accurate measurements are essential to science. As noted in Chapter 1, measurements can be made in a variety of units, but most scientists use the International System of Units (SI). The data they record sometimes has to be converted from one kind of unit to another and otherwise manipulated mathematically. This appendix extends the discussion of metric measurement and reviews some of the mathematics that you may find useful in this course or other endeavors.

A.1 The International System of Units

The standard SI unit of length is the *meter*. This distance was once defined as 0.0000001 of Earth's quadrant—that is, of the distance from the North Pole to the equator measured along a meridian. The quadrant proved difficult to measure accurately, and today the meter is defined precisely as the distance light travels in a vacuum during 1/299,792,458 of a second.

The SI unit of mass is the *kilogram* (1 kg = 1000 g). It is based on a standard platinum–iridium cylinder kept at the International Bureau of Weights and Measures. The *gram* is a more convenient unit for many chemical operations.

The derived SI unit of volume is the *cubic meter*. The units more frequently employed in chemistry, however, are the *liter* (1 L = 0.001 m^3) and the *milliliter* (1 mL = 0.001 L). Other SI units of length, mass, and volume are derived from these basic units. Table A.1 lists some metric units of length, mass, and volume and illustrates the use of prefixes.

Table A.1	Some Metric Units of Length, Mass, and Volume
Length	
1 kilometer (km)	= 1000 meters (m)
1 meter (m)	= 100 centimeters (cm)
1 centimeter (cm)	= 10 millimeters (mm)
1 millimeter (mm)	= 1000 micrometers (μm)
1 micrometer (μm)	= 1000 nanometers (nm)
Mass	
1 kilogram (kg)	= 1000 grams (g)
1 gram (g)	= 1000 milligrams (mg)
1 milligram (mg)	= 1000 micrograms (μg)
Volume	
1 liter (L)	= 1000 milliliters (mL)
1 milliliter (mL)	= 1000 microliters (μL)
1 milliliter (mL)	= 1 cubic centimeter (cm^3)

A.2 Exponential (Scientific) Notation

Scientists often use numbers that are inconceivably large or small. For example, light travels at about 300,000,000 m/s. There are 602,200,000,000,000,000,000,000 carbon atoms in 12.01 g of carbon. On the small side, the diameter of an atom is about 0.0000000001 m, and the diameter of an atomic nucleus is about 0.000000000000001 m. Because it is difficult to keep track of the zeros in such numbers, scientists find it convenient to express them in exponential notation.

A number is in *exponential notation* when it is written as the product of a coefficient and a power of 10. (Such a number is called *scientific notation* when the coefficient has a value between 1 and 10). Two examples are

$$4.18 \times 10^3 \quad \text{and} \quad 6.57 \times 10^{-4}$$

Expressing numbers in exponential form generally serves two purposes.

1. We can write very large or very small numbers in a minimum of space and with a reduced chance of typographical error.
2. We can convey explicit information about the precision of measurements: The number of significant figures (Section A.4) in a measured quantity is stated unambiguously.

In the expression 10^n, n is the exponent of 10, and the number 10 is said to be raised to the nth power. If n is a *positive quantity*, 10^n has a value *greater than 1*. If n is a *negative quantity*, 10^n has a value *less than 1*. We are particularly interested in cases where n is an integer. For example,

We express 612,000 in scientific notation as follows:

$$612{,}000 = 6.12 \times 100{,}000 = 6.12 \times 10^5$$

We express 0.000505 in scientific notation as

$$0.000505 = 5.05 \times 0.0001 = 5.05 \times 10^{-4}$$

We can use a more direct approach to converting numbers to scientific notation.

- Count the number of places a decimal point must be moved to produce a coefficient having a value between 1 and 10.
- The number of places counted then becomes the power of 10.
- The power of 10 is *positive* if the decimal point is moved to the *left*.

$$6\,12000 \quad = \quad 6.12 \times 10^5$$

Move the decimal point (here understood) *five places to the left*

The exponent is (positive) 5

- The power of 10 is *negative* if the decimal point is moved to the *right*.

$$0.000505 \quad = \quad 5.05 \times 10^{-4}$$

Move the decimal point *four places to the right*

The exponent is (negative) 4

To convert a number from exponential form to the conventional form, move the decimal point in the opposite direction.

$$3.75 \times 10^6 = 3.750000$$

| The exponent is 6 | Move the decimal point six places to the *right* |

$$7.91 \times 10^{-7} = 0.0000007.91$$

| The exponent is −7 | Move the decimal point seven places to the *left* |

It is easy to handle exponential numbers on most calculators. A typical procedure is to enter the number, hit the key [EE] or [EXP], and then enter the exponent of 10. The keystrokes required for the number 2.85×10^7 are [2] [.] [8] [5] [EE] [7].

For the number 1.67×10^{-5}, the keystrokes are [1] [.] [6] [7] [EXP] [5] [±]; the last keystroke changes the sign of the exponent. Many calculators can be set to convert all numbers and calculated results to the exponential form, regardless of the form in which the numbers are entered. Most scientific and graphing calculators can also be set to display a fixed number of digits in the results.

Addition and Subtraction

To add or subtract numbers in exponential notation using a scientific or graphing calculator, simply enter the numbers as usual and perform the desired operations. However, to add or subtract numbers *by hand* in exponential notation, it is necessary to express each quantity as the *same power of 10*. In calculations, this approach treats the power of 10 in the same way as a unit—it is simply "carried along." For example, we express each quantity in the following calculation with the power 10^{-3}.

$$(3.22 \times 10^{-3}) + (7.3 \times 10^{-4}) - (4.8 \times 10^{-4}) =$$
$$(3.22 \times 10^{-3}) + (0.73 \times 10^{-3}) - (0.48 \times 10^{-3}) = (3.22 + 0.73 - 0.48) \times 10^{-3}$$
$$= 3.47 \times 10^{-3}$$

Multiplication and Division

To multiply numbers expressed in exponential form by hand, *multiply* all coefficients to obtain the coefficient of the result and *add* all exponents to obtain the power of 10 in the result. Generally, most calculators perform these operations automatically, and no intermediate results need to be recorded.

To divide two numbers in exponential form, *divide* the coefficients to obtain the coefficient of the result and *subtract* the exponent in the denominator from the exponent in the numerator to obtain the power of 10. In the example below, multiplication and division are combined. First, the rule for multiplication is applied to the numerator and to the denominator, and then the rule for division is used.

Rewrite in exponential form

$$\frac{0.015 \times 0.0088 \times 822}{0.092 \times 0.48} = \frac{(1.5 \times 10^{-2})(8.8 \times 10^{-3})(8.22 \times 10^2)}{(9.2 \times 10^{-2})(4.8 \times 10^{-1})}$$

Apply the rule for multiplication to the numerator and denominator

Apply the rule for division

$$= \frac{1.1 \times 10^{-1}}{4.4 \times 10^{-2}} = 0.25 \times 10^{-1-(-2)} = 0.25 \times 10^1 = 2.5$$

Raising a Number to a Power and Extracting the Root of an Exponential Number

To raise an exponential number to a given power, raise the coefficient to that power and multiply the exponent by that power. For example, we can cube a number (that is, raise it to the *third* power) in the following manner.

Rewrite in exponential form	Cube the coefficient	Multiply the exponent by 3

$$(0.0066)^3 = (6.6 \times 10^{-3})^3 = (6.6)^3 \times 10^{(-3 \times 3)}$$

$$= (2.9 \times 10^2) \times 10^{-9} = 2.9 \times 10^{-7}$$

To extract the root of an exponential number, we raise the number to a fractional power—one-half power for a square root, one-third power for a cube root, and so on. Most calculators have keys designed for extracting square roots and cube roots. Thus, to extract the square root of 1.57×10^5, enter the number 1.57×10^5 into a calculator, and use the $[\sqrt{\ }]$ key.

$$\sqrt{1.57 \times 10^{-5}} = 3.96 \times 10^{-3}$$

Some calculators allow you to extract roots by keying the root in as a fractional exponent. For example, we can take a cube root as follows.

$$(2.75 \times 10^{-9})^{1/3} = 1.40 \times 10^{-3}$$

SELF-ASSESSMENT Questions

For items 1–4, express the number in scientific notation, and then select the correct answer.

1. 35,400
   a. 3.54×10^{-4}
   b. 35.4×10^{-3}
   c. 3.54×10^4
   d. 35.4×10^4

2. 43,600,000
   a. 436×10^4
   b. 43.6×10^{-6}
   c. 4.36×10^7
   d. 4.36×10^{-7}

3. 0.000000000000312
   a. 3.12×10^{-15}
   b. 3.12×10^{-13}
   c. 3.12×10^{-12}
   d. 3.12×10^{13}

4. 0.000438
   a. 4.38×10^{-3}
   b. 4.38×10^{-4}
   c. 4.38×10^4
   d. 4.38×10^6

For items 5–6, express the number in decimal (ordinary) notation, and then select the correct answer.

5. 7.1×10^4
   a. 0.00071
   b. 0.000071
   c. 71,000
   d. 710,000

6. 2.83×10^{-4}
   a. 0.000283
   b. 0.00283
   c. 2830
   d. 28,300

For items 7–14, perform the indicated operation, and then select the correct answer.

7. $(3.0 \times 10^4) \times (2.1 \times 10^5) = ?$
   a. 5.1×10^9
   b. 6.3×10^1
   c. 6.3×10^9
   d. 6.3×10^{20}

8. $(6.27 \times 10^{-5}) \times (4.12 \times 10^{-12}) = ?$
   a. 2.58×10^{-17}
   b. 2.58×10^{-16}
   c. 2.58×10^{-59}
   d. 2.58×10^{59}

9. $\dfrac{4.33 \times 10^{-7}}{7.61 \times 10^{22}} = ?$
   a. 5.69×10^{-30}
   b. 5.69×10^{-15}
   c. 5.69×10^{15}
   d. 5.69×10^{30}

10. $\dfrac{9.37 \times 10^9}{3.79 \times 10^{27}} = ?$
    a. 2.47×10^{-36}
    b. 2.47×10^{-35}
    c. 2.47×10^{-18}
    d. 2.47×10^{36}

11. $\dfrac{2.21 \times 10^5}{9.80 \times 10^{-7}} = ?$
    a. 2.26×10^{-12}
    b. 2.26×10^{-11}
    c. 2.26×10^{11}
    d. 4.43×10^{12}

12. $\dfrac{4.60 \times 10^{-12}}{2.17 \times 10^3} = ?$
    a. 2.12×10^{-15}
    b. 2.12×10^{-14}
    c. 2.12×10^{14}
    d. 2.12×10^{15}

13. $(2.19 \times 10^{-6})^2 = ?$
    a. 4.80×10^{-12}
    b. 4.80×10^{-6}
    c. 4.80×10^6
    d. 4.80×10^{12}

14. $\sqrt{1.74 \times 10^{-7}} = ?$
    a. 1.32×10^{-7}
    b. 4.17×10^{-7}
    c. 4.17×10^{-4}
    d. 1.32×10^{-4}

A.3 Unit Conversions

Chapter 1 discusses conversions within the metric system. Because almost all countries except the United States use metric measurements, we sometimes need to convert between common and metric units. Suppose that an American applies for a job in another country and the job application asks for her height in centimeters. She knows that her height is 66.0 in. An actual measured quantity is the same, no matter the unit we use to express it. The woman's height is the same, whether we express it in inches, feet, centimeters, or millimeters. We can use equivalencies (given here to three significant figures; Section A.4) such as those in Table A.2 to derive conversion factors.

In mathematics, multiplying a quantity by 1 does not change its value in any fundamental way. We can therefore use a factor equivalent to 1 to convert between inches and centimeters. We find our factor in the definition of the inch in Table A.2.

$$1 \text{ in.} = 2.54 \text{ cm}$$

Table A.2	Some Conversions between Common and Metric Units
Length	
1 mile (mi) = 1.61 kilometers (km)	
1 yard (yd) = 0.914 meter (m)	
1 inch (in.) = 2.54 centimeters (cm)[a]	
Mass	
1 pound (lb) = 454 grams (g)	
1 ounce (oz) = 28.4 grams (g)	
1 pound (lb) = 0.454 kilogram (kg)	
Volume	
1 U.S. quart (qt) = 0.946 liter (L)	
1 U.S. pint (pt) = 0.473 liter (L)	
1 fluid ounce (fl oz) = 29.6 milliliters (mL)	
1 gallon (gal) = 3.78 liters (L)	

[a]This conversion is exact. The other conversions are available with more significant digits if needed; see any edition of the *CRC Handbook of Chemistry and Physics*.

Notice that if we divide both sides of this equation by 1 in., we obtain a ratio of quantities that is equal to 1.

$$1 = \frac{1 \text{ in.}}{1 \text{ in.}} = \frac{2.54 \text{ cm}}{1 \text{ in.}}$$

If we divide both sides of the equation by 2.54 cm, we also obtain a ratio of quantities that is equal to 1.

$$\frac{1 \text{ in.}}{2.54 \text{ cm}} = \frac{2.54 \text{ cm}}{2.54 \text{ cm}} = 1$$

The two ratios, one shown in red and the other in blue, are conversion factors. A *conversion factor* is a ratio of terms, equivalent to the number 1, used to change the unit in which a quantity is expressed. We call this process the *unit conversion method* of problem solving. Because we set up calculations by examining the *dimensions* associated with the given quantity, those associated with the desired result, and those needed in the conversion factors, the process is sometimes called *dimensional analysis*.

What happens when we multiply a known quantity by a conversion factor? The original unit cancels out and is replaced by the desired unit. Thus, our general approach to using conversion factors is

Desired quantity and unit = given quantity and unit × conversion factors

Now let's return to the question about the woman's height, a measured quantity of 66.0 in. To get an answer in centimeters, we must use the appropriate conversion factor (in blue). Note that the desired unit (cm) is in the numerator and the unit to be replaced (in.) is in the denominator. Thus, we can cancel the unit in. so that only the unit cm remains.

$$66.0 \text{ in.} \times \frac{2.54 \text{ cm}}{1 \text{ in.}} = 168 \text{ cm (rounded off from 167.64)}$$

You can see why the other conversion factor (in red) won't work. No units cancel. Instead, we get a nonsensical unit.

$$66.0 \text{ in.} \times \frac{1 \text{ in.}}{2.54 \text{ cm}} = \frac{26.0 \text{ in.}^2}{\text{cm}}$$

Following are some examples and exercises to give you some practice in this method of problem solving. A variety of conversion calculators are available on the Internet. Use the key words *conversion calculator*.

Example A.1   Unit Conversions

a. Convert 0.742 kg to grams.
b. Convert 0.615 lb to ounces.
c. Convert 135 lb to kilograms.

Solution

a. This is a conversion from one metric unit to another. We simply use our knowledge of prefixes to convert from kilograms to grams.

We start here	This converts kg to g	Our answer: the number and the unit

$$0.742 \text{ kg} \times \frac{1000 \text{ g}}{1 \text{ kg}} = 742 \text{ g}$$

b. This is a conversion from one common unit to another. Here we use the fact that 1 lb = 16 oz to convert from pounds to ounces. Then we proceed as in part (a), arranging the conversion factor to cancel the unit lb.

$$0.615 \text{ lb} \times \frac{16 \text{ oz}}{1 \text{ lb}} = 9.84 \text{ oz}$$

c. This is a conversion from a common unit to a metric unit. We need data from Table A.2 to convert from pounds to kilograms. Then we proceed as in part (b), arranging the conversion factor to cancel the unit lb.

$$135 \text{ lb} \times \frac{0.454 \text{ kg}}{1 \text{ lb}} = 61.3 \text{ kg}$$

(Our answers have the proper number of significant figures. If you do not understand significant figures and wish to do so, they are discussed in Section A.4. This text uses three significant figures for most calculations.)

▪ **EXERCISE A.1**

a. Convert 16.3 mg to grams.

b. Convert 24.5 oz to pounds.

c. Convert 12.5 fl oz to milliliters.

Quite often, to get the desired unit, we must use more than one conversion factor. We can do so by arranging all the necessary conversion factors in a single setup that yields the final answer in the desired unit.

Example A.2   Unit Conversions

What is the length, in millimeters, of a 3.25-ft piece of tubing?

Solution

No relationship between feet and millimeters is given in Table A.2, so we need more than one conversion factor. We can think of the problem as a series of three conversions.

1. Use the fact that 1 ft = 12 in. to convert from feet to inches.

2. Use data from Table A.2 to convert from inches to centimeters.

3. Use our knowledge of prefixes to convert from centimeters to millimeters.

We could solve this problem in three distinct steps by making one conversion in each step, but it is just as easy to combine three conversion factors into a single setup. Then we proceed as indicated below.

$$3.25 \text{ ft} \times \frac{12 \text{ in.}}{1 \text{ ft}} \times \frac{2.54 \text{ cm}}{1 \text{ in.}} \times \frac{10 \text{ mm}}{1 \text{ cm}} = 991 \text{ mm}$$

▪ **EXERCISE A.2**

Carry out the following conversions.

a. 729.9 ft to kilometers

b. 1.17 gal to fluid ounces

Sometimes we need to convert two or more units in the measured quantity. We can do this by arranging all the necessary conversion factors in a single setup so that the starting units cancel and the conversions yield the final answer in the desired units.

Example A.3   Unit Conversions

A saline solution has 1.00 lb of salt in 1.00 gal of solution. Calculate the concentration in grams per liter of solution.

Solution

First, let's identify the measured quantities. They can be expressed in the form of a ratio of mass of salt in pounds to a volume in gallons.

$$\frac{1.00 \text{ lb (salt)}}{1.00 \text{ gal (solution)}}$$

This ratio must be converted to one expressed in grams per liter. We must convert from pounds to grams in the numerator and from gallons to liters in the denominator. The following set of equivalent values from Table A.2 can be used to formulate conversion factors.

$$1\ lb = 454\ g \qquad 1\ gal = 3.78\ L$$

Note that we could also do the conversions in the numerator and denominator separately and then divide the numerator by the denominator.

$$\text{Numerator:} \quad 1.00\ \cancel{lb} \times \frac{454\ g}{1\ \cancel{lb}} = 454\ g$$

$$\text{Denominator:} \quad 1.00\ \cancel{gal} \times \frac{3.78\ L}{1\ \cancel{gal}} = 3.78\ L$$

$$\text{Division:} \quad \frac{454\ g}{3.78\ L} = 120\ g/L$$

Both methods give the same answer to three significant figures.

▪ **EXERCISE A.3**

Carry out the following conversions.
  a. 88.0 km/h to meters per second
  b. 4.07 g/L to ounces per quart

SELF-ASSESSMENT Questions

For items 1–5, perform the indicated conversion, and then select the correct answer. You may need data from Table A.2 for some of the items.

1. 645 μs to seconds
   a. 6.45×10^{-6} s
   b. 6.45×10^{-4} s
   c. 6.45×10^{-2} s
   d. 6.45×10^{8} s

2. 1445 oz to grams
   a. 50.9 g
   b. 90.3 g
   c. 144.5 g
   d. 4.10×10^{4} g

3. 1.24×10^{5} mm to feet
   a. 10.3 ft
   b. 103 ft
   c. 407 ft
   d. 4.88×10^{3} ft

4. 12.0 fl oz to milliliters
   a. 0.405 mL
   b. 240 mL
   c. 355 mL
   d. 3.55×10^{5} mL

5. 343 m/s to miles per hour
   a. 0.0592 mi/h
   b. 12.8 mi/h
   c. 767 mi/h
   d. 1220 mi/h

Answers: 1, b; 2, d; 3, c; 4, c; 5, c

A.4 Precision, Accuracy, and Significant Figures

Counting can give exact numbers. For example, we can count exactly 24 students in a room. Measurements, on the other hand, are subject to error. One source of error is the measuring instruments themselves. For example, an incorrectly calibrated thermometer may consistently yield a result that is 0.2 °C too low. Other errors may result from the experimenter's lack of skill or care in using measuring instruments. But even the most careful measurement will have some uncertainty associated with it. For example, a meter stick can be used to measure to the nearest millimeter or so. But there is no way for a meter stick to give a measurement that is correct to the nearest 0.001 mm.

Precision and Accuracy

Suppose that five students were asked to measure a person's height using a meter stick marked off in millimeters. The five measurements are recorded in Table A.3. The *precision* of a set of measurements refers to how closely individual measurements agree with one another. We say that the precision is good if each of the measurements is close to the average or poor if there is a wide deviation from the average value.

How would you describe the precision of the data in Table A.3? Examine the individual data, note the average value, and determine how much the individual data differ from the average. Because the maximum deviation from the average value is 0.003 m, the precision is quite good.

Table A.3	Five Measurements of a Person's Height
Student	Height (m)
1	1.827
2	1.824
3	1.826
4	1.828
5	1.829
Average	1.827

The *accuracy* of a set of measurements refers to the closeness of the average of the set to the "correct," or most probable, value. Measurements of high precision are more likely to be accurate than are those of poor precision, but even highly precise measurements are sometimes inaccurate. For example, what if the meter sticks used to obtain the data in Table A.3 were actually 1005 mm long but still had 1000-mm markings? The accuracy of the measurements would be rather poor, even though the precision would remain good.

Sampling Errors

No matter how accurate an analysis, it will not mean much unless it is performed on valid, representative samples. Consider determining the level of glucose in the blood of a patient. High glucose levels are associated with diabetes, a debilitating disease. Results vary, depending on several factors such as the time of day and what and when the person last ate. Glucose levels are much higher soon after a meal high in sugars. They also depend on other factors, such as stress. Medical doctors usually take blood for analysis after a night of fasting. These fasting glucose levels tend to be more reliable, but physicians often repeat the analysis when high or otherwise suspicious results are obtained. Therefore, there is no one true value for the level of glucose in a person's blood. Repeated samplings provide an average level. Similar results from several measurements give much more confidence in the findings. For example, a diagnosis of diabetes is usually based on two consecutive fasting blood glucose levels above 120 mg/dL.

Significant Figures

Look again at Table A.3. Notice that the five measurements of height agree in the first three digits (1.82); they differ only in the fourth digit. We say that the fourth digit is uncertain. All digits known with certainty, plus the first uncertain one, are

(a) Low accuracy (b) Low accuracy
   Low precision   High precision

(c) High accuracy (d) High accuracy
   Low precision   High precision

▲ Comparing precision and accuracy: a dartboard analogy. (a) The darts are both scattered (low precision) and off-center (low accuracy). (b) The darts are in a tight cluster (high precision) but still off-center (low accuracy). (c) The darts are somewhat scattered (low precision) but evenly distributed about the center (high accuracy). (d) The darts are in a tight cluster (high precision) and well centered (high accuracy).

called *significant figures*. The precision of a measurement is reflected in the number of significant figures—the more significant figures, the more precise the measurement. The measurements in Table A.3 have four significant figures. In other words, we are quite sure that the person's height is between 1.82 m and 1.83 m. Our best estimate of the average value, including the uncertain digit, is 1.827 m.

The number 1.827 has four digits; we say it has four significant figures. In any properly reported measurement, all nonzero digits are significant. Zeros, however, may or may not be significant because they can be used in two ways: as a part of the measured value or to position a decimal point.

- Zeros between two other significant digits are significant. *Examples*: 4807 (four significant figures); 70.004 (five).
- The lone zero preceding a decimal point is there for readability; it is not significant. *Example*: 0.352 (three significant figures).
- Zeros that precede the first nonzero digit are also not significant. *Examples*: 0.000819 (three significant figures); 0.03307 (four).
- Zeros at the end of a number are significant if they are to the right of the decimal point. *Examples*: 0.2000 (four significant figures); 0.050120 (five).

We can summarize these four situations with a general rule: When we read a number from left to right, all the digits starting with the first nonzero digit are significant. Numbers without a decimal point that end in zeros are a special case, however.

- Zeros at the end of a number may or may not be significant if the number is written without a decimal point. *Example*: 700. We do not know whether the number 700 was measured to the nearest unit, ten, or hundred. To avoid this confusion, we can use exponential notation (Section A.2). In exponential notation, 700 is recorded as 7×10^2 or 7.0×10^2 or 7.00×10^2 to indicate one, two, or three significant figures, respectively. The only significant digits are those in the coefficient, not in the power of 10.

We use significant figures only with measurements—quantities subject to error. The concept does not apply to a quantity that is

1. inherently an integer, such as 3 sides to a triangle or 12 items in a dozen;
2. inherently a fraction, such as the radius of a circle equals $\frac{1}{2}$ of the diameter;
3. obtained by an accurate count, such as 18 students in a class; or
4. a defined quantity, such as 1 km = 1000 m.

In these contexts, the numbers 3, 12, $\frac{1}{2}$, 18, and 1000 can have as many significant figures as we want. More properly, we say that each is an *exact value*.

Example A.4	Significant Figures

In everyday life, common units are often used with metric units in parentheses (or vice versa), but significant figures are not always considered. Which of the following has followed proper significant figure usage?

a. A Chinese high-speed train broke a world record in 2010 for fastest unmodified commercial train, reaching speeds of up to 481.1 kph (298.9 mph), state media reported.

b. The Earth warmed by about 0.7° Celsius (1.26° Fahrenheit) over the past century

Solution

a. The quantity 481.1 kph has four significant figures, as does 298.9 mph; significant figure rules were followed.

b. The quantity 0.7° has only one significant figure, but 1.26° Fahrenheit has three; significant figure rules were not followed.

▪ EXERCISE A.4

Which of the following has followed proper significant figure usage?

a. A set of exercise room weights are rated at 45 lb (20.4 kg).

b. Fossils of an ancient human-like creature, named *Ardipithecus ramidus*, was found in Ethiopia in 1992 and shown to be 4,400,000 years old. In 2009 researchers demonstrated that *A. ramidus* was likely to be a direct human ancestor. Because it took 17 years to assess the significance of the fossils, a Twitter note said that made the fossil 4,400,017 years old.

Significant Figures in Calculations: Multiplication and Division

If we measure a sheet of notepaper and find it to be 14.5 cm wide and 21.7 cm long, we can find the area of the paper by multiplying the two quantities. A calculator gives the answer as 314.65. Can we conclude that the area is 314.65 cm^2? That is, can we know the area to the nearest hundredth of a square centimeter when we know the width and length only to the nearest tenth of a centimeter? It just doesn't seem reasonable—and it isn't. A calculated quantity can be no more precise than the data used in the calculation, and the reported result should reflect this fact.

A strict application of this principle involves a fairly complicated statistical analysis that we will not attempt here, but we can do a fairly good job by using a practical rule involving significant figures:

> In multiplication and division, the reported result should have no more significant figures than the factor with the fewest significant figures.

In other words, a calculation is only as precise as the least precise measurement that enters into the calculation.

To obtain a numerical answer with the proper number of significant figures often requires that we round off numbers. In rounding, we drop all digits that are not significant and, if necessary, adjust the last reported digit. We use the following rules in rounding.

▪ If the leftmost digit to be dropped is *4 or less*, drop it and all following digits. *Example*: If we need four significant figures, 69.744 rounds to 69.74, or if we need three significant figures, to 69.7.

▪ If the leftmost digit to be dropped is *5 or greater*, increase the final retained digit by 1. *Example*: 538.76 rounds to 538.8 if we need four significant figures. Similarly, 74.397 rounds to 74.40 if we need four significant figures or to 74.4 if we need three.

Example A.5	Unit Conversions

What is the area, in square centimeters, of a rectangular gauze bandage that is 2.54 cm wide and 12.42 cm long? Use the correct number of significant figures in the answer.

Solution

The area of a rectangle is the product of its length and width. In the result, we can show only as many significant figures as there are in the least precisely stated dimension, the width, which has three significant figures.

$$2.54 \text{ cm} \times 12.42 \text{ cm} = 31.5468 \text{ cm}^2 = 31.5 \text{ cm}^2$$

We use the rules for rounding off numbers as the basis for dropping the digits 468.

▪ EXERCISE A.5

Calculate the volume, in cubic meters, of a rectangular block of foamed plastic that is 1.827 m long, 1.04 m wide, and 0.064 m thick. Use the correct number of significant figures.

Example A.6   Significant Figures

For a laboratory experiment, a teacher wants to divide all of a 226.8-g sample of glucose equally among the 18 members of her class. How many grams of glucose should each student receive?

Solution

The number 18 is a counted number, that is, an exact number that is not subject to significant figure rules. The answer should carry four significant figures, the same as in 226.8 g.

$$\frac{226.8 \text{ g}}{18 \text{ students}} = 12.60 \text{ g/student}$$

In this calculation, a calculator displays the result as 12.6. We add the digit 0 to emphasize that the result is precise to four significant figures.

▪ EXERCISE A.6

A dozen eggs has a mass of 681 g. What is the average mass of one of the eggs, expressed with the appropriate number of significant figures?

Significant Figures in Calculations: Addition and Subtraction

In addition or subtraction, we are concerned not with the number of significant figures but with the number of digits to the right of the decimal point. When we add or subtract quantities with varying numbers of digits to the right of the decimal point, we need to note the one with the fewest such digits. The result should contain the same number of digits to the right of its decimal point. For example, if you are adding several masses and one of them is measured only to the nearest gram, the total mass cannot be stated to the nearest milligram no matter how precise the other measurements are.

We apply this idea in Example A.7. Note that in a calculation involving several steps, we need round off only the final result.

Example A.7   Significant Figures

Perform the following calculation and round off the answer to the correct number of significant figures.

$$2.146 \text{ g} + 72.1 \text{ g} - 9.1434 \text{ g}$$

Solution

In this calculation, we add two numbers and subtract a third from the sum of the first two.

$$
\begin{array}{ll}
2.146 \text{ g} & \leftarrow \text{three decimal places} \\
+\ 72.1 \text{ g} & \leftarrow \text{one decimal place} \\
\hline
74.246 \text{ g} & \\
\end{array}
$$

$$
\begin{array}{ll}
-\ 9.1434 \text{ g} & \leftarrow \text{four decimal places} \\
\hline
65.1026 \text{ g} = 65.1 \text{ g} & \leftarrow \text{one decimal place} \\
\end{array}
$$

Note that we do not round off the intermediate result (74.246). When using a calculator, you generally don't need to write down an intermediate result.

▪ EXERCISE A.7
Perform the indicated operations and give answers with the proper number of significant figures. Note that in addition and subtraction all terms must be expressed in the same unit.
  a. 48.2 m + 3.82 m + 48.4394 m
  b. 15.436 L + 5.3 L − 6.24 L − 8.177 L
  c. (51.5 m + 2.67 m) × (33.42 m − 0.124 m)
  d. $\dfrac{125.1 \text{ g} - 1.22 \text{ g}}{52.5 \text{ mL} + 0.63 \text{ mL}}$

SELF-ASSESSMENT Questions

1. A measurement has good precision if it
   a. is close to an accepted standard
   b. is close to similar measurements
   c. has few significant figures
   d. is the only value determined

2. Following are data for the length of a pencil as measured by students X, Y, and Z. The length is known to be 11.54 cm.

	Trial 1	Trial 2	Trial 3
X	11.8	11.1	11.5
Y	11.7	11.2	11.6
Z	11.3	11.4	11.5

   Which of the following best characterizes the data?
   a. Y has the most precise data, X the most accurate.
   b. Y has the most precise data, Z the most accurate.
   c. Z has the most precise data, X the most accurate.
   d. Z has the most precise data, Y the most accurate.

3. 725.8055 rounded to three significant figures is
   a. 725.806   **b.** 725.81   **c.** 725.8   **d.** 726

For items 4–6, determine the number of significant figures, and then select the correct answer.

4. 0.0000073
   a. 2   **b.** 5   **c.** 6   **d.** 8

5. 0.04000
   a. 2   **b.** 4   **c.** 5   **d.** 6

6. 80.0040
   a. 2   **b.** 4   **c.** 5   **d.** 6

For items 7–16, perform the indicated calculation, and then select the correct answer, with the proper number of significant figures.

7. 7.20 + 3.013 + 0.04327 = ?
   a. 10.26   **b.** 10.256
   c. 10.2563   **d.** 10.25627

8. 4.702 − 0.4123 = ?
   a. 4.2897   **b.** 4.29   **c.** 4.290   **d.** 4.30

9. 10.03 + 4.555 = ?
   a. 14   **b.** 14.59   **c.** 14.6   **d.** 15

10. 15.3 − 4.001 = ?
    a. 11   **b.** 11.2   **c.** 11.299   **d.** 11.3

11. 4.602 ÷ 0.0240 = ?
    a. 191   **b.** 191.75   **c.** 191.8   **d.** 192

12. 40.625 × 0.0028 = ?
    a. 0.11   **b.** 0.11375   **c.** 0.1138   **d.** 0.114

13. 8.64 ÷ 0.1216 = ?
    a. 71.1   **b.** 71.05   **c.** 71.0526   **d.** 71.053

14. (10.30)(0.186) ÷ 0.085 = ?
    a. 23   **b.** 22.5   **c.** 22.5388   **d.** 2.254

15. (42.5 + 0.459) ÷ 28.45 = ?
    a. 1.510   **b.** 1.5103   **c.** 1.51   **d.** 1.510

16. (7.06 ÷ 0.084) − (29.6 × 0.023) = ?
    a. 83   **b.** 83.3   **c.** 83.4   **d.** 83.369

Answers: 1, b; 2, d; 3, d; 4, a; 5, b; 6, d; 7, a; 8, c; 9, b; 10, d; 11, d; 12, a; 13, a; 14, a; 15, c; 16, a

A.5 Calculations Involving Temperature

As noted in Chapter 1, we sometimes need to make conversions from one temperature scale to another. On the Fahrenheit scale, the freezing point of water is 32 °F and the boiling point is 212 °F; on the Celsius scale, the freezing point of water is 0 °C and the boiling point is 100 °C. A 100° temperature interval (100 − 0) on the Celsius scale therefore equals a 180° interval (212 − 32) on the Fahrenheit scale. From these facts, we can derive two equations that relate temperatures on the two scales. One of these requires multiplying the degrees of Celsius temperature by the factor

In everyday life, the following ditty will often suffice to assess the meaning of a Celsius temperature.

THE CELSIUS SCALE
Thirty is hot,
Twenty is pleasing,
Ten is quite cool,
And zero is freezing.

1.8 (that is, 180/100) to obtain the degrees of Fahrenheit temperature, followed by adding 32 to account for the fact that $0\,°C = 32\,°F$.

$$°F = (1.8 \times °C) + 32$$

In the other equation, we subtract 32 from the Fahrenheit temperature to get the number of degrees Fahrenheit above the freezing point of water. Then this quantity is divided by 1.8.

$$°C = \frac{°F - 32}{1.8}$$

The SI unit of temperature is the kelvin (Chapters 1 and 6). Recall that to convert from °C to K, we simply add 273.15. And to convert from K to °C, we subtract 273.15.

$$K = °C + 273.15 \qquad \text{and} \qquad °C = K - 273.15$$

Example A.8 illustrates a practical situation where conversion between Celsius and Fahrenheit temperatures is necessary.

Example A.8 | Temperature Conversion

At home, you keep your thermostat set at 68 °F. When traveling, you have a room with a thermostat that uses the Celsius scale. What Celsius temperature will give you the same temperature as at home?

Solution

$$°C = \frac{°F - 32}{1.8} = \frac{68 - 32}{1.8} = 20\,°C$$

▪ EXERCISE A.8
  a. Convert 85.0 °C to degrees Fahrenheit.
  b. Convert −12.2 °C to degrees Fahrenheit.
  c. Convert 355 °F to degrees Celsius.
  d. Convert −20.8 °F to degrees Celsius.

SELF-ASSESSMENT Questions

For items 1–10, perform the indicated conversion, and then select the correct answer.

1. 25 °C to kelvins
   a. −298 K   b. −248 K   c. 248 K   d. 298 K

2. 373 K to degrees Celsius
   a. −73 °C   b. 0 °C   c. 73 °C   d. 100 °C

3. 301 K to degrees Celsius
   a. −72 °C   b. 28 °C   c. 128 °C   d. 374 °C

4. 473 °C to kelvins
   a. 100 K   b. 200 K   c. 300 K   d. 746 K

5. 37.0 °C to degrees Fahrenheit
   a. −20.6 °F   b. −38.3 °F   c. 69.0 °F   d. 98.6 °F

6. 5.50 °F to degrees Celsius
   a. −20.8°C   b. −14.7 °C   c. 3.06 °C   d. 6.31 °C

7. 273 °C to degrees Fahrenheit
   a. 152 °F   b. 491 °F   c. 523 °F   d. 549 °F

8. 98.2 °F to degrees Celsius
   a. 36.8 °C   b. 54.6 °C
   c. 72.3 °C   d. 177 °C

9. 2175 °C to degrees Fahrenheit
   a. 1190 °F   b. 1208 °F
   c. 1226 °F   d. 3947 °F

10. 25.0 °F to degrees Celsius
   a. −31.6 °C   b. −13.9 °C
   c. −3.89 °C   d. 42.8 °C

11. The temperatures, 0 K, 0 °C, and 0 °F, arranged from coldest to hottest, are
   a. 0 °C, 0 °F, 0 K   b. 0 K, 0 °C, 0 °F
   c. 0 °F, 0 °C, 0 K   d. 0 K, 0 °F, 0 °C

Answers: 1, d; 2, d; 3, b; 4, d; 5, d; 6, b; 7, c; 8, a; 9, d; 10, c; 11, d

BRIEF ANSWERS TO SELECTED PROBLEMS

Answers are provided for *all in-chapter exercises*. Brief answers are given for *odd-numbered Review Questions*; more complete answers can be obtained by reviewing the text. Answers are provided for *all odd-numbered Problems and Additional Problems*.

Note: For numerical problems, your answer may differ slightly from ours because of rounding and the use of significant figures (see Appendix).

Chapter 1

1.1 **A. a.** DQ would probably be small.
   b. DQ would probably be large.
   B. a. DQ would be uncertain.
   b. DQ would probably be large.
1.2 **A. a.** 1.00 kg   **b.** 179 lb
1.3 physical: b, d; chemical: a, c
1.4 **A.** elements: He, No, Os; compounds: CuO, NO, KF   **B.** 9
1.5 **a.** 7.24 kg   **b.** 4.29 μm   **c.** 7.91 ms
   d. 2.29 cg   **e.** 7.90 Mm
1.6 **a.** 7.45×10^{-9} m   **b.** 5.25×10^{-6} s   **c.** 1.415×10^{3} m
   d. 2.06×10^{-3} m   **e.** 6.19×10^{3} m
1.7 **A.** 500 cm^2 **B.** 1600 cm^3
1.8 **a.** 755 mm   **b.** 0.2056 L   **c.** 206,000 μg
   d. 73.8 mm   **e.** 1.11 g/mL   **f.** 73.8 mm
1.10 **A.** 1.11 g/mL   **B.** Magnesium
   C. 4.5 mL   **D.** No
1.11 **A.** 351 K   **B.** 77 K
1.12 **A.** 1799 kcal   **B.** 34 kcal

1. Science is testable, reproducible, explanatory, predictive, and tentative. Testability best distinguishes science.
3. These problems usually have too many variables to be treated by the scientific method.
5. Risk–benefit analysis compares benefits of an action to risks of that action.
7. DQ, the desirability quotient, is benefits divided by risks. A large DQ means that risks are minimal compared to benefits. Often it is hard to quantify risks and benefits.
9. The SI-derived unit for volume is liter (L). Because one liter represents a relative large quantity, volumes measured in milliliters (mL) and, sometimes, in microliters (μL) are often used in the laboratory.
11. **a.** applied   **b.** applied   **c.** basic
13. The benefits to society are very great. The risk to selected individuals is great but is managed by restricting access to penicillin by prescription and requiring the care of a physician. The DQ is high.
15. **a.** high
    b. high (but lower than in scenario a)
17. The DQ for routinely treating sore throats is low, especially if the origin of the problem is unknown. The risk of development of antibiotic-resistant bacteria likely outweighs the possible benefits of the treatment. The flu is a viral problem that does not usually respond to antibiotics so the desirability quotient for antibiotic use in that instance would likely be considerably lower than for their use to treat a sore throat of bacterial origin.
19. 100 g, 2 kg
21. Options a and b both seem reasonable.
23. 250 mL
25. 1.46×10^{9} km^3
27. Yes; the 26.3-mm i.d. tube is larger than 25.4 mm (1 inch).
29. **a.** physical property   **b.** chemical property
    c. physical property   **d.** chemical property
31. **a.** physical change   **b.** chemical change
    c. physical change

33. **a.** substance   **b.** mixture
    c. substance   **d.** substance
35. **a.** homogeneous   **b.** homogeneous
    c. homogeneous   **d.** heterogeneous
37. **a.** substance
39. **a.** element   **b.** element
    c. compound   **d.** compound
41. **a.** iron   **b.** magnesium
    c. helium   **d.** nitrogen
43. f
45. **a.** 1.0 dL   **b.** 8.5 pg   **c.** 1.05 mm
47. **a.** 55.2 L   **b.** 0.325 g   **c.** 0.27 m
    d. 2.7 cm   **e.** 0.078 ms
49. **a.** cm   **b.** kg   **c.** dL
51. **a.** 310 mm   **b.** 0.31 m   **c.** 3.1×10^{8} nm
53. **a.** 9.33 g/cm^3
55. **a.** 74.1 g
57. **a.** 344 mL   **b.** 495 cm^3
59.

Hexane

Water

Mercury

61. Yes
63. 5.4×10^{3} g
65. $-196\,°C$
67. 38.5 kcal
69. 52.6 min
71. b
73. 5.7 y
75. **1.** d   **2.** e   **3.** b   **4.** a   **5.** d
77. 590 g = 5.9×10^{2} g
79. Cabbage (lightest) < potatoes < sugar (heaviest)
81. 5.23 g/cm^3
83. 6.73×10^{-6} cm
85. 0.908 metric tons
87. **a.** 1.3 g/cm^3 **b.** 5.44 g/cm^3 **c.** 0.688 g/cm^3
89. Green chemistry is the design of chemical products and processes that reduce or eliminate the generation and use of hazardous substances from the beginning to the end of the process.
91. a

Chemistry @ Home

1. They all have slightly different densities.
2. The liquids at the bottom of the glass have a higher density than those at the top. Those liquids at the top have the lowest density of the group.
3. Yes, several of the liquids will mix together; water and alcohol are miscible meaning they will mix together. The vegetable oil and syrup will separate back out as they are oil based and immiscible.
4. The water and alcohol will not separate back out but the vegetable oil and syrup will separate back out as they are oil based and immiscible.
5. Density (weight/volume) allows you to convert between the volume of a substance and its mass (or weight). Density becomes important anytime you want to build something where weight and distribution of weight are critical. For example, you can make a "boat" out of aluminum foil and float it on water, but if you "crumple" the same piece of aluminum foil it sinks when you place it in water.

Chapter 2

2.1 **A.** 3 atoms of hydrogen to 1 atom of phosphorus
   B. 63.0 g nitrogen

2.2 112 g CaO

2.3 average Cl + I is 81.2; actual Br is 79.9 u

1. **a.** atomic: matter is made of discrete particles; continuous: matter is infinitely divisible.
   b. Greek: four elements, no atoms; modern: each element has its own kind of atom.

3. People, calculators, and M&M candies are discrete at the macroscopic level. Cloth and milk chocolate are continuous, giving the impression that they can be infinitely divided.

5. Cavendish's development of quantitative methods of establishing the proportions of atoms in a substance produced results substantiating the law of definite proportions.

7. The law of definite proportions states that elements combine in the same proportions in any compound regardless of the source of origin of that compound.

9. Law of multiple proportions

11. C has 15 oxygen atoms; the initial mixture has only 14.

13. Mendeleev used the relationship between the chemical properties of the elements and their atomic masses to create his periodic table. His organization caused him to predict the existence of yet-to-be-discovered elements when known elements would otherwise have to be placed in columns with elements whose chemical properties did not 'fit'.

15. **a.** If the container is completely sealed then its weight after one or two weeks will be the same as it weighed at the start of the experiment because all the life processes involving reactions conserve the atoms involved. Some of those atoms will appear in the form of gases, some as solids, and others as liquids but all will be retained in the container.
   b. If the mouse was housed in a wire container then any gaseous products of its metabolism would escape through the cage so the weight after one or two weeks would be less than the original weight of the mouse, its food, and its water.

17. c

19. 6.60 g H.

21. The mass of carbon in 88.20 g of propane is 72.06 g C
   The mass of C in the CO_2 that forms in the combustion cannot exceed 72.06 g according to the law of conservation of mass. The mass of C in 300.06 g of CO_2 as proposed by the student is: 81.88 g C which is more than was available in the combustion.

23. b

25. **a.** 86.8 g of hydrogen.   **b.** 688 g of oxygen.

27. 3 parts of carbon>11 parts of carbon dioxide = x parts of carbon> 14 kg of carbon dioxide or 3.8 kg. (3 parts of carbon plus 8 parts of oxygen gives 11 parts of carbon dioxide.)

29. **a.** consistent with Dalton's theory.
   b. not consistent with Dalton's theory.

31. Dalton's theory says that chemical reactions involved the rearrangement of atoms so the carbon atoms in the diamond would have combined with oxygen atoms to form a new compound and the hydrogen and oxygen atoms in water would form different combinations when water was electrolyzed.

33. d

35. The mass ratio of carbon to oxygen in carbon suboxide is (1.126) ($52.96 \div 47.04$) = 1.126). d This whole number ratio follows the law of multiple proportions.

37. If the first compound is SnO, then the second compound must be SnO_2.

39. 2:3 and 3:4; law of multiple proportions.

41. 0.08326 mol C
   5.014×10^{22} C atoms

43. 60.0000 g carbon-12
   60.0535 g C

45. Yes, the ratio of carbon to hydrogen in the three samples is the same.

47. There must be 6 F atoms for every U atom in the compound.

49. sulfur (0.623 g)
   Mass of SO_2 formed, g = (1.305 g S)(0.623 g SO_2/0.312 g S) = 2.61 g SO_2.

51. Divide 0.5836 g by 0.4375 to get 1.334. This gives a ratio of N to O of 1.334 to 1. Multiply both by 3 to get a whole number ratio of 4.002 to 3 or 4 to 3.

53. This experiment illustrates the law of conservation of mass. Although the arrangement of the atoms changed when a gas was formed, all the atoms were retained in the balloon so their mass did not change.

55. **a.** mass of Se = (32 + 125)/2 = 78.6.
   b. mass of Se = (32.06 + 127.60)/2 = 79.83.

57. The replacement of lead in paints with titanium dioxide is one example; nontoxic substitutions for lead in plastics and solders are additional examples.

Chemistry @ Home

1. Both reactions will "fizz" and a gas will bubble out of the mixture. The weight should go down for the mixture that was NOT in the bag due to the loss of carbon dioxide. The mixture that was IN the bag should remain the same weight.

2. The weight should not have changed since the carbon dioxide should be captured within the sealed bag.

3. The law of conservation of matter states that matter cannot be created or destroyed. Therefore, in the Alka-Seltzer reaction, the matter within the tablet does not disappear, but some of it is transformed in to a gas, which escapes. If we can trap that gas, as we did with the bag, then we can see that the mass is conserved, but the matter is transformed in to a different state (a gas).

Chapter 3

3.1 **A.** 33 neutrons   **B.** 131; iodine-131

3.2 **A.** $^{90}_{37}X$ and $^{88}_{37}X$; $^{88}_{38}X$ and $^{93}_{38}X$ **B.** three

3.3 **A.** 32 electrons   **B.** 3

3.4 **a.** (Be) 2 2
   b. (Mg) 2 8 2; both have the same number of outer electrons.

3.5 **A. a.** $1s^2 2s^2 2p^5$
      b. $1s^2 2s^2 2p^6 3s^2 3p^5$ (Both have the valence configuration $ns^2 np^5$.)
   B. a. $1s^2 2s^2 2p^6 3s^2 3p^6 3d^{10} 4s^2$
      b. $1s^2 2s^2 2p^6 3s^2 3p^6 3d^{10} 4s^2 4p^6 4d^{10} 5s^2 5p^2$

3.6 **A a.** (Rb) $5s^1$ **b.** (Se) $4s^2 4p^4$ **c.** (Ge) $4s^2 4p^2$
   B a. (Ga) $4s^2 4p^1$ **b.** (In) $5s^2 5p^1$

1. **a.** Crookes invented the gas discharge tube.
   b. Goldstein discovered positive particles.
   c. Faraday showed that matter is electrical in nature.
   d. Thomson determined the mass-to-charge ratio for the electron.
   e. Rutherford recognized and named the nuclear particles now known as alpha and beta particles.
   f. Chadwick discovered neutrons.

3. Both are forms of energy. Gamma rays are more penetrating.

5. Rutherford postulated that all the positive charge and nearly all the mass of an atom are concentrated in a tiny nucleus.

7. A and B, no; A and C, no; A and D, yes; B and C, yes; C and D, no.

9. While the number of protons in all atoms of a particular element is the same, the number of neutrons can vary, producing different isotopes of that element.

11. The atomic number of ruthenium is 44 and its atomic symbol is Ru.

13. The atom in which the electron moves from the first to the third shell.

15. The quantum (or quantum mechanical) model, derived from the mathematical quantum mechanics approach, described electrons as having wave properties as well as particle properties.

17. **a.** Be atoms have 4 electrons.
   b. Na atoms have 11 electrons.
   c. S atoms have 16 electrons.
   d. Se atoms have 34 electrons.
   e. Cu atoms have 29 electrons.
   f. U atoms have 92 electrons.

19. Alpha particles have the largest mass. Beta particles have a negative charge and a much smaller mass than alpha particles. Gamma radiation has no charge and no mass.
21. d
23. **a.** $^{37}_{17}Cl$ or chlorine-37 or Cl-37
    b. $^{55}_{25}Mn$ or manganese-55 or Mn-55
25. There are four different elements listed: two isotopes of sodium (Na, atomic number 11), and one atom each of neon (Ne, atomic number 10), boron (B, atomic number 5), and magnesium (Mg, atomic number 12).
27. 28
29. 2+
31. **a.** 8   **b.** 14   **c.** 28
33. **a.** Possible excited state: The $1s$ orbital holds 2 electrons, or $2s$ orbital.
    b. Incorrect
    c. Possible excited state: Two electrons have been raised from the $2s$ to the $2p$ subshell.
    d. This atom is in its ground state.
35. Neon, Ne.
37. Si has two $3p$ electrons; Ge has two $4p$ electrons; germanium is a much larger atom.
39. **a.** metal   **b.** metal   **c.** metal   **d.** nonmetal
41. Ne and Kr
43. 4
45. **a.** 15   **b.** Phosphorus   **c.** 15   **d.** 6   **e.** 0
47.

   a. Kr   **b.** Na   **c.** Br   **d.** Sc
49. **a.** $1s^2 2s^2 2p^6 3s^2 3p^6 3d^6 4s^2$
    b. $1s^2 2s^2 2p^6 3s^2 3p^6 3d^{10} 4s^2 4p^6 4d^{10} 5s^2 5p^2$
    c. $1s^2 2s^2 2p^6 3s^2 3p^6 3d^{10} 4s^2 4p^6 4d^{10} 4f^{14} 5s^2 5p^6 5d^{10} 6s^2 6p^2$
51. The period 5 elements are in group 2A (only s electrons) and group 3B (d electrons). Therefore, the elements are strontium (Sr) and yttrium (Y).
53. b
55. d

Chemistry @ Home

1. Answers vary. There should be a large list of colors when viewed with the diffraction film.
2. There are different metals in the different colored candles, which give the flames their colors.
3. When the atoms are heated electrons gain energy and transition to higher energy levels. When the energy is released as photons the colors are observed.
4. There are several potential sources of contamination, such as the wick, the wax, dyes added to the wax, etc. Also looking through the diffraction grating film is also subjective.
5. Typical results blended with information from the ColorFlame website regarding candle ingredients.

Candle	Flame color (to naked eye)	Diffraction emissions	Element identified
Red	Red	Red/Yellow/Green (possibly Indigo)	Lithium Strontium Calcium
Purple	Yellow and Violet	Orange/Green/Indigo	Potassium
Green	White with traces of Indigo and/or Yellow	Red/Yellow/Green/Indigo	Phosphorus Copper Zinc
Blue	Green/Indigo	Yellow/Green/Indigo	Copper Selenium
Orange	Yellow/Orange (intense)	Orange	Sodium

Chapter 4

4.1 **a.** :Är: **b.** ·Ca· **c.** :F̈· **d.** ·N̈· **e.** K· **f.** :S̈·

4.2 **A.** $Li· + :F̈· \longrightarrow Li^+ + :F̈:^-$

   B. $Rb· + :Ï· \longrightarrow Rb^+ + :Ï:^-$

4.3 **a.** $2 ·Äl· + 3 :Ö· \longrightarrow 2 Al^{3+} + 3 :Ö:^{2-}$

4.4 **A. a.** CaF_2 **b.** Li_2O
    B. $FeCl_2$ and $FeCl_3$
4.5 **a.** K_2O **b.** Ca_3N_2 **c.** Mg_3P_2 **d.** AlP
4.6 **a.** calcium fluoride **b.** copper(II) bromide

4.8 **a.** $:Br· + ·Br: \longrightarrow :Br:Br:$

   b. $H· + ·Br: \longrightarrow H:Br:$

   c. $:Ï· + ·Cl: \longrightarrow :Ï:Cl:$

4.9 **A. a.** polar covalent   **b.** ionic
      c. nonpolar covalent   **d.** polar covalent
   B. a. polar covalent   **b.** polar covalent
      c. polar covalent   **d.** nonpolar covalent
   C. b. < a. < d. < c.
4.10 **a.** bromine trifluoride   **b.** bromine pentafluoride
     c. dinitrogen monoxide   **d.** nitrogen dioxide
4.11 **a.** CO_2 **b.** Cl_2O_7 **c.** NI_3 **d.** S_2F_{10}
4.12 **a.** $CaCO_3$ **b.** K_3PO_4 **c.** $(NH_4)_2S$
4.13 **A. a.** magnesium carbonate   **b.** calcium phosphate
      c. ammonium acetate
   B. a. ammonium sulfate
      b. potassium dihydrogen phosphate

4.14 **A. a.** $:C≡O:$ **b.** $:F̈—Ö—F̈:$ **b.** H—C—Cl: with H above and H below

B. a. $[:N̈=N=N̈:]^-$ **b.** $\left[H—N—H \right]^+$ with H above and H below

   c. $:Ö=N̈—Ö—F̈:$

4.15 **A. a.** trigonal pyramidal   **b.** tetrahedral
     B. a. trigonal planar   **b.** bent (at both O)
     C. a. P in PH_3 **b.** O in H_2O

1. Sodium metal is quite reactive; sodium ions (as in NaCl) are quite unreactive.

3. Cl⁻ ions are not reactive; they are strongly attracted to positive ions such as Na⁺ with which they form ionic bonds.

5. a. 1+   **b.** 2−   **c.** 3−   **d.** 2+

7. a. 2−   **b.** 3+   **c.** 1+   **d.** 2+

9. Carbon and nitrogen atoms can easily form triple bonds, either with other identical atoms or with atoms of other elements. Examples are H—C≡C—H, :N≡N:, and H—C ≡ N:. Oxygen very rarely forms triple bonds although one common example is : C≡O:.

11. a. · Ca ·   **b.** : S̈ :   **c.** · S̈i ·

13. a. Na⁺ $\left[: \ddot{I} : \right]^{-}$ **b.** 2 K⁺ $\left[: \ddot{S} : \right]^{2-}$

    c. Ca²⁺ 2$\left[: \ddot{C}l : \right]^{-}$ **d.** Al³⁺ 3$\left[: \ddot{F} : \right]^{-}$

15. b

17. a. S^{2-} **b.** Potassium ion   **c.** Bromide ion
     d. F⁻   **e.** Calcium ion   **f.** Iron(III)

19. Mo^{4+} is the molybdenum(IV) ion.
     Mo^{6+} is the molybdenum(VI) ion.

21. a. Mn^{2+} **b.** Mn^{3+} **c.** Mn^{7+}

23. a matches with d: $FeCl_2$ is iron(II) chloride; c matches with h: AgF is silver fluoride; e matches with b: $FeBr_3$ is iron(III) bromide; and g matches with f: Na_2O is sodium oxide.

25. Cr_2O_3, chromium(III) oxide, and CrO_3 is called chromium(VI) oxide.

27. a matches with d: NH_4NO_3 is ammonium nitrate; c matches with h: $CaCO_3$ is calcium carbonate; e matches with b: $FePO_4$ is iron(III) phosphate; and g matches with f: $Ca(CH_3CO_2)_2$ is calcium acetate.

29. a. is silver nitrite   **b.** Li_2CrO_4
     c. ammonium sulfite   **d.** $Mg(HCO_3)_2$
     e. Cu_3PO_4 **f.** aluminum permanganate

31. H:F̈:

33. H:P̈:H
        H

35. :C̈l:C:C̈l:
       :C̈l:

37. A hydrogen atom has only one valence electron. In a covalent bond involving H, the H atom pairs this single valence electron with a valence electron contributed by the atom with which it is forming the bond.

39. a. N_2O_4 **b.** $BrCl_3$
     c. Oxygen difluoride   **d.** NI_3
     e. Carbon tetrabromide   **f.** Dinitrogen tetrasulfide

41.

a. H—Si—H (with H above and below Si)
b. :F: :F: / :N—N: / :F: :F:
c. H—C—N: (with H's around C and N)
d. H—C—H with :O: double bonded above C

e. :N—O: (with H above N, H below N, and :O: to right)

f. H—Ö—P̈—Ö—H with :O—H below P

43. a. $\left[: \ddot{C}l — \ddot{O} : \right]^{-}$ **b.** $\left[H — \ddot{O} — P — \ddot{O} : \right]^{2-}$ (with :O: above and :O: below P)

    c. $\left[: \ddot{O} — \ddot{B}r — \ddot{O} : \right]^{-}$ (with :O: below Br)

45. In order for a covalent bond between elements A and B to be polar, the electronegativity difference between A and B must be between 0.5 and 2.0. If the electronegativity difference between A and B is less than 0.5 the bond will be considered nonpolar; if the electronegativity difference is greater than 2.0 then the bond will likely be ionic.

47. a. polar   **b.** polar   **c.** polar

49. a. H—O   **b.** N—F   **c.** Cl—B (with directional arrows)

51. a. $Si^{\delta+}—O^{\delta-}$ **b.** F—F   **c.** $F^{\delta-}—N^{\delta+}$

53. a. ionic   **b.** nonpolar covalent
     c. ionic   **d.** nonpolar covalent

55. P—Cl < N—F < Si—Cl < H—F < B—F < Si—F

57. a. tetrahedral   **b.** bent
     c. pyramidal   **d.** tetrahedral
     e. bent   **f.** triangular

59. BeF_2 is linear and therefore nonpolar F⁻—Be⁺—F⁻.

61. polar
     a. Ca^{2+}: $1s^22s^22p^63s^23p^6$
     b. Rb^+: $1s^22s^22p^63s^23p^63d^{10}4s^24p^6$
     c. S^{2-}: $1s^22s^22p^63s^23p^6$
     d. I^-: $1s^22s^22p^63s^23p^63d^{10}4s^24p^64d^{10}5s^25p^6$
     e. N^{3-}: $1s^22s^22p^6$
     f. Se^{2-}: $1s^22s^22p^63s^23p^63d^{10}4s^24p^6$

63. a. nonpolar bonds; 109°; nonpolar molecule
     b. polar bonds; 120°; polar molecule
     c. polar bonds; 109°; polar molecule
     d. polar bonds; 109°; polar molecule
     e. polar bonds; 109°; nonpolar molecule
     f. polar bonds; 109°; nonpolar molecule

65. polar bonds; 120°; polar molecule

67. S—Cl nonpolar; O—H, polar

69. free radicals

71. a. XeF_4 **b.** I_3^- :Ï—Ï—Ï:

     c. SF_4 **d.** KrF_2 :F̈—Kr—F̈:

73.

Bond dipole — O (with H, H) — Bond dipole

Molecular dipole

75. The central S atom in SCl_2 is surrounded by four electron sets giving it bond angles of approximately 109°. Two of the electron sets are nonbonded electron pairs so their electron density is located closer to the S atom than is the case with the other two electron pairs the density of which is drawn towards the Cl atoms. The 'extra' electron repulsion caused by the nonbonded electron pairs forces the Cl—S—Cl bond angle to contract slightly, making it a bit less than 109°.

77. nonpolar

79. Taking K, metallic potassium, would not be a wise idea as it would react violently with the water in your mouth (saliva is an aqueous solution). Instead, the potassium your doctor prescribes is a salt containing K^+ ions, such as KCl.

81. a. Ca^{2+}: $1s^2 2s^2 2p^6 3s^2 3p^6$
    b. Rb^+: $1s^2 2s^2 2p^6 3s^2 3p^6 4s^2 3d^{10} 4p^6$
    c. S^{2-}: $1s^2 2s^2 2p^6 3s^2 3p^6$
    d. I^-: $1s^2 2s^2 2p^6 3s^2 3p^6 4s^2 3d^{10} 4p^6 5s^2 4d^{10} 5p^6$
    e. N^{3-}: $1s^2 2s^2 2p^6$
    f. Se^{2-}: $1s^2 2s^2 2p^6 3s^2 3p^6 4s^2 3d^{10} 4p^6$

83. The halogens have seven valence electrons. Forming single bonds by sharing a bond with one other atom gives them an octet of electrons.

85. $Al_2(WO_4)_3$

87. $Q_3(ZX_4)_2$

89. A central atom adopting a tetrahedral geometry is one surrounded by four electron sets. While those four electron sets complete the octet for the central atom, they are mutually repulsive because electrons are electrically negative and like charges repel one another. The most efficient way of separating the four negative areas around a central atom is to space them so that the central atom occupies the center and the four electron sets occupy the vertices of a tetrahedron.

91. molecular recognition

93. Medicinal chemists design new drug molecules to resemble biological molecules that bind to enzymes which recognize the molecules by shapes and partial charges.

Chemistry @ Home

1. SO_2 has a lone pair of electrons on the central sulfur atom, which pushes the oxygen molecules away and gives it a 120° angle. Water has two pairs of lone electrons on the central oxygen atoms, which push away the hydrogen atoms and gives the molecule a tetrahedral angle of 109.5°.

2. Tetrahedral

3. 120° angle

Chapter 5

5.1 **A.** $3 H_2 + N_2 \longrightarrow 2 NH_3$
     B. $2 Fe_2O_3 + 3 C \longrightarrow 3 CO_2 + 4 Fe$

5.2 **A.** 1.66 L   **B.** Propane; 3.2 L

5.3 **a.** 65.0 u   **b.** 76.1 u   **c.** 147.0 u   **d.** 234.1 u

5.4 **a.** 16.5% N   **b.** 41.1 %N

5.5 **A. a.** 0.874 g C   **b.** 1000 g H_2O
     c. 17.0 g $Ca(HSO_4)_2$
     B. a. 0.0664 mol Fe   **b.** 2.29 mol C_5H_{12}
     c. 14.8 mol $Mg(NO_3)_2$

5.6 *Molecular:* 2 molecules H_2S react with 3 molecules O_2 to form 2 molecules SO_2 and 2 molecules H_2C
     Molar: 2 mol H_2S react with 3 mol O_2 to form 2 mol SO_2 and 2 mol H_2C
     Mass: 68.2 g H_2S react with 96.0 g O_2 to form 128.1 g SO_2 and 36.0 g H_2C

5.7 **A. a.** 3.75 mol CO_2 **b.** 0.0354 mol CO_2
     B. Propane, 7.5 mol

5.8 **A.** 3.43 g O_2
     B. a. 974 g CO_2 **b.** 1082 g CO_2

5.9 **A.** 0.00672 M
     B. 1.09 M

5.10 **A. a.** 0.0918 M   **b.** 0.0168 M
      B. 0.00881 M

5.11 **a.** 336 g KOH   **b.** 11.2 g KOH

5.12 **A.** 24.7 mL

5.13 **A.** 89% ethanol
      B. 31% toluene

5.14 **A.** 2.06% H_2O_2
      B. 49.3% NaOH

5.15 **A.** Dissolve 11.3 g glucose in enough water to make 250 g of solution.
      B. Dissolve 11.1 g NaCl in enough water to make 1250 g of solution.

1. **a.** The smallest repeating unit of a substance
   b. The sum of the atomic masses of a chemical compound
   c. The amount of a substance that contains 6.022×10^{23} formula units of the substance
   d. The number of atoms (6.022×10^{23}) in exactly 12 g of pure carbon-12
   e. The formula mass of a substance expressed in grams; mass of one mole
   f. The volume occupied by 1 mol of a gas under specified conditions

3. Avogadro's hypothesis states that equal volumes of all gases contain the same number of molecules at fixed temperature and pressure. It explains why volumes of gaseous reactants and products combine in small whole-number ratios

5. **a.** A solution is a homogeneous mixture of two or more substances.
   b. The solvent is the substance present in the greatest quantity in a solution.
   c. A solute is a substance dissolved in a solvent to form a solution.
   d. An aqueous solution is a solution in which water is the solvent.

7. **a.** 12   **b.** 3   **c.** 6

9. 6 N, 3 P, 27 H, 12 O

11. **a.** 2 molecules of H_2O_2 produce 2 molecules of H_2O and one molecule of O_2
    b. 2 mol of H_2O_2 produce 2 mol of H_2O and one mol of O_2
    c. 68 g of H_2O_2 produce 36 g of H_2O and 32 g of O_2

13. **a.** $2 Mg + O_2 \longrightarrow 2 MgO$
    b. $C_3H_8 + 5 O_2 \longrightarrow 3 CO_2 + 4 H_2O$
    c. $3 H_2 + Ta_2O_3 \longrightarrow 2 Ta + 3 H_2O$

15. **a.** $N_2 + O_2 \longrightarrow 2 NO$
    b. $2 O_3 \longrightarrow 3 O_2$
    c. $UO_2 + 4 HF \longrightarrow UF_4 + 2 H_2O$

17.

Hydrogen gas (two volumes)   +   Oxygen gas (one volume)   ⟶   Steam (two volumes)

19. **a.** 144 L CO_2 **b.** 2.64 mL

21. 7:1

23. **a.** 6.02×10^{23} molecules of S_8. **b.** 4.82×10^{24} S atoms.

25. c

27. **a.** 169.9 g   **b.** 351.2 g
    c. 317.7 g   **d.** 104.0 g/mol

29. **a.** 1770 g   **b.** 635 g   **c.** 85.5 g

31. **a.** 0.0195 mol   **b.** 0.133 mol   **c.** 0.356 mol

33. **a.** 17.1%   **b.** 26.2%

35. **a.** 3.38 mol CO_2 **b.** 16.5 mol O_2

37. **a.** 1400 g NH_3 **b.** 200 g H_2

39. **a.** 1.95 M   **b.** 0.848 M

41. **a.** 2.75 mol NaOH; 110 g NaOH
    b. 0.101 mol $C_6H_{12}O_6$; 18.2 g $C_6H_{12}O_6$

43. **a.** 0.333 L
    b. 0.0450 mol KH_2AsO_4; volume of solution 0.64 L

45. **a.** 10.5%   **b.** 4.70%
47. 310 g NaCl. To prepare the solution, dissolve 310 g of NaCl in 3440 g of water.
49. Add 40.0 mL of acetic acid to the water to bring the total volume of the solution to 2.00 L.
51. The first equation is correct. The second equation is not correct because it is not balanced.
53. **a.** $Hg(NO_3)_2(s) \longrightarrow Hg(l) + 2\,NO_2(g) + O_2(g)$
    b. $Na_2CO_3(aq) + 2\,HCl(aq) \longrightarrow H_2O(l) + CO_2(g) + 2\,NaCl(aq)$
55. **a.** yes   **b.** $0.50\ mol\ C_2H_2$
57. number of moles of $CaCO_3 = 2.5 \times 10^3$ mol; number of moles of $CaO = 2.5 \times 10^3$ mol; mass of $CaO = 1.4 \times 10^5$ g CaO
59. $0.418\ mol\ H_2O_2$
61. **a.** 94.9% ethanol   **b.** 0.258% acetone
63. **a.** 3.57×10^{-22} g U   **b.** 722 U atoms
65. 8.25 mL
67. The number of cups of water in all the oceans is 6.10×10^{21} and the number of H_2O molecules in a cup of water is $7,89 \times 10^{24}$ so the statement is valid.
69. The balanced chemical equation for the neutralization reaction is:
    $$H_2SO_4 + 2\,NaHCO_3 \longrightarrow Na_2SO_4 + 2\,H_2O + 2\,CO_2$$
    mass of $H_2SO_4 = 5.0 \times 10^7$ g H_2SO_4.
    number of moles of H_2SO_4 spilled $= 5.10 \times 10^5$ mol $H_2\,SO_4$.
    number of moles of $NaHCO_3 = 1.02 \times 10^6$ mol.
    mass of $NaHCO_3$ required $= 8.57 \times 10^7$ g or 8.57×10^4 kg.
71. $111\ mol\ H_2O$
73. **a.** $C_6H_{12}O_6 \longrightarrow 2\,C_2H_6O + 2\,CO_2;\ C_2H_4 + H_2O \longrightarrow C_2H_6O$
    b. (1) 51.1%; (2) 100%
    c. (1) CO_2 is a byproduct ("waste"); (2) no byproduct
    d. (1) sustainable; (2) not sustainable
    e. reaction (1) does produce a byproduct, but is sustainable and does not consume valuable, non-renewable petroleum.
75. **a.** 51.3%   **b.** 52.6%   **c.** 81.5%

Chemistry @ Home

1. The greenhouse effect is demonstrated with methane + oxygen combining to form carbon dioxide and water.
2. While carbon dioxide is essential to life on earth too much carbon dioxide is contributing to global climate change. The burning of fossil fuels has made a considerable impact to the environment and will continue to cause environmental harms if we are not able to reduce our carbon footprint.
3. The law of the conservation of matter states that matter is neither created nor destroyed during the course of a chemical reaction. Although they may be combined differently the mass of the atoms in the reactants must equal the mass of the atoms in the product. This is a fundamental building block to understanding and applying chemistry it is used in practical applications of redox chemistry electrochemistry and stoichiometry.

Chapter 6

6.1   400 mm Hg
6.2   **A.** 1800 mL   **B.** 503 mm Hg
6.3   **A.** 21.5 L   **B.** −259.8 °C
6.4   **A.** 29 psi   **B.** −95 °C
6.5   **A.** 5.86 g/L   **B.** 1.29; only 0.22 times that of Xe
6.6   **A.** 922 mL   **B.** 426 torr
6.7   **A. a.** 0.0526 torr   **b.** 9.99 L
     B. 112 L

1. Both solids and liquids are difficult to compress because the particles are close together. Liquids flow because their particles are free to move; solids have fixed shapes because their particles have fixed positions.
3. The conversion from a solid to a liquid is called melting and the conversion from a liquid to a gas is called vaporization. The conversion of a gas to a liquid is called condensation, and the conversion from a liquid to a solid is called freezing.

5. **a.** Ionic interactions, NaCl.
   b. Dipole-dipole interactions, $H_2C{=}O$.
   c. Hydrogen bonding, H_2O, CH_3CH_2OH, NH_3
   d. Dispersion forces CCl_4
7. Inversely proportional to pressure and directly proportional to the absolute temperature
9. NBr_3 polar; N_2 nonpolar, NaBr ionic
11. N_2
13. He, C_2H_6, NH_3, KCl
15. Water: NaCl and Li_2CO_3; tetrachloride: C_5H_{12} and C_8H_{18}
17. $42.9\ m^3$
19. 0.497 atm
21. 3.76 L
23. 117 mL
25. 1.07 L
27. 160 °C
29. **a.** 22.4 L   **b.** 39.2 L   **c.** 5.04 L
31. 9.91 g/L
33. **a.** 47.4 g/mol   **b.** 66.5 g/mol
35. The ideal gas law is PV = nRT. If n is constant:
    a. decrease   **b.** decrease   **c.** increase
37. **a.** the temperature will decrease.
    b. then the pressure will decrease.
39. **a.** 0.172 L   **b.** 1.04 atm
41. 0.0208 mol
43. 0.00415 mol
45. 14.5 L
47. 1. Gas particles are in rapid constant motion and move in straight lines.
    2. Particles of a gas are small compared with the distances between them.
    3. Because the particles of a gas are so far apart, there is very little attraction between them.
    4. Particles of a gas collide with one another. Energy is conserved in these collisions; energy lost by one particle is gained by the other.
    5. Temperature is a measure of the average kinetic energy (energy of motion) of the gas particles.
49. **a.** size and pressure
    b. size and pressure
    c. temperature and pressure
51. 3.0 g He
53. 0.394 L
55. 44.0 g/mol
57. **a.** $68\ m^3$ **b.** 68,000 L   **c.** 132 kg CO_2
59. **a.** 380 mmHg   **b.** 38 mmHg   **c.** 7.6 mmHg
61. b, c, d
63. 1.16 L
65. Supercritical carbon dioxide is inexpensive, convenient to use, in flammable, and nontoxic, all characteristics that support its use in greener chemical processing.
67. Perchloroethylene, previously used in the dry cleaning industry, has been replaced with $scCO_2$, and methylene chloride has been replaced by $scCO_2$ for the decaffeination of coffee.

Chemistry @ Home

1. The balloon that we used was 11.5 inches in circumference at room temperature. In the warm water the balloon grew to about 11.8 inches after 4 minutes (after 1 minute it was at 11.75 inches).
2. In the cold water it shrunk to about 11.25 inches (after 2 minutes it was 11.45 inches).
3. The heat makes the air molecules inside the balloon move faster and therefore exerts a greater force on the balloon walls, making it grow. While, the cooled balloon actually makes the molecules slow down and therefore the force exerted on the walls is less and the balloon shrinks.
4. As the temperature increases, the volume will increase.
5. The pressure would increase if heated due to the increased force exert on the container and decrease if cooled due to the decreased

force. Since the balloon is not a rigid container, it will expand or contract.

Chapter 7

7.1 **A. a.** $HI(aq) \longrightarrow H^+(aq) + I^-(aq)$

    b. $Ca(OH)_2(s) \xrightarrow{H_2O} Ca^{2+}(aq) + 2\ OH^-(aq)$

  B. $CH_3COOH(aq) \xrightarrow{H_2O} H^+(aq) + CH_3COO^-(aq)$

7.2 **A.** $HBr(aq) + H_2O \longrightarrow H_3O^+(aq) + Br^-(aq)$

  B. $HClO_4 + CH_3OH \longrightarrow CH_3OH_2{}^+ + ClO_4{}^-$

7.3 **A.** H_2SeO_3

  B. HNO_3

7.4 **A.** $Sr(OH)_2$

  B. KOH

7.5 **A.** $NaOH(aq) + HC_2H_3O_2(aq) \longrightarrow NaC_2H_3O_2(aq) + H_2O$

  B. $2\ HCl(aq) + Mg(OH)_2(aq) \longrightarrow MgCl_2(aq) + 2\ H_2O$

7.6 **A.** $pH = 9$ **B.** $pH = 2$

7.7 **A.** 1×10^{-2} M (0.01 M)   **B.** 1×10^{-3} M (0.001 M)

7.8 c

7.9 Beaker III: HNO_3; Beaker II: KOH

7.10 **a.** CN^- **b.** H_2O **c.** $HSO_4{}^-$ **d.** H_2CO_3

1. **a.** Arrhenius said an acid is a substance that donates one or more H^+ ions to water. Brønsted-Lowry defined an acid as a substance that donates one or more H^+ ions to a solution. In essence, the two definitions are the same. H_2SO_4, sulfuric acid, is an example.

  b. An Arrhenius base is a compound that donates one or more OH^- ions to a solution. According to the Brønsted-Lowry definition, a base is a proton acceptor. KOH, potassium hydroxide, is an example of an Arrhenius base. KOH is also an example of a Brønsted-Lowry base because OH^- ions can accept H^+ ions to form H_2O. NH_3 is an example of a Brønsted-Lowry base but not of an Arrhenius base.

  c. A salt is an ionic compound formed from the neutralization of an acid with a base. K_2SO_4, potassium sulfate, is the salt formed by the reaction of H_2SO_4 and KOH.

3. A neutralized solution would have a $pH = 7$, and this solution would have no effect on either iron or zinc. Although both of these metals would react with an acidic solution, neither reacts in a solution with $pH = 7$.

5. We refer to H^+ ions as protons when describing acid-base chemistry. Protons are the positively charged nuclear particles that are counted when determining the atomic number of an element. The atomic number of hydrogen is 1 meaning that there is one proton in the nucleus of an H atom. Because the mass number (number of protons plus neutrons) of most H atoms is 1, most H nuclei contain only one proton. When the sole electron from an H atom is lost to form H^+, all that remains is a proton. Hence the name.

7. Neutralization of an acid occurs when an equivalent amount of base is added so that $[H^+] = [OH^-]$. Bases are neutralized when an equivalent amount of acid is added so that $[H^+] = [OH^-]$.

9. Strong bases ionize in water, producing OH^- to the extent that they are soluble. Weak bases also react with water to produce OH^- ions, but only 5% or less of the weak base species in solution undergo the reaction.

11. Strong acids and bases are corrosive and can cause burns.

13. **a.** $HClO_4 \xrightarrow{H_2O} H^+ + ClO_4{}^-$

  b. $RbOH \xrightarrow{H_2O} Rb^+ + OH^-$

15. $H_2PO_4{}^- \xrightarrow{H_2O} HPO_4{}^{2-} + OH^-$

17. **a.** $(CH_3)_2NH$ **b.** $C_6H_5NH_2$ **c.** $C_6H_5CH_2NH_2$

19. **a.** $HCOOH(aq) + H_2O(l) \longrightarrow H_3O^+(aq) + COO^-(aq)$

  b. $C_5H_5N(aq) + H_2O(l) \longrightarrow C_5H_5NH^+(aq) + OH^-(aq)$

21. $NH_3(aq) + H_2O \longrightarrow NH_4{}^+(aq) + OH^-(aq)$

23. **a.** HCl: HCl(g) is hydrogen chloride; HCl(aq) is hydrochloric acid.

  b. $Sr(OH)_2$

  c. KOH is potassium hydroxide.   **d.** H_3BO_3

25. **a.** phosphoric acid, acid.   **b.** cesium hydroxide, base.

  c. carbonic acid, acid.

27. **a.** HNO_3 **b.** H_3PO_3

29. **a.** $SO_3 + H_2O \longrightarrow H_2SO_4$, acid.

  b. $MgO + H_2O \longrightarrow Mg(OH)_2$, base.

31. strong acid

33. weak base

35. **a.** strong base   **b.** strong acid

  c. weak acid   **d.** salt

37. **a.** highest   **b.** lowest   **c.** weak acid

39. **a.** $KOH(aq) + HCl(aq) \longrightarrow KCl(aq) + H_2O(l)$

  b. $LiOH(aq) + HNO_3(aq) \longrightarrow LiNO_3(aq) + H_2O(l)$

41. **a.** $H_2SO_3(aq) + Mg(OH)_2(aq) \longrightarrow 2\ H_2O(aq) + MgSO_3(aq)$

43. **a.** acidic   **b.** neutral   **c.** acidic   **d.** basic

45. 5.0

47. 9.0

49. 0.001 M

51. The pH of milk of magnesia is between 10 and 11.

53. $HNO_3(aq) + NH_3(aq) \longrightarrow NO_3{}^-(aq) + NH_4{}^+(aq)$

  a. HNO_3, nitric acid, is the acid; NH_3, is the base

  b. $NO_3{}^-(aq)$

  c. $NH_4{}^+(aq)$

55. $Al(OH)_3(s) + 3\ HCl(aq) \longrightarrow AlCl_3(aq) + 3\ H_2O$

  $Mg(OH)_2(s) + 2\ HCl(aq) \longrightarrow MgCl_2(aq) + 2\ H_2O$

57. Bases are reported to taste bitter so soaps are likely to be basic which means that the pH of a soap solution would be greater than 7.0.

59. No. To be an Arrhenius base the OH^- group must be paired with a metal.

61. HI; $SrCO_3(s) + 2\ HI(aq) \longrightarrow SrI_2(aq) + H_2CO_3(aq)$

63. **a.** 3   **b.** 2

65. 14.0

67. A buffer solution is made from a mixture of a weak acid and its salt or a weak base and its salt. Ammonia is a weak base while sodium hydroxide is a strong base. Therefore, the combination of ammonia (NH_3) and ammonium acetate ($NH_4C_2H_3O_2$) would meet the requirement of a weak base and its salt while the combination of sodium hydroxide (NaOH) and sodium acetate ($NaC_2H_3O_2$) would not.

69. $Al_2(CO_3)_3(s) + 6\ HCl(aq) \longrightarrow 2\ AlCl_3(aq) + 3\ H_2O(l) + 3\ CO_2(g)$

71. $S(s) + O_2(g) \longrightarrow SO_2(g)$

  $2\ SO_2(g) + O_2(g) \xrightarrow{V_2O_5} 2\ SO_3(g)$

  $SO_3(g) + H_2O(l) \longrightarrow H_2SO_4(l)$

73. 1000 L

75. Montmorillonite clay

Chemistry @ Home

1. This is entirely subjective

2. Lemon Juice-2

  Vinegar-3

  Orange Juice-4

  Shampoo-6

  Red Cabbage Indicator-7-neutral

3. Tap water-8 (depends on your water source)

  Baking soda-10

  Milk of magnesia-11

  Ammonia-12

4. Add a few drops of one of the basic solutions such as ammonia, baking soda solution or milk of magnesia.

5. Possibly the pH of the water could impact your results. It is also possible that the substances could have unknown additives which could also influence your results.

Chapter 8

8.1 oxidation: a, b, d; reduction: c

8.2 reduction: a; oxidation: b

8.3 reduction: a, c, d; oxidation: b

8.4. **a.** 0   **b.** −1   **c.** +5   **d.** +3

8.5. **a.** reduction   **b.** oxidation

8.6. **a.** oxidizing agent: O_2; reducing agent: Se
     b. oxidizing agent: Br_2; reducing agent: K
     c. oxidizing agent: O_2; reducing agent: Fe
     d. oxidizing agent: V_2O_5; reducing agent: H_2

8.7. oxidation: $Co \longrightarrow Co^{3+} + 3\,e^-$; reduction: $S + 2\,e^- \longrightarrow S^{2-}$

8.8. **A.** $Zn + 2\,H^+ \longrightarrow Zn^{2+} + H_2$
     B. $Pb + 2\,Ag(NH_3)_2{}^+ \longrightarrow Pb^{2+} + 2\,Ag + 4\,NH_3$

8.9. **a.** $2\,Zn + O_2 \longrightarrow 2\,ZnO$
     b. $Se + O_2 \longrightarrow SeO_2$
     c. $C + O_2 \longrightarrow CO_2$

1. The oxidation number is increased during oxidation and decreased in reduction.

3. In an electrochemical cell the anode is a conducting material in contact with a substance that will spontaneously release electrons to the substance in contact with the cathode. The reason why electrons flow from the anode to the cathode is that the substances that form as a result of the redox reaction are more energetically stable than the reactants.

5. The porous plate between two electrode compartments allows ions to pass through, thereby completing the electrical circuit and keeping the solutions electrically neutral.

7. The case (container) of a regular carbon-zinc dry cell battery is composed of Zn which acts as the anode in the oxidation-reduction reaction. Zn is oxidized to Zn^{2+} in the reaction.

9. The reaction that occurs during the recharging of a lead storage battery is:
$2\,PbSO_4 + 2\,H_2O \longrightarrow Pb + PbO_2 + 2\,H_2SO_4$. $PbSO_4$ is converted to Pb and PbO_2.

11. Lithium has a very low density and can provide higher voltages than other metals.

13. Ag is oxidized by H_2S to produce Ag_2S which is black. Aluminum foil can be used to reduce Ag^+ back to Ag. This way the silver remains on the object rather than being abraded off with a rough cloth.

15. Through the process of photosynthesis plants are able to store energy from the sun in the form of chemical bonds in reduced forms of carbon. We consume foods which contain these compounds and reverse the photosynthetic reaction by oxidizing the carbon atoms and releasing the stored energy. We use the released energy to fuel the physiological reactions that, among other things, enable our hearts to beat.

17. **a.** The oxidation number of carbon in C is zero; in CCl_4 the ON is +4. The ON increased so C is oxidized.
     b. The oxidation number of C increases from zero to +2. C is oxidized.
     c. The oxidation number of C increases from zero to +4. C is oxidized.
     d. The oxidation of C increases from −1 to zero so C is oxidized.
     e. The oxidation number of C decreases from zero to −4 so C is reduced.

19. **a.** $Ca \longrightarrow Ca^{2+} + 2\,e^-$ **b.** $Al \longrightarrow Al^{3+} + 3\,e^-$
     c. $Cu \longrightarrow Cu^+ + e^-$ **d.** $Cu \longrightarrow Cu^{2+} + 2\,e^-$

21. **a.** Cu is oxidized; O_2 is reduced.
     b. Mg is oxidized; H^+ is reduced.
     c. The O in H_2O_2 is oxidized; Br_2 is reduced.
     d. S in $S_2O_3{}^{2-}$ is oxidized; O_2 is reduced.

23. **a.** C is oxidized so it is the reducing agent; Fe is reduced so it is the oxidizing agent.
     b. P is oxidized so it is the reducing agent; O_2 is reduced so it is the oxidizing agent.
     c. C is oxidized and is the reducing agent; H is reduced and is the oxidizing agent.
     d. Zn is oxidized and is the reducing agent; H is reduced and is the oxidizing agent.

25. Copper reduces the silver from Ag^+ to Ag.

27. MnO_2 is the oxidizing agent; Zn is the reducing agent.

29. The anode is the reducing agent; the cathode is the oxidizing agent.

31. oxidizing agent

33. **a.** $Fe \longrightarrow Fe^{2+} + 2\,e^-$ half-reaction of oxidation.
     $2\,H^+ + 2\,e^- \longrightarrow H_2$ half-reaction of reduction.
     b. $Cr^{2+}\,2\,e^- \longrightarrow Cr^0$ half-reaction of reduction.
     $Al \longrightarrow Al^{3+} + 3\,e^-$ half-reaction of oxidation.

35. **a.** half reaction of reduction; half reaction of oxidation
     $Cu^{2+} + Fe \longrightarrow Cu + Fe^{2+}$
     b. half reaction of oxidation; half reaction of reduction
     $2\,H_2O_2 + 4\,Fe^{3+} \longrightarrow 2\,O_2 + 4\,H^+ + 4\,Fe^{2+}$
     c. half reaction of reduction; half reaction of oxidation
     $WO_3 + 3\,C_2H_6O \longrightarrow W + 3\,H_2O + 3\,C_2H_4O$

37. **a.** Oxidation half reaction; Reduction half reaction
     $2\,Mn^{2+} + 3\,Pb^{4+} \longrightarrow 2\,Mn^{5+} + 3\,Pb^{2+}$
     b. Oxidation half reaction; Reduction half reaction
     $4\,S^{2+} + O \longrightarrow 4\,S^{2.5+} + O^{2-}$

39. **a.** One of the C atoms in CH_3CHO is oxidized; one of the O atoms in H_2O_2 is reduced.
     b. C is oxidized; Mn is reduced.

41. **a.** reduced   **b.** reduced

43. The unsaturated oil is reduced because the number of H atoms per C atom has increased.

45. I^- is oxidized; Cl_2 is reduced

47. The reactant, tartaric acid, is reduced to glucose in the ripening process. The C atoms in tartaric acid gain H and lose O atoms in the process.

49. oxidized

51. Fe is reduced as its ON changes from +3 to +2. Fe^{3+} is the oxidizing agent. C is reduced as its ON changes from zero in $C_6H_{12}O_6$ to +4 in CO_2.

53. **a.** $N_2 + 2\,O_2 \longrightarrow 2\,NO_2$
     b. $CS_2 + 3\,O_2 \longrightarrow CO_2 + 2\,SO_2$
     c. $C_5H_{12} + 8\,O_2 \longrightarrow 5\,CO_2 + 6\,H_2O$

55. **a.** +2   **b.** +4   **c.** −4   **d.** +4   **e.** +2

57. $F > Cl > Br > I$

59. The light grease or oil coating protects the metal tools from air oxidation.

61. $2\,CO_2 + e^- \longrightarrow C_2O_4{}^{2-}$; CO_2 is reduced

63. volume of O_2/min = 1.6 L O_2/min
     volume of O_2/day = 2000 L O_2/day

65. **a.** oxidation   **b.** $CO_2 + 24\,H^+ + 24\,e^- \longrightarrow 6\,H_2O + C_6H_{12}O_6$

67. +4; 0

69. Metals frequently act as reducing agents because they can often gain more stable valence electron configurations through the loss of electrons. Nonmetals can act as oxidizing or as reducing agents depending on the substance(s) they are paired with. For example, hydrogen peroxide, H_2O_2, can function as an oxidizing agent or as a reducing agent.

71. $H_2 + Cl_2 \longrightarrow 2\,HCl$; Cl_2

73. $2\,Al + 6\,H_2O \longrightarrow 2\,Al(OH)_3 + 3\,H_2$; Al is the reducing agent and H_2O is the oxidizing agent.

75. **a.** NAD^+ is reduced to NADH and ethanol is oxidized to acetaldehyde.
     The half-reaction of reduction is: $NAD^+ + H^+ + 2\,e^- \longrightarrow$ NADH
     The half-reaction of oxidation is: $CH_3CH_2OH \longrightarrow CH_3CHO + 2\,H^+ + 2\,e^-$
     The complete reaction is: $NAD^+ + CH_3CH_2OH \longrightarrow CH_3CHO + H^+ + NADH$
     b. The half-reaction of reduction is:
     $CH_3COCOOH + 2\,H^+ + 2\,e^- \longrightarrow CH_3CHOHCOOH$
     The half-reaction of oxidation is: $NADH \longrightarrow NAD^+ + H^+ + 2\,e^-$
     The complete reaction is: $CH_3COCOOH + NADH + H^+ \longrightarrow CH_3CHOHCOOH + NAD^+$

77. **a.** Industrial chemicals are produced on a large scale.
     b. Complex molecules are usually produced as specialty chemicals.

c. Specialty chemicals usually have a higher value in the marketplace than industrial chemicals.

d. Industrial chemicals are often the building blocks for more complex specialty chemicals.

79. Many oxidation catalysts have organic molecules built into their structures. These organic components may undergo chemical oxidation, causing the catalyst to lose effectiveness.

Chemistry @ Home

1. The zinc is more reactive than copper, which means that zinc loses electrons more easily than copper.
2. The lemon should produce close to one volt and about 2 milliamps.
3. The kiwi should produce just over one volt and about 2 milliamps.
4. The kiwi will most likely produce more volts.
5. The fruit when connected in a series you may have been enough to power the mini light bulb. While the light bulb only needs 1.5 volts it may need more milliamps than you were able to provide due to resistance from your connection of the fruit.

Chapter 9

9.1 **a.** Molecular: C_6H_{14}; complete structural:

condensed structural: $CH_3CH_2CH_2CH_2CH_2CH_3$

a. Molecular: C_8H_{18}; complete structural:

condensed structural: $CH_3CH_2CH_2CH_2CH_2CH_2CH_2CH_3$

9.2 **A.**
a.
$$CH_2-CH_2$$
$$|\qquad|$$
$$CH_2-CH_2$$

B. The cyclic structure has 1 additional C—C bond, and therefore 2 fewer C—H bonds. It is still considered an alkane because it has only single bonds, but it is not as saturated as a regular alkane.

9.4 **A.** No, there are not. There are two H atoms on one of the doubly bonded carbon atoms. It fails rule 2 and cannot have geometric isomers.
B. **a.** No isomers

b. Yes,

c. there really is no such molecule as 3-pentene, it is the same as 2-pentene. It would have the same structures as it.
d. No isomers

9.5 **a.** $CHCl_3$ **b.** CCl_4
9.6 **a.** $CH_3CH_2CH_2CH_2OH$

b.

9.7 **a.** alcohol   **b.** ether   **c.** ether
d. phenol   **e.** ether
9.8 **A.** $CH_3OCH_2CH_2CH_2CH_3$ **B.** $CH_3CH_2OC(CH_3)_3$
9.9. **a.** ketone   **b.** aldehyde   **c.** aldehyde
9.10. **a.** $CH_3CH_2CH_2COOH$
b. CH_3CHO
c. $CH_3CH_2COCH_2CH_3$
d. $CH_3CH_2COCH_2CH_2CH_2CH_2CH_3$
e. $CH_3CH_2CH_2CH_2CH_2CH_2CHO$
f. $CH_3CH_2CH_2CH_2CH_2COOH$
9.11 **a.** $CH_3CH_2CH_2CH_2NH_2$
b. $CH_3CH_2NHCH_2CH_3$
c. $CH_3NHCH_2CH_2CH_3$
d. $(CH_3)_2CHNHCH_3$
9.12 **a.** amine (NH)   **b.** amide (NH)
c. amine (N)   **d.** amine (CONH)
9.13 heterocyclic compounds: a, d
1. Carbon atoms can bond strongly to each other; can bond strongly to other elements; can form chains, rings, and other kinds of structures.
3. Isomers have the same general formula but different structures.
5. A set of six delocalized electrons
7. 1-4 C, gases; 5-16 C, liquids; 718 C, solids
9. **a.** ethanol   **b.** 2-propanol   **c.** methanol
11. Historical use: anesthetic; modern use: solvent
13. **a.** alcohol   **b.** ketone   **c.** ester
d. ether   **e.** carboxylic acid   **f.** aldehyde
15. **a.** organic   **b.** organic
c. inorganic   **d.** inorganic
17. **a.** 6   **b.** 9   **c.** 5   **d.** 5
19. **a.** C_8H_{18} **b.** $C_{14}H_{30}$
21. **a.** butane   **b.** butadiene   **c.** acetylene
23. **a.** C_5H_{12}; $CH_3CH_2CH_2CH_2CH_3$
b. $C_{10}H_{22}$; $CH_3CH_2CH_2CH_2CH_2CH_2CH_2CH_2CH_2CH_3$
25. **a.** methyl   **b.** *sec*-butyl
27. **a.** ethanol   **b.** 1-propanol   **c.** CH_3OH
d. $CH_3CH_2CH_2CH_2CH_2CH(OH)CH_3$

29. **a.**

b.

31. **a.** $CH_3CH_2CH_2OCH_2CH_2CH_3$
b. $CH_3CH_2CH_2CH_2OCH_2CH_3$
33. **a.** $CH_3CH_2COCH_3$ **b.** HCHO
c. butyraldehyde (butanal)
d. butyl ethyl ketone (3-heptanone)
35. **a.** propanoic acid   **b.** pentanoic acid
c. HCOOH   **d.** C_6H_6
37. **a.** CH_3COOCH_3 **b.** $CH_3CH_2CH_2COOCH_3$
c. ethyl propionate (ethyl propanoate).
39. **a.** $(CH_3CH_2)_3N$ **b.** $CH_3CH_2NHCH_3$
c. propylamine   **d.** ethylmethylamine
41. **a.** same   **b.** same   **c.** isomers
43. **a.** homologs   **b.** none of these
45. **a.** unsaturated; alkene   **b.** unsaturated; cyclic alkene
47. Malic acid has one alcohol group (—OH) and two carboxylic acid groups (—COOH)
49. **a.** heterocyclic; amine.
b. cycloalkane substituted with an amino group (not heterocyclic).
51. **a.** $C_{17}H_{26}O_4$ **b.** $C_{17}H_{24}O_3$
c. a phenol, an ether, a ketone, and an aliphatic alcohol.
d. a phenol, an ether, a ketone, and an alkene.
e. This is a dehydration reaction because the elements of water are removed.

53. a. $CH_3CH_2C\equiv CCH_3 + 2 H_2 \longrightarrow CH_3CH_2CH_2CH_2CH_3$
  b. $CH_3CH=C(CH_3)CH_2CH_2CH_2CH_3 + H_2 \longrightarrow$
  $CH_3CH_2CH(CH_3)CH_2CH_2CH_2CH_3$

55. a. $CH_3CH_2CH_2CH_2OH$ **b.** $CH_3CH_2CH(OH)CH_2CH_3$
  c. $CH_3CHOHCH(CH_3)_2$ **d.** $C_6H_5CH_2OH$

57. These compounds are all isomers

59. Equation is balanced as is; 731 g C_2H_6O

61. a. dispersion and (weak) dipole-dipole.
  b. hydrogen bonds The stronger hydrogen bonds cause ethanol to remain a liquid at room temperature.

63. a. HO—⟨benzene ring⟩—OH   **b.** O=⟨ring⟩=O

65. a. 6.55×10^{-4} g/mL   **b.** 1.25×10^{-3} g/mL
  c. 1.83×10^{-3} g/mL   **d.** 2.41×10^{-3} g/mL

67. b

69. Solvent is renewable and less toxic, and less solvent is used

71. Less energy is used; molecules absorb energy directly so less energy is lost to the surroundings

Chemistry @ Home

1.

Fat (1 tbsp)	Saturated (grams)	Mono-unsat-urated (grams)	Poly-unsaturated (grams)
Safflower oil	0.8	10.2	2.0
Sesame oil	1.9	5.4	5.6
Peanut oil	2.3	6.2	4.3

2. Because they are solid at room temperature, we would expect that they would have a higher amount of saturated fat and therefore a lower degree of unsaturation.

3. The trans double bonds will have similar structures as saturated fats and will pack closely to be more solid and therefore build up in the body, whereas cis double bonds create a kink in the fatty acid chain and the fat will be more fluid due to the inability to stack.

cis fatty acid

trans fatty acid

Chapter 10

10.1 $-CH_2CH(C\equiv N)-$

10.2 A.
$\left[CH_2CH-CH_2CH-CH_2CH-CH_2CH\right]$ with F substituents

B. $[CH_2CH(OCOCH_3)CH_2CH(OCOCH_3)$
  $CH_2CH(OCOCH_3)CH_2CH(OCOCH_3)]$

10.3 a. $[OCH_2COOCH_2COOCH_2COOCH_2CO]$
  b. $[OCH_2(C=O)]_n$

1. The monomer in polyethylene is ethylene, $H_2C=CH_2$, while that in polyvinyl chloride is vinyl chloride, $H_2C=CHCl$. Structurally, vinyl chloride is an ethylene molecule with one of the hydrogen atoms replaced with a chlorine atom. Polyethylene is used for, among other things, toys, plastic bags, and trash cans.

3. Polymerization in which all the monomer atoms are incorporated in the polymer; a double bond

5. styrene

7. Celluloid is a semi-synthetic material made from natural cellulose that has been treated with nitric acid.

9. Synthetic fibers are cheaper and have a wider range of properties.

11. For many applications, plastics must be separated by type, melted, and formed into new objects.

13. LDPE has highly branched molecules—a loosely packed, amorphous structure that makes it soft and flexible compared with HDPE.

15. a. $H_2C=CH_2$ **b.** $H_2C=CHC_6H_5$

17. a.

b. $[CH_2CF_2CH_2CF_2CH_2CF_2CH_2CF_2]$

19. a. $[CH_2CH(CH_2CH_2CH_3)CH_2CH(CH_2CH_2CH_3)$
  $CH_2CH(CH_2CH_2CH_3)]$

b.

21.
23. When stretched, rubber's coiled molecules are straightened. When released, the molecules coil again.

25. SBR is made by copolymerization of styrene and butadiene.

27. $[CO(CH_2)_6CONH(CH_2)_8NHCO(CH_2)_6CONH(CH_2)_8NH]$

29. $[OCH_2COOCH_2COOCH_2CO]$

31. The long chains can entangle with one another; intermolecular forces are greatly multiplied in large molecules; large polymer molecules move more slowly than do small molecules.

33. The temperature at which the properties of the polymer change from hard, stiff, and brittle to rubbery and tough; rubbery materials such as automobile tires should have a low T_g; glass substitutes, a high T_g.

35. Monomer: a; repeating unit: b; polymer: c. addition polymerization

37. $CH_2=CCl_2$ and $CH_2=CHCl$.

39.

41. $\{-CH_2-C(CH_3)_2-CH_2-C(CH_3)_2-CH_2-C(CH_3)_2-CH_2-C(CH_3)_2-\}$

43.

45.
$CH_3-CH=CH_2 \xrightarrow{Catalyst} [(CH_2-CH)]_n$ with CH_3 substituent

47. Elastomer; the golf ball

49. Because 1-butanol has an OH group on one end of the molecule only, the reaction cannot continue after the first ester forms on both ends of the terephthalic acid. The final product will be limited to a trimer of butanol–terephthalic acid–butanol or $CH_3(CH_2)_3OC(O)C_6H_5C(O)O(CH_2)_3CH_3$. A polymer cannot form.

51.

53. **a.** $+CH_2CH_2OCH_2CH_2OCH_2CH_2OCH_2CH_2O+$
    b. $+CH_2CH_2SCH_2CH_2SCH_2CH_2SCH_2CH_2S+$

55. b

57. c

Chemistry @ Home

1. The ball will bounce. The height varies you can expect it to from 12-36 inches.

2. The cross-linking of PVA and borax is a chemical reaction. The materials are combined to create a substance that has different properties from the original starting materials.

3. Depending on how much of each ingredient that you mix together, you can make something that is "goopy", slimy, or stretchy. For instance if you add more cornstarch, you will be able to bend and stretch the mix. Add less borax and you will get a "goopy" mixture. To make a slimy substance, add more glue.

4. No the ball is not biodegradable. PVA is made from carbon-based monomers that are generally derived from petroleum.

Chapter 11

11.1 **a.** $^{214}_{83}Bi \longrightarrow ^{210}_{81}Tl + ^4_2He$ **b.** $^{94}_{41}Nb \longrightarrow ^{94}_{42}Mo + ^0_{-1}e$
    c. $^{68}_{31}Ga \longrightarrow ^{18}_8Zn + ^0_{+1}e$ **d.** $^{37}_{18}Nb \longrightarrow ^0_{-1} + ^{37}_{17}Cl$

11.2 **A.** 6.25%   **B.** 500 Bq; 4 Bq

11.3 **a.** yes (3 Bq left)   **b.** no (4.0×10^{10} Bq remain)

11.4 **a.** 11,460 y   **b.** 49 y

11.5 **a.** A neutron (^1_0n)   **b.** Thorium-232 ($^{232}_{90}Th$)

11.6 Silicon-30 ($^{30}_{14}Si$)

11.7 Higher; the gas can be absorbed by inhalation and decay in the body.

1. d

3. **i.** b   **ii.** a   **iii.** c

5. **a.** Alpha particle emission (^4_2He) results in a loss of 4 in the nucleon number and a loss of 2 in the atomic number.
   b. Gamma ray emission (γ) does not change either the nucleon number or the atomic number of the product. Gamma rays are bundles of energy.
   c. Proton particle emission (^1_1H) results in the loss of one in the nucleon number and one in the atomic number.

7. False; in the period of a second half life, half of the remaining radioactive sample decays leaving 25% of the original radioactive sample.

9. amount of F-19 remaining in the sample is 0.125 of the original amount; amount of F-19 remaining 0.625 μg.

11. Technetium-99m produces gamma rays that can help with diagnosis. What is especially desirable about this isotope is that it does not release alpha, beta, or positron particles that could do internal harm and it has a short half-life (6.0 hr) so it does not linger in long in the body of the person being tested.

13. Two kinds of protection for workers dealing with radioactive materials are making certain the materials are kept and used in shielded containers (or areas), and increasing as much as possible the distance between the worker and the radioactive source(s).

15. (1) develop the conditions for a sustained nuclear fission reaction, (2) develop a process to enrich uranium to produce a sample containing 90% U-235, (3) to find an effect way of producing plutonium-239 which is another fissionable isotope, and (4) to construct a bomb based on a nuclear fission reaction.

17. Uncontrolled nuclear fission reactions can be used to cause destruction as in the case of bombs. Secondly, the same basic reactions can be controlled and used instead of fossil fuels to generate power for the general population. Third, fission reactions can be controlled and used to power sea-going vessels.

19. b

21. **a.** $^{250}_{98}Cf \longrightarrow ^4_2He + ^{246}_{96}Cm$ **b.** $^{210}_{83}Bi \longrightarrow ^{210}_{84}Po + ^0_{-1}e$
    c. $^{117}_{53}I \longrightarrow ^0_{+1}e + ^{117}_{52}Te$

23. **a.** $^{179}_{79}Au \longrightarrow ^{175}_{77}Ir + ^4_2He$
    b. $^{12}_6C + ^2_1H \longrightarrow ^{13}_6C + ^1_1H$
    c. $^{154}_{62}Sm + ^1_0n \longrightarrow 2^1_0n + ^{153}_{62}Sm$

25. $^{99m}_{43}Tc \longrightarrow ^{99}_{43}Tc + \gamma$ The reaction emits gamma radiation.

27. $^{237}_{93}Np \longrightarrow ^4_2He + ^{233}_{91}Pa$

29. Reaction for the first step: $^{107}_{47}Ag + ^1_0n \longrightarrow ^{108}_{47}Ag$
    Reaction for the second step: $^{108}_{47}Ag \longrightarrow ^0_{-1}e + ^{108}_{48}Cd$

31. 0.0625 μg for n; 100,000 years.

33. b

35. 90 days

37. 156 hr

39. 18.5 Bq

41. 25 days

43. $^{48}_{20}Ca + ^{247}_{97}Bk \longrightarrow ^{293}_{117}X + 2^1_0n$; Two neutrons were released.
    $^{48}_{20}Ca + ^{247}_{97}Bk \longrightarrow ^{294}_{117}X + ^1_0n$; One neutron was released.

45. **a.** $^{64}_{28}Ni + ^{238}_{92}U \longrightarrow ^{302}_{120}X$
    b. $^{58}_{26}Fe + ^{244}_{94}Pu \longrightarrow ^{302}_{120}X$
    c. $^{54}_{24}Cr + ^{248}_{96}Cm \longrightarrow ^{302}_{120}X$

47. **a.** Gamma radiation is the most penetrating, followed by beta radiation and then alpha radiation.

49. $^{235}_{92}U + ^1_0n \longrightarrow ^{236}_{92}U^* \longrightarrow ^{92}_{36}Kr + ^{141}_{56}Ba + 3^1_0n$
    The chain reaction continues when each of the three neutrons emitted by the fission of U-236 strike another U-235 nucleus in what is called a chain reaction.

51. **a.** 2×10^{13} cal; 2×10^{10} kcal   **b.** 2×10^8 bowls

53. $^{238}_{92}U + ^1_0n \longrightarrow ^{239}_{92}U$
    $^{239}_{92}U \longrightarrow ^{239}_{93}Np + ^0_{-1}e$
    $^{239}_{93}Np \longrightarrow ^{239}_{94}Pu + ^0_{-1}e$

55. The original U-235 that undergoes fission forms two smaller nuclei, both of which are also radioactive.

57. Many apply: Power plants control the rate of the fission reaction, so it is slow, continuous and controlled. Bombs fission reaction rates are almost instantaneous, all the energy is released at once, and not controlled. Power plants use control rods to regulate the amount of neutrons and how much material is above the critical mass, bombs have no control rods and it is all brought above the critical mass at once. People can be nearby and live during the operation of a nuclear power plant, you need to be a long ways away during the operation of a nuclear bomb! Another difference is that the level of enrichment of U-235 required for use of a uranium sample in a power plant is only 3-5% while that required for use in a bomb is 90%. Another difference is that the rate of the fission reaction in a nuclear power plant is very carefully controlled by the use of neutron-absorbing control rods while the fission reaction in a bomb is not controlled at all.

59. $^{210}_{84}Pu \longrightarrow ^4_2He + ^{206}_{82}Pb$. The reaction products are lead-206 and an alpha particle.

61. $^{223}_{88}Ra \longrightarrow ^{219}_{86}Rn + ^4_2He$
    $^{223}_{88}Ra \longrightarrow ^{209}_{82}Pb + ^{14}_6C$

63. $^9_4Be + ^4_2He \longrightarrow ^{12}_6C + ^1_0n$
    This was the first experimental detection of the neutron.

65. 7 half lives; 80 days

67. 11,460 years

69. 25 hr

71. **a.** 0.125 or 12.5%.   **b.** Uranium-238.

73. 3.2×10^7 Bq

75. plutonium = 853 cm³; coated plutonium = 131 cm³; baseball = 189 cm³; volleyball = 4900 cm³; basketball = 7550 cm³

77. I-131: concentration = 0; Green Chemistry Principle 10. Tc-99: concentration = 0.9999; Green Principles 3 and 12. For Pu-239: concentration = 0.9997; separate and use as fuel in a nuclear reactor, which is an application

Chemistry @ Home

1. The answer should be around 1,000 years
2. About 3,000 years old
3. The curve should look the same, but the amount in each column will be higher (the shape of the curve should be about the same, though).
4. The piece of candy might last one half-life or several – it is random.

Chapter 12

1. One substance enhances the effect of another; asbestos fibers and cigarette smoke
3. Montmorillonite is added to cat litter so that it will clump in the presence of moisture, making it easier to separate the litter that has absorbed moisture from that which has not.
5. Cement production requires extensive mining; the rotary kiln used in its production consumes fossil fuels; and particular matter from the crushing operations, along with smoke and sulfur dioxide from the burning of fossil fuels, make air pollution by cement plants especially serious.
7. Copper and tin are easier to extract from ores than is iron.
9. Aluminum ores are thinly distributed in clays rather than localized.
11. storing them in sanitary landfills; incinerating them; recycling them.
13. The problem is keeping the metal in a usable form and not dispersed through the environment.
15. d
17. Lithosphere: solid portion of Earth; hydrosphere: watery portion; atmosphere: gaseous mass surrounding Earth.
19. Si (15.9%) > H (15.1%) > Na (1.8%) > Fe (1.5%) = Ca (1.5%) > Mg (1.4%) > K (1.0%).
21. The rankings in questions 19 and 20 are different because of the way in which the percentages were calculated. Atom percent reflects the relative numbers of individual kinds of atoms while mass percentages reflect the relative masses contributed by each element. Because some atoms are much heavier than others, the two kinds of percentages do not agree.
23. $+\dfrac{8}{3}$ or $+2\dfrac{2}{3}$.
25. Cooking improved the flavor and digestibility of meat and grains; heating adobe bricks made stronger ceramic bricks; firing clay at high temperatures produced ceramic pots, making cooking and storage of food much easier.
27. The ratio of silicon to oxygen atoms in silica is 1:2. However, because each silicon atom is surrounded by *four* oxygen atoms, the basic unit of quartz is the SiO_4 tetrahedron.

29.

31. Micas are composed of SiO_4 tetrahedra arranged in two-dimensional sheet-like arrays. Micas are easily cleaved into thin, transparent sheets. The sheets are linked by bonds between O atoms and cations, mainly Al^{3+}. The bonding within the sheets is stronger than the attractions from sheet to sheet.
33. a
35. b
37. In the production of glass, crystalline materials are heated to a temperature at which they start to lose their repeating arrangement of atomic units (SiO_4) because the bridging interactions within the crystalline matrix break leading to an irregular three-dimensional arrangement of the SiO_4 tetrahedra,

39. Oxides of various metals can be substituted for some or all of the sand, soda, or limestone. Adding extra elements to glass changes its color.
41. Ceramics are inorganic nonmetallic solids that are usually crystalline or partly crystalline. Heating in the manufacturing of ceramics along with the flexibility of the materials used to make them means that ceramics can be tailored to specific uses. Many ceramics have been made from kaolinite clays and aluminum oxide. The more advanced ceramics originate from silicon carbide as well as tungsten carbide. Ceramic materials are particularly useful when high temperatures are present.
43. Cement is a complex mixture of calcium and aluminum silicates. The raw materials for the production of cement are limestone and clay which are finely ground, mixed, and roasted at about 1500 °C. The finished product is mixed with sand, gravel, and water to form concrete.
45. a. The ON of Cu in Cu_2O is +1. In Cu the ON of Cu in its elemental form is zero.
    b. The ON of Fe ion Fe_2O_3 is +3. In Fe the ON of Fe in its elemental form is zero.
    c. The ON of Al in Al_2O_3 is +3. In Al the ON of Al in its elemental form is zero.
47. Metals usually occur in their ores combined with oxygen (example: Fe_2O_3) or sulfur (example: CuS) in the form of ionic compounds.
    $2\ Cu_2O \longrightarrow 4\ Cu + O_2$; $Fe_2O_3 + 3\ CO \longrightarrow 2\ Fe + 3\ CO_2$; and $2\ Al_2O_3 \longrightarrow 4\ Al + 3\ O_2$ are examples of reduction reactions in which metals are produced in their elemental forms.
49. a. It increases the hardness of the resultant alloy so it can be used in more applications.
    b. Bronze   c. Bronze
51. Copper is used extensively in electrical wires because of its excellent electrical conductivity. It is also used in roofing because of its thermal conductivity and appearance. In addition it is used in plumbing pipes. Steel is a versatile material whose properties such as hardness, toughness, or corrosion resistance that can be varied by adding other metals to the alloy (see Table 12.5). Steel is used in an almost unimaginably wide range of applications including construction, engines, and prosthetic devices.
53. Al requires the most energy because it is more reactive than either of the other two metals.
55. A katana is strong with a sharp edge. The temperature of the smelting process is carefully monitored to control the carbon content of the steel between 0.5 and 1.5%. The higher the carbon content is, the harder but less flexible the steel will be. The process results in several, layered steels with different carbon concentrations so that the cutting edge is very sharp and hard, while the center is tough enough to adsorb impact without breaking the blade.
57. Balanced equation: $2\ ErF_3 + 3\ Mg \longrightarrow 2\ Er + 3\ MgF_2$
    a. Er in is reduced from the 3+ ion (ON = +3) in ErF_3 to the elemental form (ON = zero).
    b. Mg provides the electrons to Er^{3+} for the reduction so Mg is the reducing agent.
    c. Mg is oxidized, going from ON = zero to ON = +2
    d. Er^{3+} in ErF_3 is the oxidizing agent because it removes the electrons from Mg.
59. Balanced equation: $2\ EuCl_3 \longrightarrow 2\ Eu + 3\ Cl_2$
    a. Eu in is reduced from the 3+ ion (ON = +3) in $EuCl_3$ to the elemental form (ON = zero).
    b. Cl^- in $EuCl_3$ provides the electrons to Eu^{3+} for the reduction so Cl^- is the reducing agent.
    c. Cl^- is oxidized, going from ON = −1 to ON = zero
    d. Eu^{3+} in $EuCl_3$ is the oxidizing agent because it removes the electrons from Cl^-.
61. 70.0 g $InCl_3$
63. 1,200,000,000 kWh
65. 5.0 g NaCN
67. Assuming it isn't recycled, according to Figure 12.9, approximately 60-70 percent of municipal waste could be burned as fuel.

69. The three Rs stand for reduce, reuse, and recycle.

71. e

Chemistry @ Home

1. The lemon juice and vinegar should have bubbled or fizzed on the limestone, calcite, and chalk, which all contain calcium carbonate. The lemon juice is more acidic with a pH of 2.3 and vinegar usually has a pH closer to 3 which means you could get more fizzing with the lemon juice.

2. Only the rocks with calcium carbonate such as limestone or chalk will react resulting in CO_2 gas bubbles. Rocks such as quartz and granite should not have a reaction with the acids or water.

3. The experiment demonstrates the impact of acid rain on national and international landmarks made of limestone. Statues are no longer crafted only using calcium carbonate in the limestone form but combined with other building materials.

4. $CaCO_3 + C_2H_4O_2 \longrightarrow Ca(C_2H_3O_2)_2 + CO_2 + H_2O$

Chapter 13

13.1 A. 3790 g H_2O **B.** 4940 kg CO_2

1. Refrigerant; molding of plastic foams

3. Solid mineral matter left behind after burning coal is bottom ash. Fly ash goes out the smokestack.

5. Gases that trap heat in the atmosphere; CO_2, CH_4, H_2O

7. a. Ground level ozone is a powerful oxidizing agent and is highly reactive. It is a severe respiratory irritant and especially harmful to children. Ozone causes rubber to harden and crack, resulting in damage to automobile tires, and also causes crop damage.

   b. Depletion of stratospheric ozone lessens the ability of the atmosphere to intercept ultraviolet light from the sun. Rays in this part of the electromagnetic spectrum are capable of doing cellular damage and causing cancer.

9. Photochemical smog occurs when unburned hydrocarbons and nitrogen oxides, in the presence of sunlight, undergo a complex series of reactions to produce a brown haze. This type of smog is often associated with warm, sunny climates. Polluted air associated with industrial activities is often called industrial smog. It is characterized by the presence of smoke, fog, sulfur dioxide and particulate matter such as ash and soot. Most industrial smog occurs as the result of burning coal. The weather conditions associated with industrial smog are cool/cold temperatures, high humidity, and often fog.

11. Nitrogen fixation is combining nitrogen with another element to make it available to plants. One very useful form of "fixed" nitrogen is ammonia (NH_3). One reason why nitrogen fixation is important is that the process has resulted in a great increase in food production.

13. Thermosphere

15. a. $4\,Fe + 3\,O_2 \longrightarrow 2\,Fe_2O_3$ **b.** $4\,Cr + 3\,O_2 \longrightarrow 2\,Cr_2O_3$

17. Cold, damp, still

19. $S + O_2 \longrightarrow SO_2$

21. $SO_2 + 2\,H_2S \longrightarrow 3\,S + 2\,H_2O$

23. The solid lime (CaO) reacts with SO_2 gas, causing it to form a solid product, $CaSO_3$, which is easy to collect. Some scrubbers react the $CaSO_3$ with oxygen to form a more useful product, $CaSO_4$.
The reactions for this are: $CaCO_3(s) \longrightarrow CaO(s) + CO_2(g)$
$$CaO(s) + SO_2(g) \longrightarrow CaSO_3(s)$$
And, in the case of formation of $CaSO_4(s)$: $2\,CaSO_3(s) + O_2(g) \longrightarrow$
$$2\,CaSO_4(g).$$

25. high temperatures; $N_2 + O_2 \longrightarrow 2\,NO$

27. PAN stands for peroxyacetyl nitrate ($CH_3COOONO_2$). PAN, is formed from hydrocarbons, oxygen, and nitrogen dioxide, makes breathing difficult and causes eye irritation.

29. a, c

31. NO

33. By hindering O_2 transport and thus adding to the workload of the heart

35. U.S. emissions of CO have decreased from 140 million tons in 1992 to slightly more than 70 million tons in 2013. This decrease is likely due, in part, to improvements in automobile efficiency and to the efficiency of catalytic converters.

37. allotropes

39. global warming

41. In the troposphere, ozone is a pollutant associated with photochemical smog. NO enters the air in automobile exhaust and reacts with the O_2 in the air, forming NO_2. Sunlight spits the NO_2 into NO and O atoms. The O atoms combine with O_2 molecules to form O_3. Chlorofluorocarbons, CFCs, are among the atmospheric components responsible for a decrease in O_3 concentration in the stratosphere. When CFCs interact with UV radiation the bond between a C atom and a Cl atom breaks, creating a chlorine radical. This radical enters into the otherwise constant cycle that ensures the constant O_3 concentration, reacting with O_3 to decrease its concentration. One Cl radical can lead to the destruction of thousands of O_3 molecules.

43. H_2SO_4 and HNO_3

45. $6\,HNO_3(aq) + 2\,Fe(s) \longrightarrow 2\,Fe(NO_3)_3(aq) + 3\,H_2(g)$

47. Carbon monoxide from poorly ventilated heaters indoors; from automobiles outdoors.

49. The crawl space allows gaseous radon to dissipate through vents; the concrete slab traps it inside.

51. A gas; it can escape from rocks and enter houses, and is readily inhaled.

53. The warming of Earth caused by gases absorbing infrared radiation.

55. The CO_2 exhaled by humans is part of the natural carbon cycle which begins when photosynthetic organisms store the sun's energy by producing glucose from atmospheric CO_2 and H_2O. Humans fuel their existence by eating food containing the stored energy (and other important elements and compounds). In the broadest of terms the energy from food is released through essentially the reverse of the photosynthetic reaction, producing the CO_2 and H_2O that we exhale. Thus this cycle is not a big contributor to the atmospheric CO_2 level.

57. 40%

59. The warming of Earth caused by gases absorbing infrared radiation.

61. 6.9 mg/day

63. Water vapor will form clouds and may even lead to cooling by reflecting sunlight back to space.

65. There would be about two air molecules from the Buddha's breath in a breath you take today.

67. $3\,NO_2 + H_2O \longrightarrow 2\,HNO_3 + NO;\ 2\,NO + O_2 \longrightarrow 2\,NO_2$

69. The message to U.S. citizens could be that, individually, they are contributing 40% more to the atmospheric CO_2 concentration than the individuals in China.

71. a. 5.1×10^{18} kJ

   b. 5.0×10^{17} kJ; this amount is 10% of the amount of energy needed to cause a 1° temperature increase.

   c. 2×10^{17} kJ; which is about 4% of the amount of energy needed to cause a 1° temperature increase.

73. c; 3200 *t* NF_3

75. NF_3: R8: Contact with combustible material may cause fire; R20: Harmful by inhalation; R36/38: Irritating to eyes/irritating to skin. F2: R7: May cause fire; R8: Contact with combustible material may cause fire; R26: Very toxic by inhalation; R35: Causes severe burns; R41: Risk of serious damage to eyes.

Chemistry @ Home

1. The color change is immediate. The control and SPF 4 should be about the same (no difference in color – both very vibrant colors). SPF 15 should be less colored than the control and 4, and the 30 and 50 both should look less colored than 15. SPF values below 30 do very little to block out the harmful UVA/UVB rays.

2. Answers will vary.

3. The results should show that the SPF sunscreen is no longer blocking the UV rays. Recently the FDA passed regulation that manufacturers can no longer make claims that sunscreens are "waterproof" or "sweatproof".

Chapter 14

14.1 A. 800 cal; 80.0 kcal; 334 kJ   **B.** copper

1. The crude oil would not dissolve; it would float.
3. agricultural fields, feedlots
5. Microorganisms that cause disease.
7. Leaking underground storage tanks, nitrates from farm fertilizer, volatile organic chemicals.
9. Nutrients and wastes could be returned to the soil rather than allowed to enter the water system; composting toilets could replace traditional toilets; buffer zones around agricultural fields and industrial complexes could be designed to include plants that are capable of phytoremediation of the water.
11. Chlorinated hydrocarbons are unreactive and do not break down readily.
13. Water expands when it freezes because it forms a rigid hydrogen-bonded structure with relatively large holes. The ice floats, protecting the deeper water from freezing.
15. 2.48×10^4 cal
17. The difference in the specific heat capacities for solid and liquid water is due to the way that the water molecules can convert energy into motion, whether vibrational (in the case of ice) or translational (in the case of liquid water).
19. Vaporization of water (sweat) cools our bodies.
21. Water evaporates from the skin, removing heat.
23. Dust, dissolved atmospheric gases such as carbon dioxide and oxygen, nitric acid from lightning storms; various pollutants.
25. Aerobic bacteria require the involvement of O_2 in order to break down nutrients. Anaerobic bacteria can break down nutrients in the absence of O_2.
27. 50 mg/L
29. Acid rain and mine runoff.
31. The limestone that neutralizes the acid leaves calcium ions in the water.
33. 0.7 to 1.0 ppm
35. Yes. Ultraviolet light kills microorganisms.
37. 2 L
39. Bottled water is safe and convenient but very expensive relative to tap water. It may not be as safe as municipal water because although it is considered a food and therefore regulated by the EPA, it is not tested as rigorously as municipal water supplies. Perhaps the biggest drawback of bottled water is the need to manufacture the bottles, a process that requires both petroleum supplies and a great deal of energy. Recycling these bottles would help lessen the disadvantages of this product.
41. Sewage is collected in a pond; it removes solids that are allowed to settle..
43. Nitrates and phosphates are not removed by secondary wastewater treatment.
45. **a.** tertiary   **b.** primary   **c.** secondary
47. $2 HNO_3(aq) + CaCO_3(s) \longrightarrow$
    $Ca^{2+}(aq) + 2 NO_3^-(aq) + H_2O(l) + CO_2(g)$
49. $Ca_5(PO_4)_3OH(s) + F^-(aq) \longrightarrow Ca_5(PO_4)_3F(s) + OH^-(aq)$
51. **a.** 11 ppb   **b.** 140 ppm
53. No, the levels (0.009 mg Cu/L, 8 mg NO_3/L) are below the standards.
55. d
57. d
59. b
61. d
63. Chlorine is reduced in going from Cl_2 to $2 Cl^-$; it is the oxidizing agent. Sulfur dioxide is oxidized in going from SO_2 to SO_4^{2-}; it is the reducing agent.
65. dispersion forces
67. **a.** 9.5×10^3 kcal   **b.** 715 g CH_4
    c. 35.4 ft^3 **d.** $0.26
69. Polar substances tend to remain dissolved in polar solvents. Because a larger amount of substance X than of Y remained dissolved in the water, X must be more polar than Y.

71. It would probably be better if the pesticide was polar rather than nonpolar so that it would not tend to dissolve in fatty tissue and biomagnify in the food chain. The best pesticide would break down into nontoxic substances once it enters the environment.

Chemistry @ Home
1. The color fades as does the taste the more you dilute the water but you can still see a faint color even though you can't taste the sugar.
2. There was virtually no color or taste to the 6th cup. If you continued the experiment with a few more dilutions you could get to a point where there would be no color or taste changes.
3. Dilution is not an answer for pollution. It is far preferable to not create pollution in the first place. Just because the water is not colored or sweet does not mean that the contamination is entirely gone. Some chemicals can still have detrimental effects at very low concentrations.
4. Chemicals can contaminate our water supply from sediments, air and bioaccumulation. Resulting in ending up in the air we breathe, soil and plants and animals we consume.

Chapter 15

15.1 A. 39,000 J
    B. 46,800 J fluorescent bulb; 216,000 J incandescent bulb; 78.3% savings
    C. $1.24 savings
15.2 A. 183 kJ   **B.** 2700 kJ
15.3 A. 2210 kJ   **B.** 1.43 kcal

1. Nuclear fusion
3. Coal; petroleum
5. **a.** $C_3H_8 + 5 O_2(g) \longrightarrow 3 CO_2 + 4 H_2O(l) + energy$
   b. $2 C_4H_{10}(g) + 13 O_2(g) \longrightarrow 8 CO_2 + 10 H_2O + energy$
7. $C_{13}H_{28} + 20 O_2(g) \longrightarrow 13 CO_2 + 14 H_2O + energy$
9. In the complete combustion of a hydrocarbon the hydrocarbon reacts with oxygen to produced carbon dioxide and water.
11. $CH_4(g) + 2 O_2(g) \longrightarrow CO_2(g) + 2 H_2O(l)$
13. Reactions almost always proceed more rapidly at higher temperatures because the collisions between reactants are more likely to produce reactant products.
15. **a.**

   b. 1652 kJ   **c.** 996 kJ
   d. 1596 kJ   **e.** 1868 kJ
   f. total energy required = 2648 kJ; total energy released = 3464 kJ; net energy outcome = −816 kJ The negative sign indicates that more energy was released than was required so the reaction is exothermic.
17. 1.97×10^4 kJ
19. 4.44 kJ
21. The amount of energy required to reverse a reaction is the same as the amount of energy released by the reaction, 803 kJ.
23. The first law of thermodynamics says that energy is conserved, which means that the amount of energy in the universe is a constant.
25. Entropy is the measure of the degree of distribution of energy (disorder) in a system. Entropy increases when a fossil fuel is burned because larger molecules (the fuel) are converted into a larger number of smaller molecules.
27. In both cases the potassium (K) exists in a solid state. In metallic K the entropy is very low because the K atoms are not in motion and are surrounded by other K atoms. In the case of the KCl in the fertilizer the entropy is higher because the K^+ ions are surrounded by Cl^- ions and the KCl is mixed with the other components of the fertilizer.

29. The second law of thermodynamics states that heat always flows from a hot object to a cooler one. Therefore, in the case of the ice cream in a bowl, the room is warmer than the ice cream so heat moves from the warm room to the ice cream, causing it to melt.

31. Natural gas and petroleum are cleaner-burning fuels because their combustion products are primarily CO_2 and H_2O. When coal burns there is ash produced and the sulfur content is converted into SO_2 which contributes to acid rain. Coal also contains mercury which enters the air and is highly toxic. In addition, the advent of automobiles made the use of liquid energy sources (petroleum) much more convenient than solid energy sources (coal). Transporting the fuel is easier too.

33. **a.** time remaining, years = 5.0 years
    b. time remaining, years = 1.6 years

35. time remaining, years = 13.2 years

37. The advantages of petroleum as a fuel source are that it is a relatively abundant liquid which makes it accessible and more convenient to transport than coal or another solid fuel. Its combustion products are generally limited to CO_2 and H_2O which means that petroleum is generally cleaner burning than coal. Its disadvantage is that petroleum is a complex mixture of hydrocarbons that must be separated into fractions before it can be used. Petroleum sources are not as widely spread around the globe as coal beds are so there can be political issues associated with its availability.

39. Octane rating of gasoline describes the extent to which a gasoline mixture ignites before the spark plug fires, creating a knocking that can damage engines. Some types of hydrocarbons, especially those with branched chains, tend to burn more evenly and were less likely to cause knocking than other hydrocarbons.

41. Asphalt is the residue of the processing of petroleum. Using it in paving roads and highways provides a use for an otherwise "waste" product.

43. About 20% of U.S. electricity is produced by nuclear power plants.

45. The same fission reaction is used in both nuclear power plants and nuclear bombs, but the uranium used in power plants is enriched to only 3–4% U-235 whereas the uranium used in a nuclear bomb is about 90% U-235. Therefore, a power plant uses nuclear material far below the required U-235 concentration needed to create a nuclear explosion so a power plant will not explode.

47. No. The U-235 concentration required for an atomic bomb is much higher (90% vs. 3–4%) than the concentration required for the fission process in a nuclear bomb.

49. Uranium-238 can be converted to fissionable plutonium-239 by bombardment with neutrons. If a reactor is built with a core of fissionable plutonium surrounded by uranium-238, neutrons from the fission of plutonium convert the uranium-238 shield to more plutonium, effectively producing more fuel than it consumes. Even though plutonium is created from uranium-238, the process still requires energy, so the law of conservation of energy is not violated.

51. The main fuel in fusion reactors is deuterium, which is plentiful and can be obtained from fractional electrolysis of water. Also, the primary waste product is helium, which is stable and biologically inert. Plasma is a hot, gaseous mixture of charged particles (nuclei and electrons) made from atoms that have been stripped of their electrons,

53. $^{232}_{90}\text{Th} + ^{1}_{0}\text{n} \longrightarrow ^{233}_{90}\text{Th} \longrightarrow ^{0}_{-1}\text{e} + ^{233}_{91}\text{Pa}$
    $^{233}_{91}\text{Pa} \longrightarrow ^{233}_{92}\text{U} + ^{0}_{-1}\text{e}$

55. Number of mol of CH_4 = 2.2×10^7 mol CH_4
    Mass of CH_4, t = 350 t

57. A photovoltaic cell converts sunlight directly into electricity.

59. 1.3 kW = 1200 W
    Area of solar cell, m^2 = 13 m^2.
    Solar cells are not very efficient and need a very large surface area. There also needs to be a means of energy storage for nighttime and very cloudy days.

61. Biomass is plant material used as fuel. Biomass is a renewable resource whose primary combustion products are CO_2 and H_2O (plus ash). Biomass requires a large investment in land and the energy required to plant and harvest the crop. Often the crops are not located close to the areas where the energy is needed so they must be transported. Plant material is not as dense an energy source as are fossil fuels for example, because the plant molecules contain a relatively large amount of oxygen, greatly reducing the amount of energy released per gram of compound upon combustion.

63. **a.** Wind power: Advantages: Wind is clean, free, and abundant. Disadvantages: rotating blades kill birds; upfront costs of wind turbines are high but they pay off in the long run. Limitations: Wind does not blow constantly so some means of energy storage or an alternate energy source must be available.
    b. Geothermal power: Advantages: Works in summer and winter. Disadvantages: Expensive to install (but pays for itself over time). Limitations: Generally limited to areas where steam or hot water are near the surface of the Earth.
    c. biodiesel: Advantages: Can be synthesized from waste cooking oil and agricultural wastes. Disadvantages: It takes energy to create biodiesel so we can get more energy from burning biomass than from converting it to biodiesel; Large quantities of corrosive substances (sodium hydroxide and potassium hydroxide) are used to prepare biodiesel. Limitations: Technology isn't as well developed to maximize the energy gain as it will be.
    d. hydroelectric power: Advantages: Clean. Disadvantages: Reservoirs silt up and dams break, land is lost when reservoirs are formed. Limitations: Most good dam sights in the U.S. are already in use.
    e. geothermal home heating system: Advantages: Same as with geothermal power. Disadvantages: Expensive to install but pays off in the long run; Limitations: None.

65. **a.** $CO(g) + 2\,H_2(g) \longrightarrow CH_3OH$
    b. $2\,H_2(g) + O_2(g) \longrightarrow 2\,H_2O(l)$

67. This process is exothermic because the reactants release heat to the surroundings when they are mixed.

69. **a.** number of watts = 102 W
    b. $(102\text{ W})(1\text{ hp}/745\text{ W}) = 0.14$. Domesticated horses increased the availability of energy somewhat; 1 hp = 7.45 humanpower

71. **a.** Power (W) is energy (J) per second (s). In the case of the banana, energy = 7.11×10^5 J
    Time, in seconds = 7200 s
    Power = 99 W
    b. Power = 5.9×10^8 W
    Although both the banana and the hand grenade provide the same amount of energy, the hand grenade is 6×10^6 times more powerful than the banana because of the amount of time over which the same energy is dispelled.

73. The equation for the combustion of methane is: $CH_4 + 2\,O_2 \longrightarrow CO_2 + 2\,H_2O$. The molar mass of CH_4 is 16.0 g/mol and the molar mass of CO_2 is 44.0 g/mol.
    Mass of CH_4 required, 6.91 t

    Note: in the calculation above we converted metric tons to kg and then to g to use the molar mass in units of g/mol. Then we converted the answer in grams back to metric tons as asked for by the problem.

75. mass SO_2 = 3.1×10^7 g SO_2
    volume = 1.1×10^{12} m^3
    concentration of SO_2, $\mu g/m^3$ = 28 $\mu g\ SO_2/m^3$
    The SO_2 concentration does not exceed the primary national air quality standard.

77. **a.** number of = 75.2 y
    b. Americans represent roughly 4.5% of the world population. If the per capita consumption for the rest of the world increased to the per capita level in the U.S., the population would be

consuming roughly $(4)(1.32 \times 10^5 \text{ TWh}) = 5.28 \times 10^5 \text{ TWh}$. If this were the case, the available energy would last for $(9.92 \times 10^6 \text{ TWh})(1 \text{ y}/5.28 \times 10^5 \text{ TWh}) = $ less than 19 years. In either case, we are not using the energy in a sustainable way and need to find ways of replacing nonrenewable energy resources with renewable energy resources, as well as reducing our reliance on energy.

   c. The rate of energy use will likely grow instead of remaining the same, so reserves might not last the 75 y calculated in part (a). Worldwide use is unlikely to reach the U.S. level anytime soon, if ever, and so the estimate in part (b) is not at all realistic.

79. The answer is d. All the aspects of a process listed in answers a, b, and c are looked at when green chemistry principles are used to evaluate energy-generation processes.

Chemistry @ Home

1. Both reactions were chemical changes.
2. Water and the candy caused an endothermic reaction because heat was absorbed into the system.
3. Yeast and hydrogen peroxide caused an exothermic reaction because heat was given off as a result of the reaction.
4. Oxygen was the gas released with the yeast and hydrogen peroxide reaction.
5. The reaction with the candy and water would not relight the candy because oxygen is not a byproduct of that reaction.

Chapter 16

16.1 Mannose differs from galactose in configuration about C-2 and C-4.

16.2 **A. a.** H-P-N-A
      b. Histidylprolylasparagylalanine
   B. a. Thr-Gly-Ala-Ala-Leu
      b. T-G-A-A-L

16.3 **A.** 3   **B.** 24

16.4 **A.** Sugar: ribose; base: uracil; RNA
   B. Neither, uracil occurs only in RNA, deoxyribose occurs only in DNA.

1. Photosynthesis converts solar energy to carbohydrates, which provide energy to plants and to organisms that eat plants.
3. In every cell; muscles, skin, hair, nails.
5. polyamides
7. If the molar mass of a polypeptide exceeds about 10,000 g, it is called a protein.
9. Hydrogen bonds
11. DNA is a double helix; RNA is a single helix with some loops.
13. A process that produces millions of copies of a specific DNA sequence
15. Step 1: isolation and amplification
   Step 2: gene is spliced into a plasmid
   Step 3: plasmid is inserted into a host cell
   Step 4: plasmid replicates, making copies of itself
17. a, c
19. Glycogen is animal starch. Amylose is a plant starch with glucose units joined in a continuous chain. Amylopectin is a plant starch with branched chains of glucose units.
21. c, d
23. Sucrose and lactose
25. **a.** glucose   **b.** glucose
27. aldehyde and alcohol (hydroxyl) functional groups
29. disaccharide
31. Structurally, oils have more C-to-C double bonds than fats have. At room temperature, fats are solids, and oils are liquid.
33. **a.** saturated   **b.** polyunsaturated
   c. monounsaturated   **d.** saturated
35. **a.** 18   **b.** 16   **c.** 18
37. Corn oil (right); unsaturated
39. d
41. lysine and methionine

43. **a.**   **b.**

45. **a.**
   b.

47. aspartylphenylalanine
49. hydrogen bonds, ionic bonds, disulfide linkages, and dispersion forces
51. **a.** DNA   **b.** RNA   **c.** RNA
53. ribose; uracil
55. **a.** guanine   **b.** thymine
   c. cytosine   **d.** adenine
57. Each strand of the parent DNA double helix remains associated with the newly synthesized DNA strand.
59. **a.** DNA and mRNA
   b. mRNA and tRNA
61. c
63. d
65. c
67. Transfer RNA (tRNA) molecules carry amino acids to the mRNA which is the site of protein synthesis in the cell.
69. **a.** primary   **b.** secondary
71. **a.** pyrimidine   **b.** pyrimidine
73. **a.** purine   **b.** RNA
75. **a.** ~Thr-Ser-Met-Ala~   **b.** ~Thr-Ser-Ala-Ala~
77. The mRNA codon would have the three-letter base pair of CGU.
79. Water
81. d

Chemistry @ Home

1. Yes you are able to see the clear strands binding together.
2. The consistency makes it a challenge to pick the clumps up but you can do it.
3. Since DNA is unique, crime scene investigators will collect samples from crime scenes. When they find a DNA sample that doesn't match the victim, they compare it to samples from possible suspects. If a suspect has left DNA at the crime scene, they are definitely tied to the crime.
4. The Watson-Crick structure of DNA was so important because it helped answer questions such as how cells are able to divide and go on functioning, how genetic data is passed on to new generations and how proteins are built to required specifications. Many major advances have been possible thanks to this discovery.

Chapter 17

17.1 **A.** about 45% fat
   B. 75% of the maximum recommended fat intake per day; only 150 g more; difficult

17.2 **A.** Fatty acid I
   B. Fatty acid I, because fatty acid III is a cis fatty acid and not a trans fatty acid

1. energy source
3. Vitamins are organic; minerals are inorganic.

5. Fat soluble; an excess is stored and accumulated; excess water soluble vitamins are excreted.

7. Substances other than basic foodstuffs that are put into food for various reasons related to production, processing, packaging, or storage.

9. Monosodium glutamate, a flavor enhancer

11. α-tocopherol (vitamin E)

13. The methyl ester of the dipeptide aspartylphenylalanine

15. Some food additives are added to increase the nutritional value of the substance, others are added to enhance color and flavor, others to retard spoilage, to ripen or prevent ripening, or to control moisture levels.

17. a

19. Hydrolysis

21. Hydrolysis; fatty acids, glycerol, mono- and diglycerides

23. Most animal fats are solids; most vegetable oils are liquids; animal fats generally have fewer C-to-C double bonds than vegetable oils.

25. An adequate protein provides all the essential amino acids in sufficient quantities; meat, eggs, milk.

27. Corn: lysine and tryptophan; beans: methionine.

29. Yes, it has grains and beans.

31. **a.** Iodine   **b.** hemoglobin   **c.** Calcium
    d. Sodium is critical in controlling the exchange of fluids between cells and plasma.

33. Water soluble: pantothenic acid, biotin; fat soluble: phylloquinone

35. Ascorbic acid, Vitamin C; calciferol, Vitamin D_2; cyanocobalamin, Vitamin B_{12}; retinol, Vitamin A; and tocopherol, Vitamin E.

37. **a.** niacin (vitamin B_3)   **b.** thiamin (vitamin B_1)
    c. Pernicious anemia

39. **a.** fat soluble   **b.** water soluble
    c. water soluble   **d.** fat soluble

41. d

43. **a.** BHA is an antioxidant.
    b. FD&C Blue No. 2 is a colorant.
    c. Saccharin is an artificial sweetener.

45. d

47. Reducing agents, usually free-radical scavengers added to foods to prevent fats and oils from becoming rancid; vitamin E; BHT, and BHA

49. About 51% from carbohydrates; 21% from fat; 25% from protein.

51. About 81 kcal; about 56% from fat

53. 11 g saturated fat

55. c, e

57. 45%

59. 20%

61. **a.** 58% kcal   **b.** 40% kcal

63. Riboflavin and cyanocobalamin; they are water soluble and not easily stored.

65. Double bonds in unsaturated fats are more reactive than single bonds in saturated fats; unsaturated fats and oils would have spoiled more readily than saturated fats.

67. Adding beta-carotene to foods serves two purposes. First, it adds yellow color to the food, and second, beta-carotene is a precursor to vitamin A so adding it increases the vitamin content of the food as well.

69. **a.** 4   **b.** 3   **c.** 2   **d.** 1

71. Food waste can be converted to fuels through anaerobic digestion by microorganisms.

Chemistry @ Home

1. The bags with sugar and cereals (with sugar) grew the most and indicated the most active yeast growth.

2. $C_{12}H_{22}O_{11} + H_2O \longrightarrow 4\,C_2H_5{}^-OH + 4\,CO_2$

3. This will vary by cereal sample

Chapter 18

1. Natural drugs are molecules that come from natural sources which usually means that they've been extracted from plant or animal sources by physical processes as opposed to materials formed by chemical reactions. Semi-synthetic drugs are made by modifying molecules derived from natural sources to improve their therapeutic properties. Synthetic drugs are synthesized in laboratories and drug companies.

3. A drug that kills or slows the growth of bacteria; originally limited to formulations derived from living organisms.

5. Cortisol: a hormone released in the body during stressed or agitated states; prednisone: a semisynthetic hormone similar to cortisone.

7. Mediators of hormone action; prostaglandins act near where they are produced; hormones act throughout the body.

9. Ketamine, PCP.

11. a drug that produces stupor and relief of pain.

13. Brain amines are made from dietary amino acids; for example, high-carbohydrate diets produce high serotonin levels in the brain.

15. No, they help control some symptoms.

17. Ethyl alcohol and marijuana are examples of natural drugs. Aspirin, LSD, and heroin are examples of a semi-natural drugs. Hydrocodone is an example of a synthetic narcotic.

19. Chemotherapy is the use of drugs to treat cancer.

21. acetylsalicylic acid

23. Acetaminophen does not promote bleeding.

25. Amide, phenol

27. c

29. a

31. To create codeine, the phenolic hydroxyl group ($-OH$) in morphine is replaced by a methoxy group ($-OCH_3$). Codeine resembles morphine in its action but is less potent, has less tendency to induce sleep, and is less addictive.

33. $H_2N-\bigcirc-SO_2NH_2$ $H_2N-\bigcirc-COOH$

35. They are effective against a wide variety of bacteria.

37. b

39. **a.** Nucleoside analogs
    b. Non-nucleoside reverse transcriptase inhibitors
    c. Protease inhibitors

41. b

43. Yes. The nitrogen mustard HN_2 causes lung, mammary, and liver tumors when injected into mice but it can be used with some success in the management of certain human tumors.

45. 6-mercaptopurine; antimetabolite

47. A hormone is a chemical messenger produced in the endocrine glands that is released in one part of the body and signals physiological change in other parts of the body. A prostaglandin is a hormone-like lipid derived from a fatty acid. Prostaglandins function similarly to hormones in that they act on target cells. However, they differ from hormones in that they act near the site where they are produced, can have different effects in different tissues, and are rapidly metabolized.

49. two ketone groups and a $C=C$ double bond

51. it causes the uterus to expel an implanted egg and end a pregnancy at an early stage.

53. Emergency contraceptives, also called morning-after pills, can be used to prevent pregnancy after unprotected intercourse. There are two kinds of emergency contraceptives: combination pills with both estrogen and progestin (synthetic analogs of the natural substances) and pills containing only progestin. Given in high doses, emergency contraceptives half development of the uterine lining and inhibit ovulation and fertilization. Intrauterine devices (IUDs) are also used, as is RU-486. IUDs cause inflammation that makes the endometrium unsuitable for implantation, and RU-486 causes the uterus to expel an implanted egg.

55. a

57. c

59. a drug that affects the human mind and the way we perceive things.

61. a
63. b
65. c
67. a. brain damage **b.** miscarriage **c.** nausea
69. b
71. b
73.

8-methoxy 2,4-dione

75. a. 2.5 g **b.** 1.7 capsule/dose
77. four fused rings
79. fat soluble; fat is nonpolar and this molecule has only one oxygen atom and one nitrogen atom in a structure containing 17 carbon and 21 hydrogen atoms means that the large majority of bonds in the structure are nonpolar.

81.

83. 3,4-methylenedioxymethamphetamine, gamma hydroxybutyrate, Rohypnol, ketamine, methamphetamine.
85. timber rattlesnake is more toxic because less of it will cause a fatal reaction.
87. Nicotine, because it takes a smaller amount to kill the rat—2500 mg procaine; 50 mg nicotine.

89.

91.

93. *Gamma*-butyrolactone (GBL) contains a cyclic ester. Hydrolyzing the ester will convert GBL to the open chain structure $HOCH_2CH_2CH_2COOH$.

95. c, a, b
97. inhibiting the production of prostaglandins.
99. Ketoprofen; One of the oxygen-containing groups is a and the other is a carboxylic acid.
101. prostaglandins (and arachidonic acid); two alcohol functional groups; one ketone; carboxylic acid group.
103. for TDF: 4.2×10^7 kg waste; for TAF: 1.7×10^6 kg waste. The difference in the amount of waste produced is 4.0×10^7 kg

Chemistry @ Home

1. Brand 1:
$$Al(OH)_3(s) + 3\ CH_3COOH(aq) \longrightarrow$$
$$Al(OOCCH_3)_3(aq) + 3\ H_2O(l)$$

$$MgCO_3(s) + 2\ CH_3COOH(aq) \longrightarrow$$
$$Mg(OOCCH_3)_2(aq) + H_2O(l) + CO_2(g)$$
Brand 2:
$$CaCO_3(s) + 2\ CH_3COOH(aq) \longrightarrow$$
$$Ca(OOCCH_3)_2(aq) + H_2O(l) + CO_2(g)$$
$$Mg(OH)_2(s) + 2\ CH_3COOH\ (aq) \longrightarrow$$
$$Mg(OOCCH_3)_2(aq) + 2\ H_2O(l)$$
Brand 3:
$$CaCO_3(s) + 2\ CH_3COOH(aq) \longrightarrow$$
$$Ca(OOCCH_3)_2(aq) + H_2O(l) + CO_2(g)$$

2. We used vinegar (acetic acid) for this experiment. The excess gas in the stomach is typically hydrochloric acid. This is one difference. The contents of the stomach are another variable – other things can work against the active ingredient, or enhance it.
3. The tablets are made differently, with different fillers and inactive ingredients. And, therefore, they might dissolve at a different rate.

Chapter 19

19.1 A. 4.8 lb **B.** 7.4 lb
19.2 A. 70 mi **B.** 2700 kcal
19.3 A. 16.3 **B.** 174 lb
1. Meat and other animal products
3. Deplete glycogen stores and dehydrate yourself; no, it would be mostly water loss.
5. Better understanding of muscle physiology; drugs; improved equipment.
7. One method involves measuring a person's density but subject to considerable error and does not take into account the volume of air in the lungs. A second method involves using bioelectric impedance, problems with this method involve taking into account many variables such as bone density, water content, and location of fat.
9. fat metabolism produces ketone bodies which stress the kidneys; energy for brain activity is low; muscle development and construction of other critical proteins is limited.
11. Athletes need more calories. The added energy is obtained with additional carbohydrates.
13. avoid pernicious anemia.
15. Arthritis; B_6 is a cofactor for more than 100 enzymes.
17. Promotes absorption of calcium and phosphorus. The upper limit is 2000 IU; more than that can be toxic.
19. Promotes production of urine; ADH acts to retain urine.
21. No. Thirst is often a delayed response.
23. Depletion of glycogen and water loss.
25. 2.0 hr
27. 80 g
29. 20 km
31. a. Leptin protects against weight loss.
b. Ghrelin is an appetite stimulant.
33. 27
35. Weightlifting; no
37. No
39. a. Anaerobic **b.** Aerobic
41. Store needed oxygen
43. ATP can be generated rapidly and hydrolyzed rapidly.
45. No; the best way to build muscles is by exercise.
47. Anti-inflammatory; fluid retention, hypertension, ulcers, disturbance of sex hormone balance.
49. The body releases endorphins that have much the same effect as some narcotics.
51. Exercise directly affects the brain by increasing its blood supply and producing neurotrophins which enhance the growth of brain cells. Exercises involving complex motions lead to an increase in the connections between brain cells.
53. Heart disease; stroke; lung cancer; emphysema; pneumonia; cancers of the pancreas, bladder, breast, kidney, and cervix.
55. 2400 kcal/day

57. density: 0.82 g/mL. Fat because the person's density more resembles the density of fat tissue than the density of lean tissue.
59. **a.** 27% body fat   **b.** 5% body fat   **c.** Person B
    d. 1.083 g/cm³; The air in the lungs helps keep a person afloat.
61. **a.** 27   **b.** 144
63. **a.** 20.1 mL O_2 **b.** 1200 mL O_2
65. 2.1 lb
67. c

Chemistry @ Home

1. Many cereals have varying amounts of the "recommended daily allowance" (RDA) of iron. This experiment works best when there is a lot of iron for the magnet to be attracted to such as with Total, which claims to have 18 mg of iron per serving.
2. Cereals are fortified with iron as an easy way for people to meet their dietary reference intake (DRI).
3. Red meat, liver, dark leafy greens, egg yolks, beans, oysters are all possible answers.

Chapter 20

20.1 **A.** $2 NH_3 + H_3PO_4 \longrightarrow (NH_4)_2HPO_4$
    B. $ZnO + H_2SO_4 \longrightarrow ZnSO_4 + H_2O$
20.2 **A.** 1.53%   **B.** 0.59%; about 1/3 as fast as part A
1. carbon dioxide and water through the photosynthesis process.
3. Kills weed plants before crop seedlings emerge.
5. population would increase faster than the food supply.
7. C, H, O
9. lightning, bacteria, the Haber process.
11. Ammonia without water; as fertilizer.
13. the root tips must leave the plant.
15. DDT is effective against many insects, but it remains toxic long after initial use.
17. They are fat soluble and become concentrated in fats moving up the food chain.
19. Mostly to bait traps and monitor infestations to determine when best to use a pesticide.
21. Male insects are sterilized by radiation, chemicals, or crossbreeding, and then released for nonproductive breeding. Expensive and time consuming.
23. 35 g DDT
25. Lethal dose of diquat dibromide = 3.4×10^4 mg or 34 g; Lethal dose of paraquat = 8.4×10^3 mg or 8.4 g
27. Addition of a constant amount each growth period; adding $10 to a savings account each week
29. 20 months; arithmetically
31. Of the 7.7 billion acres of ice-free land, 14.9% of it is used for urban areas, roads, and mines.
    Number of acres used for urban areas, roads, and mines = 1.1×10^9 acres
33. $6 CO_2 + 6 H_2O \longrightarrow C_6H_{12}O_6 + 6 O_2$
35. **1.** b   **2.** b   **3.** d   **4.** a   **5.** c
37. **a.** N, P
    b. $2 NH_3 + H_3PO_4 \longrightarrow (NH_4)_2HPO_4$
39. $CuO(s) + H_2SO_4(aq) \longrightarrow CuSO_4(aq) + H_2O(l)$
41. Lime is another name for calcium oxide, CaO. Lime is added to neutralize acidic soils.
43. $2 KOH + CO_2 \longrightarrow K_2CO_3 + H_2O$
    $K_2CO_3 + CO_2 + H_2O \longrightarrow 2 KHCO_3$
    not organic
45. **a.** 8.7%
    b. 8.3 years
    c. changes in birth rate or death rate
47. a, b
49. d

Chemistry @ Home

1. The weed killer with the dish detergent and the salt is the most effective. The surfactant helps spread the solution over the leaves and the acidity of the vinegar (5% acetic acid) contributes to the suffocation of the plant. Salt contaminates the

soil and causes reverse osmosis starving the plants of the nutrients from the soil. Strong concentrations of salt and vinegar can cause lasting damage to the ground if not applied carefully.
2. The weed killer with the dish detergent and the vinegar is more effective than just vinegar. The surfactant helps spread the solution over the leaves and the acidity of the vinegar (5% acetic acid) contributes to the suffocation of the plant.
3. Vinegar most likely will be the least effective of the 3 weed killers but depending on the weed it can certainly still work it just may take longer than the 3 day experiment.
4. Vinegar alone is most likely the least effective of the 2 weed killers but depending on the weed it can certainly still work it just may take longer than the 3 day experiment.
5. Answer will vary

Chapter 21

21.1 **a.** nonionic   **b.** anionic
    c. anionic   **d.** cationic
1. An excellent cleanser in soft water, relatively nontoxic, derived from renewable sources, biodegradable; doesn't work well in hard water or acidic water.
3. **1.** a   **2.** f   **3.** b   **4.** c   **5.** d   **6.** e
5. Loosens baked-on grease and burned-on food, excellent glass-cleaner; vapors are irritating, toxic; don't mix with chlorine bleaches.
7. Mildly abrasive and absorbs odors.
9. It is softer and produces a finer lather.
11. abrasives
13. Sodium palmitate and glycerol.
15.

17. precipitating calcium, magnesium, and iron(II) ions, and making the water more alkaline.
19. Ca^{2+}, Mg^{2+}, and Fe^{2+}
21. $3 Ca^{2+}(aq) + 2 PO_4^{3-}(aq) \longrightarrow Ca_3(PO_4)_2(s)$
23. A substance added to a substrate to increase its detergency.
25. exchanging calcium and magnesium ions for sodium ions.
27. a molecule that carries both a positive and a negative charge.
29. Cationic surfactants have a positive charge, anionic surfactants have a negative charge.
31. I
33. All three
35. I and II ionic surfactants; III cationic surfactant.
37. hexadecyltrimethylammonium chloride.
39. Trichloroisocyanuric, sodium percarbonate.
41. In hot water they liberate hydrogen peroxide, which is responsible for the bleaching action.
43. Flammability, toxic fumes.
45. No. It is too hazardous in many ways.
47. A skin softener
49. OMC is insoluble in water and does not wash off as easily as PABA from sweat or while swimming.
51. lead(II) sulfide (galena).
53. oil, wax, pigments.
55. bacteria; brush and floss after eating.
57. **a.** sweetener
    b. protection against cavities
    c. detergent
    d. for highly sensitive teeth
    e. whitening agent and helps prevent gum disease
    f. abrasive

59. A complex mixture of compounds used as a fragrance; cologne is diluted perfume.

61. Makes the face feel cool

63. Temporary dyes are water soluble and can be washed out; permanent dyes last until the hair is cut off or falls out.

65. A reducing agent is used to break the disulfide linkages in hair. The hair is then wrapped around a rod. A mild oxidizing agent is then applied to re-establish disulfide linkages to reconfigure the hair in the shape of the rod.

67. Changing hair color from dark to lighter involves oxidizing the colored pigment to lighten it. Changing gray hair to a darker color involves permanent dyes that affect only the dead outer layer of the hair

69. II

71. I

73. $CH_3(CH_2)_{14}COOCH(CH_3)_2$

75. Top-note components tend to be small molecules with greater volatility (lower boiling points) than middle-note components of perfumes. Although the sizes of phenylacetaldehyde and 2-phenylethanol are similar, 2-phenylethanol can form hydrogen bonds while phenylacetaldehyde cannot. Therefore, the volatility of 2-phenylethanol is not as great as that of phenylacetaldehyde.

77. When combined with water, sodium hydroxide dissolves, producing considerable heat which works to melt any grease responsible for the clog. If the clog is caused by hair, the sodium hydroxide reacts with the grease, converting it to a soap which is more easily removed.

79. the alcohol that reacts with palmitic acid to form carnauba wax has 34 carbon atoms while the alcohol that reacts with palmitic acid to form spermaceti has 16 carbon atoms.

81. **a.** $CaCO_3(s) + 2\,HCl(aq) \longrightarrow CaCl_2(aq) + CO_2(g) + H_2O(l)$
    b. $CaCO_3(s) + 2\,NaHSO_4(aq) \longrightarrow$
       $Ca^{2+}(aq) + 2\,SO_4^{2-}(aq) + CO_2(g) + 2\,Na^+(aq)\,H_2O(l)$

83. c

85. **a.** bleaching agent
    b. sodium salt of palmitic acid and a soap.
    c. detergent builder
    d. wax

Chemistry @ Home

1. Soap and water works best for cleaning hands. Technique is the most important. There is no scientific evidence that hand sanitizers clean as well as or better than soap and water. Hand sanitizers should be used when soap and water is not available.

2. You could test other soaps, commercially available hand sanitizers and have more subjects to test.

3. Soap is a surfactant that reduces the surface tension of water allowing it to interact with oil and grease more easily. The hydrocarbon "tails" of the soap molecule are nonpolar and attract the oil and grease while the "head" of the soap is polar and attracted to water. The water and oil form an emulsion and the dirt can then be removed easily.

   The active ingredient in hand sanitizers is alcohol. Concentration of 60% isopropyl alcohol and above kills germs and bacteria it does not work like a surfactant and therefore is not as effective with removing embedded dirt and grease.

Chapter 22

1. Taken in small amounts, no. Larger amounts can cause liver problems.

3. The route of administration determines the speed of the poison's action, the rate at which it is detoxified, etc.

5. Mercury: occupational exposure; eating contaminated fish, etc. Lead: leaded paint chips; soldered pipes (water) and cans (food).

7. Sunlight, radon, safrole, PAHs.

9. a, b

11. disrupts the protein's ability to function.

13. Metabolic poisons prevent cellular oxidation of metabolites; carbon monoxide, nitrates.

15. Nitrate ions act by oxidizing the Fe^{2+} in hemoglobin to Fe^{3+}

17. c, d

19. Fish convert ingested mercury into methyl mercury which is extremely toxic.

21. ties up lead ions into complexes which can be excreted.

23. tabun, sarin, and soman.

25. Botulin, of example, blocks the synthesis of acetylcholine, with curare, atropine, and some local anesthetics act by blocking aceticholine receptor sites.

27. oxidizing it to less toxic cotinine.

29. No, they just catalyze oxidation.

31. Buildup of these enzymes in a chronic alcoholic leads to a more rapid destruction of testosterone which leads to alcoholic impotence.

33. 7.95 g

35. The Ames test would be an effective tool to use to make this determination.

37. Incomplete burning of almost any organic material.

39. Humans are not exposed to comparable doses; human metabolism is different from test-animal metabolism.

41. genes that trigger or sustain the processes that convert normal cells to cancerous cells.

43. A toxic waste contains or releases toxic; paint, pesticides, motor oil, medicines, and cleansers.

45. 5.3×10^{10} molecules

47. **a.** $C_{10}H_{16}O$ **b.** 4.8 g   **c.** 5 mg

49. **a.** 99.48%; 95.50%; The control group contained a few percent fewer smokers.
    b. 0.9948:1; 0.9550:1
    c. 0.96:1; the control group was a good representation of the cancer sufferer group.

51. The data in Table 22.1 indicate that one would have to ingest relatively large masses of some compounds (for example sucrose) before the dose reached the LD_{50} level, but only extremely small amounts of other substances (ricin and botulin toxin, for example) to surpass the LD_{50} level.

53. **a.** No   **b.** Yes

55. The body converts inert benzene to a carcinogenic epoxide.

57. **a.** 10.3 mL vodka   **b.** 15.4 mg/mL

59. b

61. Saving millions of dollars, improved consumer safety, and reducing the load of poisons in the environment.

Chemistry @ Home

1. Yes the seeds in the control should have the fastest growth and longest roots.

2. There was no growth at the 10% NaCl concentration.

3. There is a clear difference in growth between the 1% and 0.01% NaCl concentrations.

4. This experiment provides evidence that at 10% NaCl concentration is toxic to lettuce seeds as there is no growth. While at 1% NaCl there is considerable growth but at 0.1% NaCl there is less growth rather than more growth. The expectation would be that there would be no growth with the higher concentrations and more growth with the lower concentrations. The data shows that lettuce seeds are tolerant of 1% NaCl but not tolerant at 0.1% NaCl. The growth for .01% and .001% is similar to that of the control. The low concentrations of NaCl do not impede lettuce seed growth.

Appendix

A.1 **a.** 0.0163 g   **b.** 1.53 lb   **c.** 370 ml
A.2 **a.** 0.2224 km   **b.** 150 fl oz
A.3 **a.** 24.4 m/s   **b.** 0.136 oz/qt
A.4 **a.** No   **b.** No
A.5 **a.** $0.12\ m^3$
A.6 56.8 g
A.7 **a.** 100.5 m   **b.** 6.3 L
    c. $1800\ m^2\ (1.80 \times 103\ m^2)$ **d.** 2.33 g/mL
A.8 **a.** 185 °F   **b.** 10.0 °F   **c.** 179 °C   **d.** −29.3 °C

GLOSSARY

absolute zero The lowest possible temperature, 0 K or -273.15 °C or -459.7 °F.

absorb Gather a substance on a surface in a condensed layer.

acid A substance that, when added to water, produces an excess of hydrogen ions; a proton donor.

acid–base indicator A substance that is one color in acid and another color in base.

acidic anhydride A substance, such as a nonmetal oxide, that reacts with water to form an acid.

acid rain Precipitation having a pH less than 5.6.

acquired immune deficiency syndrome (AIDS) A disease caused by a retrovirus (HIV) that weakens the immune system.

activated sludge method A technique for secondary sewage treatment in which the sewage is aerated and some sludge is recycled.

activation energy The minimum quantity of energy that must be available before a chemical reaction can take place.

active site The region on an enzyme or a catalyst where a reaction occurs.

addition polymerization A polymerization reaction in which all the atoms of the monomer molecules are included in the polymer.

addition reaction A reaction in which the single product contains all the atoms of two reactant molecules.

adipose tissue Connective tissue where fat is stored.

advanced treatment Sewage treatment designed to remove phosphates, nitrates, other soluble impurities, and metals and other contaminants; also called tertiary treatment.

aerobic exercise Physical activity in which muscle contractions occur in the presence of oxygen.

aerobic oxidation An oxidation process occurring in the presence of oxygen.

aerosol Particles of 1 mm diameter or less, dispersed in air.

aflatoxins Toxins produced by molds growing on stored peanuts and grains.

Agent Orange A combination of 2,4-D and 2,4,5-T used extensively in Vietnam to remove forest cover and destroy crops that maintained enemy armies.

agonist A molecule that fits and activates a specific receptor.

AIDS See **acquired immune deficiency syndrome.**

alchemy A mixture of chemistry and magic practiced in Europe during the Middle Ages (500 to 1500 C.E.).

alcohol (ROH) An organic compound composed of an alkyl group and a hydroxyl group.

aldehyde (RCHO) An organic compound with a carbonyl group that has a hydrogen atom attached to the carbonyl carbon.

aldose A monosaccharide with an aldehyde functional group.

aliphatic compound A nonaromatic substance. *See also* **aromatic compound.**

alkali metal A metal in group 1A in the customary U.S. arrangement of the periodic table or in group 1 of the IUPAC-recommended table.

alkaline earth metal An element in group 2A in the customary U.S. arrangement of the periodic table or in group 2 of the IUPAC-recommended table.

alkaloid A physiologically active nitrogen-containing organic compound that occurs naturally in a plant.

alkalosis A physiological condition in which the pH of the blood is too high.

alkane A hydrocarbon with only single bonds; a saturated hydrocarbon.

alkene A hydrocarbon containing one or more double bonds.

alkyl group (—R) The group of atoms that results when a hydrogen atom is removed from an alkane.

alkyne A hydrocarbon containing one or more triple bonds.

allergen A substance that triggers an allergic reaction.

allotropes Different forms of the same element in the same physical state.

alloy A mixture of two or more elements, at least one of which is a metal; an alloy has metallic properties.

alpha decay Emission of an alpha particle ($^4_2$He) by a radioactive nucleus.

alpha helix A secondary structure of a protein molecule in which the chains coil around one another in a spiral arrangement.

alpha (α) particle A cluster of two protons and two neutrons; a helium nucleus.

Ames test A laboratory test that screens for mutagens, which are usually also carcinogens.

amide group (—CON—) A functional group in which a carbon is joined to an oxygen atom by a double bond and to a nitrogen atom by a single bond.

amine A nitrogen compound derived from ammonia by replacing one or more hydrogen atoms with alkyl or aromatic group(s).

amino acid An organic compound that contains both an amino group and a carboxyl group; amino acids combine to produce proteins.

amino group (—NH$_2$) A functional group comprised of a nitrogen atom bonded to two hydrogen atoms.

amphetamines Stimulant drugs that are similar in structure to epinephrine and norepinephrine.

amphoteric surfactant A surfactant whose active part bears both a negative charge and a positive charge.

anabolic steroid A drug that aids in the building (anabolism) of body proteins and thus of muscle tissue.

anabolism The building up of molecules through metabolic processes.

anaerobic decay Decomposition in the absence of oxygen.

anaerobic exercise Physical activity that takes place without sufficient oxygen.

analgesic A substance that provides pain relief.

androgen A male sex hormone.

anesthetic A substance that causes loss of feeling or awareness.

anion A negatively charged ion.

anionic surfactant A surfactant whose active part (water-soluble head) bears a negative charge.

anode A positive electrode at which oxidation occurs.

antagonist A molecule that prevents the action of an agonist by blocking its receptor.

antibiotic A soluble substance, produced by a mold or bacterium, which inhibits growth of other microorganisms.

anticarcinogen A substance that inhibits the development of cancer.

anticholinergic A drug that acts on nerves using acetylcholine as a neurotransmitter.

anticoagulant A substance that inhibits the clotting of blood.

anticodon The sequence of three adjacent nucleotides in a tRNA molecule that is complementary to a codon on mRNA.

antihistamine A substance that relieves the symptoms caused by allergens: sneezing, itchy eyes, and runny nose.

anti-inflammatory A substance that inhibits inflammation.

antimetabolite A compound that inhibits the synthesis of DNA and thus slows the growth of cancer cells.

antioxidant A reducing agent that retards damaging oxidation reactions in living cells or reacts with free radicals to prevent rancidity in foods.

antiperspirant A formulation that retards perspiration by constricting the openings of sweat glands.

antipyretic A fever-reducing substance.

apoenzyme The pure protein part of an enzyme.

applied research An investigation aimed at creating a useful product or solving a particular problem.

aqueous solution A solution in which the solvent is water.

arithmetic growth A process in which a constant quantity is added during each period of time.

aromatic compound A compound that has a ring structure and properties like those of benzene.

asbestos A fibrous silicate mineral composed of chains of SiO_4 tetrahedra.

astringent A substance that constricts the openings of sweat glands, thus reducing the amount of perspiration that escapes.

atmosphere The thin blanket of air surrounding Earth.

atmosphere (atm) A unit of pressure equal to 760 mmHg.

atom The smallest characteristic particle of an element.

atomic mass unit (u) The unit of relative atomic masses, equal to $\frac{1}{12}$ the mass of a carbon-12 atom.

atomic number (Z) The number of protons in the nucleus of an atom.

atomic theory A model that explains the law of multiple proportions and the law of constant composition by stating that all elements are composed of atoms.

Avogadro's hypothesis Equal volumes of gases, regardless of their compositions, contain equal numbers of molecules when measured at a given temperature and pressure.

Avogadro's law At a fixed temperature and pressure, the volume of a gas is directly proportional to the amount (number of moles) of gas.

Avogadro's number The number of atoms (6.022×10^{23}) in exactly 12 g of pure carbon-12.

background radiation Constantly occurring radiation from cosmic rays and from natural radioactive isotopes in air, water, soil, and rocks.

base A substance that, when added to water, produces an excess of hydroxide ions; a proton acceptor.

base triplet The sequence of three bases on a tRNA molecule that determine which amino acid it can carry.

basic anhydride A substance, such as a metal oxide, that reacts with water to form a base.

basic research The search for knowledge for its own sake.

battery A series of two or more connected electrochemical cells.

becquerel (Bq) A measure of the rate of radioactive decay; 1 becquerel (Bq) = 1 disintegration/s.

beta decay Emission of a beta particle by a radioactive nucleus.

beta (β) particle An electron emitted by a radioactive nucleus.

beta pleated sheet A secondary protein structure in which arrays of chains form a zigzag sheet.

binary ionic compound A compound consisting of cations of a metal and anions of a nonmetal.

binding energy The energy that holds the nucleons together in an atom's nucleus.

biochemical oxygen demand (BOD) The quantity of oxygen required by microorganisms to remove organic matter from water.

biochemistry The study of the chemistry of living things and life processes.

biomass Dry plant material used as fuel.

bitumen A hydrocarbon mixture obtained from tar sands by heating.

bleaches Oxidizing agents used to remove unwanted color from fabric or other material.

blood sugar Glucose, a simple sugar that is circulated in the bloodstream and used directly by cells for energy.

boiling point The temperature at which a substance changes state from a liquid to a gas throughout the bulk of the liquid.

bond See **chemical bond**.

bonding pair A pair of electrons shared by two atoms, forming a chemical bond.

Boyle's law For a given mass of gas at constant temperature, the volume varies inversely with the pressure.

breeder reactor A nuclear reactor that converts nonfissionable isotopes to nuclear fuel.

broad-spectrum antibiotic An antibiotic that is effective against a wide variety of microorganisms.

bronze An alloy of copper and tin.

buffer solution A mixture of a weak acid and its conjugate base or a weak base and its conjugate acid that maintains a nearly constant pH when a small amount of strong acid or strong base is added.

builder Any substance (often a complex phosphate) added to a surfactant to increase its detergency.

calorie (cal) The amount of heat required to raise the temperature of 1 g of water by 1 °C.

carbohydrate A compound consisting of carbon, hydrogen, and oxygen; a starch or sugar.

carbon-14 dating A radioisotopic technique for determining the age of artifacts, based on the half-life of carbon-14.

carbonyl group (C=O) A functional group consisting of a carbon atom joined to an oxygen atom by a double bond.

carboxyl group (—COOH) A carbon atom with a double bond to one oxygen atom and a single bond to a second oxygen atom, which in turn is bonded to a hydrogen atom; the functional group of carboxylic acids.

carboxylic acid (RCOOH) An organic compound that contains the carboxyl functional group.

carcinogen A substance or physical entity that causes the growth of tumors.

catabolism Any metabolic process in which complex compounds are broken down into simpler substances.

catalyst A substance that increases the rate of a chemical reaction without itself being used up.

catalytic converter A device that uses catalysts that oxidize carbon monoxide and hydrocarbons to carbon dioxide and reduce nitrogen oxides to nitrogen gas.

catalytic reforming A process that converts straight-chain alkanes to aromatic hydrocarbons.

cathode A negative electrode at which reduction occurs.

cathode ray A stream of high-speed electrons emitted from a cathode in an evacuated tube.

cation A positively charged ion.

cationic surfactant A surfactant whose active part (water-soluble head) bears a positive charge.

celluloid Cellulose nitrate, a synthetic material derived from natural cellulose by treating it with nitric acid.

cellulose A polymer comprised of glucose units joined by beta linkages.

Celsius scale A temperature scale on which water freezes at 0° and boils at 100°.

cement A complex mixture of calcium and aluminum silicates made from limestone and clay; mixed with water to make concrete.

ceramic A hard, solid product made by heating clay and other minerals to fuse them.

chain reaction A self-sustaining reaction in which one or more products of one event cause one or more new events.

charcoal filtration Filtration of water through charcoal to adsorb organic compounds.

Charles's law For a given mass of gas at constant pressure, the volume varies directly with the absolute temperature.

chelating Tying up metal ions by surrounding them.

chemical bond The force of attraction that holds atoms or ions together in compounds.

chemical change A change in chemical composition.

chemical equation A shorthand representation of a chemical change that uses symbols and formulas instead of words.

chemical property A characteristic of a substance that describes the way in which the substance reacts with another substance to change its composition.

chemical symbol An abbreviation, consisting of one or two letters, that stands for an element.

chemistry The study of matter and the changes it undergoes.

chemotherapy The use of chemicals to control or cure diseases.

chiral carbon A carbon atom that has four different groups attached to it.

coal A solid fossil fuel that is rich in carbon.

codon A sequence of three adjacent nucleotides in an mRNA molecule that specifies one amino acid.

coenzyme An organic molecule (often a vitamin) that combines with an apoenzyme to make a complete, functioning enzyme.

cofactor An ion or molecule that combines with an apoenzyme to make a complete, functioning enzyme.

cologne A diluted perfume.

combined gas law The single relationship that incorporates the simple gas laws.

compound A substance made up of two or more elements combined in a fixed ratio.

concentrated solution A solution that has a relatively large amount of solute per unit volume of solution.

concrete A building material made from cement, sand, gravel, and water.

condensation The reverse of vaporization; a change from the gaseous state to the liquid state.

condensation polymerization A polymerization reaction in which not all the atoms in the starting monomers are incorporated in the polymer because water (or other small) molecules are formed as by-products.

condensed structural formula A chemical formula for an organic compound that omits the bonds joining hydrogens to carbons.

conjugate acid–base pair Two molecules or ions that differ by one proton.

copolymer A polymer formed by the combination of two (or more) different monomers.

core electrons Electrons in any shell of an atom except the outermost shell.

corrosive waste A hazardous waste that requires a special container because it destroys conventional container materials.

cosmetics Substances defined in the 1938 U.S. Food, Drug, and Cosmetic Act as "articles intended to be rubbed, poured, sprinkled or sprayed on, introduced into, or otherwise applied to the human body or any part thereof, for cleaning, beautifying, promoting attractiveness or altering the appearance."

cosmic rays Extremely high-energy radiation from outer space.

covalent bond A bond formed when two atoms share one or more pairs of electrons.

cream An emulsion of tiny water droplets in oil.

critical mass The minimum amount of fissionable material required to achieve a self-sustaining chain reaction.

crystal A solid, regular array of ions.

cyclic hydrocarbon A ring-containing hydrocarbon.

daughter isotope An isotope formed by the radioactive decay of another isotope.

defoliant A substance that causes premature dropping of leaves by plants.

density The amount of mass per unit volume.

deodorant A product that contains perfume to mask body odor; some have a germicide to kill odor-causing bacteria.

deoxyribonucleic acid (DNA) The type of nucleic acid found primarily in the nuclei of cells; contains the sugar deoxyribose.

depilatory A hair remover.

deposition The direct formation of a solid from a gas without passing through the liquid state; the reverse of sublimation.

depressant drug A drug that slows both physical and mental activity.

detergent A cleansing agent, usually a synthetic surfactant.

deuterium An isotope of hydrogen with a proton and a neutron in the nucleus (mass of 2 u).

dextro isomer A "right-handed" isomer.

dietary mineral An inorganic substance required in the diet for proper health and well-being.

Dietary Reference Intakes (DRIs) A set of reference values for nutrients established by the U.S. Academy of Sciences for planning and assessing diets.

dilute solution A solution that has a relatively small amount of solute per unit volume of solution.

dioxins Highly toxic chlorinated cyclic compounds produced by burning wastes containing chlorinated compounds; once found as contaminants in the defoliant 2,4,5-T.

dipole A molecule that is polar.

dipole–dipole forces The attractive forces that exist among polar covalent molecules.

disaccharide A sugar that on hydrolysis yields two monosaccharide molecules per molecule of disaccharide.

dispersion forces The momentary, usually weak, attractive forces between molecules resulting from electron motions that create short-lived dipoles.

dissociative anesthetic A substance that causes gross personality disorders, including hallucinations similar to those in near-death experiences.

dissolved oxygen Oxygen dissolved in water; provides a measure of the water's ability to support fish and other aquatic life.

disulfide linkage A covalent linkage between cysteine units through two sulfur atoms.

diuretic A substance that increases the output of urine.

double bond The sharing of two pairs of electrons between two atoms.

doubling time The time it takes a population to double in size.

drug A substance that affects the functioning of living things; used to relieve pain, to treat illness, or to improve health or well-being.

drug abuse The use of a drug for its intoxicating effect.

drug misuse The use of a drug in a manner other than its intended use.

duet rule Hydrogen and helium may have at most two electrons in their outermost shells.

elastomer A polymeric material that returns to its original shape after being stretched.

electrochemical cell A device that produces electricity by means of a chemical reaction.

electrode A carbon rod or a metal strip inserted into an electrochemical cell, at which oxidation or reduction occurs.

electrolysis The process of using electricity to cause chemical change.

electrolyte A compound that conducts an electric current in water solution.

electron The subatomic particle that bears a unit of negative charge.

electron capture (EC) A type of radioactive decay in which a nucleus absorbs an electron from the first or second shell of the atom.

electron configuration The arrangement of an atom's electrons in its energy levels.

electron-dot symbol See **Lewis symbol.**

electronegativity The attraction of an atom in a molecule for a bonding pair of electrons.

electrostatic precipitator A device that removes particulate matter from smokestack gases by creating an electric charge on the particles, which are then removed by attraction to a surface of opposite charge.

element A substance composed of atoms that have the same number of protons.

emollient An oil or grease used as a skin softener.

emulsion A suspension of submicroscopic particles of fat or oil in water.

enantiomers Isomers that are not superimposable on their mirror image.

end note The fraction of a perfume that has the lowest volatility; composed of large molecules.

endorphins Naturally occurring peptides that bond to the same receptor sites as morphine.

endothermic Absorbing energy from the surroundings.

energy The ability to do work.

energy levels (shells) The specific, quantized values of energy that an electron can have in an atom.

enrichment (of food) Replacement of B vitamins and addition of iron to flour.

enrichment (of an isotope) The process by which the proportion of one isotope of an element is increased relative to those of the others.

entropy A measure of the dispersal of energy among the possible states of a system.

enzyme A biological catalyst.

essential amino acid An amino acid that is not produced in the body and must be included in the diet.

ester (RCOOR′) A compound derived from a carboxylic acid and an alcohol; the —OH of the acid is replaced by an —OR group.

estrogen A female sex hormone.

ether (ROR′) A molecule with two hydrocarbon groups attached to the same oxygen atom.

eutrophication The excessive growth of algae in a body of water, which causes some of the plants to die because of a lack of light; the water becomes choked with vegetation, depleted of oxygen, and useless as a fish habitat or for recreation.

excited state A state in which an atom has at least one electron that has moved from a lower to a higher energy level.

exothermic Releasing energy (usually heat) to the surroundings.

fast-twitch fibers The stronger, larger muscle fibers that are suited for short bursts of vigorous exercise.

fat An ester formed by the reaction of glycerol with three fatty-acid units; a triglyceride or triacylglycerol.

fat depots Storage places for fats in the body.

fatty acid A carboxylic acid that contains 4 to 20 or more carbon atoms in a chain.

first law of thermodynamics (law of conservation of energy) Energy cannot be created or destroyed, only transformed.

flammable waste A hazardous waste that burns readily on ignition, presenting a fire hazard.

FLaReS An acronym representing four rules used to test a claim: falsifiability, logic, replicability, and sufficiency.

flocculent A substance that causes particles to clump together and settle out.

food additive Any substance other than a basic foodstuff that is added to food to aid nutrition, enhance color or flavor, or provide texture.

formula A representation of a chemical substance in which the component chemical elements are represented by their symbols.

formula mass The sum of the masses of the atoms represented in the formula of a substance, expressed in atomic mass units (u).

fossil fuels Natural fuels derived from once-living plants and animals; especially coal, petroleum, and natural gas.

free radical A highly reactive chemical species that contains an unpaired electron.

freezing The reverse of melting; a change from the liquid to the solid state.

fuel A substance that burns readily with the release of significant energy.

fuel cell A device that produces electricity directly from continuously supplied fuel and oxygen.

functional group An atom or group of atoms that confers characteristic properties to a family of organic compounds.

fundamental particle An electron, proton, or neutron.

gamma decay Emission of a gamma ray $(^0_0\gamma)$ by a radioactive nucleus.

gamma (γ) rays Radiation that is emitted by radioactive substances and has higher energy and is more penetrating than X-rays.

gas The state of matter in which the substance takes both the shape and volume of a container that it occupies.

gasoline The fraction of petroleum that consists of hydrocarbons, mainly alkanes, with five to twelve carbons and is used as automotive fuel.

Gay-Lussac's law The pressure of a fixed amount of gas at fixed volume is directly proportional to its temperature in kelvins.

gene The segment of a DNA molecule that contains the information necessary to produce a protein; the smallest unit of hereditary information.

general anesthetic A depressant that acts on the brain to produce unconsciousness and insensitivity to pain.

geometric growth A process in which the rate of growth itself increases during each period of time.

geometric isomers Molecules having the same molecular formula that are locked into their spatial positions with respect to one another due to a double bond or a ring structure.

geothermal energy Energy derived from the heat of Earth's interior.

glass A noncrystalline solid material obtained by melting sand with soda, lime, and various other metal oxides.

glass transition temperature (T_g) The temperature above which a polymer is rubbery and tough and below which the polymer is brittle.

global warming An increase in Earth's average temperature.

globular protein A protein whose molecules are folded into compact spherical or ovoid shapes.

glycogen A polymer of glucose with alpha linkages and branched chains; stored in the liver and muscles.

GRAS list A list, established by the U.S. Congress in 1958, of food additives generally recognized as safe.

green chemistry An approach that uses materials and processes that are intended to prevent or reduce pollution at its source.

greenhouse effect The retention of the sun's heat energy by Earth's atmosphere as a result of excess carbon dioxide and other gases in the atmosphere.

ground state The state of an atom in which all of its electrons are in the lowest possible energy levels.

group The elements in a column in the periodic table; a family of elements.

half-life The length of time required for one-half of the radioactive nuclei in a sample to decay.

hallucinogenic drug A drug that produces visions and sensations that are not part of reality.

halogen An element in group 7A in the customary U.S. arrangement of the periodic table or in group 17 of the IUPAC-recommended table.

hard water Water containing excessive concentrations of ions of calcium, magnesium, and/or iron.

hazardous waste A waste that, when improperly managed, can cause or contribute to death or illness or threaten human health or the environment.

heat Energy transfer that occurs as a result of a temperature difference.

heat of vaporization The amount of heat involved in the evaporation or condensation of a fixed amount of a substance.

heat stroke A failure of the body's heat regulatory system; unless the victim is treated promptly, the rapid rise in body temperature will cause brain damage or death.

herbicide A material used to kill weeds (plants classified as pests).

heterocyclic compound A cyclic compound in which one or more atoms in the ring is not carbon.

homogeneous Completely uniform; a property of a sample that has the same composition in all parts.

homologous series A series of compounds whose adjacent members differ by a fixed unit of structure.

hormone A chemical messenger secreted into the blood by an endocrine gland.

humectant A moistening agent added to food.

hydrocarbon An organic compound that contains only carbon and hydrogen.

hydrogen bomb A bomb based on the nuclear fusion of isotopes of hydrogen.

hydrogen bond A type of intermolecular force in which a hydrogen atom covalently bonded in one molecule is attracted to a nonmetal atom in a neighboring molecule; both the atom to which the hydrogen atom is bonded and the one to which it is attracted are small, highly electronegative atoms, usually N, O, or F.

hydrolysis The reaction of a substance with water; literally, a splitting by water.

hydrophilic Attracted to polar solvents such as water.

hydrophobic Not attracted to water; attracted to oil or grease.

hypoallergenic cosmetics Cosmetics claimed to cause fewer allergic reactions than regular products.

hypothesis A tentative explanation of observations that can be tested by experiment.

ideal gas law The volume of a gas is proportional to the amount of gas and its Kelvin temperature and inversely proportional to its pressure.

induced radioactivity Radioactivity caused by bombarding a stable isotope with elemental particles, forming a radioactive isotope.

industrial smog (sulfurous smog) Polluted air associated with industrial activities, characterized by sulfur oxides and particulate matter.

inorganic chemistry The study of the compounds of all elements other than carbon.

insecticide A substance that is used to kill insects.

iodine number The number of grams of iodine that reacts with 100 g of a fat or oil; an indication of the degree of unsaturation.

ion A charged atom or group of atoms.

ionic bond The chemical bond that results when electrons are transferred from a metal to a nonmetal; the electrostatic attraction between ions of opposite charge.

ionizing radiation Radiation that produces ions as it passes through matter.

isoelectronic Having the same electron configuration.

isomers Compounds that have the same molecular formula but different structures.

isotopes Atoms that have the same number of protons but different numbers of neutrons.

joule (J) The SI unit of energy (1 J = 0.239 cal).

juvenile hormone A hormone that controls the rate of development of young organisms; used to prevent insects from maturing.

kelvin (K) The SI unit of temperature; zero on the Kelvin scale is absolute zero.

keratin The tough, fibrous protein that comprises most of the outermost layer of the epidermis.

kerogen The complex material found in oil shale; has an approximate composition of $(C_6H_8O)_n$, where n is a large number.

ketone (RCOR′) An organic compound with a carbonyl group between two carbon atoms.

ketose A monosaccharide with a ketone functional group.

kilocalorie (kcal) A unit of energy equal to 1000 cal; one food calorie.

kilogram (kg) The SI unit of mass, a quantity equal to about 2.2 lb.

kinetic energy The energy of motion.

kinetic–molecular theory An explanation of the behavior of gases based on the motion and energy of particles.

lanolin A natural wax obtained from sheep's wool.

law of combining volumes The volumes of gaseous reactants and products are in a small whole-number ratio when all measurements are made at the same temperature and pressure.

law of conservation of energy See **first law of thermodynamics.**

law of conservation of mass Matter is neither created nor destroyed during a chemical change.

law of definite proportions A compound always contains the same elements in exactly the same proportions by mass; also called the *law of constant composition*.

law of multiple proportions Elements may combine in different proportions to form more than one compound—for example, CO and CO_2.

LD$_{50}$ The dosage that is lethal to 50% of a population of test animals.

levo isomer A "left-handed" isomer.

Lewis formula A structural formula of a molecule or polyatomic ion that shows the arrangement of atoms, bonds, and lone pairs.

Lewis symbol A symbol consisting of the element's symbol surrounded by dots representing the atom's valence electrons; also referred to as an *electron-dot symbol*.

limiting reactant The reactant that is used up first in a reaction, after which the reaction ceases no matter how much remains of the other reactants.

line-angle formula A representation of a molecule in which the corners and ends of lines are understood to be carbon atoms and each carbon atom is understood to be attached to enough hydrogen atoms to give it four bonds.

line spectrum The pattern of colored lines emitted by an element.

lipid A substance from animal or plant cells that is soluble in solvents of low polarity and insoluble in water.

lipoprotein A protein combined with a lipid, such as a triglyceride or cholesterol.

liquid The state of matter in which the substance assumes the shape of its container, flows readily, and maintains a fairly constant volume.

liter (L) A unit of volume equal to a cubic decimeter.

local anesthetic A substance that renders part of the body insensitive to pain while leaving the patient conscious.

lone pair A pair of unshared electrons in the valence shell of an atom; also called a *nonbonding pair*.

lotion An emulsion of tiny oil droplets dispersed in water.

main group elements The elements in the A groups of the customary U.S. arrangement of the periodic table or in groups 1, 2, and 13–18 of the IUPAC-recommended table.

marijuana A hallucinogenic drug consisting of the leaves, flowers, seeds, and small stems of the *Cannabis* plant.

mass A measure of the quantity of matter.

mass–energy equation Einstein's equation $E = mc^2$, in which E is energy, m is mass, and c is the speed of light.

mass number (A) The sum of the numbers of protons and neutrons in the nucleus of an atom; also called the *nucleon number*.

matter The stuff of which all materials are made; anything that has mass and occupies space.

melanin A brownish-black pigment that determines the color of the skin and hair.

melting point The temperature at which a substance changes from the solid to the liquid state.

messenger RNA (mRNA) The type of RNA that contains the codons for a protein; travels from the nucleus of the cell to a ribosome.

metabolism The set of coordinated chemical reactions that keep the cells of an organism alive.

metalloid An element with properties intermediate between those of metals and those of nonmetals.

metals The elements that are to the left of the heavy, stepped line in the periodic table.

meter (m) The SI unit of length, slightly longer than a yard.

mica A mineral composed of SiO_4 tetrahedra arranged in a two-dimensional, sheetlike array.

micelle A tiny spherical oil droplet in which the hydrocarbon tails of soap molecules are embedded, with their hydrophilic heads lying along the outer surface.

micronutrient A substance needed by a plant or animal in only tiny amounts.

middle note The fraction of a perfume that is intermediate in volatility and is responsible for the lingering aroma after most top-note compounds have vaporized.

mineral (dietary) An inorganic substance required in the diet for good health.

mineral (geological) A naturally occurring inorganic solid with a definite composition.

mixture Matter with a variable composition.

moisturizer A substance that acts to retain moisture in the skin by forming a protective physical barrier.

molarity (M) The concentration of a solution in moles of solute per liter of solution.

molar mass The mass of one mole of a substance expressed in units of grams/mole.

molar volume The volume occupied by 1 mol of a substance (usually a gas) under specified conditions.

mole (mol) The amount of a substance that contains 6.022×10^{23} elementary units (atoms, molecules, or formula units) of the substance.

molecular mass The mass of a molecule of a substance; the sum of the atomic masses as indicated by the molecular formula, expressed in atomic mass units (u).

molecule An electrically neutral unit of two or more atoms joined by covalent bonds; the smallest fundamental unit of a molecular substance.

monomer A substance of relatively low molecular mass; monomer molecules are the building blocks of polymers.

monosaccharide A carbohydrate that cannot be hydrolyzed into simpler sugars.

mousse A foamy hair care product composed of resins and used to hold hair in place.

mutagen Any entity that causes changes in genes without destroying the genetic material.

narcotic A depressant, analgesic drug that induces narcosis (sleep).

natural gas A mixture of gases, mainly methane, found in underground deposits.

natural philosophy Philosophical speculation about nature.

neuron A nerve cell.

neurotransmitter A chemical that carries an impulse across a synapse from one nerve cell to the next.

neurotrophin A substance produced during exercise that promotes the growth of brain cells.

neutralization The combination of H^+ and OH^- to form water or the reaction of an acid and a base to produce a salt and water.

neutron A nuclear particle with a mass of approximately 1 u and no electric charge.

nitrogen cycle The various processes by which nitrogen is cycled among the atmosphere, soil, water, and living organisms.

nitrogen fixation A process that combines nitrogen with one or more other elements.

noble gases Generally unreactive elements that appear in group 8A of the customary U.S. arrangement of the periodic table or in group 18 of the IUPAC-recommended table.

nonbonding pair See **lone pair.**

nonionic surfactant A surfactant whose active part bears no ionic charge.

nonmetals The elements to the right of the heavy, stepped line in the periodic table.

nonpolar covalent bond A covalent bond in which there is equal sharing of the bonding pair of electrons.

nonsteroidal anti-inflammatory drug (NSAID) A type of anti-inflammatory drug that is milder than the more potent steroidal anti-inflammatory drugs such as cortisone and prednisone.

nuclear fission The splitting of an atomic nucleus into two smaller ones.

nuclear fusion The combination of two small atomic nuclei to produce one larger nucleus.

nuclear reactor A power plant that produces electricity using nuclear fission reactions.

nucleic acid A nucleotide polymer, DNA or RNA.

nucleon A proton or a neutron.

nucleon number See **mass number**.

nucleotide A combination of an amine base, a sugar unit, and a phosphate unit; the monomer unit of nucleic acids.

nucleus The tiny core of an atom, composed of protons and neutrons and containing all the positive charge and most of the mass of the atom.

octane rating The comparison of the antiknock quality of a gasoline to that of pure isooctane (with a rating of 100).

octet rule Atoms tend to have eight electrons in the outermost shell.

oil (food) A substance formed from glycerol and fatty acids, which is liquid at room temperature.

oil shale Fossil rock from which oil can be obtained at high cost.

optical brightener A compound that absorbs the invisible ultraviolet component of sunlight and reemits it as visible light at the blue end of the spectrum; added to detergents to make whites "whiter."

orbital A volume of space in an atom that is occupied by one or two electrons.

organic chemistry The study of the compounds of carbon.

organic farming Farming without using synthetic fertilizers or pesticides.

orphan drugs Medicinal products intended for diagnosis, prevention, or treatment of rare serious or life-threatening diseases.

oxidation An increase in oxidation number; combination of an element or compound with oxygen; loss of hydrogen; loss of electrons.

oxidizing agent A substance that causes oxidation and is itself reduced.

oxygen cycle The various processes by which oxygen is cycled among the atmosphere, soil, water, and living organisms.

oxygen debt The demand for oxygen in muscle cells that builds up during anaerobic exercise.

ozone layer The layer of the stratosphere that contains ozone and shields living creatures on Earth from the sun's ultraviolet radiation.

paint A surface coating that contains a pigment, a binder, and a solvent.

particulate matter (PM) An air pollutant composed of solid and liquid particles whose size is greater than that of a molecule.

peptide bond The amide linkage that joins amino acids in chains of peptides, polypeptides, and proteins.

percent by mass The concentration of a solution, expressed as (mass of solute ÷ mass of solution) × 100%.

percent by volume The concentration of a solution, expressed as (volume of solute ÷ volume of solution) × 100%.

perfume A fragrant mixture of plant extracts and other chemicals dissolved in alcohol.

period A horizontal row of the periodic table.

periodic table A systematic arrangement of the elements in columns and rows; elements in a given column have similar properties.

pesticide A substance that kills some kind of pest (weeds, insects, rodents, and so on).

petroleum A thick liquid mixture of (mostly) hydrocarbons occurring in various geologic deposits.

pH The negative logarithm of the hydronium ion concentration, which indicates the degree of acidity or basicity of a solution.

pharmacology The study of the response of living organisms to drugs.

phenol A compound with an OH group attached to a benzene ring.

pheromone A chemical secreted by an insect or other organism to mark a trail, send out an alarm, or attract a mate.

photochemical smog Smog created by the action of sunlight on hydrocarbons and nitrogen oxides, which come mainly from automobile exhaust.

photon A unit particle of energy.

photosynthesis The chemical process used by green plants to convert solar energy into chemical energy by reducing carbon dioxide and producing glucose.

photovoltaic cell A solar cell; a cell that uses semiconductors to convert sunlight directly to electric energy.

physical change A change in physical state or form.

physical property A quality of a substance that can be demonstrated without changing the composition of the substance.

phytoremediation A method of wastewater treatment that allows plants in a lagoon to remove metals and other contaminants.

placebo effect The phenomenon in which an inactive substance produces results in recipients for psychological reasons.

plasma A state of matter similar to a gas but composed of isolated electrons and nuclei rather than discrete whole atoms or molecules.

plasticizer A substance added to some plastics to make them more flexible and easier to work with.

poison A substance that causes injury, illness, or death of a living organism.

polar covalent bond A covalent bond in which the bonding pair of electrons is shared unequally by the two atoms, giving each atom a partial positive or negative charge.

polar molecule A molecule that has a separation between centers of positive and negative charge; a dipole.

pollutant A chemical that causes undesirable effects by being in the wrong place and/or in the wrong concentration.

polyamide A polymer that has monomer units joined by amide linkages.

polyatomic ion A charged particle consisting of two or more covalently bonded atoms.

polyester A polymer that has monomer units joined by ester linkages.

polymer A molecule with a large molecular mass that is formed of repeating smaller units (monomers).

polymerase chain reaction (PCR) A process that reproduces many copies of a DNA fragment.

polypeptide A polymer of amino acids, usually of lower molecular mass than a protein.

polysaccharide A carbohydrate, such as starch or cellulose, that consists of many monosaccharide units linked together.

polyunsaturated fat A fat containing fatty-acid units that have two or more carbon-to-carbon double bonds.

positron (β^+ or $_{+1}^{0}e$) A positively charged particle with the mass of an electron.

potential energy Energy due to position or composition.

preemergent herbicide A herbicide that is rapidly broken down in the soil and can therefore be used to kill weed plants before crop seedlings emerge.

primary plant nutrients Nitrogen, phosphorus, and potassium.

primary sewage treatment Treatment of wastewater in a holding pond to allow some of the sewage solids to settle out as sludge.

primary structure The amino-acid sequence in a protein.

product A substance produced by a chemical reaction; product formulas follow the arrow in a chemical equation.

progestin A steroid hormone that mimics the action of progesterone.

prostaglandin One of several hormone-like lipids that are derived from the fatty acid arachidonic acid; involved in increased blood pressure, the contractions of smooth muscle, and other physiological processes.

protein An amino acid polymer with a molecular weight exceeding about 10,000 u.

proton (H^+) The hydrogen ion in acid–base chemistry.

proton (nuclear) The unit of positive charge in the nucleus of an atom.

psychotropic drugs Drugs that affect the mind.

purine A heterocyclic amine base with two fused rings, found in nucleic acids.

pyrimidine A heterocyclic amine base with one ring, found in nucleic acids.

quantum A discrete unit of energy; one photon.

quartz A silicate composed of SiO_4 tetrahedra arranged in a three-dimensional array.

quaternary structure An arrangement of protein subunits in a particular pattern.

radiation therapy Use of radioisotopes to destroy cancer cells.

radioactive decay The disintegration of an unstable atomic nucleus with spontaneous emission of radiation.

radioactive fallout Radioactive debris produced by explosion of a nuclear bomb.

radioactivity The spontaneous emission of particles (for example, alpha or beta) or rays (gamma) from unstable atomic nuclei.

radioisotopes Atoms or ions with radioactive nuclei.

reactant A starting material in a chemical change; reactant formulas precede the arrow in a chemical equation.

reactive wastes Hazardous wastes that tend to react spontaneously or to react vigorously with air or water.

Recommended Daily Allowance (RDA) The recommended level of a nutrient necessary for a balanced diet.

recycle To make something new from something previously used.

reduce To make something smaller in size, quantity, or number.

reducing agent A substance that causes reduction and is itself oxidized.

reduction A decrease in oxidation number; a gain of electrons; a loss of oxygen; a gain of hydrogen.

replication Copying or duplication; the process by which DNA reproduces itself.

resin A polymeric organic material, usually a sticky solid or semisolid.

restorative drug A drug used to relieve the pain and reduce the inflammation resulting from overuse of muscles.

retrovirus An RNA virus that synthesizes DNA in a host cell.

reuse To use something again, especially in a different way or after reclaiming or reprocessing it.

reverse osmosis A method of pressure filtration through a semipermeable membrane; water flows from an area of high salt concentration to an area of low salt concentration.

ribonucleic acid (RNA) The form of nucleic acid found mainly in the cytoplasm but also present in all other parts of the cell; contains the sugar ribose.

risk–benefit analysis A technique for estimating a desirability quotient by dividing the benefits by the risks.

rule of 72 A mathematical formula that gives the doubling time for a population growing geometrically; 72 divided by the annual rate of growth expressed as a percentage equals the doubling time.

salt An ionic compound produced by the reaction of an acid with a base.

saponins Natural compounds in some plants that produce a soapy lather.

saturated fat A triglyceride composed of a large proportion of saturated fatty acids esterified with glycerol.

saturated hydrocarbon An alkane; a compound of carbon and hydrogen with only single bonds.

science An accumulation of knowledge about nature and the physical world.

scientific law A summary of experimental data; often expressed in the form of a mathematical equation.

scientific model A representation of an invisible process that uses tangible items or pictures.

sebum An oily secretion that protects the skin from moisture loss.

second law of thermodynamics The entropy of the universe increases in any spontaneous process.

secondary plant nutrients Magnesium, calcium, and sulfur.

secondary sewage treatment Passing effluent from primary sewage treatment through gravel and sand filters to aerate the water and remove suspended solids.

secondary structure The arrangement of a protein's polypeptide chains—for example, helix or pleated sheet.

sex attractant A pheromone released by an organism to attract a mate.

shell One of the specific, quantized energy levels that an electron can occupy in an atom.

significant figures Those measured digits that are known with certainty plus one uncertain digit.

silicone A polymer whose chains consists of alternating silicon and oxygen atoms.

single bond A pair of electrons shared between two atoms.

SI units (International System of Units) A measuring system that is used by scientists worldwide and has seven base quantities with their multiples and submultiples.

skin protection factor (SPF) The rating of a sunscreen's ability to absorb or block ultraviolet radiation.

slag A relatively low-melting product of the reaction of limestone with silicate impurities in iron ore.

slow-twitch fibers Muscle fibers suited for steady exercise of long duration.

smog The combination of smoke and fog; polluted air.

soap A salt (usually a sodium salt) of a long-chain carboxylic acid.

solar cell A device used for converting sunlight to electricity; a photoelectric cell.

solid A state of matter in which the substance has a definite shape and volume.

solute The substance that is dissolved in another substance (solvent) to form a solution; usually present in a smaller amount than the solvent.

solution A homogeneous mixture of two or more substances.

solvent The substance that dissolves another substance (solute) to form a solution; usually present in a larger amount than the solute.

specific heat The amount of heat required to raise the temperature of 1 g of a substance by 1 °C.

standard temperature and pressure (STP) Conditions of 0 °C and 1 atm pressure.

starch A polymer of glucose units joined by alpha linkages; a complex carbohydrate.

starvation The withholding of nutrition from the body, whether voluntary or involuntary.

steel An alloy of iron containing small amounts of carbon and usually another metal such as manganese, nickel, or chromium.

stereoisomers Isomers having the same formula but differing in the arrangement of atoms or groups of atoms in three-dimensional space.

steroid A molecule that has a four-ring skeletal structure, with one cyclopentane and three cyclohexane fused rings.

stimulant drug A drug that increases alertness, speeds up mental processes, and generally elevates the mood.

stoichiometric factor A factor that relates the numbers of moles of two substances through their coefficients in a chemical equation.

stoichiometry The quantitative relationship between reactants and products in a chemical reaction.

strong acid An acid that ionizes completely in water; a potent proton donor.

strong base A base that dissociates completely in water; a potent proton acceptor.

structural formula A chemical formula that shows how the atoms of a molecule are arranged, to which other atom(s) they are bonded, and the kinds of bonds.

sublevel See **subshell**.

sublimation Conversion of a solid directly to the gaseous state without going through the liquid state.

subshell A set of orbitals in an atom that are in the same shell and have the same energy; also called a *sublevel*.

substance A sample of matter that always has the same composition, no matter how it is made or where it is found.

substituent An atom or group of atoms substituted for a hydrogen atom on a hydrocarbon.

substrate The substance that attaches to the active site of an enzyme and is then acted upon.

sulfurous smog See **industrial smog**.

sunscreen A substance or mixture that blocks or absorbs ultraviolet (UV) radiation.

supercritical fluid An intermediate state having properties of both gases and liquids.

surface-active agent (surfactant) Any substance that stabilizes the suspension in water of a nonpolar substance such as oil.

surroundings Everything that is not part of the system being observed in a thermochemical study.

sustainable agriculture Farming practices that can produce food and fiber indefinitely, without causing irreparable damage to the ecosystem.

sustainable chemistry An approach designed to meet the needs of the present generation without compromising the needs of future generations.

synapse A tiny gap between nerve cells.

synergistic effect An effect greater than the sum of the effects expected from two or more phenomena.

system The part of the universe under consideration in a thermochemical study.

tar sands Sands that contain bitumen, a thick hydrocarbon material.

technology The practical application of knowledge by which humans modify the materials of nature to better satisfy their needs and wants.

temperature A measure of heat intensity, or how energetic the particles of a sample are.

temperature inversion A warm layer of air above a cool, stagnant lower layer.

teratogen A substance that causes birth defects when introduced into the body of a pregnant female.

tertiary structure The folding pattern of a protein.

tetracyclines Antibacterial drugs with four fused rings.

theory A detailed explanation of a phenomenon that is based on experimentation and may be revised if new data warrant.

thermochemistry The study of energy changes that occur during chemical reactions.

thermonuclear reactions Nuclear fusion reactions that require extremely high temperatures and pressures.

thermoplastic polymer A kind of polymer that can be heated and reshaped.

thermosetting polymer A kind of polymer that cannot be softened and remolded.

thermosetting resins Polymeric materials that harden irreversibly.

top note The fraction of a perfume that vaporizes most quickly, is composed of relatively small molecules, and is responsible for the odor when the perfume is first applied.

toxicology The branch of pharmacology that deals with the effects of poisons on the body, their identification and detection, and remedies for them.

toxic waste A waste that contains or releases poisonous substances in amounts large enough to threaten human health or the environment.

toxin A poisonous substance produced by a living organism.

tracers Radioisotopes used to trace the movement of substances or locate the sites of activity in physical, chemical, and biological systems.

transcription The process by which a segment of DNA transfers its information to a messenger RNA (mRNA) molecule during protein synthesis.

transfer RNA (tRNA) A small molecule that contains anticodon nucleotides; the RNA molecule that bonds to and carries an amino acid.

transition elements Metallic elements in the B groups of the customary U.S. arrangement of the periodic table or in groups 3–12 of the IUPAC-recommended table.

translation The process by which the information contained in the codon of an mRNA molecule is converted to a protein structure.

transmutation The conversion of one element into another.

triglyceride An ester of glycerol with three fatty-acid units; also called a triacylglycerol.

triple bond The sharing of three pairs of electrons between two atoms.

tritium A radioactive isotope of hydrogen with two neutrons and one proton in the nucleus (hydrogen-3).

unsaturated hydrocarbon An alkene, alkyne, or aromatic hydrocarbon; a hydrocarbon containing one or more double or triple bonds or aromatic rings.

valence electrons Electrons in the outermost shell of an atom.

valence shell electron pair repulsion theory (VSEPR theory) A theory of chemical bonding useful in determining the shapes of molecules; it states that valence shell electron pairs around a central atom locate themselves as far apart as possible.

vaporization The process by which a substance changes from the liquid to the gaseous (vapor) state.

variable A factor that changes during an experiment.

vitamin An organic compound that is required in the diet to protect against some diseases.

volatile organic compounds (VOCs) Compounds that cause pollution because they vaporize readily.

VSEPR theory See **valence shell electron pair repulsion theory**.

vulcanization The process of making naturally soft rubber harder by reacting it with sulfur.

wax An ester of a long-chain fatty acid with a long-chain alcohol.

weak acid An acid that ionizes only slightly in water; a poor proton donor.

weak base A base that ionizes only slightly in water; a poor proton acceptor.

weight A measure of the force of attraction between Earth (or another planet) and an object.

wet scrubber A pollution control device that uses water to remove pollutants from smokestack gases.

X-rays Radiation similar to visible light but of much higher energy and much more penetrating.

zwitterion A molecule that contains both a positive charge and a negative charge; a dipolar ion.

CREDITS

Photo Credits

Cover Solar panels in sunflower field: Henglein and Steets/Cultura/Getty Images; Earth from space: Laara Cerman/Leigh Righton/Stockbyte/Getty Images; Polar Bear: M G Therin Weise/Getty Images; Hybrid car: Robert Churchill/Getty Images; Antarctic ozone hole: NASA; Streamlined train: ssuaphotos/Shutterstock; Wind turbines: Patryk Kosmider/Shutterstock; Solar Panels concept: FrameAngel/Shutterstock; Hands and plant: Showcake/Shutterstock; Ocean Wave: EpicStockMedia/Shutterstock; Desert sand: Bildagentur Zoonar GmbH/Shutterstock; Fir trees: natalia_maroz/Shutterstock; Strawberry Farm: antpkr/Shutterstock; Chapter 1 page 1 (top left): Elenathewise/Fotolia; page 1 (bottom right): FikMik/Fotolia; page 1 (top right): Reika/Shutterstock; page 2 (top left):Creatas/JupiterImages; page 3(top right): HANDOUT/MCT/Newscom; page 3 (bottom right): Stephen Denness/Shutterstock; page 5 (bottom right): James Steidl/Shutterstock; page 8(top left): iofoto/Shutterstock; page 11 (top right): Everett Collection Inc/Alamy;page 12 (top left): Karen Tam/AP Images; page 12 (bottom left): NASA; page 13 (bottom center): Tom Bochsler Photography Limited/Pearson Education; page 13 (bottom left): Charles D. Winters/Science Source; page 17 (bottom right): Martin McCarthy/iStock/360/Getty Images; page 17 (bottom right): Tammy Bryngelson/Getty Images; page 17 (bottom left): jmatzick/Shutterstock; page 17 (bottom left): United States Mint page 19 (bottom left): Richard Megna/Fundamental Photographs; page 24 (bottom right): ollaweila/Fotolia; page 25 (center right): Pearson Education; page 28 (top right): emf_images/Fotolia; page 28 (top left): niderlander/Shutterstock; page 32 (bottom right): Elevance Renewable Science, Inc. and Wilmar International Limited; page 35 (bottom right): Terry McCreary page 36 (center right): Buquet Christophe/Shutterstock; page 37 (center left): Martyn F Chillmaid/Pearson Education; page 38 (bottom right): Harvard-Smithsonian Center for Astrophysics; page 38 (top right): Yana Kabangu/Shutterstock; page 40 (top right): Stephen Oliver/DK Images; Chapter 2 page 41 (top left): Karl Thomas - Coll. 3/all Over images/Alamy; page 41 (top right): Stockbyte/Getty Images; page 41 (bottom right): Wilson Ho; page 42 (center): seread/Fotolia; page 42 (center right): yasar simit/Fotolia; page 42 (center right): CB2/ZOB/WENN.com/Newscom; page 43 (top left): konradlew/E+/Getty Images; page 43 inset Susumu Nishinaga/Science Source; page 44 (center left) Dea/E. Lessing/De Agostini Picture Library/Getty Images; page 45 (center right): Richard Megna/Fundamental Photographs; page 45 (center left): Manamana/Shutterstock; page 45 (center): Katharina Wittfeld/Shutterstock; page 47 (center right): Georgios Kollidas/Fotolia; page 49 (top right): Matt Meadows/Photolibrary/Getty Images; page 54 (bottom left): ria novosti/Science Source; page 56 (center left): Drs. Ali Yazdani & Daniel J. Hornbaker/Science Source; page 57 (top left): Harry Taylor/DK Images; page 57 (bottom left): Harry Taylor/DK Images; page 57 (top left): Scanrail/Fotolia; page 57 (top right): Patryk Kosmider/Fotolia; page 57 (top right): tagstiles.com/Fotolia; page 57 (bottom center): Michael Shake/Shutterstock; page 57 (top right): LesPalenik/Shutterstock; page 57 (bottom right): skaljac/Shutterstock; page 58 (bottom): Libby Welch/Alamy; page 62 (bottom right): Richard Megna/Fundamental Photographs; page 62 (bottom right): Richard Megna/Fundamental Photographs; Chapter 3 page 65 (bottom left): geöffnet/Fotolia; page 65 (top right): Comstock Images/Getty Images; page 65 (top left): Rudi Von Briel/Getty Images; page 66 (top left): GL Archive/Alamy; page 67 (center right): Richard Megna/Fundamental Photographs; page 69 (bottom right): National Library of Medicine; page 70 (top left): Interfoto/Alamy; page 71 (center right): Str/AFP/Getty Images/Newscom; page 76 (bottom left): eff Hunter/The Image Bank/Getty Images; page 77 (top left): Richard Megna/Fundamental Photographs; page 77 (top left): Richard Megna/Fundamental Photographs; page 77 (top center): Richard Megna/Fundamental Photographs; page 77 (top right): Richard Megna/Fundamental Photographs; page 77 (top right): Richard Megna/Fundamental Photographs; page 77 (bottom left): Wabash Instrument Corp/Fundamental Photographs; page 77 (bottom right): David Parker/Science Source; page 79 (bottom right): Elenathewise/Fotolia; page 86 (top left): Richard Megna/Fundamental Photographs; page 86 (top left): Richard Megna/Fundamental Photographs; page 87 (top right): Colin Keates/Natural History Museum/DK Images; page 87 (top right): Yuriko Nakao/Reuters page 94 (top right): Andrey Kuzmin/Fotolia; Chapter 4 page 95 (top right): ChinellatoPhoto/Shutterstock; page 95 (bottom right): Fotocrisis/Shutterstock; page 95 (top left): Phase4Studios/Shutterstock; page 97 (bottom right): Lawrence Berkeley National Laboratory/Science Source; page 99 (center left): Richard Megna/Fundamental Photographs; page 99 (center): Richard Megna/Fundamental Photographs; page 99 (center right): Richard Megna/Fundamental Photographs; page 100 (bottom left): Richard Megna/Fundamental Photographs; page 100 (center right): Charles D. Winters/Science Source; page 102 (bottom left): Alexander Dvorak/Shutterstock; page 104 (bottom right): Eric Schrader/Pearson Education; page 120 (bottom right): Eric Schrader/Pearson Education; page 135 (bottom center): Courtesy of Meg Shanahan Photography; Chapter 5 page 136 (top right):

Jake Norton/Alamy; page 136 (bottom left): Barry C. Bishop/National Geographic/Getty Images; page 136 (top left): andibyte/Shutterstock; page 142 (center left): photodreams2/Alamy; page 147 (bottom center): Richard Megna/Fundamental Photographs; page 148 (bottom left): GENT SHKULLAKU/AFP/Getty Images/Newscom; page 152 (top left): Alistair Scott/Alamy; page 154 (bottom left): Eric Schrader/Pearson Education; page 155 (center right): Nathan Eldridge/Pearson Education; page 156 (top left): Nathan Eldridge/Pearson Education; page 163 (top right): gekaskr/Fotolia; page 163 (center right): Lucian Milasan/Fotolia; Chapter 6 page 164 (top right): Sophie Vigneault/123RF; page 164 (bottom left): Joshua Resnick/Shutterstock; page 164 (top left): CAN BALCIOGLU/Shutterstock; page 165 (center right): GTS Production/Shutterstock; page 166 (top left): Richard Megna/Fundamental Photographs; page 166 (center left): Nikita Tiunov/Shutterstock; page 167 (center right): Richard Megna/Fundamental Photographs; page 167 (center left): Richard Megna/Fundamental Photographs; page 167 (top right): Ariel Bravy/Shutterstock; page 171 (bottom center): Liv friis-larsen/Shutterstock; page 171 (bottom left): Tony Freeman/PhotoEdit; page 171 (bottom left): George Mattei/Science Source; page 177 (top right): Richard Megna/Fundamental Photographs; page 177 (center right): Richard Megna/Fundamental Photographs; page 179 (center right): Oleksiy Mark/Shutterstock; page 188 (bottom center): amalia19/Shutterstock; Chapter 7 page 189 (top left): IS695/Image Source/Alamy; page 189 (top right): schankz/Shutterstock; page 189 (bottom right): Denis Larkin/Shutterstock; page 190 (bottom left): Pearson Education; page 190 (bottom center): Pearson Education; page 190 (bottom right): Pearson Education; page 191 (center right): Richard Megna/Fundamental Photographs; page 191 (top left): Pearson Education; page 191 (top right): Tyler Boyes/Shutterstock; page 191 (top right): Denise Kappa/Shutterstock; page 192 (top left): Science and Society/SuperStock; page 193 (center right): Valua Vitaly/Fotolia; page 197 (top right): Everett Collection; page 200 (bottom left): Richard Megna/Fundamental Photographs; page 200 (bottom center): Richard Megna/Fundamental Photographs; page 200 (bottom right): Richard Megna/Fundamental Photographs; page 203 (top right): Richard Megna/Fundamental Photographs; page 206 (bottom left): Pearson Education; page 207 Getty Images; page 208 (bottom left): Michael P Gadomski/Science Source; page 215 (center right): Farsad-Behzad Ghafarian/Shutterstock; Chapter 8 page 216 (top right): Kara/Fotolia; page 216 (top left): Otmar Smit/Fotolia; page 216 (bottom left): MaxyM/Shutterstock; page 217 (center left): Paul Silverman/Fundamental Photographs; page 217 (center right): Paul Silverman/Fundamental Photographs; page 226 (top left): Peticolas/Megna/Fundamental Photographs; page 226 (center left): Peticolas/Richard Megna/Fundamental Photographs; page 228 (bottom center): Spencer Grant/PhotoEdit; page 228 (bottom right): Spencer Grant/PhotoEdit; page 229 (center right): Marianne de Jong/Shutterstock; page 230 (bottom left): Krishnacreations/Fotolia; page 233 (bottom right): Walter Drake Company page 234 (bottom left): Kzenon/Shutterstock; page 235 (top right): NASA; page 236 (top left): Richard Megna/Fundamental Photographs; page 236 (bottom left): Pearson Education; page 238 (top left): Paul Reid/Shutterstock; page 239 (top right): Pearson Education; page 239 (center right): Vovan/Shutterstock; page 244 (bottom right): Sherri R. Camp/Shutterstock; page 245 (bottom left): Jacob Kearns/Shutterstock; Chapter 9 page 249 (top left): Swell Photography/Alamy; page 249 (top right): Ril/Fotolia; page 252 (center left): Vladimir Breytberg/Shutterstock; page 256 (bottom left): Richard Megna/Fundamental Photographs; page 257 (top right): JPC-PROD/Shutterstock; page 260 (center left): Clive Freeman/Science Source; page 262 (bottom left): Pearson Education; page 266 (bottom left): Pearson Education; page 267 (bottom left): Pearson Education; page 267 (bottom right): Southern Illinois University/Science Source; page 272 (bottom left): Pearson Education; page 279 (bottom right): Qsonica; page 283 (center right): Sommai/Fotolia; page 283 (bottom right): Richard Nowitz/National Geographic/Getty Images; Chapter 10 page 287 (bottom right): BALDUCCI/SINTESI/SIPA/Newscom; page 287 (top right): Areipa.lt/Shutterstock; page 287 (top left): Jelle-vd-Wolf/Shutterstock; page 288 (top left): Brian Nolan/Shutterstock; page 290 (bottom right): Richard Megna/Fundamental Photographs; page 292 (center left): JoeAppel/Pittsburgh tribune-Review/AP Images; page 292 (top left): Richard Megna/Fundamental Photographs; page 293 (bottom right): Dennis MacDonald/PhotoEdit page 294 (top center): James Edward Bates/MCT/Newscom; page 294 (top center): Koksharov Dmitry/Shutterstock; page 294 (top right): Inara Prusakova/Shutterstock; page 294 (bottom left): Michele Cozzolino/Shutterstock; page 295 (top right): Freerk Brouwer/Shutterstock; page 296 (top left): Geoff Tompkinson/Science Source; page 298 (center left): Maridav/Shutterstock; page 298 (bottom left): IMAGENFX/Shutterstock; page 300 (bottom left): Zoonar/richterfoto/AGE Fotostock; page 302 (bottom left): Mar Photographics/Alamy; page 302 (top left): Pearson Education; page 303 (center right): Crisferra/Shutterstock; page 305 (center right): Amoco Fabrics & Fibers page 306 (bottom):

Beth Hall/Alamy; page 315 (center right): Jessica Burfield/Daf(top left): y Domestic; Chapter 11 page 316 (top right): Scott Camazine/Alamy; page 316 (top left): Custom Medical Stock Photo; page 316 (bottom left): SergeyIT/Shutterstock; page 319 (top left): Nora D.Volkow, MD/National Institute of Health; page 328 (bottom left): Library of Congress Prints and Photographs Division[LC-DIG-ggbain-36570]; page 329 (bottom right): Science Source; page 330 (center left): Simon Fraser/Science Source; page 334 (bottom left): AGE Fotostock America; page 336 (top left): Pictorial Press Ltd/Alamy; page 336 (center left): PF-(bygone1)/Alamy; page 339 (center right): Lawrence Berkeley National Laboratory page 340 (center left): United States Air Force; page 343 (center right): GeoEye Inc; page 343 (top left): AFP Photo/JIJI Press/Getty Images/Newscom; page 344 (bottom right): Steve Allen/Shutterstock; page 351 (bottom left): ACORN 1/Alamy; Chapter 12 page 187 (bottom right): Gary Gladstone/Stockbyte/Getty Images; page 352 (top right): eccolo/Fotolia; page 352 (bottom left): Joan Albert Lluch/Fotolia; page 352 (top left): Alina Cardiae Photography/Shutterstock; page 354 (top left): Galyna Andrushko/Shutterstock; page 355 (bottom right): Gary Cook/Alamy; page 355 (bottom left): Madlen/Shutterstock; page 356 (top center): American Geological Institute; page 356 (bottom center): Arizona Yale Collection# B6065 (mm scale) on p, 8, Source: Asbestos; page 356 (center): S_E/Fotolia; page 358 (top right): meadow2007/Fotolia; page 359 (bottom right): Lee Prince/Shutterstock; page 359 (top right): Nikkytok/Shutterstock; page 360 (center left): terex/Fotolia; page 360 (top left): Bruce C. Murray/Shutterstock; page 364 (center right): Kolbasov Alexander Itar-Tass Photos/Newscom; page 364 (top left): Arturo Limon/Shutterstock; page 364 (bottom left): Charles D. Winters/Science Source; page 367 (bottom left): Arne Dedert/dpa/picture-alliance/Newscom; page 367 (bottom center): vvoe/Fotolia; page 372 (top right): Dave King/DK Images; page 372 (center left): Stephen St. John/Getty Images; Chapter 13 page 373 (top left): NASA Images; page 373 (top right): frescomovie/Shutterstock; page 375 (top right): Mario Babiera/Alamy; page 379 (top right): NASA; page 380 (top left): Sergei Butorin/Shutterstock; page 381 (center right): AP Images; page 381 (top right): Science Source page 384 (top left): bluebird13/Getty Images; page 386 (center left): Jens Peermann/Shutterstock; page 390 (top left): Richard Megna/Fundamental Photographs; page 393 (right) Susan Solomon; Chapter 14 page 410 (top right): Adam Gryko/Fotolia; page 410 (bottom left): Jonutis/Shutterstock; page 410 (top left): Tischenko Irina/Shutterstock; page 411 (bottom right): Age fotostock/SuperStock page 412 (bottom left): NASA; page 418 (top): Robert Brook/Alamy; page 418 (bototm) U.S. Environmental Protection Agency; page 419 (bottom right): Alamy; page 419 (top right): Krista Kennell/ZUMA Press/Newscom; page 420 (bottom left): EyePress/AP Images; page 421 (top right): Mike Segar/Reuters; page 422 (center left): Pearson Education; page 425 (bottom left): Pavel Rahman/AP Images; page 427 (bottom right): National Institute of Dental Research; Chapter 15 page 437 (top left): Casey Reed/NASA; page 437 (top right): NASA/SDO/AIA; page 437 (bottom): Rafa Irusta/Shutterstock; page 438 (bottom left): U.S. Consumer Product Safety Commission; page 441 (top right): Greenshoots Communications/Alamy; page 441 (center right): Richard Megna/Fundamental Photographs; page 443 (bottom right): Mark phillips/Alamy; page 444 (center left): Schrader, Eric; page 445 (top right): D and D Photo Sudbury/Shutterstock; page 446 (center): Richard Megna/Fundamental Photographs; page 447 (top right): Attila JANDI/Shutterstock; page 450 (top left): Tennessee Valley Authority page 450 (bottom center): U.S. Department of the Interior Museum page 450 (bottom right): U.S. Department of the Interior Museum; page 451 John Kaprielian/Getty Images; page 452 (top center): BanksPhotos/E+/Getty Images; page 459 (top left): Larry Lee Photography/Spirit/Corbis; page 460 (bottom left): US Department of Energy page 462 (bottom left): EFDA Jet; page 464 (top right): Shutterstock; page 466 (top left): Martin Bond/Science Source; page 467 (bottom right): Videowokart/Shutterstock; page 468 (bottom left): Renewables/Denmark/Reuters; page 468 (center right): Reuters Photographer/Reuters; page 469 (top left): Steve Allen/Science Source; page 471 (bottom right): jadimages/Shutterstock; page 477 (top left): Photo courtesy Kathy Ceceri, www.craftsfor-learning.com; page 477 (center right): Gift of Curiosity Chapter 16 page 478 (top left): Soren Egeberg Photography/Shutterstock; page 478 (top right): Levent Konuk/Shutterstock; page 479 (top right): Biosphoto/SuperStock; page 482 (top left): Pearson Education; page 483 (bottom left): Biophoto Associates/Science Source; page 483 (bottom left): CNRI/Science Source; page 486 (center left): Shutterstock; page 487 (bottom left): Richard Megna/Fundamental Photographs; page 496 (top left): Swapan/Fotolia; page 499 (top right): Science Source; page 501 (top right): Andrew Syred/Science Source; page 504 (bottom left): Angela Waye/Shutterstock; page 508 (bottom right): UCLA Henry Samueli School of Engineering and Applied Science; page 511 (bottom left): Pearson; page 511 (bottom right): Pearson; page 511 (bottom left): Pearson Education; page 515 (bottom right): Beret Olsen; page 515 (top right): Beret Olsen; Chapter 17 page 516 (top left): Konstantin Yuganov/Fotolia; page 516 (top right): Alex Jackson/Shutterstock; page 517 (bottom left): Richard Megna/Fundamental Photographs; page 518 (center right): Shutterstock; page 518 (bottom center): ranplett/Getty Images; page 518 (top right): Alex Treadway/National Geographic Image Collection/Alamy; page 518 (bottom left): Marilyn Duerst; page 519 (top left): Newscom; page 520 (top left): Pearson Education; page 521 (top left): Martin M. Rotker/Science Source; page 521 (top left): Peter Arnold, Inc./Alamy; page 522 (bottom right): Pearson Education; page 522 (top right): Pearson Education; page 526 (top right): Andy Crump, TDR, World Health Organization/Science Source; page 527 (top left): Mike Goldwater/Alamy; page 528 (top right): Pearson Education; page 529 (top left): Biophoto Associates/Science Source; page 529 (center left): Wellcome Image Library/Custom Medical Stock Photo -- All rights; page 531 (bottom right): charles taylor/Shutterstock; page 535 (bottom left): GVictoria/Shutterstock; page 541 (bottom left): Maria Komar/Shutterstock; page 542 (top left): USDA National Peanut Research Laboratory/AP Images; page 543 (bottom left): Madlen/Shutterstock; page 543 (bottom left): Africa Studio/Shutterstock; page 543 (bottom left): Maksim Toome/Shutterstock; page 543 (bottom left): Artmim/Shutterstock; page 543 (center left): lchriste2/Fotolia; page 548 (center left): Pearson Education; page 550 (bottom left): Courtesy of Meg Shanahan Photography; page 550 (top right): Courtesy of Meg Shanahan Photography page 550 (center right): Courtesy of Meg Shanahan Photography; page 550 (bottom right): Courtesy of Meg Shanahan Photography; Chapter 18 page 551 (top left): unpict/Fotolia; page 551 (bottom center): Eric Schrader/Pearson Education; page 551 (top right): Radu Razvan/Shutterstock; page 552 (center left): Ray Pfortner/Photolibrary/Getty Images; page 552 (top left): mce128/iStockphoto; page 552 (top left): Karel Gallas/Shutterstock; page 552 (bottom left): Jeff Rotman/Science Source; page 554 (bottom left): Mike Kemp/RubberBall/Alamy; page 556 (bottom left): John Hill; page 557 (top right): Nigel Cat(top left):in/Alamy; page 557 (bottom right): Library of Congress Prints and Photographs Division; page 572 (bottom left): Gary J. Shulfer/Marvin Lang; page 574 (bottom left): Custom Medical Stock Photo/Newscom; page 582 (bottom left): Ildi Papp/Shutterstock; page 590 (bottom left): U.S Drug Enforcement Administration; page 591 Monkey Business Images/Shutterstock; page 602 Amy Cannon; Chapter 19 page 603 (top right): Foodpics/Shutterstock; page 603 (bottom right): Rido/Shutterstock; page 603 (top right): Aleksandr Markin/Shutterstock; page 604 (bottom left): US Department of Agriculture; page 609 (bottom right): Christopher Edwin Nuzzaco/Shutterstock; page 610 (center right): NASA/Kathy Barnstorff; page 614 (bottom left): Steve Zylius/PhotoShot; page 615 (top right): Python Pictures/Everett Collection; page 616 (top left): Robyn Beck/AFP/Getty Images; page 617 (top right): Pearson Education; page 617 (bottom right): Andresr/Shutterstock; page 618 (top left): Kathy Willens/AP Images; page 618 (bottom left): Dr. William McDonald, MD page 619 (bottom): Richard Vogel/AP Images; page 619 (top right): Greg M. Cooper/AP Images; page 622 (bottom left): Kuttig-travel-2/Alamy; page 623 (bottom center): Thomas Kienzle/AP Images; Chapter 20 page 630 (top right): SeanPavonePhoto/Fotolia; page 630 (top left): Akihiro Sugimoto/Aflo/Getty Images; page 630 (bottom left): TAGSTOCK1/Shutterstock; page 631 (bottom right): Stephanie Coffman/Shutterstock; page 632 (top left): Pearson Education page 633 (top right): Doug Martin/Science Source; page 634 (top left): NASA image courtesy Jeff Schmaltz, MODIS Land Rapid Response; page 635 (top right): Pearson Education; page 636 (top left): Arlene Jean Gee/Shutterstock; page 636 (bottom left): Sarah Cut; (top left): e/DK Images; page 637 Newscom; page 639 (top right): US Department of Agriculture; page 643 (bottom right): US Department of Agriculture; page 644 (top left): Yellowj/Shutterstock; page 648 (top left): Jonathan Pearson/Alamy; page 651 (top right): Christine Nesbitt/Africapictures.net/Newscom; page 652 Paul Looyen/123RF; page 657 (top left): KATE ANDERSON/Beyond Benign; page 657 (top right): KATE ANDERSON/Beyond Benign; page 657 (center left): KATE ANDERSON/Beyond Benign; page 657 (center right): KATE ANDERSON/Beyond Benign; page 657 (bottom left): Agriculture Dept/AP Images; Chapter 21 page 658 (top right): Ariel Skelley/Getty Images; page 658 (top left): YuriyZhuravov/Shutterstock; page 658 (bottom center): MSPhotographic/Fotolia; page 659 (top right): Richard Megna/Fundamental Photographs; page 659 (bottom right): Ken Welsh/Alamy; page 662 (bottom right): Richard Megna/Fundamental Photographs; page 665 (top center): Inc/Shutterstock; page 665 (top right): Richard Megna/Fundamental Photographs; page 665 (bottom left): Janice Haney Carr/Centers for Disease Control and Prevention; page 667 (bottom right): Alfred Pasieka/Science Source; page 667 (center right): Pearson Education; page 670 (bottom left): Pearson Education/Pearson Science; page 673 (center right): Richard Megna/Fundamental Photographs; page 674 (bottom left): ChandraPhoto/Shutterstock; page 674 (bottom center): Pearson Education; page 674 (bottom right): Genevieve Anderson; page 679 (bottom right): Pearson Education; page 682 (bottom left): Pearson Education; page 684 (center left): Elena Stepanova/Shutterstock; page 693 (bottom center): David Smart/Shutterstock; page 693 (top right): Phil Masturzo/MCT/Newscom; page 693 (center right): Fernando Madeira/Fotolia; Chapter 22 page 694 (top left): zigzagmtart/123RF; page 694 (top): Studio Porto Sabbia/Fotolia; page 694 (bottom left): Daffodils hivaka/Fotolia; page 695 (bottom left): Gérard Sauze/Fotolia page 696 (center left): Getty Images; page 696 (top left): Sufi/Shutterstock; page 700 (bottom left): Kevin Wolf/AP Images; page 701 (bottom right): U.S. Consumer Product Safety Commission/AP Images; page 706 (top center): Hand-out/ALLERGAN/Newscom; page 706 (top right): CNW Group/Allergan/Hand-out/Newscom; page 707 (top right): Picsfive/Shutterstock; page 707 (top right): Sciencesource;page 711 (bottom right): US Food and Drug Administration; page 720 (top right): Kate Anderson/Beyond Benign; page 720 (center right): Kate Anderson/Beyond Benign; Green Chemistry features: AKIRA/a.collectionRF/Getty Images; Chemistry at Home features: Yagi Studio/Digital Vision/Getty Images.

Text Credits

Inside front cover Figure, "Twelve Principles of Green Chemistry," GREEN CHEMISTRY: THEORY AND PRACTICE by Paul Anastas & John Warner (1998) Figure 4.1 from p. 30. By permission of Oxford University Press. Chapter 1 page 12 Quote: "There are two compelling reasons why society must support basic science. One is substantial: The theoretical physics of yesterday is the nuclear defense of today; ..." Kornberg, Arthur. The biologic synthesis of deoxyribonucleic acid. Nobel Lecture, December 11, 1959. Chapter 12 page 366 Figure 12.10 Population timeline from 1800-2050 Source: United Nations, World Population Prospects: The 2012 Revision. New York: 2012. Chapter 13 page 373 I saw the blackness of space, and then the bright blue Earth. And then it looked as if someone had taken a royal blue crayon and traced along Earth's horizon. And then I realized that blue line, that really thin royal blue line, was Earth's atmosphere, and that was all there was of it. And it's so clear from that perspective how fragile our existence is." Sally Ride, Sher, Lynn. 2014. Sally Ride: America's First Woman in Space. New York: Simon & Schuster. page 392 "to use proven methods of controlling indoor air pollution. These methods include eliminating or controlling pollutant sources, increasing outdoor air ventilation, and using proven methods of air cleaning." U.S. Environmental Protection Agency, "Ozone Generators That are Sold as Air Cleaners". page 398 Map: Estimated deaths attributed to climate change in the year 2000, by subregion Source: McMichael, JJ, Campbell-Lendrum D, Kovats RS, et al. Global Climate. In comparative quantification of health risks: global and regional burden of disease due to selected major risk factors.; M Ezzati, Lopez, AD, Rodgers A., Murray CJL. Geneva, World Health Organization, 2004. page 409 Figure 13.11 The ozone hole (purple) over Antarctica Ozone Hole, September 16, 2013: NASA; http://earthobservatory.nasa.gov/IOTD/view.php?id=82235 Chapter 14 page 415 Figure 14.2 Where Is Earth's Water? Data from Igor Shiklomanov's chapter "World fresh water resources" in Water in Crisis: A Guide to the World's Fresh Water Resources. page 416 Figure 14.3 The water (hydrological) cycle Source USGS: http://water.usgs.gove/edu/watercyclessummary.html. page 421 Figure 14.4 Areas of the contiguous United States where groundwater is likely to be contaminated by nitrates Source: U.S. Geological Survey Scienti c

Investigations Map 2881. Chapter 15 page 447 Table 15.3 Estimated U.S. and World Reserves of Economically Recoverable Fuels and Annual Consumption of Fossil Fuels Source: U.S. Energy Information Administration, April 2014 report; Data are as of January 1, 2013, for the year ending December 31, 2012. page 449 Table 15.4 Table: Major Components of Various Types of Coal (Minor Components Include Volatile Materials and Sulfur) Source: Data from Diessel, C. F. K. Coal-Bearing Depositional Systems. New York: Springer-Verlag, 1992. page 459 Table 15.7 Electricity Generation Using Nuclear Power Plants (Selected Countries) International Atomic Energy Agency, PRIS Database. Vienna: 2010. page 470 Table 15.8 Table: Total Primary Energy Consumption Per Capita, (quadrillion BTU's in 2011) Source: US Energy Information Administration. Chapter 17 page 534 "This statement has not been evaluated ... treat, cure, or prevent any disease." Source: Dietary Supplement Health and Education Act of 1994. Chapter 18 page 589 Table 18.5 Caffeine in Soft Drinks Source: National Soft Drink Association, FDA. page 589 "no one has ever become a cigarette smoker by smoking cigarettes without nicotine", "think of the cigarette as a dispenser for a dose unit of nicotine." Source: Philip Morris quoted in Internal Report for Philip Morris (1972), written by William L Dunn, Jr, cited in Douglas, op. cit., at 3. Chapter 20 page 638 Table 20.3 Approximate Acute Toxicity of Insecticidal Preparations Administered Orally to Rats. Sources: O'Neill, Maryadele J., Patricia E. Heckelman, Cherie B. Koch, Kristin J. Roman, and Catherine M. Kenny, The Merck Index, 14th ed. (Whitehouse Station, NJ: Merck & Co., 2006), and the Extension Toxicology Network. page 648 Figure 20.15 Energy use in modern agriculture and food production. Data from Center for Sustainable Systems, University of Michigan. 2013. "U.S. Food System Factsheet." Pub. No. CSS01-06. October 2013 Chapter 22 page 708 Figure 22.7 Chart: Ranking cancer risks. About 30% of all cancer deaths are attributed to tobacco and another 30% or so to a diet high in fat and calories and low in fruits and vegetables. Environmental pollution and food additives rank high in the public's perception of cancer causes but are only relatively minor contributors to cancer deaths. Source: Based on data from Harvard University School of Public Health.

INDEX